BERNARD SHAW
Collected Letters
1874–1897

London, 1886
(*From a photograph by Frederick Hollyer*)

BERNARD SHAW

Collected Letters
1874-1897

EDITED BY DAN H. LAURENCE

MAX REINHARDT
LONDON

Printed and bound in Great Britain for
Max Reinhardt Ltd
10 Earlham Street, London WC2
by William Clowes & Sons Ltd, Beccles
Set in Monotype Ehrhardt
First published 1965

To
the Editor's parents,
with love and gratitude

Contents

Contents

Illustrations

x

INTRODUCTION

"Put it out of your head," Shaw advised his American publisher when an edition of his collected letters was proposed in 1949. "There are billions of them," he argued, "and I am adding to them every day." Though he frequently complained that his correspondence was a crushing burden—"This correspondence is getting intolerable," he had grumbled as far back as 1891 —he enormously enjoyed letter-writing, and would devote endless hours to it, especially while travelling, carrying huge batches of unanswered correspondence in a sack into which he dipped at any opportunity. Shaw's letters are, for the most part, happy letters, reflecting the same vitality and zest for living that characterised him in his plays, his critical articles, and his public addresses, while at the same time exposing the inner life of the public man. He dictated some of his letters, or scribbled them out in shorthand for a secretary to transcribe, and many were typewritten by Shaw himself, usually in a rather clumsy manner. For the most part, however, his personal correspondence was written by hand, and how his pen flew! Page after page of narrative, criticism, or advice flowed spontaneously and in high style from his hand and brain: letters which, to borrow John Morley's description of Shaw's writing in 1885, were "pointed, rapid, forcible, sometimes witty, often powerful, and occasionally eloquent." And though Shaw must have been aware even before the turn of the century that his letters were being saved and would one day receive public scrutiny, there is never in them an element of self-consciousness, an awareness that the world is reading over the author's shoulder.

Shaw, by conservative estimate, must in his lifetime have written at least a quarter of a million letters and postcards (squeezing as many as two hundred cramped but completely legible words on a single card!), an output whose massiveness resulted in large part from his insistence on transacting personally most of his business, including the printing and publishing of his works at home and abroad; the licensing of his plays for domestic and foreign production, whether professional, stock, or amateur; the translating of his plays (on which he frequently collaborated, with the assistance of dictionaries and grammars); and even the granting of routine permissions for the quotation of his works in scholarly publications. And not infrequently the motivation for a letter was the awareness that the recipient, whom Shaw knew to be in straitened circumstances, would be able to take the letter to a dealer and instantly realise a sum of money for it.

Much of this mountain of correspondence has not survived. Thousands of letters written by Shaw in the course of his Socialistic or journalistic duties before 1900 have gone the way of the dustbin. Two world wars took their toll of correspondence (and correspondents) throughout Europe; the London blitz in 1941 pulverised the letters to Dame Sybil Thorndike and to Geraldine Spooner, with whom Shaw was infatuated briefly in early

Fabian days. Many of his letters to his printer, Messrs R. & R. Clark of Edinburgh, were in the office files commandeered for war scrap; there was no time to hunt them out and preserve them.

Many letters were deliberately destroyed. Shaw himself burned the letters he had written to Annie Besant when she returned them to him in December 1887 after they had agreed that their relationship was growing intimate to the point of becoming ''a vulgar intrigue.'' (''Reading over my letters before destroying them,'' he noted in his diary, ''rather disgusted me with the trifling of the last two years with women.'') He also destroyed family correspondence whenever it happened to return to his hand, and successfully persuaded his Dublin schoolboy friend Matthew Edward McNulty to destroy all his boyhood and adolescent correspondence.

Other incendiaries included Jenny Patterson's executor, Mrs Arabella Musters, who in 1924 destroyed all the letters that Shaw's seductress had tenderly preserved for forty years; Alice Lockett, who burned Shaw's earliest letters to her at his request, as well as her own letters which he had returned to her (but only after he had copied them all out in shorthand in a pocket notebook); and Mrs H.K. Ayliff, the widow of the director of Shaw's plays at Malvern and Birmingham, who destroyed all but one letter to her husband.

But if the percentage rate of known survival of Shaw's letters is comparatively small, the residuum available to me in the preparation of this edition has far exceeded Shaw's own expectation that a ''complete collection'' of his correspondence would run to twenty volumes. And as an edition even near this size would be commercially unfeasible—''you are no kind of publisher,'' Shaw told Edward Dodd, ''if you even entertain the idea of so unprofitable a venture as that''—it has become the editor's responsibility to select, for what will eventually be a four-volume edition, those letters which most effectively shed light on Shaw and on the things his life stood for.

Of the 691 letters selected for this first volume, 456 are hitherto unpublished, 181 were previously published in full or with minor deletions, and 54 have been published in extract only. All editorial emendations or deletions made by previous editors (notably those by Shaw in the letters to Ellen Terry, which he silently co-edited with Christopher St John) have been restored in the present edition.

In his last will and testament Shaw requested that, in the event that there should be posthumous publication of any of his writings, ''heed be taken both to the credit and the feelings of any surviving person alluded to therein but no suppressions need be made for the purpose of whitewashing my own character or conduct.'' The injunction, in regard to the present volume, is academic, for not more than two or three of the *dramatis personae* (notably Bertrand Russell) survive. No omissions have therefore been necessary. The letters completely excluded from the volume are mostly short business or personal notes which have proved to be of no particular interest or which contain materials substantially the same as in correspondence already included, and whose omission in no way ''whitewashes'' Shaw.

xii

A considerable number of the letters written between 1876 and 1890 are reproduced from manuscripts preserved in the archives bequeathed by Shaw to the British Museum. It was Shaw's habit, for purposes of record, to copy his reply on the reverse of the letter he had just dealt with. It was also his custom in these years to prepare rough drafts when dealing with business matters, revising and polishing them and preserving the work sheets as file copies. Since many of the copies and drafts were written in Pitman shorthand, which Shaw had recently adopted, transcription of shorthand became a major editorial responsibility.

Fortunately, I was able to obtain the services of a patient, persistent, and thoroughly knowledgeable Pitmanite, Miss Barbara Smoker, to cope with the complications of transcription. This, as Miss Smoker subsequently reported in the newsletter of the Phonetic Alphabet Association in 1961, entailed ''not only the interpretation of almost microscopic outlines, with never a guide line to indicate position, and often written with leaky pens in very rolling rolling-stock of the 1880's, not only the tracking down of ancient grammalogues which have appeared in no Pitman textbook since the 1870's when Shaw learnt as much shorthand theory as he considered necessary for his purpose, but also coping with flagrant inconsistencies, even where the same word occurs twice within a few lines, and with such aberrations as hooks facing the wrong way and strokes running in the opposite direction to that intended . . .'' For those Shavian shorthand puzzles which Miss Smoker and I were unable to solve, we drew upon the experience of Shaw's longtime secretary Miss Blanche Patch, who generously joined us in the British Museum to peer through our magnifying glass and clarify all but a stubborn few indecipherables.

The texts of the letters in this edition are based, for the most part, on the original manuscripts (or on microfilm or photostatic copies). In some instances, however, it has been necessary to work from previously published texts or from transcripts, exposing the editor to the same sort of pitfall as that experienced by the late E. J. West, when he edited the letters of Shaw to Reginald Golding Bright (*Advice to a Young Critic*, 1955) from a typescript provided by his publisher. Professor West, for instance, was completely baffled by Shaw's reference to an ''Italian'' essay he was about to write, and no wonder, for ''Italian'' was a copyist's misreading of ''Fabian.''

The one major correspondence reproduced here from transcripts is that with the actress Janet Achurch and her husband Charles Charrington. The originals of these letters were purchased by the University of Texas in 1958 as part of the manuscript collection of Mr T. E. Hanley, which contains the largest and finest group of Shaw's manuscripts and letters in existence. For reasons best known to himself, however, Mr Hanley included in the transaction a stipulation that Shaw's letters to the Charringtons be sealed for ten years. The texts I have published are reproduced principally from transcriptions, made in 1926 by the late Ashley Dukes for the dealer Gabriel Wells, which are now in the Shaw archive in the British Museum. Other

xiii

transcriptions by Dukes, which have been collated with the originals, prove to be so faithful in their reproduction, however, that I am inclined to believe that the Charrington transcripts are equally reliable. Unfortunately, the Dukes transcriptions constitute only about sixty per cent of the full correspondence with the Charringtons.

"Letters" in this edition is to be construed as a generic term covering all forms of communication: postcards, lettercards, correspondence cards, notes, telegrams, cables. For purposes of clarity and general readability, the headings have been styled uniformly, thus removing the danger of misreading a date; salutations and valedictions follow the form established by Shaw in holograph correspondence. In transcription of the body of a letter, the *principle* has been the Pope-inspired one, "Whatever is, is right." Obvious typos in typewritten letters and misprints in published texts have been corrected, and minor flaws (such as the repetition of the last word on one sheet as the first word on the next) have been silently obliterated. In all other respects, however, the aim has been for faithfulness to the original, including Shaw's idiosyncratic punctuation and phonetic spelling, as well as his numerous grammatical errors. After all, as he informed W. E. Henley in 1890, "I am a writer of English and not of grammar. If the grammarian cannot square his pedantries with my English, why, so much the worse for his pedantries. . . . you actually turned my living vernacular indicatives into dead, ridiculous and utterly incorrect subjunctives . . . I write as men speak: when my subjunctives come, they are memorable for ever."

And since Shaw himself frequently was inconsistent in his orthography, in his elimination of apostrophes in contractions, and in his use of quotation marks, italics, ampersands, and capital letters for a definite article in a book or play title, I have deemed it advisable not to attempt to restyle those letters for which only published texts or transcripts are available, since it is impossible to determine to what extent, if any, Shaw's original text has been tampered with.

Shaw's drawings in his letters have been reproduced photographically from the originals (with varying degrees of success) in all but two instances, the impossibility of obtaining a sharp enough reproduction from a photocopy here necessitating the substitution of careful tracings.

I have striven in my editing to be objective and unobtrusive, allowing Shaw to speak for himself and the reader to form his own judgments. All pertinent biographical material has been packaged compactly in headnotes, with footnotes being utilised solely for technical bibliographical information. Dates, especially of birth and death, have been painstakingly researched at Somerset House or in other responsible records, and many hitherto accepted dates have as a result been revised. When the other side of a correspondence has survived and permission could be obtained for its use, pertinent extracts have been incorporated in the notes.

Inevitably there has been a problem of defining the audience for a work such as this. If one aims to please the literary specialist, it will be necessary to provide minute details which the general reader may find of no particular consequence and which he will almost certainly label "pedantic." And if the primer elements are spelled out for the general reader, the bored scholar may scornfully attack this as an attempt to "popularize." Even more of a problem is how to deal with two distinctly different *national* audiences now that co-operative publishing across the Atlantic for reasons of economy results in photo-reproduction of the English edition, or importation of sheets, for the American publication. An English reader may feel his intelligence is being insulted when the editor provides an annotation for "G.O.M." in reference to Gladstone, yet this annotation may be as necessary for the American reader as one would be for the English reader coming upon "G.O.P." as a symbol for the American Republican Party. I have resolved the issue by embracing Shaw's counsel to Frederick Evans in 1895, when the latter was preparing an edition (subsequently abandoned) of Shaw's musical criticism: "I charge you by all your gods to be guided exactly and faithfully by *what YOU like*, even if it seems to you that nobody else will like it." Whether that, as Shaw insisted, will "secure a perfectly satisfactory job" is yet to be seen.

The bracketed code information which precedes each letter provides specific sources for correspondence located in public institutions or in other permanent archives. However, as several private owners of correspondence prefer anonymity, and as some letters have changed hands as many as two or three times during the preparation of this volume, I have elected to forgo identification of individual owners. Many of these donors of material will, in any event, be instantly recognised in the general acknowledgment which follows. The code also indicates any prior publication of correspondence, but I have not attempted to record the specific flaws in these texts. Instead, in my reproduction I have carefully corrected errors of transcription, restored the deletions (some of which were not indicated by ellipsis marks), eliminated deliberate distortions, and revised inaccurate dates. The texts as now published may therefore be accepted as definitive.

For generous permission to publish copyright material I should like to express my gratitude to Miss Nancy Archer for extracts from letters by William Archer; Messrs Longmans, Green for a passage from Beatrice Webb's *Our Partnership*; Messrs Macmillan for extracts from letters from Richard Bentley & Son; Max Reinhardt Ltd for extracts from letters by Ellen Terry from *Ellen Terry and Bernard Shaw: A Correspondence;* Mrs Dorinda Maxse for an extract from a letter by Henry Arthur Jones; the Public Trustee for extracts from letters by William Heinemann; Mr D. Sydenham for the reproduction of Robert Anning Bell's portrait of Jenny Patterson; Col. William M. Sharpe for extracts from letters by Alice Lockett. Extensive efforts to locate the executors of several other correspondents were unsuccessful, but I have taken the liberty of quoting briefly from their letters without formal permission on the assumption that this permission would not, in any case, have been withheld.

In the preparation of this edition I have had the liberal co-operation and moral support of two exceptional friends and colleagues: Dr Harry M. Geduld, whose researches on my behalf during the past half-dozen years have been colossal labour savers, and Mr Eric J. Batson, the most generous person I have ever known, who not only assisted with research and provided important introductions to several English Shavians, but who read all of the proofs of this volume, correcting and advising invaluably, and then undertook the gargantuan task of indexing the entire edition.* My gratitude also knows no bounds as regards Miss Margery Hoyle of the British Museum, who interrupted often, with extraordinary equanimity, her own complex job of sorting and preparing for use the correspondence in the Shaw archive in order to respond to my various appeals. To Mr Bernard Burgunder, who has been building an enviable collection of Shaw manuscripts, rehearsal copies, and books for Cornell, my thanks for extending a collector's co-operation beyond the gift of photostats and the loan of numerous pertinent materials to the purchase from dealers or by auction of those items which I indicated to him would be valuable to me in my editorial endeavours. I am also pleased to make public acknowledgment of a large debt to my very patient editor, Mr J. B. Blackley, whose advice and services, too numerous to chronicle, have been a frequent assistance and comfort to me.

I should like here to offer a special note of thanks to that much harassed, overworked, and underpaid group of people known as the staff of the British Museum, who have in a thousand ways during the past fifteen years been partners in my research successes. From Keeper and Superintendent down to desk clerk and cart-pusher, they have my gratitude and, more, my affection. At Bloomsbury: Mr S. J. Arthur, Mr J. Mackenzie, Mr J. Saborin Morris, Dr Dennis Rhodes, Mr T. C. Skeat, Mr R. F. Sutton, Mr Derek H. Turner. At Colindale: Mr P. Allén, Mr A. G. Evans, Mr A. D. Holland, Mr M. M. Martin, and Mr W. D. Wilson, as well as the late James Barnes, Mr W. A. Charlotte, Mr Taffy Davies, Mr G. E. Johnson, Mr T. Newell, and Mr J. H. Poms.

My thanks too, for the loan or gift of manuscripts, transcriptions, photocopies, books, and associated papers, or for information or research assistance and numerous other kindnesses in the preparation of Volume One of this edition, to the following:

Mr C. G. Allen, Senior Assistant Librarian of the British Library of Political and Economic Science; Miss Elizabeth Anderson of William Heinemann Ltd; Miss M. Elizabeth Barber of the Society of Authors; Professor Joseph O. Baylen; Dr Claud Beatty; Mr Jacob Blanck; Mr Andrew Block; Mrs Ann Bowden; Mr Benjamin Bromberg; Dr Harold F. Brooks; Professor and

---

* Sorrowfully I must record the death of Mr Batson on 2nd May by a tragic accident, which occurred, before he had completed the index to this first volume. I am most grateful to Mrs Phyllis Cope, who generously undertook to complete the complex task, under the awful pressure of a printer's deadline, working from Mr Batson's notes, index outline, and marked galleys.

Mrs T.J.Brown; Mr R.F.C.Butcher, Senior Library Clerk of the House of Commons Library; Mr LaFayette Butler.

Mr Herbert Cahoon; the late Patrick Carroll of the Walter Hampden Memorial Library; Mr John Carter; Mr William D.Chase; Mr Cyril Clemens; the late Sir Sydney Cockerell; Miss Sarah Courtauld; Mrs Gladys Cremer, Librarian of the Fabian Society; Mr Ivo L.Currall; Miss Elizabeth de Haas; the late James H.Drake; Mr Marston Drake; the late Ashley Dukes; Miss Janet Dunbar; Mr Barry Duncan.

Professor Joel Egerer, Curator of the Fales Collection, New York University Library; Mr DeCoursey Fales; Mr Charles Feinberg; Mr Lew David Feldman of the House of El Dieff; Miss Elsa Forman; Samuel French Ltd.; Miss Mary Garnham, Librarian of the British Drama League; Miss Freda Gaye of the British Theatre Museum; Mr Karl Goedecke; Dr John D.Gordan, Curator of the Henry W. and Albert A.Berg Collection, New York Public Library.

Mme Henriette Hamon; Mr and Mrs T.Edward Hanley; Mr Godfrey Harding; Mrs Katharine S.Harris; Mr Rupert Hart-Davis; Mrs Ruth Hart-Davis; Miss Phyllis Hartnoll; Professor George Harris Healey of the Cornell University Library; the late Archibald Henderson; Mr Edward Hingers; the late David M. Holtzmann of the Shaw Society of America; Mr Richard Hughes; the late Professor William A.Jackson and Miss Carolyn Jakeman of the Houghton Library, Harvard University; Mr David Kirschenbaum of the Carnegie Book Shop.

Mr Allan M.Laing; Mr Corliss Lamont; Professor Cecil Lang of Syracuse University; Mr Edward Connery Lathem of the Baker Library, Dartmouth College; Mr Lawrence London, Curator of Rare Books, University of North Carolina Library; Miss Philippa MacLiesh of the Society of Authors; Mr John S.Maywood, Archivist of *The Times*, London; the late Earl Mesnier; Mr Harold Mortlake; Mr A.N.L.Munby of King's College, Cambridge University; Mr M.H.Mushlin; Mrs Georgina Chaworth Musters; Miss Winifred Myers; Mr George W. Nash, Curator of the Gertrude Enthoven Theatre Collection, Victoria and Albert Museum; Mr John O'Donovan.

Miss Blanche Patch; the late Hesketh Pearson; Mr Sam Pierce of the Museum of the City of New York; Sir James Pitman; Dr F.N.L.Poynter, Chief Librarian of the Wellcome Historical Medical Library; Mr Stanley J. Pryor; Mr Louis A. Rachow of the Walter Hampden Memorial Library; Mrs Oriole Riché; Miss Monique Russ; Mr John Ryder; Professor Stanley Rypins; Mrs Vera Scriabine of the New York Shavians; Miss Ellen Shaffer, Rare Books Librarian of the Free Library of Philadelphia; the late Louis H. Silver; Miss Barbara Smoker; Sotheby & Co; Mr Maxwell W.Steinhardt; Professor E.E.Stokes, Jr; the late Hannen Swaffer; the late Arthur Swann of the Parke-Bernet Galleries.

Mr Robert H.Taylor; Mrs Joan Troost; Mr C.K.J.Underhill, Secretary of the Passfield Trust; Mr Allen B.Veanor; the late Allan Wade; Mr Alexander D.Wainwright of the Princeton University Library; the late Dorothy Walker;

Miss May Wallas; Mr John Wardrop; Professor Stanley Weintraub, Editor of *The Shaw Review*; the late Dr Octavia Wilberforce; Mrs Shirley Williams of the Fabian Society; Mrs Marguerite Willson; Miss Marjorie Gray Wynne, Rare Books Librarian of the Yale University Library.

I am indebted also to the staffs of the following institutions and organisations: the Francis Bacon Society; Cornell University Library; Edward Laurence Doheny Library of St John's Seminary; Folger Shakespeare Library; Henry E. Huntington Library; Internationaal Instituut voor Sociale Geschiedenis; Library of Congress; London Library; Morgan Library; National Library of Ireland; National Library of Scotland; National Library of Wales; New York University Library; St Pancras Public Libraries; Sheffield Central Library; University of California Library (Los Angeles); University of Chicago Library; University of Illinois Library.

But of all the institutions to whom I have applied, unquestionably the most generous has been the Humanities Research Center of the University of Texas, whose director, Dr F. Warren Roberts, with the endorsement of the Chancellor, Dr Harry H. Ransom, allowed me to draw freely on all Shaw materials in the Center, and to publish the texts of several hundred Shaw letters from the Hanley and other collections, without which this edition would have been considerably impoverished.

I should like also to acknowledge the very substantial assistance of Mr Henry Allen Moe, Dr Gorden N. Ray, and the John Simon Guggenheim Foundation by the award of a Guggenheim Fellowship in 1960–61, and the gift of a grant-in-aid by New York University from the Arts and Science Research Fund.

Finally, my thanks to all those who kindly placed at my disposal Shaw materials which, owing to limitations of space, could not be included in the edition. And, as there must be innumerable caches of Shaw correspondence which I have not yet come upon, I should be most grateful for communications from readers who may be able to direct me to those letters before publication of subsequent volumes.

DAN H. LAURENCE

New York University,
University Heights.
March 1965

Code to description of correspondence

A Holograph letter
B Holograph letter-card
C Holograph postcard
D Holograph correspondence card
E Holograph note or "Compliments of Bernard Shaw" enclosure card
F Shorthand draft or copy
G Holograph draft or copy
H Typewritten letter
J Typewritten letter-card
K Typewritten postcard
L Dictated letter, in holograph of Charlotte Shaw, signed by Shaw
M Dictated letter-card, in holograph of Charlotte Shaw, signed by Shaw
N Dictated postcard, in holograph of Charlotte Shaw, signed by Shaw
P Dictated letter, in holograph of secretary, signed by Shaw
Q Dictated letter-card, in holograph of secretary, signed by Shaw
R Dictated postcard, in holograph of secretary, signed by Shaw
S Transcription: original unlocated
T Transcription: original located but unavailable for examination
U Photographic reproduction: original unlocated
V Photographic reproduction: original located but unavailable for examination
W Facsimile publication
X Published text
Y Telegram
t Typed signature
u Unsigned

NOTE

" *Diary, BM* " *refers to an autobiographical notebook covering 1876 to 1884, now in the Shaw archive in the British Museum. All other* " *Diary* " *references are to the thirteen diary volumes kept by Shaw between 1885 and 1897, now in the British Library of Political and Economic Science.*

Code to sources of
ownership of letters in this volume

NOTE

*The placement of an "e" after a code number in the
body of this work indicates that, in prior publication,
only an extract or severely truncated text of the
letter has appeared.*

1 Privately owned
2 British Museum
3 General Collections, Humanities Research Center, University of Texas
4 T.E. Hanley Collection, Humanities Research Center, University of Texas
5 Henry W. and Albert A. Berg Collection, New York Public Library
6 Houghton Library, Harvard University
7 Yale University Library
8 De Coursey Fales Collection, New York University Library
9 Bernard F. Burgunder Collection, Cornell University Library
10 Library of Congress
11 Princeton University Library
12 J. Harlin O'Connell Collection, Princeton University Library
13 British Library of Political and Economic Science
14 Passfield Trust Papers, British Library of Political and Economic Science
15 Heal Collection, St Pancras Public Libraries
16 Sheffield Central Library
17 King's College Library, Cambridge University
18 National Library of Scotland
19 University of California Library, Los Angeles
20 University of Chicago Library
21 Free Library of Philadelphia
22 Society of Authors Archive
23 Baker Library, Dartmouth College
24 Edward Laurence Doheny Memorial Library, St John's Seminary
25 Henry E. Huntington Library
26 University of Illinois Library

27 Fabian Society
28 Internationaal Instituut voor Sociale Geschiedenis, Amsterdam
29 National Library of Wales
30 British Theatre Museum
31 Arents Collection, New York Public Library
32 William Morris Gallery, Walthamstow
33 Division of Special Collections, New York University Library

Code to sources of prior publication

101 F. E. Loewenstein, "Do You Remember, Mr. Shaw?" *Adam*, August 1946
102 Archibald Henderson, "Bernard Shaw's Novels: And Why They Failed." *Dalhousie Review*, Winter 1954-5
103 "The Love Letters of Bernard Shaw." *Esquire*, April 1958
104 Blanche Patch, *Thirty Years with G. B. S.* (1951)
105 Charles Morgan, *The House of Macmillan* (1943)
106 Bowes and Bowes, Cambridge, Catalogue 523 (1950)
107 Sotheby & Company, Catalogue of sale, 16 December 1958
108 C. Archer, *William Archer: Life, Work and Friendships* (1931)
109 *Letters from George Bernard Shaw to Miss Alma Murray* (1927); *More Letters . . .* (1932)
110 Frederic Whyte, *Life of W. T. Stead* (1925)
111 Raphael King, London, Catalogue 33 (1939)
112 H. Saxe Wyndham, *August Manns and the Saturday Concerts* (1909)
113 Archibald Henderson, *George Bernard Shaw: His Life and Work* (1911)
114 Ernest Rhys, *Letters from Limbo* (1936)
115 Clifford Bax (ed.), *Florence Farr, Bernard Shaw and W. B. Yeats* (1941)
116 Archibald Henderson, *Bernard Shaw: Playboy and Prophet* (1932)
117 Christopher St John (ed.), *Ellen Terry and Bernard Shaw: A Correspondence* (1931)
118 Raphael King, London, Catalogue 5 (1929)
119 C. E. M. Joad (ed.), *Shaw and Society* (1953)
120 American Art Association, Catalogue of Marsden J. Perry sale, 11–12 March 1936
121 Grant Richards, *Memories of a Misspent Youth* (1932)
122 Maggs Brothers, London, Catalogue 877 (1961)

123 Michael Orme, *J.T.Grein: The Story of a Pioneer* (1936)
124 Doris Arthur Jones, *The Life and Letters of Henry Arthur Jones* (1930)
125 Bernard Shaw, *Advice to a Young Critic*, ed. E.J.West (1955)
126 Frank Harris, *Bernard Shaw* (1931)
127 Paul Wilstach, *Richard Mansfield: The Man and the Actor* (1909)
128 *Actors' Society Monthly Bulletin*, February 1904
129 *Yale University Library Gazette*, October 1937
130 Ashley Dukes, "A Doll's House and the Open Door." *Theatre Arts*, January 1928
131 *Labour Leader*, 21 December 1895
132 Robert Buchanan, *Is Barabbas a Necessity?* (1896)
133 Laurence Irving, *Henry Irving: The Actor and His World* (1952)
134 Erwin McCall, *The Martyrdom of Percy Whitcomb* (1897)
135 Grant Richards, *Author Hunting* (1934)
136 St John Ervine, *Bernard Shaw: His Life, Work and Friends* (1956)
137 "The Cleveland Street Scandals." *Encounter*, September 1954
138 American Art Association, Catalogue of sale, 18 December 1928
139 *The Flying Dutchman* (Hofstra College student newspaper), 22 November 1957
140 Thomas Okey, *A Basketful of Memories* (1930)
141 Archibald Henderson, *George Bernard Shaw: Man of the Century* (1956)
142 Robert Liddell Lowe, "Two Shaw Letters." *Modern Language Review*, October 1958
143 Unsigned note, in "Occasional Notes." *Pall Mall Gazette*, 17 September 1888
144 Doris Langley Moore, *E. Nesbit: A Biography* (1933)
145 Rupert Hart-Davis (ed.), *The Letters of Oscar Wilde* (1962)
146 *The Clarion*, 13 February 1897
147 Patrick J. Hogan Jr and J.O.Baylen, "G. Bernard Shaw and W.T.Stead." *Studies in English Literature 1500–1900*, Autumn 1961
148 Mrs T.P.O'Connor, *I Myself* (1910)
149 Joseph O. Baylen, "George Bernard Shaw and the Socialist League." *International Review of Social History*, VII, Part 3 (1962)
150 Tighe Hopkins, "Anonymity?" *New Review*, March 1890
151 Janet Dunbar, *Mrs. G.B.S.: A Portrait* (1963)
152 Stephen Winsten, *Jesting Apostle* (1956)
153 "When G.B.S. Was Rejected." *Sunday Times*, 11 July 1948

PART I

1874-1876

(1874–1876)

George Bernard Shaw was born on 26th July 1856, at No. 3 Upper Synge Street, Dublin. He had two older sisters, Lucinda Frances ("Lucy"), born in 1853, and Elinor Agnes ("Yuppy"), born in 1855.

Their father, George Carr Shaw (born 1814), was a former civil servant who had sold his pension to enable him to enter into a partnership as a grain merchant. Although he was related to Sir Robert Shaw of Bushy Park and to the Recorder of Dublin, he was himself but a "Protestant merchant-gentleman and feudal downstart," as his son later acknowledged, whose awareness that several of his siblings enjoyed more prosperous circumstances and unchallengeable social positions led him to drown his self-consciousness and insecurity in drink. It was not, his son recorded, "a convivial weakness," but "a neurosis, pathological, miserable."

In 1852, after a brief courtship, George Carr Shaw married Lucinda Elizabeth Gurly (born 1830), a genteel and unworldly young woman, who had the misfortune to be seeking almost frantically an escape from a boorish, somewhat tyrannical father and the domestic slavery she had known in the home of a maiden aunt after the early death of her mother.

What she accomplished was the barter of Scylla for Charybdis. The marriage was a complete failure. The husband who had seemed to be a quite eligible if middle-aged bachelor turned out to be impecunious and unsuccessful, an alcoholic, and, perhaps worst of all, a reserved, uninteresting man, whose social withdrawal eventually led to his being dubbed "The Hermit" by his children and their friends. His only gift to his son seems to have been an extraordinary sense of the ludicrous, which manifested itself in the mockery of solemnity.

Mrs Shaw's salvation proved to be a mezzo-soprano voice of remarkable tonal purity, which she undertook to cultivate through singing lessons. The person she turned to was George John Vandeleur Lee, a crippled eccentric, well known in Dublin musical circles as an orchestral conductor, entrepreneur, and teacher, who boasted of a "Method" for singing which is supposed to have performed miracles for his mesmerised pupil. She was soon performing under Lee's direction in amateur recitals and opera performances in the Antient Concert Rooms in Brunswick Street, composing and publishing musical settings for popular verses (at first under the pseudonym "Hilda," later in London under her own name), and with increasing frequency abandoning her domestic and maternal responsibilities.

Her son's formal education was brief but complicated. Once he outgrew the influence of a governess, Miss Caroline Hill, he was turned over to a clerical uncle, the Rev. William George Carroll, for Latin instruction. Thereafter came a dizzying succession of educational "prisons": the Wesleyan Connexional School, where the pupil, according to his later testimony, learned nothing—but was recipient on two occasions of good conduct certificates; a private school at Glasthule, near Dalkey; the Central Model Boys' School in Marlborough Street (a mortifying experience for a snobbish young Protestant, for it was a Roman Catholic institution); and the Dublin English Scientific and Commercial Day School in Aungier Street, from which he departed in 1871, at the age of fifteen, to seek employment.

Shaw's genuine education came from an early saturation in music, literature, art, and drama. Vandeleur Lee and the Shaws had entered into a peculiar but innocent arrangement whereby they shared a domicile at No. 1 Hatch Street, and later a cottage at Dalkey; from the music lessons and rehearsals that filled the air, young Shaw learned to recognise and to sing or whistle, before he was twelve, all the principal works of Handel, Haydn, Mozart, Beethoven, Rossini, Bellini, Donizetti, and Verdi. He read with avidity Shakespeare, Dickens, Scott, Bunyan, Trollope, and popular "bloods" or "shockers" in penny parts. He spent hours gazing at the old masters in the Dublin National Gallery until he could identify at sight their unique styles. And he was an habitual visitor to the Royal Theatre in Dawkins Street, where for two shillings he could crowd into the pit for a glimpse of such popular performers as Barry Sullivan, Sam Johnson, or Peter Granby, emerging from the crush with "all my front buttons down the middle of my back."

The frequent change of schools, coupled with the fact that by nature he was as shy and retiring as his father, resulted in young Shaw becoming almost totally self-reliant and self-sufficient. Among his contemporaries he had only one close friend, Matthew Edward McNulty, with whom he shared his ideas and his dreams. The two studied art together, Shaw enrolling briefly for late afternoon courses in the Royal Academy of Art, and they read and criticised each other's literary endeavours. The influence of the theatre upon young George Shaw early manifested itself in now lugubrious, now roistering, but always gory verse drama. His first serious effort appears to have been a verse play, illustrated by the author, entitled "Strawberrinos: or, the Haunted Winebin." Its hero, Strawberrinos, underwent a series of breath-taking adventures

4

which were constantly capped by the supernatural skills of a sardonic demon. In the play's great incantation scene the demon sang a refrain:

> Fill the magic cup!
>   Drink it with a will;
> If it doesn't save your life
>   It is pretty sure to kill—
>   A saline draught and a big blue pill!

to which the chorus, emphatically and menacingly, echoed: "A big blue pill!"

After his withdrawal from school in 1871 Shaw accepted employment as a junior clerk in the firm of Uniacke Townshend & Co., "a highly exclusive gentlemanly estate office," he later recorded, "crowded with premium paying apprentices who, being mostly university graduates, were fully up to Shaw standards of gentility, and were addressed as Mister while I was plain Shaw."

In 1873 Vandeleur Lee came to a decision that was to have an immediate, devastating effect upon the Shaw household. Dissatisfied with the limitations imposed upon his art by Dublin's provincialism and parochialism, Lee conducted his final Dublin concert on 26th May 1873, and almost instantly deserted his native city for London. Mrs Shaw, with equal abruptness, packed her bags and followed after him, sailing from Dunleary on 17th June, deserting her husband and two of her children (for she carried only Agnes with her) on her twenty-first wedding anniversary. Shortly thereafter she sent for Lucy. Only once did she return, in March 1874, to supervise the transfer of her husband and son from Hatch Street into lodgings near by.

At last, George Shaw decided that he too had had enough of Dublin. Early in 1876 he proceeded to cut his moorings by resigning his cashier's position in the land agency. Perhaps the reason for his departure was, as he rationalised in the preface to *Immaturity*, because failure, poverty, obscurity, and the ostracism and contempt which these implied were all that Dublin offered to "the enormity of my unconscious ambition." Perhaps, however, he was motivated more simply by a desire to escape from the scene of an aborted romance, which he subsequently labelled "the Calypso infatuation," and of which he was to versify shortly after his arrival in London:

> Then farewell, oh bewitching Calypso
> Thou didst shake my philosophy well

5

> But believe me, the next time I trip so
> No poem shall tell. (BM)

He departed for England on 31st March, four days after the death of his sister Agnes, of consumption, at Ventnor, Isle of Wight.

To LUCINDA FRANCES SHAW

[A/4]

1 Hatch Street
4th March 1874. 1 o.C a.m.

[This letter, the earliest on record, to Shaw's elder sister in London corrects some erroneous impressions perpetuated by his biographers, establishing that Shaw and his father did not remove to lodgings at 61 Harcourt Street until more than nine months after Mrs Shaw had left Dublin to follow Vandeleur Lee to London (a full three years later than the date assigned by Archibald Henderson), and that Mrs Shaw, far from deserting her husband and son completely, had returned to Dublin to effect their transfer. *Out of Court* was one of several three-decker novels written by Mrs Cashel Hoey (Frances "Fanny" Johnston), daughter of Mrs Shaw's half-sister Charlotte. Shaw's appeal to Lucy for publishing information tends to confirm the belief of her biographer Henry G. Farmer that she had been selling (or attempting to sell) stories to the London journals. Matthew Edward McNulty (1856–1943) was Shaw's school companion and lifelong friend, who later became infatuated briefly with Lucy. Although McNulty entered the banking profession, he published four novels and several plays, two of which (*The Lord Mayor* and *The Courting of Mary Doyle*) were produced by the Abbey Theatre.]

Cara Lucia

I am sorry to say that I have read your letter. I shall take especial care not to do so again for you really are worthy of your parent in the matter of verbosity and far more personal. Your remarks are most offensive. Let my nose alone, better a bottle than a peony. Did the Mar mention that the cat has got mange as well as Paddy. It has no hair at all on its head which adds to its already prepossessing appearance. Mamma on arriving [in Dublin] sat down in the cab with such violence that she burst open the door which I had to hold shut during the rest of the journey [to Hatch Street]. I wish you joy of the reading of "Out of Court." In gratitude for the treat it will only be good taste to find fault with the grammar, cough loudly at the affecting passages, and whenever a character is mentioned ask absently who's this he or she was. When the book is thrown at your head you may be satisfied with the effect produced. However I did not write to say all this and merely write it as a concession to your taste for rubbish. I want to know

7

where one can get their writings published and paid for. In what journal. What is the best opening. I want this for my own sake partly but immediately for the benefit of a friend of mine, a genius, I think Agnes recollects McNulty, a corpulent youth with curly black hair. He is in want of money and wants to find out where he can get it for writing. I shall regard it as a favor if you will give me the extent of your information on the subject. I will also regard it as a favour if you will be as concise as possible, your style of communication with the mar being unnecessarily voluminous. I have found in the house a great bundle of stuff and whether it is red worsted or Agnes's hair I don't know.

yrs
GBShaw

To LUCINDA FRANCES SHAW

61 Harcourt Street
24th February 1875

[A/4]

[Vandeleur Lee and his partner Richard Michael Levey (1811–99), who edited the *Annals* (1821–80) *of the Theatre Royal, Dublin* (1880), had first produced Bellini's *La Sonnambula* at the Theatre Royal, Dublin, on 31st March 1873, with "Miss Lucy Shaw" as Amina. Lee himself conducted the performance. Whether the production was repeated in London is uncertain, but Lucy did appear in London as the Queen of Spain in Marchetti's *Ruy Blas* for Lee's amateur opera series, of which Major Wallace Carpenter was the impresario, and for which Alfred Moul (d. 1924), later a successful composer and voice teacher and director of the Alhambra, apparently served as rehearsal pianist, a task later undertaken by Shaw. Lucy, who intensely disliked Lee and was reluctant to work under his direction, soon turned professional, making her theatrical début, under the name Frances Carr, in the pantomime *Beauty and the Beast* at the Royal Park, Camden Town, on Christmas Eve 1879. Subsequently she joined the Carl Rosa Opera Company, making her first appearance as Arline in Balfe's *The Bohemian Girl* at the Theatre Royal, Huddersfield, on 23rd September 1881. Although Shaw tended always to deprecate Lucy's abilities as a singer and especially as an actress, the critic of the *Huddersfield Examiner* reported: "She has a sweet small voice of very fair compass and quality, has a pleasing manner, and gave evidence of artistic and histrionic ability beyond what might have been expected from a *debutante* . . . As the opera proceeded Miss Carr gained confidence, and sang exceedingly well . . . showing some capital vocalisation and phrasing." In 1884, as Lucy Carr Shaw, a name she retained profession-

8

ally the rest of her life, she embarked on a two years' tour of the provinces with a D'Oyly Carte company, appearing as Celia in *Iolanthe*, Ella in *Patience*, Josephine in *Pinafore*, Aline in *The Sorcerer*, and in the title rôle of *Princess Ida*.

Oughterard was the family seat of the Shaws, near Galway in Western Ireland, from 1802, and later became the home of Shaw's maternal grandfather Walter Bagnall Gurly. Ada Cavendish (1839–95), who achieved her first notable success at the Olympic, London, in Wilkie Collins's *The New Magdalen*, made frequent provincial tours. Luigi Agnesi (1833–75), a basso, was best known for his singing of Rossini in the true Italian style at Drury Lane; he died on 2nd February.]

My dear Lucy

I am much obliged to you for going to the bother of writing out all this business for me. It is just what I expected, the old story. I think you have acted with too much forbearance, or at least, too little decision. In the first place I consider Carpenter's letter simply impertinent, and I think you ought to have sat on him. If anybody wrote me a letter taking me to task in that way, I would give him to understand that I considered it a liberty rather, in point of fact convey to him the vulgar intimation that he should keep his advice until it was asked for. And poor Moul likewise. However it's too late now. As to Lee, I would decline to listen to him. We all know what his tirades are worth, and I think his coming to Victoria Grove and launching out at you as he did, simply outrageous. The sum of my advice to you is, to cultivate of all things, serene philosophy. Never under any circumstances lose temper, and never let yourself be put out. If you are, don't shew it. They have not been acting squarely with you at all, they are afraid of you, don't understand you in the least, and consequently have fallen into a wretched policy of half coaxing and half coercing, by indirect influences and threats. Now, you know what is right, just as well as I do. If you keep to that, declining to recognise any petty bits of expediency, or to humour anybody's wrongheadedness, you are quite safe. You are quite clear as to what you are doing, you know why you are doing it and so you have only to be immoveable, polite, generally amiable, and adamant. If Major Carpenter, or any other enthusiastic individual pens homilies to you, decline to receive them. If Mamma argues, call things by their proper names, be excessively polite to her, and she will at last see that there is not the smallest use in it. As to Lee, he is simply hopeless and incorrigible. Don't mind him at all. On the conducting stool, he is a talented man, anywhere else, he is to be avoided. He should engage an acting manager, and never interfere in business matters himself. His considering you the most vicious of created beings need not occasion you any uneasiness, in fact it's a compliment. Marlowe was a ruffian, a Jesuit, a thoroughly bad man, because he did not appreciate nonsense. Now, as far as the above takes the shape of "advice," I give it principally because you ask me for it. It is superfluous for two reasons. Firstly, because nobody ever takes advice. Secondly, because I have quite as much faith in your instinct as in my own, and because a man's instinct does not always fall in exactly with a woman's. As the case stands, I really don't see any difficulty at all. Why refuse the Sonnambula point blank? If it is ever done, of course you will do it. It gives you something to do. Don't pledge yourself to do it at all. But there is no reason why you shouldn't do it, that I can see except the objection to worry. Your position is, "I decline to be worried, fight away among yourselves. If you ever bring the thing to a producible state, here I am, if not, it's your own fault, only if you take the initiative and begin to worry, I withdraw." As you know these rows always evaporate, it seems to be absurd to talk seriously about them, but I think if you kept a firm straight line, and kept rigidly on the right side, half of them might be avoided. You are prone to sulkiness. Drop that, and when you *do* go to rehearsals, go as if you had some interest in the affair, and not in the Clara Doherty style, inspiring everybody present with an intense desire to knock your head against the wall. If people bother you to sing when you don't want, never resort to rudeness as I expect you sometimes do, chaff is the best expedient. So long as the point is ultimately carried it may as well be done pleasantly as not. And be sure you do carry the point, for if you don't people will think you are doing the coy maiden and want to be coaxed. You ought to laugh at Mamma more than you do. If you get sulky with her, she becomes pugnacious and obstinate, but she is easily laughed out of her ideas. In particular, if she threatens you with seclusion at Oughterard make a standing joke of it against her at once. It is a sound and fury, signifying nothing. I am going to write to her now, telling her that I have betrayed her to you so completely, that there is no use in her keeping her back up and affecting dignity. It is absurd that there should be any misunderstanding between you at all. If there is an easy chair at Brompton, cultivate it. When you collapse back into a comfortable chair and smile blandly, you really feel philosophical, and not likely to make a mountain of a molehill. I don't know whether I make you understand my view of the case exactly, for ink is an unsympathetic medium of communication. Don't forget what I say about your sulkiness & lassitude. I am certain you are often horribly aggravating, in addition to which (being my sister) you are lazy and perpetually postponing going in at anything till next week, you require some extra good humour to give airiness to these faults. Are you going to get married? In love with anyone? I fell wildly, madly, suicidally in love with the New Magdalen, Miss Ada Cavendish. I had up the most exquisite imitation of her in the part, and also of her "Charge of the Light Brigade," which was the most bewitchingly abominable recitation I ever heard. I suppose you know Agnesi's dead. You might report progress, and favour me with an odd letter occasionally if not too lazy.

yrs
GBShaw

To LUCINDA ELIZABETH SHAW

61 Harcourt Street
[A/4]   24th October [*sic*] 1875

[The content of this letter to Shaw's mother establishes that, despite its inexplicably being dated October, it was written on the same day as was the previous letter to Lucy: 24th February.]

My respected Parent

I write to tell you that you may as well drop all your dignity with Lucy. You are basely betrayed. Stunned by the torrent of deprecation weekly hurled at me by the governor, I wrote to Lucy to tell me all about it. I told her everything you said about her. I told her not to mind you when you threatened Oughterard. I told her all! All! ALL! I trust you may not catch it on her return to the maternal bosom. I trust you have not caught it already. I trust that no profane language rises involuntarily to your lips as you peruse these words. I know that you will love me as you never did before for my straightforward conduct. I feel that even now you are wishing you could kiss me. But I must forbear to dwell longer on the touching subject. Lucy, in return gave *her* statement of the case, gave a copy of her rude point blank refusal to Carpenter, and of his gentlemanly and unobtrusive reply. Permit me to suggest that in future you should adopt a more honest line of policy with respect to her, and tell her whatever you have to say plainly and in the first instance directly to her instead of taking refuge in a system of worry and indirect knagging which would infuriate Job. And don't make an awful row about these musical businesses which are always impending and always evaporating. Lee is ruined you say.

My dear mother, the same calamity has occurred on an average three hundred & sixtyfive times a year, during my experience of him. Get up the Sonnambula, *stop worrying Lucy*, act like sensible people (if possible) and you will have your Amina all safe enough, I believe. I heard from her in reply to my letter, tonight. She doesn't complain of being ill used, she simply states the case, which is confirmed by my old experience, of the usual unbusinesslike, wearisome rubbish, & vituperation of everybody and everything, which is inseparable from Lee's "acting management." What I have just now written to Lucy I repeat to you. Advise Lee to get a man to do the business part of the work for him, there are dozens of fools only too glad to be called secretaries to this & that amateur performance. Let Lee then confine himself as much as possible to the music, in that department he is unsurpassed, and he will not be ruined half so often. I may venture to remind you, although I believe Lucy will not object to do the operas, that she has a perfect right to refuse if she likes and that she was not born for the express purpose of being given parts in anything that turns up. I have been giving her some good advice, and am secretly convinced that you want it a great deal worse. Out of evil comes good, and out of all this trouble comes enjoyment for me. I laugh as I picture the dismay, the rage, the elevation of your back, with which you will greet this. I give you warning that there is no use in trying to crush me. Now don't seize a pen and start off, "My dear George, I am considerably surprised to read" &c or "I am at a loss to understand &c." If within the next week I get anything commencing like that, I shall hand it over to the governor as being more in his line than in mine. Treat it with silent contempt, I implore you. If you are anxious to know what I said to Lucy, I have no doubt she will shew you my letters and you are quite welcome to shew her this. Meanwhile I have the honor to remain, dear mother, your affectionate & dutiful son

G BShaw

To C. UNIACKE TOWNSHEND

[S/4; X/101]

[61 Harcourt Street]
23rd March 1875

[On 26th October 1871, through the influence of his uncle, R. Frederick Shaw, who was until his death Chief of the Land Valuation Office, Shaw obtained a position as office boy ("junior clerk I called myself") to a "leading and terribly respectable" firm of land agents, headed by Charles Uniacke Townshend (1829–1907). In February 1873, when "the most active and responsible official of the office," the cashier George Wilson Irvin, suddenly absconded, Shaw found himself employed as a "stopgap" until a new cashier "of appropriate age and responsibility" could be obtained. "Immediately the machine worked again quite smoothly. I, who never knew how much money I had of my own . . . proved a model of accuracy as to the money of others. I acquired my predecessor's very neat handwriting, my own being too sloped and straggly for the cash book. The efforts to fill my important place more worthily slackened. . . . My salary was raised to £48 a year, which was as much as I expected at sixteen and much less than the firm would have had to pay a competent adult: in short, I made good in spite of myself, and found, to my dismay, that Business, instead of expelling me as the worthless impostor I was, was fastening upon me with no intention of letting me go." (Preface, *Immaturity*, 1930.) After his experience with Shaw's predecessor, however, Townshend took the precaution of having the new cashier bonded, by the London Guarantee & Accident Co., on 5th March 1873. On the reverse of the draft of his letter, Shaw noted: "to C.U.T. on second renewal of guarantee. Written at his instance."]

Dear Sir

As you have consented, at my request, and in consideration of my objection to ask for private security, to accept that of a company, I beg to enclose you receipt for the renewal of same to March 1876, and to thank you for waiving your claim to a more satisfactory guarantee.

truly yours
G B Shaw

To HENRY PEASE

[G/31]

61 Harcourt Street
24th January 1876

[Henry Pease (1807–81) was a railway projector, whose father had constructed in 1825 the first railway line in England, from Stockton to Darlington. *Public Opinion*, on 22nd January, reported under the heading "Literary": "Mr. Henry Pease, of Darlington, has offered a premium of £50 for the best essay on the evils of smoking among the young." It was in the correspondence column of this London weekly news digest, on 3rd April 1875, that Shaw's first public literary effort had appeared, it being a secularist attack on the American evangelists Dwight Lyman Moody (1837–99) and Ira D. Sankey (1840–1908), who had held a revival meeting in Dublin.]

Dear Sir

In last weeks issue of Public Opinion appears a paragraph stating that you have offered a prize of £50, for the best essay on the evils of smoking; but giving no further particulars as to the conditions of competition, or the time allowed for preparing the essays.

If you will supply me with the necessary information, or let me know to whom I should apply, I shall feel much obliged.

yrs
GBShaw

To C. UNIACKE TOWNSHEND

61 Harcourt Street
[S/4; X/101]   29th February 1876

[Just when Shaw made his decision to leave Dublin for London is uncertain. Those familiar, however, with his frugal nature as a young man and his obsession for giving and receiving full value will appreciate his remaining at his post up to the very last day for which he had paid for bonding.]

Dear Sir

I beg to give you notice that at the end of next month, I shall leave your office.

My reason is, that I object to receive a salary for which I give no adequate value. Not having enough to do, it follows that the little I have is not well done. When I ceased to act as Cashier I anticipated this, and have since become satisfied that I was right.

Under these circumstances I prefer to discontinue my services & remain

very truly yours
G. B. Shaw

PART II

1876-1884

II
(1876–1884)

Immediately upon his arrival in England, Shaw joined his bereaved mother and Lucy at Ventnor, where he remained for a month. When he proceeded to London he was, as his journal indicates, "unoccupied." He applied without result to numerous friends of his relatives for employment; by September he was reduced to paying three and a half guineas for a cram course in Excise preparatory to taking a Civil Service examination. It was Vandeleur Lee who rescued Shaw from anxiety and poverty by accepting a post as musical critic to a satiric weekly, *The Hornet*, and privately arranging for his prodigy to write the notices and receive the emoluments. The deception was successfully sustained for nearly a year.

When this employment ceased, Shaw made only sporadic, half-hearted attempts to find another position, for, convinced by this time that his genius lay in creative writing, he preferred to ply his pen prodigiously, though uncommercially, while simultaneously "improving" himself through the study of harmony, counterpoint, French, and Italian. For seven months, in 1879–80, he laboured for the Edison Telephone Company, but thereafter he would not permit himself to be burdened by routine commercial employment. "If a writer has to rob his mother," William Faulkner once stated, "he will not hesitate; the 'Ode on a Grecian Urn' is worth any number of old ladies." That Shaw subscribed to the same view of artistic dedication and personal sacrifice is evident in his preface (1905) to *The Irrational Knot*: "I did not throw myself into the struggle for life: I threw my mother into it. I was not a staff to my father's old age: I hung on to his coat tails . . . Callous as Comus to moral babble, I steadily wrote my five pages a day and made a man of myself (at my mother's expense) instead of a slave."

His father might grumble: "You are an illnatured cur, that, you would not once in a way, say 6 or 12 months, drop me a few lines no matter whether you have anything to say or not" (28th March 1881; BM). His sister might encourage his mother to throw the parasite out of the house. No matter. The writing went on, until five novels were completed. They were "all jejune and rotten," Shaw informed Frederick Evans in 1895, but "if I had never written the five long novels and the bushel of articles that were refused I should not have been able to do the work that finally offered itself to me." In an interview in 1929 he informed Sewell Stokes that "one *must* learn to write first. Then, once you know your job, there is no need to bother with it any more. All you have to do is to say what you have to say, without the bother of considering how to say it." This lesson was Shaw's great accomplishment between 1879 and 1883.

In his early twenties Shaw was a provincial bumpkin, sorely conscious of his impoverished appearance (though he conscientiously trimmed his cuffs with a scissors and wore his tall hat reversed so that the brim should not bend double when he doffed it to an acquaintance), and suffering from hesitancy of speech and a general *gaucherie*. Determinedly, however, he strove to educate himself. He pored over books on etiquette in the British Museum; he forced himself to accept social invitations, such as the "at homes" of Lady Wilde; gradually he developed self-confidence and imperturbability through membership and persistent participation in debating societies. His circle of friends enlarged steadily, among them the poet Richard Hengist Horne and his wife Sophie, the young exchequer clerk and phonetician who signed himself "jeemz leki," the Alsatian *basso profundo* Richard Deck (who instructed Shaw in the voice control "method" of Delsarte), the amateur pugilist Pakenham Beatty, the physician J. Kingston Barton and his brother William, at whose home Shaw spent most of his Saturday evenings.

The greatest single influence on Shaw's life at this time, however, was the economist Henry George, whom he heard speak on Land Nationalisation and Single Tax at the nonconformist Memorial Hall in Farringdon Street on 5th September 1882. The handsome, eloquent American apostle, said Shaw, struck him dumb and instantly converted him from barren agnostic disputation to economics. Shaw read George's *Progress and Poverty* and the first volume of Marx's *Capital* (in Deville's French translation, there being as yet no English translation of the work), and he attended meetings of H. M. Hyndman's Social Democratic Federation. Eventually he rejected the "pseudo-Marxist" S.D.F. and embraced the newly founded Fabian Society, which appealed to "educated middle-class intelligentsia: my own class in fact," and which elected him to membership on 5th September 1884, and to its Executive Committee on 2nd January 1885.

From the chrysalis there now emerged the suave, persuasive, dynamic being whom London, and then the world, shortly was to know as "G.B.S."

18

Ventnor, April 1876

To MATTHEW EDWARD McNULTY

[X/152.e]

[13 Victoria Grove SW]
3rd June 1876

[McNulty, in his late years, drafted a lengthy (and frequently inaccurate) memoir of his long association with Shaw, in which he noted that he had once been requested by Shaw to destroy all the early correspondence he had received from the latter, and that he had instantly complied. Stephen Winsten, however, in his *Jesting Apostle* (1956), reproduced a portion of what was purported to be the first letter from Shaw to McNulty after his arrival in London. No source was provided for this bit of exaggerative autobiography.]

I did not burn my boats for the sake of a flame. My prospects in Dublin were stupendous. The employer's daughter would have been mine for the asking and partnership in the firm assured. The only obstacle to the fortune was that I cared neither for the post nor for the daughter, not insuperable, I admit. I was full of politics and religion and these were, as you know, forbidden. Here am I, in London, without the credentials of a peasant immigrant and I still bear traces of the Shaw snobbery which considers manual work contemptible, and on no account will I enter an office again. You are the only person in the world to whom I am a person with an identity and a soul. That is why I cling to you. Strangely enough I am not in the least depressed, but elated, if anything, because it had to be.

I have a notion hazy that mother thinks me crazy and Lucy thinks me lazy.

To PAKENHAM BEATTY

[G/2]

13 Victoria Grove SW
1st November 1878

[Pakenham Thomas Beatty (1855–1930) was born of Irish parents at Maranhão, Brazil; although he spent part of his boyhood at Dalkey, he and Shaw did not meet until they both came to London. Beatty, a dilettante with a penchant for Swinburnean poetry, educated at Harrow and Bonn, living on

19

an inheritance which he rapidly squandered, was an avid amateur pugilist. It was through him that Shaw was introduced to Ned Donnelly, Professor of Boxing to the London Athletic Club, from whom Shaw received sparring lessons, and who was the model for Ned Skene in *Cashel Byron's Profession*. On 17th March 1883 Beatty and Shaw actually applied for participation in the Amateur Boxing Championship at Lillie Bridge Grounds (Shaw, who weighed barely 10 stone [140 pounds], entered both Middle and Heavy Weight classes), but though their names appeared on the official programme, they were not chosen for competition. Shaw was very fond of the idealistic Beatty, despite his profligate ways and lack of practicality, and Beatty's influence on Shaw may be traced from *Cashel Byron's Profession* to several of the plays. Beatty's nickname, Paquito, for example, supplied the alias for Captain Brassbound, while his act of christening his son Mazzini after the great Italian revolutionist received Shavian commentary in *Heartbreak House*, when Hesione Hushabye relates that "Mazzini was a celebrity of some kind who knew Ellie's grandparents. They were both poets, like the Brownings; and when her father came into the world Mazzini said 'Another soldier born for freedom!' So they christened him Mazzini; and he has been fighting for freedom in his quiet way ever since. Thats why he is so poor." The book of poems, Beatty's first, was *To My Lady and Other Poems*, published in November.

Mrs Collier was one of several London hostesses who sought to befriend the awkward, lonely young Shaw. She may have been the E.A.Collier who sent Shaw a religious medal to wear; at the time of her letter he noted: "Received on the 21st March 1878, with a medal of the Virgin Mary enclosed. Agreed to wear for 6 mos & discarded it accordingly 21/9/78." The tiny medal, affixed to a black cord, survives in the British Museum archive, Shaw having preserved it all his life.]

Many thanks for your letter, which I received two days ago from Mrs Collier. The books have not yet been delivered so I am still in an attitude of expectancy, for keeping me in which, I trust that the printer may be punished hereafter. I hope to write to you again when I have read the poems. If you leave your present address in the meantime, perhaps you would let me know.

G B Shaw

To G.R.SIMS

[G/2]

13 Victoria Grove SW
18th September 1879

[After his first brief fling as a "ghost" musical critic for *The Hornet* (November 1876–September 1877), Shaw made no further attempt to ply his pen until late in 1878. Throughout 1879 he submitted about a dozen essays to numerous publications, the subjects ranging from orchestral conducting to oakum picking, but only two found their way into print. The first, "Opera in Italian," was accepted by the editor, Charles Mackeson, for the *Saturday Musical Review*, where it appeared, unsigned and unpaid for, on 22nd February 1879. The second, "Christian Names," was accepted by George Robert Sims (1847–1922), editor of *One and All*, who became celebrated as "Dagonet" in *The Referee*. Shaw, unaware that most London journals paid for contributions only upon publication, apparently had assumed, when the acceptance letter was unaccompanied by a cheque, that he was not to be paid for his essay. When it appeared, on 11th October 1879, Shaw received payment of fifteen shillings, the first literary money he had ever earned under his own name, though that name had still not appeared in print.]

Dear Sir

I am much gratified by your acceptance of my article "Christian Names." At the same time, as I am not an amateur, may I ask whether, in the event of my sending you any further contributions, it will be worth your while to remunerate me for them?

truly yours
G. B. Shaw

To ARNOLD WHITE

[G.u/4; X/101.e]   13 Victoria Grove SW
                                                     5th October 1879

[Arnold White was manager and secretary of the Edison Telephone Company of London, to whom Shaw received an introduction from his cousin Mrs Cashel Hoey. The novel which he was revising was *Immaturity*, which he had begun in March 1879 and which was completed on 28th September 1879 (after which it was twice revised, the final revision being completed on 3rd January 1881). Shaw eventually submitted it to ten publishers (an eleventh, Sampson Low, declined even to read it), but it remained unpublished until its author included it in his Collected Edition in 1930. It was not, however, Shaw's first attempt at a novel. Though he never revealed the fact during his lifetime, he had begun in 1878 to outline a novel, which he called *The Legg Papers*. The surviving notes reveal that the work was to be a narrative by one Priday Morgan Legg (uncle to Newcastle Legg, the hero), which was being edited for publication by the Reverend Epaminondas Gentleflower. The localities were established as the family residence at Gelston Legbury, Sockbank School, and Country View, the home of Jupiter

Beedleby, whose daughter Sylvia presumably was to have been Shaw's first heroine. The novel was abandoned almost immediately, however, and a few months later Shaw turned to the autobiographical material which emerged as his "first" novel, *Immaturity*. The presence of a central character named Zeno Legge in Shaw's short story "The Miraculous Revenge," first published in *Time*, March 1885, suggests that the plot materials for *The Legg Papers* were not entirely discarded.

The testimonial mentioned in the postscript is dated 9th August 1878, and reads:

"Mr. George Shaw served in our office from 1st November, 1871 to 31st. March 1876 when he left at his own desire.

"He entered as a youth and left us having attained to the position of Cashier.

"He is a young man of great business capacity, strict accuracy, and was thoroughly reliable and trustworthy.

"Anything given him to do, was always accurately & well done. We parted from him with regret, and shall always be glad to hear of his welfare.

C. Uniacke Townshend & Co.
Land Agents."]

Dear Mr White

After our recent conversation, I think it best to tell you what my circumstances are, as your experience will enable you to judge of my position better probably than I can myself.

When I was fifteen, I left school—where I had learnt nothing—and entered the office of a leading firm of landagents in Dublin as junior clerk, at a salary of £18 a year. In this post I sulkily distinguished myself so much that when, a year later, the cashier, an elderly man whose testimonials were quite as flattering as that which I enclose, absconded, I took his place, and kept it. Its duties were the receipt and payment of the rents, insurances, charges, private debts &c on many estates with occasional trips to the country to make collections. They acted also as private bankers, & to a certain extent, confidential agents to their clients, and hence I became accustomed to handling large sums of money and to meeting men of all conditions. I should mention that there were no bill transactions, and that therefore I know very little about this branch of business.

My post being the most active & responsible in the office, I resisted offers of promotion as being in the nature of kicking me upstairs. However, the firm desired to place a relative of theirs at the cash desk, and so I eventually became a general clerk, that is to say, I had nothing to do, and drew an increased salary for doing it. At this time, having learnt all that the office could teach me, and feeling uncomfortable in its narrow Irish atmosphere, I resigned, rejected an offer of reinstatement as cashier, and came to London, where my mother and sisters had been for some time. This was in April 1876. I at first prepared to enter the civil service, but as I was neither a linguist nor a mathematician, I had to study for a small berth. Whilst I was doing so, and getting very impatient of the society of schoolboys and the tutelage of a grinder, a friend of mine who was musical critic to a weekly paper, offered me the emoluments of the post if I would discharge its duties. I threw up my studies, and set to work to reform the musical profession. At the end of a year my friend was one of the most unpopular men in London, the paper was getting into difficulties, and complications were arising from the proprietor's doubts as to a critic who was not only very severe, but capable of being in two places at the same time. I gave up that too (making a virtue of necessity), and the proprietor presently retired, ruined.

In the last two years I have not filled any post, nor have I been doing anything specially calculated to qualify me for a business one. During the first half of that time, I was unsettled, and much in that active, but unproductive vein in which an immature man wanders about London at night, plans extravagant social reforms, reads Shelley, and so forth. I wrote a few unsuccessful articles, studied harmony and counterpoint, and wrote a novel, which I am now revising. It cost me five months labour, and I have no means of publishing it when it is finished.

My only reason for seeking commercial employment is a pecuniary one. I know how to wait for success in literature, but I do not know how to live on air in the interim. My family are in difficulties. I may be deceived as to my literary capacity, and in any case, it is as well to be independent of a fine art if clean work is to be made in it. Experience of the organisation & administration of such an enterprise as yours, which is in some sort a tangible part of civilization, would be worth working for. I have no illusions on the subject of business, and although it is exhilarating to make a clever stroke occasionally, the everyday work is too serious, in my opinion, to be undertaken for the purpose (as in landagency) of enriching an individual at the expense of the community. However, I should be loth to press you for a place in which I might not be the right man. If you can give me any hints as to what I might do with myself elsewhere, I shall be well satisfied, for I know you will be able [to] understand my position. Hitherto I have disregarded so much advice from well intentioned friends, that I am reputed almost as impracticable as another member of the family with whom you are acquainted.

Pray excuse the length of this letter. I understood that you desired to get some idea of my character, and this I could not have given you by confining myself to facts which would not distinguish me from the next fifty clerks who might apply to you. Narrative too, is a congenial form to me.

It only remains to thank you again for your exceedingly kind reception of my informal visit.

faithfully yrs
[G. B. Shaw]

P.S. The testimonial was obtained without my knowledge from Messrs Townshend more than two years after I had left them, by my father. Doubtless you know how little such documents are worth.

To HURST & BLACKETT

[G/2]

13 Victoria Grove SW
13th November 1879

[Hurst & Blackett were the first publishers to view *Immaturity*, receiving the manuscript on 8th November, five days after Shaw had completed the first revision. Kegan Paul & Co., in rejecting the novel on 25th November, informed its author that "we do not think it would stand out sufficiently among the crowd of novels so constantly issuing from the press to prove commercially successful if brought before the world"(BM).]

Gentlemen

Pray accept my best thanks for your courtesy in reading my book.

If, instead of returning it to me, you would with equal convenience forward the MS to Messrs Kegan Paul & Co. 1 Paternoster Square, you would oblige me greatly by doing so.

yours obd^{tly}
G. B. Shaw

To GEORGE BENTLEY

[G/2]

13 Victoria Grove SW
25th December 1879

[George Bentley (1828–95), publisher and author, son of the publisher Richard Bentley (1794–1871), was the editor of *Temple Bar* from 1866 until

his death. "The Brand of Cain," a tale which Shaw attempted unsuccessfully to peddle for more than five years until his only draft was lost
in the mails, concerned a woman who had committed a murder of which she
was never suspected. When an amateur photographer took her picture, in
the negative "the brand of Cain" appeared on her forehead. Shaw, at a
later date, was unable to recall how the tale ended.]

Dear Sir

At the suggestion of Messrs R. Bentley, who informed me that you
might be able to make use of a short piece of fiction, I send herewith
a MS entitled "The Brand of Cain." Should you favour me by reading
it, I would venture to remind you that, despite the gravity of the title
and style of narration, the design is altogether grotesque. Indeed,
I fear the story is too preposterous to be worth publishing in "Temple
Bar." If it be so, pray excuse my troubling you——

yours obd^{ly}
G. B. Shaw

To MR DAUGLISH

Way-Leave Department
Edison Telephone Co.
31st December 1879

[G.u/4; X/101]

[Dauglish was head of the Way-Leave Department of the Edison Telephone
Company, and Shaw's immediate superior when the latter entered employment on 14th November 1879. Shaw worked on a commission basis, his job
being to persuade property owners to permit the company to erect poles or
similar structures on their rooftops to facilitate the stringing of telephone
wires. For each consent obtained, he was paid half a crown. As can be seen
from this letter, in the first six weeks of his employment Shaw had obtained
one consent! His letter resulted in a new financial arrangement, giving him
a basic salary of £48 per annum. In February he was promoted to Dauglish's
position, at a salary of £80 per annum plus commissions, and given an office
to himself. In June 1880 the Edison Company merged with its rival, the Bell
Telephone Company, and gave a month's notice to its employees. Although
he was invited to apply for employment with the new United Telephone
Company, Shaw preferred to take advantage of the avenue of escape. On
5th July 1880 he was once again unemployed.]

Dear Sir

As I understand that you are in communication with the Manager
on the subject of the organisation of this department, I take the

25

opportunity to inform you that I am under an absolute necessity to discontinue my services forthwith. Despite the liberality of the commission allowed, I find it in practice unremunerative. [It is also rather precarious, in illustration of which, I may mention that I have as yet received only two shillings and sixpence; that my private expenses meanwhile have amounted to two guineas; and that I entered upon my duties in obedience to pressing pecuniary demands.]*

I should have requested the company to place me on a different footing, but for my reluctance to place any time out of my own disposal when the demands on it are so variable. In fact, though I find payment by commission impracticable, I hardly care to undertake the work on any other terms.

your obtsrvt
[G. B. Shaw]

* Deleted in draft.

To RICHARD BENTLEY & SON

13 Victoria Grove SW
15th January 1880

[G/2]

Gentlemen

I beg to thank you for your courtesy in submitting my MSS "Immaturity" to your reader. You cannot possibly regret the unfavourable result more than I do.

If convenient, pray return the MS to me at the above address.

faithfully yours
G. B. Shaw

P.S. Should you earnestly believe that you can render me a real service by putting this unlucky book into the fire (three other eminent firms have disdained it) you are at liberty to do so; and this shall be your justification for the same.

To MACMILLAN & CO.

13 Victoria Grove SW
1st February 1880

[G.u/2]

[Macmillan & Co. sent Shaw a reader's report on *Immaturity* on 31st January, and in its covering letter suggested revision: "The judgement is certainly one that arouses interest in your work, though we hardly feel courage to publish it as it stands" (BM). The report read : "A 3 vol. novel. I have given more than usual attention to this M.S., for it has a certain quality about it— not exactly of an attractive kind, but still not common. It is the work of a humourist and a realist, crossed, however, by veins of merely literary discussion. There is a piquant oddity about the situations now and then: and the characters are certainly not drawn after the conventional patterns of fiction. It is dry and ironic in flavour. . . . Recognising all these things, I ask myself what it is all about: what is the key, the purpose, the meaning of a long work of this kind without plot or issue. . . . It is undoubtedly clever, but most readers would find it dry, unattractive, and too devoid of any sort of emotion. And then it is very long." (Charles Morgan, *The House of Macmillan*, 1943.) On 3rd February, having received the following letter from Shaw, Macmillan rejected the novel.]

Gentlemen

My MS has arrived safely with a very kind letter from you, and a critical description of my book which could not, I believe, be more accurate.

The flatness of the novel was so involved by its design, that in writing it, I did not propose to myself to save it from appearing dull to a reader who should seek for excitement in it. This design was, to write a novel scrupulously true to nature, with no incident in it to which everyday experience might not afford a parallel, and yet which should constantly provoke in [a] reader full of the emotional ethics of the conventional novel, a sense of oddity and unexpectedness. In short, not to be ironic, but to deal with those ordinary experiences which are a constant irony on sentimentalism, at which the whole work is mainly directed. The machinery employed is an arrangement of two heros & 2 heroines, strongly contrasted and shuffling about, changing partners, and playing on one another throughout. Thus, one of my alternative titles to "Immaturity," was "A Quadrille"; but I rejected it for the same reason that led me to excise every word that betrayed the least consciousness on my part of my own design. I also cut out pages of analysis of character, because I think the dramatic method of *exhibiting* character the true one, and that analysis has been carried so far in the furthest point to which novel writing has been brought, that future advances will discard it rather than develop it.

The result is a panorama without a descriptive lecture. Now, if, in order to stamp the book as a meditation on life, I insert a lecture, I violate my own crotchets as to art workmanship. On the other hand, if I heighten the interest by unusual and exciting incidents, I abandon my design and spoil my moral. I am too raw a workman to fulfil the conditions and avoid the difficulties at the same time, and therefore, anxious as I am to get introduced to the public so as to be more at my ease with them next time, I confess that I am utterly at a loss when I attempt to plan such a recasting of the book as you suggest. I would give up the idea of publishing it altogether, but that there are portions of it (small ones, unfortunately) which I have not the heart to consign to oblivion without making some sort of plea for, particularly since your critic has relieved me of some of my worst doubts concerning them. Would it be possible to publish the book as a series of magazine papers, or in some form from which the ordinary reader would not look for his accustomed stimulants?

I hope to avail myself of your invitation to call in the course of the week, so I need not add anything more at present. I suppose you are sufficiently used to the communicativeness of young authors on the subject of their own works to excuse the length at which I have already troubled you.

I am, gentlemen,
yours faithfully
[G. B. Shaw]

To ELIZABETH LAWSON

13 Victoria Grove SW
[G.u/2]   16th January 1880

[On 15th January Shaw received an invitation, addressed to "Mr Carr Shaw," from Elizabeth Lawson, Carlton House, Cheyne Walk, to attend a dance on the 20th. Mrs Lawson was the mother of Cecil Lawson (1851–82), landscape painter, who was the prototype for Cyril Scott in *Immaturity*, and Malcolm Lawson (1849–?), musician and conductor of the Gluck Society. In the preface (written in 1921) to *Immaturity* Shaw reminisced: "I found myself invited to visit the Lawsons, who were at home in Cheyne Walk every Sunday evening. I suffered such agonies of shyness that I sometimes walked up and down the Embankment for twenty minutes or more before venturing to knock at the door: indeed I should have funked it altogether, and hurried home asking myself what was the use of torturing myself when it was so easy to run away, if I had not been instinctively aware that I must never let myself off in this manner if I meant ever to do anything in the world. Few men can have suffered more than I did in my youth from simple cowardice or been more horribly ashamed of it. I shirked and hid when the peril, real or imaginary, was of the sort that I had no vital interest in facing; but when such an interest was at stake, I went ahead and suffered accordingly. The worst of it was that when I appeared in the Lawsons' drawingroom I did not appeal to the goodnature of the company as a pardonably and even becomingly bashful novice. I had not then tuned the Shavian note to any sort of harmony; and I have no doubt the Lawsons found me discordant, crudely self-assertive, and insufferable. . . . The house and its artistic atmosphere were most congenial to me; and I liked all the Lawsons; but I had not mastered the art of society at that time, and could not bear making an inartistic exhibition of myself; so I soon ceased to plague them. . . ."]

Dear Mrs Lawson

I am certainly the most unfortunate of men, for I shall be engaged on Tuesday evening in a sordid matter of business, which will not be put off. What is worse, even if I were free, I should be afraid to accept your invitation; as I do not know how to dance, and am a more dispiriting object in a drawing room than I am—as you know—at a supper table; I could unquestionably eat if I liked, whereas I could not accomplish a waltz for the sake of the most attractive partner you could offer me, and this, for one who has the privilege of knowing the resources you have at hand, is saying everything. I should be an envious and gloomy wallflower, and in your house an unhappy guest would be an anomaly.

Nevertheless, I am very grateful to you for remembering me, and beg you to believe me, dear Mrs Lawson,

faithfully yours
[G. B. Shaw]

To GEORGE BENTLEY

[G/2]

[13 Victoria Grove SW]
5th March 1880

[George Bentley, in rejecting "The Brand of Cain" on 5th March, noted that he had marked up the manuscript "to draw attention to obvious errors." The defects, he pointed out, were numerous: "The wind-up is very bad, the commencement not good, the photographer's character must not be too exaggerated in regard to his nervousness. This is overdone when he photographs the woman. . . . Too much time can hardly be spent upon that particular scene which is well imagined." He concluded generously: "If you care to work on it, I will read it again" (BM).]

Dear Sir

Pray accept my best thanks for the favour you have done me in going so far out of the usual course as to point out the defects of a condemned MS. I shall not, however, abuse your kindness by asking

29

you to read it again, because I think the failure of the story is more radical than you suppose. The intemperance of the descriptive passages, which has very naturally offended your taste, arises from this peculiar difficulty—that the situations appear, not as they are, but as the photographer, who has vulgar ideas of effect, describes them. The description is put into his mouth in order the more easily to produce the necessary confusion in the reader's mind as to whether the incidents really happened to the photographer, whether he hysterically exaggerates fragments of fact, or whether he is simply an outrageous liar, practising on the complacent and twaddling hypochondriac who has set him talking. Hence too, the provoking barrenness of the conclusion. I perceive by your remarks that I have totally missed my aim, and produced the effect of a feeble attempt at serious romance. The effect was hardly worth the heaviness of the attempt, and I am afraid that my favourite object of avoiding second hand sentences and literary "shop" in general, looks very like amateurishness when attained, and still more like it when superficially attained only.

I mention these points to excuse myself for not acknowledging your courtesy in the proper way by setting hand to work in pursuance of your advice. If I can produce something more rational and less abortive than the "Brand of Cain," perhaps I may again trespass on your patience. In the meantime, believe me, dear sir,

yours faithfully
G. B. Shaw

To JOHN MORLEY

[G.u/2]

13 Victoria Grove SW
22nd May 1880

[John Morley (1838–1923), who became Lord Morley of Blackburn, was M.P. for Newcastle-on-Tyne (1883–95) and twice Chief Secretary for Ireland (1886, 1892–95) with a seat in the Cabinet. He succeeded Frederick Greenwood as editor of the *Pall Mall Gazette* in May 1880. On 22nd May he informed Shaw he had heard "from a common friend [George (later Sir George) Macmillan of Macmillan & Co] that you might perhaps be able & willing occasionally to write for me on this paper. If you care to entertain the notion I shall be very happy to talk it over with you some day next week" (BM). Although Morley instantly earned Shaw's gratitude for this early effort to assist the incipient journalist, his subsequent political policies made him one of the prime targets of Shaw's socialistic wrath.]

30

Dear Sir

I shall have pleasure in calling on you next week if you will be good enough to let me know the hour most convenient to you. You may name any time—morning or afternoon—without fear of embarrassing me. However, should I not hear from you, I shall call on Tuesday at 2 o'clock, but I have no reason for selecting this hour except that it may save you the trouble of writing a second time.

> I am, dear sir,
> yours very truly
> [G. B. Shaw]

To JOHN MORLEY

[G/2]

13 Victoria Grove SW
13th June 1880

[At Morley's request Shaw submitted a review of a recently published three-decker novel, *George Vanbrugh's Mistake*, by Henry Baden Pritchard (1841–88). On 2nd June, Morley wrote: "I am not sure I can use your review, but I like the style of it. Could you not send me some short middle article upon some social or other topic?" (BM) Shaw in response sent an essay "Exhausted Arts" (a facsimile of its first leaf is reproduced in *G.B.S. 90*, ed. Stephen Winsten, 1946) and a review of Henry Irving's production of *The Merchant of Venice* at the Lyceum. The "three volume pamphlet on penal servitude" which Shaw disdained to "waste powder on" was a novel, *In Her Majesty's Keeping*, by the Hon. Lewis Strange Wingfield (1842–91).]

Dear Mr Morley

In the very limited time which my present occupation leaves at my disposal, I have only been able to produce the enclosed article on "Exhausted Arts," which I am afraid you will find rather indigestible. I send also a paper on the Merchant of Venice, which I of course do not expect you to read through; but a glance into it will give you an idea of what (—besides the usual "shop")—I can do as a dramatic critic. I should prefer writing on theatrical or musical events to manufacturing random articles, which is to me much the same thing as making bricks without straw.

I expect in a short time to be offered a not very brilliant appointment which will leave me even less time for literary pursuits than I have at present. Should you advise me to accept it? I must have either one stool or the other to sit upon.

31

I should feel obliged by your returning me any papers of which you made no use. I will send you back the books you lent me, tomorrow. Wingfield's novel is a three volume pamphlet on penal servitude, and a review of it would be merely an article on that subject. The romantic part is too bad to waste powder on.

yours faithfully
[G. B. Shaw]

To JOHN MORLEY

[13 Victoria Grove SW]
[G.u/2]   15th June 1880

[Morley returned the two manuscripts on 14th June: "They are not quite suitable for this paper.... With regard to the question that you ask me, I cannot hesitate to say, that in my opinion you would do well to get out of journalism. It is a most precarious, dependent, and unsatisfactory profession, excepting for a very few who happen to have the knack, or manage to persuade people that they have it.... I wish I could have been of more service to you" (BM). Not until 1885 did Shaw succeed in publishing a review in the *Pall Mall Gazette*, by which time Morley had been succeeded as editor by his assistant, W. T. Stead.]

Dear Mr Morley

I have received your letter, and also my last two MSS, with a note from Mr Taylor, all safe.

Thank you very much for your attempt to befriend me. I am sorry for having baffled it; but I fear I am incorrigible. Instead of cultivating that unfortunate knack, I laboriously rub all signs of it out. I wonder whether the public really like it.

Should you ever require anything particularly disagreeable written about anybody, pray remember

yours faithfully
[G. B. Shaw]

To ARNOLD WHITE

13 Victoria Grove SW
[G.u/4; X/101]   5th July 1880
Sir

There is due to me by the [Edison Telephone] Company about one guinea, being the proportion of my salary from the 1st inst to the expiry of my engagement today. A further sum of six shillings advanced by me to C. Knibb, lately in the way-leave department of the Co., has not been repaid to me. His receipt therefor is amongst the papers endorsed "Official" at 77 Cornhill; but I have mislaid my memorandum of this payment, and I cannot describe it more particularly than as commission for two consents for the wire to the East India Dock. Should this claim be too informal for presentation to the Board, pray suppress it, and excuse my troubling you with it.

I am, sir,
your obedient servant
[G. B. Shaw]

[On 7th July, Shaw received payment of 27s. from Rudolph H. Krause.]

To MESSRS R. F. WHITE & SON

[G/5]

13 Victoria Grove SW
22nd July 1880

[This (and several letters in 1882) refutes the assertions of Hesketh Pearson, F. E. Loewenstein, and other chroniclers of Shaw's life that, after his departure from the Edison Telephone Company, he never again "sinned against his nature" by seeking regular commercial employment. But see letter of 18th November 1889 to Hubert Bland.

The advertisement read: "CLERK WANTED.—To Law Clerks and others.—The advertiser REQUIRES the SERVICES, in London, of an intelligent YOUNG MAN, about 20 years of age, of respectable family and fair education, of good personal appearance and address, one who desires out-of-door occupation, and a permanent and improving position. Salary to commence at 100 guineas. Address, with full particulars as to family and previous occupations, to X.X.X., care of Messrs. R. F. White and Son, 33, Fleet-street."]

Sir

With reference to an advertisement appearing in the "Times" of this date, I should be glad to learn the nature of the employment referred to.

I am 25 years of age, and have some experience in literature, in landagency (Irish), and in the establishment of the telephone system in London. I shall, no doubt, be able to satisfy you on the other points mentioned, but I cannot command private influence likely to further any business entrusted to me. [Shaw had first written, and then

33

expunged, the statement: "I shall not be likely to further any business entrusted to me by family influence."]

I am, sir,
your obedient servant
G.B. Shaw

To W. BLACKWOOD & SONS

[A/18; X/102]

13 Victoria Grove SW
22nd September 1880

[In the preface to *Immaturity* Shaw claimed that "Blackwood actually accepted [the novel], and then revoked." There is, however, no evidence in the Blackwood archive in the National Library of Scotland to corroborate this, and the only document which survives in the Shaw archive is a rejection by Blackwood, delivered through its London office manager, Joseph M. Langford (1810–84), on 28th September.]

Gentlemen

On the 24th of last March, I submitted to you, by your permission, an MS novel entitled "Immaturity." If you have had leisure to examine it, I should feel obliged by your communicating the result.

Pardon me for thus anticipating your convenience, and believe me

faithfully yours
G.B. Shaw

To J. M. FELLS

[A/1]

13 Victoria Grove SW
24th October 1880

[John Manger Fells (1858–1925), secretary of the Zetetical Society, was an accountant and economist, author of several works on industrial economy and factory accounts. James Lecky (1856–90), a civil servant in the Exchequer and Audit Department, whom Shaw met through a mutual friend, Chichester Bell, nephew of the inventor of the telephone, was an accomplished musician, author of the article on Temperament (system of tuning keyed instruments) in the first edition of *Grove's Dictionary of Music and Musicians*, a subject in which he instructed Shaw. It was from Lecky, who was interested also in phonetics, that Shaw gained his earliest knowledge of philology and received an introduction to such philological scholars as Alexander John Ellis (1814–90) and Henry Sweet (1845–1912).]

Dear Sir

My friend Mr James Lecky has requested me to communicate with you respecting a Debating Society which I wish to join, and for which, he informs me, you act as secretary.

Will you kindly acquaint me with the necessary preliminaries to membership, and oblige

yours faithfully
G. B. Shaw

To J. M. FELLS

[A/1]

13 Victoria Grove S W
25th October 1880

[The Zetetical Society was founded in 1878, on the lines of the famous London Dialectical Society, to "furnish opportunities for the unrestricted discussion of Social, Political, and Philosophical subjects." Shaw, in *Sixteen Self Sketches* (1949), claimed Lecky had "dragged" him to the meeting of 28th October 1880. "I had an air of impudence; but was really an arrant coward, nervous and self-conscious to a heartbreaking degree. Yet I could not hold my tongue. I started up and said something in the debate, and then, feeling that I had made a fool of myself . . . I vowed I would join the society; go every week; speak in every debate; and become a speaker or perish in the attempt. I carried out this resolution." The correspondence with Fells, however, establishes that Shaw had applied for membership even before he had attended his first meeting.]

Dear Sir

I shall gratefully avail myself of your offer to second my nomination by Mr Lecky for the Zetetical Soc^y. I have written to him, and may now, I perceive, leave the matter in your care, for which, as well your letter, and the ticket for Thursday evening, I owe you many thanks.

I am, dear Sir,
yours faithfully
G. B. Shaw

To J. KINGSTON BARTON

[A/5]

13 Victoria Grove S W
29th November 1880

[Dr J. Kingston Barton (1854–1941) of St Bartholomew's Hospital first met Shaw in October 1879; they soon became good friends. Shaw visited Barton,

35

first in his lodgings in the Gloucester Road, and from 1882 at Barton's home at 2, Courtfield Road, almost every Saturday evening, until in 1885 their growing responsibilities and heavy engagements drew them apart. In this letter Shaw was seeking advice for his new novel *The Irrational Knot*. The "female dipsomaniac" was an actress, Virtue Lalage (Susannah Conolly), sister of the hero of Shaw's novel. This is the first letter extant which bears the initials "GBS".]

I am in need of the following professional information, which I forgot to ask you for on Saturday last.

1. Can a female dipsomaniac, after a two years course of champagne, bring herself to the final starvation stage in so short a time as four months, on unlimited brandy?

2. Is it proper for her to get stout and bloated on the champagne, and become emaciated on the brandy?

3. What is she like near the end of the process? Is she pale or red, dry or clammy, (how is her hand on the latter point?) hyperaesthesiad, anaesthesiad or normal. For instance, if she is coming down a dark staircase at night, and meets a person with a lamp, will she be dazzled by the light, slow to become conscious of it, or merely as usual?

4. Is it right for her to complain of hunger, thirst, and internal pains, and to make desperate attempts to drink; to talk rationally, to know that she is going to die, and to be able to walk across a room.

5. If she (or anybody else, I suppose, for that matter) falls and strikes her temple violently against a stove, can she be killed at once? If not, how soon? (The sooner the better for me). If at once, how soon would a doctor be able to pronounce positively that she was dead? (N.B. An American doctor). Might not a woman killed quickly in this way, stumble up on her hands and knees for a moment after striking her head, and then drop dead? Would not her face during such an effort be very white, and her expression dazed (I ask this on the chance of your having seen something of the sort—otherwise I presume you cannot say).

6. Is a woman who has fainted, usually able to talk sensibly and remember what happened immediately before her faint as soon as she comes to? If not, how soon?

7. How long do you suppose an average woman (dipso as described —aged 29) would last alive after the inability to retain food or drink set in?

Here endeth the first lesson. I have purposely framed the above questions so that you can interline or write across them Yes—No—

3 months—red—clammy—and so forth, and return this sheet to me. In this way you will not lose much time over them, and you need not excogitate the chances very deeply, as all I want is a reasonable possibility of the conditions occurring.

GBS

To MACMILLAN & CO.

[G.u/2]

37 Fitzroy Street W
4th January 1881

[Shaw's second novel, *The Irrational Knot*, based in part on his experiences with the Edison Telephone Company and on his relationship with his actress sister Lucy, was begun in June 1880 and completed on 1st December. In rejecting the novel Macmillan did not inform the author that its reader had described it as "a novel of the most disagreeable kind. It is clearly the work of a man with a certain originality and courage of mind. There is nothing conventional either about the structure or the style; and the characters have a curious flavour and 'sapidity' about them. But the thought of the book is all wrong; the whole idea of it is odd, perverse and crude. It is the work of a man writing about life, when he knows nothing of it. . . . So far as your publication is concerned, it is out of the question. There is too much of adultery and the like matters." (Charles Morgan, *The House of Macmillan*, 1943.)

On 23rd December 1880 the Shaws had moved from Victoria Grove to unfurnished lodgings at 37 Fitzroy Street. This placed Shaw within walking distance of the British Museum, whose reading room he had frequented "a good deal for the first time" (Diary, BM) late in the year.]

Gentlemen

Pray accept my best thanks for your attention to my novel. I should feel much obliged by your forwarding the MS direct to Mr Langford, at Messrs Blackwoods, instead of returning it to me. He has asked me to place it in his hands as soon as possible, as he is leaving town; and I am anxious to avoid the delay of two deliveries.

I am, gentlemen,
yours faithfully
[G. B. Shaw]

To G. R. SIMS

[G.u/4]

37 Fitzroy Street W
10th February 1881

[No sooner had Sims accepted "Christian Names" for *One and All* in September 1879 than Shaw began to bombard him with additional contributions, including "The Brand of Cain," an essay entitled "On the true signification of the term 'gentleman,'" and a tale, "The Extinguished Lamp," which he recorded in his working notebook as "never returned." It is not unlikely that Minnie Macmullen was an early Shavian pseudonym, for on at least two subsequent occasions he signed women's names (Horatia Ribbonson and Amelia Mackintosh) to letters contributed to the *Pall Mall Gazette*, and in February 1880 he drafted an essay, "A Reminiscence of Hector Berlioz" (unpublished), which opened with the caution: "Readers are so apt to conclude that a writer who employs the first person (as I do for the sake of simplicity) must be a man, that I think it best to begin my narrative by saying that I am a woman" (BM). It is also possible that the author was Lucy Carr Shaw. Across the draft of Shaw's letter to Sims is his notation: "Received the MSS shortly after by parcels delivery."]

Dear Sir

Is there the slightest chance of recovering an MS entitled "Only Human and therefore Weak," which was sent to your office at Wine Office Court in Oct or Nov. 1879. It was addressed from 13 Victoria Grove, and was written in four "Australian" copy books. The authoress, Miss Minnie Macmullen, has asked me to try whether it can be restored to her, as she sets—as usual—considerable store by it. Pray excuse this application—I know it is somewhat unreasonable.

yours faithfully
[G. B. Shaw]

To RICHARD BENTLEY & SON

[G/2]

c/o Dr Gurly. Leyton. Essex
14th July 1881

[Dr Walter John Gurly (1835–99) was Shaw's Rabelaisian maternal uncle, a physician who had been medical officer for many years on ships of the Inman line and who had recently settled down to a general practice at Leyton. Shaw visited Dr Gurly in June to recuperate from an attack of smallpox contracted in late May, the blemishing effects of which led him to cultivate the beard he wore for the remainder of his life.]

38

Gentlemen

I am much obliged to you for reading "The Irrational Knot," and sorry that it has not repaid your trouble. I must admit the justice of your hint that my style is not general; it has been confirmed by most candid friends. Nevertheless, as you cannot be unaware of the difference between what the public like, and what they will read (and the latter is the only consideration that influences me when writing) I fear the book has graver faults, of which you have spared me a recital.

Kindly return the MSS to me at 37 Fitzroy Street.

> I am, gentlemen,
> faithfully yours
> G. B. Shaw

To SMITH, ELDER & CO.

> Care of Dr Gurly
> Leyton. Essex
> 14th July 1881

[W/153]

Gentlemen

Will you oblige me by reading a MS novel of mine [*The Irrational Knot*], for which I am desirous to find a publisher? It is of the usual length, and deals with modern society.

After the 1st prox. my address will be 37 Fitzroy Street W

> I am, Gentlemen,
> your obedient servant
> G B Shaw

To J. M. FELLS

> c/o Dr Gurly. Leyton. Essex
> 23rd August 1881

[A/1]

[Although he had participated in several discussions at meetings of the Zetetical Society, and had been toying with the manuscript of a lecture for several months, it was not until August 1881 that Shaw worked up the courage to accept a formal challenge to read a paper before the Society. The title he finally chose was "On what is called The Sacredness of Human Life, and its bearing on the question of Capital Punishment."]

Dear Fells

I shall be delighted to give the society a discourse on "The Sacredness of Human Life." I know you do not approve of this title, but I promise you that you will admit that it was unavoidable when you hear the paper, which will start a discussion on Capital Punishment, and perhaps on the Population Question too. In fact you may, if you like, announce it as 'The Sacr^d &c, with especial reference to the question of Capital Punishment.' By avoiding the direct title, I shall also avoid the history and statistics of the question, which nobody wants to be bothered with, and I shall be able to be Periscope's.

Let me know when you will require me to orate, if you know yourself. My illness is a thing of the past. In deference to the feelings of the Society, I refrained from attending the June meeting, but even then I was guaranteed quite well and safe, and I have not since relapsed. To a man who has acquired the habit of reading in bed, the chief objection to varioloid is the expense.

I shall see you next month at Philippi or elsewhere. Meanwhile let me hear what you opine of the Sacredness.

yrs ever
G B S

To G. J. VANDELEUR LEE

[G.u/2]

Leyton. Essex
24th August 1881

[Lee, who had published two earlier editions of a work entitled *The Voice* (both of which had been ghost-written for him), proposed to Shaw that the latter undertake to draft the text for a third edition. Shaw, as indicated by the extract which he copied from his reply to Lee's letter of 23rd August, accepted the commission. Although the work was never completed, the fragmentary shorthand manuscript and a typescript survive in the Berg Collection. There is evidence that Shaw plied his pen for Lee on numerous other occasions. In January 1881 Lee wrote: "Your M.S. [unidentified] and corrections are admirable. No proof will be returned to you. The enclosed [£5] is to pay for subscriptions to libraries & books that you may require to work out of [for] the result that will regenerate the musical world. When more coin is wanted I shall be glad to send it" (BM). This may have been an earlier attempt to enroll Shaw in the *Voice* project, but Shaw returned the money. In 1883 he provided a publicity release for Lee's contemplated production of *Patience*, which appeared in the *Court Journal* on 30th June, though the performance eventually was cancelled. And in 1886, a few months before Lee's sudden death, Shaw drew up a prospectus for him on "How to Cure Clergyman's Sore Throat," no copy of which survives (if it ever actually was printed). Shaw also served frequently as Lee's rehearsal pianist and general factotum, performing the duties of stage manager, for example, at an operatic performance at Londonderry House, Park Lane (Lee's home), on 1st July 1882, for the Fund for the Relief of the Distressed Ladies of Ireland.]

Extract from Reply

However, I am disposed to have a shot at it; but I will not engage myself so far as to put you to any expense in the matter. If it comes to a published book, and there is anything gained over and above expenses, I will take a share.

To PATTIE MOYE

[G/4]

D[r] Gurly. Leyton. Essex
25th September 1881

[Pattie Moye, who nominated Shaw for membership in the Dialectical Society, which he joined in October, was also a member of the Executive Committee of the Zetetical Society. Shaw was elected to the Executive of the latter society for the year 1881–82, other members of which were Sidney Webb, John George Godard (subsequently Shaw's solicitor), and Emil Garcke (1856–1930), who became one of the leaders in the development of electrical enterprises in Great Britain.]

Dear Mrs Moye

I have just received and forwarded the Dialectical papers. Many thanks for your nomination of me, and also for Miss Marshalls, which I owe to your good offices, and not as I would fain believe (for a man is a vain thing) to my own merit. I look forward to the October meeting, where I will, I hope, have an opportunity of thanking you personally.

I am, dear Mrs Moye,
gratefully yours
G. B. Shaw

To G. J. VANDELEUR LEE

[F/2]

[37 Fitzroy Street W]
16th October 1881

I have left Leyton, so your letter had to be sent back to me. If Messent has anything good going, I shall be delighted to undertake it.

Needs must when necessity (or his prototype) drives. I have made a few notes for our undertaking [*The Voice*], and am beginning to foresee that I will be able to make something of it, that may not only fetch the reviewers but also (if the chapters are advertised) the public too—or at least that young section of them who feel that they have lyric greatness in them.

GBS

To JAMES VIRTUE

[G.u/2]

37 Fitzroy Street W
21st November 1881

[James Virtue (1829–92) and Frederick Daldy were the proprietors of the *Art Journal*. Mrs Gurly was Aunt Emily, the wife of Walter John Gurly. The advice Shaw was seeking concerned the possible sale of *The Irrational Knot* to an American publisher, who subsequently rejected it "on the ground of its immorality" (BM). It is interesting to note that Shaw, having declined at this time to accept a position with the National Telephone Company and having answered in vain several advertisements for commercial positions, had contemplated emigrating to America. This, he later commented, "was probably suggested by the Bells" (Diary, BM), Chichester Bell and his wife being then in Washington.]

Sir

Will you favour me with a short interview in the course of the next few days? My aunt, Mrs Gurly, tells me that I may trespass on your time so far. By the courtesy of Mr Daldy I am already in possession of all the general information I require, but I should be glad to have the help of your experience in judging a proposal which has just been made to me. I shall not detain you long, and any hour after 11 am will be convenient to me.

I am, dear Sir,
yours faithfully
[G.B. Shaw]

To REMINGTON & CO.

[F.u/2]

37 Fitzroy Street W
26th November 1881

[In response to Shaw's inquiry concerning the cost of publishing *Immaturity* at his own expense, Remington informed him on 20th October that they were prepared to publish the novel in three volumes at a cost of £95, to be sold at one and a half guineas. The first "edition" would consist of 400 copies, and the second and third of 300 copies each. The other offer made to Shaw was by Newman & Co.]

Gentlemen

I have received your proposal to publish my novel "Immaturity," and, as far as I can judge at present, it is less advantageous than an offer made me by another firm for the same book. At what rate would you account to me for the copies sold? Do you still estimate the advertising at £25? I should like to have an exact basis for calculation, because, as I do not possess £95 (or, indeed, 95/-) I must endeavour to borrow the money on the security of the novel—not a very tempting speculation for a man of business.

I may say at once, however, that your proposal is not an encouraging one. I am told that £95 will practically secure you against loss. If that is so, what consideration do you offer for the share of 1/3 which you require? If I am to be capitalist as well as artist, might I not as well publish on commission and retain my copyright entire? Again, it is not likely that there will be any occasion to print 1000 copies at $1\frac{1}{2}$ guineas, and I presume your right to a third will be established not only in the first issue, but in the copyright, and would extend to colonial editions, railway editions, &c, should such be called for.

If the book has really inspired you with any confidence in its success, I should be very glad to sell you the copyright [for] what you may choose to offer for it, or to take a small royalty in lieu of finding £95 and having 2/3. It will be neither easy nor pleasant to borrow money in the face of the obvious remark that if the book was worth anything, some publisher would have taken it up. Let me add that if it will not pay, I had rather it remained in MS.

I am, gentlemen,
yours faithfully
[G. B. Shaw]

To REMINGTON & CO.

37 Fitzroy Street W
30th November 1881

[In their reply of 30th November, Remington informed Shaw that the copyright would revert to the author after the publication of the three "editions" contracted for. The publisher, they informed him, would expend more than

£25 for advertising, and noted that libraries paid only 18s. against the trade (wholesale) rate of 22s. 6d.]

Gentlemen

Many thanks for particulars. The offer I mentioned as having been already made to me was that I should pay £100 and receive 3/4; the other conditions being similar to those of your proposal. I think the additional 1/12 share is worth the extra £5. However, I shall bear your offer in mind if I am still disposed to publish "Immaturity" when I have the means to do so.

Pray do not imagine that I question the fairness of your proposal. Obviously, it might be varied in its apportioning of profits and expenditure without becoming less equitable. I am merely trying who will make the best bargain with me.

Kindly return the MS at your convenience, and believe me

yours faithfully and obliged.
[G. B. Shaw]

To PATTIE MOYE

[G/4]

37 Fitzroy Street W
18th December 1881

[William Marwood (1820–83) was the public executioner; he introduced the "long drop."]

Dear Mrs Moye

I send you herewith the draft of the paper which I propose to read at the Zetetical Society on the subject of Capital Punishment. I feel some compunction about inflicting it on you, but the only alternative would be a concise account of my views within the limits of a letter, and as concise accounts, however neat and pointed, are only to be understood at the cost of considerable mental application, I believe you will prefer the more diffuse and (consequently) more easily intelligible statement contained in the paper.

I will suppose, then, that you have read the paper, and that you have fairly recovered from any shock which its suggestions may have caused you. You are now in a position to argue that the alleged irrevocability of the death penalty is an objection which applies equally to the shortest term of imprisonment. Also that perpetual imprisonment involves much more suffering to the criminal and cost to the community than capital punishment. But you must, as you will presently see, paradoxically maintain, side by side with this, that death, owing to the

44

[ope]ration of The Reluctance to be Killed, remains the *extreme penalty*; for, as a matter of fact, the criminal always prefers perpetual imprisonment. This is the chief and exquisite recommendation of capital punishment over penal servitude for life. It is cheaper, more humane, more final in its efficacy to remove a source of danger to the community, & yet more terrible to the evildoer. Society is never so respectable as when it is double faced. Here are two faces for it, a face of reason to prove to the philanthropist that on the scaffold benevolence and self defence are reconciled as far as, in their opposed natures, they possibly can be reconciled; and a face of superstitious terror to make the criminal believe in spite of reason that death is the worst of evils for him. Society, in short, inflicts the maximum of pain with the minimum of remorse.

Reverting for the moment to the question of irrevocability, it would be well to be ready with the remark that Human Justice must act in an assumption of its own infallibility. Nothing less will justify it in acting to the detriment of a sentient being at all.

So far, we have made out that death is a more reasonable punishment than lifelong imprisonment. The abolitionists, sagaciously perceiving that we have proved too much, will challenge us to extend the death penalty to housebreaking, manslaughter and all crimes punishable by very long periods of imprisonment. We reply that we should certainly do so, but for the operation of the principle epitomised in the proverb "As well be hung for a sheep as a lamb." So long as we consider the pickpocket less dangerous to society than the forger, and the forger than the murderer—so long, that is, as we admit degrees of crime, just so long must we have degrees of punishment. Hence the care we took to admit that death is an extreme penalty. We must have an extreme penalty, strictly limited to an extreme crime, if we wish to give the criminally disposed an interest in refraining from extreme crimes. Now, murder has this peculiarity. It is a means of escape from the consequences of all other crimes. If housebreaking be made capital, the burglar has nothing to lose and possibly liberty to gain by shooting the policeman, the householder, and as many other obstacles to his flight as his revolver will answer for. The penalty of death for burglary was abolished for this very reason, a reason which controls all criminal codes, and which, be it observed, has no root in morality—it is a reason of pure expediency. When even shoplifting was punishable by death, the apprehension of a felon was a service of mortal danger, and the criminal classes formed haunts in cities upon which no ordinary force of police dared intrude. Hence the need of a series of punishments increasing in severity to the extreme of death, and corresponding to a series of crimes culminating in murder. It follows also that the abolitionist's work is only begun when capital punishment is abolished. They must modify the whole perspective of punishments, or else the result of the change will be that the forger, the burglar, and all those who face penal servitude for life as the inevitable result of their capture, may as well slay their captors out of hand.

It is very unusual for a debate on a subject of this kind to pass without some need for a reminder that the function of criminal law is to protect society, and not to revenge outraged morality; and that on abstract grounds there is no justification for punishment at all. But so long as society deliberately makes criminal classes, (which is exactly what it now does) it cannot do better than kill them as fast as possible.

The method of carrying out capital punishment is quite another question. National respect for vested interests is opposed to throwing the class to which hangmen belong out of employment; but for my own part I look with unspeakable loathing on the whole apparatus of homicide, from Marwood, with his atrocious virtuosity in long drops, up to the governor & chaplain, & down again to the intelligent natives watching outside for the black flag. Ugh! I beg your pardon for mentioning it.

This is all I can think on the subject at present. As it is Sunday afternoon I am writing at the disadvantage of having my sister on the one hand & my mother on the other. Miss Shaw, who is a Roman Catholic on Sabbath evenings, and a Protestant (when she is up in time) in the mornings, is playing the pianoforte. Meanwhile Mrs Shaw reads, and remonstrates at intervals with her daughter, who is neglecting an important appointment, now half an hour overdue. These remonstrances provoke retorts, and end in brief domestic storms which sweep over *Mr* Shaw, and fill his soul with malice. So perhaps you will excuse me if I am not quite clear. If there is any point on which you are doubtful, please let me know, and I will do my best to elucidate it, though you will be unjust to yourself if you suppose that your own intelligence can be in any way indebted to my warped humor. To be strong in argument one must have faith in it, whereas, to my mind, it is less a means of eliciting truth than of excusing ourselves for pretending to believe what we know in our hearts to be nonsense. With which profound remark, and an apology for the length of this letter, I am, dear Mrs Moye

yours faithfully
GBS

46

To J. M. FELLS

[A/1]

Leyton. Essex
30th January 1882

[Shaw's paper on capital punishment was delivered, as scheduled, on 8th (not 7th) February 1882 at the South Place Chapel. Sidney James Webb (1859–1947), when Shaw first met him at a Zetetical meeting in October 1880, was a stripling employed as a clerk in the City office of a Colonial broker, studying nights for the Civil Service examination which enabled him, in 1882, to enter the Colonial Office. The warm personal relationship between the two men spanned nearly seventy years, during which time they were jointly instrumental in building the Fabian Society (founded in 1884) into the most significant Socialist organisation in Britain. Shaw considered Webb "the ablest man in England," and once told Archibald Henderson, "Quite the cleverest thing I ever did in my life was to force my friendship on Webb, to extort his, and keep it" (*Bernard Shaw: Playboy and Prophet*, 1932). The lecture by Webb which did not require to be "prematurely delivered" was "Heredity as a Factor in Psychology and Ethics."]

Dear Fells

I have overtaxed the patience of the Almighty, and he has smitten me; and, through me, the Zetetical Society. He has gone for me in the throat (relaxed and horribly sore) in the joints (swollen and rheumatic) in the lungs (reverberating with the first hollow cough of phthisis, of which disease one of my sisters had the bad taste to die) and in the brain (extinguished, by Heaven! like a candle in the tempest of His wrath). I am down here in a species of quarantine, my doctor [Uncle Walter John Gurly] being uncertain as to whether I may not be in the preliminary stage of some destructive and probably fatal zymotic disease. If at the end of the week, I be still merely collapsed, he will insist on my going at once to Lincolnshire (a remote place on the east coast, of which you have perhaps heard) and abstaining from private speculation, public debate, pen and ink, and all spiritual joys, until I recover my tone. I scorn his evil auguries; but the fact remains that I would cheerfully die rather than deliver a lecture this evening (for instance) or even face the task of remodelling and enlarging my paper, which I find to be unpresentable and idiotic at present. I have still great hopes of being able to come up to the scratch on the 7th; but I do not feel justified in leaving you wholly unwarned of the peril which the occasion undeniably stands in.

Pray excuse the incoherence of this letter—I am incapable of

47

writing, and shall soon forfeit the distinction of being the only sane

Shaw

in existence.

P.S. If I fail, and Webb objects to be prematurely delivered, can you put any one else up? Or put up yourself—the very thing! Since we came to Conduit St your eloquence has been a sealed fountain.

To RICHARD BENTLEY & SON

c/o W. J. Gurley, Esq.
Leyton. Essex

[F/2]
18th February 1882

[*Love Among the Artists*, Shaw's third novel, was begun on 19th May 1881 and completed in December of the same year, while he was convalescing at Leyton. Unlike *The Irrational Knot*, which "carried me as far as I could go in Rationalism and Materialism," Shaw noted in 1946, he had taken as his hero "a British Beethoven, utterly unreasonable and unaccountable, and even outrageous, but a vital genius, powerful in an art that is beyond logic and even beyond words" (Nat'l. Lib. of Ireland). However, his composer was even less understood by the publishers' readers than his mechanic had been. "He was, it seemed, simply no gentleman." Bentley, in rejecting it, informed Shaw that the novel "is not of a sufficiently encouraging nature to enable us to make overtures to you for its publication. The work is written with a smart and apparently practised pen, but the whole story would seem to be lacking in point of interest for the general reader" (BM).]

Gentlemen

I am much obliged to you for the attention you have given to my novel "Love among the Artists," and trust that the result will not discourage you from conferring a similar favour on me on a future occasion [if] I ask you to do so. I am not without a hope that the point of my work, obscure though it seems to be, will yet strike your reader, who (if you will excuse my saying so) either underrates the capacity of "the general reader," or applies the term to a class of persons who— like himself—read little else but newspapers, and whom therefore a novelist is not concerned to please.

Kindly return the MS to 37 Fitzroy St., W, at your convenience.

I am, gentlemen,
yours faithfully
G. B. Shaw

To ETHEL SOUTHAM

[F/2]

36 Osnaburgh Street N W
24th July 1882

[Shaw, on 24th July 1882, scanning the pages of the *Daily News* for employment possibilities, came upon the following advertisement: "Wanted, a copyist, to copy MS. of a novel. State terms per folio, and number of words. —Miss Southam, Windermere." The Shaws had moved to Osnaburgh Street on 22nd April.]

Madam

You have advertised in the Daily News for a writer competent to prepare a MS of [a] novel for the press. It is somewhat difficult to state fixed terms for an undertaking of this sort—quite impossible to do so at so much per thousand words. If the MS is the work of an expert, and need only be literally transcribed, pray excuse my troubling you, and apply to the nearest law stationer, who will soon find you a copyist. If however the author is a novice, and the MS needs to be punctuated, paragraphed, revised, and, in short, so arranged as to present to the reader as nearly as possible the same effect as it should have when printed, skilled assistance will be required.

I will undertake to do this with a MS of the length of an ordinary 2 or 3 vol. novel for ten guineas. I will reproduce the novel in a fit state for the printers' hands, I will co-operate with the author to make the work as perfect as possible without interfering with his authorship. If there are any solecisms in the use of titles, blunders in allusions of the fine arts, impossible legal disputes, or such other slips as are common in fiction, I will correct them, and if it [is] desired, give a critical opinion of the work.

I am, Madam,
your obedient servant
[G. B. Shaw]

To ETHEL SOUTHAM

[F.u/2]

36 Osnaburgh Street N W
28th July 1882

Madam

There are certain considerations which make it difficult for me to satisfy by means of references my competence to assist you. Your own judgment will serve you better than that of those who are strangers to you, and personal friends of mine. If you will pull half a dozen leaves out of your MS and send them to me, I will treat them exactly as I propose to treat the entire novel (as far, that is, as my ignorance of the story will permit me), and return it to you. If you disapprove of the result, the matter can drop there. Or, if you get an inkling from it of how you might set about the rest of the work yourself, you will be perfectly welcome to the hint. In either case I will expect no payment.

Perhaps the first point on which you may need an opinion is whether it is really necessary to copy the MS. If it be a first book, you may have to publish it at your own expense. In that case the publishers would have it put into shape for you, and anything you had previously paid for such work would be wasted. Allow me to add, though it is quite beyond my province, that the hard, and to a beginner, repugnant task of revising, is an indispensable part of an author's training, and that you will do yourself an injustice if you commit it to their hands before you have done the very best you can for yourself.

If I am to make a fair copy of the book, I shall still require ten guineas; but I may be able to mark the MS in such a way that, with the aid of a specimen page which I can prepare, an ordinary scrivener might do the copying. My fee for this would be 3 guineas. If feasible it is a plan I would recommend you to adopt, as any copyist can do the mere hand work as well or better than I, and at less cost to you. In answer to your question—I have been for some years occupied in writing, reading, revising, or criticising works of fiction in manuscript.

[G. B. Shaw]

To ETHEL SOUTHAM

[F.u/2]

36 Osnaburgh Street N W
31st July 1882
(not posted till 1/8/82)

[The German tragedian was Daniel E. Bandmann (1840–1905). Shaw had viewed his production of *Hamlet* in Dublin in 1873.]

Dear Madam

It's too soon to revise your book as yet. A revision made piecemeal, without any knowledge of what is to happen in the 3rd vol., would be of little value. It would have to be done over again, when the work was finished. Besides, you would find yourself worried and discouraged by having chapter 1 pulled to pieces whilst you were composing chapter 2. However, there need not now be any question of copying the MS. Write on one side of the paper only, leave a margin at the left hand, place the lines sufficiently far apart to admit of interlined corrections, and, when writing the dialogues, put each speech in a separate paragraph with the first line indented or beginning a little to the right of your margin, thus:

"I do not know what to do with you," said Mrs Byron. "Dr Moncrieff says you are very idle and rough."

In short, make your written page resemble that of the printed novel, in every respect except that of being in manuscript. There will then be no need for copying. If a passage is corrected so far as to become illegible, a piece of clean paper can be pasted over it, and written on. At worst, the whole page can be torn out and replaced.

As you have begun the novel already, you had better use the same size paper throughout, but if you write on white paper, use the cheapest you can get (I generally use what is called "Demi," folded in quarto). Expensive paper not only makes a heavy MS, but, by its shining surface, tries the eyes severely. This is an important matter when you have to fill 5 pages a day regularly during 3 months, which is practically what you have set about doing.

Do not be too much afraid of tautology. The work of a novice often owes most of its awkwardness to efforts to avoid repeating the same word twice on a page. This is especially the case in dialogue. For instance, if you invent a conversation between Mrs Smith and Mrs Jones, you need not study such alternatives to "said Mrs S" as "replied Mrs Jones," "observed Mrs Smith," "rejoined," "remarked," "answered," and so on. Also, call your hero by his name as often as you have occasion to mention him. Do not ring changes on him as "the impassioned youth," "the young artist," "our hero," and the like. The tendency to do these things is stronger than your good taste will let you suppose at present.

Try to make the dialogue describe itself. For instance:

"The church seems such an odd profession for Harry to choose," said Mrs Smith.

Mrs Jones started and looked incredulously at her visitor, as she said, "I thought he was going into the army."

This is very bad. I would correct it as follows:

"The church seems an odd profession for Harry to choose."

"The church! I thought he was going into the army."

Omit even the "said so-and-so" if you can, and make the speech characteristic of the person who utters it. In good dialogue, such as you will find in great perfection in Shakspere and Molière, each speech provokes the one which follows, so that instead of a series of statements, or a mere catechism, you have the play of one person's mind on another's, expressing a state of feeling [which is] sprung, coaxed or startled into existence by the other. If you do not get this quality into a dialogue, cut it out and replace it by a piece of narrative. If you do get it, then you may be guilty of bad taste, bad grammar, or what you will, you will never be dull. Study all entertaining literature, from Shakspere to Miss Rhoda Broughton, and you will find this in it, whilst in the works of writers like Milton and Lord Byron, who had not the faculty of character drawing (the great novelists' faculty) you will find it absent.

Never use an adjective or adverb [unless] it is absolutely necessary to the sense or rhythm of the sentence. Let the hero love the heroine and not be passionately devoted to her, let the heroine suffer pain, and not poignant anguish, let the villain make efforts, and not desperate struggling. When you do use an adverb, do not put "very" before it. And do not qualify facts or thoughts which are too impressive in themselves to need your assistance, as I once heard a German tragedian do in this fashion:

To be or not to be, that is the *awful* question.

If you wish your adjectives to be effective, you must not cheapen them by scattering them broadcast on trivial occasions. Do not pet and dandle your favourite characters. This is one of the commonest and most objectionable habits of lady novelists.

If you write a novel without disregarding these hints except consciously and [for] sufficient reasons, you will find that this [indecipherable] is the difference between the power of expression and the habit of talking. When the book is finished, revise it carefully, and weigh every word in it. Then, if you [are] still desirous of my assistance, I will read it attentively, and give you what help I can. If I can do anything in the meantime, pray let me know.

You will find it best not to shew your MS to anybody unless you know some person whose opinion you particularly value. If a rule can be said to exist for such a matter, it is that an author's friends flatter, and her family ridicules her work.

I am, dear Madam,

yours faithfully
[G. B. Shaw]

P.S. I have written at some length in order to give you an opportunity of judging how far I shall be able to make myself intelligible to you in the event of your entrusting me with the revision of your novel.

[Whether Miss Southam eventually completed and published her novel is unknown. The only book listed in the British Museum catalogue which bears her name is a collaboration by Gertrude and Ethel Armitage Southam, entitled "*Hors de Combat*"; *or, Three Weeks in a Hospital*, published by Cassell in 1891.]

To UNIDENTIFIED CORRESPONDENT

[G.u/4]

36 Osnaburgh Street N W
24th August 1882

[Still seeking employment, Shaw answered the following advertisement: "PRESS.—Descriptive, Satirical, and Critical Paragraphist (Resident) WANTED for provincial weekly. £2 per week to commence with. State politics, &c.—P., 51, Kennington-road, S.E."]

Sir

To what locality does your advertisement in the Daily News of this day refer? If to a busy Musical and Dramatic centre, perhaps you would favour me with an interview. My views in art are tolerably catholic: in politics I am an independent radical. I have acted as critic to the Critical and Satirical Journal in London "The Hornet" and have had considerable literary experience in other directions.

I am
your obedient servant
[G. B. Shaw]

To JOSHUA HATTON

[F.u/2]

36 Osnaburgh Street N W
2nd October 1882

[Joshua Hatton was editor of Colburn's *New Monthly Magazine*. Although Shaw did not obtain the post he sought, that of re-write man, Hatton commissioned him in January 1883 to write one commercial article. This appeared, unsigned, under the title "C. H. Bennett & Co." in July 1883.]

Dear Sir

The work you describe will suit me. As to the other question— whether my way of doing it will suit you—if you will send me a specimen of the style to which I will have to write up, and some material, I will shew you what I can do.

Kindly let me know what terms I may expect in the event of my proving useful.

> I am, dear sir,
> yours truly
> [G. B. Shaw]

To THE SECRETARY OF
THE SMOKE ABATEMENT INSTITUTE

> 36 Osnaburgh Street N W
> 28th December 1882

[F/5]

[The Smoke Abatement Institute had advertised for an "active, well-educated" secretary, "some engineering knowledge advantageous, but not essential."]

Sir

I would be glad to fill such an appointment as that advertised by you in the Times of today. I am 27 years old, and have had more than 5 years experience of office routine and am a competent correspondent.

I have had some literary practice and am accustomed to public meetings which I do not mind addressing on occasion.

I am not an engineer but I have negotiated between the public and an engineering department of a Telephone company without finding myself at a loss. I am an indifferent shorthand writer.

On these points, perhaps, a personal interview would be most satisfactory to you. I may add that I am not at all particular as to the kind of work I have to do except that I prefer an active post, with not less than 30/- [a] week salary.

> I am, sir,
> your obedient servant
> G. B. Shaw

To UNIDENTIFIED CORRESPONDENT

[c. 1883]

[F.u/2]

You are, it appears, a French painter desiring to learn English. I am an English author desiring to learn to draw. Suppose we take advantage

54

of one another's disposition. If you care to ask me any question about myself, write to me in your own language, and I will answer you frankly and exactly.

yours faithfully
[G. B. Shaw]

To FRANCIS HUEFFER

[F.u/2]

36 Osnaburgh Street N W
7th January 1883

[Dr Francis Hueffer (1845–89), father of Ford Madox Ford, was musical critic of *The Times*, author of a pioneer study of Richard Wagner (1874), and editor of the short-lived *Musical Review* (1883) and *Musical World* (1886). The "Prendi" aria is from Bellini's *La Sonnambula*.]

Dear Sir

My friend Mr Vandeleur Lee informs me that I may offer my services to you as a writer on musical subjects. Any work of the kind, large or small, would be very acceptable to me at present.

I have not yet seen the Musical Review, and therefore do not know whether it is conservative or liberal. For my own part, I don't consider "Prendi l'anel ti dono" everything that music ought to be, nor the second act of "Tristan" everything that it ought not to be, nor do I shake my head over the 9th symphony and prefer the septet. On the other hand, I do not look upon Don Giovanni as obsolete tum-tum, and I have a high opinion of Mendelssohn, though I revere him somewhat less than the average British organist does. In fact, if you can imagine a modern musician very fond of "Der Ring" and not fiercely contemptuous of Il Trovatore, who is at the same time not simply an easy-going optimist, perhaps you know as much of my tastes as I can tell you in a letter without making it intolerably long. I was a musical critic once before—for about a year. What I should, I will, with your permission, leave forgotten. I slashed away indignantly at the shortcomings of musical London—got concert advertisements withdrawn from the paper and, briefly, played the deuce. So I have done little more than sown my wild oats. This was about five years ago, and I have had no practice since, having been consistently occupied in the department of literature, which I regard as my speciality. I have in this way pretty nearly ruined myself. I am now desirous of turning my knowledge of music again to account—more discreetly than before, I hope. My artistic culture is not exclusively musical. I know enough to see all the arts with a good many of the sidelights which they throw on each other. Nor is my knowledge of music merely musical. I know something of the wants of singers, orchestral players and conductors, and of the differences which crop up between them. I have sufficient technical knowledge to call things by their right names, and to arrive at some conclusion as to the merits of a work from the score when I am out of reach of a performance. I am something of an adept in the superstitions of singing mysteries.

I should not trouble you with these particulars had not Mr Lee told me that you desired to be informed as fully as possible of what I professed to be able to do. I thought I should consult your convenience best by saying as much as I could for myself without ceremony.

I am, dear sir,

yours faithfully
[G.B. Shaw]

To FRANCIS HUEFFER

[F/2]

36 Osnaburgh Street N W
19th January 1883

[At Hueffer's invitation Shaw submitted an article entitled "Music for the People." There was, however, a divergence of opinion between the two as to the validity of Shaw's arguments, and Hueffer, interviewing Shaw on 18th January, apparently accused him of being an opinionated youth with too limited a range of experience to pass the judgments embodied in his article. Six years later, in his *Star* musical column (6th December 1889), Shaw reminisced: "I remember once coming to loggerheads with the late Dr. Francis Hueffer, about fifteen seconds after the opening of our first conversation . . . I declared that English society did not care about music— did not know good music from bad. He replied, with great force, that I knew nothing about it; that nobody had ever seen me in really decent society; that I moved amidst cranks, Bohemians, unbelievers, agitators, and— generally speaking—riff-raff of all sorts; and that I was merely theorising emptily about the people whom I called bloated aristocrats. He described, by way of example, an evening at Lord Derby's house, where he had greatly enjoyed some excellent music; and he asked me whether I knew that such music was, in a quiet way, a constant grace of the best sort of English social life. I suggested that he should give me an opportunity to judge for myself

by introducing me to these circles; but this he entirely declined to do . . ."
Hueffer eventually accepted the article; it was published in the *Musical Review* on 10th and 17th March.

The music publishers to whom Shaw refers had, on publishing ten new pianoforte sonatas, "sent out a circular containing an appeal *ad misericordiam* that at least a few people would, either in public spirit or charity, take the unprecedented step of buying these compositions." Sir Joseph Barnby (1838–96) was the founder of a choral society which bore his name; he succeeded Gounod as conductor of the Royal Albert Hall Choral Society.]

Dear Dr Hueffer

I have re-read and re-thought my article on music for the people, and I am incorrigible—I won't modify a word of it, and would submit every statement in it to the most exhaustive controversy if it were worth anyone's while to debate the question. What society do you wish me to flatter? If it be court, I know nothing about that, except that state concerts are mere singing shows, inferior in interest to "classical nights" at Covent Garden. Tell Lord D[erby] I have never been at his house, but I know that he orders good music, just as he orders good champagne, I know from whom he orders it, what he pays for it, and what he gets for his money, and the conclusion I have come to is that he knows no more of the quality of the article sent him than a teetotaller would of the champagne.

Mayfair society, South Kensington and St Johns Wood society, Chelsea society, Blackheath and Holloway society, and the dwellers [on] the borders of Epping Forest—I have had glimpses of all of them, and found musicians [in] much the same proportion as there were righteous men in the cities of the plain. Add to the arguments mentioned in the article the one fact of those unfortunate piano sonatas which Rudall, Carte are endeavouring by dint of begging letters and desperate advertisements to sell an edition of. Compare that with the enterprise of publishers and picture dealers, whose arts society really does encourage to the best of its ability. As against all this, you say that the people who seek you out are musical (of course they are), and that the Prince of Wales was curious enough to go to the "Nibelung Ring" when it was performed here for the first time in London. I gave due [?] to that act of self-sacrifice, and I say again—see article.* It may be "a sweeping assertion," but that is no objection to it if it be 99/100 true, which is as true as any critical statement—not a mere platitude—is

* Shaw presumably inserted a passage here from his article when he recopied the letter from the shorthand draft.

ever likely to be. It is a sweeping assertion that every object on earth is subject to the law of gravitation, for instance.

As to your notion that music halls are an unmitigated evil, I think that *is* sweeping, in your own sense of the term. I am convinced that music halls, when they are freed from the censorship of Middlesex magistrates and their like, will do more to educate the people artistically than all the nimminy-pimminy concerts in the world. I have been at these concerts, and I have been at music halls and not enjoyed any of them; but I gained the knowledge on which I base my opinion. I have said as much for [indecipherable] and "Sally in Our Alley" as they deserve. Highly cultivated people like to be infantile in their enthusiasms occasionally; hence the esteem in which they hold old ballads. A couple of years [ago] I found myself convalescent in the country, with a piano, and a collection of our noble, pathetic, naive &c &c English songs. A little of them went a very far way. At the end of the week I was glad when someone lent me a score of The Bohemian Girl!!! Any man who takes off his spectacles and gives himself a shake will see that there are old ballads which are quite inferior—words and music—to some modern music-hall songs. On this subject, I am an advocate for music halls absolutely free from restrictions, and an unsympathetic [indecipherable] of the people's entertainment sort of thing.

In short, we will drop the article into the waste paper basket, as the indiscretion of a youth of 27 from your point of view, and from mine— no matter what. But what is it that gives the vitality to the criticism of Berlioz and Schumann, both of whom you admire? Is it a conscious, [indecipherable] calm leading to the conclusion that there is much to be said on both sides? Suppose your critic pitched into Les Huguenots as Schumann did, or into Mr Barnby as Berlioz assuredly would have done, would you not think me rather juvenile? For my part, I believe the public likes to see a fight, I think they ought to be gratified when there is battle to be done in a good cause, and I see that the journals which make [it] a rule not to touch a subject without leaving a mark on it, are those which succeed: The Westminster [Review], The World, The Saturday Review, The Figaro, The Referee &c, blackguard papers, no doubt, some of them, but all ready to fight for their opinions. I grant you that it is not worth while to fight, that most things, impartially considered, are as broad as they are long, but in this spirit is it not still less worth while to publish a journal? and criticism is mere waste of time.

Excuse me for troubling you at this length: but if you tell a conceited

58

man that he is juvenile and thoughtless, you must expect him to have it out with you. I will send you another article as soon as I can hit on a subject. Pray excuse my boldness—there is no ill-humour to it.

> yours very truly
> G. B. Shaw

To WILLIAM M. LAFFAN

[F/2]   36 Osnaburgh Street N W
                                                        9th March 1883

[William M. Laffan (1848–1909), London agent for Harper & Brothers (he later became editor and proprietor of the New York *Sun*), asked Shaw on 9th March if he would care to submit *Cashel Byron's Profession* to Harper in New York, as "they might be able to use it serially." On 31st May, when the manuscript was returned by Bentley, Shaw submitted it to Laffan. *Cashel*, Shaw's fourth novel, begun on 12th April 1882 and completed in early February 1883, developed out of his interest in pugilism, its central characters being inspired by boxer Jack Burke and trainer Ned Donnelly. Although it eventually proved to be the nearest to a popular novel that Shaw ever produced, eliciting praise from Robert Louis Stevenson and W. E. Henley, it found its way into print only when Shaw consented to its serialisation in 1885, without payment, as "padding" for a Socialist monthly, *To-Day*.]

Dear Sir

The MS to which you refer is at present in the hands of Messrs Bentley & Son. However, as nothing would surprise me more than their undertaking its publication, I will probably avail [myself] of your kind suggestion in the course of a few weeks. I am in no hurry—I have hardly waited 4 years as yet.

I am much indebted to you and to Mr Kegan Paul for shewing me this opening.

> yours faithfully
> G. B. Shaw

To RICHARD BENTLEY & SON

[G.u/2]   36 Osnaburgh Street N W
                                                        31st May 1883

[In returning *Cashel Byron's Profession* after holding it for several months, Bentley credited the delay to the fact that the novel had undergone two

6—B.S. I

readings, the last being in March. Despite Shaw's suspicions of procrastination, Bentley seems to have been genuinely interested in the novel, for George Bentley later in the year undertook to have it read a third time before it was finally rejected. Pierce Egan (1772–1849), English sports writer, author of *Boxiana*, was one of several chroniclers whose works on pugilism Shaw had perused in the British Museum as source material for *Cashel*.]

Dear Sirs

I have received "Cashel Byron" safely, and beg to thank you for the attention you have given it. I read it twice (and wrote it twice) myself, but I certainly would not have done so except under the strong compulsion of authorship, and your repetition of the experiment seems to me either a remarkable proof of your conscientiousness in judging the novel, or a flattering tribute to its interest. But why did you not send it back to me last March? Is it possible that, with your great experience, you did not know that if you looked you would never leap—that when you could no longer defer your decision, you would act on the principle, "When you are in doubt, don't." I do not ask you this with any idea of troubling you for a reply, but merely as a defence to a certain strain in your letter which seems to reproach me with having inconsiderately pressed you for an answer.

You are quite right as to the horrible blackguardism of the book, but pray remember that I have tried science and the finer arts as subjects in vain, and that the lower I go, the better I seem to please.

Should you ever contemplate a reprint of the works of the late Pierce Egan, I will be happy, in the capacity of editor, to place at your disposal the historical research which I have wasted on "Cashel Byron."

Forgive me for thus trifling with your valuable time, and believe me,

dear Sirs,
yours faithfully
[G. B. Shaw]

To G. B. WOODRUFF

[F.u/2]

36 Osnaburgh Street N W
27th June 1883

[George B. Woodruff wrote to Shaw on 23rd and 26th June, inviting him to come to Brighton, expenses paid, to be interviewed for the post of tutor to Woodruff's son, replacing a tutor who was considering the acceptance of a curacy. Shaw eventually arranged to meet Woodruff in London, but nothing came of the negotiations. This, however, was not the first time Shaw had been encouraged to enter the academic world. In 1880 a former colleague of the Edison Telephone Company, Edwin Habgood, who had gone into teaching, unsuccessfully urged Shaw to apply for the Assistant Head Mastership at his school at Normansfield, Kingston-on-Thames.]

Dear Sir

My afternoons and evenings are unfortunately engaged in such a way that I am afraid I cannot avail myself of your invitation until next week, when I will be at your disposal on any day except Wednesday evening. This state of things is unusual with me, and I regret that it should have happened exceptionally at a moment when you are doubtless anxious to form a first opinion as to whether my candidature is worth following up. If you will be in the city on Friday, I can meet you there at any hour before five.

I am, dear sir,
yours faithfully
[G.B.Shaw]

To WILLIAM M. LAFFAN

36 Osnaburgh Street N W
[F/2]   8th August 1883

[Although Harper found *Cashel Byron's Profession* of "no use to them" in 1883, they subsequently published it in their Harper's Handy Series in December 1886, offering Shaw a payment of £10 despite the fact that the novel was not protected by copyright in America. He accepted the money, but returned it on moral grounds in 1899 when he learned that *Cashel* had been "pirated" by a Harper competitor.]

Dear Sir

I have just received a letter [of 24th July] from Messrs Harper, in which they ask what they are to do with my MS "Cashel Byron's Profession," which they find is of no use to them. Shall I write to them to send it to my address, or can you conveniently get it for me? I presume you have such facilities for the transit of books across the Atlantic, otherwise I would not trespass on you.

yours faithfully and obliged
G.B.Shaw

To H. SUTHERLAND EDWARDS

[F.u/2]

36 Osnaburgh Street N W
6th September 1883

[Henry Sutherland Edwards (1829–1906) had been musical critic for the *Pall Mall Gazette*, but, as he pointed out to Shaw on 26th September, he was now writing for the *St James's Gazette*. Unfortunately, he added, he was unable to help Shaw at present.]

Dear Mr Sutherland Edwards

I have just received the enclosed post card from Mr Vandeleur Lee. The work it describes would be welcome to me at present, but I do not know how to proceed without some more explicit account of how the matter stands than Mr Lee has given me. Will you be so kind as to enlighten me?

I presume the requirement of the Pall Mall is only a temporary one, and that a critic of no particular authority may suffice. As to my skill, perhaps Dr Hueffer will be able to give you an opinion, though he will certainly not endorse me as what is called a safe writer.

I hope I need not apologise for troubling you.

[yours faithfully
G.B.Shaw]

To ALICE LOCKETT

[T/1; X/136]

36 Osnaburgh Street N W
9th September 1883

[At Leyton in the summer of 1881 Shaw met two young women, Maggie Gardner and Jane Elizabeth Lockett (1855-1943). The latter introduced him to her younger sister Alice Mary, and Shaw instantly fell in love. At the slightest provocation he would scribble impassioned verses in shorthand into his pocket notebook:

When we speak I say "Miss Lockett";
Now my courtesy I'll pocket
And indulge myself by spelling
"Alice," and not hear her telling
Me to check my mad presumption,
With an exquisite assumption
Of offended dignity
Which endears her more to me.

Recklessly I dare again
On this page with ink to rain
Alice, Alice
Alice, Alice, Alice
Alice!
Alice!
Alice!
Alice!
Alice!
Alice!
Alice!
Alice!
Alice!
Alice!
Alice!
Alice!
Alice!
Darling Alice!!! [Burgunder, Cornell]

The Locketts, daughters of Jane Hewison and Walford Charles Lockett, an engineer, of Rawstorne House, Leytonstone, were middle-class, Victorian-indoctrinated women who had been moulded at the inevitable Ladies' College (Cambridge House, Leyton). Jane had even written a novel (of which Shaw in 1882 was so sharply critical that Jane was moved to reply: "Had I known when asking you to read 'Yeast' that I was condemning you to such a severe task, I should certainly have hesitated before making such an exorbitant demand . . . forgive me for having thoughtlessly inflicted upon [you] such severe literary labour" [BM]). But although Alice Lockett's education and family background had not prepared her to cope with an aberrant genius like young George Shaw, she made a good try at it. When they first met she was twenty-three, headstrong, and possessed of a driving ambition to break away from her environment and to climb socially. At the time of their meeting with Shaw (the introduction to Jane had been made by Dr Gurly, who was the family physician), the Lockett sisters were living in Walthamstow, having moved into a smaller house following a series of disasters which included the loss of their father in 1879 and their elder brother Walford in 1880. Their mother, who had suffered a paralytic stroke, survived for only a few years. Not desiring to be a burden to their grandmother, who had undertaken their care, the girls sought professions. Jane prepared for a career in education; Alice enrolled in the nursing course at St Mary's Hospital, Paddington. Almost simultaneously she undertook a course of vocal lessons from Mrs Carr Shaw, a device which enabled her to see George Shaw at least once a week.

For more than three years Alice Lockett struggled with a dual personality which Shaw, astutely, perceived and diagnosed. Her romantic nature, coupled with an innate desire to escape from a conventional—and therefore dull—environment, made it difficult for Alice to sublimate the urge to consort with Shaw, yet when she was with the impecunious bohemian her will froze, she suffered severe pangs of conscience, and she rushed home to pen child-like defensive letters. The two quarrelled incessantly, Shaw goading Alice by attacking her weakest defences, and she seeking, by way of exculpation for the behaviour she couldn't fully control, to retaliate by wounding his sensitive ego. They returned each other's letters (or those which survived) on two occasions, and eventually they drifted apart, Alice marrying Dr William Salisbury Sharpe (1864–1947), a former house surgeon of St Mary's Hospital in 1890. In later years they remained friendly, but met only infrequently. Sharpe operated on Shaw's foot in 1898, and during the first World War, when Sharpe was on active service and her financial position was precarious, Alice borrowed a small sum of money to pay an insurance premium. She died, in 1942, at the age of 84.]

Forgive me. I dont know why, on my honor; but in playing on my own thoughts for the entertainment of the most charming of companions last night, I unskilfully struck a note that pained her—unless she greatly deceived me. I have felt remorseful ever since, and she has been reproaching herself all day for wilfully missing a train. Heavens! to regret having dared at last to be frank and kind! Did you not see at that moment a set of leading strings fall from you and hang themselves upon me in the form of golden chains? The heart of any other man would have stopped during those seconds after you had slowly turned your back upon the barrier and yet were still in doubt. Mine is a machine and did not stop; but it did something strange. It put me in *suspense*, which is the essence of woman's power over man, and which you had never made me feel before—and I was always certain of what you would do until that question of the train arose. And I repaid you for the luxury by paining you. I did not intend to do so any more than you intended to please me, so forgive forgive forgive forgive forgive me.

I cannot (or perhaps will not) resist the impulse to write to you. Believe nothing that I say—and I have a wicked tongue, a deadly pen, and a cold heart—I shall be angry with myself tomorrow for sending you this, and yet, when I next meet you, I shall plunge headlong into fresh cause for anger.

Farewell, dear Alice. There! is it not outrageous? Burn it. Do not read it. Alas! it is too late: you *have* read it.

GBS

64

Alice Lockett

To ALICE LOCKETT

[T/1; X/136]

36 Osnaburgh Street N W
11th September 1883

[Alice had written that morning: "May I ask what was the object of your letter to me? Did you think it necessary to revive the pain caused by your words of last evening? All people are not machines: some are capable of genuine feelings. You know very well you have the power of paining me, and you are not very careful in exercising it. You have done it over and over again. As I cannot accuse you of want of discrimination, I presume you enjoy the power you possess. Your letter proves what I have many times told you—that you are one of the weakest men I have ever met; and in spite of your cleverness I cannot help despising you. The warning not to trust you is a needless one: unless you have a very bad memory you will recall the fact of my having told you so often. Although you truly repudiated the idea of insincerity your letter is one of condemnation. Much more could I say, but have said too much already" (Hanley, Texas).]

Come! if you meant all you said, you would not have written to me at all. When you are with me, you have flashes of generosity. You strive to keep it down, you have tried to prove that it does not exist by a wicked letter, and yet the letter—most ungenerous of letters—owes its very existence to that generosity. Was it not weak to write to me? Not at all. It was strong. It is the Miss Lockett vein that is the weak one, and the Alice vein that is the strong one. What is the saying—I can only quote it from memory, but it begins, I think, "Unless you become as a little child." Yet you have the greatest dread of becoming as a little child: you strive to be an unapproachable grown up person, of the world, worldly. It is that grown up person, Miss Lockett to wit, who reproaches me for my weakness, fearing that weakness instinctively because it is my strength. Well, let Miss Lockett beware, for she is the dragon that preys upon Alice, and I will rescue Alice from her. I hate her with a mortal hatred. Already I have shaken her. I have (as she admits) power to pain her, and I have (as she presumes) the will to use that power. I do not respect her, do not admire her, know her for one of those to whom it was said that the first shall be last, and that she that loveth her life shall lose it. I will shew Alice what she is, and Alice will abandon her for ever. Miss Lockett says she cannot help despising me. It is false; Miss Lockett fears me, and is piqued when I dispraise her. She says that unless I have a very bad memory, I will recollect the ungenerous things she has said to me. Wrong again: I do not recollect one of them, and yet my memory is good, for I recollect everything that Alice has said to me. I know half a dozen Miss Locketts.

65

They all toss their heads in the same way, all seek their own dignity by the same hackneyed road (fondly thinking it to be a private path of their own, and utterly forgetful of that "little child's" precept), and all say the very same forced and false things to me. If I could recollect commonplaces, how could I recollect which of the half dozen uttered any particular one? But there is only one Alice, and her sayings are her own, and therefore memorable. She is the sweetest of companions, and for her sake I have sworn war against foolish Miss Lockett, who is ashamed of her and suppresses and snubs her as the false and artificial always suppresses, snubs, and is ashamed of the natural, simple, humble, and truthful. But Miss Lockett, proud as she is of her strength, is a weakling; and her complaints, her pains, her bitter letters beginning with that vile phrase "May I ask," and going on to ask without waiting for the permission that she was not sincere in begging, are the throes of her dissolution. She has no patience and no faith: I, her enemy, have patience and knowledge, and care nothing for her opinion, knowing that I must win that of Alice. I hear Miss Lockett protest: she is always ready to answer for Alice. But I know better. Have I not also a dual self—an enemy within my gates—an egotistical George Shaw upon whose neck I have to keep a grinding foot—a first cousin of Miss Lockett? And such a model of a righteous man as that George Shaw was in the days of his dominion! How resolved he was to be an example to others, to tread the path of duty, to respect himself, to walk with the ears of his conscience strained on the alert, to do everything as perfectly as it could be done, and—oh—monstrous!—to improve all those with whom he came in contact. Here was a castle of strength and rectitude for you! And here was a foundation of measureless ignorance, conceit, and weakness! Verily, until he became as a little child again and was not ashamed to fall in love with Alice (then greatly under the thumb of Miss Lockett, who was, however, much flattered by the attention of a person of superior talent) he was in a bad way.

Do you not see the trick of my swordplay and lovemaking combined. Why do I please—delight you at one moment, and stab and mortify you at the next? Simply by planting an envenomed sting in one of Miss Lockett's foibles, and then telling Alice that I am fond of her. There is nothing human and real that is not pleased by the affection even of a dog or a slave, much less of an equal. Alice is pleased, and has no second thought to poison her pleasure. Even Miss Lockett's vanity is flattered, but she thinks it due to herself to pretend that love is an infringement of her claims to respect. But her claim refutes itself.

66

Respectability is a quality, not a right. The lily does not claim white-ness—it *is* white. Alice does not claim respectability—she *is* respectable.

Farewell, dear Alice—do not shew this letter to Miss Lockett; it will only enrage her. Do not let her write to me again—write yourself. I have old letters upstairs, the very counterparts of hers—almost the same words. Pray hide our correspondence from her, hide our inter-views from her, and be tranquil, she will not trouble you long.

I write in great haste and it is past midnight, so cannot stop to choose my words.

GBS

PS If this letter should accidentally fall into the hands of Miss Lockett, she is bidden to bear in mind that it is written for Alice alone.

To ALICE LOCKETT

[T/1; X/103.e]

36 Osnaburgh Street N W
8th October 1883

[This letter is a reply to a note from Alice on 7th October: "That is right, put your own big construction on what people say, be wilfully blunt. How dense you are! You [don't] even give me the benefit of a serious mood. If you did, perhaps I might understand you" (Hanley, Texas). Charles Bradlaugh (1833–91) was England's leading secularist and a social and political reformer, leader of the National Secularist Society.]

It is better to complain that I will not be serious with you than to pretend to be perfectly indifferent. I remember a silly, prettyish Miss Lockett who would have scorned to care whether I was serious or not. Let us see whether we cannot make a wise and noble Alice out of her. I think there has been some change, although you have not yet become as a little child, and still have much of that determination to save your life which ends in losing it.

When I first met you, you were a typical atheist. Last night I heard a clergyman say of Mr Bradlaugh, "He a sceptic! Not a bit of it: he is the most cocksure man in England." I immediately thought of you, the most (to adopt the parson's vernacular) cocksure woman in Walthamstow, teaching your Sunday school class the right and wrong of everything, and explaining the acts and mission of the apostles with the complacency of a thorough-going Pharisee. When you go to your class to seek what they can teach you, you will perhaps be in a fair way to teach them something. But until then, she that will save her life shall &c &c &c.

I am sorry that I offend you by not being serious. I am sorrier that I please you still less when I am serious. I am glad that I can read between the lines of your reproaches, and make all your unmeant resentment matter for fresh meaning. And do you not think yourself an ungrateful wretch to accuse me of want of seriousness? Granted that I am a buffoon—one whose profession it is to bribe people to listen to me by literary antics such as silly tales of lovemaking and so forth. But has anyone been more serious with you than I? If you have made me feel, have I not made you think? Have I been altogether unto you as a liar, and as waters that fail? (This is Scripture, and I hope you will not profanely doubt the seriousness of *that*.) I am, as I have private reasons for knowing, opinionated, vain, weak, ignorant, lazy and so forth, and the glimpses you get of these failings do not deceive you in the least. But dare any man or woman profess themselves impartial, modest, strong, wise, and diligent? Let any such cast the first stone. Such failings are instructive to witness sometimes, and you may learn a little from them alone, not to mention the abysses of folly of which I do not know myself to be guilty any more than I know the taste of water. (We do not know the taste of water because our palates live in water. For an analogous reason, thoroughly false people are never conscious of their falsehood.) You must not expect perfection from me. By the bye, I have observed that the people who hold the abominable doctrine of original sin are those who seem most surprised when they meet with people who fall short of absolute virtue. (They don't know that there is no such thing as absolute virtue.)

Here comes a frivolous interruption to my thoughts in the shape of a very pretty young lady (I am writing at the B. Museum) who passes and vanishes. I am frightfully tired of writing—I have been slaving at it all day. Farewell, and study Figaro diligently. Mozart's music and your beaux yeux—what need I more to be happy after my day's work. Ah, if our business here were merely to be happy! (I confess I shouldn't really enjoy such a state of things. I despise happiness.)

> yrs, blind and yawning and about to go
> home to tea
> GBS

To ALICE LOCKETT

36 Osnaburgh Street N W
[T/1]   20th October 1883. 2.35 a.m.

Dear Miss Lockett

I think you were unnecessarily severe with me this evening at tea.
I cannot recall the hard things you said to me, but I yield to an impulse
to let you know that Alice, in spite of fatigue and neuralgia, looked so
beautiful when she interrupted me at the piano, that only your presence
and that of my mother prevented me from saying a thousand silly things
to her. Partly to wound you through your jealousy of her, partly because I would not persuade her that I am not so hard as you describe
me, partly because I do not care how much I hurt you provided I
please her ever so little, and partly for reasons obscure to myself which
prevent me from going to bed in peace on this my late return without
a word to her in acknowledgment of a thrill which has lasted me through
a political meeting and four hours of private debate on dry questions
of economy, I take this wicked and forbidden step of writing to you.

Am I not a coward?—knowing that you dare not answer, and cannot
resent this indiscreet scrawl. My comfort is that I am plunged so deep
in your displeasure that I can do nothing to make you think worse of
me.

GBS

To JOSHUA HATTON

36 Osnaburgh Street N W
[F.u/2]   30th October 1883

Dear Sir

Kindly send me a cheque for my article "C.H.Bennett & Co.,"
pages 352–7 of the July number of the New Monthly Magazine. Your
letter commissioning me to write the article is dated Jan. 20th.

I am, dear sir,
yours faithfully
[G.B.Shaw]

To ALICE LOCKETT

[T/1; X/103.e]

[36 Osnaburgh Street N W]
5th November 1883

Here is your letter—not that I have anything to say, but because
you expect it. At least you said so. I walked home from Liverpool St.
[Station], and got frightfully wet (I believe I am in for an attack of
rheumatic fever at least) all because you would not wait half a minute
whilst I went back for an umbrella. Wretch that you were to catch
that train, and fool that I am to put myself in the way of caring whether
you caught it or not! I will be your slave no longer: you used me vilely
when we met before, and you disappointed me horribly tonight. I
recant every word I have ever said to you, and plead temporary insanity
as my excuse for having uttered them. I am exceedingly glad that I
had not to wait another half hour at that waiting room. I detest the
entire universe. I did nothing all the time but tell you monstrous lies—
I wonder you can be so credulous as to believe my transparent flatteries.
I say the same things to everybody. I believe in my soul that you never
meant to catch that train—that you were as much disappointed as I
when you found it had not gone. As much disappointed, that is, as I
pretended to have been. In reality, I was overjoyed. You told me I was
in an unamiable humor. Behold the fruits of it. Must I eternally
flatter flatter flatter flatter flatter? When you sit bolt upright opposite me
in a railway carriage, you look like a Chinese idol. What! I feel like the
Chinaman, do I? Not in the least, I assure you. I felt a thrill of delight
when you said you were going to Glostershire. Heaven knows when I
shall recover this wetting. If ever woman was undeservedly beloved
(supposing any man could be found mad enough to love you a little at
odd moments when your complexion is unusually beautiful) you are
she.

yours
with the most profound
Indifference
and in the most entire
Freedom
from any attraction on the part of
Any Woman Living

GBS

70

To ALICE LOCKETT

[T/1; X/103.e]

36 Osnaburgh Street N W
6th November 1883

[Alice's response, on 6th November, to Shaw's provoking letter of the previous day was addressed "to the irresistible George Shaw":

"Wounded vanity, wounded pride, humiliation and ego. Your letter is expressive and fair, and much else besides. In fact it is the most eloquent epistle I have ever received from you, the answering of which gives me the greatest delight and pleasure. You think you have opened my eyes to the fact of your being a confirmed hypocrite. Nay, my eyes were never so brightened: you have owned yourself that I have never placed the slightest faith in you.

"George Shaw, you have been playing a long game, therefore your pique! You consider yourself irresistable and are piqued because your base flattery has been without the usual results. Some genuineness and manliness would find a responsive chord in my heart, but mechanical sentiment is only a bore. What woman admires a man for owning herself to be his slave? She does not even respect him.

"A man does not love a woman for her good looks or for a beautiful complexion, but for what she is. Some men are so clumsy, instead of drawing forth the most noble part of a woman's hand, they repress it. I am sorry that our friendship is at an end. You are certainly entertaining and have taught me many useful things and pleasant things, and I thank you very much. May I quote from one of your letters? 'I your enemy have faith, patience and knowledge, and care nothing for her opinion.' Where is your faith? Where is your patience? Where is your knowledge? And where is your disregard for my opinion? Your very wish to quarrel with the entire universe shows very fully that you do care. But, seriously, I am really sorry that you should give way. I suppose that you prefer to give way rather than run the chance of being blown up in a railway tunnel. Very wise! I remain in perfect condition of heart and fancy" (Hanley, Texas).]

Aha! I thought a new sort of letter would make you answer me. As you say, I have "become as a little child," and a very silly baby I have to play with. So I must not love you for your good looks and complexion (fancy the vanity of a woman praising herself in that fashion. For shame!) but for what you are. Well, what are you? Come, tell me what all these great qualities are for which I am to love you. You say you are generous and manly (which latter is nonsense). Is it generous to tell me that I consider myself irresistible (which you spell improperly)? You say you cannot respect me because I am your slave. How can you be so conceited as to believe that I am your slave? You say the writing of your letter afforded you the greatest delight, and then you go on through six pages boasting intolerably of your insight, your

71

superiority to flattery, your "true generousness" (generosity), your scorn of servility, your "good looks," your "beautiful complexion," the extent to which your spiritual nature surpasses both, the nobility of women in general, your "heart and fancy," and your scrupulous justice and gratitude even to such worms as myself so far as I deserve it. Then comes a lecture to me on the sin of vanity. I believe such a monstrous outburst of egotism never was penned. And, after being called base, clumsy (oh fury!) impatient and ignorant, I am told that I am very entertaining and instructive. Am I a dancing bear or a learned pig that I should be insulted thus? I have sometimes blamed you for being morbidly afraid lest people should suppose that you were praising yourself, and I have effected a frightfully complete cure. "Beautiful complexion!" "true generousness!"—did any man ever read or woman write such things before? But it is all my fault for telling you of them. Why don't you date your letters, and write legibly, and write on paper unblemished by vain shows of insincere grief.

Alas, my dear Alice, all this folly goes against the grain with me tonight. It is all mechanical. I could be serious, only you would not understand me then. We are a pair of children, and petulant children should be petted and kissed into good humor. I am too big to be petted; but you are not too big to be kissed, and your "beautiful complexion" has tempted me often. Enough, midnight strikes, and my head is in a tumult with matters about which you do not care twopence. But your corner is an adorable place in which to pass the evening of a busy day. You will find all about it and about your dual entity (if you understand that) made the foundation of the most sentimental part of my new book [Chapter XIV of *An Unsocial Socialist*, in which Trefusis speaks of the dual nature of Gertrude Lindsay.]

GBS

PS Oh ye, to whom she shews this letter, consider whether you have not been as great fools as I, before ye blame me. Is it my fault if she does not deserve all the hours I have given to her?

To ALICE LOCKETT

[V/1; X/103.e]

36 Osnaburgh Street N W
19th November 1883

Dearest Alice
   Goodnight!
   You are dancing through my head to this tune

and I cannot refrain from telling you so. Forgive me.

This is a silly letter to replace the one you tore up and threw out of the window. Or else it is a sensible letter to replace the silly one you destroyed. I do not know which—I only know that when we were at the piano this evening, and you—No, I will not tell you. Is not that like yourself? I am catching the infection of your reserve—your eloquent checked revelations.

I am full of remorse for saying those things to you. If I had your heart, I know I should break it, and yet I wish I had it. Is not this monstrous? Take your lesson in the morning, so that I may never see you again, I implore you; and when you have done so, and I presently beg you to come in the evening, do not listen to me.

Oh the infinite mischief that a woman may do by stooping forward to turn over a sheet of music!

I am alone, and yet there is a detestable, hardheaded, heartless, cynical, cool devil seated in my chair telling me that all this is insincere lying affection. But I defy him—it is he who lies. I have only sold my working hours to him. Hate and mistrust him as much as you will; but believe me too, and help me to snatch a few moments from his withering power.

You are going to write something in reply, but you should check yourself, suspect "the trap." You are right—put your pen aside and only look as you did tonight.

Come, away with moody melancholy; I had much better have only written the first paragraph of this letter—it contains all. One more goodnight, fatal one. I protest that it is all your fault, Alice Alice Alice Alice Alice Alice Alice Alice Alice Alice Alice Alice Alice Alice Alice Alice Alice undeservedly beloved Alice.

Am I not a wretched fool?
GBS

To ALICE LOCKETT

[T/1]

36 Osnaburgh Street N W
1.25 a.m. 23rd November 1883

Aha! So you have opened it after all. Are you not ashamed of your goodness to me.

I could not get a tram, as they were all going in the wrong direction, so had to walk the whole way. I am comfortably tired, and so hungry that I have broken through my custom, and made a hermit's supper on a few nuts and raisins which I found in the cupboard, with a cup of cocoa. Fortified by these, I hope to finish my work before retiring.

I have no stamp, so cannot post this until morning. However, it will keep. I will say no more—this shall be a proper letter, fit for your grandmother to read.

I believe I will never talk of love to you again, except when you are cross and I sarcastic. I grow too fond of you for such profane stuff.

GBS

To GEORGE BENTLEY

[F/2]

36 Osnaburgh Street N W
26th November 1883

Dear Sir

In last June I had an interview with you concerning a novel of mine called "Cashel Byron's Profession" of which you had received an unfavourable report from two of your readers. You [nevertheless] expressed your willingness to read the book and judge for yourself. If you still care to do so, will you allow me to send you the MS, which I have at last succeeded in getting into my hands again. I am anxious, whether you publish it or not, that you should derive your opinion of me as a writer from my work, and not from reports, however able. In doubtful cases like mine, they lean too much to the safe side.

yours faithfully
G. B. Shaw

To ALICE LOCKETT

[T/1; X/103.e]

36 Osnaburgh Street N W
29th November 1883

[Rt. Rev. Charles William Stubbs (1845–1912) was Vicar of Granborough in 1883. A Christian Democrat, he later became Dean of Ely and Bishop of Truro.]

Dear Miss Lockett

I think our acquaintance had better cease at once, and for ever. I will not go into particulars, as I have no desire to wound your feelings, which I have always scrupulously respected. I will merely say that though I despise falsehood and treachery, yet I wish you well and forgive you. When we next meet, let it be as strangers.

This evening, on the distinct understanding that there was no longer anything to attr—— I should say to detain me on Thursdays, I had made an appointment at Balls Pond. Outrageously and heartlessly deceived as I found I had been, I kept that appointment with my usual unselfishness and rectitude of principle. I had my reward. The Revd. Canon Stubbs, lecturing on Shelley, interested me, and Balls Pond applauded my speech to the echo. I had a long walk, which my health requires. I was not stifled in the underground railway, which I detest, nor had I to waste half an hour, longing to be back at my work, in a draughty terminus waiting for the train. No one trifled with my feelings, or told me that I was despised by them. In a word, I was happy.

Never again will I believe the professions of people with whom religion and an affectation of conscientiousness is only a cloak for the most heartless coquetry. I apply this observation to no particular individual; it is impersonal and general. My circumstances provoke it, and I leave its application to your conscience.

I relinquish our acquaintance which was never more than the amusement of an idle hour, without regret, save for having ever formed it.

yours truly
Whom?

Not I, on my soul, oh tyrannical but irresistible Alice. I will not swear that I would have promised to go to Balls Pond had I known you were coming; but, having promised, I kept my word, in spite of your constant whisper, audible through the door to me at my lonely meal in the next room, "Wait, and come with me." Aha, wretch, I am too strong for you. I snap your chains like Samson.

7—B.S. I

And pray, says you in extreme indignation, do you suppose it was necessary to apologize to me for not having come with me to Liverpool St, as if I expected you to do so, or cared whether you came or not? Have I not repeatedly told you that I prefer to go alone?

True, Miss L. I beg your pardon: I have no right to intrude on you in this fashion.

I am not in the vein for writing tonight, or else I have exhausted it over my novel. I do not know why I began this letter. I do not believe I am sorry that I went to Balls Pond instead of to Broad St, and yet I can think of no other reason. I am as monotonous as the sparrow and the dove, the linnet and the thrush, in that song of yours. And yet I do not—my heart is as sound as a brass kettle. So is yours. We are too cautious, too calculating, too selfish, too heartless, to venture head over heels in love. And yet there is something—Oh, this is an intolerable letter, an intolerable mood to write in, an intolerable hour (half past one in the morning) to write at, an intolerable pen to write with, and—I was going to add an intolerable coquette to write to, but it is false. If you were only that I cannot think I would ever have thrown away two words on you, much less spent hours with you. Pleasant and ever-to-be-remembered hours too!

Adieu, dear Alice
GBS

To ALICE LOCKETT

36 Osnaburgh Street N W
11th December 1883. 3 a.m.

[T/1]

[Across this letter Alice scrawled "Bah! I dont believe a word. I happen to know all about your engagement."]

I really had important business elsewhere tonight. I did not tell you so because I thought you would rather believe that you had provoked me to small spite than know that I was placing a matter of business before the pleasure of seeing you on your way.

What I did say, I quite meant. How had you the heart to keep such a base promise—to make good such a pitiful boast? I hope it was Miss Lockett and not Alice. What would you have thought of me had I kept the only promise I ever broke to you?

GBS

76

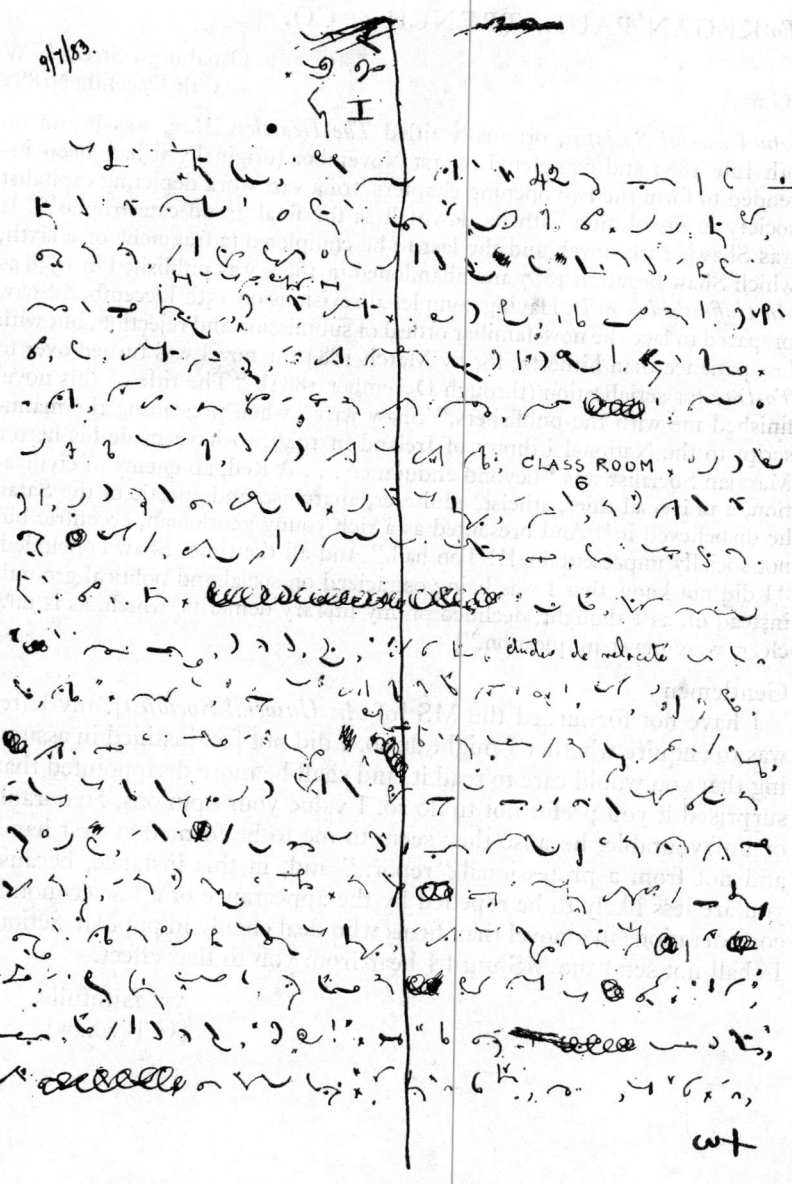

9/7/83.

CLASS ROOM,

An Unsocial Socialist
First page of shorthand draft, 1883 (*British Museum*)

77

To KEGAN PAUL, TRENCH & CO.

36 Osnaburgh Street N W
18th December 1883

[G.u/2]

[*An Unsocial Socialist*, originally titled *The Heartless Man*, was begun on 9th July 1883 and completed on 1st November (originally it had been intended to form the two opening chapters "of a vast work depicting capitalist society in dissolution with its downfall as the final grand catastrophe"). It was Shaw's fifth novel, and the last to be completed (a fragment of a sixth, which Shaw began in 1887 and abandoned in 1888, was published in 1958 as *An Unfinished Novel*). Having completed revisions on 15th December, Shaw prepared to face the now-familiar ordeal of submission and rejection, but with less patience than hitherto, for by March 1884 the novel was turned over to *To-Day* for serialisation (through December 1884). "The title of this novel finished me with the publishers," Shaw wrote when presenting the manuscript to the National Library of Ireland in 1946; to have made his hero a Marxian Socialist was "beyond endurance . . . A Red, an enemy of civilization, a universal thief, atheist, adulterer, anarchist, and apostle of the Satan he disbelieved in!! And presented as a rich young gentleman, eccentric but not socially unpresentable!!! Too bad." And all the time, Shaw concluded, "I did not know that I was being ostracized on social and political grounds instead of, as I thought, declined on my literary demerits, which, as is now clear, were never in question."]

Gentlemen

I have not forwarded the MS [of *An Unsocial Socialist*]; my letter was to enquire whether I might do so. I did not feel justified in assuming that you would care to read it, and shall be more disappointed than surprised if you prefer not to do so. I value your opinions, favourable or unfavourable, because they seem to me to be formed at first hand, and not from a professional "report," and, in this instance, because you are less likely to be repelled by the appearance of a few economic considerations in a novel than firms who deal chiefly in popular fiction. I shall not send the MS until I hear from you to that effect.

yrs faithfully
[G. B. Shaw]

To JOSHUA HATTON

[F/2]

[36 Osnaburgh Street N W]
3rd January 1884

Dear Sir

What about my article "C.H. Bennett & Co." in the July number of Colburn's? If I dont hear from you in answer to this, I shall begin to feel disappointed with the whole transaction.

yours faithfully
G. B. Shaw

To ALEXANDER SMITH

[F.u/2]

36 Osnaburgh Street N W
29th January 1884

[A.S. Smith was secretary of the Hunterian Club, Glasgow. Dr F.J. Furnivall (1825–1910), founder of the New Shakspere Society and the Browning Society, entrusted to Shaw the work of providing an index and glossary for the Hunterian Club's new edition of Thomas Lodge's works, for a fee of five guineas. Shaw slaved industriously at the project for several months, but his interest eventually palled, and as the work began to interfere with his burgeoning Socialist commitments, he tended increasingly to procrastinate. Although he eventually completed the largest portion of the work, his delays resulted in frantic appeals from the Hunterian Club and its printer Robert Anderson through July 1885, by which time Shaw managed to squirm out of the demanding and ill-paid assignment by arranging with Furnivall to assign the balance of the work to the scholar Thomas Tyler (1826–1902), editor of Shakespeare's sonnets. Sir Edmund W. Gosse (1849–1928) provided a prefatory "Memoir of Thomas Lodge," which was privately printed, for copyright, in an edition of ten copies in 1882.]

Dear Sir

Mr Furnivall has placed in my hands the Hunterian Society's reprint of the works of Thomas Lodge. It is in 19 separate parts, each having an independent pagination. As I understand that they are to be collected in 3 vols., I must devise some system of cross reference between the index and the table of contents in order to lead the reader to the particular tract to which my figures will refer. It will be useless, for instance, to send the reader to page 10 Vol. I, as there will be half a dozen pages numbered 10 in that vol. It will therefore be necessary to send me the title pages and contents, &c., of all the vols. I should

79

like to have Mr Gosse's memoir also, as its particulars ought to appear in the index. In fact, the entire collection should be in my hands, in order that there may be no occasion for additions later on. As they would be interpolations, they would be a source of expense in the printer's hands.

I am, dear sir,
yours faithfully
[G. B. Shaw]

To DOLLIE RADFORD

[A/5]

36 Osnaburgh Street N W
31st March 1884

[Caroline ("Dollie") Maitland (d. 1920), who had recently married Ernest Radford (1857–1919), a barrister, poet, and, later, secretary of the Rhymers Club, provided Shaw with some lyrics to set to music. The song to which Shaw referred in this letter was entitled "How She Comes." In September 1884 he composed the music for another of Mrs Radford's lyrics, "Ah Love, I lack thy kisses." *Progress* was a monthly journal (1883–87), edited by the secularist G. W. Foote, in which several poems by the then Miss Maitland had appeared in 1883.]

Dear Mrs Radford

I send you a setting of one of your songs for a tenor voice. It goes high enough to keep most amateur tenors at a distance; but the song would not be bright enough in a lower key. I had not time to copy it out at full length as I ought to have done; but you will be able to find your way through the repeats, though I know they are troublesome. The music is trumpery enough; but I am not a composer, and only profess to be tremendous in the third volume of a novel, so do not be too hard on my commonplaces. They will suffice to shew you the extent to which music alters the aspect of a poem. You will find, on examining the song as it stands, that it is inconclusive—leaves a "Is that all?" feeling behind it. You seem to have an extraordinary kaleidoscopic talent for stringing all manner of beautiful images and associations harmoniously together, and these, when combined with the pithiness and conclusiveness of an epigram, form perfect songs. But you are neither pithy nor conclusive. For instance, put a good epigram in verse beside the verses I have set, and you will have two opposite extremes in poetry. On the whole, I prefer your extreme for my own part; but this is not a respectable preference, being essentially that of a lazy man who does not want the trouble of thinking. I am not altogether satisfied: I believe you can do better. A large part of the charm of your verses is their prettiness, and that seems to come so naturally to you that I do not give you much credit for it. Some of the poems in Progress were fine, I thought.

Excuse my criticism. It is hardly a compliment to ask you to do so; but it seems ill-natured to fling off half a dozen disparaging remarks without expressing anything of the unfortunately inexpressible other side of the question.

yours faithfully
G. B. Shaw

P.S. If the music seems to you outrageously inappropriate to the poem, please give me an idea of how you wish them set and I will try again.

To MATTHEW EDWARD McNULTY

[A/2]

36 Osnaburgh Street N W
15th April 1884

[On 15th March the recently-founded Socialist journal *Justice* had published a letter by Shaw on economics, headed "Who is the Thief?" to which he had appended the signature "G. B. S. Larking." A reply to this letter the following week, signed "T. R. Ernest," was written by Edward Bibbins Aveling, D.Sc. (1851–98), common-law husband of Karl Marx's daughter Eleanor and translator of Marx's *Capital*. Shaw partially modelled after Aveling the artist Louis Dubedat in *The Doctor's Dilemma*. Henry Mayers Hyndman (1842–1921), leader of the Social Democratic Federation, had founded *Justice* to be "the organ of Social Democracy." Shaw, for a brief time before, and just after, he became a member of the Fabian Society in September 1884, flirted with the S.D.F., lecturing and writing for it, but he never actually became a member. R.P.B. Frost's article, "Mr. Herbert Spencer on Socialism," appeared in *Justice* on 12th April. Edwin Booth (1833–93), the great American tragedian, appeared in London at the Princess's Theatre in December 1880, in Tom Taylor's *The Fool's Revenge*.

At a subsequent date Shaw noted on the envelope in which this letter was contained: "Letter to McN. which dates the beginning of my lecturing & shews the economic muddle I was in then."]

There is no fallacy in my letter, except the assumption that my statement of the truth is a reductio ad absurdum. "T. R. Ernest" is quite right. Society shares the swag with the capitalist. When you buy a pair of trousers for fifteen shillings you probably get a larger share of the surplus value extorted from the worker than either the sweater, the merchant tailor, or even the merchant tailor's landlord.

In the instance (a purely fictitious one) given by me, I put the item of wages at 3/-. You alter it at your pleasure to 2/-, 1/-, 6^d & so forth. Well, I might as well have chosen 6^d as three shillings, just as I might have supposed the value of the table to be £150 instead of £1. I have no objection to take 6^d as the wage, but then the cost of the table to the purchaser will be brought down by capitalist competition (pace GBS Larking) to about 11/-. No matter what the other items are, so long as there is a profit of 7/- on the sale of the table at its value (£1—to be explained presently) some rival capitalist will bribe customers to deal with him by sacrificing some of the 7/- to them. If the table only costs the capitalist 10/6 (taking your figures) he can afford to sell it for 11/-, and will eventually be forced by competition to do so.

You ask what fixes the price of the table at £1. I have assumed, for the sake of argument, that £1 is the value of the table. What does that mean? Simply this. Tables do not grow ready made—neither do sovereigns. Before the table exists, trees must be felled, and the wood carted to the workshop; saws, planes, and lathes must have been made; horses must have been slain and their hoofs melted into glue upon fires which colliers have sweated to supply fuel to. In short, so many hours labor of man must have been consumed directly or indirectly in producing the table. Just so to produce the sovereign, ships must have sailed, mines must have [been] digged, smelters smelted to gold (using therein the labor of the collier and furnace maker), minters have minted, artists designed, and devil knows what else beside. Suppose from first to last it has taken twenty hours labor to produce a sovereign. Then a table worth a sovereign is a table which, from first to last, it has taken twenty hours to produce. If paper money be used, the cheque or note is simply an order on the tinker, tailor, or candlestick maker for twenty hours labor embodied in kettles, clothes, candlesticks, or whatever the table maker wants. If people could be depended on not to forge these drafts for labor, the whole business of the world might be carried on (as the greater part of it really is) without the use of coin at all.

Now you see what I imply when I fix the price of my table at £1. Observe that there is no room for profit in the transaction. I work an hour for you, and you work an hour for me.

Let us follow up the table. Its value is made up as follows. Raw material (wood) + glue + screws + wear & tear of saws, planes, lathes or other machines used in the making + paint, polish, or varnish + castors + rent, rates & taxes of a workshop for ten hours (the time in which the materials become a table) = 10/-. Let the money value of an hours labor be a shilling. Then to the 10/- must be added the labor of a table maker for ten hours = 10/-. 10/- + 10/- = £1, the value of the table. The table embodies twenty hours labor; but only ten hours of it is the labor of a table maker. The other ten hours is made up of the labor of woodcutters, carters, knackers, carters again, gluemakers, ironminers, railwaymen, smelters, railwaymen again, founders, railwaymen, screwmakers, colliers, sawmakers, planemakers &c &c &c &c &c &c, price of landlord's monopoly (teste [Henry] George), protection by police, water companies' labor &c &c &c &c—the imagination cracks beneath the load. But the result is that by ten hours additional work a table maker can produce a table.

Now note that the additional ten hours depend for their table producing power on the forespent other ten hours. Let us call the table maker Hugh de Cholmondoly—or, for shortness, Chum. Chum cannot fell trees, make planes, glue &c &c &c &c &c &c; and, if he could, it would take him some years to amass material for a table. Only in a highly socialized industrial system, with millions of men at his back, can Chum obtain his materials for ten hours work. Therefore Chum is helpless without materials. With them he can make in ten hours a table worth twenty hours work (ten of which he must pay to the producers of the material). But without them he cannot in twice twenty hours make anything whatsoever. He cannot grind the wind or store up sunlight in his pockets to let out to a darkling world at night at so much per cubic foot. *He possesses nothing but his labor force, and that is useless to him without materials to employ it on.* This is the position of the modern proletaire—of Chum also. Nature has supplied the material; but the landlord has intercepted the supply, and has sold to the capitalist what he cannot use in his own way. What is Chum to do? He must work. Why? Because his stomach tortures him until he fills it with bread, and when he asks for bread, the baker says "This loaf cost me an hours work—you must give me a useful article embodying an hours work in exchange for such embodiment." Chum is willing to work, but, as aforesaid, must have material. All the material is owned by the capitalists. Chum goes to the capitalist, and says, "I want materials to make a table—ten shillings worth will suffice." "Why should I give you materials?" says the Cap. "Who asks you to give them?" says Chum. "I will replace them, and you shall be as well off

83

as before." "I want to be better off than before," says Cap. "There is no reason why you should be unless you work as I have to do," says Chum. "But," says Cap, "you cant do without me, you know." "True," says Chum, "but neither can you do without me. Your raw material, workshop, and machinery are no more use to you without my labor (or some one's) than my labor is of use to me without your material &c. We are mutually dependent." Cap yields: Chum makes the table in ten hours, and receives for it £1, the equivalent of 20 hours labor. 10 hours of this are due to Cap, and ten to himself. He gives Cap 10/- and keeps 10/-: justice is done, Jack is as good as his master, and there is no idea of profit, nor division of classes.

But Cap cannot supply Chum with 10/- worth of material next day, because he too has a stomach, and he must give some to the baker (say 1/-). He therefore can only give Chum 9/-. Chum has to get the other shillingsworth from some other capitalist (or direct from the producer of the material paying for it out of his earned 10/-); and when he sells the second table for £1, Cap only gets back the 9/- he advanced, 1/- of which the baker must again have for the days food. Eight days later Cap (not having worked) is destitute, and must do as Chum did—work for his living. Thus, where justice is done, and an hours labor given for an hours labor, no man can live idle.

And, justice or no justice, if each man could only barely support himself by working as hard as he could all day, no man could live idle. This actually happens when nature is niggardly and the machinery of production primitive and barbarous. But in a highly civilized modern community it does not happen. A man can probably (with the help of nineteenth century machinery) produce enough in one hour to keep himself in reasonable comfort for 24. If so, by working ten hours a day he can support himself and nine idlers in reasonable comfort. Or, by contenting himself with half the comfort, he can support four idlers in twice as much comfort as is reasonable and one in once and a half as much. Or he can support one other man in monstrous luxury. To him it is all the same whether his nine hours unnecessary labor is pocketed in a lump by a rackrenting landlord or distributed between nine railway shareholders. The essential point is that a state of things exists in which a man can produce more than he consumes. In such a state of things a man can live idle if he can force another to work for him.

Go we back now to Chum and Cap. Suppose that Cap is not convinced by Chum's argument that they are reciprocally dependent. Suppose Cap says "My friend, you are mistaken. Your stomach must

84

be filled within this present week or you die. I have money enough (made for me by other Chums on the terms which I am about to offer you) to keep me supplied with all I need for years. I can starve you out. Of course, you can go to the workhouse." "Workhouse indeed!" says poor snobbish hoodwinked Chum, "Im no pauper, I aint. Im willin' to work." "Bravely spoken," says Cap. "I like to see a man honest and independent. Come into my workshop. You shall have five shillings a day (of ten hours), and permanent employment." What can Chum do but consent, since he cannot get materials on any other terms. He makes a table per day at a cost to the human race of twenty hours labor as before, and to himself of ten hours labor, value ten shillings, for which he receives five.

Cost of table *to the Community*

Labor of woodcutters, carters, knackers, sawmakers &c &c &c	s	d
10 hrs at 1/- per hour	10	0
Labor of table maker. 10 hrs @ 1/- per hr	10	0
Total £1–0–0		

One pound is the just price or value of the table, and for the present it is the market price. But see here.

Cost of Table to Capitalist.

Purchased materials embodying 10 hrs labor of woodcutters	s	
&c as above, @ 1/- per hr	10	0
Wages paid to table maker	5	0
Total 15–0		

The Cap. takes for nothing, every time he sells a table, five shillings of the value created by Chum's labor. He calls this profit, reward of abstinence, interest on capital, encouragement to him for his superior intelligence, or anything he pleases. It *is* simple robbery. What is Chum doing now? He is, instead of enjoying the produce of his labor force, actually selling that labor force in the market as a commodity. Competition regulates the prices of commodities in the market, and it presently regulates poor Chum. Whilst Chum gets so high a wage as half what he makes, it may safely be concluded that there are not many more Chums about than Cap needs to work up his material. But the population increases, Chums become more plentiful, and perhaps the invention of a machine throws a thousand or so of them out of employment. Any of them, sooner than starve, will gladly do Chum's days work for 4/6. Cap naturally buys labor as cheap as he can get it. Chum has to accept 4/6 in order to keep his place, and Cap's profit becomes 5/6 (the value of the table remaining the same). Another man offers to take 4/-. The Trades Union calls him "knobstick" and he is threatened, knocked down, kicked, and frightened off; but in the long run the Trades Union is beaten, and wages come down to the lowest figure at which Chum can keep himself going and breed fresh Chums to make profit for the descendants of Cap. Say that 3/- is that figure; and you have the state of things from which G.B.S.Larking starts. You will see that 3/-, being the minimum to which "the iron law of wages" always tends, cannot be reduced, as you suggest, to 2/- 1/6 or 6ᵈ. Cap would have reduced it before, if it were possible to do so. We now have Cap with his 7/- profit. In my letter to Justice I describe how competition will make him disgorge this, sixpence by sixpence, just as it made Chum disgorge before. In practice, of course, the two processes would run concurrently, and each reduction in price would make the pretext for the successive reductions of Chum's wages. Sometimes—nay, very often, the market price falls below the sum of the wage and the cost of material, and the capitalist is smashed. How is this possible?

Thusly. The cost of running a train from Westland Row to Kingstown is the same pretty much whether the carriages contain two hundred passengers, or are empty. If the traffic consisted of about six passengers twice a day, a coach would flourish and a railway be ruined. If it consisted of 60 passengers fifty times a day, the coach would be ruined and the railway would flourish. How would the coach capitalist be ruined [?] The railway could afford to transport people to Kingstown at a profit at less than he could afford to charge even if he forewent his profits. An organized society working a large industry can always produce more economically than small individual undertakings, on exactly the same principle as two families by clubbing together can live more cheaply than they could in separate houses, with separate attendance, rates, taxes, butchers waste &c &c. Co-operative stores first, by reducing prices, force small shopkeepers to make up the difference by longer hours and harder work (terrible to their employe's) and eventually smash them. Everywhere the large capitalists are swallowing up the small ones. Whole trades are being monopolized by single firms as the screw trade is supposed to have been by the Chamberlains; and others have passed into so few hands that the monopolists, as in the case of the American railways, find it more profitable to combine against the public than to compete. It is in this way that the capitalist system has evolved from its own essential principle of competition the instrument of its own destruction.

86

This is a tedious thing to explain, and I wish you would tell me whether you can make anything of my explanation. Do not destroy this letter, but send it back to me, as it has just occurred to me that it might be made the nucleus of a contribution for Justice or the C[hristian] S[ocialist], for which I have been asked.

I have not seen Spencer's article. There is a long comment on it by Frost this week. S. talks about the Wages Fund, an exploded pet of the old fashioned economists. You are right (and rather good) on the subject of the effect of Socialism on Individualism. When S trembles at the power of the State as monopolist in chief, he forgets that the private monopolists now exercise all the powers of a govt without its responsibilities. The railways practically govern the United States at present.

I am to lecture at the Invicta [Working Men's] Club in Woolwich— not in the open air.

I saw Booth in "The Fool's Revenge," and thought him very smart, but not spontaneous; and heavy and elocutionary when he tried pathos. Hope to see him in a better play.

You think that Scott & Dumas are obsolescent because your Dumas– Scott period belongs to the past. But look at the railway bookstalls, and judge whether the supply there does not indicate a demand.

I hope you dont mean that Fra Angelico could not draw better than most of our modern R.A.'s [Royal Academicians]. Heavens! Two in the morning.

GBS

To J. DYKES CAMPBELL

36 Osnaburgh Street N W

[A/2]   5th May 1884

[James Dykes Campbell (1838–95) in 1884 was Secretary of the Browning Society. Shaw's "speech," the drafted report of which he supplied for the Society's *Monthly Abstract of Proceedings*, was a contribution to a discussion at the 25th April meeting following the reading of a paper on Browning's "Caliban upon Setebos" by James Cotter Morison (1832–88), biographer of Gibbon and Macaulay.]

Dear Mr Campbell

I send you a report of my speech from memory. The notes you sent me made my blood run cold until I came to a few blunders which convinced me that I had not really talked such nonsense, but that your stenographer, instead of reporting me verbatim, had made a few inaccurate notes of my speech in shorthand, and transcribed them wrongly. I am a poor phonographer myself; but I think if I took down a speaker as having uttered the words "epic poet," I could make a saner transcript of my own notes than "block poet." The fellow was thinking of his own head.

I should have sent you the report sooner, but had not time to prepare it, as I was occupied with a lecture ["Thieves"] which I had to deliver last night [at the Invicta Club].

yours faithfully
G. B. Shaw

P.S. I am not sure that the parentheses in my report describe accurately what took place. The fact is that I am always so nervous when I speak, that I stand in a sort of trance, and have only a very confused notion of the interruptions with which I am often favored. Kindly correct, if necessary, in this respect.

If you care to send me a printers proof, you shall have it back by return of post. But I do not think any serious mistake is likely to occur.

To KATIE SAMUEL

[F.u/2]

[36 Osnaburgh Street, N W]
[?30th May 1884]

[Shaw received a few letters from Katie Samuel in May, principally concerned with her desire that he write a new ending (which he declined to do) for her novel *Jane Conquest*. Although her identity is uncertain, Miss Samuel's statement to Shaw that he was "affecting her peace of mind" indicates that she was another of the numerous young ladies infatuated with him during this period. He, in turn, noted in his diary that he had fallen in love with Miss Samuel "for a week or so." Later she emigrated to Canada, and was heard of only once more, in a letter from Shaw to Charlotte Payne-Townshend on 7th November 1897, in which he informed her that "My old flame" was now "a Montreal matron."]

Dear Miss Samuel

Forgetting to give you your book was perhaps the least of the 1000 stupidities which I committed last night. Worse than that, in trying to cut open the leaves without a paper knife I tore your copy inexcusably. I beg your pardon on all accounts. I have a vague impression,

88

such as a drinker might have on the morrow of an orgy, that I behaved very foolishly and chattered insanely and at random on topics thoughtlessly suggested by Monty. I even awoke this morning with a fancy that I sang an air from Stabat Mater as a species of rare treat for you, but this, thank God, must have been a dream. I have purposely delayed writing until the verge of post hour, and so must close in some haste.

yours (I cannot think of an adverb that would satisfy both of us)
[G. B. Shaw]

To ALICE LOCKETT

[T/1]

36 Osnaburgh Street N W
26th June 1884

Come at six, and have tea, saith Mrs Carr Shaw.

My train was late on Tuesday: it did not leave Hoe St until past twelve. Did I leave you abruptly, or did my power of dissembling carry me safely off? After begging you to stay a moment with the most selfish coolness I suddenly caught fire; my self command wavered, and I fled. Wretch that I am, or that you are! I do not know which. It does not matter—our longest walk was also my pleasantest.

À demain, chère Alice. Which means in English, I have the honor to remain, honored Madam, and dearest ennobler and consoler of my idlest, and (without you) darkest hours,

yours most respectfully
George Mister Shaw

PS Nothing. I have waited for five minutes for some sentence to come, in vain. Come, sir; be sensible: shut up your letter and dont make a fool of yourself. The young lady knows when she is to come, and that is enough for her. True, and enough for me, too.

To ALEXANDER SMITH

[F/2]

36 Osnaburgh Street N W
1st July 1884

Dear Sir

The Lodge Index has proved a far longer job than I anticipated;

and I have had to put it aside several times to make room for other work. It is still far from completion. I have read the whole reprint through closely, and have finished all the work which did not require any exceptionally long research. The Index which required further consideration I put aside, and the [glosses], which promise to be the most troublesome, are still before me. I am very anxious to get it over and off my mind.

If Mr Gosse's memoir contains any new facts concerning Lodge, I should like to see it, as there are one or two references in the old text which I do not understand.

> I am, dear sir,
> yours faithfully
> G. B. Shaw

To ALICE LOCKETT

36 Osnaburgh Street N W
7th July 1884

[T/1]

And they say women are sympathetic!—not that I ever said so. Why do you select the first time you find me out of sorts, with all my arrangements for the week and evening upset, to be impatient and to make everything as difficult and unpleasant for me as possible? When you try my patience, do I ever lose it? And when half a dozen cross events try it, you lose yours, and take out that small workbox tape by which you think you can measure my whole soul because you have (with much surprise and self-congratulation at your own cleverness) fitted one or two of my smaller social ways with it, to discover why I am like a baffled bear. I have lost an evening's business, found you odious, been almost rude to the innocent Jane in consequence of the flippant turn which you gave to my attempt to be frank over the difficulty, and have had for consolation a long walk with Mrs Chatterbox [Jenny Patterson]. You are always reproaching me for giving you lumps of sugar as though you were a baby. But see how you treat me the moment I am worried and forget the sugar. Well, you shall have larger lumps the next time. You will not be able to resist taking them, and yet the remembrance of this letter shall poison your enjoyment of them. I am savage beyond measure with you and everyone else. You have been a wicked failure this evening, and I have been an ill-used saint.

G. B. S.

To ALICE LOCKETT

[T/1]

36 Osnaburgh Street N W
9th July 1884

["Yes!" replied Alice on 8th July, "women *are* sympathetic, when there is real need. Take your real needs to any woman, and you will find her sympathetic. What did you write that unreal letter [for]? So full of petty fault-finding. I can hardly believe that it is written by a man, who prides himself on the possession of an unlimited depth of soul.

"What right have you to find fault with my behaviour? I am quite unconscious of anything in my conduct that you have any right to reprove. As for your conduct, it was faultless. But I suppose that you want me to pay you a compliment?" (BM)]

Enough, dearest Alice: you are only a child, and I am a fool to quarrel with you. But you are very unreasonable. Must I break my neck, or lose my sight, before you will sympathize with me? You infinitely silly one, it is my small troubles that I go to you with—what do you know of my larger needs, or how could you sympathize with them? I have spoken of them to you once or twice just to try you, and you never suspected that there was anything serious in question.

I will tell you something funny. I wrote you a letter the other day with a very pretty beginning. Changing my mind, I left it unfinished, and sent you, instead, the one you have just replied to (in spite of your vows never, never, never, so long as you lived, to write another line to me). But I quite forgot the unfinished fragment, and it remained on the table among the stationery there. This morning I found it laid neatly by my mother in the davenport. It must have amused her. Look her in the face, if you dare, at your next lesson.

Now let me reproach you with a real fault. Of all the vile handwritings and the pretty women in existence, Alice is the prettiest and her handwriting the vilest.

amued

There is a facsimile. I defy you to tell me what it means. I can tell you—by the context. It means Decided. Your h is a capital N. Your u is a capital W. Your s is a slovenly figure 8. You would write mun as uuu, and expect me to decipher it. Your a is & upside down. Your d is truly confounding. Sometimes it is el. More often u, because you seldom make the heads of your letters long enough, though you

8—B.S. I

91

decorate them with unnaturally long tails. As to the rest of the letters, I know not how you make them, for I can only guess at the words without attempting to distinguish the letters. You write long sloping heavy letters all in loops, bearing on a great wet pen as if it were a graving tool. I believe you rest your cheek on your elbow, and follow the movements of your hand with your tongue. Everything you write sounds clumsy. Do, cherished Alice, for my sake and for the sake of all who love you and read your letters, teach yourself to write afresh. All the letters in Walthamstow should not be of the same height. The ts should be taller than the as, the W, l and h taller than the ts. The tallest stroke in your writing of it is the middle arch of the m. This is because you think constantly of yourself, and never of your poor reader —in a word because you are unsympathetic—in small matters only, of course. (As if a woman incapable of sympathy on small occasions could display it in great emergencies!) Time flies. Farewell. We can talk it over further when next we walk together, until when take good care of my heart.

GBS

To ALICE LOCKETT

[T/1]

36 Osnaburgh Street N W
12th August 1884

[Mrs Carr Shaw was at this time visiting at Broadstairs, Kent, with Mrs Jane Patterson, who had a cottage there. Alice, anticipating her return, had sent a box of flowers from Moreton-in-Marsh, where she was on holiday at the home of the Rev. James William Clarke (1831–1888), a distant relative to whom the Lockett sisters referred as their uncle, and his wife Anne (1832–1912). Shaw's sentiments concerning cut flowers (later shared by his wife Charlotte) are echoed in virtually the same words by Peter Keegan in Act II of *John Bull's Other Island*.]

My dear Alice

Thank you for the flowers. My mother is not here. She will not return until Monday next at soonest. I know nothing about flowers; but I have followed your instructions implicitly. They are in the largest basin in the house. When I poured the water in they stirred uncomfortably, and did not half like it, as far as I could see. As to all the yellow and red ones, it seems a pity to have pulled them. Suppose that my mother is fond of children. Would you cut the heads off all the children you could find and send them to her to stick in vases about the room? Yet cut flowers always suggest that idea to me. However, you had one inspiration. You sent three fern leaves. They are not strong wild bracken such as used to twist round my instep when I was a child, and my feet were beautiful upon the mountains; but they have the same odour—they carry me back sixteen years to when—wretch that you are—I would not have turned from the sky or sea to look at you if you passed. I was very weak then, and am comparatively very strong now; and yet, Good Lord, what am I doing? Writing to you! No matter; I have lived a bachelor life this past fortnight, rising early, working reasonably well, and not regretting my follies. Now that you come unasked with your flowers, I am not to be blamed for turning for a few moments towards you, and saying a few words to an imaginary Alice for whose accommodation I have borrowed a face and figure from Miss Lockett of Walthamstow.

How is your dear aunt? Kindly give her my affectionate regards. This reminds me of our last walk together, and how vilely you disenchanted me afterwards. My heart hardens—I will solace myself with my ferns and their associations with the days when I had a fool's head and a boy's heart instead of, as at present, a man's head and a fool's heart (what there is of it). After all, England is a vile country. I speak not of the men and women—they are vile everywhere; but of the scenery. The Thames is pretty and green, but you cannot see the round towers of other days in the wave beneath you shining there. Farewell, and thanks for the ferns. You did not intend them; but I will set them off against many small wounds that you did intend, and would repeat if I had let you see me wince. Eternal love to Janey. As for you, when you return I will make you fall in love with me merely to shew you how clever I am.

GBS

To ALICE LOCKETT

[A/1]   [36 Osnaburgh Street N W]
                                                         [12th August 1884]

[In the second post on 12th August, Shaw received a one-line note from Alice: "Sorry I forgot to send the enclosed before A.M.L." The "enclosed" were a few penny stamps, reimbursement to Shaw for the postage he had expended on his letters to Alice. (On another occasion, she had returned one of his letters with the scrawled statement across the envelope "This is not worth a penny stamp.") Shaw's terse reply is borrowed from Ecclesiastes, 7:28.]

" Which get my soul seeketh, but I find not: one man in a thousand have I found, but a woman among all these have I not found."

Farewell, incorrigible trifler: I am awake and in earnest at last

To ALICE LOCKETT

[T/1; X/103.e]

36 Osnaburgh Street N W
19th August 1884

[Writing from Moreton on 13th August, Alice admitted: "I am sorry that your feelings were so hurt by my returning the ten stamps. I dont know why, but it is positive pain to feel that you have even spent one penny on me. That I owe you a debt of gratitude, I am well aware, that I do not wish to pay; you have to a great extent improved my character, and I am not unmindful of this. . . . That I was pleased to receive your letter, I frankly own, as it was quite unexpected. I had made up my mind never to hear from you or see you again, after your last dramatic farewell. 'Farewell, inveterate [*sic*] trifler I am awake &c &c' When I return . . . these words will be to me like a steel armour. Your hard-heartedness is infectious" (BM).]

Knowest thou, dear Alice, where my mother is? She was to have returned on Monday; but she has not come: her letters accumulate; and I have to take thought unto the morrow for butter and sugar and other grocer considerations. She has not written. She has had a taste of vagabondizing; and she likes it: she is a born Bohemian.

So you have no time for thought. Poor Alice!

Shall I write you a letter in return for your three sheets of reticences? A year ago I would have written copiously. But now I begin to reflect.

94

For the last fourteen years I have been writing letters—some thousands of them—a couple of hundred perhaps to women—and what has come of it all? Only that it is growing harder and harder to write, easier and easier to be written to. You are a novice at letter writing, I an expert. I am a novice at love making, you an expert. Let us then improve ourselves by practice. Write to me, and I will make love to you—to relieve the enormous solitude which I carry about with me. I do not like myself, and sometimes I do not like you; but there are moments when our two unfortunate souls seem to cling to the same spar in a gleam of sunshine, free of the other wreckage for a moment.

Well, let us make the most of the days of our vanity. Do you ever read Shakspere, or Swift, or Koheleth? (popularly known as Ecclesiastes).

I have sent To-Day to Janey.

Why have you and she become so abandonedly reckless of the impropriety of corresponding with me?

GBS

PS How long do you suppose it has taken me to write this little letter?

To ALEXANDER SMITH

[F.u/2]

36 Osnaburgh Street N W
29th August 1884

Dear Sir

I send the Index by parcels post. There remains the work on the proofs, and some references to be inserted as soon as I have succeeded in verifying them. The Index might be extended, but I hope I have done enough to save a little time to future dippers into works of Lodge. Readers almost always complain of too much glossary and too little index in complete editions. The reprint is certainly a very fine one.

As this is a slack time with printers I think it best not to wait for the completion of the few slips about which I am still in doubt. Kindly send me the proofs. They ought not to be paged, as the insertion of additional slips would cause over-running.

yours faithfully
[G.B.Shaw]

To ALICE LOCKETT

36 Osnaburgh Street N W
26th September 1884

[T/1]

Where is Janie? I am reminded of you, your sex, and your sister, by my proofs for To-Day, the last number of which I never sent. The October part will be out in a few days and if my mother has not sent the Sept. part, I will send the two to Janie as soon as you let me know her address. I am full of serious matters tonight, and do not know how you have continued to thrust yourself in. If you were the best, dearest, and loveliest of your sex; and I the best, kindest and handsomest of mine, how happy we should be! As it is, you are only a wretch who takes advantage of the weakest side of my character to make me continue my letter when I have said all I have to say. My mother will return tomorrow (Saturday). When we last parted I went to Leytonstone. I left in an ill humour, and went to St James' St., where, by a frantic race from Markhouse Lane I just caught a train. I walked home from Liverpool St, and was so tired through abstinence from my evening meal (your disgraceful fault) that I was unequal to the exertion of eating, and went straight to bed in the lowest of spirits. My system sustained such a shock that I was unable to rise until nearly eleven o'clock next morning.

Adieu, worldly saint. Pray for

your unworldly sinner
GBS

To JANE LOCKETT

36 Osnaburgh Street N W
12th October 1884

[W/103]

[Shaw had been sending Jane Lockett the monthly parts of *An Unsocial Socialist*. Jane, stung by the criticism of her sister's handwriting, gave vent to her feelings by recording on the letter: "I have written a curt note of thanks in answer to this, which needs a microscope it is so small" (BM). Jane, who never married, became co-director, with Miss Jane Grattan, of Parkside School for Girls at Harrogate, but was obliged to retire in 1902, due to failing sight. Although she never became completely blind, Jane learned to read braille, and in 1910 became an instructor at the Royal Institute for the Blind, Birmingham.]

Dear Miss Lockett

A word of apology for not having sent you the magazine sooner. It was partly my own fault, partly the difficulty of getting your address from Alice, and partly the impossibility of reading her handwriting when she did send it. You shall have the next number punctually. I hope you approve of the story.

yours fraternally (this is the
received Socialist ending)
G. B. Shaw

To ALICE LOCKETT

[T/1]

36 Osnaburgh Street N W
13th October 1884

[The International Health Exhibition opened in London on 8th May and ran to the end of the year. It was in connection with this exhibition, and with a Parliamentary inquiry on patent medicines inspired by it, that Shaw undertook to write, at George (later Sir George) Radford's request, an article on patent medicines. For this work Radford (1851-1917) paid him £4. 14. 6 (five guineas, less ten per cent commission), noting in a letter to his brother Ernest on 9th August 1884: "I would have remitted before but have been waiting for our clients' decision in the matter. They have succeeded in stirring up some M.P.s about the alleged grievance, and there is some prospect of legislation. Whether this will be *before* the House of Lords is let to a prosperous mad-doctor for a private lunatic asylum or after can only be conjectured." (Unpublished letter, privately owned.) Shaw never discovered if his article was published.

Alice's friend Gibney ("Giggley") has defied identification.]

I am very sleepy, very tired, and do not care sufficiently about anybody or anything to reproach you. After walking and talking energetically all the afternoon, I hurried home to tea, took it, and then hurried to Liverpool St, where I arrived at a quarter to nine. You could not possibly have caught an earlier train than the nine except by leaving the Health Exhibition before eight. I sat in our waiting room for a while, and saw the train off. I returned to the room, read a little, moped a little, and found, on rising to watch the 9.30 train that I had a terrific cramp which lamed me. I cursed my folly in being there at all until I had walked the cramp away. Then I went back once more to the waiting-room, shut my eyes, and considered myself asleep until something roused me, and I stared for some minutes at a cat which was lapping the water in the croft placed on the table for the refreshment of passengers. Then I went to sleep again, and began to wonder whether you were as tired as I, and to hope that, if you were, you were already at home and in bed. Finally I watched the 10.10 train, and then, giving you up, came back by underground to Portland Road.

When I returned here today at one o'clock, I found my mother at home. "Why have you come back?" said she. "Is the museum closed?" "I haven't been to the museum," said I. "Where have you been?" she *looked*. "With Alice," I *said*. "Well, upon my word!" she exclaimed outraged. Then, after a moments reflection, resignedly, "She is old enough to take care of herself." I told her about Giggley, and she said she had better write to you. I remarked that as you had mentioned the hour of your return, I should probably see you in the evening. On this she declared that she really would speak to you about it ("it" meaning me and not Gibney), but subsequently fell back on her previous position of deference to your independent right to arrange your own conduct for yourself. I told her what you said today when I narrated her reception of me after our holiday. So you can meet each the other's eye as best you can—I am between you both an ill-used man, told on the one hand that I am not to be trusted—on the other that it is a shame for me to go on as I do—and left catching my death in unutterably lonely railway waiting-rooms. At least they would be lonely did not my imagination people them. Adieu, faithless one. God will be very angry with you for deceiving me. Have you no gratitude to Him for your good looks?

GBS

PS I would not bear being written to in this fashion if I were you. This is only an anticipation of your own thought. You can see how superficial it is by my detecting it.

To ALICE LOCKETT

[T/1; X/103.e]

36 Osnaburgh Street N W
16th October 1884

["I am answering your letter," Alice wrote on 15th October, "not because I want to, but because I consider it most unfair . . . As far as our meeting was concerned, no decided arrangement had been made. You never are decided (I hate people to hesitate). You asked me what time I thought of returning? And I told you that I should be at Liverpool St. at half past eight, and kept my word & by the 8.32 train I went home. Since your communication of the morning, distrust had crept into my heart (confirmed by your letter of this morning), and acting upon a nature at once imaginative and impulsive, I went straight home. . . . And as I believe your Mother's friendship more [sincere] than yours, I shall listen to her & tell her the true circumstances of our last two meetings." As an afterthought, Alice added a postscript: "No amount of writing will alter my convictions, so pray do not trouble to answer this" (BM).

Elinor L. Huddart published novels pseudonymously (*My Heart and I*, 1883, under the name of Elinor Hume) or anonymously (*Commonplace Sinners*, 1885). In 1901 Shaw commented in *The Candid Friend* that he had conducted a "long correspondence" with her in his early days, and that her "fervidly-imaginative novels would have made her known if I could have persuaded her to make her name public, or at least to stick to the same pen name, instead of changing it for every book." In 1884 she resided at Uplands, Fareham (near Portsmouth).]

Demon! Demon! Demon!

Not a statement in your letter is true except the wicked and heartless one that you went home by the 8.32 train, which was the act of a fiend. You did want to answer my letter. You did not consider it unfair. There *was* occasion to write. A decided arrangement *was* made. I am never wanting in decision. I did not ask you what time you thought of returning. You did not say that you would be at Liverpool St at half past eight, but, in return to my direct question when you would be back, answered that you would leave the Exhibition at eight. Mistrust did not creep into your heart after my letter: you have no heart, and you have mistrusted me (and, with more reason, yourself also) ever since we first met. You are neither imaginative nor impulsive, and I believe you went home in a rage. I do not try my best to make anything: if I were capable of trying my best I should be a better man, and not suffer you to make a fool of me. You do not value my mother's friendship more than mine. You will not listen to her, nor tell her the true circumstances of our last two meetings, because she knows them better than you. You have no convictions to be altered by writing or otherwise.

I am not offended: I am only furious. You were quite right to go by the 8.32. Had you waited, I should have despised you (or tried to, on principle); for I respect people who always act sensibly and are devoid of the weaknesses known as "feelings." You behaved like a prudent woman, like a lady, and like a flint-hearted wretch.

Remember that when we parted that day at Jessie's, we did so for ever. I never sought to renew our acquaintance: it was you who called on me and insisted on my going with you to Edgware Road. Then, having made an absolute assignation with me, you left me to absorb a whole railway stationfull of rheumatism whilst you were at home laughing at me. Thank God (if there was any such person) I have perfect control of my temper, and, when I am hurt, can conceal my indignation.

I have another letter to write, and so must hold my hand. Adieu, dear demon.

GBS

PS Heavens! I nearly put this by mistake into the envelope of the other one, which is to Elinor Huddart! It happens that we had an appointment the other day which she was unable to keep, and I have not seen her since. Fancy her feelings if she had received this and took all the abuse to herself. I should have been lectured, too; Elinor is a serious friend, and not a trifler like Miss Lockett.

To THE EDITOR OF *JUSTICE*

[G/1]

36 Osnaburgh Street N W
24th October 1884

[This needling letter to H. M. Hyndman, which was not published, is the first on record to which Shaw signed his name in full. William Ward, 1st Earl of Dudley (d. 1885), owned large mineral deposits in Staffordshire and Worcestershire.]

Sir

As a Social Democrat, I call upon you to remove from the title page of the 41st number [15th October] of Justice the words "Organ of the Social Democracy." In that number, speaking presumably on behalf of the Social Democratic Federation, you say "If we win, we shall live to see Lord Dudley mining coal in his own pits at his own prices, and his wife making nails at ninepence a day." Here you distinctly promise that, if you win [control of the government], exploitation of labour in its most brutal form shall continue exactly as before; your former opponents being the exploited. If the Federation council do not at its next meeting expressly disclaim or retract this abominable declaration, neither the body which it represents, nor your paper, can escape repudiation by all real Social Democrats under whose notice your most deplorable expression of bad feeling may happen to fall.

I am, Sir,
yours truly
George Bernard Shaw

To HENRY HYDE CHAMPION

36 Osnaburgh Street N W

[F/2]   1st November 1884

[Henry Hyde Champion (1859–1928), first honorary secretary of the Social Democratic Federation, was editor of *To-Day* and proprietor of the Modern Press. He was tried for sedition (1886) after the Trafalgar Square riots, defended himself, and was acquitted; contributed very materially to the London Dock Strike (1889) by taking command of the pickets; emigrated to Australia in 1893, serving there as Shaw's literary agent. On 31st October 1884 he asked Shaw to edit Laurence Gronlund's *The Co-operative Common-wealth*, published in Boston earlier in the year, undertaking to pay Shaw £5 "for the editing if the book ever produces anything over the cost & advts" (BM). Gronlund, Danish-born American socialist (1846–99), authorised Champion "to alter spelling, phrases &c.," but subsequently repudiated Shaw's edition and published a rival "authorised" edition with a new preface.

William Black (1841–98) was the Scottish author of numerous three-decker novels, including *Macleod of Dare* (1878). James Edwin Thorold Rogers (1823–90) was an English economist, a Cobdenite, author of an *Economic Interpretation of History* (1888). Sir Robert Giffen (1837–1910) was an English economist and statistician, chief of the statistical department of the Board of Trade (1876–97). William Hurrell Mallock (1849–1923) was the author of *Is Life Worth Living?* (1879) and *The Reconstruction of Belief* (1905). Shaw scored Mallock's views on political economy in "Socialism and Superior Brains," *Fortnightly Review* (April 1894), later reprinted as a Fabian tract.]

You are a most bloodthirsty exploiter of labor. You must give me much more than £5. How long do you think £5 would last me?— About two hours. It is only at the rate of $4\frac{1}{4}^{d}$ a page. I want $8\frac{1}{2}^{d}$ for my services as literary artist, and $8\frac{1}{2}^{d}$ more as skilled economist. Ask W. Black and Thorold Rogers whether they will do it any cheaper. I want half of the first £40 profit made. This arrangement is enormously favorable to you. Take two hypothetical results, and see how generous I am. If the book only pays its expenses, you lose nothing, and I lose my time and labor. If it produces a profit of £1000, you will pocket 98% of surplus value out of my labor—if £2000, 99%—and so on. *The more successful the book is, the greater is your profit and the heavier my exploitation.*

Gronlund may as well save himself the trouble of correcting his proof sheets as far as the style is concerned. He knows nothing whatever about it, and is likely to make trouble for me and to muddle his ideas even more than he has done already. By God, I never read [such] English! I must leave the figures over if the letterpress is in order.

Proofs ad libitum will be needed—the last set to be paged, as it will be necessary to make an index. The index is a separate and most tedious job, requiring skill, instinct of the subtlest selective order, and patience; but I will make you a present of it, though it would be cheap at another twenty. The chief objection to giving English figures is that Giffen, Mallock and the rest will refute them. As I have never made a calculation in my life with even an approximation to accuracy, they will find the job an easy and delightful one.

G.B.S.

To DAVID DOUGLAS

[F/9; X/104]

36 Osnaburgh Street N W
20th December 1884

[David Douglas (1823–1916) was an Edinburgh publisher.]

Dear Sir

A novel of mine called An Unsocial Socialist has just finished its course as a serial through the pages of a magazine called To Day. I am anxious to see it reprinted in a cheap form. Will you allow me to send you the book to read? If you should find it worth a place in your 1/- series, I shall be very well pleased indeed to have my book so well introduced.

I am, dear Sir,
yours faithfully
G. B. Shaw

To CHATTO & WINDUS

[F/9; X/104]

36 Osnaburgh Street N W
26th December 1884

Gentlemen

Will you oblige me by reading a novel of mine entitled "An Unsocial Socialist"? It is in print having already run through a magazine as a serial.

I am, gentlemen,
yours faithfully
George Bernard Shaw

[At foot of this text Shaw noted:]

The same verb. et lit.
to Macmillan & Co.
30/12/84.

PART III

1885-1893

III
(1885–1893)

In January 1885 Shaw began to keep a diary (actually it consisted of a record of his daily appointments and finances, supplemented by a disjointed series of business memos and some occasional notes of a personal nature). He continued the practice until 1894, when "after three months effort to keep a note of my daily movements and expenditure in the same way as I have done since 1885, I finally gave up the attempt and rid my mind of it. The years during which a record has been kept are a sufficient sample of the way I lived." The fortuitously preserved record reveals, above all, how astonishingly crowded with activity Shaw's life had suddenly become. Through the generous intervention of William Archer he had obtained appointments as critic of music for the *Dramatic Review* and of art for *The World*, in addition to which he was providing a steady flow of book reviews for the *Pall Mall Gazette*. His freelance writing commitments burgeoned year after year, as did his lecture engagements.

If in January 1885 he found no audience awaiting him at St John's Coffee House in Hoxton "in consequence of W. Morris being round the corner lecturing," he was soon drawing capacity audiences at nearly one hundred lectures a year, many of his auditors being attracted, not alone by the social message, but also by what an interviewer was to describe as "a blend of bland and blond Mephistopheles with meek and mild curate." One of his bolder admirers, the tempestuous widow Jenny Patterson, soon led him to "an intimacy" on his 29th birthday which Shaw recorded euphemistically as "my first connection of the kind. I was an absolute novice. I did not take the initiative in the matter." Being besieged by female acquaintances ready to take the initiative for him was a new and pleasant experience for Shaw, and he assumed with gusto and more than a dash of smugness the rôle of philanderer which had been thrust upon him. Amusedly, he played one woman against another, stimulating agonising jealousies among them and eliciting such self-torturing communications as the following from a young lady named Grace Gilchrist: "I have felt myself these last few weeks socially estranged from you. I wished I had not parted so abruptly from you after that walk home . . . I am sure it was all a misunderstanding: I was wrong to give way to childish jealousy of other women. . . I know I have everything to learn in socialism: my faults are not my destiny, though

sometimes indeed one's faults create an adverse destiny for one."
(26th March 1888; BM.)

Romantic dalliance, however, was never permitted to interfere with Shaw's Socialist and other professional commitments, and during the decade that followed his introduction into "public" life he toiled energetically as many as eighteen hours a day, seven days a week. He made frequent lecture trips to the provinces, spoke somewhere in London on every Sunday of the year, undertook virtually every writing assignment that came his way (employing a bevy of Thackerayan pseudonyms, including G. B. S. Larking, Julius Floemmochser, Redbarn Wash, A. Donis, and the Rev. C. W. Stiggins, Jr. of Box Hill), revised and published two of his novels in book form, developed a Fabian lecture into *The Quintessence of Ibsenism*, drafted many of the Fabian tracts and, in his capacity as chairman of the Publications Committee, revised and edited most of the tracts drafted by his colleagues. He even found time to appear occasionally in amateur theatricals, as in Miss (Ada?) Radford's dramatic sketch *The Appointment*, produced as a Socialist League "entertainment" in aid of the Bryant and May Strike Fund, on 14th April 1888, in which Shaw, sharing the stage with May Morris and Ernest Radford, appeared in the rôle of Mr I. Roscius Garrick. And persistently he strove to further his self-education, participating in a Marxist discussion circle in Hampstead and an economic circle in Belsize Square, continuing sporadically with his music studies, struggling frustratedly with French, German and Portuguese ["Made a desperate attempt to learn and work through Ollendorff (a textbook developing a simplified method of learning modern languages by examples and exercises rather than by rules) from end to end, but did not find myself much the forwarder for it"].

Meanwhile his financial circumstances had improved markedly. By 1887 the Shaws had settled comfortably into a house at No. 29 Fitzroy Square, where Shaw now enjoyed, in addition to his top-floor bedroom, the luxury of a second-floor study overlooking the Square. His journalistic earnings increased annually: £150 in 1888, £197 in 1889, £252 in 1890, £310 in 1893; and this income, supplemented by his mother's earnings as a public school singing teacher, enabled the family to purchase a new piano "on the hire system" and to begin "to live a little more fully."

Shaw, by this time, had become something of a celebrity. "Everybody in London," the Labourite *Sunday World* proclaimed in 1891, "knows Shaw, Fabian Socialist, art and musical critic, vegetarian, ascetic, humourist, artist to the tips of his fingers, man of the people to the tips of his boots. The most original and inspiring of men—fiercely uncompromising, full of ideas, irrepressibly brilliant—an Irishman." The Dublin *Evening Telegraph*, acknowledging in May 1889 the accomplishments of its expatriated native son, extravagantly peppered its encomium with such descriptives as "clever author," novels of "power and brilliancy," and "thorough unconventionality and charm of style." And an interviewer for *The Pelican*, describing in 1892 Shaw's prowess as a musical critic, rhapsodised that he "makes diminished sevenths interesting. Throws positive halo round augmented ninths."

Jauntily long-striding down the street, the "ubiquitous Mr Shaw" (as he was labelled by the editor of *The Star*) cut an unconventional figure in his yellow Jaeger one-piece wool suit, topped with a brown slouch hat of the broadest of contemporary brims and the roughest of textures, his neck embraced by a red scarf, and the costume completed with gloves and swinging umbrella. "You have all seen him," noted the *Workman's Times* in 1894, "A tall, lean, icy man, white faced, with a hard, clear, fleshless voice, restless grey-blue eyes, neatly-parted fair hair, big feet, and a reddish, untamed beard."

His bearing grew more commanding, his personality more electrifying day by day. Without actively seeking the position, he presently found himself ensconced as local sage and clairvoyant, frequently appealed to for counsel, but quite prepared, when not solicited, to dispense advice gratuitously. Everybody's business became Shaw's business, and he spared no pains to educate at any opportunity—in his correspondence as in his writings and lectures. "I remember, as a youth," the journalist Hannen Swaffer recalled in 1927, "sitting in an old Tudor room in the Strand, learning economics in Shaw's class...And I realised that Shaw would have made one of the most brilliant dons any university has ever known. Theories lived while he spoke, making marks on a blackboard with chalk." Shaw had become a skilful didacticist in his journalism and in his platform orations. Only one challenge, the fusion of his literary and oratorical skills, remained to be met. He unearthed the fragmentary manuscript of the play Archer had goaded him into undertaking in 1884, and after a hiatus of nearly eight years brought the drama *Widowers' Houses* to completion. He was now a playwright.

To HENRY SEYMOUR

[F.u/2]

36 Osnaburgh Street NW
5th January 1884 [1885]

[Henry Seymour (1859?–1938) was the editor of *The Anarchist*; Shaw's article "What's in a Name? (How an Anarchist might put it)" appeared in the first number, in March. Seymour later was a pioneer in the gramophone industry, and for two decades served as honorary secretary of the Francis Bacon Society. Anarchist Benjamin Tucker's unauthorised reprint of the article in his Boston weekly, *Liberty*, on 11th April 1885, marked the first appearance of a Shaw work in America. As the subtitle indicates, Shaw had written the piece merely as a "guide" for the revolutionist Charlotte Wilson, a fellow Fabian who edited the journal *Freedom*. He was to have frequent cause to regret the indiscretion of permitting the article to bear his signature, for it was reprinted under the title *Anarchism versus State Socialism* by Seymour in 1889, and again in 1896 (for distribution, to Shaw's embarrassment, to delegates at the Trades Union Congress), and though Shaw, who was draftsman of Fabian Tract 45, *The Impossibilities of Anarchism* (1893), endlessly denied that the views were his own, he was haunted most of his life by charges, levelled by Ford Madox Ford among others, that in his youth he had been an anarchist.

John Ramsay McCulloch (1789–1864), Scottish economist, was the author of *Principles of Political Economy* (1825) and propounder of a wages' fund theory.]

Dear Sir

The article you refer to was written more to shew Mrs Wilson my idea of the line an anarchist paper should take in England than as an expression of my own convictions. Anarchist is an exceedingly elastic term, and I have not the remotest idea of what line your paper will take, or of what other writers I should find myself in company with in the event of my signing [it]: both of which one likes to know particularly well before letting one's name appear in a first number. As far as I remember what I wrote (I should like, bye and bye, to see a proof in any case before deciding) there is nothing in it that I object to commit myself publicly to; but if it is to be taken with a context of un-irrigated McCullochism on the one hand, or advocates of the "rush on the shops" on the other I do not care enough about the article to expose myself to misconstruction by signing it. I should also object to my signature appearing unless the other articles were signed with real names—unless it was the practice of the paper, in short. If you can satisfy me on these points, I see no reason for withholding my name if you really think its publication would be of the smallest use to you.

You will, I hope, excuse my plainness. Had I written the article with a view to its being signed I should have made no difficulty whatever on the point.

> I am, dear sir,
> yours faithfully
> [George Bernard Shaw]

To HAWKES & PHELPS

[F/2]

36 Osnaburgh Street N W
7th January 1884 [1885]

[Although "The Brand of Cain" had by now a history of six years of rejections, Shaw made one more effort to obtain publication for it, in October 1884, by sending it to Hawkes & Phelps of Birmingham for possible inclusion in their literary annual, *Christmas Tales*. The manuscript, however, was lost in transit or mislaid by the publisher, who informed Shaw on 6th January, in reply to his query, that to their knowledge it had never been received. It was Shaw's only copy of the tale, and he never rewrote it.]

Gentlemen

I certainly sent you by book post, on the 21st Oct. last, an MS entitled "The Brand of Cain," with a letter notifying its dispatch and replying to yours of the 14th Oct. The letter and the packet were, of course, separate. Will you kindly cause another search to be made before I apply to the P.O.

The loss of the MS is no great matter, as I can use the plot of the tale again. But if by any chance it has been stolen in transit and used, I shall run the risk of being accused of plagiarizing my own story. I am sorry you should have any trouble in the matter.

> I am, gentlemen,
> yours faithfully
> George Bernard Shaw

To MACMILLAN & CO.

[X/105]

36 Osnaburgh Street N W
14th January 1885

[Charles Morgan, in *The House of Macmillan*, reports that, in rejecting *An Unsocial Socialist*, Macmillan had written that they "would be glad to look at anything else he might write of a more substantial kind."]

Gentlemen

Many thanks for reading An Unsocial Socialist. Your demand for "something more substantial" takes my breath away. Your reader, I fear, thought the book not serious—perhaps because it was not dull. If so, he was an Englishman. I have only met one reviewer [J.M. Robertson] and one oral critic [William Archer] who really took the book in. They were both Scotchmen. You must admit that when one deals with two large questions in a novel, and throws in an epitome of modern German socialism as set forth by Marx as a makeweight, it is rather startling to be met with an implied accusation of triviality.

yours faithfully
George Bernard Shaw

To EDMUND HARVEY

[F/2]

36 Osnaburgh Street N W
16th January 1885

[Edmund Harvey, of Orange, Waterford, Ireland, wrote to Shaw on 11th January, praising *An Unsocial Socialist*, which he had read serially, and asking if it would appear as a book. John Boyd Kinnear (1828–1920) was a member of the Scottish bar and a London journalist, who later became a scientific farmer. He wrote numerous books on political and legal reform, civil government, Eastern and Irish questions. Smilash is the assumed name of the protagonist of Shaw's novel.]

Dear Sir

Many thanks for your kind letter and for Mr Boyd Kinnear's pamphlet.

I have not as yet succeeded in concluding any arrangement for the publication of An Unsocial Socialist in a single volume at a reasonable price. It can only be done by a publisher of exceptional resources, and such are apt to think that their enterprise might be better directed than in ventilating the opinions of Smilash, who bye and bye would probably confirm Mr Boyd Kinnear that until the people make their own laws it matters little where their laws are made or what the nationality of the capitalists who make them may be.

> I am, dear sir,
> yours faithfully
> George Bernard Shaw

To ALEXANDER SMITH

[F/2]

36 Osnaburgh Street N W
19th January 1885

Dear Sir

I never think of the Lodge Index without a twinge of remorse. The proofs are already corrected; but the delay arises from the incompleteness of the index. There are still some glosses to be inserted which defied my research, and will, I am afraid, take a lot of hunting up. What I have completed cost me so much more time than I had dreamt of its doing that I was forced to postpone the final searches for words. At present I am editing an American work [Gronlund's *The Co-operative Commonwealth*] which I have practically to rewrite as it goes through the press. I hope to be rid of it in a fortnight or so, and then I will make a desperate effort to get at Lodge. I wish he had never been born—I feel guilty when I think of you and the printer, but I really cannot help myself.

> yours faithfully
> George Bernard Shaw

To JOHN M. ROBERTSON

[A/2]

36 Osnaburgh Street N W
19th January 1885

[John Mackinnon Robertson (1856–1933), British journalist, politician, and Shakespearean scholar, was Annie Besant's protégé and editorial assistant on *Our Corner* in 1885. Mrs Besant (1847–1933), whom Shaw had met at one or another of the meetings of his debating societies, was a freethinker (associated with Charles Bradlaugh), who converted to Fabian Socialism in April 1885, and in 1889 became a Theosophist. *The Irrational Knot* was serialised in *Our Corner* from April 1885 to February 1887. *Love Among the Artists*, which Robertson had preferred, eventually was published in *Our Corner* from November 1887 to December 1888. The lecture on Socialism which Shaw delivered to the Dialectical Society (and on 26th February to the Liberal and Social Union) was published in the *Christian Socialist* in April.]

Mrs Besant writes to say that "Mr Robertson fancies that the Irrational Knot is the least likely of your" (my) "novels to suit us." Now I write to say that you have not read the Irrational Knot, that you ought to know better at your age than to dogmatise about novels that you haven't read, and that, by the Lord! you shant have the other one that you want. What do the readers of Our Corner care about the life of a musician? they dont know Wagner's Tristan from "Pop goes the weazel." The Irrational Knot is very long, and highly moral, and deeply interesting. A child can understand it, and a stern man can weep over it (if he likes). I am not going to be insulted before my time by being told at this stage of the proceedings that it wont suit. Run it through Our Corner, and when it is finished (in four years or so) perhaps you may get the other to follow it if you behave yourself in the meantime and refrain from telling Mrs Besant that my books are immoral and dull. I have no doubt that you have gone that length, though she is too kind to say so. No, sir: forbear these rash judgments until you have swallowed the MS, which you may expect any time in the course of the next fortnight. I must alter a few scenes—the alterations will remain to the good even if they fail to please you.

Mrs Besant suggests that I should send my paper on Socialism (Dialectical—next Wednesday) to the Corner. Unhappily it isnt a paper. I havent had time to prepare one, and shall orate extemporaneously. I shall probably write it out before re-delivering it at the Liberal [and] Social Union.

George Bernard Shaw
(Champion Moralist)

To MACMILLAN & CO.

[F/2; X/105]

36 Osnaburgh Street N W
22nd January 1885

[Replying on 22nd January to Shaw's letter of the 14th, Macmillan informed him that they had meant to send a copy of their reader's report, now enclosed, to show that his novel "had been by no means unappreciated. Our reader is not responsible for the epithet 'unsubstantial' which was perhaps not quite fortunate though we could not think of any other that would better express our meaning." The report, written by John Morley (though Shaw was un-aware of this), described the novel as "a *jeu d'esprit*, or satire, with a good stroke of socialist meaning in it." Morley had, however, apparently forgotten that he had met the author a few years earlier and that he had advised him to drop journalism. "The story," he continued, "is designedly paradoxical, absurd and impossible, as if it were one of [Thomas Love] Peacock's. But whoever he may be, the author knows how to write; he is pointed, rapid, forcible, sometimes witty, often powerful, and occasionally eloquent. I suppose one must call his book a trifle, but it is a clever trifle. . . . The present book is Ruskinian doctrine; theories with a whimsical and deliberately extravagant story, served up with pungent literary sauce. The result is a dish, which I fancy only the few would relish. . . . but the writer if he is young, is a man to keep one's eye upon" (Charles Morgan, *The House of Macmillan*).]

Gentlemen

Many thanks for your letter. I forgive your critic, although the book is perfectly serious—which is precisely why people take it as a joke. Its impossibilities are the commonplace occurrences of life. All my readers, as far as I know them, like the book; but they tell me that although they relish it they dont think the general public would. Which is the more discouraging, as this tendency of each man to con-sider himself unique is one of the main themes of the novel. Surely out of thirty millions of copyright persons (so to speak) there must be a few thousand who would keep me in bread and cheese for the sake of my story-telling, if you would only let me get at them.

However, I hope to attack you again with something more or less tremendous, if I can afford to write it.

I am very sensible of your kindness in sending me your reader's opinion, and am,

yours faithfully
George Bernard Shaw

To MARY GRACE WALKER

36 Osnaburgh Street N W
23rd January 1885

[A/3]

[Mary Grace Walker (1849–1920) was the wife of Sir Emery Walker (1851–1933), whom Shaw had met at the Hammersmith Branch of the Social Democratic Federation (from which William Morris, Walker, and others withdrew in 1885 to form the Socialist League). Walker later was associated

PART II

PIANOFORTE SOLO ... "Wanderstunden." ... ... *Heller*

KATHLEEN INA

⊲ "ALONE" ⊳

An original Comedy-Drama in Three Acts

By PALGRAVE SIMPSON and HERMANN MERIVALE

COLONEL CHALLICE	EDWARD AVELING
STRATTON STRAWLESS	... G. B. SHAW
BERTIE CAMERON	... PHILIP SYDNEY
DR. MICKLETHWAITE	J. HUNTER WATTS
MAUDE TREVOR	MAY MORRIS
MRS. THORNTON	ELEANOR MARX AVELING

REVOLUTIONARY SONG "The March of the Workers."
To the tune of "John Brown." Words by WILLIAM MORRIS
The audience are requested to join in the singing in unison.

Programme for the Socialist League production of *Alone*,
Ladbroke Hall, 30th January, 1885

(*Berg Collection, New York Public Library*)

with Morris in the Kelmscott Press, after which he and the famous book-binder Thomas Cobden-Sanderson (1840–1922) founded the Doves Press. "Miss Morris" was William's daughter May (1862–1938), with whom Shaw was for a time in love. Shaw performed the rôle of Stratton Strawless in a benefit performance of Palgrave Simpson and Herman Merivale's play *Alone*, presented by the Socialist League in the Ladbroke Hall on 30th January. The "detestable villain who plays her lover" was a young Socialist named Philip Sydney.]

Dear Mrs Walker

Never whilst I live will I steal a handkerchief again. If you knew the torments I have suffered you would forgive me. For a fortnight or so I honestly forgot it. Then I put it off until I could invent a good excuse. The longer I waited the harder it became to invent anything probable. At last I began to think I would leave the country and not give the handkerchief back at all. My rectitude decayed, and I acquired a hangdog expression which I fancied everybody noticed. One day I saw Mr Walker in the [British] Museum. He did not speak, but his eye said plainly "I thought better of you. I did indeed." Shortly after-wards I noticed that Miss Morris's manner became cold towards me. She said it was because I was always late at rehearsal, and would not keep my appointments; but one day, as I happened to come near a chair which she had just left, she hastily came back, took up a hand-kerchief which she had placed there, and put it safely into her pocket. Then I saw that she knew my guilt. This was dreadful; for I have not rehearsed a play with Miss Morris without some damage to my self-possession. I do not love her—I have too much sense for such follies; but I hate and envy the detestable villain who plays her lover with all my soul. And now she knows that I am no better than a pickpocket. Her father too, now listens to my denunciations of the hideous dishonesty of capitalism with a twinkle in his eye which only the restitution of that fatal handkerchief can wipe out. Take it, my dear Mrs Walker, and never lend me another. It is not kind to lead weak natures into temptation.

Have you a copy of the sonnet which I took from you for To-Day? It was fully arranged that it was to appear in the January number, and I attacked Champion with bitter reproaches when it failed to do so. He evaded me for some time; but I am now persuaded that he has lost it. I am to blame for not making a copy myself before sending it to 13 Paternoster Row, where everything goes astray. When I first told Champion I had a sonnet for him he became violent, and swore that it should not go in. He thought it was one of my own composition.

When he read it he changed his tune completely, and admitted its excellence.

I had to give up shewing your Furnivall poem to people, as they invariably asked me for my copy. I dont believe he half deserves it. Your verses seem to me to have beauty quite apart from the sense of the words. However, my admiration is not worth having; for I know nothing about poetry. But I assure you it is sincere.

When the handkerchief scandal has blown over a little I hope to go down to Hammersmith and deliver a new lecture in the character of

the repentant thief
George Bernard Shaw

To SWAN SONNENSCHEIN & CO.

[F/2]

36 Osnaburgh Street N W
16th February 1885

[Swan Sonnenschein & Co. was founded in 1878 by William Swan Sonnenschein (1855–1931). Among its early publications were the first English edition of Marx's *Capital*, J.M.Barrie's first book *Better Dead*, George Moore's *Confessions of a Young Man*, and a monthly journal, *Time*, to which Shaw contributed on two occasions. In 1911 the firm merged with George Allen & Co.]

Gentlemen

I have by me a novel entitled An Unsocial Socialist which has run through a magazine as a serial. It may possibly be worth reprinting in cheap form. Would you care to look through the book with a view to this.

I am, gentlemen,
yours faithfully
George Bernard Shaw

To SWAN SONNENSCHEIN & CO.

[F/2]

36 Osnaburgh Street N W
23rd February 1885

[Swan Sonnenschein, on 23rd February, agreed to accept Shaw's novel, to be published first at six shillings, then in a cheaper edition. The terms called for expenses to be borne by the publisher, and the author to receive a royalty of 5% on the first thousand, 10% on further sales. The editors suggested that Shaw make "numerous trifling alterations" which they had marked in the margins of the parts of *To-Day* sent them.]

Gentlemen:

I shall be glad to execute such an agreement as you propose for the publication of An Unsocial Socialist. Kindly send me the form. I am much obliged for the marginal corrections, and shall consider them carefully in revising the book.

yours faithfully
George Bernard Shaw

To SWAN SONNENSCHEIN & CO.

36 Osnaburgh Street N W
25th February 1885

[F/2]

[Upon examining Swan Sonnenschein's standard contract, Shaw discovered that he would have to assign his copyright in the novel to the publishers indefinitely. This he refused to do, offering only to "lease" the rights for five years, subject to renewal. This limitation of licence was a principle from which Shaw throughout his life never departed.]

Gentlemen

I can by no means persuade myself to let the copyright of "An Unsocial Socialist" pass away from me for ever. If the book be not dead this time five years I shall most probably have either changed my mind about it entirely, or be ready to do some further work upon it, if not to carry out my original design of a larger book of which it is only the first volume. I am willing that you shall have the exclusive right to publish the book for five years on the conditions named. But the copyright must remain my property, and the book come under my control again to alter, withdraw, or do what I please with. I doubt if it has five years' life in it in its present state.

Kindly explain to me anything unreasonable in this proposition of mine. As it is my commercial instinct that you should come to associate my name with profitable enterprises, I am anxious that the book should prove remunerative to you. It is my artistic instincts upon which I am disposed to take a stand. I wish to guard my right to commit suicide, as it were—to make alterations in the book that might destroy its popularity. That is not very likely, but it is quite possible that (after the five years) I might wish to effect a change which you might consider fatal and which I might regard as a necessary improvement. You will foresee that I might also, if my fame had greatly increased, propose a new arrangement at a competition price. Doubtless I should; but the efforts I should consequently make to increase my reputation would be all to the advantage of your patent while it lasted. We would also exploit it as vigorously as possible during that period, so that there would most probably be nothing left of it except a shilling edition for which no other publisher would give me any better terms. These are the only economic aspects of the case which occur to me. Your greater experience will apprise you of others, most likely. I am open to conviction, except as to the copyright.

> I am, gentlemen,
> yours faithfully
> George Bernard Shaw

To EDWIN PAGET PALMER

[F/2]

36 Osnaburgh Street N W
26th February 1885

[Edwin Paget Palmer was editor of the newly-founded *Dramatic Review*; Shaw had been recommended to him as musical critic by William Archer. Shaw's grievance stemmed from the fact that Palmer had not published an article he had submitted on the Bach Choir's performance on 19th February of a musical setting of scenes from Shelley's *Prometheus Unbound* by Hubert (later Sir Charles Hubert) Parry (1848–1918). The oratorio to which Shaw referred was a performance by Miss Caroline Holland's Choir, on 24th February, of Joseph Rheinberger's "Christophorus; or, The Legend of St Christopher." "The Inventions" refers to the International Inventions Exhibition, which opened at South Kensington in May 1885; Shaw reviewed its numerous musical programmes in the *Dramatic Review*, *Our Corner*, and the *Magazine of Music*. Wilson Barrett (1846–1904) was an English actor, playwright, and manager, who had been proprietor of the Princess's Theatre since 1881; Palmer had reviewed his *Brutus* in the last issue.]

Dear Mr Palmer

That is just what I am [a man with a grievance], and a man with a very considerable grievance too. I have a couple of grievances, in fact, a musical one and a personal one.

First, as to the musical one. A concert is given consisting of an

118

oratorio by a leading German composer, performed for the first time in England. Also of a setting of one of the greatest poems in the English language by an English composer, performed for the first time in London. Finally, a musical curiosity of great interest in the shape of two instruments largely used by Bach, and now manufactured for the first time for 150 years probably, for use at the forthcoming Bach festival and "The Inventions." I am bound to stand up for my department, and when you say that these events must give way to new pieces, I maintain that—if music is to be dealt with in the D.R. at all—the concert in question is just as important as Wilson Barrett's production of Brutus.

Next, the personal grievance. When we last did business together, you said you should want an article for "the week after next" (this week). I agreed, and went to the concert, paying for my seat. Then I spent more than a day looking up the history of the Bach choir and writing the article. I squeezed that day out with great difficulty, as I have three printers clamouring for copy from me, and have lectures to deliver tonight, tomorrow, and on Sunday. All this you will think, is nothing to you, since you are willing to pay me. But it is nonetheless intensely disagreeable to me to have to say practically "You have wasted my time, and now I am going to waste your money." Publication of the article, too, is part of the consideration which induces me to write it, and the money minus the publication is less than I bargained for.

This is quite enough of grumbling for an affair which is after all only a trifle, and neither your fault nor mine. But since you seemed a little surprised at "the grievance" I thought it better to shew you that it was not quite groundless.

In conclusion may I repeat my old advice to have nothing to do with music. Musicians wont take in a paper for the sake of an article once in three weeks or so, with all the leading events left out. Besides, the critical business is rubbish—stark raving rot.

yours faithfully
George Bernard Shaw

To SWAN SONNENSCHEIN & CO.

36 Osnaburgh Street N W
1st March 1885

[G.u/2]

Gentlemen

If by the copyright you only mean the stereo-plates, I am quite willing that they shall remain your property for all time. But at the expiration of the five years they would only serve you in this manner. Let us suppose that the five years have elapsed, and that another publisher, learning that I am receiving ten per cent on the nominal price of the book, offers me twenty. I go to you and say "You must give me 20% or I will take the book out of your hands." You, having the stereo-plates, will be better able to comply than your competitor, who would have to cast new plates, get the book on his list anew, and so forth.

As you say, it is a pity in your view, to limit the publisher's interest; but your interest is already, by the terms of form of agreement, limited by mine, as mine is by that of the community. My proposition does not limit your interest even to five years; for I can never extort more than the market value of the book. More than that, if its circulation be very languid five years hence, you can reduce the royalty, just as, on the opposite supposition, I can raise it. Only in the event of the book proving profitable to you is there the slightest chance of any firm bidding against you for it. Your greatest risk is that the book may fail at first, but that some subsequent literary achievement of mine may suddenly raise its value just too late for you to profit by it. You might partially insure against this by publishing all my subsequent achievements, so as to make on the success what you would lose on the failure. But I conclude that you do not anticipate any failure.

As to a joint property in the stereos, I have no right to any such joint property as I am not prepared to contribute towards their cost. Neither would such joint property be of the least use to me.

Can we not agree for a definite number of editions and copies, with an outside limit which I must permit, but which you need not produce unless there be a demand, the whole transaction to cease after five years?

I am, gentlemen,
yours faithfully
[George Bernard Shaw]

To EDWIN PAGET PALMER

[F/2]
[36 Osnaburgh Street N W]
[2nd March 1885]

[Palmer apologetically sent a cheque, on 2nd March, for the Bach Choir article, which he suggested he might still be able to use in the next issue; it did not appear. Subsequently Shaw used some of the material in his article on "The Bach Bi-Centenary," published in the *Dramatic Review* on 28th March. He continued to contribute signed articles and unsigned notes to the journal until early in 1886.]

Dear Mr Palmer

If you give cheques for nothing, you will ruin yourself as an editor. If I write articles merely for money, I will ruin myself as an artist. It is part of my profession to turn my back on money (which has always returned the compliment). So I return your cheque. At the same time, I do not see why I should be at the loss of my expenses; so, if you will send me postal orders for 6/-, I will pocket them without the least scruple.

The Bach article is hopelessly stale now; and I have been to nothing since, nor is there anything on this week. If the "other man" is game for an article, get it from him by all means, as it will save me the trouble of spinning out a column of trash about nothing in particular. Pray dont trouble about what you call interfering with me. I had much rather give place to a regular musical critic than stand in his way for the sake of an occasional guinea. If you will only not ask me for an article except when you really want it and have room for it, you may treat me in other respects like a mere machine. Every writer has his weakness. One is jealous; another sets an exaggerated value on his time. I belong to the latter class. As far as journalism goes, I am void of jealousy, and am glad to get out of my duties if anyone else will perform them.

How came so many misprints into the last number? You boiled down [Edward] Aveling's article into a paragraph, and then put in both the paragraph and the article. You will find that over proofs Homer himself couldnt have afforded to nod. Excuse the criticism.

yours faithfully
George Bernard Shaw

To SWAN SONNENSCHEIN & CO.

36 Osnaburgh Street N W
[F/2]   6th March 1885

Gentlemen

You have forwarded me by mistake a cheque for £3.3.0 for an
article in the March number of "Time." My contribution to that
number was, however, a story of 16 pp. ["The Miraculous Revenge"].
You are also indebted to me for a review of [Michael Davitt's] "Leaves
from a Prison Diary" in the February number. It only ran to 2 pp.
That makes £9.9.0 in all. I return your cheque, and

Am, gentlemen,
yours faithfully
George Bernard Shaw

To E. M. ABDY-WILLIAMS

36 Osnaburgh Street N W
[G.u/2]   9th March 1885

[E.M.Abdy-Williams (later Mrs Bernhard Whishaw), author of several
three-decker novels, including *The World Below* and *For His Friend*, and
later a dramatist, was, for a brief period, editor of *Time*.]

Dear Miss Abdy-Williams

Just listen to this. "We" (that is Sonnenschein & Co^y) "have consulted with the editor" (of Time) "and learn, as we had been previously
informed, that it was distinctly stated that the only payment that should
be made for the review you contributed should be a copy of the work
in question" (published at 2/-). I could have had at least four copies of
the book on the same terms from papers and magazines to which I
give all my gratuitous work; and it is quite impossible for me to express
to you how emphatically I would have refused to review Michael
Davitt for a capitalist magazine for nothing. I understood that you
asked me to do it that evening at the Fabian because, as a sort of
expert in Davitt economics, I could review the book in a short time.
We said nothing at all about payment: I concluding that there would
be no question about the usual terms. Kindly let me have a line to say
whether I may fight this out with Messrs Sonnenschein without
inconveniencing you in any way.

I am, dear Miss Abdy-Williams,
yours faithfully
[George Bernard Shaw]

To SWAN SONNENSCHEIN & CO.

[F/2]

[36 Osnaburgh Street N W]
9th March 1885

[Swan Sonnenschein, on 9th March, informed Shaw that the three guineas previously sent was the correct price for "The Miraculous Revenge" as they never paid "considerable sums" for such "make-up matter," which was often, indeed, contributed free.]

Gentlemen

I have written to Miss Abdy-Williams with reference to the statement in your letter, and have no doubt that you will find, on further consultation, that you are in error as to the review of Mr Davitt's book.

I do not understand your letter as far as it relates to my story. You say you do not pay considerable sums for "make-up matter." This seems to me doubly irrelevant. I have not asked you for a considerable sum, but for $\frac{1}{2}$ a guinea a page, the usual rate of payment for a shilling magazine, and the rate paid to the contributors to Time when it was $\frac{1}{2}$ its present price. With "make-up matter" I have nothing to do, as I have not sent you any. In these circumstances, I again return your cheque, and am,

Gentlemen,
yours faithfully
George Bernard Shaw

To E. M. ABDY-WILLIAMS

[F/2]

36 Osnaburgh Street N W
10th March 1885

[Miss Abdy-Williams replied on 10th March that it was her understanding that the Davitt review was to be remunerated by the receipt of a copy of the book for review.]

Dear Miss Abdy-Williams

You didnt [tell me distinctly], indeed! But as you evidently intended to, I shall withdraw my claim and give Messrs Sonnenschein the benefit of the review. It would not have been nice of me to interrupt you with an absurd "How much?" in a matter in which the usual terms are always taken for granted unless there is express mention of exceptional conditions. No doubt it is all my fault; but I think I may plead extenuating circumstances in earnest of your private judgment of

yours faithfully
George Bernard Shaw

To SWAN SONNENSCHEIN & CO.

36 Osnaburgh Street N W

[F/2]   10th March 1885

Gentlemen

It appears from a letter I have just received from the editor of "Time" that I was quite in the wrong as to the review of "Leaves from a Prison Diary" for which I claimed one guinea. You are very welcome to regard it as a gratuitous contribution, and I must beg you to excuse me for having stated that you owed me anything for it.

I am, gentlemen,
yours faithfully
George Bernard Shaw

To E. M. ABDY-WILLIAMS

36 Osnaburgh Street N W

[F/2]   11th March 1885

[Miss Abdy-Williams, apologising for the misunderstanding, sent a cheque, on 11th March, for £1 to remunerate Shaw for the Davitt review.]

Dear Miss Abdy-Williams

Many thanks. I accept the cheque as you probably had rather have me do so, and I remain the obliged party in the transaction

and faithfully yours
George Bernard Shaw

P.S. I append a formal receipt.

To SWAN SONNENSCHEIN & CO.

36 Osnaburgh Street N W

[X/106]   16th March 1885

Gentlemen

I want more than 10% for a fifteen years lease of "An Unsocial Socialist." As offers go, and as trade stands at present, I am aware that the offer is a reasonable one. If I thought that the relations of

124

authors, publishers, and booksellers would not alter for fifteen years, I should accept it. But I believe that within that time machinery will so diminish the cost of printing that the value of copyrights which are genuine monopolies will be greatly increased. At the same time the compositors will be ruined; and the profits of bookselling and publishing matter which is subject to competition will be so reduced that only the very large capitals will be able to stand it. Speculation in ordinary copyrights will not be worth attempting; and even the old fashioned publishers will begin to find that publishing on commission is the safest and the most lucrative. Monopoly copyrights, supplying a public demand which cannot be met by hack writers, will rise in value; and if an International Copyright Treaty be concluded (and fifteen years may take us past even that) authors of reputation and the commonest knowledge of business will deal directly with publishers in America. These considerations, and others which spring out of them, make one think fifteen years a long time. Further, I am no longer in any danger of finding no opening. I have already provided for the publication of the novel [*Cashel Byron's Profession*] which is about to appear as a serial in To-Day; and one of my juvenile works [*The Irrational Knot*] has been secured on rather better terms than I ever dreamt of getting for it by another magazine [*Our Corner*]. As it is prodigiously long, it will keep me alive modestly for some time to come. On the whole I had rather wait a year or so than close with you for ten per cent.

I am, Gentlemen,
yours faithfully
George Bernard Shaw

To WILLIAM ARCHER

[A/2]

36 Osnaburgh Street N W
16th March 1885

[William Archer (1856–1924), Scottish dramatic critic, playwright, and translator of Ibsen, met Shaw in 1883 in the British Museum reading room. They became instant friends, and Archer, who had already established a good journalistic reputation in London, generously obtained employment for Shaw as musical critic for the *Dramatic Review* and the *Magazine of Music*, as book reviewer for the *Pall Mall Gazette*, and in 1886 as art critic for *The World*. It was Archer, too, who encouraged Shaw to complete his first play, *Widowers' Houses*, though he early withdrew as collaborator. Archer's death, following an operation in 1924, evoked from the grief-stricken Shaw the most bitter tirade on the medical profession he had ever uttered.

The St James's Theatre production of *As You Like It* starred Mrs Kendal (Madge Robertson), later Dame Madge Kendal (1849–1935), as Rosalind; W. H. Kendal (1843–1917) as Orlando; John (later Sir John) Hare (1844–1921) as Touchstone; Linda Dietz (d. 1920) as Celia; Herbert Waring as Oliver; A. M. Denison (d. 1891) as Duke Frederick; and Henry Vernon as Charles the Wrestler. Hans Lien Brækstad (1845–1915), Anglo-Norwegian journalist and littérateur, was Vice-Consul for Norway from 1906; in 1888 he and Shaw discussed a project for translating Ibsen's *Peer Gynt*, Brækstad to read the play to Shaw, giving him the literal English translation, and Shaw to "put it into shape"—in verse! Shaw toyed with the work for several weeks, then abandoned the idea. *True Women* (1883) was a play translated by Brækstad from the Swedish of Anne Charlotte Edgren, Duchess di Cajanello (1849–92); it was not published until 1890. Alexander L. Kielland (1849–1906) was a Norwegian novelist and playwright, whose *Tales of Two Countries* Archer translated for Harper in 1891. The novel Archer had given to Shaw was the just-published *Skipper Worse*, translated by Henry John Moreton (3rd Earl of Ducie). Archer, however, had made an independent translation of a portion of the novel, included in an essay, "Kielland Again," published in G. W. Foote's journal, *Progress*, December 1883, under the pseudonym "Norman Britton."]

I have just been to "As you Like it." If you want matter for a Palmeresque paragraph you may describe poor Rosalind's bad cold. Exposure in the forest of Arden and an immutable resolution not to blow her nose before the audience did their deadly work; and at her exit in the third act she made a mistressly stroke of business out of them. She fainted, slipping from the neck of Linda Dietz with a beautiful stage fall in the patent collapsible manner. Orlando, with unconcealed scepticism as to the cause of the tragedy, and brutally marital blindness to its timeliness and attractiveness, bundled her off promptly. Well might she ask in the next act whether she had not counterfeited excellently. It was the only good piece of acting I saw. Such all-round abject, utter, abysmal, bottomless incompetence I hope I may never see again. The direct cause of the failure of the revival is the frightful badness of Oliver and Frederic. Had they been even presentable, Charles the Wrestler would have made a good start for the play in spite of Orlando, whose stupidity I never before fully realised. Mrs Kendal, without a cold, could be made a good Rosalind by a few hints from me. But the decadence of the stage is awful. We have our work cut out for us, I can tell you. My opinion of Shakspere has gone up prodigiously: my opinion of Victorian stage culture is below zero.

I write by this post to Sonnenschein giving him a concise sketch of the history of publishing in England from 1885 to 1900, shewing the great increase in value of good copyrights that must take place, and declining a 15 years lease at 10%. Adroitly interwoven plagiarisms from Brækstad give an air of practical knowledge to the forecast.

Brækstad, by the bye, has sent me a copy of "True Women." I read some of it between "As you Like it," and think it good so far. It smells of Ibsen.

Kielland ought to be regarded with loathing by a boa constrictor like you. He does not even preserve the order of events in the scenes, much less the order of the scenes. The chapters that did me most impress are the description of Garman's garden (Trianon overgrown with rushes &c), the kissing of Sarah by Fennefos, and—from a partly comic point of view—that scene between Worse and Randulf which you translated for Foote. Fennefos & Sarah were particularly startling in their naturalness. I left the book for you this afternoon. When I keep books long, butter, porridge, jam, cocoa, and orange juice accumulate between the leaves and disgust the next reader.

GBS

To MRS WILLIAM ARCHER

36 Osnaburgh Street N W
[A/2]   18th March 1885
[Archer had married Frances E. Trickett (1855–1929) on 23rd October 1884. The "friend from the north" was Edward Rimbault Dibdin of Edinburgh, whom Shaw met a few nights later. Dibdin (1853–1941) was art critic for the *Liverpool Courier* from 1887 to 1904; he later became curator of the Walker Art Gallery, Liverpool.]

Dear Mrs Archer

Your friend from the north shews an utter disregard of my convenience and indeed of human possibility in selecting Thursday for his visit. I have to go to the Albert Hall to the rehearsal of the Bach festival. This, which was yesterday a prospect of pleasure, is now one of sacrifice. Kismet!

Moonenschein has not yet replied. I have paralysed him for a post or two.

yours faithfully
George Bernard Shaw
(I am forming the habit of
signing the name by which
posterity will revere me)

127

To SWAN SONNENSCHEIN & CO.

[F/2]

36 Osnaburgh Street N W
24th March 1885

[Swan Sonnenschein capitulated on 21st March, stating that they shared Shaw's anticipations as to the development of the book trade "to some extent," and thought that a fifteen years' lease might be very speculative for both parties. Instead, they suggested a seven years' lease at 10% royalty, renewable for a like period at their option at 20% royalty (BM).]

Gentlemen

Thanks for your letter of the 21st inst. If your offer refers to the English and colonial copyright only I accept it on condition that you are not to sublet your assign; that is, that if you become bankrupt (avert the omen!) the agreement shall re-pass. Further, that you do not limit me in the matter of proof corrections to £5. The cost of revision has already been borne by the printers of To-Day, and I had not anticipated having to do much more work upon the novel after its set up, but I know by experience that there will be compositors' errors to correct, for most of which I shall be held responsible. If you can impress on your printers that I do my own punctuation, and that I expect them to set me up as faithfully when they consider me wrong as when they approve of my method, the bill for composition will be very small as far as it depends on me. As you have bargained for the book as it stands, I shall not hold myself at liberty to make any substantial alterations in it; but I had rather not be limited by any express agreement, lest I have the printer charging me for having given me a great deal of trouble on the pretext that it is I that have troubled him.

The only question that remains to be settled, as far as I can recollect, is that of the foreign copyrights. Should these ever have any value, I had much rather not have the trouble of negotiating them for myself; but as they involve no risk, and cost but little time to dispose of, I think I may ask for 33% of the proceeds without undue rapacity.

I am, gentlemen,
yours faithfully
George Bernard Shaw

To SWAN SONNENSCHEIN & CO.

[F/2]

36 Osnaburgh Street N W
30th March 1885

[Swan Sonnenschein's agreement form was posted on 27th March, with a letter covering all the points raised by Shaw on the 24th. With regard to corrections, however, they doubled the proposed limit to £10, noting that they would instruct the printers to retain Shaw's punctuation and would establish that they would not pay the printer for any charges on that score.]

Gentlemen

I return your form of agreement with some alterations and additions, subject to which I will execute it without further demur. They are as follows:

I have struck out 2ndly. The printed part of it amounts to nothing except that you are to publish the book in one volume, which I see no reason to insist upon. The MS clause is superfluous because it expresses a right which the law secures to you without express stipulation. As our interests are identical on this point, and your position rather weakened than fortified by the clause, we had better let well alone.

For 3rdly I have altered "shall be the property of" to "is hereby assigned by the author to." Although a copyright is personal property, I believe we have no power to declare by a deed that it is the property of anyone in particular. I have undoubtedly the power to assign my copyright; and the law will thereupon secure to you the benefit of it. The clause as it stands in print is not a covenant: it is an act of legislation.

Into 7thly I have introduced the condition of six months' notice of renewal, which I hope you will find it worth while, when the time comes, to give me.

I have added the 9thly to protect myself against a defect (from the author's point of view) in the law, whereby a publisher can virtually destroy an author's copyright by printing, whilst the agreement is in force, copies enough to stock the market after the expiry of the term.

Finally I have substituted for 2ndly the provision of a few presentation copies of which I should like to have the disposal.

I should have returned [the text] sooner, but that I already have three printers clamouring at me constantly, besides intermittent demands, so that I cannot possibly set your printer to work before next Monday morning, although I know that time is of importance at this season.

I am, gentlemen,
yours faithfully
George Bernard Shaw

To SWAN SONNENSCHEIN & CO.

[F/2]

36 Osnaburgh Street N W
6th April 1885

[The altered agreement form was posted to Shaw on 4th April, with the information that the form "is not an Assignment, which requires a wholly different wording and a different stamp; it is merely an Agreement."]

Gentlemen

Enclosed you will find the agreement signed by me. Also a few pages for the printer to start upon. I shall send a respectable supply tomorrow evening.

I put in the clause about the presentation copies not because I doubted your willingness to give them to me, but because I doubted my own willingness to ask for them. Common as such requests are, I cannot for the life of me see that they are reasonable unless they are part of the bargain.

I hope your venture will be a profitable one, apart from my share in the returns. If I could only make your fortune, your competitors would hasten to make mine.

In haste,
yours faithfully
George Bernard Shaw

To J.L.MAHON

[A/28; X/149]

36 Osnaburgh Street N W
13th April 1885

[John Lincoln Mahon, a young engineer of Irish origin, was a well-known Socialist agitator in London, associated with William Morris in the newly-founded Socialist League, of which he was the first secretary. Andreas Scheu (1844–1927), an Austrian revolutionary, was a close friend of Morris for many years. He and Mahon established the Scottish Land and Labour League, and Scheu subsequently became chief promoter of the Scottish Social Democratic Party.

The "anti-Soudanese" meeting was to protest a decision of the prime minister (Gladstone) to abandon plans for the occupation of the Sudan following the massacre of General "Chinese" Gordon and the defenders of Khartoum in late January. The ex-Khedive of Egypt was Ismael Pasha (1830–95), who was deposed in 1879. Pecksniff, Chadband, and Joseph

Surface are characters in, respectively, Dickens's *Martin Chuzzlewit* and *Bleak House* and Sheridan's *The School for Scandal*.]

Dear Mahon—or stop a bit: this is official.

Dear Sir

Your letter dated the 11th inst has just reached me. The informal consent on my part to speak at an anti-Soudanese-War meeting, to which you allude, was conditional. When Mr Scheu, in your presence, proposed that I should move, and he second, the first resolution, I said I would if the resolution were good enough. On the strength of this, the Socialist League have circulated a handbill containing two resolutions which I never saw, with a statement that they will be supported by "Comrade Shaw." Now, as I hate all fraternity mongering just as heartily as any other variety of cant, and as I expressly protested against and repudiated it at a former meeting of the League, I consider the action of the League in announcing me as "Comrade," as immoral in its way as the Nile expedition. I am G. Bernard Shaw of the Fabian Society, member of an individualist state, and therefore nobody's comrade.

You further inform me that the Committee have chosen my place as defender of the second resolution against possible opposition. If I may choose my own place, I shall prefer to provide the opposition myself. A composition of one hundred and thirty-odd words, utterly unintelligible to anyone not an expert in Socialese, and missing the special point which makes the Soudanese war indefensible and atrocious even from the point of view of those who consider capitalism justified by the degree of civilization which it imposes, does not deserve to be passed either by intelligent outsiders or adept Socialists.

As for Resolution I, you can hardly expect me to second or support a statement that the war is, after all, "only the necessary outcome of the system of commercial exploitation." The meeting will probably ask ironically "Oh, indeed! Is that all? *Only* the necessary outcome, forsooth." At least it would if it knew what commercial exploitation meant. But as a matter of fact the Egyptian war is a far lower form of villainy than commercial exploitation. The Socialist League have unfortunately an official explanation for all wars; and they have forced it upon this Egyptian affair with the result of considerably extenuating its wickedness.

On the whole I think I had better not speak. My position in the matter of the war is that the Ex Khedive was a profligate, the bond-holders his pandars and procuresses, the British army a catspaw, the

British nation a fool, and the whole transaction an instructive epitome of human nature. I leave your denunciations, your sympathizings, your dauntless resistances, your curses, your glaring outgrowths, your victims planted in the soil, and your commercial patriotism to be supported by Comrades Pecksniff, Chadband, and Joseph Surface. Damn your sentiments. Doubly damn your mixed metaphors.

Please apologize for my plainness to those members of the Council who are not my personal friends, and whose feelings I am therefore reluctant to hurt.

George Bernard Shaw

To J. KINGSTON BARTON

[C.u/1; X/107]

[36 Osnaburgh Street NW]
[19th April 1885]

[George Carr Shaw died, alone, in a lodging house at 21, Leeson Park Avenue, Dublin, on 19th April, of congestion of the lungs, in his seventy-first year. Shaw was home alone when the telegram came; he immediately relayed the news to his mother, who was visiting her brother, Dr Gurly, at Leyton. Lucy Carr Shaw, who was in Dublin at the time of her father's death, did not attend the funeral. At the top of his note to Barton, Shaw drew two staves of music, headed "Grave."]

Telegram just received to say that the governor has left the universe on rather particular business and set me up as

An Orphan

To R. FREDERICK SHAW

[A/2]

36 Osnaburgh Street N W
23rd April 1885

[The financial desperation of the Shaws led Shaw to write to his Uncle Frederick (1824–?) almost immediately upon receipt of the news of George Carr Shaw's death, to determine how much money could be realised from his father's estate. Three days later he wrote again; his uncle returned the letter with his own remarks scrawled across it. From this letter we can see

132

that Shaw himself was in a state of confusion as to family finances; it is possible here to reconstruct the picture only fragmentarily.

George Carr Shaw in 1850 had been granted a government pension of £60 per annum after a period of employment in the Dublin law courts. This he sold for £500 to a man named O'Brien (who then insured the pensioner's life for £600); the money thus obtained enabled George Carr Shaw to enter into partnership in 1852 with George Clibborn as a trader in corn. Lucinda Elizabeth Shaw, at the time of her marriage on 17th June 1852, possessed personal assets in the amount of "one thousand two hundred and fifty Six pounds Nine shillings and two pence Government three and a quarter per cent Stock Standing . . . in the Books of the Governor and Company of the Bank of England." On the day before her wedding, however, she and her husband were required by her father, Walter Bagnall Gurly (1800–85), to sign a marriage settlement whereby these assets, as well as all income subsequently to be derived from the marriage settlement of 26th December 1829 between her father and his wife Lucinda Whitcroft (1802?–39) or from the will of her grandfather John Whitcroft (1768–1843), a wealthy Dublin pawnbroker, were to be transferred to two trustees, James Wilson and Arthur Greene.

Under the terms of Gurly's marriage settlement in 1829, the children of that marriage (there were three, but one died in infancy) were to receive a sum of £4000 from the Whitcroft estate, "to be paid to them at such age or respective ages and in such shares and proportions as the said Walter Bagnall Gurly should by any Deed or instrument in writing . . . direct and appoint." By an agreement between Gurly and his two surviving offspring, on 30th October 1869, Walter John Gurly received £2500 and Lucinda Elizabeth Shaw £1500. Mrs Shaw's share, "for her own sole and separate use and free from the debts control or engagements of her husband," was parcelled out to her in amounts of £100 a year. Contrary, however, to Shaw's own later recollections and to the asseverations of his biographers, Whitcroft left no bequest to the three children of his granddaughter. Thus we are provided with a mystery as to the source of the £400 settled on Shaw's younger sister, Agnes, unless it came from Mrs Shaw's own trust, established in 1852, or from the estate of her Aunt Ellen Whitcroft (1805–62).

By June 1885 the affairs of George Carr Shaw had been sufficiently ordered to enable his son to go on a shopping spree for "the first new garments I have had for years. These will be paid for out of the insurance on my father's life" (Diary). At Jaeger's he spent the princely sum of £11. 1. 0 for an all-wool suit, a black coat and vest, collars, a cravat, and a pair of pants.

Davitt & Co. refers to Michael Davitt (1846–1906), agrarian reformer, founder and leader of the Irish Land League, whose *Leaves from a Prison Diary* Shaw had reviewed two months earlier.

This is the first recorded letter to which Shaw appended the signature "G. Bernard Shaw."]

Dear Uncle Frederick

Many thanks for information. I fear I have shocked you; but never mind—I have not humbugged you, which was the only alternative.

Suppose we realize this £130, we shall have to pay interest on it to my grandfather until his death, shall we not? or rather you, as trustee, must pay it. What I want to know is whether your liability for this interest is covered by the mortgage, or will you be dependent on us to pay it yearly? If the latter, how much will it be?—what is the rate %?

If the £260 is settled on Lucy, so much the better for me, as she would, on my mother's dying intestate, take the sum appointed, and the rest would come to me. At least such is my impression. She made the previous appointments with the intention of excluding me, and I remember pointing out to her at the time that she had done, in effect, the very reverse.

£100 just now would pay a few bills for us and keep us going for a month or so very conveniently. I am sorry I cannot take up Plunkett's I.O.[U.] at once; I hope he will not be inconvenienced by the delay. [Uncle Frederick replied: "Under these circumstances your Mother had better write me a formal letter stating that she wishes to give Lucy the benefit of £130 more for her advancement, and asking me to have a Deed prepared to that effect. My Policy on your Father's life is for £150 which leaves £20 over the Trust Money. I will pay the £100 for £15 out of that, and repay myself £5 of the money out of pocket, and I will expect your Mother to authorise me to pay myself all I advanced (for which I will send her the Vouchers) out of the £130. This will leave about £120 to send to her."]

What is the date of the odd £300 due to O'Brien? I never heard of it before. [Uncle Frederick replied: "Sent particulars to your Mother. The sum is under £300—I was guessing when I named that sum."]

I knew (from my socialistic studies of the movement of capital) that Clibborn & Shaw must have come to grief in the long run.

We are greatly indebted to you for undertaking all the arrangements. As to the troubles of the Gurly trust, I can only say that I know the family character and fully appreciate what it has cost you. Healthy old man, my grandfather!

Sorry to hear that you are not well. You will, I hope, experience a reaction after the depression of the funeral. Do not stand any of the family nonsense—they will do their best to keep down your spirits. You will find my way of looking at matters not half a bad one.

yours philosophically
G. Bernard Shaw

—Postscript to the other letter—

I made a blunder about the £130, which has, I see, nothing to do with W.B. Gurly. Still, I was under the impression that my father had to pay some small interest yearly for some money drawn out and not covered by the interest on the mortgage.

My mother believes that he made a will. [Shaw added subsequently: "Yes. Uncle F. drew it up—and sends it herewith."] At Agnes's death, he succeeded to the £400 that had been settled on her, or whatever was left of it. This he told my mother he had restored to her by will. If he did not, I presume that I succeed to this £400.

Is Scott a farmer or a landlord. If the latter, is not the security bad, thanks to Davitt and Co.? As a socialist I hope it is. As a mortgagee I hope it isnt.

GBS

To JAMES B. MURDOCH

[F/2]

[36 Osnaburgh Street N W]
[*c.* 4th] July 1885

[James Barclay Murdoch, who succeeded Alexander Smith as secretary of the Hunterian Club, wrote on 3rd July that Dr Furnivall thought Shaw was being too elaborate with the Lodge index. He apologised for having been hard on Shaw as a result of Shaw having been hard upon himself, and asked for entries under A to E by return of post.]

Dear Sir

I am at present so entangled in other work that I am at a loss to know how to make time today even when Dr Furnivall assures me that all I now can do with the Lodge glossary is insert all my desiderata with a note to the effect that they have proved insurmountable. I still cling to the idea that a fresh man could do something more. In any case, he can expedite the finish of the job which I have so scandalously delayed. Accordingly, I have written to Dr Furnivall asking him to find some zealous worker who will attack the remainder of the enterprise vigorously and bring it to a happy conclusion if possible—to a speedy one in any case. I have told Dr Furnivall that the Hunterian Club promised me 5 gns., and have authorised him to offer this sum to my successor for his trouble. I shall practically save money by this arrangement, as it will save me time enough to make more than 5 gns. in other ways.

I assure you that nothing that you have written to me requires the least apology. You have been most considerate throughout; and I feel that I have been almost outrageously the reverse. I certainly must have seemed so. I can only plead that I am the victim of economic forces in this matter.

faithfully yours
George Bernard Shaw

To JAMES B. MURDOCH

36 Osnaburgh Street N W
28th July 1885

[F/2]

[Although Dr Furnivall had transferred the Lodge index to Thomas Tyler to complete, Murdoch was dissatisfied with Shaw's altruism in offering his full fee to Tyler, which he felt would be "quixotic." He didn't believe the Hunterian directors—"little as you may think of them (perhaps because they allowed you to put off too long)"—would entertain the proposal (BM).

The Rev. William Anthony Harrison (1828?–92) of St Anne's Vicarage, South Lambeth, was a Shakespeare textual scholar associated with Furnivall in the New Shakspere Society.]

My dear Sir

Some weeks ago Dr Furnivall asked Mr Thomas Tyler, of Offord Road, London, N., to undertake the completion of the Lodge Index. Mr Tyler consented; and the matter is now in his hands. He is to have the 5 guineas, and I am to keep the set of Lodge. A letter to him, asking how soon the work is likely to be finished, will probably do no harm.

I am just as glad that the money should be put out of the question between the Hunterian Club and myself. I assure you I have no grudge against the directors; but I have always protested against being treated as a paid indexer who was not fulfilling his bargain. But the £5.5.0 certainly vitiated this position of mine; and I only allowed it to be part of the arrangement because I did not want to take an insufferable attitude of obliging the Club in the matter. I said distinctly that the sum was not large enough to be regarded as an equivalent for the trouble involved, and stipulated that I should therefore do the Index only at my leisure, postponing it always to more remunerative work. This made the bargain a fair one; and I have only remonstrated with the Club when they complained (very naturally) of the postponement which they had nevertheless agreed to. But the agreement has now been reduced ad absurdum by a change in my circumstances that leaves me no leisure, and no prospect of any. Still, I am not bound to finish within any given period; and the club is not bound to pay me until I have finished. In this ridiculous extremity, the best thing for both parties is engagement of Mr Tyler to finish the job. There is no more quixotism than is quite commonly practised by men who work on old English literature without being paid for it in cash.

Mr Tyler will probably make short work of most of my difficulties. I might have disposed of many of them myself by consulting him, or Mr Furnivall, or the Rev. Mr Harrison; but as this would have been practically asking them to do my work for me, I could not get over my reluctance to trouble them. As Mr Tyler does not propose to read Lodge through, I had better have a look at the proofs to detect misprints in names, &c.

faithfully
G. Bernard Shaw

To MRS PAKENHAM BEATTY

36 Osnaburgh Street N W
4th September 1885

[A/4]

[Edith Benigna Isabel Hutton Dowling Beatty (1852–1933), known as Ida, who had married Pakenham Beatty on 22nd February 1879, had studied the piano under Gounod, and read and spoke French fluently. For several years, until they moved in 1885 to "Teviotdale" in the Mill Hill Road (on the outskirts of London), Shaw visited the Beattys virtually every Sunday, to don the gloves and spar with Paquito, and to improve his French by trying it on Mrs Beatty, who tended to mother "old grandfather Shaw" (a sobriquet she had bestowed upon him). The Beattys had three children; their oldest, a son born in 1881, was christened Pakenham William Albert Hengist Mazzini Beatty, the Hengist being in honour of Beatty's poet friend Richard Hengist Horne, the Mazzini paying tribute to the Italian revolutionist. Shaw jocularly countered this idealistic act by dubbing the youngster Bismarck. Osborne was the family governess. *Marcia*, a verse tragedy by Beatty, was published in 1884; Shaw, under the pseudonym "L.O.Streeter" (meaning "Lives on Osnaburgh Street"), reviewed it so unfavourably in the August 1884 issue of *To-Day* that his father was moved to write from Dublin: "I am afraid Mr Streeter deserves the title of 'Ruffian' from Mr Beatty" (BM). In *An Unsocial Socialist*, the poetic drama (which Shaw had read in manuscript) became *The Patriot Martyrs*, and its author was satirised as Chichester Erskine.

Jaegerism consisted of following the "Sanitary Woollen System" propounded by Dr Gustav Jaeger (1832–1917), a health culturist who advocated the substitution of woollen clothing and bedding for cotton, linen, or any fibrous fabric. Shaw endorsed Jaeger's system throughout his life.

Sergius Stepniak was the pseudonym of Sergei Mikhailovich Kravchinski (1852–95), a Russian nihilist who had settled in London. Stepniak, active in the Socialist movement, wrote several books, including *Russia under the Tsars* (1885) and *The Career of a Nihilist* (1889). The prospectus to which Shaw refers called for the formation of a Society of Friends of Russia.]

Dear Mrs Beatty

If you Jagerize Bismarck, you had better order him a knitted tunic. You can study the general effect in the jerseys of the Salvation Army. The costume will probably expose him to insult from the youths of Mill Hill Park, with whom he can exercise himself in the art of self defence. Do not try to make him look pretty. It is my private opinion that Bismarck has had more of the charming but enervating atmosphere of the nursery than is good for him. Get him a pair of thick boots, and turn him loose for an hour or two every day. And send him, above all, to a Kindergarten, if there is a genuine one in the neighborhood. I will try and find out whether there is one, and urge the question of the fellow's education for a year or two until Paquito wakes up to it. I used to read Shakspere when I was his age. I speak with feeling, as I have observed that you and Osborne have developed a sort of smartness in him that is only one degree removed from silliness. A clever boy should be "old fashioned," and his mother should hate him—at least, whether she should or not, she always does.

The enclosed prospectus may interest Paquito. Stepniak, who received it coldly at first, has taken it up with some enthusiasm. A society with the object of diffusing information about Russia cannot be expected to feel very grateful to the diffuser of Marcia, which is a gross and wanton misrepresentation of facts from beginning to end; but if the poet will give his name and half a crown, his offence may possibly be condoned. I perceived last Sunday that your imagination drew a hideous picture of Stepniak. But you need not be apprehensive. I assure you I shall never connive at the infliction upon you of any socialist of the plentiful "scallawag" type. Stepniak is an amiable middle aged gentleman who will probably be rather afraid of you, but who will make you feel that he is worthy of your friendly and distinguished consideration. But you are not likely to see him at Teviotdale just yet.

William Morris

May Morris

Pakenham Beatty

William Archer

If I were in his place, and a stranger living a selfish, lonely, and luxuriously idle life, were to send for me to entertain him at his dinner, and shew myself to him as a curiosity, I would accept the invitation, but I would bring a heavy club along and lay that stranger out. There was a time—an aspiring bachelor time—when I would have introduced Paquito hopefully to any band of choice spirits, but now I blush to own him. His poetry, in point of ideas, is getting something too awful. You need not fear the lady you refer to, as you can at any moment foudroyer her (thanks to my treacherous indiscretion) by threatening to mention les crapauds before her husband.

grandpaternally yours
George Bernard Shaw

To MAY MORRIS

[A/2]

36 Osnaburgh Street N W
22nd September 1885

[On 20th September the police broke up a Socialist meeting in Limehouse and arrested several participants. On the 22nd, William Morris, who had attended the court proceedings, was arrested for "alleged disorderly conduct in court," brought before Magistrate Thomas W. Saunders (1814–90) of Thames police court, and acquitted. The meeting at Stepney, at which Shaw, Edward Aveling, and Annie Besant were present, was designed to organise a Free Speech protest demonstration the following Sunday; Shaw pledged himself to go to prison if necessary. The police, however, did not interfere with the demonstrators.

The rehearsal was for a Socialist League concert on the 26th. At an earlier concert, on 21st November 1884, in aid of the Social Democratic Federation (from which Morris and his Socialist League associates broke away early in 1885), Shaw and Miss Kathleen Ina had played "the two overtures" in duet.

Clementia (Mrs Peter Alfred) Taylor was a Unitarian, friend of W. J. Fox, Mazzini, and all the radicals of the day. Her home in Kensington was for many years a hotbed of "movements."]

Dear Miss Morris

I shall not be able to attend the rehearsal at Grittleton Road tomorrow, as it appears I must be at Stepney Green to assist the Vigilance Com^{tee} with my wisdom and eloquence. I have written to Mrs Taylor, and have added that I have written to you; but whether your engagement with her falls through or not in consequence I leave you to settle between you.

yours fra—faithfully, I mean
George Bernard Shaw

To MRS PAKENHAM BEATTY

36 Osnaburgh Street N W
22nd September 1885

[S/1]

[C.H. Johns was a friend of the Beattys, and another of Paquito's sparring partners. He was popular as a poetry reciter (of such works as Tennyson's "Dora") at Socialist meetings and concerts.]

Dear Mrs Beatty

I have read your letter attentively several times, each time leaving me more bewildered than before. You say Paquito has not returned, and ask me for God's sake to say what I have done with him. Then you say that he is ill in bed. All I can do is to tell you the history of last night.

Paquito, Stepniak, Champion, and I dined at the Criterion. Champion brought word that Morris had been arrested. We agreed to go after dinner to the Socialist League Hall in Farringdon Road and hear the news. Accordingly we walked thence from the Criterion, Champion and I leading, P and Stepniak behind. Champion and I walked quickly, and had to stop at the turnings to make sure that the other two were following. We could hear them most of the time above the din of the traffic, shouting one another down about Victor Hugo or the like. Near the corner of Queen St. Champion stopped to buy a paper and we were all together for a moment. Then we went into Holborn in the same order as before. Opposite Furnivall's Inn, we crossed the roadway, and when we looked about for the poet and the Nihilist, they were invisible, nor were their voices audible in the land. We waited and looked about for a while; but they had given us the slip. Stepniak, however, knows the Socialist League premises, and we concluded that he would turn up there, so we went on, and were soon in the thick of an excited meeting, at which I was relieved to see Morris, and delighted to see Her [May Morris]. Champion had to speak twice, and was much occupied. I, between following the proceedings and watching the divine profile of the most beautiful of women, soon became utterly indifferent to everything else. Neither Stepniak nor Paquito ever appeared, though Stepniak at least knew the way thither perfectly well. Whither they went, and what they did, is best known to themselves. Aveling saw them in the neighbourhood of the hall; that was the only scrap of news I could get.

You have of course learnt the particulars of Morris' arrest from the papers. I am in a state of terror about this east end business; for I have pledged myself to speak next Sunday, to get arrested, to refuse to pay the fine, and to do the month. The prospect is anything but agreeable, I assure you.

What on earth made Paquito ill? Was it the glee dinner, or did he quarrel with Stepniak? Or was it the combat with Johns, and the bowl-foaming at the American bar subsequently? Suggest to him to do a month with me. The compulsory abstinence would renovate his exhausted frame, and would greatly amuse

yours, dear Mrs Beatty, most lowspiritedly
heroically
George Bernard Shaw

To MRS PAKENHAM BEATTY

[A/5]

36 Osnaburgh Street N W
1st October 1885

[Dr Walter Tyrrell (1851–1931), a West Kensington physician, senior anaesthetist of St Thomas's Hospital, was a protégé of Shaw's friend Barton.]

Dear Mrs Beatty

I know Dr Tyrrell. He is a perfectly safe man. He has the misfortune to resemble me in point of complexion; and if he comes to see poor Bismarck he will listen to all that you have to say with a stony quietness that will make your blood run cold. But he will then treat the patient with his utmost skill, which is said by his brother doctors to be very considerable. My mother once saw him manage a difficult case, and she formed as high an opinion of him as you once held of Dr [Henry S.] Wilson. But I am afraid you will find it difficult to dispense with a local doctor. A long time ago Barton had to give up attending cases as far off as Bayswater, and Tyrrell is quite as busy. However, I of course do not know what their arrangement may be about distant cases. Do not on any account wait for Barton's return. He will be away for another week at least, and you need have no misgivings as to Tyrrell, if you can induce him to come down. I have not much faith in doctors in the present condition of their science; but I think if you tell Tyrrell that Bismarck has had several previous attacks, and that the seaside has always cured him, he will probably order you off there at once. Only remember that if you overstate your case in order to get your idea carried out, and your idea happens to be wrong, you will feel rather the worse for it if the small man succumbs to the journey and the change. I know very well that you want, not Barton's advice, but your

141

own advice given with Barton's authority. No doubt your instinct is right, and your advice is good; but if you go through the form of consulting a doctor at all pray dont cook his opinion for him by only telling him what is favourable to your own theory. You see I have some slight doubts of your firmness under a strong temptation to practise a little special pleading. I only mention them for the sake of poor much bemothered and much benursed Mazzini.

If any man hates you, *assassinate him*. Hatred is mortal: it kills at ten miles—at ten thousand miles. All the people I ever hated died. A deadly and horrible emanation comes from a hater to his victim, and slays. Happily your enemy is too utterly sunk in his own weakness to hate effectively. Happily too, a bright and rational liking is a spring of vitality in the person liked. So like Mazzini brightly and rationally. But dont love him—that will smother him. A woman's love is too much for a child: besides, there is always something fierce and selfish in it. In your place I think I should try Tyrrell.

GBS

To ALICE LOCKETT

36 Osnaburgh Street N W
8th October 1885

[T/1; X/103]

[On the evening of 8th October, Shaw met Stepniak and William Earl Hodgson (d. 1910), a leader-writer for *The Times* and the *National Review*, novelist, and fishing expert. Hodgson later described the meeting, which took place at Edward Pease's home, in a small, privately printed book, *A Night with a Nihilist* (1886).]

No, not for the smallest fraction of a second. My season is commencing: my nights are filling up one by one: I am booked for half a dozen lectures within the next month. I shall be out tonight with Stepniak and the underdone. My DR [*Dramatic Review*] copy must be done today, tomorrow an article is due for the Magazine of Music. On Saturday my contribution to Our Corner must be written. On Sunday there is a lecture ["The Attitude of Socialists towards Other Bodies"], not one idea for which have I yet arranged. Meanwhile, To-day is howling for more copy. See you this week! Avaunt, sorceress: not this month— not until next July. Not, in any case, until I am again in the detestable humour which is the only one to which you minister. Remember: I am not always a savage. My pleasures are music, conversation, the grapple of my intelligence with fresher ones. All this I can sweeten with a kiss; but I cannot saturate and spoil it with fifty thousand. Love making grows tedious to me—the emotion has evaporated from it. This is your fault: since your return I have seen you twice, and both times you have been lazy and unintelligently luxurious. I will not spend such evenings except when I am for a moment tired and brutish. Even then I will turn with relief and gratitude from moral death with you to moral life and activity with other women—with men—with the Fabians even— with my work—anywhere where all my faculties and sympathies are awake and active. I only value friends for what they can give me: if you can only give me one thing, I shall value you only for that. It is useless for you to protest—the matter is not within my will—you will be valued as you deserve, not as you wish to be valued. You have said that the most beautiful woman can give no more than she has. Do not forget that I cannot esteem the most beautiful woman for more than she is. I want as much as I can get: there is no need to force it upon me if it exists; I am only too thirsty for companionship. Beware. When all the love has gone out of me, I am remorseless: I hurl the truth about like destroying lightning.

GBS

To SWAN SONNENSCHEIN & CO.

[F/2]

36 Osnaburgh Street N W
19th October 1885

[After eight months Shaw was still quarrelling with Swan Sonnenschein over payment for "The Miraculous Revenge" in *Time*. On 7th October the publisher informed Shaw that he was in error in supposing that a shilling magazine has necessarily a definite scale of payments "regardless of the contributor's subject or standing," nor did they regulate their payments by those made by other publishers, but paid what the article was thought to be worth (BM). The "couple of essays on P.E." presumably were Shaw's letters to Swan Sonnenschein & Co., in which he attempted to teach them political economy.]

Gentlemen

The position taken by you in your letter dated the 7th is economically untenable. You say that you do not regulate your payments by those made by other publishers; but you do—you must—you cannot help yourselves. I do not know on what principle you have fixed my remuneration at four shillings and threepence a page; but it is obvious that as long as I can obtain double that rate for my work from competing editors you must double your terms if you want me to write for you. My standing and the value of my work are fixed by the operation of the market; and you are no more in a position to fix my price at four and threepence than I am to fix it at 400 and threepence. If you had offered me half a crown for the entire contribution, you might have defended the offer on the same ground as that which you have just taken.

Permit me to add that as I have waited eight months for payments, have had to sacrifice a whole morning to remedying your printer's disregard to my fairly legible copy, and have had to throw in a couple of essays on P.E. into the bargain, I consider that my demand is reasonable and my patience exemplary.

Kindly therefore send a cheque for seven guineas to

yours faithfully
George Bernard Shaw

To MRS PAKENHAM BEATTY

[S/1]

36 Osnaburgh Street N W
24th November 1885

[John E. Williams had recently served a one month prison sentence for his participation in the Dod Street demonstration in defence of free speech and the public right of assembly.]

Dear Mrs Beatty

Many thanks for your kind letter. I am not sure that I understand it all: you write with so much enthusiasm that you often introduce "its" without mentioning any subject previously, or speak of "him" and "her" without having named anyone. Also, for the sake of brevity, you omit every third word, and I am not sure that I always guess it correctly. You tell me of things done by my mother which I cannot help thinking were really perpetrated by Daisy [the Beattys' maid] or Osborne; and Paquito and Johns get inextricably confounded in a maze of relatives and personal pronouns. Pray do not think I complain; what your letters lose in perspicuity they gain in a certain naive grace which is highly characteristic of you, and therefore extremely pleasant.

If you are on speaking terms with Paquito, please tell him that I found his cheque waiting for me on my return from Leicester, and that I hope to see Champion soon, and make enquiries about the Williams subscription and the poem [Beatty's "Quia multum Amavi," which appeared in *To-Day*, February 1886].

I lecture on Sunday at the Eleusis [Radical] Club, Chelsea, so must defer my next visit to Teviotdale for a fortnight at least. Daignez, madame, d'accepter le dévouement très humble et pas du tout distingué de

George Bernard Shaw

To WILLIAM ARCHER

[A/2]
36 Osnaburgh Street N W
12th December 1885

[Archer, who was dramatic critic of *The World*, had been imposed upon by the editor Edmund Yates (1831–94) to double as art critic, signing the latter articles "F.B." (for Fred Bayham, a character in Thackeray's *The Newcomes*). As Shaw had accompanied him on a recent tour of the galleries, offering comments and suggestions, Archer felt obliged to share the payment with him and sent a cheque for £1. 6. 8 to Shaw. In February 1886 Archer persuaded Yates to appoint Shaw art critic, a post he held until December 1889.

Walter Crane (1845–1915), painter and book illustrator, was a leader with William Morris in the romantic movement in British decorative art, and associated with Morris in the Socialist movement. It was at the first open meeting of the Shelley Society on 10th March 1886 that Shaw, following a lecture by the Rev. Stopford Brooke on "Shelley as Poet and Man," is supposed to have shocked the staid members of the Society by announcing that, like Shelley, "I am a Socialist, an Atheist, and a Vegetarian."]

Your mind is in a thoroughly morbid condition with regard to the pictures. I return the cheque, and recommend more exercise and earlier hours. My moral ground is this. If you are a competent critic, you do not need my assistance. If you are not competent, you are imposing on Yates, and I cannot share the proceeds of a fraud. This, I hope, is conclusive. If it is not, I can easily find a fresh position equally elevated and inexpugnable.

Robertson has sent me a ticket for his lecture. I shall look in there on my way to an appointment down Kensington way [to visit Vandeleur Lee].

My lecture came off well enough, but I was sorry to miss you, as I laid down a formula for scientific criticism expressly on your account. It excited general loathing. Morris & Crane came, and spoke.

Furnivall has just revealed the Shelley Society to me. I thought it would be a tip; but have seen it in yesterday's P.M. [*Pall Mall Gazette*].

Damn this pen. I left my own at home (I am au Musée).

GBS

To WILLIAM ARCHER

36 Osnaburgh Street N W

[A/2; X/108.e]
14th December 1885

[Sir Henry Norman (1858–1939) and Charles Robert Morley (1853–1916), nephew of John Morley, were members of the editorial staff of the *Pall Mall Gazette*. Robert William Lowe (1853–1902) was a Scottish insurance broker and dramatic critic, to whom Archer dedicated *The Theatrical 'World'* of *1893*. These three, plus J.M.Robertson and E.R.V.Dibdin, were Archer's close friends and frequent companions. David Ricardo (1772–1823), English economist, developed a theory of rent, profit, and wages known as Ricardo's Law. Ferdinand Lassalle (1825–64), German Socialist, formulated a so-called "iron law of wages."]

I re-return the cheque, and if you re-re-return it, I will re-re-re-return it again ("again" being here, as you justly observe, tautological). The considerations which induce me to do so follow in no particular order.

1. The idea of one man sucking another's brains is a depraved individualist idea. No man has a right of property in the ideas of which he is the mouthpiece. The law does not permit a man to patent a discovery, but only an invention concreted as a machine. The ideas of your criticism are mere natural raw material which neither of us is entitled to monopolize. You have only to imagine Norman, Morley, Lowe, Robertson, Dibdin, and myself sending in our claims whenever we detect in your writings an idea to which our conversation with you led up (and which therefore would never have occurred to you without us), to perceive the frightful and anarchical impossibilism to which your proposition of private property in ideas—especially critical ideas—must lead in practice. If I am to be paid for what I suggested to you, for example, the painters must clearly be paid for what they suggested to me. This is the *reductio ad absurdum*. The devil has presented you with a depraved conception disguised as conscientiousness.

For what, then, are you to be paid by Yates? For the ideas in your article? Certainly not. Only for the skilled labour of producing with

146

hand, ink, and pen, a certain instrument for the utilization and distribution of these ideas. The reading world must feed you whilst you write for it. *Must*, mind you, solely because you wouldnt write the article if they didnt, whereas you would think away all the same, pay or no pay. But they must also feed you whilst you are going through the galleries, because otherwise you would never darken their doors. Ergo, you say, they must also feed me whilst I walk through the galleries. But they do not: they pay only one man's time—yours. Yet I go. Observe: I am under no external compulsion to go, yet I do so. Obviously then, it pays me to go without direct remuneration; and for me under these circumstances to take the cheque would be to pocket a bonus to which I am not entitled, and to shorten your life by one half. The latter point is too obvious to need detailed explanation. You are, by the Ricardo-Lassalle iron law, working at a bare subsistence wage. For the two hours (say) you spend in a gallery, you only get two hours subsistence. Of this you give me one hour, although I am already provided for (as shewn by my willingness to come for nothing apparently). Consequently you can only support life for one hour instead of the two for which you have been provisioned by society & Yates. Therefore the division shortens your life by one half, whereas I, having half as much again as I need, suffer from surrepletion.

As it is, I have the advantage of seeing the galleries for nothing without the drudgery of writing the articles. I do not like to lose the record of the art life, and yet going to a gallery by myself bores me so much that I let the [Royal] Academy itself slip last year, and should have done so this year but for your bearing me thither one day. (I perceive your manly form stooping at the catalogue desk, and moving along as if your hat had blown off and were making three or four knots before a gentle breeze.) If you decline to utilize your complimentary tickets in future for my benefit, you will be perpetrating an act—or series of acts —of wanton and fiendish malignity. Pray observe that I am not actuated by motives of generosity. You are much better off than I am, and any pecuniary consideration on my part for you would be senseless. I perceive the proposed arrangement to be unjust, and therefore I am proof against your special pleading that you are placed in "an unpleasant hole" by my obduracy. Were you to be placed naked in a blast furnace, my decision would be the same. Fiat justitia: ruat coelum. (Latin!)

Here you approach in person, evidently resolved to confer—at least it is like your footstep and shadow. "Hallo &c"

GBS

147

To MRS PAKENHAM BEATTY

[A/4]

36 Osnaburgh Street N W
23rd December 1885

[Erard & Co. manufactured pianos. *Cashel Byron's Profession* was published in February 1886, stereotyped from the pages of *To-Day*, in which it had been serialised. It was Shaw's first book.]

Dear Mrs Beatty

I believe you are doing it on purpose.

—Extract from Page 2 of your last—

"*I like Erard,* and, if I possibly can, will have one since Paquito does not object to pay £5 a quarter &c."

—Extract from Page 4 of the same—

"Any of the 3 pianos named by Mrs Shaw will do. The smallest, blackest, and softest will be my taste."

There is a point at which the most sympathetic intelligence gives way. I reach that point when I strive to reconcile those two statements in your letter. Have pity on me, and drop the subject. I have done my best.

I am afraid that I shall not be able to come to Teviotdale on the 27th after all. Sunday becomes more and more impossible as demands for lectures thicken. Les jours de Sinclair Road ne reviendront jamais

ébahi, étourdi, mais fidèle
GBS

"Cashel Byron" next month, complete in paper cover, one shilling. Review copy to American Traveller [a London journal, 1875–90].

To H. HALLIDAY SPARLING

36 Osnaburgh Street N W
24th December 1885

[C/28; X/149]

[Henry Halliday Sparling (1860–1924), who was Morris's protégé and assistant, married May Morris in June 1890. They were later divorced.]

George Bernard Shaw (Fabian serio-comic artist) at liberty for genteel leading business on the 13th & 27th prox. All other Wednesdays in January filled up.

GBS

148

To MRS PAKENHAM BEATTY

36 Osnaburgh Street N W

[S/1]   29th December 1885

Dear Mrs Beatty

My mother's memorandum went back to you, I think, in my last letter. I cannot find it.

As to your being sorry that I have "taken it up so," I cannot express my feelings. I haven't taken it up at all: I have laid it down in despair. If you would only curb your speculations as to how I am "taking it up," and make up your mind about the piano, how much faster we should all get along! In your last letter you announced two exactly opposite and reciprocally exclusive conclusions without giving me the faintest clue as to which was the final one. Now you tell me that I know exactly what you mean. What can I do but lose my temper and reply furiously that you don't know what you mean, yourself. Here is my last advice as to the piano.

Take no further notice of my mother's selections. Go down to Erard's and see whether they can give you what you want at a possible price. If not, then we can see further. But as you have a distinct idea of what you require, you must go and choose for yourself. If you won't or can't do this, then you shan't have a piano at all.

I cannot afford to go down to Teviotdale just now. This month has been a disastrous one for me financially, and I must scorn delights and live laborious days for a while in consequence. Paquito has not the remotest idea of what it is to be exploited on the piece-work system by newspapers.

Forgive rudeness. In haste

GBS

To HUBERT BLAND

[36 Osnaburgh Street N W]

[F/2]   8th February 1886

[Hubert Bland (1856–1914), Socialist writer and journalist, was one of the founders of the Fabian Society. His wife, Edith Nesbit (1858–1924), a novelist, poet, and writer of juvenile books, was also active in the Socialist movement. Charlotte Wilson had drafted a portion of Fabian Tract No. 4, "What Socialism Is."

Shaw's letter was written "in rhyme," according to a note in his diary, but the scansion is so clumsy that no effort has been made to set it (from the shorthand draft) in verse form.]

149

Dear Bland

With respect to the [Fabian] conference and the needful guarantee, you may put down my name on your list for the same and rely for a share on me. Kindly say when I must come down with the dust and how much the amount should be. If every Fabian contributes a quid, it will run to £80; but as everyone wont, youll be short if I dont somewhat overstretch this point, so book me for three, though the offer will be not quite so good as it sounds for I see very little likelihood of my finding funds to pay, and may answer your call—if I answer at all—by requesting a brief delay for my means are such that I have none too much to live on from day to day.

Mrs Wilson's tract on collectivism, as I from the first foresaw, seems certain now to end in a ruin. I think we must either withdraw or allow Mrs Bl[and] to take it in hand.

> yours ever
> G. Bernard Shaw

To MRS PAKENHAM BEATTY

[A/4]

36 Osnaburgh Street N W
10th March 1886

[Beatty had for some time been infatuated by Lucy Carr Shaw; there is evidence that, as early as 1884, he had been forcing his attentions upon her, for in August of that year George Carr Shaw wrote from Dublin: "I hope that fellow [Beatty] is not still annoying Lucy. It must be very distressing to her" (BM). In March 1886 Lucy was staying with Jenny Patterson (see next letter, to Mrs Patterson) in Brompton Square, where she was recuperating from an attack of pleurisy. Beatty called on Lucy there, but the two women were openly rude to him.]

Dear Mrs Beatty

Why felicitate me on the utterances of an insert of the press when I am so much more happy in your appreciation? But I find nothing about "Cashel Byron" in the St James's Gazette. Did you not mean the review (by my friend Archer) in Monday's Pall Mall?

Your visit to Brompton Square has produced an impression utterly fatal to the poet. I have just received a letter from Mrs Patterson in which she says "*Mrs* Beatty we shall always be charmed to see. She is simply delightful." Now what do those four lines under "Mrs" mean? Evidently a strong distinction between Mrs and Mr. It is plain that the rascal represented himself as being the victim of cruel parents, who forced him in his early youth into a detested union with a harsh,

Jane Patterson
(*From Portrait by Robert Anning Bell*)

ill-favored, parsimonious, puritanical woman of fifty, with no poetic heart to beat in unison with his own. Who would not be kind to a poet in such a predicament, however suspicious his eye might be? But now the murder is out. Don Juan is unmasked. The young, charming, and neglected wife is *en évidence*. The suggestions of the wicked eye are verified: blue spectacles even will be in vain should he have the hardihood to visit her now, which she strongly objects to his doing. Brompton Square, in fact, is up in arms against him.

Such is my interpretation of "*Mrs*."

GBS

To JANE PATTERSON

[A/1]

36 Osnaburgh Street N W
10th March 1886

[Mrs Jane ("Jenny") Patterson (*c.* 1839–1924) was a widow who had come to London from Dublin following the death of her husband. Although there is slight evidence that she knew Shaw's mother in Dublin, Shaw appears to have first met her at her London home, 5 Hans Place, in 1882. Later, when she moved to Brompton Square and began to take singing lessons from Mrs Shaw, the relationship between Mrs Patterson and the Shaws became quite intimate. Although she was more than fifteen years older than Shaw, Jenny set her cap for the young man, and after several preliminary skirmishes —"a declaration of passion," but Shaw's "Virgo intacta still" on 10th July, and "forced caresses" on the 18th—she succeeded in helping him to celebrate his 29th birthday on 26th July "by a new experience" (Diary). This belated loss of virginity produced mixed reactions in Shaw. In the first flush of exaltation he wrote a "full circumstantial account" of his affair to his friend McNulty in Dublin, but the next day he "resolved to begin a new Pilgrim's Progress" (Diary). The relationship with Jenny lasted for several years, running a stormy course as the passionate woman sought her lover's favours while he callously toyed with her affections and was cruelly indifferent to her. Only this one letter from Shaw to Jenny survives, the balance having been destroyed by her executor after her death. Although Shaw destroyed a good many of Jenny's letters, enough have survived to clarify the nature of their relationship, as in Jenny's lament of 11th May 1886: "I am a wretched miserable woman a coward I cannot open your letter. I have longed for it with all my soul I am ill laid low by crying & pain. Do not abandon me my love have pity on me. forgive the passion of Sunday it recoils in me I suffer for it now pity me and forgive me J." Or in her purring note of 29th July 1886: "Good night my love. My friend & lover I am content that there are no barriers betwixt us—that you have taken me back. I will try to make *you* content with *me*. be my friend when you will my

love when you will—but let the friend be first. Always and ever your Jenny"
(BM).

Pakenham Beatty called on Lucy again on the 10th, occasioning
Mrs Patterson to write to Shaw that neither Lucy nor she desired to know
Mr Beatty, whom she labelled "a Hass," and if he returned he would be
told they were not at home. "Will you do a kindly action & save him a
useless journey" (BM).]

As to Beatty, do as you please. Only remember that—

There are more considerate ways of getting rid of a man than shutting
the door in his face.

If a man's acquaintance has been accepted by a woman, and he has
not behaved improperly, he has a right to be dealt with in the most
considerate way.

You and Lucy have about as much reason to be frightened as a pair
of vigorous and experienced cats have to recoil before an exceptionally
nervous mouse.

And (general aphorism) people always act cruelly and stupidly under
the influence of unreasonable fear.

———————————

With regard to the "à bientôt" at the end of your note, I may say
that my diary presents an unbroken array of engagements right up to
the 23rd. I had hoped to see you on the 22nd; but an invitation to
spend that evening at Blackheath [with the Blands] has just arrived.

I am, Madam,
your obedient servant
GBS

To CHARLES J. KITCHING

36 Osnaburgh Street N W
[G/2]   11th March 1886

[Charles J. Kitching, Hon. Secretary of the Political Council, Hammersmith
Socialist Club, wrote on 10th March to say: "I am directed by this Council
to convey to you the hearty thanks of its members for the generous manner
in which you have always responded to the invitation to lecture at our Club;
and to express their high appreciation of your ability in dealing with the
various subjects you have put before them" (BM).]

Dear Sir

I hasten to acknowledge the pleasure given me by the very kind
expressions in your letter on behalf of the Hammersmith Club, and

to say how much I, on my side, am indebted to them for having invited me to occupy their platform.

I am, dear Sir,
yours faithfully
George Bernard Shaw

To WILLIAM ARCHER

[A/2]

36 Osnaburgh Street N W
16th April 1886

[Shaw helped Archer read the proofs of the latter's book *About the Theatre: Essays and Studies*, published later that year by T. Fisher Unwin. Denis Diderot (1713–84) was a French philosopher, encyclopaedist, and man of letters. The private quarrel by two performers between the lines of Molière's *Le dépit amoureux* is found in Diderot's *The Paradox of Acting*, which Shaw had read in the Walter H. Pollock translation published by Unwin in 1883. The author of *A Scrap of Paper* was Victorien Sardou (1831–1908), popular French playwright whose influence on the English stage Shaw subsequently labelled in his *Saturday Review* criticisms "Sardoodledom."]

All the points about the actor are wrong. As you recapitulate them on Slip 57 they conflict with the following facts.

1. Acting destroys morbid self consciousness by making the actor a master of the science of appearances. Just as the man is less *morbidly* self conscious than the youth, so is the actor than the man. 2. Amounts only to the fact that the actor must be particularly careful not to make an ass of himself. Expectation of applause is not constantly present to a good actor, because such a one puts a lot of work into his acting, and this work keeps his attention fully occupied. You cannot do two things at once. If you are thinking of the applause you are either not acting, or acting mechanically, like Diderot's couple who interpolated a private quarrel between their lines. An actor may of course be much mortified if, after he has done his work thoroughly, the audience do not seem to appreciate it—so may any other artist. The truth is that "the somnambulism of genius" (which is bosh) does not leave room for the eager expectation of applause which you suppose to leave no room for anything else. No 3 is not a bit more true of acting than of painting, poetry, composition, or anything else. The same remark applies to Nº 4. An unappreciated actor can persist in taking theatres and offering himself to the public just as I used to persist in writing novels and offering them to the publishers. It is true that unless he can educate the public to accept him within fifteen years, his chance will be gone for ever; but as a matter of fact every man of genius gains his verdict

within that time unless his views are so exceptional as to make him hopelessly dependent on posterity in which case he is a monstrous premature birth. 5. The supply of first places on the stage is not less in proportion to the aspirancy than in other professions named by you at the top of slip 57. You mention sculptors: go and talk to any sculptor about the commission for the Gordon statue or the Wellington statue. There are a dozen opportunities of playing Hamlet for one PRA [President of the Royal Academy] ship, or chance of a London statue or public building of the first magnitude, to say nothing of frescoes and all artistic work above the level of cabinet pictures. And surely there are heaps of chances for cabinet-picture actors & actresses.

As to Shakspere, I suspend judgment until the argument is fully unrolled. But I contend that our feeling that blank verse is artificial and flat is based on blank verse that *is* artificial & flat, or that is un-skilfully uttered so as to appear so. The ruinousness of Shakspere is only an excuse for bad performances. Given one of his tearing good plays acted and mounted as adequately as The Scrap of Paper and success is as certain in one case as in the other. But it is ten times as hard to get a decent performance of "As You Like It" as of "A Scrap of Paper": hence a London manager is ten times safer with a play of Sardou's than with a play of Shakspere's. This is the sort of thing that needs saying from time to time. You spar with the actors & Shakspere in a highly scientific manner; but it seems to me that you do not lead off enough, except in your bout with the Censor. The public needs to be roused by some destructive as well as evasive fighting.

In haste

GBS

P.S. Never mind my pencil nicks on the proof. There is only one to be attended to—that about "resulting from" which I take to be a tortology.

To DR F. J. FURNIVALL

[A/1]

36 Osnaburgh Street N W
5th May 1886

[The Shelley Society presented Shelley's verse drama *The Cenci* at the Grand Theatre, Islington, the afternoon of 7th May 1886. It was the first perform-ance of the play, shown privately due to the refusal of the Lord Chamberlain's office to grant it a public licence, on the ground that the performance of such a play would deprave the public. Shaw took charge of press relations for the production, and reviewed it in the June issue of *Our Corner*: "In indulging

154

his whim to produce something in the obsolete and absurd form which Shakspere had done so much with, Shelley no doubt believed that he was engaged upon a solid and permanent composition. In reality he was only experimenting to find a suitable form for his efforts to 'teach the human heart, through its sympathies and antipathies, the knowledge of itself; in proportion to the possession of which knowledge, every human being is wise, just, sincere, tolerant, and kind.' . . . The result furnishes an artistic parallel to Wagner's 'Rienzi.' It is a strenuous but futile and never-to-be-repeated attempt to bottle the new wine in the old skins." Sydney E. Preston was, in 1886, honorary secretary of the Shelley Society.]

Dear Dr Furnivall

In case I should not see you at the Museum today, I write to say that if you know of any spare tickets for the Cenci, I am a deserving man much in want of them. Preston sent me two balcony and two amphitheatre; but they are gone like smoke, and I want one for myself and two for my mother and sister (who has professional claims as a young actress, save the mark). Is there not a stall for so eminent a critic as

yours unreasonably
G. Bernard Shaw

To ALMA MURRAY

36 Osnaburgh Street N W
[A/1; X/109]   6th May 1886
[Alma Murray (1854–1945), wife of Alfred William Forman (1840–1925), the translator of Wagner's *Ring*, gained a reputation in London for under-taking challenging rôles, appearing in the Browning Society's revivals of *A Blot on the 'Scutcheon* and *Colombe's Birthday* and in the Shelley Society's production of *The Cenci*, which earned for her the title of "the poetic actress without a rival." She created the rôle of Raïna Petkoff in Shaw's *Arms and the Man* at the Avenue Theatre on 21st April 1894.]

Dear Miss Alma Murray

Many thanks for the tickets you so kindly spared me. I was forgotten in the first distribution of tickets, and was further impoverished by a couple of dramatic critics who had also been neglected, and whom I thought it a mistake to exclude. Much of the pressure for tickets is, I find, a run on Beatrice created by Colombe.

very gratefully
G. Bernard Shaw

To HUBERT BLAND

36 Osnaburgh Street N W
3rd July 1886
[A/4]

["Master Fabian" was the infant son of Bland and Edith Nesbit; he died in 1900, three months before his sixteenth birthday.]

Verdict

Quite astonishingly conventional but with a living, moving unconventionality, as of one with whom the conventional opinion is a faith, and not an echo. Mind: this is not condemnation; for the conventional view is very largely the right one. But there is no sympathy in it for the poor *bourgeoisie*, who are also men & brothers: there is even a touch of the rancour of Bax.

I object to the way in which the point about the children is put. People who do not see a man or woman in every child always strike a false note in singing about them. I protest against their being held up as dainties—things with clinging arms and flower soft faces. The next time Master Fabian raises his voice against the injustice of the world in apparently unmotived yelling, give him an energetic smacking and then read him pages 46 & 47 and ask his candid opinion of them.

The lecture should begin at the red ink ¶ on page 2. What precedes it is awkward. You positively must not begin an essay by "People are very fond of saying" &c. It is a most outrageously artless way of hauling on a proposition.

Be prepared to give authorities for your historical statements; and forget not, I pray you, that the horrors attributed by the persecuted to the persecutors are as untrustworthy as the tales of early Christianity or Paris Communardism.

That is all I can say.

GBS

To MRS PAKENHAM BEATTY

36 Osnaburgh Street N W
5th August 1886
[A/4]

[Mrs Beatty's "ribald brother-in-law" was Octavius Holmes Beatty (1864–1924), a barrister, poet, and dabbler in Liberal politics, who had married Margaret Spencer at Oxford on 8th July. "Jupiter Olympus" was Shaw's name for Mrs Beatty's brother, Charles Hutton Dowling, a well-known

Dublin dentist. Algernon Swinburne's poem "The Commonweal: A Song for Unionists" had appeared in *The Times* on 1st July 1886.]

Dear Mrs Beatty

My mind is quite at ease about the babes at Teviotdale since you say that Aunt Charlotte is in charge of them. Though I have never seen that lady, I have the most implicit confidence in her. Extreme bashfulness, however, and the revision of "An Unsocial Socialist" for the printer, forbids my paying her my respects in person. Were the mistress of the mansion there I would venture at all hazards. In her absence the attraction is, I confess, feeble. Besides, I cannot help feeling that if Aunt Charlotte happened to be out when I called, my position with Osborne would be a difficult one. Heaven knows what construction might not be put on my visit by your ribald brother-in-law and your irreverent poet-husband.

I saw the marriage announced in the papers with an ostentation quite the reverse of socialistic. But for my Sunday lectures I should certainly have called to exult over Paquito when Swinburne fulfilled my prophecies by turning out a miserable music-hall jingo the moment he was put to the proof in practical politics. Ha! ha!

My illness was not fatal. I got a boil upon my cheek, and Barton immediately diagnosed constitutional decay from vegetarianism. But my cheek is now as fair and soft as of yore.

Pray remember me to Jupiter Olympus, and believe me, dear Mrs Beatty, yours convalescently

GBS

To ALICE LOCKETT

[A/9]

36 Osnaburgh Street N W
19th August 1886

My dear Alice

I swear by the spirit of Nature's author, which is in the hills, which is in our hearts, which is in the innocent nibbling rabbits that sit among the fallen fir cones at the base of the obelisk hill in the autumn evening, which is in the gentlemen who shoot the rabbits for sport and the weasels that suck their blood for food, which is in the lowly worm and in the pretty redbreast that bites him in two, which is in the myriad fish in that beautiful bay, all eating one another, which is in the bored owner of the white sailed yacht and the brutalized drunkards and drudges on the grimy coal schooners, which is in the studded granite islands in the sea of heather and in the hideous crawling things that fly from the glorious light when you turn the stone over, which is in the miserable people and their miserable oppressors, which is in me who see distress everywhere and in you who see it nowhere, which is [in] the rock to which we cling for assurance that we may all go on doing wrong as there must be some good purpose in it and it will all come right in the end: I swear by it that you write the very worst hand—the absolutely wrongest and most immoral and inartistic hand ever written by woman. A weeks careful practice at the rate of an hour a day, preceded by prayer (which is a genuinely efficacious exercise to calm one's nerves—a sort of hypnotism) would spare your correspondents much suffering.

May I ask what it is to you whether I am or am not a hypocrite. Are the things I say true or not? If they are, what does it matter whether I believe them or not, or with what feelings I utter them? The things I say about myself are true perhaps for the moment, further I do not guarantee them. They do not matter. The things I say about you are more to the purpose. But I will tell you something. Whenever I say anything about you that strikes you as being particularly true and as displaying some insight, just repeat it to the first woman you meet as your opinion of her, and she will be as much struck with your insight as you were with mine. All these things are mere commonplace deductions from the constitution of human nature and the position of women in society. You remember my old talk about you and your better self: Alice and Miss Lockett! I have often said that to women, and they always feel its truth and are touched by my having discovered and believed in their better self. All men do too, and probably all dogs and cats, if they could tell us so. But most women would indignantly deny that they were not absolutely original and peculiar in this private fiction of a dual self. If you tell a human being, male or female, that he or she has more in common with the most antipathetic other human being on earth of the same age, than he (or she) can possibly have that is unique, you will offend them. Nevertheless this is so. The reason I know so much about you (and about everybody else) is that at least nine tenths of me is a simple repetition of nine tenths of you. The odd tenths (our respective individualities) are probably little developed yet,

158

we being young; and, anyhow, they bear a trifling proportion to the rest. The only advantage I have over you is that I have found this out and that you havent. You may assent to the simple proposition as an obvious truism; but in practice you cling (it comes out in little ways) to the illusion of your own individuality—

12th October 1886

I have just discovered this letter, forgotten and unfinished. Is it possible that I did not write to you when you were at Dalkey? I thought I did. This fragment of a letter is just weighty enough to be posted rather than torn up.

GBS

To SWAN SONNENSCHEIN & CO.

[F/2]

36 Osnaburgh Street N W
26th August 1886

[Although a few advance copies were distributed late in 1886, *An Unsocial Socialist* was not published until February 1887.]

Dear Sirs

The enclosed sheets of An U S are ready for the printer. If the book reaches the reviewers while the impression made by "Cashel Byron" is fresh, and before they are swamped with Xmas literature, so much the better for us all. I anticipate very little delay or trouble with the proofs, as I have spent the past fortnight in getting the sheets as right as they will come. Another such holiday would ruin me.

yours faithfully
G. Bernard Shaw

To MRS PAKENHAM BEATTY

[A/4]

36 Osnaburgh Street N W
11th September 1886

Dear Mrs Beatty

I have been both rude and busy, and have had so many letters within the last three days that I gave up all idea of answering them until the next lull in my work. They culminated in a request from a young lady that I would write to her, not because she required any information, but because she had "nothing to read." That finished me, as far as correspondence with your sex was concerned.

As to the kinder-garten, I am afraid I have exhausted all my sources of information. I will try to think of someone—Stay: I have just thought of an educational lady. She shall be written to forthwith. As to books, I should suggest "Jack the Giant Killer." When I was two months old or so, my favorite books were "The Arabian Nights," "The Pilgrim's Progress," Homer's Iliad (translated by Lord Derby), Gulliver's Travels, "The Skeleton Horseman" (in penny numbers), Shakespere, and La Rochefoucauld's Maxims; especially the last.

My mother's address is Chandos House, Broadstairs, until Wednesday. I should regard your asking her to ascertain the price of anything as an experiment fraught with danger. I have written to Mrs Patterson, asking her for the information.

On consideration, I decline to treat the manly Jupiter like a child by going through the farce of presenting him with a ninepenny novel. Let us keep our souls unsoiled by gammon.

I shall probably anticipate this letter by a call tomorrow; but I am not quite sure. I have unluckily destroyed the envelope of your last letter but one, forgetting that it contained a question about some dictionary or other. You must tell me again.

festinately yrs
GBS

To SWAN SONNENSCHEIN & CO.

36 Osnaburgh Street N W
17th October 1886

[F.u/2]

Dear Sirs

Revision of An Unsocial Socialist herewith. It did not occur to me to write a preface: I have really nothing to say, so I shall take the safe course of holding my tongue.

I think it will be well to introduce me as the author of Cashel Byron's Profession on the title page.

I presume the cover will be a plain cloth one.

Kindly let me know the date of publication as soon as you can fix it.

yours faithfully
[G. Bernard Shaw]

To ALMA MURRAY

[A/1; X/109]
36 Osnaburgh Street N W
20th October 1886

Dear Mrs Forman

I enclose to you what was enclosed to me—two papers and a card. Dr Furnivall recommended you this afternoon to read a book of mine [*Cashel Byron's Profession*]—a shilling shocker—and, in the author's presence, you could not refuse without absolute barbarity. The publishers will send you a copy, the possession of which will enable you for ever after to say "Yes: I have got it, and intend to read it." Not that I am indifferent whether you read it or not: I shall be extremely mortified if you dont; and I assure you it is one of the cleverest books I know, though I wrote it when an infant, comparatively speaking. But I feel that people must not be forced to adopt me as their favorite author, even for their own good; and it struck me that Dr Furnivall hardly respected your right to choose your own books. Anyhow, I hope you will not blame

yours quite innocently
G. Bernard Shaw

To J. R. OSGOOD

[F/2]
36 Osnaburgh Street N W
14th January 1887

[James R. Osgood (1836–92), American publisher, had become Harper's London representative in 1885. On 12th January 1887 he reported that *Cashel Byron's Profession* had been published in Harper's Handy Series in New York, and offered Shaw an honorarium of £10 for the book, which actually was in the public domain in America. James Brander Matthews (1852–1929), American author and educator, became a professor of dramatic literature at Columbia University (1892–1924).]

Dear Sir

You have my address accurately. As to the copyright, I assure you Messrs Harper had the refusal of it; and they availed themselves of it too. Anybody might have had it for 10d in 1883.

I am much obliged to you and Mr Brander Matthews.

yours very truly
G. Bernard Shaw

To J. R. OSGOOD

36 Osnaburgh Street N W
7th February 1887
[F/2]

[Shaw had begun, almost immediately after the publication of *An Unsocial Socialist*, to urge Swan Sonnenschein & Co. to take over *Cashel Byron's Profession*, which had been badly handled by the Modern Press. To avoid the cost of re-setting, it had been suggested that the English publisher consider obtaining a duplicate set of the Harper plates.]

Dear Sir

I got your letter, and put off answering it out of sheer procrastiveness. I beg your pardon: I intended to answer when I saw my publisher, and somehow that got put off too. The difficulty about a duplicate set of plates is that the American printer, with the innate weakness of his trade, has taken upon himself the repunctuation of "Cashel Byron"; and as in every alteration he is flagrantly wrong and I classically right— as, furthermore, a wrong stop is quite as painful to me as any other grammatical error, I cannot make up my mind to sanction the havoc by adopting his setting. Further, the villain has actually bowdlerised the text by substituting "——" for "damn," with the effect—upon anyone familiar with the language of the British pugilist—of suggesting something much worse. The moral injury to me from the language I have used over these unprovoked assaults on my literary offspring far outweighs that saved to the American nation by the omission of my hero's harmless expletives.

Messrs Sonnenschein, the publishers of a novel of mine which will appear presently, tell me that they have communicated with Messrs Harper, presumably through you, about advance sheets—if advance sheets are desired.

Another book of mine [*The Irrational Knot*] has just finished its course as a serial; but it is not quite satisfactory to me, and so far, I do not intend to let it be republished if I can help it. Besides, there is an elopement in it, which would perhaps shock a nation which recoils from damns. Pardon this mild sarcasm.

Let me again apologise for the delay in replying to you. I partly intended to call on you.

yours very truly
G. Bernard Shaw

162

36 Osnaburgh Street N W
8th February 1887

[S/1]

[Albertine and Florence were Mrs Beatty's sisters.]

!!!!!!!!!!!!!! Vous aussi! Vous!! Vous!!! Maudit soit Jager! Je comprends enfin. Mais n'importe: c'est ainsi partout—partout, je vous assure. Je me moque de ces accidents: femme souvent varie: cette illusion ne durera jamais pendant six mois. Oui, pure illusion—folie— n'en pensez plus.

Do you suppose I am an advocate of making children miserable? If so, would I not have recommended you to send the bairns to the nearest infant-convict prison? Instead, I take great care to discover a school with a sensible mistress and a rational system; and my reward is that I am accused of advocating dry bread and whacks! This is a mother's gratitude! No: I say that the children are tired of eternal mamma and eternal nursery and eternal c-a-t cat and b-a-t bat, and that they want change of air and scenes and faces and new varieties of mischief. If you had proposed to send them to your Telemachus school I should have interfered violently to rescue them. But surely you don't suppose that all schools are like that, or that any really decent modern school can do no better.

Albertine is very like somebody—I cannot think whom. She has not your unquenchable roguery; and she is not a cold hearted imposter like Florence, nor yet a swaggering exuberance of Nature like the Olympian Charles [Dowling]. She looks a tender and solitary soul, looking wistfully for more congenial company than her relatives by blood and marriage. Invite her to Teviotdale; and the bairns will soon see a ghost there, an all-wool ghost. Don't talk to me of romances: I was sent into the world expressly to dance on them with thick boots— to shatter, stab, and murder them. I defy you to be romantic about me (I understand your fable of my decease to be an advance in that direction) and if you attempt it, I will go straight to Paquito; tell him that you are being drawn into the whirlpool of fascination which has engulfed all the brunettes I know; express my opinion that it serves him right for having made an unmitigated ass of himself about Florence; and give him his choice between instantly knocking that insincere poetic affectation of blighted affection on the head, and seeing me arrive, clad in an irresistible new Jaeger samite, and vanquish his Florence, his Ida, his ———* and everyone else at one

* Shaw's omission.

163

dazzling flash. All these foolish fancies only want daylight and fresh air to scatter them. Once or twice, or three times at most, I may have allowed myself a moment's weakness out of sheer good nature, but only to spring upright again with added resilience.

Tell Paquito that the Socialist League have been challenged by C. Bradlaugh to pick a man to fight him at catch weight—three rounds of thirty minutes, fifteen minutes, and again fifteen minutes apiece— St Jas's Hall or anywhere in the home circuit. Customers being backward for the [John L.] Sullivan of the platform, the League has appealed to the Fabian champion, who admits his liability to defend the belt. The set-to promises to be a rare one.

Need I explain that the Fabian champion is

yours marmoreally
G. Bernard Shaw

To HENRY A. BARKER

36 Osnaburgh Street N W
[A/28; X/149]
9th February 1887

[As Shaw had informed Ida Beatty on 8th February, he had been invited to represent the Socialist League in a debate with the secularist Charles Bradlaugh, scheduled for 20th March. Shaw was to be "backed" in the debate by the Rev. Fred W. Ford of Holy Trinity Vicarage. On 15th February, H. A. Barker, secretary of the Socialist League, informed Shaw that the League preferred both oral and written debate, either in the League's journal *Commonweal* or in Bradlaugh's *National Reformer*, with E. Belfort Bax writing for the League (BM). Although the oral debate did not take place, the written debate by Bax and Bradlaugh was published in 1887 under the title *Will Socialism Benefit the English People?* Bax (1854–1926), a philosophical writer who was a co-founder with Morris of the Socialist League, later was Shaw's predecessor as musical critic of *The Star*, under the pseudonym "Musigena."]

Dear Sir

As a Socialist, I believe that it is time for us to abandon the principle of Individualism, and to substitute that of Socialism, on pain of national decay. Holding this, I am bound to maintain it in open debate against *anyone* who disputes it and whose opinion to the contrary is of weight with the public. Therefore, though for personal reasons I am anxious to avoid any course that may strain the friendly relations which

164

Mr Bradlaugh's services to the people have established between him and my colleagues as well as myself, I cannot refuse to accept the duty of debating with him if it be allotted to me by either of the bodies challenged by him. Only let it be understood that I am not the challenger, and that I did not volunteer for the defence.

As to the conditions of the debate, they may be left, as far as I am concerned, to the opposition. I should prefer an audience of undecided inquirers or individualists to one of convinced socialists; and I had rather debate at a disadvantage than give my opponent the least cause to complain of the spirit in which he was met, or the manner in which the discussion was arranged.

I presume that your executive has duly weighed the fact that I am a member of the Fabian Society only, and am not bound by the manifesto of the Socialist League.

I am, dear Sir,
yours faithfully
G. Bernard Shaw

To HENRY A. BARKER

36 Osnaburgh Street NW
[A/28; X/149]   24th February 1887
[Bradlaugh contributed the monthly "Political Corner" article to *Our Corner*; the article to which Shaw alluded was "Socialism: Its Fallacies and Dangers," in the March 1887 number.]

Dear Sir

I am afraid I should mislead Mr Bradlaugh if I were to accept, as he requires, the manifestoes of the Democratic Federation and Socialist League. I do not mind saying that they are defensible and wholesome documents; but I have just read an article by Mr Bradlaugh in "Our Corner" which convinces me that if I undertake to be bound by them, the debate will be wasted in disputes as to what they mean. If the debate is to be on the manifestoes, then Mr Bradlaugh must challenge them; express his opinion of them in a proposition; and offer to maintain that proposition against anyone who will undertake to defend the manifestoes. Whether I would undertake such a defence would of course depend on the terms of the proposition. In any case, Mr Bradlaugh would have to assume the offensive and open the debate.

But if I am to challenge the validity of the principle of individualism,

165

and Mr Bradlaugh to defend it, then I will be bound by nothing except the terms of my proposition and my controversial duties. In order to leave no doubt that my attack on individualism commits me to advocacy of the proposals concerning land and capital which make socialism practically revolutionary, I will affirm "That it is advisable to abandon the principle of individualism for that of socialism; and that this change of policy can be made effective only by complete resumption of the land, with a transfer of the existing capital of the country from its present holders to the state." If this does not commit me deeply enough, I must leave it to Mr Bradlaugh to state explicitly what further inference from the manifestoes he will expect me to adopt.

If this seems unfair, kindly write to me before communicating with Mr Bradlaugh. I do not wish to raise difficulties—only to avoid misunderstanding as far as I can.

I am, dear Sir,
yours faithfully
G. Bernard Shaw

To HENRY A. BARKER

[A/28; X/149]

29 Fitzroy Square W
10th March 1887

[The Shaws had moved to 29 Fitzroy Square on 5th March.]

Dear Sir

I have read the letter from Mr Bradlaugh which you forwarded to me. I have only to say, in the friendliest spirit, that I also see no reason to modify my last letter in any respect.

I am, dear Sir
yours faithfully
G. Bernard Shaw

To WILLIAM SWAN SONNENSCHEIN

[F/2]

29 Fitzroy Square W
2nd May 1887

[Having failed to receive any satisfaction from Swan Sonnenschein's editors concerning the proposal to republish *Cashel Byron's Profession*, Shaw proceeded to do a job of salesmanship on the publisher himself.]

Dear Sonnenschein

There is a novel of mine, "Cashel Byron's Profession," which, after many queer adventures, got out last year in the most beastly shilling form, printed from stereos taken from a monthly mag with a page of impossible size. It got well reviewed; but Champion, the publisher, was unable to take advantage of this, as he was not in a position to push the book with the trade. It was too ugly, and too long; and only 500-odd copies went off. I quite expected this; but the book served my turn as an advertisement; and I left it with Champion until he had got all that there was to be got out of his edition of it. Now, however, I have ascertained that the sale has practically ceased; and he says he will not feel aggrieved if I take it out of his hands. I have no time to bother about it just at present; but it occurs to me that you might be able to do something with it. It is not nearly so good as An Unsocial Socialist; but it is generally considered better, is a faster seller, and has been gorgeously reviewed. There are two sets of plates of it in existence: Champion's stereos, which are utterly damnable; and those made for a very neat reprint in Harper's "Handy Volume Series." These are presentable, but small; and the few errors of punctuation and attempts at bowdlerising (such as "d——" or simply "——" for damn, and the like) have been made by the American printers without the least regard to my feelings. Duplicates of these plates can be obtained; but I had rather have the book set up afresh and issued at a higher price. What do you think? It would have to be advertised to give it a fresh start, as of course it is a dead horse as far as reviewing is concerned.

I hear that you are issuing a book on socialism by Kempsomebody who seems to have been attending my lectures and turning them to account! At least Bax has some idea of the sort: I have not read the book myself.

yours
G. Bernard Shaw

To WILLIAM SWAN SONNENSCHEIN

29 Fitzroy Square W
3rd May 1887

[F.u/2]

[Swan Sonnenschein replied, on 3rd May, that the firm was so full of new undertakings that they could not undertake a reprint of *Cashel* at present, but would like to consider it again in the autumn, when they planned to start a series of cheap reprints (BM). He enclosed a copy of N. Kempner's *Common-sense Socialism*.

Many thanks for Kempner. His indebtedness to me may be only a phase of Baxomania.

Cashel will keep very well until the autumn: in fact, I never thought of anything being done with it sooner. Such a series as you suggest would be about the place for it.

[G. Bernard Shaw]

To EDWARD AVELING

[F.u/2]
[29 Fitzroy Square W]
[17th May 1887]

[On 7th May the *Pall Mall Gazette* published a letter from Shaw, "Marx and Modern Socialism," attacking the Marxian theories of H. M. Hyndman, leader of the Social Democratic Federation. Hyndman's rebuttal appeared on the 11th. A second letter from Shaw, "Socialists at Home," on 12th May led to a further outburst from Hyndman on the 16th. Shaw's third letter was rejected by the *Pall Mall Gazette*, but a letter from Annie Besant on the 24th hammered the final Fabian nail into Hyndman's coffin.

Rev. Philip H. Wicksteed (1844–1927), classical scholar, translator of Dante, and student of political economy, had clashed with Shaw over Marx's *Das Kapital* in the October 1884 and the January and April 1885 issues of *To-Day*. A three-part review by Shaw of the just-published first English translation (by Aveling and Samuel Moore) of Volume I of *Capital* appeared in the *National Reformer* on 7th, 14th, and 21st August 1887.]

My dear Aveling

I am greatly relieved at receiving a friendly letter from you whilst the world is yet reeling from the shock of my blasphemy. If you will kindly tell me how I am to face Mrs Aveling after it, I shall be more grateful than I can express. And now before I come to business, let me implore you to go slow. Remember that Newton was wrong about light—that Goethe was wrong about colors—that Darwin clearly overstressed natural selection, and then ask yourself whether it isnt at least possible that Marx was wrong about value. Even I have erred in my time.

Now—remembering above all things to go slow—hear the truth. I believe the value theory to be wrong—wrong, my dear fellow, not a doubt of it—bad as McCulloch. What is more, everybody knows the trick of it now. Mallock and the rest of them are going to kick it all about the place, identifying it with Socialism—in order to dignify them as savers of society. I foresee this because I have done more up and down fighting for Marx than any other socialist in the country. After pointing out a fatal flaw in his derivation of surplus value in Justice before that paper was a month old, I nevertheless defended him tooth and nail against stupid critics . . . [but] when I saw the storm coming I knew that the theory must be thrown overboard. I did it as gently as possible. I did not say it was wrong. I only said that socialism was not based on it, and that its refutation had been antici- pated by the socialists themselves. Then comes Hyndman, in hopeless confusion of thought, and gives me the chance I have been waiting for of publicly repudiating him as a representative English socialist. I have replied to his last letter and will keep it up as long as the editor will let me; for your notion that he is getting the best is a Marxian illusion. If my last letter goes in, I shall have repeated 3 times that socialism does not stand or fall by the Value Theory; I shall have brought the Fabian (which has all the real guts of English Socialism in it) before the public as the socialist antidote to Hyndmanism. The mob, remember, know nothing of the great Shaw joke, and take me quite seriously—or properly; however, to let you into a secret, not one of you have the least idea of what being in earnest really means. As to the Wicksteed affair, his article did not seem to me conclusive as against the Ricardian theory, and if you happen ever to see the criticism and my reply I think you will see that there was moral room for the latter.

[The draft ends here.]

To PAKENHAM BEATTY

[S/1]

29 Fitzroy Square W
27th May 1887

[Tom Codlin and Short were itinerant showmen in Dickens's *The Old Curiosity Shop*.]

Go slow, my friend, or you will be milked like a cow. If you sanction such a division of labor as the [Social Democratic] Federation getting themselves into trouble by dint of bad judgment and you getting them out by dint of good money, you will soon be a beggar. And then, by

169

the Lord, sir, you will taste the wane of your popularity. Hear the counsel of the wise man—the friend of the people—the disdainer of Codlin Leagues and Short Federations alike. Instead of wasting thirty guineas a year on sixth rate talent, spend one single guinea on the Fabian, which has been doing the work whilst the others have been snatching the credit of it with discordant chin music. I send you a couple of pamphlets as specimens of solid propagandist literature. The Fabians are not the property of a single rich man, like the [Socialist] League; and they never get into trouble by disorderly behaviour or require defence funds. The statements put forward by the Fabians have never been denied or refuted. They have never lied about their own strength. When any difficult work has been on hand—when a 70 guinea conference with the radicals and secularists has been needed —when an opponent for Bradlaugh has been desiderated—when answers to really scientific champions have been required by the Commonweal—when, in short, sensible and educated workers who mean business, either as lecturers or writers, have been indispensable —then have the braggarts turned to the Fabian for help, and have gotten it in a noble oblivion of insult and disparagement. The Fabian lecturers are famous throughout the world. Their women are beautiful; their men brave. Their executive council challenges the universe for quality, comprising as it does the eyeglassed and indomitable Bland (treasurer of the society—editor of To-Day, which is renowned for its poetry—verb. sap.), the provenly heroic Annie Besant, the blameless Shaw, a genuine working man [W. L. Phillips] in the lath & plaster line, and three other men of approved distinction and fiery devotion—the least of them an M.A. Join the Fabian, and you will find its name a puissant protector. Say to the horseleech, "I have joined the Fabian," and he will drop off as though you had overwhelmed him with salt.

GBS

To WILLIAM T. STEAD

29 Fitzroy Square W
8th June 1887

[A/1; X/110]

[William Thomas Stead (1849–1912) succeeded John Morley as editor of the *Pall Mall Gazette* in 1885. A crusading journalist with an interest in ecclesiastical matters, social questions, and international peace, he forced the Gladstone government to send General Gordon to Khartoum in 1884, and was instrumental in bringing about the enactment of the Criminal Law Amendment Act in 1885. Shaw's letter was a reply to John Ruskin's attack on 8th June on "The Functions of the P.M.G.," motivated by a review of the Rev.Charles Adolphus Row's *Future Retribution*. Shaw informed Stead's biographer, Frederic Whyte, in 1924, that the letter had not been intended for publication, and that Stead understood this.

Olga Novikoff (1840–1925) was a Russian journalist, resident in England, who sought to promote friendship between Russia and England. She was a friend of Gladstone and Thomas Carlyle. Lord Decimus Tite Barnacle and Christopher Casby are characters in Dickens's *Little Dorrit*, the former a windy peer holding a high position in the Circumlocution Office, the latter the Landlord of Bleeding Heart Yard, who grinds his tenants by proxy. "The Duke of Bedford and his agent Mr Bourne may have been in my mind," Shaw told Whyte, when he referred to "Colonel O'Callaghan" and "Mr Hosford."]

Sir

The question raised in "anxious courtesy" by Mr Ruskin is one that younger men are discussing with less patience, and perhaps with more hope. Your paper now enjoys a peculiar opportunity; it is the only existing one that has a chance of gaining the great place now going a-begging—that of leader of the Press in the march to meet the coming twentieth century. Your rivals are too blind, too deaf, too dumb, and too full of notions of literary propriety which may concern a guild of reviewers, but which, in the councils of newspaper editors as well as of statesmen, are misplaced frivolities. The future leadership is either for you, or for some one bold enough to mount on your shoulders.

Foremost among your present disadvantages is the fact that you are bound by your position to support some party in Parliament, whereas there is no party at all representative of your views. For a year or so past you have been desperately trying to smuggle your opinions into the head of some public man, in the hope that, finding them there, he may mistake them for his own. You have treated your readers to sudden articles on Lord This, the Marquis of That, and Mr the Other. After all, you say on these occasions, Lord This is a statesman. He is accustomed to weigh his words; he has a deep sense of public duty; and he is at this moment the arbiter of the fate of the Empire. What he will now undoubtedly do is—&c &c &c (here you present him with an elaborate policy). Your readers, perfectly aware that Lord This, far from being what you are trying to make him act like, is simply a bewildered blockhead, chuckle over your ruse, and are not surprised to find his lordship either too dull to understand your programme or too obstinate to be beholden to you for it. Baffled, but not discouraged, you try again with the Marquis of That, ingeniously contriving to take him seriously by contrasting him with some specially flippant member of his own party. But the Marquis of That, being patently to all the world an aristocratic cynic run to seed, without conviction enough to run a coffee-tavern, much less an empire, has no relish for your enthusiastic urgency, and would deride it if the responsibilities of office were not making him too uncomfortable even for sneering. And when you fall back on Mr the Other, either he is vindictive and will not forgive you for having been less complimentary on former occasions, or he is conceited and will not be dictated to by an evening paper, or else he is not the man you take him for. Whereupon, disgusted with yourself for having wasted a hope on any of them, you drub them impartially all round and plunge into Home Rule, a proximate and simple issue, practically difficult, but not obscure in principle.

The peculiar reputation of the Pall Mall, however, was not gained by its coolness of judgment in political matters of the Home Rule type. It is something to have brought the Jingoes to their senses about Russia, and Mr Gladstone to his senses about the exclusion of the Irish representatives from Westminster. But the word put in for Russia, and so brilliantly seconded by Madame Novikoff, compelled an assent that was at its best a sullen one, for were the Tsar personally another Angel Gabriel, we should none the less be mad to build upon the stability or good faith of a despotic bureaucracy. And Home Rule is not yet achieved. To neither of these questions, then, does the Pall Mall owe its unique position. That is wholly due to its memorable resolution to attack social abuses with the terrible weapon of truth-telling. If you sheathe that weapon, what will maintain the paper in its present place when the Afghan frontier and Home Rule are forgotten?

I venture to predict that the future is to the journal which, having gained a wide hearing, will dare to tell polite society that it lives by the robbery and murder of the poor, and to ask pardon of the poor for its tacit approval of such robbery and murder in the past. The denial of this is the great lie that is rotting our national life. Every recommendation to the poor to be more industrious, more thrifty, and more temperate, implies the falsehood that the poor are poor because they are idle, improvident, and drunken, and the rich rich because they are the reverse. Every homily to the workers on the importance of our industrial capital is intended to convey the falsehood that that capital was created by the present holders of it. The air is thick with lying on this vital question. It is useless to challenge discussion, to point to the children of the poor dying in heaps before our eyes because the fruit of their parents' excessive toil is being consumed by useless idlers, or to prove to the hilt from the most eminent "orthodox" statisticians and economists that their science neither explains it away, excuses it, nor proves it to be inevitable. Society will not listen; it does not mean to be ill-natured; but, like Colonel O'Callaghan, it must have its unearned income; and if the people will not pay, the police and the military must make them: and that is all. And, so far, the Pall Mall Gazette does not seem to object. True, you send your spirited Commissioner to Bodyke, and his "blood is up" there; but you sit here in London in the midst of worse things, and your blood seems to remain down. Now the working men who are beginning to read your paper know that your Commissioner may get his blood to boiling point any week at evictions in Bethnal Green and Bermondsey without the expense of a trip to Bodyke; and they are asking whether there is any chance of your denouncing my Lord Decimus and Mr Casby as you have denounced Colonel O'Callaghan and Mr Hosford.

If I could palm a programme upon you as you have vainly tried to palm one on Lord This and the rest of them, I should beg you to dish the Socialists by helping to get back the land and the misappropriated capital for the people by such measures as the municipalization of town rents, the nationalization of railways, the sweeping away of our inexpressibly wicked workhouse prisons in favour of State-owned farms and factories to which the wretches who now drudge in our sweaters' workshops should come for employment and due reward, and the utter repudiation of the claim of the sweater (as the incarnation of private enterprise) to be protected from the competition of the whole people organized to secure their own welfare. The truths in this matter are even harder to tell than were those of the Criminal Law Amendment Act. In branding an elderly voluptuary as a detestable satyr you have public opinion on your side; but the public opinion that is to brand, as in effect selfish thieves, many thoroughly amiable and well-intentioned men of culture, with their gentle and refined wives and accomplished daughters, all living gracefully and generously together on rent and dividends, is a living opinion that has yet to be created. That it must be created and acted upon if we are to avert the social decay which the increase of our population alone is surely bringing upon us is as certain as any deduction from economic science can possibly be. That the newspaper which does most to create that opinion is destined to be the best abused and most popular one in England is not equally certain. But that the chances are worth weighing by the

Pall Mall Gazette above all other purposes, is the opinion of many, believe me, besides

your obedient servant
G. Bernard Shaw

To DE WITT J. SELIGMAN

29 Fitzroy Square W
18th August 1887

[F.u/2]

[De Witt J. Seligman, formerly a broker on the New York Stock Exchange, was proprietor of the American journal *The Epoch*. William Archer, who had been providing Seligman with "European Correspondence," recommended Shaw as his successor. Shaw submitted two letters, which were published on 17th June and 22nd July, covering such topics as Victoria's Golden Jubilee, the Coercion Bill, Henry Irving's *Werner*, and the American Art Exhibition. But Seligman, who was paying $8 for a two-thousand-word contribution, informed Shaw that these letters were, "candidly speaking, not exactly what our readers want. . . . We would suggest touching upon the following topics in a very bright and crisp manner . . . Why Americans find it so much easier to get into the best English Society than the English do themselves? Something about the American Minister at the Court of St. James; does he entertain much?—Something about the incomes of English lords. . . . something about Guinness's Stock?—Something about the London Stock Exchange?—About the incomes of English Bankers as compared with the incomes of English property holders. . . . The income and circulation of English Dailies and Weeklies . . . How English swells who have nothing to do pass away their time" (BM).]

Dear Sir

I quite understand the sort of letter you require; but even if you were willing to dispense with my signature I could not very well do it for you myself, for several reasons; and for the life of me I cannot think of anybody just now to whom I could recommend you to apply. Mr Edmund Yates, the proprietor of The World, is probably better qualified to select such a correspondent as you want than any one else in London. Unfortunately, everybody is out of town at present. Some of the subjects you mention—Guinness Stock and Capell's, for instance —would be hopelessly stale after a fortnight's interval. Anything in the nature of a money article, to have any use or interest, would have to be wired. The circulation of London dailies and weeklies cannot be ascertained except by very intimate insiders; and as no men stand in that relation to more than one, or at most two or three papers, comparative estimates are practically impossible. The papers here are private concerns. The value of shares in them does not get quoted.

As to society matters and the entertainments of your Ambassador, the part I am taking in the socialist movement here makes it impossible for me to deal with them from the point of view of those who are chiefly interested in them. In London, at least, I am better known to the public as a Socialist than as a writer.

I am, dear Sir, yours faithfully
[G. Bernard Shaw]

To WILLIAM ARCHER

[A/2]

29 Fitzroy Square W
4th October 1887

[*Rheingold* was the working title of a play on which Shaw and Archer had been collaborating (Archer had first suggested the plot in 1884). On 6th October Shaw read the first two acts to Archer, noting afterwards in his diary: "Long argument ensued, Archer having received it with contempt" (but see also Shaw's letter of 24th February 1888 to Alma Murray). Shaw set the play aside, but returned to it in 1892; it became *Widowers' Houses*.

It is amusing to see Shaw optimistically casting the fragmentary work with most of the acting aristocracy of the West End. The Kendals and John Hare were reigning stars of the St James's Theatre. William Mackintosh (1855–1929) was a young character actor of exceptional ability. Arthur Cecil (1843–96) had made a success in a series of Pinero farces at the Old Court Theatre. George Barrett (1850–94) was the brother of Wilson Barrett and performed in the latter's acting company. Edward W. Gardiner (1862–99) was a leading man at Drury Lane and husband of Kate Rorke, who appeared as Candida in the first public performance in London of Shaw's play in 1904. Harry Nicholls (1852–1926) was a popular Drury Lane actor and songwriter. Edward O'Connor Terry (1844–1912) was noted for eccentric humour, his rôles ranging from burlesque to the gravedigger in *Hamlet*.

This is Shaw's first reference to Ellen Terry, who figured so importantly in his life and who will loom large in later portions of this volume. It is interesting to note that the celebrated actor-manager Henry Irving (1838–1905), whom Shaw later castigated unmercifully for his failure to experiment and to further the cause of the British theatre, was under consideration for a rôle in Shaw's dream cast.]

I have left the first two acts of the Rheingold at John St, in longhand. They are not supposed to be complete; but they present a series of

175

consecutive dialogues in which your idea is prepared and developed. The central notion is quite perfect; but the hallucinations with which you surrounded it are absent: you will have to put them in yourself. The bathing place is impossible; and I dont see how the long lost old woman is to be introduced without destroying the realism and freshness of the play: she would simply turn the thing into a plot, and ruin it. I think the story would bear four acts; but I have no idea of how it is to proceed. The peculiarity so far is that there is only one female character; and her social isolation is essential to the situation. Will you proceed either to chuck in the remaining acts, or provide me with a skeleton for them? You will perceive that my genius has brought the romantic notion which possessed you, into vivid contact with real life.

I should prefer the St Jas's Theatre, with Mrs Kendal as Blanche, Hare as Sartorius, Mackintosh as Lickcheese, Arthur Cecil as Cokane, and Kendal as Trench. Or Ellen Terry as Blanche, Wilson Barrett as Sartorius, George Barrett as Lickcheese, Irving as Cokane, and Gardiner as Trench. Harry Nicholls or Edward Terry might understudy Cokane; and Alma Murray might in extremity be allowed to play Blanche.

What is your opinion? I think, by the bye, that the title Rheingold ought to be saved for a romantic play. This is realism.

GBS

P.S. Never mind clerical errors: I have not read it over. And the details as to the hotel garden, the time &c, are all at sixes and sevens.

To UNIDENTIFIED CORRESPONDENT

[29 Fitzroy Square W]
21st October 1887

[X/111.e]

. . . We call the working men proles because that is exactly what they are, and exactly what we complain of their being. It is not our business to flatter them, but to point out that they are a disunited, faithless, servile crew who have only to unite, keep faith, and renounce all servility to make themselves men and citizens. They are getting to know it too, and to think just as much of the men who tell them so, as of those who try to catch their votes by telling them that they are the salt of the earth. . . .

To WILLIAM MORRIS

[A/2]

29 Fitzroy Square W
22nd November 1887

[William Morris (1834–96), English poet, artist, social reformer, and publisher, was the founder of a movement to reform Victorian styles by the manufacture of furniture, wallpaper, fabrics, etc. He started the Kelmscott Press at Hammersmith in 1890; earlier he had organised the Socialist League and edited its organ *The Commonweal*. He was the author of a utopian novel *News from Nowhere*, embodying his socialistic ideals, and numerous volumes of verse and of prose romance.

On 13th November a demonstration in Trafalgar Square had been called by London's socialist and anarchist organisations to protest against the Government's Irish policy. The various processions were attacked and broken up by the police, aided by the Foot Guards and Life Guards, under orders from General Sir Charles Warren (1840–1927), Commissioner of the Metropolitan Police. Among the participants arrested were H. M. Hyndman, John Burns, and R. B. Cunninghame Graham (1852–1936), a socialist M.P. who had deliberately provoked arrest to test the issue in court; the three received jail sentences. The result of Bloody Sunday in Trafalgar Square, however, was to secure the right of free speech on the famous site. H. B. Tarleton was a member of the Socialist League.]

I send you a supply of Fabian invitations, and a list of the meetings. The forms are only to induce people to go—not an indispensable condition of admission. Nobody asks to see them.

I was somewhat relieved to see the [Socialist] League march up to Clerkenwell on the 13th without you. The women were much in the way. The police charged us the moment they saw Mrs Taylor. But you should have seen that high hearted host run. Running hardly expresses our collective action. We *skedaddled*, and never drew rein until we were safe on Hampstead Heath or thereabouts. Tarleton found me paralysed with terror and brought me on to the Square, the police kindly letting me through in consideration of my genteel appearance. On the whole, I think it was the most abjectly disgraceful defeat ever suffered by a band of heroes outnumbering their foes a thousand to one.

I dont object to Sparling's article [written for *The Commonweal*] on the ground that it is revolutionary. I deprecate its publication because it is calculated to get him into gaol without doing any good as a set-off. I object to a defiant policy altogether at present. If we persist in it, we shall be eaten bit by bit like an artichoke. They will provoke; we will defy; they will punish. I do not see the wisdom of that until we are at least strong enough to resist twenty policemen with the help of Heaven and Mrs Taylor.

177

I wish generally that our journals would keep their tempers. If Stead had not forced us to march on the Square a week too soon by his "Not one Sunday must be allowed to pass" nonsense, we should have been there now. It all comes from people trying to live down to fiction instead of up to facts.

GBS

To ARTHUR H. MACKMURDO

29 Fitzroy Square W
22nd November 1887

[A/32]

[Arthur H. Mackmurdo (1851–1942), architect and designer, founded the Century Guild in 1882. Richard Le Gallienne (1866–1947), poet and man of letters, later succeeded Clement Shorter as book reviewer on *The Star* (see letter of 4th January 1893 to Pakenham Beatty).]

Dear Mackmurdo (not to stand on ceremony)

I strongly advise Mr Le-Gallienne to send the sonnet ["Trafalgar Square—November 13, 1887"] to the P.M.G. himself. So far from its having any better chance coming through me, it will only rouse that jealousy of his own position as the proper person to send contributions to, which even the most magnanimous editor is not quite free from. If I knew Stead personally, I might take the sonnet down and shew it to him; but I never spoke to him in my life; and [Henry] Norman, the only influential member of the staff with whom I am on intimate terms, is away in America.

If the poet is incurably bashful, I shall not refuse a second application; but I am at present advising him for his good. Nothing is to be gained, and something lost, by sending contributions to the wrong man; and—as I unexpectedly dont know my editor "to speak to"—that is all I am as far as the Pall Mall is concerned.

Kindly explain to Le G. so that he may not suppose that I am unwilling to serve him in the matter.

yrs
G. Bernard Shaw

To WILLIAM SWAN SONNENSCHEIN

29 Fitzroy Square W
28th November 1887

[F/2]

Dear Sonnenschein

I agreed long ago to the issue of "An US" at a shilling; and I have no doubt that a certain number of workmen and socialists will buy it at that price if it's brought under their notice. If a really new edition is made by the addition of a postscript which I should like to write, several people who have the book already would buy a new copy at a shilling. But nothing worth talking about will ever come out of my books unless they are advertised. "Cashel Byron" is *the* popular book; but nobody can get C.B. If it were issued uniform with An US, and one book advertised in the other, if nowhere else, they might help to sell each other. I would even consent to let out the I. Knot, which hit the secularist taste remarkably, in order to make something like a series. But I am ashamed of the whole boodle of them, and am not eager to take any more trouble about them unless someone takes them up in earnest. Guarantee me £20 a month on condition of my writing 6 novels in 6 years; and I will begin to believe that you mean business— though you will probably drop a couple of thousand over it.

Let me know whether the new chapter of A U.S. is feasible. I should much prefer to add it to a cheap edition, though I dont think it is likely to go well except [if] it is put on C.Byron's back.

It is 4 years since I gave up fiction; and I am in two minds whether I will ever return to it. Pecuniarily, at least, the failure has been too heavy.

yours
G. Bernard Shaw

To WILLIAM SWAN SONNENSCHEIN

29 Fitzroy Square W
[F/2; X/106.e]   29th December 1887

[As the original edition of *An Unsocial Socialist* had sold very poorly, the remaining sheets (amounting to more than half the edition of one thousand copies) were cased in an inexpensive binding and issued as a "cheap edition" at two shillings. For this issue Shaw provided a six-page Appendix purporting to be a letter from the novel's central character, Sidney Trefusis, to the author, clarifying certain distortions of "fact" and encouraging the author to find better employment for his talent than the writing of novels. Edward Carpenter (1844–1929), a socialist writer and poet (strongly influenced by Walt Whitman) who abjured Victorian convention and "respectability," was the author of *Towards Democracy* (1883) and *Love's Coming of Age* (1896).]

Dear Sonnenschein

I enclose the addendum for the cheap edition of "An Unsocial Socialist." It would be cheap by itself at a shilling. Might I suggest that you should put in some pages of advertisements of your socialistic publications—[Edward] Carpenter, Kempner et hoc genus omnes. I am still rather anxious to get out a reasonable shilling edition of "Cashel Byron's Profession," and to try to make it advertise the other & the other it. When Harper of New York brought out a very pretty little handy copy of it, I asked the agent—Appleton [error for Osgood?], I think his name is—whether copies could be imported or duplicates of the plates obtained. He replied that if I had no objection, either or both could be managed easily. Then I believe I examined the edition and found that it was improperly punctuated and occasionally bowdlerized in a silly way; but on the whole it was not bad, and it was undeniably neat. Is it possible to diminish the risk of an experiment with the book by getting duplicates of these plates? I am often told that there is a demand for the book but no supply. I confess I dont believe this; but if a demand arose, Cashel Byron would be as inaccessible in Champion's hands as at the North Pole. Would you care to meddle with it? Champion has no objection. I suppose there has been no sale of "An U.S." this half year. I am really sorry for having let you in for it. My novels are Magnificent; but they are not business.

Compliments of the detestable season.

yrs
G. Bernard Shaw

To WILLIAM SWAN SONNENSCHEIN

[F/2; X/106.e]
29 Fitzroy Square W
31st December 1887

[Jake Kilrain and John L. Sullivan (1858–1918) were contemporary boxing champions.]

Dear Sonnenschein

Hi! Stop! Murder! Thieves! Fire! What are you dreaming about? If Trefusis's letter is put *before* the story I swear I will set fire to Paternoster Square. It would be utterly unintelligible to anyone who had not learnt all about the book. It would discount the story, destroy the illusion, and drive me mad. Give it to a reader, and observe his lively interest, his tears, his cheers, his irrepressible laughter. No: it must come at the end; but as the last page of the novel is a left hand one, everyone will see the appendix on the right hand one. Ugh! you have made my blood run cold.

About Cashel Byron I should have explained that there are two sets of stereos in existence—Champion's and Harper's. Unfortunately Champion's were taken from the typeset for To-Day in a long octavo that proved ugly and unsaleable. There is nothing for it but to abandon them as useless. Harper's plates are for his Handy Vol. Series, and very neat. I have no copies of either by me at present. The alteration of half a dozen words would restore the American edition to the original purity of the author's edition. I could add a preface for a new edition if necessary, a propos of Kilrain, Sullivan & Co. [Here follows an account of the I. Knot &c, of no importance.]*

As to the cover for "An U.S.," I have no practicable ideas. Your books are generally happily turned out; and my notions as to catching covers are not bright. I greatly prefer yellow to pink; but there is a red that used to be called Mahdi red that would look startlingly socialistic. We used to print Fabian tickets in it; and it was a great success. But I question the policy of suggesting a sensational dynamite story when the book is so much the reverse. As to an illustration, Trefusis shooting the statue's head off is the only incident that lends itself. If I can think of anything, I will let you know.

yrs
G. Bernard Shaw

* The note is Shaw's, bracketed in the shorthand draft.

To WILLIAM SWAN SONNENSCHEIN

29 Fitzroy Square W
4th January 1888

[F/2]

[*In Troubled Times* was a popular novel on the Netherlands war of independence, translated from the Dutch of Miss A. S. C. Wallis. Francis Lowrey, until he emigrated to South Africa in 1888, was Swan Sonnenschein's partner. The "whatdoyoucallit" was the publisher's device, a rectangular panel containing a shield with the initials WSS, between two unicorns, set against an apple tree laden with fruit. George Moore (1852–1933), one of the authors published by Swan Sonnenschein, had gained attention (and a fair degree of notoriety) through his "realistic" novels *A Mummer's Wife* (1885), *A Drama in Muslin* (1886), and *A Mere Accident* (1887). The last of these was reviewed anonymously by Shaw in the *Pall Mall Gazette* on 19th July 1887.]

Dear Sonnenschein

I have not the least idea of how a 2/- edition would go. I thought the 2/- yellow railway novel was a thing of the past. How do you find the Unicorn series selling? If it is successful, I see no reason why the U.S. should not be put into it, except that it is only half as thick a book as "In Troubled Times." But my private leaning is towards the nimble ninepence for C. Byron and An U.S. The I. Knot would be better suited to the Unicorn, as it is fearfully long. Still I have no very strong opinion in the matter, as I know nothing of how 2/- novels have been going of late years.

I strenuously object, however—and here I call Lowrey to my aid—to the enlargement of your whatdoyoucallit on the cover. I invite you to study the original, with its really crisp decorative foliage in black and white at the top, and its game and skittish unicorns, who have tucked in their tails for a joke. Now turn to the revolting green and yellow affair outside. Look at the dejected unicorns, with their trotters hanging like stuffed things, and their tails between their legs. Look at the foolish formal foliage (oh, forgive me, I am alliterating like G——e M——e) and the shield spoilt in shape and proportion. Such a cover would justify a revolution. The backing is much better. But you really must get a new design for the front. The only man who can do such things really well is [Walter] Crane; and he only does his best when he is working for nothing: his cover-pages to the Pioneer, Practical Socialist and Our Corner are worth ten of Atalanta.

yours
GBS

To NATHANIEL WEDD

[C/17]

29 Fitzroy Square W
9th February 1888

[Nathaniel Wedd (1864–1940), classical scholar and Fellow of King's College, Cambridge, was secretary of the Cambridge Fabian Society. Shaw lectured at King's College on 18th February, on "Socialism: Its Growth and Necessity," with Oscar Browning (1837–1923) historical writer and Cambridge educationalist, in the chair.]

Kindly let me know particulars of my lecture—time, place, &c, as soon as they are settled. Some of our people here have friends in Cambridge to whom they wish to write, so that we may get as good an audience as possible for the money.

yrs
G. Bernard Shaw

To T. P. O'CONNOR

[A/4; X/136.e]

29 Fitzroy Square W
9th February 1888

[Thomas Power O'Connor (1848–1929), Irish journalist and Liberal M.P., founded *The Star* on 17th January 1888. His assistant editor, H. W. Massingham, hired Shaw as a political writer, but Shaw's intemperate attacks on John Morley and other leaders of the Government and his Socialist leanings led to frequent clashes with O'Connor, and on 9th February Shaw resigned from the editorial staff. He continued, however, to contribute occasional articles and notes until August 1888, when he was invited by the newspaper's musical critic, E. Belfort Bax, to cover musical events during Bax's vacation. He continued as second-string critic until Bax resigned in February 1889, when Shaw, under the pseudonym "Corno di Bassetto," undertook his now classic series of "Musical Mems."

W. H. Smith (1825–91) was a newsagent, bookseller, and, from 1886, First Lord of the Treasury and leader of the House of Commons. George Howell (1833–1910), trades union leader, was author of *Conflicts of Capital and Labour Historically and Economically Considered* (1878). Sir Robert Donald (1861–1933), a journalist who subsequently served under Massingham on the *Daily Chronicle*, became its editor in 1902. T. R. Threlfal was secretary of the Labour Electoral Association. John Burns (1858–1943), Fabian and trade unionist, was chief leader of the 1889 dock strike. A Socialist M.P. from 1892, he was known as the "Man with the Red Flag." Thomas Binning, a member of the Socialist League, was one of the founders of the Central Democratic Club (1889), of which Shaw was a vice-president. Joseph Chamberlain (1836–1914), Liberal M.P., opposed coercion in Ireland, resigned from the third Gladstone cabinet (1886) on introduction of the home-rule bill, leading Liberal Unionists in efforts to modify the bill. Henry Broadhurst (1840–1911), Liberal M.P. and a vigorous trade unionist, was secretary of the Parliamentary Committee of the Trades Union Congress (1875–90). He later became, ironically, one of the strongest opponents of efforts to convert the unions to Socialism.]

Dear Chief

This is my resignation. I am not worth my salt to the Star; and you will be more at your ease without having constantly to suppress my articles. Sooner than trample on my feelings by telling me so, you would probably allow the paper to pay me £10,000 a year for doing nothing. So I must give myself the sack; though what is to become of you and Mass^{ghm} when you have no one to guide you through the mists of sentimental Utopianism is more than I can foresee. The special Providence that protects children be your safeguard!

I may as well mention some reasons why we cannot pull together on

183

an editorial staff. Ten years ago it would have been true that I am no journalist, because I will write only on subjects that I have thought about. But today the journalist-in-chief must be above all things an apostle, a man of convictions, illusions, fanaticisms, everything that made a man impossible in the days when the Star was impossible. From these two points of view I appear a greenhorn to you, and you appear a dreamer to me. You believe in nothing (not even in me); the fourteen million wage workers with their halfpence and their school-board education are a cipher to you; nobody hates, curses, or fears you, as so many do Stead. You have no policy; you think it safe to risk a general election on Home Rule alone; you believe in the Liberal party, which, with its journalists, is only a forest of dead trees; and you estimate the effective strength of socialism at 200 men of no account. Yet you permit an insane attack by Massingham on capital by confiscating rent wholesale without any provision by Shaw for its reinvestment and readministration, which means, as even W. H. Smith will confound you by pointing out, destroying the industries of the country and flinging millions of men starving on the streets in order to overwhelm Goschen for one year with 600 millions of money to distribute desperately in panem and arcenses, and, when hell is let loose in consequence, to crush the people or be crushed in a mortal struggle to regain despotic mastery. This is what comes of mere theorizing. You cannot expect me to have a hand in such anarchism; for I am no anarchist: I am a practical politician, and, as far as any individual insect can, I know what I want, how to get it, and the forces that will compel you, when you have sewn your revolutionary wild oats, to settle down to my humdrum radical programme, whether you like it or not. If I had energy, eloquence, and physical monumentality, I should bring London up to the mark in one winter's campaign: as it is, I must wait for a better vehicle. I have tried the Star; but the pair which draws it is too young and wild, so I must wait for the next chance.

Just two words more. 1. When you mentioned Stead yesterday, I had not read the speech of G. Howells. I now perceive that his set want to play you off against Stead, who is very properly wiping his shoes on them. Pray dont think of letting them nobble you. On the contrary, write an article headed "Dastardly Dumb Dogs," and give Donald his fling against the Trades Unionists, who are, remember, only 600,000 out of 8 million adult male workers. And the best of the 600,000 are, like Threlfal, Burns, and Binning (who wrote to you the other day) all for socialism and against simple trades-unionism. 2. Tell John

Morley roundly in private that the latest principles from Voltaire & Bentham will not do for Stonecutter St, and that your Star must cross his sooner or later if he persists in his 18th century Rip-van-Winkleism. Also that the people instinctively mistrust a close shaven man. Nevertheless, in spite of razors, Chamberlain's loss of ground is only temporary; and so far from being extinct, he is certain to have a very big, if not a very longlived boom yet. And you attack him, and are tender with Broadhurst!

I shall come down in the morning as usual in case there should be any press of work; but next week I must retire into the privacy which best befits an unassuming man. Let not your unfortunate goodnature prevent you from taking me at my word. The magnitude of my personal vanity, reflected from the magnitude of my cause, places me above literary huffiness. I am celebrated for my tact in never giving offence and never taking it, though I have had no occasion to exercise this gift at the Star, you and Massingham being the two most amiable anarchists I know. Excuse prolixity.

yrs
G. Bernard Shaw

To H. W. MASSINGHAM

[A/4]

29 Fitzroy Square W
9th February 1888

[Henry William Massingham (1860–1924), T.P. O'Connor's deputy on *The Star*, succeeded as editor in July 1890 when O'Connor sold out and founded a rival paper *The Sun*. Massingham joined the *Daily Chronicle* in 1892, assuming its editorship from 1895 to 1899. From 1907 to 1923 he was editor of *The Nation*.]

Dear Massingham

I have written to T.P. withdrawing from the Star. It is a pity that the experiment has been a failure; but I think you must see that T.P's conciliatory no-policy is hopelessly incompatible with my aggressive policy. I can only relapse into reviewing novels for the P.M.G. and criticising pictures for Yates until I can get a paper of my own. T.P's attachment to John Morley is the final blow. It is impossible to attain even high mud mark in politics without taking that solemn literary obsolescence and shaking the starch out of him twice a week regularly.

I like T.P. immensely, and will probably jam him into a novel some day, if I ever write one again. The goodnatured way in which he puts his pipestopper into the volcano and trusts to his own cleverness and luck to coax it to keep reasonably quiet is irresistible. But I really cannot come there bothering him with my cranky notions, as he thinks them. You and he get on just as well without me as with me. So off I go; and civilization is respited for a while yet.

I shall look in tomorrow morning in case you should be depending on me.

GBS

To NATHANIEL WEDD

[A/17]

29 Fitzroy Square W
20th February 1888

[Wedd had handed Shaw a sovereign for expenses, but Shaw accepted only the cost of his third–class railway fare.]

Dear Wedd

I enclose 10^s/9^d change out of your sovereign. I enjoyed myself prodigiously, and finished up with flying colours at Deptford. The glimpse of university life interested me greatly: it has seized my imagination so that I almost believe that Cambridge is my alma mater and that I have spent a long life in her cloisters.

In haste (stacks of work waiting)

G. Bernard Shaw—M.A.

To ALMA MURRAY

[A/26; X/109]

29 Fitzroy Square W
22nd February 1888

[Rev. Stopford A. Brooke (1832–1916), Irish preacher, literary scholar, and Fabian Socialist, preached as a Unitarian minister at Bedford Chapel, Bloomsbury, and headed the Bedford Debating Society. Robert Alfred Potts was a scholar active in the Shelley and Browning Societies, and a frequent contributor to *Notes and Queries*. Edward Armitage (1817–96), well-known historical painter, executed frescoes in the Houses of Parliament.]

Dear Mrs Forman

Do you know anything about the art of acting? If so, would you go so far as to lecture on it to a debating society? It is a very superior debating society, with Stopford Brooke as "perpetual grand" at its meetings, and persons of culture like Potts, and of genius like myself, always present to support him. At the last committee meeting we were discussing forthcoming papers, when someone remarked that a paper on Irving had been a great success some years ago, and that we should try one on acting. I strenuously denied that the two subjects were even remotely cognate, but I finished by saying involuntarily "Miss Alma Murray." Brooke was enchanted, and gave an enthusiastic description of your appearance at the opening meeting of the Shelley Society—which had nothing whatever to do with your acting, by the bye. The rest were awestruck at the audacity of the suggestion; and the secretary, when requested to write to you, declined on the ground that he "hadn't the cheek." Cheek being a socialistic attribute, the duty of sounding you on the subject was put upon me. I by no means recommend you to consent, though from purely selfish motives I hope you will. Our meetings take place on the 2nd & 4th Thursdays in the month at Gordon Square in a noble Gothic hall with cartoons by Armitage, oak panelling, and a defective system of lighting. Is there the faintest chance of your being disengaged in April or May? The Shelley [Society], the Wagner, the Browning, and the Century Guild [of Artists] will come as one man if you give the word for a crowd, or, if you prefer a quiet address to a few hundreds or so, the issue of invitations can be limited accordingly.

I make no apology for the excessive coolness of the proposition. Faint heart never &c.

yours—(my kingdom for the right word!)
G. Bernard Shaw

To ALMA MURRAY

29 Fitzroy Square W
24th February 1888

[A/26; X/109]

[Alma Murray was rehearsing in Percy Lynwood and Mark Ambient's *Christina*, which opened at the Olympic on 8th March; it had been performed at a single matinée on 22nd April 1887 at the Prince of Wales's. On a dare by Frank Podmore (1855–1910), psychical researchist, after a meeting of the Psychical Research Society on 29th October 1885, Shaw had spent the night, accompanied by Percy Lynwood and two other men, in the supposedly haunted Ivy House, Grove Road, St Anne's Hill, Wandsworth. Shaw reported tersely in his diary: "Slept there. Terrific nightmare."

Browning's *A Blot on the 'Scutcheon*, starring Alma Murray as Blanche was performed at the Olympic on 15th March; Shaw attended the matinée with Jenny Patterson. The earlier production, under the auspices of the

Browning Society, had been performed on 30th April and 2nd May 1885, with Fores Brette as Blanche.]

Dear Mrs Forman

I shall blight the Bedford as gently as possible. Somehow, competent people never will lecture. I delivered sixtysix lectures last year on subjects which I certainly do not know half as much about as you do about acting.

I really cannot refrain from saying a word about "Christina." The authors are known to me as harmless and estimable men out of the theatre; but it infuriates me to see good gifts wasted on such stuff. At its production last year I raged over it for ten minutes to an acquaintance with whom I had once slept in a haunted house. He agreed with me, and then mentioned that he was the collaborator of Ambient. However, it served him right. I wish I could write you a real play myself; but unfortunately I have not the faculty. I once wrote two acts of a splendid play, and read them to an eminent dramatic critic. He laughed the first to scorn, and went asleep in the middle of the second; so I made him a present of the MS (to his intense indignation) and set to work to destroy the society that makes bad plays possible. What a career you will have when that work is completed!

I look forward, breathless, to the Blot. They did it once before, at St George's Hall, with, oh! SUCH a Mildred! Good Heavens!

In short, thank you for your kind reception of our proposal.

> yrs very truly
> G. Bernard Shaw

To MRS T. P. O'CONNOR

29 Fitzroy Square W
[X/148]   17th May 1888

[Elizabeth Paschal O'Connor (1856-1931) was an American, formerly employed by Harper & Brothers in New York as a manuscript reader. George Moore's *Confessions of a Young Man* had just been issued by Swan Sonnenschein.]

Dear Mrs O'Connor

Decidedly the American woman is the woman of the future, but how the American woman contrives to get on with the Irishman of the present, without driving him out of his senses by franknesses which strike me as appalling indiscretion, was the second thought which occurred to me when I met you at "The Star" sanctum, the first thought being, of course, the realization of the American woman herself personally. It is the Irishman's charm and defect that he never loses his *naïveté* as to woman, he never ventures to think that she is human; and consequently he is eternally chivalrous, which is convenient at times, but which on the whole makes him desperately conventional on the woman question, and inclined to think that her place, after she has seen to his dinner and his buttons, is a glass case, and her chief duty to hold her tongue. I cannot help intrusively surmising that the unfortunate T.P. is having the remnants of this superstition ruthlessly extirpated by the aforesaid American woman of the future. I am enviously sorry for him.

I admit that it was a fall for Trefusis when he married Agatha [in *An Unsocial Socialist*], but it was inevitable. They were one another's natural prey from the first, and when two people find that out it ends always in the same way in spite of reason, unless one or other or both is "Bespoke" before the meeting occurs.

As to the vegetarian meal, I positively refuse. I have had considerable experience of the danger of associating myself with experiments of that kind. When the victim is a man he forgives me after a time, but women are not so magnanimous; besides, your suggestion—the most extraordinary ever made by woman—that the reformed diet might have the effect of assimilating your personal appearance to mine, chills me to the soul. Imagine your becoming fair, not to say green! No, thank you! If all the women were made fair tomorrow I should retire to a monastery the day after. The fact is these bean-pies and so on are not the proper things to eat, though they are better than cow. The correct thing is good bread and good fruit and nothing else. At present it is impossible to get either except at odd times.

It is superfluous to recommend M's "Confessions" to me; I have heard them from his own lips. I doubt if there is any other such man in the world as he. I cannot describe him; he would baffle even T.P.'s descriptive talent, and I accept your phrase as the final felicity of criticism on him.

My book-writing days are over, unluckily; for the last five years I have had to live and lecture at my own expense, and I should not know how to write a novel now if I wanted to. At the present moment, by the by, I should be writing notes for the mossy-headed Massingham. How I should like to get hold of that paper just for a fortnight!

G. B. S.

I beg your pardon, I have such a habit of signing that way, that I forget and do it when better manners are needed. Pray excuse it.

To GRAHAM WALLAS

[A/13]

29 Fitzroy Square W
14th June 1888

[Graham Wallas (1858–1932), sociologist, author of *Human Nature in Politics* (1908) and *The Great Society* (1914), member of the London School Board (1894–1904), lecturer at the London School of Economics (1895–1923) and Professor of Political Science at London University (1914–23), joined the Fabian Society in 1886, served on the Executive Committee 1888–95, and was one of the "Big Four" (with Webb, Olivier, and Shaw) until he withdrew from the Society under pressure of other duties in 1904.

R. Sutton & Co. had just invited Shaw to provide a book on Socialism for its University Economics Series. In August he had a request from Havelock Ellis for a volume on rent and value for Ellis's new Contemporary Science series. Shaw accepted both invitations. He worked at the first book in brief spurts and with many lapses from October 1888 to January 1889, at which time he undertook to edit a volume of *Fabian Essays in Socialism* for the Fabian Society. The book for Sutton was never completed. The book for Ellis was never begun.

James Leigh Joynes (1853–93) was a former teacher, poet, friend of William Morris, and member of the S.D.F.]

Mrs Wilson is going to lecture on Distribution under Anarchism or something of that sort at 13 Farringdon Road tonight. If Webb is in town I shall try & get him to come there with me, as I have nothing else to do & there is nobody at home. If you are loafing anywhere near Fitzroy Square at seven I shall be coming home from the Museum to tea just then & if you look in we are sure to find brown bread, cocoa, eggs or tea about, though we will have to prepare them for ourselves.

I have got an offer to write a text book of Socialism in the University series for a royalty of 4^d a copy. As there is no money down it will be a desperate drain; but I think I ought to take the chance, as the fellow (Sutton of Ludgate Hill) must on those terms push the sale up to 1500 to save himself from a loss, and, if possible, on to 20,000 in order to become rich beyond the dreams of avarice.

I had arranged to go up the river today with Joynes; but D is not V, judging by the weather. . . .

GBS

To COVENT GARDEN MANAGER

[G.u/1]

[29 Fitzroy Square W]
[*c.* July 1888]

[This unfinished draft of a "letter" of complaint to the Covent Garden management presages similar assaults by "Corno di Bassetto" in *The*

Sidney Webb

Beatrice Webb

Annie Besant

Graham Wallas

Star on subsequent occasions. Sir Augustus Harris (1851–96), theatre manager and impresario, produced spectacular melodrama and elaborate pantomime at Drury Lane and, later, opera at Her Majesty's and Covent Garden. He did much for the cause of Wagner's music in London. But Shaw, in his *Saturday Review* obituary of Harris on 4th July 1896, insisted that "he was not a great manager; and I am not convinced that he was even a very clever one," and condemned the Press for "bowing a little too low before commercial success, and offering it the wreaths that belong to genius and devotion alone."

Sarah Siddons (1755–1831), famous tragic actress, was acknowledged queen of the London stage from 1782 until her farewell performance as Lady Macbeth (her greatest rôle) in 1812. Vincent Crummles, a character in Dickens's *Nicholas Nickleby*, was the manager of a travelling theatrical company.]

The other evening a stall at the Covent Garden Opera House was placed at my disposal by a friend who had had a serious turn after a hard season of it. I went, and began my operatic experience by refusing to purchase a book of the words at 600 per cent. profit to the vendor. I offered to hire it for the evening on the same terms as those upon which opera glasses are let at ordinary theatres; but though forty books could easily be produced and sold for the money value of one cheap glass, the attendant refused my offer. I then took up one of the bills which lay about, and found in it an invitation to complain to the manager of anything of which I disapproved. I take this opportunity of mentioning a few things.

I complain, to begin with, of Mr Augustus Harris taking upon himself to dictate to me what sort of coat I shall wear in a public theatre, merely because he happens to be the manager of that theatre. Next season, I shall purchase a stall for the most important evening I can select. I shall dress in white flannels. I shall then hire for the evening the most repulsive waiter I can find in the lowest oyster shop in London. I shall rub him with bacon crackling, smooth his hair with fried sausages, shower stale gravy upon him, season him with Worcester sauce, and give him just enough drink to make him self assertive without making him actually drunk. With him I shall present myself at the stalls; explain that he is my brother; and that we have arranged that I am to see the opera unless evening dress is indispensable, in which case my brother, being in evening dress, must take my place. If other gentlemen will public-spiritedly follow my example, the result is certain. The impertinent sumptuary regulation will disappear from the bills.

I furthermore complain that the people on the stage dont act. I do not set up to be a judge of singing; but I can compare the acting with what I am accustomed to at other theatres; and I say it is not acting at all: it is nothing but sawing the air and attitudinizing like a parcel of barn stormers as one imagines them in the days of Mrs Siddons. I also object to the scenery and stage arrangements as obsolete and ridiculous. The whole thing is out of date: I cannot stand sky borders, tragedy queens in black dresses, old men made up like Father Christmas, heroes in blue satin tunics and dove colored tights, villains in stage helmets and spangle armour, and all the other things that I have read about in Crummles, and seen the relics of in provincial theatres in my boyhood.

[The draft ends here.]

To T. P. O'CONNOR

[A/4]
29 Fitzroy Square W
13th August 1888

[Shaw had written and submitted to *The Star*, on Sunday the 12th, an article on the Report of the Pan-Anglican Synod on Socialism. John Dunn (1834– ?) was a Scot who renounced civilisation and adopted Zulu nationality, becoming right-hand man to Cetewayo (d. 1884), the Zulu chief who rebelled against British rule in 1878. The latter is exotically recreated in Shaw's *The Admirable Bashville* (1901).]

Dear T. P.

Heaven forgive you! The full text of the Synod's report on Socialism was published on Saturday evening; London was unable to sleep that night with anxiety to see what the Star would say; on Sunday I held the whole population spellbound in Regents Park with the report in my hand as a text; on Monday afternoon the Star appeared with a lively article on the Weekly News of 1622, having rejected an article on the report of the 11th Aug. 1888 as not sufficiently novel. Idiot that I am, why did I not send you an article on the Jubilee or the Inventions Exhibition? How much wiser was the man who sent you the leaderettes about John Dunn and Cetewayo! Oh, the new Journalism, the new new Journalism!

Well, no matter.

GBS

To R. SUTTON

[F/2]

29 Fitzroy Square W
22nd August 1888

[William Stanley Jevons (1835–82), economist and logician, was Professor of Political Economy at University College, London, 1876–80.]

Dear Sir

I think the book had better be quite simply "Socialism," in keeping with Mr Jevons's title "Political Economy." It would fit quite well into the heading "The University Series" or "The University Economic Series."

I am, dear sir,
yours faithfully
G. Bernard Shaw

To T. FISHER UNWIN

[S/7; W/138.e]

29 Fitzroy Square W
4th September 1888

[Thomas Fisher Unwin (1848–1935) was founder, in 1882, of the publishing house which bore his name. Son-in-law of Richard Cobden, he was a joint founder of the Friends of Russian Freedom and of the first council of the Publishers' Association. He discovered Joseph Conrad, and published W.B. Yeats's early works.]

Dear Unwin

I see that you are issuing a series of novels. Perhaps the enclosed [*Cashel Byron's Profession*] might interest you. The author referred to, whose regard for you is only equalled by his own great personal merit, has been approached on the subject by Cassells. (I mention this to impress you with a sense of the demand he is in, and of the importance of your at once seizing the golden opportunity). Cassells have not made up their mercenary minds with becoming eagerness; and the author is growing uneasy as he feels a sense stealing on him that the book is not at bottom right, or it would not have been so well received by a detestable individualistic press. He wants it out before he comes to the point of feeling bound to suppress the volume altogether. He is growing middle-aged, and feels that the works of his early youth (the book was written in 1882) hardly become the dignity of his graver years.

He is a man of moderate views, and never expects more than a simple royalty of 25% on four times the nominal price of his books. And even this he does not always get.

Think it over in the course of the coming season. No immediate communication expected.

yrs
G. Bernard Shaw

To C. KINLOCH-COOKE

[X/143.e]

[29 Fitzroy Square W]
[14th September 1888]

[Since May 1885, when William Archer had turned over to him a copy of Henry F. Keenan's novel *Trajan* to review for the *Pall Mall Gazette* (16th May; unsigned), Shaw had contributed more than a hundred book reviews to the newspaper. In September 1888, having completed a review of Robert Oliver's *Unnoticed Analogies: A Talk on the Irish Question*, Shaw submitted with it a letter of complaint to the sub-editor, Clement Kinloch-Cooke (1854–1944), "remonstrating about the sort of book sent me for review" (Diary). Kinloch-Cooke (knighted in 1905, created a Baronet in 1926), who subsequently was associated with *The Observer*, the *English Illustrated Magazine*, and the *New Review* (see also letter of 7th May 1891 to Emery Walker), published an unsigned extract from Shaw's letter on 17th September, commenting: "Here is a bitter cry from a reviewer who is exasperated at the long continuance of the silly season in the publishing trade." The omissions are Kinloch-Cooke's.

Mary Elizabeth Braddon (1837–1915) was the prolific "manufacturer" of more than seventy novels (many of them three-deckers), as well as short stories, plays, and travel guides. The Kyrle Society was a charitable institution founded in 1877 as a memorial to the philanthropist John Kyrle (1637–1724).]

Have —— or —— been yet disposed of? If not, I should be glad to get them as a relief to the slow murder of the cursed parcels of rubbish with which you blast my prime. Surely it must be dawning on editors at last that any sort of live copy is better than the mechanical literary stuff poured out on ordinary novels and minor poetry. Why condemn me to read things that I can't review—that no artistic conscience could long survive the reviewing of! Why don't you begin notices of boots, hats, dogcarts and so on? They would be fifty times as useful and interesting as reviews of the last novel by Miss Braddon, who is a princess among novel manufacturers. There ought to be legislation against this sort of thing—on the lines of the Factory Acts. I believe the mortality in hospitals is perceptibly increased by the books distributed through reviewers by the Kyrle Society.

To MRS T. P. O'CONNOR

[X/148]

29 Fitzroy Square W
16th September 1888

[Shaw's paper "The Transition to Social Democracy," read before the British Association for the Advancement of Science, at Bath on 7th September, was published in *Our Corner* in November 1888. On 8th September *The Star* had reported the speech, but not so unfavourably as Shaw intimates in this letter. He also delivered impromptu lectures on "Social Democracy" to members of the Dalston Reform Club on 15th September and the Southwark Branch of the S.D.F. the next night. The paper being prepared for 5th October was "The Economic Aspect of Socialism," read before the Fabian Society and subsequently published in *Fabian Essays in Socialism* (1889).

The Italian Exhibition, a lavish enterprise which extended over West Brompton, Earls Court, and West Kensington, ran from 12th May to 31st October 1888. The "enclosed," according to Mrs O'Connor in *I Myself* (1910), was "a brilliant article by Tighe Hopkins, suggested by a paragraph in 'For Maids, Wives, and Widows' my weekly column in 'the Star.'" Tighe Hopkins (1856–1919) was a journalist and novelist (Shaw reviewed his *For Freedom* in the *Pall Mall Gazette*, 7th May 1888). Shaw had met Hopkins at the home of Jenny Patterson on 12th January 1886, recording in his diary that Hopkins "was bent on seduction, and we tried which should outstay the other. Eventually he had to go for his train."]

Dear Mrs O'Connor

I take it that you are back from Kreuznach by this time. I too am back—from Bath—upon which expedition (I was three hours and a half there) I spent a fortnight's hard work and a pound in present cash, only to be maligned and misrepresented in "The Star" and to return in a state of destitution with my Italian Exhibition project faded into an impossible dream. No, madam. Share the splendour of West Kensington with the giddy Massingham if you will, and leave to sterner, grimmer uses the slave of the world's destiny and of his own genius.

I walked home from my lecture at Dalston last night to save a tram fare—think of that and blush! Probably I shall walk home from the New Cut tonight for the same reason. Last month I earned £6, 12s. The month's rent is £5. I have another paper to prepare for October 5th, equal in difficulty to the Bath one, and equally paid in the gratitude of posterity. I have two books commissioned, payment by royalty after they are published—and you talk of the Italian Exhibition! Ha, ha! Do you know what the Italian Exhibition costs? Our tickets, third class, including admission, half-a-crown if they would cost a penny. One programme between us, a penny. The Blue Grotto, threepence (for you—I should wait outside as I have seen the imposture already); sixpenny seats at the Coliseum—one shilling; threepenny seats at the Mandolinists—sixpence; shilling seats at the Marionettes—two shillings; Switchback Railway, one turn—sixpence. Refreshments, say fourpence, as we could be scrupulously economical. Loss of time, reckoned at "Star" rates of payment—half-a-crown apiece. Total, twelve shillings and twopence! So that even if I borrowed ten shillings from you to start with (which an Army Reserve man in the S.D. Federation tells me is the cheapest plan of managing an affair of this sort) I should still be two shillings and twopence out of pocket. Two shillings and twopence to gratify the whim of a giddy young woman who proposes (monstrous conceit) to take my education in hand! *My* education! You a baby, still looking with wide-open, delighted eyes at the glitter of West European whitewash and advising maids, wives, and widows with the artless wisdom of an incomparable and unique *naïveté—educate me*! Stupendous project! No, I learn from everybody, and what I learn I teach, but I am nobody's pupil, though I should be glad indeed to meet my master. You will find very few people in London who know anything, but those who do have learnt it all from me! All of which is as much as to say that for the present I am tied, neck and heels, to stump and inkpot, and mustn't introduce the statue to its original yet awhile.

Meanwhile, I hope you are well, as this leaves me at present—thank God! (if there were one) for it. This is the Irish formula, and faultless in its way.

I judge by a fervour in the leading article that the editor of "The Star" is again at his post. Convey to him such kind regards as can pass between two hardened worldlings.

Of the enclosed I very grievously suspect Master Tighe Hopkins—but you began it.

G.B.S.

To THE EDITOR OF THE STAR

[A/1]

Sky Parlor
19th September 1888

[A series of brutal murders of women, accompanied by hideous mutilations, in the Whitechapel district of London's East End began on 31st August, continuing with alarming frequency into 1889. The murderer, known only as "Jack the Ripper," was never apprehended. On 19th September *The Star* published a leading article on the crimes (there had been only two murders at this date), and for several days the columns of the paper overflowed with letters on the subject "Is Christianity a Failure?" Shaw contributed two pseudonymous letters (a favourite device of his) to the controversy, neither of which was accepted by the editor.]

Sir

Why do you try to put the Whitechapel murders on me? Sir Charles Warren is quite right not to catch the unfortunate murderer, whose conviction and punishment would be conducted on my father's old lines of an eye for an eye, which I have always consistently repudiated. As to the eighteen centuries of what you call Christianity, I have nothing to do with it. It was invented by an aristocrat of the Roman set [St Paul], a university man whose epistles are the silliest middle class stuff on record. When I see my name mixed up with it in your excellent paper, I feel as if nails were going into me—and I know what that sensation is like better than you do. Trusting that you will excuse this intrusion on your valuable space,

I am, Sir &c
J.C.

To THE EDITOR OF THE STAR

[G/4; X/139]

[29 Fitzroy Square W]
[20th September 1888]

Sir

I am a native of a country where Christianity is unknown. Having heard much of the English Protestant form of your religion in the course of my travels, I have devoted myself to its study—from men, not from books—since I entered England. My conclusion is that your question is hardly worth considering, as only a very small proportion of the population have any religious beliefs at all. Those who have are nearly all called Christians; but they have not all the same belief: there are at least as many creeds as there are classes. Among the poor, for instance, the Salvation Army spreads a vivid conceit (as your great poet Shakespere would say) of the horrors of hell and the ecstasies of heaven, so that the uncertainty as to whether the individual is "saved" —or destined for heaven—or not, is intensely exciting. Here the hope of heaven makes the people content to bear their deep poverty.

Higher in the social scale there prevails the conception of a terrible divine wrath and vengeance, only to be propitiated by human sacrifice begun by the supreme immolation of Christ and continued daily in the mortified ascetic lives of his followers. Much of the gloom and aversion to fine art which characterizes the lower middle class is undoubtedly due to this terrible creed, which makes Sunday the especial scourge of childhood. Still higher up, in circles where the mind and artistic senses are highly cultivated, hell is disbelieved; only the more pleasing and amiable parts of the Bible are held to be valid; and the divine power is personified by the gentle and humane Jesus of Nazareth.

Besides these are also Christian Socialists, who look to the establishment of the Kingdom of heaven on earth by a Christ in whom may be discovered a general agreement with the doctrines of the American Mr Henry George. But among the most advanced classes, Christianity shades into an indefinite optimism without any belief in the supernatural. I am told by some that the beliefs in a personal God, and in an imperishable organ called the soul, which survives the body and is subject to reward or punishment according to the acts performed during the life of the body, are no vital part of Christianity and are rejected by many true Christians. But others of my acquaintance regard the slightest expression of doubt on these points as blasphemous in the highest degree, and will passionately declare that the sceptic is no Christian, but an atheist whose soul shall dwell in tormenting fire for ever.

This want of agreement among Christians is so striking that to a foreigner it does not seem possible to discuss whether Christianity is a failure whilst the word means so many different beliefs. Of the irreligious majority of the English people I notice that great numbers go to church because it is one of the duties which are included in what is called "respectability." There is such a general belief in luck and witchcraft, that nearly all the citizens avoid walking under ladders; gamble incessantly in stocks and shares and on the turf; and buy immense quantities of charms called patent medicines. Their wives also hold the priests and doctors in great respect. It is also evident from the hanging law and from the general consensus of opinion that death is the greatest of evils, that the doctrine of the immortality of the soul, like that of returning good for evil, is only formally professed and not really believed in.

It is my intention to write a book upon England for the instruction of my own countrymen; and I hope to learn much from this greatly interesting correspondence upon Christianity in the Star newspaper.

your obedient servant
Shendar Brwa

To THE EDITOR OF *THE STAR*

[A/1]

[29 Fitzroy Square W]
[20th September 1888]

[After attending a preachment on Socialism by the Bishop of Rochester at St John the Evangelist's Church, on 20th September, Shaw proceeded to send a conventional "correspondent's report" to the *Pall Mall Gazette*, which appeared in the issue of the 21st, and another of his pseudonymous letters to *The Star*, whose editor treated it, apparently, with as much disdain as he had the letters on Christianity written just previously. It was not published.

Edward Stuart Talbot (1844–1934), Bishop of Rochester, was a moderately high churchman who was an ardent supporter of social reforms. Rev. Stewart D. Headlam (1847–1924), Christian Socialist minister, Fabian, member of the London School Board, and founder of the Guild of St Matthew, which sponsored the Bishop's lecture, is best known as the samaritan who obtained and put up the bail money for Oscar Wilde at the time of his arrest in 1895. Rev. Henry Cary Shuttleworth (1850–1900), also a Christian Socialist and Fabian, was Rector of St Nicholas Cole-Abbey.]

Honored Sir and Editor

Having bin for the fust time in my life to church for to hear the Bishop of Rorchester preach I take the liberty of letting you know what passed, thinking that perhaps you never seen a Bishop and no more had I til this very evening. Honored Sir I would not have gone not being opinionated that way except for the Reverend Mr Headlam which they told me would fight the Bishop on sight and the Reverend Mr Shuttleworth of Nicholas Coal Abbey would be his bottleholder, the same being not true but a plant as fighting is not allowed in Church,

199

so those two gentlemen they only looked at him as much as to say what they'd do when they got him outside. He sat to the left of the table that was railed in to put the money on (we all settin well outside with the singers all in white between us and it) and Reverend Hedlam he was with two seconds on the right, more in the corner like. The Bishop had a red necktie and was as hard as nails and proper stiff, I can tell you. He saved hisself up for the sermon, and put all the work on Headlam and Shuttleworth. Headlam read out about all the gold and silver in the palace, thousands and thousands, and the Bishop looked as proud as Punch of owning it all. Then Shuttleworth done a cruel lot of praying; and the boys sung a sam like mad, cutting out the running for the organ, which done a good finish. The organ had windows, and the gentleman kept opening and shutting them so that sometimes you couldnt hear yourself and sometimes you couldnt hear him. The singing was the best of it to my taste. Then the Bishop he up a ladder and preached about socialism; but he warnt used to it, and when I sez "Hear hear" to encourage him, he stops and sez "This is a church" sez he, as if I didnt know. It was a treat to hear him giving everybody a setting down all round. First he give it to the man that said "Master: speak to my brother that has kep back half my property" or words to that effeck. Then he give it to the lord that said it wornt no business of his. Then he give it to the police, and said Christ hadnt nothing to do with them. Then he give it to the Socialists straight, and said that equal property would spile personal ambition, and that wolves was wolves and when caught would disappear as such. Then he give it to the capitalists and said they must all be done away with. Then he give it to us for cheering him. Then he give it to a man named Marks for being a Christian Jew. Then he give it to a lot more for being Germans. Then he said co-operation was salvation and if you'll believe it before the words was well out of his mouth he give it to the co-operators like anythink. Then he let Phil. Officer have it for preaching the survival of the fittest; Phil. didnt like it, I tell you, whoever he was. Then he says "Blessed are ye poor; for yours is the Kingdom of Heaven." Then he says, quite genteel, as he hoped he wornt wearying us; but we was bashful to answer afraid he'd give it to us again. Then he touches up the Gild of St Matthew, as the collection was for, for mixing in politics. Then he takes a snooze for about forty winks with his head in his hands; and we sings a hymn very quiet, so as not to wake him. Then he hears the money chinking, and comes down the ladder prompt to take it at the table. Then he blesses us as if the whole place belonged to him; and out we sneaks hot foot. I must say I never see a man come up more to my notion of a Bishop as him. I wish I was one. Hoping you will ascuse the liberty,

I am, Sir,
yours respectfully
Jem Nicholls

P.S. The church was the big un in the Waterloo Road, near the railway bridge.

To HAVELOCK ELLIS

[C/8]

29 Fitzroy Square W
6th October 1888

[Henry Havelock Ellis (1859–1939), scientist and man of letters, conducted researches in psychology and sociology of sex, the results of which were recorded in seven volumes (1897–1928) constituting his monumental *Studies in the Psychology of Sex*. D. Gordon was editor for the firm of Walter Scott, publisher of the Contemporary Science series which Ellis was editing (see headnote to letter of 14th June 1888 to Graham Wallas).]

Excuse my delay—I have been so busy over a paper for the Fabian that I had no energy to spare for anything else. It's over now.

It seems to me that selling for a period comes to the same thing as selling an edition, and is more satisfactory. How many copies is an edition according to Scott's (or Gordon's) notion? Could you not put me in direct conflict with him, so as to save worrying you with all the chaffering. Of course he will accept a reasonable arrangement; but I want to make an unreasonable one.

GBS

To T. FISHER UNWIN

[S/7; X/136.e]

29 Fitzroy Square W
19th November 1888

Dear Unwin

No thank you: no more novels for me. Five failures are enough to satisfy my appetite for enterprise in fiction. I have no intention of lowering myself to the level of Bruce's spider. The success of future attempts must be guaranteed beforehand by a cheque for £500 for seven years copyright. Otherwise the attempts will not be made.

Seriously, I have no longer either time or inclination for tomfooling over novels. And your repudiation of "Cashel Byron" is a positive relief to me; for I hate the book from my soul.

I have just run a really pretty novel through "Our Corner," which you ought to read if you ever come across the volumes of that moribund magazine; but it would be of no use to you professionally. "Love among the Artists" is the name. When you are tired of saleable novels, and want to read something really dainty, you will find it the very thing for you.

G.B.S.

To JIM CONNELL

29 Fitzroy Square W
[A/4]   11th December 1888

[Jim Connell (1852–1929), member of the Deptford Radical Association and later active in the Independent Labour Party, was a journalist who contributed regularly to Keir Hardie's *Labour Leader* and author of the lyrics of the Socialist song "The Red Flag." Connell had invited the Fabians to put up a man to stand for Deptford for the County Council.]

Dear Mr Connell

I am afraid the Fabian cannot supply you with a candidate. Some of us are civil servants; some have no qualification; some, like myself, have no money; others, like Hubert Bland, have had enough of elections for the present. I shall bring the matter forward at the council meeting on Thursday; but I see no chance of anything coming of it.

Our socialist work, you see, compels us to live from hand to mouth, and that pretty closely too.

I heard something about Hyndman standing for Deptford; but I suppose his qualification has lapsed.

yours faithfully
G. Bernard Shaw

To AUGUST MANNS

29 Fitzroy Square W
[X/112]   19th December 1888

[Shaw's unsigned notice of the Crystal Palace concert of 8th December so interested conductor August Manns that he wrote on the 15th to "The

Musical Critic of *The Star*" to do him the favour of identifying himself.
"I am aware," he wrote, "that this request may appear a little bold and
strange, but then I take it for granted that professional etiquette will prompt
you to forgive an old Musician for this display of special curiosity" (BM).
Manns (1825–1907) was a German bandmaster and conductor (knighted in
1904) who led the Saturday Concerts at the Crystal Palace from 1855 to
1901. He fostered the work of German composers, notably Schumann.]

Dear Sir

Your right to know the name of the writer who ventures to criticize
you in a public newspaper is unquestionable. He is, however, a person
of no consequence whatever—one who occasionally indulges himself
with a Saturday trip to the Palace on the strength of being able to earn
the price of his ticket (a considerable sum to him) by a stray notice in
the *Star* or perhaps the *Pall Mall Gazette*. He has no position or
reputation which entitle him to the smallest consideration as a writer
on music. Musical critics, as you know, are of two sorts, musicians who
are no writers and writers who are no musicians. The *Star* adventurer
belongs to the second class, and he was never more astonished and
flattered in his life than when he learned that his irresponsible sallies
had attracted your attention. If his name were one to speak for itself,
he would not intrude upon you with the explanations, but would
simply enclose the card of one who is at least musical enough to feel
deeply indebted to you and to sign himself,

yours, most respectfully
G. Bernard Shaw

To JIM CONNELL

[A/4]
29 Fitzroy Square W
1st January 1889

Dear Mr Connell

I am afraid I should have absolutely no chance in Deptford without
the support of the Liberal as well as the Radical Association. Now if
the Liberal Ass^on will not accept Bland, they certainly will not accept
me, as I should have to make exactly the same conditions as he
mentioned, i.e., no expense to himself, and no more Liberal candidates
to be put forward than there are seats. Can you not force them to run
Bland along with Phillips?

If I could pay my own expenses I should not be so particular about

15—B.S. I

the risk of defeat; but it is impossible for me to throw away other men's money, time and votes in order to figure as a candidate. Why not send a strong remonstrance to the Liberal Ass^cn? It is clearly their business to put another man up unless they have arranged with the Conservatives to put in Phillips and a Tory, which the state of the register may possibly justify them in doing. But if there are two conservatives up, then they should certainly run a second Liberal. Suppose you suggest to them that if they dont take on Bland, you will put up a much more extreme man on your own account?

yrs
G. Bernard Shaw

To ISABEL SANDHAM

29 Fitzroy Square W
8th February 1889

[A/4]

[Mrs Isabel Sandham became a member of the Fabian Society later in 1889, and served as Secretary of the South-Western Group. In April 1891 she was elected to the Fabian Executive Committee. Benjamin F. C. Costelloe (1855–99), barrister, journalist, and Fabian lecturer, became a member of the London County Council (1891–99). Mrs Costelloe was Mary Pearsall Smith (1864–1945), an American, who subsequently deserted her husband and their two small daughters. After Costelloe's death, she married the art connoisseur, Bernhard Berenson.]

Dear Madam

I shall be happy to speak for the Women's Com^tee of the Chelsea Liberal Association on the 22nd March at a meeting to discuss the condition of the workers. But why dont the women get women to speak? Mrs Costelloe is an able speaker: why have *Mr* Costelloe? Why have me, when there are half a dozen women who could do what I am wanted to do?

It will be impossible for the different speakers to announce separate subjects for their speeches. The meeting will be held to discuss some subject; and each speaker will address the audience on that subject. If a resolution is to be moved, do not announce my name until I have had an opportunity of reading it.

If I speak, I need not, as I have explained, be announced to speak on "Socialism"; but it must be understood that I come to speak as a Social-Democrat, and will probably make that thoroughly understood in the course of any speech I may deliver. The Com^tee cannot have me without Social Democracy: indeed, I am not known politically in any other connexion.

yours very truly
G. Bernard Shaw

To ISABEL SANDHAM

[A/4]

29 Fitzroy Square W
9th March 1889

Dear Mrs Sandham
In that case I vehemently, violently, flatly, firmly, point-blank refuse. Imagine getting up in cold blood to devastate a pleasant party by speechifying. No: one cannot be friendly & social as well as oratorical; and if Costelloe's sense of humor is so feeble as to allow him to get up and interrupt the proceedings so incongruously, I strongly advise you to vote against him at the next election. I dont mind coming for the purpose of enjoying myself, or for the other purpose of doing a stroke of work. But as to interfering with the enjoyment of others by dragging in politics where nobody wants them!—not I.

I hope I have your sympathy in my view of the matter.

Is it not exasperating—the way that people do a good thing & then deliberately spoil it?

yrs very truly
G. Bernard Shaw

To ISABEL SANDHAM

[A/4]

29 Fitzroy Square W
13th March 1889

[Shaw addressed the Women's Committee of the Chelsea Liberal Association on the 22nd March, as requested. He was, however, the only speaker, and recorded in his diary that he "pitched into them and into the Liberal Party to their great astonishment."]

Dear Madam
Very well: if I am ordered to come, I must. But this is really enough to drive a man out of his senses; for I solemnly protest that I wrote with the friendliest feeling.

205

I should have written yesterday; but the editing of the Fabian Essays, coming upon me with a quantity of other work, has driven me into a state of being a week late with everything. Apparently, it has also deprived me of the power of writing proper letters. I can only plead my distracted circumstances, and throw myself on your forbearance.

yours, snubbed
G. Bernard Shaw

To WILLIAM SANDERS

29 Fitzroy Square W
[X/113]   23rd March 1889

[William Stephen Sanders (1871–1941) was Secretary of the Election Committee of the Battersea Branch of the Social Democratic Federation (not the Liberal and Radical Association as Shaw erroneously states in his letter, the confusion stemming from the fact that the two groups had held a joint conference to select a parliamentary candidate). Sanders later became a Fabian; he served as the Society's secretary from 1914 to 1920, and as honorary treasurer thereafter. He was elected Labour M.P. for North Battersea in 1929.]

Dear Sir
   I wish it were possible for me to thank the Battersea L. and R. Association for their invitation, and accept it without further words. But there is the old difficulty which makes genuine democracy impossible at present—I mean the money difficulty. For the last year I have had to neglect my professional duties so much, and to be so outrageously unpunctual and uncertain in the execution of work entrusted to me by employers of literary labour, that my pecuniary position is worse than it was; and I am at present almost wholly dependent on critical work which requires my presence during several evenings in the week at public performances. Badly as I do this at present, I could not do it at all if I had parliamentary duties to discharge; and as to getting back any of the old work that could be done in the morning, I rather think the action I should be bound to take in Parliament would lead to closer and closer boycotting. As to the serious literary work that is independent of editors and politics, I have never succeeded in making it support me; and in any case it is not compatible with energetic work in another direction carried on simultaneously. You must excuse my troubling you with these details; but the Association, consisting of men

206

who know what getting a living means, will understand the importance of them. As a political worker outside Parliament I can just manage to pay my way and so keep myself straight and independent. But you know, and the Association will know, how a man goes to pieces when he has to let his work go, and then to run into debt, to borrow in order to get out of debt by getting into it again, to beg in order to pay off the loans, and finally either to sell himself or to give up, beaten.

If the constituency wants a candidate, I see nothing for it but paying him. If Battersea makes up its mind to that, it can pick and choose among men many of whom are stronger than I. And since it is well to get so much good value for the money as can be had, I think poor constituencies (and all real democratic constituencies are poor) will for some time be compelled to kill two birds with one stone, and put the same man into both County Council and Parliament. This, however, is a matter which you are sure to know your own minds about, and it is not for me to meddle in it.

Some day, perhaps, I may be better able to take an extra duty; for, after all, I am not a bad workman when I have time and opportunity to show what I can do; and I need scarcely say that if the literary employers find that there is money to be made out of me, they will swallow my opinions fast enough.

I am, dear Sir,
yours faithfully
G. Bernard Shaw

To NATHANIEL WEDD

[A/17]

29 Fitzroy Square W
10th April 1889

[Hermann Vezin (1830–1910), American-born actor, scored a major success in February 1889 when he substituted for the ailing Irving in *Macbeth* at the Lyceum. He created the rôle of Fergus Crampton in Shaw's *You Never Can Tell* in 1899.]

Dear Wedd

If you are in town on Friday, will you look in at Bloomsbury Hall, Hart St W.C. any time after eight. The Fabians are giving a "social evening" at which they desire your company. Evening dress not compulsory though admissible on the plea of ordinary attire being unpresentable—recitations, music &c Alma Murray & Herman Vezin —refreshments (contract at 9ᵈ a head)—suburban aristocracy—samples of proletariat (carefully selected)—omnibuses at 11.30. Come if you can. I have exhausted my stock of regular cards, but will send on one as a reminder if a fresh supply reaches me in time.

yrs
G. Bernard Shaw

P.S. R.S.V.P. if you cant come.

To WILLIAM ARCHER

Hotel de Vienne. Brussels
18th April 1889

[C/2]

[Shaw sailed on 17th April for Belgium, his first visit to the Continent. He arrived in Antwerp on the morning of the 18th, and in a single day toured the city, proceeded to Mechlin, and reached Rotterdam in time to visit the theatre. During the next five days, accompanied by George Radford (whom he had met aboard the channel steamer), Shaw visited The Hague, Amsterdam (where he attended a "very successful" Dutch production of Ibsen's *A Doll's House*), Utrecht, Haarlem, and Rotterdam, returning to London on the 24th. Jean Sully Mounet (1841–1916), known as Mounet-Sully, was a famous French tragedian who performed from 1872 at the Comédie Française.]

My worst forebodings have been realized. I have seen nothing that I was not already tired of except the Musée Plantin at Antwerp, which nobody seems to care about, and which is worth a dozen such whitened dogholes as the Cathedral. These cathedrals are all rot: none of them are finished; the building of a certain sort of tracery at a prodigious height to get a lace work effect is a mere trick; and the insides are ugly and full of vile modern stained glass. I thought the San Carlo Borromeo church at Antwerp the most horrible experience of my life until I went into the picture gallery, which is a pretty nightmare to cross the ocean to see. Antwerp is exactly like Limerick, only duller. I spent an hour in Mechlin; saw the cathedral and another barrack of the same army; and fled howling to Brussels, where I went to the Theatre de la Monnaie and was driven out after one act by Mounet Sully declaiming Oedipus with a lot of the Français people. The weather has been magnificent; but Nature conspires with you in vain to palm off the Continent on me as a success. My only piece of luck was not seeing the descent from the Cross, because of Easter. Off to the Hague on Sat^y, and back Wed^y morn^g.

GBS

208

To DAVID J. O'DONOGHUE

29 Fitzroy Square W

[A/5]

9th May 1889

[David J. O'Donoghue (1866–1917) and Francis A. Fahy (1854–1935) had published a series of articles on "Ireland in London" in the Dublin *Evening Telegraph* in April and May, in which Shaw was chronicled as "the reviewer of the *P.M.G.*" from 1885 to 1888. Fahy was a poet, author of *Irish Songs and Poems* (1887). O'Donoghue, a journalist, edited *The Humour of Ireland* (1894), which contained extracts from the "Corno di Bassetto" articles. Joseph Fitzgerald Molloy (1858–1908) was the author of several novels; Shaw reviewed his *A Modern Magician* in the *Pall Mall Gazette* (5th December 1887). Samuel Carter Hall (1800–89) was an Irish-born novelist and editor of the *Art Journal* (1839–80). Florence C. Armstrong and Mrs Catharine Drew wrote novels; the former also published verse. John Cashel Hoey (1828–92), Agent General for Victoria, was the second husband of Shaw's cousin Frances Johnston. Sir Charles Gavan Duffy (1816–1903) was an Irish Nationalist tried for treason-felony in 1848; he emigrated to Australia, where in 1871 he became prime minister. Harry Furniss (1854–1925) was a well-known cartoonist, on the staff of *Punch* (1880–94).]

Dear Sir

Thanks for your letter and the cutting from the Evening Telegraph. The article interests me the more as I have sometimes wondered at the remarkable number of literary Scotchmen, and the very few literary Irishmen my own fortune has brought me into contact with. Your list far exceeded my knowledge: still, no list of the kind, short of the Recording Angel's, ever is absolutely complete; and if I were you, I should, before republishing, send a copy of the article to a few of the people named in it, and ask them could they and would they supply any omissions that might fall within their private knowledge. Fitzgerald Molloy, for instance, was secretary to S. C. Hall for a long time; and he is now a busy member of "the Salon." He must know nearly all the Irish literary people. Besides Mrs Cashel Hoey, whom you have mentioned (she is a cousin of mine), there is Miss Florence Armstrong, an art critic and story writer, and Miss Drew. Cashel Hoey, by the bye, was one of Gavan Duffy's group of agitators & writers in the old days; I took the liberty of borrowing his name for Cashel Byron. Furniss was a schoolfellow of mine at the Wesleyan Connexional School in Stephens Green, where the boys were almost all not Wesleyans, but Protestants. He is the only schoolfellow I have found in the ranks here.

I was of course not *the* critic of the PMG: there was no such thing

209

possible, as the paper published at least two reviews a day; and I contributed about three a month. I seldom reviewed poetry, though once or twice a batch of minor poets fell to my lot. Mr Fahy was not one of my victims. One of the most active of my reviewing colleagues was William Archer, who is a Scotchman; but all the long reviews of distinctly Irish quality during the 1885–8 period may, I think, be set down either to me or to Oscar Wilde, whose reviews were sometimes credited to me. His work was exceptionally finished in style and very amusing.

Dr Edward Aveling, who writes plays under the name "Alec Nelson," claims to be an Irishman; and Mrs Besant also is persuaded that she comes from our native land.

If I can help you to any information in the course of your labors pray do not hesitate to shoot.

yrs
GBS

To CLEMENT SHORTER

[S/4]

29 Fitzroy Square W
23rd May 1889

[Clement King Shorter (1857–1926), journalist, literary critic, and editor, was on the staff of *The Star* when Shaw first met him. In 1889 he became assistant to editor John Latey Jr (1842–1902) on the *Penny Illustrated Paper*, to which Shaw agreed to contribute a weekly column, "Asides." Two of these were published, on 1st and 8th June, signed "No Gentleman," but when Latey rejected the material submitted for the third week, Shaw cancelled the agreement.]

How now, Clement Shorter! Art mad? I wrote that I was seized with symptoms of mortal disease, and might not live to complete my contract. Hell to your soul, you unfeeling villain, is my life to be made a jest of in this fashion? Do you expect me to get up naked out of my grave and write columns of penny illustrated bumfodder?

On Monday things looked so bad—so like sickening for a bad illness, that I felt bound to warn Latey that there was a chance of my failing. However, I have beaten the fever and got off with a bad throat; so I shall pull it off this week, I expect.

G.B.S.

To GEORGE STANDRING

[A/24]

29 Fitzroy Square W
31st May 1889

[George Standring (1855–1924), editor of *The Radical* and printer to the Fabian Society from 1885, did not become a member of the Society until February 1893. Jules Magny (1845–1927) was a French Socialist journalist, author of *Histoire d'un morceau de verre* (1873), translator, and (from 1890) a Fabian.]

My dear Standring

I am engaged to Bland for Sunday afternoon up to lecture time; and as I put him off last Friday when we had arranged a walk, I hardly like to put him off again. Does Magny frequent the British Museum? I no longer do so; but I could meet him there for an hour some afternoon before this day week, if we cannot clear up matters at Hatcham. In the evenings I am in the clutches of the opera (kindly believe in God for a moment that we may invoke his curse on that detestable institution). Or if J.M. will send me his translation I will read it carefully, elucidate any point that seems wrong, and return it in good time. In fact I will do anything in reason to accommodate him.

yrs
GBS

To JULES MAGNY

[A/4]

29 Fitzroy Square W
4th June 1889

[Magny had undertaken to translate Shaw's paper "The Transition to Social Democracy," delivered before the British Association at Bath on 7th September 1888; it appeared in *La Revue Socialiste* in August and September 1889. Shaw provided Magny with 8½ pages of notes on his translation, incorporated in the following letter. The first two notes are reproduced, to provide the reader with a sample of Shaw's detailed approach to the material.]

Dear M. Magny

The following are the points that struck me in reading your translation: I have in each case put a dot in the margin opposite the line referred to. Wherever you have made a pencil alteration I shall say something about it except where your first version seems to me all right. Excuse my vile French.

Page 3—"j'ai toujours constaté que ce coquin &c." The meaning is—"je n'ai jamais entendu parler d'un homme qui, dans cette situation, a osé soutenir que c'est un devoir &c."

Page 4—"tres peu centralisées même en vue de desseins purement politiques." I dont know whether "même" would do this; but it seems to me to clear up a certain ambiguity in the sentence as it stands—"Démon étranger" refers to the term used by the Chinese, who describe all foreigners as "foreign devils." I dont know whether the expression is quoted in France. . . .

This is all I have to say except to thank you for having given so much pains to my paper. Excuse my stopping abruptly: I have to rush off to my evening's work.

Bon voyage!
G. Bernard Shaw

To GEORGE STANDRING

[29 Fitzroy Square W]
[c. 4th June 1889]

[A/4]

[Isaac Watts (1674–1748) was a theologian, author of over 600 hymns, the most famous of which is "O God, our help in ages past." Jack Cade was an Irish political rebel, one of the historical personages in Shakespeare's *Henry VI, Part 2*; Shaw quoted his speech "But then are we in order, when we are most out of order."]

I went over Magny's translation, and enjoyed myself in correcting his French. My quotations from the book of Job & Dr Watts had utterly floored him; and he translated "Jack Cade" as "le bourreau." But wherever he had a fair chance, he did very well; and you would hardly have known me in my French dress, I looked so solemn and academic. He seems to be a very good sort of fellow.

yrs
GBS

To JULES MAGNY

[A/4]

29 Fitzroy Square W
7th June 1889

[Georges Boulanger (1837–91) was a controversial French general, known as the "Man on Horseback."]

Dear M. Magny

I shall not have a moment to spare from my work until Monday, when I hope to go through the rest of your translation and send it on to you according to your instructions.

I forgot to mention one point. On page 262 of Our Corner, in the 10th line from the foot, there occurs the phrase "expensive sham-fight." A sham-fight is the sort of thing they do at a review, mere show and blank cartridge—*style Boulanger, cheval noir*, "*en revenant de la revue*" &c—you understand.

As to *la question pécuniare*, that does not concern me at all. The ideas in the paper are no more mine than anyone else's: the labor of expressing them in French has been yours, and the remuneration (if any) must be yours also. Pray use your own discretion in the matter.

I shall call the attention of the Star to La Justice.

yrs
GBS

To WILLIAM ARCHER

[A/2]

29 Fitzroy Square W
11th June 1889

[Shaw attended the first performance of Ibsen's *A Doll's House*, produced by Charles Charrington and starring his wife Janet Achurch, at the Novelty Theatre on 7th June. As Archer, who was dramatic critic of the *Manchester Guardian*, would not review his own translation, Shaw substituted for him as reviewer. On the 8th the two men had a lengthy discussion of the play. On the 11th Shaw saw it again.

Sir Hubert Llewellyn Smith (1864–1945) was an economist who later became Permanent Secretary to the Board of Trade and chief economic adviser to the Government. Charles Booth (1840–1916), a sociological writer, had recently written (with several assistants) *Life and Labour in East London*. One of Booth's assistants was Beatrice Potter, who in 1892 became Mrs Sidney Webb.

"Julius Floemmochser" was a pseudonym Shaw had appended to a letter in *The Star* on 1st February 1889, in which he had attacked the French actor for being "no actor at all, but only that horrible speaking automaton, an

213

elocutionist," who held illusion and histrionics subservient to perfect elocution. This was a reply to an A.B. Walkley review of a French company appearing at the Royalty Theatre.]

I noticed a good many shortcomings tonight that escaped me before, & that ought to be remedied somehow. The cardinal one is that the situation in the second act is not made clear. The audience does not understand her [Nora's] idea that Helmer will take the forgery on himself. When she exclaims "He will do it" they dont know what it means. I asked my neighbor—who was intensely interested—at the end of the act whether he understood this; and he was quite in the dark. His companion (Lleyewellyn Smith of Toynbee, who did a lot of the work for that book of Booth's on East London) knew; but he had read the play; and he agreed with me that the point did not come out in the acting. In several places, the piece wants playing up. In spite of Julius Floemmochser I am alive to the necessity of perfect diction when an attempt is made at realism in the pitch of conversation. I was in the fourth row of the pit, which is not unreasonably far back; but I lost several lines, and was conscious of a great relief when they spoke out or made their words tell. One unfortunate pittite at last cried out respectfully but imploringly "Speak up"; and my sympathies were entirely with him. One of the scenes which needs to be brought out is that between Nora [Janet Achurch] & the nurse. Mrs Linden [Gertrude Warden] is fading into nothing; and I have come to the conclusion that Krogstad [Royce Carleton] is bad, an opinion which I found shared by Stepniak. They are all relapsing into their ordinary stage tricks now that they are at their ease & the strain of the first night off. Miss A actually bowed to the applause on her entrance, a proceeding which so ruined the illusion—she was the only one who did it—that I have resorted to the "last device of a coward," an anonymous letter, begging her not to do it again. If she shews it to you—mum!

Charrington is better: the exit is greatly improved.

GBS

To JULES MAGNY

29 Fitzroy Square W
12th June 1889

[A/4]

[The Eiffel Tower, 984 ft. high, built by French engineer Alexandre Eiffel (1832–1923), had been erected in the Champs de Mars for the Paris Exposition of 1889.]

Janet Achurch

Janet Achurch and Charles Charrington in *A Doll's House*
(Novelty Theatre, June 1889)

Dear M. Magny

To continue my notes:—

[Four pages of notes follow.]

This is all I have to say about the paper except to congratulate myself on getting it so well translated.

What a curious nation the French are! They have had the highest tower in the world open to the public for weeks; and yet nobody has committed suicide from it yet. If it were in London there would have been a perfect shower of Englishmen from it, head-foremost, in the first week.

yrs truly
GBS

To JANET ACHURCH

[T/1 (A/4)]

29 Fitzroy Square W
17th June 1889

[Janet Achurch (1864–1916), daughter of William Prior Sharp of Manchester (her mother died at her birth) and granddaughter of Mr and Mrs Achurch Ward, well-known performers at the Theatre Royal, Manchester, made her theatre début at nineteen in a curtain-raiser at the Olympic. After a few appearances with Geneviève Ward's company, she toured with her second husband Charles Charrington [Martin] (d. 1926), with F.R.Benson (playing all the standard Shakespeare leads, including Desdemona, Ophelia, and Lady Macbeth), and with Herbert Beerbohm Tree. *A Doll's House* was her first major success. To produce it, the Charringtons had obtained the funds for a week's engagement at the Novelty by signing with Williamson, Garner & Musgrove for a joint engagement to tour the antipodes for two years at £25 a week, and had then mortgaged the salary. Although their Ibsen experiment brought them instant acclaim, they were unable to delay their departure for Australia, and the production was withdrawn on 29th June.

On the evening of 16th June Shaw had sat beside Janet Achurch at the *Doll's House* celebration dinner in the saloon of the Novelty. It was their first meeting. "Interesting young woman," he noted in his diary. Shaw's lecture, which bore the improbable title "Acting, by one who does not believe in it; or the place of the Stage in the Fool's Paradise of Art," was delivered before the Church and Stage Guild on 5th February. A "verbatim" report, drafted by Shaw from memory, was published in the *Church Reformer* in March 1889. Among the "indignant" members of the profession present were Oscar Wilde, playwright Edward Rose, and William Archer.]

Dear Miss Achurch

I send you the two books. "Cashel Byron" is supposed to be my

215

classic—my masterpiece—my one complete work of art. Consequently it is in print and I need not trouble you to send it back to me. The other, my fifth and last attempt, was a failure; and as I possess no other copy, if you deprive me of it you will impoverish me much more than you will enrich yourself. It was intended to be a great work. I wrote two huge chapters; discovered that I had nothing more to say; and thereupon gave up fiction & took to Socialism, publishing the two abortive chapters as Book I & Book II of a complete novel, which is, of course, no more complete than I was.

Kindly consider that for years past every Sunday evening of mine has been spent on some more or less squalid platform, lecturing, lecturing, lecturing, and lecturing. At the end of last month I caught a chill for the first time in my life. It ended in a bad throat: I nevertheless had to orate four times in the following week. That settled me. I had to stop positively for a fortnight, and so I got last Sunday free. Otherwise I should not have been able to go to the Novelty; for if you once put off a lecturing engagement for any private consideration whatever, you are lost. But just imagine how old and hackneyed one gets at this sort of thing; and then imagine the effect of being suddenly magnetized, irradiated, transported, fired, rejuvenated, bewitched by a wild and glorious young woman who, fortified against all reprisals, by a happy prior attachment, simply amuses herself by ruthless and careless manslaughter. Under such circumstances the wisest man presents a miserable spectacle of infatuation; and I therefore plead for an indulgent construction of my motives and character. In short, though I shall always be happy to talk any quantity of insincere nonsense to amuse you, yet I, too, have histrionic powers, and can play the serious man on occasion, if no better actor is to be had.

I send you also a lecture I once delivered on Acting, my only public utterance in connection with that art. It was received with inexpressible indignation by all the members of the profession who happened to be present.

My mother has just looked into the room to observe casually that this is the 37th anniversary of her wedding. This does not interest me in the least; but it reminds me of her very Irish criticism of Miss Janet Achurch. On the first night of the Doll's House she looked intently at that gifted actress, and then said, with intense conviction: "That one is a *divil*." But it is necessary to know Irish locutions to appreciate this.

G. Bernard Shaw

To JULES MAGNY

[A/4]

29 Fitzroy Square W
23rd July 1889

[Benôit Malon (1841–93), French politician, was editor of *La Revue Socialiste*. Shaw left for his first visit to the Bayreuth Wagner Festival on 25th July, and returned to London on 4th August after breaking his journey at Nuremberg, Frankfurt, Mainz, Coblenz, and Cologne. His reports on Bayreuth appeared in *The Star* on 1st, 2nd, 6th, and 7th August.]

Dear M. Magny

So long as it is understood that the article will eventually appear, a few months sooner or later can make no difference. Tell Malon that it will soon be reprinted in "Fabian Essays," which will be instantly translated into every known language, living or dead, thereby leaving him lamenting for not having been beforehand.

"Love among the Artists" was finished. It is true that the absence of any conventional winding-up of the story made people believe that the death of "Our Corner" had broken it off short; but the fact is that the book, which I wrote as long ago as 1881, ended exactly as it appeared in print. It was a lame conclusion; but I simply stopped when I had nothing more to say. The customary ending—the marriages of the heroes & heroines—takes place in the middle of the book. But surely it isn't worth translating. Every nation can produce novels enough & to spare for itself.

I start for Bayreuth in a couple of days & shall not be back for nearly a fortnight.—Your English is perfect.

GBS

To EMERY WALKER

[A/1]

29 Fitzroy Square W
5th August 1889

[Walker did the process engravings of the illustrations for Shaw's "Wagner in Bayreuth" article in the October *English Illustrated Magazine*. The firm of B. Schott's Sons controlled the Wagner copyrights. The singers at the Bayreuth festival included Fritz Friedrichs, Amalie Materna (1845–1918), who had created at Bayreuth the rôles of Brunnhilde (1876) and Kundry (1882), Heinrich Gudehus (1845–1909), Therese Malten (1855–1930), and Ernest Van Dyck (1861–1923), who was a favourite in London, especially noted for the rôle of Parsifal. The Wheatsheaf was a vegetarian restaurant in Rathbone Place.]

Dear Walker

It is now seven; and I have made no perceptible impression on my arrears; so I give up the notion of going to Hammersmith.

The enclosed are playbills of three of the performances (only these three operas are being done). With them I send a photolithograph of a page of the pianoforte score of Tristan, as hawked about Bayreuth at a penny. Now I propose that you put these three bills together thus:—

and photo them down to the size that will just go across the Ill. Eng. page. Tristan, by the bye, should be in the middle, between Parsifal & die Meistersinger. On the back you will find a plan of the seats; & I think this ought to be reproduced too on an intelligibly large scale.

Schott ought to be willing to oblige, as the article will help to sell Wagner's works, the copyrights of which are all in his hands. He might get over fresh copies of the bills, *uncreased*, in packages of music from the head quarters at Mainz—that is, Schott's head quarters. If more portraits are wanted, I would suggest Friedrichs and Materna, not in character; Gudehus either in private or at full length as Walther singing the prize song in the last act of Die Meistersinger; and Malten as Kundry (first act & second act) at full length—also a head of Van Dyck as Parsifal. Or, as Gudehus would take up a lot of room at full length, it would be good fun to have his head in private side by side with his head as Walther, the make-up being amusing in this comparison.

I should like to know at once whether illustrations to this extent would be indulged in. For instance, if Malten's portrait as Kundry in the second act were put in, I could refer to it in the text as an example of the German backwardness in the matter of stage costume. Besides, by George, there is no time to lose if the things have to be got from Germany and engraved. I should have brought them over myself on the chance of their being useful; but a difficulty arose at the last moment (I did not see Malten & van Dyck until the last evening) and

Archer assured me that the Nuremberg shops were full of them. But when I got to Nuremberg, there was nothing but the photos of the theatre, of Wagner himself, and of some bad drawings purporting to represent the stage pictures. I shall be at the Wheatsheaf tomorrow at two in case you are that way.

GBS

To HENRY S. SALT

29 Fitzroy Square W
7th August 1889

[C/5]

[Henry S. Salt (1851–1939), former Eton master, vegetarian, writer, and secretary for thirty years of the Humanitarian League, had moved into a labourer's cottage "at a hole called Tilford" in the wilds of Surrey. Shaw had visited the Salts there in 1888, trudging four miles from the railway station in a downpour, and taking his revenge in a devastating article, "A Sunday in the Surrey Hills" (*Pall Mall Gazette*, 25th April 1888). It was James Leigh Joynes, the brother of Salt's wife Kate, who had introduced Shaw to Salt. He was in ill-health for several years before his death.]

I did not originate the reference to the river; but when Webb spontaneously brought it out, I smiled and held my peace. I am convinced that a searching statistical examination would disclose an unexampled death rate for Tilford, due not so much to typhoid fever as to mere weariness of life.

I returned from Bayreuth on Sunday evening. J L J should have come with me had he been equal to Wagnerizing. Mrs Salt ought to go. By starting tomorrow she can just catch the last complete set of performances. Cost—only about £16 per head.

GBS

To MARCUS B. HUISH

29 Fitzroy Square W
8th August 1889

[A/25]

[Marcus Bourne Huish (1843–1921) was editor of the *Art Journal* and author of many books on art. Shaw eventually contributed an article on the painter J.M. Strudwick (1849–1937), published in April 1891.]

Dear Sir

I must apologize for not answering your letter at once; but I was over at Bayreuth when it came, and have only just returned.

I have no doubt I shall find something to write an article on for the Art Journal; but as for suggesting a subject now, that is just what I am constitutionally incapable of doing. Can you relieve me of the initiative; or would you mind leaving the subject open?

yours faithfully
G. Bernard Shaw

To J. STANLEY LITTLE

29 Fitzroy Square W
[A/4]   26th August 1889

[James Stanley Little (1856–1940), author, editor, and honorary secretary of the Shelley Society (1886–87), organised in 1892 the Shelley Centenary celebration at Horsham with Joseph John Robinson (1858–1939), a Sussex justice of the peace and editor of the *West Sussex Gazette*. He was active in the Incorporated Society of Authors and was associated with the movement for the reform of the Royal Academy. *What is Art?* and *What the Boy Thought* were both published in 1884.]

Dear Stanley Little

I have been all over the place from Putney to Bayreuth for a month past; and my correspondence has fallen into abysmal arrear. Today I have an afternoon to spare for writing thirteen letters.

Your "What is Art?" is stimulating. It is refreshing to find a man who can go it at this rate. If you conscientiously rewrite it every few years, revising until you have got the final expression of yourself on each occasion, you will someday have a fine work out of it. At present a lot of it is too hotheaded on matters that are not worth getting into a rage about. However, I am no critic of Art: I hate the whole confounded cultus, which is only a huge sponge to sop up the energies of men who are divinely discontented. If the dockhands came to me tomorrow and said that they were going to start burning and demolishing, but could not make up their minds what to start on, I should recommend them to go for the works of art first as for their most dangerous rivals in the attention of the thoughtful.

[Cecil] Lawson was a genius: I met him a few times about 11 or 12 years ago; and he suggested to me one of the characters in my first novel—an appalling mass of jejune MS which has never seen the light of the compositors case. That is, the character is a rude caricature of him: I do not mean that he suggested it verbally.

Your "What the boy thought" I shake my head at and pass by. A most unworthy literary gambol. Where do you expect to go to when you die?

I sometimes come to a dead standstill for want of a holiday & a country walk; for they work me like a dog on Sundays orating out of doors & indoors. Are there any walks in your neighborhood [Horsham, Sussex]? And can one, for a moderate third class fare, go and come on the same day?

The Press-cutting people [Romeike & Curtice] have sent me nothing from Public Opinion yet.

GBS—otherwise Shaw

To TIGHE HOPKINS

[A/9; X/150.e]

29 Fitzroy Square W
31st August 1889

[Hopkins had asked Shaw for an opinion on signed versus unsigned articles for a contribution called "Anonymity?" which he was preparing for the *New Review* (November 1889 and March 1890). Shaw knew two Runcimans, and it is uncertain to which he refers in this letter. John F. Runciman (1866–1916), secretary of the Fabian Society's Southern Group, later became musical critic of the *Saturday Review*. James Runciman (1852–91), his uncle, an amateur boxing enthusiast and friend of W. E. Henley and Robert Louis Stevenson, had recently corresponded with Shaw urging the dramatisation of *Cashel Byron's Profession*.

Andrew Lang (1844–1912) was the well-known Scottish poet and man of letters. Thomas Babington Macaulay (1800–59), writer and statesman, was a frequent contributor to the *Edinburgh Review* and author of a *History of England* (1848–61). Herbert Spencer (1820–1903), rationalist philosopher, was the creator of a System of Synthetic Philosophy. Charles Stewart Parnell (1846–91) was the Irish Nationalist leader and M.P. Arthur James Balfour (1848–1930), English statesman, was at this time Chief Secretary for Ireland; he later became prime minister. Andrea Ferrara was an eleventh-century broadswordmaker and armourer at Belluno (*c.* 1585). Edward Linley Sambourne (1844–1910), illustrator and cartoonist, was on the staff of *Punch*.]

Dear Hopkins

In vain all these friendly remonstrances. Cashel Byron was but a sermon, after all. Why preach it over again? No sir: you shall have something better than "An U.S." some of these days; but it will not be in the form of a novel. Some time ago I tried novelizing again, and

221

wrote a chapter & a half [*An Unfinished Novel*, published in 1958]; but I could not stand the form: it is too clumsy and unreal. Sometimes in spare moments I write dialogues; and these are all working up to a certain end (a sermon, of course) my imagination playing the usual tricks meanwhile of creating visionary persons &c. When I have a few hundred of these dialogues worked up and interlocked, then a drama will be the result—a moral, instructive, suggestive comedy of modern society, guaranteed correct in philosophic & economic detail, and unactably independent of theatrical considerations. Meanwhile, *I live*. Point out to me any "brilliant" person who can say as much. I repudiate brilliant promise, fiction & political economy as ends. My business is to incarnate the Zeitgeist, whereby I experience its impulse and universality, and it experiences the personal raptures of music.

I perceive that I have not made altogether a bad shot at Runciman's character. Hum!

I have not profoundly considered the subject of signed articles; but I am, roughly & practically speaking, in favor of signatures, because, though I am the most conscientious of men, I write more carefully, and with a keener sense of direct personal responsibility for the soundness of my utterances, when what I write appears over my signature. Furthermore, I write with greater freedom when I bear the whole responsibility myself. Again, I like to get credit for my own brilliancy, because this secures to me personally the full "rent" of my ability, whereas, when I write anonymously, it is absorbed by the newspaper proprietor. This, however, has nothing to do with the public, who are by no means concerned to enrich me at the expense of the proprietor, or to enrich him at mine, so long as they have to find the money equally in both cases. It only explains why I, like all specially dazzling writers, am interested in extending the signature system as far as my best work goes. Another reason for the dazzlers liking it is that it protects them from being discredited by the work of their imitators. There is a pseudo Lang on the Daily News whose articles must sometimes make the flesh of the original merry Andrew creep lest the uncritical public should mistake the copy for the model. Then there are the deadly vendettas that arise out of reviews. When I used to review for the Pall Mall, the barbarous amusement of skinning minor poets alive was in vogue; and an *auto da fe* took place once a month or so with a batch of them, the executioner being sometimes Oscar Wilde, sometimes William Archer, sometimes myself. As only our elementary vices were brought into play; and as the literary manifestations of these are much alike in all men at a couple of pounds

222

a column, there was no saying, in the absence of signatures, which was the real torturer on these occasions; and to this day there are men who hate me for inhumanities perpetrated by Archer or Wilde. No doubt the mistakes compensated each other in the mass; but this did not happen in their incidence on us individually, as the tendency of men to ascribe injuries to persons who know them led to each of us being credited, within his own circle of acquaintances, with the reviews of the whole three. In more serious reviews I have known several instances of the reviewer feeling bound to write to the author confessing his name and address, though this naturally occurred only when the review was dictated by an overwhelming sense of duty, in which case it was invariably a surpassingly disagreeable one. All these private considerations bias the opinions of professional journalists on the subject.

From the point of view of abstract morality it has to be remembered that many newspaper articles are social & not individual products. The journalistic "we" in Macaulay's essays is a fiction because the opinions expressed are not those of the Edinburgh Review editorial staff or of the class to which that staff proposed to act as mouthpiece: they are Mac's own. But the ordinary working journalist, who simply offers his services as a finder and arranger of words for any opinions that may be in want of them and able to pay for them, would, by signing his article, presume on a distinction that the public do not make in literature. Nobody concludes that the carpenters & masons who build a Conservative club are themselves Conservatives, nor will any Baptist compositor refuse a job on a book of Herbert Spencer's. But a writer is supposed to approve of the purport of what he writes; and the radical who writes conservative articles is considered a prostitute. In practice, of course, men are constantly modifying their work to suit the papers which employ them. The whole question of how far that modification should go, is part of the whole question of how far boycotting should go and how far toleration. If I were a watchmaker I should consider myself bound to make a watch for any fellow citizen who ordered it, without going into his political or social opinions. But if somebody ordered an infernal machine apparatus from me, I should feel equally bound to find out what it was wanted for before I consented to make it. In the same way, though Yates does not refuse to employ me as art critic because I am a socialist, he would certainly refuse to employ me as political leader writer. And I do not refuse to write art criticism for him, though I should certainly refuse to write Unionist leaders if he asked me. But I do not say that a Home Ruler, if a journalist, might not sink his opinions as completely as a compositor or reporter, and write, on principle, what he was paid for writing, whether it was Parnellist or Balfourist in its tendency. But he could not honestly write in the first person singular, or indeed in the first person at all; and though he might sign his name and argue that his signature to the workmanship of a Unionist article no more proved him a Unionist than Andrea Ferrara's mark on a sword blade proved him a duellist & assassin, yet who would make such a distinction in the present elementary condition of public opinion on such matters? To cover such cases there would have to be a double signature. Thus, when the editor means the article but doesnt write it, and a professional journalist writes it but doesnt mean it, it could be signed Buckle *inv.*: Brown (or Robinson) *scrip*. And if I wrote an article in favor of Socialism, I could sign it, in the manner of Linley Sambourne, Bernard Shaw *inv. et scrip.*

My practical conclusion is that since a man who writes without conviction in the third person is generally a pest and a bore, and seldom now gets really important work to do, his signature is uncalled for, & his sphere is that of pure news. All articles expressing individual opinions should be signed, without exception. Papers which hide the identity of their contributors are generally ashamed of them.—Will this do?

yrs
GBS

To JULES MAGNY

[A/4]

29 Fitzroy Square W
2nd September 1889

[William Clarke (1852–1901), political journalist and lecturer, was a member of the Executive Committee of the Fabian Society (1888–91). Other contributors to the *Fabian Essays in Socialism* were Annie Besant, Sydney Olivier, Hubert Bland, and Graham Wallas.]

My dear Magny

Thanks for the Revue Socialiste. I have not had time to read it yet. Excuse my not writing sooner; but I am a bad correspondent, my firm principle being never to do today what can be put off till tomorrow.

Sidney Webb has some intention of revising his "Progress of Socialism" for publication in England. It is rather long for a magazine article. You will see by the enclosed that we are getting out a volume of eight essays, all of which would, I think, be well worth translating. If Malon likes my Transition article, he would be sure to like William Clarke's paper on the Industrial Aspect of Socialism. Webb's essay also contains a mass of information.

Besides the Transition article, there is another of mine on the economic basis of Socialism which is, as far as I know, the only demonstration of the origin of "surplus value" by a socialist which is based, not on Karl Marx's Ricardian theory of value, but on the modern theory which has superseded that of Ricardo, and which was supposed by the professors to be fatal to the socialist theory of exploitation.

> In haste, which pray excuse,
> yrs
> GBS

To EMERY WALKER

[C/1]

29 Fitzroy Square W
12th September 1889

[Shaw was seeking a publisher for the *Fabian Essays*. The Fabian Society eventually published the volume at its own expense, which proved a profitable decision.]

I have written to both of 'em already. Putnam has not replied.

If Longmans or Macmillans would publish it *here* on commission for 10%, we should be very well pleased. F. Unwin demanded 20% which was rather too much of a good thing. I believe the book will get boom[ed] tremendously if it is energetically put about. There is nothing like it in the market & it is *commercially unproducible*.

Can you specially recommend a binder?

All Sundays booked up to 1st Dec.

> GBS

To WILLIAM ARCHER

[A/2]

29 Fitzroy Square W
22nd October 1889

[On 18th October Shaw recorded in his diary: "I did a thing that has been in my mind for some time—wrote to Edmund Yates asking him to give the art-criticship to Lady Colin Campbell, as it is no longer worth my while to do so much work for so little satisfaction, not to mention money." Yates replied to Shaw on the 20th, admitting "you have been cavalierly treated by having your articles so frequently omitted—and often and often I have tried for a rearrangement of the paper in order to include your work, and have held my blue pencil quivering in the air before it swooped down for your excision. . . . But if it can be managed, anyhow, I have no idea of loosening my hold on you; I am far too proud of your cooperation" (BM). Shaw submitted his resignation shortly thereafter, though he continued to make an occasional contribution. Later in the year he applied, unsuccessfully, to T. Wemyss Reid for the art-criticship of *The Speaker*, which was to begin publication in January.

Lady Colin Campbell (d. 1911) was the plaintiff in a sensational series of court actions which resulted in her obtaining a judicial separation from her husband, youngest son of the 8th Duke of Argyll, on grounds of cruelty. Subsequently she earned her living as a journalist, and succeeded Shaw as art critic of *The World*.]

You may be interested and amused by the fact that I went for Yates at last on Friday in four glorious pages beginning "Your treatment of me as art critic is monstrous, scandalous &c &c &c" *crescendo molto alla fine*. My proposal was that he should hand over the job to Lady Colin Campbell, who could include the exhibitions in her "Woman's Walks" and to save the £29 odd per an. which I absorb, & which doesnt pay me. Edmund, in reply, is gracefully magnanimous, munificent, pleasantrative, proud of the connection, remorseful for inevitable editorial stinginess as to space. He offers to put all the minor exhibitions on to Lady C.C; to take eight articles a year on the big exhibitions at the usual rate; and to pay me besides £52 a year as retainer. After this I cannot complain as to money; but I am hanged if I know what to say. Taking £52 a year for refusing to write about pictures more than 8 times a year is out of the question; and if I offer, as I probably shall, to undertake the 8 articles alone, leaving myself free to do what I please in other directions, I shall lose the run of the minor shows, which are really necessary to keep one *au courant* with the art world. And yet I cannot afford to go to them on the old paragraph system.

Can you suggest anything? I am tolerably clear about my reply—i.e. refuse the £52; offer to do the eight articles for him; warn him that if some other paper offers me a free run for its money I will transfer my services; and make it clear that the only way to "retain" me is to give me a column a week as well as a pound. All this of course to be put with the tact for which I am famous. But I am not so clear about it as to be indisposed to consider any other view of the case that may occur to you; for I have been so up to the neck in the final throes (mixed; but never mind) of "Fabian Essays" that I have not had time to lay my mind to the thing fairly.

If you can spare the time so soon let me have a line by return, as Y's letter languishes unanswered.

GBS

P.S. Advice to accept the offer as it stands will be rejected as a base dictate of Caledonian prudence.

To SERGIUS STEPNIAK

[A/8]

29 Fitzroy Square W
17th November 1889

[Sir Walter Scott (1826–1910), founder of the Walter Scott Publishing Co., issued a revised edition of *Cashel Byron's Profession* (1889), the "cheap" edition of *Fabian Essays in Socialism* (1890), and *The Quintessence of Ibsenism* (1891).]

Dear Stepniak

Scott has just sent me a copy of "The Career of a Nihilist," for which I shall expect you to thank me, as I intend to send it back to you. The fact is, I bought one of the first copies sold in London: the man was opening the package containing it as I entered the shop; and I arranged with the Star to give me decent space to review it in. But since then, Massingham, the assistant editor, has written to me to say that he has read the book, and is so pleased with it that he wants to do the review himself. I have therefore gracefully retired in his favor; and as I know by experience that you are the person most likely to want a spare copy, I shall send mine by parcels post to you as soon as I hear from you. All I want is a post card to say whether you are still at 13 Grove Gardens.

I have not had time to read further than p. 59, which is too soon for any opinion worth delivering.

yrs
G. Bernard Shaw

To HUBERT BLAND

29 Fitzroy Square W

[X/144]   18th November 1889

[Bland had lectured to the Fabian Society on 15th November on "The Protest of Literature and Sentiment." During the discussion which followed, Wallas had made a statement to which Bland took offence. Mrs Carr Shaw had, since January 1886, been singing mistress at the North London Collegiate School, founded by Frances Mary Buss, famous Victorian advocate of liberal education for women. Prior to that, Mrs Carr Shaw had taught at the Clapham High School. Charles Kingsley (1819–75), clergyman and novelist, was closely identified with Christian Socialism, and the author of *Alton Locke* (1850) and *Yeast* (1851), showing sympathy with the Chartists. Lord George Bentinck (1802–48) was a turf enthusiast who devoted himself to the improvement of horse-racing.]

What I said was that before a man gets to a consciousness of his spiritual self he has to pay a certain price. Of course such language is damnably unscientific; but then as we have not yet discovered the phraseology of the spirit of will, the thing cannot be put scientifically. The ordinary man, leading the ordinary life, never becomes conscious of the will or impulse in him that sets his brain to work at devising ways and reasons. He supposes his life to be a mere matter of logical consequences from a few bodily appetites and externally appointed "duties" with their attendant pains and penalties. If he believes in his soul, it turns out to be a purely materialistic conception of some intangible organ in him that will preserve his individual consciousness after death and play a harp or roast eternally according to certain conditions fulfilled during his life. If such a man is to attain consciousness of himself as a vessel of the Zeitgeist or will or whatever it may be, he must pay the price of turning his back on the loaves and fishes, the duties, the ready-made logic, the systems and the creeds. He must do what he likes instead of doing what, on secondhand principles, he ought. And of course, there is a devil of a fight to acquire the power to do what you like and to get fed and clothed for doing it. You and I, according to the most sacred secondhand principles, should be prosperous men of business, I for the sake of my poor dear mother, who in her old age, has to live on a second floor and eke out the domestic purse by teaching schoolgirls to sing, you for the sake of your clever and interesting wife and pretty children. In bygone days, when I had nothing to shew for myself except rejected MSS. and was reproached over and over again, more or less directly, with being an idle, lazy, heartless, selfish scoundrel, and I myself was too young to

228

have my eyes quite open, I would absolutely go now and then to look after some opening which I had no real intention of taking, but which I still thought it necessary to find some external reason for not taking. No doubt you have done the same thing in one form or another. Now I have no faintest hesitation left. The secondhand system on which I "ought" to have been a stockbroker has absolutely no validity for me. My one line of progress is from writing stories, reviews, and articles, more and more towards writing fully and exhaustively what I like. And of course, my mother, the victim of my selfishness, is a hearty, independent, and jolly person, instead of a miserable old woman dragged at the chariot wheels of her miserable son, who had dutifully sacrificed himself for her comfort. Imagine Mrs Bland as the wife of a horrible city snob with a huge villa, a carriage, and several thousand a year, which is exactly what, on moral principles, it was your duty to have made her. You and I have followed our original impulse, and our reward is that we have been conscious of its existence and can rejoice therein. The coming into clearer light of this consciousness has not occurred to me as a crisis. It has been gradual. I do not proceed by crises. My tendency is rather to overlook changes in myself, and proceed on absolute assumptions until the consequences pull me up with a short turn.

Wallas made my blood run cold for a moment; but he really did not mean it. He was full of the meannesses of Kingsley and the profligacy of Bentinck; and it was about that he was speaking when, by what seemed like an intentional stroke, he made it appear for a moment that he was talking about you in the most personal way. This triumph of dialectics was quite unintended. I attacked him about it when he sat down and he was unmistakably taken aback and probably thought that I was giving an ingenious twist to what he said. Obviously, I think, it was too bad to have been done on purpose; you would have been justified in appealing to the exec. as a court of honor; for that sort of thing would make debating impossible on ordinary lines. However, you passed it off very happily; and the bulk of the audience did not catch the apparent innuendo.

There can be no doubt that the paper was a great success. The Coleridgian part was vital and very well done I think. You must have put a lot of elbow grease into it.

G.B.S.

To THE EDITOR OF *TRUTH*

29 Fitzroy Square W
[X/137]   26th November 1889

[On 20th August 1889, George Daniel Veck (who described himself as a minister) was arrested as an accomplice in the operation of a house of male prostitution at 19 Cleveland Street. Several members of the aristocracy were involved as being clients of the house. The trial was swift and quiet, and the newspapers timidly refrained from any discussion of the incident. It was Henry Labouchere, proprietor of *Truth*, and his editor Horace Voules (1844–1909) who broke the silence. When Ernest Parke (1860–1944), deputy-editor of *The Star* and proprietor of the weekly *North London Press*, followed suit in the latter journal, he was prosecuted for criminal libel by Lord Euston, one of the young aristocrats whose name he had mentioned as a frequenter of the Cleveland Street house. Parke received a jail sentence of one year. Before and during his trial, until the *North London Press* ceased publication in February 1890, Shaw undertook to write the leading articles as a favour to Parke.

Norfolk Island, a territory of Australia, was from 1788 to 1855 a penal colony. Auberon Herbert (1838–1906) was a crusading journalist, editor of *Free Life*. George William Wilshere, Baron Bramwell (1808–92), was a Lord Justice; he drafted the Common Law Procedure Act (1852). Leonard Courtney (1832–1918) was a writer for *The Times*, professor of political economy, and statesman. Onan (Genesis, 38) was Judah's son, whose evasion of his obligation to his brother's widow caused his death. Oneida Creek was the scene of an American communal experiment, founded by John Humphrey Noyes in 1848, involving eugenic mating.

Shaw's letter was rejected by *Truth*.]

Sir

I am sorry to have to ask you to allow me to mention what everybody declares unmentionable; but as a majority of the population habitually flavor their conversation with it to the extent of mentioning it at every sixth word or so, I shall not make matters much worse by a serious utterance on the subject. My justification shall be that we may presently be saddled with the moral responsibility for monstrously severe punishments inflicted not only on persons who have corrupted children, but on others whose conduct, however nasty and ridiculous, has been perfectly within their admitted rights as individuals.

To a fully occupied person in normal health, with due opportunities for healthy social enjoyment, the mere idea of the subject of the threatened prosecutions is so expressively disagreeable as to appear unnatural. But everybody does not find it so. There are among us highly respected citizens who have been expelled from public schools for giving effect to the contrary opinion; and there are hundreds of

230

others who might have been expelled on the same ground had they been found out. Greek philosophers, otherwise of unquestioned virtue, have differed with us on the point. So have soldiers, sailors, convicts, and in fact members of all communities deprived of intercourse with women. A whole series of Balzac's novels turns upon attachments formed by galley slaves for one another—attachments which are represented as redeeming them from utter savagery. Women, from Sappho downwards, have shewn that this abnormal appetite is not confined to one sex. Now I do not believe myself to be the only man in England acquainted with these facts. And I strongly protest against any journalist writing, as nine out of ten are at this moment dipping their pens to write, as if he had never heard of such things except as vague and sinister rumours concerning the most corrupt phases in the decadence of Babylon, Greece and Rome. All men of the world know that they are constantly carried on by a small minority of people, just as morphine injecting or opium smoking are constantly carried on; and that wherever the passions are denied their natural satisfaction (as on Norfolk Island, for instance) the alternative will become correspondingly general unless it is prevented by stringent surveillance.

I appeal now to the champions of individual rights—to Mr Herbert Spencer, Mr Auberon Herbert, Lord Bramwell, Mr Leonard Courtney, Mr John Morley, Mr Bradlaugh and the rest—to join me in a protest against a law by which two adult men can be sentenced to twenty years penal servitude for a private act, freely consented to and desired by both, which concerns themselves alone. There is absolutely no justification for the law except the old theological one of making the secular arm the instrument of God's vengeance. It is a survival from that discarded system with its stonings and burnings; and it survives because it is so unpleasant that men are loth to meddle with it even with the object of getting rid of it, lest they should be suspected of acting in their personal interest. If the conduct which its abolition would remove from the category of crime is indeed intolerably repellent to society, persons addicted to it can be boycotted—"hounded out," as the phrase goes. But it is worth mentioning that society, instead of acting up in any such way to its overcharged protestations of horrors, only laughs contemptuously. You, Mr Editor, or I, or any man who knows London life, could without a moment's hesitation, point out at least one gentleman and one lady as to whose character in this respect there is no more doubt than there is as to that of the latest absconder against whom a warrant is out; but we do not find that their social acceptance is much, if at all, less than that of their untainted peers.

231

We are now free to face with the evil of our relic of Inquisition law, and of the moral cowardice which prevents our getting rid of it. When the corruption of children (which is quite on a different footing, and is a legitimate subject for resolute repression) made it necessary the other day to expose a den of debauchees, the Press was paralyzed with superstitious terror; and not a word was said until you, fortified by your parliamentary position, let the cat out of the bag. My friend Mr Parke, promptly following it up, is menaced with proceedings which would never have been dreamt of had he advanced charges—socially much more serious—of polluting rivers with factory refuse, or paying women wages that needed to be eked out to subsistence point by prostitution. One result of this is that the scandals can no longer be ignored by the general Press. The only question now is, shall they be discussed with sane straightforwardness and without affectation; or are they to be darkly hinted at and gloated over as filthy, unmentionable, abominable, and every other adjective and innuendo that can make them prurient and mischievous? If the latter, the discussion will do more harm than all the practices, from the subterfuge of Onan to the peculiar continence of Oneida Creek, which might be persecuted as "abominations" with as much reason as the *poses plastiques* of Cleveland St. For my own part, always reserving the right of the children to careful protection against debauchees, I protest against the principle of the law under which the warrants have been issued; and I hope that no attempt will be made to enforce its outrageous penalties in the case of adult men.

yrs, &c
G. Bernard Shaw

To JULES MAGNY

29 Fitzroy Square W
6th December 1889

[A/4]

[William Saunders (1823–95), a member of the London County Council, was leader of the English Land Restoration League. *Fabian Essays in Socialism* was published in December. To everyone's surprise, the entire edition of 1000 copies sold out within a month and a second impression was hurriedly ordered. The work proved to be a steady seller, going through several editions (Shaw or Webb provided it with new prefaces on four occasions); it remains in print to the present day.]

Dear Magny

I would suggest a more economical distribution of the copies of the Review. It is not necessary to send separate copies to Hyndman & to the S.D.F. The one to Hyndman (who, as far as literature is concerned, *is* the S.D.F.) will suffice. Again if Webb receives a copy and I receive a copy, it is hardly necessary to send a third impersonally to the Fabian Society, which has no library & no journal. Mrs Besant, too, is on the Fabian executive; but she should have her copy with a request that she should introduce it to the notice of the "National Reformer." A copy to T.P. [O'Connor] would be simply wasted; but one to H.W. Massingham, as the Social Democratic editor of the Star, would secure a notice. He is nominally the assistant editor; but it is he who really forces the socialist programme into the Star in spite of T.P., who is merely a Home Ruler & does not believe that socialism is a real political force. Now if they will send a copy to Massingham with an adroit letter conveying that the fact of his being the real progressive power at Stonecutter St is *a matter of continental reputation* (and of course not mentioning me) he will be enormously flattered, and will probably take care that the Review is noticed.

W. Saunders does not know that he is a socialist; and he is such a thorough John Bull that I cannot imagine a French magazine interesting him much. His clientèle consists of [Henry] Georgites, who all mistrust socialism, especially when it is explained in French.

E. Belfort Bax has just undertaken the editorship of a magazine called "Time," published by Sonnenschein, Paternoster Square E.C. If he is not already a subscriber a copy might not be wasted on him.

Why not try a copy on the Pall Mall Gazette? They devote a page every month to the reviews; and they might, out of mere love of novelty, include the R. S.

H.H. Champion, 13 Paternoster Row E.C. represents a certain set among social reformers, and edits the Labor Elector. None of the copies sent to the Fabian or the S.D.F. would come under his notice.

"Fabian Essays" are now in the hands of the bookbinder. W. Clarke's essay is one of them.

Sidney Webb has just demenagé. His new address is 4 Park Villas East. N.W.

GBS

To T. WEMYSS REID

[A/4]
29 Fitzroy Square W
14th January 1890

[T. Wemyss Reid (1842–1905) was a Scottish journalist, manager of Cassell & Co. (1887–1905), and editor of *The Speaker*, which first appeared on 4th January. Shaw's reference is to his unsigned leader, "The Whigs Find a Speaker," in the *North London Press* on 11th January. "The True Radical Programme," Fabian Tract No. 6 (1887) was drafted by Shaw. Spencer Compton Cavendish, Lord Hartington (1833–1908), was a Liberal M.P., who, with Joseph Chamberlain, formed the Liberal Unionist Party (1886); he was opposed to Gladstone's home rule policy, favouring coercion. George Viscount Goschen (1831–1907) was a supporter of Hartington in the formation of the Liberal Unionist Party.]

Dear Sir

Good Heavens! I did not disclaim personal opinion, but personal feeling. Do you take me for a rascal—or at least a greater rascal than I really am? When you throw your Speaker right across my line of march, I must charge at it; for I, alas! have no power to select my antagonists: all I can do is to disclaim private malice in cases where the last word before the onslaught has been a friendly one.

But if you have the power to select your antagonists, why not select me? You know exactly what next Friday's Daily News leader will say; and yet you will read it. You dont know what next Friday's North London Press will say; and yet you wont read it, although it is the expression of a force (not an individual one) which has driven your party like sheep all the way from Nottingham in 1887 to Manchester in 1889. If you think I am pretending to be wise after the event (and there is nothing that sixpence will not think of a halfpenny) invest a penny in "The True Radical Programme" published by the Fabian Society immediately after Nottingham. Compare it with the Daily News of the period; and you will understand why I write with this unaccountable flush of victory on me. The fact is, Webb & I and half a dozen other men who know their own minds and can live on £150 a year, have out talked you, out written you, out worked you, brought your official ring climbing down in all directions with speeches on "social reform" and then set Radical London laughing at their ineptitude.

I have tried to open your eyes to this, and to the fact that your enemies are not before you, but behind you. Last week I made the Speaker the occasion of the first open avowal of the deliberate & irreconcileable hostility between the New Radicalism & the old. You refuse to read it. Then read the Star & watch the struggle between *our* Social Democratic editor & *your* Home Rule Liberal editor. When you have grasped the situation, will you join Goschen & [will] Hartington join us? Home Rule is not eternal; and when it is settled, the *via media* vanishes.

I must not take up your time further. I shall look for your answer from time to time in the Speaker.

yrs

G. Bernard Shaw

To GRAHAM WALLAS

[A/1]

29 Fitzroy Square W
21st January 1890

[Hugh Holmes Gore, a member of the Bristol Town Council and a Fabian, was a leader of the Bristol Sunday Society, whose Sunday school Shaw attended while visiting Bristol the weekend of the 18th to 20th to lecture on "Socialism in Real Life." Sydney (later Baron) Olivier (1859–1943) was one of the early Fabians, serving on the Executive Committee from 1887 to 1899, and a lifelong friend of Shaw and Webb. He became Governor of Jamaica (1907–13). James Rowlands (1851–1920), who had lectured to the Fabians earlier in the month, was M.P. for East Finsbury (1886–95) and Secretary of the Leaseholds Enfranchisement Association. Adolphe Smith (1850–1925), one of the pioneer Socialists in London and a Fabian for many years, was special correspondent for *The Times* and, for over forty years, Special Commissioner of *The Lancet*.

Henry R. Beeton was a stockbroker, at whose home a group that included Shaw, Philip Wicksteed, Herbert S. Foxwell, and Francis Y. Edgeworth had been meeting fortnightly since 1885 to discuss economic questions. This group eventually evolved into the Economic Club. Foxwell (1849–1936), a conservative, was Professor of Political Economy at University College, London, and a lecturer at the London School of Economics, founded in 1895 by the Webbs. Edgeworth (1845–1926), economist and statistician, was Professor of Political Economy at Oxford, and also lectured at the L.S.E. Stanton Coit (1857–1944), American-born ethical culture leader, was president of the West London Ethical Society.]

Your congested liver, whatever else it may have done, has considerably improved your handwriting; but its effects on your spelling have been disastrous. I believe all our livers want shaking up. When you get on your legs again you had better start fencing with [Benjamin] Costelloe. If you do, and can fix the precise spot in him which believes in a god, just snip the button off your foil and stick it well through at that point.

[Emery] Walker wants to know whether there is any prospect of your turning up on the 6th March to lecture at Hammersmith. I have told him that you expect to be beginning again just about then. I was to have lectured there next Sunday; but I have had to substitute [William] Clarke to enable me to go down to Nottingham & do your lectures there. Webb will be at Oxford, setting things right at that seat of learning.

I found the virtuous Gore still coming it over Bristol to an extraordinary extent. His method seems to be the wholesale abuse of his position as a man whom you dont like to refuse when he asks you to do anything. The unscrupulousness with which he asks everybody to do everything takes away my breath. The river at the [Clifton] suspension bridge point bangs the Rhine into a cocked hat. Bax's heroine who jumped over "without sustaining constitutional injury" now leads strikes & is a noted character. She is, however, sensitive on the subject of arostatics; and I ascertained, for Bax's discomfiture, that she took to her bed for nearly a week after her jump. On Sunday morning I went to the Sunday School, where we sang Morris's chants to popular airs, & I conversed speciously on Trade Unions with an amalgamated engineer. An afternoon party to introduce me to the brotherhood & sisterhood was hell, as we stuck in corners & were too shy to mingle. My lecture was second rate; but it was good enough for them: they applauded like mad. The local atheist sat all by himself and defiantly yelled "Hear Hear" whenever the others looked glum or puzzled. On the whole, I like H.H.G.

Olivier's outlines are vague after the influenza: he looks like a plaster statue after an attempt to wash its face by a stupid housemaid. He came down to the Rowlands meeting to say that the Essays were practically sold out, and now *il s'agit de* print another thousand. Rowlands appealed for indulgence on the score of a headache & cold. When he was done, Mrs Besant exposed him; I bashed him down; Webb buttered him up; and Adolph Smith made a heroic revolutionary speech, without a ray of reason in it, which just saved Rowland's bacon, as it gave him something to reply to. As to the rest of us, he declined combat, happily remarking that there was no difference between us except one of principle, we being in favor of Land Nationalization, which he could not give his adherence to, as he advocated taxation of ground rents. He was imperturbably good humoured, and so was able to remove his *débris* with credit.

236

At Beeton's Wicksteed turned up. He had been working out the fact that if a man undertakes productive operations which require a great many tools, they will not be productive at all if he has not tools enough. With a few simple curves he managed to extract from this position a degree of mental confusion that bids fair to last us the whole season. Beeton declared that the point was most original; and we all regretted the absence of Foxwell & Edgeworth, who carefully stayed away to avoid the announced sociology. I spoke to Beeton as to the change that would inevitably come over our meetings if he went in for you & for sociology. He, much alarmed, voted for sticking to the curves & the blackboard & I said I would convey this to you. Stanton Coit turned up & did not utter a syllable the whole evening; but one Robert Hammond, of Hilldrop, Highgate, a Sheffield candidate, was bluster-ous, several times snatching the chalk from Wicksteed & improvising curves of his own. He says he is game to have the sociology at his own house if you will come. He evidently wants tips for Sheffield.

[James] Runciman writes that Fabian Essays have knocked him endways—that he sees now that things which he had settled long ago in his mind were settled in sheer ignorance & that he has thrown away his chance in life &c &c &c.

GBS

To CHARLES CHARRINGTON

[T/1(A/4)]

29 Fitzroy Square W
28th January 1890

[Janet Achurch and Charrington were still in Australia. Later they toured New Zealand, Tasmania, India, and Egypt, not returning to England until 1892. Arthur Bingham Walkley (1855–1926) was dramatic critic of *The Star* (1888–1900), under the pseudonym "Spectator," and of *The Times* (1900–26). Shaw's *Man and Superman* was dedicated to him. Brandon Thomas (1856–1914), actor and playwright, is best known as the author of *Charley's Aunt* (1892). Shaw's unsigned review of *The Gold Craze* appeared in the *Manchester Guardian* on 2nd December 1889. Amy Roselle (1844–95) had made her début in E. A. Sothern's company; she appeared frequently with her husband Arthur Dacre (d. 1895), leading man to Modjeska. Sir Walter Besant (1836–1901), was the author of numerous popular novels, several of which were concerned with social conditions.

The Scarlet Letter, dramatised from Hawthorne's novel by "Alec Nelson" (Edward Aveling) was produced by Charrington, with Janet Achurch as Hester Prynne, at the Olympic on 5th June 1888. Kate Rorke (1866–1945) was leading lady to Sir John Hare and Sir George Alexander. She created the rôle of Candida in the first public performance of Shaw's play in London at the Court Theatre, 1904. Florence O'Driscoll (d. 1939), an Australian, was a Chartered Civil Engineer, journalist, M.P. for South Monaghan (1892–95), and Parliamentary Whip. Shaw had met him in London a few years earlier. Ada Rehan (1860–1916), Irish comedienne, emigrated to America where she was leading lady to Augustin Daly for many years. After her retirement, she became companion to the American poet Amy Lowell. Shaw made an unsuccessful effort in 1901 to induce Miss Rehan to undertake the rôle of Lady Cicely in *Captain Brassbound's Conversion*; eventually it was played by Janet Achurch and, later, by Ellen Terry.]

Dear Charrington

This is return of post as nearly as I can get to it. My hours that make my days, my days that make my years, follow one another pell mell into the maw of Socialism; and I am left ageing and out of breath without a moment of rest for my tired soul. However, this is no news for you. But if I had time I would have the law on them, damn them, for overcharging my letter; for I weighed it & stamped it with my own hand, according to Act of Parliament.

I published some of the matter contained in your last. In sending your first account you did not make sufficient allowance for the inveterate pessimism & diffidence of Archer, who proceeded to draw, in the Pall Mall [Gazette], a picture of the failure of The Doll's House which positively plunged London into gloom. Your letter relieved my mind so much that it seemed important to me that the public mind should also be relieved. I therefore proceeded to *souffler* Walkley, the dramatic critic of the Star, who duly announced in his next *feuilleton* that the accounts published had been misleading, and that the Doll's House was, in Australia, a greater success than it had been in London. I then attacked Archer privately; but he shook his head and declared that he had noticed that actors were no judges of the success of a piece. When I cited the impression made at the Novelty I found that he had gradually convinced himself that the play ran there for about three nights amid a hail of dead cats, sixteen-a-shilling eggs, brickbats & gingerbeer bottles, and that on the fourth night there was no audience. The climax was his telling me that my own judgment was of no value, partly because I am a lunatic, but chiefly because my head was turned by my first conversation with a pretty actress. In transports of rage at this, I replied in unmitigated terms; compared him to Helmer; and finally, grown quite reckless, taunted him with having sent to the pretty actress the notice which he had promised his wife to throw into the

238

wastepaper basket. That evening I was terrified by a visit from Mrs Archer, who came, as I thought, to have it out with me; but it turned out to be only a revival of Archer's old bilious headaches, and a consequent need for me to take his place at the production of Brandon Thomas's "Gold Craze" at the Princess's. The "Gold Craze," in which Amy Roselle trailed a long robe of white China silk through the primeval forests of the Congo, was an expensive & ghastly failure. However, this is by the way. The main point is that Miss—Miss—Miss —I forget the name: the lady who played Nora to your Dr Rank at the Novelty—if she happens to be writing to Archer, should roundly rate him for belittling her success & Ibsen's; and should urge him to be not faithless but believing. For all this time the man is writing his World *feuilletons* in the most unsettled way, and is lavishing his time & substance on translations of Ibsen which he is editing for Scott at a ridiculously low price. And the more Ibsen-mad he gets (he has never been the same man since June last) the more he declares that Ibsen is bound to be a dismal failure.

Have you seen the prodigious sequel to The Doll's House in the "English Illustrated" for January, by Walter Besant? I cannot describe it: I am not artist enough with my pen. The Ibsenites here turned up their noses & said it was beneath notice; but it struck me as being of enormous importance as a representative middle class evangelical verdict on the play. Besides which, the ball must be kept rolling on every possible pretext, so that by the time you come back, everybody who has not seen the Doll's House will feel quite out of it, especially in the provinces. So I made a dash, and wrote a sequel ["Still after the Doll's House"] to Besant's sequel, obtaining a perfectly free hand by presenting it free gratis & for nothing to Bax, who has become editor & part proprietor of "Time." It appears in this number (Feb). I send you the two sequels, Besant's & mine. The worst of it is that my sequel is declared to be beneath the level even of Besant's—to be slosh, rubbish, dull dreary Philistine stuff &c &c &c. It is "not even comic" they say. They are all wrong: it is first rate; but the dramatic form hides its merit from them: they want more description to explain how Nora said the things to Krogstad. Besides, they have not taken in Besant's sequel, upon which mine depends wholly. These criticisms are of course confined to those who have seen the proofs; but they are tolerably unanimous, Mrs Aveling [Eleanor Marx] having led them off, & Archer agreeing with her to the point of begging me for the sake of my reputation not to publish it. But two people to whom I *read* it rose to the stimulus of the living word, & evidently felt the effect I intended to produce. Anyhow, there will be discussion, and repetition of Doll's House Doll's House Doll's House here, there & everywhere, which is the desideratum.

Rosmersholm & the Lady from the Sea have been published here. Rosmersholm was written expressly by Providence for you & your wife. You were created & brought together for no other end than that you should play it. Others could do this bit well & that bit cleverly; but you alone can sustain the deep black flood of feeling from the first moment to the last. This is the power that makes me remember, out of dozens of forgotten matinees, "The Scarlet Letter" as I remember the Bayreuth performance of Tristan & Isolde. Never read any criticism but this: it is the only one that really concerns you.

I should like to see you as Shylock, but would not cross the street to see Mrs Forgetfulness as Portia, which I could play myself on my head. Isabella in Measure for Measure would draw me. When you become a past master of your art, try Leontes in A Winter's Tale. It is better business than Othello, as will be demonstrated some day—why not by you? [Frank] Benson is playing Shakespear here with fair success. I saw his Midsummer Night's Dream. He played Lysander; but neither he nor anyone else in the company except Kate Rorke (Helena) rose above mediocrity. It is not the illiterate, indifferent, professional mediocrity, but the literate, amateur, enthusiastic mediocrity; and so, on the whole, as the thing was staged with some taste, it was fairly enjoyable. Kate was not a bit Helena; but she spoke musically & looked well, for which be all her sins forgiven her. I have been so busy of nights that I have seen nothing else that would at all interest you to hear of.

I saw the [Unwin] edition de luxe of the Doll's House the other day for the first time. I put aside a guinea to get a photograph of Nora & help off the enterprise when I first heard about it; but when the dock strike came I said "Danton, no weakness" and sent my sovereign to the east end—or rather your sovereign; for as I had already resolved to part with it, the sacrifice cost me nothing except the photograph; and if she thinks I care about that she is very much mistaken. Women are nothing to me. This heart is a rock: they will make grindstones for diamonds out of it when I am dead. But the photographs published, though not ill selected, are not those I would have chosen. Archer has a frameful on his wall. One of them, Nora holding the tambourine aloft, has a touch of the woman at her completest and noblest. Photographically, you look too young to inspire confidence as a medical man, though you looked responsible enough on the stage.

240

By the bye, Archer particularly wants to know *did you pray* at the end of the Doll's House when you did Helmer?

Our book "Fabian Essays in Socialism" is going off pretty well here. The first thousand disappeared like smoke.

I have escaped the influenza; but it has sent me touring to the provinces delivering lectures for men who are down with it, and overworked me generally.

Give my compliment to Florence O'Driscoll if you see him again. His memory is as green as his beard is red.

"Cashel Byron" was reported a failure in October last. Only 2500 copies gone—should have been 10,000 at least. Have not heard of it since. I cannot do novels now: I have grown out of it. My next effort in fiction—if I ever have time to make one—will be a play. Someday I shall write a piece for you and Janet Rehan—or is it Ada Achurch?— my memory is a wreck.

"Time" is now practically in the hands of the Avelings, who run it for Bax. Suppose you do an article—"Our Adventures with the Doll's House in Australia," it would be sure of a refuge there even if the other magazines (which pay better—Time is doing business at rates varying from nothing to five shillings a page) hardened their hearts against it, which I dont think likely.

Farewell for the present: may the wellspring of your powers never run dry.

GBS

To T. P. O'CONNOR

[A/4; X/136.e]

29 Fitzroy Square W
5th February 1890

[Although Shaw threatened to resign as *The Star*'s musical critic in February (in an effort to prod O'Connor into increasing his salary), he did not withdraw until May, when he had concluded arrangements with Edmund Yates to transfer his services to *The World*. On 15th May O'Connor wrote to Shaw: "I am extremely glad to hear that you have got the excellent offer of the World. Though I do not think you treat me quite fairly, that does not alter my regard for you, and then I make large allowance for the latitude in their private relations of those who preach the fraternity of all mankind. Take the offer by all means . . ." (BM).]

My dear T.P.

The giving up of the Musical Mems will be a gigantic—a Himalayan

241

mistake. However, a wilful man must have his way. I have already finished this week's column. Next week's shall be valedictory.

Reviewing is hell. I had enough of it on the Pall Mall. I can do the best literary causerie in London (not a word about books in it); but nothing short of twelve guineas a week would tempt me to begin it. I hate literature. If I tumble to the ground I shall avail myself of this soft place which you have made for me so as to avert the painful spectacle of Corno di Bassetto left sitting on his bottom; but I think I shall pull through without a larger dose of adversity than I need to shake me out of my present grouse. Nothing so fatal to an artist as a regular income.

I shall do a reprint from the Star of "Wit & Wisdom from C. di B." or something of that sort.

If you become an irreclaimable Whig, we shall exchange fearful blows as time goes on, but none below the belt. Besides, I shall knock the stuffing out of Honest John [Morley] & convince you even before you find him out.

GBS

To UNIDENTIFIED CORRESPONDENT

29 Fitzroy Square W
11th February 1890

[G/2]

Dear Sir

I have now read your pamphlet. You have got unusual literary power; but you lack skill, intellectual training, and discretion. Your sentences are often ambiguous, awkwardly punctuated, and even ungrammatical; and you have actually had stereoed 26 pages in which I have spotted nearly three dozen misprints offhand. It is only by scrutinizing every letter & weighing every word and stop anxiously that you will ever become a workmanlike writer & get a style of your own. Not, you understand, by aiming at "style," but by laboriously seeking until you find the exact expression of your own thought. If you examine the cautious, formal, but conscientious wording of Carlyle's early writings, you will see with what hard work he attained to the freedom & directness as well as the force of his mature style. Now, you have tried to jump head over heels into *his* style (not your own) at once; and although you have not made such a desperate bungle of it as your cheek deserved, yet you have done nothing but say at second hand what he said at first hand—and said so well, that there is not the least occasion for you to come forward & finish the job, especially as things, bad as they are, are better in your time than they were in his. The world does not now want to be told that society is rotten: it wants to know how it came to be rotten and what it should do to get sound. There is no use in telling it that the sparrows are all fed and that you are Christianity and Democracy & so forth. It knows better. Doubtless if you were a great poet, or a great prose writer with a style of your own, it would accept you as microcosmically all that you declare yourself, for the sake of reading your book. But at present it will see at a glance that you are simply a young man made very sensitive by privations of all sorts constantly racking a hungry talent; that you are fresh from discovering that the majority of your "brothers," as you call them, are fools (you haven't as yet half sounded their incapacity for your ideals); and that you have become excited over Carlyle's books & are lashing out into a clever imitation of his pamphlets. This will not interest it in the least: it is accustomed to it & a little impatient of it. Until you can amuse it, interest it, fascinate it by your artistic skill & the novelty of your originality, it will concern itself no more about your impulses & sufferings than if you were a tramway horse.

If you can starve it out, keep from drink, & hammer away, you may find yourself a coolheaded skilled writer or preacher some of these days. To begin with, I advise you to drop exhortation & cultivate information & accuracy. But if you depend on other people's advice, you will do little good. A man of your sort is, and must remain, alone in the world. I worked at literature for nine years without earning a pound; and at present I can do little more than scrape along as a bachelor, vegetarian, teetotaller, non smoker &c. My "fame and influence" are quite illusory from the public's point of view.

I hope I have not expressed myself too roughly.

yours truly
G. Bernard Shaw

To H. W. MASSINGHAM

[A/4; X/136.e]

29 Fitzroy Square W
28th February 1890

Dear Massingham

I have been driven by destitution to make up my Star accounts; and I find that the paper owes me no less than £7.0.1 since the 30th March

1889, for expenses, although most of the items are on the cheapest scale. This does not, by the bye, include the expenses of the *première* at Amsterdam, or Bayreuth, or Bristol, or anything outside London & Sydenham. £1.5.0 of it, however, is for admissions to the Crystal Palace, because they did not send the usual season ticket, though they did send stalls for the concerts. I think they ought to be asked again: if they dont respond it would be obviously cheaper to buy an ordinary guinea season ticket. Why not sarcastically offer to pay them for a transferable season ticket for the use of the paper. They do much for papers without a tenth of the Star's claim on them.

I find that it is impossible for me to continue as I have been doing lately. This week I have had to attend five concerts; have advanced fourteen shillings from my exhausted exchequer; and have written the Bassetto column, all for two guineas. It cannot be done at that rate. If the column is to cover all the concerts, it is worth five guineas. If not, I must send in a notice nearly every morning & get decently paid for it. The English Illustrated, the New Review, the Art Journal & the [Scottish] Art Review are all on for getting work from me. The Bassetto business stops the way & so is—at its present figure—a losing game.

For weeks like the present, in which the Eight Hours Question is deliberately & pointedly shelved & the front page a blasphemy against the Fabianism which made it famous, I shall expect double terms. Why the devil couldnt that have been reserved until North St Pancras was safe? Do you suppose that St Pancras is Partick [a district of Glasgow, considered a "safe" constituency for Labour]?

GBS

To T. P. O'CONNOR

29 Fitzroy Square W

[A/4]
4th March 1890

[The Nottingham and Manchester programmes were the reform policies evolved and advocated by the Liberal Party at annual conferences in those cities. James Stuart (1843–1913) was Liberal M.P. for Hoxton (1885–1900). In the by-election at North St Pancras on 4th March, the Liberal Unionist candidate, Thomas H. Bolton (1841–1916), a solicitor supported by *The Star*, was elected to parliament. The *People's Press*, staffed largely by Fabians, had absorbed the foundering *North London Press* during Ernest Parke's imprisonment. Shaw subsequently wrote two unsigned leaders for it, on 10th May and on 26th July 1890, the first being an attack on John Morley, O'Connor, and the Land Purchase Bill.]

Dear T.P.

Hang it all, you must not go on in this fashion merely because I have been doing all I can to ruin you for the last two or three months. If Massingham goes, my going with him will (1) double the *éclat* of his martyrdom, and (2) be an additional proof of your alleged bad editing. He foresaw what you would do when he sent on that letter; and he knows that at the two guinea rate I can afford to go better than to stay.

Now there is a difference between M's line of battle with you and mine. From the first you have known my line. When you elected to stand in with Morley, it was as obvious that I must fight you like mad, as if I had elected to stand in with Balfour. But I was not bound to any personal malice; & I have not felt any. I have raged freely round and declared that you were an idiot, that the Gladstonians were taking advantage of your indifference on the social question to buy you, and that they would infallibly bilk you, since political parties only pay debts to those whom they fear, and the Liberals have nothing to fear except from the Social Democrats who have already kicked them from the Nottingham programme of '87 to the Manchester programme of '89. But these are the commonplaces of political warfare. Massingham has gone beyond this, and is fighting with both hands by attacking not only your policy, but your diligence in fulfilling your Stonecutter St official functions. With that I have nothing to do. In the article which you brought before the directors' meeting, and which of course was an immense success with them (read a few more & they will make me editor straight off), you will not find the faintest suggestion that editor No. 1 was less active or interested than No. 2. Therefore I submit that your giving me the sack is a breach of our articles of war. Bassetto is outside the controversy; and as to your saying that his articles are unsuitable, you might as well say that Shakspere is undramatic. Look at your Friday circulation.

I propose, then, if you dont mind, to hold on until your difference with M. is settled. He is now in high spirits, riding for a fall—for paragraphs, interviews, and the position of the man whom no advanced Radical journal can do without. In the background there are large schemes—Stead hungering for his daily meal of leader &c—the Star drooping without its magic Fabian atmosphere on the first page and its Bassetto enchantments inside—an election followed by a Liberal majority wallowing in treachery to Ireland, to the London Radicals, & to all who put trust in them and who are not unprovided uncles or

245

nephews of the official ring. Then you have to deal with Stuart, Webb, the washerwoman and other corks bobbing up & down on the flowing tide. At the last moment you may realise that a victory over M. would be a victory of Samson between the pillars. M. may even beat you if the directors realise it through anything going wrong today in North St Pancras. Anyhow, I do not want to quarrel with my *five* guineas a week until I am convinced that the Star is irrevocably done for, when I shall clear out for my own sake. But I am damned if I will go on after this month for two guineas. You know as well as I do that work at once so conscientious & brilliant cannot be kept up at such rates.

I still say, as I said two years ago, that you are a lost man if you stop punishing the mere Liberals for a moment. *Events have hitherto confirmed everything I said.* You are making a present of the greatest opportunity of your life to Stuart, Massingham & Stead. I am surprised at you.

yrs sincerely
G. Bernard Shaw

PS. I am not now writing the articles in the People's Press (late North London).

To UNIDENTIFIED CORRESPONDENT

[A/5]

29 Fitzroy Square W
6th March 1890

[The recipient of this letter carefully cut his name and address from the foot of the last leaf. Fabian Tract No. 5, drafted by Sidney Webb and revised by Shaw, was published in May 1887, and was frequently revised and reprinted thereafter. Michael G. Mulhall (1836–1900), Irish statistician, was the compiler of a *Dictionary of Statistics* (1883).]

Dear Sir

I send you herewith a couple of statistical tracts published by the Fabian Society. In the first paragraph of No. 5 ("Facts for Socialists") you will find Mulhall's estimate of the annual production *per head* as £20.10.0 in 1840, £26.4.0 in 1860; & you can compare these with the estimate of £35 per head for 1881. As to the way in which, with private property, the increase of population produces poverty in spite of growing productive power, you will find that explained in the first Fabian Essay. You will also find, however, under the heading "Illth" that figures compiled largely from the Income Tax returns of rich men are not to be depended on as indices of social wealth. Still, no one, as far as I am aware, seriously contends that we have reached the limit beyond which every additional mouth swallows more than its attached pair of hands can add to our stores of subsistence.

The problem of population faces all parties, whether they are socialists or ordinary politicians accepting private property as eternal. Even those who are convinced that there is room for hundreds of millions more men, are not thereby relieved from the necessity of considering *how rapid a rate of increase* we can afford to reach this end. Though every man wants more money, he can starve himself by saving too fast to leave himself enough to spend. Similarly, though a country may want twenty millions more people, it would be ruined if every living couple began producing twenty children at intervals of a year.

A little consideration of the obvious economics of division & concert of labor will shew you that up to a certain point 2 men will produce more than twice as much as one, 6 men more than two isolated groups of 3, and so on. In the cotton industry a single man can now do what it took 200 men to do a century ago. But the limit to the quantity of raw material available makes it evident that this increase cannot go on *ad infinitum*. Theoretically, a time must come when men would be manufacturing all the raw material as fast as Nature could reproduce it. After that a growth of population would mean new hands to lighten the work, but new mouths also to share a stationary product. Before that point was reached, people might have already urged that instead of more babies it would be well to have more luxury & more elbow room. Or even after it was passed, they might say: "No matter: let us put up with simpler fare & wear our clothes a little longer before casting them off for new ones, and we can take out the saving in more babies." Consequently, if you represent the increase of population by the extension of a line (A.B) and the product per head by perpendiculars to it, a line drawn through the tops of the perpendiculars will describe a curve representing the growth of the return to labor as the number of hands brought to bear upon it increases. Such a curve would rise; reach a maximum; and fall. Roughly, you would say that D.G, the

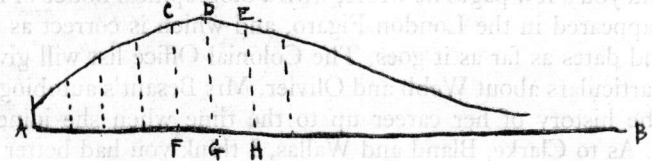

maximum of the curve, was the point at which to regulate population so that it should remain constant instead of increasing; but practically the point chosen might be C F or E H, since, though neither of these is the maximum of the curve of material wealth, either might be the maximum of the curve of happiness produced by material wealth plus human society.

yours truly
G. Bernard Shaw

To JULES MAGNY

[H/4]

29 Fitzroy Square W
14th April 1890

[Magny was writing a series of articles on the Fabians for the *Revue Socialiste*. These appeared in October 1890 and in February, May, and October 1891. Olivier's lecture on Zola, delivered on 18th April, was the first in a series of seven Fabian lectures on "Socialism in Contemporary Literature." Shaw closed the series on 18th July with a paper on Ibsen. The "biographical" sketch of Shaw in the *London Figaro*'s "Coming Men" series, on 10th August 1889, was an *auto*biographical sketch, though it may have been revised by the editor. Annie Besant's *Autobiographical Sketches* was published in 1885.

Shaw and Webb had visited Paris on 3rd to 8th April; their activities were reported by "Corno di Bassetto" in *The Star* on 11th April. Shaw had gone primarily to attend the "Soirée Musicale et Littéraire du Vendredi Saint," in which Sarah Bernhardt performed the dual rôles of the Virgin Mary and Mary Magdalen in Edmond Haraucourt's "mystery," *The Passion*.]

Dear Magny

I am really ashamed of having so neglected my promise as to the information you want about the Fabians. Olivier held out delusive hopes of the completion of the enclosed scrap of Fabian history before Easter. I intended to send it to you, finished or not, before leaving town for my holiday, which I spent in Paris, but in the rush of letter writing on the last day I forgot it. Olivier is now so busy with his paper on Zola, that it is useless to go at him again. For the present all I can do is to send you a few pages he wrote, with a biographical notice of myself which appeared in the London Figaro, and which is correct as to the facts and dates as far as it goes. The Colonial Office list will give you some particulars about Webb and Olivier. Mrs Besant's autobiography gives the history of her career up to the time when she joined the Fabian. As to Clarke, Bland and Wallas, I think you had better apply

248

to them individually for information. This would enable you to make a sketch which you could submit to us for correction—we should be forced to correct it for our own sakes as soon as we saw that it was actually going into print. This is the only plan of getting the thing done that occurs to me. There is no use in depending on us: we are so busy that we are sure to keep promising and putting off and apologizing and finally doing nothing.

Webb and I decorated the wreaths at the Fosse des Federés with our visiting cards. It struck me that the time has come when it might be possible to get a handsome international subscription for a monument there. Webb innocently asked the way to the "Fosse des Communards"; but the official declined to entertain that expression and insisted on the term Federal. Was this a very shocking solecism on our part?

yours truly
G. Bernard Shaw

To JULES MAGNY

29 Fitzroy Square W
[H/4]   16th April 1890

[The Fabians held their meetings in Willis's Rooms for many years; large meetings, special lectures, and dinners were held in the St James's Hall Restaurant. The office of *The Star* was in Stonecutter Street. Cesar de Paepe (1842–90), a Député de Bruxelles, was the author of *Le Suffrage universel et la capacité politique de la classe ouvrière* (1890).]

Mon cher Magny

Pourquoi pas venir au Fabien Vendredi soir et amener Standring pour faire briller son esprit par contact avec celui d'Olivier. Il y'a des longues années que nous n'avons vu notre Georges chez nous. Il se borne de faire une fortune colossale de l'imprimerie de nos brochures; mais il nous tient dans une telle méprise que jamais ne s'est il fait voir ni à Willis's Rooms ni à St James's Restaurant. Aussi il m'a flanqué des lettres dérisoires a Stonecutter St, alléguant que mes anecdotes sont "nonsens lepreux."

Mon sejour à Paris a produit des effects funestes sur mon Français. D'abord j'ai parlé avec difficulté, mais dans une façon absolument classique. Maintenant je parle très courrament mais aussi tout-à-fait a l'Anglaise. Les Parisiens sont très ignorant de leur langue natale. Ils

249

m'ont prié de parler Anglais quand j'ai essayé de m'expliquer en style du pays.

Je n'ai pas encore lu Cesar de Paepe; mais sur votre suggestion je ferai a point d'en faire.

Mes soirées sont très occupées avec des meetings, concerts, Carl Rosa operas &c; mais j'espère de me rendre chez vous avant que le diable m'enlève pour faire des critiques a l'enfer.

Au Fabien vous serez toujours le bienvenu. Standring aussi, s'il daigne nous honorer.

Est ce que vous pouvez comprendre cette lettre? Moi, je ne peux pas quoique je viens de l'ecrire.

Mes souffrances de mal de mer étaient atroces. J'ai retenu mon socialisme seulement.

tout à vous
GBS

To WILLIAM ARCHER

29 Fitzroy Square W
[H/2]   27th April 1890

[The "drunkard" was Pakenham Beatty, whom Shaw had found that afternoon "just recovering from delirium tremens" (Diary). The article lost under the wheels of a train and rewritten was an unsigned review of Sir Frederic Cowen's opera *Thorgrim*, published under the pseudonym "By Reuter" in *The Hawk* on 6th May.]

I was prevented from coming to tea by the plight of my drunkard, who, still in a state of horror, was surrounded by his whispering relatives, who were assembled as if for a funeral. I dispersed them with roars of laughter and inquiries after pink snakes &c, an exhibition of bad taste which at last converted the poor devil's wandering apprehensive look into a settled grin. I then took him out for a walk, and endeavored to relieve his mind of the strong illusion that nothing can ever tempt him to taste liquor more. Tomorrow he goes to a retreat at Rickmansworth, to be reformed. When we got back to the house it was too late for the train before the 7, which does not reach Paddington until 7-20. In the train I wrote an article; but I jumped out before the train stopped; and the damned thing fell under the wheels and was *coupé, haché*, like the two men in [Zola's] "La Bête Humaine." So I had to hurry home and write it over again.

250

I am to send all Ibsen's works to Rickmansworth to help in restoring the lowered moral tone of the patient. They forced him to make his will in the crisis of his agony; and he cannot get rid of the notion that the next thing must be his funeral.

GBS

To J. STANLEY LITTLE

[C/4]

29 Fitzroy Square W
19th May 1890

[Harry Furniss's *Royal Academy Antics* had been published that week. Frederick Goodall (1822–1904) was a Royal Academy artist whose work Shaw abhorred, and whom Horace Voules wanted him to "puff." A fighting interview with Voules on 16th May had led to Shaw's resignation as art critic.]

Am simply smothered, between pictures for Truth & music for the World. On Sundays I have to harangue the proletariat—am booked right up to the end of June; so Saturday to Monday is not for such as I. When the season slackens I will try to get down some day. I have got Furnisse's book. Truth is quarrelling with me because I dont admire Goodall!!! My connection with the paper may not survive the language I have used in consequence.

In hot haste
GBS

To W. E. HENLEY

[A/15]

29 Fitzroy Square W
1st July 1890

[William Ernest Henley (1849–1903) was a poet, dramatist, and editor of the *Scots* (later *National*) *Observer*, to which Shaw had contributed an unsigned article on Hans Richter (1843–1916), who had conducted the first performance of Wagner's *Ring* cycle at Bayreuth in 1876. Shaw subsequently contributed an unsigned article on Sir Arthur Sullivan (6th September), and perhaps others.]

Edward John Trelawny (1792–1881), English sailor and adventurer, was a friend of Shelley and Byron. *Deacon Brodie* (produced at Prince's Theatre on 2nd July 1884) and *Robert Macaire* (unproduced; published 1892) were written by Henley in collaboration with Robert Louis Stevenson (1850–94). Sir Charles Wyndham (1837–1919), actor-manager who produced the best-known plays of Henry Arthur Jones, rejected *Candida* in 1895 because it was "twenty years ahead of its time." Sir Herbert Beerbohm Tree (1852–1917), famous actor-manager, was the original Higgins, in 1914, to Mrs Patrick Campbell's Eliza in *Pygmalion*.]

My dear Henley

Archer dealt faithfully; but I had heard of that deplorable darkness as to Wagner, and so had to overcharge my article to receive your mis-guided watering down. On the whole, you have done your spi- I mean your watering most artistically, and without lacerating my feelings; for though your "perhaps a little passe" was maliciously intended, it reads like a keen Wagnerian sarcasm. However, there is one point on which I have a grievance. I am a writer of English and not of grammar. If the grammarian cannot square his pedantries with my English, why, so much the worse for his pedantries. I was amazed to find you the slave of the creature to such a depth that you actually turned my living vernacular indicatives into dead, ridiculous, and utterly incorrect subjunctives—you, who have such a fine artistic feeling for language when you write verse. You destroy the social character of my prose by thus distorting it to fit a school-manufactured abstraction. I write as men speak: when my subjunctives come, they are memorable for ever. Get thee behind our Henley, oh Procrustes.

I had better not do the other articles for you. It is only trifling with the subject to get me to write for you if you are an anti-Wagnerite, or, for the matter of that, a Wagnerite either. Let the Wagnerite get on his Rozinante (the critical essay) and make Wagner his Dulcinea to be tilted for with the old literary lances in the good old slashing style. Then you can get on your steed and tilt for Dulcinea Berlioz against him. You might as well tilt for Dulcinea Poe against Dulcinea Ibsen, as far as I am concerned; for the whole Dulcinea system only makes me laugh. I could write good articles enough on the subjects you name; but you would not like them; and why should I rasp your nerves when there are plenty of fellows who will be glad of the job, and will do it to your heart's content? I have as much musical writing as I can stomach on the World; what I should like to do in my spare time is political writing. I thirst for the blood of the Liberal party; and if ever your sham fight with them becomes a real one, you may come to me for a lead. I understand the business; and you, Lord bless your innocence, have had to invent your own politics for yourself, as you compose poems, except that the poems come naturally.

By the bye, James Runciman lately struck up a correspondence with me on the strength of a blathering prizefighting novel which I wrote in my verdant days, and which took his fancy. He is a great admirer of yours (so am I, in a way) though you have, it appears, quarrelled in the usual course. He has got that Trelawnyish, boyish, Alone-in-the-Pirates'-Lairish note that you and Stevenson sound occasionally. And this reminds me that I once went with Archer to see a play of yours called Deacon Brodie, which had this very note for its theme, as I understand it. The play impressed me: I should not be surprised if it turned up trumps some day. It was a pity that Irving did not get hold of your Robert Macaire (which Archer lent me) before he played the part at the Lyceum. The old version [by Charles Dumont] had absolutely no literary side at all: it might almost as well have been a ballet. It struck me that Wyndham might, if prompted, take it into his head to put your version up at the Criterion, or Beerbohm Tree at the Haymarket.

G.B.S.

To ISABEL SANDHAM

[H/4]

29 Fitzroy Square W
12th August 1890

[Shaw and Webb had left for the Continent on 29th July, visiting Brussels, Frankfurt, Munich, Oberammergau (where they attended the Passion Play on 3rd August), Stuttgart, and Strasbourg, returning to London on 10th August.]

Dear Mrs Sandham

I forget whether your time at Boulogne is expired; but I suppose I am safe in directing this to Chelsea in any case. On Sunday evening I returned from Oberammergau after twelve days absence. You should have come with us: I thought of you as we went up the Rhine (which depends altogether on a pleasant party for its interest); and my general conclusion was that in your place I should take the children out to bathe, let go the rope, forswear duty (which is only an excuse for enslaving a woman, just as "discipline" is an excuse for enslaving a soldier), and make the rest of my life one long Bayreuth. However, perhaps Webb and I would have bored you; and it is certain that you would have found Parsifal very inadequately represented by a performance lasting eight hours, with the rain falling all the time, and all the covered seats taken before your arrival.

I suppose Wallas, whom I have not yet seen, has told you something of my famous Fabian paper on Ibsen. In a year or so I shall have all the world, socialist and individualist, against me. My expositions of Ricardo's law of rent were applauded enough; but now that I have opened fire from the depths of my innermost soul against their confounded ideals of Truth, Duty, Self-Sacrifice, Virtue, Reason and so on, they fall off from me.

You ask whether it is only at the seaside that I suffer from loutishness. Well, not often elsewhere. But wherever it occurs, the symptoms are horrible. I hide myself under a cloak of perfect gentility; I write polite letters; I pay compliments; I chivalrously take off my hat when I am in the presence of a lady; I become a walking lie. Pray that you may never see me in that condition if you wish to preserve any sort of toleration for me.

I need hardly say that I want a rest badly after my holiday; but there is no prospect of any such thing now: the Fabian winter course of lectures and the provincial campaign alone would forbid it, even if there were not my madly squandered travelling expenses (twenty mortal pounds sterling) to be retrenched somehow.

GBS

To WILLIAM ARCHER

[H/2]

29 Fitzroy Square W
17th August 1890

[Archer was in Bavaria. Hans Holbein (1465?–1524) was the famous German historical painter. Fritz von Uhde (1848–1911) was a German religious and genre painter. Ary Scheffer (1795–1858) was a Dutch-born French figure and portrait painter. Sir Joseph Nöel Paton (1821–1901) was a Scottish painter of allegorical, fairy, and religious subjects. Hilmar Tönnesen is a character in Ibsen's *The Pillars of Society*. Herbert Burrows (1845–1922), a leading member of the Social Democratic Federation, was later converted, like Annie Besant, to theosophy. His attack on Shaw, "Socialism of the Sty," had appeared in *Justice* on 26th July. Ibsen had been living in exile in Munich for several years due to his dissatisfaction with Norway's stand in politics; he returned to Oslo in 1891. Inexplicably, Ibsen's interview with the Munich correspondent was not published in the *Daily Chronicle* until 28th August.]

I have written nothing about the Passion Play except a paragraph in my World article, which has been borrowed from me by somebody. However, I can give you the gist of it without waiting to get another copy and send it on. I first said that though you had come fast enough to Bayreuth, where you had no business, you had refused to come to the Passion Play, and had recommended me to spend the cost of the trip on a bicycle instead. This was my apology for trespassing on your province. I denounced Meyer [Josef Mayr, who portrayed the Christ] as a stick, grumbled at his perpetual pose as the Man of Sorrows, objected to his not letting himself go, and being such an insufferably superior person that the wonder was, not that they crucified him, but that they stood him so long. I admitted his skill and endurance as a poseur, but pointed out that all the Oberammergauers were experts in that department (they teach it in the school there) and based my dis-satisfaction on the want of feeling in his dialogue, of humour in his repartee, on his quoting texts instead of holding human intercourse, and so on. I called him the Christ, not of the elder Holbein, nor of Von Uhde (modern realist), but of Ary Scheffer and Sir Noel Paton. I swept away John and the B.V.M. [Blessed Virgin Mary] in the same condemnation. Their notion of being divine was simply not being human nor anything else, for fear of being irreverent. I praised the acting of the secular people, especially of Pilate, Nathanael, Caiaphas, Judas, and several of the minor characters. My criticism of the play was that the excision of the devil for the sake of gentility had spoiled it by weakening the motive of Judas's treachery. I also opined that the fatalistic apathy of Christ before Pilate and Herod was inadequately motivirt. This, with a detailed criticism of the music, was all I said, at no greater length than I have said above.

Oberammergau seems to be run by two women who speak all known languages, and run the Burgomaster's office and the post office alter-nately. We were much disheartened when we arrived and found our-selves in the middle of a lamenting, seatless, lodgingless horde of English and American trippers; but when we at last got up the stairs of the Rathaus and into the office, Webb had no sooner got out the words "Bitte, Vebb—" than our billet was handed to a boy guide and off we went in triumph. Webb had written to the Burgomaster; and we had arrived on the day we named. This apparently settled the affair for us, though we had had no reply. Webb's letter was couched in terms which are only used in Germany in addressing the Emperor. We were unlucky in applying too late to have covered seats reserved for us: we could only get five shilling ones, much superior to the ten shilling places for seeing and hearing, but roofless. However, as it was a most beautiful Saturday afternoon, we rejoiced in having saved five shillings apiece. Our rejoicing was shortlived. At about eight in the evening a horrible dust storm suddenly charged into the village, turning the balmy eve into a scene of darkness and confusion, in which men and women wildly held their hats on, bent their heads, shut their eyes nine tenths, and in that condition rushed about looking for their lodgings in the unaccustomed streets. By the time we were abed, the dust was succumbing to rain. In the morning it was raining as if it had no idea of leaving off; and what is more, it did not leave off. I was sustained from 8 a.m. to 5 p.m. only by the consciousness that Caiaphas (the Burgomaster) was getting as wet as I was, and that the sou'wester, unique in central Europe, was an unprecedented success.

If you leave Munich by the early (not the midday) train for Oberau, you will get to the village in time to have an afternoon there, and to see enough of it to make you content to return to Munich immediately after the performance. The best way to spend the afternoon on Saturday is to ascend the Alpine peak with the cross on the summit. The path is up through the trees beside the peak on the right. The last ten minutes of the ascent presents a mild feat of cragsmanship. If you slip, you break your neck; and the Matterhorn can do no more for you than that. There is edelweiss, and a view, and generally an American at the foot of the cross, which owes its flashing appearance to a plating of tin. Altogether it is a useful, lung opening, fifty minutes climb. I did it alone, Webb preferring to sit among the trees at the base, writing an article on municipal death duties for the Speaker.

At Munich the modern pictures in the Exhibition are worth seeing; and the Passion Play throws a light on the old German pictures in the Pinacothek. We left Munich by a very early train (seven or thereabouts); broke our journey at Augsburg; went on in the afternoon to Ulm (glorious cathedral, satisfactory restaurant called Goldener Löwe, and delightful feeling about the town in the evening light); and went on to Stuttgart, where we slept and put in a whole day, which it was not specially worth except for the rest. Then to Strassburg, where I paid two marks for an order to go to the tiptop of the cathedral spire. I outfaced agonies of terror that no typewriter can describe until the municipal steeplejack who accompanied me invited me to ascend by a naked flight of steps, each of the size and shape of a small slice of cheese, to a pinnacle, and there to stand like one of the statues and admire the view. And this, mind you, on the outside of the steeple, at a height that makes me sick to remember. How much higher I could have gone for the money I dont know; for we were still thirty or forty feet from the horrible apex of the thing; but I said "Ist genug" with what dignity I could muster, and admired the view with an intelligent-foreigner air from where I was. And yet when, after a fearful descent, I was safe in the street, I had a craving to try again—a remorse at having given in, that would have ended in my going another two marks, and leaving my invaluable brains on the pavement of the Munsterplatz if we had stayed another week there. We got home after a night in Brussels, and a stay of a few hours at Lille. The sou'wester proved a sovereign preventive of seasickness. I escaped without a qualm, both going and coming. The water was uncommonly smooth.

If you go to see Ibsen I wish you would explain a matter to him which concerns me. The Daily Chronicle published a half column or so of sensational extracts from my lecture; and its Munich correspondent thereupon went to Ibsen and told him that the London Social Democrats had been claiming him as one of themselves, and exploiting his reputation to bolster up their theories. Naturally Henrik was infuriated, and declared that he had nothing to do with the dogmas of the Social Democrats. Will you tell him if you get the chance that the true state of the case is that an eminent socialist critic made his plays the text for a fierce attack on the idealist section of the English Social Democrats, comparing them and their red flag to Hilmar Tonnesen and his "banner of the ideal." Also that the effect was to bring down on the critic the fiercest denunciation from the organ of the Social Democratic Federation, which calls me a pig incapable of understanding Beethoven's sonatas, and repudiates my socialism as "socialism of the sty." I did not read to you this section of the paper, as its interest was too purely Fabian; but the following scraps from it will shew you how it ran.

"I now come to the bearing of Ibsen's thesis on ourselves as Socialists. Ibsen himself has made no such application; for he is not a socialist: he was born in the year 1828, and formed his political opinions whilst socialism was still the most outrageously idealistic of all the new "isms." ——* The only ideal that is specially obnoxious to us as practical socialists, and that Ibsen has directly attacked, is the ideal of Law and Order. Property and Theft he lets alone; and Laissez-faire he would probably endorse, not as an ideal, but as a tolerably safe rule to adopt when Tom, Dick, and Harry begin to call themselves Society and The State, and start meddling with the moral deportment of individuals. His attitude towards Democracy I have

* The ellipses are Shaw's.

257

dealt with in describing "An Enemy of the People." His opinion of the Fabian Society is not known—probably it has not yet been formed, since he does not read English &c &c. —— Ibsen and Morris both hold mainly to the point that as long as people deliberately let themselves be idealized into doing what they dont like, thereby not only making themselves unhappy, but creating a social pressure on other folk to do the same, no mere turning of the wheels of public machinery will set them free. —— With Ibsen's thesis in one's mind, it is impossible to think without concern of the appalling adaptability of Socialism to idealist purposes. —— We (the socialists) are perhaps little troubled with the pet ideals of middle-class England, such as the honor of a gentleman, the glory of the nation, or patriotism, which Dr [Samuel] Johnson, prophetically inspired for the moment with Ibsenism, described as 'the last refuge of a scoundrel.' Still less are we tainted with those ideals of duty and discipline which are used to cloak the abject slavery of the soldier. Above all, we are fairly free from that arch-ideal called God, which concentrates into a single concept all the essential evil and incidental good of idealism. But Socialism itself as an 'ism' or ideal is as capable of mischief as any of these. —— My Socialism may thus lead me to compromise my principles, to trample on the red flag, and to be proved a traitor by Mr Herbert Burrows; but I cannot help that, anymore than I can help the other series of crimes which I am accused of under the laws of conduct laid down by the genteel idealists, who have satisfactorily proved over and over again that I have committed every conceivable atrocity, from breaking my mother's heart to damning my own soul. For the life of me I cannot see that the chains of socialistic idealism are less burdensome than those of genteel idealism, or that they lead to less obstructive and hurtful conduct."

I set great store by the setting-right of Ibsen about this matter; and even if you dont see him I wish you would drop him a line to say that his interviewer got hold of the wrong end of the stick, and that any hasty strictures of his on Social Democracy, based on the assumption that it is as dogmatic and unpractical in England as in Germany, will be represented here as repudiations of the very section which is trying, and so far with remarkable success, to rid socialism of the dogmatism, sectarianism, and absolutism of which he complains.

You may add, if you please, that I am extremely sorry that my total ignorance of Norwegian prevented my calling on him during my stay in Munich to explain his plays to him.

The Fabian, by the bye, is getting known in Germany. A recent work by a German author mentions the Fabian as the really important motor in English Social Democracy.

GBS

P.S. In the interview with the Daily Chronicle man, Ibsen again declared that "The Doll's House" was founded on fact—that Nora was a real person who had actually walked out & slammed the door.

When will you be back in England?

Walkley writes his column now from Boulogne, which he calls "Oberammergau sur mer." I got a card from him from Somme, in which he says that the Star obituary portrait of Cardinal Newman [on 12th August] was really a portrait of Lafontaine as "L'Abbe Constantin" which once adorned a Spectator column.

To W. H. DIRCKS

[X/114]

29 Fitzroy Square W
3rd September 1890

[Will H. Dircks was editor and reader of the Walter Scott Publishing Co. in Newcastle, which had just published a cheap edition of the *Fabian Essays* in paper wrappers. Scott also had a London branch. Edward R. Pease (1857–1955), a stockbroker in whose rooms the Fabian Society was founded, became paid secretary of the Society in 1890, a post he held until 1913. Scott's Camelot series of classical works was edited by Ernest Rhys.]

Dear Dirckes (it is you, isn't it?)

Tell the London house finally to go to blazes. If people want a copy of the Essays in cloth, tell them to send Pease four and sixpence, and they shall have one by return of post. The body of political economists understand perfectly that you cannot, in the face of the competition of speculative binders with no royalty to pay, afford them any royalty whatsoever; and they now see that they should have listened to the voice of Shaw, who maintained that it was possible to get a royalty of twopence on the shilling edition from you by standing out for it. THE EXTRA HALFPENNY WHICH YOU NOW OFFER IS NOT A ROYALTY ON THE TWO SHILLING EDITION AT ALL, BUT THE IDENTICAL HALFPENNY WHICH YOU SHOULD HAVE GIVEN US ON THE PAPER COPIES. However, we magnanimously make you a present of this, bearing no malice, and desiring your speedy enrichment. But when you propose a perfectly new arrangement as if it were a mere incident of the old one—when

259

furthermore, it is an arrangement which we dont desire and never contemplated—when it is expressly devised to kill the edition which we reserved our right to run for ourselves, then you get to the end of the Fabian patience, and we refuse with objurgations. If you want to run a library edition of the Essays, make us a proposal to that effect. We might not object to allowing you to print a half crown edition on large paper, provided you gave us sixpence a copy or so. Dash it all, do you take the Fabian for a sheepfold?

Personally, I have lost all faith in you because I believe the artistic sense to be the true basis of moral rectitude; and a more horrible offence against Art than what you have put above [Walter] Crane's design on the cover of the Essays, has never been perpetrated even in Newcastle. I reject your handbill with disdain, with rage, with contumelious epithets. You must reset the authors' names in the same type as "PRICE ONE SHILLING"; and the words "Essays by" must on no account be in a different type. To aim at having as many different founts as possible on the same sheet is worthy of a jobbing printer at work on a bookmaker's handbill; but that you, who turn out your Camelot title pages so well, should condescend to such barbarism simply destroys my faith in human nature. And why put Simpkin & Marshall in? Better put "all booksellers." If one of the bills falls into the hands of the trade (which is not what they are wanted for) a reference to your London house will shew them whither they must go. Of the hellish ugliness of the block of letterpress headed "What the Press says" I cannot trust myself to write, lest I should be betrayed into intemperance of language; but I would suggest that the whole should be reset so as to make room for the extracts which I have marked in the enclosed sheet of press notices, from the Methodist Times (which might take the place of the Church Reformer), the Scots Observer, the Pall Mall Gazette, and the Academy. The italic type used in the notices from the Daily News and Scottish Leader appear to me unspeakably revolting.

Some time ago, you mentioned something about changing the cover of "Cashel Byron," and introducing a design of some pugilistic kind. This is to give you formal notice that if you do anything of the sort without first submitting the cover to me, I will have your heart's blood.

yours respectfully
G. Bernard Shaw

To E. D. GIRDLESTONE

[H/12]

29 Fitzroy Square W
10th September 1890

[Edward Deacon Girdlestone (1829–92), a Fabian who helped to organise the Birmingham Fabian Society, was the author of *Christian Socialism versus Present-Day Unsocialism* (1887). His earlier work, *Society Classified*, was praised by John Ruskin in *Fors Clavigera* (1876) as "the most complete and logical statement of economic truth . . . that I have ever seen in the English language." Shaw left London on 20th September on a lecture circuit that included Birmingham, Manchester, Hyde, Kendal, Rochdale, Salford, and Carlisle, returning on 3rd October.]

Dear Mr Girdlestone

I enclose a draft of the sort of thing that is used for posters. A chairman is indispensable; and if you cannot get the Mayor to undertake that duty, put the name of his deputy in as large letters as if he was a still more important person. Would [Thomas F.] Walker, the Land Nationalizer, take it? He is in sympathy with us—has given us gold. If you have to take it yourself, mind and put your name in the most immodest type the printer possesses. In private there's nothing so becomes a man as &c. &c. &c.; but in public business self assertion is the cardinal virtue. If you dont like the title of my lecture, I can change it; but it seems to me to be calculated to bring an audience on the warpath.

I am not sure that I shall not have to ask you to harbor me over Tuesday night. On Wednesday I lecture at Staleybridge, and thereafter every night in various parts of Lancashire until the 2nd October, by which time I expect to be a mere wreck. It seems absurd to go back to London on Tuesday; and as to spending the night at Staleybridge, I doubt whether I would find that as interesting as staying with you. So if the thing is feasible, you might cautiously broach it to Mrs Girdlestone, and see how she takes it. However, I am assuming that the Monday meeting is still contemplated. Of course if it is given up, that alters matters. I am so at my wits' end with pressure of work that the temptation to return to town immediately after the Sunday meeting would be very strong if I had no business in Birmingham on the Monday.

Your title "Socialism, & the Fabian expression of it" would not do for a poster. FABIAN SOCIALISM would be better for that. But if we have a Cobden Hotel conference on Monday, it would do capitally. For a more public effort it is better to strike the keynote of practical political business at once.

261

I do not smoke, though I am not intolerant of that deplorable habit in others. I do not eat meat nor drink alcohol. Tea I also bar, and coffee. My three meals are, Breakfast—cocoa and porridge; Dinner—the usual fare, with a penn'orth of stewed Indian corn, haricot beans, or what not in place of the cow; and "Tea"—cocoa and brown bread, or eggs. But I never starve for want of special preparations.

I am afraid I shall not be able to get down on Saturday, or even much before the appointed time on Sunday; but we can settle that later on. Many thanks for your hospitality; it has put my mind much at ease.

yours truly
G. Bernard Shaw

PS. I am not M.A., nor otherwise decorated, all attempts to educate me proved utter failures.

To JULES MAGNY

29 Fitzroy Square W
12th September 1890

[A/4]

Dear Magny

On the 21st September I start at Birmingham on a Fabian lecture tour—thirteen lectures within thirteen days—ending at Longsight (near Manchester) on October 3rd. I have engagements next week on the 15th, 16th, 17th & 19th (see enclosed—come if you can). Consequently, if we are to foregather before I go to the provinces, it must be either on Thursday the 18th, or on Saturday the 20th.

Standring will just complete the Holy Trinity. Always glad to see him.

Je suis extenué de surtravail. Si vous saviez comme je suis paresseux! C'est épatant.

Eh bien!
Par exemple!
Sacrebleu!
Mille millions!
Vive la Révolution!
Sentiments les plus distingués!
GBS

To E. D. GIRDLESTONE

29 Fitzroy Square W
18th September 1890

Dear Mr Girdlestone

As you are villainously provided with Sunday trains at Birmingham, I shall take the 10, a.m. from Euston, arriving in Birmingham at 1.50. Mrs Girdlestone's instructions will enable me to make my way to Harborne. I am afraid this will be abominably inconvenient as far as your Sunday dinner is concerned, as I shall not, I suppose, reach your house much before three; but it seems inevitable. However, I am so far independent of cooking that I can make as good a dinner off brown bread & cheese, with a glass of milk & an apple or any other handy fruit, as if I had Mark Antony's kitchen at my disposal.

Mrs Girdlestone must be careful not to provide too much milk, as when I like anything I have a doglike habit of taking as much of it as I can get. It is advisable to restrict me to a glass and a half at most.

GBS

To EDWARD R. PEASE

[S/2]
chez E. D. Girdlestone
Harborne. Birmingham
22nd September 1890

Dear Pease

I write to urge the Committee tomorrow not to make an idiot of itself about those Essays. If they accept that threepence, and sanction a two shilling cloth edition, the shilling edition is done for. What has happened is this. When Scott made the original arrangement, he did not suppose that the book was important enough to tempt people at a higher price than a shilling. He then found that it was a much bigger thing than that, and that it would bear two shillings easily. The two shillings of course would shorten the circulation; but still it would pay better, as obviously ten copies sold for £1 leave a bigger margin for profits than fifteen sold for 15/-. The country booksellers will make exactly the same calculation; and the result of our consenting to the change will be that our paper edition will disappear from the market, and be replaced by a cloth edition of comparatively limited circulation. The explanation of Dircks's repeated assertions that our refusal will

263

cripple the circulation is simply that Dircks, though an estimable person in his private capacity, has succumbed morally to the economic influences of his Barabbassian trade. And even if he were so far forgetting his duty to Scott as to tell us the truth, the royalty is ridiculously small. True, there is the alleged competition of the outside binder; but to that I say, Let him bind away; and let us compete with him by shoving the paper copies as well as we can. I do not myself believe much in the outside binder. If it were a real danger, Scott could not afford to give us any extra royalty at all in competition with people producing bound copies free of extra royalty. I therefore urge that we tell Dircks flatly and finally that we refuse a two shilling edition on any terms whatsoever; but that if he would care to try a half crown edition on rather larger paper ("Great Writers" fashion) and to give us a royalty of sixpence, we might entertain it. But we must not bind ourselves to accept it. In my opinion it would be better to have no cloth edition except our own; and I regard the half crown suggestion as an extreme concession to Scott, & one of doubtful wisdom from a Fabian point of view.

If any of the plates have suffered in printing, we should insist on immediate restoration. Damaged copies on sale are insufferable.

I have failed in my plans as to lodging in Manchester. Shall wire you my address as soon as I have one. I addressed a meeting last night of a few hundred people, who listened glumly for an hour & twenty minutes to my eloquence, which was rather damaged & flattened by my having pumped myself out in efforts to sap the moral foundations of Girdlestone, who has invented a brand new ideal called ISOPHILY. Another meeting tonight, at which the Birmingham Fabian will be formally inaugurated. They seem rather on for intercepting all our Manchester lecturers now that they have begun. It might be worth considering how far this is possible.

I was to have had an advance of £10 for my expenses. Eventually my mother advanced it from the Fitzroy Square cashbox. Funds being low, you had better let her have it back again in the course of this week, lest I find her an emaciated corpse on my return.

GBS

264

To EDWARD R. PEASE

[S/2]

27 Ducie St. Manchester
25th September 1890

[Emma Brooke (d. 1926), daughter of a Cheshire cotton spinner, was introduced to Socialism and the Fabians by a former schoolmate, Charlotte Wilson. She served on the Fabian Executive Committee 1893–96, and was the author of several novels, published anonymously, including *The Super-fluous Woman* (1894) and *Transition* (1895), the latter of which contained a fascinating portrait of Sidney Webb. D'Arcy W. Reeve (d. 1926), a wealthy Liberal who later became a Fabian, frequently contributed funds for the Society's lecture campaigns, and provided the Society's first office at 276 Strand in 1891.]

Dear Pease

Unless the committee has concluded a secret profit sharing arrangement with Scott, it certainly deserves the cake for gratuitous folly. I can only say that if they had had as much trouble over the book as I, they would have thought twice about making a present of half our cloth edition rent to a publisher who has done less for us than any publisher ever yet did for an author of repute since the world began. What an ass Scott was not to stick to his original position that he ought not to be expected to pay a royalty at all! And I—I!—with a reputation for knowledge of character to lose, told this wily tradesman that the Fabians were not sheep! We have supplied the brains, the money & the advertisement; and he, without an effort, humbugs us into an agreement that would not impose on Miss Brooke. Ass that I was to trust my copyright to a council of pigeons! And what moral right, in Satan's name, had Bland, Olivier & Wallas to indulge their magnanimity without ascertaining whether Mrs Besant & Clarke were on their side or on that of Webb & myself? By the Lord, I have a mind to join the [Social Democratic] Federation—I can hear Scott & Dircks roaring with laughter at our greenness even at this distance from Newcastle. Idiots! Gulls! Tapioca heads!

Considering that Mrs Shaw advanced £10 to the Fabian, and that there appears to be no doubt that I am engaged for a fortnight's lecturing, she will probably be edified by the cautious business instinct which foresees that I may be struck by lightning on the seventh day, or possibly abscond with the gold. Was this the reaction after the romantic transaction with the bold borderer?

In Heaven's name, has the Fabian gone mad, or did D'Arcy Reeve send a hogshead of brandy as well as a promise of £50?

265

I have no particulars as to Rochdale (27th), Manchester & Salford Co-op (29th) or Barnsley (1st). Please let me know what you can. Staleybridge put me off on the pretext of an exhausting Flower Show. Staleybridge shall hear from me on the subject.

I have spoken at Webb's lectures yesterday & the day before. Can take on a job on Sunday evening if necessary, but do not particularly desire it, as I have a heavy open air harangue for that morning.

G.B.S.

To E. D. GIRDLESTONE

[A/12]

27 Ducie St. Manchester
26th September 1890

My dear Girdlestone

Seventyfive [people attending the Birmingham Fabian meeting] is immense—tremendous: it must be followed up at once. I have written to the Executive the following proposition. That William Clarke (who is for many reasons the best man for the purpose, and who is quite free from that faint but unmistakeable flavor of brimstone which clings about me) shall take Birmingham on his way to Preston just as I took it on my way to Manchester. That the London Society shall make a grant-in-aid of £15 for advertising the meetings. That both the Sunday & Monday orations be included in the posters as public meetings of the B.F.S. And that Webb & Wallas shall subsequently address the Soc^y . . . [portion of letter missing].

If I had time or energy enough now (I am overwhelmed with correspondence about lectures &c) I would defend my moral position to the death. Virtue, morals, ethics, are all a noxious product of private property. Our enemy is not essentially the landlord or capitalist: these are but accidental forms of the true enemy—the Good Man. Virtue is only a mask for the revolting features of Unhappiness. Let us be religious, if you will, but not virtuous, not moral, not good— anything but that. My only boast is that in these days when it is so easy & cheap to be a Christ, I have ventured to follow the poor, despised, but always right Devil. Ask Mrs Girdlestone whether I have not chosen the better part.

GBS

P.S. When I get back to London, I will send you my paper on the Seven Deadly Sins, if you would care to read it.

To BEATRICE POTTER

[H/14]

29 Fitzroy Square W
6th October 1890

[Beatrice Potter (1858–1943) married Sidney Webb in 1892. The Webbs (to whom Shaw invariably referred as "Darby and Joan") produced several important collaborative works, including *The History of Trade Unionism* (1894), the Minority Report of the Poor Law Commission (1909), and *Soviet Communism* (1935).]

My dear Miss Potter

This is the most unreasonable thing I ever heard of. Why, I find that it would cost me seventeen shillings for railway travelling alone; and where do you suppose that is to come from after an autumn during which the Fabian *corvée* has reached unprecedented proportions? I dare not think on what I have spent since the end of July without earning anything to make up for it. And now you, with the insouciance of a millionaire, calmly order me down to tell you about Lancashire. Never—by Heaven, never will I suffer any created woman to lead me about in this fashion. No: you may reduce the rest of the Fabian to slavery—they prattle from morning to night about Beatrice Potter in a way I despise—but if I am to go through my amusing conversational performances for you, you must come up to town: this lion is untameable. Besides, what do you think is to become of my lectures, or are they too to be imperiously set aside for you? To think that I should have lived to be sampled—to be sent down on approval or return—to be inspected by daylight by a fastidious young lady in search of an eligible Socialist Society to join! No: if you are not satisfied with the palm test, you must take your chance with me as a colleague—buy your pig in a poke, so to speak.

I am much discouraged over Lancashire. The men there want a thorough rousing. They are slaves through and through, standing up with a certain air of sturdiness for their rights as INFERIORS, but accepting the position of inferiors abjectly. My addresses were magnificent—most of them; but they need to be multiplied by dozens to be of much use. Half the value of the campaign was lost for want of a secretary and organizer on the spot, during the lectures and beforehand. Someday you will have to do this for us. Meanwhile, practise yourself in speaking; and turn no more Fabian heads with your wiles.

In uttermost haste
G. Bernard Shaw

To E. D. GIRDLESTONE

[H/12]

29 Fitzroy Square W
13th October 1890

[Rev. Lléwellyn Wood (d. 1929) was Vicar of St Nicholas, Birmingham.]

My dear Girdlestone

The miscarriage of the £15 scheme must be regarded as a piece of ill luck for the moment. The fact is, we were all hurried and out of temper through the breakdown of the secretarial department; and we practically damned everything and everybody instead of setting about our business with proper deliberation. The thing to do now is to get as good a meeting for Clarke as possible, and send him back, as you sent me back, with a strong impression of the importance of the Society. Then let us know what it has cost you; and between Pease, Clarke, and myself, something more may be done. The £5 was voted rather as a contribution to the expenses incurred in connection with my visit than for Clarke's. This, however, is between ourselves. If Clarke has a good show, and is pleased with himself, he can hardly refuse to support a proposal that we should stand half the expenses of the two meetings, which would come to £15.

As to our controversy on morals, my position is not in the least a joke. I do not deny that my sense of humor is strongly excited by the confusion and dismay which my sentiments excite in the ordinary rationalist moralist. But I enjoy it, not because his sensations are painful, but because they are obviously agreeable, although he thinks it his duty to protest that he is shocked. Follow your system logically to the end; and you will find yourself a dynamiter in politics, a vivisector in science, and in theology a St Paul. Balfour is a trained moralist; and it is precisely his moral basis which fortifies him to do his duty in Ireland. And if you turn his system hind side forward, and set up reckless selfishness as a principle (which is what—unable to escape from systems—you conceive me as doing) you will find that the practical result will be exactly the same. Or if you split the difference, and set up the Isophilitic principle, coercion will stand just as firmly on that as on the others. You put these ridiculous system-burdens on your back, and then think that they are carrying you. We see the same ethical systems producing the extremes of maleficent and beneficent conduct as applied by different men under the same circumstances; and we see the same conduct referred to the most widely different materialist and idealist systems; and yet you tell me that these systems are our only refuge from moral chaos—to which I have not the smallest

268

objection. As for your normal and universal, there are no such real categories. You get your normal simply by ignoring the abnormalities. Thus you can identify chalk with cheese by abstracting everything except what is common to the two, as weight and bulk, for instance; and I admit the necessity of performing such abstraction for the purpose of fixing a parcels post tariff. But when you go on to spread chalk on my bread, and tell me that my refusal to eat it means moral chaos, then I laugh at you; and you, in revenge, tell me that I am a paradoxer who must have his joke. Similarly, if you tell me that selfishness is a bad principle, I admit that it is so qua principle (not qua selfishness); but if you go on to say that the working classes are going to take over the land and capital of the country in a spirit of pure self sacrifice, or for any other reason than that it will benefit themselves, then I lacerate the very soul of Wood by my derisive heehaws. This making a virtue of everything is the radical vice of personal character in England. Those who are compelled to exercise self denial by bludgeon and bayonet declare that self denial is a virtue. Put the weapons into their own hands; and they will bash and perforate the policeman and the soldier, not for their own sakes, but for the great principle of Human Solidarity, or Isophily, or the Good of the Community, or Justice, or what not? I am amazed at a man of your calibre demoralizing (to express myself in terms of your own position) the mob with such monstrous, such soul corroding, such patent hypocrisy as this. Observe how easily I can PROVE that you are a rascal. Such is logic.

By religion I mean a common faith that binds men together. The bond between you and me is a religious one. Morality makes you my deadly enemy (it is your DUTY to burn me at the stake) and unites you as a brother to Balfour. Wood did not appeal to me because he talked gammon. He appealed to the duties and the Christianity of his rivals of the Establishment. A three year old curate could have knocked his whole speech into a cocked hat. The man recoiled from me because I dealt with realities, one breath of which from his pulpit would deprive him of his livelihood. He talked about the Church, poor devil, as if he did not know, as we all knew in our hearts, that there is no such thing as a Church, and never was, and never will be. When he put his intellectual box of toys on the table, I knew he would be hurt if I refused to play with them; and I was sorry for him; but what could I do: did I go down there to play? As for you, the play comes after the work: you are flagrantly unmoral in your real life, though you amuse yourself by trying to fit your actions into the old framework.

As for Mrs Girdlestone's rigid rules, I undertake to prove to her, on my next visit, that those rules bind her to elope with me. If she refuses, I shall conclude that the fact of her being fonder of you than of me has more to do with the rigid propriety of her conduct than the rules.

GBS

To ERNEST RHYS

[X/114]   29 Fitzroy Square W
                                              16th November 1890

[Ernest Rhys (1859–1946), author and editor, founded Everyman's Library. Felix Moscheles (1833–1917) was an artist who was active in the cause of international arbitration and peace. He was president of the London Esperanto Club. Natalia Janotha (1856–1932) was a well-known Polish concert pianist.]

Dear E.R.

I have tried all my photographs on the papers for processing purposes with disastrous results except the enclosed, which, though not a desirable album ornament, is the only one that presents a few characteristic black and white lines in combination with an unmistakeable Shaw hat. The only other one I have to spare is a good photo; but the results of processing it the other day in a Northumberland paper were unspeakable.

The latest about Mrs Besant is that she has withdrawn herself formally from the Fabian & S.D.F., presumably to devote herself wholly to Theosophy.

Webb's address is 4 Park Village East. N.W. He is convalescing satisfactorily, I understand.

Can I give you any information? If you would like to have your article checked as to matters of fact, send it to me.

The more I learn about other men's methods, the more I perceive that nobody except myself ever dreams of taking the trouble to attain really exhaustive literary expression. In fact, I am quite the most extraordinary man in London; and you are quite welcome to give this fact on my own authority.

G.B.S.

P.S. The photograph was taken one Sunday in Cadogan Gardens by Miss Charlotte Roche, a niece of Moscheles the painter. I remember that Janotha also fell a victim to the lens on that occasion. Miss Roche has photographed innumerable socialists and musicians.

To JOHN BURNS

[A/2]

29 Fitzroy Square W
24th November 1890

[*The Salt of the Earth*, published as the Christmas extra number of *The World* on 19th November 1890, was a collaborative "novel" conceived by Major Arthur Griffiths (1838–1908), journalist, illustrator, and authority on European prison systems and the history of London jails. The collaborators were Griffiths, Archibald Forbes, C. J. Wills, Emma Sara (Mrs F. Harcourt) Williamson, and Shaw, who provided the sections on Socialism. Forbes (1838–1900) was a journalist and war correspondent. Charles James Wills (1842–1912) was a novelist and journalist.]

Dear Burns

The Christmas number of the World is out. Dont buy it, as it contains nothing to enliven its doglike trash except a description of you, the value of which you may judge from such touches as "the harsh Scotch intonation" of your voice. As my name has been mentioned by the press as one of the authors, and as I did actually write about three pages of it (the only three readable ones in it) you may as well know that when the rough plan of the thing was submitted to me I told the author (Major Arthur Griffiths) that it was ignorant rubbish; that I would not have helped at all had it not been better to rescue at least a couple of pages from Archibald Forbes & Co. than to let them have it entirely to themselves; and that I have refused to be paid for the work or to touch the unclean profits of the thing in any way.

GBS

To ALMA MURRAY

[A/1; X/109]

29 Fitzroy Square W
25th November 1890

[Florence Farr (1860–1917), the wife of the actor Edward Emery (1861–1938), brother of Winifred Emery, was a young actress with whom Shaw later fell in love. Miss Farr, who was also an author, created the rôle of Blanche Sartorius in the initial performances of Shaw's first play, *Widowers' Houses*, at the Royalty in December 1892, as well as the rôle of Louka in *Arms and the Man* at the Avenue in April 1894. She became a Vedantist in her last years, and died of cancer in Ceylon, where she was principal of a Hindu girls' college.

John Todhunter (1839–1916), Dublin physician and writer, was the author of several plays. His *A Sicilian Idyll* had just been performed in St George's Hall, on 1st July. Herbert Waring (1857–1932) was the original Helmer in the Achurch-Charrington production of *A Doll's House* in 1889, and later performed in Henry Arthur Jones's *The Masqueraders* and Henry James's *Guy Domville* for Sir George Alexander. Marion Lea (*c.*1861–1944), the wife of the dramatist Langdon Mitchell, was an American-born actress who, in partnership with Elizabeth Robins, pioneered in Ibsen drama at the Vaudeville Theatre in 1891. Louis N. Parker (1852–1944) was a popular playwright and composer, who specialised in dramatic translations and adaptations. Lt-Col Charles Archer (1861–1941) collaborated with his brother William Archer on the translations of *Rosmersholm* and *Peer Gynt*. His biography of William Archer was published in 1931. Ibsen's "new play" presumably was *The Master Builder*.]

Dear Mrs Forman

A rumor has just reached me about your Ibsenite plans which suggests to me that you may be a little in the dark as to activity in other quarters: They tell me that you have designs on Rosmersholm. Well, Miss Florence Farr, who lately played in Todhunter's Sicilian Idyll, is going to do Rosmersholm with Waring as Rosmer; and I am the person who persuaded her thereto. She first intended to try Ellida; but I relied on you or on Miss Marion Lea for that, and induced her to read Parker's translation of R., which immediately finished her con- version. Todhunter offered to help her on condition that your rights in Parker's version were not infringed, he having evidently a great regard for you. Now Parker's version, praiseworthy as it is, is out of the question for stage use: it contains line after line that no audience would listen gravely to. William Archer, however, came to the rescue with his brother's translation, revised by himself; and this he has placed at Miss Farr's disposal for the occasion. She is already studying the part from his proofs. If you wish to do Rebecca, that is the transla- tion you must use, as Archer practically cannot be touched as the Ibsen translator *par excellence*. But since Miss Achurch has "created" Nora, and Miss Farr will "create" Rebecca, why do you not set to at once to get up a performance of The Lady from the Sea, and "create" Ellida? Archer's translation will be available in a few weeks; and in the meantime there is Mrs Aveling's, which is a very good one—far superior to her "Enemy of the People," which was not a success. Miss Marion Lea, who lately talked of forestalling you in the part, has retired; but there will soon be others in the field if it is left unoccupied. The truth is, you should have done it long ago, even if you had been driven to a back drawingroom and a company of amateurs.

I do not know yet whether there is anything to be done with Ibsen's

Florence Farr

new play, as it has not been published yet. I believe [Edmund] Gosse will translate it; but it will of course be translated independently by Archer, whose reputation as a critic, and the prestige of his personal relations with Ibsen, with the fact that Norwegian is one of the languages of the Archer family, make him by far the most desirable ally you could have in the matter.

Perhaps you know all this already; but as we all feel that the Ibsen campaign must not proceed by stolen marches, I have thought it best to make sure of your being informed.

yours sincerely
G. Bernard Shaw

To JULES MAGNY

29 Fitzroy Square W
25th November 1890

[A/4]

[Annie Besant, newly converted to theosophy, had sent a letter of resignation to the Fabian Society. The *Sunday Chronicle* was a Manchester paper in which Shaw's article, "How Socialists Have Grown Practical," appeared on 16th November.]

Mon cher Magny

Pease, who is very anxious to avoid doing anything to Mrs Besant just now at which she could take offense, begs me to get her consent before giving you a copy of the letter. I am writing to her by this post, pointing out to her that as the letter has been made public by reading it aloud at the meeting, the only effect of withholding it from the press would be that inaccurate paraphrases of it would be made from memory. Your failure to saisir le motif was not altogether P's fault, as Mrs B. did not give any reason. Evidently it is Theosophy; but she does not say so.

I have not seen the Sunday Chronicle. Can you tell me where one can buy it in London? B. is Bland. I had an article in the paper myself, headed by a horrible portrait, the Sunday before last.

I lecture at the Hatcham Liberal Club on "Alternatives to Social Democracy" on the eleventh Jany. May I look in on you *en route*? I did not settle the title of the lecture when I wrote to them; so you can give it as above if the subject is mooted in your presence.

I have conveyed your message concerning la Société du P.S. [Progrès Sténographique] to Pease, who will communicate it duly to the Fabienne.

273

Delighted to enlist you formally in our ranks. All that is necessary is to fill up the enclosed form and send it on to Pease.

yrs
GBS

To E. D. GIRDLESTONE

[H/12]

29 Fitzroy Square W
12th December 1890

[Shaw's two letters in *The Star*, on 20th and 27th November, were rejoinders to a "Parnell Must Go" outcry resulting from the divorce action brought by Capt. William Henry O'Shea (1840–1905) against his wife Katharine (1845?–1921), in which Parnell was cited as co-respondent. The Voltaire quotation is from his *Oeuvres complètes* (1785–89), Vol. 48, in which he tells of the famous French critic, the Abbé Pierre-François Desfontaines, defending himself before the Count Marc-Pierre d'Argenson on the charge of publishing libels. The Abbé exclaims, "Après tout, il faut bien que je vivre," to which the Count replies, "Je n'en vois pas la nécessité."]

My dear Girdlestone

And all this logic to find a ground for calling me a beast. Why, with half of it you could have proved me a Messiah had you been that way willed. What can I say except Saul, Saul, why persecutest thou me? If I had said "natural and therefore right," or if you had said "natural and therefore wrong," we might have a rare game of dialectical chess; and your Berserker fit might pass off harmlessly. But since I did not say it, what then? Are you resolved that I shall be a beast whether or no?—even if you have to turn Voltairean, and say, "Je ne vois pas la nécessité."

I do not know whether you saw my second letter in the Star. Nobody has made even a pretence of answering it. I enclose a copy of it—the only one I have. Let me have it again if you conveniently can—that is, without burdening your life with precautions against losing it. You will see that here is no question of Libertarianism and Necessitarianism, but first an utter demolition of Mrs Besant's absurd argument about cutting a man in two halves, and second, a plain presentment of the difficulty that just as you must have a good property law before you can safely hold the thief up to reprobation, so you must have a good marriage law before you can do likewise to the adulterer.

GBS

274

To SYDNEY OLIVIER

[H/13]

29 Fitzroy Square W
16th December 1890

[Olivier was in British Honduras, where he was serving as Acting Colonial Secretary; he did not return to London until April 1891. The Fabian manifesto under consideration was not issued. Robert E. Dell (1865–1940), a Fabian, was an international journalist who later settled in Paris. Joseph Oakeshott (1860–1945), honorary secretary of the New Fellowship, was a member of the Fabian Executive Committee from 1890 to 1902. He drafted several of the tracts, including No. 14 (*The New Reform Bill*) and No. 39 (*A Democratic Budget*). Richard Pigott (1828?–89) was the forger of letters ostensibly written by Parnell, designed to implicate Parnell in the Phoenix Park (Dublin) political murders. Frederic Hudson, a Fabian, was a solicitor, of the firm of C. J. Smith & Hudson. William Clarke was always at loggerheads with Shaw, as was Bland with Webb. Clarke's "bitter portrait" of Shaw appeared in *The Echo* on 9th December.]

This is to warn you about the Manifesto. You will have to draw it up discreetly, that is, boldly; for the Fabian seems on the eve of an eruption. The seismological signs indicate that we are all spoiling for a fight. What is more, the revolt is going to be against the Webbite opportunism. Bland, now that the Liberal party is in the dust, and an election at hand, is on for a Tory majority and twenty really advanced men in the House. Dell sides with him, and has already promised to take the chair for Hyndman at a meeting at Chelsea. Clarke has published an extraordinarily bitter portrait of me in the Echo, which not only conveys the impression that I am to be thoroughly mistrusted, but, what is of more public importance, deals with the Fabian as with a set of quidnuncs whose political influence is not worth discussing. In reply to a vigorous remonstrance which I addressed to him on the head of this performance, he writes me a string of commonplaces as to 19 out of 20 people seeing me as the Echo painted me, but finally letting the cat out of the bag by a complaint about his isolation among men who have no "ultimate aims," or whose ultimate aims differ from his. Then there is myself, feeling that if this sort of thing goes on, I shall at last be driven overboard to lighten the ship, and feeling also that the growing tendency on the part of my colleagues to put on an air of belonging to the Church of England and to allude explanatorily to my unfortunate Irish derivation whenever I happen to express THEIR opinions frankly, is not calculated to keep their souls in quite as good preservation as it keeps mine. Then comes Webb, and explains to me

275

that in England public feeling discountenances adultery, telling me this as if it were a well known fact that in Ireland adultery is regarded as identical with respectability. With these observations he couples the usual English suggestion that the obvious course was for Parnell to retire, he being a person of no moment in the Liberal game of Home Rule. Wallas improves all occasions by flying out at the people he dislikes, and aspiring fretfully towards a Blandless universe. Add to this the longing of Oakeshott to breathe a higher moral atmosphere, the defection of the soul-unsatisfied Mrs Besant, and the nebulous mass of new and unknown Fabians whose Liberalism probably only differs from the ordinary genteel variety in respect of a certain sentimental frivolity (like Mrs Whatshername, for example) and you have moral chaos. To shape it into anything like a coherent party will need some plain speaking, and a fearless facing of the risk of decimating us by searing away the people who never should have joined us. Our present game of holding our tongues lest we should discover our own disunion cannot go on any longer. The problem then is to devise a manifesto which will satisfy the impatient spirits without breaking the backs of the weak.

I think such a manifesto should emphatically repudiate the Liberal party and denounce Gladstone in express terms. We have had a startling object lesson in temporising. The nation, as far as it feels anything, is disgusted more or less consciously by the miserable exposure of trimming and hypocrisy over this Parnell case. Nobody now believes in either party: Parnell has done for the one what Pigott did for the other; and the only man who is left on his legs now is Hyndman. We must fall back on the Workers' Political Programme to shew that we also said so all along; and we must proclaim ourselves, not an advanced guard of the Liberal party, but a definitely Social-Democratic party, prepared to act with the Radical party as far as that party pursues its historic mission of overthrowing Capitalist Liberalism in the interest of the working classes, but utterly hostile to it as far as it is only the tail of the National Liberal Federation. And we should hint at holding a Social-Democratic Congress shortly. But however we do it, let us burn our boats at once.

I am not sure that we ought not to drop our public meetings if necessary for a season in order to devote ourselves to internecine shindy. Complaints came up today from Hudson and another assuring us that we had left the recruits without instruction, and that though they had been highly amused by our field nights with Bland & Co, they had failed to get that economic instruction for the sake of which they joined. They want, they say, more discussion of the sort raised by Wallas's paper.

All of which I recommend to your attention as you sleep

by the deep when the starry winds do blow.

GBS

P.S. I may add that I write under the influence of a strong feeling that we are heavily responsible for the utter damnation of H.W. M[assingham], if not for that of Michael D[avitt]. We encouraged H.W.M. to temporize when he should have walked out with his soul alive, merely because it was convenient for us to get a par. in the Star occasionally.

To JULES MAGNY

29 Fitzroy Square W
16th December 1890

[A/4]

[In 1891 Shaw expanded his Ibsen lecture into *The Quintessence of Ibsenism*, which was published in October 1891 by Walter Scott.]

My dear Magny

The paper on Ibsen which so infuriated [Herbert] Burrows was not heard by Bland: he was not in London when I read it. I hope soon to get it into print. When Ibsen's new play appears, I shall complete my paper by an analysis of it, and then set to in earnest to get it published.

I really hardly know how to describe my position intelligibly in a few words. I attack the current morality because it has come to mean a system of strict observance of certain fixed rules of conduct. Thus, a "moral" man is one who keeps the ten commandments; and an "immoral" man is one who breaks them. Among the more thoughtful classes this evil (for such I hold it to be) is intensified by the addition to the ten commandments of sentimental obligations to act up to ideal standards of heroism. Now what Ibsen has done is to call attention to the fact that the moment we begin to worship these commandments and ideals for their own sakes, we actually place them in opposition to the very purpose they were instituted to serve, i.e. human happiness. His plays are simply dramatic illustrations of the terrible mischief and misery made every day, not by scoundrels, but by moral people and idealists in their inexorable devotion to what they call their "duty." The merit of my Ibsen paper lies in its discovery of this clue to Ibsen's

277

meaning, and in an analysis of the plots of the plays so conducted as to bring this meaning out in a striking way.

Following up this line of argument on my own account I have protested against the "moral" bourgeois who is brought up to believe that it does not matter how much harm he does provided he does it according to rule, and that it is wrong to violate the rule in order to do good. I contend that the question which the recording angel will ask is not "Were you chaste?" "Were you truthful?" "Did you respect the sacredness of property?" "Did you keep the commandments?", but simply, "Did you prevent any happiness that you might have caused, or cause any suffering that you might have prevented?" On this ground a strictly truthful Russian Nihilist who had thought it better to send all his comrades to Siberia than to tell the police a lie, would assuredly be damned, whilst one who had deceived the police by a string of falsehoods would be hailed as a saint. This is what my bourgeois critics call paradoxical: of course it is nothing but the plainest common sense. My conclusion is that you cannot be moral by rule of thumb, that the search for golden rules of conduct and fixed modes of duty is as chimerical as the search for the philosopher's stone, and that we must always act under the full responsibility put upon us by the knowledge that if our "morality" causes evil, it is no more to be excused for its own sake than "immorality."

As to "les séductions de la femme," I believe opinion is divided between the people who regard me as a saint or a statue, and those who suspect me of being an Irish Don Juan who will eventually compromise Socialism by some outrageous scandal of the Parnell sort. Both opinions are equally romantic. I strenuously object to the marriage laws as they stand today, and am for granting divorce where both parties consent to it, on sufficient guarantees being given as to the children &c. I also object to the family as a legal institution on the ground that the equality of the wife and child is destroyed by making the husband the unit of the State, with powers over them which are often grossly abused. These views get stigmatized as mere libertinage; and my free expression of them does not improve my private character in the eyes of those who take the Don Juan view of me. The truth about my private character is this. I have an Irishman's habit of treating women with a certain gallantry which implies that I am respectfully submissive to their irresistible charms, and this national habit, which an Irishwoman understands perfectly, and takes for what it is worth, is rather apt to be taken seriously in matter-of-fact British circles. In fact, in this as in many other ways, I am as much a foreigner here as you are. Like most lovers of art, I am fond of women; but I never bought one on the street for my pleasure. When I was young, I was so poor and so shy that I had to give up all idea of marriage or of going into society and seducing duchesses. When you are unknown, and shabby, and penniless, and awkward, and at the same time fastidious and proud, you shrink from attempting a role which requires at least some pocket money and a presentable hat. I preserved my virginity by mere force of circumstances until I was nearer thirty than twenty, which is enough to give a man a saintly air for the rest of his life. Since then I confess there has always been somebody; but my affairs of that sort have been neither numerous nor heartless: I am too busy and preoccupied to make opportunities for myself; and when Providence makes them for me, it is not always possible to take advantage of them. Society, after all, only facilitates the relations it sanctions by marriage; and unless a man is a rascal who seduces his friends' wives and is prepared to practise on the credulity of innocent young enthusiasts who take every socialist for a saint, he cannot lead a very wild career.

I must finish hastily: a Fabian committee is waiting for me. I hope the above hasty sketch may help you to judge how far it may be desirable to amend the sketch in the *Revue Socialiste*.

G.B.S.

To JULES MAGNY

[A/4]

29 Fitzroy Square W
18th December 1890

Mon cher Magny

Malheureusement j'ai dechirée votre lettre. J'en suis bien desolé. Or rather I tore up the paragraphs and preserved the letter, meaning to do just the reverse. What's to be done now?

The passages about self sacrifice represent me correctly. However, I have been led to discuss it publicly by the stress laid by conventional idealists like [W. T.] Stead on the beauty of self sacrifice in Woman. He declares that a true woman finds in self sacrifice "the supreme satisfaction of her soul." In my Ibsen paper occurs the following:—"Of all the idealist abominations that make society pestiferous, I doubt if there be any so mean as that of forcing self sacrifice on a woman and then pretending that she likes it; and if she ventures to contradict the pretence, declaring her no true woman."

I have also protested against the practice of making saints of people who, like myself, abstain from the ordinary pleasures of society because they have no taste for them. Formerly it may have been difficult to live in a modernized Jesus Christ style; but now it is easy, convenient and cheap; and if a man makes a merit of it he is pretty sure to be a humbug.

I give these instances because the views you stated, if uttered à propos des bottes, would sound stale and trite.

I claim to be a voluptuary rather than an ascetic: I do without beef-steak because I hate it; but never deny myself a Beethoven symphony performance if I can help it.

It was really confoundedly stupid of me to destroy your MS.

GBS

To CLEMENT SHORTER

29 Fitzroy Square W

[A/1]   9th January 1891

[Shorter was now editor of the *Illustrated London News*. Shaw did not review the musical books, but he contributed musical articles on a few occasions late in 1891 and in 1892. Although he was "free for art criticism," Shaw never returned to this field professionally except for one unhappy experience, in May 1891, when an article he had agreed to write for *The Observer* on the Royal Academy Exhibition was cut, re-edited, and filled with "puffs" (see letter of 7th May 1891 to Emery Walker). Olive Schreiner (1855–1920) was the author of *The Story of an African Farm* (published pseudonymously in 1883) and *Dreams*, which had just appeared in January 1891. Shorter had criticised the latter work in his "Books and Bookmen" column on 8th January.]

Dear Shorter

Send the musical books straight along; and I will do you an occasional *causerie* on them if you like. BUT what about your musical critic? How on earth is he to keep himself abreast of the literature of his subject if his books are to be filched by an interloper? I think you had better offer him the job. It may not suit him to accept it: in that case, you can fall back on me. Of course, if it has always been the I.L.N. practice to send only actual music to the musical critic, and have the literature of music dealt with by another hand, you need not change that plan unless you like. But if your man has the requisite double

apacity for literary and musical criticism, I think you will see, in view
of the importance to you of building up a devoted staff round you,
hat you ought to recognize that capacity by proposing the occasional
auserie on musical books to him. Pray think this over carefully before
you decide. You must not make an initial editorial mistake on my
ccount. Besides, I shall be flattered by your changing your mind if
you do it at my suggestion.

I am free for art criticism this season. Newspaper proprietors please
note.

They tell me that you were surprised at being offered the editorship
of the I.L.N. Mere modesty of genius, I assure you: your succession
was as plain as a pikestaff after your exploits in rejuvenating the P.I.

I was inexpressibly shocked by your disparagement of Olive
Schreiner's volume in the Star. You ought to walk to South Africa &
back with peas in your shoes by way of penance. What were you
dreaming of? The book is a treasure.

GBS

To E. D. GIRDLESTONE

29 Fitzroy Square W

[A/12]   16th February 1891

[F. Marion Crawford (1854–1909) was a best-selling American novelist.
Shaw's *New Review* article was "Politics," a contribution to a symposium on
"The Socialist Ideal" in the January issue. Archibald Grove, the editor, had
"cut the reference to my atheism . . . in spite of his express agreement not
to alter it" (Diary).]

My dear Girdlestone

—I had almost begun "Saul, Saul, why &c." But where is your
logic? Marion Crawford says that the art of paradox can be learned in
five minutes. But the art of writing my New Review article cannot be
learned in five years. Ergo, the article is not paradoxical.

How is it that you so completely forget me when you sharpen your
pen and go out hunting? Have we not lived together for a couple of
days, and found ourselves in perfect sympathy with one another? It is
true that your favorite amusement is moralising, whilst I prefer playing
the piano; but what of that? I remember that you had two big lamps,
with clockwork wheels inside them which you used to wind up with
great enjoyment. One of these, you informed all and sundry, was the

281

light of Reason, the other the light of Duty. But the inner light of your own beneficent will was so radiant that the flames of these clumsy pieces of mechanism only cast shadows on me when you held them between us, wherefore I always blew them out and enjoyed your radiance all the more because you seemed to be puzzled when the blowing out process, instead of leaving us in the dark, made everything brighter than before. But the moment I went away you lit them up again, wound up the clockwork, and began to find me a very shady character indeed. But never mind: next time I go down to Harborne, puff, puff, out they both go; and you will find it just as impossible to believe all the things you write about me as I to believe that you believe them. I always think of you as perfectly unreasonable & unprincipled in all your motives, in spite of your pugnacity, and the elaborate rationalization by which you make its gratification a duty.

Remember me to Mrs Girdlestone, who understands the whole matter far better than you do.

GBS

To C. LEWIS HIND

[A/1]
29 Fitzroy Square W
16th February 1891

[Charles Lewis Hind (1862–1927), author and journalist, was an assistant editor of the *Art Journal*. He later became editor of the *Pall Mall Budget* (1893–95) and *The Academy* (1896–1903).]

Dear Hind

I return the proof, which I have gone over with Strudwick; so that it can now go to press. A couple of the errors made by your printers were diabolically ingenious: they changed "transcendent expressiveness" into "transcendent oppressiveness," and began a sentence "And I &c" instead of "Had I," thereby of course reversing the sense. They do these things on purpose. However, all is now seen to & remedied.

I do not know whether Huish is given to editing signed articles: I presume he is not so lost to all sense of fellowship as, for example, William Henley is. But if you have reason to suspect him of such malpractice, take an opportunity of telling him that editors who presume to paint my lilies seldom die in their beds, and invariably go to hell almost immediately after their decease.

I am sorry the article is no better than it is. Most of it was written in the train on my way to lecture at Yarmouth [on 8th February in the Gladstone Hall, on "The Evolution of Socialism and the Landlord's Share"], when I was heavily run down with work of one sort or another. However, it is presentable, if not first rate.

GBS

To T. FISHER UNWIN

[S/7]

29 Fitzroy Square W
4th March 1891

[Thomas Humphry Ward (1845–1926), husband of the novelist, was editor of *The Reign of Queen Victoria* (1887) and Macmillan's "English Poets" series. Justin McCarthy (1830–1912), Irish writer and politician, was the author of a four-volume *History of Our Own Times* (1879–80), enlarged in 1897. *Love Among the Artists* was published by Herbert S. Stone of Chicago in 1900; it did not appear in an English edition until 1914.

Unwin Brothers, a printing firm at Chilworth, had been involved in a union wage dispute since 1889. When the chairman, Edward Unwin (1840–1933), refused to permit Charles J. Drummond, secretary of the London Society of Compositors, to attend a conference in 1889 to discuss "fair wages," Shaw withdrew *Fabian Essays in Socialism*, which Unwin Brothers were to print, and gave the printing job instead to Arthur Bonner (d. 1939), son-in-law of Charles Bradlaugh, who ran a "fair house." Although Unwin Brothers offered to hold a meeting with Shaw and Annie Besant to prove that they did not pay unfair wages, Shaw refused to attend such a meeting unless the union representative was recognised.

Joseph ("Jo") Pennell (1857–1926), American artist who wrote art criticism for *The Star* under the pseudonym "Artist Unknown," became well known subsequently as an illustrator. *Rosmersholm*, starring Florence Farr, was produced at the Vaudeville on 23rd February; Shaw was in the first-night audience. The purpose of his visit to the play on 3rd March was to escort Miss Farr home, a practice in which he had been indulging with increasing frequency in recent weeks.]

My dear Fisher Unwin

Your letter of the 16th January has just come to hand, so to speak. My funeral, and the expiration of my copyrights, will come long before I find time to attend to my own business.

The only project of which I want particularly to remind you is the Century History to be published in 1900, on the 1st January. I am quite serious about this; and I should like to know whether you have ever thought it over. Nothing more startling, more actual, more absorbingly interesting, more certain to raise a tremendous discussion and make its publisher immortal can be imagined than a really adequate history of England from the industrial revolution up to the present time. No mere litterateur of the ordinary type can write it, or even conceive what there is to write. No ordinary publisher can see the chance either: his notion is something edited by Humphry Ward, or faked up by Justin McCarthy. The opportunity is one which only comes once in a lifetime; for by the time the year 2,000 comes round you will be a comparatively old man, with hardly any appetite for great enterprises. Well, Graham Wallas is now delivering a series of [London] University Extension lectures on this very subject; and he has put a prodigious quantity of work into them. At the present moment he probably knows more about it than anyone else in the world of his age. From now to 1900 he will be in the very flower of his energy, not too young and not too old; he is deeply interested in the work; he is a man of such admirable social qualities that it will pay you to lose ten thousand pounds in any enterprise that will associate you with him, since he will be able to pass you into heaven when St Peter, without his good word, would certainly insist on your going to the place reserved for all publishers; and finally he has the capacity for taking infinite pains which produces permanent work in literature. If his personal popularity and reputation as a speaker increase for the next ten years at their present rate, he will be able to bring a name worth a good deal of money to the enterprise when the time is ripe for it. I have no doubt that if a capitalist, or combination of capitalists, were to take time by the forelock and retain him on such terms as would enable him to carry out the work without absolutely starving himself, he would enter into the scheme with a will.

However, I am not very sanguine about the affair as a capitalist speculation. It is far too honest to attract the birds of prey who are always ready to back up anything that is obviously futile and unclean. Therefore it seems to me that if you are not rich enough to undertake it yourself, the book will have to be published at the author's expense in a small way about the year 1917, and remain undiscovered for ten or twenty years. What is your opinion?

I have nothing to suggest as far as my own work is concerned. I have no time to prepare it; the Fabian business and my own hand-to-mouth journalistic jobbing leave me without a moment for literary work. It is really all your fault. I have no time to go fooling round offering MSS to the eminent firms who regretted that Cashel Byron was not a sufficiently interesting work to warrant them in producing it. I want to republish "Love among the Artists" from Our Corner, as it is good enough not to disgrace me, and my reputation is now sufficient to make its publication a safe if not a brilliant operation. But I cannot stop to make up the money to get it printed myself; and you most unjustifiably refuse to do your duty except on condition of putting the work into the hands of a firm whose proceedings are emphatically condemned by the organization of the trade to which the workers they employ belong. If you employ a Union house for my books, it will probably secretly sublet the contract (for a commission) to a non-union house; so that Chilworth can rejoice all the same over the baffling of Drummond. Hang it, if these people were friends of yours I could understand your backing them; but brothers!—brothers are natural enemies by the law of nature. I do not mind discussing the question with the Chilworth exploiters; but Drummond, or some other expert representative of the Union must be a party to the conference.

I also want to reprint the cream of Corno di Bassetto from the Star, and to issue Shaw's Tales from Ibsen, uniform with Lamb's Tales from Shakspere; but here too I am deterred by your family, except as to Ibsen, which Scott (who is "a fair house") wants.

I had hoped to see you at Pennell's on Thursday; but I find I shall have to go to Rosmersholm instead.

G.B.S.

To WILLIAM ARCHER

29 Fitzroy Square W

[C/2]
14th March 1891

[H. W. Massingham had replaced Archer as reviewer of the first performance of Ibsen's *Ghosts* (translated by Archer) for the *Manchester Guardian*. It was the inaugural production of the Independent Theatre (Théâtre Libre), founded by Jacob Thomas Grein (1852–1935), Dutch-born dramatic critic.]

Massingham turned up for the M.G. I forgot to post my answer to your letter, and had to telegraph; but I infer that the telegram was not delivered before you left.

The performance was simply a tremendous success; and I fully expect that today the gloves will be off & the fighting agog in earnest.

GBS

285

To T. FISHER UNWIN

[S/7]

29 Fitzroy Square W
19th March 1891

Dear Unwin

With this I leave the three volumes of Our Corner containing "Love among the Artists." I thought it best not to send it to the city, as you are never there, and probably do nothing—after the city fashion—when you *are* there.

Archer most strenuously advises me to let these early novels of mine die. So that is one adverse critical opinion to begin with.

I looked over a few of the Corno di Bassetto columns the other day. Such sickening, vulgar, slovenly slosh never blasted my sight before. I cannot believe that there is enough good stuff sunk in this mud to be worth diving for.

I have actually attacked the Ibsen essay—put in 14 hours work on it last Monday. When ready for the press it will contain at least 25,000 words. Scott is immensely on to it: I have just received a postcard from him to say that a formal proposal will come tomorrow for its publication. It seems to me that as he has so much capital invested in Ibsen, the book must be worth more to him than to you. I suppose you are not particularly sweet on it. If you are, send me by return of post a cheque for £5,000, with an agreement securing me a 66-2/3% royalty, not to commence until the sixteenth copy.

G.B.S.

To CHARLES CHARRINGTON

[T/1(H/4)]

29 Fitzroy Square W
30th March 1891

[Marie Fraser, an actress of limited talents who thereafter rapidly disappeared from the theatre, had revived *A Doll's House* at Terry's on 27th January 1891. Elizabeth Robins (1862–1952), American-born actress and novelist (under the pseudonym "C.E. Raimond"), was shortly to become famous as an Ibsen experimenter. Sir Frank R. Benson (1858–1939), well-known actor-manager, later organised twenty-six of the annual Stratford-upon-Avon Shakespeare festivals. Charles Hudson (d. 1897) was an actor and dramatic author. Clement Scott (1841–1904), dramatic critic of the *Daily Telegraph* and adaptor of French dramas, was a violent anti-Ibsenite and leader of the critical "establishment."

John Todhunter's *Alcestis* was performed at Hengler's Circus in 1879. Thomas Thorne (1841–1918), an actor-manager, was lessee of the Vaudeville

286

Theatre. The Playgoers' Club was founded in 1884 by Heneage Mandell and Carl Hentschel; Shaw had participated in a discussion of *Ghosts* on 23rd February. Mrs Theodore Wright (d. 1922), a Fabian who was London's first Mrs Alving, was little known to the theatre, but had been familiar to members of most of the advanced social and political bodies in London since the days of the International.

Moncure D. Conway (1832–1907), American clergyman, editor, and author (Shaw reviewed his *Pine and Palm* in the *Pall Mall Gazette*, 19th March 1888), was pastor of South Place Chapel, 1864–97. Sir Edwin Arnold (1832–1904), editor of the *Daily Telegraph*, was better known as the author of the Buddhist poem "The Light of Asia" (1879). George Moore's letter on *A Doll's House* appeared in *The Times* on 18th March. The "lesser Nora" was Janet Achurch's daughter, born in Melbourne in 1890, named after the *Doll's House* heroine. She died in 1914.]

Dear Charrington

Lord knows where you will be when this reaches Melbourne; but if I wait until I learn your address, the lull of Easter Week, which enables me to get a letter or two written, will have passed.

In my last letter I stopped on the brink of Miss Marie Fraser's Doll's House, of which Archer, I understand, has given you particulars. For my own part I must penitently confess that I never quite realized how good your Doll's House was until I saw how bad that one could be without anything that could have fairly been called carelessness or incompetence in the ordinary sense. Miss Robins was nearly as sympathetic a Mrs Linden as Gertrude Warden was an unsympathetic one —if you can believe such a thing; but the rest were quite hopeless; there was a subtle absurdity about all the others which was present dimly even to their own minds, barring poor Nora, who was desperately in earnest, and desperately bad, though she deserved to have that carefully hidden from her. The only vivid thing she did was a fierce "I'm going to take off my doll's dress," which was effective, as far as anything that is quite wrong can be effective.

The next thing was Rosmersholm at the Vaudeville, with Florence Farr (whom I had turned from her original intention of playing the Lady from the Sea) as Rebecca. Benson was Rosmer, and Hudson [was] Ulric Brendel. Archer was so disheartened by the rehearsals that I had the greatest difficulty in inducing him to come; and at the last moment I was terrified myself at having thrust Florence on such an enterprise. But the thing went after all. Rebecca lacked certainty of execution both with voice and action; but she got through by dint of brains and a certain fascination and dimly visible originality. Hudson played Brendel as a low comedy drunkard. Benson, from want of faith in his part, forced his playing; but he did not distinctly fail except in the last act, which did not get for a moment on to the plane on which alone the catastrophe is credible. The third act was a great success; and the last one, though it was an utter staggerer, silenced the scoffers, the curtain falling amid a curious dumfounderment. There was a second performance through which they all crept very humbly, the criticism having roused them to a sense of their own smallness; and out of their humility a sort of dim photograph of the play as it was meant to be was arrived at. The end of the third act again made a great effect; and though Benson was still unable to manage the last act, Miss Farr this time brought off the exit to the millrace well. Clement Scott lauded her to the skies; but she is not prostrate with a sense of not knowing even the rudiments of her profession which will probably end in her knowing a good deal about them (N.B. I am in love with Miss Farr; but for Heaven's sake do not tell Mrs Charrington. Quand on ne peut avoir ce qu'on aime, il faut aimer ce qu'on a.)

As in the case of Marie Fraser's matinee the house was well filled for the first performance. Paper had to be resorted to at the second, though not to any monstrous extent. The takings were, in round numbers, £90 at the first, and £50 at the second performance. The affair was financed by John Todhunter, who wrote the "Greek play" which was done some years ago at Hengler's, and "A Sicilian Idyll," in which Miss Farr made a bit of a hit. He lost about £10 over the affair. Miss Farr got nothing but her dresses and the kudos; Benson got 20 guineas and a share of the profits (which did not come to anything, of course); Hudson got 10 guineas, and the others from three to eight. Thorne was much struck by the takings, and is asking whether there is a good Ibsen part available for him.

Concurrently with the Rosmer performances in the Playgoers' Club, an assemblage of barloafing front-row-of-the-pit-on-a-first-night dilettanti were holding sittings on Ibsen, in the form of adjourned discussions on a paper of Aveling's. I attended on two nights; and Mrs Aveling and I, being of course seasoned socialist mob orators, were much in the position of a pair of terriers dropped into a pit of rats. A few days afterwards Miss Robins, calling on Clement Scott, found him much agitated because he had just learnt that a man named Bernard Shaw had got up in the Playgoers' Club and thanked his almighty God that Ibsen would be the end of Scott and all his works. Which, except for my Almighty God, was really very much what I actually had said in criticism of a silly letter which he contributed to the discussion.

288

But the battle did not begin in earnest until the production of Ghosts. You already know from the papers about Grein and his Theatre Libre. The Play was a most terrible success. After the first act the applause was immense. After the second, a third of the applauders were startled into silence. After the third four fifths of them were awe-struck. When Grein came out, very nervous, to make his speech, a lady in the stalls said naively, "Oh, is that Ibsen?" throwing her neighbors into convulsions. Then a man in the gallery cried out to Grein "It's *too* horrible," and was instantly met with a sarcastic shout of "Why dont you go to the Adelphi?". The play was by no means seen at its best. Mrs Alving was played by Mrs Theodore Wright, who has been reciting and acting in an amateur way all her life. She was married formerly to Austin Holyoake, the publisher of the National Reformer (Bradlaugh's paper); and she subsequently married Theodore Wright, a well known member of Moncure Conway's agnostic congregation at South Place Chapel, and now a member of the Fabian. She was also intimate with the Karl Marx circle, in which she met Eleanor Marx, now Mrs Aveling. So you see she had the advantage of being on familiar ground with Mrs Alving's infidel treatises. She played very well indeed, though her application of the conventional stage method to the final situation, with advances and recoils and screams and general violent oscillations between No—yes—I cannot—I must &c&c&c, only proved, interestingly enough, that it cannot be done in that way. Engstrand [Sydney Howard] was also capital. Regina [Edith Kenward] was not the right sort of girl for the part; Oswald [Frank Lindo] was unspeakably unnatural; and Manders [Leonard Outram], whose make-up got him the credit of being "splendid," was not really good, though he did nothing that was unintelligent or in bad taste.

Next day there was the devil to pay in the papers. Scott, with my God Almighty rankling in him, went stark raving mad, and produced not only a column of criticism but a leading article (in which Sir Edwin Arnold probably had a hand) in which he compared an Ibsen play to "a dirty act done publicly," "an open drain," and so on, demanding that the Independent Theatre should be prosecuted, suppressed, fined, and deuce knows what not. Most of the other papers followed suit; and now the Royalty people are afraid to let Grein have the theatre again. Nothing will shake Archer's insane resolution not to write about performances of Ibsen's play because he is pecuniarily interested in the translations; but I contrived to prevent the World from being gagged, not only by lugging Grein into my musical article by the head and shoulders, but managing to get Lady Colin Campbell to do a special article by Archer's permission in which she played up heroically. George Moore also made an attack in the Times on the Philistines; and Grein wanted me to meddle in this correspondence; but I determined to take matters more seriously; and I am now giving up my Easter holiday in order to prepare for the press my Ibsen essay, which will, I hope, do something to revive the discussion just when it will be dropping off, and which will certainly give Scott food for reflection, as I have made his article partly the text of my discourse. I expect to get the essay, which is long enough to make a fair sized book, through the press in the course of next month.

This ends the tale of the accomplished Ibsen performances, but not of the projected ones. Miss Robins and Miss Marion Lea are going to do Hedda Gabler, with Miss R. as Hedda and Miss L. as Thea, at the Vaudeville for a whole week of matinees. Miss Marie Fraser talks wildly of doing "The Wild Duck" and "The Lady from the Sea" alternately in London and the provinces, she playing Hedvig and Miss Farr Ellida. Wilson Barrett announces "Pillars of Society" at the New Olympic; and, in short, the idea is in the air that there is money in Ibsen. However, you need not be flurried if your friends implore you to come back at once to make hay while the sun shines. It is true that the opportunity offered by the Ibsen boom to novices at scratch matinees will soon be as completely a thing of the past as amateur performances of Richard III; but it is just then that the turn of the skilful and distinguished actor will come. The long run system is being broken through now in all directions by all the actor managers who have any personal force; and since I suppose you intend to venture in that capacity when you return, it seems to me far more important that you should come back an accomplished artist, with a repertory of some extent and variety, than that you should rush home to catch the Ibsen boom. I am not of course speaking of a permanent establishment, and without prejudice to your letting us see you again for a season in London in Ibsen or anything else you may have ready. But if I were in your place I know I would sacrifice London and Ibsen and everything else for practice enough to enable me to play everything as consummately as Irving, for instance, plays Charles I. A man's consummation of his own powers is so much slower and later an affair than a woman's that it is more in her interest than in yours that a visit to London, if not a settling there, is advisable at present. However, it is of no use to plan these things overwisely: they generally settle themselves according to circumstances.

Give my compliments to the greater and the lesser Nora. Archer will probably write to you again, as he has got a typewriter and is still in the stage of playing with the new toy. I am half dead with clattering on this old machine; so farewell until we meet on the Rialto, unless indeed your return should be postponed longer than we expect, in which case you might drop a postcard to shew that you are still alive and responsive.

G.B.S.

To ELIZABETH ROBINS

29 Fitzroy Square W

[A/33] 20th April 1891

[Shaw had just attended the first performance of *Hedda Gabler* in London, produced by Elizabeth Robins and Marion Lea. His letter was written that evening between the acts of *Traviata* at Covent Garden. Charles Sugden (1850–1921), who played Judge Brack, was better known as co-respondent in a famous divorce action brought by the Earl of Desart than as an actor, having, until 1887, appeared under the stage name of Charles Neville. William Archer's translation of *The Pillars of Society* had been produced by W.H.Vernon at a special matinée at the Gaiety on 15th December 1880, this being the first recorded production of Ibsen in England. When it was revived on 17th June 1889 at the Opéra Comique, Elizabeth Robins played Martha Bernick.]

Dear Miss Robins

In company with a large and intelligent contingent of Fabians, I saw Hedda today from the back of the pit. I do not know whether you noticed that the last two acts produced a much more decisive effect than the first two; but it certainly was so as far as the pit was concerned, the reason being that a great part of the first half of the play was not satisfactorily audible. Between the second and third acts I found that my companions knew nothing about General Gabler's pistols, and had formed the most extravagant conjectures about Lovborg and the old story concerning him. The fact is, you did not sufficiently consider the effect on us of the law of nature by which the resonance of a human body is considerably reduced when it sits down. Most of the seated conversations were inaudible. Remember: I am only speaking of the back of the pit: John Burns, who was in the gallery, told me that every word was well heard there. There was no difficulty with Brack or Tesman [Scott Buist]: you, Miss Lea [as Thea Elvsted], and Lovborg

291

[Arthur Elwood] were the offenders. What is wanted is not loudness, but a little more deliberate intention and distinctness.

I was violently disappointed by your altering "do it beautifully," which ought by this time to have been a catchword throughout London, worth £1000 as an advertisement. The omission of the bit of dialogue about your figure in the first act was perhaps natural (as a contribution to the great feminine problem of how to play Hedda, Nora, Rebecca &c, with Ibsen left out); but it made your agitation when left alone on the stage quite unintelligible.

Do you think you could persuade Tesman to make his performance quite perfect by not calling you HEADER?

If you could mention my complaints to Miss Lea, be careful not to set her forcing her voice, which is a very peculiar and telling one when she does not smother it with emotion and sitting down, but would be spoiled by the slightest strain. The only part of her play that I disagreed with was at the end, where, instead of getting busy and almost happy with Tesman over the notes, she was lachrymose and useless looking.

Sugden must be afraid of that remark about your ancles. He rushes at it and makes it unnatural, and therefore artistically unpleasant, which is a needless aggravation of its general unpleasantness.

I hope you will not mind my offering these comments. You may safely accept all the compliments you get about the play and the part. I never had a more tremendous sensation in a theatre than that which began when everybody saw that the pistol shot was coming at the end. Now that it is over, I may confess that I was afraid that you would be too sympathetic; for I have never forgotten the way in which you suffused that part in "Pillars of Society" with emotion—a thing that must have been really yourself and not your acting. But, as it turned out, you were sympathetically unsympathetic, which was the exact solution of the central difficulty of playing Hedda.

yours very truly
G. Bernard Shaw

To T. FISHER UNWIN

29 Fitzroy Square W
[S/7]
22nd April 1891

[The "Hedda Gabler difficulty" refers to the publication by W. H. Baker & Co. in 1891 of a translation of *Hedda Gabler* by Edmund Gosse, which Ibsen had authorised and which conflicted with Archer's commitments to Scott.]

Dear Fisher Unwin

I am at present able to do nothing but gasp after the effort to finish the Ibsen book. All correspondence went by the board during the last three weeks of the struggle. Hence my neglect to answer your letter.

First, as to the Bassetto papers, I found that a sensible charwoman, seeing a great heap of old Stars lying about, had disposed of them as waste paper. It is true that enough is left to fake up a Pseudonym volume; but I hardly feel equal to the job just at present. A festoon of dusty old columns hangs over the gaspipe above me as I write; but the dog is not disposed to return to his vomit immediately after the Ibsen feast. Besides, most of it is wretched stuff: in the few strips I have looked over there are not two paragraphs that I would reprint. On the whole, as Walkley wants to make a book of his Spectator articles, and I have promised not to spoil his market, I think we had better leave di Bassetto to rot peacefully in his grave.

The Ibsen MS is not a very large affair. In the type and style of Archer's translations as published by Scott, it would make a book of only about 120 pages. However, I think you had better let it alone, as it seems to me that since any sensation it may make will help to sell the translations, in which Scott has much more capital invested than you have in The Lady from the Sea, it must be better worth Scott's while than yours to publish for me. The MS is at present in his hands to enable him to estimate the cost of manufacture &c. We have come to no agreement as yet; but I have no doubt we shall soon do so. I am in a certain degree bound to Scott, provided he offers me no worse terms than anyone else: partly because he has behaved handsomely to Ibsen in the Hedda Gabler difficulty, and partly because he published Cashel Byron, of which immortal work I regret to say he has sold, up to the 31st March last, only 3193 copies. Obviously he can afford to offer anything that you can afford to offer, and even more, because of the reaction on the translations, and also because, having been disappointed in the novel, he has the faith and the interest in me which a publisher always feels in an author who has bled him. (The shilling edition of the Essays—20,000 of them all sold at one volley—must have recouped him a bit, by the bye).

Someday I shall probably make up a volume of my musical articles in The World—that is, if I ever again find time to go back on old work. I am really too dead beat to entertain anything seriously at present.

The Fabian Society is contemplating a review of its own at last. People have been urging us about it for a long time; and the other day one particularly urgent individual [D'Arcy Reeve] planked down £500

293

as a start towards expenses. If you have another £500 to spare, you might let us have it at 6% *negative* interest, which, however, you might compound for by telling us how much we ought to have in hand to see us safely over a year's trial with a shilling review like Grove's, paying normal rates to contributors, but getting the editing done for £150 or £200.

Instead of returning "Love Among the Artists" to me, will you send it to Mrs [Florence Farr] Emery, 123 Dalling Road, Ravenscourt Park, W. She awaits it with an expectancy which the first few pages will rapidly cool.

G.B.S.

To WILLIAM ARCHER

29 Fitzroy Square W
[A/2]   23rd April 1891

[Archer had at last determined to break silence and to discuss the current Ibsen productions, of which he was translator, in his drama column in *The World* on 29th April.]

On page 2 of the MS, four lines from the bottom, you had better strike out "under the joint management &c" which gives the sentence the air of an advertisement. There is a certain elaborate House-of-Lords unnaturalness about the whole article which can be remedied by striking a word out here & there. For instance, why do you Desire to record Emphatically the deep impression made by the Production &c &c, instead of saying "I want, then, to record the deep impression made upon me by Hedda Gabler last Monday afternoon at the Vaudeville"? And again, "that fact, I say [my lords & gentlemen]* is not without its interest as a human document." Cant you say "that fact, I hope, has its interest as a h.d."? It is this unlucky half page that flavors all the rest: if you alter it as I suggest, the spell will be broken completely.

Common decency demands that you should modify the claim to normal impartiality in your first sentence, which should end "—any approach, not to impartiality, which I hope I know better than to pretend to in any case, but to freedom from flagrant & immediate personal and even pecuniary bias."

You have, in your remark (p. 5, two lines from foot) about the

---

* The square brackets are Shaw's.

294

respectable British householder, gloriously missed the real point of the conventional objection. Why, man alive, it is Thea, whom you so naively praise, and not Hedda, the modern Lucretia, who preferred death to dishonor, at whom the householder holds up his hands (*vide* daily papers).

With these reservations I approve immensely of the article. There is no reason why Yates should not print it. I could quite understand his objecting to your *not* noticing Ibsen plays & thereby cutting his paper clean out of the theatrical movement; but he cannot, without wantonly picking a quarrel with you, suppress this article. Why the deuce should you anticipate such a vagary on his part?

My "feminine" point in the letter to Miss R. was à propos of her cutting out the cause of her agitation in the first act and yet leaving the agitation in. My contention is that the women who are mad to play Rebecca, Hedwig, Hedda, Nora &c, recoil from the jar of the peculiarly Ibsenite passages. Ibsen says, in effect, "Here is a beautiful part for you to play, on condition that you face a laugh or two, a jar or two, a misunderstanding or two, in giving it to the unprepared public in all its completeness & reality." And immediately they set to work to see how they can get the beautiful part & yet escape the condition by cutting out all the bits that raise the laughs & the jars & misunderstandings. This I call the great feminine problem because all the beautiful parts are women's parts. Perhaps it was unfair as seeming to infer that the men were any less cowardly than the women; but I did not mean it so. The truth is that all the performances lately have been very poor specimens of the moral courage of the stage hero & heroine: they have shirked pretty nearly everything that could be shirked. Mrs Theodore Wright is by far the pluckiest of the lot.

I am off to Wolverhampton this afternoon to lecture [to the Wolverhampton Trades Council on "The Capitalists' Share"]. Hanley on Friday [another lecture, "Distribution of Wealth"], and back again on Saturday morning.

GBS

To FLORENCE FARR

[A/4; X/115]

In the train——
1st May 1891

[Jenny Patterson, whose frequent travels in the 1870's and 1880's took her to Italy, Australia, and the Near East, had just returned from Egypt. Discovering that Shaw's friendship with Florence Farr Emery had developed into a quite amorous relationship, she had had a "fearful scene" with Shaw

295

on 27th April. Her jealousy increased in intensity in succeeding months, and reached its climax on 4th February 1893 when, according to the diary, "In the evening I went to F.E.; & JP burst in on us very late in the evening. There was a most shocking scene; J.P. being violent & using atrocious language. At last I sent F.E. out of the room, having to restrain JP by force from attacking her. I was two hours getting her out of the house & I did not get her home to Brompton Sq. until near 1, nor could I get away myself until 3. I was horribly tired & upset; but I kept my patience & did not behave badly nor ungently. Did not get to bed until 4, & had a disturbed night. I made JP write a letter to me expressing her regret & promising not to annoy F.E. again. This was sent to F.E. to reassure her." The incident, which Shaw graphically recreated in Act I of his play *The Philanderer* later that year, brought to an end his turbulent relationship with Mrs Patterson.]

I have not time to write at all unless I can snatch a scrawl in this way whilst I am running about.

I also am fascinated by your proposal, oh my other self—no, not my other self, but my very self. Now is it all over and utterly dead, as if it had never been. We are mere acquaintances, my dear Mrs Emery, just as we were that day at Merton. And so we are FREE—to begin it all over again. I am a beggar once more; and once more I shall come into my great fortune. I am again an unscrupulous egotist with a remorseless will; and again shall I be moralized & have my backbone sweetly stolen away. We shall even have Rosmersholm again—but that reminds me of another matter.

There is nothing that drives me to such utter despair as when I make some blundering & unsuccessful attempt to make you see some technical point that my mother can teach to any idiot in a few lessons; and you shrink as if I were disparaging your artistic gifts. You do not know the importance of some of these tricks as regards health, economy of physical force, self containedness and the like. If I break in on your artistic vein to urge them, it is because I have an extraordinary desire to make the most of you—to make effective & visible *all* your artistic potentialities—not seven eights or nine tenths, but all. And not, observe, merely as an actress, but as a woman. Your ability to act must only be a mere consequence of your ability to live. You are so real to me as a woman that I cannot think of acting being to you anything more than a technical accomplishment which I want to see carried to a high degree of perfection. For the born actress I have a certain contempt: for the woman who is a consummate artist I have a deep fellow-feeling. The one is a sham: the other a reality completely expressed. There is thus a certain sense in which I would have you despise acting as a "vocation." It is the work that comes to your hand,

and you must do it as well as it can be done; but you must always be the mistress of your art & not the slave of its intoxications & excitements. In my own art I am ready, if only time be given me, to answer for the workmanship to the last comma; and now, if "inspiration" comes, it does not half escape me: I know how to seize it and knead it so as to exhaust all the nutriment in it.

When Archer says [in *The World*] you want grip, he misses the problem in your case. You will never proceed by way of grip, but by sustained beauty of touch. But touch on what? On a conception of your part so complete that it accounts for every moment of Rebecca's time whilst she is on the stage. That is what demands such frightful labor of invention—such years of time. At present there are innumerable gaps & holes in your conception: it is whilst you are passing through these that your "grip" is lost. Yet these gaps with you are not absolute blanks. They are rather places where you fail in intensity of realization & certainty of execution. You fade rather then vanish. And at all times, you yourself are there, never quite insignificant. I am always reassured when I see you: even when I am not satisfied, I am not disappointed: there is no air of failure in anything you do. And I am not impatient—only frightfully afraid that you will get impatient with me and my criticisms.

I saw [Hermann] Vezin at the Academy private view today, & he has not made up his mind about Rosmer. I urged him strongly to do it, though I foresee that he will be troublesome in certain ways, through not quite taking the part in. Still, he will have artistic qualities that will be invaluable to you.

I shall get to bed now without staying to discuss that other relation. At this moment I am in a contemptuous fury & vehemently assert that your Christmas estimate of it was the right one. Not for forty thousand such relations will I forego one forty thousandth part of my relation with you. Every grain of cement she [Jenny Patterson] shakes from it falls like a block of granite on her own flimsy castle in the air, the work of my [her?] own imagination. The silly triumph with which she takes, with the air of a conqueror, that which I have torn out of my own entrails for her, almost brings the lightning down upon her. Imagine being told—but I cannot write it. Damnation! triple damnation! You must give me back my peace.

If you are disengaged tomorrow afternoon, will you come to Prince's Hall (*not* St James's, mind) on the enclosed ticket [for Eugène Holliday's pianoforte recital]. The hart pants for cooling streams.

GBS

To FLORENCE FARR

[A/4; X/115]

29 Fitzroy Square W
4th May 1891

[Shaw "got away early" from a Fabian Society meeting on 4th May to call on Mrs Emery, "but found the place in darkness. Wandered about disappointed . . ." (Diary).]

Miserable, ill starred woman, what have you done? When my need was at its highest, my weariness at its uttermost, my love at its holiest, I found darkness, emptiness, void. I cannot believe now that we shall ever meet again. Years have passed over me—long solemn years: I have fallen in with my boyhood's mistress, Solitude, and wandered aimlessly with her once more, drifting like the unsatisfied moon. Tears have dropped from my heart—tears of mortal disappointment, reminding me of the days when disappointment seemed my inevitable & constant lot. I have lost my faith in all the achievement & confidence since that time: whatever my dreams may have been, I have slept where I was born, in the valley of the shadow. How could you do this thing? Are there no subtle fluids, no telepathic wires, to tell you when the chapter of accidents sets me free from my chains? This was to have been the happiest of all my great happinesses, the deepest and restfullest of all my tranquillities, the very inmost of all my loves. And I was robbed of it in the moment of embracing it by your caprice, your wanton caprice—you told me you had nothing to do. And I contrived so ingeniously, so patiently; sent my mother to the opera; induced a colleague to break an engagement I was bound to keep with him; left one meeting early and gave another the slip; and for what? Wretch! selfish, indifferent, heartless wretch! A million reproaches on you for ever and ever. Farewell: all the happiness I owe you is cancelled and the balance is now on the other side—a huge balance, incalculable, unliquidatable. You can never repay me.

GBS

To MISS VIVIE ROCHE

[C/4]

29 Fitzroy Square W
4th May 1891

[On Sunday, 3rd May, members of all London's socialist and labour organisations held a Labour Day Demonstration in Hyde Park to promote an eight-hour working day. Several Fabians, including Shaw, made speeches.]

Dear Miss Roche

I am sorry I could not come to see the banner; but this was Academy week in addition to all the musical work, & it was as much as I could do to make time to go to the park. I am still giddy with the rush of the last three days.

yrs very truly
G. Bernard Shaw

To EMERY WALKER

[A/3]

29 Fitzroy Square W
7th May 1891

[Shaw, seeking new employment as an art critic, had been recommended by Emery Walker to Clement Kinloch-Cooke, now employed by *The Observer*, who engaged his services. Shaw's "first notice" of the Royal Academy exhibition appeared in *The Observer*, unsigned, on 3rd May 1891, but it was so mutilated as to impel its author to submit an immediate resignation. Kinloch-Cooke had served as secretary to W. T. Wyndham-Quin, fourth Earl of Dunraven (1841–1926), when the latter was Under-Secretary of State for the Colonies.]

Just a hasty line to explain the row about the Observer. Cooke is such an unspeakable greenhorn that when he got my article—which I need hardly say was a very good one—he could not make head or tail of it. So instead of sending to me, he helplessly handed it to his "proprietor," who proceeded to mutilate it, interpolate scraps of insufferable private view smalltalk, break it into paragraphs in the wrong places, season it with obvious little puffs of his private friends, and generally reduce its commercial value (not to speak of its artistic value) about 1800%. If you look at the article, you will see at a glance the broken fragments of Shaw sticking ridiculously in the proprietary mud. You can image my feelings on seeing good work spoiled in this fashion by a couple of duffers, not to mention that I nearly killed myself last week in getting through the Academy, which takes a great deal of careful consideration as well as drudgery of picture inspection, and through my World business & the Sunday [Eight Hours] demonstration with a lecture in the evening ["Alternatives to Social Democracy," to the Southwark Branch of the S.D.F.]. My first impulse was to tell Mister K. C. that a man who was so ignorant as to behave in a silly & offensive way without knowing it ought to devote himself wholly to Dunraven secretarizing & to let editing alone. However, I forbore, as the poor devil evidently thought that he was proceeding in the most reasonable way. I wrote him an exceedingly paternal letter, telling him plainly what he had done, and washed my hands of the affair.

[Ernest] Radford has just written to me to know whether he can take up the job without interfering with me; and I have wired him to go ahead. You must warn R. (who is much more prone to make rows than I am) that K.C. wants the commonest sort of work, & in fact prefers it to careful work. You might also give K.C. a hint that if you are to introduce capable men to him, you expect them to be treated with ordinary consideration. He has really behaved damned badly, & will do it again if he is not brought to his senses by a sound snubbing. Just imagine the letters that will pass if he treats Radford's article as he treated mine!

I suppose you dont happen to know any editor of mature age who would use up my elaborate scheme for the unwritten second article. Anyhow, I havent time to write it now.

In haste
GBS

To E. C. CHAPMAN

29 Fitzroy Square W
29th July 1891

[A/4]

[E. C. Chapman was a secularist who had heard Shaw address the Camberwell Branch of the National Secular Society on "Freethought, Old and New," on 26th April. Rev. Benjamin Waugh (1839–1908) was a Congregational minister, co-founder of the London Society for the Prevention of Cruelty to Children (1884). Jean-Baptiste de Monet, Chevalier de Lamarck (1744–1829), was a French naturalist, forerunner of Darwin, who proposed a theory that changes in environment cause changes in the structure of plants and animals. Samuel Butler (1835–1902) attacked Darwin's law of natural selection in a series of works, one of which, *Luck or Cunning?*, had a profound influence on Shaw, who reviewed it in the *Pall Mall Gazette* on 31st May 1887. John Henry (Cardinal) Newman (1801–90), English theologian, was an Anglican leader of the Oxford movement who became a convert to Roman Catholicism. The *National Reformer*, founded in 1860 by Charles Bradlaugh, was the journal of the National Secular Society.]

Dear Sir

I am sorry to have left your letter of the 27th April so long unanswered; but my profession makes it impossible for me to do much in the way of correspondence between Easter and the close of the season towards the end of July. The delay makes it necessary for me to send you back your letter, as otherwise you would hardly remember the points you raised in it.

(a) I agree with you that the motto "We seek for Truth" sufficiently indicated the distinction between the old positive method of the Secularist and the theological method of the Christian. But that does not dispose of my objection that we do not seek for truth in the abstract. The Rev. Benjamin Waugh seeks for facts that will support his will-to-believe that secularists are worse men than Christians. Our friend John Robertson seeks for facts that support his will-to-believe that Materialist-Rationalists are the only honest Secularists, and that all others are hypocrites and time servers. The result is that neither Waugh or Robertson have ever discovered one of the glaring facts that contradict them; and you have Waugh, in perfectly good faith, informing the world that the people who ill treat children are mostly secularists, whilst Robertson, in equally good faith, makes the statements about Socialists with which you are no doubt familiar. I contend that nothing can be more trivial than the assumption that the easy proof that both Robertson & Waugh are liars has any value whatever. They have made statements which are false, with the rebutting facts staring them in the face. Therefore Robertson can amuse himself, if he likes, by *proving* Waugh a liar, just as I could amuse myself, if I liked, by *proving* Robertson a liar. But I happen to know that Robertson is an honest man; and those who know Waugh testify the same of him. Therefore all I ask both men to do is to give up pretending that they "seek for Truth." Every man sees what he looks for, and hears what he listens for, and nothing else. At this moment, every object within range of your eyes appears double to you except that which you are looking at. Nevertheless you not only do not know this, but even when you are told of it, you experience the greatest difficulty in seeing it. In my opinion, until Secularists become so alive to the intellectual analogue of this fact, that they discard their motto as ridiculous, they will never rank, intellectually, as a grown up body. Your citation of [Charles] Darwin (c) does not, I think, tell against this position. Darwin searched with extraordinary diligence for facts to support his theory of natural selection. Surely you do not contend that he was equally eager in discovering the facts that support the Lamarckian theory of functional adaptation. Writers like Samuel Butler have had no difficulty in convicting him of gross partiality towards his own theory. And yet you will not easily find a more unquestionably honest investigator than Darwin.

(b) As to men becoming Freethinkers against their will, that is, to me, simply unthinkable. I can "prove," if you like, that boys learn to smoke against their will because it makes them sick & gets them punished; but I am afraid you will only laugh at me if I do. All that can be said is that as the freethinking will gradually grows and supplants the superstitious will, there is a period in which the conflict of the two produces a very painful struggle in the man, the forces being sometimes so evenly balanced that the slightest circumstance will turn the scale, the same man being a sceptic at 2 o'clock on a fine afternoon and a remorseful Christian at 2 in the morning with a thunderstorm raging. Everyone knows the boastful atheist who sends for the clergyman the moment the doctor shakes his head. But in the long run the freethinking will outgrows & supplants its rival wholly; and the recreant, either in his own person or in that of his posterity, becomes as indifferent to the devil as Luther became to the Pope. My whole point is that the process is not one of logical conviction, but of growth.

(d) Much as I admire Olive Schreiner, I am not sure that it was not the girl rather than the strong woman who wrote [in *Dreams*] that sentence about every step towards truth (or disillusion) being a tread on your own heart. I have found it otherwise. It is rather a fetter shaken off. I never gave up an old belief without feeling inclined to give three cheers and jump into the air like the swineherd [Gurth] in Scott's novel [*Ivanhoe*] when his master made him a freeman.

(e) I think you will find, on reflection, that we have no more case against theism than theists have against atheism. Newman shewed that our line of argument led to an insufferably repugnant conclusion. When we replied that we found the conclusion congenial, he had nothing more to say. Similarly, all we can do is to shew that his reasoning led to insufferably repugnant conclusions. The Newmanite replies that the conclusions appear to him to be perfectly satisfactory. What more have we to say? The irresistibility of a chain of logic lies, not in the logic, but in the acceptability of the conclusion to the person addressed. For instance, corporal punishment is an abominable practice to my mind; but the reasons for it are "irresistible" to those who approve of it.

(f) I evidently did not make my illustration about the British Museum books clear. It is an old and second hand one; and I thought it would be familiar to many of my hearers. The physiology of thought and action, so far, gives no explanation of consciousness. If I touch you with an unpleasantly hot or cold material, you draw back. If I touch a sensitive plant with my finger it shrinks back & crumples up. The

302

same effect is produced with consciousness in the one case, and without it in the other. If you take a plunge into the sea, you unconsciously close your pores against the cold. If you go out on a cold day, you consciously put on an overcoat. Science can give you reason why you should not make & put on an overcoat without knowing it just as you shut your pores. In the same way science can explain why and how books are written; but it cannot account for the process being accompanied by consciousness. Therefore, *as far as science goes*, all the books in the world might have been written (except those which are written without consciousness) without the knowledge of the authors. Knowledge, in this sense, is conscious consciousness. Of course this position is only taken as a *reductio-ad-absurdum* of the sufficiency of rationalized physical science as an explanation of life. And rationalized physical science is Materialism, in spite of Robertson's ingenious efforts to widen the word into a sense in which nobody ever uses it or ever did or ever will use it. The moral for Secularists is that a basis of physical science no more justifies dogmatism than a metaphysical basis does.

(g) The cogency of my Fabian Essay argument depends on the fact that men are not Materialists. I have never seen the logic of the dynamiter refuted, nor that of the vivisectionist. But this is a *reductio ad absurdum* of logic regarded as a prime motor, not a justification of dynamite or vivisection. Similarly, I admit that there are excellent reasons for going to war, and for retaliating upon persons who injure us. Yet I am, on the whole, strongly opposed both to war & retaliation.

You will, I hope, accept this hasty reply as better than no reply at all. In a book of mine which is now in the press, entitled "The Quintessence of Ibsenism," I have dealt with the subject more carefully. I have thought of describing my experiences as a Secularist lecturer in an article in the N.R.; but I doubt if it will be possible for me to find the needful time. A feeling that the line taken by the N.R. about my lectures was only widening the breach between Socialists & Secularists decided me to drop the subject. I am sorry for this; since I am confirmed in my suspicion that Secularism is falling behind the time through the incompatibility of its middle class intellectual prejudices with the working class movement; but all the time I have to spare is required for the direct propaganda of Socialism, and I cannot undertake a campaign for the rejuvenation of Secularism singlehanded.

yours faithfully
G. Bernard Shaw

To W. S. DE MATTOS

[A/27]

29 Fitzroy Square W
30th July 1891

[William S. De Mattos (1851-?), a Cambridge University Liberal who was converted to Socialism and an indefatigable organiser, was Lecture Secretary for the Fabian Society; he later emigrated to British Columbia. Henry Hunt Hutchinson (1824-94), an elderly Fabian who was Clerk to the Justices of Derby, had contributed funds to underwrite Fabian lecture tours of the provinces in 1890. On his death he left the Society a trust of about £9000, which enabled the Webbs to found the London School of Economics. Robert Blatchford (1851-1943), who was known by the pseudonym "Nunquam," was a socialist journalist on the staff of the Manchester *Sunday Chronicle*; he founded *The Clarion* in December 1891.]

Dear de Mattos

I rather overlooked one passage in Hutchinson's letter to me which seems to indicate his willingness to finance another autumn campaign. He writes:—

"I am clearly of opinion that my last year's contribution was, and is, no mistake. It has done its work well; and I am more than satisfied, and ready to do it again. The field is ready to the harvest; and I hope the laborer will be there, after the dogdays, strong and ready to go in."

What do you make of this? If you write to him, remember that he is wildly enthusiastic about Nunquam. His address is 90 Green Hill, Derby (*H.* Hutchinson).

yrs
GBS

To PERCY BUNTING

[A/20; X/142]

29 Fitzroy Square W
30th July 1891

[Sir Percy Bunting (1836-1911), social reformer and founder (1883) of the National Vigilance Association, was the editor of the *Contemporary Review*. Shaw did not go to Bayreuth that year, but he expatiated on "the lesson of Bayreuth for England" in *The World* on 12th September, advocating a Wagner theatre on Richmond Hill. The Venice trip was a tour of Italy with the Art Workers' Guild in September 1891 (see letter of 23rd September to William Morris).]

Dear Mr Bunting

Does the Contemporary ever meddle with music? My reason for asking you is that ever since I found that all the Bayreuth tickets were

304

Hammersmith Terrace, 1891
(*From a photograph by Emery Walker*)

gone, I have felt that I must go there at all hazards. Parsifal Van Dyck engages to find seats for me. I now want an excuse in the shape of a magazine article for spending the money, which I cannot afford, as I stand committed to a trip to Venice as well. However, I would rather stay at home than repeat the usual Bayreuth article, with illustrations, portraits &c. What I want to do is to deal at large with the lesson of Bayreuth for England, to compare Covent Garden &c. If I find that I have anything of this sort to say when I come back, would you care to have an article?

I need not start until the 13th August; but as Van Dyck is waiting for my reply to his offer I should be glad to know as soon as possible.

yours faithfully
G. Bernard Shaw

To EMERY WALKER

29 Fitzroy Square W
[A/3]   11th August 1891

[Massingham did not accompany the Art Workers' Guild on its two-week excursion to Italy.]

Dear Walker

Will you pass the enclosed cheque for £15.10.6 through your bank (I do not run to a banking account myself) and pay my £10 [deposit] out of it. You may as well keep the balance of the £13.10.10 (or whatever it is) and pay that for me as well when it is called for. The balance you can let me have at any convenient time.

Massingham wants to join the expedition. Can this be managed, or have they as many people as they want? He is a suitable fellow & would make good company. I am writing to him by this post to tell him to send you £10 by return if he is in earnest about it.

You had better set up in business as a photographer. Archer, who has been much misused and retouched by both Barraud and Elliot & Fry, and who is much struck by your portraits of myself and Wallas, wants to know whether you could be persuaded to photograph him.

GBS

PS. If Massingham sends you the money, you can return it with a polite regret that the number of the expedition is already reached & cannot be extended, if you do not care to nominate him.

To FLORENCE FARR

c/o H. S. Salt
Oxted. Surrey
[A/4; X/115]   20th August 1891

[Shaw had been giving Florence Farr elocution and vocal lessons, using *Rosmersholm* as an exercise book. His diary entry indicates that the first sentence of his letter must be taken literally: "In the morning I went out and lay down among the thistles on the brink of a sandpit, keeping off the rain with my mackintosh and writing . . ."]

I am at present grovelling among the thistles & bees on the brink of a sandpit. The rain was trying to dislodge me an hour ago, & now the sun is having a turn. Nothing could have been less successful with me than the country air. I am only just recovering from the misery into which I was plunged by a sleepless night in a bed about 5 ft 2 in. long in the restless, demagnetized atmosphere of this pretentiously rural place. If I hold out until Saturday afternoon I shall have endured the utmost that nature can sustain.

Prithee persevere with the speaking: I found with unspeakable delight last time that you were beginning to do it quite beautifully. There is much more to be done, of course, much ill usage in store for you, but success is now certain. You have reached the stage of the Idiotically Beautiful. There remain the stages of the Intelligently Beautiful & finally of the Powerfully Beautiful; & until you have attained the last you will never be able to compel me to recognize the substance of that soul of which I was shown a brief image by Nature for her own purposes.

The heat grows insufferable: I must up & away. Yet last night the country was covered with icebergs.

GBS

To SIDNEY WEBB

Stafford
[A/14]   1st September 1891

[Shaw had embarked on a provincial lecture tour on 28th August, which included Reading, Oxford, Dorchester, Great Milton (F. York Powell in the chair), Walsall, Stafford, Wolverhampton, Newcastle, Longton, Hanley, and Northampton. Sir Cornelius M. Warmington (1842–1908) was a barrister and member of the Senate of London University, who was running for Parliament. William Hines (d. 1904), a chimney sweep and trade union agitator,

306

who had just joined the Fabians, instantly organised a successful Oxford branch. Powell (1850–1904) was a lecturer and tutor of Christ Church, who in 1894 became Regius Professor of Modern History at Oxford. Despite Shaw's optimism about the Walsall anarchists being docile, six of them were arrested in 1892 for manufacturing bombs and four (Charles, Cailes, Deakin, and Battola) were sentenced to penal servitude. Kate Dodd was secretary of the Reading (Berkshire) Branch of the Fabian Society.]

Dear Webb

Have you seen the extracts headed "Gladstonians & Socialists" from the London letter of the Manchester Courier? The Pall Mall [Gazette] also said things about the Lewisham election to the same effect. Will you write a letter to some suitable London paper explaining that Warmington, so far from being pushed by the Fabians &c, deliberately made it impossible for them to support him by sticking to Leaseholds Enfranchisement, & drawing the moral that it is useless for Gladstonians to bid for the support of labor speakers whilst they have labor measures in one hand & reactionary Whig measures in the other. I wrote to W, as we agreed, on the subject; and so did Wallas. W. cannot therefore contradict any statement to the effect that he lost the aid of the "eloquent speakers" whose absence some Gladstonian paper deplored the other day by going in for L.E. A letter from you would be sure to be inserted & quoted just at present.

You ought to do a trip to Oxford & get Hines to drive you about the villages speechifying. On a fine day it is very pleasant; and it is a capital way of getting quietly into the way of talking to the agricultural laborer in the open, an art to which you now, I suppose, stand committed in view of possible rural candidatures. Hines has enthusiastic recollections of your Russell Club performances; and his gift for overwhelming opponents & interrupters with sheer insult is unique. York Powell, who put me up, is a very good fellow. His rooms are about the prettiest in Christchurch; and he does not keep one in the least on the stretch in the manner of hosts. I believe that by following up the work with Hines we could collar the whole countryside.

Walsall was an utter failure. It rained so hard that the meeting was out of the question. I could only get up on a chair in the street with umbrella & macintosh, & ask a few people who stopped to stare, to come to the club & listen to me. About 15 came. The whole game is spoiled by this club calling itself The Anarchist-Communist Club. They mean absolutely nothing by it; but of course it isolates them & breaks their back just as completely as if they did.

In Reading I stood in the street & jawed for an hour & a half. I

307

believe a Fabian named Miss Kate Dodd was present: she should be consulted as [to] the effect produced, as she is an active & intelligent person, they tell me.

Wolverhampton tonight. I have just ascertained that the meeting has been planned with a view to police interference & the offering me up as a victim in the cause of free speech. Pleasant prospect this.

The Potteries people have taken halls & announced a charge of a penny for admission, with 6ᵈ reserved seats. It will be interesting to see how this succeeds.

Back late on Sunday night.

GBS

To EMERY WALKER

[C.u/3]

29 Fitzroy Square W
11th September 1891

[The Art Workers' Guild paid a visit to the National Gallery on the 12th. William Archer and Shaw visited Walker the morning of the 13th to have Archer's photo taken.]

Archer will have to return to his place on Sunday & catch an after-noon train later on for Cobham. So he wants to come down pretty early, and to get away before dinner.

Are you coming to the National Gallery tomorrow to have your mind improved? Do not forget to put a tin of insect powder in your bag. Some of the Italian hotels are world-famous for their

To WILLIAM MORRIS

[A/3; X/140.e]

Venice
23rd September 1891

[The Art Workers' Guild tour, which began on 16th September, included Milan, Verona, Venice (for a week), Padua, Mantua, and Pavia; the tourists returned to London on 4th October. Henry Longden Sr (d. 1920), a metal worker who was an early member of the Art Workers' Guild, was one of the founders (in 1888) of the Arts and Crafts Exhibition Society, of which Walter Crane was president. Henry Holiday (1839–1927) was a stained-glass designer and artist, whose work graces Salisbury Cathedral and St Luke's Hospital, New York. Sir Francis L. Chantrey (1781–1841) was a sculptor and portrait painter. Joseph Turner (1775–1851) was the famous English landscape painter and water-colourist, several of whose paintings (*c.* 1843–44) had Venice as their subject. Sir Sydney C. Cockerell (1867–1962) was secretary to William Morris and the Kelmscott Press (1892–98); he later became director of the Fitzwilliam Museum, Cambridge.

The views expressed in this letter were subsequently embodied in Shaw's essay, "On Going to Church," in *The Savoy*, January 1896.]

Dear Morris

I write to you partly because if I do not, Walker will; and he will tell you anything he thinks will please you, regardless of his private mind; but chiefly because I must work off my growing irritation and escape for a moment from the fearful solitude created by these 27 men, most of whom have taken up art as the last refuge of general incompetence. On reflection, I doubt if this remark will bear examination: I suppose it is in the nature of such an expedition that we should all appear fools to one another now and then. But about 20 out of the 27 seem to me to be capable of admiring everything except beauty. They will admire a thing because it is early Gothic, because it is Rennisongce, because it is by someone they have read about, because it is one of the thousand odd objects which Ruskin has described as "the most entirely great work of art in the world" &c. &c. &c. &c. They are a godsend to the photograph sellers, the tinkers, & the fruiterers. They buy halfpennyworths of figs, melons, & poor little grapes, and swear that they never tasted such lusciousness. They stare at turners & coppersmiths, and buy the antiquities which the blackguards are making under their very noses. Even Walker has just paid 3½ francs for a three-spouted brass thing supposed to be a lamp, but really a sort of candlesnuff incense burner which would stink him out of Hammersmith Terrace if he attempted to use it. The ring at the top is bent, and the stand is damaged and dirty. These evidences of age console him for the flagrant modernity of the combustion chamber, or whatever they call it.

The Venetian municipality has placed at our disposal a person supposed to be a young architect, whom I rather suspect of being a plain clothes policeman set to watch that we do not steal bits of mosaic, or cut our names in the monuments. He takes no interest in us; is ill

309

at ease and desperately bored by our exclamations of "Che beau maison!" (on my honor this is verbatum), "Très bellissimo," "Most interesting" "Chi a dipinto questo scoolptoor?" and so on. Longden senior, whose French is so execrable that even I can detect solecisms in it, carries on in the most enterprising way with curators of galleries who receive us. As to our special architect here, he refers all our questions to the attendants, and hardly makes a pretence of ever having been in the place before! And I have an uneasy suspicion that we take advantage of collectivity to bilk the wretched sacristans unmercifully in the matter of tips. The Art Workers' Guild will be known henceforth as a body which expects a man to shew round 20 persons for one franc. At least I infer this from the difference between the faces of the sacristans whom I tip, and those tipped by our unfortunate organizer, who has to be mean for us all. Sometimes a party of five art workers take a gondola for two hours, and offer the gondolier a franc and a tip of 25 cents. They regard his protests as an attempt to impose on them.

As to my own impressions, I can only say, so far, that Italian architecture appears to me to be inferior to northern architecture. It is wonderfully spontaneous and happy; but it is not organic: it is flagrantly architecture for the sake of ornamentality. The proportions are often knocked off with the greatest luck, and the general effect handsome, distinguished (or rather grand), joyous, and so on; but the thing does not grow in the great way, nor can I see much tracery that could not be "restored" (if destroyed) without loss of quality by the Venetians today. The cathedral at Milan [the Duomo] disgusted me: it struck me as representing the result of giving a carte blanche order for the biggest thing of the kind that could be done. Every sort of decoration is heaped up and elaborated and repeated. There are windows miles high & acres broad, with nothing in them but hundreds of little piffling pictures like pages out of Cassell's Illustrated Family Bible— not even a joke in them except the stealing of Adam & Eve from Coreggio's Venus & Mercury in the National Gallery. I greatly prefer St Pauls, which at any rate is the work of an architect [Sir Christopher Wren], whereas at Milan there were all sorts of artists employed to get over the difficulty of there being no architect. The only great church I saw in Milan was an old one called San Ambrogio, with the altar—made of gold, jewels, filigree, mosaic &c—shut up in Chubb safe doors, which they opened after energetic chaffering for 10 francs for the lot of us. This was a Romanesque church; and it and one at Verona called St Zeno are the only places I felt happy in on the way here. At San Ambrogio there was plenty of free & beautiful work in

310

the capitals of the pillars in the courtyard, and in the carving of the panels in the choir stalls. At the Brera I saw lots of fragments of stone with this free & fresh work on them. The director there, though a very pleasant and genuinely enthusiastic old boy, never said a word about it, though he was very proud of a pretty statue of Gaston de Foix, which Henry Holiday & Chantrey could have turned out between them to perfection. Here in Venice the churches I have seen—the Frari (which Walker *will* call the Friary), San Giovanni e Paolo, S. Rocco—are nothing but enormous barns, with a sort of ribbed vaulting in the apse which looks exactly like modern cast iron construction. Of course there are here and there monuments, carvings &c, which are beautiful; but they are all as separate from the building as the pictures are. I have not put my nose inside St Marks yet; but the outside disappointed me: I expected above all things color, and it is *scraped clean*. Besides, I believe most of the best artworks the Venetians have, they stole to start with. Then they got rich, and ladled out money for their palaces & tombs & the like. The extraordinary difficulty of building in the sea, necessitating the most thorough & careful foundation work, made the Venetian people able to rise to the money with magnificent work of a kind—Tintoretto & Paul Veronese being the greatest in that kind—but somehow they did nothing architecturally that gives me the sensation I remember getting many years ago when I saw St John's Chapel in the Tower of London (I had never troubled myself consciously about it before). Splendid walls, splendid windows, splendid stairs, splendid pinnacles, but no vital, unanswerable, convincing arches, vaultings, and growths of stone into one great rooftree. So, somehow, Italy seems to me a humbug. In S. Zeno there is a most beautiful sort of porch—a canopy on two exquisitely slender but sufficient pillars—and a fine tower. But even in these earliest & finest churches, the organic nature of the porch & the arches is not carried far: it is small in proportion to the barn which is already there, though the barn is finely balanced in its own shape, unlike these monstrous Venetian affairs.

This is a generalization of my first hasty impression, which may be a quite insufferable one, in which case it will in due time right itself. Somehow there is a painful element in the whole affair which throws me back on my old iconoclastic idea of destroying the entire show. For it is a show and nothing else. Neither the Italians nor the trippers on whom they sponge have any part or lot in the fine things they see. They didnt make them; couldn't make them; consequently cant appreciate them even when they are ready made for them. The people here who are chock full of Ruskin are just as bad as the authorities who cut out illuminated capitals from old MSS & paste them on millboards in frames for exhibition. And they are much worse than the blank Philistines, who shew a healthy preference for the penny steamers, the sunsets & the Lido. The first day we were here was a very fine day & it convinced me completely that the only painter who had the least notion of what he had to paint was Turner. I saw at once, of course, the things all the common painters are driving at—the clear atmosphere, the olive complexions & so on—but I saw, too, that they never came within 100 miles of reaching it.

However, I do not believe that a permanent, living art can ever come out of the conditions of Venetian splendour, even at its greatest time. The best art of all will come when we are rid of splendor and everything in the glorious line. Then by all means let them restore & ruin & cut up missal pages & scrape & do what they like. The old bricks are of no use in building up the new art, as far as I can see, though at Milan I was surprised to find how not only the "style" of the great painters, but the very figures they painted were gradually evolved from man to man from Cimabue & Giotto to Titian.

A Venetian has just come in. He declares that Walker's lamp must be old, because it would have cost more if it had been new. I must leave off so that I may talk to him & be polite. Now that I think of it, my apologies should be rather for the unconscionable length to which I have run over stale matters.

You should see Walker & Cockrell. Their faces & necks are mere mosquito pastures—all red spots. I have protected myself by burning pastilles which make a fume so noxious that I have all but succumbed to it myself. I have also been fortunate in discouraging fleas, which soon abandon the settlements they found on me. The fact is, I perspire freely. My keys, for instance, get quite dulled with rust in a short time. I am convinced that the damp gives the fleas rheumatism, which must be a hideously unpleasant complaint for an insect which has to jump for its life every few seconds. Hence they soon quit me.

Walker says he will write as soon as he can settle down to it—also that he has not been inside S. Maria Salute, as the outside is enough for him.

GBS

312

To FLORENCE FARR

247 Moorside Lane. Birmingham
[7th October 1891]

[A/4; X/115]

[Shaw visited Birmingham on 6th to 8th October to hear William Morris's address on the pre-Raphaelites at the Municipal Art Gallery, which opened a loan collection exhibition. The pseudonymous appellation for Florence Farr, linked with the reference to her "beautiful eyes that are still blind," suggests that Shaw had in mind Mrs Anna Williams (1706–83), a blind Welsh poet befriended by Dr Samuel Johnson, in which case his reference to himself as Walker could be an association with John Walker (1732–1807), a professional lecturer on elocution who also enjoyed Dr Johnson's patronage. "Hooky Walker," however, was a popular Victorian derisive exclamation meaning "Ridiculous! Incredible!" in response to a statement that was either not to be trusted or obviously exaggerated. Joseph Mazzini (1805–72) was the famous Italian revolutionist. The effusion of this letter reflects not only the influence of the pre-Raphaelite exhibition, but also the oratorios *Elijah* and *Messiah* which Shaw had heard at the Birmingham Festival that week.]

My dear Mrs Williams

This is to certify that you are my best and dearest love, the regenerator of my heart, the holiest joy of my soul, my treasure, my salvation, my rest, my reward, my darling youngest child, my secret glimpse of heaven, my angel of the Annunciation, not yet herself awake, but rousing me from a long sleep with the beat of her unconscious wings, and shining upon me with her beautiful eyes that are still blind.

Also to observe incidentally that Wednesday is the nearest evening that shews blank in my diary.

yours truly
Joseph Mazzini Walker

To ELIZABETH ROBINS

Great Northern Express
Somewhere beyond Grantham. 3.45 p.m.
19th October 1891

[A/33]

[Shaw's "difficult paper," delivered to the Fabians on 16th October, was "The Difficulties of Anarchism," subsequently published as Tract No. 45 under the title *The Impossibilities of Anarchism* (1893). The Halifax lecture on Labour Representation the night of the 19th drew an audience of 400. *Denise*, by Alexandre Dumas fils, first seen at the Comédie Française in 1885, was produced in an English translation at the Lyceum by Henry Irving on 11th June 1886.]

313

Dear Miss Robins

I do not really know how to apologize; but it has just occurred to me that in putting off answering your letter last week I totally forgot that I was also putting off forwarding your letter to Mrs Theodore Wright. I earnestly hope that I have not done irreparable mischief by this outrageous oversight. The moment the train will allow me I shall telegraph instructions to my mother to forward the letter at once. I can only say in my defence that though I often have to leave my letters over for a week or so, I seldom achieve such a masterpiece of inconsiderateness as this has been. It is the fault of a very elaborate & difficult paper which I had to read at the Fabian last Friday. This threw over my World article to Saturday & Sunday; and the result was that I was at high pressure all the week—so completely preoccupied that the only thing I remembered about your letter was that I had an excuse for writing to you when the rush was over. And now that it *is* over I have nothing to say but this awful confession.

I address this to the Opera Comique, as I have not your letter with me. I am en route for Halifax, where I lecture this evening, returning tomorrow afternoon.

In order to bring *Denise* up to date, you should get me to play Thouvenin & to rewrite the part from my own point of view. But this is the only departure from the original that ought to be tolerated. If you avail yourself of [Clement] Scott's version, make him discard his "adaptations" and give you a translation instead—an English equivalent, as exact as he can get it. The moralizings of Dumas fils will be much better understood than those of Ibsen, though the poetry of H.I. [Henry Irving] will be badly missed.

yours, much out of countenance
G. Bernard Shaw

To WILLIAM ARCHER

[H/2]
29 Fitzroy Square W
25th October 1891

[Archer had written "The Quintessence of Ibsenism: An Open Letter to George Bernard Shaw" for the November issue of the *New Review*. Robert W. Buchanan (1841–1901), poet and novelist, was the author of the famous attack on the pre-Raphaelites, "The Fleshly School of Poetry," in the *Contemporary Review* (1871). Buchanan, who addressed Shaw variously as "Jehovah Junr" and "Dear Timon," was also addicted to open letters, and later published two of these ("The Jester as Moral Pioneer" and "The 'Translation' of Bottom the Realist") on Shaw in the *Sunday Special* (3rd and 24th April 1898).

Arthur Schopenhauer (1788–1860), German philosopher and chief expounder of pessimism, was the author of *The World as Will and Idea* (1818; English transl. 1883). *Emperor and Galilean* (1869–73), a massive poetic work by Ibsen, consists of two dramas on the subject of the apostasy of the Emperor Julian.]

[Archibald] Grove has just sent me your open letter with a suggestion that I should write a reply to it. On reading it over I have formed a strong opinion that you ought without further ado to burn it. Everybody will expect something specially good from you on the subject; and this is quite exceptionally bad. Its badness is twofold. In the first place it entirely omits the really serious question of the review—that is to say, whether my interpretation of Ibsen is right or wrong, or how much right and how much wrong, and if wholly wrong what Ibsen's meaning actually is. As to this there is nothing in the letter, absolutely nothing. You must have something at the bottom of Walden Pond, if you ask the public to dive into it. Either the language of The Wild Duck means something or nothing. If something, is it something particular, or is it the ordinary meaning—is Relling simply Clement Scott or Buchanan? If the latter, why has it puzzled and revolted Clemmy? If the former, am I right or wrong; and if wrong, put your finger on the error. And if you do put your finger on it, shew whether it is common to myself and Ibsen (in which case I should be right in my interpretation, though we should be both wrong in our philosophy) or whether it has led me to miss Ibsen's meaning. That is the job which the book presents to the illustrious W. A. from the public point of view. Instead of doing it, you have written a criticism of *me*, leaving it to be inferred that you do not demur to the identity between Ibsen's philosophy and what you call mine, and that you dismiss them both as worthless.

The worst of it is that your criticism of me is nothing but a mere crudity. It is like a country parson's criticism of Socialism. Socialism is an attack on property : that is enough for him; how could we get on without property; we should have universal theft and anarchy: in a week things would be as they were &c, &c, &c. Now there is no poorer dialectical game than that which proceeds by each party assuming that the other means what he cannot possibly mean—that he is an idiot, in short. This is what the parson does; and this is what you do. You see an attack on Reason; and you immediately go ahead to shew how impossible it is to do without reason. That is what everybody does in the first five minutes, and what nobody has any excuse for doing in the second five. When you have once thought out the position that the real and of course eternally indispensable function of Reason is to devise the means for the satisfaction of the will, whereas the essence of Rationalism is to set it up as being the prime motor of human action— the steam instead of the engine—you will then find not only that the book is precise on the point, but that it contains the most emphatic and explicit warning against the error you have fallen into. In the place where you call me an ingenuous sophist, you blunder in an amazing manner into the reductio-ad-absurdum of your own assumption about the extinction of reason. My book is closely reasoned from cover to cover. Precisely, says you: therefore you have not got rid of reason after all. Exactly, I reply; and now, in the name of Reason itself, may I ask you which of us you suppose that stone has brained?

The phrase about the age of reason going its way after the age of faith, by the bye, is not a rhetorical flourish, but an allusion to Tom Paine's proclamation of the Age of Reason as the successor to the Age of Faith. And he meant that Reason was to ascertain the Divine Will instead of taking the Church's word for it.

What you say of the Voltaire point is hopelessly fudged by your overlooking my careful limitation of the meaning of his "necessity" to logical necessity. The whole gist of my criticism of him is that he did regard lack of logical necessity as lack of real necessity. If you can shew from other writings and sayings of his that he was not really under any such confusion, and that he saw eye to eye with Schopenhauer on the point, then you will throw a new and startling light on his character. And, observe, you will then have changed the complexion of his "Je n'en vois pas &c.," from a fundamentally honest though mistaken home truth to a brutal quibble. You accuse me of quibbling, by the bye. You will always find that when one man has a tight grip of the meaning of a word, and another man has a loose and perpetually shifting one, the latter always accuses the former of quibbling. I defy you to pick out one passage in which I have used the Voltairean "necessity" in any other sense than the one expressly claimed for it at the outset. So there!

As to Schopenhauer, you have seized only the vaguest generalization of his synthesis—so vague that it seems identical with your equally vague generalization of mine. In vain have I warned you in the book itself against confusing his metaphysics with his philosophy. I have taken his distinction between the intellect and the will, a natural fact which has always been preached (as I have pointed out) in one form or another,

316

but which he undoubtedly brought clearly into the light of modern thought. That does not make me a Schopenhaurist, or Ibsen one. His pessimism, and his conviction that the will was the devil and the intellect the divine saviour, marks him off from me and from Ibsen in the clearest and most fundamental way. You might just as well call me a Herbert Spencerist because I accept the doctrine of evolution. My whole book is a protest against the Genganger, the dread of the Will and the blind faith in the intellect. And as to pessimism, not only ought the last page of my first Fabian Essay to publicly absolve me from all suspicion of it, but the Quintessence first disposes of it by implication on the simple ground that it *is* an ISM, and then deals with it explicitly in the pages dealing with the survivals in Ibsen's mind of the old middle class pessimism as shewn in Emperor & Galilean &c. The fact is, you have done just what you think I did: you have fished one notion out of Schopenhauer, or rather out of his reputation, and you call that Schopenhauerism. In any case, the second and third sentences of your third paragraph simply mean that I have given "my" doctrine a wantonly obscurantist air by using the terms of a philosophic synthesis which marked a great advance towards lucidity of thought. Of course you dont mean this; but just conceive the confusion of mind you must have attained in order unsuspectingly to leave such holes in your article.

Your objection that the distinction between the Will and the Reason is not new (after which you go on, as usual in such cases, to deny that it exists) brings the letter down to the level of the Noodle's oration. I do not say this merely because I have not only pointed out the antiquity of the distinction myself, but mentioned the most familiar and convincing forms of its recognition before Schopenhauer's grandfather was born. It is because Ibsen has put forward as novel certain consequences of it which have been so completely overlooked that our moral standards have become seriously corrupted. That is where the novelty is; and that is where it is claimed. Now if you mean to say that the novelty is no novelty—that the criticism of life in Ghosts or the Wild Duck is stale and trite, then you are an ass; and matters are so far irremediable. But if you have only missed the point, then you have merely made an ass of yourself, which is remediable by suppressing your oversight.

Another Noodle's Oration phrase, and a quite inexcusable one, is "showman of a moral waxwork." It is a base desertion of Ibsen—a deliberate going over to the haters of light who cant about art for art's sake. And it is a most unworthy and inadequate treatment of my very

317

careful demonstration of the point at which Ibsen's delight in the exercise of his artistic faculty came at last under complete subjection to his impulse as a moralist. (And observe, the artistic faculty may work harder under the compulsion of the moral impulse than in freedom, just as the reason is far keener as the servant of the will than when it is merely taking exercise in the academy.)

It is impossible for me to go on any further. I have already cursed you up hill and down dale for forcing me on a very busy day to say all this over again which I have so laboriously said before merely because you will go fooling over a serious bit of thinking. Out of the depths of a pessimism induced by your actual observation of the fact (for statistics see "Facts for Socialists," one penny) that out of every five men in the country four live uncomfortably, one dishonorably, and most of them miserably both one and the other, you find yourself under such a necessity to whittle down and disparage any clear statement whatever, that you proceed to inform the world that the will to live now means the will to live nobly, or at least comfortably. Now if there were any sort of satisfaction to you in this, I would not attempt to baulk you in it. But since it is only your way of swearing you will ne'er consent; since it will do you no credit and me no good; since it includes Ibsen in the depreciation of what has been said as not worth saying; and since the occasion is one on which you will be expected to put forward your sharpest and closest dialectical power—since finally it is all the blastedest evasion, misunderstanding, and nonsense, I most vehemently recommend you to either cancel it or do it over again.

In hottest haste
GBS

To WILLIAM ARCHER

[A/2]

29 Fitzroy Square W
26th October 1891

This crackbrained proposal really finishes me. You must have your way as to publishing your letter; but no public reply from me is possible. Quem Deus vult asinare, prius dementit. An awful silence will fall on your little world when the New Review appears: your friends will breathe only by stealth. I write to Grove to say, No answer.

Evidently your underlining means that I am a Rationalist because I deal in rational ideas. Doubtless I am also a Positivist because I deal with positive facts, and you a Chiropodist because you have corns.

If you like, you may put my reply at the foot of your letter in these terms—"Oh William Archer, William Archer: where are your brains? G.B.S."

GBS

[Archer drafted a reply on the reverse of Shaw's letter of the 26th, in which he reminded Shaw "I have always said you would end by being Pope, & now I'm sure of it. Better order your triple crown at once. Only not content with being infallible yourself you insist on everyone else being infallible, & want to have all bad reasoning burnt by the common hangman. Very likely my reasoning *is* bad; but I insist on my inalienable right to reason badly if I please. And let me add that if all your unborable revolutionists are going to be infallible logic-machines, I think they'll have a mighty dull time of it. But that's a contingency I face with equanimity. The probability is that neither of us is anywhere near right, but it's very likely that you have the right end of the stick & I the wrong. All I want you to do is to pull.

"Of course I think you're doing precisely what you think I'm doing. If there ever have been rationalists idiotic enough to make reason the motor in human conduct, why worry about them at this time of day? I say you are setting up an idiotic rationalism (which may or may not have some sort of historic foundation) & thinking you've done a mighty fine thing when you've knocked it down again. I don't think I'm quite as bad as that, for the position I attribute to you (whether it's yours or not) is not idiotic, only injudicious. In a word, I accuse you of deifying the mainspring of the watch & reviling the regulator; you accuse me of deifying the regulator & ignoring the mainspring; of course the latter blunder would be the more imbecile of the two; but 'who deniges of it, Betsey Prig'? [The reference is to Dickens's *Martin Chuzzlewit*.]

"As to answering or not answering, the difference between us is this: I want you to accept the Socratic method of working towards truth, you howl because I haven't put all Ibsen & all myself into a newspaper article (for you know it wasn't intended even for a Review) with Herbert Spencerian precision. And remember, I'm not casting myself for Socrates—Socrates, I take it, is the fellow who comes best out of the skirmish, & as you're a practised debater & I'm not, it would be more shame to you if that wasn't you. As a matter of fact your position is not Socratic but Clement Scottish— you say 'Yah, here comes a beastly pessimist—the only thing I can do is to 'eave 'arf a brick at him, & as I dont care to do that I'll do nothing.'"]

319

To WILLIAM ARCHER

[H/2]

29 Fitzroy Square W
7th November 1891

[Frank Harris (1856–1931) was at this time editor of the *Fortnightly Review*, in the November issue of which Archer had contributed to a discussion on dramatic criticism, "The Free Stage and the Drama." Harris gained fame when he acquired the *Saturday Review* in 1894; he also gained the lifelong friendship of Shaw, who was his dramatic critic from 1895 to 1898. Mary Anderson (1859–1940) was an American-born actress of great beauty but limited talent, who retired from the stage after her marriage in 1889 to Antonio de Navarro. Leporello is valet to Don Giovanni in Mozart's opera.

Shaw, in a moment of confusion, posted this letter to Harris, who returned it on 11th November with the comment: "I will confess to a sense of mystification upon reading the enclosed letter of yours, which none the less afforded me much amusement. I tried to look upon it as the eccentricity of a clever writer, but failed to comprehend its drift. I felt as Alice may have felt in Wonderland" (BM).]

I have just had a letter from Frank Harris asking me to put my oar into the discussion on criticism. I have refused on the ground that I have said all that need be said in the appendix to the Quintessence. The magnanimity of this resolution consists in my abstaining from exposing the monstrous hypocrisies of your own article. When I see you posing as the incorruptible Archer, assuring the public with an air of primeval simplicity that you would not know how to set about getting half a crown for a notice if you wanted to, and that no monk knows less of teas with pretty actresses than William the Anchorite, I really feel a moral revulsion. How if I were to tell the world that I have hardly once dropped in on you unexpectedly at Queen Square without disturbing a tete-a-tete between you and some pretty actress or another; so that your stock excuse became that I did it on purpose, having got wind of the appointment? Marion [Lea] la bionda today: Elizabeth [Robins] la bruna tomorrow. Have you forgotten Hampstead Heath and Mary Anderson? do the photographs of the fascinating Janet [Achurch] no longer plaster your walls? is your table already cleared of the gift books of the irresistible [Ada] Rehan, the reward of your shameless recantation? If Leporello, with his catalogue in his pocket, had ever come upon an article by Don Juan expressing an artless surprise that no pretty woman ever tried to "get at" him, he would have felt much as I feel over the Fortnightly. I can see all those beauteous eyes winking as they read your audacities, and their owners making private notes not to believe men who wear incorruptible collars. The amazing, staggering,

320

breath bereaving part of it all is that I actually believe that you thought
you were perfectly sincere in what you wrote. Why, man alive, there
is not an ambitious actress in London whose first move is not to get at
William Archer. And they do it with perfect security under cover of
your theory that the thing is impossible and consequently never
happens. Your theory that your name has never been publicly connected with Ibsen's, and that you have in fact hardly ever alluded to
that obscure foreigner, is nothing to your pretty actress theory.

I have just received the New Review article. The oftener I read it,
the more flagrantly does it proclaim itself pure Clement Scott. Its
hideous superficiality has destroyed my faith in your intellectual
solidity as completely as the Fortnightly has destroyed my belief—
what was left of it—in your moral integrity. A man who can assert that
the only safe way to work the L & M Railway is to draw up an absolute
and unalterable time table, and start the trains at the appointed speed
and hour without regard to earthquake, landslip, accident, snowfall,
fog or certain death (since the human mind is incapable of any other
guidance except blind idealistic adherence to the letter of the time-
table) is a man who ought not to be at large. Now either you mean this,
or you are incapable of seeing that an ordinary time-table is no violation
at all of the principle that "circumstances alter cases," in which case
you are a manifest idiot. Altogether the article is one which you will
have to live down.

If you would like to print the first part of this letter in the next
Fortnightly as a reply to your article, I have no objection whatever. In
fact, I think it ought to be done in the public interest.

Walkley says he is bringing out a book. Why did you let him throw
away his copyright permanently?

GBS

11th Nov. 1891

Has anything more unspeakably awful ever happened than my sending this to Harris & his letter to you?

To WILLIAM ARCHER

29 Fitzroy Square W
[A/2]   9th November 1891

[Louis Frederick Austin (1852–1905), secretary to Henry Irving, was also
the dramatic critic of the *New Review*. William Davenport Adams (1851–
1904), head of the Reviewing Department of the *Globe* from 1885, was

literary and theatrical critic for several London papers. Joseph Knight (1829–1907), theatre historian and editor of *Notes and Queries*, was dramatic critic of *The Athenaeum*. "Thomson" was Sidney R. Thompson, who replaced Shaw as musical critic of *The Star*, signing his articles "Piccolo." Giulia Ravogli was an Italian prima donna, hailed as one of the greatest dramatic sopranos of her day.]

Horror on horror's head: I have put your letter into Harris's envelope —and such a letter! Description would be futile: you must read the letter when he sends it on in order to realize the awful situation. I am really very sorry. Fortunately, he will probably take it to be pure chaff.

Your point about anti-Ibsen criticism needing no hypothesis of corruption to explain it is one which I quite catch. I ought to, considering that you have stolen it from my appendix (see page 160, lines 6–16). In your letter, you say, waking up suddenly to a sense of real life, that people have often tried, and do continually try, to chicken and champagne you. In the article you solemnly declare that no one has yet thought it worth while to make the slightest attempt to buy your good will. Which of these two positions is the apriorist and which the realist one? You also say in your letter that corruption, *as regards Ibsen*, does not come into play. What, then, is your view of, for instance, the terrific row made by Yates when Lady C[olin] C[ampbell]'s article on Ghosts got into the paper during his absence at Bath? Was it his conscientious Puritanism or his countryhouse circulation that was imperilled then? Or do you suppose that this was a solitary and accidental incident? Or have you forgotten it? Further, there is in your article no limitation of your denial of corruption to criticism of Ibsen, any more than there is in my appendix.

The fact is, you have not yet realized that what you have read about and talked about as "getting at" critics, is just what is happening to you and me and Lady C. & Austin & Davenport Adams & Knight & Massingham & all the rest that you know. You are like Agatha in "An Unsocial Socialist," regarding yourself as an exceptional person whose experiences do not belong to the common categories. You have, in short, talked prose all your life without knowing it. The other evening, at the Shaftesbury, Thomson of the Star came up to me with tears in his eyes (positively) and shewed me "her last gift." It was a handsome cigar box which Giulia Ravogli had given him on her departure. Poor Thomson was as void of all guile in the matter as you were when you were taking tea with Miss Robins. To him it only meant that he liked Giulia and that she had been kind to him. To the public it meant that "Piccolo" had been got at. In Thomson's place I being an older man, should have returned the cigar case. In your place I should have taken tea with Miss Robins—possibly have gone to greater extremities, but my article in the Fortnightly should have been a graceful explanation of how the corruption actually worked—how different it was from the fancy picture of gross bribery & blackmail painted by apriorists. And I should not have flatly contradicted either George Moore or the author of a document so very carefully drawn up and so scrupulously based on observation of facts as the appendix to the Quintessence.

Seriously, I think that page 671 of the Fortnightly is a most outrageous piece of trifling—not to say petulance. You should join the Fabian & get a little realism knocked into you.

GBS

To SERGIUS STEPNIAK

[C/1]

29 Fitzroy Square W
9th November 1891

[Stepniak was serving as a sponsor of child prodigy Max Hambourg, who later became famous as the pianist Mark Hambourg (1879–1960). Shaw reviewed the concert on 2nd December in *The World*: "Another prodigy, young Max Hambourg, gave a pianoforte recital at Steinway Hall, and once more played Bach better than any other composer on his program. With such a training as Eugene Holliday has had from Rubinstein, this Russian lad might astonish the world some day; but he does not seem to be exactly in the way of getting it at present." Bernhard Stavenhagen (1862–1914), a pupil of Liszt, was a well-known concert pianist and conductor.]

Dear Stepniak

I have just been looking over Hambourg's programme. There are half a dozen shocking misprints in it which should be remedied. And I think the first item is an artistic mistake. Nobody now cares very much for Beethoven's early concertos: Stavenhagen has been playing them lately without much effect. With a second piano substituted for an orchestra they are utterly spoiled. Such a makeshift is only permissible in private practice: it ought not to be done in public merely to shew that the boy can play the notes. I strongly recommend the substitution of a sonata.

G. Bernard Shaw

To WILLIAM ARCHER

[A/2]

29 Fitzroy Square W
10th November 1891

[Frederick G. Tomlins (1804–67) had been the dramatic and art critic of the *Morning Advertiser*. Georges Ohnet (1848–1918) was a French novelist and dramatist; Pinero's *The Ironmaster* was an adaptation of his novel *Le Maître de forges*. Thomas Archer (1885–1918), known to all as "Tomarcher," was William Archer's only child, killed in action in World War I. Henrietta Hodson (1841–1910), an actress, was the wife of the Rt Hon. Henry Labouchere (1831–1912), proprietor of *Truth*; she appears to have been the person responsible for the attempted "puffs" of Frederick Goodall in Shaw's art critiques. "Norman Britton" was the pseudonym signed by Archer to his contributions to the secularist monthly *Progress* (1883–84). Sir Henry Hawkins, Baron Brampton (1817–1907), was a judge who, presiding over many murder trials, acquired the nickname "Hanging Hawkins." G. W. Foote (1850–1915) was a secularist writer, lecturer, and outspoken editor of *The Freethinker* and *Progress*, who succeeded Charles Bradlaugh as head of the National Secular Society. Sir Frederick Wedmore (1844–1921), author and editor, was chief art critic of *The Standard* for many years.]

Yes; but look here. You havent said that chicken and champagne dont matter: what you have told the public is that they dont exist. And that is precisely why I have made so much of this occasion. Hitherto the difference between us has always been, not as to facts, but as to how much the facts mattered. But now, for the first time, you have misstated the facts themselves. It is one thing to say to George Moore, "My good sir, you are quite mistaken if you suppose that we critics spare [Frank] Harris or [Charles] Whyndham one jot because they have chickened and champagned us," and quite another to say, "You are an ignorant liar: critics are never chickened and champagned; and if I wanted a liver wing or a glass of dry Monopole tomorrow, I should not, after all these 12 years, know where to turn for it." Now that I have had the trouble of sticking to you like a bulldog for about a week, I have forced you to come down to reality and, as you say, to agree with me as to the facts. But is it possible that you do not see that if you published this letter of yours in the Pall Mall [Gazette] tomorrow, it would be received with amazement as a complete confession of the utter falsehood of your description of your personal experience in the Fortnightly?

I insist on the point because I have been watching your writing, and find that whilst it has lately gained considerably in eloquence, freedom, and wilfulness in the better sense, it is also getting unscrupulous &

careless. Letting yourself go on the generous side, you also let yourself go on the ungenerous side without making up and verifying your case with your old caution. A few years ago it would have been impossible for you to have conducted a controversy with Moore in such a fashion as to enable him to put you in the wrong at every step of the argument, whatever the merits of your conclusion might be.

Take the case as to me, too. Formerly you stuck to your facts; and though I sometimes thought you saw too few of them at a time, or weighed them unjudgmatically, or grouped them badly, yet I never felt that you were misleading people, and never felt the smallest impulse to contradict you, knowing pretty well that you would finally come unconsciously round to my view in the course of time, when the kaleidoscope had shifted a bit, just as I have sometimes come round to yours. But now you have said the thing that is not—you have drawn a romantic portrait of yourself which is not true, exactly as [Clement] Scott draws maudlin groups of himself, Tomlins & Co. which are not true. And you have also offered me the indignity—of which I mildly complain, on principle—of dismissing me contemptuously with a blow beneath the belt by denying the facts on which my deduction was based, and thereby pretending to convict me of pure deduction.

As to the Ghosts incident, let me first call attention to the extraordinary jump you have made from the position that undue influence was nil in the special case of Ibsen, to the position that Ibsen is so specially obnoxious to editorial influence that it is unfair to argue from it to ordinary plays. This by the way, as a revelation of how your grip slips. But the main point to be grasped is that if you mean, by your "negligable quantity" that in the vast majority of cases the play raises no question of morals or politics, and that neither critic, editor nor proprietor has an axe to grind in the matter one way or another, then I grant you the first part, and admit, as to the second, that it is rather the abstract sense of danger in speaking out than any definite bias for or against the play in question that operates. And even in this I am making the shallowest of concessions; for a moment's reflection will convince you that though a drama by [Robert] Buchanan or Ohnet apparently raises no moral question—and really as well as apparently does not do so in the mind of the conventionally moralled critic—yet you and Walkley and all the abler men have a fundamental quarrel with the Ohnetesque morality which you never dream of raising seriously, simply because, in your case, of Mrs Archer and Tom. Under the circumstances it is not worth doing. But if you were in as independent a position as Samuel Butler, you would think it worth doing, and would do it, if not thoroughly, at least far more than you do now. Suppose you were a critic of commonplace ability—one who could be dismissed and replaced without loss to your paper, as is necessarily the case with most critics. Suppose the only berth that offered itself was one on the Sunday Times, or a private secretaryship to Irving. Would you ever think of telling the whole truth about a Drury Lane or Lyceum performance? Suppose by chance you had not translated Ghosts, and you had had Lady Colin's job, and Yates had been in town. Would you have ventured to say, Either my criticism goes in or I go out? You know that I lost about £100 a year for refusing to criticise in the private interests of Mrs Labouchere. Do you doubt that Mrs Labouchere interferes in the dramatic criticism as well, considering her past? Most men lose their sense of the omnipresent corruption just as they lose their sense of the taste of water, which is always in their mouths; but I think, if you quite seriously examine your career as a writer from the days when you signed Norman Britton to the Fortnightly Review period you will see that you have had to trim your work to suit your paper, Pall Mall, Pioneer, World, [Manchester] Guardian or what not. You now do it instinctively, without feeling it, as I do myself. But compare my Fabian Essays and my Quintessence with my World articles, bold as the last affect to be; and you will find the butter on my mother's bread and my own sticking to my fingers. What would my writing be if I had a wife and family, and had no more ability than any of the men who are craving for my berth today? This is not Stupidity: it is Poverty and Servitude. I prostitute myself as honestly as I can; but I am bought and sold for all that. I do not take a £10 note for a notice; nor does Judge Hawkins take a £50 note for a favorable summing up; nor would [Joseph] Chamberlain take £1000 for backing a private Bill. And so, by putting your standard at our level, you may say that criticism, the Bench, and Parliament are pure, just as you can express your satisfaction with Helmer because he is so far superior to Uriah Heep. You know two journalists who may fairly be called uncompromisingly honest in their utterances. One is [John M.] Robertson: the other is Foote. Both of them are a good deal honester than I am, because, although they do not publish more extreme opinions, yet they have to serve them up without Shaw sauce; and it was a strong sense of this that provoked Robertson to say, in the N.R. [*National Reformer*], that I never said anything that was not palatable to my audiences. Think of all the compliances you have made that they have refused to make; and say is it fair to hold yourself and the rest of the critics, from Wedmore down to Scott, up as uncorrupted and incorruptible. The pretension is valid at Ohnet's standard. Is it so at Ibsen's standard? Or at any standard worth setting up?

However, I have run away from my point that, granting that only a narrow upper margin of dramatic literature raises any controversy at the ordinary standard, no ordinary critic dare, for his livelihood's sake, strike a blow for the anti-idealist side.

By the bye, you have got Voltaire on the brain (vide recent World par.). The saying "that which is too silly to say, one sings it" is in the first act (I think) of Beaumarchais' Mariage de Figaro. Just think of what you have come to when I have to set you right on points of French dramatic literature.

GBS

To WILLIAM ARCHER

29 Fitzroy Square W

[H/2]   13th November 1891

[Antipholus is one of the twin brothers involved in the mistaken-identity plot of Shakespeare's *A Comedy of Errors*. Shaw is quoting Joel Chandler Harris's Uncle Remus in the final paragraph.]

Much obliged for the fancy portrait of yourself on the old lines. Artistically drawn, but not in the least like the original. Have invariably proceeded—with satisfactory results—on the assumption that it was a fancy sketch.

Meaning of the phrase about generous and ungenerous simply that you have lately praised more effusively and blamed more abusively than you used to—that you write to express your feeling without the old preoccupation as to the abstract merits of the case. Meaning re Ohnet, that his plays are vitiated by "idealist" morals, and that this is the real objection to them.

You must observe that in my remarks on compromise, or corruption, or what you choose to call it provided you consistently mean the operation of external causes in inducing a man to suppress, modify, or veil his opinions, I was not delivering a series of moral judgments. The question at issue is not for a moment whether there are some rascally editors and critics. There are black sheep in every flock. The question is, assuming a man to be upright, independent and clean handed, will he under existing circumstances criticize without fear or favor. I say

327

no. In such concessions as he makes he may feel quite justified—may feel that he would demand them if he were in the editor's (or other concessionaire's) place. But it is one thing to say that the critic is not to blame for making certain concessions: it is quite another to assert that the concessions are not made, or to infer that because they dont matter individually they dont matter socially. In saying that you are not to blame and that Yates is not to blame and that you sympathise with Yates and that he would have let you go further than another writer whom he could have more easily done without, you do not for a moment prove that the World is incorrupt. All you shew is that the corruption is not the fault of the editor and critic.

Again, take the comparison of your case and that of G. W. F[oote]. It shews at once that you are muzzled, because F., though himself muzzled in other directions, bluntly says things which you are glad to have said, and which you would probably say yourself sometimes if there was no reason to the contrary. But it does not at all shew that G. W. F. is a nobler character than you. He occupies the most eminent position that his ability and opportunity brought within his reach. In spite of what I said about Shaw sauce I should laugh at Robertson if he claimed to be a braver man than I because my style of swordplay, which he cannot manage, is a safer one than his. We all go as far as our styles will carry us. All four of us get further than the rank and file of our competitors by dint of our exceptional ability. If we cannot get beyond a certain point, it is obvious that the rank and file of the critics get turned back far sooner. The man who gets as far as he wants to go— to say all that he wants to say—must be so completely of the color of his environment that his being a critic as distinct from a mere reporter is hardly conceivable.

Do not suppose that when I insist on my view of a question that I am reproaching you for not being a Shaw. The notion of two Shaws corresponding with one another is one which staggers even me. Your pugnacity, wit, knowledge &c are undoubtedly mixed in different proportions to mine, and the result is both quantitatively and chemically different. I sometimes, when a good side of you comes out by chance against a bad side of me, feel apologetic for the difference; but as we clearly could not stand one another if the difference were abolished, whether by the Archerization of Shaw (with Mrs Archer in the background wondering which was the real Antipholus) or the Shawation of Archer, let us rejoice that it exists. But as to our putting our brains to as good a use as they are capable of, it is as plain as a pikestaff to me that our environment is too many for us in several ways, including

328

some that are pernicious both to ourselves and our neighbors. But I grant you that what we come in conflict with is not opposing faiths in art or religion. It is simply proprietary interests, all powerful, and vested in the darkness of mind of the people.

I do not think that there is anything in the notion that your "layin low and saying nuffin" may have been more baneful to you than if you had upset the apple cart. But I wonder whether you defrauded your parents of a necessary part of their education? For instance, if the same thing should happen with Tom, would you not rather he spoke out than shut you out of his life that way?

GBS

PS I shall be at the Wheatsheaf tomorrow at two. I have a fearful cold, and paid my sixth visit to the dentist [Dr W. J. McDonald] yesterday. I have taken annoyingly to getting my teeth drilled.

To C. THOMAS

[A/23]

29 Fitzroy Square W
11th December 1891

[C. Thomas was an employee of Messrs Robson & Son, printer of *The World*.]

Dear Mr Thomas

I shall try to fake up some reviews on Sunday & let you have them on Monday morning. But I had a sort of breakdown on Thursday from overwork—at least what is overwork to a man naturally so lazy as I am. If it comes on again, I must absolutely drop it. However, I shall try to take it easy tomorrow; and I do not propose to put any very severe labor into the "Christmas Music" business. I cannot see what the paper wants with more advertisements: it has too many already. 90% of them ought to be put down by law: they are only incentives to waste of money.

GBS

To T. FISHER UNWIN

[S/7]

29 Fitzroy Square W
1st January 1892

[The Century Company of New York was publisher of *The Century Dictionary: an encyclopedic lexicon of the English language*, in six volumes,

329

1889–91. Shaw's review of A.B. Walkley's *Playhouse Impressions* appeared in
The Star on 9th January.]

Dear Fisher Unwin

Who are the Century Company? The Chronicle review of the
Dictionary reminds me of their existence. I still hold to my "idea" of
a Century History 1800–1900, to be written by Graham Wallas (who
has already fulfilled half my prophesies by his success as a lecturer on
history) and to be published in 1900. It appears to me that, apart from
the hopelessly fossilized condition of the English firms who are in a
position to undertake ten year enterprises, America has now such a
huge reading public that by 1900 all the monumental books of reference will come from there. The appropriateness of the title of the
Century Co. to a Century History is obvious. Therefore, since you
are insensible to the merits of my project, tell me who is the right man
to approach, and I will attack at headquarters myself.

I have reviewed Walkley's book to the extent of a whole column of
the Star. The corrected proof went in yesterday marked "not to be
used until Jan. 11th." The 9th is Saturday, on which days his own
column appears.

yrs
G.B.S.

To MATTHEW EDWARD McNULTY

29 Fitzroy Square W

[H/4]   27th January 1891 [1892]

[McNulty had published a letter in *The Star* on 22nd January, asserting that
The Mountebanks by W.S. Gilbert and Alfred Cellier (1844–91), the composer of *Dorothy* (in which Lucy Carr Shaw had appeared), was a plagiarism
of an unpublished and unproduced libretto for a comic opera which McNulty
had submitted to Cellier. McNulty's "prima donna" was Lucy Carr Shaw,
with whom he had been corresponding. A. Goring Thomas (1852–92) was
the composer of the opera *Nadeshda* (1885), which Shaw had assailed in the
Dramatic Review (25th April 1885). The criticism of Shaw's novels in the
February *Novel Review* (formerly *Tinsley's*) was of his own authorship.
Bashville is the lovesick footman of Lydia Carew in *Cashel Byron's Profession*.
Ruy Blas is the romantic hero of Victor Hugo's play (1838). Claude Melnotte
is a character in Edward Bulwer Lytton's play *The Lady of Lyons* (1838).]

Come back, rash man: you are making an ass of yourself in this
business. I have cross-examined your prima donna; and her evidence

330

is conclusive against you as to Cellier's not having opened your libretto (if he ever did) until long after Gilbert's book was in his hands, virtually complete. The description of your libretto in the [Daily] Herald disposes of all resemblance between it and The Mountebanks. The "Tamorras" are not Anarchists, nor do they allude to any political or social question: they are the good old Gilbertian brigands whom we have known all our lives. You have insanely *imagined* Gilbert's book before reading it. But even if you were able to establish the most extraordinary coincidences between the two books—and you havent really established one; for the clockwork is as old as clockwork itself— you are bound to admit that Gilbert's statement that he read his book to Goring Thomas last February is either a downright lie (which is impossible) or else disposes of the charge of plagiarism. I may observe that there has just appeared in the first number of The Novel Review a criticism of my novels which points out that the glove fight in Cashel Byron is a reproduction, with some variation of detail, of the wrestling match in As You Like It, and that Bashville is only Ruy Blas and Claude Melnotte over again. Get this instructive review and read it: it is accompanied by a portrait of me.

If you get yourself handsomely and ingeniously out of this mess, making it clear that your book remains valid for some other composer, and adroitly exciting curiosity by giving one or two telling extracts, you may score a devilish good advertisement and get set up in the librettist business eventually by it. Per contra, if you persist in an impossible contention, you will get marked as a man deficient in good sense and sociability, which means damnation. In any case be very wary about saying anything actionable; for Gilbert is touchy, rather litigious, and has a much longer purse than yours.

This is unsympathetic; but it is infallible.

GBS

P.S. There has been no difficulty here about getting the librettos— I ascertained that at the theatre, where I got the one I sent you. Dont mention Lucy on any account. She is a hostile witness, in effect.

To FLORENCE FARR

29 Fitzroy Square W
[H/4; X/115]   28th January 1892

I spent last evening arranging old papers and thinking. Result:— when the thinking was over it was going on to three o'clock—time to go to bed. Otherwise I should have written.

Now listen to me, will-less girl. When you tell me that I best know what I am, I assent, not with humility, but with towering head striking against every star and raising great bumps on them; so that astronomers reel amazed from their telescopes. Cubits high and fathoms deep am I the noblest creature you have yet met in this wood of monkeys where I found you straying. Some of them thought you a pretty female ape; others thought you a goddess: the first asked you to play with them; the second asked to be allowed to worship you: you could not say No to either. Then come I, the man, and make you my woman on your stopping me as I wandered lonely through the forest and asking me to look earnestly at you. For many years had I wandered alone, sufficient to myself: I will, at a word, wander on again alone. But what will you do—return to the monkeys? It is not possible: self-sufficient must you also become or else find no less a man than I to be your mate.

There are two sorts of genius in this world. One is produced by the breed throwing forward to the godlike man, exactly as it sometimes throws backward to the apelike. The other is the mere monster produced by an accidental excess of some faculty—musical, muscular, sexual even. A giant belongs properly to this category: he has a genius for altitude. Now the second order of genius requires no education: he (or she) does at once and without effort his feat, whatever it may be, and scoffs at laborious practice. The first order finds it far otherwise. It is immature at thirty, and though desperately in need of education (being less a child of Nature by so much more as it is advanced in evolution) can find nothing but misleading until it laboriously teaches itself. I am a genius of the first order; and so are you; but I know my order and the price I must pay for excellence, whereas you are always appealing to the experience of the second order to justify your own self-neglect.

You are wrong to scorn farcical comedy. It is by jingling the bells of a jester's cap that I, like Heine, have made people listen to me. All genuinely intellectual work is humorous. You can create your part in a farcical comedy: in Rosmersholm you can only offer yourself as an imitation of something created by Ibsen. I wish to see you an accomplished actress. When you get your part in the first piece, I insist on your reading it over to me. When you are a highly skilled hand, and all difficulties about want of engagements and money disappear, then we will consider further.

Now I must fly, only stopping to say that I challenge any analyst to find one base ingredient in my regard for you; but I will not face the judgment bar at the end of my life with you if I am unable to meet the question, "Why did you suffer her to do her work badly?"

your taskmaster
GBS

To ALMA MURRAY

[H/1; X/109]
29 Fitzroy Square W
15th February 1892

Dear Mrs Forman

At the risk of putting you out of all patience, I write to ask whether I must really proceed with the commission given me by the Shelley Society (merely to find a cast for the Cenci—the simplest thing in the world, of course) on the assumption that you are out of the question for Beatrice. I know of course that if such a calamity can be brought about by mortal means, the Independent Theatre may be relied on to achieve it; but I find it extremely hard to reconcile myself to accepting what they tell me is now the inevitable. Furnivall declares that you said that there would be no difficulty in getting plenty of people who would be only too glad to get the part, and who would do it better than you. If you really said that, you must have been in a mood to say anything. Name one of these gifted aspirants for me, and I will trouble you no more. There was a rumor of Vezin intending to refuse his old part; but on my writing to him for confirmation, he replies "What rot!! I should be delighted to have the chance of playing Cenci again." Is it possible that you have none of this feeling about Beatrice? I heartily wish I could offer you an opportunity of playing it without any but perfectly sympathetic associations and under completely satisfactory artistic conditions; but you will understand that the feebler the general conditions are, the more anxious I am to secure the strongest individual conditions as to the chief parts.

Excuse my importunity. I feel that I can say nothing that you must not have already considered; but as I said before, I somehow cannot feel convinced without a word from yourself directly that I am really to go and search for a makeshift Beatrice. I have not dared to hint to Vezin that there is any question as to who is to play with him. Is there no hope of a repetition of the old success?

yours very truly
G. Bernard Shaw

333

To ALMA MURRAY

[H/1; X/109]

29 Fitzroy Square W
18th February 1892

[Laura Johnson was a young actress who had received tutelage from Hermann Vezin and Madame Modjeska. She and Vezin were touring with Ben Greet's company, another young member of which was Mrs Patrick Campbell. Charles Wilmot (1839–96), actor-manager, was lessee of the Islington Grand.]

Dear Mrs Forman

Thank you for reviving me—after crushing me with your refusal—by the hint that there is a likelihood of your playing Beatrice under your own auspices. I should not have dreamt of urging you to play it under ours if it had occurred to me at the time that there was any alternative.

However, I write mainly to let you know exactly how Vezin is situated. He is on tour, and returns on the 23rd May, when he begins a final fortnight at the Standard. He is of course playing the legitimate drama with Miss Laura Johnson, of whose genius he becomes more and more convinced as he goes on. This puts him out of the question as Cenci until the latter half of June—a serious delay. Also there is the difficulty raised by the new covenant in the lease of the Grand at Islington, whereby Wilmot is bound not to allow the theatre to be used for the performance of unlicensed plays. To wait until the hot weather sets in, and then to take our luck in some deserted theatre, under such discipline as the Independents are capable of establishing, is to me so uninviting that I have resolved on the desperate course of asking Beerbohm Tree to give us the Haymarket and play Cenci to Miss Florence Farr's Beatrice. If Tree accepts this simple-minded proposal, and you subsequently play Beatrice to Vezin's Count, then Shelley will have been centenarized to his heart's content, and Vezin will not be disappointed. Failing that, we must wait for Vezin. But before he commits himself to us, you ought to let him know of any scheme you may have which might give him the opportunity he desires under far more agreeable conditions than we are likely to provide him with. In the interest of my clients the S.S. [Shelley Society] and the I.T. [Independent Theatre], I am prepared to throw Vezin over to the extent of getting Tree in his place if I can thereby secure a theatre and performance early in the season. But I dont think it would be compatible with the friendly relations between us if I were to let him pledge himself to us in ignorance of the fact that there was a better alternative available—that is, to ally himself to you in organizing a

334

really independent performance to which the S.S. people might be forced to subscribe if their own plan failed. Perhaps my imagination is enlarging unwarrantably on your hint; but as I am in favor of your playing Beatrice in any case, I conclude that you will not mind my shewing you all my cards. So, as all Ibsen's heroines say sooner or later, "Now you know."

yours sincerely
G. Bernard Shaw

To J. STANLEY LITTLE

[C/4]

29 Fitzroy Square W
21st March 1892

I dont know Tree's address but if I come across it (I think Todhunter knows it) I will send it on.

Nothing but reviews of fiction nowadays. Have you seen the Novel Review, of which I send you a choice sample? They *can't* succeed; it's impossible.

Advantage of printing play outweighs, in my opinion, risk of piracy. Print one side of paper only, leaving left hand page blank, & have it marked as Proof for private use & not for publication, or something of that sort.

GBS

To LORD RUSSELL

[A/4]

29 Fitzroy Square W
11th April 1892

[John Francis Russell (1865–1931), the brother of Bertrand Russell (who succeeded him as 3rd Earl), was an electrical engineer who became a barrister: he later enlisted as a Fabian. William Alexander Hunter (1844–98), Liberal M.P. for North Aberdeen, had recently introduced a Bill in Parliament to amend the divorce law; it was subsequently rejected. Arnold Toynbee (1852–83), a sociologist and economist, was a pioneer in the social settlement movement. Two years after his death, the first social settlement in the world, Toynbee Hall, Whitechapel, was erected in his honour. Russell presumably addressed Shaw in care of the settlement.]

Dear Lord Russell

I am not the Shaw you knew at Balliol. It is so hard to get any political party to risk meddling with the marriage laws, that I doubt if anything serious will be done until the increase in the number of women able to earn their own living leads to an increase in the number of free unions, known to all the friends of the parties, but not supposed to be. If people only realized before marriage that they might come to dislike one another, and that to have to live with one whom you dislike is penal servitude of the worst kind, they would face anything in the way of social ostracism sooner than run such a risk. But as a matter of fact there is no need to be found out by people who do not want to find you out, and who will wink at anything provided it is not officially mentioned. Consequently I am inclined to think that the upholders of the marriage contract will eventually be forced to lighten & loosen the chains in order to prevent their falling out of use altogether.

I am of course quite in favor of Hunter's Bill.

Excuse my delay in answering your letter. As I am not a Toynbeeite, it took some time to reach me; and I have been overwhelmed with business of one kind or another ever since.

yours faithfully
G. Bernard Shaw

To E. D. GIRDLESTONE

[C/12]

29 Fitzroy Square W
12th April 1892

There is not a man living who is not in favor of equality of opportunity, justice, and everything that is proper & sublime, consistently, of course, with an independent income for himself. J.M. [John Morley] is the worst of all political scoundrels—the conscientious, high-principled scoundrel. Robespierre was a mere trimmer in comparison.

I send you a copy of the Novel Review, which you should have had a month ago but for my laziness & the pressure on my time.

GBS

To JANET ACHURCH

[T/1 (A/4)]

29 Fitzroy Square W
21st April 1892 (in the train)

[The Charringtons had revived *A Doll's House* at the Avenue, on 19th April, with Charrington shifting rôles from Dr Rank to Torvald Helmer.]

Dear Mrs Charrington

Will you excuse my scribbling a letter in a train; it is my only opportunity. I was at the Avenue on Tuesday, and I have just been shewn the onslaught made by Clement Scott in yesterday's Telegraph. You will understand that C.S., during your absence, has been grievously abused by Archer, Walkley and myself, and is now the recognised leader of anti-Ibsenism. Nevertheless he has not hitherto been ill natured about the performers—rather ostentatiously the reverse, in fact; and I dont doubt that his criticism expresses his real mind. However, I do not set overmuch store by it, as I have come to the conclusion that the dramatic critics here have lost all sense of what acting is. They look at plays—Lady Windermere's Fan is an instance—in which there is one actress supported by a crowd of people not one of whom is better than a fairly good walking gentleman or lady; and they write columns about it without one line to shew that they have perceived any shortcoming. Therefore dont attend to any of them; but listen with the greatest respect to MY opinion.

First—so as to keep the main interest to the last—as to the performance in general. Charrington is a complete failure as Helmer. It is not his fault; it is that the part is not in his nature. I always told you that his strong point was that he played with conviction. What is wanted for Helmer is complacency *without* conviction. Charrington has conviction without complacency; and the result is disastrous to the play. It is a case of congenital incapacity—there is no remedy but to send for Waring & return to the old Dr Rank. Charrington's real chance is Rosmer.

As to Nora, the difficulty about her is that she had no artistic conscience. During her travels her voice has become much more powerful —quite Hyde Parkian in its pedal notes, in fact; but she has scandalously neglected to cultivate the beautiful, reposeful, quietly expressive, infinitely inflectionable normal voice, neither raised nor lowered, which is the great charm of a fine speaker. She explodes into fortissimos during which she forgets all about the tone—forgets the one constant tender care which never deserts the great artist. When she quoted the imaginary will of the imaginary old gentleman in the first act, she raised her voice and ground out the words from her chair so harshly—

337

so wickedly without the free, beautiful, fine laughing ring which should have been there—that it took the united strength of my three companions, the *ouvreuse*, the acting manager, the fireman, and a commissionaire to hold me down and restrain me from hurling an opera glass at her head. I refuse to tolerate any Nora who tightens her lower lip like an india rubber band, and then speaks by main force, exulting in the strength of her youth. I am not to be propitiated by any increase in tragic power, however striking. Anybody can be tragic if they are born so; but that every stroke shall be beautiful as well as powerful, beautiful to the eye and ear; that is what I call art. Talking of the eye reminds me to say that if a woman cannot swing in a rocking chair by the mere undulation of her balance, without getting her feet on the ground and pushing off from them like an Oxford stroke at the boat race, she ought to be perched on an office stool all through the scene and forbidden to get down.

The end of the second act was painful; and I go to the theatre to be *moved*, not pained. The tarantella began at the pitch which it should only have touched for the 1/100000000th of a second at the end. I believe you deliberately seized the scene round the waist and ran away with it until it was spinning fast enough to run away with you. You were excited—a most unpardonable thing in an artist.

On the other hand—but no matter about the other side. I admit that your comprehension of the part is extraordinary, and that you make it live in the most glowing, magnetic way. But Nora may be Nora, and even Norissima—I am not denying that you are Norissima— and yet she may cruelly starve and baffle the artistic appetite—the appetite for beauty and grace. My lacerated heart accuses you of first shewing that you could, if you pleased, make every tone in your voice a caress or an inspiration, and then *squawking*—positively squawking: of first moving like an angel and then tightening your chin, your wrists and your ankles in order to achieve a stupendous *bounce* out of mere cruelty to me. These things will drive me mad someday.

The play which has proved most popular here, next to the Doll's House, is Hedda Gabler, which, as you have Miss Lea for Thea, you ought to try. But beware of Charrington as Lövborg. The play is always misunderstood because people imagine that Lövborg is in earnest when he takes the pistol, and really means to kill himself, instead of merely gratifying his propensity, as a male coquet, for making scenes.

In fact he does nothing all through the play but make scenes; and what I am afraid of is that Charrington's confounded air of conviction and sincerity will get the scenes taken as earnest.

338

I must conclude hastily—my time is up. I have had to tumble out what I have to say very roughly. Make allowances for the circumstances; and believe, if you please, that though my critical sensibility has been frightfully sharpened by incessant exercise during your absence, my admiration is in nowise abated.

yrs sincerely
G. Bernard Shaw

P.S. I hope you got a copy of "The Quintessence of Ibsenism." I ordered one to be sent to you. If not, let me know; so that I may repair the omission.

To H. B. SAMUELS

[A/23]
29 Fitzroy Square W
24th April 1892

[Harry B. Samuels, one of the anarchists who had gained control of the Socialist League and its organ, *Commonweal*, had inherited command of the journal during the imprisonment of its editor, David J. Nicoll, who had been found guilty of publishing a violent article, after the Walsall anarchists' trial, denouncing the Home Secretary, the judge who tried the case, and the inspector of police who conducted it. Nicoll was sentenced at the Old Bailey on 2nd May 1892, by Lord Coleridge, to eighteen months' hard labour for incitement to murder. Fred Charles was one of the Walsall anarchists. Henri Coulon (1855–?) was a French author of books of jurisprudence on marriage and divorce; he wrote *De la liberté de la presse* (1894).]

Dear Samuels

I am overwhelmed with applications for political articles, and have had to let two provincial Fabian enterprises collapse without helping them. But what would be the use of my contributing to the Commonweal? It is now only supported by the Anarchists; and if I were to write an article on it, they would fill it with their refutations and criticisms of me for weeks afterwards, and kill the paper stone dead. Besides, why should I help a cause which only ends in getting you all into the hands of the police? If I could have stopped the Commonweal months ago I should have done so, since I saw how it must end. If you succeed in keeping the paper going, I hope you will make the readers understand that they can do no good by serving themselves up on toast to the police for saying things that they only imagine they mean, and making bombs that they havent the slightest real intention of using.

Poor Nicholl, who is incapable of even hurting an opponent's feelings, will be quite as severely handled for talking nonsense about torches and daggers as if he were actually in the habit of using them. Even you, who have much more sense than Nicoll & Charles put together, had a very narrow escape once from being prosecuted for something you said in your account of the Leeds strike. So mind you dont go putting your head into the lion's mouth. If he snaps, off goes your head: if he doesnt, people will suspect you of being a spy; so you will lose by it anyhow.

However, you did not write to me for advice, but for help. I am sorry I cannot give it. Under the circumstances I dont think you can reasonably blame me.

If you belong to any club that takes in Truth, you ought to look at it to see what they say about Coulon.

yours truly
G. Bernard Shaw

To JANET ACHURCH

[T/1 (A/4)]

29 Fitzroy Square W
6th May 1892

Death & distraction, it is midnight; and your letter has only just reached me. I could kill you—I could almost kill myself. You must have known that I had to go out at five: this is your revenge for the train letter. Never was there anything so heartless. I will complain of you to Charrington—I will have satisfaction—I will tear up by the roots all the fibres you have ever stirred in me—I will throw away my heart & soul and have my inside fitted with brass machinery and mill-stones.

Let me be calm: why should I care. I DONT care. I am perfectly composed—indifferent. I regret extremely that an engagement should have deprived me of the pleasure of answering your kind letter in person. I trust you are well—and Mr Charrington—and your daughter. The weather is cold, but fine; and the crops are well advanced.

I must go to a concert tomorrow at three. I have an engagement in the evening. I am Laocoon in the toils. From four to five, from seven to eight, from five to seven, would it be of any use my calling then?

GBS

To JIM CONNELL

[A/4]

[Connell wrote on 6th June, enclosing a copy of a letter he had sent to
Justice dissociating himself from the attack on Shaw and Webb in the current
issue. Bax's paper on value, read before the National Liberal Club on
11th May, had just been published in the *Personal Rights Journal*, followed
by a symposium to which Hyndman, Shaw, and others contributed; Shaw's
article appeared in the July number. World's End, Chelsea, was the open-air
meeting place of small groups of radicals; on several successive Sundays the
police had attacked speakers there. A committee of radical organisations was
formed in January 1892 to arrange a monster demonstration, *à la* Trafalgar
Square. Shaw was delegated by the Fabian Society to oppose the demonstration; when his suggested amendments to the demonstration resolution were
defeated, the Fabians withdrew. With the assistance of Sir Charles Russell,
several Fabians met with the Home Office to discuss the issue, which they
were able to resolve without conflict. The demonstration was not held.
Sir Charles Russell, M.P. (1832–1900), later Baron Russell, was counsel for
Parnell in the Pigott forgery inquiry; he became Lord Chief Justice of
England. The Fabian Election Manifesto, drafted by Shaw for the General
Election in July, was issued as Fabian Tract No. 40.]

My dear Connell

More power to your elbow! Bax told me before your letter came that
you had come down on Justice like several thousand of brick. However,
neither Webb nor I ever supposed that the paragraph represented the
feelings of anyone but H.M.H[yndman], whose style we recognized.
Besides, there was a reason for the attack. Some time ago there was
a "Political Economy Dinner" at the National Liberal Club, at which
Webb took the chair; Bax read a paper on Value (the old sore subject);
and Hyndman and I were invited guests. The result was a battle royal,
in which H.M.H. not having you to take care of him, and knowing
about as much of abstract economics as a pig does of a holiday, got
rather roughly handled, although Webb did his best to smooth matters.
So he went home and relieved his feelings by firing off that shot in
Justice. I suppose I should have let him alone; but there were a lot of
men there who understood the subject, and who were rather on the
sneer at Socialist economics; so I did not see why H.M.H. should be
allowed to give away our reputation merely because his feelings are so
easily hurt. Besides, I have given up trying to keep on good terms with
him since that World's End affair, his account of which in Justice
would only be appreciated by those who were present at the meeting &
knew what actually happened.

Talking of the World's End, Sir C. Russell is still full of your speech at the Haggerston Club.

I will shew your letter to Webb. He will be glad to see it as a sort of shake-hands, though, as I have said, he would not dream of blaming anyone except H. M. H. for the paragraph.

> In haste—getting out the
> Fabian Election Manifesto—
> yrs compatriotically
> G. Bernard Shaw

To ELLEN TERRY

[U(C)/10]

29 Fitzroy Square W
19th June 1892

[Dame Ellen Terry (1848–1928) was at this time leading lady to Henry Irving at the Lyceum. She had written to Edmund Yates, soliciting the attendance of his musical critic at the concert of her protegé, Miss F. Elvira Gambogi (d. 1940), at the Lyric Club on 24th June. Yates passed the request on to Shaw, who replied personally, thus initiating the now-immortal Shaw-Terry correspondence, which, however, did not develop in earnest until 1895. The two did not meet personally until 16th December 1900, at the Stage Society's performance of *Captain Brassbound's Conversion*, in which Janet Achurch appeared in the rôle Shaw had written for Ellen.

Miss Gambogi failed to achieve eminence as a singer, and subsequently turned to teaching and composing. Matthew Gregory Lewis (1775–1818), best known for his Gothic romance, *Ambrosio, or the Monk* (1796), was the author of a poem, "The Captive," which Ellen Terry recited at Miss Gambogi's concert. Nathaniel Vert, a concert agent, managed several leading artists, including Hans Richter.]

Dear Miss Terry

Many thanks; the paragraph is in the printer's hands.

In the programme, Monk Lewis's name ought to be given either as "Monk" Lewis, or Matthew Gregory Lewis. Monk is only a nickname. I mention it on the chance of your not knowing it.

Will you be so good as to let Miss G. know that whenever Vert acts for her, the World will get no tickets unless she sends them herself. I remember hearing Miss G. in 1887. Do you think she was *really* only 17 then? Naturally I do not expect any answer to this question.

> yrs very truly
> G. Bernard Shaw

342

Ellen Terry

To GRAHAM WALLAS

[A/13]

29 Fitzroy Square W
21st June 1892

[The tract Shaw mentions here actually is No. 41, *The Fabian Society:
What it has Done; & How it has Done It*, a paper which he had read before
the Fabian Society on 6th February 1892. It was published in August. The
"Tory money affair" refers to the section "Tory Gold at the 1885 Election,"
in which Shaw discusses the acceptance by the Social Democratic Federation
of Tory funds for the election campaigns of two of its London candidates in
1885. The leaflet on voting drafted by Shaw was *Vote! Vote!! Vote!!!*
(Fabian leaflet No. 43), issued the following week.]

I enclose the proof of Tract 42. If you look through it, the Exec.,
which evidently does not want to be bothered with it, will be satisfied.
We ought, I think, to hold it back until after the election, as the raking
up of the Tory money affair could do no possible good to any of the
advanced candidates, and would look rather like a deliberate attempt
to injure the S.D.F. men.

I drafted the leaflet about voting last night in the train & sent it to
Standring; but it did not come off very well. Our publications ought
not to be perpetual Shaw.

We ought to tackle the Income Tax question soon. I believe the
practical difficulties of Eight Hours will prove a joke compared to the
differentiation of the I.T. After the election we must take a clean sweep
ahead & go at Socialism. We have spent quite enough time in teaching
people the A.B.C. of electioneering; and now that the fruits of our
experience are in black & white in the Manifesto & the History, we
can leave them to the operation of the press.

GBS

To EMERY WALKER

[C/3]

29 Fitzroy Square W
22nd June 1892

[Walker was secretary to the Committee of the Society for the Protection of
Ancient Buildings, known as "the Anti-Scrape." Shaw campaigned in Dover
in behalf of Major E. G. Edwards of Kingston, Canada, a Fabian candidate for
parliament.]

I am so frightfully pressed for electioneering speeches just now that
I see hardly any chance of getting to the S.P.A.B. Indeed I have already
promised to speak at Dover on that night if possible. I should like to

come, as, since my trip to Italy, I have definitely made up my mind
that all ancient buildings ought to be demolished as soon as possible.
I am still sound on the restoration question; but this logically involves
the repudiation of preservation, which always means restoration &
nothing else.

GBS

To ELLEN TERRY

[X/117]

29 Fitzroy Square W
24th June 1892

[In his review in *The World* on 6th July, Shaw reported: "Miss Gambogi's
concert was abruptly finished, for me, by Miss Ellen Terry, who projected
herself into a recitation with such superb artistic power that I was quite
unable to face the feeble superficiality of ordinary concert business after it,
and so hurried out of the room. Miss Gambogi is too young as yet to have
much grip of her talent, which is, besides, by no means precociously
developed; but she has natural refinement, good looks, and an engaging
personality, reminding one occasionally of Trebelli." Zelia Trebelli-Bettini
(1838–92), Paris-born mezzo-soprano, was one of London's best-loved
singers until her retirement in 1889. Two of her most popular rôles were
Cherubino in *The Marriage of Figaro* and Zerlina in *Don Giovanni*.]

Dear Miss Terry

I went to the Lyric Club today, and listened to your young Italian
friend. The only thing I can do is to give you my exact opinion, which
you can take for what it is worth, and communicate to her or not, as
you may think best. In every respect except the purely musical one,
you will understand the position better than I do myself. To begin
with, you know that you do not hold your present position because you
possess this, that, and the other personal attraction, but because you
have made yourself one of the six best actresses in the fourteen thousand
millions of people (I think that is the figure) in the world. And you
therefore know that nothing short of being one of the six best singers in
the world would enable your novice to get praised as you get praised.
At the concert, for instance, although I was morbidly alive to every
weakness in Lewis's poem, guessing all the bads and sads beforehand,
and being tickled beyond measure by the line beginning "My language
&c," yet you brought tears to my eyes, not, you will understand, by
the imaginary sorrows of the lunatic (sorrow does not make me cry,
even when it is real) but by doing the thing beautifully. My whole
claim to be a critic of art is that I can be touched in that way. Now

your friend did not touch me in the least. I liked her at once: she is very amiable, very clever, and very good-looking. But—and now the murder is coming out—she is not interesting as an artist. She sang the bolero from [Verdi's] The Sicilian Vespers prettily and fluently, just as she would, I dare say, repeat one of Ophelia's speeches if you taught it to her. What is more, she sang it intelligently. You know, however, that this is not enough. The quality of execution that makes apparently trivial passages interesting, the intense grip of one's work that rouses all the attention of an audience: these she has not got to anything like a sufficient degree to make a career for her; and what is more, she will never acquire them in drawing-rooms or in the Lyric Club. What she does is not convincing to me: it is only a development of that facility in music which clever children acquire when they are brought up in a musical atmosphere. You must know how children who grow up amid theatrical surroundings catch up a certain familiarity with stage ways which inexperienced people easily mistake for genuine artistic talent. Bedford Park is full of such imps, who will nevertheless be hopelessly beaten in the long run by comparatively unpromising competitors. Now singing is to your signorina partly what acting is to the imps: more a picked-up habit than an art. She has got to turn the habit into an art—to put purpose into it—to make it the means of realizing herself, concentrating herself, throwing herself completely and exhaustively into action—I cannot express it; but you will perhaps recognize what I mean. I therefore think she ought to work on the stage if she can obtain an opening. All her drawingroom beauty and charm will vanish at once behind the footlights; and she will have to remake herself, build herself up from the foundation, instead of taking herself down from a peg as she was hung up by Nature, and wearing herself at the Lyric Club before audiences more or less packed. She has a certain resemblance to Trebelli both in facial expression and musical style; and she might, if she worked hard enough, succeed her as Cherubino, Zerlina, &c. Her voice is all stifled by singing into carpets and curtains: it wants large spaces to develop in; and what is true of her voice is true also of herself. She will never be a dazzling vocal executant any more than Trebelli was: her success, if it is to come at all, will be in sympathetic, intelligent dramatic singing. The most unpromising thing about her is her grace in her present uncultivated state. When Nature intends anyone to be a highly cultivated artist, she generally forces them on by condemning them to fiendishness or loutishness until they fulfil her intention. However, there must be exceptions to this, except perhaps as to the fiendishness.

345

I really must not make this letter any longer: you must be out of patience already. My verdict briefly is that as a drawingroom singer the signorina is no better than many others; and I would not walk a hundred yards to hear her sing again. But if she takes good care of herself and her voice, ten years work on the stage may make something of her. There is a certain humanity about her, to the development of which I should be sorry to prophesy any limit. At the same time, if she prefers to take things easy, and sing and compose in her present fashion, she may, with her social talent, get on very peacefully and comfortably, which you will perhaps tell her is better than being a great artist. If you do, you will be guilty of a most awful falsehood; but you must settle that with your own conscience.

My chief concern about this letter is the likelihood of its putting you to the trouble of acknowledging it. If writing is a trouble to you (my own correspondence drives me stark mad) pray do not mind me, or at least do not go beyond saying "Thank you for nothing" on a postcard.

yours very truly
G. Bernard Shaw

To ELLEN TERRY

29 Fitzroy Square W
1st July 1892

[H/1; X/117]

[Ellen Terry, replying on 29th June to thank Shaw, had confessed: "I didnt like you when you first wrote to me. I thought you unkind, and exceedingly stiff and prim. Now I beg your pardon most heartily." Richard D'Oyly Carte (1844–1901) had been impresario of the Gilbert and Sullivan operas since 1875. Helen Lenoir (d. 1913), Carte's London secretary, became his second wife in 1888. The Royal English Opera House was built by Carte in 1890 to house English grand opera (it is now the Palace Theatre); its inaugural production, on 31st January 1891, was Arthur Sullivan's *Ivanhoe*. Lenore Snyder (1870–?), Indianapolis-born prima-donna, made her London début at the Savoy as leading lady of *The Nautch Girl*.

In an address before the Liverpool Philomathic Society on 14th October 1891, Henry Irving had made an attack on *The Quintessence of Ibsenism*, commenting, "I understand from this authority [Shaw] that one of the qualifications for playing Ibsen is to have no fear of making yourself 'acutely ridiculous' and I can easily believe that this exponent of Ibsen is not troubled by that kind of trepidation . . ." (*Liverpool Daily Post*, 15th October 1891.) Shaw's hasty trip to Bradford was to campaign for Fabian candidate Ben Tillett before polling-day, 3rd July.]

346

Dear Miss Terry

Just a hasty line—something sensible. Do you know Doyly Carte or Mrs Doyly Carte, who was Miss Lenoir? They always have several companies touring in a small way with their Savoy repertory; and they are the only people in the comic opera line in London, as far as I know, with whom the signorina's niceness would not be a disadvantage. Besides, there are the possibilities of the New English Opera House, and of Carte's turn for operatic speculation. They might give her something to begin with. You ought to be able to make her speak English as well as the Dutch prima donna at the Savoy, Miss Snyders.

I am unfortunately quite unable to help her myself. As a musical critic I must not ask the most microscopic favor from any musical artist or entrepreneur.

I really did not mean to be stiff. Consider my awful situation. I had no right to go an inch beyond the business on which Yates wrote to me. I was presuming on the chance of your never having heard of me; but I was also running a considerable risk of your writing something of this kind to Yates :—"Sir: I wrote to you to ask you a trifling favor. In return, you have exposed me to a communication from the vilest of mankind, an enemy of religion and society, a shameless spouter of sedition in the streets, a wretch whose opinions about the womanliness which is the glory of my sex have made hardened profligates blush, a champion of the monster Ibsen, and one whom, to crown all, Mr Irving held up to public execration at a banquet in Liverpool for calling me an ignoramus. Henceforth, Mr Yates, we are strangers. I am, Sir, your obedient servant, Ellen Terry." Lots of people take that view of me, and go out of their way to print it. And from their point of view, it is perfectly true, all except the calling you an ignoramus, a calumny for which I will one day be even with Irving, who had better never have been born than quote my books without reading them.

I write in great haste, as I am up to my eyes in the election, my spouting propensities making me for the moment a much courted person. I am off to Bradford for a couple of days tomorrow; and I thought it better to suggest Carte in case you should take steps at once. I hope this letter is intelligible—I hardly know whether I am on my head or my heels. I am delighted beyond reason that my last letter was a good one. If the others were really stiff (which I am disposed to deny) your replies were angelic.

The stage is waiting for me at the corner of the square—open air meeting.

GBS

To ELLEN TERRY

29 Fitzroy Square W
5th July 1892

[U(H)/10; X/117]

["*Did* you call me an 'ignoramus'?" asked Ellen Terry on 4th July. "Well, I forgive you for speaking the truth. But I must ask Mr Irving to tell me all about it." Shaw's reference, in *The Quintessence of Ibsenism*, was not to Ellen Terry specifically, but to "the senior generation of inveterately sentimental actresses, schooled in the old fashion if at all . . . quite out of the political and social movement around them . . . intellectually *naïve* to the last degree. The new [intellectual] school says to the old, You cannot play Ibsen because you are ignoramuses."

Nance Oldfield, a one-act comedy by Charles Reade (1814–84), author of *The Cloister and the Hearth*, was first performed by Ellen Terry at the Lyceum on 12th May 1891. Alfred Cecil Calmour (1857–1912), formerly an actor in Irving's company, was the author of *The Amber Heart*, which Irving and Ellen Terry had been performing since 1887. Miss Gambogi, Ellen reported, "cleared £100 by that concert, the first money the poor girl has ever had." Elizabeth Robins had recently appeared in *Karin*, translated by Mrs Hugh Bell from the Swedish of Alfhild Agrell, at the Vaudeville on 10th May. Janet Achurch had become ill after her strenuous tour of the East; she never fully recovered her strength, and was more seriously stricken in 1895.]

One letter more—positively the last, as writing to you is only a form of self-indulgence.

The word ignoramus occurs in the book which I send you herewith. I will not tell you the page; but I may say that it is so far from the beginning that I doubt if any human being has held out long enough to reach it, except a few who began at the end and read backward. When I wrote the book I had a terrible grudge against you, and I have it still. It arose in this way. I do not often find time to go to the theatre; but I go when I can. One day I went into an afternoon performance, and found a poor ungifted, dowdy, charmless young woman [Rose Meller] struggling pathetically with Ibsen's Lady from the Sea. She was doing her best; and I thanked my stars that I was not a dramatic critic, and had not to go home and tell her that after all her study and toil she had done far more harm than good. That was the first act of my little experience. Act 2 was another visit to another theatre. There I found the woman who OUGHT to have played the Lady from the Sea— the woman with all the nameless charm, all the skill, all the force, in a word, all the genius—playing—guess what? Why, a charade the whole artistic weight of which would not have taxed the strength of the top

348

joint of her little finger. And the silly public delightedly applauding. Worse than that, traitors calling themselves critics were encouraging her—allowing their brains and consciences to be cajoled away by her beauty—talking fatuously of her child's play as if it had been the best she was capable of. I was furious. If I had been a god, and had created her powers for her, I should have interrupted the performance with thunder, and asked in a fearful voice why she was wasting the sacred fire of which I had made her trustee. But I knew that she had made her powers for herself, and could be called to account by nobody for the use she made of them. So I sat helpless, and went off in impotent rage. Since then I have never heard Nance Oldfield praised without vowing vengeance. And yet Charles Reade was better than Calmour. Oh, the Amber Heart, the Amber Heart, the Amber Heart! My wrath returns on me as I think of it all. Ask you a favor! Never, by all that ought to be sacred to both of us as artists, not the smallest—not even the greatest.

I congratulate Miss Gambogi on the £100, but much more on having no father or mother, so that she can spend it all on making herself an artist, and be quite free into the bargain. To have friends, and to have no relations: do you call that a disadvantage? Happy girl! And I have helped her to clear a hundred pounds! Do you hear that, oh Rosmersholm Rebecca [Florence Farr], ruined by two enormously successful Ibsen matinees, and now honestly buckling-to at six lines in a *lever de rideau* [Ernest Cosham's *The Home Coming*, at the Comedy Theatre] to pay for your lodgings? Think of it, oh Hedda-Gabler-Karin [Elizabeth Robins], staring gloomily at the bank book that registers the cost of your courage and skill. What would you give for the half of it just now, oh cleaned-out and invalided, but still indomitable Nora [Janet Achurch]? And you, oh vanished and forgotten Ellida, I wonder have *you* a hundred pounds to bless yourself with?

And you, Nance Oldfield, what have you done to set against the records of these hardly used ones? Why (says you) created my incomparable self, sir. True, irresistible Ellen, quite true. That silences me. Farewell.

GBS

To G. W. SPRY

29 Fitzroy Square W

[A/4]

12th July 1892

[G. W. Spry was lecture secretary of the North Kensington branch of the Social Democratic Federation. H. R. Taylor (1873?–1906), of the S.D.F., was a parliamentary Labour candidate for North-East Bethnal Green in the General Election in July.]

Dear Sir

I did not mean to convey to you that I resented the attacks in Justice on my own account. As you know, they are nothing new; and I have never let them prevent me from lecturing for the S.D.F. But they have been specially mischievous to our cause of late: for instance, Taylor's position at Bethnal Green was made quite impossible by the fact that Justice, in the very thick of the election, attacked all the people on whose help Taylor was depending, and recommended the workers not to vote for the other Labor candidates. Now the rank & file of the Federation could have put a stop to this sort of thing long ago if they had wished to. Individually the members have always been ready to tell me that they disapproved of the way in which Justice was edited, and that they thought it did more harm than good. But they never refused to sell it, never passed a resolution condemning any of the attacks, never took any step to shew that they were in the least in earnest in their disapproval. I used to laugh the matter off, and take no notice. But now that the Labor movement is coming into public prominence, and is being criticised and watched as it never was before, we cannot afford to trifle with each other any longer; and I have determined to bring home the responsibility of the S.D.F. attacks on the Fabian Society to the men of the S.D.F. whenever they ask me to speak for them. Not that I am unwilling to speak; but that I do not see why men should expect me to be at their disposal whilst they are supporting & circulating the bitterest attempts to discredit me with the working classes. It shews that they do not take themselves, nor their paper, nor their cause seriously.

I understand, then, that Sunday the 24th is off. But pray explain to the Branch that I have not refused to speak for them—that it is they who have put themselves in such a position that they cannot accept my offer. I cannot honestly say that I am sorry to be out of the engagement; for I really do not see how the S.D.F. is to face the public after this election. It pledged itself publicly to run about a dozen candidates in London with money ready banked for the purpose. It has actually run one, by dint of sending round the hat, and getting £100 from the Workmen's Times. Result, 106 votes. Believe me, I do not mention this ill naturedly, to cast it in your teeth; but I do ask you whether it would not be better for the N. Kensington Socialists to give up all the superior pretensions which have ended so poorly, and throw in their lot with the Radicals in the district, pushing on Socialism on Fabian lines. Remember that Socialism must be established, if it is to come at all, by the whole working class of the country, and not by the members of any particular Federation or Society. The whole secret of the Fabian success is that the Fabians know that Socialism is not going to be patented and set going by the Fabian Society. And the whole secret of the S.D.F. failure is that the S.D.F. thinks that the whole nation is going to join it and hand over the job of managing the land & capital to the council up at the Strand. It seems to me that unless the S.D.F. completely changes its policy, it will not be able to keep a single really able workingman leader in its ranks.

yours faithfully
G. Bernard Shaw

To HUBERT BLAND

[C/4]

29 Fitzroy Square W
16th July 1892

[Shaw was still revising and enlarging his history of the Fabian Society, which became Tract No. 41. John C. Foulger of Peckham, former partner of H.H. Champion in the Modern Press and publisher of *Cashel Byron's Profession*, was an early Fabian. The Clerkenwell branch of the Social Democratic Federation, defying the S.D.F. manifesto calling on the workers to vote for none but Social Democratic candidates, and "going Fabian," caused the election by *three* votes of Dadabhai Naoroji (1825–1917), the Liberal candidate for Central Finsbury; Naoroji thus became the first Indian member of parliament.]

I really dare not put a word into the tract about "The Need of a New &c." I was firmly convinced that I wrote it myself until Webb assured me that he, *and not Olivier*, was the author. Besides, the genuine original Fabian in To Day was Foulger, who debated Evolution v Revolution with Hyndman in the old days. I have tried a new title & a postscript, which I will exhibit when Standring has them ready. I imagine there is as much of you, me, and Webb in the tract as Olivier, Wallas & Co can reasonably be expected to stand. Have you seen that the Clerkenwell S.D.F. went Fabian at the election & upset the whole Justice apple cart, since the Council dare not expel them chock-a-block.

GBS

351

To J. STANLEY LITTLE

[A/4]

29 Fitzroy Square W
25th July 1892

[The Shelley centennial celebration at Horsham eventually was held on 4th August. Shaw's report of the event, "Shaming the Devil about Shelley," appeared in *The Albemarle* in September. Franz August Koenigstein (1860?–1892), known as "Ravachol," was an Anarchist-Communist and dynamitard, associated with bomb outrages in Spain and in Paris, who had been guillotined on 10th July. *Queen Mab*, written when Shelley was eighteen, was surreptitiously published in 1813; it attacks marriage, commerce, Christianity, royalty, etc. *Laon and Cythna* is a symbolic poem written in 1817, in which the hero and heroine are brother and sister; it was revised in 1818, eliminating the incestuous element, and retitled *The Revolt of Islam*.]

Dear Stanley Little

If by any chance I go down to Horsham on the 8th it will be as a casual spectator of the proceedings. There is to be a Shelley celebration by the Freethinkers at the Hall of Science here on the 4th, and I shall make my speech at that. If I spoke at Horsham I should say that the Shelley library was the damndest nonsense from the Shelleyan point of view, since it could not possibly occupy the position in the country which it claims if it contained, as it ought, the most complete collection outside the British Museum of works on Atheism, Free Love, Republicanism, Socialism and the like. The whole affair will be simply a conspiracy to persuade the silly Sussexers that Shelley was a model Churchman & country gentleman who attained great distinction in literature. If there is one man in the district who has the gumption to get up and ask the audience whether they know that Shelley was expelled from Oxford as an atheist, and that he ran away from his wife with the daughter of an atheist anarchist [William Godwin], and that he taught that it was just as natural and proper for a man to sleep with his own sister as with any other woman, your library will come tumbling down about your ears before the foundation stone is laid. No doubt it will be a glorious lark to know all this, and yet to see Sussex gaping reverently whilst [Edmund] Gosse & Co "confine themselves as much as possible to the literary side of Shelley's genius." It will be like a commemmoration of Ravachol on the strength of his mechanical & surgical dexterity, without any allusion to his applications of it.

No: a free library is always an advantage; and I am quite willing to see P.B.S. made the pretext for establishing one; but as my whole

352

reputation, such as it is, is that of a burster-up of such games as this Horsham one, I cannot reasonably be expected to lend a hand.

When the library is founded, one of the first things that will happen will be the exclusion of Queen Mab from its shelves, and the substitution of the Revolt of Islam for Laon & Cythna.

I have half a mind to speak on the village green, if there is one, on the political side of Shelley's teaching.

You will not mind my obduracy, I hope. I think you are justified, under the circumstances, in behaving like a most double-dyed villain sooner than let the Centenary pass without having anything gained; and that is just why I refrain from coming down and blowing the gaff on you.

GBS

To ALMA MURRAY

29 Fitzroy Square W
4th August 1892

[X/109]

[The chairman of the Horsham meeting was Robert H. Hurst (1817–1905), a Justice of the Peace and a former M.P. for Horsham. The "radical" Shelley meeting in London that evening, in the Hall of Science, was chaired by G. W. Foote, who eloquently recited "Men of England"; the principal speaker was Dr F. J. Furnivall.]

Dear Mrs Forman

You really ought to have recited today before the exodus to catch the 5.17 train. I came over from Cobham to hear you, and had to be content with seeing you only, though I admit that that was more than worth the journey. I had to get up to town to speak at a Shelley meeting at the east end, which, to my great astonishment, was a remarkable success. I was called on for an account of the Horsham meeting; and I repeated the chairman's speech almost verbatim without the slightest exaggeration. You should have heard the screams of ecstasy with which it was received. The audience received two recitations with great relish: if you had been there they would have brought down the building.

The Cenci performance collapsed most disgracefully. Is there any hope in that dark hint you gave me about your intention of repeating Beatrice?

yrs sincerely
G. Bernard Shaw

353

Cher ~~Citoyen~~ Citoyen

Voilà mes réponses à votre catéchisme. Il faut ~~avoir~~ pas de l'indulgence ~~pour mon style britannique~~ : j'ai fait de mon mieux ~~pour~~ ~~m'expliquer au moins intelligiblement. La politique~~ ~~que j'ai exprimée~~ ~~en~~ ma réponse à la question 17 est celle ~~~~ ~~~~ de toute ~~doute~~, Anglaise qui ~~pendant~~ la moindre influence ~~~~ ici. C'est à elle que la Société Fabienne doit ~~son remarquable succès~~ ; ~~~~ à regretter que ~~~~ Blind et Singer, pendant ~~~~ Angleterre ~~~~ par ~~~~ tout à fait ~~~~, comme quelque chose accomplie. ~~~~ On s'étonne ici de l'ignorance des Socialistes étrangers ~~~~ ~~~~ Anglais : il semblent ~~~~ tous leurs renseignements ~~~~ ~~~~ le plus impossible. On est tenté ~~~~ de croire que tout Socialiste ~~qui~~ ~~~~ ne trouve ~~~~ de ~~vrai~~ ~~~~ en constatant sur le champ correspondant ~~~~ pour tous les pays de l'Europe. J'espère que ~~~~ votre enquête aura ~~~~ ~~~~

To B. GUINANDEAU

29 Fitzroy Square W
[G.u/1]   12 Aôut 1892

[B. Guinandeau, a member of the editorial staff of *La Justice*, had written
from Paris on 3rd August, asking if Shaw would answer a series of questions
on British socialism. Shaw's reply does not seem to have been published.
August Bebel (1840–1913), leader of the German Social Democrats, was the
editor of *Vorwärts*. Paul Singer (1844–1911) was a German politician,
member of the Reichstag (from 1884), and a leader of the Social Democratic
Party.]

Cher Citoyen

Voilà mes réponses à votre catéchisme. Il faut avoir de l'indulgence
pour mon style brittanique: j'ai fait de mon mieux pour m'expliquer
au moins intelligiblement. La politique constitutionnelle que j'ai
esquissée en ma réponse à question 17 est celle de toute Société
Socialiste Anglaise exerçant la moindre influence ici. C'est à elle que la
Société Fabienne doit son remarquable succès; et dans l'interêt de
l'entente cordiale internationale, il est à regretter que Bebel et Singer,
pendant leur séjour récent en Angleterre, aient, par un malentendu
tout-à-fait extraordinaire, publiquement denigré cette politique comme
quelque chose de purement academique. On s'étonne ici de l'ignorance
des Socialistes étrangères sur le Socialisme Anglais: ils semblent tirer
leur renseignements aux sources le plus impossibles. On est tenté de
croire que tout Socialiste qui se trouve en dehors du vrai mouvement
se constitue sur le champ correspondant Anglais pour tous les pays de
l'Europe. Les journaux bien instruits sur ce sujet, comme, par example,
la Revue Socialiste, sont très rares.

J'espère que votre enquête aura pour effet de faire disparaître les
conceptions erronées ainsi répandues.

sincèrement à vous
[G. Bernard Shaw]

To JOHN BURNS

29 Fitzroy Square W
[A/2]   12th August 1892

[Burns, at this time, was head of the trade unionists' Progressive Party. In
the 1892 General Election he was elected M.P. for Battersea. The Fabian
Society reprinted in 1893, from the *Nineteenth Century*, Burns's *The*

Unemployed (Tract No. 47). The Fabians and the Progressives worked closely together, their policies being largely identical in the area of municipal affairs. Pandeli Ralli (1845–1928) was M.P. for Bridport (1875–80) and for Wallingford (1880–85); he later became a Justice of the Peace. A labour conflict between the newly-established trade union of postmen and the Postmaster-General had resulted in much agitation, charges of sweating, and eventually a mass firing of postmen and telegraphists. There were two discharged Post Office "fellows" in the news at this moment—Cleary and Cheesman; which one Shaw had in mind is uncertain.

Newcastle held a by-election in August; the local Fabian Society did not support either candidate. W.H.Utley, a London journalist, was Fabian lecturer and organising secretary for Lancashire and northern England. Robert Gascoyne-Cecil, 3rd Marquis of Salisbury (1830–1903), was prime minister until, by a vote of No Confidence on 8th August, he was forced to resign, enabling Gladstone to form his fourth Government.]

Dear Burns

I have been thinking over what you told me; and I think it looks like a formidable Unionist intrigue, with [Henry Hyde] Champion at the wires. Keir Hardie, or whoever is pulling his strings, seems to be calculating that the situation is such that whatever man takes the initiative, the others must follow him. That, however, is a game that two can play at; and you can play it better than anybody, because you are the brazen head that the country is waiting to hear speak. There are three questions on which your action will be watched.

1. Is Ralli to be backed against [John] Morley at Newcastle?
2. Is an autumn session desirable?
3. Is the Post Office fellow (not the wrong 'un) to be reinstated?

To take 3 first, I have a fancy for it as a good opportunity to break silence in the house with a statesmanlike explanation of the complete change of front on the part of progressive politicians towards the civil service. Formerly civil servants were all creatures & nominees of the classes: they were dreaded not only as bureaucrats but as hangers-on of the aristocracy. Their corruption & incompetence was the great argument against all State interference with industry. Now Democracy & competitive examination has changed all that: the civil servant is an independent citizen, far safer from corrupt political pressure than the private employee. Further, we look to a great extension of State & municipal industry (this is the opportunity for that reference to "the ultimate aims of the Labor party" which is sure to make a little sensation coming from you); and unless the fullest liberty of political action and trade combination be maintained for public employees, the inevitable spread of municipal Socialism would be destructive to that

356

personal liberty of which none feel the vital importance more than the Socialists themselves. (Ahem!) Consequently it is for the Labor party to make a determined stand on this point—insignificant as it may appear to those members of the Liberal party whose education has been exclusively Whiggish—and to insist on the immediate abrogation of all departmental regulations curtailing freedom of political action & trade combination among civil servants, with, of course, the reinstatement of the dismissed men. What do you think of this line? It seems to me that it would make an amendment to the address which would utterly snuff out Hardie's commonplace & hopeless splutter about the autumn session.

As to No 1, about Morley, it seems to me quite clear that if Ralli refuses 8 Hours & the Labor programme, Hardie can only save himself from figuring as a Unionist catspaw by declaring at once that Morley must be supported, and that, too, decisively. What is wanted now is a vigorous lead. I am writing to Utley to get the Fabian questions put to Ralli at once, and to let you know the result. Unless Ralli will pledge himself to vote against Salisbury & with the Labor party on so many questions (including 8 hours) as to clearly outweigh his unsoundness on Home Rule, the workers should be told authoritatively—meaning by John Burns—that since they have neglected their opportunities of putting up a Newcastle workman & chucking both Morley & Ralli, they have now nothing for it but to vote straight for Morley & do their duty next time by being ready with a Labor candidate. And this might be accompanied by a broad hint to Champion & Co. that if they worked for Ralli, there would be an end of their influence in the movement except as avowed Unionist agents. But if Ralli bids the reserved price, then he ought to be supported vigorously—spoken for in Newcastle—backed for all that Labor is worth. Anything is better than action by halves at this moment. However, as Ralli probably wont come up to the scratch, that is not worth bothering about just now.

As to No 2, the autumn session, it is delightfully indifferent except as an opportunity of showing K.H. that he cannot commit you to amendments that he moves without consulting you. It wont pass; and though there is a notion about that an autumn session is the correct Radical card, nobody really cares whether you support, oppose, or simply walk out of the house.

I am writing hastily and without much consideration; but I have gone ahead, knowing by experience how much easier it is to think a subject over when some other man holds it up, as it were. My ideas may be all damned nonsense; but they will do to start a discussion

357

between Burns and the M.P. for Battersea. Whatever policy you adopt, make Massingham back it up.

Tell Mrs Burns that I got out of my trouble with my companion [Florence Farr] by immediately making a great grievance of her having been shy of coming up to be introduced. I thus got into the position of the injured party before she had time to start on me; and we were friends again before we were half way back to Hammersmith.

Dont bother to answer: I know what a curse correspondence is. The old rule was, Never write a letter and never burn one. Mine is, Never keep a letter & never answer one.

GBS

To SIDNEY WEBB

[A/14; X/141.e]

29 Fitzroy Square W
12th August 1892

[M. Maltman Barry, sub-editor of H. H. Champion's *Labour Elector*, was a mysterious figure in radical circles, said to have been a spy for Karl Marx and, later, for Lord Randolph Churchill. Joseph Burgess (1853–1934), who wrote under the pseudonym "Autolycus," was a mill-hand who became editor of the *Workman's Times*. James Shaw Maxwell, who was a Fabian for a brief period, was newly-elected secretary of the Independent Labour Party. Georges Clemenceau (1841–1929), French statesman, became premier of France in 1906.

William Hines had several daughters, four of whom (Emily, Ada, Annie, and Kate) were Fabians. The "ghastly mess" in Parliament refers to the brass band which accompanied Keir Hardie to Westminster when he took his parliamentary seat, and to the tweed cap he insisted on wearing, both of which gave some offence to his colleagues and to a fastidious public. Rev. John Trevor (1855–?), founder of the Labour Churches, had encouraged friends to form a Manchester branch of the I.L.P. Shaw's *Sunday Chronicle* article, "After the Election," was published on 7th August. Sir Thomas Milvain (1844–1916), Conservative M.P. of Durham City, was defeated at Newcastle that month.]

Webb, me bhoy: a wurd wud yiz.

I have just had a chat with Burns; and everything is at sixes & sevens in the House at our end of it. The most significant news is that Champion is at work (and presumably Maltman Barry) behind Keir Hardie. Burns declares that the Workman's Times money was provided through Champion, and that Burgess & Shaw Maxwell (who is doing a weekly

358

labor article in the Echo) are having their strings pulled extensively. He says that K.H. has broken all their compacts not to act without consultation, and that what he (JB) has said at their confabs has been published as "interview" in a Glasgow paper through Maxwell. Burns even says that he believes that Hardie's motion for the autumn session, as to which J.B. was not consulted, was suggested by Chamberlain. Whether there is anything in this does not matter: there is, in my opinion, evidence that the Unionists, aided by Champion, are going to try hard to collar the Labor men.

Burns disapproves of the autumn session; is much struck by Gladstone, who seems to him a lion among a pack of curs; and does not know what to do. I have suggested to him to take advantage of the platonic character of the autumn session proposal to go against it and show K.H. & Co. that they cannot commit him to anything they please on his allegiance to Labor; and to seize the question of the dismissal of the Post Office officials to make his debut in the House & give it a discreet glimpse of the ultimate aims of the Labor party by way of justifying a claim for the total reversal of the old anti-bureaucrat policy of the Whigs.

I was talking to Utley today. He says that what the office wants is another clerk who can write shorthand, and a typewriter. He says the correspondence takes too much of the secretary's time. Probably he is right.

La Justice, Clemenceau's paper (meaning that C. gets so much a year for the use of his name) has sent me 28 printed questions which it is addressing to the leaders of mankind on the subject of Socialism. They undertake to publish the answers; and I have accordingly embodied the Fabian policy in a set of answers which will certainly gain me the next vacant fauteuil at the Academie. I have also, in the letter accompanying the answers, complained of the ignorance of the English movement among foreigners, smacking Bebel & Singer in the eye for their *dénigrement* of our programme, and concluding—"On est tenté de croire que tout Socialiste qui se trouve en dehors du vrai mouvement se constitue sur le champ correspondant anglais pour tous les pays de l'Europe." The correct address of this kindly passage is 65 Chancery Lane, the residence of Edward Aveling Esq. Magny, who acted as reviser, says that my French style, though un peu Britannique, and invariably wrong in the genders, is otherwise masterly.

I hear from Oxford that de Mattos is ravishing every maiden in the country, and that even the tolerant Hines took umbrage when some seven or eight of his daughters had succumbed. I will not answer for

359

the accuracy of this statement in detail; but York Powell writes to me privately urging the importance of dissociating ourselves from the satyromaniac W. S. de M, who has, it appears, handsomely apologized to Hines. What more could a gentleman do?

I am seriously of opinion that what is wanted here is a salon for the social cultivation of the Socialist party in parliament. Will Madame Potter-Webb undertake it? Now that we are not at hand to cut out the work, the whole affair in parliament is getting into a most ghastly mess. Besides, we must all go into the House in a body next time; and the sooner we form a secret society with that aim, & select our constituency, the better. I am, you see, slowly reviving after the utter prostration into which I fell at the end of the season; and now

> "In me, too, might ariseth
> And the place is perilous."

On the 14th Sept. I go off to Florence, returning to London (though also to Florence, strange to say—that is her name) on the 2nd October. Wallas is on the fiords, Bland on the Medway, and Oakeshott on the marry.

I have preached an open air sermon & an indoors one—the former in heavy rain—at the Labor Church, Manchester. Trevor says he could not help starting the Independent Labor Party there—that the workers are Tories to such an extent that the permeation racket cannot be worked there. I also wrote an article in the [Manchester] Sunday Chronicle on the elections, explaining the animus of the Labor party against Morley on the extremely *post hoc* ground that his "honest" attitude irritated those who recollected how he had compliantly left Bradlaugh to fight the Oath question [in parliament, 1880–86]. Some excuse was really wanted. If Milvain is the flogging man, by the bye, I think I shall cut into the Newcastle business with a clear declaration that Morley must be supported against him. Keir Hardie's game is sheer Unionism. My estimate of K. H. is that he is a Scotchman with alternate intervals of second sight (during which he does not see anything, but is suffused with afflatus) and common incapacity.

You had better destroy this letter, though it is worth fully four & sixpence as an autograph. We ought, by the bye, to have a letter destroying compact in the inner ring.

GBS

P.S. On Tuesday about 40 female clerks in the G.P.O. took a room in the Memorial Hall & got me to lecture them on Socialism. They were bored by the subject but fascinated by the lecturer.

To ALMA MURRAY

[B/1; X/109]   29 Fitzroy Square W
                                                  16th August 1892

[E.F.S.Pigott, Earl Lathom (1824–95), was licenser of plays in the office of
the Lord Chamberlain.]

Dear Mrs Forman

   It is impossible to get the Cenci licensed. We tried our best; but
Pigott is evidently determined not to take the responsibility. It was
said that he was quite ready to wink at an invitation performance; but
when Beerbohm Tree was on the point of lending us the Haymarket,
an interview which he had with Pigott completely changed his tone:
he remained sympathetic, and offered to lend us the scenery &c; but
it was quite evident that he had been effectually bound over by the
censorship. I believe Pigott persuades the managers that if they do not
support him they will be put under the control of the County Council,
which they particularly dread. Unless Pigott is succeeded by a more
liberal licenser or else abolished altogether I see no chance of getting
the Cenci out of the Index.

                                                         GBS

To SIDNEY WEBB

[A/14; X/141.e]   29 Fitzroy Square W
                                                  22nd August 1892

[Shaw, Burns, Champion, and other Socialists contributed a series of letters
on the political situation to the *Daily Chronicle* in August. Shaw's first two
letters, on 20th and 24th August, concerned John Morley's Newcastle
campaign; a third, on 25th August, was a reply to Champion. James Arthur
Forgie was secretary *pro tem* of the Newcastle Fabians. Timothy Michael
Healy (1855–1931) was an Irish Nationalist M.P. and vigorous advocate of
home rule. George Shipton (1839–1911), by trade a builder, was long-time
secretary of the London Trades Council, whose efforts produced important
and far-reaching reforms in the labour laws. E.J.Howell (1877?–1959) was
a clerk in the Fabian Society office and bookshop manager from 1892 until
his retirement in 1939.]

   I have drafted the circular to the Trades Councils about the November elections, also a paragraph for the [Fabian] News. Will you tell
Utley when the circulars ought to be sent: it strikes me that it may be
too soon yet. November is a long way off.

I have just forgotten to send in my claim to get on the register. Next year I shall write a letter in the Chronicle urging all Liberals & Radicals to purposely omit to send in their claims, so as to force the Government to introduce monthly registration in order not to find all their supporters off the register at a General Election.

Yesterday, at Massingham's, Burns came in. We meant to have a great political council; but we mostly relaxed & frivolled. (By the bye, remind me when you come back, to tell you the story of the clergyman & the dentist. It doubled up both M. & B.) I asked Burns how he accounted for Champion subsidizing him. He said that the intention was unmistakeable. It was to get a secret to hold over him. He declares that Champion laid down the following program to an informant of his, whose name he will not reveal. "I [Champion]* will be in the next Parliament, where I will be the Parnell of the Labor party. Keir Hardie will soon crumple up: I can do as I like with him. Burns will make his first speech to the biggest house ever assembled to hear a 'maiden'; and he will make a success of it. But he will not face the disclosure that he ran with my money; and so he will come my way." Which calculation (discoverable in Shaw Maxwell's articles [a series of paragraphs on 17th August] in the Echo) Jack has smashed at one blow by his letter ["Mr John Burns's Election Expenses"] to the Chronicle [on 18th August].

My own Chronicle letter re Morley has the disadvantage that everybody is interested in suppressing it—Morleyites, Ralli-ites, Independents, Irishmen and all. And yet, since all the waverers are Ishmaelites, the letter would not have gained them over on any other terms. I have therefore written to the Newcastle Fabian suggesting that they should reprint it & circulate it among the Elswick men &c. Forgie, the secretary, had pleaded to Utley that if they took any definite action it would split them; but I have told him to split away, and thank his Maker for so good an opportunity of getting rid of the non-Fabian socialists in his society, also of planting the Fabians as the sane socialists of Newcastle. But as I rather doubt whether it will be possible for him to follow this heroic advice, I have also written to Florence O'Driscoll, M.P., telling him that, whether they like my letter or not, they had better circulate it among the Impossibilists if they mean Morley to win. I cling to O'Driscoll a little because Davitt has so utterly botched the job of mediating between Labor & Home Rule at Newcastle. O'D. swears that the Irish party furnish us with a trustworthy phalanx of 70 roaring democrats. Tim Healy he holds up as a veritable Hyndman.

* Shaw's brackets.

362

When I failed to enthuse over Tim, he said, "Ah, if y' only knew that Mannnn!" He actually wanted to telephone for him to come and give me ocular proof of his devotion to the red flag. O'D. is no fool, however; and when he comes to know a little more, he may be useful to us.

Today I examined every pub. in St Martin's Lane; but George Shipton's name was not on any of them. Evidently the license has not changed hands yet. But it is still hardly possible that G.S. would not have contradicted the report if it be false. Utley says that 3 members of the T.C. have spoken of it to him as a matter within their private knowledge.

Champion has been blackballed at the Democratic Club.

I saw [A.C.H.] Grahame of the Poplar Branch today at the office. He had been looking for Burgess to tell him that he had made an Ass of himself re the election money; but Burgess, not being just then *chez lui*, had escaped his fury. I am to go down to Poplar to warn the group against Tory wiles.

Utley has got a typewriter on approval from a too enterprising canvasser. I think we ought to get one, not because Pease is a captain of industry, but because Howell writes an utterly unpresentable hand. There are now so many typewriters coming into the market that we might, by taking them all successively on approval, keep ourselves supplied for a year free of charge. Utley, by the bye, is kept exceedingly hard at work; and so much of it is office boy's work that it cannot be economical to have him at it. I have sounded him on the subject of Manchester; and he seems agreeable. Suppose we decide to have practically two secretaries—one in London & one in Manchester: for which of the two places do we need the better man? Pease says he will be back at 276 on Thursday. The office needs to have some money spent on it. The carpet is in rags; there is no shipshape accommodation in the way of letter filing; and the outer office is not handsome enough to impress visitors, nor disordered enough to give the idea of an American torrent of business.

De Mattos still keeps writing about lectures on our behalf in all sorts of places, Kendal among them.

GBS

To SIDNEY WEBB

29 Fitzroy Square W

[A/14; X/141.e]   25th August 1892

[Bryant & May is a firm of match manufacturers, the working conditions in whose factories were then a constant target for reformers. Thomas Burt (1837–1922), Labour M.P. for Morpeth, was president of the Newcastle Trades Union Congress in 1891. Charles Fenwick (1850–1918), a working miner, was Labour M.P. for Wansbeck. James Havelock Wilson (1858–1929), Labour-Liberal M.P. (1892), had founded the National Sailors' and Firemen's Union in 1887. Herbert Henry Asquith (1852–1928), later Earl of Oxford and Asquith, was at this time Home Secretary; he became prime minister in 1908. Henry Matthews, Viscount Llandoff (1826–1913), had been Home Secretary at the time of the Trafalgar Square demonstration. George William Russell (1853–1919), a member of the London County Council, was a Liberal politician. There were two Commissioners (rather than Commanders) of Woods and Forests in August 1892: George Culley and Sir Robert Nigel Kingscote (1830–1908).

The "G.O.M." (Grand Old Man) was Gladstone. Edward Grey (1862–1933), later Viscount Grey of Fallodon, was at this time Under-Secretary for Foreign Affairs. Sir Arthur H.D. Acland (1847–1926), Liberal politician and educationalist, was M.P. for Rotherham. F.C. Baum, a Fabian, had been elected to the London County Council in March 1892. Alfred R. Dryhurst (1859–1949), a Fabian, was for many years a member of the British Museum staff, serving as Assistant Secretary from 1908 until his retirement in 1924.]

I enclose the whole Morley correspondence. I have no doubt now that I was right to cut in. You will see that my first letter is a convincingly plain statement of the whole case, except for a grossly disingenuous reference to the seven hours in the Northumberland mines, which is clearly due to your influence. Karl Pearson unexpectedly cut into the discussion in a highly Socialist-of-the-Study style. Finally Champion denied being a Unionist; but I think my letter of today re Bryant & May has knocked him out on that point. On the whole all the letters I have received go to convince me that I have succeeded in doing all that could be done to weaken the Champion-Barry combination & to make the election as damaging to the official ring as is consistent with saving Honest John. If Morley gets in, well and good, he gets in after a sufficiently undignified hustling; and our influence with the Irish party & the Radicals is greatly increased. If he is beaten, will you instantly write a letter to the P.M.G. drawing the moral. Point out that the utmost the Labor leaders can do is powerless, even when fortified by the opposition of known Tory wirepullers, to overcome the feeling of the new electorate against reaction in industrial

364

questions. Shew that Morley had a splendid democratic program, a great reputation, a special claim as the messenger of peace to Ireland, and that he was backed by the old Labor leaders (Burt & Fenwick) the new labor leaders (Burns & Wilson) the Irish-Labor leader (Davitt) by Fabianism (Shaw) &, in short, by everybody except C[unninghame] Graham, who is nothing if not a *Frondeur* and by Keir Hardie, who is nobody, and [who] did not attempt to follow up his opposition. And yet it was impossible to swing the advanced vote round to the opponent of Eight Hours & the belated champion of "liberty" for adult male labor, although his opponent was the feeblest of reactionaries on all other points. Rub it in well. I cannot do it, because there has been quite enough of me in the matter. Send the letter up in time for Saturday's PMG if possible. Subject, of course, to your better judgment, or Mrs Webb's: we do not as yet know in London which power is supreme.

Re Trafalgar Square, which I stupidly forgot in my last letter, can we get at Asquith, whose temper & the official instinct will probably lead him to make an ass of himself by acting à la Matthews. What he must do is to accord permission with delight. The word must then be given for all Radicals & Liberals "To the Square"; Russell & other London members must speak; and the whole affair must be turned into a great celebration of the Downfall of Coercion & the Re-establishment of Freedom of Speech by the G.O.M. This will swamp the S.D.F. and enable the Com^r of Woods & Forests to do just what he pleases afterwards in the way of preventing "abuse" of the right of meeting in the square by the unemployed pending the transfer to the Co. Council of the custody of the place. This is so plainly the right thing to do; and a provocation of a repetition of Bloody Sunday or (at least) the Worlds End business is so clearly the wrong thing, that the Government is quite certain to adopt the latter unless Asquith is well talked to. Can Mrs Webb undertake this diplomatic mission. I think I once saw Beatrice Potter, in an Indian blanket, fascinating Asquith. Could she get his scalp now, think you?

Whatever mess there is now, we must be in it: otherwise, as in 1883–7, Hyndman & Champion will have the field to themselves. When you want to get in at the pit door, you must wedge yourself into the heaviest crush: the moment the pressure relaxes, you know you are in a back eddy, comfortable, but not getting in. It is all very well for Grey, Acland & Co, who have reserved seats, to lie low: we must use our elbows. (Be careful not to present this letter to Herbert Burrows as a specimen of my handwriting. It would be much misunderstood.)

Champion's smartness has certainly proved pretty thin this time; but it is always worth while to get well advertised as the recognized dealer in the loaves & fishes. Trevor, of Manchester, shewed me a letter from Wilson which revealed incredible abysses of venality on the part of the Labor stalwarts of Middlesbro'.

I can get no further re Shipton until his name goes up. I shall, however, constitute myself Angel-of-the-Passover in ordinary for St Martin's Lane, & let you know if the blood of the lamb gets sprinkled. As to Baum, what can we do? He shewed a considerable want of sense in speaking for Taylor after bringing all the extremists down on him for his complaisance in the opposite direction.

I have made the points you emphasise in the T.C. circular & paragraph. As you are so much more conscious of the personalities of the TCs than I am (I frankly dont believe they exist) I think you will be able to improve the circular. I shall tell Utley to send you a proof.

I go down to Abinger tomorrow to stay a day with the Dryhursts. On Saturday I shall probably cross over to Oxted & see the Salts. Did I tell you that my Italian tour—Cholera permitting—will take me away from the 14 Sept. to the 2nd Oct.?

GBS

PS. Please return the Chronicle correspondence & the enclosed letter from O'Driscoll.

To GRAHAM WALLAS

[B/13]

29 Fitzroy Square W
20th September 1892

[This letter reflects the Fabian Society's propensity for educating its members. Emil Behnke (1836–92), a well-known vocal teacher and lecturer, was organising a voice-production course at the time of his death; the project was revived two months later by Mrs Agnes Larkcom-Jacobs. Correspondence classes in Economics were also instituted. And in October 1892, the "University Extension," in the Essex Hall, was inaugurated with two courses of ten lectures each by Bernard Bosanquet ("Plato and the Beginnings of Philosophy") and John Rae ("The Progress and Present Position of Socialism"). Miss Mary Lacey gave a course of six lectures on "The Tudor Period" in the same month, in connection with the Oxford University Extension.]

If Behnke is dead there is an end of the elocution project; for I dont know anybody else who would meet our requirements.

Let me know Webb's Edinburgh address if it reaches you: I presume he has left Glasgow. Also when you intend to resume your cycling lessons.

Bland is quite right about the need for making up our minds about this N.I. [National Independent] Labor Party, which is nothing but a new S.D.F. with Champion instead of Hyndman. There is also the Church question coming up.

That University Extension Fabian scheme of yours is really a most outrageous one. My toleration is large; but the action of the intelligent & aspiring young working man being led by the Fabian to the shrine of History, with Miss Lacy as pythoness, is too much even for me. It is the most complete case of Satan finding mischief still for busy hands to do that ever I heard of.

GBS

To AMY LAWRENCE

29 Fitzroy Square W
[B/4]
26th October 1892

[Miss Amy Lawrence, concerned by the efforts of a new landlord to increase her rent, had written to Shaw for advice. A Girton College student, she joined the Fabian Society in July 1893.]

Dear Miss Lawrence

When the rates are raised on a grocer, he does not increase the price of sugar. If he could, he would raise it without waiting to have his rates raised. If the Income Tax is doubled next April, your landlord will not double the rent of your rooms, because he is getting all you can afford out of you at present. Nevertheless if the tax were applied in such a way as to relieve you of some expense in connection with your lodging which you now bear, he could raise the rent & leave you no richer (though also no poorer) than you were before. But if it were applied to give you some benefit that you had simply done without before because you couldnt afford it, obviously that would not enable you to pay more. Generally speaking, a landlord can only raise rent under such circumstances when the tax laid on the landlord is taken off the tenant; so that at worst, the tenant is as well off as he was at first. If you study political economy you will learn at greater length that a tax on rent cannot be shifted, and that all taxation even now falls finally on rent. The lease has nothing to do with it, except of

367

course that a leaseholder is secure against having the rent raised on him until his lease expires.

There is no reason why you should not get up more lectures. All that about treating one shamefully is nonsense, as of course you know. Why not ask Mrs Sidney Webb (Miss Beatrice Potter) 10 Netherhall Gardens, Hampstead, N.W.

GBS

To GRAHAM WALLAS

[B/13]

29 Fitzroy Square W
28th October 1892

[Fred Hammill (1856–1901), a member of the Fabian Executive Committee (1892–95), was a prominent worker with Keir Hardie in the Independent Labour Party. The right of public meeting in Trafalgar Square was finally resolved at the end of 1892; a Shaw letter on the subject appeared in the *Pall Mall Gazette* on 16th November.]

I hurried along Drury Lane this evening after the Com^{tee}, but could not find you. Bland scored this evening as far as surprising me went: I had not the least idea, until [Robert] Dell let the cat out of the bag, that a concerted attack was being made on our flank.

I have asked Pease to find out whether Hammill is going to attend the Trafalgar Sq. Com^{tee} on Sunday, with a view to seeing you there in case he cannot turn up.

GBS

To AMY LAWRENCE

[A/1]

29 Fitzroy Square W
1st November 1892

Dear Miss Lawrence

I think you will find my explanation sufficient if you follow it up. You say that if your landlord were to double your rent you would either leave or put up with one room instead of two. That is a very simple way out of the difficulty for you; but what's to become of your landlord when his rooms are unlet? He is now presumably getting from you the most that anybody will pay him for them; for if anyone else would pay £10 more he would turn you out and take that person as his tenant.

368

Therefore if he raises the rent he simply empties his house and cuts off his own income. I can shew you sets of rooms—very desirable ones—which have been empty for five years because the landlords persist in asking £100 a year when the market value is only eighty.

You pay 1/6 of your income in rent, whilst others pay 1/4. The Duke of Westminster could get a splendid mansion for 1/400 part of his income. But that means that the incomes are high, not that the rents are low. Houses are not any dearer to rich people than to poor: on the contrary, they are cheaper, because rich people are "desirable tenants."

If you cut a fine street, like Shaftesbury Avenue or Victoria St, through a slum, up will go the rents on the frontage of that street. If you make a park, up will go the rents on the frontage of the park. But in these cases the actual value of the sites and houses has been raised; and the people who cannot afford to live in fine streets or on park fronts must turn out. But if you follow up this turning-out process, you will see that it does not do any harm. Suppose a big company bought up Guildford St [Miss Lawrence's address], and rebuilt it with piles of flats worth £30 a year more than you can afford to pay. Well, you would turn out. But the increase in the number of flats would lower their price. The Guildford St speculator, in order to get people to move into his new flats, would have to give them a little better value than they got in their old quarters. And when their old quarters were vacated, the old landlords would have to reduce rents in order to get fresh tenants. And this would go on right through the whole series of grades of dwellings; so that you, though compelled to leave the improved Guildford St, would nevertheless find rooms as good as those in Guildford St used to be at a lower rent.

The house you are in has evidently actually risen in value during the term of the lease, so that it is now beyond the means of your landlord. But unless you are now paying less than the market value of your rooms, the new landlord ought to be willing to retain you as tenant if he does not propose either to improve the house by laying out capital on it or else turn it into a single dwelling without lodgers.

I only mentioned "doubling the rent" as a convenient illustration. The same economic argument applies to all cases of raising rent, from decupling it down to adding sixpence a year.

You will observe that though I have explained your case as to the park front, it was not really a case in point. If you put a tax on a haberdasher, that will not enable him to get a farthing more for a cotton bodice than before. But if the tax were applied to improve the neighborhood to such an extent that he filled his shop with woollen jackets

369

instead of cotton bodices, of course he would charge more for the jackets than for the bodices, though nobody would say that the tax had therefore raised the price of clothing.

I know that my explanations will puzzle you if you are not accustomed to economic problems. Remember that you must follow everything up in economics. It is not enough to say, "Oh, if my rent were raised I should leave: that is all." You must consider the position of the landlord when you have left & a long string of other things into the bargain.

In haste, which please excuse.

yours sincerely

G. Bernard Shaw

To JOHN LANE

29 Fitzroy Square W

22nd November 1892

(Address for the moment to care of Sparling, at

8 Hammersmith Terrace.)

[A/1; X/118.e]

[John Lane (1854–1925), London publisher of the *Yellow Book* and of the works of Oscar Wilde, Richard Le Gallienne, William Watson, and Florence Farr, was co-founder with Elkin Mathews of the Bodley Head publishing company in 1887. *Widowers' Houses,* advertised as "An Original Didactic Realistic Play in Three Acts," was produced by the Independent Theatre on 9th December 1892 at the Royalty, under the direction of Herman de Lange, with Florence Farr as Blanche (a rôle which, ironically, was modelled after Jenny Patterson). The play eventually was published by Henry & Co., in May 1893, as No. 1 in the Independent Theatre Series, edited by J. T. Grein.]

Were you serious about publishing that play of mine? I am not sure that it would be a very gorgeous investment; but I suppose a limited edition at a high price would be bought by a certain number of idiots who would not buy anything of mine for a penny or a shilling. However, you can judge for yourself: my chief object in writing to you is to remind you that if the play is to be printed, it will need all the send-off it will get from the criticism and discussion of the performance; and as this is to take place (if it does not fall through) on the 9th Dec., we must literally rush into print. A simple and not too expensive way of making an *édition de luxe* of it will be to illustrate with photographs of the cast in costume. The leading lady is a very goodlooking woman, I might remark. It ought to be a quarto—not too large, but just large enough.

Your suggestion came into my mind this afternoon for the first time with full force. To confess the truth, the chief attraction to me is the opportunity of presenting a copy to each of the actors, who are all playing for nothing. So dont set too much store by my favorable view of the chance of a sale.

yours faithfully
G. Bernard Shaw

To A. J. MARRIOTT

c/o H. H. Sparling
8 Hammersmith Terrace W
14th December 1892

[S/1]

[A. J. Marriott, socialist author and poet (*Song of Brotherhood between the English and Irish People*, 1888), met Shaw when they were both members of the South St Pancras Liberal Association. Shaw proposed him for Fabian membership in February 1894.]

Dear Marriott

The drains are up at Fitzroy Square, thanks to our friend the sanitary inspector; and I am staying out here in consequence. Your letter is by far the most interesting I have had about the play. I have collected rents in Ireland, including some weekly ones from very poor people; and I know something of the utter want of any sense of duty in the matter on both sides. But I have, of course, no experience of London tenements, though human nature is much the same everywhere.

Let us have a chat by all means some evening during the slack time at Christmas. I should enjoy it. I have such an inhuman heap of letters to answer that I can say no more at present; we can pursue the subject when we meet.

Someday I will talk out about the population question with a vengeance.

G. Bernard Shaw

To CHARLES CHARRINGTON

8 Hammersmith Terrace W,
as the drains are up at Fitzroy Square
14th December 1892

[T/1 (B.u/4)]

[James Welch (1865–1917) played Lickcheese, the collector of rents. He also created the rôles of Major Petkoff in *Arms and the Man* (1894) and the Waiter in *You Never Can Tell* (1900). William Moy Thomas (1828–1910) was the dramatic critic of the *Daily News*. According to a report in the *Labour Leader*, 5th May 1894, Shaw not only "appeared before the curtain" on opening night but "delivered a lecture on Socialism to the astonishment of the ordinary play-folk and the delight of his friends. One of the papers next day announced that Mr G.B.Shaw had delivered a lecture on Socialism at the Royalty Theatre last evening, and after giving a report of what had been said, added as a kind of afterthought, 'The lecture was preceded by a play entitled *Widowers' Houses*.'"]

Dear Charrington

If you have seen "Widowers' Houses" you will understand that it was altogether too experimental to be put on anywhere except at the I.T., least of all at the theatre of any manager for whom I had a ray of personal regard. All that could be done with it would be about three matinees run by some manager who had a theatre and a staff eating their heads off in the afternoon. The third matinee would perhaps bring the performance up to the level of a bad dress rehearsal. However, I have proved myself a man to be reckoned with. I have got the blue book across the footlights. I have made Welch's reputation and blasted Florence Farr's. I have established the fact that Moy Thomas is the greatest dramatic critic of the age, and that Archer & Walkley are a pair of idiots. I have appeared before the curtain amid transcendent hooting & retired amid cheers. And I have spent so much time at rehearsal that I am stark ruined, and am ruefully asking myself whether a continental trip for my health would not have been far more economical than all this theatrical glory. For of what value was it to me when J.A.C. was not there to see. As yesterday's matinee was for the managers, I took it for granted that you would be there. I will try hard to get over to see you in the course of the next few days, tomorrow if no musical performance claims me—failing that, Monday. I am staying for the moment with H.H.Sparling.

372

To WILLIAM ARCHER

[C/2]

29 Fitzroy Square W
14th December 1892

[Archer's review of *Widowers' Houses* appeared in *The World* on 14th December. Five months later, when Archer reviewed the published text of the play in *The World* (4th May 1893), he offered the startling opinion: "It is a pity that Mr. Shaw should labour under a delusion as to the true bent of his talent, and, mistaking an amusing *jeu d'esprit* for a work of creative art, should perhaps be tempted to devote further time and energy to a form of production for which he has no special ability and some constitutional disabilities. A man of his power of mind can do nothing that is altogether contemptible. We may be quite sure that if he took palette and 'commenced painter,' or set to work to manipulate a lump of clay, he would produce a picture or a statue that would bear the impress of a keen intelligence, and would be well worth looking at. That is precisely the case of *Widowers' Houses*. It is a curious example of what can be done in art by sheer brain-power, apart from natural aptitude. For it does not appear that Mr. Shaw has any more specific talent for the drama than he has for painting or sculpture."]

I have come to the conclusion that Moy Thomas (who sat it out again yesterday, every line) is the greatest critic of the age, and Massingham entirely right in his estimate of you and Walkley. A more amazing exposition of your Shaw theory even I have never encountered than that World article. Here am I, who have collected slum rents weekly with these hands, & for 4½ years been behind the scenes of the middle class landowner—who have philandered with women of all sorts & sizes—and I am told gravely to go to nature & give up apriorizing about such matters by you, you sentimental Sweet Lavendery recluse. Get out!

GBS

To ALFRED NUTT

[B/3]

c/o William Morris
Kelmscott House. Lechlade
25th December 1892

[Alfred Trübner Nutt (1856–1910), head of the publishing firm of David Nutt Ltd, was a noted folklorist, founder of the Irish Texts Society in 1898.]

Dear Sir

I have only succeeded in getting together one complete MS of the play, which I am correcting, fitting with a preface &c. I must hold on to it until the job is finished. Meanwhile I have had a couple of offers for its publication—three, in fact. One of them is from a firm in which Mr Grein, of the Independent Theatre, is interested. They propose to try a half crown edition, with a sixpenny royalty; and I am rather inclined, on Grein's account, to accept this if I can satisfy myself that the firm in question has the requisite circulating machinery. Do you think you could do better for me than this? The reason I ask you to bid for a pig in a poke is that the quality of the bacon is hardly in question this time. Three months ago the play would certainly not have been worth publishing. Today a heap of articles and notices (my own collection of press cuttings runs over 130, and is far from complete) has presumably created some curiosity about the work; and it is the value of the curiosity that is now in the market. It is on this basis, and not on that of the literary value of the MS (as to which I have my own unalterable opinion) that I want an offer.

yrs faithfully
G. Bernard Shaw

P.S. I return to town on Wednesday; so that my address is still 29 Fitzroy Square. W.

To PAKENHAM BEATTY

8 Hammersmith Terrace W
4th January 1893

[A/4]

[The "poor little sensitive plant" was Richard Le Gallienne, who, as "Logroller," was the book reviewer of *The Star*, in which newspaper Shaw had unfavourably reviewed his *English Poems* (published by Elkin Mathews and John Lane) on 27th October 1892. On 3rd November Le Gallienne had replied:

> "Poor little book, that only yesterday
> Fluttered new born in delicate array,
> How bruised and broken in the mud you lie,
> Surely some elephant was passing by;
> Or those mad herds of Galilean swine
> Have hoofed across that pretty page of thine.
> A nightingale the Minotaur hath torn,
> So seems my little murdered book this morn.
> Bury it gently where no eye may see,
> And for its epitaph write "C. di B."

374

Sir William Watson (1858–1935), a poet considered by many of his contemporaries to be the successor to Tennyson, had recently been adjudged insane. The *Fortnightly Review* article, "What Mr Gladstone Ought to Do," was a contribution to a symposium on the Home Rule Bill in the February issue. Fabian Tract No. 47, John Burns's *The Unemployed*, was edited by Shaw.]

Why all this fury against a poor little sensitive plant like Richard? Why, his fighting weight is not two and a half ounces: a rough word would drive him to suicide. You do not suppose that he is a rough knuckled, thick skinned ruffian of the Trelawny type, do you? He was horribly hurt when I took his valentines and love letters, over every one of which I have no doubt he dropped a tear of quivering sensibility, and crumpled them up in my horny fist; and I shouldnt have done it if I had not thought that he was getting spoiled. As it was, I wrote the review in such a way as to sell his book; and sure enough his publisher tells me that after my review & the one in the St James's Gazette, he sold 1250 copies! What do you think of that for a volume of minimus poetry? I know he complains of me; and his little poem in the Star was pathetic in its squeak of pain. I would willingly make him some amends for having hurt his feelings if there were any opening for doing so; but as there is none, I leave him to grow older & stronger.

That reminds me, by the bye, that we are now arrived at years of discretion. As middle aged buffers we must not pick quarrels with young men, or take up their hasty challenges. If you have not by this time mellowed sufficiently to have a deep and genuine Shelleyan horror of violence, then it is the office of a friend to trip you from behind, sit on your head, and deliver you over to the custodians of the poet Watson. It is really shocking to find you actually brooding over a trifle like Le G's harmless conceit. You must awake from these evil dreams.

I am at present so overwhelmed with a Fortnightly article, a pamphlet on the unemployed for the Fabian, the publication of my play with a preface &c, besides my ordinary overwork that you might as well be in Russia as at Ealing as far as your accessibility is concerned. However, I will make an offer. Reserve next Wednesday afternoon, and I will struggle out of the net as far as Asheton. If the frost lasts we might do a skate. I tried last night on the lake at Grove Park, Chiswick, and did my little bit literally on my head.

GBS

To EDWARD R. PEASE

[C/4]

29 Fitzroy Square W
9th January 1893

[Shaw replaced Hubert Bland as a representative of the Fabian Society, on 13th January, at the Foundation Conference of the National Independent Labour Party at Bradford. When Shaw's credentials were challenged as faulty by the Fabian opposition, he accepted the decision of the Conference that he be barred from the proceedings to the extent of withdrawing from the floor of the house. However, he "promptly took up a strong enfilading position in the gallery, from which he bombarded us so violently with his interruptions that on the following day we admitted him to our deliberations in sheer self-defence" (*Sir James Sexton: Agitator . . . An Autobiography*, 1936).]

Bland's defection is too frightful. I can do nothing in the way of calling a meeting for Thursday; but if you can communicate with the Fabian at Bradford, you may tell them that I shall be available on Thursday evening, if that will be of any use. Can I have my expenses in advance: I am stony broke just now, owing to having forgotten to provide for my Income Tax.

GBS

To EDWARD R. PEASE

[H/1; X/119]

29 Fitzroy Square W
11th January 1893

[Frank Podmore had proposed Fabius Cunctator as the Fabian Society's "patron saint" and had coined its temperate slogan; hence "Podmorius Cunctator." The Fabian Election Manifesto (Tract No. 40), 1892, was bound in dark red wrappers. Sir William Pollard Byles (1839–1917), son of the founder of the *Bradford Observer*, was a social reformer and radical M.P. for Shipley. Miss Isabel Priestley (later the wife of the author Bart Kennedy), assistant secretary of the Fabian Society (1892–95), became a member of the Executive Committee in 1895. Shaw had been typewriting his articles and much of his correspondence, since 14th March 1890, on a second-hand Bar-Lock typewriter purchased from H.W.Massingham.]

Dear Pease

Your esteemed cheque for £3 on account of expenses has come to hand, and shall be duly vouched for the auditors. If you will let me know at your convenience when the Fabian last settled up with me for

376

expenses, I will undertake to advance unliquidated claims far exceeding any conceivable arrear of even my subscription, without trenching on this trip.

In cases where a nice sense of personal dignity leads a lecturer to treat your request for details of expenses with scorn, the proper course is to pass over the incident with imperturbable politeness, and to take particular care that the defaulter never again sees the color of the Fabian money. "For the right moment you must wait patiently &c" (vide Podmorius Cunctator). I imagine we shall find it a cheap way of getting rid of the sort of lecturer whom we cannot very well get rid of in any other way.

The printed credential raises a nice question of the constitution of the Society. I must fortify myself with a copy of that constitution and some tracts. Will you, on receiving this, precipitate yourself with the utmost instantaneousness on the bewildered Howell, and bid him forthwith post me a copy of the rules &c, a last annual report, the History of the Fabian, and the blood red Election Manifesto, addressed Care of W.P.BYLES ESQ. M.P., Oakfield, Bradford, so that I may receive them on my arrival there. As we are overloaded with the Manifesto, and as it is an exposition of the line I propose to take at the Conference, I think it might be well to send down a supply for distribution among the Fabians (who have forgotten it all by this time) if not among the delegates at large. But dont send the stock to me, as I am a bad colporteur.

My present intention is to go uncompromisingly for Permeation, for non-centralized local organization of the Labor Party, and for the bringing up of the country to the London mark by the supplanting of Liberalism by Progressivism. I feel like forcing the fighting as extravagantly as possible; so as to make it clear to all the new men that the Fabian is the lead for them to follow as soon as they have found out S-M [Shaw Maxwell] & Co. If you listen attentively on Friday you will probably hear the noise of the debate in the distance.

Ask Miss Priestly what she would give to be able to type like this.

I am, Sir
your obedient servant
GBS

29 Fitzroy Square W

[S/1]   30th January 1893

[William P. Johnson (1866–1923), secretary of the National Union of Shop
Assistants, had been an I.L.P. delegate from Manchester to the Bradford
conference. Shaw's article, "The Bradford Conference: From the Fabian
Point of View," appeared in the *Workman's Times* on 28th January. The fourth
clause of the suggested constitution submitted by the Manchester delegates
called for all members of the I.L.P. to "pledge themselves to abstain from
voting for any candidate for election to any representative body who is in
any way a nominee of the Liberal, Liberal-Unionist, or Conservative Party."
Hall probably was Benjamin T. Hall (1864–1931), a Fabian, who was chairman of the Deptford Labour Party.]

Dear Johnson

Delighted to hear from you, though for the moment I can do no
more than reply in a few hasty words.

That article of mine is culpably goodnatured. If you knew all I
might have said and didn't say, you would be astonished at my moderation. But, hang it all, you do know enough to see that we (the Fabians)
have taken things very amiably. You Manchester fellows have done
your very worst to us. You did all you could to keep us out of the Conference; and when we got in you warned it against our "insidious
reasoning," meaning, in plain English, our dishonesty. At the General
Election, when we had planked our last shilling at West Bradford to
defeat [Alfred] Illingworth and get in [Ben] Tillett, Blatchford
deliberately made a furious attack on us in the Clarion at the critical
moment, with the result that Tillett was beaten and Illingworth was
victorious by 300 votes, a hotheaded sacrifice of Independent Labour
to mere anti-Fabian prejudice. Your confounded 4th Clause destroyed
the Manchester Fabian Society by driving every man who was worth
his salt out of it. Wherever your influence has reached, we find ourselves received with suspicious hostility, just as we were at Bradford,
where only for us the I.L.P. would have presented the country with a
feeble Liberal programme of the Broadhurst-Howell pattern. When
it comes to hard business, you are none of you worth a cent. You run
away terrified from the wirepullers whom we are always in handygrips
with, as we must be if we are to outwit them and outfight them. You
twaddle about your principles and your ideals and your purity to an
extent that would nauseate a chaplain to a girls' school. Worst of all,
you get beaten at the polls, drubbed, smacked, discredited, polly-
wogged by Liberals and Tories with equal ease. Even when you have

378

saturated the I.L.P. with your abhorrence of Permeation, Permeation walks on your countenances without an effort. By God, Johnson, I blush for you—I am ashamed of Manchester—I apologise to the British nation for associating Socialism with men who set about making the millenium as children set about making a mud pie. And yet you tell me that I was hard on you in the W.T. Get out!

As to teaching history and economics, what we have found in the Fabian is that the man who learns them without also learning politics, trade, and the world, is ten times more unmanageable and obstructive than the ordinary rule-of-thumb Radical. Did you not see Aveling, who is saturated with Marx and history and what are supposed by Socialists to be economics (bless their innocence!) supporting that idiotic denunciation of piece work, which I said nothing about because I could not, with all my "cynicism," believe that the Conference could be so incredibly ignorant of north country Trade-Unionism as to pass it. History and Economics be blowed!

If I had time I would put in every week's W.T. an article which would send all Manchester into epileptic convulsions until they began to shew a proper sense of the colossal superiority of their fathers the Fabians.

Mind you get Hall or somebody in at the next General Election on the Liberal + Labour vote. Never mind the shock to your principles: if you are not prepared to be damned for the cause in the next world you won't do much for it in this.

yrs impenitently
G. Bernard Shaw

To ELIZABETH ROBINS

[A/33]

29 Fitzroy Square W
5th February 1893

[Shaw had interviewed Elizabeth Robins on 4th February, at the end of which, according to his diary note, she "got rather alarmed .... and swore she would shoot me if I said anything she did not approve of." The interview was not published. Miss Robins was rehearsing Ibsen's *The Master Builder*, which she presented at the Trafalgar Square Theatre on 20th February.]

Dear Miss Robins

Will you just look at this rough sketch of the interview you were good enough to give me on Saturday, and say what you think of it.

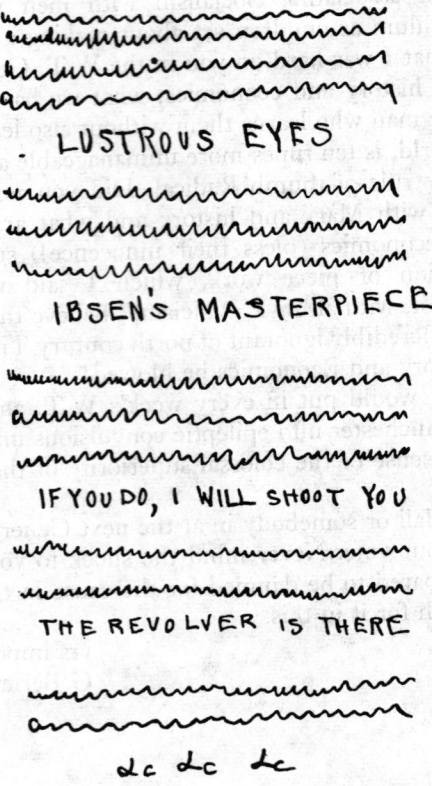

SENSATIONAL HEADINGS ad. lib.

LUSTROUS EYES

IBSEN'S MASTERPIECE

IF YOU DO, I WILL SHOOT YOU

THE REVOLVER IS THERE

&c &c &c

Never in my life have I had such a professional success. You were clay in the hands of the potter. I have interviewed beautiful women before; but none of them were ever so noble as to threaten to shoot me. It would make any ordinary man's fortune. And I am going, for your sake, to sacrifice it all—or at least to reserve it for my autobiography.

Now let me give you some advice. 1. Never let an interviewer put you on your guard: it is only his way of putting you off it. 2. Never let him know or see anything that is not for publication. 3. Either barricade the front door or surrender at discretion. 4. Remember that you can be interviewed or not interviewed, as you please; but you cannot be both interviewed and not interviewed at the same time.

5. Remember that the interviewer, in spite of his unfamiliar technique, is a practised comedian. 6. Remember also that all interview*ee's* say exactly the same things, and that the interview*er* knows them by heart, whereas the interviewee is necessarily a comparative novice. 7. Remember that the published interview will be a mass of misinterpretation & that the reproduction of your portrait will be a hideous failure. 8. If the interviewer makes any difficulty about letting you see proofs, do not argue the point, but just write quietly for them to his editor. 9. Get interviewed as often as you can by good interviewers & let them say what they like so long as their copy is entertaining. 10. (& chiefest) Always *interview yourself* if you can.

I could never have convinced you of the impolicy of your frightful and quite undeserved mistrust of me except by mystifying you as I have done. Now select a nice rehearsal for me and let us have a talk with [Herbert] Waring; and I will promise not to play any more pranks on you.

yours sincerely
G. Bernard Shaw

To WILLIAM P. JOHNSON

29 Fitzroy Square W
13th February 1893

[S/1]

[Shaw's letter, "Cry-Baby Stalwarts," in the *Workman's Times* on 18th February, was a reply to Pete Curran (1860–1910) of the I.L.P. on the Bradford conference. W.S. De Mattos, Shaw's fellow delegate at the conference, had also been refused admission by the Standing Order Committee, of which Johnson was a member.]

Dear Johnson

I have sent [Joseph] Burgess a letter for the W.T.—more egotistical than ever. Have you noticed that one result of the Fabians constantly telling the world how clever they are is that the world is beginning to believe them, and, of course, to pretend that it found out the cleverness for itself. Study us, my boy, and learn how to bounce; for it is only by bouncing that our little stage army can conquer the country.

I know quite well that it was the arrival of [Robert] Blatchford and the Manchester contingent at the last moment that saved de Mattos and myself. That was what I meant by "gallant opponents" in my article. I also quite agree with you that the Fabian had no real *locus standi*; and if you had consistently objected to the S.D.F. men as well and kept their vote out of the division, you would have carried your point. But you would also have ruined the I.L.P., since, in the absence of Burns and his Labour League, it was only the presence of the Fabian that saved the credit of the Conference with the south of England. But as the Conference did not know that, our getting in and having our own way with the programme was a triumph of Fabian cheek.

Halifax was lost, confound it, by sheer want of business experience on our side.

G. Bernard Shaw

To ELIZABETH ROBINS

[B/33]

29 Fitzroy Square W
20th February 1893

[On 20th February Shaw and Archer attended the matinée première of *The Master Builder* (translated by Archer and Edmund W. Gosse), in which Miss Robins appeared as Hilda Wangel and Herbert Waring as Halvard Solness. Shaw had lectured on the 19th to the Liberal Club, Lincoln, on labour politics.]

There is no saying what the papers will come out with tomorrow morning; so I had better send you my certificate of the perfect success of the play as far as I am concerned. It held me and moved me from beginning to end. I thought the dolls scene particularly pathetic. So never mind if they scoff. Waring is not quite able to carry through the second act: he has not the mystery, the fascination for it; but he never acted better. Why does he make up like John Burns? I shall say nothing about Hilda, as she is an ungovernable person off the stage and would take anything I could say in bad part. Her conduct presents only one extenuating circumstance—she sent me a ticket as a sort of atonement for having treated me very badly.

I rushed up from Lincoln to hear the play & was full of the cathedral whilst Solness was talking shop.

Get the curtain down a little faster at the end.

GBS

382

To WILLIAM ARCHER

[B/2]

29 Fitzroy Square W
23rd February 1893

[*The Strike at Arlingford*, by the Irish novelist George Moore (1852–1933), was produced by the Independent Theatre at the Opéra Comique on 21st February. Baron Lionel de Rothschild (1808–79), Conservative M.P., inherited from his father the leadership of the famous House of Rothschild. James Livesey (1831–1925), head of a firm of civil and mechanical engineers, was one of the earliest advocates of the use of steel. Louise Michel (1830–1905) was a French anarchist agitator who resided in London from 1886 to 1895. John Reid is the central character in Moore's play. Philos Ingarfield is a character in Henry Arthur Jones's *The Crusaders* (1891).]

I do not know whether it is altogether fair for me, as a rival dramatist, to blow the gaff on Moore; but dont let yourself in for endorsing his strikology. He has confused the master collier class (ironmasters, manufacturers &c) with the financial class, & has taken Lionel Rothschild as his model when he should have taken Livesey. Steinbach's speech, "if only we were as well organised as they" is too ludicrously opposed to the facts to be fully appreciated by anyone who does not know how the masters out-organise the men in every colliery district. The confusion of Trade Unionism with Socialism and with Louise Michellism is utter and inextricable. The notion of sending for the military under circumstances which would have ensured their presence in considerable strength weeks beforehand is another blunder. In fact, from the realistic point of view, the whole play is utter non-sense: it was so unreal to me that it bored me to distraction. The first act only needed some practical knowledge to be made very amusing, especially the deputation. Moore's counterpoint is weak; he runs too much into duets. A master of polyphony like myself would have made a fine concerted piece out of that quartet & chorus. John Reid was simply Ingarfield over again. *Do* blow up the I.T. about the acting: even my lot, though they had not had half the rehearsal, did better than poor Moore's. I have written to him to warn him that his sociology is not what it might be, & to put him on his guard against leaving in that brutal speech about the public house in Manchester, where they are starving just now.

GBS

383

To OSCAR WILDE

[X/145.e]

[29 Fitzroy Square W]
28th February 1893

[Oscar Wilde (1854–1900) and Shaw were not close friends, but they had met on a few occasions, and shared an interest both in drama and in socialism, Wilde having published a significant essay, "The Soul of Man under Socialism," in the *Fortnightly Review*, February 1891. Wilde had sent Shaw a copy of *Salomé*, "in purple raiment," on 23rd February, in gratitude for *The Quintessence of Ibsenism*, which he considered to be "written well and wisely and with sound wit . . ." After reading *Widowers' Houses*, he informed Shaw on 9th May: "I like your superb confidence in the dramatic value of the mere facts of life . . . and your preface is . . . a real masterpiece of trenchant writing and caustic wit and dramatic instinct" (*Letters of Oscar Wilde*, ed. Rupert Hart-Davis, 1962). This extract from Shaw's letter (the original being unlocated) was taken by Mr Hart-Davis from the J. B. Stetson sale catalogue, Anderson Galleries, New York, 1920.]

Salome is still wandering in her purple raiment in search of me, and I expect her to arrive a perfect outcast, branded with inky stamps, bruised by flinging from hard hands into red prison [*i.e.*, post office] vans, stuffed and contaminated . . . I hope soon to send you my play *Widowers' Houses* which you will find tolerably amusing.

To JANET ACHURCH

[T/1 (B/4)]

29 Fitzroy Square W
3rd March 1893

[The Charringtons produced an English translation of Richard Voss's *Alexandra* at the Royalty on 4th March, inaugurating an experimental repertory season. Shaw and George Moore had attended the dress rehearsal. Jane Hading (1859–1941), a leading member of the Comédie Française, created the rôle of Claire in Ohnet's *Le Maître de forges*.]

I cry off the tragedy: I can write nothing beautiful enough for you. And I can no longer allow myself to be in love with you: nobody short of an archangel with purple and gold wings shall henceforth be allowed to approach you. Do not suppose that I am infatuated by the red wig: Jane Hading in Le Maitre de Forges was just as beautiful: I am actually less enamoured than before, because my admiration elbows out the commoner sentiment. I speak as a critic, not merely as a miserable two legged man. It was a masterpiece of conception in that *genre*, and a

384

masterpiece of execution both for beauty of style and success of expression. Do not read the papers: you must have roused all the powers of darkness to the most desperate resistance: in the discomfort of being made to feel that their hoofs and horns want cutting they will certainly rail at you. Do not let Archer put you out of conceit with your curious punctuation: it is all right—your internal music is not at fault: *I* say that everything was beautiful, and that you are the sufficient justification of all the shortcomings of the play.

Poor Moore howled with rage after the first act at the thought of having been robbed of you in his play. Well he might.

Now for Rosmersholm. I will stand no more of that wretched old Doll's House. There is no going back now.

GBS

To ELIZABETH ROBINS

[B/33]

29 Fitzroy Square W
3rd March 1893

[George R. Foss (1860–1938), an actor-manager, was stage manager and assistant to Shaw in the first production of *Arms and the Man* in 1894. Athol Forde had also created the rôle of Kroll in Florence Farr's production of *Rosmersholm* in 1891. John Beauchamp (1851–1921) was a popular character actor.]

I was at the performance this afternoon, and have to report that it was not, except in one respect, an improvement on the first. Waring appeared to me to have been listening to everybody's kind advice & to have allowed himself to be distracted from his own original conception, with the result that he was more stagey than before and had less grip & conviction, in the first act especially. There were faint traces of the same thing in the others; and Foss was not an improvement on Forde. However, I was probably much cooler and more critical and generally harder to please. All the modifications made for the sake of playing faster were to the bad: whenever people say "too slow" they really mean "too fast to sink in," or "too empty of action & significance of playing."

Your own playing was much better—surer, intenser, triumphantly convinced and convincing. I confess to a complete renewal of my admiration for your great artistic power; and my critical troll is deeply grateful to your artistic troll. It was really a noble and beautiful

385

performance. At the same time I hasten to relieve you from any sense of being disarmed against your will by assuring you, in our personal, non-artistic and non-critical relations, of my unmitigated defiance, and resentment of the wounds you have dealt to my justifiable vanity.

Perhaps some accident happened in the first act. I thought I heard you say to Beauchamp, when you were putting down your luggage, "What SHALL we do?"

GBS

To WILLIAM ARCHER

[40 Queen Square WC]
Friday afternoon [24th March 1893]

[H.t/2]

[Shaw called on Archer on 24th March, and "as he was not in, wrote a letter on his typewriter for him" (Diary). Archer's article was "The Theatres," which appeared in the May issue of the *English Illustrated Magazine*. The "preface" by Archer was secured by the device of quoting at length Archer's history of the *Rhinegold* collaboration as reported by him in *The World* on 14th December 1892. Carl Edvard Brandes' *A Visit*, translated by Archer from the Danish, had been produced at the Royalty on 4th March 1892. It was announced for publication in the Henry & Co. Independent Theatre Series, but did not appear.]

I leave the article, which seems to me good enough in spite of its inhumanity, except on one point. The explanation of the success of the translations on the stage is that in middle class social and political life Norway is the microcosm and England is the macrocosm. As I have often told you, if you would only join the local caucus, you would see at once that An Enemy of the People comes home to Holborn as closely as A Doll's House comes home to Brixton and Holloway, which are just as narrow and provincial as Norway. Ninetyfive per cent of an Ibsen play is as true of any English town as it is of Christiania; and the odd five per cent is not sufficient to make the performance in the least puzzling. Probably this is less true of France; but modern commercialism levels all nations down to the same bourgeois life, and raises the same problems for realist playwrights, though not for romantic ones. This is what destroys the whole parallel between Molière and Co. (as far as translation is concerned) and Ibsen; and I think you owe it to your reputation to shew that the difference is within the sphere of your consciousness in the article. Even apart from realist plays the drama is

386

more international than you represent it; for most of the adaptations—especially the most successful ones—are very close translations. It is the ultra adapted ones that fail.

The note about the theatres on page 76 of the MS had better come out, because the description of the Novelty is, I think, distinctly libellous, and the other two instances are more of the nature of apologies.

The tone of the article generally is one of devilish malignity towards the unfortunate Scott and the rest. They may deserve it; but when Widowers' Houses celebrates its six hundredth night, Scott will have his revenge.

I leave you the two sheets of W.H. which were missing from the set of proofs I sent you before. There are two points to admire: first, the ingenuity with which I have secured a preface by William Archer without running any of the risks which destroyed poor Jones; and second, the sublime preface by Grein, with its adroit allusion to the play 'setting the machinery of public opinion in motion and SUPPLYING BRICKS' &c. The proof of the final sheet is unique, and will be readily saleable for ten guineas in view of the champion misprint which has produced the sentence beginning on the last line of page 121.

I make no apology for lifting your copy out of the World, as I confined myself strictly to that part which is clearly made out of my own flesh and blood.

Please let me know whether you are going to publish A Visit in the series (or anything else) as I see I shall have to do the whole volume, advertisements and all, myself.

G.B.S.

To WILLIAM ARCHER

[B/2]

29 Fitzroy Square W
27th March 1893

[George Dandin is the tradesman hero in Molière's comedy of the same name; his frequent comment on the humiliations he suffers is "Vous l'avez voulu, George Dandin."]

I am writing to Grein to alter the advertisement of the 2nd vol. of the I.T. series on the ground that you are resolved not to have any other play in the same book with "A Visit." I suppose that is all right. I am also writing to Moore asking him whether he is still bent on taking "The Strike" to Scott.

387

About that first act [of *Widowers' Houses*], I am prepared to admit that it is no great shakes, except that Cokane is a creation, and my one French critic was right when he said that "la composition de cette lettre à laquelle Sartorius est appelé à collaborer pendant que les deux amoureux s'en vont reflirter dans le fond du jardin, constitue une scène de réelle et bonne comédie, au dialogue piquant et serre." Your objection to both is bad taste pure and simple; but as for the rest I do not press its excellence, provided you allow for the inevitable postponement of the glimpse of the under world to the second act caused by your own insistence on my beginning on the Rhine. "Tu l'as voulu, George Dandin."

GBS

To PAKENHAM BEATTY

[S/1]

29 Fitzroy Square W
4th April 1893

[Lucy Carr Shaw had married actor Charles Robert Butterfield (whose stage name was Cecil Burt) on 17th December 1887.]

Haven't the least idea of Lucy's address. I think she is in Birmingham with one of her husband's sisters. Write to her here and ask her: she gets her letters sent on from time to time.

Brahms is just like Tennyson, an extraordinary musician, with the brains of a third rate village policeman.

GBS

To EDWARD R. PEASE

[C/4]

29 Fitzroy Square W
18th April 1893

[At the instigation of William Morris a Joint Committee of Socialist Bodies was formed by the Fabian Society, the Social Democratic Federation, and the Hammersmith Socialist Society in January 1893. Morris, H. M. Hyndman, and Shaw undertook to draft a joint manifesto, which was published on 1st May. The Joint Committee was foredoomed to failure by the inability of Hyndman and the Fabians to agree on a defined policy, and in July the Fabian Society withdrew its delegates. See also letter of 15th December 1895 to Walter Crane.]

388

I find I cant go to the Joint Committee next Thursday. With a view to Webb's signature to the Manifesto, it would be well if he could take my place. Somebody ought to raise the question of a prefatory note to the Manifesto explaining the circumstances of its appearance.

GBS

To WILLIAM P. JOHNSON

[S/1]
29 Fitzroy Square W
24th April 1893
[Johnson's article, "The Fourth Clause," had appeared in *The Clarion* (Manchester) on 25th March.]

Dear Johnson

I intended to reply to your letter of the 2nd March, but never found time until it was out of date. What struck me in it was the impression made on you by "the patience, courage, and tenacity," shewn by the people during the strike, and your protest against their being regarded as "a mass of puppets with a few intellectual bosses to pull the strings." But I do not regard them in that way at all. What makes you think so is the open way in which I distinguish between the technical skill of the thinker and tactician who provides the masses with a policy, and the qualities in the masses which lead them to want a policy. Let me illustrate my point in this way. The masses want boots. Working men are constantly denying themselves something in order to get a pair of boots for one of the children. They shew patience, courage and tenacity in their pursuit of boots. But they don't know how to make boots. They must go to the bootmaker for them. This does not mean that they are puppets bossed by the bootmaker; on the contrary, it is their demand for boots that pulls his strings and sets him in motion. It is just the same in politics. The people want a policy (at least about $\frac{1}{1000}$th per cent. of them do); but they can't make one: they must go to the thinker and tactician for it. He may cheat them, more or less, just as the bootmakers do; but in the long run they find out the political shoe that fits them, and insist on having it. In offering them the Fabian make of shoe, I don't question their capacity or loyalty; I only assume what everybody knows as a plain matter of fact, namely, that they can't make the shoe themselves, and must suit themselves at the Fabian shop or the I.L.P. shop or the S.D.F. shop or the Liberal or Tory shops, whichever best understand their need. You offer them your own

389

special make of shoe, which I object to on the ground that it is too small for the average foot, and has a peg sticking up through the sole into the flesh, said peg being the 4th Clause.

In the W.T. [on 22nd April] my remarks about excluding Trade Unionists and Co-operators were not levelled at the I.L.P., but at the S.D.F., which has violently attacked them in the south. I did not see your note in the Clarion—I wish I had. I cannot get the Clarion here, and would never see the W.T. if they did not send it to me from the office.

As to what you can do on the Committee, my reply, of course, is Permeate. As Wallas says "Postulate, Permeate, perorate." Get up a "Facts for Manchester," like our "Facts for Socialists" or "Facts for Bristol." The Liverpudlians have made a start with a good leaflet of this kind. Use our Questions for Candidates at all local elections. Get a complete set of our tracts, including our Election Manifesto of last year, and steal everything that fits Manchester out of them. Say very little about the I.L.P. and a great deal about the Labour Question until you have stoked up public feeling a bit. Select your Parliamentary candidate carefully. Have your man on the Liberal caucuses and the Trades Council. When the question of the Liberals selecting their candidates comes up, insist on their adopting a Labour candidate in at least one of the divisions. Force them into the position of either adopting your man or else standing publicly convicted of having driven Labour out of their ranks by refusing to recognise its just claims. Sound the Clarion *fortissimo*. If you do it vigorously and adroitly, you will get in one man for Manchester on the Burns-Keir Hardie plan. This is the way, and the only way. You must, I need hardly say, begin by abolishing the 4th Clause and evicting all the stalwarts, besides voting for my appointment as Labour Dictator for ten years certain at the next Conference.

G. Bernard Shaw

To PAKENHAM BEATTY

29 Fitzroy Square W
[S/1]   24th April 1893

[Pierre Loti's *The Book of Pity and of Death*, published in France in 1891, had recently been issued in an English translation made by T. P. O'Connor.]

Just received "Le Livre de la Pitié et de la Mort" in morocco raiment, much too fine for my dustheap. I shall certainly give it to the next woman I fall in love with: They all like poets' autographs. I have never read anything of Loti's—will report when I have tasted the sample. Thanks in her name who will someday caress the morocco with the five teeth of the redbeard's favourite comb.

GBS

To FLORENCE FARR

[A/4; X/109]

29 Fitzroy Square W
27th April 1893

[The Charringtons produced *Adrienne Lecouvreur* by Eugène Scribe and Ernest Legouvé (adapted by Henry Herman) at the Royalty on 26th April. It survived only for a few performances. Herbert Flemming (1856–1908), young leading actor, also appeared with the Charringtons in *Alexandra*, *A Doll's House* (as Krogstad), and Brandon Thomas's *Clever Alice*. *The Iron Chest* (1796), a tragedy by George Coleman the Younger, based on William Godwin's *Caleb Williams*, had been revived by Irving at the Lyceum in 1879. The Abbé was played by C.P. Little, the Duchesse by a Miss Ashton, and the Princess by Florence Farr. Templar Saxe (1865–1935), formerly understudy to the musical-comedy star Hayden Coffin, was better known as a vocalist than as an actor.]

The unspeakable absurdity of that performance is only surpassed by the unparalleled blastedness of the play. Even the two men in the gallery who had got their orders from Flemming, and who strove so heroically to make a reception for him, were paralysed as the play jingled its poor old wires along. Why do they not strike out all those painful allusions to the crowded state of the house and to the histrionic capacity of the people on the stage.

The last act is simply ridiculous. Irving in The Iron Chest, gnawing at the boards and saying "Whep me, ye grenning fiends" was modern and plausible in comparison. Janet was transcendently bad. In the scene in the dark, & the recitation scene, I thought she was letting you get ahead out of pure consideration for me; but the finale destroyed that romantic illusion. To her infinite credit, the more she tries to make the play live, the more ghastly & ridiculous become its antics. Charrington comes off best. The Abbé is like a jack-acting amateur. Saxe's coat & the Duchesse's gloves are badly in want of cleaning; and you ought to powder your own hair & go about every day as an old woman whilst the piece lasts, the wig being only fit for a Salvation Army drum-stick.

391

In the first scene you are insufferable. You wave your arms about like a fairy in a transformation scene, obviously *pretending* to make an impossible toilet. You must invent something real to do, or else simply put on the patch intently, carefully, resolutely (as becomes a poisoner-potential) and then study yourself thoughtfully in the glass, like an artist in the art of dress. If you decide at any time to do nothing, shut your mouth, and compose yourself, and *do* nothing. As a *grande dame* you should never be at a loss and never in a hurry. You should speak a little at least with your lips, and not say "supposeitisnotformebutfor another" so as to strike the house dumb with its utter want of any intention or meaning. As to the way you tighten your upper lip, and bunch up your back, and stiffen your neck, and hold on by your elbows, that is, I admit, necessary to prevent you falling forward on your nose, and it is good for the calves and lumbar muscles, which are developed by the strain. I sacrifice this advantage on the platform & in the street by balancing my torso on my pelvis, and my head on my torso, so that they stand erect by their own weight. This lazy practice would also enable me, by a very slight movement of my head, to draw back with some dignity from Saxe in the first act, at the flower incident.

In the passages of action you manage to make a sort of success. So could anybody, I conclude. In the recitation scene Janet gives away the scene by bad stage management. The old style—the Princess & the audience grouped R, and Adrienne beginning L in profile and crossing as she grows more vehement—was far better. You should not put the cap on openly by rising to receive the charge. You should insult Adrienne by not attending to her, turning your face to the audience, playing with your face as you feel that she is approaching you, but not looking at her until she has finished the last line she hurls at you, when you should spring up & face her for the first time. Your rising earlier spoils her speech, which is already hampered by the small room & unimposing arrangement of the tableau. I wish I could get over to-morrow to go over the part with you, especially the first scene, which is very badly talked; but it's impossible. Friday & Saturday are jam full. On Sunday I have to lecture at Bow at half past seven.

The sooner the play disappears, the better for the reputation of the Charringtons & their enterprise. But you rather score off it; and I advise you to make the most of it while it lasts.

GBS

392

To ELIZABETH ROBINS

[C/33]

29 Fitzroy Square W
28th April 1893

[*Alan's Wife*, produced by the Independent Theatre at Terry's Theatre on 2nd May 1893, was adapted from a Swedish story by Elin Ameen. The authorship of the controversial drama was not disclosed, and for years was the subject of conjecture. Among the candidates were Archer, Lucy (Mrs W. Kingdon), Clifford the novelist (Shaw's first choice), and Elizabeth Robins (Shaw's second choice). Actually it was the work of Florence Bell (1852–1930), later Lady Hugh Bell, although Miss Robins was responsible for some revisions.]

Whoever wrote that play, it is of the Kingdom of Clifford from beginning to end—superstitious atheism—sensational anti-Goddity all over. Wallas has made a bet that it is Mrs C.

GBS

To WILLIAM ARCHER

[H/2]

29 Fitzroy Square W
11th May 1893

[Elsie Mackenzie, a singer whose concert Shaw attended on the evening of the 11th, was the sister of Sir Hector Mackenzie (1856–1929), a schoolmate and life-long friend of Archer, who became chief pathologist of St Thomas's Hospital. *Frou Frou* (1869), by Henri Meilhac and Ludovic Halévy, had been produced, in their own adaptation, by the Charringtons at the Manchester Comedy Theatre in December 1886. A translation of *La Joie fait peur* by Delphine de Girardin (1804–55), who wrote under the pseudonym "Charles de Launay," was produced at the Royalty on 30th June 1891. There is no evidence that Shaw viewed either production.]

You shew a deplorable want of grasp of the business talents of your compatriots. Miss Elsie has cultivated me with the greatest care ever since Hector introduced me to the household some years ago. She called, consulted me, and bound me over to attend the concert weeks ago. I abstain from returning the ticket so as not to deprive you of your excuse for not going.

You are perfectly right in your sketch of the right treatment of *Alan's Wife*. A woman capable of thinking for herself on questions of life and death would, obviously, quarrel with such a softheaded old mother and would have gusty times with her husband.

393

I believe the real difference between us is caused by the play being real to me in a way that it is not to you, or to the author. To you the incident is imaginary. Now to me it is comparatively common. Women do, as a matter of fact, polish off invalids and children on the ground that it is the most sensible and humane thing to do. Infanticide on that and other grounds is not a thing that women confess to; but every coroner knows how frequent it is. As to women who, if they dont exactly give Oswald the morphia, nevertheless deliberately and affectionately read the doctor's instructions backwards, you would not doubt their existence if you wore a sympathetic looking collar instead of giving your head the appearance of being stuck in a jam pot, and so repelling the confidence of clever women. Such women are not in the least like Jean, and never do it in Jean's way. They dont get hung; and they dont repent: on the contrary, they are invariably proud of having done the right thing. The tragedy, if there is tragedy, lies in the fact, and not in the fuss that is made about it. To represent a woman killing her child in such a way as to convince nine tenths of the audience that she is suffering from puerperal mania, and then getting hung for it, is to my mind shirking the problem as completely as it can be shirked without ignoring it altogether.

If I were to treat the subject, I should represent Jean as a rational being in society as it exists at present; and I should shew her killing the child with cool and successful precautions against being found out. I should then represent her mother and the parson and all the neighbors as being morally certain that she had done it, and herself as keeping up no greater pretense to the contrary than might be needed to save her neck. And I should represent their theories as to their own horror and her remorse as breaking down signally in practice, leaving her, when she had recovered from the natural grief produced by the sawing episode and so forth, the happiest and most sincerely respected woman in the parish. I should, by the bye, have married her to the parson, and, out of the struggle between the poor little chap's piety and his common sense (enlightened by his love), made a roaring good part for [James] Welch. When I think of that wasted opportunity, I feel more than ever contemptuous of this skulking author who writes like a female apprentice of [Robert] Buchanan.

The reason I cannot rush publicly into the controversy is that I should be unable to dissociate the problematical aspect of the play from its artistic aspect. You admire the execution, its large simplicity and so on. I dont. You may call *East Lynne* largely handled if you like, or the end of *Frou-frou*, or *Le Joie fait peur*, or anything else that

394

uncorks the eye of the emotional actress, with almost as much chance of gaining my full assent. But I quite admit that the picture is painted with a full brush, and is a remarkable example of the fact that the sort of work that has hitherto been supposed proper to the novel only will do on the stage as well as and a good [deal] better than the shoppy stage style. But I still think that the pathos and the ideas are most horribly common; and as to the character creation, what bungler could not fake up that dreadful old woman and her gossip, not to mention the minister who, thanks to Welch, looked like a character until he opened his mouth and twaddled. These opinions I must, as a comrade Independent, keep to myself.

As to what you say about greenness, freshness, youth, susceptibility to enjoyment and so on, I can only say, with Rossetti, that

> The thumb as it goes
> To the end of the nose

conveys my opinion of this quintessence of the Clement Scott illusion. Why the devil dont you write a play instead of perpetually talking about it? You can do it well enough if you will only face making an ass of yourself in the preliminary trials, as you had to when you learnt to cycle. I've all but finished another play [*The Philanderer*] myself, quite as promising a failure as Widowers' Houses, but a step nearer to something more than talk about what plays ought to be. Just think of all the horrors you could revel in for the mere sake of telling Nature that you knew her real character and were not afraid to look her in the face.

What a chap you are!

GBS

To PAKENHAM BEATTY

[S/1]   29 Fitzroy Square W
                                                          19 May 1893
[R. Gueraut, to whom Beatty was lending a sum of money, apparently was a librarian at Christ Church, Oxford.]

Letter safely to hand—have telegraphed Powell for instructions & received his sanction for sending the relief direct to Gueraut, which I have done, substituting orders for cheque so as to avoid revealing name. However, unless you very particularly wish the contrary, I shall tell

Powell, who ought to know, as I shall expect him to see that G. pays up in due time. No charity: he must pay up if he starves for it—Thanks for the [Loti] book: it is full of the sweet odour of a well spent life. I wept over pp. 8–9.

G.B.S.

To ELIZABETH ROBINS

29 Fitzroy Square W
5th June 1893

[A/33]

[Miss Robins was producing a series of twelve Ibsen performances at the Opéra Comique, subsidised by purchase of season-tickets, including *Hedda Gabler* (which Shaw attended with May Morris on the evening of the 5th), *Rosmersholm*, and a double bill of *The Master Builder* and the fourth act of *Brand*. Shaw's unsigned interview with Lady Colin Campbell appeared in *The Star* on 2nd June.]

These lines, oh most beautiful, in great haste.

When Thea says she thinks the woman in Lovborg's life was the red haired opera singer, you say "No doubt" or something to that effect with a crudely stagy affectation of insincerity. This is caused by the effort on your mind of your wirework shoulder pieces, which are an outrage.

In the third act, when Brack makes the speech to which you reply "Then he hadn't any vine leaves in his hair," you say it cynically, without any marking of the first stroke of the disillusionment. This totally destroys the effect of the entire play.

In the same act, later on, there is a gross blunder in the stage management. Lovborg sits down crushed L; and Thea immediately does the same R. The effect is, of course, comic.

When Tesman says—referring to the resuscitation of the "child," "I owe it to Eilert's memory," he ought to say it with a certain troubled significance, since you and he know that the book was murdered.

Miss [Marie] Linden is nothing like so good as Marion Lea. [Lewis] Waller is all very well in his way; but he fails entirely to overcome the subtlest difficulty of the part—that of conveying somehow to the audience that he has not the slightest intention of shooting himself, and that poor Hedda is being duped.

That feather boa, which you made fashionable before, will load you at the day of judgment with the blood of many slaughtered birds.

396

I shall say nothing complimentary about Hedda. You are too exacting. I have flattered you beyond the utmost appetite of the next vainest woman in the world, heaping up praises that would have sounded exaggerated if divided among the Virgin Mary, Duse, and Cleopatra. But you always find I crumple one of the million roseleaves, and turn and rend me for it. Now I give you up in desperation, and speak only to find fault. I may as well be hung for a sheep as a lamb.

Why did you not get me to ask to be allowed to interview you? I did a very pretty interview with Lady Colin Campbell for the Star the other day; and I should have flattered you more than I did her. What have I ever done to you that you should so brutally shew your mistrust of me? Granted that I am odious, yet I can be made use of. I can invent the interview without inflicting myself on you, and send it to you for correction. Have I ever persecuted you or worried you further than by merely existing out of your sight? Good Heavens! what have my crimes—my intrusions—been? You say "Come here, dog: you are wanted"; and I come obediently and am presently threatened with a pistol & terrified out of my life. You send me for a cab, and contemptuously reward me with a lift, during which, being so near you, I cannot help being in love with you in a poetic and not in the least ignoble way; but though I do not venture on the faintest expression of my impulse, you discover it by a sort of devilish divination, and instantly I am seized and flung out of the vehicle into the mud, with wheels flying over me this way and that and horses dancing & stumbling on my countenance.

I have finished another play, with four good parts for men and three for women—the chief of the three a superb one. Aha! I do not know how to write for the stage, do I not? We shall see, injurious Elizabeth, we shall see.

GBS

To JANET ACHURCH

[T/1 (A/4)]

29 Fitzroy Square W
7th July 1893

[Shaw wrote a description, on 6th July, of the wedding procession of the Duke of York (later George V) and Princess Mary of Teck; it appeared, unsigned, in *The Star* that afternoon.]

The history of the enclosed indelicacy is as follows. On Thursday I went from your house to Mrs Sparling's, 8 Hammersmith Terrace W.

She is better known as May Morris, daughter of William of that ilk, and an embroidress of fame. I mentioned, on being called on to give an account of my wanderings after the royal wedding, that I had been to see you; and this led to questions about your enterprise, to which I replied that it had left you and Charrington in very considerable difficulties. She said she had met you once at somebody's—Mrs Horner's, or some such name. The subject then dropped; but she must have seen that it was rather on my mind, as indeed it was; for today she asked me whether, if she cashed a deposit receipt for £10 which she happened to have lying idle, you would, as a matter of freemasonry between one artist and another, borrow it from her and pay her when you are next in luck. I said I'd try; and she then and there produced the enclosed notes. I imagine, though she did not directly say so for obvious reasons, that she would like me to let you know that she is not an opulent patroness of the arts, but a worker like yourself, only, for the moment, with £10 to the good instead of to the bad. Her husband is a literary man who is not as yet altogether a self-supporting institution; and she lives in a quiet little house, with an embroidery factory cumbering the drawing-room from nine to five, on the river near this end of Chiswick Mall.

Under these circumstances it seems to me that you need not hesitate to take her at her word. But if you do, you are bound in honor not to use any of it to pay your debts with. It is for enjoyment and use, not for transfer to some creditor. At least that is how it strikes me.

If you are offended, take it out of *me*, not out of her. But there is no occasion for anything of the sort. Still, just as the idea of your not having plenty of money rankles in me like a screw propeller cutting up the centre of my heart, which is absolutely wrong and uncomradely in me; so you may, equally unreasonably, be angry with me. If so, let us forgive one another.

After all, ten pounds is ten pounds, isnt it? Damn the whole monetary system!

GBS

To GRAHAM WALLAS

[H/13]

29 Fitzroy Square W
20th July 1893

[Harry B. Rogers, secretary of the Battersea branch of the S.D.F., was running for the London County Council in a by-election at Battersea on 22nd July. He was defeated by R. F. E. Willis (d. 1905), a Fabian who was backed in the election by John Burns. Ernest E. Williams was one of the Fabian delegates to the Joint Committee of Socialist Bodies. It was his motion in November 1893, that the Fabian Society renew its delegation to the Joint Committee, which climaxed the "mutiny" to which Shaw refers in his letter of 8th September 1893 to Wallas. The motion was defeated, and Williams shortly thereafter withdrew from the Executive Committee.]

Will you make a point of being at the Executive tomorrow so as to be ready for any difficulty that may arise over the report of the Joint Committee. We had a very unpleasant evening of it there. In future we must go in force or else we must withdraw from it altogether. Hyndman made a desperate attempt to pass a resolution in favor of Rogers; but Morris fortunately refused to put it on the ground that the bodies had not had notice. H.M.H. then moved urgency, but that also Morris refused. He then wrangled over the wording of the minutes with the evident object of claiming for Rogers that the Joint Committee were in favor of his candidature and that a resolution would have been passed to that effect but for a purely technical difficulty. He also fought hard to get the resolution about our supporting Socialist candidates passed; and here of course Williams and De Mattos took his part against me. He eventually got it referred back to the constituent bodies in an amended form which comes to exactly the same thing. Olivier declared in favor of it, though he voted as instructed; Hammill did the same. None of them seemed to see the game; and I was in the disadvantageous position of apparently wrangling with Hyndman for the sake of wrangling. If we dont either bring all our debating power to bear on that Committee or else clear out of what is and always has been a false position, we shall get up to the neck in the tactics of the S.D.F.

As I shall have to leave the Executive early, try to attend punctually and bring on the Joint Committee report at once. It is a great pity that we did not give the society a lead by supporting Willis. Hyndman let out that he is going to run a candidate against Burns at the next general election, and as the local Fabians act now they will probably act then. We must play up for our side. I suggest that if you are asked to speak for Willis you should do so, or even go down unasked, unless there are points against Willis that I know nothing of.

I am sending a manifold of this to Webb.

GBS

[At the head of the carbon copy to Webb, Shaw added: "Hold this up to the window & read through the paper. I accidentally put the carbon paper in upside down."]

To AUGUSTIN HAMON

29 Fitzroy Square W
31 Juillet 1893

[S/1]

[Augustin Hamon (1862–1945), French Socialist-Anarchist author and editor, became Shaw's French translator in 1904. Shaw attended the International Socialist Congress at Zürich early in August; his reports, signed "From a Special Correspondent," appeared in *The Star* on 8th to 14th August.]

Cher Monsieur

Merci bien! la Daily Chronicle vient de m'envoyer le livre et la brochure que vous avez eu la bonté de m'offrir. En ce moment je pars pour la France en route pour le prochain congrès à Zurich. Ce petit tour achevé, je me donnerai le plaisir d'étudier "La France Sociale et Politique," qui m'a vivement interessé au premier coup d'oeil.

Je ne suis pas attaché à la Daily Chronicle, quoique j'y ai contribué quelques revues. H.W.Massingham, le feuilletoniste parlementaire, est membre de la Société Fabienne, et vous servira peut être. (Excusez mon style Britannique)

yours very truly
G. Bernard Shaw

To WILLIAM ARCHER

29 Fitzroy Square W
21st August 1893

[A/33]

[Piona was a mystical land of plenty, conceived in the imagination of Archer's young son Tom. Sir Edward Tyas Cook (1857–1919) had been assistant editor to W.T.Stead on the *Pall Mall Gazette*; he succeeded Stead as editor in 1890, but resigned when the paper was purchased by William Waldorf (later Viscount) Astor. When George Newnes founded the *Westminster Gazette* in January 1893, Cook was appointed editor. Arthur W. Pinero's *The Second Mrs Tanqueray* had been produced on 27th May 1893 at the St James's Theatre, starring Mrs Patrick Campbell and George Alexander.]

I somehow dont feel that the Music Halls need a report sufficiently to justify an editor in rising to the occasion. Of course if we were to follow it up and eventually publish a conspectus of the art of the day—music halls, concerts, opera, & theatres—there might be some interest in it for the bookmakers of posterity. But I dont feel that we should have any real grip of the subject, because we have no experience of it. If we had been constant music hall goers for the last 20 years, then we

400

could really apply the historical method & produce something valuable; but as we have probably not made twenty visits between us in our lives, we should have to fall back on apriorism and bare description of what is not worth describing. However, if you have a call, I am willing to go round and help.

The restless energy with which you are throwing yourself into all manner of controversies suggests to me that you are going mad. Or rather, you have at last thrown off the restraints that used to keep up your character for sanity, and are recklessly exhibiting yourself to the public in your true character of a Nihilist. The cynical lunacy of your fundamental propositions used to be veiled partly by your own reserve, and partly by the air of sobriety given to your logical superstructure by the contrast with my superficial extravaganza on a hidden bed rock foundation of reality and common sense. But your letter to the Chronicle and other recent exploits of yours are blowing the gaff. Further, by throwing all your energy & excitability into trifles, you are forcing yourself to find adequate material in them to work on, and as they dont in themselves provide this you magnify them imaginatively until they are big enough to exercise all your powers; and then you wrestle with them to the great astonishment of the public, which sees you struggling with grasshoppers as if they were giants. All these terrible combats with Walkley & others on behalf of Wilde, Pinero, [Frank] Harris &c. &c. &c. belong to Piona and not to the wake-a-day world. Le Gallienne, otherwise twaddly enough, is right in complaining that you shew no sense of proportion, the reason being that you are wreaking all your powers on small jobs with a magnifying glass in your eye. I therefore return to my old position as to your business in the world. All this trouncing of Walkley out of positions which he does not really hold, and which you manufacture out of his obvious carelessness of expression, is waste of time—mere cat's-cradle work, which will soon bore even the few who now care to watch it. When the Westminster Gazette started, Cook said to me, as an objection to my suggestion of a dramatic feuilleton, that nobody really wanted the "My dear A.B.W. business"; and I am inclined to think that he was right in hesitating to dedicate a column of the paper to—possibly—an interminable controversy about nothing. When that confounded preface to Alan's Wife appears, it will land you at the extreme limit of human patience. Sooner or later—unless you wait until it is too late—you will have to turn your dramatic instinct into its legitimate channel, and write plays yourself. If you spend the next six months in writing a play, it will no doubt not be a *very* first rate one; but at all events it will be more respectable than the product of all the hours you have spent over the question of whether Walkley saw a streak of red paint or not. It is already quite evident that unless you take your part in the production of "the new drama," you will be driven by the inner necessity of justifying yourself to yourself, to abuse it frantically, and to champion the reactionary drama against it. The one fact that is clear about Alan's Wife is that you should have written it yourself. You would then have had the right to put a preface to it. Instead of that you leave it to another, and then, with a monstrous want of sense of the position, come forward to explain and defend and justify your own undone work in front of the unhappy person who did it. If Walkley has only the gumption to see this opening he can send you to the bottom with a single shot; and for my part I hope he will. Defend yourself and your own work and your own plays by all means; but do have the good sense to drop the pretence that Pinero & the author of Alan's Wife & the rest of them are all William Archers, and that therefore you are the proper person to answer for their notions. No matter how cleverly you do it, the fictitiousness of the whole position makes it tedious.

You could very easily provide Grein with a horrible drama for next season on purely mechanical lines, and from that you could go on to improve the quality of your horrors until you did something in the tragic line. You will have to become as a little child again and consent to make an ass of yourself publicly by making your debut as dramatic author; but surely that will be better than "My dear A.B.W." ad. lib., with the proceeds invested in Australian banks.

You will admit—as far as you are at present capable of admitting anything—that I am an extremely patient man; but the years are flying. I told you about eight years ago that you had "a good education, instead of which you went about stealing turnips." Your answer was to go and get married—checkmate for years to come. In about four years, I mentioned the subject again, only to find Tom Archer and the Australian banks in complete command of the situation. Now, after four years more, I again suggest that it is time to begin. As journalists we have had our turn; and if there is nothing higher before us—if the future, as Mrs Tank [i.e., Mrs Tanqueray] says, is only to be the past entered through another gate—why, then, the lethal chamber is the proper place for us.

GBS

402

To WILLIAM ARCHER

[B/2]

c/o Sidney Webb
The Argoed. Monmouth
30th August 1893

My address is as above for the moment. I dont know how long I shall stay—perhaps into next week, perhaps only to the end of this.

Your reasons for not doing your duty by your own dæmon are so conclusive that they would have shut up Shakspere if they had occurred to him.

I have finished the first act of my new play [*Mrs Warrens's Profession*], in which I have skilfully blended the plot of The Second Mrs Tanqueray with that of The Cenci. It will be just the thing for the I.T.

GBS

To EDWARD R. PEASE

[C/4]

The Argoed. Monmouth
31st August 1893

[Fabian Tract No. 48, *Eight Hours by Law*, drafted by Henry W. Macrosty and revised by Shaw, was issued in January 1894.]

Will you call on Wallas to make a report on the Eight Hour tract at the Executive. Webb agrees with me that it is an important document, containing at least the real working solution. Properly boomed in the press on top of the Trade Union Congress, it ought to revive the demand for 8 Hour literature sufficiently to sell itself. If there is not money enough, a par. should be put in Fabian News saying that the tract is ready, but is being held back for lack of funds.

GBS

To JANET ACHURCH

[T/1 (B/4); X/136.e]

The Argoed. Monmouth
4th September 1893

[Shaw and Janet Achurch were, at this time, writing separate dramatic treatments of the same work. In a letter published in the *Daily Chronicle* on 30th April 1898, Shaw explained: "As to 'Mrs. Warren's Profession,' it came about in this way. Miss Janet Achurch mentioned to me a novel by some

403

French writer [De Maupassant's *Yvette*] as having a dramatisable story in it. It being hopeless to get me to read anything, she told me the story, which was ultra-romantic. I said, 'Oh, I will work out the real truth about that mother some day.' In the following autumn I was the guest of a lady [Beatrice Webb] of very distinguished ability—one whose knowledge of English social types is as remarkable as her command of industrial and political questions. She suggested that I should put on the stage a real modern lady of the governing class—not the sort of thing that theatrical and critical authorities imagine such a lady to be. I did so; and the result was Miss Vivie Warren . . . Mrs. Warren herself was my version of the heroine of the romance narrated by Miss Achurch. . . . I finally persuaded Miss Achurch, who is clever with her pen, to dramatise her story herself on its original romantic lines." The Achurch version was called *Mrs. Daintree's Daughter*.]

Rejoiced to hear that you are having change of air. I am hanging on down here, the place being amazingly beautiful in all directions. The play progresses bravely; but it has left the original lines. I have made the daughter the heroine, and the mother a most deplorable old rip (saving your presence). The great scene will be the crushing of the mother by the daughter. I retain the old roué, but keep him restrained by a continual doubt as to whether the heroine may not be his daughter. The young lover's father, an outrageous clergyman, is in the same perplexity, he also being an old flame of the mother's. The lover is an agreeable young spark, wholly good-for-nothing. The girl is a quite original character. The mother, uncertain who the girl's father is, keeps all the old men at bay by telling each one that he is the parent. The second act is half finished and wholly planned. How does your version progress?

GBS

To GRAHAM WALLAS

The Argoed. Monmouth
[A/13]   8th September 1893

[The Trade Union book was Sidney and Beatrice Webb's *The History of Trade Unionism*, which Shaw extensively revised.]

Dear Wallas

I have no fear of the mutiny re the Joint Committee: they said the same thing about our withdrawal from the Unemployed affair. If there is anything said at the next Exec. about a private meeting to discuss the affair & move a vote of censure, play up for it as hard as you can. Say that it is important that we should have the sanction of the Society for our action in order to shut up the S.D.F.'s twaddle about our not representing the Fabians. We can dispense with the complete number of signatures if necessary, and offer them battle. Then, if they come on, we must go down and strew their mutilated corpses on the blast. If we shew a moment's hesitation we are done for: if we rush yelling and exulting on the enemy they will not stir again for the whole session.

The alternative before the Society will be either to acquiesce in our withdrawal, or else to be represented on the committee by five Hyndmanites. I wont serve, you wont serve, Webb wont serve, and Bland wont serve; and we can give a private meeting three such powerful speeches explaining why not, and what the consequences of leaving Hyndman without the check of our presence would be, that we could certainly sweep a decent meeting if we were commonly tactful.

We must, however, satisfy the legitimate aspirations of the ardent spirits by getting out a furious attack on the Government, rallying labor to put third candidates in the field. Get this about if you can among the irreconcileables; for they know that if we do the hitting it will be much harder than anyone else's & will so be persuaded to wait for what will happen. I am writing to Sparling about this, with a view to the Democratic Club connexion.

I am not quite sure whether I shall come up next Friday or not. I am working over the Trade Union book. It is a tough and a long job; but it is straightforward & satisfactory work, as all my excisions & rearrangements & bits of framing have so far carried convictions.

Webb has a blazing bad headache & cant write.

GBS

To EDWARD R. PEASE

[A/27]

The Argoed. Monmouth
12th September 1893

Dear Pease

Will you submit the enclosed to the Pub. Com^tee with a view to having it multiplied and sent out with all the press copies of the tract [No. 46, B.T.Hall's *Socialism and Sailors*]. Also make them pass a standing instruction that a similar letter, with suitable variations in the second sentence, be sent out with every future tract. We dont get half as much press notice as we ought.

I shall not be back until next week.

GBS

To FREDERICK WHELEN

[C/4]

29 Fitzroy Square W
27th September 1893

[Frederick Whelen (1867–1955), who became a Fabian in December 1892, was a political lecturer and writer, cousin of publisher Grant Richards. In 1898 he founded the Stage Society, and in 1908 the Afternoon Theatre. In Shaw's diary the speech is recorded as having been delivered on *15th* November to the London Reform Union in Chelsea Town Hall.]

Dear Whelen

My business as musical critic makes it impossible to pledge myself to weeknights for lectures; but if you dont mind risking an off-chance of having to find a substitute for me at the last moment (say three days or so beforehand) you may put me down for "How to make London businesslike" on the 16th November. Let me know when and where the lecture is to take place whenever it is convenient to you.

yrs
G. Bernard Shaw

To JANET ACHURCH

[X/120]

6th October 1893

[On 6th October Shaw called on the Charringtons, "amusing myself on the way by composing a rhyme to put into a copy of the Quintessence of Ibsenism which I was bringing to Janet. But they were out; so I left the book and came home" (Diary).]

To Janet Achurch from G. Bernard Shaw.

A memory that never lessens
　　Lies in this little book enshrined;
How I extracted this Quintessence
　　To keep me in your mind;
For through the void in which not one beam
　　Of sense was seen by young or old
You flashed, a light'ning, living sunbeam
　　And changed the rayless notes to gold.

406

To BEATRICE WEBB

[A/13]
29 Fitzroy Square W
6th November 1893

[H.W. Massingham had joined the Fabian Society in March 1891, but finding himself in sharp disagreement with the policies outlined in its political manifesto "To Your Tents, Oh Israel!" (drafted by Shaw, assisted by Webb, but signed "By the Fabian Society"), published in the November issue of the *Fortnightly Review*, he resigned his membership and attacked the Society in his leaders in the *Daily Chronicle*. At the Liberal and Radical Union council meeting on the evening of 6th November, Shaw recorded, "I spoke recklessly, without tact or temper, and probably did more harm than good" (Diary).]

Dear Mrs Webb

I enclose Massingham's second letter to add to your collection. I dined with him yesterday, and as he had not received my card the night before, he was so amazed at my [making an] appearance that he yelled with laughter. He is in a perfectly fluid condition and would, I believe, be much happier in our bottle than in anyone else's. I suggested that he should look us up on Saturday evening; and I think he wants to; but he expressed strong misgivings about his reception, and said he "could not face an irritated woman." As he cannot very well assume that his old invitation remains unaffected by his Chronicle sallies, I suggest that you write him a reassuringly goodhumored note to the effect that you hope that his feelings as expressed in print will not cut him off from our Saturdays.

I am half afraid that the reaction against the Manifesto may score at the L & R.U. tonight. However, we shall see.

GBS

To GEORGINA SHAW

[A/29]
29 Fitzroy Square W
13th November 1893

[Aunt Georgina (d. 1911), the widow of R. Frederick Shaw, now resided in London. She had written to her nephew to request that he obtain some publicity in "his" paper for one of her friends, who had invented a wire mattress.]

I like that expression of yours—*my* paper. *My* paper, indeed! I am further than ever from having any paper or any press influence. My only interest in wire mattresses at present is in the idea that they might be convenient things to lie down and die on out of sheer weariness.

I wish I had been able to have a chat and post you up in my affairs at the Arts & Crafts [Exhibition]; but I was in a fearful situation— beset on all sides & insensible to every consideration but that of speedy escape.

GBS

To GRANT RICHARDS

[X/121]

29 Fitzroy Square W
13th November 1893

[Grant Richards (1872–1948), at this time secretary and assistant editor to W.T.Stead on the *Review of Reviews*, founded his own publishing firm in 1897. He published Shaw's *Plays Pleasant and Unpleasant* (1898) and several other early works.]

Dear Sir

As usual, the Stereoscopic people have taken a decent photograph and then deliberately ruined it by rubbing every line and mark out of the face, which looks like a piece of dirty drawing paper. Please, in the interests of reasonable art and common sense, do not have it repro- duced. There are three alternatives. 1. Don't portray me at all, which I should prefer to any encouragement of this abominable retouching business, which I have always denounced as an art critic. 2. Use the excellent wood cut you published in the R. of R. last January (I think) and which was done for the Ill. London News. 3. Reproduce the en- closed untouched photo, which you can see at least represents a human face with the traces of a human life on it instead of the slab of wet dough which the Stereoscopic people have felt bound to produce. It has never been reproduced before and even a half successful print of it would be better than an entirely successful print of the other.

yours very truly
G.Bernard Shaw

To JANET ACHURCH

[T/1 (A/4)]

29 Fitzroy Square W
2nd December 1893

[The lecture to the Pioneer Reform Association on the 3rd was "How We Become Atheists." The lecture to the Eleusis Club, Chelsea, on 17th

December was "The Political Situation" ("It was a bad one," Shaw recorded, "much too long, the invariable result of not being fresh"). After writing this letter on the 2nd, Shaw visited the Charringtons after all, at which time "Janet read me as much as she has written of her play—the original Mrs Warren—which she has recommenced and is going to finish in collaboration with Lady Colin [Campbell]. Charrington read part of the second act of his play [see headnote to letter of 16th March 1896 to Charrington], and I read the existing fragment of mine [*Arms and the Man*]— an urge of play reading over which we all made merry" (Diary).]

I enclose a notification of a lecture which I have to deliver tomorrow in your neighborhood. It will take place in a phrenologist's shop & will be as poky, ridiculous & dismal as anyone could desire; but there will be no Socialism in it, no statistics about gas & water, & possibly there may be a funny discussion. Mind: I don't invite you to come, or advise you to come, or accept any responsibility whatever for your coming. I wouldn't come myself if I could be dispensed with. But since you so ardently desire to hear me, I keep my promise to inform you of a chance of doing so without travelling across London. On the 17th, however, I shall be at the Eleusis Club in Kings Road, in my regular legitimate tub thumping political capacity, so that if the fire is particularly comfortable tomorrow evening you have an excellent excuse for not leaving it.

I have made a desperate attempt to begin a real romantic play for F. F. in the style of Victor Hugo. The first act is nearly finished; and it is quite the funniest attempt at that style of composition ever made. I am told that I have unconsciously reproduced the bedroom scene from [Victor Hugo's] *Marion de L'Orme*, which I never read.

GBS

To EDWARD R. PEASE

29 Fitzroy Square W

[A/27]   4th December 1893

[It was the policy of the Fabian Society to issue proofs of tracts to its members for criticism; this allowed for the resolution of differences of opinion at private members' meetings before publication. Shaw had been for several years chairman of the Publishing Committee.]

Dear Pease

I have done the 8 Hour tract [editing] myself. I found that all the important alterations had been arrived at independently by Macrosty,

Webb & myself; so I have had no trouble in accepting them. I have carefully collated [R. F. E.] Willis, Miss [Mary L.] Cameron & [T. M.] Watt as well; so that you can assure them that nothing has been disregarded or overlooked.

I have not time to make a copy of the revised proof to keep. It would be a frightful thing if it went astray; so I think you had better have a copy made before you post it to Standring, in view of the recent losses of letters. Tell Standring to send back the corrected proof with the revise & let me see both of them.

I am writing to Webb about it.

GBS

P.S. I return the collated proofs in a separate cover.

To GRANT RICHARDS

[29 Fitzroy Square W]
[X/121]   8th December [1893]
Dear Sir

I am very sorry to have given you unnecessary trouble; but I thought you wanted the photographs for "process": I had no idea that you were going to have them cut. The one I sent you is an abominably difficult one to copy with the graver; and accordingly it has beaten your engraver rather badly. The Stereoscopic full face one, on the contrary, is easy; and the objection against the photograph—the hideously false texture of the flesh—does not apply to the engraving. So by all means use A, which I return. It is a sufficiently good likeness, and, what is more to the purpose, not a bad engraving, in spite of a certain amount of rather cheap white line work in the cheeks, effective enough, but not calculated to delight experts as much as black lines cut by Albert Durer. My objection to the Stereoscopic work had no reference at all to the ferocity of the expression; if they had produced a really good picture of either a tiger or a lamb, you should have been more than welcome to put my name underneath it as an excuse for publishing it. I protested against it solely because it was a botched, stippled, falsified, vulgarized abomination as a work of art. Your engraver, being an artist, has undone the mischief done by the Regent Street tradesman, and I hope you will not waste his work by hesitating to publish A. I am extremely obliged to you for the trouble and cost you have been at to meet

410

my views on the subject. Believe me, I should never have dreamt of raising any difficulty over the mere matter of my personal appearance.

yours very truly
G. Bernard Shaw

To LOUISE S. LIEBICH

[X/122]

[29 Fitzroy Square W]
8th December 1893

[Mrs Franz Liebich, Debussy's friend and biographer, and her husband had given a Chopin "lecture-recital" at St James's Hall, which Shaw had made the subject of his article in *The World* on 6th December: "I must apologize to Mrs Liebich for making her lecture the text of so ponderous a discourse on lecturing, for her discourse was far more entertaining than the ordinary private concert; but if the musical lecture is going to become an institution, it is my business to pounce on its weak points, with a view to its improvement, and, finally, to such perfection as it is capable of."]

Dear Mrs Liebich

I am much obliged to you for your kind letter, and for the very good-humoured way in which you have taken the part of my article which exacted from you that terrible condition of being allowed to figure in a whole column of a journal which lives by its circulation, the condition, namely, that you must amuse the public a little. The net result, when I do that with an artist, is: the artist remembers me in connection with a very disagreeable sensation and hates me for ever after; whilst the public remembers the artist in connection with an agreeable sensation (forgetting the particulars) which is the essence of popularity.

I hope to have the pleasure of meeting you and Mr Liebich some day; but Sunday would be the busiest day in the week for me (my World article being generally left to the last moment, Sunday's last post) if the other days were not generally twice as busy. The fact is, I have to be at so many places that I never can go anywhere. Musical criticism, though it takes all my time, is quite a minor activity of mine. I have my article to write, four picture exhibitions to criticise, a political conference to attend, and a lecture to deliver before Sunday night. Do you wonder that I cannot avail myself of your kind invitation?

[yours sincerely
G. Bernard Shaw]

To J. T. GREIN

29 Fitzroy Square W
12th December 1893

[X/123]

[The Independent Theatre did not produce *Mrs Warren's Profession*, Grein having considered the work too provocative even for a private showing. The play was first presented by the Stage Society at the New Lyric Club on 5th June 1902, with Fanny Brough as Mrs Warren, Madge McIntosh as Vivie, and Granville Barker as Frank.

Rutland Barrington (1853–1922) was for many years a member of the D'Oyly Carte Company. Alexes Leighton (d. 1926) was a supporting actress who had appeared in Pinero's *The Times* in 1891. Mrs Bernard Beere (1856–1915), a popular London actress-manager, had recently appeared in Oscar Wilde's *A Woman of No Importance*.]

Dear Grein

You ask me for particulars about the play. Well, its title is "Mrs Warren's Profession." It is in four acts, with six characters, none of them being minor parts. The heroine, Vivie Warren, will be played by Janet Achurch; the hero, Frank Gardner, by Bernard Gould; the villain, Sir George Crofts, by Charrington; and the other three as Heaven may direct. The most important of the three, and in fact the leading part in the play, is Mrs Warren, Vivie's mother, old enough to have a daughter of twenty-three or thereabouts, a woman of bad character, proprietress of two *maisons tolérées* in Brussels, and of similar establishments in other continental cities. She must be an actress of considerable power, and of some humour. Then there is an amiable old bachelor, Praed, who could be played by anybody who can play Cayley in "The Second Mrs Tanqueray." Also a stout, pompous clergyman, father of the hero, with a fairly good comic part. Rutland Barrington is the sort of man for it.

The great difficulty is Mrs Warren. Archer suggests Miss Alexis Leighton, whom I have not seen, or at least do not recollect. Some one else suggests Mrs Bernard Beere. I should be content, myself, with Mrs Patrick Campbell. The part is a vulgar one; but unless the vulgarity is the artistic vulgarity of a refined actress, just as the immorality must be the artistic immorality of a woman whom the audience respects, the part will be unendurable. She has only a few easy and effective scraps of comedy in the first and third acts—nothing that need cost an hour's work to get up. In the second act she has a very powerful scene, and another in the fourth, both curtains being shared by her with the heroine, who is the feeder on both occasions. There is a reputation to be got out of the part.

412

I wish we could fatten up Welch for the parson; but as it stands the part would be of no use to him.

I do not think there is the least chance of the play being licensed. How will this affect our chances of getting a theatre? The stage of the Opera Comique would hardly be deep enough for the scene in the second act, I'm afraid.

yours sincerely
G. Bernard Shaw

PART IV

1894-1897

IV
(1894–1897)

Shaw had long been convinced that he could not create dramas that should delight the public because he "had no taste for what is called popular art, no respect for popular morality, no belief in popular religion, no admiration for popular heroics"; and until he was thirty-five his journalistic successes provided sufficient income to obviate the necessity to experiment with iconoclastic drama.

Then criticism began to pall. "In my weekly columns, which I once filled full from a magic well that never ran dry or lost its sparkle provided I pumped hard enough," Shaw noted in the preface to *Plays Unpleasant* (1898), "I began to repeat myself; to fall into a style which, to my great peril, was recognized as at least partly serious; to find the pump tiring me and the water lower in the well." A younger generation was knocking at the door, and the ageing critic listened to these vigorous raps "with penurious alarm." It was time for a bold decision. He had made, he recalled, a rough memorandum for his own guidance "that unless I could produce at least half a dozen plays before I was forty, I had better let playwriting alone." By 26th July 1896 the quota had been met—with one play and a fraction of a second to spare.

Meanwhile, the sudden death in 1894 of the editor Edmund Yates had impelled Shaw to resign from the staff of *The World*; seven years of musical criticism for London papers without respite had proven a severe strain on his attention ("especially after the first half hour of our absurdly long concerts," he commented in his diary), and it was gratifying to be the recipient at this moment of a few hundred pounds, royalties from the British and American productions of *Arms and the Man*, which released the fledgling dramatist from immediate financial dependence on journalism. In less than a year, however, Shaw succumbed to a tempting offer by Frank Harris to serve as dramatic critic for the *Saturday Review*. He seemed, in fact, to be constitutionally incapable of slowing his pace.

His social entanglements also accelerated, growing increasingly complex. He was in the midst of an affair with Florence Farr. He was struggling frantically with Janet Achurch in a vain effort to rescue her from drug addiction. And his friends, convinced that what he needed to set him right was a wife, secretly conspired to pair him off with an artist, Bertha Newcombe, who was all too eager to endorse their scheme.

417

Then, in January 1896, while visiting Beatrice and Sidney Webb, Shaw was introduced to Charlotte Payne-Townshend, the "green-eyed Irish millionairess," and for the next two years wooed her in puckish fashion, while deliberately creating the impression that she was the predator and he the unwilling, luckless victim.

Was ever woman in such fashion wooed?—by a vegetarian who dined, ever on the run, on apples, nuts, macaroni, brown bread, and cocoa; who penned articles in suburban train carriages while travelling to and from Socialist lecture engagements or theatrical performances (occasionally losing his manuscripts under the wheels as he emerged at his station), or who scribbled plays in shorthand in pocket notebooks at odd moments, leaning against the Embankment, standing beneath a fog-shrouded gas lamp at a street corner at midnight, sprawled beside his bicycle in a country meadow surrounded by cud-chewing bovines, or seated nonchalantly on a park bench under an umbrella in pouring rain.

Back and forth he darted each afternoon and evening, from the Fabian office in the Strand to Miss Payne-Townshend's flat in Adelphi Terrace and on to the British Museum reading room, conferring there with Yeats, Butler, Gissing, Archer, Bertrand Russell, and Marie Corelli, or poring over government "blue books" and researching on local drainage or on public lavatories in his capacity as a newly elected Vestryman of the Parish of St Pancras. Then back to Miss Payne-Townshend's, and off again to the theatre or a meeting, returning finally, after a brisk night walk which took him past Miss Payne-Townshend's now-darkened bedroom window, to his study in Fitzroy Square. There he worked until the small hours of the morning under the flickering light of a colza reading lamp, while his eyes smarted and teared, until the pain drove him to resort to an eyeshade or sunglasses for the reading of his *Plays Pleasant and Unpleasant* in galley proof, and to the use of green-tinted, non-glare paper for his manuscripts and correspondence. And when he had difficulty waking in the morning (even the alarm couldn't rouse him), he impatiently accused himself of laziness!

Shaw's health in these years was in a constantly precarious state, for he drove himself as if demons were pricking at him. By the end of 1897 he had come dangerously close to physical destruction, and the effects were shortly to make themselves known. He was also, though he may not yet have realised it, at the threshold of an important new phase of his life. In a few brief months he would retire from professional criticism—and from forty-two years of bachelorhood.

To EDWARD R. PEASE

The Argoed. Monmouth
[B/27]   8th January 1894

["To Your Tents, Oh Israel!" was expanded by Shaw for publication in January 1894 as Fabian Tract No. 49, *A Plan of Campaign for Labor*. Its "practical proposals for labor representation" made it one of the most controversial documents ever published by the Society.]

Dear Pease

I hope to get back to town on Wednesday in time for the Publishing Committee. The Manifesto is all right: the additions (Newcastle Program, Massingham, Davitt &c) were expressly ordered by the meeting. The "tons of revolutionary principles" came out because on examination it made bad sense with the preceding matter, the only relevant part of which had to be shifted to another page. Tell all & sundry that they need not bother about the changes: they are all unanswerably necessary, improving, and quite consonant with instructions. After spending 4 whole days drudgery on it I am the only person who has any authoritative knowledge of the subject.

GBS

To FREDERICK WHELEN

29 Fitzroy Square W
[B/4]   29th January 1894

[Whelen had invited Shaw to stand as a parliamentary candidate in Chelsea, backed by the Fabian South Western Group.]

My dear Whelen

Gramercy for the offer; but we mustnt waste our resources on forlorn hopes. I cannot see that there is any chance of winning Chelsea, or of holding it if it were won by a fluke. If there were, I should suggest your boldly adventuring yourself, as you are a resident and can make a local reputation much better than I could.

Perhaps I shall see you on Thursday at Mrs Sandham's, though I am not sure that I shall be able to come.

GBS

To JOHN BURNS

[C/2]

29 Fitzroy Square W
22nd February 1894

If you can spare the time to look in at Webb's tomorrow evening, it will be a charitable deed to come. We want to shew you the sort of calculation on which we ventured the Fabian Manifesto & to get your opinion generally as to whether anything can be done with the Parliamentary Com^{tee} [of the Trades Union Congress]. Something that Broadhurst said makes me rather anxious about the situation. Make Massingham come, anyhow, alive or dead, if you cant come yourself.

G. Bernard Shaw

To HENRY ARTHUR JONES

[S/2]

c/o H. S. Salt. Oxted. Surrey
20th March 1894

[Henry Arthur Jones (1851–1929) was, in 1894, second only to Pinero as a leading London dramatist. Shaw met him at Archer's home on 4th May 1885, and for many years they were close friends, Jones having, according to his daughter, "a deep and strong attachment" for Shaw. At the outbreak of World War I, however, Shaw's attitude toward the war and his defence of Ireland against England outraged Jones, who attacked Shaw violently, to the extent of instigating his banishment from the Dramatists' Club. Shaw made a generous effort, in Jones's last years, to renew the friendship, but Jones, though deeply touched, could not bring himself to accept a reconciliation.

Florence Farr had leased the Avenue Theatre for a season, financed anonymously by Miss Annie E. F. Horniman (1860–1937), a wealthy young theatre patron, who subsequently built and equipped the Abbey Theatre, Dublin, and founded the famous repertory company at the Gaiety Theatre, Manchester. Although Florence Farr had negotiated with Shaw for *Arms and the Man* (originally called *Alps and Balkans*), he did not consider the play ready for production, and she opened her season on 29th March with a double bill consisting of John Todhunter's *A Comedy of Sighs* and W. B. Yeats's *The Land of Heart's Desire*. The critical reaction on the 30th, however, was so unfavourable that Shaw, that evening, found a telegram summoning him to the theatre immediately. "Went down and found F. E. and Helmsley (the acting manager) with 'Widowers' Houses' open before them, contemplating its production in despair. I dissuaded them from that and after some discussion took my new play out on to the Embankment Gardens and there and then put the last touches to it before leaving it to be typewritten" (Diary). By 11th April *Arms and the Man* was in rehearsal.

420

Alma Murray

Sir Henry Irving

Henry Arthur Jones

Elizabeth Robins

Jones's familiarity with the Avenue stemmed from the fact that three of his plays—*The Crusaders* (1891), *The Middleman* (1891), and *Judah* (1892)—had been produced there. "I'm very glad you are writing for the stage," he replied on 21st March, "it is such a splendid safeguard of one's sanity." As for financial advice, "The Rule," he noted, "is to get as much as you can, though I fear it somewhat smacks of conventionality—I mean the rule, not your play"(Texas).]

Dear Jones

As there is no Trade Union of dramatic authors, and I am going into the business, I can only avoid blacklegging by asking you what are the list prices, so to speak, for the work. The management at the Avenue makes me a proposal as follows. 5% on gross receipts for 50 nights, 6% thereafter; £25 down certain, to be repaid out of percentage if the play runs; and the management to retain the "British rights" for a term of years. To this I reply that I will dispose of nothing but the London rights for the run, reserving provincial rights and everything else, but foregoing the advance of £25 and offering to forego all fees whatsoever if the play fails. Under these circumstances what percentage ought I to demand in the event of a success? I do not want to run down prices by asking too little, or, on the other hand, to be unreasonable. Archer says 6 or 7 per cent. is about the mark. What do you say? Two lines on a postcard will suffice.

As far as I can ascertain, the Avenue holds, when full, £200 (you know all about it) and the expenses will be about £100 a night.

I am loth to put you to the agony of writing even a postcard, since I presume you share my hatred of correspondence. But the cause of Trade Unionism is sacred.

yrs sincerely
G. Bernard Shaw

To GRAHAM WALLAS

[C/13]

c/o H.S.Salt. Oxted
24th March 1894

[Constance Clara Black (1862–1946), who married the writer Edward Garnett (1868–1937), was the translator of many Russian novels by Turgenev, Tolstoi, and Chekhov. Shaw had known the Black sisters (Grace, Clementina, and Constance) ever since the early 1880's; Grace had been in love with him, and Constance's son David Garnett (b. 1892) has claimed (in *The Golden Echo*, 1954) that Shaw once told him he would have proposed to

Constance if he could have afforded marriage. Mrs Garnett was elected to the Fabian Executive in May 1894.]

Mrs Garnett has done nothing for the Fabian; and there is not the smallest reason to suppose that she has any other object in Executiving than to be in the fashion. However, I have no objection whatever to her coming on; she and I were acquainted formerly. But I wont manifest in her favor or in anyone else's without much further consideration. There is, I hear, some question of getting our names to use as supporters &c. If I am not to do that for Galton &c, I shall certainly not do it for Constance. What is your view?

GBS

To ALMA MURRAY

[B/1; X/109]

29 Fitzroy Square W
30th March 1894

Dear Miss Alma Murray

The fiasco last night at the Avenue has made it necessary to produce a play of mine with all possible speed, as the only way of rescuing the enterprise. There are two young women's parts in it, one that of the heroine and the other that of her servant, who is, however, a sufficiently important person (she has two important scenes) to make it possible for a leading lady to play her without any sacrifice of dignity. I want Miss Farr to play, *not* the heroine, but the servant. If I can persuade her to do this, and to crown her magnanimity by allowing you to play the heroine, will you consent to be approached on the subject, or have you any decisive objection or prior engagement that puts you out of the question? The lady does not swear, nor does she throttle the servant like the heroine in my other play. She has to make herself a little ridiculous (unconsciously) once or twice; but for the most part she has to be romantically beautiful or else amusing in a bearably dignified way. She is a Bulgarian, and can, I suppose, wear extraordinary things if she wishes.

You will understand that I may fail to induce Miss Farr to face the risk of being complimented on her wisdom in giving up her lead to you. Your terms may be too high—a dozen things may baffle me in my design. But if I succeed, will there be any objection on your side?

yrs sincerely
G. Bernard Shaw

422

To ALMA MURRAY

[B/1; X/109]

29 Fitzroy Square W
16th April 1894

Dear Miss Alma Murray

The Wagner concert tomorrow will prevent my attending the rehearsal; so I had better let you have a couple of points that struck me this evening. When you interrupt the challenge scene, Bluntschli tells you not to be alarmed—he wont hurt Sergius—he has acted as sword instructor &c &c. The phrase that stabs you in the speech is "In the morning I shall be off home & never see you again." That is what makes you forget all about the duel & shew your feelings in the next speech— "I never said &c." The point seemed to me to want marking. By the bye, will you point out that "In the morning" should be "In an hour," as he has already received the telegram. In the pocket-picking scene, the line "Ah, how can you say that to me, father?" ought to be in the most pathetic edition of the noble attitude & thrilling voice, leading up to the Judas kiss.

A little more malice is wanted in the "Were they angry with you for running away from Sergius's charge" & so on; and in the second act, "The little beast" should come at the end of a sort of reverie or blue study during which you pay not the least attention to the mother's scolding.

How capitally the scene in the third act with Bluntschli went this morning!

yrs sincerely
G. Bernard Shaw

To JOHN LANE

[C/7]

29 Fitzroy Square W
16th April 1894

Dear Lane

Has your experience of Lady Windermere's Fan &c. led you to suppose that publishing plays is worth while? Is there anything to be done with this play of mine which is to be produced on Saturday evening by Miss Farr?

In spite of your better feelings you will probably be glad to hear that I have had to pay [the penalty of having the work sell poorly] for allowing Grein to publish the other play [*Widowers' Houses*] as well as to produce it. His firm never advertised it even once; and the sale, which was only effected by great perseverance & determination on the part of the purchasers, was 150 copies! Ah! had I but listened to thee!

yrs sincerely
G. Bernard Shaw

To C. T. H. HELMSLEY

[A/4]

29 Fitzroy Square W
17 April 1894

[Charles T. Hunt Helmsley (1866–1940), manager of the Avenue Theatre, later was general manager for Sir George Alexander at the St James's Theatre. *Arms and the Man* opened at the Avenue on 21st April. The "Bulgarian admiral" was a Russian, Esper Aleksandrovich Serebryekov, who, upon learning he was suspected of Nihilist sympathies, jumped ship and escaped to England. Sir Henry Norman (1858-1939), who became a Baronet in 1915, was a member of the editorial staff of the *Daily Chronicle* in 1895. He retired from journalism in 1899.]

Dear Helmsley

Among the people who are to add lustre [to] the first night are Stepniak & the Bulgarian admiral who gave me the local color. They will go together; so will you send either a box or three good seats to Sergius Stepniak, 31 Blandford Road, Bedford Park W. Also 2 to C. Charrington, 9 Overstrand Mansions, Battersea Park S.W., taking care to put Mrs Charrington somewhere where her beauty will not be lost. Sidney Webb, 41 Grosvenor Road, Westminster Embankment S.W, might possibly bring a cabinet minister if he has a box; but anyhow let him have two good places. Olivier should be looked after; also Graham Wallas (one seat) 32 Gt Ormond St. Queens Square. W.C. I presume Oscar Wilde & George Moore will be looked after; and I particularly want provision to be made for Henry Arthur Jones (at full length) and Mrs Jones, Townshend House, North Gates, Regent's Park N.W.

As to the press, I want Archer to have two seats. Also Henry Norman, 27 Grosvenor Road S.W, and H.W. Massingham, Pleasant View, Nightingale Lane S.W, and Ernest Parke, The Star, Stonecutter St E.C., all three powerful journalistic allies of mine. A couple of places ought to be sent to T.P. O'Connor M.P. either to the Ho. of Commons

424

or to the Sun Office—unless you have his private address, which I have lost. Walkley might have a second seat if there is one to spare: his wife would probably like to come. A seat for Jules Magny, 4 New Cross Road S.E, is important. He represents the Foreign Press Association & spreads my reputation assiduously throughout the continent. Joseph Pennell, 14 Buckingham St, Strand W.C. should have two seats.

If there are *three* decent seats left after all this, they might be sent to Hubert Bland, 2 Birch Grove, Lee S.E.: Mrs Bland will be worth a thousand posters in Blackheath, & they are both active journalists.

This is all I can think of at present. I shall mention three or four hundred more presently.

In haste, yrs ever
G. Bernard Shaw

To GEORGINA SHAW

[A/29]

29 Fitzroy Square W
22nd April 1894

[Unfortunately, Shaw had forgotten to provide tickets to *Arms and the Man* for his London relations (a not infrequent occurrence throughout his life), and Aunt Georgina apparently had taken him to task for this.]

My dear Georgina

Why didnt you ask me? I forgot everybody except the people who reminded me vigorously of their demands. If you only knew what rehearsing and producing a play is when it comes in addition to un-interrupted ordinary work, you would never dream of trusting to an author's memory or to his feelings. I was not at the theatre yesterday until 8.30; so I did not get your letter until it was too late to repair the omission, which, believe me, I greatly regret.

I enclose the only card I have for the affair this evening.

yrs sincerely
G. Bernard Shaw

To WILLIAM ARCHER

[A/2]

29 Fitzroy Square W
23rd April 1894

[This letter was written after midnight the night of the 22nd–23rd. Shaw had not yet seen Archer's review of *Arms and the Man*, but it is obvious that Archer had communicated to him much of the substance of the review, in which he had likened the *chassés croisés* of Shaw's play to Gilbertian

425

426

extravaganza, and had stated that in the second act "we find ourselves in Mr. Gilbert's Palace of Truth." The play, he reported, was "a fantastic, psychological extravaganza, in which drama, farce, and Gilbertian irony keep flashing past the bewildered eye. . . ." Sir William Schwenck Gilbert (1836–1911) had written *The Palace of Truth*, a cynical "fairy" extravaganza, in 1870, prior to his famous collaboration with Sir Arthur Sullivan.]

I must really clear that Gilbert notion out of your head before you disgrace yourself over Arms & The Man. You have a perfect rag shop of old ideas in your head which prevent your getting a step ahead.

Gilbert is simply a paradoxically humorous cynic. He accepts the conventional ideals implicitly, but observes that people do not really live up to them. This he regards as a failure on their part at which he mocks bitterly. This position is precisely that of Sergius in the play, who, when disilluded, declares that life is a farce. It is a perfectly barren position: nothing comes of it but cynicism, pessimism, & irony.

I do not accept the conventional ideals. To them I oppose in the play the practical life & morals of the efficient, realistic man, unaffectedly ready to face what risks must be faced, considerate but not chivalrous, patient and practical; and I not only represent the woman as instinctively falling in love with all this even whilst all her notions of fine-mannishness are being outraged; but I dot the i's by making him say in audible words—"You mean, dont you, that I am the first man that has ever taken you *quite* seriously &c"—"Now that you've found out that life isnt a farce, but something quite sensible & serious &c" and so on. You will not find a trace of this in Gilbert, and only some broken glimpses of it in Ibsen, who is by old habit a pessimist. My whole secret is that I have got clean through the old categories of good & evil, and no longer use them even for dramatic effect. Sergius is ridiculous through the breakdown of his ideals, not odious from his falling short of them. As Gilbert sees, they dont work; but what Gilbert does not see is that there is something else that does work, and that in that something else there is a completely satisfactory asylum for the affections. It is this positive element in my philosophy that makes Arms & The Man a perfectly genuine play about real people, with a happy ending and hope & life in it, instead of a thing like [Gilbert's] "Engaged" which is nothing but a sneer at people for not being what Sergius & Raina play at being before they find one another out. Every touch in Engaged is false: not one speech or action in it is possible. In the first act of Arms & The Man there is not one speech of Bluntschli's that is not faithful in fact & spirit to the realities of soldiering. All the effect is got out of facts stated in the simplest terms. The chocolate, the effect of a third day under fire, the dirt, the sleepiness, the cavalry charge are pro-saically accurate. The effect is produced by an adroit contrast of their reality with the unreality of the woman's notions. If you could only rid yourself of the intense unreality of your own preconceptions, and of your obsession by the ideals which you grow pessimistic over, you would not find that an effect due to the ridiculous obviousness and common sense of realism breaking through the mist & glamor of idealism, was a mere mechanical topsyturvyism.

But my chief object in writing this letter is to call your attention to the fact that last night, whether it leads to a commercial success or not, totally shatters your theory that I cannot write for the stage. Your notice of Widowers' Houses was one of the stupidest things you ever perpetrated, except perhaps your notice of Arms & The Man, which will no doubt explain matters virtually on the old ground that I am a supernatural being. Now the theory of *my* dramatic incompetence was part of a general theory involving *your* dramatic incompetence too. If you write a play, which you can do if you will sit down sincerely to amuse yourself, it will get produced as easily as Arms & The Man. And I still think that you ought to try. You dont intend to spend the rest of your life reviewing for the P.M.G., do you?

GBS

To WILLIAM ARCHER

[B/2]

29 Fitzroy Square W
23rd April 1894

[Shaw had now received an advance proof of Archer's review, which was published in *The World* on 25th April, and in which Archer had written: "Mr. Shaw is by nature and habit one of those philosophers who concentrate their attention upon the seamy side of the human mind. . . . To look at nothing but the seamy side may be to see life steadily, but is not to see it whole. As an artist, Mr. Shaw suffers from this limitation. . . . He not only dwells on the seamy side to the exclusion of all else, but he makes his characters turn their moral garments inside out and go about with the linings displayed, flaunting the seams and raw edges and stiffenings and paddings." Of Raïna, Archer commented: "Here [in the second act] we have a girl who, in the course of some six hours, transfers her affections (save the mark!) from a man whom she thought she had adored for years, to one whom she has only once before set eyes on." He referred to Raïna as having a "bloodless frame," and accused Shaw of a "peculiar habit of straining all the red corpuscles out of the blood of his personages."

428

Elizabeth Thompson (1844–1933) was a Swiss-born English painter of military and battle scenes.]

Come, what did I tell you? Your first column, in which you describe things sanely and objectively, is capital. Then you strike on "the seamy side," the good old seamy side, and immediately the whole notice goes to pieces. It might have been written—from that point on—by a Bulgarian idealist. Do you think war is any the less terrible & heroic in its reality—on *its* seamy side, as you would say—than it is in the visions of Raina & of the critics who know it from engravings of Elizabeth Thompson's pictures in the Regent St shop windows? And so on as regards the whole material of the play.

Your "transfer of Raina's affections" is a masterpiece of obtuseness. I offer to submit the point to your wife as arbitrator. The reference is to be "Did Raina love Sergius & then *transfer* that love to Bluntschli; or did she, after imaginatively living up to an ideal relation with Sergius, and conceiving a sub-conscious dislike for him under the strain, fall in love for the first time with Bluntschli?" Mrs Archer will tell you straight off that the latter is the true solution, and that it is written large on the play, staring your amblyopia out of countenance. (I am convinced, by the way, that Mrs Archer used to be just like Raina). Poor Sergius, struggling with your idiotic view of the seamy side, and heroically marrying Louka because he *will* not be a coward and a trifler (as per that idiotic view) is patent even to a man's understanding, if the man's eyes are open. You ought to be ashamed of yourself for applying such a word as "bloodless" to a man who is bleeding from fifty wounds to his spirit—a perfect Banquo's ghost.

GBS

To HENRY ARTHUR JONES

S/2; X/124]

29 Fitzroy Square W
24th April 1894

[Charles Overton (1858–98), Australian-born actor, was London representative for the American theatre manager Albert Marshman Palmer (1838–1905), who, at this time, was manager of Wallack's Theatre, New York. Shaw's "No use in wishing you success" refers to the forthcoming production of Jones's *The Masqueraders* at the St James's Theatre on 28th April.]

My dear Jones
I got your telegram with great pleasure on the first night of Arms and The Man. With signal ingratitude I am now going to give you some

further trouble at a moment when my own recent experience teaches me that no man of the feeblest altruism would take up a moment of your time.

The trouble is, American rights. Overton wants to buy them for Palmer. His offer is £100 down; play to be produced within a year; Palmer to have U.S. and Canadian rights for five years; my royalties to be 5% on $4000 a week, 10% on the next $2000, and 15% on anything over. He is evidently very keen on the bargain and pressed the £100 cheque repeatedly on me today. But I declined and said I would draft the agreement for him myself.

Now I have no doubt that I could get £150 down if I stood out for it; but about that I do not care, as I can perfectly well afford to wait. What staggers me is the application of the sliding scale. At the Avenue I get 5% when the receipts do not exceed £100 a night (a rather common circumstance so far), $7\frac{1}{2}$ when they do not exceed £150, and 10% after that. This is quite a different thing from 5% on £100 of the receipts, $7\frac{1}{2}$% on the excess up to £150 and 10 on the balance, which is the system proposed by Overton for his 5, 10, and 15. I should prefer 10% all round. At the Avenue, too, I have only given a license for the bare run of the theatre and nothing more, whereas Palmer ties me up for 5 years. Overton, however, assures me that these are the usual terms; and I have allowed him to assume that I will close with him on that understanding.

Can I do better? Am I being had? I have to ask you because you are the only person I know whose business faculty inspires me with the smallest confidence. To enable you to answer with Yes, No, or a figure, I enclose a sheet of questions, as if you were a parliamentary candidate. It will save time. No use in wishing you success when asking you a favor. Besides, *you're* safe.

yrs sincerely
G. Bernard Shaw

To JANET ACHURCH

29 Fitzroy Square W
25th April 1894

[T/1 (B/4)]

Janet Achurch had replaced Marion Terry in Sutton Vane's *The Cotton King* at the Adelphi.]

Put my letter in the fire: I have now recovered my touch with you

430

and see plainly that you meant nothing of the sort. I dont know why I wrote it—probably I instinctively felt that there was an opening for a good stage effect. But I am sometimes very suggestive in my stagey moments; and I hope I did it well. I wish you had a good vegetarian cook, or that I could get Mrs Besant to make a Theosophist of you. She once went in for high feeding & stimulants, on medical testimony that it was "necessary" for her; but the Brahminical regimen has been a complete success with her.

I can tell you all the rest when next we meet.

GBS

To CHARLES OVERTON

[A/1]

29 Fitzroy Square W
25th April 1894

Dear Mr Overton

I have been applying my mind in earnest to the question of American rights for the last day and a half; and I think I can get better terms out of Palmer on one or two points.

First, the sliding scale, which I at first took to be a series of percentages on gross receipts and not on successive increments, is not good enough. It ought to be 5% on $3000, 10% on the next thousand, and 15% on all above. But I should prefer a level 10% all round.

Second, I think it would be better, instead of agreeing for five years, to make an agreement from year to year, the renewal being conditional on the piece being played not less than 100 times in the year. My object in this is to get the play back into my own hands the moment Palmer has had enough of it. I have suffered much from publishers locking up my literary capital during the last two or three years of an agreement.

Third, it should be a condition that my name as author should be attached to all announcements, and that the play be performed according to my text, without interpolations or alterations.

On the other hand, we may as well drop the question of the advance. The £100 down is really no inducement to me; and yet I could not very well refuse, if I took it, to make some concession on the sliding scale. I do not want to touch a farthing that has not been paid down by the public at the doors. In my case to deal in advances would be to throw away all the advantage I hold from being independent of dramatic authorship as far as my livelihood is concerned.

431

As to my suggestion about selling outright, we may drop that also. On reflection it is clear to me that Palmer could not, as a good business man, make me an offer that would tempt me.

I have discussed terms with you so far on the understanding that we should close at whatever was the usual thing, I being then quite in the dark on the subject. I have now done my best to inform myself by consulting those of my friends who are dramatic authors or experts in the matter; and though it is clear from what they said that you have done your best to make a good bargain for both parties at once, I prefer to take all my advantage from a good percentage instead of from advance + percentage.

Let me know how this strikes you. I can then draft the agreement, unless we cry off.

yours faithfully
G. Bernard Shaw

To CHARLES OVERTON

29 Fitzroy Square W
28th April 1894

A/6]

Dear Mr Overton

Dont be angry: that's only my way of doing business. Tell Palmer I've cried off. What do you say to my terms?

yrs faithfully
G. Bernard Shaw

To R. GOLDING BRIGHT

29 Fitzroy Square W
30th April 1894

[A/1; X/125]

[Reginald Golding Bright (1874–1941), at this time an office clerk aspiring to be a journalist, subsequently became manager of the London office of the American play-agent Elisabeth Marbury, and the husband of Mary Chavelita Dunne ("George Egerton"). Shaw had participated in a debate on "Criticism, Corruption and the Remedy" at the Playgoers' Club on 22nd April; Golding Bright presumably was in the audience. He was also present in the gallery of the Avenue on the opening night of *Arms and the Man*, where,

432

some time during the performance, he was moved to express his dissatisfaction with a remark in the play by hissing. When Shaw appeared for a curtain call after the performance, Golding Bright uttered a loud "Boo!"—which inspired Shaw to utter the now-famous response, "My dear fellow, I quite agree with you, but what are we two against so many?"]

Dear Sir

Your letter has only just reached me. They did not forward it from the theatre, expecting a visit from me every day.

There is no way of becoming a dramatic critic. It happens by accident. For instance, I have never been offered a post of the kind, though I should have been quite willing to take it any time these last eighteen years. But when the accident happens, it happens to a journalist. It is to men who are already in the profession, and known as men who can write and who know the ways of papers, that editors turn when a vacancy occurs. If you work for a paper as a reporter or paragraphist, and are keen on theatres, you can generally do a stray notice on an emergency which makes you known to the editor as having a turn that way. Then, if the dramatic critic dies, or goes on another paper, or drops journalism, you have your chance of succeeding him, if you have shewn the requisite capacity. That is the regular way. But you may induce some friend who starts a paper, or becomes editor of one, to give you a trial straight off; but that is a matter of pure luck, with, of course, the skill to take the luck when it comes. Remember, to be a critic, you must be not only a bit of an expert in your subject, but you must also have literary skill, and trained critical skill too—the power of analysis, comparison &c. I have had to go through years of work as a reviewer of books, a critic of pictures, a writer on political & social questions, and a musical critic, in order to qualify myself for the post I now hold on the staff of The World. You must not think that because you only heard of me for the first time the other day or thereabouts that I got such reputation as I have cheaply. I came to London in 1876, and have been fighting for existence ever since. Even my little platform performance at the Playgoers' Club was the result of about fifteen years practice of public speaking, mostly under the humblest circumstances. I tell you this lest you should be discouraged and embittered by thinking that you are meeting with exceptional and unfair difficulties. In London all beginners are forty, with twenty years of obscure hard work behind them; and, believe me, those obscure twenty years are not the worst part of one's life, nor need you nor anyone be afraid to face them.

I still hold to it that a man who thinks a dramatic performance worth waiting at the pit door all day for is a lunatic. The front row of the pit

433

is worth something; but it is not worth that. However, I only give you my own valuation. If your enthusiasm makes it worth the trouble to you, I have no right to object.

All the views which you attribute to me concerning Mr Irving and Mr Tree and the "new school" have, if you will excuse my saying so, been put into your mind by newspaper paragraphs written by people who have not the slightest knowledge of me or my views. There is nothing that annoys me more than all this nonsense about new schools & the new drama & the rest of it. I suffer from it considerably, as it leads people to construe purely dramatic passages in my plays as interpolations of what are supposed to be my political views. But even if the play did contain any such interpolation, I should not admit your right to make a disturbance on the head of it. If the Fabians in the gallery were enjoying my play, as I am glad to say that the gallery still does now that there are no longer any Fabians in it, why did you carry your disapproval of a purely imaginary allusion to the Royal Family to the point of making them lose patience with you? Have they ever disturbed you in the enjoyment of the patriotic and loyal sentiments with which popular military melodramas are freely spiced? We have both been present, I have no doubt, at first nights of plays containing a good deal that is exceedingly repugnant to my political & moral opinions. I dont think you have ever found me interrupting an actor or annoying my neighbors on that account. I simply do not go to the sort of plays I dislike.

In conclusion, let me assure you that I did my best to put before you a true picture of what a brave soldier who knows his business really is. I heartily wish you could bring me an audience of veterans—of men who know what it is to ride a bolting horse in a charge, or to trust to the commissariat for food during a battle, or to be under fire for two or three days: they would not have taken my chocolate &c &c for silly jokes, as I feel a good many of the audience did.

yours faithfully
G. Bernard Shaw

To CHARLES OVERTON

29 Fitzroy Square W
[A/1]   8th May 1894
My dear Overton

Get out: Palmer has been to see the play, and has told you just what I told you about it all along. Thank you all the same: your competition

434

has been most useful to me: I shouldnt have brought my man [Felix Mansfield] to terms half so easily without it.

We shall deal over my next play, I hope, now that you know the sort of man I am.

yours ever
G. Bernard Shaw

To ALMA MURRAY

29 Fitzroy Square W
[A/1; X/109]   11th May 1894

My dear Miss Alma Murray

What—oh what has become of my Raina? How could you have the heart to play that way for me—to lacerate every fibre in my being? Where's the poetry gone—the tenderness—the sincerity of the noble attitude and the thrilling voice? Where is the beauty of the dream about Sergius, the genuine heart stir and sympathy of the attempt to encourage the strange man when he breaks down? Have you turned cynic, or have you been reading the papers and believing in them instead of believing in your part? I have no reproaches deep enough for you; for those men cannot act unless you make them act: it is not in human nature; and the utter failure of the play today—for it was an utter failure, in spite of the laughs at those jokes which are as obvious as sitting down on a bandbox—was all your fault. When you are right the play cannot fail: when you are wrong, it cannot succeed. Oh, that first act! that horrible first act! could anything expiate it? I swear I will never go to that theatre again. Here is my heart, stuck full of

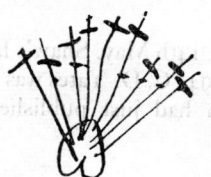

swords by your cruel hands.

yours, agonised
G. Bernard Shaw

["I am truly sad at heart," Alma Murray replied, "to think I have so deeply wounded you. You know I told you *before* the matinee that I thought it time you came & saw us all & 'pulled us together,' but alas I did not know I was

435

such a guilty person. I have altered one or two points I confess & generally find them go better with the audience. I suppose it is these comedy touches you object to. I will do my best to take them all out & if you really mean you will never go to the theatre again perhaps you will come here & tell me exactly where it is I hurt you most. Is it only in the first act?" (*Letters from George Bernard Shaw to Miss Alma Murray*, 1927.)]

To ARTHUR WAUGH

[A/4]

29 Fitzroy Square W
16th May 1894

[Arthur Waugh (1866–1943), sub-editor of the *New Review*, eventually became managing director of the publishing firm of Chapman & Hall. Shaw's article, "A Dramatic Realist to His Critics," published in the July issue of the *New Review*, was a frontal attack on criticism of Shaw's military references in *Arms and the Man*.]

Dear Sir

By a desperate effort I send you the MS of the bulk of my article, and will try to get the rest finished tomorrow. I greatly regret that I have not had time to turn out something better: the state of the MS will give you an idea of how much of it has been scrawled in vehicles. I must try to improve it a little in proof.

yours faithfully
G. Bernard Shaw

To C. D. YATES

[G.u/2]

29 Fitzroy Square W
30th May 1894

[Edmund Yates had died on 14th May. Shaw's last critical notice appeared in *The World* on 8th August 1894. C. D. Yates was one of Edmund Yates's four sons. Sidney R. Thompson had just published a critical monograph on Hector Berlioz.]

My dear Yates

I thought it possible that a command might be taken by Major Griffiths, of whose editorship I have had experience to the extent of a World Xmas number.

Will it cause any serious inconvenience if I take the opportunity to drop out of the post of musical critic? When I left The Star I was succeeded in that capacity by Mr Sidney Thompson, of 14 Russell

436

Chambers, Bury St W.C., whose articles signed "Piccolo" consoled the Star readers for my secession. Since that time he has devoted himself more exclusively to musical criticism than I have been able to do. He has visited France & Italy for all the most famous representations of the past few years; and this experience, with his own cleverness & a certain bright & attractive personal note in his criticism, seems to me to mark him out as the best man, all things considered, for the purposes of The World. I may add that he does not, as far as I know, share my political views or take the least interest in them. My own stock in him lies in the fact that he is one of the cleverest of the young men who followed me up when I went first ahead in musical criticism.

I shall, of course, keep my department going until fresh arrangements are made, if the editor desires it.

yrs sincerely
[G. Bernard Shaw]

To ALMA MURRAY

[H/1; X/109]

29 Fitzroy Square W
1st June 1894

[Clare Greet (1871–1939) was a young actress (no relation to Sir Ben Greet, though she studied under him) who later performed frequently with the Stage Society. There is no record of her having substituted for Florence Farr in *Arms and the Man*, but she subsequently created the rôles of Rummy Mitchens in *Major Barbara* (1905) and Megaera in *Androcles and the Lion* (1913).]

Dear Miss Alma Murray

I went to the Avenue tonight for a while under the impression that Miss Greet was playing Louka. This ended, not in my seeing Miss Greet, but in seeing the last two acts of the play again.

I have now to entirely withdraw all my former observations, which you will please attribute to temporary aberration. It is quite impossible that you could ever have played Raina otherwise than beautifully. Besides, your Raina is now something of your own, which I admired from the back of the pit like anyone else in the theatre. I shall not now accept your invitation to call and talk the part over, because whenever any woman gives me the pleasure your playing tonight did, I cannot help falling violently in love with her; and I can no longer support the spectacle of Forman's domestic happiness. He is a most intolerable

437

usurper and monopolist; and the advantage he has taken of the mere accident of his knowing you before I did appears to me to be altogether unjustifiable.

Lest you should think that I was in too good a humor to make my appreciation worth much, let me add a criticism in proof of the vigilance of my faculty. The incident of Raina's coming upon Bluntschli in the second act and losing her presence of mind so completely as to betray herself by her exclamation "Oh! the chocolate cream soldier" is not intelligible as you play it. I don't object to your treatment, as it belongs to your feeling about the part; but it gives away the situation. Nothing but a bouncing exclamation of surprise, quite sudden and spontaneous, followed by a very evident moment of confusion as you realize what you have done, will make the audience understand what has happened. If the steps had been placed according to my design there would have been no difficulty; you would have burst upon Bluntschli and the audience the instant you stepped through the door, with the light full on you. As it is, it seems to me that the only way would be to make you descend the steps first, and then bring Bluntschli suddenly upon you round the corner. Anyhow the exclamation wants to be taken more *con esplosione*, as Meyerbeer put it. But I am quite content to let the point go, as I do not at all dislike your play at the moment; indeed, I am disposed to say, if it does not make the effect I aimed at [,] so much the worse for the effect.

yours contritely
G. Bernard Shaw

To MAJOR ARTHUR GRIFFITHS

[G.u/2]

[29 Fitzroy Square W]
2nd June 1894

[Shaw's only professional association with Griffiths had been in connection with the group-written novel, *The Salt of the Earth*, in 1890. His dissatisfaction with the collaboration, which resulted in his refusal to accept payment for his share in the project, appears to have had its source in a contretemps concerning the amount of the remuneration, coupled with a refusal by Griffiths to accept any of Shaw's suggestions for the development of the novel.

Theodore Child (1846–92), an Oxford graduate and London journalist, who was Paris correspondent for *The World*, died of cholera in Persia. It was

438

in Child's short-lived English-language journal, *The Parisian*, published in Paris, that Henry James's "A Bundle of Letters" first appeared in 1879.]

Dear Maj[or] G[riffiths]

Not a bit of it: there is no objection in the [least] on my part [to] serve under you. I have no patience with that sort of boycotting; nor have I any misgiving as to our getting on together excellently. As to that Xmas number, you certainly landed me most refreshingly over it; but I did not take it at all in bad part. Even if you propose to deal in future on the understanding that you will hold yourself free to land me again whenever it suits you, I am quite ready to take you on at those terms and to look after myself without being personally unpleasant. Why then should we fail to hit it off in a relation which involves no conflict of our interests?

You will now want to know why, in that case, I resign the moment you take the editor's chair. I reply, that I do it for obvious reasons of the most sordid character. Let me put the situation fully before you. You know exactly what Yates was; and you will see, if you consider the matter for a moment from any point of view, that he and I suited one another extraordinarily well. He felt, without perhaps knowing it definitely, that what the clubs & the country houses & the respectable middle classes want is blasphemous, seditious, licentious, completely emancipated, thoroughly human & unmoral papers, made perfectly presentable, and guaranteed as the correct social thing. This is what is summed up under the title "journal for men & women" (therefore not virginibus puerisque). How to keep our entrée to the countryhouses for the purpose of rescuing the wretched inhabitants for a few hours a week from God, Mrs Grundy & the Seven Deadly Virtues: that was, & is, the World problem. When Yates engaged me he did not ask me any questions as to my speculative disbeliefs; but the opinions of Archer, myself, & Theodore Childs were as obviously identical on leading social topics as if we had all passed a rigid test examination to qualify ourselves for entrance to hell. Yates's selection of us shewed that whether he was fully conscious or not, he could be depended on to feel his way in the right direction; and also that his instinct included an appreciation of the backing of real character which is necessary to save an unconventional paper from lapsing into blackguardism. Add to this that valuable quality which we have all been describing in the papers as his loyalty, and which meant security of tenure for us, and you have all the conditions which tempted us to stick to Yates & The World without considering too closely, as we got on in our profession, whether the old salary was the top of our new market.

439

Now for the present position. The fact that some years ago I agreed to fill a page of the World every week for £260 a year, and that I never revised the bargain as the growth of my professional reputation made it less & less eligible for me, is no reason why I should make the same bargain with you today. In the Xmas number affair you shewed me two things: first, that the World *esprit de corps* does not run as between your set on the staff and mine, and second—which is more to the point—that you are likely to reverse Yates's policy & proceed on the assumption that society likes the sort of loyal, constitutional, jingo, pietistic slosh it has to pretend to like. Now I do not say that there is not a demand for such stuff; but I do say that your subscribers dont want it, and that if they did, any hack writer of the younger generation can supply it in a less old fashioned style than the men to whom you are likely to continue Yates's loyalty. I may mistake your point of view; but surely that is what is on the cards and you yourself dealt them to me in the only deal we ever had together.

Now for the practical upshot of all this. If I continue to face the weekly return of those two columns—which is getting more & more like facing a succession of knockdown blows—I must have either ten pounds per article, or £8 a week on the same terms as to vacations as I now have [at] £5. The reason I did not say this at once, instead of talking about resignation, is that it is not worth your while to pay so much. A younger, fresher man, like Sidney Thompson for instance, who is in a hurry to get married, will be glad to do the work for £5; and the difference between his writing & mine—assuming it for arguments sake to be a difference for the worse—wont cost you £3 worth of subscribers. Further, he would be safe for the next ten years, improving all the time; whereas I can hardly be relied on from one year to another. Therefore, instead of proposing a bad bargain to you, I suggested my withdrawal & the engagement of Thompson straight off.

If you still care to talk matters over, let us make our appointment for the end of next week. That will give you time to turn this letter over in your mind; and it will leave me free to cope with some pressing business in connection with my dramatic ventures.

You will, I hope, excuse me if any of this sounds disagreeable. It is difficult to be genuinely explicit without jarring a little here & there; but I assure you I have no ill feeling at all in the matter.

yrs sincerely
[G. Bernard Shaw]

440

To RICHARD MANSFIELD

[A/21]

29 Fitzroy Square W
5th June 1894

[Richard Mansfield (1854–1907), Berlin-born actor of English parentage, appeared on the English stage from 1877 to 1882, when he emigrated to New York, where he became a leading actor-manager. His most successful productions were *Dr Jekyll and Mr Hyde*, *Beau Brummel*, Shaw's *The Devil's Disciple* (1896), and Rostand's *Cyrano de Bergerac*. His brother Felix Mansfield (1852–?), who served as his agent and business manager, negotiated the formal contract for *Arms and the Man* with Shaw on 9th June 1894.

Shaw's self-drafted contract with Mansfield for *Arms and the Man* was a one-year licence for performance in the United States and Canada, by which the author was to receive "£10 per centum of the gross receipts." The Shavian attention to detail may be discerned most clearly in Clause 5: "At all performances of the comedy the text as contained in the prompt copy supplied by the Author to the Manager shall be spoken without intentional interpolation or alteration saving only such reasonable curtailment as may be necessary to bring the performance within the limits of time customary in the place of performance for plays of its class." (The draft memorandum of agreement is in the Berg Collection, New York Public Library.)]

My dear Mr Mansfield

Enclosed you will find a draft of the Shylockian bond which I propose. Your brother suggests that in a contract some consideration should pass; but that does not apply to an agreement of this kind any more than to the letting of a house or an agreement with a publisher. Kindly look through it at your convenience & let me know whether it will do.

yours very truly
G. Bernard Shaw

To RICHARD MANSFIELD

[H/21; X/116]

29 Fitzroy Square W
9th June 1894

[Despite Shaw's blandishments, Mansfield played Bluntschli when *Arms and the Man* opened at the Herald Square Theatre in New York on 17th September 1894, with his wife, Beatrice Cameron (1868–1940), appearing opposite him as Raïna. Sergius was performed by Henry Jewett (1862–1930), an Australian actor who emigrated to America in 1892, where he scored an instant success as leading man to Julia Marlowe.]

My dear Mansfield

I am sorry you were snatched away before I could pay you a second visit. I have just executed the agreement in the presence of Felix, who will send you the two copies: one with my signature for you to keep, and the other for you to sign in the presence of a witness and return to me. In this way you will have a copy executed by me, and I a copy executed by you, which will give us the satisfaction of pretending that we are both very careful and accurate men of business.

I again want to impress on you the fact that the novel flavor of Arms and The Man involves a certain struggle with the public. Unless you play in it, it will be just what it has been here: that is, a notable artistic success costing the management between three and four thousand pounds. Do not entertain the notion that the play has not been properly worked. There is not a dodge that has not been tried. All that is wanted is an actor with a strong personal following in a theatre with an established clientèle. Producing the play "under the personal superintendence of Mr Richard Mansfield" will only emphasize the fact that you are not going to play in it. Even playing Bluntschli is not much use, since he will be safe in weaker hands: what is wanted is a man who will take over the piece with a sure grip when the Swiss drops out in the second act, and who will play up to the height of the expectations created in the first act—a man who will strike the imagination of the house at once, and lift that flirtation scene with Louka into one of the hits of the play. From his first entrance to the end, Sergius is practically never off the stage except during the one comedy scene between Raina and Bluntschli early in the third act. All Sergius's scenes are horribly unsafe in second rate hands, whereas Bluntschli and Raina *cannot* fail, though they can of course be played more or less well.

I expect to have your prompt copy ready in a few days. When it reaches you, you will, I hope, see the importance of Sergius and Louka to the success of the play. By the way, Sergius is a very improbable name for a Bulgarian: Would you like to change him to Marko?

yours faithfully
G. Bernard Shaw

442

To HENRY ARTHUR JONES

[S/2; X/124]

29 Fitzroy Square W
11th June 1894

[Sigmund Lautenberg, who since 1887 had been the managing director of Berlin's Residenztheater, had just undertaken the management of the Neues Theater. *The Lady Slavey*, a musical play by George Dance and John Crook, was first performed in Northampton on 4th September 1893, and toured the provinces for a year before opening in London. The provincial manager willing to risk producing an "advanced" play was a man named Louis Weighton. Rehearsals for the provincial tour commenced on 21st August 1894, with A. E. Drinkwater (1852–1923), father of John Drinkwater, in the leading rôle.]

My dear Jones

This is about as near return of post as I can get to acknowledge the copy of The Masqueraders you sent me. I am rather curious to see it on the boards, as there is a certain fanciful quality in it that attracts me; and I want to see how much of it they succeed in getting across the footlights. I like the fairy tale in the bar of a country hotel, the fantastic woman, the star-gazer, and the vaporous brother. The comedy is of course first rate: you have never appreciated yourself fully in that department, or you would have given us more in the way of unmixed thoroughpaced comedy. The rest I forgive you for, though I believe you faked up that atrocious nurse for the express purpose of infuriating me. And there is such a lot to be done on the stage with the real hospital nurse. My real soldier in Arms and The Man would not have been in it if you had risen to the occasion. Every one of that woman's allusions to duty elicited a howl of rage from me. She morally outrages my tenderest sensibilities.

I have just had a visit from Sigmund Lautenburg of the New Theatre, Berlin. He has come to London under the impression that the two great successes of the year in England are Arms and The Man and The Lady Slavey, now being played in Nottingham. I explained to him that Nottingham is not a district of west central London, and that Arms and The Man, with its splendid advertisements and its applicants for stalls turned away nightly, has only twice drawn as much as half the cost of sending up the curtain, and has on two other less happy occasions in Whit week and the cab strike gone down to £14. Having thus placed him on his guard against the wiles of London, I got the paper and told him where to go to see the really successful pieces, and who were the leading authors. As he wrote to me a few weeks ago I have made inquiries about him and found that he is *the* man to do Berlin business with; so if he calls on you or otherwise opens negotiations about The Masqueraders, be good to him for my sake, as I am greatly touched by his illusions on the subject of my eminence, and on his complimenting me on my strong resemblance to Jesus Christ. He is at De Kayser's [Royal] Hotel, Blackfriars Bridge, in case you should know him already.

We put [Charles] Wyndham into a delicate situation the other day. When you arrived I was in the act of reading to him an extremely advanced farcical comedy of mine called The Philanderer, he having shewn a very proper sense of my gifts after witnessing the Avenue Show. As I know that you are doing a play for him, I felt disposed to wink at you through the crack of the door. For Heaven's sake don't write him anything that will run long.

Your advice in business matters has been quite invaluable to me. I enclose a duplicate of the draft agreement for America, from which you will see that I did exactly what you told me. For the provinces I have arranged for ten per cent. in the half dozen big cities, and seven and a half in the thirty next in order of importance, and five per cent. in the rest. I have no faith in its success in the provinces, especially as it has failed here so signally with the pit and gallery; but since the provincial success of A Woman of No Importance the notion has got about that there is business in "advanced" plays on the road; and I have found a man willing to risk it.

I shall have a brilliant article in next month's New Review on Arms and The Man, giving all my authorities for the military realism (there is not an original notion in the whole affair from beginning to end) and stating my position as regards cynicism and all that sort of rubbish.

By the way, talking of that, how frightfully pessimistic your play is! Hang it all, Regent's Park, with all its drawbacks, is better than Andromeda. Why don't you chuck up these idiotic moral systems according to which human nature comes out base and filthy? It's the systems that are wrong and not we. I believe in the good old Molière-Labiche-Sheridan line; they would have been very well contented with myself and Walker and Morris and the rest of us, and not have sighed for any Andromeda.

yours sincerely
G.Bernard Shaw

444

To WILLIAM T. STEAD

29 Fitzroy Square W

[A/1; X/147]   16th June 1894

[Stead, who had a fanatical dislike for the stage, considered acting a sinful
occupation; like many reformers, however, he had no first-hand knowledge of
the thing he condemned, as he had never been to the theatre. Wagner's story,
"An End in Paris" (1841), provided the inspiration for Louis Dubedat's
"artist's creed" in the death scene of Shaw's *The Doctor's Dilemma* (1911).
Stead's "memorial" urged upon the government the sponsorship of an
international armaments suspension.]

Dear Mr Stead

I return the memorial, signed. But allow me to point out that you
have not, as far as I am aware, come to see my play, "Arms and The
Man," in which, for the first time, soldiering has been treated on the
stage with some reference to its reality. As the June Review of Reviews
is now out, and the play will only run to the 11th July, when the agreement under which the theatre is taken expires, I am in a position to
suggest that you should sit out a performance at my invitation without
incurring any suspicion of wanting to supply a serious deficiency in
the Review by becoming the subject of "The Play of the Month,"
which is quite as important in its way as the book of the month. It is so
long since Ober Ammergau that you must be ripe for a second visit to
the theatre by this time; and if you will at any time signify your willingness to venture into the Avenue, you shall have all the seats you want
with every possible dispatch.

Wagner, the composer, once wrote a sketch called "The End of a
Musician in Paris," in which the hero, on the point of death, says his
creed, beginning, "I believe in God, Mozart and Beethoven." Now you
were brought up to believe in God, but not in Mozart and Beethoven,
whereas I was brought up to believe in Mozart and Beethoven but not
in God. I submit with the utmost docility to your determination to repair the deficiencies in my education on the theological side; and I
think you ought to occasionally try the influence of art, just to see what
it is like. If you were going to preach a sermon on war, I would come
to church to hear you. Why not come to the theatre to hear my sermon?
That is, of course, if it would not bore you too much.

yours sincerely
G. Bernard Shaw

445

To ARTHUR WAUGH

[V/1]

29 Fitzroy Square W
18th June 1894

[William Heinemann (1863–1920), publisher of the *New Review*, founded in 1890 the publishing house which bears his name. A drama enthusiast, and himself the author of several plays, he published Pinero, Maeterlinck, and Ibsen, as well as novels by Henry James, H. G. Wells, and Joseph Conrad. Although Heinemann discussed with Shaw the possibility of publishing *Arms and the Man*, the play first appeared in Grant Richards's edition of *Plays Pleasant and Unpleasant* (1898).

The editor of the *Yellow Book* was the American novelist Henry Harland (1861–1905). Shaw's "engagement," however, never was fulfilled. When Aubrey Beardsley, formerly art editor of the *Yellow Book*, helped to found a rival publication, *The Savoy*, Shaw contributed an essay "On Going to Church" to the first number, in January 1896.

Arthur Waugh, in *One Man's Road* (1932), recalled that, although he had written the "timorous letter" which elicited Shaw's angry response, he was merely following the order of Archibald Grove, who considered the article to be "brilliant but long."]

Dear Sir

Have you any conscience—any remorse—any moral sentiments of any kind? You delay an article of mine for a month on the pretext that it is too valuable to be cut down & that you had not left room for it in the June number. You thereby inflict the utmost inconvenience upon me, by defeating the scheme which Mr Heinemann & I had formed for publishing my play with the article as a preface. Further, by deferring the considerable advertisement which the article would have given the play, until the end of the season, you cause me considerable pecuniary loss. In spite of this, I allow you to keep the article and thereby defer for a quarter the fulfilment of an engagement with the editor of *The Yellow Book*, who offers me higher terms than your scale. And you now have the inconceivable audacity—the unabashed and flagitious callousness—to make fresh difficulties at the last moment on the ground that you have, with my article in type before you since last month, again made up your number without regard to its length. Where were you born?—where educated?—where do you expect to go to when you die?

I have gone through the article very carefully, and made the final proof corrections. I have reduced it in length by exactly one line; and I make it a positive condition that the article goes in this month precisely as it stands in the enclosed proof, or else is returned to me in final settlement and conclusion of all dealings between me and the New Review.

446

You can cut out what other article you please—you can double the size of the July number—you can triple the price—you can eat the whole edition and die of indigestion, leaving the editor [Archibald Grove] to replace you by some person with an elementary sense of responsibility —but you shall not tamper with that article.

If you are still unable to realise the situation, I beg of you to refer the matter to Mr Grove or Mr Heinemann before acting on your own responsibility. It is incredible to me that they would permit any contribution to the New Review to be treated as you—without any sort of excuse or apology—propose to treat me.

yours truly
G. Bernard Shaw

To MATTHEW EDWARD McNULTY

[A/4]

29 Fitzroy Square W
2nd July 1894

[McNulty's novel was *Misther O'Ryan: An Incident in the History of a Nation*, published by Edward Arnold. *Arms and the Man* achieved a run of fifty performances before it was withdrawn on 7th July. Between the London and American productions in 1894 Shaw earned royalties of £341. 15. 2, enabling him on 6th November, for the first time in his life, to open a bank account. One of the "distinguished" visitors to the play was the Prince of Wales, who, according to St John Ervine, "was offended by its satire" and left the theatre muttering "of course, the fellow is a damned crank!"

Vera was McNulty's daughter. Kate Gurly (d. 1915) had lived with the Shaws for many years. In her childhood she fell from a horse, broke her back, and grew up hunchbacked. An unhappy woman, addicted to heavy drinking, she was converted to Roman Catholicism before her death.]

It was weighing on my mind rather that I ought to take some steps to put the National Observer, the Pall Mall &c &c, on to your book, as I saw that they would play up for you handsomely. I am relieved to find that they have discovered you unprompted.

Arms & The Man comes off on Saturday, having been manufactured into a London success at a net loss of about £4,000. Roughly speaking, it has extracted some £1500 from the public pocket; and numbers of very clever and distinguished people have come repeatedly (for nothing). The curious thing—to an outsider—is that this is the case with most London successes.

On what terms have you published your novel? I suppose you wont

447

get anything out of it; but that is all the more reason for you to stick to your copyright. I never let a thing go for more than five years.

I had forgotten the crime of Vera's baptism, which seems a trifle compared to the outrage of vaccination. Why on earth didnt you rejoice in the failure of the first attempt? The whole business is a peculiarly filthy piece of witchcraft, which will probably be exploded even in parliament soon in view of the last report of the Commission. Good Heavens! how much oftener would you have poisoned the child if this dose had failed? Her drawing bears a healthy resemblance to many other drawings that have been shewn to me by friends who have become parents, though I admit that there may be talent there.

I have taken the very serious step of cutting off my income by privately arranging to drop the World business at the end of the season; and now, if I cannot make something out of the theatre, I am a ruined man; for I have not £20 saved; and Lucy and Kate Gurly (my mother's half sister) are now members of the family. I am about to begin the world at last.

GBS

To WILLIAM T. STEAD

[A/1; X/147]

29 Fitzroy Square W
4th July 1894

Dear Mr Stead

What a man you are—to talk of making a round of the theatres, as if they were brothels! Why, how many years do you suppose it takes to learn how to see and hear in a theatre? However, if you begin, you had better begin with the most serious attempt yet made to treat the theatre as a temple—I mean, of course, Bayreuth. I have just had an offer of tickets for the first four performances this year at par (£1 apiece)—July 19, Parsifal, 20th, Lohengrin, 22 Tannhauser, & 23 Parsifal again (it is the regular thing to do Parsifal twice). Will you take these tickets if I can still secure them for you? Remember, in Parsifal the Holy Ghost descends, and the hero's feet are washed with a woman's tears and dried with her hair. Ober Ammergau was a miserable, genteelified, Sir Noel Patonesque Sunday School piece of illustrated Bibleism: Bayreuth is very different.

What do you say?

yrs sincerely
G. Bernard Shaw

To GRANT ALLEN

[A/1; X/121]

29 Fitzroy Square W
6th July 1894

[Grant Allen (1848–99), Canadian-born writer and journalist, uncle of Grant Richards, was Professor of Mental Philosophy and Logic at the Government College in Jamaica (1870–76). After his return to England he became a leader-writer for the *Daily News* and author of more than two dozen books, including *Physiological Aesthetics*, a biography of Darwin, and several successful novels. In his article "The New Hedonism," in the *Fortnightly Review*, March 1894, Allen defined the "new hedonist" as a "moral" man in that he fights against "the narrow and vulgar morality" of the old ascetics. "Self-development is greater than self-sacrifice," he claimed.]

Dear Grant Allen

Do you mean us to strike you off the Fabian roll or do you not? I have stood between you and this doom until I am positively ashamed of you. Confound it, do you know what you cost us in postage and printing every year? Do you ever look at the tracts that are sent you, or calculate how much time they cost literary men who are poorer than you are? Do you know how many hours a week the committee work of the society costs? Do you know how many poor devils of workmen write to us when they can no longer spare us a few shillings to ask us to strike them off, so as to save our stamps? Meanwhile you are working up our stuff into Westminster articles & periodically writing to the Atheneum to announce that you have sold yourself to the devil for money (of which we never see the color). The executive committee burst into a downright fury today when your name was again brought up as a defaulter; and the secretary flatly refused to write to you again. Is this the New Hedonism? Have you any honor, any conscience, any survivals of shame left in you? I persuaded the committee to instruct the secretary to hold his hand until next Wednesday, & undertook in the meantime to write to you. This gives you at least time to resign. *Do* wake up.

yours out of all patience
G. Bernard Shaw

449

To WILLIAM T. STEAD

29 Fitzroy Square W
8th July 1894

[A/1; X/147]

[Shaw departed for Bayreuth on 16th July, stopping over at Darmstadt, Würzburg, and Nuremberg, and returned via Ostend and Dover on 26th July. Dr William Ashton Ellis (1853–1919), a physician, was the pioneer translator of Wagner's prose works into English, a dedicated scholar who would have starved in his late years if Shaw had not been instrumental in procuring a Civil List pension for him.]

My dear Stead

This is most noble of you; I believe you wont regret it. I enclose the four tickets, which were purchased on the 9th March last, and were the best then left available. The theatre holds about 1000 people; and only one of your seats (652) is far enough back to be more than half way from the stage to the royal boxes, which bring up the rear. All the seats are equally good as far as being in full view of the whole stage is concerned; and the acoustics conditions are perfect; but the very high numbers are the least desirable because of the distance from the stage.

Your being "an utter barbarian" is a great advantage. Wagner stands or falls by the success of his appeal to "the folks"—that is, to the unsophisticatedly receptive natural man. If you want to read up on the subject, read Wagner's "Communication to My Friends"—the part concerning Lohengrin & Tannhauser—translated in W. Ashton Ellis's Wagner's Prose Works in English, Vol. I, Kegan Paul, Trubner &c. If you have any difficulty getting it from the London Library or wherever you borrow books, let me know & I will see whether I cannot hunt you up a copy. *Parsifal* you had better deliver yourself up to without further preparation than reading the text. You can get the books of all the operas in the Bayreuth shops for about a shilling—English translations.

To secure lodgings, write to the Wohnungs Committee, Bayreuth, describing what you want & what days you will arrive and quit. The office is in the railway station. When you get out of the train you give your name at this office; and they hand you a card with full particulars of where you are to go. For a clean room in the main street, high up over a shop, I have paid eighteen shillings for a week, including breakfast. As you can get the same accommodation in Berlin for a month for about the same money, you will be highly welcome on these terms. Of course, there are hotels, if you prefer them.

You wont want to arrive in Bayreuth until the morning of the 19th nor stay there after the fall of the curtain on the 23rd unless you go Wagner mad, and make frantic bids [for tickets] for all the subsequent perform-

450

ances. I write all this in case I should be unable to hit you off by a visit. The season is pretty heavy on my time just now. I am going to drop out of The World now that Yates is gone. Next winter the greatest music critic in Europe will be silent on the subject unless he gets an extremely handsome inducement to go on.

yours sincerely
G. Bernard Shaw

P.S. Let me know if I can give or get you any further information.

To GRANT ALLEN

[B/1; X/121]

29 Fitzroy Square W
10th July 1894

Dear Grant Allen

The Fabian palm being oiled, its indignation (simulated for the purpose of extracting money) will subside. You will receive the official acknowledgment of your bounty in due course.

I have entered the [luncheon] engagement at the Savile [Club] for the 27th at 1.30 (can they feed a vegetarian?) in my diary; but I can only hope I shall be in London to keep it, as I must presently be off to Bayreuth. However, as I intend to come straight back after the performance on the 23rd., there is no reason why I should not be up to time. I can then let you into the secrets of a London success in the theatrical line.

yrs ever
G. Bernard Shaw

To C. T. H. HELMSLEY

[A/1]

29 Fitzroy Square W
12th July 1894

My dear Helmsley

I find that out of Arms & The Man I have made £90 and your acquaintance. This is handsome payment, thanks to the latter item, which will, I hope, long outlast the former. When you take a theatre of your own, just bring me pen and ink, a ream of paper, a bottle of gingerbeer, and a few beans, and you shall have the most brilliant play of the century to open with.

yrs ever
G. Bernard Shaw

29 Fitzroy Square W
12th July 1894

[A/4; X/116]

[George R.Foss, who was stage manager for *Arms and the Man*, had served as assistant to Shaw in the staging of the play (Shaw's first directorial effort).]

My dear Foss

I should long ago have acknowledged the specifications of the scenes you sent me for the new prompt books of Arms & The Man. In putting in all the stage movement of the play, which is as much an integral part of its authorship as the text itself, I was confronted with an account in black & white of how much it owed to you; and in preparing a play which I now have in hand for the stage I find that I have learned a great deal of my business from you. Our personal acquaintance has been so pleasant and unceremonious that I have always taken your skill and interest in the work as a matter of course, along with your great goodhumor and forbearance whenever I was inclined to persist in making a mistake in spite of you; but I should be sorry to let the occasion pass altogether without a word to shew that I quite knew how well off I was in having your help. I hope Arms & The Man is not the last enterprise in which we shall be associated.

Dont bother to acknowledge this letter: it is not meant formally enough for that.

yours sincerely
G. Bernard Shaw

To BEATRICE WEBB

bei Herrn Kapper, hintere Damallee 1
Bayreuth
20th July 1894

[C/14; X/141.e]

[Madame Roland (Jeanne Manon), condemned by the Revolutionary Tribunal in 1793, is supposed to have asked, at the foot of the guillotine, for pen and paper, which were denied to her. Sydney Olivier's wife Margaret (1861–1953) and Agatha Thornycroft were sisters; Sir William Hamo Thornycroft, R.A. (1850–1925), was a well-known sculptor. Alice Stopford (Mrs J.R.) Green (d. 1929), a friend and neighbour of the Webbs, was a historian and member of the first Senate of the Irish Free State; she worked for the defence of Roger Casement. Mandell Creighton (1843–1901), Bishop of London, was a long-time friend of Beatrice Webb. His daughter

Beatrice (1874–?), active in the management of London's board schools, later became a Deaconess of St Hilda's, Ootacamund, India.]

Being for the moment rather bored at an open air restaurant up on the hill here in the middle of the day; and having, unlike Madame Roland at the foot of the scaffold, a fountain pen and a post card about me; being, furthermore, a wanderer far from home, I find my thoughts turning, not to Fitzroy Square, but to Thee, if you will allow me that expression, in which, not to be invidious, I will include your satellite Wallas and your sun Webb, I being a mere comet and—confound this sentence, I cannot get out of it; it is like a peroration. Well, the Oliviers are here; and the Thorneycrofts are here; and Mrs Green is here, apparently under the protection of a gentleman; and the bishop is here; and I am going to stalk the Bishop's daughter between the acts this afternoon. I nearly killed myself yesterday in trying to get an account of the first performance off to the Star by the 8.45 post, the last act beginning at 8.30. Keep your eye on that paper. I hope to send further bulletins later on.

GBS

To JOSEPH EDWARDS

[A/4]

29 Fitzroy Square W
28th July 1894

[Joseph Edwards, a Liverpool Fabian, was the editor and publisher of the *Labour Annual*, which was about to make its first appearance. Shaw's letter was written across the back of the printed prospectus, which he had taken the trouble to proofread and revise.]

Dear Edwards

All I can suggest is that in future you might lay a little more stress, in an explanatory way, on the utility of a year book. The fact is, Labor men, from want of business training, are often amazingly ignorant of the use of books of reference &, generally speaking, of what I may call labor saving office furniture. They keep letters & press cuttings & the like (which they never can find when wanted) for the sake of preserving the information as to dates, addresses &c, which you would put in order for them in the annual for a shilling a year. Make this clear to them & they will *feel the want* of the book, which is the great thing.

I am so busy this week that I could not answer you by return as I should have liked to have done. With best wishes,

yours sincerely
G. Bernard Shaw

453

To ARNOLD DOLMETSCH

[B/24]

29 Fitzroy Square W
4th September 1894

[Arnold Dolmetsch (1858–1940), a French musician who settled in London, specialised in collecting, constructing, and performing upon ancient musical instruments. Shaw's *World* notice of 4th July and his article "The Musical Revolution" in the September *Musical Courier* were concerned with Dolmetsch's manufacture of a clavichord for the Royal College of Music.]

Dear Mr Dolmetsch

Will you excuse my not answering your two letters at the end of last June. It is impossible for a musical critic to do anything in June except go to performances & write about them. However, I managed to follow up the article in the World by another in the New York Musical Courier, a copy of which I have asked its London agent & correspondent to send you when it appears: I will very gladly avail myself someday of your kind invitation to look through your workshop. Just at present, however, I shall not have any opportunity of doing so, as I start for Italy tomorrow & shall be away for at least three weeks.

I am leaving The World; but no doubt I shall write from time to time on music in the magazines.

yrs very truly
G. Bernard Shaw

To JULES MAGNY

[A/1]

Florence
17th September 1894

[Dr Henri Polak (1868–1943), a Dutch Socialist who resided in Amsterdam, was president of the Amalgamated Netherlands Diamond Workers' Union, a journalist, and translator of Shaw's *The Impossibilities of Anarchism* in 1895. Polak had recently been elected president of the Foreign Press Association. Joseph Mazzini Wheeler (1850–98), a journalist, collaborated with G.W. Foote on several secularist works and compiled a *Biographical Dictionary of Freethinkers* (1889). Van Gogh emigrated to New York in 1895. Shaw had left London on 5th September for an Italian tour with the Art Workers Guild, visiting Basle, Pallanza, Milan, Florence, Pisa, Genoa, and Como; he returned on 23rd September.]

Dear Magny

Will you tell our friend Pollag (or is his name spelt Polak?) that Otto Wichers van Gogh, who is, I believe, desirous of getting some

454

assistance from the Foreign Press Association, is known to me as a journalist and the author of some plays which have been performed by the Independent Theatre (Freie Bühne) of Berlin. He is a Freethinker, and was banished by the Swiss government for a pamphlet called "Rettet die Kinder." Mazzini Wheeler introduced him to me on his arrival here. His pecuniary position must be rather desperate—in fact, I know it is; but when a man is bundled neck & crop into a strange country with no resources for an entirely disinterested attack on what we call bourgeois opinions, the difficulties of his position are no fault of his own; and I must say that he made no attempt to use Wheeler's introduction as an adventurer would have done. He seems a very decent fellow; and if the F.P.A. can help him, they might easily find a less deserving applicant.

He asked me to tell Polak what I know about him; but I dont know P's address, so write to you instead.

I shall be back in England next week.

yrs sincerely
G. Bernard Shaw

To JIM CONNELL

29 Fitzroy Square W
1st October 1894

[A/4]

Dear Connell

Another journal [*The New Age*]! I spend half my life in holding out hopes of copy to new socialist & labor papers—hopes which are never fulfilled. It is not possible for me to do anything in time for the first number [4th October]; and, frankly, the most I could do later on would be to send a stray contribution which would by no means justify a man of your tender conscience in announcing me as one of the staff, so to speak, of the venture. I need hardly say that experience has left me absolutely cynical as to the financial success of any such magazine; and the longer I live, the more I doubt the wisdom of giving the oppressed proletarian anything that he won't pay for.

Now can you tell by this letter whether I have promised to contribute or not?

yours fraternally
William Ewart Gladstone

455

29 Fitzroy Square W

[S/1; X/126.e]

28th October 1894

[Henry Thomas Buckle (1821–62), English historian, adopted a scientific manner of writing history, with attention to physical conditions, climate, soil, etc. His great work was his *History of Civilisation in England* (1857–61).]

My dear Marriott

I do not know how many years it is since you undertook to make me read Buckle's History of Civilisation, and lent me your copy with that object. You must have despaired more than once of ever getting your three volumes back, much less inducing me to apply myself to them. But you will be glad to hear that I finished the last volume yesterday, having read every word of the three, notes and all, with the attention they deserve. And I assure you I am extremely obliged to you for making me do it. Out of the millions of books in the world, there are very few that make any permanent mark on the minds of those who read them. If I were asked to name some nineteenth century examples, I should certainly mention Marx and Buckle among the first.

As you have read both, you will have been struck by the fact that they both start from the same general view that the particular form of civilization in any place, including its laws, religion and customs, depends really on the economic conditions: that is, on its climate and on the ease or difficulty with which its food can be produced. But Marx followed this up in a direction produced by his interest in labor and his sympathy with its oppression. Buckle followed it up in a direction produced by his sympathy with freethought and its oppressions. Marx was the champion of the slave, Buckle the champion of the sceptic. The result was that in spite of their determination to be strictly "scientific" and to read everything connected with their subject so as to get at all the facts of it, you have Marx coming out as a thorough Collectivist, declaring that since the industrial organisation must be the real government, it had better be made the nominal government too, and so brought under the control of the people: whilst Buckle comes out a thorough Individualist in the old sense, declaring that "to maintain order, to prevent the strong from oppressing the weak, and to adopt certain precautions respecting the public health, are the only services which any government can render to the interests of civilisation." It is quite curious to see Buckle, who on some points sees further than Marx, yet on this industrial question sticking at the point of mere Manchester School free trade, which Marx left so far behind.

Naturally we too, as freethinkers, are delighted by Buckle's chapters on the history of Spain under ecclesiastical government, and of the Scotch intellect in the seventeenth century. Here he piles up his evidence just in the manner of Marx telling the story of modern Capitalism: the effect produced is one of overwhelming dislike of the whole thing, and complete conviction of its inevitable downfall. And his intense belief in the value of doubt, "the great principle of scepticism," the need of constant innovation, the unreality of mere formal or legal changes in our institutions when they are not merely the carrying out of changes in the minds of the people—all these convictions of his, hammered in as they are with just the right sort of *homely* historical examples to appeal to the man of everyday experience, are quite after my own heart, and after yours too, if I may judge by the passages you have marked. I wish, by the way, that the I.L.P. and the S.D.F. would take to heart his saying that the study of history will shew, "what men seem only recently to have begun to understand, that, in politics, no certain principles having yet been discovered, the first principles of success are compromise, barter, expediency."

By the way, there is a touching description at the end of the third chapter of the third volume, of "the historian." It is evidently Buckle's picture of himself.

Buckle does not strike me as a very brilliant literary artist. He explains everything very clearly and carefully, and thinks his way conscientiously down into a sentence until he has got the exact point of it; and when his feelings are deeply touched he makes an earnest and often successful attempt to be very impressive in his style. But he does not shew any of those powers by which a great artist with the pen (as distinguished from a good straightforward workman) throws all sorts of sidelights on his narrative by flashes of irony, humor, poetry, wit, tenderness and so on. It says a great deal for him that he makes you value him so highly that you take serious pains to read him carefully through in spite of the fact that he has hardly anything fascinating in his manner of writing. Marx was much more of a genius in this way. But Buckle's weaknesses are more pardonable than Marx's. For instance, both of them make a great display in their foot notes of their immense research and erudition. But the foot notes make it clear that Buckle read all his books with interest and sympathy, not quoting anything until he had taken pains to master the point of it; whereas Marx can hardly be said to have read anything except the bluebooks on which he bases his case. No doubt he turned over the leaves of a great many books and pamphlets sufficiently to make some contemptuous quotation or allusion, or to accuse the author of plagiarism; but he was evidently incapable of tolerating anybody who did not share his sensitiveness on the labor question, and simply could and would not take the trouble to make out their drift. Buckle rises above controversy much oftener than Marx—perhaps because he did not realise as keenly as Marx did the frightful conditions against which he was battling.

I cannot post this letter to you immediately, as I am waiting to get your latest address from the Fabian list of members which will be sent round presently. Tomorrow I start north for a week's hard work on the platform. On my return I hope to send you this letter with the three volumes and my very sincere thanks for having made me read them.

G. Bernard Shaw

To RICHARD MANSFIELD

[X/127.e]

[29 Fitzroy Square W]
[Undated: October 1894]

[Although *Arms and the Man* received a generally favourable critical reception in New York following its première on 17th September, it survived for only sixteen performances. Mansfield, however, retained it in his repertory in New York and on tour for the balance of the season. The excisions in the text of this fragment were made by Paul Wilstach, who published it in his *Richard Mansfield: The Man and the Actor* (1909).]

. . . Of course it doesn't draw; whoever supposed it would? It has produced reputation, discussion, advertisement; it has brought me enough money to live for six months, during which I will write two more plays. So take it off in the peaceful conviction that you have treated it very handsomely and that the author is more than satisfied. . . . Judging by the reception of "Arms and The Man," I cannot doubt that if you were to play "The Philanderer," you would be lynched at the end of the first act. It exudes brimstone at every pore. . . . I should like very much to see you as Bluntschli. If you will come to London I will even go so far as to sit out "Arms and The Man" to see you. . . .

To J. CUTHBERT HADDEN

[A/1]

29 Fitzroy Square W
15th November 1894

[J. Cuthbert Hadden (1816–1914), an organist, was editor of the *Scottish Musical Monthly*, Edinburgh. Shaw's article, "How to become a Musical

Richard Mansfield as Captain Bluntschli in *Arms and the Man*
(Herald Square Theatre, New York, September 1894)

Critic," appeared in the December issue. In the School Board elections in November, Stewart Headlam and Graham Wallas were successful candidates. Shaw ran for the St Pancras Vestry, but was defeated.]

Dear Sir

I enclose the article—the best I can manage under a very heavy pressure of work brought on me by the local elections here. It is extremely difficult to be a dramatic author, a journalist, and a candidate for the vestry all at once, especially with School Board meetings clamoring for platform speeches at every turn. However, I hope the article is readable. Will you be so good as to make sure that it does not go to press until I have corrected a proof.

> yours faithfully
> G. Bernard Shaw

To HENRY ARTHUR JONES

[X/124]

29 Fitzroy Square W
19th November 1894

["Jo" was the critic Joseph Knight, who wrote a preface to Jones's *Judah* when it was published in 1894. The play, first produced at the Shaftesbury Theatre on 21st May 1890, had been highly praised by most of the dramatic critics.]

My dear Shakespear

Ben Jonson, as you say, is an excellent judge of a man; but on the whole I should prefer your autobiography to his biography.

Far be it from me to rage against Jo; he and the rest have treated me devilishly well, all things considered; but the fact remains that Joseph's observations on *Judah* are supremely uninteresting. One wants to know what *you* have to say about it.

Judah amused me. It consists of clever preliminaries; and when the real play begins with the matrimonial experiment of Judah and Vashti, down comes the curtain as usual. Come: I will write plays for the next ten years at £150 apiece, as the outside of my hopes for fees; and then the public will be ready to hear the solution of the problems you so fancifully pose it. You will find me making a terrible pace for you in a few years, if you don't run away from Townshend House and take to vegetarianism, sandals, and the pilgrim's bowl.

> G. B. S.

To R. GOLDING BRIGHT

[A&B/1; X/125]

29 Fitzroy Square W
19th November 1894

[Shaw eventually accepted on 4th December Frank Harris's offer of the dramatic critic's post on the *Saturday Review*, at a weekly salary of £6. Robert Hichens (1864–1950), who replaced Shaw as musical critic for *The World*, was the author of the anonymously-published satire *The Green Carnation* (1894) and *The Garden of Allah* (1905). Frances E. McFall (1862–1943) was a popular novelist and feminist, who wrote *The Heavenly Twins* (1893) under the pseudonym "Sarah Grand."]

Dear Sir

Your letter surprised me, because, as it happened, I had just sent your name to an editor who wanted a dramatic critic; and it seemed odd that we should think of one another simultaneously. However, as the position in question—that of the criticship of The Saturday Review under Frank Harris—was one which could only as a very bold experiment have been given to a comparatively untried hand, Harris was probably more disposed to damn my eyes for refusing the berth myself than to entertain my suggestion of an alternative.

By all means make the Sun pay you. But if you can afford it, let the account run until it is large enough to save the appearance of worrying about a trifle—say until it is over a couple of pounds or so. Never allow a regular commercial newspaper to get copy from you for nothing; but never, either, if you can avoid it, show any anxiety about being paid. Take it as a matter of course that what is worth publishing is worth paying for.

The title "Mrs Jarman's Profession" is a curious illustration of the influence of Paula Tanqueray [who had masqueraded under the name of Mrs Jarman]. The real title is "Mrs Warren's Profession." The name Jarman never came into my head, nor is there any authority for it except some association of ideas in Grein's head which led him to give the wrong name to his interviewer.

My separation from The World is permanent. I made up my mind to take the opportunity of Edmund Yates's death to escape from musical criticism, which is not so amusing to the writer who has written a long article on the subject every week for seven years as it is to his readers. I have an article on musical criticism in a forthcoming number of The Scottish Musical Monthly. I will ask the editor to send you a copy.

My successor Mr Hitchens (or whatever his name is) seems to me to write cleverly & pleasantly enough. You must give up detesting everything appertaining to Oscar Wilde or to anyone else. The critic's first

460

duty is to admit, with absolute respect, the right of every man to his own style. Wilde's wit and his fine literary workmanship are points of great value. There is always a vulgar cry both for and against every man or woman of any distinction; and from such cries you cannot keep your mind too clear if you wish to attain distinction yourself. You know the sort of thing I mean: you have heard it about Whistler, Sarah Grand, Ibsen, Wagner—everybody who has a touch of genius. Excuse this scrap of sermon: I would not intrude it upon you if I did not know by experience the great difficulty of forming and holding to a genuine original opinion of public men on their own merits when so many fools are chattering about them in all directions.

Keep up your courage: from what you tell me you are getting on very well as far as the papers are concerned. But you ought to write a couple of books on the drama. Burn them afterwards by all means; but write them. I started by writing five books, one after the other, without producing the least impression on an apparently implacable destiny.

I am overwhelmed with work in connection with the Schoolboard & Vestry elections & have only time to send this hastiest of scrawls.

yrs faithfully
G. Bernard Shaw

To HENRY ARTHUR JONES

West Cliff Hotel. Folkestone
2nd December 1894
(Beastly wet day)

[S/2; X/124]

[The just-completed play was *Candida*. Shaw did not begin another play, however, until the summer of 1895 when he set to work on *The Man of Destiny*. Rev. Jeremiah Joyce (1763–1816), for many years secretary of the Unitarian Society and a minister of advanced political views, published his *Scientific Dialogues* in 1807. David Garrick (1717–79), noted actor-manager of the Drury Lane Theatre, made his own free adaptations of Shakespeare.]

My dear H.A.J.

Here I am at the seaside between the finishing of one play and the beginning of another, just the time to send back the ball to you.

All that you say is quite true statically. Dynamically, it is of no virtue whatever. Like you, I write plays because I like it, and because I cannot remember any period in my life when I could help inventing people and scenes. I am not a storyteller: things occur to me as scenes, with action and dialogue—as moments, developing themselves out of their own vitality. I believe you will see as I go on that the conception of me as a doctrinaire, or as a sort of theatrical Joyce (of *Scientific Dialogues* fame), is a wrong one. On the contrary, my quarrel with the conventional drama is that it is doctrinaire to the uttermost extreme of dogmatism—that the dramatist is so strait-jacketted in theories of conduct that he cannot even state his conventional solution clearly, but leaves it to be vaguely understood, and so for the life of him cannot write a decent last act. I find that when I present a drama of pure feeling, wittily expressed, the effect when read by me to a picked audience of people in a room is excellent. But in a theatre, the mass of the people, too stupid to relish the wit, and too convention-ridden to sympathise with real as distinct from theatrical feeling, simply cannot see any drama or fun there at all; whilst the clever people feel the discrepancy between the real and theatrical feeling only as a Gilbertian satire on the latter, and, appreciating the wit well enough, are eager to shew their cleverness by proclaiming me as a monstrously clever sparkler in the cynical line. These clever people predominate in a first night audience; and, accordingly, in "Arms and The Man," I had the curious experience of witnessing an apparently insane success, with the actors and actresses almost losing their heads with the intoxication of laugh after laugh, and of going before the curtain to tremendous applause, the only person in the theatre who knew that the whole affair was a ghastly failure. The same thing is occurring now in Boston, Philadelphia, &c— there is about as much of me in the affair as there is of Shakespere in Garrick's "Katherine and Petruchio." Here and there, of course, I come across a person who was *moved* by the play, or by such portions of it as got played any better than a pantomime opening; but for the general paying public there needs a long fight, during which my plays will have to be produced in spite of all economic considerations, sometimes because the parts are too fascinating to be resisted, sometimes because Pinero is not ready with his commissioned play, sometimes because I am willing to forgo an advance, sometimes because Nature will not submit wholly to the box office.

Now here you will at once detect an enormous assumption on my part that I am a man of genius. But what can I do—on what other assumption am I to proceed if I am to write plays at all? You will detect the further assumption that the public, which will still be the public twenty years hence, will nevertheless see feeling and reality where they see nothing now but mere intellectual swordplay and satire. But that is what always happens. You must remember my musical experience. I remember well when even cultivated musicians could hear no melody in Lohengrin, not to mention Die Meistersinger, and when they thought Spohr's and Mendelssohn's oratorios, and "Mozart's 12th Mass" the summit of musical sublimity and profundity. The public is still as great an ass (to speak in that way) as it was then; but it now knows that Wagner's work is all melody and feeling, and that the other stuff is nine tenths formality and twaddle. Consequently I am absolutely confident that *if my work is good* (the only assumption on which I can go on with it) all the miracles will happen, and it will be quite well worth my while to make £150 a play, or even to make nothing and starve, or play Wagner to your Liszt in the sense of borrowing all your spare cash.

And now as to the barrenness of politics. What conviction can you really have as to their barrenness unless you have fallen in love with them and found that no child came of their embraces?—or unless you have actually worked in the arena with politicians all through their apprenticeship. You have to swallow all the formulas if you are to know what they really taste like and what effect they have on the constitution. Politics are just as much a part of life as gambling or poetry; and it is extremely instructive to see how impotent the political opinions which men *think*, are to produce action, and how potent the political prejudices which men *feel*, are to produce it. I am a politician because life only realises itself by functioning energetically in all directions; and I find on the platform and in council opportunities for functioning away like mad with faculties that would otherwise be atrophied from disuse. My passion, like that of all artists, is for efficiency, which means intensity of life and breadth and variety of experience; and already I find, as a dramatist, that I can go at one stroke to the centre of matters that reduce the purely literary man to colorless platitudes.

Do you now begin to understand, oh Henry Arthur Jones, that you have to deal with a man who habitually thinks of himself as one of the great geniuses of all time?—just as you necessarily do yourself. We may be deceiving ourselves; but why add to the heavy chances of that the absolute certainty of such a deception as would be involved in the notion that we thought ourselves common fellows with a bit of talent.

Have you ever considered the case of Dickens carefully? Don't you think his last (and greatest) works would have been much greater if he had had something of the systematic philosophical, historical, economic, and above all, artistic training of Goethe? I grant you it is a

463

difficult question; but surely so fine a spirit could have been rescued from the reproach of being a Philistine, a guzzler, and an ignorantly contemptuous reporter-politician?

G. Bernard Shaw

To R. GOLDING BRIGHT

29 Fitzroy Square W
2nd December 1894

[B/1; X/125]

[Golding Bright's "notice" was a review of Clement Scott's adaptation of Sardou's *Odette*, at the Princess Theatre. The full text of the review, with Shaw's revisions, is reproduced in Bernard Shaw, *Advice to a Young Critic*, ed. E. J. West (1955). Sydney Grundy (1848–1914) was a popular dramatist whose play *The New Woman* had been produced at the Comedy Theatre in September 1894. Shaw's first dramatic notice in the *Saturday Review*, on 5th January 1895, was of Grundy's *Slaves of the Ring*. The "celebrated letter" by Shaw on the Empire controversy, published in the *Pall Mall Gazette* on 16th October 1894, concerned prostitutes plying their trade in the Empire Theatre promenade.]

Dear Sir

The best service I can do you is to take your notice and jot down on it without ceremony the comments which occur to me. You will find first certain alterations in black ink. In them I have tried to say, as well as I can off hand, what you were trying to say: that is, since it was evident you were dodging round some point or other, I have considered the only point there was to make, and have made it. It came quite easy when I had altered your statement about Frenchmen at large to what you really meant—the conventional stage Frenchman. Always find out rigidly and exactly what you mean, and never strike an attitude, whether national or moral or critical or anything else. You struck a national attitude when you wrote that about the Frenchman and Englishman; and you struck a moral attitude when you wrote "She has sunk low enough in all conscience." Get your facts right first: that is the foundation of all style, because style is the expression of yourself; and you cannot express yourself genuinely except on a basis of precise reality.

In red ink you will find some criticisms which you may confidently take as expressing what an experienced editor would think of your sample of work.

You have not at all taken in my recommendation to you to write a book. You say you are scarcely competent to write books just yet. That is just why I recommend you to learn. If I advised you to learn to skate, you would not reply that your balance was scarcely good enough yet. A man learns to skate by staggering about and making a fool of himself. Indeed he progresses in all things by resolutely making a fool of himself. You will never write a good book until you have written some bad ones. If they have sent you my Scottish article, you will see that I began by writing some abominably bad criticisms. I wrote five long books before I started again on press work. William Archer wrote a long magnum opus on the life and works of Richard Wagner, a huge novel [*The Doom of the Destroyed*], and a book on the drama [*English Dramatists of Today*, 1882], besides an essay on Irving [*Henry Irving, Actor and Manager*, 1883] and a good deal of leader work for a Scotch paper [*Edinburgh Evening News*] before he began his victorious career on The World. He also perpetrated about four plays in his early days. (By the way, you mustn't publish this information). You must go through that mill too; and you can't possibly start too soon. Write a thousand words a day for the next five years for at least nine months every year. Read all the great critics—Ruskin, Richard Wagner, Lessing, Lamb and Hazlitt. Get a ticket for the British Museum reading room, and live there as much as you can. Go to all the first rate orchestral concerts and to the opera, as well as to the theatres. Join debating societies and learn to speak in public. Haunt little Sunday evening political meetings and exercise that accomplishment. Study men and politics in this way. As long as you stay in the office, try and be the smartest hand in it: I spent four and a half years in an office before I was twenty. Be a teetotaller; don't gamble; don't lend; dont borrow; dont for your life get married; make the attainment of EFFICIENCY your sole object for the next fifteen years; and if the city can teach you nothing more, or demands more time than you can spare from your apprenticeship, tell your father that you prefer to cut loose and starve, and *do it*. But it will take you at least a year or two of tough work before you will be able to build up for yourself either the courage or the right to take heroic measures. Finally, since I have given you all this advice, I add this crowning precept, the most valuable of all. NEVER TAKE ANYBODY'S ADVICE.

And now, to abandon the role of your guide, philosopher and friend, which I don't propose to revert to again until you report progress in ten years or so, let me thank you for the paragraph in the Sun, which was quite right and appropriate. I have no more news at present, except that I have nearly finished a new play, the leading part in which

465

I hope to see played by Miss Janet Achurch, of whose genius I have always had a very high opinion. It is quite a sentimental play, which I hope to find understood by women, if not by men; and it is so straightforward that I expect to find it pronounced a miracle of perversity. This is my fifth dramatic composition. The first was "Widowers' Houses," of Independent Theatre fame. The second was "The Philanderer," a topical comedy in which the New Woman figured before Mr Grundy discovered her. The third was "Mrs Warren's Profession," a play with a purpose, the purpose being much the same as that of my celebrated letter to the Pall Mall Gazette on the Empire controversy. The fourth was "Arms and The Man," which was so completely misunderstood that it made my reputation as a playwright both here and in New York. The Independent Theatre has already announced "Mrs Warren's Profession" for its forthcoming season. "The Philanderer" was written originally for that society; but on its completion I threw it aside and wrote another more suitable for the purposes of the society—Mrs Warren. Wyndham asked me to do something for him on seeing "Arms and The Man"; and I tried to persuade him to play The Philanderer; but whilst the project was under consideration, Wyndham made such a decisive success with "Rebellious Susan" that he resolved to follow up the vein of comedy opened by Henry Arthur Jones to the end before venturing upon the Shawian quicksand. But this involved so long a delay that I withdrew the play, and am now looking round to see whether the world contains another actor who can philander as well as Wyndham. As I have always said that if I did not write six plays before I was forty I would never write one after, I must finish the work now in hand and another as well before the 26th July 1896; but I hope to do much more than that, since I have managed to get through the present play within three months, during which I have had to take part in the Schoolboard and Vestry elections, to keep up my work in the Fabian Society, to deliver nearly two dozen lectures in London and the provinces, and to fire off various articles and criticisms. The fact is, I took a good holiday in Germany, Italy, and in Surrey; and I accumulated a stock of health which I am dissipating at a frightful rate. The Christmas holidays will come just in time to save my life.

If any of this stuff is of use to you for paragraphing purposes—and remember that the world will not stand too much Bernard Shaw—you are welcome to work it up by all means when it suits you. Only, don't quote it as having been said by me. That is an easy way out which I bar.

I find that you have got an atrociously long letter out of me. I have been blazing away on the platform this evening [at Kentish Town, on

"The Limits of Democracy"] for an hour and a half, and ought to be in bed instead of clattering at this machine.

yours, half asleep

G. Bernard Shaw

To PAKENHAM BEATTY

29 Fitzroy Square W

3rd December 1894

[B/4]

[William Archer read his translation of Ibsen's *Little Eyolf* to a group of friends on the afternoon of 3rd December, prior to its publication the following week. Although H. W. Massingham asked Shaw to review the work for the *Daily Chronicle*, he eventually rejected Shaw's review and published his own notice on the 12th.]

Sorry I had to put you off today; but I really am giddy & headachy & livery with rushing about from one place to another; and I had this afternoon to attend a private & confidential reading of Ibsen's new play for the purposes of reviewing it red hot of publication. I then had to address 2 vestry election meetings. You should see the candidates! We have to kidnap them in the streets, and daze them into submitting to be brought into the hall and nominated under the impression that they are being pressed for a coroner's jury. It is a crime for a man in your position not to serve: you could, at your worst, talk the heads off most of them.

I have the same game on hand tomorrow evening; and in the afternoon I have to meet Frank Harris on bread & butter business connected with the Saturday. On Wednesday evening, by the Lord, it is you who will have to stand by me. I must have beans, ginger beer, and the latest scandal about Johns and the rest to soothe me. I shall fly to Ealing to leave care behind me. Go on the vestry, my boy; and put Mrs Beatty on the Guardians; and you will be astonished at the indifference with which you will offer the stoneyard to all your embarrassed relatives.

GBS

To WILLIAM ARCHER

29 Fitzroy Square W

6th December 1894

[B.t/2]

[Archer had asked Shaw to provide a preface for his annual volume *The Theatrical 'World' of 1894*. The 1893 volume had been dedicated to Archer's friend Robert W. Lowe.]

467

There is one serious objection to my doing the preface; and that is that I have hardly been half a dozen times to the theatre (including all that I saw of "Arms and The Man") in the course of the year. I should have to make that fact the text of my discourse, I suppose. Further, I have always been of opinion, and am still, that the custom of getting Jones to write a preface for Smith's book is a very idiotic one. I remonstrated strongly with H. A. J. the other day for publishing *Judah* with a preface by Joe Knight. Not that I objected to Knight, but that I wanted to know what Henry Arthur had to say about his own work, and not what Joseph thought of it—as to which there was evidence already in the Athenaeum and elsewhere. Your last dedicatory preface to Lowe was interesting: I heard people talking about it with considerable feeling, though personally I thought it deficient in profundity of sentiment. But it did not at all explain your point of view as a critic. It seems to me that such a book is incomplete without a general review of the dramatic movement of the year; and this can only gain charm by being put in the form of the critic's confession as to how far he has been compelled to throw himself into one or other of the parties which are inevitably formed for progress or conservation whenever a movement takes place. I know your enormous reluctance to realise your own experience in this fashion; but it is assuredly a thing you must do, whether you write it down or not, if you are to progress in consciousness—which is the only sort of progress possible to a critic. Why not use such an excellent opportunity as the annual preface to the Theatrical World for this purpose? It is easier this year to get me to do something; and next year and the year after there may be a sparkler or two still left to fall back on. But think of the inevitable time when, if you keep up this silly shirking practice of getting an alien preface, you will have to fall back on the nobodies who will consider that they are laying you under a large obligation by writing something of which you will be secretly ashamed. This appears to me to make out a heavy case against the preface. If in spite of it you persist in calling in outside aid, call in mine sooner than anyone else's by all means; but the right man for the work is clearly William Archer and nobody else.

I sympathise with you so entirely—in the sense of knowing how you feel about it—that on Monday, in spite of Massingham's appeal for my presence and support, I two or three times almost made up my mind to spare you the agony of my appearance on the scene. But I think you will admit that it was desirable to get as much horse power as possible into the discussion of the play on your reading it, and that this was no less important in view of my own review than of Massingham's. I have always been one of the most indulgent of fathers to you up to the point at which your petulances and protervities are clearly spoiling good business. At that point, I cannot be blamed for asserting that I, too, have my validity in the universal scheme.

By the way, so far from backing my proposal for a page of reviews you received it with pathetic dismay, and plainly impressed on Massingham that he would be doing the most cruel violence to your finest feelings if he thus exposed your darling naked in the slave market to be priced by a horde of filthy reviewers. If you doubt this, ask him.

Why don't you set yourself to find out what you mean when you say that I never saw or felt a play in my life? You are quite right in-so-far as you mean something, and something which I quite understand; but you know perfectly well that the something is not that I never saw or felt a play in my life. If you were to say that the Adelphi theatre was not in the Strand, I daresay I should find out what you really meant by that statement; but I should also suspect you of not having precisely cornered your own meaning, judging from your very loose expression of it. You must find a more plausible Shaw formula, if it were only to save you from open disaster in criticising my plays. It is true that what are to you the solid and permanent elements in "Little Eyolf" are to me the illusory and transitory ones, and that the solution which you announced as conventional and disappointing is as real to me as the solution that breakfast brings to my morning's appetite—and by the solution, remember, I do not mean the mere material dress of the matter—the huts and the boys and so on—but the new feeling which these indicate. The transition from the passionate, idealistic world of love and hate (two names for the same thing), lust and murder, sacrifice and expiation, virtue and vice, and all the rest of it, to the real, creative, material world, comes just in that way. And the entry into the second costs the plunge into the first. Perhaps it may a little disappoint you, after the fantastic solution of Peer Gynt, and the no-solution of Rosmersholm, that a real solution is only found in something that brings the great Ibsen into line with Monsieur Tout-le-monde; but that, in my view, is the final *pièce de conviction*.

I shall not need the book (at least not indispensably) for my review, which is already finished and sent to the printer. But I should like to study that point about the letters, as I can see at present no function for them except that of explaining Asta's objection to live with the Almers before the play begins. This does not seem sufficient: besides, why should she not be his sister in reality? It would improve the case instead of damaging it.

469

I write by this post to Heinemann to ask him when I may let my review loose.

G.B.S.

To R. GOLDING BRIGHT

[A/1; X/125]

29 Fitzroy Square W
14th December 1894

[George Alexander produced and starred in Henry James's *Guy Domville* at the St James's Theatre on 5th January 1895.]

Dear Sir

The paragraph does not refer to "Mrs Warren's Profession," which has not yet been submitted to the Censor. I do not know what it refers to. It sounds like Henry James & Alexander; but I have heard nothing about it.

This year license was refused by Mr Pigott to a play [*A Freedom in Fetters*] by Mr Sydney Olivier, who, as an upper division clerk in the Colonial Office, ranks as a more highly qualified man than Mr Pigott, whose appointment is a matter of patronage, and who might quite possibly be an illiterate person, whereas an upper division civil servant has to pass a very stiff examination. The license was applied for by Miss Farr, who wished to produce the play at the Avenue Theatre. Mr Olivier attempted to discuss the question with Mr Pigott, but found him to be an ignorant and prejudiced opponent of the movement begun by Ibsen. It was quite useless to talk to him: he was well intentioned enough, but incapable. This is the only recent example of Censorial despotism with which I am acquainted.

Do not write a book for the purpose of burning it. Write it on the assumption that it is going to be published and to be useful & successful. Then see what will happen. Probably you will be unable to find a publisher; and you will have learnt so much by the effort of writing it that you will go on afresh & pass it by. But don't burn it, even if you become ashamed of it. Keep it in a drawer somewhere. At thirty, you will be impatient of the stuff you wrote at twenty; but at forty, you will recover some of your respect for the dreams of your youth. Besides, it may turn out worth publishing. One never knows. The one certain thing is that you must write, write, write every day for several years if you are to become a master workman in your profession.

As to your suggestion that perhaps I was better able to afford such exercises than you, I can only say that the difference between us appears to be that your father is fairly well off, whereas mine was poor and embarrassed. If your board and lodging are guaranteed, you may consider yourself a king. If you had seen me about twelve years ago, you would have seen a grimly shabby figure. For about nine years after I came to London I made nothing & wrote a good deal. Then for five or six years I made about £150. Then for a few years I made nearly £300. At present my income has gone back to its old figure—o. So you see money does not matter so much. A prosperous stockbroker would consider my career a dismal one; but as a matter of fact if you consider the variety of my interests and activities, the friends I have made (not to mention the enemies), the consideration I enjoy, and the degree of personal efficiency I have acquired, you will, I think, see that if I had devoted myself to making several thousand a year as a stockbroker, I should have made a very bad bargain. And remember that I began as much handicapped by poverty, shyness, awkwardness, and all the miseries of weak immaturity as anybody could have done. You have probably twice my opportunities & advantages, if not ten times. The fact is that everybody has to stand the same racket more or less—more if he is penniless, less if he has a father who guarantees a roof and a meal. So go ahead: the world's your oyster.

GBS

To JANET ACHURCH

[T/1 (A/4)]

West Cliff Hotel. Folkestone
22nd December 1894

[Beatrice Lamb (1866–?), who began her career as a member of Beerbohm Tree's company, had been steadily gaining stature for several years as a leading lady in popular comedies and drawing-room dramas. Olga Brandon (1865–1906), an Australian actress of Russian parentage who had made a spectacular success in *Judah*, had thereafter appeared mostly in second-rate melodrama.]

Here I am, taking the sea air with Wallas. The sea air travels at the rate of 120 miles an hour and goes through clothes, flesh, bone, spirit and all, so that one walks against it like a naked soul, exhilarated, but teeming at the nose. We are in an immense hotel, with 180 rooms and a few guests, who have nothing to do, and are miserable exceedingly having come down expressly to be happy. I shall begin a new play presently. The last having been so happily inspired by you, I look about Folkestone for some new inspiratrice, but in vain: every woman in the place either strikes me cheerfully prosaic at a glance, or else makes me boil with ten-philander-power cynicism. Everybody is quoting [R.L.] Stevenson's dictum about the height of happiness being attained when you live in the open air with the woman you love. Convinced as I am that love is hopelessly vulgar and happiness insufferably tedious to those who have once gained the heights, I nevertheless find that these material heights—these windswept cliffs—make me robustly vulgar, greedy and ambitious. If you by any chance tumble off the heights yourself ever, you will understand how vigorously despicable I am under these circumstances. The ozone offers an immense opportunity to any thoroughly abandoned female who would like to become the heroine of a play as black as "Candida" is white.

By the way, what about "Mrs Warren's Profession"? Must Vivvums, too, wait? We never thought of that. Excellent part, by the way, for Beatrice Lamb, who is rather like the resolute, educated modern young woman. And I begin to feel a distinct hankering after Olga Brandon for Candida, or perhaps Mrs Bernard Beere. Should be glad to have your views down here, where I have leisure to consider them.

I am, as you will observe, in an entirely worthless humour. That is the result of health, fresh air, plenty of food, early rising, long walks and the rest of the bracing delusions.

GBS

To WILLIAM ARCHER

West Cliff Hotel. Folkestone
[A/2]   28th December 1894

[Henry V. Esmond (1869–1922), actor and playwright, appeared in George Alexander's productions of *The Second Mrs Tanqueray* and *The Masqueraders*. Shaw was in error about the availability of *The Dramatic Year Book*, edited by C.S. Cheltnam, which appeared only once, in 1892, although it was intended to be an annual.]

I return to town tomorrow afternoon to take up the duties, fairly forced on me by Harris, of dramatic critic to the Saturday Review; so do not send on any more proofs to Folkestone. It is questionable whether it is quite decent for a dramatic author to be also a dramatic critic; but my extreme reluctance to make myself dependent for my bread and butter on the acceptance of my plays by managers tempts me to hold to the position that my real profession is that by which I can earn my bread in security. Anyhow, I am prepared to do anything which will enable me to keep my plays for twenty years with perfect tranquillity if it takes that time to educate the public into wanting them.

I read "Candida" to Alexander before I came down here. He instantly perceived that it was Marchbanks' & Candida's (that is, Esmond's & Janet's) play and not his. He said he would produce it if he could get down to the poet's age; but he would not play Morell. He had acted that sort of part, he said, until people were declaring that he could not act. By so doing he has made money enough to make him independent of playing anything but parts which will give him, as he put it, a property in himself as well as in his theatre. This, being intelligent, delighted me, and I took off "Candida" in high spirits. However, as he said he wanted to act a clever man, I suggested The Philanderer, who is an extremely clever man. He asked me to let him read it. I sent it to him & have not heard from him since. He said he wanted a play, because neither Jones nor Pinero were ready. He meant ready to step in on the failure of Henry James's play; but naturally he did not say so.

I am desperately floored by your confounded proofs [of The Theatrical 'World']. A year or two ago, when there was some question of republishing my World articles, I looked through a few of them, and found them, apart from the context of time and place for which they were originally designed, quite impossibly dull, stale and ineffective. I will not go so far as to say that your articles are so affecting; but they are sufficiently damnable. Who now cares for a discussion of the probability of the plot of [Sydney Grundy's] "A Bunch of Violets"? What further use to [D'Oyly] Carte is your attempt to make yourself agreeable, kindly & tolerant over such a ghastly and foredoomed insanity as [Michel Carré and André Messager's] Mirette? Is it tolerable to have Ibsen and Duse, not to mention myself, cut into strips by two-thousand-word lengths of mere regurgitation of the year's refuse, which is sufficiently chronicled elsewhere in the Dramatic Year & the files of the Era? I am in utter despair: I dont know what to write by way of preface. If your laziness had led you to follow my example & leave the articles buried, I could not have complained; but I am now more than ever convinced that you should either let your year's work alone or else rearrange it all as an annual article having the same excellence as its parts originally had as weekly articles. You tell me that the experiment of last year was not a financial success. I tear my hair and desperately

473

ask you, why should it? I declare before high Heaven that [Walter] Scott is a fool, and you a shirk, to publish a book that is no book. If it paid you you would have some excuse, but it doesnt.

I am also greatly hampered in even trying to think out a preface by the overwhelming obstacle which you make so light of—that I have not seen the plays you deal with. I must at least try to see the New Woman & rebellious Susan when I come up.

I have read a Scott novel down here. On my trip to Italy last September I read "Catriona." And, making all due allowance for the inferiority of "Catriona" as a specimen of R.L.S., and for the fact that "Old Mortality" is not one of Scott's failures, I cannot see the sense of forcing the comparison between the two men as everyone is doing just now. I wonder what Stevenson's work would have come to if he had lived to bring it to its full realisation. His death [on 4th December] seems to me a complete cut-off of a man who had never got to close quarters with life & who was only beginning to peep carefully over his palisade of cleverness at it.

Here ringeth the table d'hôte bell.

GBS

To UNIDENTIFIED YOUNG AMERICAN WOMAN

[X/128]

[29 Fitzroy Square W]
[Undated: 1895]

I am much obliged to you for the kind expressions in your letter about the "Quintessence of Ibsenism." It is always interesting to have a woman's opinion of anything written about women, when she can be persuaded to express it sincerely. It may perhaps interest you to know that one of my latest works is a play asserting the full strength of the domestic position for women. You call yourself an undomestic woman; but I suggest to you that a lack of aptitude for household management is too negative a qualification to take an effective stand upon. A positive aptitude for something else is better; but such a positive aptitude gets recognized nowadays; for instance, women of ability in the professions, or in politics or business, (or even in fashion and pleasure) do not find it impossible, or even unreasonably difficult, to delegate their domestic duties and pursue their careers. The really hard position for the moment is that of the domestic woman, whose enormously valuable services, both to society and to her own household are accepted and even exacted

474

as a matter of course, as if they were the least she could do in return for the privilege of being fed and clothed and housed and protected. Except when the death of a man's wife occurs at such a time that he has to pay a stranger to discharge her household and parental duties until he goes back to the cheaper plan by marrying again, it is very hard to convince him that his wife is a productive worker; and the woman, unfortunately, is harder to convince than he is, no doubt because she does so many things, and does them in such an amateur way (not being directly and avowedly paid for them) that she does nothing well, and therefore has no belief in herself.

I therefore am strongly of opinion that the undomestic woman, when she has once secured her position by escaping from domestic servitude as men escape from unskilled labor; that is, by mastering a trade or profession, can maintain her own individuality to the full extent of her own strength (we are none of us very strong in that way, man or woman) with infinitely less difficulty than the domestic woman.

So it is not for your own hand that you will have to fight so much as for that of the domestic woman from whose ill paid, ill organized, ill recognized, and consequently ill executed industry, you, as an undomestic woman, will presumably emancipate yourself.

I say this because without it my little book might possibly lead you to overlook it. Someday, if I ever have time, I will try to make a second edition of the Quintessence cover more of the "Womanly Woman" case than it does at present.

yours sincerely
G. Bernard Shaw

To R. GOLDING BRIGHT

[B/1; X/125]

29 Fitzroy Square W
11th January 1895

[Thouvenin is the *raisonneur* (*i.e.*, the dramatist's mouthpiece) in *Denise* by Alexandre Dumas *fils*. Eleanor Calhoun (1865–1957), the ingénue of Grundy's *Slaves of the Ring*, was a young American actress who had gained favour in London when she succeeded Olga Brandon in *Judah*. She married Prince Lazarovich-Hrebelianovich of Serbia in 1903. John Gilbert Hare (1869–1951), the son of Sir John Hare, deserted the stage in 1904 for a career as a bacteriologist and pathologist.]

Dear Sir

The worst of this paragraphing business is that it deals so much with persons and brings you across all manner of personal dislikes and quarrels which cause your work to be thrown aside through no fault of your own. For instance, Runciman, the musical critic of the Saturday, who is perhaps the best of recent editorial finds in the way of a critic, was for a time working for the Sun. They actually dismissed him out of sheer inability to know a good man when they had got hold of them. Being a good man he has character enough to make enemies. So has Frank Harris. So have I. A paragraph about all three of us has several chances against it in any newspaper office in London. As you probably saw, I ran the gauntlet in The Star successfully, though I do not know who the paragraphist was. I think you would do well to invest a few shillings (only three, I think) in a huge volume called Sell's Dictionary of the world's press, Fleet St, near Fetter Lane, and study it carefully with a view to seeing what you could do in the way of manifolding your paragraphs and sending them simultaneously to several papers throughout the country. I have not had experience enough of this sort of journalism to advise you as to details; but it seems to me that this is a thing that an enterprising man ought to do. If you could persuade your father to equip you with a Remington or North typewriter (these are the best for such rough handling as manifolding requires) as part of the necessary outfit of a young man desirous of being up to date in an office, you could make at least ten copies of a paragraph with carbon paper, and send them simultaneously to ten different papers in ten different districts, with, of course, a chance of two or three of them being inserted. You could offer a weekly column of theatrical gossip and news at a low price—say ten or fifteen shillings—to a number of papers whose circulations do not overlap, and whose day of publication is the same, and try to make it pay by getting more than one paper to take it. But be careful to see that the proprietors of the papers you approach are different, as there are some provincial newspapers which are practically duplicates issued by the same firm in widely distant parts of the kingdom. Even if you don't succeed, you will pick up a certain knowledge of the press, and you will find out the sort of questions you ought to put to the men who do make this sort of thing pay. It is always worth while to do a thing the wrong way in order to find out how not to do it, which is an important step towards finding out how to do it.

I am much obliged to you for your appreciation of my Saturday articles. In a way your opinion of Grundy's play is fairer than mine, as you take the thing on its merits, whereas I am partly fighting against the leading of the drama further in a direction which I believe to be, for the present, the wrong direction. And I greatly dislike the clumsy device (as it seems to me) of "the reasoner" introduced to explain the play—the Thouvenin of Dumas *fils*. The courage that struck you as to the ending was discounted for me by two things. First, the wretched claptrap about "the thin red line," which, as you may imagine, did not seem very courageous to the author of "Arms and The Man"; and second, the stupidity of the conclusion that there is no solution of the difficulty of unhappy marriages, whereas there is a perfectly simple solution in reform of the divorce laws. In some American States, South Dakota for instance, those four people could have re-sorted themselves quite easily. It is quite a feature of stageland and the aloofness of our theatrical people from real life that dramatists are always propounding as Sphinx-enigmas questions that every practical man knows the answer to, whilst they skip light-heartedly over situations which in real life raise the most appalling difficulties. As to the acting, poor Brandon Thomas of course did what he could, and did it very well, to pull off an impossible part. I saw the play on the second night; and Miss Calhoun, though not bad as far as she went, certainly did not do as much as she might have done with that one scene which was all that justified the existence of the play, and was in fact the root of it. You must not dismiss Gilbert Hare as beneath contempt. Suppose your father bought The World, and handed over the theatrical column to you, you would at first probably disappoint the readers who were accustomed to Archer's work. But if you turned out a fairly presentable column, and really did your blood best, correcting every sentence carefully and taking your work earnestly, all the good men who had been through the mill would admit that you had a right to your trial. If you want to enjoy masterly acting twenty years hence, you must be very tender to the apprentices and journeymen of today.

I doubt if I shall republish my Saturday articles. I never could be persuaded to do so with my World articles. Taken out of the atmosphere of the week in which they were written, they lost half their freshness.

G.B.S.

To JANET ACHURCH

29 Fitzroy Square W
[T/1 (A/4)]   25th January 1895

[Lewis Waller (1860–1915), popular London actor, had appeared in several of the recent Ibsen productions, including *Ghosts* (Oswald), *Hedda Gabler* (Lövborg), *Rosmersholm* (Rosmer), and *The Master Builder* (Solness). He became lessee of the Haymarket Theatre in January 1895, opening with Wilde's *An Ideal Husband*, in which Sir Charles Hawtrey appeared as Lord Goring, and Julia Neilson (1869–1957), frequently Waller's leading lady, as Lady Chiltern. Charles Hawtrey (1858–1923), a well-known actor-manager, who excelled in farce and light comedy, showed interest in *The Philanderer*, *You Never Can Tell*, and other Shaw plays, but never produced any of them. Janet Achurch had appeared, in April 1893, in Brandon Thomas's *Clever Alice*, with J.M.Barrie's *Becky Sharp* ("a scene from Thackeray") as curtain-raiser. Victor Hugo's drama *Le Roi s'amuse* (1832) was adapted by Francesco Mario Piave as a libretto for Verdi's *Rigoletto*.]

I have made an appointment with Waller to read "Candida"; but I shall read Eugene for all he is worth, as to sacrifice him would be to sacrifice the play. The only chance is in the fact that Waller is at an earlier phase of actor-management than Alexander, and may play for a managerial and financial success at the cost of playing Morell. But I am not sanguine. If he refuses, I shall try him with the Philanderer (Hawtrey in the title part) sooner than leave that stone unturned; and if he sees money in that, Miss Neilson is clearly out of the question for Julia, a part which I still think you could do yourself good by playing, as it would put you to the height of your cleverness and technical skill to play it; and these are the qualities for which you most need to gain credit. Nobody has seen you play a really keen comedy part, finished up to the finger nails. Clever Alice & Becky Sharp were only tomfooleries. Besides, with Paula Tanqueray in everyone's head as a great acting part, the public & the critics will have their cue for Julia. If you could pull off that part well, you would have no more trouble with Pinero: I know exactly what he thinks about you at present. What he thinks is all wrong; but you must do a piece of fine filagree work to convert him.

I am not surprised about Mrs Daintry. Waller's perfectly right; the ending is not the sort of thing for his audience. Besides, it is not really good drama: it is only good acting. After the revelation about the daughter, the play, dramatically speaking, stops as completely as "Candida" stops after the Erklarung in the third act. When the curtain goes up again, the only question is, how is the affair to be wound up? It is soon clear that butchery is to be the solution; and the first hint at the morphia brushes away the last shred of curiosity about the drama: all that remains is to see you die, as one waits to see Camille or Adrienne die. This makes the play one for a Bernhardt to star in, not for a West End manager to run for the amusement of a smart clientele, who begin (thank Heaven!) to look on stage poisonings much as they do

478

on broadsword combats. "Mrs D's D" is, after all, only "Le Roi s'Amuse" turned inside out: your one really original point—a genuinely tragic one, with a real last act in it—was the mother's discovery of the daughter's worthlessness; and that you cut out. You know I told you that you hadn't written your play. I am not sure that you had not better save it up for yourself for the days when you will be Bernhardting round the world. However, we can talk about it when we meet, if I am in a sufficiently disagreeable humor.

Tell C.C. I have received the play & will read it as soon as I can.

GBS

To R. GOLDING BRIGHT

[B/1; X/125]

29 Fitzroy Square W
30th January 1895

[Oscar Wilde's curtain speech after the first performance of *An Ideal Husband* on 3rd January had evoked much comment and criticism in the press. The "correct statement" in *The World*, on 30th January, was that George Alexander "has not, as the paragraphists have been busily paragraphing, accepted . . . *Candida*. On the contrary, Mr. Alexander declined it, with regret, finding himself unsuited for the part of the young poet, who is, in a certain sense, its hero."]

Dear Mr Bright

This is just the sort of case in which children are atrociously cruel to their parents. The first thing to do is to clear your mind of all protest against the position of your father's wife. No matter who or what she is or was, or whether you and your brothers and sisters like or dislike her, your father's claim to be happy with the woman he prefers and to marry her and put her interests before those of everyone else is indisputable. Of course it is a very disagreeable turn of events for the family; but it is not a grievance. If you take it in bad part, you will do pure, unmitigated, useless harm, since the marriage cannot be undone (even if it were reasonable to demand that it should); and besides, by making your father's relation with his children resentful and miserable, you will throw him more helplessly than ever on the sympathy of his wife, and almost drive him to make an unfair division of his property in her favor when he dies.

£50 a year is a fortune to a man in your position. You can't take hansoms on it, nor patronise the three and sixpenny lunch and the seven and sixpenny *table d'hote* at the Criterion on it, nor go to the stalls on it, nor live in a Whitehall Court flat on it; but you can keep yourself on it much better than most city clerks can keep a wife and family on it. With such an endowment you haven't the ghost of a claim on your father, though you must bid a long farewell to the style of living indicated by a house in the country and an income of £2,000 a year. I presume the Regent's Park Terrace menage is beyond your new means; so you better at once look for a cheap room as near the British Museum as you can get it and arrange with the landlady for your breakfast. Then select a cheap restaurant, or study the art of dining cheaply at Gatti's, for instance. Get a ticket for the museum library, and study the drama there up to eight every night with all the advantages of communal heating, lavatory accommodation and electric light, with a comfortable seat, unlimited books, and ink and blotting paper all for nothing. When you are settled in this groove with your necessary expenditure well within the fifty, write to your father, and tell him that he may now cut off the supplies altogether; excuse yourself pleasantly for having perhaps made a little unnecessary friction over the second Mrs Tan—I mean Bright; and wish him every domestic happiness and farewell. By cutting the cable before the supplies are exhausted you will prove that you are not merely making the best of a bad job, but boldly tackling the world as an independent man, in which character your father will not after be able to help respecting you. And I assure you you will write ever so much better after having shewn your mettle *to yourself* as well as to your father, who will begin to value you the moment you are able to do without him, possibly with favorable effects on his will, though I need hardly say that a calculation on that need not trouble a man of your years.

Excuse my giving you good advice: I have no doubt you get plenty of it. But what can I say on the case, as you put it to me, but what I have said?

You are really too hard on Wilde. His "I have enjoyed myself very much" was an Irishman's way of giving all the credit to the actors and effacing his own claims as author.

All the paragraphs about Alexander having accepted a piece of mine are wrong. The only correct statement of the case is that in this week's World.

yours sincerely
G. Bernard Shaw

To ARNOLD DOLMETSCH

[B/24]

29 Fitzroy Square W
31st January 1895

[Henry T. Finck (1854–1926), the musical critic for the New York *Evening Post* (1881–1923), was a champion of Wagner, Chopin, Liszt, and Edward MacDowell. Herbert P. Horne (1865–1916), an architect, writer, and connoisseur, was an editor of the *Century Guild Hobby Horse* (1886–93) and a frequent contributor to the *Saturday Review*. Shaw and John F. Runciman visited Dolmetsch's studio in West Dulwich on 6th February.]

Dear Dr Dolmetsch

Now that I have taken to dramatic criticism I find that the theatre keeps me away from concerts almost as completely as the concerts used to keep me away from the theatre. I was quite unable to get to the Salle Erard on either of your evenings.

I hope they sent you a copy of the article I wrote for the international number of that big American musical paper. It provoked the American critic Fink to attack me for my ignorance of the marvels of that majestic instrument the modern GRAND PIANOFORTE, which is to the obsolete tinkling, jingling, harpsichord or clavichord as the ocean steamer to the savage coracle &c. &c. &c.—you know the sort of stuff. Some day, when I have time, I will make Mr Fink wish he had never been born rather than spread himself in this fashion over a subject of which he knows nothing.

My chief regret at the discontinuance of my musical work is that I lose the power to help you to make your work known quickly. My successor on The World, Mr R. S. Hichens, seems a clever and sympathetic critic: perhaps, if you do not already know him, he might respond to an invitation [and] maintain the interest which the World musical column has so often shewn in the revival of the clavichord and the old chamber instruments generally. My musical colleague on the Saturday Review is a very able young man, enormously interested in Purcell, named J. F. Runciman. He is a skilled professional musician and a slashing journalist; and he could be of more use to you on the Saturday than even Mr Horne, who does not deal with concerts. Now I have a suggestion to make. You once asked me to call on you some afternoon and see your workshop. Shall I avail myself of your invitation, and try to persuade Runciman to come with me? Or do you know him already?

yours sincerely
G. Bernard Shaw

481

To EDWARD R. PEASE

[C/4]

29 Fitzroy Square W
4th February 1895

[Sidney Webb, who had been London County Council member for Deptford since 1892, was standing for re-election as a Progressive candidate. He won by an increased majority.]

The Leeds people must wait until the C.C. elections are over. A glance at my diary would convince you that I am hopelessly overdone— no less than ten evenings this month are already booked for public orations alone, without counting theatrical & private-public engagements.

I am afraid I shall not be able to get to the Pub[lication] Com[mittee] on Wednesday.

GBS

To CLEMENT SHORTER

[B/1]

29 Fitzroy Square W
14th February 1895

[Sir William J. Ingram (1847–1924) was managing director of the *Illustrated London News* and *The Sketch*, both of which were edited by Shorter until he resigned in 1900 to found *The Sphere*.]

My dear Shorter

I am such an incorrigibly amiable man that when you try to persuade me to undertake some fresh work I cannot help blinding myself for the moment to its utter impossibility. What you want is good G.B.S. stuff, and, like everybody else, you persist in thinking that I have nothing to do but turn on the tap at any time and pour it out at the rate of a thousand words an hour. That is not the true state of the case by a long way. If I were to take your offer, I should never have a moment to spare from journalism; and very soon my copy, whilst doubling its length, would lose half its value. You are virtually asking me, for the sake of an extra three guineas a week which I don't in the least want, to relinquish the drama, the political platform (almost), and everything that my Saturday Review work buys me time for. I ask you, not as an editor, but as a man of letters and a philosopher, is it reasonable? And would it be fair to Harris, who pays me a retainer of six pounds a week to start with, and who always wants some extra work done in the political or reviewing line, to destroy his monopoly of the G.B.S. signature,

482

not for your sake, but for that of Ingram, who ought long ago to have offered me a ten years agreement at a thousand a year for the exclusive right to my services? Besides, there are lots of fellows who can now do better G.B.S. than I can, and who would be glad of the chance. The whole difficulty is the money difficulty. Take any promising young man and give him at least £5 a week, and make him understand that he must earn it, and that as your representative he must hold his head high; and he will blossom presently like a magnolia in a hothouse. That is the right way to do it: the wrong way is to offer me three guineas for the skim milk after Harris has had the cream. High rates, treatment of contributor as distinguished man, and exclusive services: that is the secret of editors like Yates. However, all this will come in better when you command a journal of your own; but meanwhile, cost Ingram as much as possible in order that he may esteem you the more highly.

I did four and a half years of picture work for the World; and, to tell the truth, it would not be easy under any circumstances to induce me to go back to that. I hate going back: I want to conquer fresh territory.

> yours impracticably
> G. Bernard Shaw

To CHARLES CHARRINGTON

[T/1 (A/4)]

29 Fitzroy Square W
18th February 1895

[Charrington's first-hand knowledge of pawnbrokers was put to good use in Fabian Tract No. 91, *Municipal Pawnshops* (1899), of which he was the draughtsman.]

Dear Charrington

It seems to me that you are throwing away a providential opportunity of getting rid of the incrustations of home life. Surely their hypothecation has been a relief to you and an infernal nuisance to the pawnbroker. Let him sell them: he is bound by law, I think, to pay you any surplus he may make on the transaction. Or, if he has been friendly, pay him the interest and beg him to sell the things for you and at least remove them from your life even if he cannot make something for you by the transaction. He will have nothing to complain of then: and you will be freed for ever from the intolerable burthen of useless property.

> In haste,
> ever yrs
> G. Bernard Shaw

483

To RICHARD MANSFIELD

[B/21; X/141.e]

29 Fitzroy Square W
22nd February 1895

[Elisabeth Marbury (1856–1933), American author, play-broker, and literary agent, had undertaken, in 1894, at Mansfield's suggestion, to handle Shaw's royalty payments. Later, however, Mansfield complained to Shaw that, as Miss Marbury represented the Frohman theatre trust, it was impossible for her to be impartial in her dealings with him. Despite Mansfield's arguments, Shaw remained Miss Marbury's client, an undated note from him (*circa* 1894–95) assuring her that she was looking after his interests quite satisfactorily:

"Rapacious Elisabeth Marbury

"What do you want me to make a fortune for? Don't you know that the draft you sent me will permit me to live and preach Socialism for six months? The next time you have so large an amount to remit, please send it to me by instalments, or you will put me to the inconvenience of having a bank account.

"What do you mean by giving me advice about writing a play with a view to the box office receipts? I shall continue writing just as I do now for the next ten years. After that we can wallow in the gold poured at our feet by a dramatically regenerated public" [X/116].

Charles Frohman (1860–1915) and his brother Daniel (1851–1940) were American theatrical managers. Charles, known as "the Napoleon of the Drama," developed the Empire Stock Company (whose stars included Maude Adams, Julia Marlowe, and William Faversham). The leading figure in the group of managers known as the Theatrical Syndicate, he produced plays in New York and London by the leading dramatists of the day until his death in the *Lusitania* disaster. His Shaw productions included *Captain Brassbound's Conversion* (New York, 1907) and *Misalliance* (London, 1910).

Samuel French (1818–98), founder of the American play publishing company which bears his name, and who had bought out the firm of Thomas Hales Lacy in 1872 to create a London branch, served as agent for many dramatists, particularly in the handling of amateur rights. Shaw, who considered French's agency charges exorbitant, agitated against the firm in the Society of Authors for many years (Shaw's correspondence with the Society of Authors concerning French's fees will be supplemented in Vol. II, by a rebuttal provided by Mr Cyril W. Hogg, a member of the British firm of Samuel French from 1901).

A. C. Gunter's *Prince Karl* and T. R. Sullivan's adaptation of Stevenson's *Dr Jekyll and Mr Hyde* were two of Mansfield's most popular successes.]

My dear Mansfield

Listen, I implore you, to the case for Miss Marbury. I elected her on your nomination; I made her personal acquaintance; I nearly drove

484

her distracted by insisting on a power of attorney of my own devising; I interested her in my peculiar ways; I spent both time and thought on the arrangement; and the result has been entirely satisfactory to me: she has not given me the faintest cause for complaint. I knew all along that if I required her assistance in negotiating with the Frohmanns, I could have it; but she never pressed this on me in any way; and she played a scrupulously fair hand in respect to you, taking pains to assure me that you had done everything that could be done for the play; that the way in which you scored every point in the part was extraordinary; and that you were sacrificing better paying business to give it its utmost chance as far as you were free to do so. In London last year, everyone said, "Why didn't you give the play to Frohmann: *he* would have run it for three months &c. &c." if she had wanted to roll his log. But no hint of the kind dropped from her. So far, since if I am to be loyally served, I must stick by my agent as I expect her to stick by me, I must not throw her over. It is all very well for you to be Napoleonically capricious; but I am not Napoleon. I am only Richelieu.

On the other hand, you do not feel sure that she does not let the Frohmanns see plays addressed to you in her care. But could you feel safe in this respect with any agent? I should not. I should never dream of sending a play to you through her or French or anybody else in the business. All agents read plays; talk about them; and (if necessary) shew them; and the way to guard against this is not to change from one agent to another, but to get the plays sent to you direct, and to return them in the same fashion. In my case, however, the danger does not arise. I always make my own contracts and deal direct with managers. An agent's commission would be sheer loss to me. Very likely if I were to send Miss Marbury *The Philanderer*, she would offer to get me a contract from Frohmann on terms pecuniarily better in some immediate respects than you can offer with due regard to Prince Karl, Jekyll-Hyde and the rest of Bluntschli's rivals—including, of course, a substantial advance on which she would take a handsome commission. If she didn't, I should begin to doubt her business ability. But I don't propose to let her into the transaction at all. I shall send the play straight to you; and you can read it for your amusement. If it strikes you as worth producing in New York, we can settle together as we did about *Arms and The Man*. This limits Miss Marbury to her business of relieving you of the trouble of remitting me my royalties, and of getting me good exchange. She does this very well; and I know her, whereas I don't know French, in whose moral superiority I don't in the least believe, especially as he is old-established. You know what they are, all of them. Besides, if you don't like *The Philanderer*, which I think extremely probable, it would suit me very well to have the fact of its existence known to Frohmann. So by all means continue to send the supplies through her. On other points we shall deal without intermediaries.

Now let me ask you whether you can play a boy of eighteen—a strange creature—a poet—a bundle of nerves—a genius—and a rattling good part. The actor-managers here can't get down to the age. The play, which is called *Candida*, is the most fascinating work in the world—my latest—in three acts, one cheap scene, and with six characters. The woman's part divides the interest and the necessary genius with the poet's. There are only two people in the world possible for it: Janet Achurch, for whom it was written, and Mrs Kendal. If Janet creates it here, will you pay her fare out and back and give her 300 dollars a week or so for the sake of covering yourself with new and strange fascinations as the poet? By the way, there's probably money in the piece; but it's a charming work of art; and the money would fly somehow.

The Philanderer is a dangerous play with a clever but ignominious leading part. The leading woman, also ignominious, must be beautiful, passionate, and a perfect terror in the way of temper. Unless there has been plenty of chatter in New York about Ibsen, "the new woman" &c, the play, which is highly topical on these points, won't do there. In any case I gravely doubt whether it will be of any use to you.

You are aware of course that a play must not be produced in America unless it has been copyrighted by a performance here.

I write in haste, overwhelmed with political work. England is becoming worse than America in the matter of local elections. I am afraid there is no chance of my getting across the Atlantic this year. If you Philander, you will have to divine the handling of the play.

The blessed American Post Office lately sent me back a letter I sent you about one or two little matters in the text of Arms and The Man. Not finding you at your former address in New York, they simply returned it as "not known." Just imagine the English P.O. returning a letter addressed to Henry Irving as "not known"!

yours sincerely
G. Bernard Shaw

P.S. Since "Candida" is such a cheap and simple play, why not fly over here in the thick of the season; take a theatre for half a dozen matinées; play the poet to Janet's Candida; set all London talking & wondering; & disappear in a flash of blue fire? That would be immensely in character.

486

To JULES MAGNY

29 Fitzroy Square W

[C/4]   25th February 1895

[Magny was translating Shaw's "The Economic Basis of Socialism," the first essay in *Fabian Essays in Socialism*.]

Dear Magny

You must translate "shadow grasping" literally, I suppose. It comes from the fable of the dog with the piece of meat in his mouth. He saw his own image in the water; grabbed at the reflection of his piece of meat; & of course lost the reality.

"On the make" is slang for having an interested motive—wanting to make money.

I dont know whether aristocratie foncière is the same as county family. I should think it is. The county families are the families of the landed gentry, squires, lords of the manor, justices of the peace, masters of hounds &c &c.

I will send you Widowers' Houses in a day or two. I want to read it through again to see whether there is anything to correct.

GBS

To RICHARD MANSFIELD

29 Fitzroy Square W

[A/21; X/116]   27th February 1895

[Although Mansfield seriously considered *The Philanderer* for production, he was not completely satisfied with the play. "It is an extraordinary thing," he informed William Winter (1836–1917), dramatic critic of the New York *Tribune*; "it turns Ibsen inside out, and the spectacle, as a result, is not a pleasant or agreeable one" (Winter, *Life and Art of Richard Mansfield*, 1910). When his brother Felix urged him to accept *Candida* instead, he dropped the earlier play and turned his attention to the new one, though he had not yet received a copy of the manuscript. In his reply (dated 15th February, which is obviously an error) to Shaw's letter of 22nd February, he stated: "I should *very* much like to see 'Candida'—may I? I still play youths of 18. The only trouble is I look too young for the part" (BM).]

My dear Mansfield

I send by this mail prompt copy of The Philanderer, addressed, like this letter, to Wells, Fargo & Co. I have gone through it, and corrected it. You will find the stage business sufficiently full to enable you to get

487

into order at the first rehearsal—it always saves fully three wasted rehearsals to have a fully worked out plan to begin from, whether it is adhered to in every detail subsequently or not. If you dont like the play, wire me at once the single word "declined" so that I may be saved the trouble of the copyrighting performance here. I am relying on your date of Easter Monday as the first American performance.

The company must be very metropolitan and presentable if the play is to succeed. And the play is the doubtful point: if it succeeds, the parts can't fail. The man who plays Craven must be a handsome, genial old boy of whom the public are thoroughly fond. Julia must be full of passion & beauty. Paramore must be rather rigid and well conducted—a model conventional leading man. Cuthbertson is a caricature of Clement Scott, whose double you must have somewhere on the New York press. Charteris must be played by you—by YOU, Richard Mansfield, not Lancelot nor another—else the contract's off. The atmosphere must be well dressed, easy, refined: you must pamper the company and not bully them.

In hot haste for post
G. Bernard Shaw

P.S. I'll send on contract & so forth presently.

To CHARLES CHARRINGTON

[T/1 (B/4); X/136.e]

29 Fitzroy Square W
1st March 1895

[Shaw's obituary attack on the licenser of plays, E.F.S.Pigott, who had died on 23rd February, appeared in the *Saturday Review* on 2nd March, captioned "Down with the Censorship!" The same issue contained his unsigned leader, "To-Day's Warfare," on the County Council elections. At the Humanitarian League conference on 1st March, Shaw participated in discussions of "Slaughter House Reform" and "Cruel Sports."

Yorke Stephens (1860–1937) created the rôle of Bluntschli in *Arms and the Man* at the Avenue Theatre in 1894. As his plan to go into management at this time proved abortive, *The Philanderer* was shelved, and had to wait ten years for its first professional performance. Shaw had forgotten that he had once chosen E.W.Gardiner as a possibility for Harry Trench in *Widowers' Houses* (see letter of 4th October 1887 to Archer). Bernard Gould was the stage name of the *Punch* caricaturist Sir Bernard Partridge (1861–1945), who was the original Sergius in *Arms and the Man*. Edward Rose (1849–1904), an actor and dramatist, adapted *The Prisoner of Zenda* and other

adventure novels for the stage. *The Woman Who Did* (1895), a novel by
Grant Allen which attacked the double standard of morality, was castigated
by the critics as being sexually scandalous.]

I could not answer your letter before, because I have had to work
until I became sick—positively and literally sick—this week. I have
replied to Clement Scott's article on Pigott last Monday, wherein he
called me a liar ("allegations that are as coarse as they are untrue") by
the most abusive article ever written on a recently dead man, finishing
up with as inhuman an onslaught as was ever made on a living one of
Clement's weight. Also I have written an elaborate article on the County
Council election. Further, I have gone all over the stage business and
dialogue of The Philanderer, corrected numerous and fearful errors in
the prompt copy, and sent it off in time to catch Thursday's boat at
Queenstown for New York, where it is to be produced by Mansfield on
Easter Monday. This was in pursuance of wild telegrams from that
eminent actor. Having achieved these feats since Monday, I went and
delivered speeches at the Humanitarian Conference; partook of a
dinner with the Humanitarians, made another speech; went home with
Olivier and a violent headache; got sick as aforesaid; and crawled off
this morning to apply my favorite remedy, the excavation of another
tooth. To sit in an easy chair, hypnotised by keeping my mouth wide
open, and soothed by the buzzing of the drill as it flies round inside my
tooth, all the time watching another man working hard, is extraordinarily restful to me. I think it is because the yielding up of oneself
utterly to be operated on by another instead of operating on the minds
of others produces such a complete change of attitude and suspension
of the overworked faculty, that I feel the greatest regret now that the
dentist [Dr W. J. McDonald] says I am for the present in perfect
repair.

There is a new theatrical project in the air to which to you in dreadful secrecy impart I will. Yorke Stephens, Kate Rorke, and E.W.
Gardiner (whoever he may be) want to go into management. If they can
get the Vaudeville, that is what Kate would prefer. And they make an
excellent start by asking me whether I cannot give them a play. Naturally I reply that I have the very thing for them in the Philanderer,
which Yorke Stephens may as well add to Bluntschli as one of his crea-
tions. But of course they want another play or two in hand before they
plunge. Yorke is taking the Philanderer down to Brighton over Sunday
to read it there; and if he approves, I shall probably have to read it to
the trio next week. Shall I, in that case, mention that Mrs Daintry
is in stock? Kate Rorke would play it very well; and as Y.S. is bent on

finding a part for Gould, there is your middle aged sentimentalist fitted to the life.

Rose writes to me that there has been a flagrant case of a refusal of a license by the Lord Chamberlain this week.

I am told, not at first hand though, that the capital which the mysterious backer [Annie Horniman] of "Arms and The Man" proposes to put down four years hence is no less than quarter of a million. We had better all spend the interim in writing plays with magnificent leading parts for Miss F.F.

Permit me to remark that you produce the greatest mental confusion by answering letters addressed to your talented wife as if they were addressed to yourself in the course of a grave disquisition on art. I object to have my gibes served up cold as general propositions. However, I find your criticism very interesting (as might be expected, you have as great a craze for criticism as I have for acting).

I have not often formulated the lessons of my apprenticeship as a writer; but I did once write down in a notebook something like this: *You cannot be an artist until you have contracted yourself within the limits of your art*. Now the effect the artist produces on others is that of unlimitedness; and it is this great mystery and infinitude which attracts us all to art at first in these days. But when you get to practice an art you find that the unlimited length before you is of exactly the same nature as the unlimited length before a horse in a circus. You start at the north end of the ring, and with immense galloping and jumping of hurdles you get to the south side. Call the north end Giotto; then the east end is Michel Angelo, beyond whom the course seems to stretch into the vastest eternity, exploring which, with your back turned on Giotto, for whose little childish art you have an inconceivable contempt (which you had already acquired, perhaps, north east at Lippi and Botticelli) you push ahead, to find yourself presently in such a damnable bog of blathering unreality and manual clumsiness that you are glad to bear north again and come back PreRaphaelitically to Giotto again. And it is the same from Chaucer to Shakespear and on to Pope and back again in a hurry to Morris; or from Palestrina and the old contrapuntists to Beethoven and Berlioz and back in a hurry to the absolute music of Brahms, or a thousand other routes which it would take too much reflection to construct accurately. I have worked critically over quite enough of them to have formed an estimate of the merits, from the point of view of my own feeling of course, of the various points of the circle. I have my feeling for the exquisitely cultivated sense of beauty— an almost devotional sense—and the great pains and skill of execution

490

which produces work of one kind, and for the bold ideas, the daring unscrupulous handling, the imaginative illusions that produce another kind. And I have a leaning towards the former that you dont sympathise with, although some bit of work resulting from it may here and there captivate you. I prefer a woman knitting to Ajax fighting the sheep, because I know that although very little will come of the knitting, nothing will come of the fighting. So do you, in acting, because you know all about the histrionic Ajax, but in literature you still have a notion that there is a future for Ajax, and that I am opposing my limitations to his infinity. I assure you he can't get out of the ring any more than I can; and as to your crowds, they are very fine things; in [Rossini's] William Tell and [Wagner's] Rienzi you have very stirring dramas of the crowd: Hauptmann's "Weavers" also suggests good business in that direction: but when you see a man like me, trying to do fine counterpoint in even so few as three real parts, as in Candida, or in seven, as in the finale of The Philanderer, never tell him he ought to go and write choruses instead. I grant you the work is not so skilful as if I had been more years at it; but there is no more worthy sort of work to try for. It is as good as I can get it at my present stage; and therefore I dont say, like Janet, "This is all wrong," because if I could see that it was all wrong, I should muddle at it until I got it right, or else get round the difficulty on some other tack; and as to saying "I dont know anything about this" I never hear Janet say it without a lively impulse to take the poker to her, or at least swear. Just listen to her when she talks about acting. She cites her own work; she stands over it; she is as self-confident as you please. She goes on, in fact, exactly as I do about writing. Why? Because she has been doing every day for years and years on the stage what I have been doing every day for years and years with my pen. It is astonishing what work she does with the pen under these circumstances; but her inexperience comes out in the parts she is not interested in much herself. She does not get work enough on to them: she has not accumulated and intensified the habit of finishing literary work all over. It is really to revive her own flagging interest at certain places that she drags in these sketches, which are mostly sketches of mere peculiarities, or of a theoretic person like the Wilde who makes notes on his shirtcuffs (as if A Woman of No Importance would be produced in any such silly way) without the solid detail of humanity underneath which you find in Polonius. Janet would have done only the fussy, funny part of Polonius: she would never have taken the trouble to have put in all those sides of him—the father of his daughter, the father of his son, the master of his servant, the shrewd old man of the world, which round him off so wonderfully. You must let me schoolmaster Janet in my unsympathetic way, however it may wring your heart, because you are a very unfit person to educate her. You are rather like Hedda Gabler in respect of your having discovered so much of what was shoved down your throat as virtue to be a fraud, that you idealise the repudiation of the seven deadly virtues. Now in art this does not do. You must plod away diligently in the station of life to which your vocation has called you, making the work always as good as you can, turning methodically from the fine sentence of which you have corrected the grammar to the punctuation of the next, like the ant or the bee or the good boy, or any other disgusting character in books for the edification of youth. In fact, you must conquer the domain of virtue before you make the devil a present of it; and it is as the family chaplain that I am going to be useful to Janet, who has many shocking little vices which must be cast out with prayer and fasting before she attains to perfect literary freedom. But indeed I shall, I think, always disparage her writing, since at the bottom of my soul I dont believe in any mortal achieving excellence in two arts with unrelated techniques. I should like her to attain the possible limit of perfection as an actress, and then to write her own life. Writing plays is all very well as an amusement whilst she is disengaged; but I am not sure that if I were she, I would not spend my time in working over Shakespear and all the drama I could lay hands on, and copy out the parts with stage business, inventing the action and practising the vocal effects. I am always afraid that she will miss the summit of her art through her not having had my inestimable advantage of having no facility, being very awkward and self conscious, and above all, being ugly, uninteresting and unpresentable. I got nothing for nothing; had to slave and plod for bare life to make myself at all current; and the result is the brilliant red-bearded creature you now see. Nature gave Janet a success half ready made, and enabled her to do things with impunity for which I should, so to speak, have been pelted from the stage and sacked next morning. I want a revival of the art of beautiful acting; and I know it to be impossible without tremendous practice and constant aiming at beauty of execution, not through a mechanical study of poses and pronunciations (though every actor should be a plastic and phonetic expert), but through a cultivation of delicate feeling, and absolute renunciation of all the coarser elements of popularity. And I must lay my plays out for that. You have no idea, I believe, of the limitations under which I write, the constant search for the right sort of distinction, whether of style, or thought, or humor, or vulgarity—how very nicely I have to ascertain

492

the truth in order that I may find the true error with such precision as to make it appear that it was the first thing that came into the head of the character into whose mouth I put it. Of course that is no more than my business; and you are quite right to take it for granted, and proceed to grumble at what I have *not* done; but it is none the less indispensable; and Janet must not be encouraged to skip over it in her literary efforts. It produces undistinguished bits in her work underneath that natural charm of dialogue which sometimes gives it so pretty an air.

You may depend on it, I will get my plays performed all I can, whatever I may say to Wyndham in another connection. Also, I will let emotion and passion have all the play I can in my characters. But you must recollect that there is distinction even in emotion and passion; and that the finer kinds will not run through the wellworn channels of speech. They make new intellectual speech channels; and for some time these will necessarily appear so strange and artificial that it will be supposed that they are incapable of conveying emotion. They said for many years, remember, that Wagner's endless melody was nothing but discord.

GBS

P.S. I will bring along "The Woman Who Did" presently. It is an amusingly boyish book.

To JANET ACHURCH

29 Fitzroy Square W
[T/1 (C/4)]   3rd March 1895
[Shaw lectured on 3rd March to the Camberwell Branch of the S.D.F. on "The Fabian Society," and on 4th March to a Hampstead social group known as The Argosy.]

I learn that you and Miss Charrington honored me with a call on Saturday. You should have gone to New Cross Road, where, in a dismantled shop without a fire, and with the light of heaven obscured by election bills, you would have found me shivering in charge of one of Webb's committee rooms. The election has been a most almighty smash. I am glad it is over. On Tuesday or Wednesday perhaps, I will repair to Overstrand and tell you the news, if there be any to tell. I have just done the wretched hour of lecturing & arguing in a little den full of tobacco smoke in Camberwell; and I have to lecture tomorrow in polite society in Hampstead; but after that I hope to have a few evenings free. You seem to have got on capitally with Beatrice Webb.

GBS

493

To RICHARD MANSFIELD

29 Fitzroy Square W

[B.t/21; X/141.e]   9th March 1895

[Mansfield had hired Janet Achurch, at a salary of $250 a week, to play
Candida. She sailed for New York on 16th March, accompanied by a young
Scandinavian actor, Albert Gran, who had been discovered by Felix
Mansfield. Gran later appeared in Mrs Patrick Campbell's revival of
Sudermann's *Magda* (1900) and in several of the Stage Society's productions.
T. W. Robertson's *Caste*, first produced in 1867, had been revived in February
1894 by Forbes-Robertson.]

My dear Mansfield

I am somewhat horrified to learn, from the American news in this
day's Era, that Mrs Mansfield has been hurt. I hope it is nothing permanently serious.

I write in great haste to catch the post. Felix, whose hair grew greyer
and greyer at each successive telegram, and is now white as snow, has
secured Miss Achurch and will start with her for New York this day
week. It is a good move, because the real reason why she got so little
to do here was that our actor managers have a not unnatural reluctance
to be played off their own stages by their leading ladies. You will not
be in any danger of that; and she will be immensely helped by having to
stand up to real acting.

I am working away as hard as I can at the stage business of Candida.
I will get the parts copied out here if there is time as well as the script;
so that there may not be a moment's delay in getting to work at the
other side. Meanwhile I had better tell you what you will want for the
play. There are six parts only. One of them is an old man, vulgar, like
Eccles in Caste, only not a drunken waster, but a comfortably well off
vestryman who has made money in trade. He must be a genuinely funny
low comedian, able to talk vulgar English—drop his Hs and so forth.
And he must be really a middleaged or elderly man and not a young man
made up old, which is one of the most depressing things known to the
stage. Then there is a young woman of the standing of a female clerk,
rather a little spitfire, a bit common, but with some comic force and a
touch of feeling when needed. She must not be slowtongued: the part
requires smart, pert utterance. If you know any pair who could play
Eccles and Polly Eccles thoroughly well, you may engage them straight
off for Candida. Then there is a curate. Any solemn young walking
gentleman who can speak well will do for him. The other three parts
are, yourself, Janet, and your leading man, who must be equal to a very

494

strong part which would be the star part if there were not the other part to relegate it to important utility. The character is a strong, genial clergyman (Candida's husband) with much weight and popular force of style. I have not seen the Scandinavian whom Felix is bringing out; so cannot say whether he looks likely to suit the part.

I must break off: it is post hour. There will be plenty of time to arrange the dresses and the one scene, which presents no difficulty. The Philanderer must now wait: it would be madness to produce it before *Candida*. I will keep Candida for you in London, and am quite disposed to hold over other plays for you if you can arrange to conquer the two worlds within a reasonable time. More of that afterwards.

G.B.S.

To JANET ACHURCH

[T/1 (A/4)]
29 Fitzroy Square W
12th March 1895

[Ethel Dickens (1864–1936), a granddaughter of Charles Dickens, operated a typewriting service in Tavistock Street. The play at the Strand was F. W. Sidney's farce *A Loving Legacy*, which Shaw did not trouble to review. Despite his avowed intention to "shirk" the Fabian committee meeting on the 13th, he managed to attend before proceeding to the Garrick Theatre for the opening of Pinero's *The Notorious Mrs Ebbsmith*, which proved to be one of Mrs Patrick Campbell's greatest successes. Shaw reviewed it in the *Saturday Review* on 16th March.]

I found myself totally unable to write my political article today, but fortunately not unable to take things just a little easy. In the evening I got the promised prompt copies from Miss Dickens. On glancing through them I find that they need careful correction; and this I have been unable to give them tonight, as I have had to go first to a meeting & then to the Strand theatre, which has replunged me into my wrecked condition. So instead of sitting up all night & destroying myself I shall go to bed & send you this letter instead of the play as promised. I have written to cry off the political article; and I intend to shirk the Fabian committee, and so leave tomorrow with nothing to be done but overhaul the prompt copy for you thoroughly, go down to Miss Dickens's to fetch the other copies & the parts, and go to the Garrick in the evening. If you would like to call here any time after or before your visit to the lady who is going to the dentist, you will find me much in the condition of Bluntschli in the first act of Arms & The Man. I shall go out to get much lunch & to call at Miss Dickens's (who won't be ready for me until late in the afternoon) but I could make a point of getting back here about five. However, I do not want to drag you up here unless it would be more convenient for you to put in the time between your appointment & the Criterion in town than return to Battersea. If you dont come, I shall send the prompt copy by post—indeed I shall do that anyhow to save you the trouble of carrying it. On Thursday I shall precipitate myself on the Saturday article on "Mrs Ebbsmith"; and if I can get it finished early enough, I will go right on to Overstrand (with your permission) as Olivier, whom I met tonight, has asked me to be present at the reading of his play.

I detail my woes because I am in extreme need of being petted. I am the most frightened, discouraged, impotent creature at present in England. But I shall get into bed before half past twelve for once; and in the morning I shall be on my way back to the most insolent self sufficiency. Goodnight.

GBS

To CLEMENT SCOTT

[G.u/2]

29 Fitzroy Square W
12th March 1895

[After accusing Scott, in his *Saturday Review* article of 2nd March, of having written the obituary notice of the late censor, Pigott, in the *Daily Telegraph*, Shaw discovered that the notice actually had been written by Lionel Monckton (1862–1924), musical critic of the newspaper and, later, composer of *The Arcadians* (1909) and *The Quaker Girl* (1910). Shaw's graceful retraction appeared in his article of 16th March.]

Dear Mr Scott

What I am prepared to do, naturally, is to climb down in the Saturday, though I wish I could do it so as to drop heavily on Lionel Monckton's best hat, the villain. I will not add any expression of regret to you privately because I am quite the reverse of sorry to learn that the assault against which I defended myself does not come from you. Not that it was anything to complain of or to bear malice about; but it was distinctly a sort of challenge to fight on the question, and one which I could not very well refuse to take up, considering the influence of the Daily Telegraph and my own very strong feeling that the Censorship is a political abuse of the most mischievous kind.

496

I confess I took into consideration when I wrote the article, the possibility that you had not written it, because I knew that you were, or had very recently been, at Hyères; and I also knew that Monckton had acquired an extraordinary virtuosity in imitating your work. In this instance, he appears to have gone a step further, and to have actually written in your character, assuming not only your style, but your opinions on the censorship, and even your experience as a playgoer and an adapter. I went carefully through your evidence before the royal commission before I wrote my article; and, on the whole, it seemed to me that it was better to assume that you, as dramatic critic of the paper, were responsible, than to adopt the formula of "a writer in the Daily Telegraph," as everybody would have concluded that you were the writer in question, and you would have had no opportunity of disclaiming. The notice really carried all the weight of your signature. I therefore shuffle all the blame on the shoulders of anonymous journalism and the tendency of younger writers to copy their favorite masters' styles. I only wish you would carry your disclaimer to the length of allowing me to cite you as an ally in my campaign on behalf of the freedom of the drama.

Why do you not insist on the Daily Telegraph attaching your initials to all your notices without exception? If I have broken down the Saturday Review superstition on that point by the simple process of saying "No signature, no Shaw" you, in your much stronger position, might give the ultimatum of "No signature, no Scott." There are so many young lions who can write my own style better than I can, that mere self preservation drives me to limit my responsibility to my own sins. And what will you say when you find the recording angel debiting you with Monckton's account?

You will find a reference to the matter in next Saturday's Saturday, though "The Obnoxious Mrs Ebbsmith" will probably prevent me from giving as much space to the subject as I perhaps ought.

yours very truly
[G. Bernard Shaw]

To RICHARD MANSFIELD

[B/21; X/141.e]

29 Fitzroy Square W
16th March 1895

[Kate Phillips (1856–1931), who was at one time a member of Irving's company, was currently appearing in a revival of Grundy's *Sowing the Wind*. Mrs (later Lady) Bancroft was Marie Wilton (1839–1921), wife of the actor-manager Sir Squire Bancroft (1841–1926). She had returned to the stage in 1893, after several years of retirement, to appear in a revival of B. C. Stephenson and Clement Scott's *Diplomacy*.]

My dear Mansfield

I have seen them off; and though on my return here I tumbled on my bed and slept like an exhausted dog for an hour, I am still too shaky to work this machine rationally. I see brick color with one eye and a blueish orange with the other. They all snivelled at the station. Janet was so affected that she did not know what she was doing, and took an affectionate farewell of Felix under the impression that he was Charrington, who, on his part, lifted Gran in his arms and kissed him in the full persuasion that he was little Nora. She, poor infant, was with great difficulty coaxed up to crying point, Felix having inconsiderately given her emotions the wrong turn by presenting her with a colossal box of Bluntschli's speciality. Your nephew Alfred, scorning such weakness, vanished before the train did; and I revelled in the callousness induced by having had all the softer feelings worked out of me.

Felix, in addition to my blessing, which is probably not copyrightable in America, has the full score of Candida and the band parts (all except the first violin, which Janet took to study on the way, and which she will no doubt lose), conscientiously read through and corrected by me—a labor which will leave its marks on my constitution until the last trumpet. It has been impossible for me to send out the contract with them: it must wait until next week. Terms, practically the same as before, except for a stipulation about the cast to secure to Janet the vested interest in the part which I promised her during its gestation. The understanding is that if it succeeds in New York, I am to hold the London rights for you for, say, a year, on the New York terms. However, I shall make fresh demands for London as to the cast. Unless you manage to get a very unlikely supply of talent for the New York production, it will be better for us all to cast the piece here strongly from the London point of view: that is, with some well known leading man (Waring, for instance) as Morell, Kate Phillips as Prossy (unless Mrs Bancroft would like to try it), and a popular low comedian as Burgess. I saw Gran this

498

morning at the station, and was very favorably impressed by him; but he is too young, and not English enough, to play Morell here. The question of age is quite exceptionally important in this instance. You may, by sheer skill, succeed in making yourself appear a boy of eighteen in contrast to a man of your own real age; but beside a man of half your age made up for double that figure, the artificiality would be terrible. Gran has the pleasant frank style, and something of the physique for the part; and if he can hide his accent, his foreignness would not matter in New York, where the Church of England parson is an unknown quantity; so that I should not at all demur if you thought, after reckoning him up, that he would do Morell for you at the 5th Avenue [Theatre] as well as the best other man available; but for this country Morell must be ultra-home made.

If you find at rehearsal that any of the lines cannot be made to go, sack the whole company at once and get in others. I have tested every line of it in my readings of the play; and there is a way of making every bit of it worth doing. There are no points: the entire work is one sustained point from beginning to end.

In some respects I want my stage management and business stuck to with tolerable closeness. For instance, in the second act there are certain places where you must efface yourself whilst Burgess and Morell are spreading themselves. This is essential to the effect of your breaking in again. I have put you on a chair with your back to the audience during the first of these intervals; and I urge you not to alter this, as I have very slender faith in your powers of self suppression (I don't question your goodwill) if the audience can see what in my present shattered condition you will perhaps excuse me for calling your mug. Later on, though you have hardly anything to say except the flash "That's brave: that's beautiful," it is important that your face should be seen. The passage where you put your hand on your heart with a sympathetic sense of the stab Morell has suffered is cribbed from Wagner's *Parsifal*.

If the play is not successful, fatten Janet, engage a Living Skeleton, buy a drum, and take to the road.

If it is successful, play Oswald in Ibsen's "Ghosts." Try Lovborg in Hedda Gabler anyhow: nobody has ever touched the part here; and Janet would be a perfect Hedda.

I can no more. I hope Mrs Mansfield has quite recovered from her shaking.

By the way, unless there is a great Bernard Shaw catch-on over Candida, as to the likelihood of which I am rather sceptical, the

Philanderer had better lie quiet for a while. What a part Julia would be for Mrs Patrick Campbell, with Hare as the Colonel!

Compliments to the expatriated. My next play will be called Arabia Felix (name of the heroine) in compliment to your brother.

Miss Marbury says that the grave holds no secrets deeper than those of the returns entrusted to her.

yours—wrecked

G. Bernard Shaw

P.S. I asked you long ago whether you had any Bluntschli photographs. If you have, send me one, and let me have your New York address.

To WILLIAM ARCHER

29 Fitzroy Square W

18th March 1895

[B.t/2]

[Dick Phenyl, a barrister, is a leading character in Pinero's comedy *Sweet Lavender* (1888). *The Hobby Horse*, also by Pinero, was produced in 1886. Eustace D. Hartley (d. 1897) and his wife Margaret were Fabians.]

The "division of wealth" passage is all right. If only he [Ibsen?] had used the word "distribution" he would have cleared the reef.

I am greatly dissatisfied with my article on the play. I was in the middle of the worry and overwork thrown on me by the necessity of getting *Candida* ready for the boat on Saturday, with the parts all corrected and the full score provided with a minutely detailed plan of the stage action and so on. The production of the play on Wednesday rushed me mercilessly, as the paper has to be ready to catch the foreign mails on Friday afternoon; so that I was quite unable to get into a sympathetic, humane mood, and could only express the—in short, what I did express. However, I should not at all mind seeing Pinero driven back into the comic line. It is in that line alone that he shews the smallest fertility. Mrs Ebbsmith, like the other two would-be serious plays, not only shews awkwardness, constraint, and impotence on its intellectual side, but apparent exhaustion and sterility on its inventive side. All the characters in it bundled together, and squeezed in a wine press, would not produce blood enough to make Dick Phenyl. "The Hobby Horse" is a masterpiece of humor and fancy in comparison. It seems to me that it is only by the frankest abandonment of himself to his real tastes and capacities that he can do anything worth doing now

500

on the stage. But he won't do that, because he is a Jew, with the Jew's passion for fame and effect and the Jew's indifference to the reality of the means by which they are produced. A man who, at Pinero's age and in his position and with his secure bank account, could bring himself to that Bible business, is hopelessly damned. You might as well try to fertilise a mule. We shall have to take these plays of his for exactly what they are, without trying to appeal for better to a will which he simply hasn't got in him. After all, I don't know that I could have done anything more for him than what I did; and that was to alter the words "silly and cowardly" to "less sensible and less courageous."

I think you are wrong about his pioneering. He is, and always has been, a camp follower and not a leader. That sort of man, in his lust for effect, sometimes tries to catch the public imagination by bizarrerie; and since genuinely original and faithful work always strikes the mob at first as bizarre, the real bizarrerie may accidentally help to secure a hearing for the work that is mistaken for bizarrerie. You have of course the champion instance of Meyerbeer (a Jew) leading up in this way to Wagner, who abhorred him and all his works. But I believe myself that the gain is wiped off with a heavy balance to the bad by the loss. Pinero is only cutting the grooves deeper that I wish to lift the drama out of. To the man who is touched and fascinated by Pinero, Shaw will be the merest sand and sawdust, all the more irritating because it would appear so very easy to give my subjects the Pinerotic effect. In the long run, of course, he can do me no harm; but in the meantime I am bound, not to be grateful to him as my John the Baptist, but to let him have his show goodhumoredly whilst it lasts. And in speaking of myself here, I do not mean myself individually, but my school, or rather the school to which I belong, which is the great classic school.

I am going to hear Olivier's play on the 27th at Miss [Emma] Brooke's in Hampstead. Is there any other fixture—at Hartley's, for instance? But you needn't trouble to answer this, as I am sure to hear from Olivier himself.

I suggest that you should reconsider your position concerning Mansfield and Peer Gynt. I have put it into his head that if he succeeds as Eugene he should follow it up with Oswald, and that as nobody has ever made anything in England of Lovborg, he should try his hand at Hedda Gabler with Janet. I still fail to see any better man to back.

G.B.S.

To JANET ACHURCH

29 Fitzroy Square W
[T/1 (B/4)]   20th March 1895

[Herbert Flemming had appeared on 15th March in the Independent Theatre's single performance, at the Opéra Comique, of a translation of J.C.de Vos's *A Man's Love*.]

I see that the mail goes tonight, and that the next one is two days off. Therefore I interrupt my Saturday Review work to send you a hasty line on one or two matters which I forgot to mention to you.

First, and most important, you are, immediately on receipt of this letter, to send for a barber, and have your head shaved absolutely bald. Then get a brown wig, of the natural color of your own hair. Candida with gold hair is improbable; but Candida with artificially gold hair is impossible. Further, you must not be fringy or fluffy. Send to a photograph shop for a picture of some Roman bust—say that of Julia, daughter of Augustus and wife of Agrippa, from the Uffizi in Florence —and take that as your model, or rather as your point of departure. You must part your hair in the middle, and be sweet, sensible, comely, dignified, and Madonna like. If you condescend to the vulgarity of being a pretty woman, much less a flashy one (as in that fatal supper scene in Clever Alice which was the true cause of the divine wrath that extinguished you for so long afterwards) you are lost. There are ten indispensable qualities which must underlie all your play: to wit, 1, Dignity, 2, Dignity, 3, Dignity, 4, Dignity, 5, Dignity, 6, Dignity, 7, Dignity, 8, Dignity, 9, Dignity, and 10, Dignity. And the least attempt on your part to be dignified will be utterly fatal.

Observe, Janet Achurch, what you have to do is to play the part. You have not to make a success. New York must notice nothing: it must say "Of course," and go home quietly. If it says "Hooray" then you will be a mere popular actress, a sort of person whom I utterly decline to know. You must confine yourself strictly to your business, and do that punctually and faithfully, undisturbed by any covetings of success for yourself or me or the play. It does not matter whether the play fails or not, or whether you are admired or not: it is sufficient if you gain the respect of the public and your fellow artists, which you cannot fail to do if only you will keep yourself to the point. If Candida does not please the people, then go on to the next play without being disconcerted. This is the way to win the two main things needed: quiet sleep and efficient digestion.

Don't take any *undigested* advice. On any point you are more likely

502

to be right than anyone else once you have considered it. I urge you to go to church once a day at least to tranquillise your nerves. If you feel inclined to cry, go and meditate and *pray*. The religious life is the only one possible for you. Read the gospel of St John and the lives of the saints: they will do everything for you that morphia only pretends to do. Watch and pray and fast and be humbly proud; and all the rest shall be added to you.

Charrington has burst out into an exceeding splendor of raiment, like a bridegroom. He has just been here devising a telegraph code for you. I went to see Flemming at the Independent Theatre after we parted at Waterloo, and have written a long notice of him for the Saturday [23rd March] which will please him and perhaps be of some use to him. He was so amazingly like you in his play that I have serious thoughts of getting him to play Candida at the copyrighting performance, unless I can persuade Ellen Terry, who has just written me a letter about another matter. Tree, writing from Chicago, wants the Philanderer; but no doubt Mansfield has mentioned that to you.

I said something to Charrington about getting Marion Lea to play Prossy; but I did not mean it seriously, as I think that there would be no room for her in a company with you and Mrs Mansfield in it. I mention this as a matter of prudence; for Mansfield is so Napoleonic in his swoops at any suggestion that he is quite capable of telegraphing to her straight off. I shall write to him by the next mail. It is on the verge of six o'clock; so I must break off and make for the post.

Remember—the religious life. No ambition, and no golden hair. I know that you will understand my advice, and take it—for ten minutes or so.

GBS

To JANET ACHURCH

[T/1 (B/4)]

29 Fitzroy Square W
23rd March 1895

[The "religious woman" at the Novelty Theatre on 16th June 1889 was the famous Norwegian concert pianist Agathe Backer-Gröndahl (1847–1907). Shaw's interview with her appeared in *The Star* on 13th July 1889.]

My dear Janet

I have at last got an evening to myself, and a grave mood in which we two must go apart and talk to one another seriously. I am not tired now; and tomorrow, consequently, I shall be restless: this moment comes between the two states. Did you think I was joking in my last letter when I talked about religion? If so, you were wrong. The other day—Thursday—I went down to Richmond and met there, by appointment, F. [Florence Farr], who had written at last rather bitterly about my apparent avoidance of her. We strolled about the park all the afternoon, from seat to seat (she being rather weak with influenza); and I chatted and chatted and she laughed and laughed in her obliging way and we had something to eat at the Swiss café and went to her sister's in Bedford Park by tramtop and I told her all the news and she told me all the news, about her bicycling, and her literary doings, and the quarter million, which she confirmed with aggravating unconcern, as if she were mentioning that her nephew would be ten years old in four years; and she had nothing in the world to say to me, and I had nothing in the world to say to her. Pleasanter company one could not desire— good humored, adaptable, no trouble, easily amused (frightfully easily), beautiful grey eyes and so on. But what is there lacking in her, and in all the other women of her class one meets? Not brains: she is a clever woman. Not knowledge: it is impossible to mention anything she does not know. Not affection: she would respond gratefully enough to any tenderness shewn her. Why, then, the frightful vacuity, the levity, the shallowness, the vulgarity, the pointlessness that makes me wish, in Richmond Park, that I could have half an hour with the trees and the earth and the sky over the Thames Valley, half an hour of comparatively deep communion? It must be that she has no religion. For the really religious people, you will have observed, are not empty. They have dignity, conviction, sobriety and force. However impossibly narrow and stupid the mere articles of their creed may be, it is obvious that they are respectable, efficient, and able to do without happiness. And they can do extraordinary things, from early churchgoing to martyrdom. Presently the race develops a degree of intelligence to which their reverence for the miraculous—their belief in it because it *is* miraculous—is impossible. You then get two sorts of people: irreligious people, whom no amount of culture can make otherwise than worthless, and artists, who find in their art an irresistible motive. But the artists, having to make extraordinary exertions and sacrifices, cannot do it without extraordinary resources. They must have either *recreation*, in the literal sense of that profoundly significant word, or else stimulation. Now recreation is the secret of the religious life—of the old cathedral building. You go in there and pray or meditate, and are profoundly rested and recreated. You do this every day; and you need no

504

stimulants, no meat, no spirits, no enjoyments: you live the heavenly life, and die at a stupendous age, unexhausted in spirit. But you do not lead the heavenly life by abstaining: you abstain because you live the heavenly life. It is not a case of stopping whisky, but a case of beginning manna. Charrington has always been right in seeing that my gospel, regarded as a mere gospel of abstinence, was a false one. You cannot act on beans and water: if nothing better than that is available, you must take to whisky, morphia, and hell fire if no better may be. But there is always religion if you can reach it—the religion of Beethoven's ninth symphony, the religion which rediscovers God in man and the Virgin Mother in every carpenter's wife, which sweeps away miracle and reveals the old dogmas as the depths of which everyday facts are only the surface, which sanctifies all life and substitutes a profound dignity and self-respect for the old materialistic self. This is the most recreative of all religions: with it you can live on half a bean a day, if that is all that your bodily wellbeing requires.

Now I wonder do you think this nonsense? Most women do, except the votaries of the supernatural religions. To them I am a mere atheist; and when I come to the women who have thrown off the old religions, I find myself between the women like F., who has no religion at all, and is therefore hopelessly ineffectual, and the woman who acquires positive force from ambition, greed, jealousy, passion, and all the stimulants. Sometimes there is a relapse into some form of supernatural religion adapted to the stage of intellectual development at which the Bible ceases to appear inspired. Then the stimulants stop; and recreation begins and makes abstinence possible. Mrs Besant the Secularist eats and drinks largely, and becomes stouter and coarser every year. Mrs Besant the Theosophist becomes a teetotaller and vegetarian. Janet Achurch, an ambitious young devil of an actress, meets me at a dinner at the Novelty Theatre. I meet her first on the stairs below, and observe at a glance that she has no soul. I sit next her at dinner and observe further, before ten minutes have passed, that she empties her glass quite thoughtlessly as often as it is filled, and will have drunk too much before the end of the evening. I accordingly tell her at once that I love her, which is nine tenths profane gallantry and only one tenth germ of a truth thereafter to develop; but there is a religious woman in the room, whom I profoundly respect. In the later hours we adjourn to the stage; and the religious woman plays the piano like a great artist, most nobly and beautifully, I being the only person present who knows that all the others, who are great dramatic geniuses, much occupied with their own eminence, can do nothing at all comparable to the lady who plays. She is sober as a judge: Janet is excited: she is quiet and distinguished: Janet is raffish. All this I tell myself pitilessly; for Janet fascinates me. Janet goes off across the world; and I celebrate the Norwegian pianist in critique and interview. Janet fascinates me even in Australia; and I write to her occasionally. My jealous Julia [Jenny Patterson] suspects me, and tells me terrible things—about Flemming, about debts, about champagne. I treat them with derision, and secretly know them to be all true. People have to fight their way through such things: I wonder will Janet. She returns; and I go to the first night of the Doll's House, in which, by this time, I have lost all interest whatsoever as a play. There is Janet, fighting her way through by brute force and stimulants. She succeeds; but Clement Scott makes a curt remark about the stimulants, which remark is in a sense true. There is force, interest, power, badly abused but still power, fascination amid rapidly closing-in ruin; but none of the beauty, the devotion, the dignity with which the Norwegian played Beethoven's concerto in E flat. I sometimes think over the matter coolly, and check my tendency to think that genius *must* beat all abuses, by deliberately recalling many an instance in which stimulants had beaten genius. Finally the millstones catch Janet and grind her remorselessly. I break through the fascination and get to a more human feeling for her. I have been no saint myself—have hunted after one form of happiness occasionally. Janet *recreates* me with an emotion which lifts me high out of that. I become a saint at once and write a drama in which I idealise Janet. I have a horrible fear that if I lecture her, she will detest me; but her soul, which has come to life, or rather awakened from its sleep since the night of the Novelty Theatre, is worth wrestling for; and I do brutal things—put money into her pocket secretly in order purposely to produce a scene with her husband. Janet at last wakes to the emotion under which I have abstained; and for a while she rapidly begins to draw on rich stores of life, becomes beautiful, becomes real, becomes almost saintly, looks at me with eyes that have no glamor of morphia in them, and with an affection that is not hysterical, though in the middle of it all she stabs me to the heart by dyeing her hair a refulgent yellow. The question is, how am I to make Janet religious, so that she may recreate herself and feel no need of stimulants. That is the question that obsesses me.

Now you have my theory brought home to yourself. Now you know what I conceive as wanting for Candida, and what Eugene means when he says, "I no longer desire happiness: life is nobler than that." That is the language of the man recreated by a flash of religion.

It is drawing near post hour—12 midnight on Saturday to catch the

German mail tomorrow morning. Let me hastily add that I have purposely abstained from worrying about your acting. Charrington is so nervous as to your interests that he is almost convinced that if you breathe the way you do at home, it will be an ungraceful trick. But you cannot help yourself by taking care not to do this or that. If only you occupy every moment of the play with Candida, you will not drop into any tricks that do not belong to her. And the time for pupilage is past: you must be left now to your own vigilance and conscience as an artist. Sweep all concern about little tricks and mannerisms away from your mind; and be generous to yourself as well as to the rest—for you must be generous to them, and make their points for them if necessary, since they will all be in much greater danger than you. In short, dearest Janet, be entirely magnanimous and beautiful in your thoughts and never mind the success of the play or of yourself. Believe me, it is not success that lies in our hands—yours or mine. Success is only an aspect that certain results of our work—not the work itself—bear in the eyes of others. Take it quietly and see what will happen.

There is a great deal for you to forgive in this letter. I have rambled into it without intending it: indeed I have quite got away from what I supposed I was going to say when I began.

GBS

To RICHARD MANSFIELD

[B/21; X/129.e]

29 Fitzroy Square W
27th March 1895

[The copyright performance of *Candida* took place at the Theatre Royal, South Shields, on 30th March. The parts were read by members of the *Arms and the Man* touring company, including Lilian M. Revell (who later became A. E. Drinkwater's second wife) as Candida, Drinkwater as Marchbanks, and George Young as Morell. Aurélien-Marie Lugné-Poë (1869–1940), French actor-manager of the Théâtre de L'Œuvre in Paris, staged Maurice Maeterlinck's *Pelléas et Mélisande* (1892), *Rosmersholm* (1893), Wilde's *Salomé* (1895), and *Peer Gynt* (1896). In 1923 he produced *Pygmalion* in Paris, at the Théâtre des Arts. Shaw met Lugné-Poë and Maeterlinck during their London visit in March 1895.]

My dear Mansfield

I wish I had time to write; but I haven't. I hoped to get an interview into "Town Topics" before Easter; but I am afraid I shall not be able to write it. This copyrighting performance (program of which I enclose) with all its attendant arrangements and expenses, and a thousand other things besides my literary work (you haven't the least idea what a lot of it I have to do to earn £6 a week and act as referee by cable in your combats with Janet) has left me without a moment. For Heaven's sake star everybody who wants to be starred. Star the callboy; see that everybody else in the theatre has his name printed in letters three inches longer than your own; bribe the press to interview the entire staff; publish albums of their photographs taken at various periods of their march from the cradle to the grave; polish Janet's boots and cast Mrs Mansfield for old women exclusively; only act and make them act within an inch of their lives. It is good business to star Janet; what is the use of giving a woman fifty pounds a week if you are not going to run her for all she is worth? Star her until she begs you for God's sake not to raise any more expectations. She comes from Manchester: she will grab everything you try to keep from her. Treat her as the Roman soldiers treated the woman who asked for the gold things on their arms: crush her beneath the weight of your shield. Give her everything she dares ask; and make her understand that she has got to prove herself worth it on the 15th April. The performance must come off then: it is all over the press here already; and if it breaks down it will be impossible to avoid explanations. Never mind starring yourself: you are, or ought to be, *hors concours*. I told Janet to offer to be content with a line in diamond type in the bill, and then win her position: if she cannot rise to that, why, have a new fount of type cast for her, six feet high, and paint the town hell color with her name. These follies drive me stark mad: I hereby authorise you to announce her as the authoress of the play, if that will please her.

Lugné-Poë and the Theatre de L'Oeuvre are playing here—Ibsen and Maeterlinck: shabby and misunderstood, but artistically first rate. Man of genius, by the Lord.

No fair play here for you or anyone else. Who wants fair play? London is a fortress in which every man must, as an outsider, batter a breach for himself. Then in, sword in hand. Success, achievement, fruition, is death. Fortunately, they fight you from behind barricades in every street when you have carried the wall; so that there is always an obstacle, and, consequently, an object in life.

All the same, no nonsense this time about an August season. The season is over by the middle of July. Don't be in a hurry: Candida can wait until next year if it proves worth going on with at all. Immer Muth!

In haste
G. Bernard Shaw

508

MISS JANET ACHURCH

BEGS TO ANNOUNCE A

NEW PLAY

WRITTEN EXPRESSLY FOR

MISS JANET ACHURCH

ENTITLED

CANDIDA

CANDIDA ... MISS ACHURCH

SUPPORTED BY
R. MANSFIELD AND OTHERS

DO NOT
MISS JANET ACHURCH

509

P.S. Hand over royalties on Candida to Elisabeth as usual. She has the requisite authority to bind and to loose in the matter of receipts.

P.P.S. I must register a telegraphic address. My neglect to do so has already cost you about five pounds, I am afraid. When I have settled it with the postal authorities I will cable it to Miss Marbury, who will impart it to you.

—Draft Poster—

[See illustration on page 509.]

To JANET ACHURCH

[T/1 (B/4)]

29 Fitzroy Square W
30th March 1895

[The interview for *Town Topics* (New York) was not published. The lyric sung by Shaw to Janet served also as a serenade by the fickle dramatist to Mrs Patrick Campbell (*Saturday Review*, 7th March 1896) and to Ellen Terry (letter of 15th May 1898). It is from an unidentified ballad which was a favourite of Shaw's mother.

In an interview with Janet on 18th May 1895, the *New York Dramatic Mirror* reported: "Mr. Mansfield engaged Miss Achurch for three years at a salary of $250 a week, and it was understood that she was to be given leading roles only. When it came to decide what was a leading role, Miss Achurch found that the contract she had signed gave Mr. Mansfield the power to cast her for parts she did not like. She, therefore, proposed to him to tear up the original contract, and make another, giving her absolute power to refuse any part she did not see fit to play. This new contract was to expire on June 1 of this year, and fifty dollars a week was to come off Miss Achurch's salary. To this proposal Mr. Mansfield assented, and that is why the English actress is going back to London so soon."]

I am sending by this mail an interview to "Town Topics," which they may or may not insert. I am so addled by want of exercise, and ceaseless clatter, clatter, clatter at this machine, that I am incapable of writing anything that has not a hysterical air about it. My Saturday article, which ought to be a specially perfect one—all about Ibsen and the Theatre de l'Oeuvre, with remarks on Miss Robins and Miss Farr and so on—is full of idiotic misprints, which I was too tired to be able to notice in the proof. I have a frightful feeling that my previous letters have been all morbid. However, no matter. The spring is germinating; this mail finishes all I can do with regard to "Candida" in America;

the copyrighting performance is over at last; the Easter holiday is at hand; life rises in me and conscience wanes; and there is animation in my style even as I sing

> But what are vernal joys to me?
> Where thou art not, no spring can be.

I shall never be able to begin a new play until I fall in love with somebody else.

Charrington called yesterday. He said you wouldn't sign a contract, he was sure of that; you would rather not bind yourself. But my own feeling is that you had a stronger interest in getting a contract than Mansfield has in giving it to you. Suppose "Candida," as is probable—more probable than any other event—is a success on the first night, a "*succes d'estime*" for the following fortnight, and then vanishes from the New York stage. Mansfield, in disgust at the whole business, may say that *you* have failed, and that you are not worth the fifty pounds a week. Then you will sail out of his theatre, and make a dash, with your usual energy, at all the other managers, and at possible backers, who will all be sufficiently polite to your beaux yeux to hold out hopes. You will have fifty projects on hand in a fortnight; you will spend every farthing you possess in anticipation of their success, though they will all be utterly unreal and impossible; you will send for Charrington and Nora and pay their passages out with the last farthing you can raise; finally, when the schemes are all obviously bankrupt, you will, by a desperate effort, borrow a thousand dollars, take a theatre, put up the Doll's House, and return in a week to exactly the same position in New York as you were in in London when the doors were closed at Terry's. This means that you will be in a worse position; for one is not allowed to do that sort of thing twice in this world. You may reply that there is *Mrs Daintry*; but I retort that you could not possibly get money enough to give Mrs Daintry a fair chance, and that the mere mention of the play reminds me of how unfit you are to take care of your own interests, since you have given away two thirds of it for nothing.

On the other hand, if you get your two years contract, what will happen then? You will of course stipulate for leading parts (with a reasonable regard for Mrs Mansfield); and you will then be sure of work and fifty pounds a week for two years, during which you can save and look about you with a view to campaigning on your own account afterwards. No doubt two years seems a long time to you, who have been accustomed to start operations in a fortnight; but how have they succeeded? What are you afraid of in the transaction? Is it that Mansfield

511

will not pay you? He must; he cannot exist without considerable property as a theatrical manager; and whilst the property is there, the law can force him to pay your salary. Or is it that he will give you no parts, and prevent you by injunction from playing for anyone else? Do you think people behave that way when it costs them fifty pounds a week?

But you may be dreaming that "Candida" will be such a success that it will place New York at your feet. It won't; and even if it does, it will not place Boston and Chicago and so on at your feet without Mansfield. It will really be a success of the combination of yourself with Mansfield; and it is absolutely impossible for it to justify you in feeling sure that you would maintain your lead without him. You may say that Fröhmann or somebody will say "Come and be my leading lady at a hundred a week." Well, the chance of that contingency is just good enough to enable you to extract a two years contract from Mansfield *now*; but it is not good enough to risk going without a contract for. Besides, it was Mansfield, not Frohmann or another, that gave you your chance; and he is entitled to the full profit of it if it turns out well. And he has "Candida," subject, it is true, to the condition of playing it fifty times a year with you in the title part, but morally entitled, if you go to another manager for purely commercial reasons, to demand the substitution of—say Ellen Terry. What plays have the other managers got that would shew you to the fullest advantage?

All this you must ponder carefully. In telling Mansfield to let you have your own way, I am running the great risk that he will comply, and that your way will be the old ruinous way. The summing up of the case is this. Either you intend to make your career in America as some manager's leading lady, or you intend to make it as your own entrepreneur. Well, you cannot begin the latter at once because you have no money; and you must once for all give up the old plan of throwing your friends' savings into enterprises that are as ill considered as enterprises conducted with other peoples' money usually are. Therefore, you *must* work for a salary for a few years at least. Are you going to let the certainty of a two years engagement at fifty pounds a week (excellent pay) slip through your fingers on the chance of "Candida" being successful enough to bring you a better offer?

That's the question you have to face. I don't advise you one way or the other; I simply take care that the case in favour of a contract shall be put clearly before you. Probably Charrington will put the other side with equal eloquence.

GBS

To JANET ACHURCH

[T/1 (B/4)]
29 Fitzroy Square W
3rd April 1895

I had looked forward to writing you a long letter; but your cable to Charrington saying that Candida is withdrawn has dropped here with explosive force, Charrington being all for an immediate departure as a stowaway on the next liner to New York. However, I shall cable to Mansfield; for he *must* produce "Candida" now, and produce it at once too, or else there will be forty thousand fiends to pay; for the newspaper boom here is immense—two interviews with me this week, paragraphs innumerable, quotations from the passage about you and Ellen Terry in my preface to Archer's book, altogether such an outburst of interest that the fact of the advent of Candida under Mansfield's management with you in the title part is nailed into the public mind. [Clement] Scott ignores it and announces another project of Mansfield's. If there is any failure, he will jump at the chance of alluding to "misleading statements" and so forth; and then woe to those who trifle with me; for the explanations will lose none of their picturesqueness if I have to make them. It will be an advertisement for me and the play in any case, one which may perhaps end, if Mansfield leaves me in the lurch, in the rapid production of "Candida" here, with "The Philanderer" on top of it. When I learn that you are not busy rehearsing with all your might, remorse leaves me.

I forget whether I told you that the clause in the agreement relating to you runs as follows:

"The Manager shall engage Miss Janet Achurch and shall cast her for the title part of Candida at all performances given under this agreement and shall not permit Miss Janet Achurch to perform publicly in America on any occasion prior to her appearance as Candida."

I went to Onslow Square to see Charrington last night (the cablegram came this morning). He seems very comfortable but did not approve of my praising Elizabeth Robins in my Saturday article as much as I did. Cannot make him understand Fabian politics; he wants you to advance as an individual; I want to create the impression that an army is on the march. I don't want him to go over, because he is spoiling for a fight, and will tell you all the things you want to be told, and give you the advice you want to take, whilst I, alas!, shall be playing Candida, the scolding mother, making myself hateful, refusing the money when there is money to be refused, and so on. Wretched lot mine among all you children, with nobody's lap to cry on when I am worried to

513

distraction. If only I could be myself and at the same time be a fool ruining you and myself and everybody else, but making you happy and making things move at the same time. Charrington is right because he *is* a fool, Parsifal the incorrigible, hating what he doesn't like and loving what he likes, fighting the one and grudging it its crust, backing up the other in the teeth of all justice. Oh, million million million millions, how I should like to get one good grip of you and throw you over the next house, across the Atlantic, away irrecoverably into space. For it is you, wretch, you are making all these difficulties, who else can it be? Those who hate you make difficulties for you; and you remove them. *I* remove difficulties from your path; and you make them—pile them up faster than I can hurl them away. No matter: I will best you in the long run; the great Boyg does not fight, he conquers.

Nora has a commodious nursery, plan of which I subjoin. She was watched over by an elderly lady who sat nursing a white cat until Charrington and I went up and relieved guard. Nora declined to take any notice whatever of us; Charrington tried her with a kiss; but she received it without a pretence of interest; she was sufficiently conscious to have opened her eyes to look at me if she had felt the smallest curiosity; but she didn't, which I take to be a sign of healthy devotion to her slumbers. She sleeps in sheets, with a calico cover to her pillow, instead of wool; consequently she lies with her small rosy hand stretched out to the side of the bed, and tosses about occasionally. Her countenance is not yet deeply lined with care; but there was the faintest possible contraction about her brow. This you may possibly attribute to grief for her absent mother; but I am absolutely convinced that it was concern lest she should be disturbed to kiss me.

I must be off now to catch the post and to cable Mansfield. If Charrington has to go I will save him from the horrors of the steerage; but I shall keep him here if possible by suggesting that the money might be better spent, if the worst happens, in bringing you back.

GBS

[Accompanying the letter was a diagram of Nora's nursery, with a note: "In this diagram A indicates photographs of you, most of them bearing marks of having been partially chewed by Nora, at one time or another. Mimi [Janet's sister?] appeared later on, in furs, looking brilliant to the verge of impropriety."]

To JANET ACHURCH

29 Fitzroy Square W
5th April 1895

[T/1 (B/4)]

[The performance of "Living Pictures" at the Palace Theatre, consisting of posed reproductions of art works, came under the attack of the National Vigilance Association. Shaw's *Saturday Review* article of 6th April was a reply to an address by William A. Coote (1842–1919), secretary of the N.V.A. The *New Budget* interview, on 11th April, was "Mr Bernard Shaw and His New Play." The interview in *The Realm*, on 5th April, was "Candida: A Talk with Mr. Bernard Shaw." Harry Jackson (1836–85), actor and stage manager, was well known as a music-hall mimic. Mansfield's "Napoleon show" was Lorimer Stoddard's play *Napoleon Bonaparte* (1894). Israel Zangwill (1864–1926), author and dramatist who specialised in Jewish themes, is best-known for his novel *Children of the Ghetto* (1892). Sir Bertram McKennal (1863–1931), a sculptor, later designed the war memorial at Islington, the tomb of Edward VII at St George's Chapel, Windsor, and the coinage for George V.]

My dear Janet

I have played my last card, and am beaten, as far as I can see, without remedy. I have done what I could; I have scamped none of the work, stinted none of the minutes or sixpences; I have worked the press; I have privately flattered Mansfield and abused you; I have concentrated every force that I could bring to bear to secure you a good show with Candida. Can I do anything more? And how long must I keep my temper with these rotten levers that break in my hands the moment the dead lift comes? It is the distance that has defeated me. If only I were in New York, with one hand on his throat, and the other on the public pulse through the interviewers, I would play him a scene from the life of Wellington that would astonish him. Never has man yet made such a sacrifice for a woman as I am making now in not letting fly at him by this mail. But I have so laid things out to force him for his own credit to keep faith with me, that I cannot be certain that he may not tomorrow realize that he had better do Candida after all. He will get letters of mine that are on their way, and may guess from them that my smile has a Saturday Review set of teeth behind it. He may lose heart over whatever other play he intends to open with. He may receive a visit from an angel in the night warning him that Charrington is on the seas after his scalp. If I fire a shot now that cannot strike him for eight days, it may strike you by upsetting some new arrangement made in the meantime. I am tied hand and foot—not a bad thing for a man in a rage—and can only grind my teeth to you privately. If this were a big mis-

515

fortune I should not mind: if you had dropped all the existing copies of the play accidentally into the Atlantic, it would have wrinkled my brow less than it would have wrinkled the Atlantic: the infuriating thing is that it is an annoyance, and no misfortune at all. I have my play; I have you for the part; I have a huge extra advertisement; I have not a single false step to regret all through. But this only sets my conscience perfectly free to boil over with the impatience of the capable workman who finds a trumpery job spoiled by the breaking of the tool he is using. Besides, my deepest humanity is revolted by his skulking in his throne room and refusing to see you and treat with you as one artist of the first rank with another. The compromise he has made is simply a payment to you to give him the power of preventing you from appearing in New York this season. —But this is waste of time: let me talk sense.

By this mail I write to Miss Marbury, my agent (Empire Theatre Building, 40th St. and Broadway), instructing her to get the script and parts of Candida, and the script of The Philanderer from Mansfield, if he has not changed his mind by the time my letter arrives. I have further instructed her to give the parts to you, and to send me back the script. You will therefore have the set of parts as well as a prompt copy in your possession, in case of need. But as I still think Candida a valuable chance for you, I will not let you throw away the first performance of it except on a thoroughly serious occasion. C.C. starts tonight for Liverpool to join the Cunarder which sails tomorrow. He insists on going as an emigrant; and as there seems to me to be something in his contention that he will be too seasick to care where or how he travels—oh, here he is; and he is not going after all: your cablegram has stopped him. (Pause for conversation.)

· · · · · · · ·

I am just as glad that he is not to spend the next week in unspeakable wretchedness on the sea. Yesterday he said that he would see you, anyhow. You have no doubt noticed that when he is moved, his countenance swells in an alarming manner. It swelled slightly when he said this; and when I remarked, with a quite unintentional coolness and matter-of-factness, "Yes: it will be a relief to her to see you" (meaning that you would have someone else than the maid to tell your troubles to), he echoed the word "Relief!" with a distinct expression of surprise at so gross an understatement of the position. On the whole, I am glad his departure is postponed. Mansfield will escape having his head punched, which is a disappointment; but then you will perhaps manage better on your own judgment. So far, you seem to

516

have made the very best of the situation; and when you shew yourself a capable woman (especially in a matter which I have bungled) the ocean in my heart is moved by a delightful tidal wave. Charrington has shewn me all your letters: at least he has read them to me. He is under the impression that he has only read the business parts, omitting the domestic and sentimental episodes; but in this he is deluded, I think: it all slips out. In return for which I carefully conceal from him what I write, lest he should realise that I have been worrying and blaming and anticipating the worst from you. How infinitely I am repaid for my trouble by my disappointment, oh blessed Janet!

Do you notice that my spirits have gone up? Well, when I began I thought that a very special article I had sent to the Saturday about the "Living Pictures" and the Puritans had been suppressed because no proof had arrived; but the proof came whilst C.C. was here; and my irritable fear of nothing is dispelled.

If you wish to try a last chance, send for the unhappy Felix, and ask him whether he quite realises what it means to make an enemy of me. I send you the New Budget interview; and if I can get the Realm one in time for the mail I will send that too. I have dozens of newspaper notices about the production in New York. I have backed Mansfield for all the booming I am worth, and got him as much advertisement as Pinero's reputation could have brought him—more, in fact, for if the play had been Pinero's, the notices would have been all Pinero and no Mansfield. I have spent money and time without doubt or grudging on the business, backing Mansfield as if he were the Bank of England. I have his letters and his telegrams pledging him to produce the play and play the part. And what I have done I can undo. I can follow up every one of those interviews with another interview on the much more interesting subject of the breakdown. I can explain that Mansfield is all very well in a part like Bluntschli, where he has nothing to do but sit down and score *my* points, or in a variety entertainment borrowed from the music hall repertory of the late Harry Jackson, consisting of imitations of Napoleon, but that when it comes to real drama, in which he has to hold his own against artists of standing from London, he runs away, after trying to induce the artist of whom he is afraid to throw the play over by making insolent and absurd conditions with her. I can refuse to allow him to play Bluntschli in London on the ground that what is good enough for barnstorming in the States is not good enough for a London West End Theatre. I can force him either to play Bluntschli a hundred times a year in America or to give it up altogether. I can, if he dares come here with his Napoleon show and Jekyll and

Hyde rubbish, do him such exact and conscientious justice in the Saturday as he will not love me for. I can make Zangwill and all the other young authors whom he is courting in London fully impressed with a sense of what I got by treating him as an artist and a gentleman. I can, in short, do everything that he would do if he were in my place, including an action for damages.

All this, you will understand, is lowlived nonsense; but if things are still bad when you get this, you may, if you would like to amuse yourself, try the effect of it on Felix's nerves. Tell him that I am very fond of you and a great admirer of yours; and that I am furious at Richard's treatment of you. I don't know whether he has brains enough to see that a man who *can* do all this, and *won't*, is even a less eligible element in his future than a man who could do it and would. Anyhow, ask Felix what he would take to come and ask me for another play, or even to call on me just at present.

And so farewell for the moment. I was to have met the McKennals at Onslow Square last night; but I had to interview Massingham first at the Chronicle office, and so did not arrive until they had departed.

I hope you rescued my last letter from its imaginary destination at the New Copenhagen Hotel.

GBS

To JANET ACHURCH

[T/1 (B/4)]

29 Fitzroy Square W
13th April 1895

I have just come up from Beachy Head, where I am spending Easter week [with the Webbs, Wallas, Charles Trevelyan, and Bertha Newcombe], for one night to see a piece at the Adelphi [*The Girl I Left Behind Me* by Franklyn Fyles and David Belasco]. I find a letter from you waiting for me—the one in which you describe Mansfield's Bluntschli and so on: also his objection to put his head on Candida's knees, which I propose to get over by putting his head beneath Candida's feet presently. I have just ten minutes before post hour to send you a line.

Miss Marbury has, I suppose, told you, as I asked her to, that you can now cable to "Socialist, London," which is my registered address. I have sent you a couple of cables—no, perhaps only one—addressed "Candida, New York"; but C.C. did not tell me to put Via Commercial

518

on it. Anyhow, it was only about the letter which I addressed to the New Copenhagen Hotel instead of New Amsterdam.

C.C. told me the other day that you cabled him about shewing "Candida" to Mrs Kendal [appearing in repertory at Abbey's Theatre, New York]. Ah, if you dare, Janet Achurch, IF YOU DARE. Shew it to whom you please; but part with it to nobody; and remember, no Janet, no Candida. You had better get some intelligent manager to engage you and Esmond and Waring for the winter season to produce the play.

This is a horribly slow method of corresponding: letters are obsolete before they arrive.

At Beachy Head I have been trying to learn the bicycle; and after a desperate struggle, renewed on two successive days, I will do twenty yards and a destructive fall against any professional in England. My God, the stiffness, the blisters, the bruises, the pains in every twisted muscle, the crashes against the chalk road that I have endured—and at my age too. But I shall come like gold from the furnace: I will not be beaten by that hellish machine. When you return, you will be proud of my ability to sit gracefully on a wheel; and you need not trouble about my health.

Oh, the spring, the spring, and Janet miles and miles away.

C.C. telegraphs that he is coming at midnight to see me. He will tell me a lot of news no doubt. I will write again when I get back to Beachy Head.

GBS

To CHARLES CHARRINGTON

[T/1 (A/4)]

Beachy Head Hotel. Eastbourne
16th April 1895

Telegram just received from Mansfield "Am opening Garrick with Arms Man [on 23rd April] will produce Candida if I need not appear." The benevolent object here is to produce the play with a bad cast, and by making it a failure, at one stroke prevent any other manager from getting it and prevent Janet from making a success in New York. I have not yet made up my mind whether to cable, or to leave Miss Marbury to carry out her instructions & get the play from him. Probably I shall cable to her & not to him at all. The effect will be, anyhow, that he may not now produce the play on any terms whatever. Am posting this bit of news to Janet. Back tomorrow evening.

GBS

519

[In reply to a cable from Shaw on 16th April, Mansfield returned the manuscript of *Candida* to Elisabeth Marbury, and wrote to Shaw in extenuation: ". . . I had hoped for a stunning—live work from you. I felt sure you would follow Arms & the Man with a knock out blow—you have—but you've hit the wrong man. My faith was so great that I engaged Miss Achurch on the strength of it—and at a time when I need every farthing I can muster, she has cost me hundreds without making the slightest return.

"You are probably at this moment greatly enraged with me for not being still more obliging and throwing away a thousand or so. (I wish I could.) In a year you will have calmed down. In two years you will have thanked me. I think you owe me a great play" (BM).]

To JANET ACHURCH

[T/1 (B/4)]

29 Fitzroy Square W
19th April 1895

[Henry Lee (1857–1910), an actor and impersonator, was billed as a "Protean artist." A statement in *The Era* on 13th April that Shaw "insists that the lady shall receive £50 a week for her services" led to a reply by Shaw, on 20th April, substantially as indicated here to Janet (and with the same error of a salary of £50 a *month*). Minnie Seligman (1869–1919), an American actress described by the theatre historian C.D. Odell as "ever striving toward a goal she never reached," had appeared in New York in A.C. Gunter's *My Official Wife* and Robert Buchanan's *Lady Gladys*. Shaw's draft of the reply to Mansfield which he quoted to Janet is identical in wording except for substitution of "unchanged" for "where it was" (BM). Acton Davies (1870–1916), youthful dramatic critic of the New York *Evening Sun*, had interviewed Janet (see letter of 30th April to Janet).]

My dear Janet

I came up from Beachy Head on Wednesday (this is Friday); went to the theatre [*Delia Harding* by Comyns Carr, at the Comedy]; worked some fourteen hours or so next day, also including theatre [*The Ladies' Idol* by Arthur Law, at the Vaudeville]; and today have had to correct two important proofs and answer the letters which have at last arrived from the brothers Mansfield, besides a lot of other business. So, as usual, your letter is squeezed into a hurried half hour before the Fabian Executive.

First, I want to put before you the argument about that Comédie Française clause in Mansfield's proposal, because I am afraid that you may throw away some of the advantage of your position by not quite

520

realising its utter absurdity. At the Comédie Française, the artist has a share, a pension, and a status as a member of the most famous theatrical company in the world. Mansfield, in offering you a post in his company as the equivalent of this, was openly trifling with you. In his theatre there is no share, no pension, and no status, since he has not a single classical play in his repertory, and his "Napoleon" belongs to the class of work which Henry Lee is now doing at the Palace Music Hall here ("Great Men, Past and Present"), whilst his "Prince Karl," "Beau Brummel," and the rest are one-man entertainments requiring only the "character acting" which is now falling into disrepute in England as mere entertainer's work. "Arms and The Man" is his only modern play; and the author of that has now withdrawn all his other MSS from Mr Mansfield and positively refuses to permit any other play of his to be produced by him. You need not hit so hard as this except in an emergency; but it is better to let you know the full weight of the weapon in case of need.

A paragraph has been going the rounds here stating that I not only insisted on your being engaged for Candida, but stipulated that you should have 50 pounds a month. I do not usually contradict the mistakes of the press in these matters; but as the inference here would be that the £50 is an artificially high salary given under pressure from me, I have written to the Era pouring vitriol on the blunderer in such a way as to bring out clearly that your salary is a matter of your market value, and that I should no more dream of meddling about it than you presumably would interfere in the matter of my royalties. I also wrote privately to the Weekly Sun man asking him to take some opportunity of contradicting the report. He telegraphs begging for more information. The Era letter will no doubt be in tomorrow's issue.

Yesterday a cablegram came from Richard as follows:—"Since you insist [which I didn't: I positively forbade]* will produce Candida now cable Marbury deliver manuscript." To which I replied, "Withdrawal final." This morning another telegram came, this time from Miss Marbury:—"Will you authorise me to place Candida with good actress Minnie Seligman on terms named £100 advance 5 per cent first £600 7½ per cent next £400 ten above weekly gross reply by wire immediately." Which I did, as follows:—"Paralogize palmitic without Achurch," which, being translated through Lowe's cable code (which you had perhaps better get, as it is useful for American messages, and cannot be confused with the Unicode Latin words) means "Offer declined nothing can be done at present without Achurch." This

* The square brackets are Shaw's.

caused me a heart pang, not because of the hundred pounds, but because of the brutality of calling you Achurch instead of my darling Janet.

By the way, have you added anything to the private code we arranged? I have nothing in mine after VERETRUM.

Now as to the letters from Richard and Felix. It was just as well that Felix wrote; for his letter was written with the sweetest consideration for my feelings towards you, and I was therefore able to read it to Charrington, whereas Richard's, the existence of which I concealed from C.C. in order to avert his rushing out by the next Cunarder and having Richard's blood, was childishly indiscreet in its allusions to you. He accuses you of being fuzzy haired, of purring, of being businesslike, of smoking, of sitting on the floor, of combing your tawny locks with your fingers, of clawing your neck and scratching the air with your chin, and of being unfallable-in-love-with on all these accounts. On the subject of your acting, he maintains an eloquent silence. This, by the way, is much the most sensible part of his letter, which I wish I had time to quote more extensively. The play is not a play—it is all talk— it is lacking in all essential qualities—the stage is not for sermons— the American public would not stand it—and so forth, the whole being intersentenced with the most pathetic expressions of eternal friendship and admiration: for example, "Go on, Shaw: Beatrice and I are with you: you will always be welcome as a brother. We want a great work from you." Felix pleads nobly for his brother, and writes a really respectable letter, with four postscripts, as follows, 1. Beatrice was charmed with your letter. 2. Beatrice says you have just hit Dick's position at home to a T (I had said that he was an abject domestic slave). 3. Beatrice says she *must* have a play. 4. Beatrice says "Come over." 5. Beatrice sends love. My reply to Richard, which goes by this mail, is as follows, "My dear Mansfield, Your letter has arrived at last. I confess that I waited for it with somewhat fell intentions as to my reply; but now that the hour of vengeance has come, I find myself in perfect goodhumor, and can do nothing but laugh. I have not the slightest respect left for you; and your acquaintance with my future plays will be acquired in the course of visits to other people's theatres; but my personal liking for you remains where it was." I wrote kindly to Felix, but gave him a remorseless analysis of the whole case. Do not shew this to anyone. I am getting jealous of Davies; and so is C.

GBS

[Although the "indiscreet" letter from Mansfield to which Shaw referred above is dated 14th April, this presumably is an error, for delivery could not have been made in five days. The full text of the remarkable document reads:

"My dear Shaw.

"If we,—by we I mean Beatrice and I,—had lost a very near and dear friend we could not have sorrowed more than when we discovered 'Candida' to be of the impossible.

"It has been read—read—read—read,—and reading it would revive our courage,—*rehearsed* and hope, faith & even charity dropped below zero. My personal regard for you (—which reckoned by the average consideration one male being will bear for another in these business times is really extraordinary—) could carry me a long way into the domain of folly and would undoubtedly have slipped me across the frontier in this instance—if dire necessity, and a crisis, hadnt just in the (to you perhaps) unfortunate nick of time built a doublerow prickly-pear hedge which won't let 'Candida' thro'. Shaw—my light is perhaps very small and very dim—a mere farthing rush or a tallow dip—but viewed by it, and I have no other to view it by,— your play of Candida is lacking in all the essential qualities.

"The stage is not for sermons—*Not my stage*—no matter how charming— how bright—how clever—how trenchant those sermons may be—

"*Candida* is charming—it is more than charming—it is delightful, and I can well see how you have put into it much that is the best of yourself—but —pardon me—it is *not* a play—at least *I* do not think that it is a play— which thinking does not make it any more or any less of a play—it's just only what I think and I happen to be skipper of this ship at this time of thinking. Here are three long acts of talk—talk—talk—no matter how clever that talk is—it is talk—talk—talk.

"There isn't a creature who seeing the play would not apply Eugene's observations concerning Morell's lecturing propensities to the play itself. If you think a bustling—striving—hustling—pushing—stirring American audience will sit out calmly two hours of deliberate talk you are mistaken— and I'm not to be sacrificed to their just vengeance.

"It isn't right to try and build a play out of a mere incident. Candida is only an incident—it doesn't matter how you wad it or pad it or dress it or bedizen it—it's an incident—nothing more. All the world is crying out for deeds— for action! When I step upon the stage I want to act—I'm willing to talk a little to oblige a man like you—but I must act—and hugging my ankles for three mortal hours won't satisfy me in this regard. I can't fool myself and I can't fool my audience. I will gather together any afternoon you please a charming assemblage at our Garrick Theatre and read your play to them or play it—as best we may—but I can't put it on for dinner in the evening— people are not satisfied with only the hors d'oeuvres at dinner—where is the soup & the fish & the roast & the game and the salad and the fruit? Shaw— if you will write for me a strong, hearty—earnest—noble—genuine play —I'll play it. Plays used to be written for *actors*—actors who could stir and thrill—and that is what I want now—because I can do that—the world is tired of theories and arguments and philosophy and morbid sentiment. To be frank & to go further—I am not in sympathy with a young, delicate, morbid and altogether exceptional young man who falls in love with a massive middleaged lady who peels onions. I couldn't have made love to your Candida (Miss Janet Achurch) if I had taken ether.

"I never fall in love with fuzzy-haired persons who purr and are business-like and take a drop when they feel disposed and have weak feminine voices. My ideal is something quite different. I detest an aroma of stale tobacco and gin. I detest intrigue and slyness and sham ambitions. I don't like women who sit on the floor—or kneel by your side and have designs on your shirt-bosom—I don't like women who comb their tawny locks with their fingers, and claw their necks and scratch the air with their chins.

"You'll have to write a play that a *man* can play and about a woman that heroes fought for and a bit of ribbon that a knight tied to his lance.

"The stage is for romance and love and truth and honor. To make men better and nobler. To cheer them on the way—

"Life is real. Life is earnest. And the grave is not its goal.

. . . . . .

"Be not like dumb, driven cattle
"Be a hero in the fight!

"Go on, Shaw; Beatrice & I are with you—you will be always as welcome as a brother.—We want a great work from you.—

"Candida *is* beautiful—don't mistake me—we both understand it and we both appreciate it—There are fine things here—but—we are paid—alas—Shaw—we are paid to *act*.

"Yours, Shaw, truly

Richard Mansfield

"I am perfectly aware that you will not read this letter—you will gather that I am not about to produce Candida—& there your interest will cease—you would like to have Candida presented—if *I* don't present it—*I'm* damned—but also—I'm damned if I do. Ah Shaw Wir hatten gebauet ein stattleches Haus. I don't want to ruin it all" (BM).]

To R. GOLDING BRIGHT

[H.t/1; X/125]

29 Fitzroy Square W
22nd April 1895

Dear Mr Bright
    As usual my letters have been standing over unanswered for a long time; and I am later than I intended to be in congratulating you on having so promptly and energetically faced and dealt with the situation created by your father's action. To tell you the truth I was curious to

see whether you would have stuff enough in you to tackle it; for though it seems a simple matter enough, yet with a great many men—especially men of the artistic and literary temperament—a call for action ends like the first scene of the third act of Peer Gynt, where Peer sees the man chop his finger off to escape from military service.

> "Ay, think of it—wish it done—*will* it to boot—
> But *do* it—! No, that's past my understanding!"

I congratulate you especially on the fact that all your friends and relations regard you as a madman. That is an indispensable beginning to a respectable, independent life.

In your first letter you express yourself as rather staggered by my statement that a woman like Paula Tanqueray is the same at three as at thirtythree. That, however, is quite true. Rousseau dates his sexual susceptibility "from his birth," three years earlier than I have allowed for Paula. And there is no question of her being "corrupt, immoral in thought and idea": that is begging the whole question of morality. She is different from Ellean; but so is a poet different from a mathematician. If you take the mathematician's temperament as a moral standard, of course the poet stands condemned; but why should you? If you take Ellean as the standard, Paula is condemned; but again, why not take Paula as the standard, and condemn Ellean as cold, unnatural, selfish and so on (which is what the Paula sort of woman invariably does)? A critic must not take sides in this way without very careful consideration; for it takes all sorts to make a world; and if you could make every woman a Saint Elizabeth, the result would be practically as disastrous as if you made every woman a Catherine II.

Your defence of Paula will not, I think, hold water. Let me remind you of it, by the way, as you have probably forgotten it by this time. You say, "She was, so far as study and observation can teach me, (not bad, Master Reginald, for a pure effort of your imagination) the daughter of a well-to-do, respectable man, probably a dignitary of the church. Chance threw her into the company of a fast set; and moral ruin followed slowly but surely—facilis descensus Averni." But why did she join the fast set? We are all thrown into the company of fast sets. We are all thrown into the company of slow sets too, and of religious sets, and political sets, and artistic sets, and fashionable sets, and sporting sets, and gambling sets, and hideously debauched sets. But none of them rush at us and enlist us by a pressgang. We have to seek them out, to shew our sympathy with them, to make ourselves congenial company for them, before we can get into them. If Paula

525

was the daughter of a dignitary of the church, it must have been far easier for her to become a district visitor or half a dozen other respectable things than a prostitute. Why then did she become a prostitute? Because she was built that way, and for no other reason. I dare say your father is at this moment sorrowfully explaining to some friend that you were as sensible as possible at seventeen, and that you were well started in a city office, but that you unfortunately got into a set of theatrical loafers called the Playgoers' Club, and that they seduced you from the paths of business and corrupted you slowly but surely, and so on. But you know very well that the Playgoers' Club didn't come to you: you went to it because you are built that way, just as Paula went off in Mr Jarman's yacht instead of going into Ellean's convent, which was presumably equally within her reach. It is true that the whole female sex is driven towards prostitution or towards marriage for money (which is the same thing) by economic pressure which, in the case of very poor women, is almost irresistible; but that does not account for the difference between one woman and another in such matters, though it accounts for some of the difference between a man and a woman.

A remark of yours about the difficulty of indulging in a Saturday Review at a cost of sixpence a week suggests to me that you have not realised the advantages of Communism yet. At the Charing Cross end of St Martin's Lane you will find a free library, with a newspaper room in the basement. You have nothing to do but walk in and read all the papers without any formality whatsoever; and when you are done, you can go to the floor above and read all the magazines. We are trying to get a library for St Pancras; but we were beaten at the last poll. With the British Museum reading room round the corner, and this library within twelve minutes walk, you are five hundred a year richer than Shakespeare.

I cannot bring myself to republish my articles. They appear very entertaining in the context of the events of the week in which they appear; but just because they are good journalism, they are bad literature. I don't think the actress-manageress is going to do much good, because, obviously, she will want plays with good parts for the woman and bad parts for the men; and so, though we shall have two sorts of bad plays instead of one—the actress manageresse's play at half the theatres and the actor-manager's play at the other half, we shall be as far as ever from the genuine drama. My preface [to *The Theatrical 'World' of 1894*] is not an advocacy of the changes which I see coming, but simply a statement of them.

526

I shall go at Grein about the throwing open of the gallery at the I.T. If they really do that, it is a scandalous affair. Probably the truth is that the doorkeepers neglect their business and desert their posts.

yours sincerely
G.B.S.

To JANET ACHURCH

[T/1 (B/4); X/130]

29 Fitzroy Square W
23rd April 1895

[The third leaf of this letter was reproduced in facsimile in *Theatre Arts*, New York, January 1928.]

Charrington has just been here, with the dire news that you want to lecture on Ibsen. Now if you get a chance of making a speech under auspicious circumstances in New York, by all means do so. If there is any artistic club that you can address, get them to ask you to address them. Dont let it be a dinner, because after-dinner speaking is difficult and inconvenient; and the audience is always half drunk. But dont get a lecture agent to announce you as a lecture with a charge for admission; and dont let yourself be put into position of a professional lecturer for a moment. There must be no money in the transaction.

Suppose, then, that you are in for a speech, what had you better do? To begin with, dont write your speech. If you attempt to read a lecture on Ibsen, you will embarrass yourself and bore your audience to distraction. If you havent sufficient courage and simplicity of character to chatter away pleasantly to an audience from a few notes and your own experience, then let the platform alone. You can, without much preparation, get a very entertaining turn on some such lines as the following.

First, you hope nobody expects that you are going to deliver a lecture. For that, it is necessary to be a critic, an essayist, a student of literature, like the clever gentlemen who write about the drama for the New York papers. Besides, you are not conscious of your art as these gentlemen are. You took to the stage as a duck takes to water. When people want a lecture on swimming they dont go to a duck for it, but to a professor, who probably doesnt know how to swim at all. In the same way, if people want a lecture on the drama or the stage, they must not come to you for it, but to one of the dramatic critics. Not that you mean to suggest that they cannot act: on the contrary, it is

527

clear from the way they write that they are all accomplished actors; and you would go a long way to see a performance of a classical play with all the parts filled by critics. The subject that you are really going to talk about is yourself—a favourite subject of yours. Perhaps they (the audience) think that an impertinence—oh, it is very kind of them to disclaim that feeling; but you are sure some of them think so; and if they dont, they ought to. But you have a justification ready.

The justification is that the actress really does take a very important part in the history and development of the drama. The drama progresses by a series of experiments made on the public by actors and actresses with new plays. The public may determine the result of the experiment; but the public never makes the experiment. It does not come to you and say, "Produce a play of Ibsen's, and see how we will like it." The initiative comes always from the actor or actress, who says, "I do so long to play Nora, or Hedda Gabler: and I must try whether the public will support me in it." If Ibsen had not interested *us*, the actors, his plays would be still on the bookshelf; and I should have been celebrated for my impersonations of Pauline Deschapelles [in *The Lady of Lyons*], and Adrienne Lecouvreur, and all sorts of nonsensical heroines instead of for my Nora in A Doll's House. So you see it really does matter what *we* like and what *we* think; and that is my excuse for getting up here today to give you a piece of my mind. If any lady or gentleman present will write a play with a part in it which I feel I *must* play, that play will be performed some day, even if everyone else in Europe or America said worse things of it than Herr Max Nordau says of Ibsen. (Here endeth the exordium).

Now you (the audience) perhaps want to know why I am bent on thrusting plays like Ibsen's on the public when there are so many excellent plays, by Shakespear and other clever people, which were good enough for Mrs Siddons and ought to be good enough for me. Well, I can't tell you why any more than I can tell you why I have different ideas from my grandmother. Perhaps the change may be for the worse; but that doesnt alter the fact that there is a change, and that the change is taking place in you as well as in me. If I were to revive some of Mrs Siddons's most popular parts for you, you would be the most astonished audience in America before it was half over. You would find the sentiment of the play as much out of date as its rhetoric, so much so that you would think me mad in producing such a work at the present day. Now what all the world feels about the plays of a hundred years ago, a few people feel about the plays of twentyfive years ago. I need not tell you that an actress has to play many parts in many plays of which she has no very high opinion. Sometimes the author has not written one single line right: the actress has to invent the part for herself, and play it *between* the lines, or else speak her words with a pathetic intensity that makes you forget that the actual words do not mean anything pathetic at all, affecting the public as Sarah Bernhardt affects people who do not know a word of French, or Duse people who do not know a word of Italian. Sometimes the author has only succeeded in a single scene, though that scene may be worth producing the play for. Then some bits of a play wear out faster than others. In Shakespear there are parts—like that of Helen in "All's Well" for instance—which are still too genuine and beautiful and modern for the public; but there are also many passages which are tedious and impossible, though we all pretend to like them. These are terrible bits to get over on the stage when they cannot be cut out: when I come to them I am only *pretending to act*, which is the most horribly dishonorable feeling you can have on the stage, though perhaps that will not be easily understood by people who think that acting is all pretence. But I assure you that is how I feel; and the result is that a part that I can play from beginning to end with conviction attracts me more than the most popular play in which my faith is imperfect. Consequently I get strong preferences for one play over another; and I will try to make the nature of my preferences clearer to you by comparing certain passages in those modern plays which shew the influence of the great movement of the past half century for the better education and greater freedom of women, by passages from other plays which date in feeling from before that movement.

Now here I (G.B.S.) must leave you (Janet) to make up the real stuff of your speech for yourself. The idea is to quote the sham womanly stuff from The Lady of Lyons, Adrienne, and so on, and contrast it with passages from Ibsen's plays. A comic performance of the death scene from Adrienne would be good. Do it exactly as you do it on the stage, telling them previously that they must not laugh, and assuring them that what you are going to do is to the eighth of an inch what you have so often set the house weeping with. They will probably laugh like anything. Then give them the sharp, businesslike death scene at the end of Hedda Gabler. Allude to Dickens's Esther Summerson [in *Bleak House*] and Agnes Wickfield [in *David Copperfield*] as the sort of thing that women dislike, and shew how the women on the stage are making constantly for the sort of work which, even when it makes them unamiable, at least makes them unamiable human beings, which is better than making them amiable impostors.

You might then, very carefully and slyly, point out, on the lines of my preface to Archer's book (proof of preface enclosed in lecture of C.C.'s which goes to you by book post this mail) how the men on the stage dislike the plays in which the women's parts are real parts, and how women are being driven into management by this, with the likelihood that we shall presently have half the theatres managed by actor-managers, with no chance of a good woman's play being produced, and the other half managed by actress-manageresses, with the women [men?] at the same disadvantage, and the drama thus worse off than ever. The moral ought to be the desirability of management with artistic aims, the object being the production of the best plays and not the exhibition of this or that performer. And be sure to disclaim, in as amusing a way as possible, any pretence on your own part to be fit to be trusted with management on those lines. Say that wherever you are in charge, they may depend on having actress-management at its worst.

If you can get an invitation to address a society of women, speak on acting as a profession for women, and shew them as many stage tricks as possible. Remember, you cannot give yourself away too completely to please an audience; nor is there any method by which you can convey so strong an impression of the modest amiability of unconscious strength. You must honestly not try to make a success in the stage sense on the platform.

The post hour is come; and—thanks to this confounded project of yours, which you will have abandoned before this reaches you, probably, I have not had time to say a word to please myself. You are a hard taskmistress for an unfortunate literary man.

I went to Battersea Park yesterday to bicycle; and Nora came to see me fall. Florence was there, caracoling on her machine with surpassing elegance, to the admiration of all the park. The Webbs also struggled. But I must stop.

GBS

To JANET ACHURCH

29 Fitzroy Square W
[T/1 (B/4)]   30th April 1895

[The Acton Davies interview with Janet was reprinted in the *Weekly Sun*, London, on 28th April. Following Mansfield's statement to Janet, "You're a new woman. You play Ibsen. I detest new women who play Ibsen," Shaw had interpolated: "Mrs. Mansfield has played Nora in 'A Doll's House' in New York."]

On Saturday evening your Evening Suns came, to C.C. and myself respectively. C.C. is uneasy about this interviewing—shrinks from the vulgarity of it, recoils from the American newspaper dramatization of his idolized Janet. As for me I swore because you were late for the Sunday papers, and then dashed out and sent off a copy of the interview by express messenger to the Weekly Sun at the eleventh hour, with the vulgar but satisfactory result that the interview was reprinted at full length the next day with a little word interpolated by me to explain the allusion to Mrs M's performance of Nora. It was altogether too good to be lost; nothing could have been neater.

On the Sunday I lectured at Morris's place at Hammersmith [on "Great Men: Are They Real?"]. C.C. appeared in the audience; took copious notes; but remained mute. I did not see him afterwards, as he was at the back of the room, and the crowd was so great that I could not get down to him until he was half way home. On Monday he went off to Cambridge; and I have not seen him since.

On Monday morning Mrs Harris (our domestic assistant) came in and said that Mr [Felix] Mansfield was downstairs and wanted to know whether I would see him. As the usual course is for him to come up without misgiving, this proceeding was eloquent of his unhappy position. I received him with boisterous good humour; and he wrung my hand with the fervency of a man whose mind is relieved of a ton of lead. There were no explanations. I assumed remorselessly that I knew all about it and he did not force a discussion on me. In the afternoon I had an interview with Miss Marbury, who is quite a foot broader than she was before, and Daniel Frohmann. She also had nothing to tell me that I did not know; in fact, C.C. and I know more than either Felix or Elisabeth of the inwardness of the matter. The only amusing thing was that poor Felix, having been thrust into battle with Miss M. and being, as he supposed, bound to present a warlike front to her on Richard's behalf, was packed off to London in the same boat to countermine her (and *us*, probably). He arrived on board before her, and found Richard's valet there. On haughtily demanding the business of this menial, he learnt that he had been sent by Richard with a mammoth offering of flowers for Elisabeth, with the most affectionate and courtly inscriptions. Felix, thus gone back on, was furious, and promptly began to load Miss Marbury with enquiries after her health, offers of assistance and so on. But she (as I learnt from her after hearing the first part of the story from Felix) naturally supposed that this was only part of the plot to soften her—"to smother her in twopenn'orth of roses" as she put it—and treated Felix with the utmost

531

cruelty. Both she and Daniel were highly impressed with the smartness with which you handled your case. I like Frohmann, and feel for his wretched necessity to keep his confounded stock company employed. Did you let him see Mrs Daintry?

Felix told me that he used to ask at the New Amsterdam Hotel every day whether Charrington had arrived. I imagine that if Felix's sight is long enough to recognise Charrington in the street at a sufficient distance, he will vanish down a side street with a startling velocity.

The latest development of newspaper intelligence here expresses itself in comments on "the dispute between Miss Janet Achurch and Mr Bernard Shaw on the one hand, and Mr Mansfield on the other."

As it is now some two months since I have heard from you, I decline to prolong this letter.

By the way, you will find any further newspaper booming wasted now. There has been enough to make the necessary effect; and more than enough is too much.

GBS

To JANET ACHURCH

29 Fitzroy Square W

[T/1 (A/4)]   3rd May 1895

[Acton Bond (1861–1941), Canadian-born actor, had appeared with Irving at the Lyceum in 1892 in *Henry VIII*, *King Lear*, and *Richelieu*, but was better known at this time in the provinces than in London. In 1903 he was the organiser of the Ellen Terry Jubilee Benefit at Drury Lane.]

The paragraphs about Felix asking you to return Richard's letters and your refusing have been reprinted in the Sun here of last Wednesday. That is all the news. It is impossible for me to keep up a correspondence with a woman who never writes to me. There will be a mail in tomorrow, I suppose: and if I hear nothing then, F.F. shall be Mrs Bernard Shaw at the earliest date thereafter permitted by statute. She, by the way, is touring in the Channel Islands and at Basingstoke with Acton Bond, playing Esther in "Caste."

GBS

To EDWARD R. PEASE

[C/4]

29 Fitzroy Square W
15th May 1895

Totally forgot committee—don't know why or how.

I will take the [East India] dock gates on the *morning* of the 26th. Subject, Practical Socialism or what they [the Poplar Labor Electoral Association] please.

GBS

To ARTHUR S. CLARK

[B/1]

29 Fitzroy Square W
18th May 1895

[Fred Terry (1863–1933), actor-manager, was a brother of Ellen Terry. For several years he was a member of Beerbohm Tree's company, later appearing with John Hare and Forbes-Robertson.]

Dear Sir

At thirtyeight you should have written half a dozen plays if you intend to become a dramatist by profession. And you must not write them with a view to reforming your fortune, or with any other view than the production of a work of art that satisfies your own judgment and fulfils the purpose created by your instinct as a dramatist. You are mistaken in supposing that plays are not read. Not only managers, but actors who are waiting to become managers until they have a few good plays in hand, spend their days in drudging through manuscripts, 99% of which are hopelessly bad. But they naturally turn first to the plays with promising titles; and "The Vegetarian" is quite impossible. I have no hesitation in saying that unless that title is a purposely misleading one, the play *must* be a bad one. The only advice I can give you is not to waste any thought or anxiety on the play you have finished, but go on and write another, & then another & so on until you have either learnt the business or discovered that you have not the necessary turn for it. Refusals mean nothing: a play may be a masterpiece and yet not suit this or that particular manager. Besides the actual managers, you may take it that almost every "leading man" in London—Fred Terry, Yorke Stephens, Forbes Robertson, Arthur Bourchier, &c. &c. &c. would read anything on the chance of picking up something good enough to start with. There is also a great demand for good one-act "curtain raisers."

yrs faithfully
G. Bernard Shaw

533

To JANET ACHURCH

29 Fitzroy Square W
24th May 1895

[T/1 (B/4)]

[After the expiry of her Mansfield contract, Janet remained in New York
long enough to appear (as Shaw had predicted) in *A Doll's House* and a
double-bill of Herman Merivale and F.C.Grove's *Forget-Me-Not* and
Langdon Mitchell's *In A Season*, at Hoyt's Theatre during the week of
3rd June, under the management of Frederick C.Whitney. Her leading man
was Albert Gran. 37 Redcliffe Square was the Charringtons' current London
address; they rarely remained at one residence for longer than a few months,
and more than a dozen addresses are recorded for them and expunged in
Shaw's address books (BM). Charrington became a member of the Fabian
Society in April 1895. Jean-François Millet (1814–75) was a French genre
and landscape painter of the Barbizon school. Mansfield had produced
Louis N.Parker's *The King of Peru* at the Garrick Theatre, New York, on
7th May.]

Since you demand it, I will take my chance of this letter reaching
you before you leave America; but my experience of the extraordinary
vagaries of the transatlantic mails makes me feel that it is rather a
chance, in spite of the ten or eleven days available.

I was bicycling in Battersea Park yesterday afternoon with Trevelyan,
when Charlie came along. He had been toting Nora to Redcliffe
Square, Miss Dickens [the governess] having incurred the displeasure
of that establishment by some indiscretion or other. (By the way, you
are not to appear cognisant of these domestic matters until they reach
you through the ordinary official sources). He seemed in excellent
spirits, the day being pleasant. He is going to lecture—bless his heart,
as you would say—at the Hackney Radical Club and at the Hammersmith Socialist Society; and this I think a good thing on the whole, as
he ought to make an above-the-average public speaker, although among
the Fabians he will probably be an Impossibilist of the Impossibilists.
I take a lively interest in him, and have often speculated for a minute
or two on the questions you put in your letter.

As you say, he has a good deal in him. But if you study any human
being affectionately you will find a good deal in them: that is only
your discovery of what a wonderful deal it takes to make even the most
ordinary sort of human being. You do not yet realise, I imagine, what
a tremendous lot a man must have in hand before he begins to score.
Life is like whist in that respect: it seems surprising that a man and
his partner should be clever and lucky enough to win six tricks and yet
not score at all; but that is the nature of the game: "it takes a great

534

deal of merit to make even a small success"; and all the solid successes have an immense deal of uncounted work behind them. When you have said that Charlie has "*so much* in him—depths unfathomable," you have said nothing at all: any mother will plead the same for her ugly duckling, and plead it truthfully too; for we all have "depths unfathomable" in us, since it must have taken millions of ages to evolve even a human idiot. And that is why you have half a mind to tear up your plea: you instinctively feel its inadequacy, though you feel, too, that it expresses something that it is cowardly to suppress merely because it seems sentimental and vulgar. All the same, the inner fastidiousness is the strong side of you; for the valid thing to be expressed—to wit, your affection—boots nothing; and the inadequacy *does* make it sentimental and vulgar. If you were married to Fleming, you might say exactly the same thing for him. So let us leave aside the merits of Charlie's nature, since his chances would not be worth discussing at all unless he were clearly a man of exceptional qualities. The question is, whether he will hold his own among the exceptional men—whether he can out Herod Herod.

When you say that you would give all your hopes to see him *win*, you compendiously express everything that is base in your way of regarding him. You talk of his life as if that were something altogether to come. His life is already half lived. If you regard it as a failure— if your feeling is that here is Charlie an unappreciated failure, and there is George Alexander an overrated success, both so by the intolerable injustice of destiny; so that you feel desperately determined to strain every nerve to redress the injustice and make Charlie another George Alexander, why then you can do nothing for him but make him miserable. For it is in the nature of things impossible for a man to feel his own strength and dignity steadily unless he feels it biting on the convictions of others who are in contact with him. When Millet was accepting the obligation to be "successful," and was painting naked women, or trying to do it, in the West-end manager style, his wife, by saying "Come along and starve," did all that she could do for him. The result was that he lived as great a failure as Charlie pretty nearly all the rest of his life from your point of view, though from his own and his wife's he was a great painter, as the world found out in a hurry when he died. It seems to me that you are always wanting Charlie to paint naked women, because—and here is the essence of the thing— painting naked women, so to speak, is really a fine art and a means of genuine success for those who have the right sort of brilliant talent for it; *and you are one of those people*. With him Art, and the joy of life,

535

and all the rest of it are mere talk: he has no capacity for enjoyment of outward things. The fine clothes you gave him incommode him: he wears them so that you shall not be able to reproach him for neglecting so obvious a means to getting an engagement. A pipe, a glass of whisky, a caress from a respectable woman: that is all he cares about, although he torments himself about other things through mistaking them for what he really wants: that is, the propagation of his own ideas. He is a born preacher, a worker in ideas, a critic of thought and conduct. Now with you, it is this preaching side that is all talk. You *have* capacity for happiness. You like fine clothes, beauty, excitement, luxury, lots of money, action, objective and immediate results. That is why he likes you—why I, who am also of the preaching sort, like you. But look at the frightful hamper and friction that comes of your trying to drag one another each in the other's way. Believe me, since you cannot sympathise with him in the Madame Millet fashion, having your own way to go, the best thing you can do is to live out your own life in your own way, and leave him to do the same. By the time his projects come to anything, your time will be past: you are a woman of the present: he is a man of the future, as far as anything he can do is likely to open a road to an actress.

What you can do for him, if you have insight enough, is to keep his real nature steadily in sight, and not let yourself be led away by those self assertions of his against his own conscience—that conscience which he is so determined not to be enslaved by. It is all very well for *you* to tell lies; to borrow money that you not only know you can't repay, but wouldn't if you could; to fling away the money of your affectionate friends on desperate enterprises as recklessly as that of rich speculators who would not give a farthing to an ugly woman; and to raise your own hopes and those of others by treating every stray suggestion, however visionary, as a realised project. But that sort of thing is fatal to Charrington. It is unnatural to him; and consequently it is at bottom abhorrent to him. It is of course in the very grain of his nonconformist conscience to do things just because they are abhorrent to him—to refuse to let himself be paralysed and intimidated by formal scruples when your fate and his are at stake. But that is all nonsense. Whilst he appears to be making your interests the excuse for gratifying his own inclination to be unscrupulous, he is really martyring himself; and what would really make him happy would be to have your opposition as an excuse for being virtuous. Do what you like yourself—lie, borrow, cheat, have love affairs by the dozen, live splendidly whenever you can, if you like; but never let him do anything

536

that is not quixotically honorable. And don't expect him to take an interest in your brilliant operations on your own behalf. He has done so little for you in your career that he is deeply impressed by the need of letting you make your own way in your own fashion; but all your splendacious making of new friends and your sallies in the papers are only right for you, not for him. It is utterly contrary to his nature to advertise; and he has just the same feeling about your interviews as he has about my criticisms: he thinks such things, however clever, ought not to be. In the depths of his soul, in the abysses where love and friendship do not disturb his innermost judgment, my weekly article is a weekly act of prostitution; and your dazzling booming of yourself is the same thing. The journalist, the emotional actress—you have heard him talk about them in the abstract. Well, my dear Janet, I am a journalist, and you are an emotional actress; and unless you can draw the inevitable conclusion without a moment's misgiving, and value him for his feeling towards the emotional actress without in the least ceasing to value yourself as—among other things—an emotional actress, you will never get on with him. He is really working his way to that human and social attitude himself; but he is probably quite convinced that if he told you that your enthusiastic advertisement of him in that last interview sent a shiver down his back, you would be cruelly hurt, and would treat him to a tearing bit of emotional acting on the spot.

The moral of it all is, leave him free and be free yourself. Make your own success; and don't drag him into it, because success is against his grain. And leave him to his "failure," into which you may, I think, depend on him not to drag you, since he knows well that it is against *your* grain. Only, if you cannot see that this failure is really the sort of way in which a man like him succeeds, then, as sure as fate, you will lose him; for no man can bear to have a distorting mirror on his dressing table, no matter how pretty the frame may be.

With reference to the money you owe me, give yourself no trouble about it. When I lent it to you I knew full well that you would regard its repayment as a sacred duty; that you were touched by my lending it; that it was more than mere money to you; but oh, my dear silly Janet, I never supposed for a moment that I should ever see that money again. I do believe that if you had everything you wanted, and a thousand pounds to spend besides, and every prospect of getting as much more next month, and if you suddenly heard that I was in great want of money, it would give you exquisite pleasure to send me not only that money but a couple of hundred to boot. But that project of saving by strict economy at the hotel, in order to prosaically relodge that money for me in the London and County Bank! What have you ever done that gives you the right to suppose that I believed in that? No: that must go with the other expenses of the failure of the "Candida" project. Nevertheless there is no reason why I should utterly demoralise you. When you are next well provided with money, you might spare ten pounds to repay May Sparling what she lent you when I had no "Arms and The Man" royalties to draw upon. I have once or twice been inclined to send it to her as from you or through you; but as I have no reason to suppose that she particularly wants it, there is no sufficient justification for the element of treachery in such a proceeding. My only reason for wanting it repaid is that I have an uneasy sense, which you will understand, that the money was lent as much to me as to you. There is no hurry whatever about it, obviously; but I want you to put it in List C of your debts. List A contains the debts you don't intend to pay; List B the debts you do intend to pay; List C the debts you really *will* pay.

Come, have I been candid enough? Some day, perhaps, it will be less true than it is today. I wish you were a Mrs Siddons (whose grave they have been restoring here). She slaved in the provinces and came up to London and failed and went back to the provinces for years and came up to London again, a very respectable and honest woman, and succeeded for ever. However, as a mere personal matter, I should like you to contrive to be Janet as well. If only I could make you appreciate yourself, all would be safe. Wretch that you are!

I have just had a long letter from Mansfield. He says Parker's play has failed, and wants another with nobody else but himself in it all through to make a lot of money with. He pours forth his troubles with all his old naïveté, as if nothing whatever had occurred with which I could not fully sympathise. I really believe that half what we suspect to be policy on his part is nothing in the world but utter incapacity to *attend* to anybody but himself.

I must be off to the Fabian Executive.

GBS

To SYDNEY C. COCKERELL

[C/1]
29 Fitzroy Square W
24th June 1895

I was just about to accept your invitation for Wednesday [the 26th] with avidity when a confounded ticket came in for the Vaudeville

[Robert Buchanan and Charles Marlowe's *The Strange Adventures of Miss Brown*] for that evening. Life just now is impossible: there is some confounded performance every night in all sorts of languages. I had rather have a quiet evening than an afternoon on the river with a rush back to town and the theatre afterwards: so let us put it off for a bit until things slacken: the end [of the season] now draws near.

G.B.S.

To JANET ACHURCH

c/o Sidney Webb
The Argoed. Monmouth
[T/1 (B/4)]   8th July 1895

[Shaw was spending the summer with the Webbs. "C.T." was Courtenay Thorpe (1854–1927), a member of Charrington's company, who subsequently appeared as Marchbanks, opposite Janet, in the first public performance of the play at Aberdeen on 30th July 1897. Shaw noted, in the *Saturday Review* on 15th May 1897, that Thorpe "accomplished the remarkable feat of playing Helmer in the afternoon and the Ghost in 'Hamlet' in the evening, and doing both better than we have seen them done before." *Madame Sans-Gêne*, by Victorien Sardou and Émile Moreau, had been performed by the celebrated French actress Gabrielle Réjane (1856–1920), in her first London appearance, at the Gaiety on 23rd June 1894. A translation by J. Comyns Carr was produced in 1897 by Sir Henry Irving, with Ellen Terry as Catherine.]

Your extremely slimy impression of C.T. puts me quite off him. So let him rest.

I find that the new play [*You Never Can Tell*] is not coming. Instead, I keep fiddling at the little one act thing [*The Man of Destiny*] I began that morning in Regent's Park, with Napoleon in it, of all people. I will finish it anyhow, as I want to see whether I can write a good curtain raiser. Forbes Robertson ought to play Napoleon in order to forestall Irving in "Madame Sans Gêne." It is a perfectly idiotic play—or rather scene—but good acting, especially if the woman is a good comedian and very fascinating. It's half finished: the worst of it is over.

After 24 hours perfect weather, it is raining again like March & December rolled into one. I am pursued here by a horrible appetite, and am becoming a gross and pig-like person. It is a vile country for bicycling: yesterday morning I was charging down a ruinously steep lane when a heap of stones capsized me and I razed twelve feet of hedge from the face of the map with my left temple & shoulder. But the main objection to the place is its distance from Onslow Square. The plans for the American tour are all nonsense: tout vient à qui sait attendre.

GBS

To WILLIAM ARCHER

The Argoed. Monmouth
6th August 1895

[A/2]

[Archer was interested in purchasing a bicycle for his son, and Shaw had discussed the matter with Charles Friswell & Co., bicycle manufacturers, of Newgate Street, London.]

In the absence of any shadow of an argument in favor of the deliberate debasement of Tom's bicycle, I decline to do him that wanton injury. You might as well send him to bed with a tallow candle and snuffers on the ground that he is too young for the modern article. In five years he will want a new machine. He will then delight himself with whatever the latest thing will be, and he will partly defray the cost by selling the old one, which will only be saleable on condition of its having been quite up-to-date when it was new. A solid tyred machine would not be worth fifteen shillings the day after it was purchased; it would disappoint Tom more than no bicycle at all, besides demoralising him by giving him the habit of putting up with obsolete and inferior things instead of being always abreast of his epoch; it would disgust the manufacturer, who would take no interest in supplying a universally despised article; it would be a bad machine even of its own kind, the art of building for solid tyres being a decaying one; it would rob its owner of the amusement of using the inflator (on which Tom lays great stress) and prevent him from acquiring the accomplishment of repairing punctures: in short, it would add to the disadvantage of its direct and obvious inferiority, every conceivable contingent dis-advantage. Your peculiar modesty would on these grounds undoubtedly entitle you to a solid tyred bike for yourself (why not a hobby horse, to carry the principle through?); but I entirely object to that virtue being imposed on Tom. He conveyed to me, within the due limits of his instinctive delicacy, that the air tyre, blown on to the wheel like a bubble, as it were, was *the* thing; and I am resolved not to prove unworthy of his confidence. I have told Friswell that in every respect

540

save the mere luxuries of superfluous nickel plating & the like, I expect him to come up to the mark; and he has undertaken that Tom shall toe the 1895 line. Tom's attitude on the question seems to me sound and intelligent: his father's, feeble & superstitious. I consider that I am giving him an excellent start in life; and I trust he may never learn that his unnatural parent attempted to put him back by five or six years out of mere wanton shrinking from the front seats. Impress on him the motto "Always up to date," and bid him take warning by you and me, who at forty are only where we ought to have been at 22 if only we had had the courage.

GBS

P.S. Ought I to come up to town any time during Aug & Sep for theatre openings & the like? This is a bad place for news. If anything important threatens, drop me a card.

GBS

To EMERY WALKER

The Argoed. Monmouth

[C/1]   9th August 1895

[At the request of Benjamin Tucker, editor of *Liberty* (New York), Shaw had written a devastating critique on Max Nordau's *Degeneration* (1892–93; Engl. transl. 1895) in the form of an open letter to Tucker. It was published, under the title "A Degenerate's View of Nordau," on 27th July 1895. A revised version was issued in 1908 as *The Sanity of Art*.]

Dear Walker

I send you herewith a copy of Liberty containing my article on Nordau, which you might shew to Morris & Cockerell & anyone else within your reach who cares to read it. I must send to America for some more copies: meanwhile I am compelled to make the few I have got cover as much ground as possible.

yrs ever
G. Bernard Shaw

To CHARLES CHARRINGTON

The Argoed. Monmouth

[T/1 (B/4)]   14th August 1895

[J. W. Gleeson White (1851–98) was editor of *The Studio* (1893–94) and of *The Pageant* (1896–97). Two stories by Charrington, "Lady Bramber's

541

Ghost" and "A Sturdy Beggar," were published in one volume by
Constable's in October 1896; no story by him appeared in *The Pageant*.
Alexander Texeira de Mattos (1865–1921), translator of Zola, Chateaubriand,
and Maeterlinck, was secretary of the Independent Theatre and an editor of
Henry & Company. He married the widow of Oscar Wilde's brother
William.]

It occurs to me that in case Gleeson White should collar that story
of yours for the Pageant, you may as well bear in your private mind the
fact that the publishers, Henry & Co., are really De Mattos, Grein &
Co.

I have just written like a father to the provincial Bluntschli [A.E.
Drinkwater], who is deep in my debt over "Arms & The Man," to
tell him that he must either pay up or else shew me some reasonable
prospect of his doing something more with it than making all the
provincial managers resolve privately to book no more dates for plays
of mine. As a third alternative I have suggested that he might drop the
affair altogether, tear up our agreement, & leave the play unfettered in
my hands on condition of my crying quits as to the money. If he
closes with this, I think I shall hold the play until some decently capable
company can be found to undertake a tour with a Shaw—or mainly
Shaw—repertory.

My respects to your lady wife & honorable daughter. It rains, rains,
rains here in a way that would take the stiffening even out of Noah.

GBS

To FREDERICK H. EVANS

[A/23]

The Argoed. Monmouth
14th August 1895

[Frederick H. Evans (1852–1943) was a London bookseller, bibliophile, and
amateur photographer, whose camera work was much admired by Shaw.
Evans had approached Shaw with the idea of editing and publishing a
collection of Shaw's musical criticisms in *The World*, but the project
eventually was abandoned. John Ruskin, having decided in 1871 to become
his own publisher, underwrote the costs of printing *Fors Clavigera* and set up
his pupil and assistant George Allen (1837–1907) as his agent and publisher.
From this arrangement the publishing firm of Allen & Unwin, Ltd,
developed. Shaw followed Ruskin's example with his own English editions
from 1903 until his death, contracting with Constable & Co., Ltd, to serve
as his distributing agent.

[Simpkin, Marshall, Hamilton, Kent & Company was a wholesale book distributor and publishing house, which frequently distributed works, underwritten by the authors, on a commission basis. "The Religion of the Pianoforte" appeared in the *Fortnightly Review* in February 1894. The *Pall Mall Budget* contributions included "The Bayreuth Festival" (2nd, 9th, and 16th August 1894) and an article on Siegfried Wagner, "His Father's Ghost" (15th November 1894).]

My dear Evans

You will see by the above address that I am not visible in London just at present—perhaps shall not be until October unless some important event at the theatres brings me up for a few days.

As to the blue pencilling, I only urge you to go by the quality of the stuff, and to retain and delete nothing out of consideration for the adverse critic. If you take out everything that the critics will misunderstand and dislike, you will expunge everything that is valuable in the articles. I charge you by all your gods to be guided exactly and faithfully by *what YOU like*, even if it seems to you that nobody else will like it. That will secure a perfectly satisfactory job.

I want you to consider the question of publishing very seriously. I object to publishers: the one service they have done me is to teach me to do without them. They combine commercial rascality with artistic touchiness and pettishness, without being either good business men or fine judges of literature. All that is necessary to the production of a book is an author and a bookseller, without any intermediary parasite. The reviewers and editors will look at my name, not at the publisher's. Therefore I propose that you and I, as honest and necessary persons, I the author and you the bookseller, do follow the wise & lucrative example of Allen and Ruskin, and, with the help of Providence (technically known as Simkin & Marshall) carry this thing through ourselves. I have, out of the spoils of "Arms & The Man," just about enough money lying in the bank to pay for the manufacture of a book; and I had much rather go to work in this way than deal with a publisher unless he were to offer me a sum of money that would ensure him an exemplary loss unless he did his very utmost by the book.

As to the price, I have tried popular prices without success. My public is small and select. My own notion is that if people will go past half a crown net for a book they will go—and expect to go—to six shillings gross: that is, four & sixpence net. However, you are likely to know more about that than I do. I have much less remorse about making people pay a price for a book which shews that they really want it and intend to read it, now that the spread of Free Libraries makes it possible for really poor people to get decently got-up books.

I think I had better keep the Nordau essay intact for separate publication. Now that I think of it, there is the Fortnightly article "The Religion of the Pianoforte," an old English Illustrated Bayreuth article, and some Pall Mall Budget contributions available in case the first venture proves encouraging. Or we might do a dramatic volume. If only I could keep up the supply of capital by writing plays, we could go down to posterity together. I am growing out of journalism, though it has kept me up to the collar in a fashion. Let me hear what you think of my plan: the post is always welcome here, & your handwriting (Remington, I suppose) doubly so.

yrs sincerely
G. Bernard Shaw

To JANET ACHURCH

[T/1 (A/4)]

The Argoed. Monmouth
16th August 1895

[Bertha Newcombe, an artist who was an illustrator for the *English Illustrated Magazine*, with a studio in Cheyne Walk, and for some years a Fabian, was another of the women who fell in love with Shaw. He visited her studio frequently (she painted him as "The Platform Spellbinder" in 1893) and maintained a friendly relationship with her for several years, but apparently never considered her a potential marital partner, though Beatrice Webb and others were certain they would marry, and even seem to have conspired to bring the two together.]

Great heavens, Janet Achurch Charrington, what have you been doing, what have you been saying about me? Here, in these peaceful regions, is a sudden explosion of discussion as to my moral character. Letters from Bertha to me and to Beatrice, letters from Beatrice to Bertha, long wild screeds with nothing intelligible in them except such passages as:—

"I shall see Mrs. Charrington again [AGAIN, mind you]* tomorrow. She is a good woman; and I like her and respect her; and since &c &c &c * * * * * * * What I heard was such a revelation to me that the world seems suddenly to have come to an end. I feel dazed and must rearrange my ideas and take you away from the position you have occupied in my life. * * * * * —but knowing that

* The square brackets here and below are Shaw's, as are the ellipses.

544

you really admire and wish to do just & honorable things, that you choose a lower way of life, *that* I do not understand. [Here comes several noble minded extracts from Liberty on Nordau, after which Bertha proceeds as follows:—] You say all this: you *preach* it really and then I hear all that I have heard from Janet. What can I think? How is it possible to think of such writing as anything but hypocrisy, and to feel anything but contempt for it?"

What on earth have you been telling her? Everything that could explain such an explosion she knows perfectly well already. You must have romanced quite recklessly to bring down all this on my devoted head.

The weather has changed. Fierce sunshine and a heavy heat are upon the land; there has been a multitudinous birth of insects; the trees and flowers have begun to burn in a stealthy sort of way with rich colors. Nature, in short, is having a fit of abandoned profligacy. This seems to have spread to Bertha's studio & affected the conversation there.

My little Napoleon play progresses very slowly, and grows more ridiculous from page to page. The fun of it to me is that the character is not Napoleon at all, but Mansfield.

Ha! post hour.

GBS

To JANET ACHURCH

The Argoed. Monmouth
24th August 1895

[T/1 (A/4)]

[C.P. Little (d. 1914) was a comedy actor and journalist who had recently appeared in *The Case of Rebellious Susan* and *The Ladies' Idol*. Herman de Lange (1852–1929), who had directed *Widowers' Houses* in 1892, played Giuseppe to Granville Barker's Napoleon in the first London production of *The Man of Destiny* in 1901. The "confounded" Fabian paper was "The Political Situation," read on 4th October in the Essex Hall. *The Son of Don Juan* was a play by the Spanish dramatist José Echegaray (1833–1916), whose *Mariana* was performed by Elizabeth Robins in 1897. Mansfield appears not to have produced the play after all. *Prude's Progress* was a popular comedy by Jerome K. Jerome and Eden Phillpotts, which had been running in London since May.

Thomas Hardy's "Jack Ketch piece" was his one-act play *The Three Wayfarers*, which had been produced by Charrington (who played the hangman) at Terry's Theatre on 3rd June 1893, for a single week, on a quintuple bill which included plays by Conan Doyle, Mrs W.K. Clifford and W.H. Pollock, Lady Colin Campbell, and J.M. Barrie. Janet's short story,

545

"The Lucky Man," appeared in the *English Illustrated Magazine* in December 1895. Mrs Webb's sister was Margaret Hobhouse (1854–1921); her son Stephen (1881–1961), who later became a Quaker, was a conscientious objector during World War I, and co-author, with A. Fenner Brockway, of *English Prisons To-day* (1922).

In 1928 Bertha Newcombe, after reading this letter, provided the following note for Ashley Dukes, who proposed at the time to publish the correspondence:

"As, in a letter from 'The Argoed' dated Aug. 24 1895 Shaw refers to his acquaintance with me I think it only just that I should be allowed to state, what seems to me after nearly 40 years to be a fairly true account of our friendship. Shaw was, I should imagine, by preference a passionless man. He had passed through experiences and he seemed to have no wish for and even to fear passion though he admitted its power & pleasure. The sight of a woman deeply in love with him annoyed him. He was not in love with me, in the usual sense, or at any rate as he said only for a very short time, and he found I think those times the pleasantest when I was the appreciative listener. Unfortunately on my side there was a deep feeling most injudiciously displayed & from this distance I realise how exasperating it must have been to him. He had decided I think on a line of honourable conduct—honourable to his thinking. He kept strictly to the letter of it while allowing himself every opportunity of transgressing the spirit. Frequent talking, talking, talking of the pros & cons of marriage, even to my prospects of money or the want of it, his dislike of the sexual relation & so on, would create an atmosphere of love-making without any need for caresses or endearments.

"But in what he says in this letter, he is not fair to me. Love-making would have been very delightful doubtless, but I wanted, besides, a wider companionship, and as I was inadequately equipped for that, except as a painter of some intelligence, he refused to give more than amusement. Shaw has not a gift of sympathetic penetration into a woman's nature. He employs his clever detective power and pounces on weaknesses & faults which confirm his pre-conceived ideas. He imagines he understands. I objected to my emotions being divided into compartments and still retain my opinion that the emotion of love can be a fusion of body, spirit & mind.

"Nevertheless I acknowledge now that the hand of Providence with Shaw's consent & guidance intervened with good results on his behalf in warding off any possibility of a marriage with me" (transcript, BM).]

I have just finished the first draft of "The Man of Destiny," as I provisionally—perhaps permanently—call my one-act play. It is not exactly a burlesque: it is more a harlequinade, in which Napoleon and a strange lady play harlequin & columbine, and a chuckle headed, asinine young sub lieutenant (capital part for Little) and an innkeeper (equally capital part for De Lange) play clown and pantaloon. The dialogue is

546

all pure Shaw—nothing Candidesque or human—neither of you will like a line of it. It is in the style of Arms & The Man rather—

Great Heavens, I have just rescued it from a frightful fate. I am lying in a field, writing in any old note book with a fountain pen. A foal came up behind me that time & was just stretching down for a mouthful of the little book with the play in it when I became aware of him. And now he won't go away. I must move into the next field. * * * * * * * *

So you see I have not enlarged our repertory at all; and when I have completed the play—put in the stage business and read up and supplied the history & geography & invented the pretexts for the dramatic action (which is all in blank still) it will be time to set to work on a confounded paper with which I have to open the Fabian season on the first Friday in October.

Everybody seems bent on recommending me to marry Bertha—a fact fatal to her hopes (if it is fair to accuse her of hopes). The feeling, as I understand it, is that there is a fearful danger of my marrying somebody, and that it is perhaps more prudent to pair me with Bertha than to run the risk of my being borne off by someone worse. Now my own view is that since she is neither strong enough nor disorderly enough for a lawless life, nor cold & self sufficient enough to enjoy a genuinely single one, she ought to marry someone else. She is only wasting her affections on me. I give her nothing; and I do not even take everything—in fact I don't take anything, which makes her most miserable. She has no idea with regard to me except that she would like to tie me like a pet dog to the leg of her easel & have me always to make love to her when she is tired of painting. And she might just as well feel that way to Cleopatra's needle. When I tell her so, it only mortifies & tantalises & attracts her & makes her worse. If you told her so, it would be intolerable. So I wish somebody would come along & marry her before she worries herself into a state of brokenheartedness.

—(After lunch indoors)—

I have just received a copy of the New York "Home Journal." It contains an article on my Nordau letter, and a reprint of your Sketch interview, with the part about Mansfield summarised as being the same as that already given by you. Also a paragraph to the effect that Mansfield will open the Garrick in October with "The Son of Don Juan."

Drinkwater has written to me to say that he will see Weighton about giving up "Arms & The Man." He is evidently quite willing to jump at getting out of his arrears, which come to Heaven knows how much.

547

At the same time I am afraid his tour has hopelessly spoiled the date market with the provincial managers. His address is 1 Ladbroke Crescent, Notting Hill W. His having a "Prude's Progress" tour on hand suggests that his resources are larger than I thought. I fancy Miss Lilian Revell has embarked pecuniarily in his enterprise—at least she did so, in spite of my efforts to dissuade both of them, in "Arms & The Man." I suggest that if you open a new "Arms & The Man" prospect to him he may elect to pay up and stick to it. Would it not put you in a stronger position if the rights in the play were in my hands and at your disposal? Besides, how are the conflicting claims of the four principals (Achurch-Charrington & Drinkwater-Revell) to be adjusted? I have no faith whatever in any project that you undertake in desperation: it means fighting when you are weakest. The moment you get that feeling that something *must* be done, that four years of inaction are the limit of endurance, then do nothing. When the fit passes, and you feel quite disposed to wait ten years if necessary, then you will be in the proper magnetic condition for impressing capitalists and making favorable arrangements. By the way, have you read Echegaray's "Mariana"? C.C. scoffs at it; but it struck me as being a good star play for a woman; and if Mansfield makes a success of "The Son of Don Juan," then it might make up a six night repertory along with Nora, Candida, [G.E. Lessing's] Emilia Galotti, Alexandra, and a triple bill of "The Man of Destiny," [R.L. Stevenson and W.E. Henley's] Admiral Guinea, and Hardy's Jack Ketch piece. All three would be in the serious key of a company which might be utterly unable to touch The Philanderer.

If I recollect "The Lucky Man" aright, it is a very substantial five pounds' worth; but it is lucky to get anything at all for it as a beginning. There is no American copyright: you would have to get it set up and printed in America in order to obtain a copyright. So don't bother Shorter about it. If he publishes it in one of his papers, you will both have the right of preventing each other from republishing it separately for 23 years to come, the net result being that if ever you want to publish it in a volume of stories, he will let you do so as a matter of course by the literary equivalent of "kind permission." However, if you have any means of planting stories in America, why not do so? American papers are supposed to pay better than English ones.

We had a whole string of thunder storms here yesterday. I got a headache after getting wet in one of them on my way back from seeing Wallas off, and it was in the reaction of this that I finished the play this morning. I am not absolutely convinced that I am having a holiday at all. Long bicycle rides, ending with a crushing walk pushing the machine up this 800 foot mountain, take as much out of me as they put in, though my nerves must be tolerably healthy judging from the small provocation on which I risk my life by putting up my feet & flying headlong down hills with bends in them which make it impossible to see from the top whether the way is clear. The valleys are so beautiful in the evening that I get some *recreation* from them in spite of everything; but I somehow want a deeper solitude and a more intimate communion than is possible here. Not that this is anybody's fault; but it is so. Mrs Webb has a sister here whose little boy turns instinctively to the anarchical side of me, and is intensely anxious to have his flesh made creep by stories of devils, dwarfs, wild beasts and all manner of horrors, so that he can enjoy the luxury of not daring to lie awake at night. Wallas presented an anxious problem, as he is getting very uneasy in the bonds of socialism, and we all had fearful and prolonged arguments & pleadings which had to be steered carefully clear of ending in strained bonds & possibly broken ones. Sometimes I have felt that if I could bicycle over to Onslow Gardens and spend a couple of hours under the trees there talking to you, it would be a relief. Here I have to present a strong & alert front to everybody. The Webbs pet one another as if they were honeymooning (as usual). Mrs Williams [the domestic?] pets the boy & is petted by him; I preserve a grave superiority to these weaknesses, but feel secretly willing to ride any distance to be petted too. I only want ten minutes petting to set me up for a month; but I want that reasonable quantity, not deep down, but just on the surface, which is, as you know, the sensitive place. That is the worst of being hard & shallow.

And that is all I can say now. I must start off for a ride—alone this time, as the Webbs are tired.

GBS

To FREDERICK H. EVANS

The Argoed. Monmouth
[A/5]   27th August 1895

[Joseph M. Dent (1849–1926), founder in 1888 of the publishing firm which bears his name, published the Temple Library, the Temple (pocket) Shakespeare, and, later, Everyman's Library. He was the first publisher to employ Aubrey Beardsley as an illustrator. John Lane's Keynote Series was initiated in 1893 with George Egerton's popular *Keynotes*, which inspired

549

the title for the series. Shaw's special correspondence on the Trades Union Congress appeared in *The Star* from 2nd to 7th September.]

My dear Evans

This [specimen page] is famous: more power to your elbow! There is no need to go in for fancy printing in the style of Dent: in fact I don't like it. Artistic printing is just as cheap as inartistic: it is simply a matter of choosing the type and arranging the page. My principles are old face type—Caslon's if possible, the largest type set solid instead of the smallest leaded, broad margins below & at the sides with narrow ones above and in the middle, and, indispensably, that the printer shall be "a fair house" in the Trade Union sense. I like a fat type, to color the page well, and a light, tough, non-shiny paper.

As to the title, I always take the one that has been licked into shape by a thousand tongues, where such a title exists. I never yet met a man who did not speak spontaneously of my "World Articles" when he spoke of them at all. So we will call it "World Articles on Music" by Bernard Shaw (George is now mere waste of ink) with your imprint as suggested. Stick in the passage from the Nordau article by all means if you hanker after it. I must write a preface and interpolate all sorts of comments throughout the book, as a lot of it is probably quite wrong. I shall pay the piper myself if I run to it, as I don't share your enthusiasm for Shaw & had rather not exploit it just yet for anything but work. If I get my money back, we can try again with the Saturday stuff. Suppose I am able to pay the whole bill, how will you take your returns? As bookseller you take your commission; but how as editor? Will you have an extra commission, or a first charge on the receipts for a specified sum or how or what? Don't stint yourself of the un-hatched chickens. I am a first rate business man, and make splendid arrangements, which nobody ever keeps.

Novels be blowed! I have the *papier mâché* moulds of "An Unsocial Socialist," suitable for presentation to an asylum for the blind, as the story can be read from them with the fingers. "Cashel Byron" ought to be out of print by this time, as I shut up my agreement with Scott when the term expired and made no fresh arrangements. I withdrew it from Scott because Lane wanted it for the Keynote Series; but I never had time to follow that up. I wrote five novels altogether: the first was the biggest, but the mice ate most of it; the next two "The Irrational Knot" & "Love Among the Artists" appeared as serials in an extinct magazine (Mrs Besant's "Our Corner") and have never been dug up. They are all jejune & rotten: I shan't write any more of them. Then there are a lot of Fabian papers and scattered articles on Social-

550

ism, including a few *jeux d'esprit* in the Bassetto style. Someday I shall lend you a collection of my old Pall Mall reviews to look over: there may be a spark or two of wit & wisdom in them. There are no less than five plays, without counting "Widowers' Houses." By the Lord, we must someday have a "complete works," library edition, in seventeen volumes, no gentleman's library complete without it. The worst of it is that the great bulk of it is very poor & flimsy & provincial in contrast to what I have done for the last few years.

By the way, my Fabian tracts, though they can be bought for a penny or twopence apiece, would probably do quite well for inclusion in a volume of essays, as no amount of pamphlet circulation seems to touch the ordinary literary-Mudie circulation. For instance, my "Impossibilities of Anarchism," a really good thing of its kind, has never been reviewed.

I want to write a big book of devotion for modern people, bringing all the truths latent in the old religious dogmas into contact with real life—a gospel of Shawianity, in fact. Also an erotic book, which would pass for a sort of novel in the Sentimental Journey manner. Also more plays. Since I came down here I have finished the draft of a one act piece about Napoleon, a very Shawesque curtain raiser. On Saturday next I go to the Trades Union Congress at Cardiff (address Park Hotel, Cardiff, from the 2nd to the 7th Sept.), which I shall probably special-correspondent for The Star; then back here to write a paper on the Political Situation to open the Fabian season at Essex Hall on the 4th Oct; and then back to town to go back into harness & try to run down the constable again.

I typewrite on a Bar Lock; but they now all imitate the Remington type so closely that there is no telling. I think no more of my typewriter now than a schoolboy does of a slate pencil: my new toy is my bicycle. Do you bike?

GBS

To T. FISHER UNWIN

[S/7]   The Argoed. Monmouth
                                           27th August 1895

[*The Life of Napoleon Bonaparte* by the Columbia University historian William Milligan Sloane (1850–1928) was serialised in the *Century Magazine* (New York) from November 1894 to October 1896.]

Dear Fisher Unwin

Out of the vacacitude of the densest historical and geographical ignorance I have been writing a little one-act piece here about Napoleon. Wallas tells me that the Century has been publishing a series of papers about Napoleon's life which will give me all the personal and historical detail I want up to date. If this is so, will you instruct the Paternoster establishment to send me down the numbers containing the Napoleonic articles, with an invoice therefor, and you will greatly oblige

yrs ever

G. Bernard Shaw

To JANET ACHURCH

The Argoed. Monmouth

[T/1 (A/4)]   31st August 1895

[Miss Elizabeth H. Gabler was, of course, Elizabeth Robins. Arthur Bourchier (1863–1927), an actor-manager who had been the prime mover in the foundation of the Oxford University Dramatic Society, was manager of the Royalty Theatre (1895–96), and later of the Garrick. His wife was Violet Vanbrugh (1867–1942), who had toured with the Kendals, under-studied Ellen Terry, and performed with Augustin Daly's company.]

First, make a note that I shall be at the Park Hotel, Cardiff from Monday to Saturday; so that you may address the half dozen letters which I should like to have from you during that period accordingly.

You must have rather astonished Shorter, because Bertha, having a notion that he was not one of your admirers, did not tell him who you were. You must not send the story to America if it is to appear in the English Illustrated: practically you must make up your mind either to sell to an American editor or an English one, but not to both, because they won't arrange to bring out their periodicals on the same day, and if the publication is not simultaneous one or other of the copyrights is voided. If I recollect the length of the story aright, Shorter has nobly sustained his reputation for getting copy & drawings cheap; but do not betray any dissatisfaction; for it would be worth your while to pay him £5 to publish the story as by Janet Achurch in the E.I. Do not hesitate to throw away half a dozen stories if necessary in order to get fairly on the market.

But do you really mean to take to literature? If so, do you realise that it means sitting down every morning from ten to one (say) as regularly & steadily as Irving goes down to the Lyceum & acts in the evening? It means turning out copy as fast as the baker sends the bread, and growing your brain into the shape and condition proper to the professional pursuit of literature. What is more, it means, unless you are careful, the growing of your body into the literary shape, which is not effective on the stage, especially for young parts. Still, it would be better than doing nothing but worrying about having nothing to do. Only, do it regularly as a business or let it alone. Probably you would feel much more free to enjoy yourself & postpone thought & care for the afternoon if you had done your stint (say a thousand words) in the morning. And it seems possible to me that if you were to write fiction and elaborate the stage business of it, so to speak, in some detail, it might even exercise your imagination & suggest new ideas to you for what is, after all, your real profession.

By the way, there is an amusing study of my character from my hand in [the July issue of] The Palmist. I have asked them to send you a copy. The palmist, working from a cast of my hand, is struck by a "curious extension of the mount of Saturn in the direction of the line of the heart" (I quote from memory) and draws conclusions therefrom. The said curious extension is really a sort of broad flabby corn or callosity which you may have noticed on my right hand. The palmist, I regret to say, accuses me, as you do, of atrocious cruelty.

And now, since it passes the time for you and interests you, let us build the usual air castle in the way of theatrical business. I have now filled in the stage business of nearly three quarters of "The Man of Destiny." It is all stage business of the good old Napoleonic kind, hand in breast, hands behind back, trots up and down the room, curt speeches and so on. The woman has a good comedy part, with opportunities for beauty touches if she is capable of them. She must be fascinating; and *she must look well in a man's uniform.* Such are the opera bouffe depths to which I have descended. The whole affair is a contest of wit between Napoleon & the woman, & ought to make an attractive *lever de rideau* with two attractive people in it. The question is where am I to find an actor who will be excited instead of revolted at the idea of anticipating Irving? Tree is too tall & has not the concentration & suddenness of manner for a stage Napoleon. Would Esmond do it? Added to his bill at the St James's it might make all the difference between failure & success; and it would be a safe advertisement anyhow. And then—Eugene. Can it be worked, think you? With a view to the uniform, and the extreme immorality of the play, I think I shall suggest Miss Elizabeth H. Gabler for the woman's part. It would confirm her worst opinion of me. I doubt whether you would care for the part, though of course you could work it up. However, I have never seen you in it when writing it: indeed I haven't seen anyone in it: it is a pure fantasy. Within reasonable limits I should not make any difficulty about the leading lady if I could get the right man into it. And since I insist on you for Candida, I do not want to create the impression that I do so, not on artistic grounds, but on the usual personal ones. Esmond, for instance, might do as he liked as to this little play if it would lead to his doing what I like as to Candida. At the same time, if he were spontaneously to suggest that you might do for the lady (who is nameless, by the way, like a first citizen or second murderer), I should secretly rejoice, though C. C. would tear his hair, as you could not make a success of it except by treating it in a way peculiar to yourself, and apart from the comedy lines on which it is laid out. Failing Esmond, there seems nobody but Bourchier. His wife would enjoy the play; but his Napoleon would be a curious performance. Hare would be a capital Napoleon; but I suppose he would not brave etiquette so far, nor Alexander, nor Wyndham (who, as Buonaparte, would convulse the town).

Weighton & Drinkwater both jump at the chance of wiping off their arrears to me by surrendering "Arms & The Man." So far, the Shaw repertory is ready for the capitalist. By the way, if it ever comes to forming a company for the road, we shall miss the faithful Flemming.

Bertha is an idiot. She has mistaken her annoyance at my preventing Mrs Webb from asking her down here for moral disapproval of me. Sometimes I feel remorseful at having deprived her of the extraordinarily beautiful and moving aspects that Nature puts on here occasionally; but I suppose if she were here she would be thinking about her affairs of the heart instead of about her business. As for me, I am having no holiday at all; I have all the sensations of being worked stale from which these two months should rescue me; and I—I, George Bernard Shaw—have actually suffered from something which in anyone else I should call unhappiness. I would give anything for a moment of really sacred solitude, and perhaps twice as much for a moment of really sacred intimacy. The frightful sensation of being always on guard with another man's wife, which I escape in your case by openly and recklessly adoring you, seems to me to develop itself here to a perfectly devilish intensity. Beatrice's nature is so hostile to mine that in spite of all the admiration, esteem, kindly feeling and other dry goods that abound between us, it is only by holding my edge steadily at the most delicately felt angle to her grindstone that I can avoid becoming hateful to her. The strain on my attention is as fatiguing as writing two Saturday articles a week. Even she, though it is I who do the holding, and though she can always relieve any strain by bathing her heart in Webb's endearments, has to admit that we embarrass each other frightfully when we are alone together without some subject of keen and immediate interest to discuss. As an Irishman, an irregular artistic person, an anarchist in conduct, and above all, a creator of an atmosphere subtly disintegrative of households, I am antipathetic to her. And there are all sorts of discrepancies between her attitude to Webb & mine, too minute to be analysed here, but all felt by her, and all tending to the point of my valuing him more highly than she does (apart from love), and, just because she does not value him as much as I do, valuing her less than I value him. "I think" she said the other evening, when we were all amusing one another with personal criticisms, as our way is,—"I think Shaw regards me as a very useful wife for you." Now if you consider this speech you will see that it implies that I see a certain distance between herself and Webb, and that I stand closer to him myself, and therefore am an influence tending to make him conscious of the distance & thrust them asunder. Thus the un-embarrassed good understanding between myself and Webb makes the understanding between myself & Beatrice depend on our being con-stantly more or less on our guard, and resolutely friendly & remorseful for being unfriendly. Of course I could put forth my subtleties and bring her to a point of view where we could really understand one another if only she were a perfectly free woman; but that would involve an intimacy with her even closer than Webb's (you will understand that I am not here dealing with any sexual or physical intimacy) because there are no such obstacles of temperament between her and Webb as there are between her and me, and he can therefore never be forced to get down & back into the very foundation of her mind as I should have to do. If I did this, she would no longer be in any really special personal sense Webb's wife: the marriage, spiritually, would dissolve and vanish. The knowledge (conscious or unconscious) of this would prevent her from allowing me to take the first steps, and equally prevent me from taking them because we are not in love with one another, and nothing short of that could nerve us to such an enterprise. And so we spend our holidays together, & admire & esteem one another, and get on one another's nerves frightfully. Imagine what this is to me, spoiled as I am by the freedom and happiness of my intercourse with you.

Tomorrow morning (Sunday) I ride off to Cardiff on bikeback. I am not sure that it is not this abominable machine that has destroyed my nerve. The hills are so bad that it sometimes takes an hour & a half to go five miles; and each ride ends by shoving the thing up 800 feet through impossible lanes to this Argoed-Ararat. The other evening, after riding over thirty miles up hill & down dale, and finishing by fifteen miles at full speed to escape being overtaken by darkness (I had left my lamp at home), I was so abominably tired after pushing the thing up the lane that when I mounted to try and ride a level bit, I tumbled off. I thought I was alighting on a grass strip by the way side; but it was a briar bush which let me gracefully down to the bottom of a deep ditch. The bicycle fell over me across the top of the ditch, and as I lay there looking up peacefully at the moon through the spokes of the wheel and the laced thorntwigs of the briar, I felt blessedly happy and at rest. It required the strongest exertion of my common sense to get up and force myself on to the house. That was on Thursday; and I have not ridden either today or yesterday. Tomorrow I shall be fresh for the thirtyfive miles to Cardiff; and then business, Trade Union Congress, special correspondence for The Star, and Richard himself again.

GBS

P.S. Let me hear how the Hammersmith affair [Charrington's lecture on "A People's Theatre" to the Hammersmith Socialist Society on 1st September] comes off.

To T. FISHER UNWIN

[S/7]

The Argoed. Monmouth
9th September 1895

[Shaw's review of Echegaray's *Mariana* and *The Son of Don Juan*, published by Unwin in the Cameo Series in translations by James Graham, appeared in the *Saturday Review* on 27th April 1895.]

Dear Fisher Unwin

I see on referring to your letter that the Napoleon Centuries were sent on by rail. I shall make enquiries at the station about them.

It is very good of you to declare your readiness to become my publisher; but believe me, you deceive yourself. If I sent you anything, you would open it with joyful anticipation, finish reading it with dismay and utter disappointment, and only proceed with it to spare my feelings. I should feel the meanest of mortals if, after nearly sixteen years experience of the effect I produce on publishers (my first book was finished in 1879) I were to take advantage of your personal good

556

nature to involve you in a very doubtful speculation. Just as your letter arrived, I was engaged in a negotiation with an enthusiastic Shawite bookseller who has actually compiled a volume from my musical criticisms (knowing that I would never take that trouble myself) and wanted me to get it published in the ordinary course. But I will get the book manufactured at my own cost & risk & hand it to him to sell. If it pays its way, well & good: if not, nobody is the worse except myself.

By the way, is there any public as yet which reads plays? When you sent me the Echegaray volumes I wrote them up in the Saturday & urged them on the notice of Richard Mansfield, the actor. I see now that he declares his intention of opening the Garrick (New York) next season with "The Son of Don Juan." Do those Cameos sell? I noticed that Heinemann, after trying a 6/- Mrs Tanqueray, relapsed into the old 1/6 for Mrs Ebbsmith; and I know that these cheap Pineros only sell to amateur clubs. But if I thought that people were picking up the French trick of reading dramatic works, I should be strongly tempted to publish my plays instead of bothering to get them performed.

> yrs ever
> G. Bernard Shaw

To EDWARD R. PEASE

[C/4]
The Argoed. Monmouth
11th September 1895

Dear Pease

I cannot see my way to a [lecture] tour just now. I must get back to town and into harness about the end of next week; and meanwhile my time is full. Put them all off until next year.

> GBS

To JANET ACHURCH

[T/1 (A/4)]
The Argoed. Monmouth
16th September 1895

[Bertrand Russell (b. 1872), the third Earl Russell (from 1931), mathematician, philosopher, and leading exponent of pacifism, received the Nobel Prize for Literature in 1950. Shaw attended *Romeo and Juliet* at the Lyceum on 23rd September (see letter of 1st November 1895 to Ellen Terry).]

So you like cycling stories. Well, here is another. On Thursday afternoon I was flying down a steep hill on the Chepstow Road, with my feet up on the rests, going at a speed that took the machine miles beyond my control. A friend of ours named Russell, a brother of the Lord Russell whose wife has been making him famous by her suit for restitution, was in front of me; and Webb was behind me. Seeing the road clear before us, I gave myself up to the enjoyment of a headlong tearing toboggan down the hill. Imagine my feelings when I saw Russell jump off and turn his machine right across my path to read a signpost! Or rather imagine what I would have felt if I had had time for speculation. I rang my bell and swerved desperately to the right: he looked round and backed with his machine to the right—my right—also. Then—smash. In the last second, I managed to make a twist to the left which prevented my going into him absolutely at right angles; but the catastrophe was appalling enough in all conscience as it was. Russell, fortunately, was not even scratched; but his knickerbockers were demolished—how, I don't know. The footrests were snatched from his machine, which was upset and rattled about. My front wheel, which took the whole shock, behaved nobly; for it was still usable in a staggering way, being rounder than an hourglass but not quite so round as a garter. As for me, I flew through the air for several yards, and then smote the earth like a thunderbolt, literally hip and thigh—also shoulder, very hard, and wrists. "All right," I shouted (as if there were any hurry about it now) "I am not hurt" and bounded up, pulling myself all together instinctively. "You *must* be," said Russell, glaring at me in consternation. But apparently I wasn't: for as Webb shot past us I picked up my bike and trundled it up the hill. At the top, I felt sick, and the hills and clouds and farmhouses began to tumble about drunkenly. I sat down by the roadside. Webb suggested water. I got worse, and stretched myself flat on my back. Webb suggested brandy, seeing (as he afterwards informed me) that my lips were violet. But I scoffed at these delusive remedies, and lay as the dead. In ten minutes I got up, mounted my staggering bike after jumping on the wheel until it became moderately round, and rode to our destination (Tintern Abbey) and back to the Argoed—about 15 or 16 miles. I was not cut, my gloves having saved my wrists, and not very much bruised. But my muscles were diabolically wrenched, and my nerves considerably astonished. In the evening, the persistent funny laughing sort of pain from the strained muscles gave me shivering fits and slight nausea. Cold water made me tremble; I almost felt tempted to shirk my tub, like a child. However, that wore off next day. My sight was good and steady and my hand didn't shake, so I concluded that I was not damaged after all. The bike went off to London for repairs. I thought I could get on excellently without it for the rest of my holiday; but this afternoon I rode to Goodrich Castle and back on Webb's machine with Beatrice, 22 miles. I had made up my mind that I was rather shaken and that my nerves would not stand flying any more hills; but my patience gave out at the second one. I stuck up my feet and took it whizzing. I then concluded that the seriousness of the smash was all my imagination. Still I am not thoroughly convinced yet that I was not killed. Anybody but a vegetarian would have been. Nobody but a teetotaller would have faced a bicycle again for six months.

It is now settled that we start for London on Saturday next. If my bicycle is ready by that time I will ride home with the Webbs by way of Stonehenge and Basingstoke, arriving in London on Monday afternoon in time to go to the theatre (it's a first night somewhere, isn't it?). If the machine is still in hospital, I shall come up by train and be in town for Drury Lane on Saturday night. So let me have a line to say whether you have any engagement for Sunday, in case I should be in town on that day.

GBS

P.S. Did the Palmist not come? They wrote to me from the office to say that it had been forwarded in accordance with my instructions.

P.P.S. News just arrived that the bicycle is back—£3.15.0. This will give you a livelier idea of the extent of the ruin than any eloquence of mine. The machine being here, I will ride back to London (which means arriving on Monday afternoon) if the weather is good.

To PAKENHAM BEATTY

The Argoed. Monmouth
17th September 1895

[B/4]

[Charles Maddock Stuart (1857–1932) was first headmaster of St Dunstan's College, Catford, 1888–1922. The Rt. Hon. James Stuart (1843–1913) was Professor of Mechanism at Cambridge, 1875–89, and Labour M.P. for Hoxton, 1885–1900.]

If you hear rumors of my death, contradict them. I have had a most awful bicycle smash—the quintessence of ten railway collisions—

brother of Earl Russell of conjugal rights fame dashed into at full speed flying down a hill—£3.10.0 damage to machine—got up within the prescribed ten seconds, but had subsequently to admit knock-out—Russell bereft of his knickerbockers but otherwise unhurt—lay flat on my back for ten minutes, but then rose and rode 16 miles back on a wheel the shape of an hourglass—have got over it and flown down other hills since—will ride back to London via Stonehenge on Saturday Sunday & Monday next.

By the way, what about that boy of yours? Is there anything in the notion that he has the Dowling turn for mechanics? Because if he has, there is within reach about the best engineering school in the world for boys up to 17 or thereabouts—St Dunstan's College, Catford Bridge, Lewisham. The fee is £12 a year; but they spend three times that sum on every boy out of their endowments. 200 or 300 boys there, easy to get in by simply applying, thoroughly up to date, looked after by Technical Education Board of County Council (Webb, with whom I am staying, is chairman of the Board), headmaster C.M.Stuart, brother of Professor Stuart M.P. for Hackney. Of course they do not confine themselves to engineering; but that is their strong point. Do, in the name of all that's sensible, avoid laying up a heritage of woe for your old age by letting the boy drift into the world without a profession & training. Remember, it is no longer an affair of years now: *it's a question of minutes*: he has not sixty seconds to spare. And if the distance is a difficulty, move to Lewisham or Lee or thereabouts: its just as pretty as Ealing & probably cheaper.

GBS

To EDWARD R.PEASE

The Argoed. Monmouth
[C/4]   17th September 1895

[Shaw was one of the speakers at a meeting in the Club and Institute Hall, London, on 8th October to enlist assistance for the London Socialist Scouts. "The Political Situation: A Fabian View" appeared in the *Daily Chronicle* on 5th October.]

Dear Pease

I can only promise conditionally. If I am free of dramatic duty I will take on the Scouts. As far as I can foresee, I am not specially likely to be engaged on any of the dates named: first nights are generally either Thursdays or Saturdays.

I expect to get back to town on Monday.

GBS

PS. Ask the executive whether they will empower me to give a copy of my paper in advance to the Daily Chronicle to be printed as a verbatim report (if I can persuade Massingham to do it) also whether in that case I may have a couple of typewritten copies (carbons) prepared at the Society's expense. Can we afford such luxuries?

To FREDERICK H. EVANS

[S/1]

29 Fitzroy Square W
25th September 1895

[Benjamin Tucker did not "justify" his lines (*i.e.*, space words to align at the right-hand margin) in *Liberty*, hence the "blank verse" appearance. Richard Mansfield was stricken with typhoid in late July, and for nearly three months hovered between life and death. He returned to the stage on 25th November, in Philadelphia, in *Beau Brummel.*]

I can't reprint the Nordau essay after making a present of the first bite to Tucker. Besides, I intensely enjoy making people swallow Liberty & the blank verse printing & so on. That number of Liberty will be worth 15/- someday.

Mansfield, the American Bluntschli (hero of "Arms & The Man") is down with typhoid fever. If he expires, goodbye to my chance of getting the arrears of royalty on which I am depending for the manufacture of *our* book!!!!!

G.B.S.

To CHARLES CHARRINGTON

[T/1 (A/4)]

29 Fitzroy Square W
7th October 1895

[J. T. Grein had become London representative of Wellenstein, Krause & Co., Dutch East India merchants, a post he held until his retirement in 1922. Dorothy Leighton (Mrs G. C. Ashton Jonson) was co-founder with Grein of the Independent Theatre, and the author of *Thyrza Fleming*, produced by the I.T. on 4th January 1895 at Terry's Theatre. *Einsame Menschen* was not by Sudermann, but by Gerhart Hauptmann (1862–1946). The I.T. had acquired rights to the play in 1894, but it was not produced. Although Ibsen's *Little Eyolf* was subsequently announced for production, a disagreement with William Heinemann, who held the copyright, resulted in his withdrawal of the play (see letter of 18th February 1896 to Heinemann, and the latter's reply). It was eventually produced by Elizabeth Robins in November 1896.]

Dear Charrington

The following piece of news is to be kept a dead secret until the 26th: at least such is the condition on which it has been imparted to me. Grein, who represented, along with a partner, a Dutch firm, has been promoted to the sole representative on the withdrawal of the partner. The Dutch firm, however, exact (very properly) that their representative shall not appear as managing director of such a very shady joint stock company as the I. T. Limited, though they don't mind his amusing himself with it unofficially. Therefore, at the shareholders' meeting on the 26th, Grein will retire, and Dorothy Leighton will have to be provided with another co-director. She consulted me today as to where she could find one, being apparently quite at a loss. I said that you were the only person I knew of who was fit for the job— suggesting you speculatively, of course, without pretending to have any idea how it would strike you. She did not seem to consider the fact of your not being a member as an obstacle; and I imagine the thing is at your disposal if you care to undertake it. Dorothy's idea is to give one performance a year to keep the thing alive and avert winding up. There is £400 left in the till. And she would gladly take the opportunity to get rid of De L[ange], who contrived, with his usual tact, to offend her over "Thyrza Fleming." There are no plays available except one of Suderman's—"Einsame Mensche," I think, is its maiden name.

I told her there was no longer a *raison d'etre* for the I.T. Still, a season consisting of "Little Eyolf," if Elizabeth could be brought into the combination for one turn, and "Mrs Warren" for a good scandal, would be enough to keep the institution alive for another year and provide a good use for some of that £400.

Dorothy Leighton was very anxious to know whether your prudence could be relied on. She evidently feels that she should be helpless in the hands of a co-director who really knew the business, and is consequently afraid of getting one who would stake the whole treasury on a single cast.

GBS

To CHARLES CHARRINGTON

[T/1 (C/4)]

29 Fitzroy Square W
10th October 1895

I seem to have been rather too fertile of suggestions this time; for the alternative I placed before Dorothy L. was a co-director of her own sex with some experience of management, like Miss Robins and Miss Farr. Today I am rather taken aback by a letter from Grein in which he declares himself in favor of the Miss Farr suggestion. He is undoubtedly right if he wants to keep the I.T. dependent on him personally, as F.F. would not edge him out by mere force of gravitation as a stronger director certainly would. I wonder whether she would take it.

As there will be nobody at the shareholders' meeting except the people Dorothy packs it with, anything that can be arranged with her can probably be passed.

GBS

To FREDERICK H. EVANS

[B/4]

29 Fitzroy Square W
15th October 1895

[Shaw's lecture on 1st December was "The Political Situation," delivered in Battersea to the Labour League.]

I'll go up and see you some evening—I want to look at your photographs &c. Unluckily they have nailed me somewhere for a lecture on the 1st. Dec.: otherwise I should go to Kelmscott to see your slides. I think next Saturday is a first night at the theatre; and on Sunday I am always on the stump. Shall we say next Tuesday, between 7 & 9 (By the way, I am a teetotaller & never eat anything after 7; so don't buy a bottle of whisky or anything else for me).

We can talk then about the book. I won't let you risk anything on it—I know too much about my books for that; but I daresay I shall manage somehow after a while. It is part of the bargain, however, that you figure as editor, though you are quite welcome to write a preface repudiating my proceedings if I cut too deep into the stuff you have selected. Would it be possible to issue a first series & then, if that succeeded, a second series later on, possibly with some sort of classification—sacred & profane, ancient & modern, or something of that sort.

GBS

563

To CHARLES CHARRINGTON

[T/1 (C/4)]

29 Fitzroy Square W
19th October 1895

I have just had a talk with Grein; and it seems to me that Dorothy must have stood out for a male partner. At all events nothing was said of F.F.; and it was assumed throughout the conversation that you were to be the new co-director. Grein's counsel, his guidance, his inspiration will ever be magnanimously at your service if you should be overweighted by his mantle. I am to see him on Wednesday or Thursday. Apparently the job is very much on instead of off.

GBS

To ELLEN TERRY

[U(A)/10; X/117]

29 Fitzroy Square W
1st November 1895

[Beatrice Stella Tanner (1865–1940), who married Patrick Campbell in 1884 (he died in 1900), made her first professional stage appearance in Liverpool in 1888. By the time she and Shaw met in 1897, Mrs Campbell was one of London's reigning stars and acknowledged beauties, having scored triumphantly as the mad Astrea in G.R. Sims and Robert Buchanan's *The Trumpet Call* at the Adelphi in 1891, followed by *The Second Mrs Tanqueray* and *The Notorious Mrs Ebbsmith*. It was not until 1912, however, when Shaw wrote *Pygmalion* for her, that the famous Stella-Joey relationship came into being.

At the time of this letter Mrs Campbell was appearing with Forbes-Robertson at the Lyceum in *Romeo and Juliet*. Shaw, reviewing the production in the *Saturday Review* on 28th September, had reported that, though "she danced like the daughter of Herodias," Mrs Campbell's performance was "immature . . . at all the exceptional points . . ." There was, he added, "not a touch of tragedy, not a throb of love or fear, temper instead of passion: in short, a Juliet as unawakened as Richard III . . . Nothing of it is memorable except the dance—the irresistible dance."

Eleanora Duse had appeared in *Antony and Cleopatra* at the Lyric Theatre on 19th June 1893. Florence St John (1855–1912), a light-opera singer, had recently appeared in revivals of Audran's *The Mascotte* and Offenbach's *Madame Favart* at the Criterion. Lucy Carr Shaw had toured with her in 1883 in Offenbach's *Lurette* and *Barbe-Bleu*.]

My dear Miss Terry

This lonely critic's den, on which you have shed a ray from a newspaper wrapper, is wonderfully warmed up by it. It came just when it was wanted. I had just finished a magnificent article, not on the theatre, but on "Churchgoing" (of all subjects!) for a new quarterly; and the effort, complicated by the inexorable swing round of The Saturday Review weekly criticism, had left me *sore* with labor. At that exact moment your impulse to pet me for a moment came to hand, with heavenly effect.

I am interested in the bicycling, having lately tamed that steed myself; but I utterly refuse to concern myself with your Beatrices & Portias and the like. *Anybody* can play Shakspere: you are wanted for other things. Mrs Pat. Campbell entrances all London as Juliet, with a skirt dance. At the end, to shew that she is not going to give herself more trouble than she can help, she takes the dagger, and with a superb laziness, props it against the tomb and leans against the point, plainly conveying that if it will not go in on that provocation, it can let it alone. Then she lies down beside Romeo and revolves herself right over him like the roller of a mangle, leaving his sensitively chiselled profile perceptibly snubbed. Nothing will persuade me that Shakspere ever carries a modern woman with him right through: even Duse could do nothing with Cleopatra; and Mary Anderson, before whom the art of acting fled abashed (Lord have mercy on us, miserable sinners!) did as well as anybody else in Perdita. By the way, if you *will* let Shakspere steal you to decorate his plays with, why not play Hermione? Leontes is a magnificent part, worth fifty Othellos (Shakspere knew nothing about jealousy when he wrote "Othello"), as modern as Ibsen, and full of wonderful music—"I have tremor cordis on me" & so on.

To my great exasperation I hear that you are going to play Madame Sans Gene. And I have just finished a beautiful little one act play for Napoleon and a strange lady—a strange lady who will be murdered by someone else whilst you are nonsensically pretending to play a washerwoman. It is too bad—I tell you you can't play a washerwoman. Besides, your place is not *after* Rejane. I was asked to do an English Madame Sans Gene as an opera, for Florence St John. That was suitable enough: I said I'd do it if I had time, which I never had (time meaning will). If they had asked me to do it for Ellen Terry, I would have obliterated them from the surface of the globe. Will your tomb in Westminster Abbey have nothing but reproaches for an epitaph?

G.B.S.

29 Fitzroy Square W

[A/1; X/125]   4th November 1895

[The rôle of Mrs Warren eventually was created by Fanny Brough, in 1902. The suggested "interview" did not appear.]

Dear Sir

Will you excuse an answer scribbled in a metropolitan train. The paragraph you send me is (from its point of view) accurate enough. The actress alluded to is Mrs Theodore Wright, to whom I proposed the part of Mrs Warren. She was greatly startled when I read it to her; but the suggestion that she considered it a play that ought not to have been written will, I hope, be met presently by the announcement that she has consented to play the part. She has not done so yet, because she is only acquainted with the first two acts (an accidental visitor interrupted my reading of it to her); but she is at any rate quite open to consider it.

The play is a cold bloodedly appalling one; but not in the least a prurient one. Mrs Warren is much worse than a prostitute. She is an organism of prostitution—a woman who owns & manages brothels in every big city in Europe & is proud of it. With her gains she has had her daughter highly educated and respectably brought up in complete ignorance of the source of her mother's income. The drama, of course, lies in the discovery and its consequences. These consequences, though cruel enough, are all quite sensible & sober, no suicide nor sensational tragedy of any sort. Nobody's conscience is smitten except, I hope, the conscience of the audience. My intention is that they shall go home thoroughly uncomfortable. I can at least guarantee that any person who goes to gratify any prurient curiosity will be completely disappointed, as I am not a pandar posing as a moralist. The play has horrified everyone who has heard it, but only as an honest treatment of such a subject ought to horrify them. I want to make an end, if I can, of the furtively lascivious Pharisaism of stage immorality, by a salutary dramatisation of the reality. Miss Janet Achurch at once offered to play the part of the daughter, in whom I have sought to put on the stage for the first time (as far as I know) the highly educated, capable, independent young woman of the governing class as we know her today, working, smoking, preferring the society of men to that of women simply because men talk about the questions that interest her and not about servants & babies, making no pretence of caring much about art or romance, respectable through sheer usefulness & strength, and playing

566

the part of the charming woman only as the amusement of her life, not as its serious occupation. What do you think of that as a program for a heroine? To soften the prospect I may add that her lover will be a youth of infinite charm, absolutely good-for-nothing, and absolutely pleasant. The Independent Theatre will find no difficulty in filling the parts. If the play were as vile as has been suggested, neither Miss Achurch or any other artist would touch it. Why should they, since it could do them nothing but harm?

It may interest you to know that although I had little leisure during my autumn holiday in South Wales with the Sidney Webbs, I managed to complete a one act play the hero of which is Napoleon Buonaparte—the Napoleon of the first Italian campaign, aged 27. The other characters are a strange lady, a sub lieutenant, and an innkeeper; and the whole is in the high comedy vein of "Arms & The Man." I have made no attempt to get it produced, as my position as dramatic critic makes it very difficult for me to take the initiative in any negotiation with our managers.

You can use all this information at your discretion, except that Mrs Theodore Wright's name must be kept back until she has actually consented to play Mrs Warren. Make an interview of it if you like, though I should like a peep at it before it goes to press in that case, as I am writing in haste without much consideration.

If you want to know anything about me at any time, don't hesitate to ask. I hope your plucky start has turned out well.

yrs sincerely
G. Bernard Shaw

To CHARLES CHARRINGTON

29 Fitzroy Square W
[T/1 (C/4)] 4th November 1895

[R. C. Carton's *The Squire of Dames* (adapted from *L'Ami des femmes* by Dumas *fils*) was produced at the Criterion on 5th November. George Alexander had just been arrested on an accusation by a police officer of "intercourse with a prostitute in the ordinary pursuit of her trade." Shaw came to his defence in a letter, "The Charge against Mr George Alexander," in the *Daily Chronicle* on 7th November, in which he noted that "the circumstances as described by Mr. Alexander [of being accosted by a woman of the streets, and, moved by her plight, of offering her charity] up to the point of the intervention of the policeman have occurred to me more than once . . .."

Janet Achurch had appeared for a week in a revival of *The New Magdalen* at the Métropole, Camberwell, on 28th October, immediately after which she became ill, suffering from what she diagnosed as a touch of pleurisy.]

I look for a line from you in the morning, concluding meanwhile that no news is good news. I expect I shall have to go to "L'Ami des Femmes" tomorrow night, though no tickets have arrived so far.

I hope G.A. will get safely out of that wretched mess at Chelsea. Don't tell J. about it. If I may judge from the shock it gave me, it will only throw her back.

GBS

To CHARLES CHARRINGTON

Chronicle Office. 12.45 a.m.
[T/1 (B/4)] 6th November 1895

Here I am correcting a proof. I snatch a moment to implore you to go easy with that accursed anti pyrine. It was recklessly used in the first influenza epidemic and there was a considerable row about it afterwards, its effects being most objectionable. People recover from pleurisy: they dont recover from poison. I am in despair at the discovery of your medical mania. That is always the way: you have only to search an emancipated man's mind long enough to come upon an abyss of superstition somewhere—nowadays generally "scientific."

GBS

To CHARLES CHARRINGTON

29 Fitzroy Square W
[T/1 (B/4)] 8th November 1895

[Janet had grown progressively worse for several days, but it was not until J. Kingston Barton was consulted on 10th November that it was determined she had contracted typhoid fever. "Her illness," Shaw noted laconically in his diary, "occupied me a good deal during the last two months of the year, partly because of its bearing on all possible plans for the production of Candida, & partly because I have come into relations of intimate friendship with the Charringtons during the past 2 years or so." But from an unpublished memoir by Bertha Newcombe, written for Ashley Dukes in 1928, we get a better indication of Shaw's emotional involvement: "Then came [Janet's] illness, and for a time I had the doubtful pleasure of being a witness of Shaw's devotion & anxiety, as he would come and report her condition & his friendly actions for her comfort & that of Charrington, who, when he heard that the illness was typhoid, completely broke down. [Shaw] would tell me of the wretchedness of the household, the want of proper nursing, and how he himself sat for hours holding Janet up in his arms on her pillow . . . Then came a day when he came to tell me that he had been forbidden her room & that her death was possible. He had told me long before how he felt towards death. Anxiety, sorrow, and all efforts at prevention would naturally be undertaken, but after the inevitable end he would, as David did, rise, wash & anoint himself and, putting death behind him, grasp Life again. He said to me, 'Should Janet die, I should *never* forget her.' He then characteristically spent a quite cheerful evening with me & even told me that he had had a delightful time & enjoyed himself" (transcript, BM).]

The devil, the devil, the devil! Everything is going to hell—uncle [Walter Gurly] drunk, paralytic, collapsing and threatening to leave me his cursed [Carlow] property and debts—sister declared by my mother to be going mad—Kate Gurly a wreck—all, damn them, *robbing* Janet and you at the moment when we need our resources most for ourselves. This is not a time for anxiety or tenderness: I no longer care how anybody is: clearly I must fight and bite and work like a shark toothed vice if I am to be of any use.

If Janet is obstinate in the common feminine persuasion that wool will tickle her, better not worry her: people have got well before this in linen sheets. But there are such things as Jaeger sheetings, sold both by the yard and in cut sheets of various sizes. Shall I get some; and if so, what is the size of the napery now in use?

By the way, Barton's address is 2 Courtfield Road (J. Kingston Barton) close to Gloster Rd. station. He is such a swell now that he may have already more patients than he can attend to; but he is not a bloody fool, which is a great point to the good with a doctor. I am full up myself to the last minute today. I feel too savage to ask how Janet is; but you may as well volunteer a card, if it does not worry you too much.

GBS

To R. GOLDING BRIGHT

[A/1; X/125]

29 Fitzroy Square W
11th November 1895

[Pierre-Augustin Caron de Beaumarchais (1732–99), French playwright, was the author of *Le Barbier de Seville* and *Le Mariage de Figaro*, comedies which inspired the operas by Rossini and Mozart. Alfred de Musset (1810–57), French poet and dramatist, wrote *Lorenzaccio* and *Un Caprice*. Émile Augier (1820–89), French poet and dramatist, was the author of several comedies of manners and social satire, including *Le Mariage d'Olympe* and *Les Fourchambault*. Dion Boucicault (1822–90), Dublin-born actor and playwright, who was a leading performer on the New York stage, wrote *The Colleen Bawn*, *The Shaughraun*, and *London Assurance*. Thomas William Robertson (1829–71), dramatist brother of Mrs Kendal, was best known for his "cup-and-saucer drama," including *Ours*, *Society*, and *Caste*. Colley Cibber (1671–1757), actor, dramatist, and poet laureate, is remembered today primarily for his "improvements" in *Richard III* and for his *Apology for the Life of Colley Cibber, Comedian* (1740).]

Dear Sir

I must content myself with a hasty line. It is very possible that the Licenser will object to "Mrs Warren's Profession." It is not as yet settled whether the I.T. will give an invitation performance of the play without troubling him (as was done in the case of "Ghosts") or apply for a license & risk the dropping of the project through his refusal. Until this is settled, I think the point had better not be raised. The date is not fixed; but "Mrs W's Profession" will come *after* "Little Eyolf," not before it.

All this overtime in the city is very objectionable from the point of view of health as well as leisure. For the moment I see no escape except by getting another berth, or some journalistic work.

As to what to read, read anything you feel curious about. It's quite possible that your real interest may not lie in the theatre at all. But in any case, read dramatic literature, not histories or criticisms of it. Read three or four of the most famous plays of Molière & Victor Hugo; and sample Beaumarchais, Voltaire, De Musset, Augier, & Dumas fils, until you know their styles. Read all Goethe's plays & a lot of Schiller's. Read a rhymed play of Dryden's, a play of Wycherley's, some of Congreve's, several of Sheridan, a Boucicault & a Robertson. Read Aeschylus, Sophocles, Euripides & Aristophanes (the Greek literature is very short). Get translations if you don't know the languages. Read them with a notion of their chronological order. Read Ibsen all through. Also Cibber's apology & any memoirs of actors that you can unearth. That will do for a beginning.

If you meet me anywhere, introduce yourself to me, if you don't mind.

In haste
G. Bernard Shaw

570

To CHARLES CHARRINGTON

[T/1 (A/4)]

29 Fitzroy Square W
28th November 1895

[The "cursed thing" was a pamphlet, *Short Summary of the Position and Prospects of the Independent Theatre*, drafted by Shaw, for the reorganised I.T., of which Charrington had been appointed Managing Director in October. As amended by Dorothy Leighton (and bearing her name as author), it was issued just before Christmas. The Camden was an historical society founded in 1838, superseded in 1901 by the Royal Historical Society. The Selden is a society, founded in 1887, to promote study of the history of law. Shaw likened the I.T. to the "private societies" which supplied their supporters with "copies of high-class books . . ."

Aubrey Vincent Beardsley (1872–98) was a black-and-white artist, ornamental illustrator of *The Yellow Book*, Wilde's *Salomé*, Pope's *Rape of the Lock*, and Malory's *Morte d'Arthur*, whose striking originality had a strong influence on the art of his period. The "Beardsley business" concerned the preliminary pictorial circular for *The Savoy*, issued by the publisher Leonard Smithers. Shaw, in Grant Richards's *Author Hunting* (1934), explained: "Beardsley made a charming design of a Pierrot stepping out on to the stage to announce the paper. Smithers foolishly objected that it suggested flippancy and that John Bull would like something serious. Beardsley revenged himself by substituting a monumental John Bull for the Pierrot. Eighty thousand of this were circulated before George Moore's scrutiny detected that John had been represented in a condition of strained sexual excitement. All the contributors thereafter met and informed Smithers that he must 'withdraw' the circular. Not having any of the 80,000 left he agreed; and peace was restored."]

Dear Charrington

I think I have got this cursed thing right at last. Should have finished it last night if I had not collapsed with a bad headache. The forlorn hope attitude is abandoned; and I have mentioned Archer in such a way that it will not be possible for him, if he sees it, to instantly demand the suppression or alteration of every second sentence in the document.

I have left the details about shares and so on to be filled in. When it is printed, let me see a proof before it goes to press (dont get it printed at an "unfair house," by the way). I think Miss Robins ought to be shewn a proof & asked permission to allow her name to be used.

There are blanks for the date of Vernon's adaptation of "Pillars [of Society]," & for the total number of plays given by the I.T. The latter must be carefully counted: Grein is hopelessly inaccurate. The two crosses in the margin at p. 1 & p. 4 mean that I am not quite certain

38—B.S. I.

571

about the accuracy of the titles "Camden" & "Selden" or about the spelling of [Mrs Hugh Bell's] "Karin."

The allusion to the critics at the end will only offend the irreconcileables: all the others will think that they are among the "above suspicion" ones.

Dont let them spoil it. I had rather write another play than do the job over again.

Sorry I can't bring it over & see the invalid; but I am in the thick of this Beardsley business, the post of fighting man in chief having been conceded to me with unanimity by the scandalised contributors.

GBS

To ELLEN TERRY

29 Fitzroy Square W
28th November 1895

[U(A)/10; X/117]

[Ellen Terry and Henry Irving were on tour in America, this being their fifth visit.]

My dear Miss Terry

Very well: here is [the typescript of] The Strange Lady for you, by book post. It is of no use now that it [is] written, because nobody can act it. Mind you bring it safely back to me; for if you leave it behind you in the train or in your dressing room, somebody will give a surreptitious performance of it; and then bang goes my copyright. If the responsibility of protecting it is irksome, tear it up—I have a vague recollection of curl papers in "Nance Oldfield," for which it might be useful. I have other copies.

This is not one of my great plays, you must know: it is only a display of my knowledge of stage tricks—a commercial traveller's sample. You would like my "Candida" much better; but I never let people read that: I always read it to them—they can be heard sobbing three streets off.

By the way—I forget whether I asked you this before—if that villain Mansfield plays "Arms & The Man" anywhere within your reach, will you go & see it & tell me whether they murder it or not. And your petitioner will ever pray &c &c.

G. Bernard Shaw

572

To JOSEPH EDWARDS

[C/4]

29 Fitzroy Square W
29th November 1895

Dear Mr Edwards

When next you are revising the biographies in the Labor Annual, please bring me up to date by mentioning that in January 1895, I joined the staff of The Saturday Review under the editorship of Frank Harris, and immediately became as famous as a dramatic critic as I was under Edmund Yates in The World as a musical one—or something to that modest effect. I find it enormously convenient when people ask me for my biography, to refer them to the L.A. I hope its been a success.

yrs faithfully
G. Bernard Shaw

To FREDERICK H. EVANS

[C/4]

29 Fitzroy Square W
5th December 1895

["Socialism for Millionaires" appeared in the Contemporary Review in February 1896. It was subsequently revised and issued, in 1901, as Fabian Tract No. 107.]

Dear F.H.E.

I hasten to answer your card of the 18th ult., taking it about two months before its turn for the sake of being businesslike. I have had all my spare time taken up by an article on Churches for the Savoy, one on Socialism for Millionaires (not yet finished) for the Contemporary, a circular for the I. Theatre, and a heavy pile of dawdling. This has prevented me from opening the World parcel yet; but when the Contemporary job is over, I shall get to work on it like a giant.

GBS

To T. FISHER UNWIN

[S/7]

29 Fitzroy Square W
6th December 1895

[The printing works of Unwin Brothers, at Chilworth, had been totally destroyed by fire on the night of 23rd–24th November. Unwin announced in *The Times* on 26th November that the fire would not interfere with the issue of his publications.]

Dear Unwin

It's no use—I am kept so busy over fresh work that I cannot make time to prepare the old for publication. It will end in a posthumous edition of my collected writings.

As to plays. I cannot make out the law as to stage rights. The point is, do I forfeit my American stageright if publication precedes performance? If I could secure both copyrights & stagerights intact here and in America I should be strongly tempted to try a volume of dramas.

yrs sincerely
G. Bernard Shaw

P.S. By the way, I hope you did not suffer by the fire. As to the Brothers, serve 'em right!

To EDWARD R. PEASE

29 Fitzroy Square W
6th December 1895

[C/4]

Dear Pease

I'm afraid it's no use: I must keep my weeknights free. Anything like a course of lectures would be very difficult, especially now, with Xmas approaching, and all the current plays failing one after another (which means first nights of new ones).

GBS

To AMY C. MORANT

[29 Fitzroy Square W]
13th December 1895

[X/131]

[Amy Constance Morant, one of the "new women," who had studied economics and moral and political philosophy at Bedford and Newnham Colleges, was an organiser for the Women's Liberal Federation and a member of the S.D.F. and I.L.P. In the *Labour Leader*, on 30th November, she had challenged "our friend, the enemy, G. Bernard Shaw, Fabian" to a public debate on "The Place of Woman in the Community."]

574

Dear Miss Morant

This time you appear to be right. I accept the correction without reserve. As to the challenge, which I saw for the first time the day before yesterday, it is so unprovoked, so irrelevant, so utterly senseless, motiveless, whimsical, bravadoesque, and Miss Morantish in the craziest sense that I flatly decline to be drawn by it. I claim exemption from all that side of your activity. I used to do things of that sort myself, but now I am timid, middle-aged, stale, and serious; and the provocative, the mischievous, the risky, the dramatic, have no charms for me: they only frighten me. Challenge some fresher or foolisher man if you like, but be sensible with me, or I will avoid you like the plague.

yours sincerely
G. Bernard Shaw

To WALTER CRANE

29 Fitzroy Square W
15th December 1895

[X/116]

[Wilhelm Liebknecht (1826–1900), German journalist and politician, founded (with the assistance of Karl Marx) the Social Democratic Labour Party in Germany (1869). For an earlier reference to the "united Socialist" effort, see letter of 18th April 1893 to Pease. John C. Horobin (1855–1902), Principal of Homerton College, had run successfully as a Progressive in the Hackney contest during the last School Board election. Rose (Mrs Thomas) Jarvis was a Fabian who ran as an S.D.F. candidate for Hackney in the same election, but was defeated. She and her husband had resigned from the Fabian Society in May 1895.

Benjamin Tillett (1860–1943), a principal organiser of the Transport Workers, played an important part in the 1889 dock strike and later ran the London dock strikes of 1911 and 1912. He became Labour M.P. for North Salford in 1917. Alfred Illingworth (1827–1907) was a worsted-spinner who became Liberal M.P. for Bradford (1880–85) and West Bradford (1885–95); he defeated the Fabian-sponsored Tillett by 557 votes in the 1892 election.]

My dear Crane

In your letter to the Fabian Society you say a word about a United Socialist party. I have not time to argue out the whole position for you formally; and fortunately it is not necessary with you; so let me just fling down a few of the points which need to be taken into consideration.

The line of cleavage between the people who are socialists in England, and those who are not, does not coincide with or even lie in the same direction as that between those who call themselves socialists and those who do not.

The discrepancy is not only due to the fact that many people are socialists without knowing it, and that many others who know it decline to take a name so associated with impossible superstitions (just as most of us object to call ourselves Christians), but also to the fact that a large majority of nominal socialists—penny-a-week men enrolled on the spur of the moment after a rousing speech—have no idea of Socialism, and in fact oppose it violently when it is reduced to practical measures. For example, when the Works Department of the County Council takes its staff to Battersea to make a sewer, the cry of local jobs for local men is raised as vigorously by the socialists as by anybody else.

Consequently, any united Socialist party which could now be formed would greatly misrepresent the real strength of Socialism in the country, and misrepresent it, too, by underrating it enormously.

Experience has shown that it is not possible to carry union further than a supper club. The moment a resolution is proposed bearing on practical politics, the union breaks at once. You would get a vote of sympathy with Liebknecht through without any trouble, but nothing more. The opinion, lately spread, that the conditions have altered since the failure of the last attempt to unite has not the least foundation. The history of that attempt was as follows: Scheu mooted the project at a moment when he had been practically out of the movement for a long time, and when it had outgrown his knowledge considerably. A special meeting of the Fabian Executive was held to confer with him. We pointed out to him what would happen if he tried to force the Fabian and the S.D.F. into the same sack. Scheu does not like cold water, and he went away impatient and feeling outwitted. He then proposed the union to the Hammersmith Socialist Society, declaring that a united Socialist party would exclude the Fabians and so let the world know that they were not real socialists. The H.S.S. took up the idea of union with ardor, but repudiated the notion of excluding the Fabians. Scheu then went off in dudgeon and dropped the project, which was carried on by the H.S.S. Of course when they called on us to form a joint committee, we did not like to refuse; and the S.D.F. equally did not like to refuse. The committee was formed—5 from the S.D.F., 5 Fabians, 5 members of the H.S.S. The Fabians relied on the support of the amiable and platonic H.S.S. to get a majority over the S.D.F. The S.D.F. made exactly the same calculation. It was jealously ordained that no resolution could be passed by the committee until the constituent bodies had had notice of it and instructed their delegates how to vote after due discussion. The first thing was to issue a manifesto to shew our agreement on general principles (which meant that we did not agree on anything in particular). I suggested certain lines for it. The S.D.F. promptly objected. Morris's little manifesto of the H.S.S., a capital document in its way, was also set aside. So a sub-committee of three—Hyndman, Morris and Shaw—was appointed to draw up a new one. We had many jolly evenings on that pretext; but at last we had to go to work. Morris drafted a manifesto. I objected to everything in it that was characteristically S.D.F.; and Hyndman objected to everything that was characteristically Fabian, except that I got him to give way on the subject of municipal socialism, which he wanted to denounce. Finally nothing was left but a string of the old phrases and a few ambiguities by which Hyndman meant one thing and I another. This worthless document was published in due course; and then the joint committee began to come to close quarters. We soon found at the Fabian executive that all our meetings were taken up by discussions of the resolutions which the S.D.F. had given notice of at the joint committee. They were generally attempts to get an anti-Fabian vote from the "United Socialists." We dared not allow a meeting to pass without some of our best men being there to look after our interests; and our best men complained furiously at the waste of their time, they being already overworked. The business of our society fell into arrear. The H.S.S. looked on in pained surprise whilst those of us who saw each others' game in the S.D.F. and Fabian fought apparently for the mere love of fighting. At last, just before a bye-election for the County Council at Battersea, Hyndman came down and tried to persuade the committee to disregard the rule about notice, and pass an urgency resolution against the man whom Burns was supporting, and in favor of a socialist who had been stuck up at the last moment by the S.D.F. without the ghost of a chance of success. Morris was in the chair, and refused to allow the resolution to be put. Then Hyndman and I unmasked our batteries and went for one another tooth and nail. He said, frankly enough, that the position of the S.D.F. was that they would be happy to have the support of the joint committee in anything they did; but that they would go their own way just the same whether they got that support or not. This was virtually the position of the Fabian too; and the H.S.S. would have been in the same corner but for their abstention from practical political activity. After that, the Fabian leaders flatly refused to attend the committee any more, the whole affair being a worrying imposture, and the "unity" being a sham. The society therefore withdrew from the committee, which

577

thereupon virtually ceased to exist. A vote of censure on the executive for this was duly moved, and the society rejected it by an overwhelming majority.

There is an idea abroad, as I have said, that this need not happen again, especially if Hyndman and myself are kept in order. It need, and must, most inevitably, if the experiment is repeated. All the assurances that are being given now were given then. The theory of the S.D.F. really is that it is the only genuine socialist society, and that the Fabians are not socialists at all. The introduction of the Independent Labor Party would aggravate the discord instead of resolving it. Take a single case—that of the Hackney contest at the last Schoolboard election [22nd November 1894]. The Fabian Society stood in with the general democratic compact, and got two of its members selected as candidates —Stewart Headlam for Bethnal Green and Graham Wallas for Hoxton, the third division falling to Horobin, a non socialist. The S.D.F. flouted the compact, ran Mrs Rose Jarvis on their own account, canvassed for votes in all three divisions, denounced Wallas and Headlam as impostors (Burrows leading for the S.D.F. and Tom Mann for the I.L.P.) and were duly beaten with every possible ignominy for their stupidity and bad faith. That situation will reproduce itself at the next election. If a United Party is in existence, the S.D.F. will try to get a vote in support of their candidate from it, and some of the I.L.P. will support the S.D.F. The Fabian will oppose, also with some I.L.P. support. There will be a division; and whatever the result of the division may be, it will make an end of the pretence of unity: further, it will have no effect, because neither party will withdraw its candidates in obedience to the vote of the United. And think of the waste of time, the debates, the recriminations, the bad blood, all for nothing, all in search for mere formal assertion of a union that has no relation to the facts of life.

On the other hand, suppose we simply talk of union, and do nothing but have suppers at Wedde's or the club occasionally. Then there will be no debates, no friction, no waste of time. As before, the Fabian will help the S.D.F. and the I.L.P. when they are not making fools of themselves. They blackguard us in their papers and speeches, and denounce us as Liberals—except when we exposed the late Liberal Government in our famous Fortnightly manifesto, and then the S.D.F. promptly joined in the Liberal howl against us, just as Davitt did. They always let us lead the attack and do the work when it comes to close quarters with the politicians. We really began the I.L.P. business by guaranteeing the returning officer's fees for Tillett when he attacked

Illingworth's seat at [West] Bradford in 92. I.L.P. and S.D.F. alike take our money at elections, use our literature, our speakers, and all our resources freely, and then refresh their self-respect by vilifying us. We don't mind of course; but is it fair to ask us to go and sit in a sham council with them and listen to their windy nonsense? Let me bring it home to you in this way. All these fellows will tell you that Socialists are agreed, not only on economics and politics but on art; and they will coolly cite you and Morris as the exponents of their views on that subject. Now suppose they all became amateur artists as they have become amateur politicians and administrators, and suppose further that they were to invite Morris to place the Kelmscott Press under the direction of the United Party, and to request you to submit your plans and designs for the year to their approval. You would not feel any worse or swear any harder than Webb, and his wife, and Wallas, who have devoted themselves to economics, politics, investigation and administration as you have devoted yourself to art, feel when they are asked to enter into partnership with a body of S.D.F. branch delegates of the usual type.

I don't say that this is the whole case: it is only one side of it—the side you are most likely to overlook. It will at least explain why I try to dodge and evade the unity proposal in every possible way except as regards a purely discussing body—one that would enable representative Socialists to exchange ideas, but not to pass resolutions. And it seems to me that the supper club is the safest means so far of managing that. Have you any fresh lights on the subject?

yours sincerely
G. Bernard Shaw

To CHARLES CHARRINGTON

[T/1 (A/4); X/136.e]

29 Fitzroy Square W
15th December 1895

Dear Charrington

I have been lazily relying on you to let me know if the financial situation became strained; but my faith in you is destroyed by the disappearance of the symbol of your union with Janet. The enclosed will make a difference to the bank, not to me, as I expect to weather Xmas without sinking within ten pounds of bottom—in fact if I get in my cheques from the Savoy, Chronicle and Saturday, I shall be affluent enough to meet further emergencies. When Providence begins to play such cards against us as typhoid fever it is useless to waste delicacy and forbearance on it.

I am prepared to observe the strictest duplicity on the subject with Janet if necessary.

You need not be anxious as to the effect of Bertha's proceedings. Illness demoralizes instead of quickening the sympathies: Janet positively gloats over poor Bertha's anguish. I plead in vain for a little consideration for her.

GBS

To DOROTHY LEIGHTON

[A/4]

29 Fitzroy Square W
16th December 1895

[Aimée Daniell (1856–1936), better known as Mrs Oscar Beringer, was a Philadelphia-born dramatic author, wife of the well-known composer and musician. Her one-act play *Salvé* had received a single I.T. performance on 15th March 1895.]

Dear Mrs Ashton Johnson

I return you the proof, which still needs the insertion of the number of plays produced by the I.T. (p. 4 line 5).

The passage about the Camden & Selden Societies is all right: I have looked them up.

On page 3, the allusion to Mrs Oscar Beringer is not fair. There was no "immense success" in comparison with the others: on the contrary, the performance was not repeated, as most of the rest were. Further, the inclusion of the names of the cast would give the greatest offence to the unmentioned members of the other casts, whereas if we stick to the rule of only mentioning the *entrepreneur*, nobody will feel aggrieved. The insertion of "(not the adaptation)" is only to fill up the line for the printer and save overrunning.

On page 6 I think the sentence about Heinemann ought to be struck out. He is not an example of the reinforcement by a union of all the artistic talents to which the paragraph refers. He is not "co-operating": he is only securing his $7\frac{1}{2}\%$. The mention of him adds nothing whatever to the attractions of the I.T.; and Archer will probably be justly disgusted at seeing a compliment to himself (which is deserved) bracketed with an obviously insincere one to H.

580

I have disconnected the new sentence about Grein from the one about Charrington by retaining the full stop, in order to avoid suggesting either to Charrington or the public that Grein's remaining in touch would have anything to do with the stage arrangements.

If you disagree with my deletions, you can dot them under and "stet" them. If not, the document may go to press, I think, as soon as the number of plays produced by the I.T. is ascertained & filled in.

It is most important that the letter should be circulated to all the critics *this week* if possible. They are desperately hard up for copy just now & will be glad to write about it; but in another week or so they will be swamped by the Xmas productions.

yrs sincerely
G. Bernard Shaw

To JANET ACHURCH

29 Fitzroy Square W
23rd December 1895

[T/1 (A/4)]

[Alnaschar is the beggar in the *Arabian Nights* who indulges in visions of riches and grandeur. The Hon. Rosalind Frances Stanley (1845–1921), who married George James Howard, ninth Earl of Carlisle, was the promoter of a democratic franchise for women, and was active in the temperance movement. The mother-in-law of the Greek scholar Gilbert Murray (1866–1957), she was Shaw's model for Lady Britomart in *Major Barbara*. "Aunt Mary" appears to be a cryptic reference to Murray's wife, Lady Mary Henrietta Howard (1865–1956). The Charringtons had been interested since 1893 in producing Murray's play *Carlyon Sahib*. By February 1895 the possibility had been raised of staging the play under the aegis of the I.T. Shaw had been shown the manuscript early in 1895 and, according to Janet in a letter of 4th February to Murray, "admires it exceedingly." (Unpublished letter, courtesy of E. C. Lathem.)]

My dear Janet

(Look here, Charrington: you're not to read this: it is absolutely between myself and Janet). I am going to make myself disagreeable; but that is my chief business in life. I am uneasy, appalled, sceptical to the marrow about the future. I have submitted to horror upon horror during your illness—to animals and birds boiled to a jelly, to brandy and milk, to poison after poison. But now you are getting well; and you have made a deep impression on me by two things; first, by detailing to me a plan of campaign for the I.T., which is nothing but the old plan of campaign, which again means building castles in the air on a foundation of half a brick each, and cemented with Alnaschar dreams and good solid Manchester mendacity; and second, and far more terrible, by drinking a third of a tumbler of brandy with half a teaspoonful of soda water in it when a third of a tumbler of soda with half a teaspoon of brandy would have sufficed. What's to be done? Do you remember the scene in "Our Mutual Friend," where Rogue Riderhood is run down by a river steamer, pulled out, and laid, apparently drowned, on the bed in the Three Jolly Porters—how his daughter sits by his bed, and sees, for once, everybody kind to him and helpful about him—also how, as he comes to, all his villainy comes to also, and the people fall off from him and the daughter sees that he is coming back to his brutal old self. Now don't jump to the conclusion that the comparison is between his drowning and your illness: it's worse than that: it's between his drowning and your whole period of your being under water since the collapse [in 1893] at Terry's. It seems to me that as this I.T. scheme develops, and your hopes rise, all the innocence of the Battersea period is vanishing, and you are coming back to your weak wicked old self, your brandy and soda self, your fabling, pretending, promising, company promoting, heavy eyelidded, morphia injecting self. I see you already in Aunt Mary's brougham, rushing off to Lady Carlisle (who disbanded all her equipages when the Home Rule split broke up her political life and friendships), to tell that proud daughter of the Stanleys anything that will cheat her out of £150. And Murray will see through the whole thing and tell her. And all this when it seems possible at last to give an Ibsen performance without asking for a single gift (you *like* gifts, you wretch), and to write to Lady Carlisle and tell her that though she promised you the money, you have the performance ready for her for nothing, though the obligation is none the less. Does it ever occur to you that if you became the leading English actress you would have to represent your art with dignity among Stanleys and other such people, and that you would be severely handicapped if they remembered how you had called in Aunt Mary's brougham and told them fibs and tried to get money out of them. However, it is useless to remonstrate. You will *appreciate* the magnanimity of soul which I recommend; but you won't practise it. Therefore I must act myself—I, who haven't a wife and child, and have not the means of excusing myself. If the I.T. can get the money to do "Candida" properly, it shall have "Candida" (unless I hit on a better way). But if the least farthing of the money has to be touted for—that's the hideous right word—*touted* for by you—

582

if any shareholder is seduced into subscribing by the sight of as much as a lock of your hair or a cast off glove of yours—if there is to be any gift in the matter except *our* gift of our work, then I swear by the keen cold of this northern wind on my face and the glowing fire of it in my bones, there shall be no "Candida" at the I.T. You may contribute to its success as much as you like by making people love you, or fear you, or admire you, or be interested, fascinated, tantalised, or what not by you. But if you coin the love, fear, interest, admiration or fascination into drachmas, then I cannot have any part in the bargain. If Rothschild or the Prince of Wales want boxes, they know where they can be bought, just as they know where the Saturday Review can be bought. It is inconceivable that such measures should be congenial to you when your mind is properly strung; and you will get better all the faster if you put them behind you.

The new drama [*You Never Can Tell*] is shaping itself slowly—at least the people are coming to life. There will be a good part—as heroic as Magda—for the younger woman, and a fine part for her mother. There will be the father too; and the tragedy will be between the father and the daughter. Now, no matter who plays the father, the daughter shall never during my lifetime be played by a woman who drinks brandy. She must be a beautiful woman, a sober woman, and a woman of entirely noble spirit. If that's impossible, then I will do what I am often tempted to do—publish my plays and appeal to the imaginations of those who are capable of reading them without wasting myself on trying to have them performed without utter profanation.

It is a curious thing to me that you should express such remorse about trifles and follies that everybody commits in some form or other, and that strong people laugh at, whilst you are all the time doing things that are physically ruinous and planning things that you ought to hang yourself sooner than stoop to. There is only one physical crime that can destroy you—brandy: only one moral one—Aunt Mary's brougham.

I cannot lock up the brandy—but I can poison it. You *must* stop now: the change in your appearance shews that you are just at the point where that accursed stimulating diet must be dropped at all hazards. All through your illness you were beautiful and young; now you are beginning to look, not nourished but—steel yourself for another savage word—bloated. Do, for heaven's sake, go back to the innocent diet of the invalid—porridge made of "miller's pride" oatmeal and boiled all night into oatmeal jelly, rice, tomatoes, macaroni, without milk or eggs or other "nourishing" producers of indigestion. You *can't* drink

brandy with wholesome food; and if you take exercise you won't want
so much morphia. Eat stewed fruit and hovis. If you have any difficulty
in digesting walnuts (for instance) nibble a grain of ginger glace with
them and *chew* them and you will have no trouble. You will eventually
strike out a decent diet for yourself. Anyhow, save your soul and body
alive, and don't turn me into granite.

GBS

To ROBERT BUCHANAN

[29 Fitzroy Square W]
[X/132.e]   [Undated: late 1895]

[In March 1896 Buchanan issued a self-published pamphlet *Is Barabbas a
Necessity?* which was a Byronic attack on publishers. In it he noted that he
had received a letter from a "distinguished man of letters" to whom he
had sent a proof copy, in 1895, of his long poem *The Devil's Case*, "and whom
I chose for that confidence because I knew him to be diametrically opposed,
both in character and experience, to myself." Buchanan did not divulge the
writer's name, but assured his readers that "he is a man well known for
intellectual honesty and practical beneficence, a man for whom I have the
very highest respect, short of sympathising in the least degree with his
opinions. These are his words, and they are very remarkable words, coming
as they do from an enthusiast in the cause of social progress." Shaw confided
to Henry Salt that the letter was intended to be merely by way of illustration
in an argument that it is not the inevitable misfortunes, but the evitable ones,
that are most distasteful in life. (See "Salt on Shaw," revised by Shaw, in
Stephen Winsten's *Salt and His Circle*, 1951.) Buchanan published the
extracts without authorisation, and later wrote a letter of apology to Shaw
for having taken this liberty (BM).

Sir Hall Caine (1853–1931) was the author of several romantic novels,
frequently with a religious theme, including *The Manxman* (1894), *The
Christian* (1897), and *The White Prophet* (1909). Richard Claude Carton
(1856–1928), actor (until 1885) and playwright, was the author of numerous
popular comedies, including *The Home Secretary* (1895) and *The Tree of
Knowledge* (1896).]

I observe that you are superstitious, that you want "solutions,"
that you are driven to pessimism by your failure to find them, and that
you are highly susceptible to the fullness and oppression of heart
caused by love and death to men of strong sentiment. The reason we
get on together in our correspondence is because I am as much as
possible the reverse of all this. I have lost my father and my sister,

584

with whom I was on excellent terms; and I assure you their deaths disturbed me less than a misprint in an article. If my mother dies before me, I am quite sure that I shall not be moved by it as much as I was moved by your poem on the death of your mother. The inevitable does not touch me; it is the non-avoidance of the evitable, the neglect of the possible, the falling short of attainable efficiency, clearness, accuracy, and beauty, that set me raging. I really care deeply for nothing but *fine work*, and since nobody can help me in this, no less can greatly affect my self-sufficiency. . . . There is nothing anti-social in all this; quite the reverse. Usually this sort of thing is so terrifying and repulsive to men that they would rather believe that it is a mere affectation of mine to cover what they call "a good heart"—meaning the weaknesses (usually produced by whiskey, more or less) which they would like to believe common to all the race. But in my heart of hearts I utterly despise all this sort of special pleading. When a man whimpers to me about Goethe's coldness and selfishness, I pity him. . . . There! that's the real *Simon Pure*, with all his goods in the shop window. You may recoil as much as you like, and protest that there is a heart of gold in the back parlour, like Hall Caine's, or Carton's, or poor old Thackeray's; I only reply, do my work, if you can, with that sort of heart, made of gold that any cheesecutter will slip into!

To JANET ACHURCH

[T/1 (A/4)]

29 Fitzroy Square W
14th January 1896

[The article on Jones's play was a review of *Michael and His Lost Angel* in the *Saturday Review* on 18th January. The article eventually written by Shaw for the Melbourne *Argus* was "The Theatre in England," published on 28th March.]

A most fearful tragedy has happened to me. It is impossible that I should see you for a month at least; so all idea of your coming back to town or my going down to St Leonards must be abandoned. Today I went to get my hair cut. The man asked whether I wanted it short. I said "Yes," and was about to add certain reservations when he suddenly produced an instrument like a lawnmower, and in an instant my golden locks fell like withered grass to the floor and left my head like the back of a Japanese pug dog. Nothing escaped except a little wiglike oasis on the top. I say wiglike; for the climax of the horror was that, unknown to me, those auburn tresses with which you are familiar, concealed a grey—nay, a *white*—undergrowth, which is now an overgrowth. People ask me now what fearful shock I have experienced to turn my hair white in a single night. There must be some frightful mistake about my age: I am not in my fortieth year, but in my sixtieth. For God's sake tell me that you believe that it will grow red again—at least that you hope so.

I have already written my article on Jones's play (not, of course, on the performance); and I regret to say that in spite of myself I have protested against its ideas almost vehemently enough to satisfy Charrington. By the way I have exposed him to the risk—not very serious, I fear—of degrading himself by dramatic criticism. The Melbourne Argus people wrote to me for a £10 article on the British drama. I said "perhaps" and "presently" and made difficulties, but suggested that Charrington would be a good man to make their London dramatic correspondent. I hope he did not molest the editor when he was in Australia.

[Shaw drew a sketch here.]

That is what I should look like if the fellow had shaved me as well.

GBS

To R. B. HALDANE

29 Fitzroy Square W
20th January 1896

[C/18]

[Richard Burdon Haldane (1856–1928), later Viscount Haldane of Cloan, was a lawyer, philosopher, and statesman. A Liberal who later became a Labourite, he was M.P. for Haddingtonshire 1885–1911. George Montagu Harris (1868–1951), a Liberal who contested South St Pancras unsuccessfully in 1895 and 1896, later was active in local government movements and wrote several important books on the subject. The "Eighty" Club was founded in 1880 to promote the Liberal cause in that year's general election, and continued to function for many years thereafter. Augustine Birrell (1850–1933) was a political leader and man of letters, author of *Obiter Dicta* (1884), and Chief Secretary for Ireland 1907–16.]

My dear Haldane

There is a bye-election on here; and I have promised to speak on Wednesday evening for Harris, one of the seedlings of the 80 club. This rescues me from Birrell & D. Johnson. At seven I shall join your board at Whitehall Court. Do not kill anything for me, because I simply won't eat it.

yrs ever
G. Bernard Shaw

To R. B. HALDANE

29 Fitzroy Square W
22nd January 1896

[C/18]

[Shaw frequently confused the dates and hours of his social and business engagements, much to the distress of his associates. He eventually dined with Haldane on 5th February to meet H. H. Asquith and Arthur Balfour. Stepniak had been struck by a railway engine at Chiswick, on 23rd December 1895, as he was crossing the tracks, and died instantly. Robert Spence Watson (1837–1911), a political, social, and educational reformer, was president of the National Liberal Foundation, 1890–1902, and treasurer of the Society of Friends of Russian Freedom from its inception in 1890. John Bright (1811–89), orator and statesman, was a Liberal active in the movements for financial reform, electoral reform, and religious freedom.]

My dear Haldane

When is that dinner to come off? I got it wrong, and called this evening with a raging appetite, not having tasted food since breakfast.

Did you know Stepniak? He has left his widow without any resources; and we are getting up a Stepniak Memorial which will be, under some pretence or other, a provision for Madame S., if she can be prevailed on to accept it. Spence Watson is treasurer & we have all sorts of respectable people in it besides our own riff raff. May we put your name on the General Committee? We want Liberals especially, as Stepniak was, as far as Russia was concerned, the only Liberal left in England since Bright died.

yrs ever
G. Bernard Shaw

To PAKENHAM BEATTY

29 Fitzroy Square W
23rd January 1896

[S/1]

[The Rowdy Ove presumably was Beatty's brother-in-law Charles H. Dowling. Prince Pëtr Aleksevich Kropotkin (1842–1921), Russian geographer, revolutionist, and social philosopher, was a leader of the anarchist movement in London, 1886–1914.]

Stepniak contributions should be sent to E.R. Pease, Fabian Society, 276 Strand, W.C. Give him the Rowdy Ove's address, so that we may circularise him. The matter is very troublesome: Steppy left his wife without a cent; but the blood of the Russian aristocracy, when it takes to the cause of the people, boils at a hint of money. Pooh Bah not in it with Kropotkin & Co. We are pretending that we are endowing a translation of his works.

He was slain through pure dare devilry—wanted to perform the feat of bounding across before the train, and, being older than he thought, was caught, Achilles-like, by the heel.

G.B.S.

To EDWARD R. PEASE

[C/27]

29 Fitzroy Square W
27th January 1896

[Harriot Stanton Blatch (1856–1940), daughter of the American woman-suffrage leader Elizabeth Cady Stanton, was briefly a member of the Fabian Executive (1894–95). Tract No. 67, *Women and the Factory Acts*, was based on a lecture by Beatrice Webb to the Fabian Society on 10th January 1896.]

Mrs Stanton Blatch pours forth vials of vitriol on me and insists that Mrs Webb is wrong about the Factory Acts, and is bluffing the society. Will you send her a proof of the tract at once, if possible; or, if it is too late for proofs, a copy of it. I am writing to beg her to point out any error before we commit ourselves. Probably Webb has got it right; but we may as well submit it to Mrs Blatch, since she accuses me of conspiring with the Webbs to rush it through without letting even the lady members of the Exec. see it.

GBS

To WILLIAM ARCHER

[A/2]

29 Fitzroy Square W
29th January 1896

[Charles Hudson, appearing in Wilson Barrett's *The Sign of the Cross*, which opened at the Lyric on 4th January, had written a letter in defence

588

of the play to Archer, who had been critically severe with it in *The World*. Archer published the letter, and Shaw wryly commented on it in his *Saturday Review* article of 1st February. George Henry Lewes (1817–78), philosopher, literary critic, and common-law husband of George Eliot, was the founder of the *Fortnightly Review*, in the February 1896 number of which Archer published an article, "George Henry Lewes and the Stage." Barry Sullivan (1821–91), a romantic actor who specialised in Shakespearean parts, and who was better known in the English provinces and in Ireland than in London, was Shaw's boyhood theatre idol. Ignace Jan Paderewski (1860–1941), Polish pianist, composer, and statesman, was a popular performer in the London concert halls during the latter part of the century.

Archer had published an unsigned review of the first number of *The Savoy*, under the heading "A Yellow Book Hinterland," in the *Daily Chronicle* on 25th January. In it he commented: "Mr. George Bernard Shaw's pronouncement 'On Going to Church' is a readable review-article —nothing more. Every new virus with which Mr. Shaw is vaccinated "takes" violently, but, mingling or clashing with former inoculations, is apt to produce amazing complications. At present, Mr. Shaw is in the hot fit of Ruskinian cinquecentism, which he must perforce bring into harmony with Schopenhauerism (attenuated through Wagner), Fabianism, vegetarianism, Shelleyism, and a dozen other 'isms', superimposed upon the fundamental and congenital Shawism. The result is the gratifying discovery that the Church, purged of Christianity and re-edified according to Ruskin, is the true public-house of the modern world, to which our vegetarian progeny will resort for that stimulation which, oddly enough, is not to be found in lentils alone."

Shaw was thoroughly familiar with the works of the preacher John Bunyan (1628–88), whose *Pilgrim's Progress* (1678) was his favourite book, and the revolutionist Thomas Paine (1737–1809), and frequently cited them in his own writings. "Ça ira" was a famous French revolutionary song, believed to have originated in the hopeful reply of Benjamin Franklin to a question as to the prospects of the American republic in its war of independence.]

Hudson has by no means risen to the level of being beneath notice, though you cannot very well notice him. I am not alluding in any way to the "Sign of the Cross" question, or to you. I have simply flicked the insect off the window pane in passing, *pour encourager les autres*.

The article on Lewes is interesting. His failure on the stage was probably of the nature of the failures of musicians & composers as pianists. He had not the trained and hardened face and speech muscles of the actor who has been at it for years. It was not a question of *optique du theatre*: the evidence is that he looked all right, which he wouldn't have done if he had missed the scale of the picture even in his conception of the action. Barry Sullivan thought him a poor weak creature, I expect, just as Paderewski might think Arthur Sullivan a poor weak creature if he were challenged to play against him. If he could have beaten Barry at making faces and repeating the alphabet, he'd probably have beaten him as an actor.

The review in the Chronicle was most disgraceful. It should have been signed Norman Britton. Where do you expect to go to when you die? You talk of the beauty of 13th (not 14th) century work as "Ruskinism," as if it had no objective reality—as if I criticised with my imagination, as you do, instead of with my laboriously sharpened eyes and ears. I have been for years trying to educate you out of the common rationalistic secularism of the N.S.S. [National Secular Society]; and here you relapse into the most benighted and splenetic phase of it at the mere mention of a beautiful church. You will presently lose your temper with somebody for declaring that Bunyan wrote better than Tom Paine, or for preferring "Onward, Christian soldiers" to "Ca ira." I urge you to leave prayer and belief outside when you enter San Zeno: you evidently believe that the building would be wasted unless scientific lectures were given there by Foote. You are so inveterately imaginative that you cannot believe that any effect is due to a real cause, or that any cause produces a real effect. However, you must waken of yourself: there is no use shouting at you. See you tomorrow, I presume.

GBS

To JANET ACHURCH

[T/1 (A/4)]

29 Fitzroy Square W
29th January 1896

[*Sodom's Ende* (1891) was a play by Hermann Sudermann (1857–1928), German playwright and novelist; Shaw did not attempt to adapt it. *Michael and His Lost Angel* was withdrawn on 25th January after ten performances. Shaw, mourning its closing in his 1st February notice in the *Saturday Review*, described it as "the best play its school has given to the theatre." Cissie (Marie Cecilia) Loftus (1876–1943) was better known at this time as a music-hall performer of admirable impersonations than as a dramatic actress. Her first husband, Justin Huntly McCarthy (1861–1936), was a novelist, historian, and dramatist, whose most famous play was *If I Were King* (1901).]

I have seen Charrington today. His looks are not *altogether* satisfactory: he carries himself like a tired man—or was he always like that? You must coddle him for a while until he quite makes up the arrears of

590

sleep and recuperation he ran up during that infernal fever. Otherwise he seems jolly enough.

Flemming wants "Arms & The Man" for South Africa. I have explained to him that he would be promptly lynched if he tried it in Johannesburg at present.

Alexander wants me to adapt "Sodom's Ende." I am struggling to read your copy of it before replying.

The withdrawal of "Michael and His Lost Angel" has broken the confidence of the theatrical Government completely. The hour of the Opposition is at hand.

What do you think of Cissy Loftus for the rat wife? She is ambitious to succeed as an actress: I watered that seedling notion with a sentence in my notice of her imitations [*Saturday Review*, 27 July 1895]. I can see her in it; and it would rouse considerable interest. Justin Huntly McCarthy would also stimulate the press.

I had rare scenes with the poetess-dramatist [Florence Farr] before she left for France, mostly in operatic Italian. The red beard is now irresistible. In spite of the shears of the haircutter I am transfigured; I work spells; even Florence, once callous, has strange awakenings and cries over me—positively cries. My heart sends out invisible rays in which all other hearts tremble without knowing why. Who has kindled those rays? I hear that you return next week; but I am not impatient: my store of happiness is not nearly exhausted. Even if you were to spread your wings and fly away to other worlds, I should die at ninety quite content, with the air of the rose valleys still on my withered face, and my treasures still piled up there present & actual to me.

Here am I, the god who *has* been happy, among people who say "I want to be happy just once." The result, though, is alarming—desiring nothing further, I have become a sort of sublime monster, to whose disembodied heart the consummation of ordinary lives is a mere anti-climax.

Do you know anyone who will buy for twopence a body for which I have no longer any use? I have made tolerable love with it in my time; but now I have found nobler instruments—the imagination of a poet, the heart of a child, all discovered through the necessity—the not-to-be-denied inmost necessity—of making my way to an innocent love for Janet. Had there been no river between us, what wretched makeshift might I not have thoughtlessly accepted? Now set up a thousand other obstacles, a million other impossibilities, and I will get over them all by discovering a plane on which they do not exist. In the old days saints and abbesses used to say "Wait until we die: we shall meet in heaven." Stupid of them, when it is so simple to become an angel on earth.

Enough of common sense: I must relapse into the usual nonsense. I am writing an article for the Melbourne Argus declaring that the whole mischief here is that nobody can act.

To practise R (trilled), repeat L. M. N. R: this will, if you leave your tongue loose, bring it into the right position. Then try, first eer, ér, èr &c, and ree ré, rè &c; and then such combinations as BRee, bré, brè &c, and eebr, ébr, èbr &c, proceeding with CR, DR, FR, GR, PR, SR, TR. The terminal RD is very important; and then there is RF (serf) RP (harp) RT (art) &c. Also of course, such combinations as SP, TH, BL, CL, DL, FL, GL, PL, SL, TL, & so on, compiling them out of the alphabet in order.

GBS

P.S. Heinemann's letters are of no importance, except so far as we can make them help us if the I.T. people try to be stingy in the mounting [of *Little Eyolf*].

To WILLIAM ARCHER

[C/2]

29 Fitzroy Square W
2nd February 1896

[Sarah Thorne (1837–99), actress-manager, toured in repertory for many years, and was manager of the Theatre Royal, Margate, considered a veritable nursery for young talent. Janet Achurch, at the start of her career, had toured in Miss Thorne's company. Mopsemand is the Ratwife's dog in *Little Eyolf*.]

Look here: we must go to headquarters and consult Ibsen about the ratwife. I find that Charrington has your notion—a witch out of Macbeth, red handed from the murder of her lover (Sarah Thorne for preference) with a savage bulldog. I am convinced that this would turn the whole thing into a horrible melodrama. I am for a tiny woman with a small far away voice, four hundred years old, with strange eyes; and I find, on anxious inquiry, that I am not alone in my notion. Mopseman is clearly a beautiful little black Spitz. The point is so important, considering the immense difference to the feeling & effect of the play, that I think Ibsen should be consulted. But mind you put the case fairly. I think photographs of Cissy Loftus and Sarah Thorne might help the old man to an unbiassed decision.

GBS

To BERTHA NEWCOMBE

29 Fitzroy Square W
[A/4]   4th February 1896

[Mabel Collier, who lived in Chelsea, was another of Shaw's numerous lady friends. Nelly Erichsen (d. 1918), a young artist with a studio in Manresa Road, Chelsea, was currently doing illustrations for short stories in the *English Illustrated Magazine*; she later illustrated more than twenty books, including Thomas Okey's *Venice and Its Story* (1903) and several volumes in the Highways and Byways series, besides translating (with Edwin Björkman) many of Strindberg's plays. Shaw read *Arms and the Man* to Nelly and her friend Fanny Johnson on 4th February, a fact which he did not mention to Bertha. The Rt. Hon. Charles Philips Trevelyan (1870–1958), eldest son of the historian Sir George Otto Trevelyan, was a Liberal M.P. (1899), and, later, a pacifist-internationalist member of the Labour Party.]

I am in the difficulty of having no news for you. You do not surprise me when you tell me that the account given by your parents of their meeting with me differs from mine. When did parents ever tell their daughters the truth?

I particularly wanted to keep that bag. It was so pretty! But Mabel would have it. I argued, pleaded, demonstrated, wept; but it was no use. She said she'd be D A M N E D if I should keep it—that you had given it to her and that she meant to have it. I offered her thrice its value in gold, and a new & better case into the bargain; but no: she said she could not bear to think of my possessing anything of yours. Then she burst into tears; said she was the most unhappy woman alive; seized the bag forcibly; and rushed out distractedly in the direction of the river. I have not heard of her since.

Your attempt to discredit me with N.E. has had a most ludicrous upshot. On Monday she invited me to afternoon tea. I washed & brushed myself most carefully & went. When I got there, lo! a chaperon—a sly little woman who was drawing N. on millboard. N's introduction clearly meant, "I am sorry to disappoint your evident hope of finding me alone; but I have no intention of trusting you to that extent." Naturally, our constraint was fearful. Presently the little woman began to smile slyly as she surveyed us with confidential good-nature. She hurried up the tea; and then, before we could intervene, nodded at us in a "I know you want to get rid of me" way; snatched up her things; & deserted her hostess, leaving us in the most miserable confusion & consciousness. For an hour & a half we clung to Wagner, Shakspere & other topics (including you); and I tried hard to behave myself, although the breaking off of the end of the sofa reminded me

593

rudely that I had lapsed into my habit of sprawling and lolling. However, we parted on fair terms with an understanding that I might turn up on Monday afternoons when I had nothing better to do. I must get her to take me to the Grafton Gallery: your departure [to study in Paris] is a serious blow to me in the matter of picture seeing.

No arrangements for Easter are yet concluded. Trevelyan booked me for a cycling tour in Normandy & the continent generally; but the Webbs have backed out of it as too expensive; and I shall probably have to follow their example.

If you are not strong enough to go to Madrid on your own responsibility, father or no father, I shall really give you up.

What are you doing in the way of study? Whose atelier are you in?

I have finished the first act of the play—with another extraction, this time under gas. Nellie is disgusted at it.

GBS

To WILLIAM ARCHER

29 Fitzroy Square W
[C.u/2]   7th February 1896

The Charringtons are at 148 Oakley St, Chelsea, provisionally. I have sent on your card.

Charrington's idea of the ratwife is of course unassailable, and by no means inartistic. On the other hand his objection to Cissy is entirely wrong. He has never seen her, but has deduced her from her heredity, with appalling results, and denounces my notion as nothing but a pantomime fairy. However, I ask nothing better if the pantomime is a good one and the fairy an artist. My suggestion is really based on the position that Cissy has beauty, genius, and a quaint personality that *touches* an audience. These are treasures; and to be turned aside from them by mere logic seems to me the height of Philistine folly. Treat the play logically & realistically, and it will be horrible—brutal. This will delight you and Charrington, the fundamental aim of both of you being the shewing up of the villainy of creation. But it will make the New Drama a message of wrath. Why not at least pay Ibsen the compliment of asking has he any instructions to give? Your point about the Norwegian for Ratwife does not convince me in the teeth of the speeches put into her mouth, & her fascination for the child. That's what indicates the fairy.

594

To T. FISHER UNWIN

[S/7]

29 Fitzroy Square W
11th February 1896

[After receiving Shaw's letter of 6th December 1895, Unwin had appealed to the American literary agent Paul Reynolds (1864–1944) for advice on copyright. Reynolds, in turn, had contacted the publisher George Haven Putnam (1844–1930), one of the leaders in the international copyright struggle, who wrote a lengthy opinion. A copy of this reply had now been sent by Unwin to Shaw.]

Dear Fisher Unwin

I return Putnam's letter, which rather confirms my notion that nobody does exactly know how the law stands. I have made a note explaining the confusion into which Putnam apparently fell for a moment between the protection of a novel from dramatisation through its *copy*right, and the case of a play which can be performed from the printed copies without illegal copying. I am still very doubtful as to the case of a play published in either England or America before performance. For instance, all Ibsen's stage rights are voided here except those which Heinemann so ingeniously secured by his performances of the last two or three plays in Norwegian at the Haymarket Theatre before they were translated.

The only play of mine which has been performed in England and America is "Arms & The Man." It would not make much of a book; but with a preface by the brilliant author, and a reprint of my article in the New Review (on the military questions raised) by way of appendix, it would make a respectable Cameo.

Do you think there is really any chance of its being worth my while or yours to publish the play? You will remember that Heinemann, after trying Pinero's "Mrs Tanqueray" at 6/-, came down again to eighteenpence for paper covers and half a crown for cloth, mostly for sale to amateur clubs. He sticks to Ibsen at five shillings a play. What do you think? What do you propose?

yours sincerely
G. Bernard Shaw

595

To PERCY BUNTING

29 Fitzroy Square W

[H/20; X/142]   11th February 1896

My dear Bunting

Bless my soul, you will have to pay me a lot more than that unless you will accept the article ["Socialism for Millionaires"] as a gratuitous contribution [to the *Contemporary Review*]. The article is seven-thousand words long. At eleven guineas, that is £1.13s. per thousand, which is what an ordinary journalist gets from a London daily for unsigned review work of the rapidest kind. I am expected to do this frightfully laborious, slow work, in which solid disquisitions on the heaviest subjects, from political economy to classical music, come out as if they were the airiest *jeux d'esprit*; and I assure you that after twenty years hammering at it, I cannot make £500 a year. At £1.13s. a thousand I should not make £250. My regular terms for newspaper work are £3 per thousand words, with a minimum of £5. The Chronicle pays me that with melancholy resignation; the American and Australian papers pay it eagerly, with a liberal interpretation. If you feel incredulous when I say that it is the hardest earned money on the press at present, all I can say is, try to produce the same effect yourself, and see what it will cost you in mere labor, even to produce a middling specimen like "Socialism for Millionaires."

As it is altogether my fault for not warning you that my terms were above the average, I should very willingly take your cheque and say nothing if it were not that I have found out that the one thing I must not do is to make differential rates in favor of any particular paper or magazine. Editors who want me to write for them, and who know what I get from the Saturday Review (£312 for nine months work) positively count the words in my longer articles and prove to me that I am taking less from the Saturday than they are offering me. On the other hand I do not like to ask you to pay £21 when you calculated on £11 through my omission to settle terms beforehand, especially as a review of the standing of the Contemporary is probably worth much more to me than I am worth to it. I really do not care a rap about the money, and make this remonstrance very much against the grain; only there is something fundamentally unfriendly in having a grievance and not outing with it.

yours sincerely

G. Bernard Shaw

596

To BENJAMIN R. TUCKER

[A/1]

29 Fitzroy Square W
15th February 1896

[The *Home Journal*, a New York weekly paper, later became *Town and Country* and, eventually, *McCall's Magazine*. The article in *Town Topics*, also a New York weekly, was "How to Become a Man of Genius," which appeared on 6th December 1894. Morris Phillips & Company is probably an error for the firm of McClure, Phillips & Company, which published *McClure's Magazine*. Morris Phillips (1834–1904) was the author of the guidebook *Abroad and at Home: Practical Hints for Tourists*, issued by Brentano's in 1891 and frequently reprinted.]

My dear Tucker

I am afraid it is impossible for me to find time for a regular article for the Home Journal. For instance, I cannot manage one now. For a long time past Town Topics has been urging me to contribute; but I only succeeded in squeezing out one article for them, for which they paid me £8. My ordinary terms, paid under protest by the London Daily Chronicle (which accompanies every cheque with an intimation that our connexion is now at an end, and complains bitterly when I cheerfully act on that understanding) and with enthusiasm by Australian & American papers, are £3 per thousand words, with £5 as a minimum. From the Saturday Review I get £312 a year for nine months work. And I need hardly add that I do not make a third of the income expected by men who rattle off their copy at anything from 20/- to 40/- a thousand in good stock phrases and on business principles. Such is the pecuniary position at present.

As to the solidity & respectability of the H.J., that need not stand in the way. Not that I ever bother about the proprietors' principles much: a Shaw article is a Shaw article, and there is an end—the matter is really no more under my control than the color of my eyes is—but the fact is, I have always found that the more respectable the paper, the better I suit it. My achievements as a journalist are not written in the pages of the socialist, radical & freethinking papers, which are mostly so steeped in intolerance and cowardice as to be quite unsuspicious of their own state, but in The World, the Saturday Review & so on. The reason is that the readers of these papers will not stand being treated like children, as the great nonconformist middle classes will, and the editors who get hold of them are consequently always tolerant, with a good deal of common sense, and a spice of mischief. And proprietors are a good deal led by precedent. If Morris Phillips & Co come to you

597

and say: "How's this, Mr Tucker? You have accepted an article from a Mr Shaw denying the existence of God & advocating Free Love." You will reply, "Well, I confess I was rather shocked; but as Mr Shaw was a prominent writer on the London World for many years, and is now on the staff of the Saturday Review, and has his articles printed in the Fortnightly & Contemporary & so on, I thought it better not to interfere. You see we must march with the times." To which M.P. & Co will reply, "Oh, in that case, all right. Write to Mr Shaw & say how pleased we are with his brilliant work. After all, there really is some doubt as to the precise nature of the Origin of All Things; and as to the other point, we have all been young men, Mr Tucker. Good morning."

Some day, if I can manage it, I will send you a sample article. Meanwhile, many thanks.

For telegrams my address is "Socialist, London." It may interest you to know that this was suggested and positively forced on me by the Post Office authorities. Not that I was reluctant; but I didn't suggest it myself, and I *did* suggest several alternatives.

yrs ever
G. Bernard Shaw

To T. FISHER UNWIN

29 Fitzroy Square W
16th February 1896

[S/7]

[Sudermann's *Heimat* (1893), under the title *Magda*, had been performed in London in June 1895 simultaneously by Eleonora Duse (in Italian) and Sarah Bernhardt (in French). A translation by Louis N. Parker, also called *Magda*, was produced at the Lyceum on 3rd June 1896, starring Mrs Patrick Campbell.]

Dear Fisher Unwin

I don't see my way at that rate to give the time to writing the preface & seeing the play through the press; nor is there anything in the enterprise worth your bothering about. It is the usual difficulty: I can make more money by writing articles, and make better provision for the future by writing new plays.

One of the difficulties about the Cameo, or any other series, is the discount difficulty. I have always had sixpence royalty on a half crown book; but I have always urged the publisher to make it half a crown net, though he mostly prefers not to do it.

598

Why not undertake an edition of Sudermann's plays? Scott seems to do well enough with Archer's Ibsen translations. Get Janet Achurch, who speaks German like a native, & writes capital English dialogue (see her magazine stories) besides being famous in connection with the new drama, to undertake the translation, and the scheme will paragraph like mad. After Duse & Bernhardt in "Heimat" the only wonder is that nobody has thought of this already.

> yrs sincerely
> G. Bernard Shaw

To WILLIAM HEINEMANN

[H/5]

29 Fitzroy Square W
18th February 1896

[Rhoda Halkett may have been the daughter of Archer's friend George Roland Halkett (1855–1918), an artist who became editor of the *Pall Mall Magazine*. She appeared with Beerbohm Tree's company at Her Majesty's Theatre in 1898. William Morris's *Freeing of Pharamond* was a dramatic interlude in his verse "masque" *Love is Enough* (1872). Elizabeth Robins had appeared (apparently not to advantage) in the title rôle in *Mrs Lessingham*, a play by "George Fleming" (Constance Fletcher), which opened at the Garrick on 7th April 1894 for a six weeks' run.]

Dear Heinemann

Look here: I am getting anxious about this "Little Eyolf" business. Here is £400—fourhundred shining golden solid sovereigns—sent down from the Mount to be fooled away on anything we please. It is not likely that such an opportunity will occur again in the whole history of the human race. Matters concerning it have now come to this, that it will be spent either on Ibsen or on me—ME—moi qui vous écrit. Unless you have a new and licensable drama ready to plank down, a play of mine will have to go up, failing "Little Eyolf."

Further, if "Little Eyolf" is not done now, the Lord only knows when it will be done. I take it that Miss Robins did all that was possible to get it put up by one of the regular managers, and failed. It has not been worth their while to finance it as managers; and it has not been worth yours to finance it as publisher for the sake of the reaction of the performance on the sale of your Ibsen publications. Therefore for the present the position is that the play must be produced with that £400 or not [be] produced at all.

599

The only obstacle now in the way of acting on this is the eternal susceptibilities of the artists involved. I am writing to you now chiefly because I seem to have created the first difficulty of this kind myself by putting a spoke in the wheel of Miss Rhoda Halkett with the I.T. directorate. Miss Halkett called on me when she came over here; so that I knew what she was like. When Charrington, before he had seen her, suggested her for Asta, I repudiated the idea vehemently—laughed it to scorn—and when he afterwards mentioned that you and Grein were in her favor, I only remarked that I, too, was in her favor, she being pretty enough to knock you, myself, Grein, and a dozen other men of poetic temperament endways, and that that was just exactly why she was eternally out of the question for Asta. If she plays in "Little Eyolf" she must play Rita or nothing; and as Rita is bespoke, it seems to me that it must be nothing. Miss Leighton agreed with me; and Charrington, when he saw her, also agreed; though, as a practical manager, he is naturally not so convinced by off-the-stage appearances. Besides, as she is evidently a capable woman, and no duffing amateur, we might be driven back on her if all the competent women with suitable personalities were to fail us, though I am convinced that she would falsify the whole effect of the play. Observe, I speak from the depths of a very keen *ap*—not *de*-preciation of her qualities. If it would relieve matters at all to explain to her that *I* am the enemy, I am quite prepared to fight it out with her, although I am very anxious not to offend her, as there is a play of mine called "The Philanderer," which may eventually come to the I.T., and which has a devil of a part for her in it.

Now for the question, who *ought* to play Asta? As to that, I have no doubt in my mind at all. If only we could recapture the Elizabeth Robins of Martha (in "Pillars of Society") and of Karin, there you would have the beautiful Puritan charm, the "St Elizabeth" sanctity, the pure toned voice, the unstagey beauty of movement which would make Asta tell so well against Miss Achurch's Rita. Unfortunately Miss Robins herself is not conscious of this charm or of its value; and she would probably be highly offended if she were appealed to on the strength of it. Indeed I do not know how much of it remains, for she seems to me to have been possessed with seventyseven thousand million devils ever since she played Hedda Gabler; and I hear of her making inquiries about Morris's "Freeing of Pharamond" and the deuce knows what other follies in the way of dramatic projects. I am told of her noble conduct in handing over "Little Eyolf" to the I.T.; but what the world wants from her is not noble conduct but acting.

600

You have treated her handsomely about the rights in Hedda and The Master Builder: can you not, by some unheard of extremity of flattery, persuade her to condescend to Asta for the sake of increasing your revenues by an unprecedented sale of copies? I can do nothing: my intervention would only annoy her. Archer, whom she likes, is by constitution only effective when there is something to be prevented, not when there is something to be done. If it's quite out of the question —if she will not bear being told that she is missing a chance which she cannot afford to miss after that confounded Mrs Lessingham business (not that that was her fault)—then I see nothing for it but to make a desperate attempt to get Mary Anderson back for one night only.

I proposed Cissy Loftus for the Ratwife; and I still think I was right; but I was hooted down by Archer and Charrington.

By the way, Janet Achurch is very familiar with German and writes dialogue in English very cleverly. Why dont you bring out an English edition of Sudermann's plays, translated by her?

yours sincerely
G. Bernard Shaw

[Heinemann, in his reply on 25th February, expressed annoyance at what he considered to be Shaw's meddling: "I did not answer your letter of the 18th, because I was informed by Mr. Charrington that only he had any status to plan or decide or administer the affairs of the Independent Theatre. But your second letter convinces me that you have so entirely misunderstood my attitude towards the Independent Theatre in the past and also at present—and more especially towards you personally—that I think I must give you the reasons which compel me to withdraw 'Little Eyolf' altogether." The reasons offered were: (1) that Shaw had given the distinct impression that he wanted the Ibsen play out of the way so that his own play might be produced; (2) that Shaw and the I.T. directors had placed him, with regard to Miss Halkett, "in the light of showing improper favouritism"; (3) that Shaw and the directors "interpreted a perfectly innocent misunderstanding, which arose out of the amiable weakness of one of the Directors in not saying 'no' at the proper time, and which involved me in a promise to have the lady in question *tried* at a rehearsal (with no *undertaking* that she should act the part), into a demand on my part that she should act, or the play not be produced . . ."

Heinemann's anger seems, however, to have resulted principally from Shaw's suggestion (in a missing second letter) "of *mala fides*, or that I haven't known my own mind." Since Charrington had been dilatory about sending a corrected draft agreement for production of the play, Heinemann considered himself free "to cancel the whole thing," adding "I hope I am thereby making way for your play, and thus doing you a service." As far as the public was concerned, he concluded, "it will not be left without a performance of 'Little Eyolf' much longer, and I hope myself to be able to produce it, if no more suitable person in the theatrical world is found to do so" (Berg, N.Y.P.L.).]

To WILLIAM ARCHER

[B/2]

29 Fitzroy Square W
19th February 1896

[Meg Merrilies is an old gipsy woman in Sir Walter Scott's novel *Guy Mannering*.]

What is this I hear about your selection, for Asta—Asta the pure and flatchested—, of the voluptuous Rhoda Halkett? Can you be serious? Or do you want two Ritas in the play? I have submitted to the Meg Merrilies ratwife; but a Venusbergian Asta is too much.

The proposal of a tentative rehearsal is worthy of a parliament of bats. How could you take a part away from a capable woman like that if you once gave it to her? Siete tutti ammiliati: she has bewitched you all with her prettiness.

Can you not induce Elizabeth Robins to play it? Can't you open her eyes to the mistake she is making in letting it slip?

GBS

To CHARLES CHARRINGTON

[T/1 (A/4)]

29 Fitzroy Square W
19th February 1896

[Edward S. Willard (1853–1915), a well-known actor, had recently appeared under his own management at the Garrick in Augustus Thomas's *Alabama* and Jerome K. Jerome's *The Rise of Dick Halward*.]

(This page was written on Wednesday evening).

My dear Parsifal (Parsifal was "der reine Thor, durch Mitleid wissend").

I read Archer's letter with great gravity until I came to the last sentence, when its effect evaporated in a wild shriek of laughter.

"I have told Miss Halkett that I should write you to this effect."

Ha! Ha! ha! ha! ha! ha! ha! ha! ha! ha! ha! ha! ha! HA-AH!

602

Well done, Rhoda. He has told you that he would write to this effect.

Great Bayreuth Festival in the early days of spring. Venus—Miss Rhoda Halkett. Tannhäuser: Mr William Archer. Parsifal—Mr Charles Charrington.

Holy Elizabeth: he is in the Venusberg. He is, as Parsifal has acutely observed, but a boy, and her rounded figure has caught him. He has told her that he will write to this effect. I kiss her rounded figure, and recommend to him another quotation from "Parsifal," as follows:— Kundry (laughing harshly) Ha! ha! Bist du Keusch?

20th February 1896

Your letter is one of those self-revelations of yours which enchant me. The arrogance of your boast that you are a fool is superb. "Der reine Thor," nothing less! Well, admitting that you are potentially that, I deny that you are as yet "durch Mitleid wissend" (Janet will translate). You are in the swan shooting stage, drawing your bow on everything that flies.

No: if you were a fool, you would be "a success." I remember once being struck by an observation made by a member of one of your companies. He said that the only thing that stood in your way was the fact that you were the most infernal villain he had ever met. In this he was perfectly right. What was in his mind was not any mere circumstance such as your having acted this or that part badly, or given him a cheque that was not honoured, or misrepresented your circumstances, or the like, but that you did not wish him well—did not want him to get on—wanted to force him to work through your will instead of through his own—aimed finally at the destruction of him and all his species.

Let us make this more definite by taking cases that we both know well. Florence, for instance! Why is she no friend of yours? Why had you not the handling of that Avenue season? Not in the least because you hadn't paid her her salary when she was pretty poor, but solely because you hated her, humiliated her, looked at her artistic ambitions with pure murder in your eye, only let her play, with anguish and loathing in your soul, in an emergency which forced her on you. If you had been "a fool, enlightened by compassion," you would either have shrunk from engaging her, or, having engaged her, you would have taught her all you know, helped her, encouraged her, rehearsed her, exercised all your cleverness to save her from being crushed when it might have been necessary to let her down, and parted from her with a sense of having posted a friendly sentry to warn you of the next opportunity for you.

Take another case, Elizabeth Robins. Elizabeth says you can't act, that you haven't a single qualification for the stage, that your nature is radically anti-artistic. You say precisely the same thing about Elizabeth Robins. Both of you, instinctively perceiving that the only effect of your reciprocal verdict on me is to make me wink internally, reject me morally as a journalist, corrupted by that Opportunist pursuit. The result is that we cannot get Elizabeth for Asta, though she would do it better than anybody else within our reach. 6 of one of you: half-a-dozen of the other!

So far, all this is child's play. Now we approach the difficulties of the subject—the higher metaphysics of it. A man is spiritually all one piece: he doesn't hate one person and love another except with a hatred and love that are fundamentally one and the same passion. That you hate Janet goes without saying. She is everything that is antipathetic to you: the everything is summed up in the one withering term, an emotional actress. But here you suddenly find your logic spiked on the fact that you not only love what you hate, but find it an inmost necessity that it should love you. You seize it, and immediately begin a strange struggle. First, loving Janet, you try to identify her with yourself in your mortal quarrel with the rest of the world. Second, hating her, you wrestle with her incessantly, until at last you are left with no refuge in her affections except her instinctive perception of the higher metaphysics, and her "Mitleid."

Again, I come in. I am a journalist, a flatterer; I like all the people you hate; my instinct is to turn failure into success, not to expose success as a failure. You hate me inevitably. And yet here again the higher metaphysics take this unexpected turn, that not only does your hatred prove no obstacle to our being friends; but, more surprising still, you, the incarnation of envy and jealousy, find your point of sympathy with me in my fantastic love for your wife, although I am a most dangerous rival to you because my love is not oppressive, as yours must necessarily be as long as the element of hate lurks behind it. Besides, observe the suitability—the journalist and the emotional actress!

Now let us get back for a moment to the practical business plane. I am a shifty journalist. Janet is an emotional actress—drinks, takes morphia, unsound character and so on. Archer is a knave, and grows daily more knavish. Elizabeth Robins is ugly and cannot act. Heinemann is a Jew, with all the consequences of Judaism. Morris is a fool whose

604

instinct it is to go back instead of forward. Duse is a product of puffery. And so on through the rest of the accursed race.

There is no disputing all these descriptions. But then, what is Charles Charrington on that plane? I will tell you—a liar, a swindler, a promoter of bogus dramatic schemes, a drawer of worthless cheques, a devilish ugly fellow, a bad actor, a failure, a ruffian who uses his pretty wife, whose career he has ruined, to wheedle Saturday Review articles and cheques out of that ass Bernard Shaw (by the way, I am game for another tenner if the moving is too much of a squeeze), in short, a thoroughgoing rascal. Deny one syllable of it if you can. You cannot dismiss it as "a mere vulgar tu quoque." You cannot stand outside your own law if it is a true one. If Archer is a knave, Florence a whore, and the rest of the world made to match them, then we are all damned together; and your own place is in the seventh circle [of Dante's *Inferno*, reserved for the violently malicious].

So you see your quarrel is fundamentally with yourself. You will never get a step further until you are "durch Mitleid wissend" beyond the possibility of ever accepting the Martin theology (which is at the bottom of all your theories) again. How long the mills of the gods must grind you before they grind you exceeding small enough to become indeed "der Reine Thor," I don't know. (You can afford to wait because we, who like you, do not judge you as you, who hate us, judge us.)

Meanwhile, I submit the following propositions:—

1. That although treating people like human beings may not always produce the result which the selfish interests of the operator lead him to expect, there is no other possible way of treating them.
2. That what is wanted to make Janet successful is not any increase of her own powers, which are already more than sufficient, but an entourage of successful and brilliant persons.
3. That it is therefore your business to concentrate all your efforts on the success of those who play with her and of her manager (except when his initials are C.C.).
4. That when you have made everybody else a success on the stage, and filled the pockets of every rascal off it, you will find your neglected Janet the apex of the pyramid. There! that is enough for one sermon.

Stay—one more stab in a vital part. Janet never looked so happy, or so well, or so fresh from hopeful activity, as when she enjoyed those few blessed months away from us. Imagine the delight of that breathing space—no Charlie, no Nora, no Flemming, no Mimie, no Shaw. Did you realise what a fool she was to come back? A fool, "durch Mitleid wissend."

Oh, Charrington, Charrington, the Lord help us all!

. . . . . * .

We shall meet at Philippi, Westminster, on Sunday, I presume. I have written to Jones to ask him to recommend the appointment to Esmond's favourable consideration if he has a chance. I have written to Dorothy [Leighton] suggesting that she should ask not only Heinemann, but Elizabeth Robins, if the latter will give sufficient guarantees for my personal security. We must get together and talk as much as possible. I am anxious that you should appear in "the world of opportunism and expediency." Once there, you say, you are lost. This reminds me of the memorable stage wheeze—"If they discover me, I am lost," with the reply: "On the contrary, if they discover you, you are found." Let them all come, Rhoda and all. They may be out of the world of acting as you see it: that only proves that you don't see it as it is: it was made, like the world in general, without consulting you, confound you.

It is not so difficult to arrange people's ideas when they are once convinced that you wish them well. They are only too glad to be saved the trouble of doing it for themselves, with the additional luxury of being admired and liked and helped and all the rest of it. They will all go your way the moment you cease to desire their destruction. Your detection of Heinemann's desire to realise the ideal of the English gentleman is Luciferesquely clever: but unless you treat the gentleman as the real human being, you insult him. Better jump on him with your own unrestrained notions. I am forced to do that because I cannot manage *people*. I can only manage schemes and ideas and arrange the drama of the thing. The moment I have to deal with people who don't like me and whom I cannot win over, the limits of my tact make themselves felt. I play the deuce unless I can win by brute force of brains.

I must really go to bed now. This letter ought to keep you interested in yourself for at least a week. The first page of it was written yesterday, before I saw you today.

What demon sent Willard across our path today? I really feel my entrails twisting about at the notion of his being like that in Morell.

GBS

* The ellipsis is Shaw's.

To HENRY ARTHUR JONES

[X/124.e?]

[29 Fitzroy Square W]
20th February 1896

I am going to read *Candida* at Mrs Ashton Jonson's (Dorothy Leighton's) on Sunday evening. Do you think Esmond could be persuaded to come? I believe Mrs A. J. is going to invite him at a venture. If you happen to meet him in the meantime, tell him that the part of the poet is very considerably ahead of Little Billee [in *Trilby*].

To T. FISHER UNWIN

[S/7]

29 Fitzroy Square W
24th February 1896

Dear Fisher Unwin

If I ever publish "Arms & The Man" I shall treat it to not only an introduction, but probably to an appendix as well. The American copyright is, if anything, *more* important than the English, as the play has been much more widely made known there, and the Americans rather fancy me.

But what is the use of vexing our souls about it? It's evidently not worth publishing: you are at your old benevolent game of occasionally publishing a friend's book for amusement. I'll take the will for the deed until I have something for you with real business in it.

yours sincerely
G. Bernard Shaw

To WILLIAM ARCHER

[A/2]

29 Fitzroy Square W
6th March 1896

[Buchanan's leaflet was a brochure announcing future publications under his own imprint.]

I have just had a visit from Miss Halkett. She is in some distress because Heinemann won't see her. I expect he is now, after his spluttering flourish of her colors, going to shew us that *he* has no interest in her—not he, and that his acquaintance with her is of the slightest.

He has written to Charrington, who is to impart the gist of the communication to me this afternoon.

As to the bike, I must try and find out what is possible. The absolute crack machines of the moment are the Elswick (19 Great Portland St) and the Osmond (3 Holborn Viaduct). Their net price, new, with gear case, saddle &c, complete is £25.; and they make no second grade machines. It might be possible to get second hand ones (1895) for £15 or so; but the agents are apt to shake their heads and swear that an Osmond or an Elswick never comes back once it leaves the shop, so rapturously do the riders cling to them.

Humber, however, makes Beeston machines (the best), Wolverhampton machines, and (I think) Coventry machines; and it is generally possible to get an offer from them of something nominally second hand at a reasonable price. J. K. Starley (not Starley Bro⁵) also caters for the average man; and his machines are good, sensible ones. The Premier people work the payment-by-instalment system energetically.

I suggest the following alternatives. 1. A friend in the trade (any hardware trade) who could order a machine "for export." Mrs Emery has a convenient pal of this description, I think. 2. Approach [Henry] Norman on the subject of his admiration for the American bicycle, which may move him to buy one if he can trade off his "Referee" on you. It is a fairly new machine, as he sold its predecessor (a Starley Rover) to Webb last summer. Pennell might know of something, by the way.

Prices are high just now in consequence of the prodigious boom. Except you light on a rosy private contract, you will not get anything new for £12.10.0 that will be worth buying.

Did Buchanan send you his pamphlet [*Is Barabbas a Necessity?*] as well as the leaflet? It (the pamphlet) contains a private letter of mine. B. is in immense spirits, "clinging in desolation and despair to a faith in God."

GBS

To ELLEN TERRY

[U(A)/10; X/117]

29 Fitzroy Square W
9th March 1896

[The leper reference from II Kings is to the play *Godefroi and Yolande* by Irving's son Laurence, which was first produced in Chicago. After reading *The Man of Destiny* and finding it "delicious," Ellen had embarked on a campaign to induce Irving to produce it. Shaw's insistence on a royalty or percentage reflected his suspicion that Irving might seek to "buy" the play as a means of bribing the dramatist-critic. In a letter to Christopher St John, editor of the Terry-Shaw correspondence (1931), he wrote: "Irving's princely manner of buying literary courtiers was well known to me. The sequel proved that Irving, though contemptuously willing to pay me for control of the play, never had any serious intention of producing it."]

Ellen Terry: what do you mean by this? Have you no respect for my years, my talent, my reputation, my feelings, that you play these games on me? Here is a newspaper—a miserable American newspaper— containing a monstrous statement that you insist on playing the part of a—a—no: I cannot write it, speak it, think it. Far be all such horrors from you for ever and ever and ever!

"And he went out from his presence—a leper white as snow."

How could you have the heart to threaten me with such a thing? Do you want me to go out from your presence also white as snow, blanched by a tormented, wounded heart? Wretch! perverse, *aluminium*-hearted wretch! I do not know any other way of expressing the lightness, the hardness, the radiance of that centre of your being.

Ugh! It is not an idea, but a pain too deep for surgery.

Let me shake it off. To business!

Dear Madam

My attention has been called to certain marginal notes made by you upon a copy of the Chicago Tribune dated the 25th ult°. Among other flattering and irresistible expressions, whose probable insincerity I forgive in consideration of the exquisite pleasure they give me, I note a statement, apparently referring to my Napoleonic play, that "H.I. quite loves it, and will do it finely." Now I have to observe on this, first, that if the matter is one of love, the only initials I care for are not H.I., but E.T.; and second, that if H.I. has any serious intentions I should like to know whether they are honorable or not. For, having no idea that His Immensity had any sort of interest in the play—having sent it to you, I swear, out of pure vanity, to steal another priceless millionth of an inch of your regard by shewing you what a clever fellow I am—I might at any moment have parted with it to Mansfield or another, both for England and America. It has had one or two very narrow escapes, chiefly through my own laziness. Will you therefore befriend me to the extent of letting me know seriously whether H.I. wishes me to hold the play for him, as its production by him would of course be quite the best thing that could happen to it. If so, there is one thing that he ought to know, as he is commonly supposed to prefer to buy plays from the author. As long as I remain a dramatic critic I can neither sell plays nor take advances. I must depend altogether on royalties and percentages on actual performances. Otherwise, you see, I should simply be bribed right and left: already I could increase my income considerably by making "adaptations" for managerial shelves. It is bad enough to have my conscience telling me that with regard to you, towards whom it is my duty & my point of honor to be sternly impartial, I am hopelessly won over—won without a struggle—; but what would you think of me if I were accessible to money? At the same time, I am boundlessly accessible to the meanest commercial considerations when I can grab at them in an effective attitude of incorruptibility. You will detect at a glance the adroit mixture of flattery and business in this letter. I am eager for business— keen on it—because it will be an excuse for more flattery—because I can gratify my desire to talk nonsense to you under cover of filling my pockets. I *must* attach myself to you somehow: let me therefore do it as a matter of business. Gold, be thou my idol henceforth!

By far the best way to exploit my reputation (small, but intense) would be to produce the piece in New York. They think more of me in America than in England, thanks to "Arms & The Man." But then I should not be able to rehearse it—to teach you and H. I. how to act—to see you every day for ever so long. Besides, if the play starts in America I shall have to get up a copyrighting performance here.

But it is all nonsense: you are only playing with me. I will go to that beautiful Mrs Patrick Campbell, who won my heart long ago by her pianoforte playing as Mrs Tanqueray, and make her head twirl like a chimney cowl with my blarney. *She* shall play the Strange Lady—she and the passion worn Forbes [Robertson]. Yes, it shall be so. Farewell, faithless Ellen!

GBS

To CHARLES CHARRINGTON

29 Fitzroy Square W
16th March 1896

[T/1 (A/4)]

[*Sister Helen* may have been the play that Charrington was writing (see headnote to letter of 2nd December 1893 to Janet Achurch).]

Dear Charrington

Before you go committing yourself to Morell, I want to put before you the case on the other side—the case which has always prevented me from looking to you for Morell as I look to Janet for Candida.

Imprimis, you are only attracted by the universal human element in the man, and not by his specific individuality. That's very dangerous to begin with; and I am by no means sure that you would not overcome the obvious misfit of Eugene's age and build more successfully than that of Morell's character & temperament.

Morell is a very glib, sanguine, cocksure, popular sort of man. His utter want of shyness; his readiness to boss people spiritually; his certainty that his own ideas, being the right ideas, must be good for them: all this belongs to the vulgarity which makes him laugh at Eugene's revelation, and talk of "calf love." It is nothing to the point that he is also goodnatured, frank, sympathetic, and capable of admitting Candida's position finally when it is presented to his *feeling*, in spite of the fact that he would have disputed it hotly had it been presented to him as a purely intellectual position. That rescues him from the odium which would otherwise attach to him as, intellectually and normally, a clerical bounder; but it does not assimilate him in any way to the parts which lie nearest to you. I can see you well enough in the heartstricken passages; but I do not see you facile, cheery, spontaneous, fluent, emphatic, unhesitating and bumptious in the early scenes with Prossy & Burgess & Eugene (before the explosion) in which the whole specific part of his individuality has to be fixed; I don't hear your boisterous cheery laugh, which should not be refined out of the part merely because I have to refine it out myself in reading the play from sheer incapacity to get quite into that coarse part of his skin; I don't see Candida carrying conviction when she tells you that you are the idol of a Victoria Park congregation, the contrast in everything to the hunted Eugene; I don't see you as the spoiled child, the superficial optimist, the man who, in spite of his power of carrying everything before him by the mere rush and light & warmth of his goodnature & conviction, is stopped by the least resistance.

Granted that all this could be got over by sheer acting, is there the smallest likelihood of your making such an arduous and unnatural effort as the feat would require? And suppose you failed—suppose your Morellism carried no conviction to the audience—have you considered how complicatedly damning the failure would be both to yourself and Janet? If you stood quite alone, the effect of a return to the stage with the particular sort of failure—the failure that spoils a play sympathetic enough to make the audience angrily resent its being spoiled—would be bad enough from your own point of view as an individual unattached actor. But there is something worse to be apprehended. If people get the idea that they can't have Janet without also having you thrust into a part for which you are unsuited, it will be all up with Janet and with you. And that is just what I am afraid of. The Doll's House was all right when you played Rank the Unfortunate. It was all wrong when you played Helmer the Smug & Self Satisfied. Now Morell is really nothing but Helmer getting fair play. The question, therefore, is not whether you can get through Morell passably by putting in a few stomach tones, and (by indulging in *genuine* emotion) making yourself diabolically ugly at the moment when Candida is telling you that the women cannot look at you without adoration, but whether you could play him with such absolute conviction, fitness, and spontaneity that all question as to the propriety of your *casting yourself* for the part would fall to the ground without a word.

My own opinion on the point has already been completely betrayed to you by the fact that I have never treated the part as your property, in spite of the very discouraging quality of the practicable alternatives to you. Take any of those alternatives—Waring or anyone else—let us call him XYZ. XYZ will not exactly fail: he will only underplay; and all the papers will treat him with great politeness. *You* will either fail or succeed; and if you fail, the result will be damnation. XYZ's underplaying will not hurt Janet: it will have absolutely no reactions of any importance. Your failure, if you fail, will have the most disastrous reactions in all directions, on her, on the I.T., on me, on yourself as a manager as apart from an actor, and devil knows what else besides. Consequently you present yourself, as compared with XYZ, as a frightfully risky Morell at a point in our game where we cannot afford to throw away a single chance. Now what probability is there of your being as transcendently better a Morell, if you succeed, than XYZ, as to justify you in casting yourself for it at such odds? Hast thou these things well considered?

It seems to me that unless a play comes along with a leading part very specially suited to you, your best policy at the I.T. is to produce a series of plays very carefully, playing small parts yourself, Hare fashion, until you have made your ground sure, and thoroughly allayed all suspicions of actor-managerism. And I should not, in your place, let myself be turned aside from that except on very strong provocation.

I have, in my usual fashion, put the negative side of the case with all possible force, leaving you to supply the positive one. Why, except as a means of livelihood, a man should desire to act on the stage when he has the world to act in, is not clear to me save in the cases of men who are only effective under stage conditions. I write plays, Lord knows why; but I do not go on the stage because the stage would make me ridiculous. Somehow, I have come to class you in my consciousness, not as a stage actor, but rather as one of my Fabian gang to whom the popular performers & executants are only the marksmen and fencers, not the generals in the battle. Consequently I am too far out of sympathy with your impulse to act to be altogether a safe and loyal counsellor for you in the matter. Honestly, I should not care a damn if you never acted again so long as you were getting things done as we want them done. It is quite otherwise with Janet. Acting is her destiny. It cannot be put aside in her case as I can put aside, for instance, my own fondness for music, which made me desire to be a singer and player. Nature gave me slow, clumsy fingers and a mongrel, worthless voice, two effectual corkers to such vanity. And I did not care enough about my fancy to overcome these as I overcame the obstacles to my becoming a speaker & a writer. If I had cared enough I should have overcome them. Consequently I have no foregone conclusions as to this person being a born actor & that person a born duffer. I have no doubt you could make yourself a fine actor if you chose to; but do you really think that that is your choice? Has not your interest in art become a much wider and deeper one than the narrow interest of the pure executant, and does not that point to wider activities? Shakespere & Goethe tried acting, but did not after all do much at it. Or, to bring all this to the point, is it of anything like as much importance that you should seize the chance of playing Morell as that Janet should seize that of playing Candida?

Such are the points I want considered before we do anything rash. Meanwhile, on the business question, I am not particularly disposed to let the I.T. have Candida on Independent lines. There is no conclusive evidence that it is outside the scope of ordinary theatres, like Mrs Warren or The Philanderer. If the I.T. chooses to make me a proposition for a dozen matinees on the best business terms it can afford (said terms not to be at the expense of the cast) I shall consider it. Otherwise they must put up with The Philanderer, which would, I think, be a very appropriate & interesting production. My notion of business terms is 10% on the receipts when they are under £1000 a week, & 15% when they are above it. I blow cold for the moment because I want to see whether Esmond's interest in it is worth anything.

"Candida" produced under ordinary conditions, with a commercial and prestiginous success for Janet, plus The Philanderer at the I.T. managed as a comedy success (succes de scandale) by you, would suit us all better than an I.T. "Candida" alone.

GBS

P.S. On thinking it over, I don't think "Sister Helen" half a bad notion.

To EDWARD R. PEASE

29 Fitzroy Square W

[S/2]   20th March 1896

[Theodore Wright (1840–1912), pioneer Socialist and Fabian (since 1888), was the author (under the pseudonym "Frank Fairman") of a popular work, *Socialism Made Plain* (1888), containing a preface by William Morris. His wife was the actress who had appeared in *Ghosts* (see headnote to letter of 30th March 1891 to Charles Charrington). The Referendum resolution drafted by Shaw was one of the Fabian "Draft Resolutions for the International Socialist Congress" published in the April *Fabian News*. The Congress was held in London from 28th July to 1st August in St Martin's Town Hall. Shaw attended as the Fabian delegate representing Dublin.]

Dear Pease

Draft of Referendum resolution for International Congress enclosed.

One important piece of business I have forgotten until it is perhaps too late. Wallas is (or was) going to lecture at Toynbee Hall, practically to an S.D.F. audience, on the Feeding of the School Children. We want a tract on this very badly, as Wallas apparently has a practical solution through the Poor Law authorities to oppose to the mere cry of the S.D.F. He agreed with me in a recent conversation that the best way to get his stuff into writing would be to send a reporter to Toynbee Hall to take him down verbatim. I, or somebody else, could then make the tract out of the report. Unfortunately I have let several days slip without remembering this; but if it is not too late, you might find out from him what the date of his discourse is, and get Theodore Wright to put you on to a trustworthy verbatim reporter (he might even do the job himself). The Execs will be safe, I should think, to sanction the expenditure; if not, I should be almost disposed to guarantee the money myself & make Wallas & Webb go shares sooner than let the chance slip. On finishing the tract we could appeal to the exec. to grant us the price of the report as part of the expense of preparation, if they failed us the other way.

GBS

To JANET ACHURCH

29 Fitzroy Square W
[T/1 (B/4)]   24th March 1896

[The method by which Mrs William Archer had been relaxing Shaw was a system of nerve training conceived by Annie Payson Call (1853–1940), a mental hygienist of Newtonville, Mass. Archer had reviewed her book *Power through Repose* (1891) in the *Illustrated London News* on 11th April 1891, and Mrs Archer had been inspired by the work to master the system and become one of its strongest advocates and practitioners, eventually founding the Langley Nerve Training Colony, at which Shaw spoke on "Nerves" on 20th June 1925.]

I enclose a letter about "Candida."

I hope I did not make myself disagreeable last night. On my way back I called on the Salts and played a duet or two. Mrs Salt complained considerably of me: said she believed I had been practising scales (an unheard-of accusation); said I was in a destructively electrical condition and made her feel that she wanted to cry; said that if I undressed in the dark when going to bed, sparks would come out of me; and generally made me conscious of a grinding, destroying energy, and a heart transmuted to adamant. If I had realised that I was like that, I shouldn't have come: I am really only fit for intercourse with sensitive souls when I am broken and weary. Mrs Archer has been relaxing me joint by joint; but I am still hardly safe without a chain and muzzle. I am off to the Orange Grove [a vegetarian restaurant in St Martin's Lane] to seek the nearest possible thing to a meal of flints and nails. You must forgive my ferocity: it is 9/10ths imaginary; and the remaining tenth is strength gained by feeding on your regard for me.

GBS

To ELLEN TERRY

29 Fitzroy Square W
[U(A)/10; X/117]   26th March 1896

[W.S.Penley (1851–1912), an actor-manager, had scored a great success as Lord Fancourt Babberley in his own production of *Charley's Aunt*, which achieved a run of 1466 performances before it was withdrawn in December 1896. Pippin III (d. 768) was the King of the Franks. Mrs Anna Ruppert was a notoriously bad actress who had made her London début in 1894 in the title rôle in Clement Scott's adaptation of Sardou's *Odette*. Shaw's choice of

Penley and Mrs Ruppert for *The Man of Destiny* was designed to be a ludicrous example of miscasting. William Terriss (1847–97), formerly a member of Irving's company and equally at home in Shakespeare and in popular melodrama (of which he was a leading practitioner), was murdered at the stage-door of the Adelphi Theatre, on 16th December 1897, by a knife-wielding lunatic named Richard Archer Flint (1865–?), known as "Mad Archer," who had once been employed as a supernumerary at the Adelphi, and whom Terriss had assisted pecuniarily. The play Shaw eventually wrote for Terriss, who rejected it, was *The Devil's Disciple*.

Shaw's stage directions for Gloria's angry approach to Valentine, in Act III of *You Never Can Tell*, were founded on Ellen Terry's "business," in W. G. Wills's *Olivia*, when Olivia struck Thornhill.]

Do you see this?

Well, that is a Röntgen [X-ray] photograph of my heart, taken immediately after your telegram declaring that "The Man of Destiny" cannot possibly be performed until the 31st December 1897 (that is what next year means). What laziness! what procrastination! what indifference! Nothing to be done but put an advertisement in the paper, send round the corner for a stock scene and a few foreign looking uniforms, call a rehearsal or two, and engage an extra force of police to cope with the crowd at the doors. And yet you tell me it cannot be done for two years. Do you suppose that a trumpery toy of that sort can be put away in a drawer all that time, and then be taken out and enjoyed as if it were the brightest of novelties. Not a bit of it. Next year, when you look at my script, you will ask yourself with a sinking of the heart, whether that flimsy stuff is what you thought a part worth playing, and H. I. will ask you what you meant by committing him to such tomfoolery. I myself will writhe at the thought of an exposure of my folly on the stage as I writhe when I am asked to republish one of my novels (I once wrote novels). I hate the play already now that my Strange Lady has faded away into the unreal Future. There is no Future: there is only the Present. Do you suppose I will let you treat me as you treat Shakspere—play me centuries after I am dead? No: I will make no bonds and bargains for next year: by then my gold will have turned into withered leaves in your portmanteau. Let 1896 perform its own plays: If you do not want me until 1897 you had better have an 1897 play—I have an idea for a little play about King Pippin and his wife, with a lovely medieval French court for a stage setting—and let "The Man of Destiny" be done by Penley and Madame Anna Ruppert in London, and in America by Mansfield, who has had the audacity to ask me for another play, after heaping villainy on me over my "Candida." I see that he was sagacious enough to pit Shaw against Shakspere by putting up "Arms & The Man" at Chicago against Macbeth, and that you did *not* give your understudy a chance by going to see my play. Alas! you do not really love me.

Terriss (this is a secret) wants me to collaborate with him in a play the scenario of which includes every situation in the Lyceum repertory or the Adelphi record. The best act is "The Bells." He is arrested either for forgery or murder at every curtain, and goes on as fresh as paint and free as air when it goes up again. I talked it over with him whilst he was dressing for a matinee at the Adelphi. I noticed that his chest was black and blue. He caught the expression of pity and horror in my eye as I caught sight of the bruise, and said, with a melancholy smile, "Ah yes, Ellen Terry! You remember the third act of "Olivia" at the old Court? I was Thornhill. The marks have never come off: I shall carry them to my grave." I did not tell him that I also had received heart wounds in those days which I shall carry to my grave. Neither, by the way, did I decide in favor of the collaboration. But I seriously think I shall write a play for him. A good melodrama is a more difficult thing to write than all this clever-clever comedy: one must go straight to the core of humanity to get it, and if it is only good enough, why, there you have Lear or Macbeth.

The most depressing rumors are about here as to the next Lyceum production—"Julius Cæsar" or some such obsolete rubbish, with Wilson Barrett as Pontius Pilate. Will nothing persuade H. I. that Queen Anne is dead? There is Peer Gynt ready to his hand—can he read it without swearing to be the first man to drown that cook and peel that onion on the English stage? And how beautiful you would be as Solveig! Million millions! is H. I. blind, is he deaf, or is he no actor at all, but only a Shakspere-struck antiquary like Mary Anderson (whose autobiography is just out) that he passes by the great chances of his life as if they were pieces of orange peel laid in his path expressly to capsize him?

But of what use is it to talk? We have no theatres, no drama, no actors, no nothing. And you will play nothing for me until next year, like the old tavern sign "Credit given Tomorrow." Very well, then; but the delay raises my terms. This year, three pounds (as your

617

telegram offers) of sterling gold. But next year the three pounds must be equal pounds of your fair flesh, to be by no means cut off and taken in what part of your body pleaseth me, but to accumulate to my credit until the fortyfifth performance or so, when I will take it all in a lump, if I may libel it by such a very undescriptive word. But even then I shall only have the shrine, useless unless the inner lamp shine on me. For one ray of that every year you shall have all the plays in the world & be a thousandfold underpaid.

Great Heavens, my work, my work, my work! How is that to get done if I turn from it every moment to write to you!

GBS

To BERTHA NEWCOMBE

[A/4]

Stocks Cottage. Aldbury. Tring
31st March 1896

[Mary Augusta (Mrs Humphry) Ward (1851–1920), niece of Matthew Arnold, was a popular novelist (*Robert Elsmere*, *The History of David Grieve*), founder in 1880 of a London settlement house which subsequently became known as the Passmore Edwards Settlement, and opponent of woman-suffrage. Janet Penrose Ward (1879–1956), who married the historian George Macaulay Trevelyan, was active for many years in settlement work and other social reform activities. Shaw, at an early age, had been introduced to Trollope's novels by his seagoing uncle Walter Gurly, who had carried home to him cheap pirated editions from America. Herbert L. (later Viscount) Samuel (1870–1963), Liberal politician, was an intimate friend of the Webbs. P. A. J. Dagnan-Bouveret (1852–1929) was a French painter under whom many young British artists studied in Paris.]

Heavens! I had forgotten you—totally forgotten you. Here I am in a lonely cottage on a remote hillside. It is late at night: Wallas (to whom Mrs Humphry Ward lent this place for Easter) has gone up to town to look after the education bill and will not be back until tomorrow. I arrived yesterday night; this morning I rode to the railway station for newspapers on my bike; then worked at my drama until lunch; after that meal went for a walk with Wallas; after his departure called at the great house on Miss Janet Ward and her governess and sparkled at them over a cup of milk & hot water like a penny squib; then went off biking to a place called—in an unsuccessful attempt to christen it after one of Scott's novels—Ivinghoe, and from that round by other places to Tring & home, having tired myself by hard riding enough

618

to greatly enjoy the fire within and the immense darkness, silence &
solitude without. I could find no book here fit to read except "The Last
Chronicle of Barset" which I had not read these 25 years past; and I
have been renewing my acquaintance with the Rev. Crawley & Lily
Dale & Johnny Eames and all the rest of them with some astonishment
at the excellence of my memory of them. I used to feel that Trollope's
pictures of English society were good just as you often feel that a
portrait is a good likeness without knowing the original; and now that
I do know the original I am confirmed in my good opinion. If Trollope
had gone an inch deeper he would have come to the universal, epic
humanity that is common to all classes & periods: as it was, he just got
deep enough to make his people lifelike without getting out of the
specific stratum that gives historical value to his work. —Yes, my dear
Bertha: I know you don't want to hear criticisms from me. But I will
not be dictated to by any woman when my pen is in my hand: I shall
write as I please. —I gave up the idea of joining the Trevelyan trip
because I could not afford it. Trevelyan & Samuel handsomely offered
to take me on as a guest; but I resolved to come here instead. ✍ (This
is the Kelmscott Press way of indicating a new paragraph) Miss
Erichsen has gone off to Cheshire to paint a portrait. She offered me
one date at the studio; but I could not go. ✒ Your studio talk about
Dagnan & the other idiots is most exasperating: the model with the
baby is the only interesting part of it. How is it possible for a woman
who has known & spoken to me—familiarly, even—to return to these
childish idols? ✒ I find I forgot something that you asked me to do in
the postscript of your last letter but one—something about Lugné-Poë.
It is now too late; but what could I have done? You may play me as a
trump card for all I am worth; but I cannot play myself. ✒ "Little
Eyolf" has been withdrawn from the I. Theatre by Elizabeth Robins
(virtually), who will produce it in October in partnership with Waring.
As you may imagine, Janet will not be in the cast. The I.T. have therefore asked me to give them "Candida" for 8 matinées spread over a
month. I have startled them by attaching to my consent the condition
that they shall get £1000 for the enterprise (really £800). They point
out that I thought their capital of £400 enough for "Little Eyolf," &
that they understood me to have a soul above money. I smile
enigmatically, and hold to my demand. Janet is therefore making an
effort to get the capital herself. There have been gusts of ice & sulphur
lately, it seems. I had a fit of sardonic laughter at my own follies, and

was accused of cruelty, sacrilege, blasphemy, insult, iconoclasm, Satanism—as you would compendiously say, of being horrid. 'Twas ever thus, Bertha. Your sex likes me as children like wedding cake, for the sake of the sugar on the top. If they taste by an accident a bit of crumb or citron, it is all over: I am a fiend, delighting in vivisectional cruelties, as indicated by the corners of my mouth. ∅ My correspondence with Ellen Terry, the blarneying audacities of which would fill you with envy could you read them, has ended in an offer from Irving to buy the Napoleon play. On my refusing to sell, he offered to give me £3 a night for it. I stipulated for production this year; this was declared impossible & next year proposed, upon which I suddenly and elusively slipped away from business into a thousand wild stories and extravagances and adorations (I really do love Ellen), which are at present on their way to her. The fact is, I suspect Irving regards my shewing her the play as a familiar means of securing my share of the bribery current in my profession: at least this is just as likely as not. He has no doubt bought many a play without the faintest intention of ever performing it. You must keep my counsel in these matters.

I return to town early next week, probably. I must go to bed now. Goodnight.

GBS

To JANET ACHURCH

Stocks Cottage. Aldbury. Tring
4th April 1896

[T/1 (A/4)]

[Graham Wallas's sister presumably was Mary (d. 1922), the wife of the philosopher John H. Muirhead (1855–1940). His niece was Helen Wodehouse (b. 1880), Mistress of Girton College, 1931–42, and author of several books on philosophy and religion. A translation by Thomas Common (1850–1919) of *Nietzsche contra Wagner*, Vol. I of the contemplated Collected Works of Nietzsche (of which only two volumes were issued) by Henry & Company, was reviewed by Shaw in the *Saturday Review* on 11th April.]

Here I am drafting stacks of letters in reply to a sackful of the unanswered communications of the last six months. I send them up to Fitzroy Square to be typewritten and despatched; but even with this lightening of the manual labour my soul is weary, spite of country air and such bicycling as the weather allows. Therefore, for a moment at least I must write to someone I love and tell her some lies to relieve the well considered truths and criticisms I have conscientiously served out to more distant correspondents.

Miss Marbury sends me a newspaper cutting announcing that Mansfield has engaged himself to Charles Fröhmann for four years for a share of the receipts and a guaranteed minimum salary of 100,000 dollars— £20,000, which seems incredible. The idea is, apparently, to run him as a great Shakespearean actor—the Irving of America. He announces that he will presently drop his old repertory of Prince Karl &c.

Anything further about "Candida"?

The inmates here are Wallas, his sister, and his niece. The Webbs are coming next week. I spent the morning bicycling through the park with another Janet, an intelligent, athletic young woman of fifteen, Mrs Humphry Ward's youngest daughter. Imagine my being 25 years older than a person of full intellectual age and competence. On such occasions I realise the full significance of the singular fate which has led me to play with all the serious things of life and to deal seriously with all its plays.

Farewell: I am done: I can write no more: my brain rebels: I cannot even get out of the hollow style in which I have had to write eleven other longish letters.

The translation of Nietzsche's work—the first volume, at least—is out. If C.C. gets a chance of borrowing it, tell him to do so. He would enjoy some of it.

I can no more. I shall come up next week for the production [Clo. Graves's *A Mother of Three*] at the Comedy [on 8th April].

GBS

To ELLEN TERRY

[U(A)/10; X/117]

Stocks Cottage. Aldbury. Tring
6th April 1896

[Shaw's total royalties from Mansfield in 1896 are recorded in his diary as £139. 10. 6. The play's prior earnings (London, New York, and provincial) amounted to £341. 15. 2 in 1894 and £246. 5. 0 in 1895. The Shakespeare quotation (imprecise) is from *Much Ado About Nothing*, I, i, 219.]

There is a song of Schubert's ["Lied des gefangenen Jägers," op. 52, no. 7] in which the gentleman (who is, I think, [Sir Walter] Scott's Imprisoned Huntsman translated and retranslated and translated back again from English to German) wants "to sun himself in Ellen's eyes." That is what I am going to do for a while this evening in my Easter cottage. The weather has frowned; but Fortune has smiled. Ten splendid things have happened: to wit, 1. a letter from Ellen Terry; 2, a cheque for my Chicago royalties, swollen by the dollars of the thousands of people who were turned away from the doors where Ellen was acting and had to go to "Arms & The Man" *faute de mieux*; 3, a letter from Ellen Terry; 4, the rolling away of the clouds from the difficult second act of my new play, leaving the view clear and triumphant right on to the curtain; 5, a letter from Ellen Terry; 6, a beautiful sunset ride over the hills and far away, thinking of Ellen Terry; 7, a letter from Ellen Terry; 8, a letter from Ellen Terry; 9, a letter from Ellen Terry; 10, a letter from Ellen Ellen Ellen Ellen Ellen Ellen Ellen Ellen Ellen Eleanor Ellenest Terry.

Who has told you that Mrs Pat Cat is to have my Strange Lady? He lies in his throat, whoever he is. And yet I suspect Henry Irving—oh, I suspect him. Why, you ask, should everybody think everybody else corruptible? Because everybody *is* corruptible: is not that simple? He would buy me in the market like a rabbit, wrap me up in brown paper and put me by on his shelf if I offered myself for sale—and how else does a critic offer himself except by writing his little play, or his adaptation or what not? And it would be such a sly way to send it to you. Oh, twenty thousand million devils—! But it is not so; and it was not so; and indeed God forbid that it should be so—you see the devil can quote Shakspere for his own purpose. If he wants to do the play the least bit in the world, why, I know his value, and will reserve it for him though the next best man covered his offer ten times. But if not, do not let the rabbit be bought and wrapped up. He will not produce it for your sake: no man ever does anything for a woman's sake: from our birth to our death we are women's babies, always wanting something from them, never giving them anything except something to keep *for us*. After all, why should he be fond of people? People are always talking of love and affection and the like—just as they talk of religion—as if they were the commonest things in the world; but the Frenchman was nearer the truth when he said that a great passion is as rare as a man of genius. Has he ever loved you for the millionth fraction of a moment?: if so, for that be all his sins forgiven unto him. I do not know whether women ever love. I rather doubt it: they pity a man, *mother* him, delight in making him love them; but I always suspect that their tenderness is deepened by their remorse for being unable to love him. Man's one gift is that at his best he *can* love—not constantly, nor

622

faithfully, nor often, nor for long,—but for a moment—a few minutes perhaps out of years. It is because I have had a glimpse or two that I am such a hopelessly impious person; for when God offers me heaven as the reward of piety, I simply reply, "I know. I've been there. You can do nothing further for me, thank you."

You boast that you are a fool—it is at bottom, oh, such a tremendous boast (do you know that in Wagner's last drama, "Parsifal," the redeemer is "der reine Thor," "the pure fool"?) but you have the wisdom of the heart, which makes it possible to say deep things to you. You say I'd be sick of you in a week; but this is another boast: it implies that you could entertain me for a whole week. Good heavens! with what? With art?—with politics?—with philosophy?—or with any other department of culture? I've written more about them all (for my living) than you ever thought about them. On that plane I would exhaust you before you began, and could bore you dead with my own views in two hours. But one does not get tired of adoring the Virgin Mother. Bless me! you will say, the man is a Roman Catholic. Not at all: the man is the author of Candida; and Candida, between you and me, is the Virgin Mother and nobody else. And my present difficulty is that I want to reincarnate her—to write another Candida play *for* you. Only, it won't come. Candida came easily enough; but after her came that atrocious "Man of Destiny," a mere stage brutality, and my present play brings life and art together and strikes showers of sparks from them as if they were a knife and a grindstone. Heaven knows how many plays I shall have to write before I earn one that belongs of divine right to you. Someday, when you have two hours to spare, you must let me read Candida to you. You will find me a disagreeably cruel looking middle aged Irishman with a red beard; but that cannot be helped. By the way, you once spoke to me, although, as you were evidently woolgathering at the time, you won't remember the circumstance. It was at one of the performances [of *Ivanhoe*] at the new opera house which is now the Palace Music Hall. You were in the stalls; so was I; and it happened that we were almost the last persons to leave and were kept standing together for a moment waiting for the doorway into the corridor to clear. I was highly conscious of your illustrious presence and identity, but of course took care not to appear conscious. You seemed very much in earnest and even affected about something; and my theory is that you were in imagination impersonating some unfortunate young village girl of lowly station—Hetty in "Adam Bede" perhaps, and that you suddenly took it into your head that I was the squire, or perhaps the parson. At all events you most unexpectedly raised your eyes to mine for a moment and said, with the deepest respect, "Good evening, sir." I nearly sat down on the floor in confusion; but by good luck I managed not to wake you out of your dream. What I did was to instinctively fall into your drama (whatever it was) by saying "Good evening" so exactly in the manner of the squire acknowledging a salutation from the gamekeeper's daughter (a most respectable, promising, well conducted young woman), that you passed unsuspectingly on up the avenue, with the squirrels and rabbits scampering away as you approached; and I watched you until you turned into the path leading to the dairy and vanished. I suppose you don't happen to remember, in the course of your transmigrations, meeting a squire or parson with a red beard and a nasty expression about the corners of his mouth?

But I must not ask you questions, as you have written me enough to live on until you come back; and your precious forces must not be wasted in writing letters to me. I wish this ink—a penny a bottle at the village shop—were blacker and my writing bolder. If you have a magnifying glass, it will all come out beautifully legible.

The Independent Theatre people, having had "Little Eyolf" snatched back from their grasp by Miss Elizabeth Robins (who will produce it next October, probably, in partnership with Waring), want to produce Candida. Janet wants me to consent. I must be cruel only to be kind; and I insist on their having £1000 to finance it with, even for eight matinees spread over a month. They have only £400; so I think I am safe for the present; but they may get the money. If so, Candida may be the first thing you see on your return to these shores. But then, alas! I shall have no excuse for reading it to you.

GBS

To JANET ACHURCH

[T/1 (A/4)]

[Stocks Cottage. Aldbury. Tring]
14th April 1896

Since Charrington is coming down tomorrow I send you a line to ponder in his absence.

First, I have finished the second act of the play—finished it triumphantly on Sunday morning. On reading it over I find some transitions which no actress could be expected to follow without a little gentler management; but on the whole I have carried out my design. And now, if I had the very *faintest* idea of the next act, I should be happy.

624

Second, instead of inventing that next act I have jumped over its head on to the melodrama for Terriss. You remember a vague idea I had for the first act? Well, I have completed the scenario of not only that act, but the second and third, each of them being dramas in themselves with tremendous catastrophes. I have no longer any doubt of my being able to carry out that project with considerable force.

The only question with me now is one of time—life—health. It may possibly be that my growing certainty that I can be a dramatic poet if I concentrate myself on it, may be a symptom of decay; but it obviously will not do to proceed on that assumption. During all these years I have acquired a certain power of work, and hardened myself to stand unscraped by many knife edges that cut ordinary folk. But ability does not become genius until it has risen to the point at which its keenest states of perception touch on ecstasy, on healthy, self-possessed ecstasy, untainted by mere epileptic or drunken incontinence, or sexual incontinence. Well, in the rose valleys; on the plains of heaven, I was not incontinent; but I was ecstatic. For the moment I got far beyond any former rapture; and there was no rebound, no reaction, no bill to pay: for many days the valleys and plains were still in sight; and I never lost the ground I had gained afterwards. In a later experiment I threw all this away with such reckless, prodigal irresistible completeness, that I stood utterly drained of my ecstatic mood, only to find the naked skeleton of my force diabolically strong and resolute. I was not sorry: I felt sure after that that "Candida" was not the beginning of weakness and mollycoddledom.

But that very toughness in my skeleton makes me anxious about you. The step up to the plains of heaven was made on your bosom, I know; and it was a higher step than those I had previously taken on other bosoms. But he who mounts does not take the stairs with him, even though he may dream for the moment that each stair, as he touches it, is a plank on which he will float to the end of his journey. I know that the floating plank image is false and the stair image true; for I have left the lower stairs behind me and must in turn leave you unless you too mount along with me. I cannot change my pace (if I could I would quicken it) or alter my orbit; and if they take me away from you, I must accept the fact and make new combinations and plans based upon it. Consequently I rather want to rouse all your pride and determination not to be left behind. I think your present position is at bottom your own fault. You have not concentrated yourself on your art and trained yourself to the pitch at which your qualifications could no longer be resisted. You have few real convictions about fine art, because you have only a copious, easy, visionary imagination of it, instead of a hard knowledge founded on repeated sense-contacts with works of art, and eventually becoming a sort of sixth sense of it. The result has been a loss of ground with your loss of mere girlish charm, and that terrible lack of health instinct and beauty instinct which frightens me more than anything else about you, since it has let you play such appallingly deteriorating tricks with morphia and the like. You don't feed yourself or train yourself as regularly and scientifically as I do, though it is not my business as it is yours, and I am a frightfully lazy and untidy man in my home life and personal habits. I don't believe you have ever made a really elaborate and thorough study of your personal appearance, or of the art of personal beauty and costume, to the extent of achieving what should be the first qualification of an actress, absolute independence of her natural prettiness, or aptitude for "looking well in anything" or the like nonsense. I don't believe you have ever repented in your heart of the golden hair dye, or of the appalling circus dress in "Clever Alice." You still "fake" your costumes, accepting what will give you an air of being brilliantly or gracefully dressed, instead of going straight for the solid reality, the real distinction, of beautiful fabrics, delicate colors, and first rate workmanship. You may arrive at these accidentally in the random pursuit of your imaginary creed of beauty of dress; but you may also arrive at the most naive solecisms. An instance of this is my old grievance of your imaginary enthusiasm for music, which led to the absurd appearance of an idiot in the orchestra playing scraps of Mendelssohn's G Minor concerto on an old piano, and later on to piccolo solos which would have disgraced a barn. I have been wondering for some time whether Nora is going to have an entirely imaginary education. This is dangerous, because you cannot afford to solve all problems by simply ordering the dearest of everything, which is perhaps the safest way of getting the best of everything when you are not a real connoisseur (or connoisseuse). I want to make you uncomfortable about it all—to shew you that there are removable as well as irremovable difficulties in your way, and to remind you that as the position you are aiming at is a most tremendous prize, you will hardly get it on cheaper terms than Cæsar's: provide against every possible foreseeable contingency, and then await the toss-up of Fate. It is all very well to have genius; but genius may be either wholly realised in artistic knowledge and faculty, as in Duse's case, or it may only be a not very intensely cultivated stage still eked out by great natural charm, which is the commoner case. Now I want to see you (from the point of view of a critic) a great deal more of an artist

626

and great deal less of the beloved and beautiful Janet. You should take all that from us and give it to the stage in an elaborately manufactured form and not as raw material.

I do not write all this without perfectly realising the great obstacles in the way of carrying out such a program. But there are always excellent reasons for not doing things: only, if the reasons prevail, the things are not done. At the bottom of all my misgivings about you is your want of confidence in yourself, a diffidence which often puzzled me when I was most impressed with what you could do. The explanation, I take it, is that we cannot feel what our natural endowments are doing any more than we can taste the water in our mouths: it is only those powers which we have conquered by labor that we are conscious of and gain confidence from; therefore I take it that you have not worked hard enough.

I hope these complaints and disparagements will not make you unhappy. I know myself so fatally well-prone to overrate the powers of the people I like, but, when I once find them out, turning like a shot and accommodating myself to the new estimate of them with appalling and merciless suddenness. Here am I, after 20 years drudging away, at last venturing to tell myself that if I *begin* writing for the stage, I will master the business by the time I am fifty or so. I *know* I will get deeper into it than I now have any idea of, and that I will come to understand the requirements of the art in a way that I do not now. Suppose I should make some such frightful discovery as that you, with a surplus of every qualification except one (as yet undiscovered), totally lack that one. And suppose it should turn out that this one is an indispensable one, and that others, more thinly endowed otherwise, possess it! I know I should drop you instantaneously out of my reckoning, and that your career thenceforth would lie in other men's plays. Dear Janet: I do so want a rare comedian combined with my emotional actress; and you are damnably uninterested in me on that side—But it is one a.m: and I must not begin another sheet. Answer this.

GBS

P.S. Wallas and I return to town on Friday. Letters later than the first post should be sent to Fitzroy Square.

627

To WILLIAM ARCHER

[C/2]

29 Fitzroy Square W
15th May 1896

[Lugné-Poë's production of *Peer Gynt* was postponed until November.]

Have you heard anything about Lugné Poe's project of doing "Peer Gynt" next Wednesday at the Theatre d Oeuvre? Bertha Newcombe, who is in Paris, writes to ask whether I am coming over *supposing* they do it, & offers me a ticket. I have a sort of temptation to go, if half a dozen extra inducements were thrown in. Have you heard about it; and have you any idea of going?

GBS

To JIM CONNELL

[A/4]

29 Fitzroy Square W
22nd May 1896

My dear Connell

I really don't know what advice to give you. We are all—our generation, I mean—at the age at which every journalist who has not become an editor or become highly skilled in some very special line of journalistic work, realises that the sooner he gets out of it the better for himself. I have wielded my own pen for years past with such vigor that my introduction is certain death to its victim—if my friends cannot do without my work, they can at any rate console themselves by slaughtering those whom I recommend. In fact you may take it as a general rule in London that nothing is so dangerous as an introduction, because no man knows a friend from an enemy when once he has attained a position in which it is necessary to be civil to him anyhow; and unless he has attained this position nobody thinks his introduction worth having.

The only paper I know which is friendly to the S.D.F. is the Weekly Times & Echo. All the papers now want stories & sketches: only one has to keep persistently offering them for two years before hitting on a hole in the stone wall. I should imagine you would be able to do smart work as a descriptive reporter: it is not easy to find a man who can give light, humorous, and yet sensible accounts of public occasions like meetings, coronations, trials & so on. You might pop in a specimen to the Star, Sun, Daily Mail or the like & ask the editor to let you try

628

your hand. Then there is the London letter business—writing a column of London gossip (the more descriptive reporting, founded on actual sightseeing, in it, the better), and selling it cheap to several provincial papers simultaneously.

But if you ask me how one gets one's foot in for this sort of work, I reply, God knows! It always happens by pure accident: you might as well ask me how to get run over without intending it. All I could say would be that a certain percentage of people somehow do get run over; and similarly a certain percentage of people do tumble into work as journalists. I did not get into regular work myself for about nine years, during which I wrote five long books & a stack of articles of which not one ever was accepted save a footling little thing ["Christian Names"] for which I got fifteen shillings. And to this day I am dependent on a quite special class of work which no ordinary journalist could or would do, since it is laborious and—considering the time it takes—not lucrative in comparison with rapid general work. I have written for a paper [*The World*] for four years, and become one of its most talked-about contributors, without visiting the office often enough to become known by sight to the clerks. The surest way for one journalist to help another is to hand him over a spare job; but my job is not transferable. Consequently I cannot for the life of me tell you what to do, except, first, to turn your attention seriously to crossing-sweeping before you plunge into the abyss of Fleet Street, and second, if you must try your luck, to simply keep pegging away without counting rebuffs, offering & offering the best work you can do, carefully avoiding introductions but not avoiding journalistic acquaintances—above all, making a careful study of the elderly, drunken, Irish journalist of the old school (he's always Irish and always drunk) and making it quite clear that you have nothing in common with him except his native facility in literature.

You will observe that I have not lost my old talent for writing long letters that come to exactly nothing; but it is more friendly to do that than not to write at all.

yours sincerely
G. Bernard Shaw

To R. GOLDING BRIGHT

29 Fitzroy Square W

[A/1; X/125]   10th June 1896

["Whatever Wyndham may have said" refers to his rejection of *Candida*, which Shaw had read to him at the Criterion Theatre on 2nd December 1895. Marlborough House, in Pall Mall, was the residence of the Prince of Wales (later Edward VII). Henry James Byron (1834–84), actor-manager, was the author of several popular farces, the most successful of which, *Our Boys* (1875), achieved a record-breaking run of 1362 performances.]

Dear Bright

No: there's no ring: there never really is. Since "Arms & The Man" I have written three plays, one of them only a one-act historical piece about Napoleon. The first of these was "Candida"; and there are obvious reasons for its not being produced—my insistence on Miss Achurch for the heroine, the fact that the best man's part in it is too young for any of our actor managers (Esmond appears to be the only possible man for it), and the character of the play itself, which is fitter for a dozen select matinées than for the evening bill. The second—the Napoleon piece—has practically never been offered to anybody, because Ellen Terry took a fancy to it, and Irving proposed to produce it and play Napoleon. But I want this kept strictly private, as it may easily come to nothing, like other projects that get talked over and are afterwards crowded out by the march of events. The third play is only just finished. The only manager who has seen it (in rough draft) is Daniel Frohmann, who is perfectly friendly & is as likely as not to produce it in New York if we come to terms, whilst there is no backwardness on the part of our managers in wanting to see it. Considering that my plays are difficult, that nobody believes there is much money in them, that even their commonplaces—what you and I would think their commonplaces—strike our managers as curiously novel and advanced, and that all managers like to be courted a little and are perhaps offended by the reticence which my position as critic imposes on me in this respect—not to mention the infuriating effect of my criticisms occasionally: taking all this into account, I have nothing to complain of; indeed the wonder is that they are so attentive and so interested in my attempts. The fact is, the business of a manager is too desperately difficult and hazardous to admit of any trifling with rings or the like. Whatever Wyndham may have said or advised about a play not his own, I have not the slightest doubt that if I brought him a play tomorrow with which he could see his way to even three months' good & certain business, he would jump at it, though it were calculated to

630

send all the inmates of Marlboro' House into convulsions. A manager is kept so desperately sharply to business by the terrible drain of from £500 to £1000 a week going remorselessly on all the time, and his knowledge (derived from bitter experience) of how easily the receipts may drop from £100 a week to practically nothing, that he is forced to consider only what the public wants from him; and if you find him giving them what they don't want, and withholding what they do want, you may always take the straightforward explanation that his judgment is at fault. It is true that in the theatrical profession people are always talking Machiavelli, so to speak, and devising imaginary diplomacies and boycotts and compacts and the deuce knows what not; but at the first whiff of a success in prospect, all this is flung to the winds. The opinion of the Prince of Wales had absolutely no effect on "Arms & The Man." Nothing affected it, not even the cab strike. Every night some twenty or thirty pounds worth of people solemnly walked in and paid their money, the total receipts for the run being £1777 (I always remember it because of the sevens). The cost was probably five or six thousand. The astonishing thing, to an outsider, is that this result, of which no secret has been made, does not really impress managers as being particularly disastrous: theatrical business means making one success pay for half a dozen failures, and the half dozen failures seldom come off as well as "Arms & The Man" when allowance is made for the absence of a regular clientèle such as can always be depended on for a minimum at the Lyceum or Criterion. Wyndham, for instance (who has been very friendly to me), would probably look at it in this way. "If this fellow Shaw can pull in a couple of thousand pounds 'on his own,' and I can always pull in so much on *my* own, no matter what I play in, and the Criterion can always pull in so much on *its* own as a theatre with a reputation as a safe place to go to for a jolly evening with people who dont know one author or actor from another, then, next time I run short of safe plays and am forced to risk an experiment, I stand to lose £2000 less, in the worst event, than if I ventured with a quite untried man." But of course as long as he has plays at hand with which he feels quite safe, he will not produce mine, which seem to him to be quarter of a century ahead of the public. So you see there is no more a ring against me than there is against Ibsen or Sudermann. Twenty years ago Grundy complained fiercely that there was a ring, because no manager would touch his plays as long as there was one by Byron to be had, or else the then inevitable adaptation from the French. Nowadays no manager will produce one of my plays as long as there is one by Grundy available—or Jones, or Pinero, or Carton &c. Twenty years

631

hence, if I prove a success as a dramatist, nobody will produce a play by a beginner of 1916 as long as there is a play by me on the market. There is no ring—there never is, never has been, never will be, although there always seems to be one to the younger generation battering at the door.

The news about "Mrs Warren's Profession" is no longer true. There is no question of its immediate or remote production. The facts are rather funny, in a way. My first three plays, "Widowers' Houses," "The Philanderer," and "Mrs Warren's Profession" were what people call realistic. They were dramatic pictures of middle class society from the point of view of a Socialist who regards the basis of that society as thoroughly rotten economically and morally. In "Widowers' Houses" you had the rich suburban villa standing on the rents of the foul rookery. In "The Philanderer" you had the fashionable cult of Ibsenism and "New Womanism" on a real basis of clandestine sensuality. In "Mrs Warren's Profession" you had the procuress, the organizer of prostitution, convicting society of her occupation. All three plays were criticisms of a special phase, the capitalist phase, of modern social organization, and their purpose was to make people thoroughly uncomfortable whilst entertaining them artistically.

But my four subsequent plays, "Arms & The Man," "Candida," "The Man of Destiny" (the one-act Napoleon piece) and the unnamed four act comedy just finished, are not "realistic" plays. They deal with life at large, with human nature as it presents itself through all economic & social phases. "Arms & The Man" is the comedy of youthful romance & disillusion; "Candida" is the poetry of the Wife & Mother—the Virgin Mother in the true sense; & so on & so forth. Now for the funny part of it. These later plays are of course infinitely more pleasing, more charming, more popular than the earlier three. And of course the I.T. now wants one of these pleasant plays to make a popular success with, instead of sticking to its own special business & venturing on the realistic ones. It refuses to produce "The Philanderer" (written specially for it) because it is vulgar and immoral and cynically disrespectful to ladies and gentlemen; and it wants "Candida" or one of the later plays, which I of course refuse to let it have unless it is prepared to put it up in first rate style for a London run on ordinary business terms. Consequently there is no likelihood of any work by me being produced by the I.T., although "Mrs Warren" is still talked of on both sides as eligible. You must understand, however, that we are all on the friendliest terms, and that I am rather flattered than otherwise at the preference of my friends for those plays of mine which have no purpose except the purpose of all poets & dramatists as against those which are exposures of the bad side of our social system.

Excuse this long & hasty scrawl. I let you into these matters because the man who gossips best in print about them is the man who knows what is behind the gossip.

yrs sincerely
G. Bernard Shaw

To ELBERT HUBBARD

[C/5] 29 Fitzroy Square W
15th June 1896

[Elbert Hubbard (1856–1915), American editor, printer, and homely philosopher, was the founder of the semi-communal Roycroft Shop at East Aurora, New York. He published "On Going to Church" in his *Roycroft Quarterly* in August 1896, then issued the essay as a small volume.]

Dear Sir

I have just discovered a mislaid, and I regret to say, unanswered letter of yours dated the 28th April, referring to my article on "Church Going" in the Savoy Magazine. As the magazine is not, as far as I know, copyrighted in the United States, the articles in it are as much at your disposal as the sermons of Jeremy Taylor or the plays of Shakspere. If my wish has any weight with you, you will either reprint the article word for word as it stands or else let it alone. Further than that my interest in the matter does not go, as I can give you no exclusive rights & therefore can claim none.

yrs faithfully
G. Bernard Shaw

To ELLEN TERRY

[U(A)/10; X/117] 29 Fitzroy Square W
5th July 1896

[The "eminent London manager" was George Alexander, who had succeeded H. B. Conway as Faust in the Lyceum production on 9th January 1886 (having earlier appeared as Valentine). Shaw viewed the Ring cycle at Bayreuth on 19th to 22nd July; his reviews of the productions were published in *The Star* on 22nd to 25th July. The part Shaw had "once learnt" and "actually played" was Stratton Strawless in *Alone* (see letter of 23rd January 1885 to Mary Grace Walker). He had also performed (complete with costume and wig) the rôle of Chubb Dumpleton in the copyright performance of Edward Rose's *Odd, to Say the Least of It*, at the Novelty Theatre on 6th November 1886.]

Dear and esteemed Lady

May I venture to call your attention, now that your tour is over, and you have absolutely nothing to do but tremble at the prospect of learning Imogen, to my unhappy case. Probably you have forgotten all about me; but you used to write to me years ago, when you were in America, playing a leper, or lepress, and otherwise wringing my very heart.

My condition is this. I have finished a new play, of such extraordinary cleverness that an eminent London manager, who once played Faust to the most beautiful of all Margarets, writes, after reading it, "When I got to the end, I had no more idea what you meant by it than a tom cat." Now if I have soared in my later works beyond human comprehension, I can only fall back on my earlier ones. What I want to know is whether there was really anything serious in your notion that my Napoleonad would be added to the Lyceum Knight's Entertainments. Or are you only a flattering storytelling Scheherezade? I do hate people who can't make up their minds: they remind me of myself.

Not that I particularly want to know, after all; but I am about to celebrate my 40th birthday; and I *will* be grown up; I *will* be serious; I *will* be businesslike. Good Heavens, do you realise that I may die in the workhouse (I have often thought I should like to die there, by the way) if I do not look after my affairs. I am going to Bayreuth for the first set of performances (19th 20th 21st & 22nd); I am rushing back to the International Socialist Congress here; then to Brittany on business & holiday; then to Italy on holiday & business; then back to chains & slavery. I must—I *shall* settle my business before I go. Where is that play? where is that agreement?—am I an insect, to be treated in this fashion? You said next year, I think—the 1st January—or was it the 31st December?

Come, I will teach you the part without your opening the book once. I will get a tandem bicycle; and we shall ride along over the celestial plains, I dinning the part into your head until you pick it up as one picks up a tune by ear. That is how all parts should be taught and learnt: in my ideal company there shall not be an actress who can read. I once learnt a part (and actually played it too)—learnt it from the book. What galley slavery it was! I had rather write ten articles, or a thousand

634

plays. Imagine learning live emotion—live thought—from dead matter—linen rag and printer's ink.

Just Heaven, is this business? No. I repeat, then, I demand, I insist, I—I forget what I insist on: what I want is only to kiss your hands, which cannot be insisted on.

But I grow unbusinesslike: farewell!

G. Bernard Shaw

To CHARLES CHARRINGTON

[T/1 (C/4)]

29 Fitzroy Square W
11th July 1896

[The "accursed document" was Charrington's annotated proof copy of the Report to the International Congress (Tract No. 70), drafted by Shaw on behalf of the Fabian Society, which was under discussion at the members' meeting on 10th July.]

That accursed document of yours, which, aggravated by your thrice accursed air of keeping your temper under very trying circumstances, and acting with studied consideration, almost drove Olivier and myself to madness, was in such a form, that I could not possibly get any of its amendments adopted. I rode down in the afternoon to consult with you, but missed you. When I got to the executive, I was handed over your paper among others, which I had hastily looked through on my knee in the middle of the executive business. As there was no way of finding out from your alternative version what were amendments and what not, except by a careful comparison of the two line by line, which was physically and temporally impossible under the circumstances, I had to give it up as a bad job after hastily reading through it to see whether you had spotted anything vitally wrong. As minister in charge of the bill I had of course to fight everything except the changes we had either made ourselves or agreed to accept. The result, however, was satisfactory on the whole; and you and the rest of the malcontents had a rare time baiting us against the clock, confound you.

GBS

To JANET ACHURCH

[T/1 (C/4)]

29 Fitzroy Square W
11th July 1896

[Charrington had appeared at the Princess Theatre, in October 1894, in the Australian bushranger play *Robbery under Arms*, by Alfred Dampier and

Garnet Walch, and, as Archer noted in his review in *The World*, had "played a very abandoned ruffian . . . with uncompromising and picturesque vigour."]

You really must join the F.S. and succeed Mrs Besant as its oratress to defend me. C.C. employs the lowest arts of the demagogue against me. To the amazement and consternation of the whole executive he was suddenly joined (at his artfullest and worst) by Beatrice Webb!!! Look to it, Janet, look to it. If he hadn't openly revelled in his villainy in the manner of "Robbery Under Arms," and revolted the meeting, he might have played the very deuce.

I hope to confront the traitor at his evening meal tomorrow.

GBS

To FLORENCE FARR

[A/4; X/115]

[123 Dalling Road. Ravenscourt Park W]
[*c*. 13th–15th July 1896] 9.45

I started early this afternoon to have a glorious ride with you from 4 to midnight. The glory, unfortunately, got concentrated into a much shorter period. After lunch, as I was coming to the foot of the Haymarket after passing the National Gallery, a railway van came out of the Haymarket and made for Cockspur St. Suddenly the horse shied and plunged up towards the Nat. Gallery on his wrong side. I was going pretty fast and I hit him with the nicest accuracy in the middle of the breastbone. I went down in a forest of horse's legs, van wheels and whirling bicycle machinery; but with a nimbleness surprising in one of my years I made a twist, a roll, a bound and a spring all in one. As I did it, crack, smash, split, snap went all the bones of the bike, and as I shot on my feet the tail of the van rushed past me, and from underneath it came an amazing iron spider with twisted legs and umbrella-blown-inside-out wings which had once been my bike. Then crowd, police, frantic enquiries, names and addresses exchanged, driver of van too unspeakably relieved at finding that the smashed thing under his van was not me to deny that he was in the wrong: finally a certain indignation at my heartless composure. The van took the ruins of the bike away; and I walked off—to realise, presently, that my right knee and leg, on which I had come down, was beginning to stiffen. So I drove to the Charringtons' (having reasons for avoiding Fitzroy Sq.) and was stuped and nursed by Janet and treated as a bad accident case until about an hour ago, when I took a cab here & found that you had given me up & gone off to [F. York] Powell's.

I shall wait whilst I write a letter to the Great Western inviting them to make good the ruin wrought by their horse. I am a little shaken, I suppose, but not so much as by the smash last year in Wales. If I rest my leg I shall, I hope, be all right in time for Bayreuth.

Sorry to have wasted your afternoon; but I did not realise that I was going to keep you waiting so long—I thought half an hour would be sufficient for surgical operations at Charrington's. The sooner I am in bed, the better.

My trip to Brittany is off, I believe. We (the Webbs & I) will probably go to the east coast.

GBS

To EDWARD CARPENTER

[C/16]

29 Fitzroy Square W
29th July 1896

[Carpenter was editing a volume, *Forecasts of the Coming Century* (1897), for which Shaw provided the essay "The Illusions of Socialism." Shaw's special correspondence on the International Socialist Congress appeared in *The Star* from 27th July to 1st August.]

I decline to consider anything seriously. I have rushed from the thick of Bayreuth into the thick of this confounded Congress, doing a long article in The Star every day on both; and I must postpone all reflection until I get away to the country next Saturday. My address thereafter will be The Rectory, Stratford St Andrew, Saxmundham, Suffolk. Let us hope the article will be forthcoming: I can say no more. Tell Kate Salt not to be an idiot, but to buy a fresh set of tickets and hurry off to Bayreuth at once.

GBS

To MRS RICHARD MANSFIELD

[A/21]

The Rectory. Stratford St Andrew
Saxmundham. Suffolk
4th August 1896

[Beatrice Mansfield was in London on a brief visit. Shaw was the guest of the Webbs (who had leased a summer cottage jointly with Miss Charlotte Payne-Townshend) from 1st August to mid-September.]

637

My dear Mrs Mansfield

Do not be afraid of my misunderstanding matters: I may be aggravating occasionally; but I am intelligent. I chiefly want to learn from you whether Richard is contemplating a descent on these coasts; and, if so, what he proposes to play. Occasionally I hear of his plans in this direction; but they are always on the most nonsensical basis—usually as if the only difficulty to be settled were a personal one between the Prince of Wales and Beau Brummel. All that is of course mere romance. Beau Brummel is of no use here, nor is the old starring repertory of Prince Karl, Jekyll & Hyde, & so on. What is wanted is a good play, a good company, handsome appointments, and a first class, solid, responsible air. Also plenty of money to lose without turning a hair, and no debts to be left behind. This, imperturbably repeated for several years, without any explosions of genius, will eventually secure a position in London; but London cannot be taken by storm. After fifteen years London will begin to concede a reputation—twenty are needed for an unassailable position, which, once gained, can be held as long as . . .

[Balance of letter is missing.]

To MRS RICHARD MANSFIELD

[A/21]

Stratford St Andrew. Saxmundham
8th August 1896

[Clyde Fitch's *Beau Brummel* (1890) was Mansfield's most popular success in America. *Beau Austin*, produced at the Haymarket Theatre in 1890, was by W. E. Henley and Robert Louis Stevenson. *Rosemary*, by Louis N. Parker and Murray Carson, had been produced by Wyndham at the Criterion on 16th May 1896. Ibsen's *The Pretenders* (1864), translated by Archer, did not obtain a production in London until 1913. Mansfield, although an American, began his career in minor rôles in London, and toured the provinces in Gilbert and Sullivan. It was not until he returned to New York in 1882, however, that he attained a theatrical reputation. He brought his company to London in 1888–89, offering much of his standard repertory (*Prince Karl, Dr Jekyll and Mr Hyde*, Feuillet's *A Parisian Romance*), and appearing for the first time in *Richard III*, but his season was neither a critical nor a financial success, and he never ventured another British appearance.]

Dear Mrs Mansfield

That is just like Dick—to persuade himself—that "everybody wants Beau Brummel and is sure of its success." The fact is that nobody wants it here; nobody has ever heard of it or cares two straws about it; and everybody will associate it with "Beau Austin" and make up their minds beforehand that it will be a vapid 18th century play. The people who *have* heard of it will be prejudiced against it on that account, as the whole theatrical public is now looking eagerly *forward*, tired of the past and disgusted with the present. Even Irving is negotiating for a play of mine—a one-act piece with Napoleon and A Strange Lady as the chief figures—it would have suited Richard to perfection if he had not gone and committed himself to the Eve of Waterloo [Lorimer Stoddard's *Napoleon Bonaparte*], and all the rest of it.

There is another consideration. Is not B.B. one of those plays in which the hero is very old in the last act, and dies? This sort of thing is getting riskier and riskier in London. It was always the merest stage nonsense; and now people are beginning to find it out. In "Rosemary," for instance, Wyndham, from whom the public will stand more than they would from any other actor, did an octogenarian last act; but he was careful not to die nor to force the situation in any way. In tolerating that sort of thing London is far more grown-up than America.

There is—mere accidental "catches-on" apart—only one way to succeed in London for an *actor*, as distinguished from a businesslike showman; and that is as a careful and highly skilled workman. The Americans have susceptible imaginations; but they have neither eyes nor ears. If an imaginative, audacious, wilful, rather eccentric man *suggests* to them that he is a great actor, they will see a gigantic genius in him. The English have no imagination—at least they are not the slaves of it. But they have eyes and ears; and thorough excellence of execution, distinction of style, refinement and beauty of speech and action, and delicacy of judgment, will, if it can afford to knock at the door long enough, finally win a safe and permanent market here. In the long run the question is one of quality and quality alone, however this or that event may seem for the moment to contradict this. Wyndham, Hare & Irving have the best positions in London solely because they are the best executants. Wyndham alone can make a success of a bad play—if it is not too bad. Now if Richard will believe this and stick to it and act on it—if he will put out of his head all fancies about cabals & intrigues and jealousies (not that they don't exist; but that they are absolutely ineffectual except as a test of the strength of character that ignores them), and simply attack London with finished work in the spirit of a conscientious, determined workman, he will finally succeed. He will not succeed the first time or the second, because nothing but experience can teach him what London wants, or how indifferent it is even to the most original & clever manifestations of what it does not want; but he will always leave an impression, just as he did before, and the impressions will be cumulative. Of course if he is jealous of his plays, and jealous of his company; if he reads newspaper notices and rages over them; if he breaks his bargains and neglects his financial obligations; then matters will be much harder for him. But if only he maintains his professional point of honor, and gets the reputation of being up to the mark artistically and commercially, he will be allowed the most demoralising latitude in every other respect. Irving would never dream of treating anyone as Richard seems to have treated almost everyone here who has had anything to do with him—he understands his public obligations and the temper of London too well, but for that very reason he can do practically what he likes.

Forgive my sermonising—if I don't say it, nobody else will. I offered Irving my Napoleon play for nothing if he would produce Ibsen's "Pretenders" (playing Bishop Nicholas) or "Peer Gynt." It would be worth Richard's while to lose £10,000 by doing either whilst Irving is playing Shakspere to curates. Anyhow a new play is indispensable—a *modern* play. I don't believe in "B.B."

yrs sincerely
G. Bernard Shaw

P.S. If it helps you at all to discuss these things in letters, don't hesitate to make use of me as a correspondent as much as you please. I am always glad to hear from you.

GBS

To EDWARD CARPENTER

Stratford St Andrew. Saxmundham
19th August 1896

[C/16]

["Socialism at the International Congress" appeared in the September number of *Cosmopolis*.]

What a man can do I will. Since I came here on the first I have had exactly one idle day—a long bicycling excursion. I have had to toil over my play [*You Never Can Tell*] to get it ready for the stage & to write an article for Cosmopolis on the Congress. But I hope to dispatch the play finally to the typists tomorrow; and then I will steal a week to turn out something for you. There won't be any solid stuff in it: I have made no technical investigations & have absolutely nothing fresh to communicate: it will be a pure sermon & nothing else.

GBS

640

To ELLEN TERRY

[U(A)/10; X/117]

Stratford St Andrew. Saxmundham
Date uncertain—1896 [*c.* 20th–26th August]

[Ellen's eyesight was failing; in her letters she frequently complained of her "plague-y eyes," and philosophically contemplated blindness and the encroachments of age. On 10th July she had stated, "I fear only the character of *the Mother* becomes me."]

There are no clocks and no calendars here; but surely it must be September by this time. If not, keep this letter until it *is*, and then read it.

By the way, do you know what people do with their eyes in my family? I was taught solemnly when I was a child to dip my face into a basin of cold water every morning, and open my eyes under water. Do this twice a day, and you will be able to pick up pins from the carpet when you are ninety. It was a favorite performance of my grandmother's.

The negotiations concerning "The Man of Destiny" did not get very far. I proposed conditions to Sir H.I. Sir H.I. declined the mental effort of bothering about my conditions, and proposed exactly what I barred, namely, to treat me handsomely by making me a present of a £50 note every Christmas on condition that nobody else got the play, with an understanding that it should be produced at some date unspecified, when the tyrannical public would graciously permit the poor manager to indulge in it. To this I replied by proposing three alternatives. 1. My original conditions (virtually). 2. That you should have the play to amuse yourself with until you were tired of it without any conditions at all. 3. That *he* should have a present of it on condition of his instantly producing works by Ibsen. The effect of this on his mind was such that I have not heard from him since. Only the other day there suddenly flashed on me something that we have been forgetting all along—"Madame Sans Gêne." If you are really bent on playing that ridiculous washerwoman, there is an end of The Man of Destiny, since H.I. cannot play two Napoleons, mine and Sardou's, on top of one another. Why on earth did we not think of this before? I see the hopelessness of dissuading you from the washtub. You will certainly be the very worst laundress that ever burnt holes in the drama; but that is just what attracts you: you like to play at your profession on the stage, and to exercise your real powers in actual life.

It is all very well for you to say that you want a Mother Play; but why didn't you tell me that in time? I *have* written THE Mother Play—

641

"Candida"—and I cannot repeat a masterpiece, nor can I take away Janet's one ewe lamb from her. She told me the other day that I had been consistently treacherous about it from the beginning, because I would not let the Independent Theatre produce it with a capital of £400! What would she say if I handed it over to the most enviable & successful of her competitors—the only one, as she well knows, who has the secret of it in her nature? Besides, you probably wouldn't play it even if I did: you would rather trifle with your washerwomen & Nance Oldfields & Imogens & nonsense of that kind. I have no patience with this perverse world.

—Bother: they insist on my stopping writing & bicycling off to Ipswich with them. *I* don't want to go to Ipswich.

GBS

To ELLEN TERRY

Stratford St Andrew. Saxmundham
28th August 1896

[U(A)/10; X/117]

[Ellen was studying the rôle of Imogen in *Cymbeline*, which was to open at the Lyceum on 22nd September. The Thomas Carlyle reference is a mis-quotation of *Sartor Resartus:* ". . . you discover . . . like the Lothario in *Wilhelm Meister*, that your 'America is here or nowhere'. . ." (Chapter IX, "The Everlasting Yea"). Another variation appears in Shaw's review of De Musset's *Lorenzaccio* (*Saturday Review*, 26th June 1897). Mrs Moscheles, who had just visited Ellen, was the wife of the artist Felix Moscheles. The "Irish millionairess" was Charlotte Frances Payne-Townshend (1857–1943), whom Shaw had first met at the Webbs' on 29th January 1896, and who had joined the Fabian Society the following March. On 16th September 1896 Beatrice Webb recorded the following description of Miss Payne-Townshend in her diary:

"In person she is attractive, a large graceful woman with masses of chocolate-brown hair, pleasant grey eyes ('They are green,' she observed, on reading this entry), *matte* complexion which sometimes looks muddy, at other times forms a picturesquely pale background to her brilliant hair and bright eyes. She dresses well; in flowing white evening robes she approaches beauty. At moments she is plain. By temperament she is an anarchist, feeling any regulation or rule intolerable, a tendency which has been exaggerated by her irresponsible wealth. She is romantic but thinks herself cynical. She is a Socialist and a Radical, not because she understands the collectivist stand-point, but because she is by nature a rebel. She has no snobbishness and no convention; she has 'swallowed all formulas' but has not worked out

Charlotte Payne-Townshend

principles of her own. She is fond of men and impatient of most women; bitterly resents her enforced celibacy but thinks she could not tolerate the matter-of-fact side of marriage. Sweet-tempered, sympathetic and genuinely anxious to increase the world's enjoyment and diminish the world's pain" (Beatrice Webb, *Our Partnership*, 1948).

The phrase "great catch for someone" quoted by Shaw probably originated with Beatrice, who had thought Charlotte "would do very well" for Graham Wallas, only to find at Stratford that, within a few days, Charlotte and Shaw were "constant companions . . . scouring the country together and sitting up late at night!"]

Do you know, I should not at all mind giving him the play to do as he likes with if that were practically possible; but it isn't—at least, not on terms that I could propose and he accept. We may all admire one another, enjoy one another, love one another, enter into all sorts of charming relations with one another; but all this is the mere luxury of human intercourse: behind it all, if it is to be really worth anything, there must be a certain deep and sacred respect for one another that we are free neither to give nor to withhold. It stands as an inexorable condition that we must not violate. It does not vary according to brains or beauty or artistic talent or rank or age or education; and the difference between the wise of heart and the fool is nothing but the difference between the person who feels it & acknowledges it and the person who doesn't. It is the primal republican stuff out of which all true society is made. (The lecturer here took a glass of water, and moistened his tonsils amid applause). Now do you not see—you who are a wisehearted person, for which be all your sins forgiven unto you—that this respect prevents me from offering Irving a present of my rights just as effectually as it prevents me from violently robbing him of his? People who respect each other always make strict and fair agreements, reserving their rights, each for the other's sake as well as for his own. What would you think of a man of property who took advantage of your daughter being in love with him to marry her without a settlement?

There is another way of looking at it. You say H.I. is cautious, as well he may be; but that is a reason for his making very careful agreements. Quite the most reckless thing he could do would be to accept an understanding that he is to do as he likes with the play. For, observe, ladies & gentlemen (here the speaker assumed a forensic attitude) the author cannot divest himself of his rights without formalities more guarded and elaborate than any customary agreement need entail. I might play false at any moment. I might die; and my heirs might instantly sell their inheritance to Wilson Barrett. Miss Ellen

643

Terry might alter her present indulgent attitude towards me, and drive me to acts of jealousy, revenge & despair. *He* might die. If he made a will leaving me the play, his wife might die; he might marry again; and then the will would be invalidated.

In short, all manner of the most nonsensical complications might arise from our being too lazy & petulant to make up our minds as to what we mean to do. As for me, I had rather die than make up my mind about anything for my own sake; but I am in the hands of Necessity, and so is he. It seems to me that the sensible thing to do is to stop worrying him about it. As long as the negotiations consist in writing letters to you & getting answers to them, I am quite willing to negotiate; but that is very poor fun for him. You will find that what will happen will be that he will play Napoleon in "Madame Sans Gêne"; and Mansfield, who burns to contest his supremacy, will play my Napoleon against him. Mrs Mansfield has just been over here on the warpath; and I feel pretty sure that a second descent on London is in contemplation. I cannot very well refuse to let Mansfield play "Arms & The Man" here, though he has only the American rights; and the program will be freshened considerably by a new play. That will be the end of all our dreams about the Strange Lady. Poor Strange Lady!

To tell you the truth I have had a shock down here. In the evenings they make me read plays to them; and the other night I had to fall back on my Opus 2, a comedy called "The Philanderer," now some years old. It turned out to be a combination of mechanical farce with realistic filth which quite disgusted me; and I felt that if my plays get stale at that rate, I cannot afford to postpone their production longer than I can help.

It is downright maddening to think of your slaving over Imogen. Of course you can't remember it: who could? Unless you really want to say the things a character in a play says, your soul is not interested, and without that sort of interest memory is *impossible*. To learn Imogen requires a Bishop's wife, not *you*. Great Heavens, doesn't it make you fear that your faculties are decaying & your memory failing when you find that the lines wont come to you *eagerly*, but must be fixed into your head with hairpins, without any security for their sticking? Well, that is because Shakspere is as dead *dramatically* as a doornail. Your only chance of learning him without intolerable effort is to learn him *by ear*; for his music is unfailing. Never read your part: get somebody to speak it to you over and over again—to urge it on you, hurl it at you, until your mere imitative, echo faculty forces you to jabber it as a street piano forces you to hum a tune that you positively dislike. And when

644

you have finished with Imogen, finish with Shakspere. As Carlyle said to the emigrant "Here and now, or nowhere and never, is thy America"; so I say to you "Here (at Fitzroy Square) and now is thy Shakspere." Time flies; and you must act *something* before you die.

Curiously—in view of "Candida"—you and Janet are the only women I ever met whose ideal of voluptuous delight was that life should be one long confinement from the cradle to the grave. If I make money out of my new play I will produce "Candida" at my own expense; and you & Janet shall play it on alternate nights. It must be a curious thing to be a mother. First the child is part of yourself; then it is *your* child; then it is its father's child; then it is the child of some remote ancestor; finally it is an independent human being whom you have been the mere instrument of bringing into the world, and whom perhaps you would never have thought of caring for if anyone else had performed that acci-dental service. It must be an odd sensation looking on at these young people and being out of it, staring at their amazing callousness, and being tolerated and no doubt occasionally ridiculed by them before they have done anything whatsoever to justify them in presuming to the dis-tinction of your friendship. Of the two lots, the woman's lot of per-petual motherhood, and the man's of perpetual babyhood, I prefer the man's, I think.

I dont hate successful people: just the contrary. But I dread success. To have succeeded is to have finished one's business on earth, like the male spider, who is killed by the female the moment he has succeeded in his courtship. I like a state of continual *becoming*, with a goal in front and not behind. Then, too, I like fighting successful people; attacking them; rousing them; trying their mettle; kicking down their sand castles so as to make them build stone ones, and so on. It develops one's muscles. Besides, one learns from it: a man never tells you anything un-til you contradict him. I hate failure. Only, it must be real success: real skill, real ability, real power, not mere newspaper popularity and money, nor wicked frivolity, like Nance Oldfield. I am a magnificently successful man myself, and so are my knot of friends—the Fabian old gang—but nobody knows it except we ourselves, and even we haven't time to attend to it. We have never stopped to pick up Atalanta's apples, and can only afford a country house for our holidays because one of us has a wife with a thousand a year. This time we have been joined by an Irish millionairess who has had cleverness and character enough to de-cline the station of life—"great catch for somebody"—to which it pleased God to call her, and whom we have incorporated into our Fabian family with great success. I am going to refresh my heart by falling in love with her—I love falling in love—but, mind, only with her, not with the million; so someone else must marry her if she can stand him after me.

What a holiday this has been! I never worked so hard before in my life. Four hours writing in the morning; four hours bicycling in the afternoon every day.

I live in Fitzroy Square, on the second floor in a most repulsive house because I can't afford to live anywhere better within reach of my bread & butter.

I know Mrs Moscheles.

What do you mean by Hampton Court? Have you a place down there; or do you only drive about with H.I.? I once or twice have met you on Richmond Terrace or thereabouts with him, like two children in a gigantic perambulator, and have longed to seize him, throw him out, get up, take his place, and calmly tell the coachman to proceed. I can get down to Hampton Court any fine Sunday on my bicycle and read you "Candida" (if you really care about it—Mrs Webb says that C. is simply a woman of bad character, neither more nor less) if you will say where.

And now these epistolary follies must be suspended until Imogen is off your mind. I suppose I shall have to come up to town to slate it.

Farewell, then, until after Cymbeline, oh divine quintessential Ellen of the wise heart: we shall meet at Philippi, or in the Elysian fields or where you will.

GBS

To ELLEN TERRY

[U(A)/10; X/117]
Stratford St Andrew. Saxmundham
6th September 1896

I really don't know what to say about this silly old "Cymbeline," except that it can be done delightfully in a village schoolroom, and can't be done at the Lyceum at all, on any terms. I wish you would tell me something about Imogen for my instruction. All I can extract from the artificialities of the play is a double image—a real woman *divined* by Shakspere without his knowing it clearly, a natural aristocrat, with a high temper and perfect courage, with two moods—childlike affection and wounded rage—; and an idiotic paragon of virtue produced by Shakspere's *views* of what a woman ought to be, a person who sews, and cooks, and reads improving books until midnight, and "always reserves

646

her holy duty," and is anxious to assure people that they may trust her implicitly with their spoons & forks, and is in a chronic state of suspicion of improper behaviour on the part of other people, especially her husband, with abandoned females. If I were you I should cut the part so as to leave the paragon out and the woman in; and I should write to the Times explaining the lines of the operation. It would be a magnificent advertisement.

There are four good lines in the part. First—

"—how far it is
To this same blessed Milford"

which, like that whole scene, you will do beautifully.

Second, the exit speech, with its touch of vernacular nature:—

"Such a foe! Good heavens!"

Third, to leave the comedy lines for the more painful ones:—

"I'll hide my master from the flies."

Fourth, the only good line of pure rhetoric in Mrs Siddons's style:—

"Fear not: I'm empty of all things but grief."

Only, Shakspere, like an ass, spoils that line by adding, in words, all that the delivery of the line itself ought to convey. The words "Thy master is not there, who was, indeed, the riches of it" should not be spoken. If anyone says you left them out you can retort "I did not speak them; but I did not leave them out."

If you utter all that rubbish about false Eneas and Sinon's weeping, I will rise, snatch the nearest family Shakspere, solemnly throw it at your head, and leave the theatre. The moment Pisanio says "Good madam, hear me," cut him short with "Come, fellow, be thou honest"; and say it with something of the deep admonition which makes me remember your "Shylock: there's thrice thy money offered thee" since years & years ago. And when you have fairly started cutting the miserable attorney's rhetoric out of the scene, do it with a bold hand. Dont trouble about the Paragonese "Some jay of Italy" stuff, or the wretched, impossible logic chopping. And oh, my God, DON'T read the letter. You *can't* read it: no woman could read it out to a servant. (Oh what a DAMNED fool Shakspere was!) You must manage it in this way. In the second scene of the third act, let Pisanio begin by reading the letter, from "Thy mistress, Pisanio, hath played the strumpet &c" down to "lie bleeding in me." Then let him break off and exclaim "How! Of adultery! &c" down to "O my master: thy mind to her is now as low as were thy fortunes." Then let him resume the reading of the letter to

647

the end, when he will find himself with just the right cue for "How! That I should *murder* her. . . . *I! her!* . . ." & so on. The audience will not forget what is in the letter after that; and when Pisanio hands it to you in the fourth scene, you can *play* the reading of it with the certainty that the audience will have the clue in their imaginations burning hot. The pantomime will be easy to you—it goes this way—the horrible shock of the first sentence—"*I* false !"—then the slow, significant look at Pisanio, the man who is to kill you (it is the majesty of death that raises you for a moment from your horror)—then the return to the subject of the accusation & the slipping away of consciousness. Then cut all the rubbish out of the scene which follows, thus :—

P. "What shall I need to draw my sword? The paper
   Hath cut her throat already. What cheer, madam?

I. False to his bed, &c (the whole speech, uncut)

P. Alas, good lady (Imogen has nothing to do with this speech & should go straight on without hearing it)

I. *I* false ! Thy conscience witness, Iachimo ! (Everything can be conveyed in these 4 words)

P. Good madam, hear me—

I.   (turning on him with solemn sternness)
   Come, fellow, be thou honest.
   Do thou thy master's bidding &c &c (the whole speech uncut)

P.   Hence, vile instrument !
   Thou shalt not damn my hand

I. (sharply, not much impressed by his rhetoric at such a pass)
                        Why, I must die;
   And if I do not by thy hand, thou art
   No servant of thy master's. Prythee despatch.
   The lamb entreats the butcher: where's thy knife
   &c &c.

All this will mean an intolerable load off your memory and off the real side of Imogen. Archer will complain in The World of the violation of the Bard's integrity; and I will declare in the Saturday Review that your dramatic instinct and delicacy of feeling have never guided you more unerringly than in rescuing the live bits of Imogen from the bombazine trappings of the Bishop's wife.

There is another point which puzzles me—in that other big scene—that nice Elizabethan morsel of the woman waking up in the arms of a

648

headless corpse. I cannot for the life of me follow the business of that long speech without getting the words "A headless man" in the wrong place. For instance, you wake up, you sit up, half awake & think you are asking the way to Milford Haven—*the blessed Milford*, since for the moment you have forgotten your unhappiness. You lie down to sleep again, & in doing so touch the body of Cloten, whose head (or no head) is presumably muffled in a cloak. In your dim, half asleep funny state of consciousness, you still have the idea that you mustn't go to bed with anybody else but Posthumus, and you say "But soft, no bed-fellow." Then, in rousing yourself sufficiently to get away from this vaguely apprehended person, you awaken a little more at this very odd, dreamlike thing, that the bedfellow is covered with flowers. You take up a flower, still puzzly-dreamy, and look curiously at it. It is *bloody*, and then in an instant you are broad awake—"Oh gods & goddesses! &c." But it is quite clear that you must not know that "this bloody man" is headless, as that would utterly spoil the point later on. He looks simply as if he had swathed his head in his cloak to sleep in. It is the blood under the flowers that makes him so horrible to be alone with. When you utter the prayer "if there be yet left in heaven as small a drop of pity as a wren's eye, feared gods, [give me]* a part of it," I suppose you kneel and cover your eyes with your hands in the hope that when you remove them your prayer will be answered and the nightmare gone. You take down your hands & dare to look again. "The dream's here still. Even when I wake it is without me as within me, not imagined—felt." Now in the text, what follows is "A headless man!" This is what I cannot understand; and I believe it is an overlooked relic of some earlier arrangement of the business. For see how it plays if you omit it. Your attention is caught by the garment of Posthumus; you go on with the recognition step by step (confound those classical allusions; but they can't be helped); at last you lift the cloak to see the face, and then—"Murder in Heaven!" you go tearing, screaming, raging mad, and rave your way to the swoon as best you can (a nice thing to play every night for 100 nights). But if you leave in the words "the headless man" the sequel is spoiled, and you are represented as being surprised at finding no face on a man, who, as you have already observed, has lost his whole head. Therefore, I submit, that "headless man" sentence must be left out.

These, dear madam, are the only ideas I have on the subject of Imogen. I daresay you know your own business better than I do; but no

* The square brackets are Shaw's.

matter: your consciousness of your own view will only become more definite and determined if it contradicts somebody else's.

So you see I have no objection whatever to an intelligent cutting out of the dead & false bits of Shakspere. But when you propose to cut *me*, I am paralysed at your sacrilegious audacity. I always cut myself to the bone, reading the thing over and over until I have discovered the bits that can't be made to playact anyhow. *All* of Napoleon can be done, if only the right touch is found. If a single comma is omitted, that will be because the actor has been beaten by the author. And I always like to beat the actor, and to beat the public, *a little*: it is the only way to keep screwing up the standard. I own I have certain misgivings about H.I. as Napoleon. Swift, brusque brute force, concentrated self assertion, and the power of letting the electricity discharge itself in the meaning of the line, instead of in the look & tone of the stage figure, are all just what he has not got. His slowness, his growing habit of avoiding his part and slipping in an imaginative conception of his own *between* the lines (which made such a frightful wreck of "Lear"), all of which are part of his extraordinary insensibility to literature, are all reasons why he should avoid me, though his feeling for fine execution, and his dignity & depth of sentiment, are reasons why I should *not* avoid him. However, when "Cymbeline" is off his mind, I shall make him say Yes or No about "The Man of Destiny." Meanwhile, I shall begin another play— a melodrama. After that I will write a real comic opera, to revive *that* industry a bit; and then I shall do whatever may come next.

You will observe how strictly I confine this letter to business. After the 22nd I decline further responsibility for my actions.

GBS

To ELLEN TERRY

[U(A)/10; X/117]

Stratford St Andrew. Saxmundham
8th September 1896

[Ellen had now sent Shaw a copy of Irving's acting version of *Cymbeline* containing her own annotations. Frank Tyars (1848–1918) was a dependable actor who, according to Christopher St John, was "indispensable to Irving as a sympathetic coadjutor in parts which had to be played to enhance the effect of Irving's own creation." "Child Rowland to the dark tower came" was Edgar's song in *King Lear*; it inspired Browning's poem (1852). Frederick Harrison (1853–1926), a former actor, was manager of the Haymarket Theatre, associated from 1896 to 1905 with Cyril Maude. Maude

(1862–1951) had made his theatre début in America (1884) in *East Lynne*, later appeared with Wyndham, Lily Langtry, Alexander (*The Second Mrs Tanqueray*), and Forbes-Robertson (*The School for Scandal*, 1896) before going into management.]

I have read carefully through that copy; but, worse luck, I must either write hurriedly or miss the post, as some people have arrived here and I have had to spend a lot of time mending punctures in female bicycle tyres. Therefore brief and blunt must I be, O Ellen. Fortunately there is not much to say. Our brains evidently work in the same way. At the same time I begin to doubt whether you can really be an actress. Most of 'em have no brains at all.

You have only once slipped out of the character in your plan; and that is in the scene between Imogen and Iachimo in the 2nd Act. Imogen is an impulsive person, with quick transitions, absolutely frank self expression, and no half affections or half forgivenesses. The moment you abuse anyone she loves, she is in a rage: the moment you praise them she is delighted. It is quite easy for Iachimo to put her out of countenance by telling her that Posthumus has forgotten her; but the instant he makes the mistake of trying to gratify her by abusing him—"that runagate"—he brings down the avalanche. It is just the same with Cloten: she is forbearing with him until he makes the same mistake. And Iachimo has nothing to do but praise Posthumus, and lay the butter on thick, and she is instantly as pleased as Punch, and void of all resentment. It is this that makes her pay him the extra-special compliment of offering to take the chest into her own bedroom, *a thing she would never have done if she had not forgiven him* quite thoughtlessly—honest Injun. Therefore there is no subsiding storm, no "wary of him," no "polite—words, words, words." The words:—

> such a holy witch
> That he enchants societies to him.
> Half all men's hearts are his"

humbug her completely. The sun should come right out through the clouds when she says "You make amends."

You are unerring everywhere else.

On page 4, the speech "O the gods! When shall we see again?" is really two separate speeches. When Posthumus puts the bracelet on your arm, look for a moment with delight at the present if you like; but that doesn't matter: the great thing is that you shiver with love at his touch on your arm, and say "O the gods!" as a sigh of rapture. It is when that subsides that you ask the question a woman always does

43—B.S. I

ask—it being the nature of her sex never to be satisfied—"When will you come again?"

On the same page (4) comes the first quick transition. "I beseech you, sir, harm not yourself with your vexation" is thoroughly petulant and full of temper, Cymbeline having not only sent Posthumus away, but called him "thou basest thing." What she really means is "You may save your breath to cool your porridge, you old wretch."

On page 33—the last line—throw up your engagement and bid H.I. farewell for ever sooner than allow Pisanio to make "and too much too" a comic aside. It is a perfectly serious, tender, *nurselike* thing to say—any Irish peasant would say "and too much too, darlint," quite naturally. I hasten on, lest I should use bad language.

I still think you should let Tyars read the letter. My reasons are that if you read it so as to convey your own feelings on seeing it you cannot also read it with the decision and point needed to enable the audience to take in the force of Posthumus's instructions to Pisanio. Further, I have a particular liking for the absolute truth of effect produced by the *acting* of the reading only, without the clumsiness of an aside, not to mention the force of effect derived from the audience's foreknowledge of what is happening to you; so that they can watch you without listening to the verbal instructions. However, I don't press that. Shakspere preferred to convey the foreknowledge by Pisanio's speech in the former scene, and the fact that his knowledge of his business was always a clever half knowledge (the result of a hurry to get things done anyhow) is only known to me. So read the letter by all means; but just take another look at my way of cutting the following scene. At all events you *must* cut out "to pieces with me!" (p. 38) as it is not [only] unintelligible as it stands, but actually suggests a quite wrong idea. In the original it means "Now that there is another woman, to pieces with poor me!" As you have it, it represents Imogen as inviting Pisanio to carve her up like a chicken, which is ridiculous & spitefully out of character. And "Come: be honest—look" is nothing like so beautiful or impressive as "Come, fellow, be thou honest: do thou thy master's bidding &c." To cut out such fine bits & leave in such tawdry trash as "slander whose tongue outvenoms all the worms of Nile" is idiotic. The tearing of Posthumus's letters from her bosom seems to me very poor business—at least for you. Cut out the Roman courtesan on page 39: she belongs to the Bishopess side of the part, as you have noted.

But do *not* cut out the "clouted brogues" on p. 52; but rather "put thy shoes from off thy feet, for the place on which thou standest is holy ground." And I adjure you do not cut out the prayer to heaven for "as small a drop of pity as a wren's eye" (54): you will find it a blessed re-lief (prayer is better than crying for that purpose) and to kneel and pray with your eyes covered will be beautiful. On p. 63, do not let them cut the speech of Lucius, "I do not bid thee beg my life, good lad; and yet I know thou wilt." It belongs to *your* part, your reply being important as a bit of play.

Generally speaking, the cutting of the play is stupid to the last ex-tremity. Even from the broadest popular point of view, the omission of the grandiose scene about England and Cæsar for the queen, Cloten & the Roman, is a mistake. Cloten's part is spoiled. Every part is spoiled except "the governor's"; and he has actually damaged his own by wantonly cutting off your white & azure eyelids laced with blue of heaven's own tinct. Posthumus's exit on page 32 is utterly spoiled by a fragment of another scene stuck in in the wrong place, lest Posthumus should complain that Iachimo was jealous of him & would not let him have that scene. The prudery of the cutting is silly: Pisanio says "dis-loyal" instead of adultery; Iachimo discreetly omits the lines "where, I profess, I slept not &c"; and Cloten's irresistibly turned remark that if Imogen doesn't like his serenade "it is a vice in her ears which horsehairs and calves' guts, nor the voice of unpaved eunuch to boot (a quite delightful bit of writing) can never amend"—is sacrificed to please the curates for whom the Lyceum seems chiefly to exist.

Forgive these splenetic remarks; but really H.I.'s acting versions of Shakspere are past all bearing. The man has no artistic sense outside his own person: he is an ogre who has carried you off to his cave; and now Childe Roland is coming to the dark tower to rescue you.

This letter I positively forbid you to answer: I should not have written it if it did not bear on your present business.

Did I tell you the name of my new play—"You Never Can Tell." The Haymarket people—Harrison, Cyril Maude & Co—appear to be making up their minds to ruin themselves with it.

Hark, hark, the lark—no, the post. This hurried kiss—adieu!

GBS

To ELLEN TERRY

[U(A)/10; X/117]

Stratford St Andrew. Saxmundham
16th September 1896
(last day—leave tomorrow)

[James Leander Cathcart (1800–65) was an old-style actor whom Shaw claimed to have seen, as a boy, in Barry Sullivan's touring productions in

653

Dublin, though he was only nine-and-a-half years old when Cathcart died. Charles Kean (1811?–68), a son of Edmund Kean but inferior to his father as an actor, excelled only as Hamlet and Louis XI. William Charles Macready (1793–1873), whose Lear was considered to be unrivalled, was a famous actor-manager whose quarrel with a rival actor, Edwin Forrest, in America (1848) set off the Astor Place riots and resulted in his hasty return to England. Wardour Street was at the time notorious for antique shops that sold spurious products.

On 17th September Shaw, Miss Payne-Townshend, and the Webbs left on a brief bicycling tour from Felixstowe to Harwich, Braintree, and Hertford, before returning to London on the 21st. In her letter of 9th September, Ellen had asked Shaw to call her "Nell (or Nellen) . . . Ellen! Ugh! It suggests a tartan and sword."]

This will never do. read *no* letters (except mine) until after the 22nd. The one thing that is quite certain about Mrs Siddons's "Yes" is that she did not get it out of the letter of an amateur, or even a professional eighty years out of date. What is more, if you did it exactly like Mrs Siddons, you would do it wrong, because you are not Mrs Siddons; and even if you are a worse actress—which cannot be proved—there is all the more reason why you should put her completely out of your head. Of course, if any trustworthy person remembers that Mrs Siddons made a great effect in such and such a line, it is quite worth considering where the tender spot she found in it lies, and then touching it in your own way; but very likely you would find that the spot—if you detected it at all—was one that has lost its tenderness with the wear & tear of the imagination & the growth & change of the human spirit since her time. Just imagine Duse (now *that's* acting if you like) playing Magda at Drury Lane in 1815. The thing is not more impossibly preposterous than Mrs Siddons playing Imogen at the Lyceum in 1896; and it is this absurd and monstrous effect that your good old people want you to produce. Did you ever see Cathcart playing Iago exactly as he used to rehearse it for Charles Kean? Nay, more horrible still, did you ever see Henry Irving, 20 years ago, trying to get Macready-Barry Sullivan effects in "Richelieu"? Or would you like me to rewrite "The Man of Destiny" in blank verse? Clear all superstitions out of your mind: there is nothing before you but Ellen Terry and Imogen, and the only letters that concern you are those which I shall write when I am 99 or so begging the newest leading lady of that time to do the wren's eye exactly as Ellen Terry did it (for you must die before me and get my rooms ready for me in heaven & tell the cook about my vegetarianism)—or, better still, the letters of the old men who are now boys, and whose first

654

Imogen you will be. If you have the heart to fob them off with anything out of Wardour St—anything that is not the very ownest own of your sacredest self—you are a wretch.

After all, how easy it all is! You will have a huge house, all convinced beforehand that whatever you do will be the right thing, all idiotically loyal and enthusiastic and devoted, except a few with a deeper and *not* idiotic feeling, and yet none of them expecting more than you can give them by merely existing as you are. There will be no traditions, no comparisons, no compulsion to retain a scrap of the dead, stupid, rhetorical, stagey past. As for me, I shall be there on the first night (for the Saturday Review must have its article on "Cymbeline" all in type on Thursday) with my nostrils writhing in scornful derision of the whole wretched show. *I* shan't expect anything from you: my expectations, on my honor, will be so cynically tiny that you cannot help surpassing them—surprising, delighting me. All the other nasty critics will be like that too; and it will be easier for your pride to annihilate us than for your soft side to face the nice ones, who will believe everything you do beautiful, even if you introduce a skirtdance out of jealousy of Mrs Pat's Juliet. Of course competition paralyses you; but what great artist *competes*? As the Boyg says to Peer Gynt, "the great Boyg does not fight: he conquers." After all, the real thing that you fear is your own criticism; but don't *waste* fear on it. Cæsar, Napoleon, all the big achievers have said the same thing: guard against everything you can foresee, and then take your chance. Take your own Imogen as if it were *the* Imogen, and play it for all you are worth; and don't relax your determination or look back disconcertedly on a missfire in this or that line until the last word is out of your mouth and the curtain down. Then go home to bed, and sleep comfortably with *your* part of the work done. However, you know all about this as well as I do: only it is aggravating to have you talking about so small a business as Imogen (however large it may loom in the amateur imagination) as if you could possibly be unequal to it. Don't you see that the real difficulty is that *there is not enough in it*—not enough to absorb your whole power of work and fill your embrace & occupy every corner of your energy and affection—that Imogen, an old mechanical thing with a few touches of simple nature, is too cheap for you instead of too big? Good Lord! did you ever see Duse play Shakspere? I did—Cleopatra! It was like seeing her scrubbing a scullery. Don't deceive yourself: what you have to do on Tuesday is to be a mother to Shakspere—to cover his foolishnesses and barrennesses, and to make the most of his little scattered glimpses of divinity. If you cannot believe in the greatness of your own age & time & inheritance, you will fall into the most horrible confusion of mind and contrariety of spirit, like a noble little child looking up to foolish, mean & selfish parents.

Oh, if people only would be modest enough to believe in themselves!

Ha! there rang the bell for grub. I am hungry. I leave this place to-morrow (Thursday) and shall spend Thursday night at the Bath Hotel, Felixstowe. Thereafter as God pleases until Monday (or perhaps Tuesday) and then Fitzroy Square.

Must I really give up calling you Ellen after twenty years? Impossible: Ellen Terry is the most beautiful name in the world: it rings like a chime through the last quarter of the 19th century. It has a lovely rhythm in it. Not like Jorj, which is so horribly ugly and difficult that all attempts to call me by it are foredoomed to failure. I am, and always have been, and ever shall be, by pre-eminent brevity & commonsense, simply

SHAW

To FREDERICK H. EVANS

In a Primeval Forest in Suffolk
[A/4]   17th September 1896

Dear Evans

By an exceptionally poor bit of luck I happen to be out of reach of London until Monday or Tuesday. I should cut my tour (bicycling) short & hurry up to London at once if I were not with a party. Can you manage another Sunday? I am specially beautiful now after my holiday —during which, by the way, I have worked like a nigger.

yrs ever
G. Bernard Shaw

To CHARLOTTE PAYNE-TOWNSHEND

[?Hertford]
[Undated: assigned tentatively to 21st September 1896,
but may be of April or May 1897]
[A/2]   7.30 a.m.

[Edvard E. Lehwess, a friend of the Webbs, was a doctor of philosophy and jurisprudence, whose speciality was international legal problems.]

They have, with hellish craft, taken advantage of the absence of my watch to make me get up half an hour too early—no fires, no breakfast,

656

no refuge, no nothing. Also they have put into my hands a tragic communication from you which—my spirits having gone up in the country
air—makes no impression at all on me. *My* grievance is that I have had
no experience, curious, terrible or otherwise. I have slept most pro-
saically, and am the better for it. Did Lehwess—well, I shall see what
he looks like.

I am not quite conclusively satisfied that you are as much the better
for the country as you ought to be. Physically no doubt you eat &
assimilate and escape neuralgia. But you look as if you had returned
to your old amusement of eating your heart. I like it not. Million
thunders, you must get something to do: I have a mind to go upstairs &
shake you, only then I should lose my train.

Ha! there goes Lehwess, looking immensely satisfied with himself.
And I hear breakfast. Farewell.

GBS

To ELLEN TERRY

Underground—smoke, fog, filth,
and joggle-joggle—
[U(A)/10; X/117]   21st September 1896

[*The Area Belle* (1864) was a curtain-raiser by William Brough and Andrew
Halliday. The Secretary of State to Duse was Laurence Alma-Tadema
(d. 1940), daughter of the famous painter, who was a novelist, poet, and
co-founder with Paderewski of the Polish Victims Relief Fund (1915). On
14th June 1895 she had written to Shaw: "I have had the pleasure of translating [the review of *Magda*] to my friend Madame Duse this morning . . .
your article gave her very sincere delight" (BM). The "account of myself"
in an American magazine was an interview by Clarence Rook (based on
written replies to a questionnaire) which appeared in the Chicago *Chap-
Book* on 1st November.]

I have been bicycling about since Thursday—got your last letter but
one at Felixstowe—did not get your very last until I reached Fitzroy Sq
an hour or so ago, sopping like the policeman's helmet in The Area
Belle when it is fished out of the copper. What with changing & bathing
& getting the mud off the bicycle & unpacking & hastily opening my
accumulated letters I have had no time to sit down to yours, but must
perforce eat it standing up, like refreshments at Swindon. As to answering it, all I can do is to scrawl this in the hideous underground
train on my way to the theatre at Camberwell, where they have a real

657

first night [G. W. Appleton's *The Co-Respondent*], if you please—new and original & all the rest of it.

Now I shall have to change at Aldersgate, and this will get all crumpled & blotted.

Ha! safe in the other train at last. And now, unfortunately, I have nothing to say.

Oh quite as much as a wren's eye, I assure you. I always have, ever since I first saw you. But that's nothing; for there have [been] ever so many others from that point of view, whereas there has been only one Ellen Terry.

As to missing fire, why of course—don't you understand the development of your own art yet? Why don't you read the Saturday Review? you would learn all about it. Damn this train: I can't write with its bumping & banging about; and here we are at the Elephant already. By the way, I write most of my plays this way.

However, as I was saying about missfires. Missfires belong to the elementary stage of "making points." When you were a small baby—a very small baby—long before you could be trusted by yourself and were born—you had no bones. Then little stars & points of bone began to appear in you like the specks of butter in churned milk. These points multiplied and grew until they all integrated into a complete little skeleton, upon which Ellen Terry was built. Now that is how you become an actress. At first you try to make a few points & don't know how to make them. Then you *do* know how to make them & you think of a few more. When they miss fire, you are greatly put out. But finally the points all integrate into one continuous point, which is the whole part itself. I have sat watching Duse in Camille, analysing all her play into the million or so points of which it originally consisted, and admiring beyond expression the prodigious power of work that built it all up. And now, said I to myself, I will shew what criticism is; and I gave my analysis duly in the Saturday. And sure enough there presently comes a majestic letter from a Secretary of State. The Signora Duse, it declared, was unaccustomed to be even conscious of the unspeakable littlenesses which her work called forth, whether in praise or blame, from the insects of the Press. But the S.D. could appreciate merit even in abject occupations; and as I had shewn some power of at least understanding the very hard work which the S.D. had devoted to her art, she permitted herself for a moment to betray a consciousness of the Press, and even to thank me. I was prodigiously pleased; but what I want to know is, does she corrupt every critic in the same way—just like you in *your* way?

658

Now Duse sometimes misses fire. I saw her great opening performance of Magda at Drury Lane—everything came off like mad. I couldn't help going in to see it again when I accidentally found myself near the Savoy at a matinee of it—I positively and actually paid for my stall, a stupendous phenomenon. But observe, this time Duse, being frightened, or imagining herself ill or what not, had steeped herself in morphia, & was visibly swimming in it. Result—all the great passages escaped her—slipped through her wretched fingers; and yet it was a great performance. She played for all she was worth at that moment; and it was more than enough for anyone who had not seen the sober performance. Well, as I said before (you will have noticed that I am always saying the same things over & over again—I have no doubt I have told you the Duse story at least 30 times) if you play Imogen tomorrow for all *you* are worth under the circumstances, you can't fall below a good weekday performance, even if you are not in the vein for a regular Sunday one. Why be greedy? what would the golden moments be worth if they came always? There is always a great charm nowadays in you. I remember once feeling inclined to throw things at your head. It was during the revival of "Olivia" at the Lyceum. As it happened, you did not play well the night I saw it: compared with the old Court Olivia it was stale and spoiled. You no longer walked in the fear of the Lord, which is the beginning of wisdom. But all that seems gone now: you suffer & conquer in your work again. The agony, the dread, is the price of the success—would you cheapen it if you could?

As to not mentioning you in public, I understand the feeling; but I am not convinced. Before the world I must deal sincerely with you, however light a turn I may give my sincerity: I owe that to your dignity as an artist and to my profession. But in private I only want to please you, which makes me a liar and an actor. But you understand all this; only you are not quite as proud as you should be of the fact that you are a fully self-possessed woman and therefore not really the slave of love. You would not delight in it so if it were not entirely subject to your will—if the abandonment were real abandonment instead of voluntary, artistic, *willed* (and therefore revocable) rapture.

But I am drivelling. All this is scrawled in trains, between acts, in fragments, to amuse you at breakfast. You will find that the grandchildren, like all children, have the qualities conventionally ascribed to old age. The ideal old person is a child, the ideal child is forty, the ideal woman is a man, though women lie low & let that secret keep itself.

Now I have got home; but it is midnight; and I must go to bed betimes to be prepared for the slaughter of Cymbeline. Your account of the cast is appalling. Can *none* of them act? Oh, your apologies for them! your apologies for their existence!—do you realise what an incompetent profession it is?

I am surprised to hear that you saw "Arms & The Man." They told me that your infants all came to see it, and vainly endeavored to persuade you to venture. So I concluded that you had not ventured. By the way, when I used to read the play before it was produced, people used not to laugh at it as they laughed in the theatre. On my honor it was a serious play—a play to cry over if you could only have helped laughing.

Of course I am a vegetarian—did you suppose I was in the habit of chewing the dead bodies of animals? Ugh! And yet I confess I once did it habitually, as recently as fifteen years ago; but not since then. I cannot tell you what I am best at; for best is a rank that I have not yet attained. I will send you an account of myself presently: there is one coming out in an American magazine; and next Sunday the best amateur photographer [Evans] in London is going to try to make a pretty portrait of me. If the interviewer, who is a very clever fellow, hits me off at all, you shall have the magazine & a copy of the photograph together. The interview will let your imagination down astonishingly; but the effect of the portrait will depend on the expectations you have formed. I am apprehensive about the effect of that nasty expression about the corners of the mouth. You will catch that expression vividly in the Saturday at the end of the week. For I shall corruptly praise you no matter what you do; but oh, won't I take it out of the rest?

It's past one: I am almost asleep.

A thousand successes!—you will break my heart if you are anything less than P E R F E C T.

GBS

To CHARLOTTE PAYNE-TOWNSHEND

29 Fitzroy Square W
[E.u/2]   21st September 1896

The enclosed belongs to your [bicycle] pump. I forgot to give it to you.

What a lonely evening, and a cold going to bed!

To ELLEN TERRY

29 Fitzroy Square W
[U(A)/10; X/117]   22nd September 1896

[Ellen had written that morning: "I shall do nothing to-night. It's not because I've left my effects to chance. I've settled what I want to try for but I'm *all earth* instantly I get on the stage for this part. No inspiration, no softness, no sadness even. Tight, mechanical, *hide-bound*. I feel nothing. I know some of myself. In a few days it will all be different. I think it is the result of physical weariness. My head is tired. I cant care, cant think, cant feel. *Can Not*. After the carefullest thinking and practising every detail of my blessed work, something comes upon me. (This is when things go well and right. It has nothing to do with my will.) I feel exquisitely, and then, then, I realize the situation (in the play) and all is golden.

"But no 'gold' to-night. Only dull mud. I cant help it, dear fellow. You see it has nothing to do with me. If I ever act well, it's accident. It's *divine*, isnt it?"

The reference to what Irving "did for Lear" is clarified by Shaw in his review of *Cymbeline* in the *Saturday Review* on 26th September: "Shakespeare at his highest pitch cannot be set aside by any mortal actor, however gifted; and when Sir Henry Irving tried to interpolate a most singular and fantastic notion of an old man between the lines of a fearfully mutilated acting version of 'King Lear,' he was smashed." Irving, it should be noted, had been knighted in 1895, being the first actor thus honoured.]

Now Lord bless the woman, this is too much. Pray how long, oh stupidest, do your inspirations last? From nine in the morning until 12 at night perhaps! And do they ever come twice a day? Of course not. Then, if you felt ready for Imogen at breakfast, pray what chance would you have of feeling ready for her after dinner? Rather pray that your happiness does not come one second before the call boy—pray for it as you would pray for a bad last rehearsal, since misfortunes do not come twice running.

But mind, inspiration or no inspiration, tonight or never Imogen must be created. Next week is nothing to me or to anyone else: Napoleon might have won the battle of Waterloo a week later. It is not your business to be happy tonight, but to carry the flag to victory. It doesn't matter whether you are tired, frightened, hurt, miserable: it wouldn't matter if you hadn't slept for a week and were heartbroken and desperate. Tonight will never come again: your enemy, *his* enemy, will be there in the stalls; and woe betide the Lyceum and its traditions & reputation if you do for Cymbeline what he did for Lear! If you come on with seventyseven sharp swords sticking in your heart, I should still say you must play as if you were never to play again even if every word drove one of the swords an inch deeper. Therefore set your heart like iron, Ellen, and fight for your side tenderly—that is, strongly. Tomorrow never comes. "Cannot—tomorrow" is no answer to "Must—today."

After all, do you suppose you play the worse when you are not enjoying yourself? Ask the audience, and they will tell you that you play better. Ask *me*, and I will tell you that every mood has its value; and that the failure of inspiration, though it may take the happiness out of a few passages that are little secrets between some half dozen of us, gives force to other & perhaps harder passages. But whether or no, you are in for it now; and if anyone dares encourage you, WITHER him. A newspaper correspondent telling Nelson on the morning of the Nile to keep up his spirits would not be more monstrous than anyone encouraging you now. I am going to do my small duty; and you are going to do your greater one. Who talks of happiness until the day is over? And so—*avanti!*

Hitherto, you have only *coaxed* me. Tonight you must CONQUER me. I shall fight to the last, as if you were my mortal foe, but oh, with such a longing to be conquered.

And now I think I shall go out & get some lunch.

GBS

To R. GOLDING BRIGHT

29 Fitzroy Square W
22nd September 1896

[H.t/1; X/125]

[The enclosed cuttings reported the forthcoming production of a Shaw play (unidentified) at the Haymarket under the management of Frederick Harrison and Cyril Maude. The romantic "Zenda type" play was *Under the Red Robe*, adapted by Edward Rose from Stanley J. Weyman's novel. Archer's series of lectures on Thomas Betterton, Colley Cibber, David Garrick, and John Philip Kemble, under the title "Four Stages of Stage-History," had been delivered at the Royal Institution in May and June 1891.]

Dear Bright

I have only just returned from the country for "Cymbeline." I worked hard all through the holidays, but did not succeed in answering my letters.

I enclose some press cuttings, which you may as well contradict in

662

order to prove your omniscience to The Sun. The new play, of which I gave you the first particulars, is entitled "You Never Can Tell." Like all my plays it contains some very tempting parts, one of which has fascinated Cyril Maude. But nothing whatever has been settled; and the announcements enclosed are altogether premature. The play is still in my hands; and you may safely conclude that it will remain there until it leaves them for production. The decision of the Haymarket management to produce a romantic play of the Zenda type seems to indicate that they have reconsidered any notion they may have had of a new departure in drama. At any rate, there is one person who will not be surprised if "You Never Can Tell" is produced elsewhere; and that person is the author.

The question of the Napoleon play at the Lyceum will be decided when "Cymbeline" is out of the way. I will let you know as soon as there is anything to publish. As the matter stands at present, Irving has made me an offer of which I have no reason to complain. But I have proposed certain conditions to which he is unaccustomed, and which he is perhaps slow to understand, though they are of no particular consequence to him; and this has hung up the affair until there is more time to consider it.

It was true enough about the bicycle accident. One afternoon in the middle of July, I was riding in Pall Mall East when a Great Western Railway van, coming out of the Haymarket, turned up Pall Mall on its wrong side owing to the horse shying at something, and charged me point blank. It was a pretty piece of tournamenting. I went ahead gallantly, and hit the horse fair and square on the breastbone with my front tyre, fully believing that the most impetuous railway van must go down before the onslaught of Bernard Shaw. But it didn't. I hit the dust like the Templar before the lance of Ivanhoe; and though I managed to roll over and spring upright with an acrobatic bound just clear of the wheels, my bike came out a mangled, shrieking corpse. It was rather exciting for a sedentary literary man like myself; but I gather from your opinion of my Bayreuth articles the following week that I was none the worse for it internally.

Yes: the Star articles on the International Congress were by me.

I very strongly advise you to practise public speaking: it will be of great use to you. If you look in the lecture lists in the Sunday papers, or in "Justice," you will find plenty of announcements of meetings at halls and workmens' clubs about London or in the open air, where you can go and join in the discussion. I do not know what the debating societies, literary societies, and amateur local parliaments of today are—

663

such things never last more than four years, and the ones I frequented are dead—but there must be as many of them about as ever. The Playgoers' Club is not exactly what you want; but why do you not form a genuine debating society inside it. If there are half a dozen young fellows who really want to talk out their opinions without the humbug of the big Sunday night celebrity hunting functions, they can easily agree to meet somewhere once a week, and take it in turns to get up a subject for discussion and put some work into it—not merely air their opinions and shew their cleverness, but work up some information for the use of the rest. For instance, Archer once delivered a series of lectures at the Royal Institution which contained a lot of information about the development of the stage from the old platform in the inn yard to the modern framed picture stage. He might even consent to come down and talk for an hour to a little knot of fellows about it. As a rule, you will find that the better the man, the more willing he is to do a thing of that sort, and the less disposed to waste his time on windy functions like the Sunday full dress debates. However, that is by the way. Join or attend all the societies for discussion you can find, and speak every time, no matter how humiliating the result may be. Buy [Sir Reginald F. D. Palgrave's] "The Chairman's Handbook" (or look it up in the Museum) so as to learn the technical order of public meeting. Most public men pick it up as they go along, and never to the end of their days know it properly; but it is as well to be instructed in the matter, so as to be ready to take the chair if you are asked. From casual debating you might go on to delivering addresses; and be sure you don't write them out or learn them by heart: make a few notes and speak extemporaneously from them. And don't despise or funk the street corner: it is an indispensable part of a speaker's education.

You ought to join the political association of your district, Liberal or Conservative, according to your opinions; but you had much better begin as a Socialist and have a good generous revolutionary time before settling down. Call at the Fabian office, 276 Strand, and tell Pease, the secretary, that you want to be advised how to begin. And bring a shilling to buy tracts with. If we are too slow for you, try the S.D.F. and serve a year or two under the red flag. You will make a blazing fool of yourself; but you won't regret it.

G.B.S.

To ELLEN TERRY

[U(A)/10; X/117]   29 Fitzroy Square W
                                              23rd September 1896

[This is a reply to Ellen's note of the same day, informing Shaw that the
critics "let me down very kindly . . . I'm glad they were kind. They love
me, you know! Not for what I am, but for what they imagine I am." Shaw's
Saturday Review article on the 26th was entitled "Blaming the Bard."
Despite his threats, however, Shaw's comment on Irving's performance was
rather complimentary: "I witnessed [his Iachimo] with unqualified delight:
it was no vulgar bagful of 'points,' but a true impersonation, unbroken in its
life-current from end to end, varied on the surface with the finest comedy,
and without a single lapse in the sustained beauty of its execution." Irving,
in a curtain speech following the first performance of *Cymbeline* on the 22nd,
had announced that his productions for the coming season would be *Madame
Sans-Gêne* and *Richard III*. Joseph Hurst was Irving's box-office manager.]

Yes, that is all very well, but the real event is yet to come—the event
that London is waiting for—to which the Lyceum business is the
merest insignificant preliminary—that is, G. B. S.'s article in the Saturday. I have to do that unaided and alone: nobody writes *me* sixteen or
seventeen nice letters a day to encourage me—but no matter. If there is
a thing I hate, it is ingratitude. Some people think of nobody but themselves. But I say no more.

My article is half written; and oh! isn't it nasty! All the natural
malignity which I have been suppressing for weeks on your account is
now simply boiling over. So it is to be "Madame Sans Gêne" after all.
Oh VERY well, Sir Henry Irving. A home made Napoleon isn't good
enough for you, isnt it? Very good: we shall see. And you are
going to play Richard III, are you? Then I think I know who is going
to play Richmond: that's all.

I shall begin that article over again tomorrow: it's not half nasty
enough.

I was greatly shocked by your entrance last night. You must have
spent hours before the glass, getting up that success of personal beauty,
merely to écraser Mrs Pat. Do you think, at your age, it is right?

I consider the way you went on with Posthumus positively indecent.
Who is he, pray, that he should be made love to in that fashion? I consider myself to the full as goodlooking a man.

Look here: I shall go again in a week or two. I am not satisfied: there
is a crumple in the roseleaf here and there. You made one AWFUL
mistake. You actually bawled out the words "a headless man!" before

you had half seen him. Good heavens! you mustn't do that: it's ridiculous. You must simply start in horror, give the audience time to see in your face what is the matter, and then say "a headless man" in a frozen whisper. If you must make a noise, screech like mad when you start. Then it will be all right.

In playing Shakspere, play *to* the lines, *through* the lines, *on* the lines, but never between the lines. There simply isnt time for it. You would not stick five bars rest into a Beethoven symphony to pick up your drumsticks; and similarly you must not stop the Shakespeare orchestra for business. Nothing short of a procession or a fight should make anything so extraordinary as a silence during a Shaksperean performance. All that cave business wants pulling together: from the line about " 'tis some savage hold" to "Such a foe! Good Heavens!" you ought to get all the business of peeping & hesitating & so on packed into the duration of the speech, spoken without a single interval except a pause after the call. Otherwise it drags. Mind, I don't propose that you should omit or slur anything, but only that you should do it with the utmost economy of time.

The scene of the waking up should be moonlit: full bank holiday sunlight is too prosaic to make Imogen's dreamy condition & the uncanny effect of the mysterious body covered with flowers credible. On the other hand the low light in the scene where you read the fatal letter is not good. Somehow, at the Lyceum, the scenery is always imagined pictorially instead of dramatically.

How extra-OR-dinarily young & charming you have made yourself by that American trip! Or is it all tricks? Hurst put me five rows further back than usual. Heavens! am I the victim of a conspiracy?

Oh my article, my article, how am I to keep my style fresh if I sit up all night writing to you now that it is all over & I can be of no further use.

Can you recommend some horribly ugly person for the Strange Lady, now that Iachimo has deceived me? The villain! he has locked my play up for exactly a year. All your fault, yours, yours, yours, yours, and nobody else's. Ought to be ashamed of yourself.

GBS

666

To SIR HENRY IRVING

[A/30; X/133]

29 Fitzroy Square W
23rd September 1896

Dear Sir Henry Irving

May I take it that your announcement of Sardou's Napoleon disposes of mine as far as the Lyceum is concerned and that I am free to submit the piece, for the first time, in other quarters?

After your very kind expression of interest in the play, I do not like to act in the matter without a final word from you.

yours sincerely
G. Bernard Shaw

To ELLEN TERRY

[U(A)/10; X/117]

29 Fitzroy Square W
25th September 1896

[Ben Webster (1864–1947), husband of Dame May Whitty (1865–1948) and father of the noted Shakespearean director, actress, and writer Margaret Webster (b. 1905), was a member of Irving's company for several years. Shaw paired Webster and Ellen's son, Edward Gordon Craig, as "desperate failures as the two noble savages" in *Cymbeline*; "their utter deficiency in the grave, rather sombre, uncivilized primeval strength and Mohican dignity so finely suggested by Shakespeare, takes all the ballast out of the fourth act . . ." Hawes Craven (1837–1910) was chief scenic artist at the Lyceum from 1878 to 1902; he excelled in landscape and, according to the D.N.B., "developed scenic realism and stage illusion to their fullest legitimate limits." Shaw's new play was *The Devil's Disciple*, which he had begun to outline in shorthand just before leaving Aldbury on 14th April; the outline commences: "Ishmael [Dick Dudgeon]—Better than his people and therefore rated as worse" (BM).]

Now this is positively my last letter—the thing is getting ridiculous.

The article is finished & gone irrevocably to press. A mass of pounded, smashed, lacerated fragments, with here and there a button or a splinter of bone, is all that is left of your unhappy son, of H.I., of Shakspere, of Webster, and of the Lyceum stage management. On the latter point I want you to consider the article carefully with reference to that headless business. I am furious with myself for having omitted to urge upon you the importance of the scenic setting—I ought to have known that without a vigorous protest you would be put off with something between

Bellinzona & Tintern, and two nice young men out of a studio, instead
of a land of lions, murderers and hobgoblins, with dreadful lonely dis-
tances and threatening darknesses. Why should you ask for a drop of
pity on a nice pretty warm comfortable reassuring lovely day in the
country, with "tea for tourists" obviously just round the corner? Great
Lord, if I were a scene painter I'd have painted such an endless valley
of desolation for you that at your appearance in its awful solitudes, lost
and encompassed by terrors, everybody would have caught their breath
with a sob before you opened your mouth. I should like to see Hawes
Craven offering that cosy little hill and millstream to Mrs Siddons. The
idiot! You would rank as the greatest actress in the world if only you
were not surrounded by fools, duffers, blockheads, people with heads
like croquet balls, solid all through. How would Iachimo like to play
his scene in one of the bedrooms in Maple's shop window, with a nice
new portmanteau to hide in?

Ellen: art is one and indivisible. If ever you play Shakspere again,
dictate the scene plot before you think of anything else—even of your
dresses.

Sir H.I. does not see why Sardou's Napoleon should exclude mine.
He summons me to conference tomorrow (Saturday) at midday. I shall
see him with the Saturday article (which he will get up at five in the
morning to read) up to the hilt in his heart. Unfortunately, he will have
the satisfaction of getting the better of me in personal intercourse. In
correspondence I can always maintain an iron consistency. In conversation I shall get interested in *him*, & forget all about the importance of
my rubbishy little play. What with the article & the interview combined,
it is I, and not he, who will need to be taken to Richmond & petted.
But women have no sense of justice in these matters. I hope his cousin
will bore him to distraction.

Very well, you shan't meet me in the flesh if you'd rather not. There
is something deeply touching in that—did you *never* meet a man who
would bear meeting and knowing? Perhaps you're right: Oscar Wilde
said of me "An excellent man: he has no enemies; and none of his
friends like him." And that's quite true: they don't like me; but they
are my friends, and some of them love me. If you value a man's regard,
strive with him. As to *liking*, you like your newspaper—and despise it.
I had rather you remembered one thing I said for three days than *liked*
me (only) for 300,000,000,000,000,000 years. How would you like to be
an *amiable* woman [Florence Farr], with semicircular eyebrows?

"Candida" doesn't matter: I begin to think it an overrated play,
especially in comparison to the one I have just begun. You simply

668

couldn't read it: the first scene would bore you to death and you would never take it up again. Unless I read it to you, you must wait until it is produced, if it ever is. However, that can be managed without utter disillusion. You can be blindfolded, and then I can enter the room and get behind a screen and read away. This plan will have the enormous advantage that if you don't like the play you can slip out after the first speech or two, and slip back again & cough (to prove your presence) just before the end of the third [act]. I will promise not to utter a single word outside the play, and not to peep round the screen.

GBS

To R. GOLDING BRIGHT

[C/1; X/125]
29 Fitzroy Square W
25th September 1896

I have unluckily no news this week, as all appointments are put off until next, except one with Irving tomorrow. But as it seems that both he & the Haymarket people wish to hold on to the plays, and I cannot very well make difficulties if they are in earnest (which they now seem to be), you had better modify anything you may wish to say in the sense that the announcements in the St James's [Gazette] &c were premature insofar as nothing has been finally settled, but that it is likely that the news *will be* true by the time it is confirmed by the omniscient Sun. Say nothing about the Lyceum until the affair is quite settled.

GBS

To R. GOLDING BRIGHT

[A/1; X/125]
29 Fitzroy Square W
26th September 1896

[Ernest Alfred Bendall (1846–1924), dramatic critic of *The Observer* and the *St James's Gazette*, later became joint-examiner of plays for the Lord Chamberlain. On 27th September Golding Bright announced in the *Weekly Sun* that Irving had finally decided the previous day to "appear in the course of this or next year as two Napoleons—Sardou's . . . and Mr. Bernard Shaw's . . ."]

Dear Bright

I enclose the news. If you don't get it into tomorrow's Sun, you will be late, as Irving will give it to Bendall on his own account.

669

I have hastily thrown it into paragraph form; so that if it comes in the rush of going to press you can send it to the printers without delaying to recast it.

I believe there was an Irving interview in the Chronicle (which I did not see) in which he referred to this play without naming me or it. He said, I understand, that I offered it to him; but as a matter of fact I didn't, as I consider myself barred from that by my position as critic except in the case of managers who have taken the initiative by inviting me to shew them my plays. I don't want that said; but then I don't want the other thing said either; so if you can burke any statement about my offering plays uninvited, do so. It was Ellen Terry who managed the affair.

Observe that I have just declared that Irving has no literary judgment (see the Saturday Review). And on the same morning he accepts a play by me! A neat dilemma—either my criticism is wrong or my play is bad.

Yes: bicycling's a capital thing for the literary man. I am delighted to hear of your holidays abroad instead of that cursed city office—I was once in an office myself. Also that you are now on your journalistic feet, and able to oblige me materially in letting my news out.

Let me give you a piece of advice. When a Shakspere play is coming out—or a Sheridan one, or any old published one—buy a copy & *stage manage* it yourself, marking all the business. *Then* go and see it, and you will be astonished at the grip you will have of it & how much you will learn about the stage from your mistakes & *theirs*.

yrs ever
G. Bernard Shaw

To ELLEN TERRY

29 Fitzroy Square W

[U(A)/10; X/117]   2nd October 1896

[Winifred Emery (1861–1924), the wife of Cyril Maude, had appeared as Lady Windermere in Wilde's play, and was shortly to achieve her greatest success as Lady Babbie in Barrie's *The Little Minister* (1897). Edward Gordon Craig (b. 1872) had been a member of Irving's company since 1889; he was subsequently to gain a reputation as one of the theatre's most original (and controversial) scenic designers. Ellen had gone to the Lyceum on 26th September determined to attend the interview between Irving and Shaw, but had lost courage at the door of the office and fled.]

670

This is a nice way to behave. You coax everything you want out of me—my notions about Imogen, my play, and a beautiful notice in the Saturday, and then instantly turn on your heel and leave me there cursing the perfidy of your sex. However, it opened my eyes to the abject condition I was drifting into. I positively missed your letters—I, *I*, Bernard Shaw, MISSED the letters of a mere mortal woman. But I pulled myself together. I will not be the slave of a designing female. Henceforth I shall regard my morning's mail with the most profound indifference, the coldest calm. Let me tell you, Ellen Terry, that you make a great mistake in supposing that I am that sort of man. I am not: why should I be? What difference does it make to me whether you write to me or not? You should curb this propensity to personal vanity. This well ordered bosom is insensible to your flatteries.

Oh my dear blessed Ellen, let me stop talking nonsense for a moment. This play of mine which the Haymarket people want to do—"You Never Can Tell" (what do you think of the name, you who are so clever?) —contains parts for two twins, a boy & girl of seventeen or eighteen. The boy must be attractive, with a smart diction, an inimitable self possession, a refined gravity when mocking his elders, and an exquisite impudence. The other twin is Winifred Emery, who is youth personified (having no soul) and will hit off the callous prettiness of the sister to perfection. She does not want to play the heroine, her public reason being magnanimity, her private one that she doesn't understand the part & doesn't want to. Suggests Mrs Pat for it, to the horror & anguish of poor Harrison, whom I cruelly tell that I must have either Mrs Pat or Elizabeth Robins. However, the boy is the difficulty. I suggested Esmond; but I suspect they have got to cross purposes with him by postponing his play to mine after announcing that they would open with it. I asked them whether E.G.C. would do. They said disconsolately that they believed he went about the country playing Hamlet. I suggested that he might be capable of acting in spite of that; but as none of us had seen him do anything like what we wanted, and Winifred does not want too young a boy (being a mature girl) nothing came of it. I do not know whether you are one of the mothers who believe that their sons can do everything, or one of those who believe their sons can do nothing; but saving your maternity, do you think he would do you credit in a piece of smart comedy work? If the Esmond proposition falls through, and you will guarantee him up to the mark & capable of impersonating an extremely airy young modern gentleman of eighteen (at most) I am quite prepared to press him unless somebody likely to be the millionth of an inch better comes along, in which case your tears, your entreaties, your prayers will be in vain. There's a mother's part too—not a bad one—but if *you* will throw up Imogen & come to the Haymarket, you must play Gloria, the heroine. I anticipate an exceptionally brilliant failure this time.

You cannot read "Candida": you know very well that you have been strictly ordered not to read until your eyes are better. Wild horses shall not tear that script from me, especially after your atrocious conduct in being at the Lyceum that Saturday and not coming in. There was no danger of your kissing me: no woman, however audacious & abandoned, would *dare* take such a liberty with a man of my majestic presence. I liked Henry, though he is without exception absolutely the stupidest man I ever met—simply no brains—nothing but character & temperament. Curious, how little use mere brains are: I have a very fine set; and yet I learnt more from the first stupid woman who fell in love with me than ever they taught me.

I *won't* WONT, WONT, WONT, WONT, WONT, WON'T let you read "Candida." I *must* read it to you, if I have to do it through the keyhole. But I, too, fear to break the spell: remorses, presentiments, all sorts of tendernesses wring my heart at the thought of materialising this beautiful friendship of ours by a meeting. You were quite right not to come in on Saturday: all would have been lost. In some lonely place, by starlight—stop: I am getting idiotic. Miss Terry: your servant!

GBS

To ELLEN TERRY

[U(A)/10; X/117]

29 Fitzroy Square W
5th October 1896

[William Morris died on 3rd October. Shaw's articles were "William Morris as a Socialist" (*Daily Chronicle*, 6th October) and "Morris as Actor and Dramatist" (*Saturday Review*, 10th October). The lecture on 4th October to the Hornsey Socialist Society was "The Respectability of Socialism." Clement Scott's *From "The Bells" to "King Arthur"* had been reviewed by Shaw in the *Saturday Review* on 30th May. In her letter of 5th October Ellen informed Shaw that she believed her son "could do everything," and that if he "were given a free hand with Peer Gynt everyone else would believe in him, as well as his mother."]

I am at my wits' end—telegrams every five minutes asking for articles about Morris, and a million other worries. Last night I had to orate at

Hornsey; and a young lady got up afterwards and said, "I don't think what I have to ask belongs to the subject of the lecture; but will Mr Shaw tell us when his play will be produced at the Lyceum?"

Happy Morris! he is *resting*.

You remember the publication of Scott's criticisms of the Lyceum the other day. Well, I reviewed it: that was all. Not worth reading—dead and gone journalism.

When I read your remark about Peer Gynt, I fainted away stone dead. In Heaven's name, how old is E.G.C.? What puts such audacious ideas into his infant head? If you're serious, he must be either much too good or much too bad for me. I expect it will end in my having to teach him his alphabet.

I have just been asked to stay at Radlet from Saturday to Monday—for the 25th. What am I to do—read you "Candida"?—or did you say Radlet, or am I dreaming?

Oh, I can't write, I can't think, I am beaten, tired, wrecked. I should like to get away from this wretched place to some corner of heaven, and be rocked to sleep by you.

What did you say about Morris?—do *you* want an article about him? Look in the Chronicle tomorrow, and ask me no more questions: my brain won't work. I haven't energy even to tear this letter up.

GBS

To WILLIAM ARCHER

[C/2]

29 Fitzroy Square W
6th October 1896

I see you find fault with Ellen Terry for not making Imogen a Scotchman in the scene with Iachimo. As a matter of fact she had elaborated a remarkable scheme for playing the scene unforgivingly; and I induced her to give it up by pointing out three things. 1. That the sudden transition was a marked part of the character & was repeated over & over again elsewhere. 2. That Imogen could not possibly make the offer to take the chest into her bedroom consistent with the least suspicion or resentment. 3. That with Cloten & the king & everyone else Imogen is the same—in a childish fury the moment anyone disparages Posthumus, and in a childish ecstasy the moment anyone praises him. She is a most unguarded person, quite unsuspicious & terrifyingly courageous. You haven't half studied her.

GBS

673

To JULES MAGNY

[H/1]

29 Fitzroy Square W
6th October 1896

[At the Fabian members' meeting on 6th October, J.Ramsay MacDonald introduced a motion on behalf of himself and twenty-four other members that Tract No. 70, the *Report on Fabian Policy* presented to the International Socialist Congress in July, be withdrawn. The resolution, opposed by Shaw, Webb, and Bland, was defeated 108 to 33.]

Dear Magny

I hope you thoroughly realise the importance of the Fabian meeting next Friday at Cliffords Inn. The motion of which you have had notice "that Tract 70 be withdrawn from publication" is nothing more or less than a motion that the whole Fabian policy which it has taken us so many years to build up shall be publicly disavowed and recanted by the society. I and the rest of "the old gang" wish to embrace the opportunity to ask the society for a decisive affirmation of its adherence to that policy, and whichever way you intend to vote, I beg you to attend and give your verdict one way or the other in order that the meeting may be a thoroughly representative one.

yours sincerely
G.Bernard Shaw

To FLORENCE FARR

[B/4; X/115]

29 Fitzroy Square W
12th October 1896

[Florence Farr had just published a small volume, *Egyptian Magic*, under the pseudonym "S.S.D.D." (Sapientia Sapienti Dono Data), which was the name by which she was known in the Golden Dawn, an occult society.]

Lost wretch: I have not yet recovered from your announcement that you are the true author of Ibsen's life work. How can I or anybody or anything console you now? You would not believe in my doctrine of working at some reality every day; but you none the less worked every day at your unreality. And now you think to undo the work of all those years by a phrase & a shilling's work of exoteric Egyptology.

As for me, I can wait no longer for you: onward must I go; for the evening approaches. To all your flowermaidens I have given more than you gave me, and offered more than any of you would take. My road is the highroad; your bypaths and shortcuts only lead backward. I have often looked down them & sometimes laughed, sometimes warned you vainly. Now a great horror & weariness comes on me. I cannot help anyone except by taking help from them; and you cannot help me. You have brains & imagination—the means of deceiving yourself, without faith, honor, heart, holiness—the means of saving yourself. I have the greatest regard for you; but now to be with you is to be in hell: you make me frightfully unhappy. What *is* "the true relation" between us? The relation of the North Pole to the South. Forgive me; but you have driven me to utter desperation: I can no longer be satisfied to suffer & shake my fist at the stars.

GBS

To ELLEN TERRY

[U(A)/10; X/117]

29 Fitzroy Square W
12th October 1896

[Shaw's "attack of sentiment" was brought on by Ellen's recollections of William Morris. Arthur Roberts (1852–1933), whom Shaw characterized as "a buffoon of almost superhuman powers" (*Saturday Review*, 9th March 1895), was for many years a favourite in the music halls and pantomime; he later appeared frequently in light opera and musical farces. This letter, as well as several others between October and December, indicates that Janet Achurch was pregnant. There is, however, no record of her having had a second child, and as she undertook in January 1897 to appear in Manchester as Cleopatra to Louis Calvert's Antony, opening on 15th February (at virtually the moment she should have been preparing for her accouchement), it must be surmised that she had miscarried.

Edith Ailsa Geraldine Craig (1869–1947), the daughter of Ellen Terry, began her career in the theatre as a child, subsequently joined the Lyceum company, and in 1897 appeared as Prossy in the Charringtons' touring production of *Candida*. In later years she deserted acting for costume designing, stage-managed her mother's American tour in 1907, and founded a theatrical group, The Pioneers. It was at Edith Craig's suggestion that the Terry-Shaw correspondence was first published.]

Oh dear! you've given me an attack of sentiment. "And he shall give thee thy heart's desire" [Mendelssohn's *Elijah*]—that has been singing through my head until I have had at last to betake myself to the piano & let it out, with a good deal more to the same effect.

Well, now it's over, let me be sensible. Let me correct, coldly and accurately, the statements in your letter. It is quite impossible that my Saturday articles—about Arthur Roberts, for instance—should take the place of my letters to you. But you are right: I shall not write every week—not even every day, because good letters are rare & cannot come as regularly as the laundress. Besides, one must not weary you. Mind, I am not to be your lover, nor your friend; for a day of reckoning comes for both love and friendship. You would soon feel like the Wandering Jew: you would know that you *must* get up and move on. You must enter into an inexorably interested relation with me. My love, my friendship, are worth nothing. Nothing for nothing. I must be *used*, built into the solid fabric of your life as far as there is any usable brick in me, and thrown aside when I am used up. It is only when I am being used that I can feel my own existence, enjoy my own life. All my love affairs end tragically because the women *can't* use me. They lie low and let me imagine things about them; but in the end a frightful un-happiness, an unspeakable weariness comes; and the Wandering Jew must go on in search of someone who can use him to the utmost of his capacity. Everything real in life is based on *need*: just so far as you need me I have you tightly in my arms: beyond that I am only a luxury, and, for luxuries, love and hate are the same passion.

I have wandered into describing myself as a luxury. This means that I am talking nonsense. What news have I for you?

Oh, I forgot. At the Fabian I have had a heroic victory. I rashly boasted beforehand that my side would be victorious—that the enemy would be smashed, annihilated, routed, scattered. And it all came off: *they were*. I made a tearing speech, and was insufferably pleased with myself. You are not interested in the Fabian, I know; but I mention this just to give you a glimpse of the street corner Socialist of whom you may have heard. If Teddy (that's what you call E.G.C., if I recollect aright) ever catches Socialism, and announces his intention of spending his Sunday mornings at the Triangle, Limehouse, calling on the passersby to overthrow society, encourage him. A year at the street corner is an invaluable training to a young man, especially if he wants to play Richard III.

And now as to all my love affairs. One [Florence Farr] is just perish-ing under a bad attack of the Wandering Jew. Then there is my Irish lady with the light green eyes and the million of money, whom I have got to like so much that it would be superfluous to fall in love with her. Then there is Janet, who, on hearing of the Irish rival, first demanded, with her husband to witness my testimony, whether I still loved her, and then, on receiving the necessary assurance, relented and informed me that she had been faithless to me (with the said husband) to the extent of making "Candida" impossible until after next February, when she expects to become once more a mother. And then there are others whom I cannot recollect just at present, or whom you don't know anything about. And finally there is Ellen, to whom I vow that I will try hard not to spoil my high regard, my worthy respect, my deep tenderness, by any of those philandering follies which make me so ridiculous, so troublesome, so vulgar with women. I swear it. Only, do as you have hitherto done with so wise an instinct: keep out of my reach. You see, nobody can write exactly as I write: my letters will always be a little bit original; but personally I shouldn't be a bit original. All men are alike with a woman whom they admire. You must have been admired so much and so often—must know the symptoms so frightfully well. But now that I come to think of it, so have I. Up to the time I was 29, actually twentynine, I was too shabby for any woman to tolerate me. I stalked about in a decaying green coat, cuffs trimmed with the scissors, terrible boots, & so on. Then I got a job to do & bought a suit of clothes with the proceeds. A lady immediately invited me to tea, threw her arms round me, and said she adored me. I permitted her to adore, being intensely curious on the subject. Never having regarded myself as an attractive man, I was surprised; but I kept up appearances successfully. Since that time, whenever I have been left alone in a room with a female, she has invariably thrown her arms round me and declared she adored me. It is fate. Therefore beware. If you allow yourself to be left alone with me for a single moment, you will certainly throw your arms round me and declare you adore me; and I am not prepared to guarantee that my usual melancholy forbearance will be available in your case.

But I am really getting idiotic. All this time I have been trying to recollect something—oh, to be sure. The photographs! I return them with many thanks. The young man is excellent—good chin, good mouth, not too long upper lip, good brow, and plenty of head above his

ears. (A donkey has all his head below his ears, thus— ; whilst

Ferdinand Lassalle, the cleverest man of the century, was like

this— . His ears were where his collar should have been.)

If he [Gordon Craig] has a nimble tongue, he will make a good actor or a good anything else: perhaps he ought to be something else. There is not suffering enough in his face for the hero of "Candida"; but he might *act* that. Is the young lady Ailsa Craig? I don't recognise her, though I saw Ailsa in Pinero's play [*Bygones*, 1895] & remember her very well. I shall finish this letter by instalments in the course of the week. By the way, what place did you say? Was it Radlett?

GBS

To JUSTIN HUNTLY McCARTHY

29 Fitzroy Square W

12th October 1896

[B/5]

[McCarthy's new play had been announced as *The Philanderer*, but in recognition of Shaw's prior claim, he altered the title to *His Little Dodge* a few days before the opening performance on 24th October.]

My dear McCarthy

I saw the statement, but it did not carry any conviction to me: I put it down as one of the usual blunders. But why not use up the title? My play is the dullest filth: it will probably never be produced; and if it is, some other name will do. I will hand it over to you (the name, I mean) with pleasure—my only feeling about it is that I had rather you used it for an original play instead of wasting it on an adaptation. Still, if the original play is not ready, it is not worth saving the title up. Besides, a title like that is not a fair subject of private property. The Philanderer, the Pirate, the Shop Girl and so on, should be as free to all the world as the Marquis of Granby, the Green Man & the Goat & Compasses.

I read over my play about a month ago, and was disgusted with it. Don't hesitate to take advantage of that fact if you have the least fancy for the name: I really set no store by it, whereas I *do* set some store by your having the best name for your play.

yrs ever

GBS

To FLORENCE FARR

29 Fitzroy Square W

13th October 1896

[B/4; X/115]

You wretch—to write me a nasty letter just when a really sympathetic, original woman would have written a particularly nice one. After

678

all these years, too, with the advantage of my precepts! I am ashamed of you. I blush—I apologise to posterity for your conduct. You are incorrigible. Is it *my* fault? Have I not tried & tried & tried, lectured, protested, warned, implored? Do you want me *for ever*, greedy one?

GBS

To FLORENCE FARR

[J/4; X/115]

29 Fitzroy Square W
14th October 1896

Serve you right!

I hereby warn mankind to beware of women with large eyes, and crescent eyebrows, and a smile, and a love of miracles and moonshees. I warn them against all who like intellectual pastimes; who prefer liberty, happiness and irresponsibility to care, suffering and life; who live for and in themselves instead of for and in the world; who reject the deep universal material of human relationship and select only the luxuries of love, friendship, and amusing conversation.

I declare before creation that you are an idiot, and that there never has been, never can be, is not now, nor in any yet to be discovered fourth dimension of time ever shall be, so desperate and irreclaimable an idiot, or one whom Destiny has mocked with greater opportunities.

I renounce spiritual intercourse with you. I condemn you during all our future meetings and bicycle rides, to talk instead of listening. I may possibly, being the greater intelligence, learn something from you. From me you can learn nothing. Worse, you can mislearn.

GBS

To ELLEN TERRY

[U(A)/10; X/117]

29 Fitzroy Square W
16th October 1896

[William Archer's criticism of Ellen's interpretation of Imogen appeared in *The World* on 7th October. The subsequent criticism of Ellen and Shaw was not published. Shaw's "portrait" was a photograph by Frederick H. Evans. "And your eyes?" Ellen had written that morning; "*Look at me!*" Frederick Hollyer, a noted London photographer, was one of the pioneers

679

of "natural" camera portraits. The artist for whom Shaw was posing was Nellie Heath, a young woman who had studied under Fred Brown (1851–1941) at the Slade School and, more recently, under Walter Sickert (1860–1942.) She submitted the completed portrait to the annual exhibition of the Royal Society of Portrait Artists, but it was rejected.]

Just after my last letter was posted, when I was on the point of falling asleep, I suddenly recollected that your eyes were not strong, and that I had been inflicting a ream of tiny crabbed writing on you. Forgive me: man is by nature inconsiderate.

Here am I after spending the last hour—how, do you think? Why, in remonstrating with William Archer. First, he complains of your not making Imogen a vindictive Scotchwoman—a point on which I turned you right into his line of fire. I wrote him an abusive letter about it; and now he sends me the MS. of his next week's World article, all in refutation of my letter, and in disparagement of your reading of the scene with Iachimo. He says he will destroy it if I object "personally." I have objected in the most personal terms I can command. Would you ever suppose that man to be a walking mass of shy sentiment, striving to express himself and only succeeding in cavilling over trifles?

The eyes of the portrait are averted purposely. The consequences of their looking at the spectator might be fearful. Suppose Edy picked it up by chance! The fatal spell would operate at once: I should have her here by the next underground train, insisting on my flying with her to the ends of the earth, and utterly disregarding my feeble protests that I adore her mother. I'll send you some other views as soon as I get proofs from Evans. What I want you to admire is the skill with which he has lighted the head so as to get rid of the usual photography look about the background. His interiors of churches are particularly fine; but he is now trying his hand at portraits. He is an odd little man, a wild enthusiast about music and acting. He adores Duse and worships you. I asked him had he ever taken you: he gasped at the notion of such bliss, but added misgivingly that Hollyer told him you were an unmanageable genius, and wouldnt keep quiet. If ever you want an unprofessional portrait, you may count on him, if he does not die of nervous anticipation immediately after arranging a sitting.

The play [*The Devil's Disciple*] progresses—the new one—the melodrama—such a melodrama! I sit in a little hole of a room off Euston Road on the corner of a table with an easel propped before me so that I can write and be painted at the same time. This keeps me at work; and the portrait, for which I have to pay the artist's top price for millionaires (£5), is to make her fortune when exhibited. I do not usually allow myself to be got round in this fashion; but this girl did it without an effort. I suppose I am a great fool; but I shall turn the sittings to account in getting on with the play. As for her, she is delighted, and thinks me a most interesting & celebrated old man to have for a sitter.

So you see everybody sees me; but I never see you. I shall go to "Cymbeline" again, I think; but then you will be busy, and that will make me busy too—string me like a bow into the keenest observation, whereas I want—but no: I don't want anything. How could I look Edy in the face?

I am really sorry about the ears. They are a Shaw speciality. They stick straight out like the doors of a tryptich; and I was born with them full size, so that on windy days my nurse had to hold me by my waist-band to prevent my being blown away when the wind caught them.

Ah well, farewell—at least good night. I am glad I still have that deep shivering sigh left, ridiculous as it is. (I really am an ASS).

GBS

To CHARLOTTE PAYNE-TOWNSHEND

[Y/2]

[Euston Road post office]
17th October 1896

ALL CLEAR NOW   YES A THOUSAND TIMES

SHAW

To CHARLOTTE PAYNE-TOWNSHEND

[B/2]

29 Fitzroy Square W
21st October 1896. 2 a.m.

[On the 21st Shaw attended *Love in Idleness*, by Louis N. Parker and Edward J. Goodman, at Terry's Theatre, and on the 24th he viewed McCarthy's *His Little Dodge* at the Royalty. H.M.Hyndman, in a letter published on 20th October, had been hypercritical of Shaw's obituary of Morris. Shaw's response appeared on the 21st, and Hyndman's rebuttal on the 22nd. As was almost invariably his custom, Shaw permitted his opponent to have the last word.]

Ah! twentythousand tons off my heart; but what a frightful way to drag it off!

Theatres tomorrow [*i.e.*, night of 21st October] & on Saturday. Otherwise at large.

Hyndman attacks me furiously in the St James's Gazette for "squirting my acidulous mendacity in the face of the dead."

My——but no: I positively will not write any more silly letters. When will—but no matter.

And how soon will—but I suppose you won't stay longer than you can help.

Long past two & not yet in bed. What a night! —after last night—if only you hadn't been in pain.

GBS

To CHARLOTTE PAYNE-TOWNSHEND

[C/2]

29 Fitzroy Square W
21st October 1896

Have had to offer Haymarket people their choice of my spare evenings. No reply yet. Fabian Exec. on Friday, 5 to 7.

I—but no. Not here.

GBS

To ERWIN McCALL

[X/134]

29 Fitzroy Square W
22nd October [1896]

["Erwin McCall" (pseudonym of John Basil Barnhill), an agnostic who edited *The Eagle and the Serpent* (1898–1903), a journal of "egoistic philosophy and sociology," was an ardent Nietzschean. He later emigrated to the United States, where he debated with Eugene Debs and other Socialists and briefly edited the *American Anti-Socialist* (1912–14). The manuscript was a small work entitled *The Martyrdom of Percy Whitcomb, Socialist and Agnostic*, published in 1897 with Shaw's letter reproduced in a "Prefatory Correspondence between George Bernard Shaw and the Author."]

Dear Sir

I have read all the passages in your manuscript to which you have called my attention. I do not know any publisher who would be in the least likely to publish it for you. As far as I can judge, the case is ingeniously argued and well—even eloquently—expressed; but the whole

682

book, fundamentally, is pure folly; and I advise you to put it by and write a sensible book. Let me explain what I mean. When a logical criticism of the world, from the point of view of any system of thought or ethics, reduces the world to absurdity or crime, then it is the system, and not the world, which has been reduced to absurdity; and the whole criticism, however ingenious, may safely be discarded as idle. Unfortunately, most people persist in believing that it is the world which is at fault, although happily few of them elaborate their criticisms further than to grumble at their vexations. Your Whitcomb [who "became a convert to Egoism"] is of no mortal use for literary purposes except to figure as a character in the comedy of the type of "Le Bourgeois Gentilhomme" of Molière's, whom I recommend to your very careful consideration if you desire a pleasant tutor in the art of seeing the humour of a protest against the world being built the wrong way.

yours very truly
G. Bernard Shaw

To ELIZABETH ROBINS

29 Fitzroy Square W
23rd October 1896

[B/33]

[Miss Robins had announced forthcoming productions of Ibsen's *Little Eyolf* and Echegaray's *Mariana*. The first, in Archer's translation, was staged at the Avenue Theatre in a series of matinées commencing 23rd November; the second opened at the Court Theatre on 22nd February 1897.]

Dear Miss Robins

I have just, by the merest accident, come upon one of the Ibsen-Echegaray circulars. May I suggest that the same accident had better happen to every critic in London as soon as possible. The Sunday papers in particular are most important—especially The Weekly Sun. I have only just barely had time to be indiscreet: another 24 hours, and there would have been a week lost.

You see it is absolutely impossible to keep a secret in London, even if it were ever advisable; but it is quite possible to make the critics feel slighted at not being let into it. I hope you have told Scott all about it. Don't depend on Archer: when you tell him not to mention a thing, he actually obeys you. I have remonstrated with him again & again for this—in vain.

Remember, there are only 5 Sundays left before the performance;

and each Sunday should have its paragraph. Excuse my interfering; but really somebody must take care of these things. If I don't, nobody else will. Otherwise I should not intrude.

GBS

To R. GOLDING BRIGHT

[A/1; X/125]

29 Fitzroy Square W
23rd October 1896

[Shaw had apparently communicated to Golding Bright the same intelligence about Winifred Emery and Mrs Patrick Campbell as that which he had written to Ellen Terry on 2nd October. In his paragraphs on the 18th, however, Golding Bright had confused the relationship, in *You Never Can Tell*, between Gloria and Dolly. There is no evidence that Mrs Campbell ever was seriously considered for a part in the play, but Shaw did attempt to interest her and Forbes-Robertson in *The Devil's Disciple*, which he read to them on 18th February 1897, and which appears to have been the occasion of the first actual encounter of the actress and the dramatist.]

Dear Bright

The paragraphs last week were gorgeous, especially a slip at the end, which must have thrown all London for a radius of a mile round Mrs P.C. into convulsions. You said she was to play Winifred Emery's M O T H E R—Great Heavens, man: it's her *sister*.

The news now is that Ibsen is to the fore again. His new play [*John Gabriel Borkman*] is expected over in a few weeks; and this has so waked his disciples up to the scandal of "Little Eyolf" being still unperformed, that Miss Elizabeth Robins has flung herself into the business with all her energy; and it may now be taken as settled that "Little E" will be produced before the end of November, at a series of subscription performances, with Miss Robins as Asta and Miss Janet Achurch as Rita, that is to say, with the strongest Ibsen cast yet seen in London. Echegaray is also to have a turn. I—G.B.S., *moi qui vous parle*—devoted nearly a whole article to Echegaray's "Mariana" when it was published here, and pointed out that it ought to be snapped up as a star part by some enterprising emulator of Bernhardt & Duse. Miss Robins has taken the hint, and promises "Mariana" after "Little Eyolf." She has also declared, in a signed circular, that if the performances produce any profit, she will use it as the nucleus of a fund for the performance of plays which are too good to be commercially practicable. This means, in plain English, that she does not believe in the Independent Theatre, and is going to set about its work as if it did not exist. In the face of its prolonged inaction *we* can only say "Serve it right"; but what do Mr Grein, and Mr Charles Charrington, and Miss Dorothy Leighton say?

Of course this is nothing new for Miss Robins, to whose enterprise & devotion we already owe our acquaintance with "Hedda Gabler," "Karin," and "The Master Builder."

yrs
GBS

To ELIZABETH ROBINS

[B/33]

29 Fitzroy Square W
24th October 1896

Dear Miss Robins

It is very unfortunate that it is not possible to wait until March [to produce *Little Eyolf*]. I greatly doubt whether business of so exclusive a kind will last until Xmas; but even if it does, how is Miss Achurch to play such a frightful part up to within six weeks of her inevitable retirement? However, that cannot be helped now.

It seems to me that in addition to subscriptions you might open a guarantee fund. For instance, I don't want seats, as my entry is secured by my position on the press; or I can pay at the doors in any case; but I would guarantee £10 towards preventing a deficit falling on you, if necessary; and perhaps others would do the same on the understanding that the enterprise had certain limits—that is, that you would not, after clearing yourself, go on playing against the guarantee (though you are welcome to do that as far as I personally am concerned—or perhaps I should say that I am willing to leave that to your own judgment without conditions).

Lugné Poe plays "Peer Gynt" on Thursday week in Paris. If I could persuade Archer to come with me I should be tempted to go. A couple of articles on an Ibsen performance of that magnitude would help a good deal.

Helmsley, who managed for Miss Farr at the Avenue, is a good man; but I suppose he is not available. London is full of wasters & impostors clamoring for such a job. Unless you can get a good man, it might be worth while trying a woman. Miss Farr herself might be of some use.

685

She can't act; but she is an intelligent woman of business, and honorable in money matters.

The I.T. ought to back you to the extent of taking places for their subscribers.

yrs sincerely
G. Bernard Shaw

To ELIZABETH ROBINS

[29 Fitzroy Square W]
[Undated: assigned to 24th October 1896]

[C/33; X/151]

P.S.

Miss Payne Townshend
    41 Grosvenor Road S.W.

ought to receive circulars. She is a rich, unencumbered, and public spirited Irish Lady, and a great admirer of "The Quintessence of Ibsenism."

GBS

To CHARLOTTE PAYNE-TOWNSHEND

29 Fitzroy Square W
27th October 1896

[B/2; X/151]

[Charlotte had gone to Manchester with Beatrice Webb the previous day to attend a conference of the National Union of Women Workers. From there she proceeded alone to Ireland, not returning to London until 10th November.]

I'm unspeakably hurried and worried—oh for ten minutes peace in the moonlight at Stratford! Keep me advised of your address; keep me deep in your heart; write me two lines whenever you love me; and be happy and blessed and out of pain for my sake.

I'm glad you're gone: London, & the cessation of our open air life and our bicycling was making you wretched. I had rather you were well a thousand miles away than ill in my wretched arms.

In haste—farewell

GBS

686

To JANET ACHURCH

[T/1 (A/4)]

29 Fitzroy Square W
30th October 1896

Dearest Janet

Forgive me: I am not in the least penitent: but I beg your pardon. I noticed that you were unusually beautiful: that your eyes were like moons in a very wet fog; that your moral nature was totally submerged and your wits sensitively and rapaciously alert; that, though most cunningly coherent, you were stark raving mad; and that Charrington was in his martyrdom phase. I knew of course that this was as likely to be maternity as morphia; but I was so mortally afraid that you would help yourself out pharmaceutically with Rita and the baby that I resolved to make a violent onslaught on the assumption that you either had or were going to desolate my existence.

I have been reading "Little Eyolf" at odd moments, desperately trying, for your sake, to find any real drama in it; but I find nothing but some perfectly obvious acting, which you can do on your head without any suggestions from me. The thing is a pure study—a clinical lecture on morbid psychology, with a suggested cure at the end (seaside air and orphanage work); and its performance seems to me to be purely a matter of address and acquired finish of execution, not of ideas or inspiration. However, no doubt you've got much further into it than I: if you can enlighten me, *do*.

So you have found me out again. You always find me out and deplore the flaws in my noble nature when I am faithless and row a few strokes in somebody else's boat. But how is your ship to be of use to me, or I to it, unless I command the whole fleet?

Besides, dear Janet, I *daren't* be devoted now. The appeal of your present experience to my sympathy is too strong to be indulged. So don't be angry with

Shaw, Limited

To CHARLOTTE PAYNE-TOWNSHEND

[B/2; X/151]

29 Fitzroy Square W
1st November 1896

[Paul Bourget (1852–1935), French critic, poet, and novelist, was a friend of Henry James, whose work he influenced. Keir Hardie was contesting a parliamentary seat in a by-election at East Bradford; he was defeated.]

How much longer do you intend to stay away? It is about three weeks since I heard anything of you. Having accordingly totally forgotten you, I was reminded of Derry today by finding a description of it by—of all people—Paul Bourget, in a sketch of his called "Neptunevale" in that [September 1896] number of "Cosmopolis" in which my article [on the International Socialist Congress] appeared.

I write dozens of loveletters now by using up all the things that came into my head to say to you at Stratford. Unfortunately this, though an enormous success with all the others, is not available for letters to you.

I have been up until 3 every morning for a fortnight, and am a miserable spectacle in consequence—can't *feel* & therefore can't write as I want to write to you. I'm going to Bradford tomorrow to speak for Keir Hardie. If I don't get a letter from you to read in the train I shall blight the election.

GBS

To CHARLOTTE PAYNE-TOWNSHEND

Great Northern train
9.45 a.m. London to Bradford
2nd November 1896

[A/2; X/151.e]

[Sally (Satty) Fairchild, a member of a well-known Boston family, had met and become a close friend of Ellen Terry during one of the latter's American tours. Shaw saw much of her and Edith Craig during the latter part of 1896.]

A beautiful still night, the darkness too pale to be illumined by many stars; dying colours visible on the horizon, night clasping a fainting day upon its breast.

That's Miss [Emma] Brooke, whose novel [*Life the Accuser*] I have with me to while away the journey. It has exasperated me beyond measure, because I felt quite charmed by your sunset until Miss Brooke started at the same thing. Let it be a warning to you—an awful warning.

I really begin to doubt whether England *is* a beautiful country. To-day it simply looks cold and dull: the most interesting thing in the landscape is

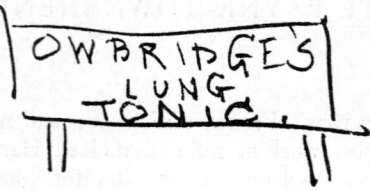

and I have no idea what to say on behalf of Keir Hardie. Oh, if I could only talk to you without writing—without forming sentences—without setting that fatigued machinery going! Why do you choose this time of all others to desert me—just now when you are most wanted?

Imagine the condition of a man who feels like this before 11 a.m.!

You might just as well have stayed here & come to Bradford with me. Here I am with three third class passengers.

This is the man opposite me. Good God, I have nothing to look at but that man for 3 hours, except OWBRIDGE'S L.T. I could accept a collision with glee if I could be certain that the man's head would be twisted off & hurled with a bang against the LUNG TONIC board.

This is the second man. He thinks he's reading the paper; but really he is falling asleep.

I regret to say that I can't draw the third man, because he has looked over my shoulder & discovered what I am doing. He is *posing* in antic-ipation of his turn with such inexpressibly ghastly results that I dare not attempt to limn him for you.

689

Stop: I have him. Observe his intellectual air. He knows I've done

it & is dying to get a peep; but I've baffled him. Now that I've turned
over the page he can peep his fill. (He does: I believe he's reading this.
Ha! ha! Ho! ho! He daren't pretend to notice the insult).

The landscape improves: we are passing into a zone where the early
November colors—no, this reminds me of Miss Brooke.

Only for Ellen Terry, who is quite angelically consolatory, and Nelly
Heath, who is painting my portrait, & Sattie Fairchild, who makes me
read my plays to her, and Ailsa Craig, who chaperones Sattie, I should
be utterly lonely without you. Janet carries out your worst theories of
maternity: all her animal forces are thrown into a sort of liquid suffu-
sion & eruption, & she's stark mad. The other day she got hold of
Bertha & simply tortured her—telling her that we (you & I) were engaged, & that it was an excellent thing for me, & that she would much
rather see me married to you than any other woman &c &c &c, whereupon the distracted Bertha wrote me such a letter that I confirmed the
news, gave her the date & full particulars as to the huge sums you were
settling on me, our arrangements, the house we had taken & the deuce
knows what else. Whereupon Bertha came & bullied me personally; de-
claimed against the perfidy of Janet & of Beatrice; said it was so disgusting that *I*, of all persons, should stoop to think about money & so on.
All this, mind, though she knew it was all nonsense. It irritates me, this
way of regarding you as an excellent settlement for me, as if you were a
house, or a sinecure. I revenge myself by giving the most Monte-
Christian accounts of your wealth & gravely admitting that it would be
certainly an excellent chance for me. They dont understand that I have
come into the fortune you have brought me already—£50,000 a week
for 6 weeks at Stratford. You can give all the other currency to whom
you please, & make me pay into the bargain.

690

Aha!—blue sky—sun!

What shall I say for Keir Hardie?

The three *miserables* have given up all pretence of reading. Even Pearson's Weekly drops from the nerveless hand of the man opposite. And I—I shall also abandon myself to my thoughts—since you *won't* come & keep me company.

After all, I *don't* care: your letter is a happy one. *Be* happy: if they love you at Mitchelstown; so do I also here in this deplorable train. A thousand blessings grow up about you & rain down on you.

GBS

To CHARLOTTE PAYNE-TOWNSHEND

[A/2; X/151.e]

29 Fitzroy Square W
4th November 1896

[Joseph Sheridan Le Fanu (1814–73), Irish novelist and editor of the Dublin *Evening Mail* (1839–58), was the author of the suspense novel *Uncle Silas* (1864). The photographs were of Charlotte's ancestral home in Derry, Rosscarbery. Shaw's letter, "The East Bradford Election," appeared in the *Bradford Observer* on 9th November.]

Now was there ever so sentimental a woman as this! You quote Lefanu on the miseries of your country and then send me photographs of the palatial splendors in which you weep. This, too, is the way you care for me—as an imaginative luxury. No matter: I wish I were with you among those hills: there are two laps in which I could rest this fagged head of mine now—Nature's and yours. I would shew you then with great eloquence that all Ireland's failures have been due to her incapacity for believing in success or happiness—for talking like Lefanu whilst Irishmen are going out into all lands & putting them on as a shepherd putteth on his garment. As long as Ireland produces men who have the sense to leave her, she does not exist in vain. The address of *my* Ireland at present is 10 Adelphi Terrace. By the way, you do not say whether you are returning thither or to Webb's.

I came up from Bradford by a slow train after the evening's meeting, starting before 10 & not arriving at Kings ✠ until half past three. It was cold; and yet I had a sort of fatigued happiness. I spoke badly & did no good, except by getting the editor of the Bradford Observer to promise to insert a letter from me on the election.

I wrote a letter to you on the journey down, but did not post it until

691

my return in the small hours. Probably it had to follow you on from Mitchelstown. I shall go to Paris for "Peer Gynt," which stands postponed now to Monday. So perhaps I shall have to travel on Sunday; but if I can manage it I will try to put off going until I have seen you. Not that it matters—it is my instinct to put off my delights—but still! I wish—but this is all nonsense. I want to tell you lies face to face—close.

Imagine! past forty and still going on like this. I hope when I am past sixty I shall be going on like it, and for you, even though you shall have been a thousand times faithless and have forgotten me with a nice husband in a first rate position in the county. But you may pretend as you please: you will find him very stupid after me.

GBS

P.S. I have a curious fancy to go to Derry without going to Ireland —by long sea or balloon or something, & spending just one evening there with you. But I am afraid you need not give any orders about my reception.

To ELLEN TERRY

29 Fitzroy Square W
[U(A)/10; X/117]   4th November 1896

[Irving's revival of *Richard III* opened at the Lyceum on 19th December; it received a full-scale Shavian bombardment in the *Saturday Review* a week later.]

I must write three words in reply; but I am getting uneasy about your eyes: it can't be good for you to write so much. I believe I ought to break off the correspondence. I would, too, if I were sure you wouldn't at once find out how easy it would be to forget me.

I see that I saw Edy's future rather than her present. Somehow I expect you have spoiled them a bit—probably succeeding handsomely with the man, and overshooting the mark a little with the woman and making her cynical. I have a morbid horror of any ill treatment of children; but I believe that love and the more touching sorts of happiness are wasted on them: they are really not capable of them—nobody is until they've earned them. In my own case I am afraid that though I was not ill treated—my parents being quite incapable of any sort of inhumanity —the fact that nobody cared for me particularly gave me a frightful self sufficiency, or rather a power of starving on imaginary feasts, that may

692

have delayed my development a good deal, and leaves me to this hour a treacherous brute in matters of pure affection. But I am quite sure that people with happy childhoods usually say—what is incomprehensible to me—that their childhood was the happiest part of their lives. Tell Edy that the two things that worthless people sacrifice everything for are happiness and freedom, and that their punishment is that they get both, only to find that they have no capacity for the happiness and no use for the freedom. You have a ready example to point this piece of maternal wisdom. You are not in the least free: you are tied neck, wrists & ankles to your profession and your domestic arrangements, and your happiness has been picked up in casual scraps on your way to your work. Edy on the contrary is quite free & has nothing to do but be happy. Yet who would choose her life instead of yours? Tell her to go and seek activity, struggle, bonds, responsibilities, terrors—in a word, life; but don't mention me as the prompter of this highly edifying lecture.

Teddy with two children—at his age! I give him up. You've ruined him. What use can the children be to him?—how can he feel their weight on his arm?—if you support them? You don't agree with me: you know all that, and know that there's another side to it? Well, shall I marry my Irish millionairess? She, like Edy, believes in freedom, and not in marriage; but I think I could prevail on her; and then I should have ever so many hundreds a month for nothing. Would you ever in your secret soul forgive me, even though I am really fond of her and she of me? No you wouldn't. Good: then you love me better than you love Ted. Let me add, though, that I shared (and deepened) *my* mother's poverty—that is, lived virtually at her expense—for long enough. I began my literary career by writing five big novels and a host of articles which nobody would publish. My earnings for nine years were exactly fifteen shillings. So perhaps Ted is a genius like me. But has he produced the five books, or only the two babies?

After all, this worldly wisdom is great nonsense.

Since Imogen is in such good condition, and my millionairess returns from Ireland on Sunday, I think I'll treat her to a stall (can't very well take a millionairess to the pit) when I come back from the Parisian "Peer Gynt," now fixed for Monday next. Oh yes, I daresay you would; but how would you believe that I was in earnest about going if it didn't cost me anything?

By the way, make H.I. go carefully over Richard III and recut it.

[Balance of letter is missing.]

693

To ELIZABETH ROBINS

[A/33]

29 Fitzroy Square W
4th November 1896

[The "affectionate" greeting to Heinemann was facetious, for there had been no communication between the two since Heinemann's angry letter to Shaw of 25th February 1896.]

Dear Miss Robins

I return Scott's letter—forgive me for not writing to acknowledge it: I am always trying to prevent myself from writing to you; and this time, being superhumanly busy and worn out, I succeeded.

The letter is exactly what I expected from Scott. He is the most sympathetic critic in London, myself perhaps excepted; and yet you expect the worst from him—with the same exception.

I cannot persuade Archer to come to Paris with me & take advantage of "Peer Gynt" to boom Ibsen. The performance has been put off to Monday. I will go anyhow if it is humanly possible; and meanwhile I will say something about "Little Eyolf" in next Saturday's Saturday.

It would be well, I think, to get Rita understudied. Fate forbid that it should prove necessary; but it is useless to blink the fact that the risk is greater than usual in her case. Or perhaps it would be better to get the ratwife understudied, and, in case of accident, get Mrs Pat to read the part of Rita. The audience would consider that better value—quite an event. But this idea you had better keep locked up tightly unless an emergency compels you to use it. Mrs Pat would certainly not do it premeditatedly.

Give my affectionate regards to Heinemann if he should ask after me.

yours sincerely
G. Bernard Shaw

P.S. Unluckily the Weekly Sun man—the principal—is a rabid anti-Ibsenite. He damps down the paragraphs of *my* man into rather coldly communicated news. However, it doesn't matter.

To ELLEN TERRY

[U(A)/10; X/117]

29 Fitzroy Square W
5th November 1896

[Shaw had received some new photographs from Ellen. Charlotte's sister was Mary Stewart Payne-Townshend (1859?–1929); in 1885 she had married

694

Colonel (later Brigadier-General) Hugh Cecil Cholmondeley (1852–1941), who commanded the London Rifle Brigade (1890–1901), fought in South Africa (1900), and commanded the 173rd Infantry Brigade in World War I. Charlotte's "broken heart" was the result of an infatuation for Dr Axel Munthe (1857–1949), Swedish physician and author of *The Story of San Michele* (1929), whom she had met in Rome in April 1894.]

Yes: I'll give them away—if I want to.

Oh why, *why*, WHY did you send me that one with your back turned. Are you not satisfied to be my good angel—must you be my everyday angel (cant write bad angel—dont believe it) as well? Those with your eyes in them are divine: it's like looking at the stars. But to turn your soul and your intelligence away from me and shew me nothing but how beautiful the outline of your cheek is, and the base of your neck, just to give me that lost feeling of unfulfilment—oh, wretch, you will provoke heaven too far some day, and then—stop: these things become detestable unless they are said plainly & bluntly.

I hereby testify that I, G.B.S., having this day inspected a photograph of Miss E. T., have felt all my nerves spring and my heart glow with the strongest impulse to have that lady in my arms, proving that my regard for her is a complete one, spiritual, intellectual, and physical, on all planes, at all times, under all circumstances, and for ever.

The reading tonight [of *You Never Can Tell*] was an appalling failure. The play's no use: I looked for my gold and found withered leaves. I must try again & again & again. I always said I should have to write twenty bad plays before I could write one good one; and yet I am taken aback to find that number seven is a phantom. I've been happy all the evening, but dead. I couldnt read; and there was nothing to read anyhow. Sattie saw that I was a mere rag: when Edy was gone she spread me out on the hearthrug on my back and relaxed me—you know the [Annie Payson Call] system: it means simply petting a tired man. There was what you call the warmth & peace of home, *your* home. If only you had taken off my burden I should have slept like a child. No: *I* shall never have a home. But do not be alarmed: Beethoven never had one either.

No: I've no courage: I am, and always have been, as timid as a mouse. Really & truly.

She doesnt come back until Tuesday. And she doesnt really *love* me. The truth is, she is a clever woman, with plenty of romantic imagination. She knows that what she lacks is physical experience, and that without it she will be in ten years time an old maid. She knows the value of her unencumbered independence, having suffered a good deal from family bonds & conventionality before the death of her mother [in September 1891] & the marriage of her sister left her free. The idea of tying herself up again by a marriage before she knows anything—before she has exploited her freedom & money power to the utmost—seems to her intellect to be unbearably foolish. Her theory is that she wont do it. She picked up a broken heart somewhere a few years ago, and made the most of it (she is very sentimental) until she happened to read "The Quintessence of Ibsenism," in which she found, as she thought, gospel, salvation, freedom, emancipation, self respect & so on. Later on she met the author, who is, as you know, able to make himself tolerable as a correspondent. He is also a bearable companion on bicycle rides, especially in a country house where there is nobody else to pair with. She got fond of me and did not coquet or pretend that she wasnt. I got fond of her, because she was a comfort to me down there. You kept my heart so warm that I got fond of everybody; and she was nearest & best. That's the situation. What does your loving wisdom say to it?

GBS

[Ellen's reply to this letter on 6th November was:

" 'Plainly and bluntly' you are a great silly Dear in the *me* part of your letter (but that part doesnt count). If *she* does not dote upon the quintessence of *you*, she'd better marry your book! . . .

"But somehow I think she'll love you quick enough. I *think* so, but it's what's in herself I can tell her, not what is in you. How very silly you clever people are. Fancy not knowing! Fancy not being sure! Do *you* know you love her? 'Cos if so, that would be safe enough to marry on. For if it came to the last second and she didnt love *you*, she couldnt kiss you, and then you'd know quick enough! I'm supposing she's a woman, not a—a—(I dont know what to call the thing I mean)—a 'female that never knows'! Those are often married things, and they have children, and there are many such, but I pity their husbands.

"It is borne in upon me that if she is your lover and you hers, I ought not to write to you quite as I do. She might not understand. I should understand it if I were the SHE, but it's because I'm not clever. I never was, and sometimes, looking at you all, I hope I never shall be!

"One thing I am clever enough to know (TO KNOW, mind. I know few things, but I know what I know). It is this. You'd be all bad, and no good in you, if you marry anyone unless you know you love her. A woman may *not* love before marriage and really love afterwards (if she has never loved before). We all love more after union (women I mean, and surely, oh surely men too). *But a man should know. . . .*

"I wonder I havent doubted you were earnest in asking me about this at

696

all! Mind I believe you are speaking 'sad brow and true man.' Too sad. It makes me unhappy for you, and so I write. But now I think I wont be with you quite so much. Do tell me, have you asked her to be your wife? (Does she know that has a lovely sound?) If you have—! If not, why dont you— 'use Sunlight soap and dont worry.' (See advertisement.)

"Patience is rich. 'How poor is he who has not patience!' (Misquoted from the Shakspere you love.)" The misquotation is from *Othello*, II, iii, 376.]

To BERTHA NEWCOMBE

[C/4]

29 Fitzroy Square W
6th November 1896

[Shaw eventually departed for Paris on 11th November, residing in the same lodging house as Bertha. He viewed *Peer Gynt* on the evening of the 12th, but did not see the Coquelin production, departing early the following morning in order to attend two Fabian meetings later in the same day. Benoît Constant Coquelin (1841–1909), famous member of the Comédie Française, had just taken over management of the Théâtre de la Porte-Saint-Martin, where in 1898 he created his most successful rôle, Cyrano de Bergerac.]

I ought to arrange, if I go, to stay a second night to see Coquelin in [Eugène Brieux's] "Les Bienfaiteurs." I have no news as to date of "P.G." I wonder will you have the gumption to telegraph. I certainly shant start without positive information.

GBS

To CHARLOTTE PAYNE-TOWNSHEND

[B/2; X/151.e]

29 Fitzroy Square W
7th November 1896

I am all in the dark as to Paris—cannot find out for certain when the performance is to take place. If I learn tomorrow that it is to be on Monday, I'll start at once.

No: you don't love me one little bit. All that is nature, instinct, sex: it proves nothing beyond itself. Don't fall in love: be your own, not mine or anyone else's. From the moment that you can't do without me, you're lost, like Bertha. Never fear: if we want one another we shall find it out. All I know is that you made the autumn very happy, and that I shall always be fond of you for that. About the future I do not concern myself: let us do what lies to our hands & wait for events. My dearest!

GBS

To GRANT RICHARDS

29 Fitzroy Square W
8th November 1896

[A/4; X/135]

[Richards had just established his publishing firm early in the year. The seven plays enumerated by Shaw eventually made up the two-volume *Plays Pleasant and Unpleasant* published by Richards in April 1898 in an edition of 1240 copies of each volume. The work was issued simultaneously in Chicago by Herbert S. Stone, but a sale of only 734 sets of the two volumes in America between April and December 1898 hardly confirmed Shaw's assertion that there was "much more to be made out of my name there than here . . ."]

Dear Sir

As far as I have been able to ascertain—and I found my opinion on what I have been told by Heinemann, Lane & Walter Scott of their experience with dramatic works by Pinero, Wilde, George Moore, &c— the public does not read plays, or at least did not a very few years ago. Have you any reason to suppose that it has changed its habits?

I have by me three realistic plays, including the one published by Messrs Henry, as to which there need be no difficulty, as it is as dead as a doornail. One of them is a frightful play; but it ought to be given to the world somehow: indeed, it may perhaps be performed by the Independent Theatre to an invited audience. At least they are always hankering after this.

I have also three plays which are works of dramatic art purely, and which include "Arms & The Man." But the other two have not yet been performed; and it would be better to wait until after their production before printing them.

Another little play, which is to be performed at the Lyceum, I will probably publish through the theatre; but there is no reason why its sale should be restricted to the inside of the house after the first run.

One quite indispensable condition is simultaneous publication in America. Indeed there is much more to be made out of my name there than here at present.

yours faithfully
G. Bernard Shaw

698

To BERTHA NEWCOMBE

[C/4]

29 Fitzroy Square W
9th November 1896

Very well: I shall start on Wednesday morning, and arrive at the Gare du Nord at seven. If you are there, well & good (do come if it's fine). If not I will find my way, possibly on foot or by a brown bus, if I am in the humor to vagabondise. I shall only bring a handbag. Shall require a bed (without sheets) for Wednesday & Thursday nights. Letter from L-P [Lugné-Poë] this morning certifying that in coming on Monday I shall not deceive myself. Return on Friday.

GBS

To CHARLOTTE PAYNE-TOWNSHEND

[D(two cards)/2; X/151.e]

29 Fitzroy Square W
9th November 1896

[This letter anticipated Charlotte's return from Ireland on the 10th.]

I am still here: "Peer Gynt" stands postponed to Thursday; so I start on Wednesday morning, and hope to return on Friday evening. The worst is that I must finish (& begin) my Saturday article [a review of George Grove's *Beethoven and His Nine Symphonies*] tomorrow; and Heaven only knows how soon or how late that will be accomplished. But I will contrive to see you somehow, at all hazards: I *must*; and that "must," which "rather alarms" you, TERRIFIES me. If it were possible to run away—if it would do any good—I'd do it; so mortally afraid am I that my trifling & lying and ingrained treachery and levity with women are going to make you miserable when my whole sane desire is to make you hap—I mean strong and self possessed and tranquil. However, we must talk about it. Webb gave me a tremendous lecture about it on Sunday; and I must tell you about that. My one hope is that you are as treacherous as I am. No matter: let's meet, meet, meet, meet, meet: bless me! how I should like to see you again for pure *liking*; for there is something between us aside and apart from all my villainy.

I've had my hair clipped as close as a horse's; so prepare for a revolting shock.

I'll call after lunch—between 3 & 4, probably. If you are out, I'll call again in the evening after my last meal. Or no, stop (idiot! I thought

I should get it all on one card) I forgot that there is a Fabian publishing committee at 4.30. It may be impossible for me to get the article sent off in time to admit of my calling between lunch & that hour. So if I do not appear by 4 (which would only leave me 15 minutes) I may try again between 5.30 & 6, after the committee. It will be a rush, I suppose: I want to buy a handbag for the journey, as I need take very little luggage. But as to the afternoon don't let me hamper you in any way. So long as I can come in the evening & have you all to myself, with all the work over and done, until bedtime, I don't care how you disappoint me in the daytime. Oh lies, lies, lies, lies, flattery & luxury & longing: can any good come of it? If you only will keep tight hold of yourself & be to yourself the centre of the universe—if only you will. Stratford was so happy: better a million times leave it as it is than spoil it. Unless you have the nerve to use me for your own development without losing yourself.

Well, well, well, well: we will talk it over most wisely—tomorrow, tomorrow, tomorrow.

GBS

To CHARLOTTE PAYNE-TOWNSHEND

29 Fitzroy Square W
10th November 1896

[B/2]

Forgive me this one night of selfish *blessedness*. I really was happy. You always surpass my expectations.

Until Friday.

But I wish there was nothing to look forward to, nothing to covet, nothing to gain. I am satisfied, satisfied, satisfied deep in my heart. The rest is mere greediness.

Good night—"ah no, the hour is ill" &c &c &c &c &c &c &c.

GBS

To CHARLOTTE PAYNE-TOWNSHEND

29 Fitzroy Square W
16th November 1896

[A/2]

Thanks. P.G. would have done tomorrow—hope you finished it. Cold much **worse**—fatal consummation highly probable.

700

Shall see you tonight.

The [messenger] boy insists on an answer—says he darent go back to you without it; but I prefer now to say all I have to say in person.

G.B.S.

To ELLEN TERRY

[U(A)/10; X/117]

29 Fitzroy Square W
16th November 1896

[Irving finally presented *Madame Sans-Gêne* at the Lyceum on 10th April 1897. *Peer Gynt* was not seen in London professionally until the Old Vic production of March 1922. "Tuesday morning novices" possibly refers to the practice of giving a matinée performance with the understudies, or with young people wanting to go on the stage in the days when there were no drama schools.]

Ah, at last a line, oh faithless, jealous, exacting, jilting Ellen. You push me into the abyss and then desert me for falling in.

Well, I have been to Paris, and seen "Peer Gynt" done in the sentimentallest French style with tenpenceworth of scenery, and the actor manager in two nameless minor parts [Solveig's father and the travelling Englishman, Mr Cotton]. And how did it go? Not, like Cymbeline & Co, by dint of everybody in the theatre making believe with all their might that they were witnessing a great work, but *really*. The scene where Solveig joins Peer in the mountains touched everybody to the marrow. The scene of the mother's death (with the lights going wrong, and everything as ridiculous as possible) was so enormously effective that if H.I. had been there, he'd have abandoned Richard III and substituted P.G. on the spot. Any of your Tuesday morning novices would have passed for a great actress in Solveig, the part is so interesting. The Strange Passenger got a round of applause; the Button Moulder was immensely appreciated; the house caught its breath & then came down with a gush when poor old played-out Peer said he would bury himself under the inscription "Çi git personne." What *is* Henry Irving thinking of, and what are *you* thinking of, that you are going to waste the precious remaining years of your careers on "Madame Sans-Gêne" and baby comediettas like "The Man of Destiny"? However, if you won't do it, you won't. Only, *it will be done*, if I have to play it myself. Considering that *anybody* can get a reputation by playing Ibsen nowadays, whereas Duse herself cannot make

Shakspere interest anybody above the level of a curate—but what is the use of saying all this to the one person who doesn't believe it. And by believing it, I don't mean merely holding up your hand and saying "Credo" (always an interesting attitude): I mean acting on the assumption that it is true.

Excuse me, Miss Terry, I grow tedious. Proceed with Madame Sans Gêne, by all means. I look forward to it with infinite interest.

Réjane's cast-off clothes on my Ellen! That will be charming—charming.

"Never has Miss Terry been so winsome as in this, her latest, assumption of the rôle of the merry laundress &c &c &c. The production was characterised by all that gorgeousness which we are accustomed to associate with the Lyceum &c &c &c."

Quite so.

Can you hear my teeth grinding, miserable woman?

Even Mrs Pat plays the ratwife sooner than not play at all.

Let us change the subject.

Your advice went straight to the mark. The moment I read that exhortation in your beautiful large print to sit in devout silence and feel beautiful and *do nothing*, I was up like a lion. Aha! were you made what you are, oh heartwise Ellen, with unshrivelled arms and fulfilled experience, by men who *spared* you, and sat in corners seraphically renunciating? And must a woman who is nervous, and sensitive, and sleeps badly, and longs for healthy rest, be *honorably* charged for a very simple remedy the modest price of £5000 a year & her hand in marriage? What kind of swindler and fortune hunter do you take me for? I swooped on Paris, and swooped back like a whirlwind ; and now, dear Ellen, she sleeps like a child, and her arms will be plump, and she is a free woman, and it has not cost her half a farthing, and she has fancied herself in love, and known secretly that she was only taking a prescription, and been relieved to find the lover at last laughing at her & reading her thoughts and confessing himself a mere bottle of nerve medicine, and riding gaily off.

What else can I be to any woman except to a wise Ellen, who can cope with me in insight, and who knows how to clothe herself in that most blessed of all things—unsatisfied desire.

Farewell—the post is at hand; and this must away tonight.

Oh, I am all alive—possessed with a legion of spirits—alive, awake, all at your inspiration.

702

What do you say now?

Ha! ha! ha! ha!!!! In mockery for all illusions—in tenderness for my dear Ellen.

GBS

To CHARLOTTE PAYNE-TOWNSHEND

[B/2]

29 Fitzroy Square W
17th November 1896

[Charles Lamoureux (1834–99), French violinist and conductor, established the Nouveaux Concerts (later called Concerts Lamoureux) in Paris in 1881.]

I have to go to the Lamoureux concert tomorrow night, to the Comedy Theatre [R.C. Carton's *A White Elephant*] on Thursday, and I forget where on Friday & Saturday. If your sister is coming up in the afternoon I could call between five & six, after the Fabian Publishing Com^tee. Or at midnight after the concert, if she would prefer that.

I have a ticket (admitting two) for the private view of Dagnan Bouveret's Lord's Supper at the Goupil Gallery on Thursday. Do you care to see it?

I am in the blackest depths, waiting grimly for a ray of heavenly light. But quite hard & happy, ironically, sardonically, gimleteyedly happy. I have squandered on you all the material out of which my illusions are made. And now I count what I have discovered, before the illusions return. And I don't find that I have made you feel anything, except nervously. You don't love me the least bit in the world. But I am all the more grateful.

GBS

To CHARLOTTE PAYNE-TOWNSHEND

[A/2]

29 Fitzroy Square W
18th November 1896

[Shaw's article was "Peer Gynt in Paris," published in the *Saturday Review* on 21st November. Charlotte's "baby" was her sister Mary Cholmondeley, to whom Charlotte generally referred as "Sissy." The Chicago *Chap-Book* contained the interview mentioned to Ellen Terry on 21st September.]

After all, I must send you the ticket. My article is not finished; and I foresee that I shall be so late that the light will be gone. Why will

703

you not take your baby?—there is nothing a lady from Shropshire likes more than to be at a private view, inaccessible to the vulgar shilling; and I hate private views—should never have dreamt of going except as a pretext for going somewhere with you.

I think they sent me a letter saying that they would give me a season ticket at the private view. In case by any chance they offer you such a thing, get it in my name, unless (as is likely enough) it is nameless, or unless you would like it in your own to go and see the picture again.

Go in the morning, whilst it's light. I will go with you some other day, or I will call after my belated lunch and go for a walk, or anything you please.

What an exacting woman you are! Is this freedom?

That Lamoureux orchestra is worth hearing as a French piece of musical machinery.

I have to go to the Comedy tomorrow.

I send you a copy of the Chap Book with a caricature of me by Max Beerbohm and an interview by Clarence Rook.

GBS

To CHARLOTTE PAYNE-TOWNSHEND

[B/2]

29 Fitzroy Square W
23rd November 1896

I quite failed to run the gauntlet successfully during the second interval [of *Little Eyolf*]. Miss Erichsen & Massingham finished me after the others had left me only a few minutes.

My mother wants to see "Little Eyolf" on Thursday or Friday. If you have spare stalls on that day & nobody else to give them to, give them to me for her.

Let us see it again someday—that dress circle was odiously stuffy.

I have only a second before post hour.

I shall be disengaged after 4.30 tomorrow.

GBS

To ELLEN TERRY

[U(A)/10; X/117]

29 Fitzroy Square W
30th November 1896

[The Ibsen articles were the *Saturday Review* notices of *Peer Gynt* and *Little Eyolf*, the latter having been published on 28th November. The notes appended to the published text of *The Devil's Disciple* in *Three Plays for Puritans* (1901) offer evidence of Shaw's "reading up the history of the American War of Independence."]

I must write at least three lines to you. Do not be afraid of wasting my time: you are, on the contrary, saving my life. Here is the proof.

1st. I finished my play today—what do you think of that? Does that look like wasting my time? Three acts, six scenes, a masterpiece all completed in a few weeks, with a trip to Paris and those Ibsen articles thrown in—articles which were so overwritten that I cut out & threw away columns. Not to mention the Bradford election.

2nd. I am the centre of a boiling whirlpool of furious enquiries from insulted editors, indignant secretaries of public bodies (wanting orations) all over the country, the management of the Haymarket, & innumerable private persons, who have written me letters upon letters, enclosing stamped envelopes, reply paid telegram forms, and every other engine for extracting instant replies in desperate emergencies. For months I haven't answered one of them. Why? Because I could write to no one but Ellen, Ellen, Ellen: all other correspondence was intolerable when I could write to her instead. And what is the result? Why, that I am not killed with lecturing and with the writing of magazine articles. (What the pecuniary result will be presently I decline to think; but now that the play is finished (in the rough) I shall try to earn a little supplemental money—not that I really want it; but I have always been so poor as to coin that nothing can persuade me now that I am not on the verge of bankruptcy.) I am saved these last inches of fatigue which kept me chronically overworked for ten years. The Socialist papers denounce me bitterly—my very devotees call me aristocrat, Tory, capitalist scribe & so on; but it is really all Ellen, Ellen, Ellen, Ellen, Ellen, the happiness, the rest, the peace, the refuge, the consolation of loving (oh, dearest Ellen, add "and being loved by"—a lie costs so little) my great treasure Ellen.

What did I want so particularly to say?—oh yes: it was this. I have written to Terriss to tell him that I have kept my promise to him & have "a strong drama" with a part for him; but I want your opinion; for I have never tried melodrama before; and this thing, with its heroic sacrifice, its impossible court martial, its execution (imagine W. T. *hanged* before the eyes of the Adelphi!), its sobbings & speeches & declamations, may possibly be the most monstrous piece of farcical absurdity that ever made an audience shriek with laughter. And yet I have honestly tried for dramatic effect. I think you could give me a really *dry* opinion on it; for it will not tickle you, like "Arms & The

Man" & "You Never Can Tell," nor get at your sympathetic side, like Candida (the heroine is not the hero of the piece this time); and you will have to drudge conscientiously through it like a stage carpenter & tell me whether it is a burlesque or not.

But now that I think of it, all this is premature. The play only exists as a tiny scrawl in my note books—things I carry about in my pockets. I shall have to revise it & work out all the stage business, besides reading up the history of the American War of Independence before I can send it to the typist to be readably copied. Meanwhile I can read it to Terriss, and to other people, but not to—well, no matter: I don't ask that the veil of the temple shall be rent: on the contrary, I am afraid, in my very soul, to come stumping in my thickbooted, coarse, discordant reality, into that realm where a magic Shaw, a phantasm, a thing who looks delicate and a boy (twelve stalls and a bittock off) poses fantastically before a *really* lovely Ellen (Remember, I have stood where I could have stolen your hairpins without unbending my elbow, and you were talking like mad all the time). But when the thing *is* typed, then you will read it for me, won't you? Perhaps before then I shall have been forced to break the spell by teaching you the words of The Strange Lady.

What shall I write next?—comic opera?

Ask Janet whether I am not a patient teacher when words have to be articulated by an undisciplined actress.

I have sat up again to write to you. Now the fire begins to burn low; and Iachimo in his trunk gets intolerable pins & needles. This grim cold is good for me, I suppose, since I am by complexion & constitution a Northman; but you I hope are warm as a summer island lying fast asleep in the Mediterranean. This sounds like a flower of literature; but I have bathed in the Mediterranean; and it was 80° Fahrenheit.

Now I have finished my play, nothing remains but to kiss my Ellen once and die.

GBS

PS What telegraphic address have they given you?

To CHARLOTTE PAYNE-TOWNSHEND

[29 Fitzroy Square W]

[E.u/2]   [Undated: assigned to 1st December 1896]

[Ellen Terry's letter of 1st December had contained a postscript: "Won't you bring her to see Cymbeline before Imogen goes away? If you do, let it be on Thursday Friday or Saturday—& *tell me first*." Shaw forwarded this portion of the letter to Charlotte, adding a note. The lecture on 2nd December was "The Jevonian Theory of Value" at the Economics Club.]

I think this must refer to you. What do you say?
(The play's finished)
(I lecture tomorrow night).

To ELIZABETH ROBINS

[B/33]

29 Fitzroy Square W
1st December 1896

[In his review of *Little Eyolf* Shaw had written: "Of Miss Robins's Asta it is difficult to say much, since the part, played as she plays it, does not exhibit anything like the full extent of her powers. Asta is a study of a temperament—the quiet, affectionate, enduring, reassuring, faithful, domestic temperament. That is not in the least Miss Robins's temperament: she is nervous, restless, intensely self-conscious, eagerly energetic. In parts which do not enable her to let herself loose in this, her natural way, she falls back on pathos, on mute misery, on a certain delicate plaintive note in her voice and grace in her bearing which appeal to our sympathy and pity without realizing any individuality for us. . . . those who have not seen Miss Robins play Hilda Wangel have no idea of what she is like when she really acts her part instead of merely giving an urbanely pictorial representation of it."]

Dear Miss Robins

Thanks for the tickets. I could not come; but I had the seats filled duly.

Never tell a critic that you haven't read his notice. First, because every actor tells him that, and he doesn't believe it. Second, because it annoys him. Third, because it is the stupidest thing you could possibly say to him. Fourth, because (in my case) you *ought* to have read it. Fifth (also in my case) because such remarks are lost on my insufferable self sufficiency.

I don't believe (yet) in Ibsen at night. Let the Avenue lessees speculate in it if they want to; but don't undertake anything except to play Asta & allow them the use of the stage right for a handsome salary, leaving Mrs Pat, Janet & the rest to make their own terms.

But I do believe in Wednesday & Saturday matinees all through the season, like the Popular Concerts. Lots of people want to see The Master Builder. Lots more the Doll's House. Lots more Hedda Gabler.

707

Could you not keep together in that way for a while? It would not interfere with routine professional work at night. The matinee & the suburban audience—the concert audience—are the keys of the situation.

You must play Hedda again in any case. Asta is ladylike—the last weakness of your Americanism. Who would pay any attention to me if I were a *gentleman*?

yrs sincerely
G. Bernard Shaw

To ELLEN TERRY

29 Fitzroy Square W
5th December 1896

[U(A)/10; X/117.e]

[Ellen had written of *You Never Can Tell* on 4th December: "I daresay there are folk who would think the old gentleman's teeth business was unpleasant. When I read it, I myself thought it was—unpretty, and I dont like ugly things. I remember you stay so long, so many pages, on the subject. . . . Then too, a pretty young lady like Miss Emery is one thing, but an old grumpy man—well, I think I *would* alter it if I were you." Janet Achurch did not leave the cast of *Little Eyolf* until after the evening performance on the 6th.]

Wretch: you thought that play might be bettered, and you did not say so. You thought two pennorth of flattery all that the occasion demanded. And you pretend to be my friend!

Have you heard of Mrs Pat's *coup d'état* at the Avenue? The "Morocco Bound" [play] syndicate have taken up "Little Eyolf." They had arranged to give Janet £25 and 3% on the receipts over £500, when Mrs Pat underbid her, apparently by offering to share in lieu of a salary; and poor Janet learnt just before the curtain went up on Friday that she was out of the cast & her part given to Mrs P. for the rest of the run. A nice surprise for a woman in her condition, wasn't it? Miss Robins, who has passed the week in a state of hysterical outragedness because Janet made her own terms with the syndicate instead of allowing her (Miss R) to get the £25 & pay her (J) £15, abetted Mrs Pat in this, and now finds Mrs Pat starred all down the Telegraph without a word of Miss Robins as Asta. You can imagine how pleasantly they all get on together under these circumstances. However, it's an ill wind that blows nobody any good. Miss Florence Farr comes in for the Ratwife.

708

Very well: I'll come on Thursday to see Imogen. The difficulty is that you won't see Miss T. unless she shews herself to you. She is, normally, a ladylike person at whom nobody would ever look twice, so perfectly does she fit into her place. Age certainly not less than 37, & looks 40. Perfectly placid and proper and pleasant—does not condescend to be anything more. And takes it all off like a mask when she selects you for that intimacy, which she does in the most coldblooded way. She is not cheap enough to be brought round to your room and *shewn* to you; she isn't an appendage, this green eyed one, but an individual. No prejudices—has too much respect *for* you to put up with anything less *from* you. In a dressing room interview you can do nothing effective except by playing the charming woman of experience & talent receiving with affectionate interest, condescension, and a lovably artless childishness of delight, a young creature just venturing into the life you are queen of. You'd feel instantly with her that such a line would be actressy and that the dressing room was the wrong *scene* for the right line. No: I wont go round to your room; and you know that perfectly well, you tantalising fiend, or else you wouldn't have suggested it.

Mind you tell me something serious about "The Philanderer." How would you like to play Julia?

GBS

To CHARLOTTE PAYNE-TOWNSHEND

[A/2]

[10 Adelphi Terrace WC]
5th December 1896. 3 o'clock

[Shaw was assisting the Webbs by revising and editing sections of their book *Industrial Democracy*, published in January 1898. See also his letters to Ellen Terry of 28th May and 27th July 1897.]

If you look at the Telegraph there with the pencil stuck through it, you will see that Janet has been thrown over handsomely at the Avenue. All the arrangements were by way of being completed—Janet to have £25 a week & a percentage—when Mrs Pat. struck in with an offer to play Rita herself. Janet's feelings may be imagined. I have just told her that it is an excellent thing for her & have bullied her for being upset about it; and she has carried herself with sufficient gallantry in the face of the enemy.

But it occurs to me that you might, if your engagements will permit, step in and give her a hand this afternoon, in this way. She has to play twice, in the afternoon & evening; and she will not have time to go back to Chelsea between the two. She says she is going to the Solferino, a café in Rupert St or thereabouts, where she cannot really rest, and where she will fidget & talk & calculate the prices of the things in the bill & drink brandy & soda & generally worry herself into the worst condition for the second performance. Now if you were to send round a note to the stage door of the Avenue, asking her to come here & simply rest, it would be an angel's message, a friendly demonstration at the right moment & a very practical service also. Tell her that you are busy and cannot talk to her or allow her to bring Charrington or anyone else who would talk—that you will hear of nothing but a comfortable room & some harmless grub for her—say that Charrington can come for her later on if he likes—you understand what is wanted.

If this is impossible or inconvenient or distasteful, there is no harm done, as she has of course no expectation of any such haven of refuge. Whilst I was at lunch, my mind, working in the direction of a disinterested excuse for calling here, struck out this benevolent idea—characteristic of my sweet disposition. As you are out I am having rather more disinterestedness than I bargained for; but no matter. I am going straight back to Fitzroy Sq to work at Webb's chapter, & will return at 8 (*after* supper) unless you wire me of any alteration in the arrangements.

GBS

To ELLEN TERRY

[U(A)/10; X/117]

29 Fitzroy Square W
7th December 1896

[*The Manxman*, adapted by Wilson Barrett in 1894 from Hall Caine's novel, and one of his most successful productions, had been revived at the Lyric on 16th November. *Journeys End in Lovers' Meeting* (1894), a one-act play by " John Oliver Hobbes " (Pearl Craigie) and George Moore, was in the Lyceum repertory. Frank Kemble Cooper (1857–1918) was for many years a member of Irving's company; it was he who, as Laertes, had led Ellen Terry as Ophelia on to the stage of the Lyceum, on 30th December 1878, in her first appearance with Irving's company. Sam Johnson (1831–1900), whom Shaw as a boy had seen when he performed low comedy rôles in the stock company of the Theatre Royal in Dublin, was another veteran member of the Lyceum company.

710

Ellen had written on 7th December: "What do you mean by saying (in re The Philanderer) it is dull and bestial? It's perfectly wonderful . . ." But in reply to Shaw's question whether she would like to play Julia, she answered: "Heavens no! I couldnt. Comedy is my 'line,' and Julia is a very tragedy."]

Oh, bother the MSS., mark them as much as you like: what else are they for? Mark everything that strikes you. I may consider a thing fortynine times; but if you consider it, it will be considered 50 times; and a line 50 times considered is 2 per cent better than a line 49 times considered. And it is the final 2 per cent that makes the difference between excellence & mediocrity.

Do you know, that Manxman affair is really a good bit of work of its kind. If you were a critic you would know how one jumps at an opportunity of praising a man who will probably be wasting his ability in making a donkey of himself next time. And I wish you would send for W.B. to rehearse "Journeys End." I don't say he could make Cooper act—no man can accomplish [im]possibilities—but he might at least devise some means of making those two look as if they had a fourteenth cousin's aunt's grandmother's house maid twice removed who had once walked out with a callboy. Mind: I am not going to have Cooper for the lieutenant & Sam Johnson for the innkeeper in "The Man of Destiny"—dont think it.

The right men, by the way, would be Little & De Lange.

I cannot make up my mind about "The Philanderer." Sometimes I loathe it, and let all my friends persuade me—Janet & Archer being the most vehement—that it is vulgar, dull, & worthless. Sometimes I think that it is worth playing. *Now* I say that if it is good enough for you it is good enough for the rest of the world.

She *shan't* be brought round to your dressing room as an appendage of mine—to be exhibited as my latest fancy. Will you never understand what I mean when I say that I can respect people's humanity as well as love their individuality. I should feel nice standing there between you. Of course she is greatly interested in you, as everybody else is; and she is quite capable of understanding your feeling. But you must manage it for yourself if you want to see her. Her address is Miss Payne Townshend, 10 Adelphi Terrace W.C. She has delightful rooms overlooking the river, over the London School of Economics (door round the corner, opposite the Caledonian Hotel). On Saturday, hearing that Janet, between the matinee & the evening performance, had no refuge but the Solferino, she promptly went to that haunt, yanked Janet (who was half dead) out of it, took her to Adelphi

Terrace, put her to bed, and delivered her punctually in magnificent condition for the performance.

I shall miss the post if I add another word.

GBS

To ELLEN TERRY

29 Fitzroy Square W
8th December 1896

[U(A)/10; X/117]

["I wonder if I'm going to be blind," Ellen mused in her letter of that morning. "You would come and see me then, my dear, wouldnt you? I would ask you to come and lie to me then and tell me that you love me. You have an ear for music and could make your voice sound sincere." As for her looking at Miss Payne-Townshend, Shaw might "rest quietly in the certain knowledge that I shall not even look through the curtain at you (or her)."

Lena Ashwell (1872–1957), later Lady Simson, who was then appearing as the Prince of Wales in *Richard III*, became one of Shaw's favourite actresses and good friends, creating the rôle of Lina Szczepanowska in *Misalliance* (1910). It was her description of her father, Commander Pocock, which provided Shaw with the inspiration for Captain Shotover in *Heartbreak House*.]

Just three lines. When you say those things about your being blind, I feel a deadly twitch that drags me all down into a writhing shuddering heap. Never write to me again; never speak to me ever at all; but keep your prosaic blessed eyes and don't torment me with the frightful beauty & mystery of a lovely blind woman.

If you don't look at her I will never forgive you. Oh, I can't explain; and you understand perfectly well. I want you to meet one another without any reference to me: I hate these contrived occasions. Well, never mind: wait until you can do something for her, or she for you: I can always wait: that's my secret—even wait for Thursday night. Only, *do* look at her; and yet how can you? F 18 & 19 is six rows off.

Yes, Lena is a fascinating squawker. If only you can convince her that it is not possible to stand on her heels & point up to the flies with both big toes simultaneously!

I must stop: I have nothing to say, or rather no time to say it in. I love you. You are at liberty to make what use you please of this communication. Of course I will love you after Thursday; but the point is that I love you *now*.

GBS

To CHARLOTTE PAYNE-TOWNSHEND

[B/2]

29 Fitzroy Square W
9th December 1896
[*i.e.*, early in the morning of 10th December]

[Shaw had visited *Little Eyolf* the evening of the 8th to see Mrs Patrick Campbell in her first performance as Rita. His criticism of her performance, under the title "Ibsen without Tears," appeared in the *Saturday Review* on 12th December. "Mrs. Patrick Campbell," he wrote, ". . . has seen how unladylike, how disturbing, how full of horror even, the part of Rita Allmers is, acted as Miss Achurch acted it. . . . [She] succeeded wonderfully in eliminating all unpleasantness from the play. . . . Her performance was infinitely reassuring and pretty . . . There was not a taste of nasty jealousy . . . Goodness gracious, I thought, what things that evil-minded Miss Achurch did read into this harmless play! And how nicely Mrs. Campbell took the drowning of the child! Just a pretty waving of the fingers, a moderate scream as if she had very nearly walked on a tin tack, and it was all over, without tears, without pain . . ."]

I enclose the ticket for the Lyceum. I have been working for twelve hours, with no variety except lunch and the publishing committee. Theatre last night, and after it a frightful altercation with Archer until about 2 o'clock; then home to broken, screwed up, murderous slumbers. Better to sit up with you, oh best beloved, than with Archer, confound him!

I will join you in the theatre, unless you find me there before you, which is not probable. My stall is F.18. F is the sixth row from the stage.

I presume Janet enjoyed Mrs Pat's incompetence. On Tuesday she read her part furtively and by snatches in the first two acts—openly in the third.

I am as tired as the Ratwife.

GBS

To CHARLOTTE PAYNE-TOWNSHEND

[B/2]

29 Fitzroy Square W
15th December 1896

There is a publishing committee tomorrow at 4.30. If I go on to you from that I shall probably be with you before six; but if you do not want to be in so early I can turn into the library & wait, or otherwise fill up the time. I shall have to go over to Webb's later on, for a while at all events; unless you deliberately and purposely practise enchantments to unman & prevent me.

The infant [Mary Cholmondeley] is unbearable—I'll threaten her with a deputation from the Humanitarian League. Can't you send her across to the Caledonian Hotel?

GBS

To PHILIP WEBB

[A/3]

29 Fitzroy Square W
29th December 1896

[Philip Webb (1831–1915), an architect and close friend of Emery Walker and William Morris, was co-founder with Morris of the Society for the Preservation of Ancient Buildings (1877). The article requested by Shaw was desired to be an attack on the decision of the Dean of Peterborough to hire a well-known architect, John Loughborough Pearson (1817–97), to restore the west front and to rebuild the central tower of Peterborough Cathedral. Shaw eventually drafted the article himself; it appeared, credited to "Architect" in the table of contents, in the *Saturday Review* on 2nd January 1897, under the title "Must Peterborough Perish?"]

My dear Webb

The Saturday Review will be glad to have a letter or an article from you about Peterborough. If you are too busy to undertake the job yourself, I will make a rough draft for you to correct & touch up, if you will instruct me to that effect by return of post. The Saturday goes to press on Friday morning; and copy should be sent in on Thursday afternoon at latest. I only proffer my services as journeyman in case you are unable to find time to do all the manual work yourself (I presume you have the bad habits of an architect); for I believe you would do the job with just the right touch.

Speaking as a journalist, I believe that what the public wants above everything is some security against the West Front tumbling on their heads. If some qualified person like yourself would point out clearly that the art of relining church towers & walls has been discovered & brought into safe and certain practice of late years, and that there is now no more necessity for pulling down and rebuilding a rotten tower than there is for repainting an old picture merely because the canvas or panel is perishing, that would have more weight than any amount of sentiment which very few people really feel.

714

Further, the nature of the pecuniary interest of the architect in the matter should be frankly stated. For instance, that a relining job, not being in the routine of ordinary contract building, but requiring constant and resourceful direction from hour to hour, makes it impossible for the swell architect whose life is one long delegation, and whose art is the art of getting commissions and never being on the spot. The public wants to know *why* Pearson's opinion isn't as good as yours; and the only reason that will convince them is a money reason.

An article which would allow the public virtually to overhear what you would say to the Dean if you had him in a corner and were quietly & unmaliciously talking to him for his good, would be just the thing.

yours sincerely
G. Bernard Shaw

To FREDERICK WHELEN

[C/4]   29 Fitzroy Square W
                                                             1st January 1897
[The "confounded article" was "General Retrospects: Socialist," for *Politics in 1896*, edited by Whelen and published by Grant Richards.]

What is that confounded article to be about? A survey of 1896 from the Socialist point of view, isn't it—10,000 words long or thereabouts? It will be the most infernal drivel. When do you go to press? I have been frightfully rushed by the theatres and by Peterborough Cathedral unfortunately, or I should not be in this helpless state of arrear.

GBS

To CHARLOTTE PAYNE-TOWNSHEND

[B/2]   29 Fitzroy Square W
                                                             1st January 1897
[Shaw went to Manchester on the 9th, lectured to the Ancoats Brotherhood on the 10th on "Repairs and Alterations in Socialism," and returned to London on the 11th January.]

I forgot to remind you last night that tomorrow (Saturday) is a first night at the Avenue [Huan Lee's *A Man about Town*, with music by Alfred Carpenter]. It begins—confound it!—at 8.30.

If anyone invites you to lunch on Sunday at a distance, accept; for I am convinced that you stay too much at home just now. I can go to Emery Walker's: he has asked me to come if I feel inclined. I am going quite mad myself for want of exercise and change of air—this article for Whelen is a hideous disaster. I feel almost reconciled to the trip to Manchester.

Our arrangement is that I am to come tomorrow afternoon and occupy myself with the American war and other follies, isn't it?

GBS

To CHARLOTTE PAYNE-TOWNSHEND

29 Fitzroy Square W
7th January 1897

[B/2]

[The *Academy* article on Archer's translation of *John Gabriel Borkman* appeared on 16th January. Charlotte had procured a copy of Edward Barrington de Fonblanque's *Political and Military Episodes in the Latter Half of the Eighteenth Century: Derived from the Life and Correspondence of the Rt. Hon. John Burgoyne, General, Statesman, Dramatist* (1876). This was the volume from which Shaw derived most of his facts on the American war of independence for *The Devil's Disciple*. The performance at the Prince of Wales's Theatre on the 8th was F. Boissier's *A Pierrot's Life*, billed as "a play without words," with music by M. Costa.]

I send you this with my last breath. It is past one a.m.; and I have worked continuously since I came down to breakfast, save only during my lunch at six. I had everything cleared off, and had sworn to do nothing except lecture at Manchester before next Saturday article when messengers began to arrive from the "Academy," & at last I promised a review of "John Gabriel Borkman" before Wednesday. Also Hawtrey sent for "The Philanderer" & compelled me to root it out and write to him.

Thanks for flowers & Fonblanque. My mother kept shewing me choice floral specimens until I all but threw the typewriter at her.

There is an afternoon performance at the P. of Wales tomorrow. I'll call at Adelphi Terrace afterwards if I dont hear from you to the contrary.

I'm quite giddy: another fifty years of this and I shall die of it. I nearly fled to you after lunch this evening; but I had sufficient grit left to pull myself together & deny myself that indulgence.

GBS

716

To MRS RICHARD MANSFIELD

[A/21; X/141.e]

29 Fitzroy Square W
8th January 1897

[Baron Chevrial, a character in *A Parisian Romance*, was one of Mansfield's most popular rôles; he performed it in his farewell appearance at the New Amsterdam Theatre, New York, on 23rd March 1907. Alberto Randegger (1832–1911), composer and conductor of the Carl Rosa Opera Company (1879–85) and the Norwich Musical Festival (1881–1905), was an intimate friend of Mansfield's mother, the opera singer Ermina Rudersdorff. Mansfield at the age of sixteen had sung one of Randegger's songs, "The Young Mountaineer," in his first stage appearance at a benefit in Swampscott, Mass., in 1873.]

My dear Mrs Mansfield

I have arrived at the end of the year with a frightful debt of correspondence against me. I cleared off all my arrears last Easter during my holiday. Since then I have broken down utterly. Every letter that could wait for a moment of happy leisure—and some that couldn't—has waited, and waited in vain. But then I have written much more than 100,000 words to everybody in the Saturday Review; and I've written two plays, not to mention various articles. At this moment I am simply beaten by three weeks continuous work—you can see it in my handwriting. I crawl to you for sympathy.

My last completed play (Op. 8) is called "The Devil's Disciple," and is just the play for America, as it occurs as an incident in the War of Independence. It is exactly the play for Richard—a splendid leading part, powerful life and death situations, any amount of singularity and individuality, simple enough for a village, and subtle enough for New York. Need I add that he is just the last person in the world to whom it would be of any use offering it? Besides the hero there is an older man—a Presbyterian minister of 50 who holds his own with the hero all through—and a very clever and effective part (General Burgoyne) in the last act. In both, the actors would make successes; and Richard would object to that. He couldn't play with an eyeglass, or a limp, or work in Chevrial or Cibber's Richard or Randegger or any of his pet nonsense. He couldn't be Richard Mansfield acting: he would have to be my man living. In short, he would have to be born over again; and though that may conceivably happen to him someday, just at present he would treat "The Devil's Disciple" exactly as he treated "Candida." Why don't you run away from him with somebody, just to give him a shock? I will send you a copy of "The D's D." someday, just to shew

717

you what I can do in melodrama. I can't do it just now because I have not time to work out the stage business so as to have the MS ready for the typist; but later on I hope to have a copy to send, unless you see it performed first, or let me read it to you on one of your visits.

"The D's D's" predecessor, "You Never Can Tell," is a four act comedy, and is *tout ce qu'il y a de plus* Shawesque. It requires a brilliant company—eight parts, all immense, the leading man a fine comedian. It is to follow the Red Robe at the Haymarket; and I have promised to keep the American rights unsold until after the production, both Frohmanns being in the field for it.

Irving is to produce "The Man of Destiny" in the course of this year. I have reserved the first turn in America for him with it up to the end of 99; but after that, though he can always play it when he wants to, his rights are not exclusive.

Give my respects to Richard. He wrote me a letter in August which created a sensation in the country house I was staying at, as it was so amusing that I read it aloud at breakfast. They all voted him the most original & interesting of geniuses. If only he had any conscience! Are there signs of the growth of one yet? It would be such a convenience for me.

yours sincerely
G. Bernard Shaw

To CHARLOTTE PAYNE-TOWNSHEND

29 Fitzroy Square W
9th January 1897

[B/2]

[Charlotte was spending a few days at Keyham Hall, Leicester, the home of her sister (the "infant"). Charles Hughes, an advocate of endowed theatres, had formed a Manchester branch of the Independent Theatre, with its own committee, to perform I.T. plays locally. Hughes was responsible for the Calvert-Achurch revival of *Antony and Cleopatra*.]

Thanks for the shawl. Far from recuperating, I contemplate Nature a shivering wreck. Imagine four hours [in a] train in such weather as this!

I withdraw my testimonial to the legibility of your handwriting. I will give a sovereign to anybody who can decipher that telegraph address. There is nothing even remotely like anything I can guess from it in the Postal Guide.

718

My address is c/o Charles Hughes. North Aspect. Kersal. Manchester.

I shudder when I think of your journey, and of the infant freezing in your first embrace.

Ugh! Let us make haste back again.

GBS

To CHARLOTTE PAYNE-TOWNSHEND

29 Fitzroy Square W
11th January 1897

[B/2]

Not a poodle, I implore you. If the instinct to have something to pet is uncontrollable, have (or hire) a baby, not a dog. I half expected to be received on my return with a letter announcing a prolongation of your visit; but this is more horrible than anything I could have imagined. To take a dog from a country house and pen it up at the top of a house in London, thereby condemning it to disease and everybody else to a life of preoccupation about taking the beast out, is positive imbecility, monstrosity, idiocy, wanton perversion & waste of life and feeling. I implore you, pause and reflect. If I am to have a rival, let him be at least human. Good God, what an idea! D O N ' T.

GBS

To ELLEN TERRY

29 Fitzroy Square W
11th January 1897

[U(B)/10; X/117]

[Ellen had recognised Shaw's handiwork in the Peterborough article. "If you didnt write that," she commented on the 9th, "you stood at 'Architect's' elbow. Anyhow his are my sentiments, but how comes it it's all put in a Shawesque manner?" Mansfield had included *Arms and the Man* in his repertory season at the Garden Theatre, New York, in November and December 1896, and Shaw had unexpectedly received about £93 in royalties.]

I forgot to say that I was not at "Architect's" elbow: he was at mine. Of course I wrote it (coached by Philip Webb); and you are the only person in London who has had the brains to find it out.

You are the only person in England, in the world, in the universe.

Oh, such piles of work—getting finally rid of that infernal article for

719

the political book (undertaken for money, before Mansfield rescued me from indigence), writing a review of "Borkman" (H. I. is irreclaimable) for the Academy, and the inevitable Saturday. A nice week. Promise to let me kiss just the tip of your little finger before Easter next year; and I will get through ten such weeks without a groan.

GBS

To JANET ACHURCH

29 Fitzroy Square W

[T.u/1 (B/4)]   11th January 1897

[Louis Calvert (1859–1923), son of the actress Mrs Charles Calvert, was a popular actor in London, the provinces, and the United States, who excelled in Shakespeare and costume drama. His greatest success, however, came when Shaw cast him as Broadbent in *John Bull's Other Island* (1904) and Undershaft in *Major Barbara* (1905) at the Court. *Antony and Cleopatra* was produced at the Queen's, Manchester, on 15th February, and later was transferred to the Olympic, London, on 24th May for a run of eleven performances.]

In frantic haste—just back from Manchester and up to my neck in work.

Hughes, who is a great pal of Calvert's, told me in dreadful secrecy that Calvert had offered you £20 and dresses. Take it: it is handsome under the circumstances (prices from 3d to 3/- only); and I think Calvert has a Shakespearean future in Manchester. Pose as a patriotic Manchester woman, full of enthusiasm for your cradle.

I have heard nothing from Hawtrey.

Helen [Kinnaird], late of Troy, now of Hyde Park Mansions, wants a play with an adventuress in it—will produce at a matinee with a view to subsequent exploitation if successful. I have smiled and assured her she is too nice for Mrs Warren. She objects, not to its morality, but to its vulgarity. Not at *all* stupid, isn't Helen.

To CHARLOTTE PAYNE-TOWNSHEND

29 Fitzroy Square W

[D/2]   15th January 1897

[Charrington lectured to the Fabian Society that evening on "A Municipal Theatre," opening with the observation that the only concern about theatres now shown by municipal authorities in England was to get people out of them.]

If you don't come to the Fabian, at the close of the meeting I shall go straight down to the Embankment and plunge into the flood. I can't go to the terrace to supper: the executive agenda is ten miles long, and the usual retirement to Gatti & Rodesano's [Restaurant] will be part of it—possibly the most important part, after this long interval. *Do* come to the meeting—think of Charrington's feelings if you don't hear his Municipal Theatre lecture. Besides, I forbore yesterday evening & the evening before on the distinct understanding that I should see you today. I have several things of the most pressing importance to say to you.

GBS

To CHARLOTTE PAYNE-TOWNSHEND

[B/2; X/151.e]

29 Fitzroy Square W
18th January 1897

[The pantomime was *Aladdin*, arranged by Oscar Barrett, at Drury Lane. In his notice on 23rd January Shaw called it "the best modern Christmas pantomime I have seen." William Albert Samuel Hewins (1865–1931), political economist, historian, and politician, was the first director (1895–1903) of the London School of Economics, founded by the Webbs with the financial assistance of the Hutchinson Trust and Miss Payne-Townshend.]

I have asked the Saturday people to get me tickets for the pantomime tomorrow—the matinée, which begins at 1.30. I have not received them yet; but possibly they will turn up in the morning.

There is a publishing committee on Wednesday. I will come afterwards and patronise Hewins.

I am delighted to hear that the neuralgia has gone. It lifts a weight of 90,000,000,000,000,000,000 tons from my heart.

GBS

To ELLEN TERRY

[U(A)/10; X/117]

29 Fitzroy Square W
27th January 1897

["I've lately met with the most extraordinary cases," Ellen wrote on 28th January, "showing the effects of the word according to Ibsen upon a young

family and their friends, and I hold converse now and again with you, but cant answer myself for you. I wish you would take more points of view."
The dates of Ellen's letter and Shaw's reply do not synchronise, indicating that one is misdated. Marie Corelli (1855–1924) was a popular novelist, whose most famous work, *The Sorrows of Satan*, in a dramatisation by Herbert Woodgate and Paul M. Berton, had been produced at the Shaftesbury on 9th January. William Morris's *Sigurd the Volsung* (1876) was an epic poem based on the Icelandic Volsunga Saga.]

No, I really can't write to you whenever I want to—how should I earn my living?

My nice flimsy bluish book that I got to write to you in is mislaid; so I have to use this vile thing. It's impossible to write in easy chairs & corners except in a book.

No: my knee isn't really bad: only it won't work properly. The bit of cartilage will presently get absorbed, or tumble out of the way, and then I shall be all right.

In this world you must know *all* the points of view, and take One, and stick to it. In taking your side, don't trouble about its being the right side—north is no righter or wronger than south—but be sure that it is really yours, and then back it for all you are worth. And never stagnate. Life is a constant becoming: all stages lead to the beginning of others. The Lyceum business, on its present plane, cannot be carried any further than it has been carried: consequently we have now reached *a beginning*. H.I. may think that he is free to abandon the drama to Wilson Barrett & Marie Corelli; but he isn't. The theatre is my battering ram as much as the platform or the press; and that is why I want to drag it to the front. My capers are part of a bigger design than you think: Shakspere, for instance, is to me one of the towers of the Bastille, and down he must come. Never mind your young families: omelettes are not made without breaking eggs; and I *hate* families.

Did you ever read Morris's "Sigurd the Volsung"? If so, do you remember Regin the dwarf, who taught the people all the arts and lived on and on, the new generations not knowing that he had taught anything, and ascribing all his work to Bragi & the rest of the gods. Well, what I say today, everybody will say tomorrow, though they will not remember who put it into their heads. Indeed, they will be right; for I never remember who puts the things into *my* head—it is the Zeitgeist. So I will give H.I. a bronze bracelet with this inscription:—

"It is not for your silver bright
But for your leading lady."

Your reproaches are undeserved: I have not been unfaithful to you. But I am like the madman in "Peer Gynt" who thought himself a pen and wanted someone to write with him. I want to be *used*, since use is life. You had no use for me except to write to you & be written to. Well, I wrote, and read. That was wise of you. But the green eyed one was also wise in her way—the way that was your way when you were at her stage of the journey. She used me too, and so far widened my life. I am not for all hands to wield; so I do not throw away my chances. You say you do not compete: well, you need not. *I* do not compete with all the men you love (more or less—I am convinced that with you a human relation is love or nothing): there I am, not possibly to be confused with any of them, and ten times better realised because of the knowledge you have gained from them than if you knew nobody but me. Just so are you not injured by the filling-up with Emeralds (schöne grüne Augen) of that castle of my life which you left unfilled.

This philosophy rather appalls the Green Eyed One with a sense of having no hold on me.

It is hard upon six; and I must fly to the post. If K. [Kate Gurly] takes the letters, she will improve the occasion at the public house. She goes anon to the west of Ireland.

For today, adieu, ever most dearestly adoredest.

GBS

To CHARLOTTE PAYNE-TOWNSHEND

29 Fitzroy Square W

[B/2; X/151.e]   28th January 1897

[The seats for the revival of *Olivia* were sent by Ellen Terry. Charlotte, however, declined to attend. In his notice of *Olivia* in the *Saturday Review* on 6th February, Shaw referred obliquely to Charlotte as "a modern lady who, when I mentioned the play the other day, dismissed it with entire conviction as 'beneath contempt' . . ." The reading was at the home of the artist Henry Marriott Paget (1856–1936), brother-in-law of Florence Farr.]

I have 2 stalls for the Lyceum on Saturday (first night of "Olivia") on condition that *we*—you and I and nobody else—use them. Can you come? If not, let me know as soon as possible. But I decline to entertain the idea of your not coming.

I have undertaken to read "The Devil's Disciple" to certain people, including York Powell, on Sunday evening; so don't reserve it for me—any three or four others will do instead.

GBS

To ALMA MURRAY

[B/1; X/109]

29 Fitzroy Square W
1st February 1897

[Except for a brief appearance as Rosalind in a revival of *As You Like It* at Camberwell in 1897, Alma Murray had been absent from the stage since 1894.]

My dear Mrs Forman

I thought of you when I was racking my brains to cast that play; but there is a leading lady—Miss Emery—in possession at the Haymarket; and she has seized on the only really pretty part. There is a sister to that part; but I cannot quite fit you into it. And the two have a mother, whose part will take a good deal of quiet acting; but she *must* be 43 at least. And that's all.

I assure you I need no reminder in your case. Whenever we get a drama that requires acting it will not be easy to do without you. At present they want *duffers*—and get them.

yrs sincerely
G. Bernard Shaw

To C. LEWIS HIND

[A/1]

29 Fitzroy Square W
3rd February 1897

My dear Hind

When you demanded that Ibsen review I purposely refrained from mentioning my terms, because I guessed that you could not very well run the Academy on the opulent basis of the more popular papers. Will you therefore treat the review as a friendly contribution. You may think that it would be friendlier still of me to pocket the cheque and say nothing; but a moment's reflection will convince you that if a man once refuses to take what's going, and demands special terms, he must go through with it. For some years past I have insisted on a minimum of £5 for merely dipping my pen in the ink, contributions of any length to be computed at £3 per thousand words. When it doesn't run to this I get out of the difficulty—if I have special reasons for writing—by doing the job for nothing. This is perhaps a worse sort of blacklegging than lowering my terms; but I only do it under peculiar circumstances.

724

I am loth to appear in the character of the cabman holding out his shilling with "Wot's this?" on his tongue, & scorn in his eye; but you will understand that I foresaw the contingency and so have no grievance.

yours sincerely
G. Bernard Shaw

To CHARLOTTE PAYNE-TOWNSHEND

[B/2]

29 Fitzroy Square W
4th February 1897

If tomorrow is at all a reasonable day I shall go to the [Royal] Academy at 12 or thereabouts unless I hear from you to the contrary.

Kate is safe in Galway. She departed in a state of unparralleled inclination—indeed she did not depart, but was sent off like a parcel.

Miss Hood's woman won't do: a letter from her today, enclosing a photograph, settles the question. She demands treatment as an equal and use of piano. To this there is no objection; but to what it implies—that is, sitting with my mother and talking to her—there is every objection. Our servant is welcome to the most honorable construction that the haughtiest civil servant could demand; but she must be a servant and not a person exchanging domestic assistance for society and a place in a family. The rest when we meet. I shall wait until 11.30 tomorrow for a message. If it does not come, I shall go to the Academy.

GBS

To ROBERT BLATCHFORD

[X/146]

[29 Fitzroy Square W]
[c. 7th February 1897]

[Blatchford, editor of *The Clarion*, had published an article on *John Gabriel Borkman* on 30th January. Shaw's criticism of it was published on 13th February, together with a rebuttal by Blatchford, which necessitated a second letter from Shaw, published on the 20th, in which he commented: "You have taken me aback slightly by publishing my letter, which would have been more considerately worded had I intended it for the general eye." Edward Francis Fay (1853-96), a widely known and loved writer for *The Clarion*, under the pseudonym "The Bounder," had died on 25th October.

725

John Austin (1790–1859), professor of jurisprudence at London University (1826–32), was the author of *Province of Jurisprudence Determined* (1832).]

My dear Nunquam

Thanks for sending me the article; but I have read it all before, in the *Standard*, the *Referee*, the *Illustrated Sporting and Dramatic News*, the *Hawk*, the *Queen*, the *Gentlewoman*, and a dozen other papers. Just look at pages 89–92 of my "Quintessence of Ibsenism," and you will see the company you keep. I shall add the *Clarion* to the list in the next edition if you wish.

When you tell me what you believe in, you produce no effect on me, because I know better than you what your real beliefs are. You say you believe in the sincerity (in the sense of truthfulness) of friendship. You don't: your article on Fay was an act of friendship, and it was a lie from beginning to end. You never told Fay what you thought of him, because he could not have borne it any more than Foldal or Borkman could bear the same revelation. If you met a woman strong minded enough to have learnt from experience the transience of physical affection, and to prepare for its evaporation whilst recognising the necessity of such affection to herself and others, you would be forced to recognise her superiority; and if you met the original of Shakespeare's merciless picture of Ophelia, you would despise her as a puppet with her father and brother, a liar with her sweetheart, and a creature with nothing in her head for madness to let out but a thoroughly unwholesome imagination, the result of suppressed sex passion, commonly called "purity."

You will never be worth your salt as a reviewer of high-class literature until you learn to face the world without imposing your trumpery little moral system on it. As long as you can say that you believe in the sincerity of friendship, you don't believe in friendship, but in sincerity. What you call a good woman is not a real woman, but a woman with certain moral qualities; your ideal friend is that by-word "the candid friend." In both cases you put the moral condition before the actual living reality; and what is the result? (1) That you are compelled to describe your fellow-creatures as "fools, knaves, weakling cranks, freaks, and wrecks" when you meet them in fiction, and, when you meet them in real life, to lie about them as you lied about Fay, and would lie again to-morrow about any other man or woman in the movement in order to square them with your notions of how your friends should be proved "good." (2) Speaking to the young men who swear by the *Clarion*, you call the greatest living master in your own calling "a weak, puerile bungler, uttering new and nasty smartnesses,

726

which would be discreditable to an amateur dramatist in his first attempt at a play." You could be forgiven more easily for any other folly than this. If you made it a reproach to Ibsen that he began life in an apothecary's shop, that he was for years desperately poor and shabby, or that his dramas are not patronised by the Prince of Wales, you might still, if these points were conceded to you, write like a man on the rest of the subject. But you only object to the claims of rank and wealth because they conflict with the claims of the morality on which you base your own orders of merit. You insist on political equality only to bring into greater relief the most odious of all inequalities, those based on goodness, purity, honesty, truth, sincerity, and the rest of your inhuman ideals. Our abominable criminal system, our abominable cult of virtuous indignation, our abominable home system in which the dwellinghouse is a petty prison and the parent a petty judge and private executioner, are all built out of your ideals. At best, they may help people to think wrongly in an elementary way on moral questions just as an abacus in an infant school may help children to add and subtract rightly; but you cannot review poetry and philosophy of the first class with a little frame of red and blue ideals.

Until you understand this, you will not have changed your mind about society in the least. You discovered, when you came to look into the world's affairs, that the present industrial system involves the robbery and ill-treatment of the workers; and as you had always been against robbery and ill-treatment, you turned against our industrial system. But you will find, if you study such works as Austin's Jurisprudence, that it is quite possible for a man to know perfectly well that our system involves the most frightful hardships and inequities, and yet not only support it on sincere humanitarian grounds, but be convinced—*reasonably* convinced, mind—that a revolt against it is the result of incomplete intellectual mastery of it—in short, of half knowledge. I have no hesitation in saying that if you carry your intellectual training and study of politics and economics to Austin's point you will, on your present moral basis, arrive at exactly his conclusions. You are only a Socialist because you think individualism is immoral; and you have jumped at that conclusion because you have never taken the trouble to master the case for Unsocialism and inhumanity. For whatever else they may be, they are not immoral; whereas Socialism is as immoral as Ibsen's plays.

You will not mind my talking back to you thus freely. I claim such authority to speak on the subject as a man may derive from years of

hard labour at the criticism of art works of the highest class. The
difficulty of the subject also prevents me from being as easy in my tone
as one usually is in a letter to a friend; but you will understand that I
have to do this job in too great a hurry to do it *nicely*. In haste,

yours sincerely
G.Bernard Shaw

To ELLEN TERRY

[X/117]

[29 Fitzroy Square W]
[Undated: assigned to 1st March 1897]

[The letter is incomplete. Lionel Mackinder (1869–1915) was a young
actor who, until this time, had appeared mostly in revues and light opera.
He was killed in action, in France. Ellen had written on 28th February,
enclosing a "queer letter" from a man in ill-health soliciting £10. Ellen had
a cottage, which she had offered to Shaw for a vacation, at Winchelsea, a
short distance from Henry James's Lamb House at Rye.]

. . . Mackinder for Phil, with, of course, Maude for the waiter and
Winifred Emery for Dolly. I daresay it will be all "werry capital"; but
though I shall do all I can at the rehearsals, I feel at present as if
nothing could induce me to witness the performance.

Your letter has just come. Of course you know my advice beforehand
—DONT. The gentleman is not slimy like the usual begging letter
writer: his frank opening "I wish you would lend ("*lend*" mark you!)
me £10" is so good that I am half disposed to advise you to send him
five shillings as a tribute to his cheek, and tell him why. But he betrays
himself later on. There is no mistaking the approach of death and the
longing for it, followed by "I Trust God I shall yet live to &c. &c."
And the clergyman's letter, and the want of food and so on! No, dear
Ellen: if you want to spend £10, get ten sovereigns and skid them out
from the beach into the sea: they will do no harm then, and they will
twinkle prettily in the sun if you make them ricochet successfully. Or
if you want to "do good" with them, send them to one of the heaps of
people who are disinterestedly in that business, and know how to do it.
But *never* give it to a beggar, especially a beggar who begs well (practice
being the secret of excellence in that as in other departments of acting).
You need have no remorse in this instance: the gentleman's cant is
unmistakable: he wont starve and he wont die; and I dont mind
wagering that he wont work either. As to his sanity, I guarantee it.

728

You cant even answer him, because if you lecture him, you must send him the money to shew that you are not taking a moral attitude to save your own pocket; if you write kindly, your sympathy is mere hypocrisy without the money; if you write "Dear Sir—No—yours truly, Ellen Terry," which would be quite proper, you will hardly feel that to be an improvement on silence. The waste paper basket is the proper place for all such appeals.

Winchelsea is too far off; and I swear I will never go there as I have gone to Barkston Gardens, only when you are away. You are the most utterly heartless wretch I have ever met.

What birthday did you say? 59th was it?

GBS

To ELLEN TERRY

[U(A)/10; X/117]

29 Fitzroy Square W
3rd March 1897

[Ellen was vacationing at Margate, studying *Madame Sans-Gêne*. Shaw had sent a typescript of *The Devil's Disciple* to her Margate address, 1 Paragon. Charlotte Payne-Townshend and the Webbs had secured a cottage at Dorking (which Shaw in several letters confused with Woking) in Surrey, for the quarter from April to June.]

Ellen: are you quite sure that you're not very ill? You should have got that play a couple of days ago: is it possible that you have been unable to—ah! I have it! Million million millions! There's no such address as 1 Paragon, and you trusted to the Post Office finding you out eventually, whilst you remained secure from my—but suppose you should really be ill. Why should I get suddenly anxious? A thousand things come into my head: your handwriting has not been steady: the wind has gone to the north and is now a dreadful March wind: you are alone in that bleak corner of the coast without anybody to smother you in sympathetic nursing.

I can't write. I am full of vague apprehensions—at least I should be if I ate meat or drank tea or did any of the usual foolish things (except loving you). The odd thing about being a vegetarian is, not that the things that happen to other people don't happen to me—they all do— but that they happen differently: pain is different, pleasure different, fever different, cold different, even love different.

Dont worry about Sans Gêne: let it be put off: Richard III will draw enough to pay forfeits until you are well.

729

I cannot think that March is quite the best—but I am talking like an old woman. Of course the sea air is good for *you*, always. Miss P.T. has secured the house at Woking: that would be the place for you, I feel sure. Wonder how Mrs Webb would like it!

Stupid and impatient that I am, why was I in such a hurry to know you? If only I had waited I should have been a fresh interest for you now. Whereas by this you are quite tired of my letters. The only possibility of novelty in me now is to talk to me. Is there really and truly such a place as 1 Paragon in Margate?

Dearest & beautifullest: do write & pretend that you're quite well.

GBS

To ELLEN TERRY

[U(A)/10; X/117]

29 Fitzroy Square W
5th March 1897

[Ellen had informed Shaw that Henry Irving was coming down to Margate to visit her.]

Oh indeed! *He's* going down on Sunday, is he? Well, of course there's no reason why he shouldn't if you are well enough to receive him, even though you are not well enough to read my play. Why should I object? It's nothing to me, is it? Oh dear me, no: I assure you you are quite mistaken if you think *I* care. I am not that sort of person—quite the opposite, as you would know if you understood my real nature. I trust he will enjoy himself. Poor fellow, he looks as if some sea air would do him good: it's only to be expected at his age.

Of course that nurse tries to prevent you from writing to me. All these nurses have begun by being advanced young women and going to hear me lecture. Jealousy—simple jealousy and nothing else. She will burn that play if you are not careful, and perhaps intercept my letters as soon as she finds out which is my handwriting. Do you think I would send you the play if it would not do you good. Read it at once: it has a nice happy ending, and a breath of my heart's affection for you is imprisoned between every pair of leaves. Or stay—no—keep it until Sunday; and get Henry to read it to you; and then you can tell me which part suits him best.

I have simply stopped working, except for the inevitable Saturday article. I have been clearing up my table—*such* a job—two long days'

730

work; but the green cloth has been reached at last. Even my bedroom table is clear. Whilst I am dressing & undressing I do all my reading. The book lies open on the table. I never shut it, but put the next book on top of it long before it's finished. After some months there is a mountain of buried books, all wide open; so that all my library is distinguished by a page with the stain of a quarter's dust & soot on it. The blacks are dreadful; for my window is always wide open, winter and summer. This work of cleaning up rests my mind, tires my back, & begrimes my face and hands. And now I begin to recuperate like mad. A few days ago I met Florence Farr. She was horrified; said I looked my age; pointed out that my moustache and two great tufts of my beard were grey. Today they are bright scarlet: a keen sap of mischievous energy rises through all my capillaries: in a day or two more I shall be 29 again. This must be also coming to you: the air from which I can extract middle aged vigor must be full of flowering youth for you. I no longer believe that you are ill: I can hear a distant noise like wind in the ferns, which must be stirring of your pores as they open and straighten to take in the first delicate draught of spring. Oh, if I were in Margate, I would squeeze them all shut again with one mighty embrace.

My mother calls to remind me that I have promised to post her letters in time. Yours too must go, with a radiating aurora of love for my Ellenest Ellen.

GBS

To ELLEN TERRY

29 Fitzroy Square W

[A/1; X/117]   7th March 1897

[The "remarkable infant" was Gordon Craig's eldest child, Rosemary, whose photos Ellen had sent. Duse had appeared in an Italian translation of *Camille* at the Lyric Theatre on 24th May 1893. Marion Terry (1853–1930) was a sister of Kate (mother of John Gielgud), Ellen, Florence, George, Charles, and Fred Terry—one of the most celebrated theatrical families on record. Marion, who had also appeared with Irving (notably as Margaret to his Faust in 1888), played leads in *Guy Domville*, *Lady Windermere's Fan*, *Michael and His Lost Angel*, and Barrie's *Quality Street* (1902).]

Bless me! that's a very remarkable infant. Just look at the energetic expression of her feet in the reading one and the "Kill Claudio" one.

The reading one is very good: it shews the character in its initiative, aggressive, wilful aspect; but the one with the cap on, dressed for walking, is equally interesting, as it shews the *social* side of her—the receptive, sensitive, endearing side. Only, they should not smother her up like that in a stiff extinguisher of stuff an inch thick, with fur round her throat. They will make her "a delicate child" in no time at that rate. Let her neck alone & give her lissome clothes (all wool) so that she can use her spine & not go propping that extinguisher on her ankles with her spine & ribs held like an open umbrella. And teach her to hate and forswear fur for the nasty smelling, savage, cruel, thoughtless, bestial thing it is.

I observe that she has plenty of room between her eyes (shewing amiability & brains & character); that she is very unmistakeably her grandmother's granddaughter (would you really say granddaughter on the stage?—Henry would, most conscientiously—or gran'daughter?); that she has great nervous energy & sensibility; that she has splendid *working*, *living* hands & feet, and not silly little ornaments; that she is much older and wiser than her father, and will probably spoil you as you spoiled him; and that she will be strong enough to make it impossible for anyone to hang her keys on her nose, in spite of a certain Terry tendency in this direction which has very nearly got the better of her gran'aunt Marion. And to think that this fellow-infant of mine will never know me except as "an old gentleman" named *Mister* Shaw! And will speak of you as "Granny" to future generations! What tragic lines that pet impostor of yours, William Shakespere, could have written on this profoundly foolish theme!

Does H.I. really say that you are in love with me? For that be all his sins forgiven him! I will go to the Lyceum again & write an article proving him to be the greatest Richard ever dreamed of. I am also touched by his refusing to believe that we have never met. No man of feeling *could* believe such heartlessness.

I did not see the paragraph you mention; but I saw another describing how you rushed on the stage after seeing Duse act Camille, & fell weeping into her arms. And yet you read my plays—much greater achievements than Duse's—and you do not rush to me and fall weeping into *my* arms. Well, no matter, since you are well again. Sleep soundly, since when you lay awake you thought of everything & everybody before me—oh, I have noted the order very feelingly. No room for more.

GBS

To ELLEN TERRY

[U(A)/10; X/117.e]

29 Fitzroy Square W
8th March 1897

[Shaw gave an outdoor lecture on "The Use of Political Power" at the East India dock gates on the 14th, sponsored by the Poplar Labour League.]

Just time for three lines. Get anyone but me to read that play to you *if you dare*. What do they know about it? I don't believe all the brutal environment of that little story is real to you; but it is to me. Ted isn't brutal enough for Richard's outbursts of savagery. "Candida"— a play which you've forgotten, but which you once read—has the part for him. The woman's part is not so difficult where she has anything to say; but the listening to the court martial—the holding on to the horror through all the laughing—that will be the difficulty. No: I wont rewrite that last act unless you tell me exactly how: I'd rather write you another play.

Mrs Webb & Miss P. T. want to know whether you would really come to Woking, and, if so, whom you'd like to have to meet you—a bishop or a politician or a philosopher. I can be sent up to town if necessary (I fancy I see myself going—*just*). They want to watch our embarrassment when we meet.

I am in a ridiculous difficulty with Miss P. T. She insists on coming to my lectures on Sundays in all sorts of holes & corners—dock gates next Sunday morning. I have noticed that these experiences make her very unhappy. At first I thought she was bored and tired and incommoded simply; but now it appears that my demagogic denunciations of the idle rich—my demands for taxation of unearned incomes— lacerate her conscience; for she has great possessions. What am I to do: she won't stay away; and I can't talk Primrose League. Was there ever such a situation?

What ought I to do with that play? That is, if Forbes won't have it?

Take care of your reviving strength. I presumed on mine the other evening to ride eight or nine miles at wild speed on the bike; and the next morning I was again a wreck.

Post hour—ever dearest—

GBS

733

29 Fitzroy Square W
13th March 1897

[U(A)/10; X/117]

["H.I. did not 'demand' the knighting for *himself*," Ellen wrote that morning. "But he resented the followers of his calling being left out in the cold." Irving, in his Royal Institution speech on 1st February 1895, had begun by putting forward "a formal claim to have acting classified *officially* among the fine arts," and thus had, in effect, demanded that he, as leading actor of the British stage, should be knighted. Shaw devoted an entire article, "Why Not Sir Henry Irving?" (*Saturday Review*, 9th February 1895), to the lecture and its significance; "let me plead against any envious and base-minded view of this claim," he wrote. "Mr. Irving is entitled to an entirely honourable construction: we owe him an unhesitating assumption that his jealousy is for the dignity of his art and not of himself . . ."

Sir Frederick Leighton (1830–96), later Baron Leighton of Stretton, a classical painter whose strength lay in his sense of design and feeling for rhythm, which he shared with Watts, was for many years president of the Royal Academy. In his article "Madox Brown, Watts, and Ibsen" (*Saturday Review*, 13th March 1897), Shaw had likened the younger actor-managers, the "knights expectant," to Leighton, and Irving to the painter and sculptor George Frederick Watts (1817–1904), who had been Ellen Terry's first husband.

" 'Gentleman!' Oh that word!" Ellen had exclaimed in her letter. "SOME DAY define the term . . . To *me* 'Gentleman' has always meant the highest and best."]

She explains to me about the knighthood—to ME! Do you know, oh woman of little faith, that when H.I. formulated his demand at the Royal Institution, it was I, and nobody else, who understood and appreciated his position, and explained it to London when everyone else was either toadying or sneering.

And so you don't know what a gentleman is. Oh my third act, my third act! Ellen: Burgoyne is a gentleman; and that is the whole meaning of that part of the play. It is not enough, for the instruction of this generation, that Richard should be superior to religion & morality as typified by his mother and his home, or to love as typified by Judith. He must also be superior to gentility—that is, to the whole ideal of modern society. Leighton's plan was to give an elegant air to life, to soften and beautify what could be softened and beautified by fine art and fine manners, to help the deserving but not quite successful subjects by a little pretence, and to ignore all the horrors. Burgoyne pleads all through for softening and easing the trial by reciprocal politeness and

734

consideration between all the parties, and for ignoring the villainy of his gallows, the unworthiness of his cause, and the murderousness of his profession. The picture is completed by the band playing Handel's music, and the Christian clergyman reading the Bible to give the strangling an air of being an impressive ceremony. Oh, *can't* I make you understand, you who are a woman *in excelsis*, and—here! listen to this.

My dear Miss Terry, to me "LADY" has always meant the highest and best. As the most perfect lady in England, you must ever command my respect and devotion.

That sounds nice and cordial, doesn't it? How am I to make you fully conscious of yourself? You wouldn't let Leighton paint your portrait. Why not, if a gentleman is the highest and the best? Surely Leighton would have made a perfectly gentlemanly picture of you. Watts was—*is*—an idealist of the finest as well as a gentleman and artist. Well, why did he not hold you? Bless your dearest eyes, my secret is that I learn from what you *do*, knowing that that is the reality of you. The dear silly old fashioned things that *you think you think*: at these I laugh, though never at you.

Why do I worry you about these things? Well, what else can I do for you? Others have wakened your love: *that* wouldn't interest you. Beauty, success, lovely ways that enable you to play with men and women as Sarasate plays with a violin: all that you have gone through. My only chance is to awaken your wisdom, which is still asleep, and so stops at the end of my second acts. But indeed I think I shall die lonely, as far as my third acts are concerned.

I was perfectly serious about Woking. They—Mrs Webb & Miss P.T.—discussed the idea a whole Sunday afternoon. I never deceived you about that or anything else; and I never laugh at anybody (this is the holy-serious truth). But Mrs Webb has insisted on the lady at Woking leaving out 12 teacups instead of 6; and she, terrified at the notion of much company, is trying to back out of her bargain. I think, however, she has gone too far for that. If you come, bring 4 copies of Sans Gêne besides your own, and we'll get up rehearsals for you. We can all act better than the Lyceum company.

I see that my watch has stopped, and that I have lost the post. If it does not rain I will bike to Barkston Gardens & drop this into the letter box; and tomorrow you will see on your doorstep a red stain wrung from my heart by the longing to go in—like Peer Gynt at the end.

I have also to go to the Haymarket to see the scene models for that wretched comedy.

In the morning to the Dock Gates, to harangue the *flaneurs* of that region until the public houses open.

On Monday to Manchester to see Janet's Cleopatra. *She* will let me see her off the stage.

I am being pressed to publish my plays. I think I will, and give up troubling the theatre. I only took to it to get closer to somebody; and she is the one person who will not endure my presence. Serve me right!

GBS

To CHARLOTTE PAYNE-TOWNSHEND

[A/2]

29 Fitzroy Square W
15th March 1897

[Shaw apparently departed for Manchester the very next day, for his notice of *Antony and Cleopatra* appeared in the *Saturday Review* on the 20th.]

I am certainly the most unfortunate of men. Neither Janet nor Hughes nor any of the Manchester people have written to me; and now you suddenly descend on me with the eminently cheerful proposal that I shall travel down to Manchester with you and then rush off to all these people and do my business with a pleasant consciousness that you are wandering about the streets by yourself, or reading the timetables in a hotel, or, more likely, drowning in the Irwell. It is the last straw: I won't go. I was prepared to set my teeth and make that cursed journey as a matter of business, partly to see "Antony," partly to discuss with Janet the possibility of a combination with [Forbes-] Robertson for Manchester, or any other opening of the kind, concerning the "Devil's Disciple." Now I am not only left in uncertainty as to whether she has received my letter (she is quite likely to have changed her lodgings) or not, but all my plans for doing all I want to do—interviewing Janet & Calvert & Hughes—perhaps putting up for the night with Hughes at Kersal—between the fall of the curtain & the 10 o'clock up train next morning are ruthlessly shattered by your sudden charge into the heart of the position. Of course you solve the difficulty by the usual proposal to part at the church door, so to speak. The exasperation of having *that* offered is all that is needed to whiten my hair. The devil take Manchester and Antony and Shakespere and the whole institution of sex!

My expedition being thus shattered, defeated, wrecked, I am left with three alternatives. One, to abandon Manchester altogether, which would, however, be a sacrifice of my business to my fury. The second, to go down tomorrow by the 10.10 from Euston, if I can rouse the local forces by—Now triple D A M N A T I O N ! here is a telegram from this idiot of a woman "When do you come down?" Reply paid. I shall reply "Never, by God!" I suppose, then, she *hasn't* got my letter. And she gives no address. Have women *any* brains? Million million millions!!!

I know what I'll do. I'll go down on Saturday if Hughes will put me up from Saturday to Monday. Then there will be time to confer with everybody on Sunday; and I shall have two nights abroad. There! *that's* settled. I shall now proceed to indite letters to Manchester which will cause the inhabitants of that region to creep into the smallest mouseholes, and hide there for six hours at least.

Now are you satisfied with the utter devastation you have wrought? I break off to *scream* with rage.

GBS

[Postscript on back of envelope] I shall sit at the feet of Hewins this evening as usual. GBS

To ELLEN TERRY

[U(B)/10; X/117]

29 Fitzroy Square W
after the play—25th March 1897

[Both Shaw and Ellen had attended the opening of Henry Arthur Jones's *The Physician* at the Criterion Theatre.]

Dearest and Everest—I could not go any nearer to you tonight (even if you had wanted me to—say that you did—oh say, say, say, say that you did) because I could not have looked at you or spoken to you otherwise than as I felt; and you would not have liked that in such a host of imperfectly sanctified eyes and ears. I was on the point, once or twice, of getting up and asking them all to go out for a few moments whilst I touched your hand for the first time.

I *saw* the play—oh yes, every stroke of it. There was no need to look at you: I felt your presence straining my heart all through.

Think of that, dear Ellen, even when you had that wicked, cruel, Indian-savageous, ugly, ridiculous plumage in your blessed hair to warn me that you have no heart. Ah, if only—well, nonsense! Good night, good night: I am a fool.

GBS

To MRS RICHARD MANSFIELD

[A/21; X/141.e]

29 Fitzroy Square W
26th March 1897

[Charles F. Coghlan (1838?–99), actor and dramatist, had played opposite
Ellen Terry in Bulwer-Lytton's *The Lady of Lyons* (1875), and was leading
man to Mrs Langtry for several years. He also achieved considerable success
in the United States, which he toured on at least three occasions.]

My dear Mrs Mansfield

I have neither answered your last letter nor sent you the play; but
I have sent it to Richard, or rather the irrepressible Felix has.

I am somewhat remorseful for abusing Richard to you; but what is
one to do? It would take a steam hammer to forge him into the proper
shape for carrying out his own purposes. You think I haven't seen him;
but I have, both on the stage and off. I know him perfectly well; and
as I should like to see him do all that he is artistically capable of—I hate
the eternal *waste* of power that goes on in our theatrical system—I shall
continue to heap all manner of taunts and insults on him until he begins
to take himself and his business quite seriously. At present a feather
will turn him aside from anything he undertakes: he will stop to fight
a schoolboy on his way to Pharsalia or Waterloo. He sends Felix to bid
for fashionable put-up plays that are of no more use to him than a silk
hat is to Coriolanus, or to propose adaptations, by men who have never
written a line for the stage, of books which he hasn't read, but the titles
of which have struck his imagination. Every such whim leaves him
three or four enemies here. Add to these the constant stream of actors
& acting-managers who have been with him—all with the same stories
about him, not altogether malicious (they don't usually dislike him), but
with the same moral in every case—that he is an interesting man who is
not to be depended on for five consecutive minutes. In England
especially he has no chance against the dull men who are to be depended on. In short, he is a spoiled child; and as he is *your* spoiled child,
you are the proper person to abuse him to.

As you say, I have no faith in anything or anybody. I am savage
about "Candida" because it was Richard's business to have made a
good deal out of that play and out of Miss Achurch, instead of letting
her make a good deal out of him, giving him nothing for it, and having a
grievance against him into the bargain. It was a mere matter of management, including the management of *me*. He should never let himself be
associated with a break down of any kind. He should establish himself
as the maker of success—other people's success; the founder of

738

reputations—other people's reputations; the Bank of England of the whole profession. Then he wont have to fight his way to the centre: he will *be* the centre. But he doesn't see this: he thinks that anybody can manage but that only a genius can act; whereas the truth is that anybody can act, but that only an able man can manage.

By the way, if Coghlan is in America he ought to play Burgoyne. I mustn't begin another sheet. How do you like the play?

yrs sincerely
G. Bernard Shaw

To CHARLOTTE PAYNE-TOWNSHEND

[A/2]

29 Fitzroy Square W
27th March 1897

Ten thousand million devils! I have made a horrible mistake: the accursed sons of hell have sent me the second ticket for *Tuesday* night. It has only just flashed on me that they had played me this dog's trick, and on looking at the miserable thing I find it is only too hideously true. Oh, if I only knew some person subject to homicidal mania: he (or she) should have that ticket.

However, if I stop to curse, you may upset all your Monday arrangements for nothing. I am too furious to be sorry, yet. I hope the performance will be a bad one, and the play [Pinero's *The Princess and the Butterfly*, at the St James's Theatre] worse; for then—*then*—THEN—THEN we shall see whose God is the Lord.

Will you go on Tuesday?

DAMN!

GBS

To GRANT RICHARDS

[B/4; X/135]

29 Fitzroy Square W
27th March 1897

[Richards published a new edition of *Cashel Byron's Profession*, with minor revisions, in 1901, the volume also including Shaw's dramatisation of the novel, under the title *The Admirable Bashville*, and "A Note on Modern Prizefighting."]

It is my private belief that half the bookselling trade in London consists in the sale of unauthorized Cashel Byrons. However, I presume Scott has some copies of his stock left. I shall ask him how many presently.

I suppose the thing may as well be republished. I read the copy you sent me. The comedy in it amused me; but the fundamental folly of the thing sickened me.

I'll bring round "The Philanderer" on Monday. I wish we could get six plays in one volume. I propose to call the issue "Plays, Pleasant & Unpleasant." Vol. I. Unpleasant, 3/6, Vol. II, Pleasant 5/-. Both together, half a crown. If we could get all six into one volume, I should have the unpleasant ones printed on light brown paper (Egyptian mummy color) in an ugly style of printing, and the pleasant ones on white paper (machine hand made) in the best Kelmscott style. Nobody has ever done a piebald volume before; and the thing would make a sensation.

G. Bernard Shaw

To ELLEN TERRY

[U(A).u/10; X/117]

29 Fitzroy Square W
9th April 1897

[The New Century Theatre was a private subscription society, founded by Elizabeth Robins, William Archer, H. W. Massingham, and Alfred Sutro, which was patterned after the Independent Theatre. Its first production was *John Gabriel Borkman*, at the Strand Theatre on 3rd May.]

Oh Ellen, dear Ellen, give up that unimportant Sans Gêne and come and pet me, console me, tell me you have loved me at odd moments. I have been working sixteen hours a day at work that nobody should ever touch after lunch, and the sight of somebody more exhausted than yourself will do you good. I had to read "You Never Can Tell" to the Haymarket company today—two hours and forty minutes—it's too long: I shall have to spoil it to suit the fashionable dinner hour. Oh, there's been no end of work about everything, from breakfast to three next morning, and not a word—not a look from Ellen. And I shall have to swear that there was never anything so enchanting as her Sans Gêne, and that those who have only seen Rejane little know &c. &c. &c. &c,

and that Sardou is this that and the other, whilst all the time I am as sore as a beaten carpet, and never want to enter a theatre again, and don't want you to act in any plays but mine—don't want you to act at all—want you to come and hide with me somewhere and nurse me back into full life and villainy again.

And you—you think you have a terrible business in hand when it might as well be Penelope in "The Area Belle" (I love Penelope: Penelope is loved by me) or Nance Oldfield, for any trouble it will give you. You'll do it on your head, and on my heart.

They haven't invited me this time [to the opening of *Madame Sans-Gêne* on 10th April]—"Miss Terry's strict orders, and Mr Bunnard Shorr was not to be admitted"—but I'll set the Saturday Review at them tomorrow and extort my seat by the majesty of the press. Or if you don't want me to be there I'll go away to the country if you'll come too. There must be an understudy available. I am growing impatient of the stage: it keeps a row of footlights between us.

Have you seen the prospectus of the New Century Theatre? You will see about it in the Saturday—but I forgot: you have given up reading it, fickle, faithless wretch that you are: I have only asked you for five minutes of your regard and you've cut me off with three. I am going to hit out with my usual treachery at this folly of collecting money for our Janets & Elizabeths to give matinees with and calling that the New Drama. We must get up a big subscription and make H.I. give a certain number of performances for it, or, if he won't, George Alexander.

Don't tell me you're tired: you are not half so tired as I am, nor so lonely nor so sore. *Don't* go to the Lyceum: stay at home and write to me: what does a first night matter? What is their silly curiosity to my heart's need?

No: I shall only bore you. Success attend you, heaped up and overflowing, whatever you play, whatever you do. You may chop off all my fingers and toes for a necklace, and have my heart as a locket if you will only say that you like them better than diamonds.

To ELLEN TERRY

[U(B)/10; X/117]

29 Fitzroy Square W
10th April 1897

I've been there, I've been there (I calculate that you are reading this after the performance, though I'm writing before it.) I offered

741

Hurst his choice of two methods of admission for me—one the usual stall for the Saturday Review, the other a hatchet and revolver plied by myself. He capitulated and gave the stall, but said it was very hard on the governor to have the likes of me representing the papers when everyone knew it was only Miss Terry I came to see. You want laughs—you shall have them—the welkin shall shiver at my heehaws, if only you don't soften my heart and give me strange pains in my inside, as you always do.

Well, what a tremendous success it has been, hasn't it? All thrown away on Sardou—might have been Shaw.

I have just learnt the result of my reading the play to the Haymarket Co.—just what I expected—Dolly precipitately abandoned and Gloria pounced on by the leading lady. I am to be played by everybody but my Ellen, who is too busy with Sar—where is my typewriter?—I am impatient for Saturday's revenge. Oh play *me*, Ellen; *me*, ME, ME, ME, ME, ME, not Sardou or another. Now go and have a blessed sleep after it all.

GBS

To ELLEN TERRY

[U(A)/10; X/117]
Lotus. Tower Hill. Dorking
12th April 1897

[Evelyn Millard (1871–1941) was a member of Alexander's company at the St James's Theatre from 1894 to 1896, where she was acclaimed for her Princess Flavia in *The Prisoner of Zenda* (1896); she later toured with Beerbohm Tree, and went into management in 1908. Eva Moore (1870–1955), wife of the actor H.V. Esmond, served her apprenticeship in J. L. Toole's company, later became a popular ingénue and leading lady in light comedy. Jean-Léon Jaurès (1859–1914), French politician, was leader of the Socialists in the Chamber of Deputies and editor of *L'Humanité* (1904–14) until his assassination.]

I have taken to running down here between the rehearsals of "You Never Can Tell." Miss Millard was offered the part of Gloria, it being arranged then that Winifred Emery was to play Dolly. But Miss Millard refused it—I don't know why. Immediately after that came the reading of the play by the author. Miss Winifred was present on the occasion, and very soon began to prick up her ears. Presently she wrote "I shall play Gloria" on a scrap of paper and passed it to

742

Cyril Maude. This settled the question of Gloria and left Dolly for Eva Moore, who is engaged at the theatre and will do very well. We rehearsed the first act today. Oh, if only they *wouldn't* act. They are tolerable until they begin that; but then—! Well, their sorrows have only begun, poor things. They think me a very harmless author so far. Wait until I begin silently and unobtrusively to get on their nerves a little.

I shall devote all my Saturday article to Sans Gêne. It's a dreadfully bad play in many ways. Can you do nothing with that prince of dunder-heads—Cooper? He spoils your business most hideously—can't give you a single line right. Can you not insist on his at least telling you about the divorce in such a tone as to give some color to your anxiety lest he should be giving in about it. He should deliberately fool you for the pleasure of getting a demonstration out of you—should rather grumblingly explain the disadvantages of Sans Gênism and put it to you as a reasonable woman whether he can be expected to stick to you under the circumstances. Instead of that the idiot declaims as if he were waving his wounded honor like a banner. His make-up is utterly wrong—like Laertes imitating Hamlet. He should be a burly, bull-fighter, quartermaster sort of non-commissioned officer on promotion.

H. I. is amusing as the old stage hand making a part out of nothing—a Gladstonian sort of performance, and very clever. His play with his right hand—lifting it from the shoulder and shaking it with all the joints loose at every word—is exactly that of Jaures, the French Socialist, a tremendous speaker.

Edy ought to have a lot more work now to complete her apprentice-ship; but where is it to be had except on tour in South Africa? She has a remarkably beautiful voice, and is very clever and capable; but she is too sane to be a hysterical leading lady and too young for heavy parts of any value. Altogether very hard to fit, which shews that she ought to plunge into the rough & tumble of the business & fit herself to everything except the sort of thing that would spoil her voice. Nothing would please me better than to find an opening for her; but my apparent "influence" in such matters is just like yours: an invisible set of chains. If only she had nobody to help her she would get on fast enough; but with a secure position at the Lyceum, Ellen Terry for a mother, Bernard Shaw for a friendly critic & a dozen other over-whelming chances, what prospect has she? It's like trying to win a swimming race with ten life belts on.

I must fly to catch my train. When do you come to Thames Ditton?

GBS

743

To ELLEN TERRY

Lotus. Tower Hill. Dorking

[U(A)/10; X/117]

16th April 1897

[*Good for Nothing* (1851) was a comedy-drama by John B. Buckstone, revived at the Haymarket Theatre in 1889. William Mackintosh (1855–1929), who played Fouché in *Madame Sans-Gêne*, had appeared for many years with Mrs John Wood and the Kendals, and played Dogberry in Irving's production of *Much Ado About Nothing* in 1891. Marie Madeleine (La) Guimard (1743–1816), French dancer and star of the Paris Opéra, was notorious for licentiousness, and for the production of legally prohibited plays in her private theatre. Joseph W. Comyns Carr (1849–1916) was a popular dramatist who frequently adapted novels or French plays for the English stage, notably Meilhac's *Frou Frou* (1881), Thomas Hardy's *Far from the Madding Crowd* (1882), and *Madame Sans-Gêne*. The detailed story of the *You Never Can Tell* rehearsals was jocularly reported in Cyril Maude's *The Haymarket Theatre* (1903) in a chapter contributed anonymously by Shaw.

Siegfried Wagner (1869–1930), composer, conductor, and stage director, was the son of Richard Wagner. He and his mother Cosima (1837–1930) directed and managed the Bayreuth Festival until their deaths. Dorothea Baird (1873–1933), who created a sensation as Trilby in Beerbohm Tree's production at the Haymarket in 1895, was married to Irving's elder son, Henry Brodribb Irving (1870–1919). Shaw was elected as a Moderate to the Vestry of St Pancras Parish, without a contest, in 1897. He served as Vestryman and Borough Councillor until 1903. Fabian Tract No. 82 was *The Workmen's Compensation Act*, drafted by Charles R. Allen Jr. of Manchester, edited and revised by Shaw.]

You are making a most unnecessary fuss over your ridiculous Sans-Gêne. There's nothing in the *execution* of that part that presents any difficulty to you beyond the mere labor of it. Once you *understand* it you have jumped over the gulf that lies between it and Nan in Good for Nothing, or anything else that you could do on your head. As a matter of fact you played it very well, knocking off the exact shade of every phrase to perfection; but why shouldn't you? No doubt you'll do it more comfortably to yourself when you are no longer afraid of fluffing; but it won't make a penn'orth of difference to the public. I suppose it was you who fluffed in the prologue (quite early in it); but the impression conveyed was that Mackintosh was the offender—I suppose you didn't give him his cue, & he waited long enough to be detected before he made up his mind that he was not going to get it.

On the book, which arrived so dilapidated that I have had to patch the outside page to prevent total disintegration I have nothing to say

744

that you have not anticipated. The cut on page 17 is a mistake: Lefebvre's ferocity needs the reminder of the stab to make it plausible. On p. 26 "La Guinard" should be "La Gui*m*ard"—at least there was a famous dancer then called Madeleine Guimard, who was so thin that they compared her dance between two satyrs to two dogs fighting for a bone. On p. 28 it is, of course, impossible to say "Do you suppose that I walk with my head downwards, like a turnip," but you might very well say, "Well, do you suppose I walk on my head." On p 35 "That was my object" (Oh Comyns Carr, Comyns Carr!!!) is absurd: it should be "I meant her to." At the foot of p 37 "What for?" is the best phrase, I think. On 41 it is too literary to say "a true man, *who has*," &c. &c, *but who* dare not" &c. I suggest "a true man, with the right to ruin himself for her sake, but not to ruin her for his own." Also, by saying "you will go now & not come back" you throw away a point. I have scribbled an amendment at the foot of the page. However, the part is not in the words, or in Sardou's play: both are only a pretext for the real character to be embodied by you.

By the way, shouldnt Neipperg be pronounced Nyperg, not Neeperg? Or is it misprinted? My recollection of the spelling is Neipperg.

So you would like to see me at rehearsals. Well, you soon shall. "The Man of Destiny" is due this year: there is no penalty for breach of the agreement: consequently H.I. is on his honor. The scenes at the Haymarket are not on the surface, but in the recesses of the hearts of the unhappy company. I sit there and stare at them. I get up and prowl. I sit somewhere else, but always with a dreadful patience and dreadful attention. It is useless to correct more than one speech per person per day; for I find that the result of my interposition—consisting of saying the thing as it ought to be said—(Heaven knows what my way of doing it may sound like to them!)—is invariably to paralyse them for five minutes, during which they are not only quite off their part, but utterly incapable of expressing any meaning whatever. So far we have only gone over the busy funny scenes repeatedly: all the big scenes for Gloria & so on are yet before us. Maude & Brandon Thomas will succeed no matter how they take their parts: that is all I can see at present. What is a Lyceum rehearsal like? Does H.I. work out all that business (see Sans Gêne blank pages) at home, or does the prompter take it down as it turns up & works out in rehearsing?

Did I say "find an opening for Edy"? I apologize. I withdraw. I abase myself—you wretch: that was precisely what you ordered me to keep my eyes open for. She wants an opening ten times more than if she had no mother. Do you remember—or did you ever hear of—the obscurity of Mozart's son? An amiable man, a clever musician, an excellent player; but hopelessly extinguished by his father's reputation. How could any man do what was expected from Mozart's son? Not Mozart himself even. Look at Siegfried Wagner. Ellen Terry's daughter! Awful! Is Ted anything of a comedian? *I* want comedians.

Suppose this "You Never Can Tell" succeeds sufficiently to make it practically certain that a dozen matinees of a new cheap play by me would pay their way. Well, get somebody to finance a dozen matinees of "Candida" for Janet on condition that Ted plays Eugene and Edy Prossy—I told the Independent Theatre people that I'd let them do it if they could bank £1000. Or let them buy a fit-up and play "Arms & The Man" & "You Never Can Tell" in the provinces. (I have *all* the British rights of "Arms" & all but eleven No. 1 towns for "You Never Can Tell.") Or let H.B. Irving & Ted, Dorothea Baird & Edy start a "Next Generation" theatre & play Othello & Iago, Emilia & Desdemona, on alternate nights. Or let them make up a nice little repertory & go round the world with it—that's the way to get trained now.

It's no use: I have nothing sensible to suggest. Teddy, though ~~hypersenti~~ hypersensitized (got it that time!) and petulated by more luxury than was good for him in the way of a mammy seems highly and nervously intelligent. He wants ten years of stern adversity—not domestic squabble—to solidify him. Pity he's married: why should he be a breeder of sinners?

What a Good Friday we're having! Rain, wind, cold, skating on all the ponds, icicles hanging from the eaves and George Bernard the shepherd blowing his nail.

When are you coming into this neighborhood? I can bike over to Thames Ditton—if only I dare. Don't let us break the spell—*do* let us break the spell—don't, do, don't, do, don't, do, don't—I resolved to let the end of the line decide it like Gretchen's flower, and it has decided nothing.

Cut out the Neipperg business from "Sans Gêne" altogether, and there will be time to play "The Man of Destiny" before it.

GBS

P.S. They're going to elect me to the St Pancras Vestry (more public work); and I'm spending Easter on a Fabian Tract—"Employer's Liability." That's why I'm so prosaic.

To ELLEN TERRY

[U(B)/10; X/117]

Lotus. Tower Hill. Dorking
17th April 1897

[Bram Stoker (1847–1912), Dublin-born author of the bloodcurdling novel *Dracula* (1897), was from 1878 business manager and adviser to Irving. He published his *Personal Reminiscences of Henry Irving* in 1906. Paul Cinquevalli (1859–1918), one of the world's greatest jugglers, was then appearing in the pantomime *Aladdin*.]

Dearest Ellen

Look out for squalls. I have just received from Stoker a cool official intimation that Sir H.I. has changed his mind about producing "A Man of Destiny." My answer goes by the same post as this card. I am in ecstasies: I have been spoiling for a row; and now I have Mansfield to fight with one hand and H.I. with the other. Hooray! Kiss me good speed; and I'll toss them all about the stage as Cinquevalli tosses oranges and dinner plates.

By the way—no, not by the way, but mainly and chiefly and all importantly—are your eyes really bad again? I hope not from the very depths of me.

GBS

P.S. Don't bother about the Man of Destiny. Watch the fun & chuckle. Leave them to me. Ha hah!!!

To ELLEN TERRY

[U(A)/10; X/117]

Lotus. Tower Hill. Dorking
21st April 1897

[Shaw, explaining the contretemps in 1931, claimed that an irreconcilable quarrel between Irving and himself had arisen out of his *Saturday Review* notice of *Richard III*. Irving, he wrote, " believed that this unlucky article was a thinly veiled accusation of drunkenness on the stage. It contained such phrases as 'He was not, as it seemed to me, answering his helm satisfactorily; and he was occasionally out of temper with his own nervous condition' and 'He made some odd slips in the text, notably by substituting *you* for *I*.'" The published Shaw-Terry correspondence, he pointed out, would show that he was "entirely innocent of the construction which was put on these remarks." He had, in fact, laboured under the misapprehension that Irving had taken umbrage at Shaw's criticism of *Olivia*. In any case, "not being a man of insinuations and hints and stabs in the back," Shaw "would, if he had thought that Irving was drunk, have said so unequivocally, or said nothing."

Francis Albert Marshall (1840–89), playwright, opera librettist, and dramatic critic, edited the "Henry Irving Edition" of Shakespeare in eight volumes (1888–90).]

This is at heart a tragic business, Ellen; but we cannot help it. My only anxiety is lest you should become involved in it. Of course I knew all about it: a good surgeon knows when his knife touches a nerve; and a good critic knows the same with his pen. There was a terrible thing in that "Olivia" notice—not, as everybody thinks, my saying that Vezin's vicar was the better of the two, or that your Olivia was better without him, but that it was a relief to get rid of him for a moment at the Lyceum. It was not so brutal as that; but as he does not understand critical points, and treats all intellectual positions as mere matters of feeling, he probably took it in that way and was hurt by it; and he will perhaps think it unfeeling of you not to be angry with me for saying it. So be kind to him, and if he is clever enough to tell you on that afternoon drive—as I should in his place—that he is giving up the play because he is jealous of me about you, take his part and console him: it is when a man is too much hurt to do the perfectly mag-nanimous thing that he most needs standing by.

As for me I promise not to quarrel: I'll fight if I have to; but that is quite a different thing: it makes no bad blood—clears it away, in fact. The worst of the business is that it has gone far beyond our control. The announcements have been made, and taken up so far that on the first night of "Cymbeline" (was it?) his speech was interrupted by someone calling out "What about Shaw's play?" and my friends promptly remonstrated with me for employing people to advertise me in this shameless fashion. So the papers will want to know why the play has been dropped; and what explanation is there but the true one? I have told him (via Stoker) that he must stand to his bargain or break faith, there being no penalty clause in the agreement to secure an honorable retreat; and that is the beginning, middle & end of the situation. If he withdraws from his pledge on no other ground (trans-parent excuses apart) than that his acceptance has made no difference in my criticisms, then the obvious conclusion is that he meant to buy me. Besides, it is the only sign that the public has had of any rapproche-ment between the Lyceum and the younger school; and he will find that he cannot deal with me quite as he used to with Frank Marshall & the rest. Not from any malice of mine, mind: believe me, that is the danger of me, that I am not likely to put myself in the wrong with you standing between us, or indeed *anyhow*, because I rather like him and—

but enough about the business. Don't be anxious: I'll behave nicely and nothing particular will happen. I can't begin another sheet because I have my article to write & nothing to write about. And my news—oh the rehearsals!—I could tell you pages of my sufferings. "Sans Gêne" alas! will make you unhappy because it has none of the water of life in it; but it's only mechanical reaction: don't be cast down. Give me only till the rehearsals are going smoothly & I'll make the sun shine somehow. I shall be in town tomorrow.

GBS

To JANET ACHURCH

[T.u/1 (B/4)]
29 Fitzroy Square W
27th April 1897

[The Independent Theatre had been promising its subscribers a production of *The Lady from the Sea* for more than three years. Janet had agreed to appear as Ellida, but changed her mind and insisted that *Candida* be done. Neither play was produced. Instead, the I.T. revived *A Doll's House* with Janet (but not Charrington), at the Globe on 10th May, and *The Wild Duck* with Charrington (but not Janet) on the 17th. The Charringtons then toured, under the auspices of the I.T., in *A Doll's House* and—Shaw having by this time relented—in *Candida*, the latter opening in Aberdeen on 30th July 1897.]

My dear Janet

The more I reflect on your observations this evening the more flagitious does your conduct appear to me. You have given me no reason worth a farthing for not keeping your engagement to play Ellida. All the difficulties were as obvious when the prospectus was issued as they are today. I am convinced that you stand to lose more by a breakdown in your promises and arrangements than by anything that can happen to you in acting an Ibsen play. *You* can't take the ground that Ibsen is not good enough for you. The substitution of "Candida" would not be at all a nice transaction for me under the circumstances, even if I were idiot enough to let you throw it away. It is quite possible to withdraw "The Lady from the Sea" frankly on the ground that it has not proved possible to do it justice; but you had much better do a new part. Your genius for ruining all your enterprises can be reserved for something bigger than this I.T. affair which you can condescend to play for without identifying yourself too closely with it. Many thanks for sending me the satchel. It got me out of a parlous difficulty.

To ELLEN TERRY

[29 Fitzroy Square W]

[U(A)/10]   29th April 1897.

[After two weeks of rehearsals of *You Never Can Tell*, Shaw withdrew the play, claiming later that "the ruin and disgrace" of Harrison and Maude "could only be averted by a heroic sacrifice" on his part (Maude, *The Haymarket Theatre*, 1903). Her Majesty's Theatre, newly built by Beerbohm Tree at a cost of £55,000, from the profits of *Trilby*, opened on 28th April with a dramatisation by Gilbert Parker of his novel *The Seats of the Mighty*. For the occasion, as Shaw informed his *Saturday Review* readers on 1st May, the poet laureate, Alfred Austin (1835–1913), had written a "straightforward and businesslike" piece of "sycophancy in rhyme" which Mrs Tree recited "with an absence of conviction that was only emphasized by her evident desire to please us all." Maud Holt (1863–1937), who became Mrs (later Lady) Tree in 1883, appeared in many of Tree's productions, but did not confine herself to her husband's company. On 3rd May she appeared at the Strand as Mrs Wilton in the New Century Theatre's production of *John Gabriel Borkman*.]

I have some faint hope that I am going to get rid of this Haymarket business after all. They now *do* see clearly that the Valentine-Gloria scenes mean failure under existing circumstances; and thereupon they have fallen back on the old wild hope that if only Shaw would use his brains to deshawize his own plays—if only they could have what they want in Shaw without what Shaw wants in them—how splendid that would be! So they have said very nicely and sympathetically that if I don't do this with "You Never Can Tell" (that is: virtually cut Valentine & Gloria out & replace them with a new patent Gloria) the play cannot be produced, and I shall lose my great chance of that splendid opportunity for a young and brilliant man, a first rate production at a first rate theatre in the Jubilee season that will never come again in all our lifetimes. They might as well offer me a beefsteak. I have embraced the opportunity of escaping a "brilliant success"; and now my one hope is that they are as much in earnest as I am; for I have had enough of wasting time on success that might have been employed in producing something real. This Jubilee business makes me sick— ugh! last night at Her Majesty's! shall I ever get the cynical taste of it off my teeth? Ellen, if you ever do what Mrs Tree did—recite Poet Laureate sycophancy with a grin of loyal rapture—I'll go into a monastery.

Where do you spend your Sundays now? Did you say Thames Ditton?

750

What do you suppose Janet wants me to do? She sees that she will not be able to do much with The Lady from The Sea with fifteen & sixpence worth of Independent Theatre scenery; so she wants to withdraw it & throw "Candida" into the gap. *You* ought to have done that Lady (not that she's at all Ibsen's best) long ago. If you gave Janet the Koh i noor she would pawn it for half a crown the first time she forgot her purse and wanted to take a cab home. I have refused with iron brutality, with insanely reproachful results.

I observed to Harrison yesterday, experimentally, that I was not for the moment on good terms with H.I. He immediately let himself loose and shewed that he knew all about it. Now that I have heard it from somebody else than you, I'll write to him; so don't be surprised if he forgets his part tonight. I hope to get back to Dorking this evening until Monday. I can think of you better there.

GBS

To SIR HENRY IRVING

[A/30; X/133]

29 Fitzroy Square W
29th April 1897

Dear Sir Henry Irving

The murder is out: they tell me that you consider that my criticism of "Richard III" implied about you what it said about Kean. I reply flatly that it *didn't*: if I had thought so, I'd have said so bluntly or else said nothing at all. Such a construction never occurred to me, and was certainly not conveyed to any of the people who spoke to me about the article. Now that the thing is suggested to me I can see that if you had that sort of reputation, the article might have been misunderstood; but who told you that you had? You underrate your immunities.

I am sorry that the article should have caused you any uneasiness; but my vanity as a critic is severely wounded by your very cheap estimate of the sort of work I do. If you knew the trouble your performances give me—you are in some ways the most difficult subject a critic can tackle, and quite the most exasperating for an author-critic—you would be astonished at my patience and amiability.

At all events, however strongly you may still resent the article (which I stand by to the uttermost comma—especially the part about Shakespeare) don't resent it on *that* score. I never dreamt of such a thing.

yours sincerely
G. Bernard Shaw

751

[Irving's reply to this letter was : "... You are absolutely wrong in your polite insinuation of the cat out of the bag—as I had not the privilege of reading your criticism—as you call it—of Richard. I never read a criticism of yours in my life. I have read lots of your droll, amusing, irrelevant and sometimes impertinent pages, but criticism containing judgment and sympathy I have never seen by your pen" (Laurence Irving, *Henry Irving: The Actor and His World*, 1951).]

To ELLEN TERRY

[U(A)/10; X/117]

Lotus. Tower Hill. Dorking
4th May 1897

Why don't you write to me sometimes, you wretch? This weather makes the birds sing incessantly, but not a note can it get out of you.

Here's a pretty instalment of the wrath to come. Yesterday evening, at Fitzroy Square, comes the inevitable interviewer with a cutting from the Daily News (evidently inspired) stating that Sir H. I. had sent me back my play to teach me better manners. Thereupon the smartest of the New Journalism editors scents a duel, and wants me to return H. I.'s fire in his paper. Not being able to tell the man that such a display of my famous marksmanship, though highly delightful to the public, would get me into trouble with my Ellen, I had to shuffle, and finally declined to say anything for publication except that the play had *not* been returned to me and that the agreement to perform could not be broken without a breach of faith impossible to the high contracting parties. So they had to be content with that for the present. What is going to happen?

Mansfield's coming over—not to act, though, as far as I know.

Saw Edy yesterday at "Borkman."

GBS

To R. GOLDING BRIGHT

[A/1; X/125]

Lotus. Tower Hill. Dorking
7th May 1897

[John Drew (1853–1927), an American matinée idol, was leading man in Augustin Daly's company, and the uncle of Ethel, Lionel, and John Barrymore. The enclosed press cutting was an extract from the "Dramatic and

Musical" column of the *Glasgow Herald* for 4th May, reporting that "Sir Henry Irving has, I hear, relinquished his intention of playing Napoleon Bonaparte in . . . A Man of Destiny. . . . [He] had previously accepted the piece, but now finds the character unsuited to him, and, moreover, as there is little chance of producing any half-programme work at the Lyceum for many months to come, he has thought it best to return the manuscript to the author with, it is understood, a handsome compliment and a present." Lincoln Springfield (d. 1950), chief reporter for *The Star* (1888–92) and a member of the editorial staff of the *Pall Mall Gazette*, had become news editor of the newly-founded *Daily Mail* in 1896.]

Dear Bright

I had better let you into all the mysteries of my plays. The fact is, nothing of mine is going to be produced at all. "The Red Robe" will probably be run through the season at the Haymarket; and the public will be left to infer that it will be followed in the autumn by "You Never Can Tell." But the truth is that two of the leading parts proved too much for the resources of the Haymarket. The lady could not possibly have got through without strong support from the gentleman; and the gentleman (your friend the dentist) was hopelessly beaten by his part, which would have required Wyndham or John Drew at least to handle it. So I went to Harrison and put it to him that we had better drop the business quietly. He was very loth to admit that such a breakdown could be possible, especially as the scenery was in hand and nine tenths of the play shaping very cheerfully. But at last he recognised that the other tenth was out of the question. So we gave it up as a bad job; and now "You Never Can Tell" is not likely to be seen until it is published. But I have settled with Harrison that this story is not to be published, as it would be very hard both on the actor who was cast for a part that was (as I foretold) quite beyond him, and on the others who would have done very well. We have simply said (truly) that the Red Robe has looked up again, and that the rehearsals of "You Never Can Tell" have been discontinued for the present. I let you into the secret so that you may know what you are about in the matter and not commit yourself to announcements that won't come off. But whilst you rearrange the background of your mind, don't let the public see anything.

Another collapse is over the Lyceum play. Irving declares that my article on "Richard III" meant that he was drunk, though of course the reasons he gives for publication are those in the enclosed press cutting. The statement that he has paid me a compliment & made me a present is, under the circumstances, enough to make a saint swear.

753

In a few days, failing any friendly arrangement with Irving, I shall tell the whole story, probably in an interview in the Daily Mail; and a very amusing story it will be. I shall have to do the interview myself, I expect; but if you care to tell Springfield that you believe you can get an interview out of me on the subject I shall bear you out unless Irving changes his attitude.

I enclose another sheet or two, containing as much as I want mentioned just now.

In haste,
yrs ever
G. Bernard Shaw

—Things you may mention—Work it up as *news* in your own way, not as communicated by me to the paper in the first person—you will know how to manage it.

1. I have been elected a member of the St Pancras Vestry. At the first general election of Vestries under the Local Government Act of 1894 it was urged that public spirited men of some standing should come forward & offer to serve. I condescended to do this and was ignominiously defeated, my sympathy with Labor being considered disreputable by the workmen of St Pancras. Now the Conservatives and Unionists and Moderates and other respectables of the parish have returned me unopposed in spite of my vehement protests that I have no time for such work. I recognize, however, that there is better work to be done in the Vestry than in the theatre, and have submitted to take my turn.

2. I have resolved to accept an offer made me by Mr Grant Richards for the publication of my plays. I am not a disappointed dramatist, as the curiosity and interest shewn in my plays by managers, and their friendliness & accessibility for me, have exceeded anything I had any right to expect. But in the present condition of the theatre it is evident that a dramatist like Ibsen, who absolutely disregards the conditions which managers are subject to, and throws himself on the reading public, is taking the only course in which any serious advance is possible, expecially if his dramas demand much technical skill from the actors. So I have made up my mind to put my plays into print and trouble the theatre no further with them. The present proposal is to issue two volumes entitled "Plays, Pleasant and Unpleasant." Vol I, "Unpleasant" will contain "The Philanderer" and the appalling "Mrs Warren's Profession" with perhaps a reprint of "Widowers' Houses." Vol II, "Pleasant," will contain "Arms & The Man,"

"Candida," and "You Never Can Tell." Possibly also "The Devil's Disciple" and "The Man of Destiny."

I decline to say anything more at present about Sir Henry Irving and "The Man of Destiny" except that the story, when I tell it—and I shall probably tell it very soon—will be quite as amusing as a Lyceum performance of the play would have been. None of the paragraphs in circulation convey the remotest approximation to the truth; and the statement that Sir Henry has returned the MS "with a handsome compliment and a present" is a particularly audacious invention. This is enough for one week, I think.

To SIR HENRY IRVING

[H/30; X/133]

29 Fitzroy Square W
10th May 1897

[The contemplated production of *The Man of Destiny* with Forbes-Robertson and Mrs Patrick Campbell did not eventuate. A day or two after this letter was written, Shaw's manuscript was returned to him by Bram Stoker with a curt note of rejection. A letter followed from Irving, drafted for him by his secretary, L.F.Austin. The nature of its contents is revealed in Ellen Terry's letter to Shaw of 11th May: "When H. read me his letter to you last evening I screamed with laughter when he came to 'callous to the feelings of others,' and 'lost the consciousness of vulgarity.'"]

Dear Sir Henry Irving

Now that we are beginning to deal seriously, we shall get this matter settled fast enough.

Here is the position. I don't want you to play "The Man of Destiny" if you don't like. Only, you mustn't *suppress* it: you must either take it or leave it. And, if you elect to leave it, you must play fairly to my public position as I have played loyally all through to yours. The public have been suddenly informed that the reports that you had accepted a play of mine were false, and that what has really happened is that I have sent in a play to the Lyceum and had it rejected. The Era hastens to rub this in vigorously; and though a certain London-letter writer [for the *Glasgow Herald*] explains that you changed your mind, he adds that you have paid me a handsome compliment and made me a handsome present—in other words, that you have bought the critic of the Saturday Review, and had him cheap. Such a presentation of the case, if uncontradicted, will disgrace both of us professionally; and sooner than leave the least whiff of it in the air, I will give

London another version in a style that will secure its eager attention. But the contradiction ought to come, not from me but from you; and if it does not take the shape of an emphatic public statement that the play will be produced, and an implied dignified rebuke to the tattlers, then we must at once concert some explanation of the abandonment of the play that will be entirely creditable to both of us, and which will leave me instantly free to deal with the play in other quarters.

I suggest the following plan. Forbes Robertson has just written to me about a project of ours which I shall have to discuss with him this week, whilst he is in town to play at the Metropole. Well, he and Mrs Campbell can play "The Man of Destiny" for me well enough—I should have suggested it to them before but for those prior claims which you are at present so irreverently playing pitch and toss with. Now if you want to get rid of the play in a highly effective and Charlemagnanimous manner, let me arrange the transfer with Forbes and flood next Sunday's papers with "The Truth About the M. of D."—to wit, that the latest instance of your well known interest in the fortunes of your younger colleagues, especially your old lieutenant F.R., is that you are handing over my play to him with my reluctant consent, and that this is the foundation of all the rumors.

If you can think of anything better than this, let me know. But the thing must be settled at once—Fate is peremptory. The public is listening; and if we don't seize the moment to speak, we shall not get the chance again. If you don't move, I shall. Weathercocks are steady in a storm; and I'll supply a raging one if necessary.

I should waste your time and save my own if I called to talk. I am an expert at that too, and can talk your head off and Stoker's as well, with half the trouble it gives me to write to you. Ask Cyril Maude.

I beg you to let me have your final decision or indecision at once. In a week Forbes will have left town and my press powder will be getting damp. A reply by return will reach me here; but I shall probably go down to Dorking by some train in the forenoon. Address Lotus, Tower Hill.

In haste, haste, post haste—what the devil possessed you to worry me at this busy time with this storm in a teacup?—

yours sincerely
G. Bernard Shaw

To ARNOLD DOLMETSCH

29 Fitzroy Square W
10th April [May] 1897

[A/24]

[The copyright reading of *The Devil's Disciple* took place in the Bijou Theatre, Bayswater, on 17th April. Shaw, billed as "Cashel Byron," performed the rôle of the Rev. Anthony Anderson.]

Dear Mr Dolmetsch

Not until this morning, when I saw the Bach article in the Saturday Review, did I realise how unpardonably I have behaved to you. I am somewhat comforted to see that the harpsichord triumphed [at the Bach Choir concert]; but I am none the less deeply ashamed of myself.

The fact is, I suddenly got news from America that a play of mine which has never been performed here was about to be produced in New York. Now unless a play is first performed in England, the author loses his rights in this country just as Gounod lost the rights for "Faust." I therefore had to throw everything else to the winds to get up a little performance here to comply with the law. This came on me at a moment when I was working at high pressure to prepare for my play at the Haymarket; and on that Saturday everything went out of my head except the scramble over the plays. Under these circumstances you will perhaps forgive me for my failure to appear. I attached great importance to the appointment; and only a really serious emergency could have swept it so completely out of my mind.

I am looking over my letters received during the past fortnight; and almost every one of them convicts me of some shocking neglect or bad manners.

yours sincerely
G. Bernard Shaw

To MATTHEW EDWARD McNULTY

Lotus. Tower Hill. Dorking
(really written in the train)
10th May 1897

[A/4]

Listen.

One of my plays, entitled "Mrs Warren's Profession," is "immoral" (Mrs W. is a procuress). It is so startling in this respect that there is no likelihood of the Censor licensing it; and if he once refuses, everyone

757

connected with any performance of it will be liable to a fine of £50. Therefore it must not be submitted to him. But I want to publish it, and if I publish before it is performed, my rights of representation (as distinct from copyright) will be forfeited, the law on the subject being mere idiotic chaos. Now the only way to circumvent this difficulty is to get the play performed out of the Lord Chamberlain's jurisdiction. Ireland is in that happy condition. What censorship there may be there—from the Castle or elsewhere—I don't know; but as a matter of fact I believe that if I were to engage one of the obscure little theatres in Dublin at which amateurs perform (there used to be one somewhere east of Westland Row) no question would arise as to whether the piece to be performed was licensed or not. If necessary I should announce Hamlet, with "to be preceded, at such & such an hour, by 'Mrs W's Profession,'" as if it were an old farce. You understand the sort of performance. A few people gabble through the play, reading the parts. There is no scenery, only a raising & dropping of the curtain. The hour selected is the most unlikely one possible. No announcement is made except that half an hour before the play begins a very modest poster is stuck on the door in view of the passer-by, with "Admission: One Guinea" at the foot of it. One person (a confederate, of course) comes in and pays the guinea, of which a box office return is solemnly made. Legally, this constitutes a public performance & saves the stage right as effectively as if the play had been produced with full honors at the Lyceum. I stagerighted my last play "The Devil's Disciple" here in London the other day in this fashion for about 30/-.

Now it occurs to me that if you were to take "Mrs Warren" in hand, you might do this trick for me in Dublin, or get it done, or, if it can't be done, find out the why & wherefore for me.

My address is still 29 Fitzroy Square. London W; but some friends of mine have taken a house at Dorking for this quarter where I stay except when I have to come up to town on business. So write to Dorking.

I write in haste, much joggled by this accursed train.

I shall send you a copy of the play as soon as it is typewritten.

G. Bernard Shaw

To ELLEN TERRY

[U(A)/10; X/117]

Lotus. Tower Hill. Dorking
11th May 1897

["A. A." was Allan Aynesworth (1865–1959), a member of Augustin Daly's company (1893–95), who had also appeared as Algy in *The Importance of Being Earnest* in 1894. Aynesworth had been cast as Valentine in *You Never Can Tell*, and Shaw (as he recorded in 1903) "had from the first contended that one of the scenes lay outside Mr. Aynesworth's peculiar province. There can be no doubt now that Mr. Shaw deliberately used his hypnotic power at rehearsal to compel Mr. Aynesworth to fulfil his prediction." Ellen had informed Shaw on 9th May that she had "tumbled out of" her tricycle recently "and it shook me pretty badly . . . My Stars and Stripes! how stiff my whole right side is, even now."]

On getting down here I was much alarmed by your telegram, as my one anxiety in this business is to avoid entangling you in the warfare. I do most strictly and peremptorily entreat you not to touch it in any way, or, if you do, to take a part entirely sympathetic to H. I. He is heavily overweighted in the contest, and is making one mistake after another in trying to get out of a position into which he has wedged himself hopelessly. If he had come to me and said, "Look here: I want to get out of doing this play; and I want at the same time to express my intense irritation at your expense" I should have cheerfully found a way out for him and drafted him a letter to write to me which would have given him the keenest satisfaction. But he does not know me or trust me or like me well enough for that. And that is why you can do nothing with him just now. It is utterly impossible that he should understand me as you understand me. Do you remember that even you, when you knew no more about me than H. I. does now, and when you had to write to me about that Italian girl (what became of her?), thought me a disagreeable and *wounding* person. It has taken me about fifty thousand love letters since that to convince you that I am only a brute nor'-nor'-west; and H. I. hasn't had any love letters, and is precisely under the same impression of my malevolence as you were under then. Anything that you say in my favor, far from convincing him, will only strike him as an act of treachery to himself. Do not be anxious—do not, at all events, betray the least anxiety. When two men fight, they find out one another's value wonderfully quickly; and the mild tussle now in progress is quite sufficient to educate Henry on the subject of Bernard better than the most tactful special pleading on your part. At present he has less respect for me than I have for myself; and I have more respect for him than he has for himself. He has been trying to trifle with me; and he does not know that what has brought him up standing in that is the firm grip of a friendly hand, and not an attempt to trip him up. He sent for Austin *because* he knew that Austin could not afford to tell him that he has no case, and would teach him a literary thrust or two at me. All that is nothing to the purpose; and he knows by this time that I know what [it] is worth. Don't let it disturb you for a moment: sit quiet and wait patiently: I shall get what I deserve, depend on it; and he *shan't*; so you need not be anxious about him.

I have quite taken in Edy's facility for arranging life in amusing narratives. I was talking to her at the Strand [Theatre] a week ago. I suggest that her version of the A.A. business ought not to be discredited, as it is much the most humane one. It would take a very big man to say, in A's position, that his part had beaten him, even if he could see that it had. If he says it was my fault, it will ease the situation for him and do me no harm. I feel rather remorseful about him, though he certainly *is* a duffer—how could he be anything else with his training, poor fellow!

Oh that tricycle, that tricycle! I told you that it was a dangerous contrivance; but you *would* have it that it was safe because it stands by itself like a perambulator when you're not on it. If you had been biking you would simply have jumped off and sworn at that old woman instead of nearly killing her and yourself as well. And if you *did* get a toss, you would ride it off in a mile or two. You should see the appalling accidents we have all lived through here—we four, Webb, Beatrice (Mrs W.), Miss P.T. & myself. On trikes we'd have been slain. No room for more. Write to *me*: dont talk to H.I.

GBS

To ELLEN TERRY

[U(A)/10; X/117]

Lotus. Tower Hill. Dorking
12th May 1897

[Ellen had revealed in her letter of 11th May that Irving had intended to perform *The Man of Destiny* on a double-bill with Sydney Grundy's *Guilty* (an adaptation of Richard Voss's *Schuldig*).]

Oh my dear, dear, dearest Ellen, I'm beaten. Forgive me; but your Henry is not a hero off the stage; and now that everything is ready to my hand for his discomfiture I find that I cannot bring myself to do any of the things I might do. He proposed originally that we should deal with one another "as two men of honor." Alas! that is not what a man of honor usually says; but I disregarded that ungenerous reflection and trusted him—or rather I gave him the power to behave like a confidence-trick man if he liked, which he has accordingly done, not because he is exactly a rogue, but because his self absorption makes him as incapable as a baby of suffering the slightest cross without petulance, or understanding obligations and treaties. I have tried to make the best of him; but there is no best: I have suddenly given him up; and now it's all over.

All that about his managerial plans is nonsense. I foresaw it all; and though he fought hard not to be tied to production this year, he finally undertook it in full view of all his arrangements. There has been no change: [his] accident only prevented "Richard III" from running uninterruptedly up to "Sans Gêne." He did not fail in his contract with Sardou, because Sardou did not deal with him "as between two men of honor." Even now he has returned the play without returning my agreement, the counterpart of which, though I should have had it for stamping within fourteen days, has *never* been sent to me. I have telegraphed to him for it. I am sorry about the Strange Lady; but I will have nothing to do with him now, least of all anything in which you are involved. It is a pity; for his bill of Shaw and Grundy could easily have been arranged if he had asked me to make any ultimate date movable to the end of a run if necessary. But it is better as it is: he would have behaved like a baby sooner or later; and *I* shouldn't have spoiled him. There is no use in wasting the play: J.F.R. & Mrs Pat. may as well do it as nobody; but I shall trouble myself no more about the theatre. I don't care, and never did care who plays Napoleon (it was written for Mansfield); but I should have liked you to play the Strange Lady; and since your infant has put a stop to that, it may be played by Mrs Pat's dresser for all I care.

Vengeance I leave to Destiny. You remember about Beaconsfield's plan. I am sorry to have lost my regard for him. Mind, *you* must not take his part now. I declare him unworthy of my Ellen.

GBS

To ELLEN TERRY

Lotus. Tower Hill. Dorking
13th May 1897

[U(A)/10; X/117]

[The interview was a detailed account of the negotiations with Irving, drafted by Shaw and given to Golding Bright. It appeared in the *Daily Mail*, exactly as written, on 15th May.]

There ought to be in today's Daily Mail or Star or some such paper an interview with me. My uncertainty arises from the fact that instead of doing the business myself directly, I have used it to give a chance to a young journalist in whom I am interested. I wrote the dialogue of the interview and gave it to him, telling him to fill in the scenery and business, and giving him the names of a few papers which have applied to me for information. I told him to get it in today (Saturday) at latest; and I think the Daily Mail is the most likely choice for him to make. But the railway station is two miles off and I am full of work; so I must wait until the afternoon to discover what has happened. I go up to town to see Hare's re-entry at the Court [in a revival of Pinero's *The Hobby Horse*], back tomorrow morning, up on Monday to the Globe [a matinée of *A Doll's House*] and Adelphi [William Gillette's *Secret Service*] & so on.

You will find nothing quarrelsome in the interview: we all come out of it with haloes of glory round our heads. The management of it being in my hands I of course play H. off the stage; but I dress him well and allow him to make a point or two. I promised you not to quarrel, and I won't: besides, were I to let the public see that I have private reasons for destroying him, I never could criticise him again without suspicion of partiality. But that shall not save him: no, by all that is Inevitable, he shall lag superfluous and perish miserably from the profession he has disgraced. You made two pencil marks—just two—in that copy of the Man of Destiny, and when I saw them the sky blackened over his brainless head. Your career has been sacrificed to the egotism of a fool: he has warmed his wretched hands callously at the embers of nearly twenty of your priceless years; and now they will flame up, scorch his eyes, burn off his rum bathed hair, and finally consume him.

Yes: I know he has a play of Grundy's. He assured me with his finest manner that the statements to the effect that he had plays on his shelves were false. He tries to hide himself from himself with a rampart of lies; and he got behind it to hide himself from me. That was why he became an actor—to escape from himself. You became an actress to realise yourself. Hence it is that all his performances have to be accepted

762

subject to the initial drawback that they are utterly incredible and impossible, whilst you, even when you act badly, are a human reality to begin with. Oh Ellen, Ellen, this infinitesimal actor-nothingness whimpers over the things I have said of him; but if he knew the *things* I have *not* said, he would shudder and die.

I have had a talk with Forbes. Mrs Pat. is ill—nerves, disappointment, alarm at engagements not coming and money going (this as I *guess*: the chivalrous Forbes gives not his lady away). But even there, with Mrs Pat. to right of us, Mrs Pat. to left of us, Mrs Pat. on easel and mantelshelf and wall, *you* were in the middle; and for that I forgave him his Mrs Pat. and let him read "The Man of Destiny." He wants "You Never Can Tell"; and why should he not have it? To *want* anything: that is to be a slave. I want nothing but you, and so am nobody's slave but yours.

Nevertheless you shall play for me yet; but not with him, not with him, not with him.

GBS

To ELLEN TERRY

[U(A)/10; X/117]

Lotus. Tower Hill. Dorking
16th May 1897

[Lilian Vavasour is the heroine of Tom Taylor's *New Men and Old Acres* (1869). Although the part was written for Ellen, it was played by Mrs Kendal in the original production at the Haymarket Theatre. Ellen, however, played the part with great success in the revival at the Old Court Theatre in November 1876. Mamillius, the young son of Leontes and Hermione in *A Winter's Tale*, was the rôle in which Ellen made her first stage appearance, at the Princess's Theatre, on 28th April 1856. Shaw deliberately pushed the dates back to exaggerate Ellen's age, even substituting Edmund Kean (1787–1833) for his son Charles, in whose company Ellen had made her début.]

Damn the play, dearest Ellen: I don't care two straws about *that*. And with you, to you, I shall be just like other people. Therefore I heap execrations on his infamous head, whilst in The Daily Mail it is "one gentleman to another." I do *not* pity him. "Tear falling pity dwells not in this eye" [*Richard III* (IV, ii, 66)], least of all for my detested rival. I know that he thinks he has done well because he has done meanly; and for that I would pity him, only the thought comes that the crafty wrinkle in his overrated countenance which years of such base exultation have graven there may have been touched by Ellen's lips; and then I stretch my maddened hands to clutch the lightning. Also I know he thinks it does not matter; but at that I laugh—in 1888 John Morley thought that the Fabian Society did not matter; and as the Liberal party felt towards the Fabian Society, so the Lyceum felt later on towards the Ibsenites.

Yes: it would have been so nice of me to give him my friendship and trust *again*, in order to prove to you that I give them to every foolish person who doesn't want them, and that therefore they are not worth *your* having. I grant you he would nurse the play better (longer) than anyone else, like a Lapland mother, who *never* weans her boys. He would have nursed it, the selfish villain, until your grandchild was old enough to come and laugh at you in that opera-bouffe hussar's uniform. Do you know that I asked him to make it follow Imogen because you can with perfect dignity put on a man's dress in a Shaksperean play, and immediately after that nobody would mind your doing it again, whereas to do it without any such preparation in a silly little play like "The Man of Destiny" would look like a mere romp. But his ineffable pigheadedness could take in no idea that did not concern himself; and even on his own account it did not occur to him that my jealousy of your dignity might have its counterfoil for him in an objection to his age. That is the aggravating thing about it: you *ought* to be too old for the part, if you are really as old as you boast of being in all the books of reference, whereas he, who equally ought to be able to carry off Napoleon's years still, never looks under fifty except when he is playing Lear.

Oh, you thought I couldn't be spiteful, madam, and small, and petty, but I *can*. Ha! ha! Everybody said it to me when I told them it was the young Napoleon. "Good God!" they shrieked, "do you remember his Romeo? It's imPOSSible." And nobody ever dreamt that you played Mamillus in the year 1822 to Edmund Kean's Leontes, or that I fell in love with Lilian Vavasour at the old Court in 1862. And you, *you*, YOU tell me I should have taken your play to this idiot and said "Do it when you can." Ah Ellen, Ellen, when you see two considerations in my head, there are never less than twenty there. You have contracted your conceptions to suit *his* head—that narrow little cutlet of a forehead that peers and guesses at *my* Temple of Reason. You should live here, where we have to stretch our foreheads like concertinas to grapple even with one another's small talk.

I have promised to join a cycling party, and they shriek for me.

Are you coming to the Wild Duck tomorrow?

Of course you've seen the Daily Mail; but I send you a copy to make sure.

Ever dearest, be beautiful & happy, for ever and ever out of abundance of life.

GBS

PS. Did he shew you *my* letters to *him*, as well as his to me? Ha ha-a-a-a-a-a-a-!

To JANET ACHURCH

[T/1 (A/4)]

Lotus. Tower Hill. Dorking
20th May 1897

[The just-completed article, "Ibsen Triumphant" (*Saturday Review*, 22nd May), was Shaw's notice of *The Wild Duck*. The article on "next Saturday week" (29th May) was a review of Janet and Louis Calvert in *Antony and Cleopatra*, which opened in London at the Olympic on the 24th, under the auspices of the I.T., and which Shaw described as "an afternoon of lacerating anguish, spent partly in contemplating Miss Achurch's overpowering experiments in rhetoric, and partly in wishing I had never been born."

Andrea del Sarto (1486–1531), the "faultless" Florentine painter, was renowned as a colourist and as a master of chiaroscuro. His wife was Lucrezia del Fede. Shaw's reference to her is based apparently on Browning's poem, in which Sarto describes her as a despicable woman, with neither heart nor intellect, who destroyed the man who had sacrificed for her his soul and the higher interests of his art.

Wilson Barrett's production of *Othello* opened at the Lyric on 22nd May, but Shaw did not attend until the 24th. Charles Brookfield (1857–1913), actor, playwright, and later joint-examiner of plays for the Lord Chamberlain, was noted for his comic impersonations of social types. He had appeared in *An Ideal Husband*, *The Home Secretary*, and *A White Elephant*.]

I have been up in town since Monday, never out of the theatres except whilst I was at work on my article. *That* finished, I come down here and find your letter—your paralyzing letter. Do you suppose I did not know that "The Wild Duck" was his [Charrington's] chance? And you—*you*—YOU did your best to spoil it for the sake of flaunting as Cleopatra in that absurd provincial entertainment. You are a monster, a moral monster. How is he to be got out of your clutches: that is what I want to know? It is clear that you are not going to act any more: it is all Sara Bernhardt now—no brains, no pains, none of the distinction and freshness of thoughtful, self controlled work, nothing but letting

765

yourself go and giving it to 'em hot and strong now that you have found that they will stand it. Oh wait, wait, WAIT until next Saturday week, Janet Achurch. Andrea del Sarto's wife was not in it with you.

I have not time to do more than a hasty scrawl. Let me know what has happened in the way of business—how much money have the matinees drawn? The truth, mind: no attempts to make out that "A Doll's House" drew more than "The Wild Duck"—it was not *half* as interesting.

I go up on Saturday afternoon to Wilson Barrett's "Othello."

Yes: I note that you never will desert Mr Micawber. Oh, if only he could be induced to desert you!

Grant Richards tells me he sent [to the I.T.] for his money back, and that Bertha did the same when Cleopatra was announced. Quite right, too, *quite* right. I ask myself (as Brookfield says) how you can have the audacity to write to me after behaving so.

GBS

To GRANT RICHARDS

Lotus. Tower Hill. Dorking
21st May 1897
[A/4; X/135]

[R. & R. Clark, Ltd is an Edinburgh printing firm of outstanding reputation. In 1946, when Clark's celebrated its centenary, Shaw wrote to its director William Maxwell (1873–1957): "So the great printing firm of R. & R. Clark is 100 years old . . . It seems to me to have been ordained by Providence to be ready for me when my time came. At all events ever since it printed my first plays . . . in 1898, it has been as natural a part of my workshop as the pen in my hand" (*Alphabet and Image*, December 1948).]

Thanks for Philanderer.

Clark is all right—a first rate house. I enclose a letter which you can hold as your certificate of your compliance with my Fair Wages Clause.

Yes: separate introductions to the volumes by all means, and separate portraits if you like. Evans has an assortment which includes both tragic & comic masks.

The best people to give the portrait to are Walker and [Walter] Boutall, 16 Clifford's Inn E.C. Emery Walker, the senior partner, will look after me like a brother. He is the guide, philosopher & friend of many publishers in the matter of illustrated books; and you ought to make his acquaintance anyhow. He is also a first rate authority on printing, and personally an almost reprehensibly amiable man.

If you have a copy of one of Walter Scott's volumes of Ibsen's plays you will see how the style of thing I want works at three plays to the volume. In Scott's edition the block of letterpress is not properly set on the page; but otherwise it is not so bad.

In drafting the agreement I should have made the five years start from the date of publication.

Nov. will do as well. Probably we shall have to add something about the American business when we find out what can be done. In it I take it that you will not meddle in the publication there yourself, but virtually act as my agent and take a percentage on what you can get for me. Or have you any other plan?

"The Man of Destiny" is quite available if there is room for it.

"The Quintessence" has been skimmed a good deal. Hadn't you better wait and see whether I sell well enough?

I am writing by this post to Henry & Co. [for a clearance on the reprinting of *Widowers' Houses*].

yrs ever
G. Bernard Shaw

To ELLEN TERRY

[U(A)/10; X/117]

29 Fitzroy Square W
24th May 1897

Come: what new infidelity is this?—how long am I to be deserted?—I have not had a line these three months. Who is my rival?—is it Henry, or that stupid Cooper, or the grandchild? Or are you angry? Or tired of me? Well, remember that you have not *quite* exhausted me: there is one play, the best of them all, which you haven't seen ("Mrs Warren's Profession"), and which I am preparing for the printer. Throw this disagreeable dog a bone, and you shall have a proof as soon as it is set up—I mean a printer's proof. I do not want to give any of that volume to the public until it has gone to you first. That is sentimental; but I have a headache after "Antony & Cleopatra" (Oh Lord!) and yet must turn out again to see "Othello." One touch of your finger on my forehead would cure me; but of course you choose this moment to desert me. Miss P. T. has found me out: after about a year of fascination she tells me that I am "the most self-centred man she ever

767

met." Just at present I am Ellen-centred; but the sun is hidden by clouds of silence. Well, I must wait, I suppose. You will get tired of him, whoever he is; and then you will be sorry you starved me.

Did you see a wild article in a new paper called "The Comet" declaring that Wilson Barrett is the greatest of English actors who is kept back by a dastardly press conspiracy organised by H.I.? Oh my head! I must away to my stall of torment, unconsoled. Cruel Ellen. Poor

GBS

P.S. I return to Dorking tomorrow. Up on Wednesday afternoon for the VESTRY!!!!

To JOHN BURNS

Lotus. Tower Hill. Dorking
28th May 1897

[A/2]

[The Princess of Wales (later Queen Alexandra) had inaugurated a fund to entertain at dinner 330,000 poor people in honour of Victoria's Diamond Jubilee, and on 24th and 30th June the Prince and Princess of Wales visited their "humble" guests during the meal, which was provided in public buildings throughout London. The London School Board election was scheduled for November, and the Fabian Society and other Socialist groups were preparing themselves for battle. The Fabians supported the Progressives and helped to win a strong majority on the Board, including four Fabians.

The Joint Socialist Policy Conference was held in the Fabian office on 2nd April, during which a plan was formulated and embodied in a resolution for the formation of a court of appeal to adjudicate between rival Socialist candidates standing for the same seat at any contested election. As might have been anticipated, nothing came of it. W.J.Barwick of Hanley and C.F. Davis of Kentish Town were members of the S.D.F. Executive Committee. George Lansbury (1859-1940), a lifelong Socialist, was M.P. for Bow and Bromley (1910-12), editor of the *Daily Herald* (1913-22), and leader of the Parliamentary Labour Party (1931-35).]

Dear Burns

It isnt the Guardians: its the Vestry. I have nothing to do with it. I addressed no meetings; I took no steps; I did what I could to provoke the wirepullers to drop me. No use: the Moderates rallied round me; the extra candidates were bullied into withdrawing; and I was elected without a contest on a compromise which enabled both sides to claim me.

My first proceeding was to make an alarmist speech declaring that the Princess's Jubilee Feed would lead to a Moscow catastrophe if we were not careful. To stop my mouth they promptly put me on the committee; and now I shall be able to buy up all St Pancras with two-shilling tickets for soup. What a glorious engine of parochial corruption it will be!

As to the Schoolboard business I am not at all easy about it, because the I.L.P. have at last succeeded in reviving that notion of a Joint Committee of Socialist Bodies; and a Committee has actually been formed of 3 Fabians, 3 S.D.Fers & 3 I.L.Pe ers. I got delegated to the one meeting as yet held. Keir Hardie proposed that the Committee should be a Court of Appeal to decide between rival Socialist candidates at elections. Foreseeing that at the Sch.B. election it would be absolutely necessary to insist on strict discipline & shut down on all independent candidates whatsoever, Socialist or not, I did what I could to defeat this; and the S.D.F. (Barwick, Davies & Lansbury), seeing that the Fabians would hold the scales in such a court between them & the I.L.P., backed me. But my colleagues (Bland & Pease) did not see the gravity of the situation & thought that I was making mischief & fomenting anti-fraternity (so I was). When the matter was referred to the Fabian Executive, an unlucky chance made the attendance small, & I lost my proposal (to decline) by one vote. So I had to accept the position of not having the confidence of the executive, and to withdraw from the Joint Committee, trusting to the S.D.F. to prevent anything being done. I think that when it comes to the point the Fabians will come right again & stand by the Progressive organization as the only one that can do anything but throw away seats; but for the moment they are not alive to this. Besides, all party ideas are discredited at present—after the Employers' Liability Bill, a Liberal Party attitude is impossible, and as a Tory one has always been out of the question, we seem to be getting genuinely mixed and independent at last.

I am staying down here with the Sidney Webbs until the 24th June. Their new book [*Industrial Democracy*] will contain a lot of interesting political theory—most of it more heterodox than Marx.

yrs sincerely
G. Bernard Shaw

29 Fitzroy Square W

[U(A)/10; X/117]   28th May 1897

No ill! A thousand ills. I never see my Ellen; I hardly ever hear from my Ellen; when she writes to me she does not post her letters: at all events she reproaches me with not answering letters I never got, and not doing things she asked me to do in petitions which never reached me. That is 999 ills; and the other is that what with the preparation of the plays for publication, and the ever returning Saturday windmill sail that strikes me down before I have stumbled to my knees after the last blow, and the Fabian with its two weekly committees, and now on top of it all the Vestry with *its* two committees, and the Webbs's great new treatise on Democracy which I have to help in revising, I cannot even write to you because I am afraid of boring you with the beaten-out fag end of my brains—because I can't feel my heart in my pen then. Of course it is all right: it is good for me to be worked to the last inch whilst I last; and I love the reality of the Vestry and its dustcarts and H'less orators after the silly visionary fashion-ridden theatres; but the machine-Shaw is not quite perfect yet: just now I am worried because I have forgotten something, left something undone, something un-satisfied, and that is YOU and nothing else. And yet if it would be a blessed thing to have you, it is the next blessedest thing to want you—better than being hard and hellish, as I now am for longer and longer stretches because I have not time or opportunity to exercise my heart.

I can't send "Mrs Warren" yet because it isn't printed. Miss P. T. has learnt to typewrite & is making me a typed copy from my original almost defaced scrawl; and this copy I am revising and filling in with business for the printer. It's much my best play; but it makes my blood run cold: I can hardly bear the most appalling bits of it. Ah, when I wrote that, I *had* some nerve. And yet it's only three or four years ago—five at most.

I have written *such* a nasty article ["Mainly about Shakespeare"] for tomorrow—nasty for Henry, nasty for Janet, nasty for Wilson Barrett. I've used Janet & H. I. as bolsters to bang one another with, recalling the old days when H. didn't know how to do the grand style, and comparing Janet in Cleopatra to him.

I go back to Dorking tomorrow morning by the 10.30 train. Had to come up tonight for the Fabian. Must come up again on Monday for a Vestry committee—Princess Dinner Fund—a ghastly, wicked, wasteful folly. But these things will give my letter a dry taste. If only I could bring you down with me. There's nobody there but Mrs Webb, Miss P.T., Beatrice Creighton (Bishop of London's daughter), Webb & myself. Alas! *four* too many. I wonder what you would think of our life—our eternal political shop; our mornings of dogged writing, all in separate rooms; our ravenous plain meals; our bicycling; the Webbs' incorrigible spooning over their industrial & political science; Miss P.T., Irish, shrewd & green eyed, finding everything "very interesting"; myself always tired and careworn, and always supposed to be "writing to Ellen." You'd die of it all in three hours, I'm afraid. Oh, I wish, I wish—

G.B.S.

To JANET ACHURCH

[T/1 (A/4)]   Lotus. Tower Hill. Dorking
                                             29th May 1897

Oh stupidest of created women, how can I answer such letters! I ask myself how I have ever consented to know a moral void—a vacuum. I am cured of arrogance: I no longer pretend to have written either "Candida" or the [*Saturday Review*] Wild Duck article: I admit that you wrote them both. But mark the result of my humility. If "Candida" is ever done, it shall not be done by subscriptions collected for the performance of a play by Ibsen. Oh, stupid, stupid, stupid, STUPID woman: can you see *nothing* when the footlights are in your eyes?

Before you do Cleopatra again you must study those big tirades: there is no use in shirking them and gabbling. I mean that stuff beginning "From my cold heart let heaven engender hail"—impossible nonsense, all of it, but all the more dependent on its sound and rhythm. And the scene with the messenger is an Irvingite imposture—a reading of your own stuck in between the lines, which you stumble over & kick out of your way as best you can. Oh, it was all Irving, every bit of it, except your tragic glaring with your eyes, which was Robins or anybody. It's no use: you're going to have your way at last, to tear and rage and be a success. Thank Heaven, I am going to publish—to renounce the theatre and all its works. Janet was an illusion; the reality is Mrs Crummles [an actress in Dickens's *Nicholas Nickleby*].

Give my compliments to Calvert on the success with which he has flattened himself out. But why did the idiot not seize the opportunity to play Hjalmar? He would have made his mark in that: Antony can no

771

more make a mark on London than a stone on the round pond in Kensington Gardens.

I am worried out of my life between my publisher clamoring for MS, and "Mrs Warren," and the Fabian, & the Vestry, and the Princess's dinner fund (I am on the St Pancras Committee of that ghastly folly) and the Saturday Review, and Cleopatra, and Heaven knows what not. And this is the moment you choose to desert the one safe course of doing exactly what I tell you and nothing else. I *knew* there was mischief in that "Lady from the Sea" prospectus when you shot it out without telling me.

Charrington turned up at the Fabian last night with a glassy eye, and a lethargic mien. He surveyed us malevolently during the lecture & then rose, and after a brief struggle with sleep and his consonants, poured forth an impassioned sermon which amazed the executive & excited the rank & file to wild applause. I thought at first that you were ill and had been keeping him up at night; but on a closer inspection I found that he was harmlessly inebriated, though in full possession of his faculties. I ask myself is all the world going mad.

GBS

To ELLEN TERRY

[U(A)/10; X/117]

Again in the train.—joggle, joggle
11th June 1897
—night—third class—after
a Fabian meeting—on my right
Webb—on my left—no matter

[The Sarah Siddons Memorial in Paddington Green, sponsored by the Shakespeare Reading Society, was unveiled on 14th June; Irving made the dedication speech. S. Murray Carson (1865–1917), actor-manager and playwright, was for many years a member of Wilson Barrett's company; he had earlier appeared as Napoleon in W. G. Wills and G. G. Collingham's *A Royal Divorce* (1891). Three performances of *The Man of Destiny* were given, at the Grand Theatre, Croydon, on 1st to 3rd July. Carson also produced *The Devil's Disciple*, for the first time in England, at the Princess of Wales's Theatre, Kennington, on 26th September 1899. The Strange Lady in *The Man of Destiny* was played by Florence West (1862–1912), the wife of Lewis Waller; she had appeared in *An Ideal Husband* and *The Manxman*.]

I got a frantic notion at the Comedy Theatre the other afternoon that you were in the house. I thought there was a Lyceum party in a

772

box because I met Cooper in the corridor. Cooper is quite a pretty, amiable looking, chubby fellow off the stage, with a complexion as charming as wig paste. Perhaps it *is* wig paste. Why can't he be taught to act? Has he NO intelligence?

Well, it was a false alarm: you were not there. I haven't seen you for so long that I have half a mind to accept my invitation to the Siddons Memorial unveiling. Oh, why isn't it the St Pancras Vestry instead of the Paddington?—I'd make a speech & drive Henry mad. An innocent friend of mine [Emery Walker] met him at dinner the other day, & said cheerfully, "When are we going to have Mr Shaw's play?" H. observed that I was a clever person, but disrespectful to dignitaries; and my friend hastened to say that he was a great friend of mine, whereupon H. said to himself "Dive, thoughts, down to my soul," and changed the subject. The other day a man [Frederick Harrison] said to me, "Irving *was* drunk in Richard." "How do you know?" says I. "I had it from his son," says he. Such are our children, Ellen. I don't know which of the two young rascals it was, but both of them probably inherit enough of their parent's impishness to be unable to resist the joke of giving him away, with or without good grounds.

The first moral lesson I can remember as a tiny child was the lesson of teetotallism, instilled by my father, a futile person [you would have thought him].* One night, when I was still about as tall as his boots, he took me out for a walk. In the course of it I conceived a monstrous, incredible suspicion. When I got home I stole to my mother & in an awestruck whisper said to her, "Mamma: I think papa's drunk." She turned away with impatient disgust & said "When is he ever anything else?" I have never believed in anything since: then the scoffer began: then was sown the seed which so annoys Henry when it comes up in my articles. Oh, a devil of a childhood, Ellen, rich only in dreams, frightful & loveless in realities. And still I have to dream of my Ellen & never touch her. Well, let them unveil Mrs Siddons; but beware that another actress too is not unveiled that day—snatched from the platform, borne from the despairing Henry & the shrieking vestry away into the land of dreams, over the plains of heaven, to my home, wherever that may be.

Oh Ellen, Ellen, Murray Carson is going to do that play at Croydon on the 28th; and the Strange Lady will be a strange lady indeed. (12th June 1897). Who she will be I know not—care not. I am powerless:

---

* The clause which the present editor has enclosed in brackets does not appear in the original letter; apparently it was inserted by Shaw in the manuscript of the Terry-Shaw correspondence in 1931.

one must not behave like a child. But I hope it will fail, ludicrously, hideously, horribly. Stay, no: I hope the lady will fail as she deserves to, and that Carson may succeed so magnificently that he will be made a Jubilee baronet—not a miserable knight.

—(Later)—

Wonder could Edy do the Strange Lady!

Lord, what a supernal night it was last night in the train & coming home. A ten inch moon, a limelight sky, nightingales, everything wonderful. Today, the same clearness & an Italian heat. For the first time for months, I've loafed—read scraps of things—done nothing. I'm tired in all my bones. I finished the revision of "Mrs Warren" yesterday. And now I *must* do some work. But—to sustain me in it—keep on loving me (if you ever did) my Ellenest—love me hard, love me soft, and deep, and sweet, and for ever and ever and ever.

GBS

To ELLEN TERRY

[U(A)/10; X/117]

The midnight train—gets to Dorking at 1 (a.m.) 14th–15th June 1897—stopping just now, but will joggle like mad presently

[The interview "G. Bernard Shaw the Vestryman" (a written reply to a questionnaire) appeared in *The Londoner for St Pancras* on 18th June.]

Do you read these jogged scrawls, I wonder. I think of your poor eyes, and resolve to tear what I have written up: then I look out at the ghostly country and the beautiful night, and I cannot bring myself to read a miserable book: I *must* talk to you: nowhere else, no time else, can we be so perfectly alone. Yes, as you guess, Ellen, I am having a bad attack of you just at present. I am restless; and a man's restlessness always means a woman; and my restlessness means Ellen. And your conduct is often shocking. Today I was wandering somewhere, thinking busily about what I supposed to be high human concerns when I glanced at a shop window; and there you were—oh disgraceful and abandoned—in your 3rd Act Sans Gene dress—a mere waistband—laughing wickedly, and saying maliciously: "Look here: restless one, at your pillow, at what you are really thinking about." How can you look Window & Grove's camera in the face with such thoughts in your head & almost nothing on. You are worse than Lilith, Adam's first wife.

Oh fie, fie, let me get away from this stuff, which you have been listening to all your life, & despise—though indeed, dearest Ellen, these silly longings stir up great waves of tenderness in which there is no guile. You were right about my letters: only it is not boredom, but exhaustion. That is the worst of letters: I must say something: I can't in pen and ink rest these bruised brains in your lap & unburden my heart with inarticulate cries. When I can think, when I can write, then my ideas fly like stones: you can never be sure that one of them will not hurt you—my very love gets knit into an infernal intellectual fabric that wounds when I mean it to caress; and when I am tired & foolish I am flat & apparently bored. Sometimes that happens to my articles; and then I am terrified indeed, and must work fiercely to remedy it. When *you* complain, I am terrified another way, thinking that the end has come—for I have only one thing to say to you, and it must get tedious sooner or later. I am particularly tedious at present in this midnight solitary journey, wanting to sleep, and yet to sleep with you. Only, do you know what the consequences would be? Well, about tomorrow at noon when the sun would be warm & the birds in full song, you would feel an irresistible impulse to fly into the woods. And there, to your great astonishment & scandal, you would be *confined* of a baby that would immediately spread a pair of wings and fly, and before you could rise to catch it it would be followed by another & another and another—hundreds of them, and they would finally catch you up & fly away with you to some heavenly country where they would grow into strong sweetheart sons with whom, in defiance of the prayerbook, you would found a divine race. Would you not like to be the mother of your own grandchildren? If you were my mother, I am sure I should carry you away to the tribe in Central America where—but I have a lot of things to say & we are at Redhill already.

I shall find a letter from you when I get back to Lotus, shall I not? Reigate we are at now; and it's a quarter to one. In ten minutes, Dorking station; in seventeen minutes thereafter, Lotus, and a letter. *Only* a letter, perhaps not even that. O Ellen, what will you say when the Recording Angel asks you why none of your sins have my name to them?

What, no letter! not even this morning. Oh very good, madam, *ve*-ry good. Sorry I troubled you, I'm sure. Busy these times, no doubt. Of course: don't mention it. Where are my vestry papers? Nothing like prosaic local work—yes: I'll do an interview with "The St Pancras Londoner" about the dust destructor and the contractor system. After all, it is in the morning that one has one's wits about one—at night, fatigue & late hours & joggling trains upset a man and make him drivel. Still, there is such a thing as common politeness; and to leave most important letters from a vestryman unanswered, unnoticed—well, no matter.

GBS

To ELLEN TERRY

[X/117]

[29 Fitzroy Square W]
[Undated: assigned to 2nd July 1897]

[The letter is incomplete. *La Femme de Claude*, by Dumas *fils*, had been performed in London in French by Bernhardt, at Daly's Theatre, on 17th July 1894, and in Italian by Duse, at the Drury Lane Theatre, on 5th June 1895.]

. . . Is it not curious that the one thing not forgivable in an actor is *being* the part instead of playing it? Duse plays La Femme de Claude with an impossible perfection, and yet never touches the creature with the tips of her fingers.

. . . Nothing annoys me more than the want of self-respect in the English people in artistic matters which makes them believe that French acting is necessarily better than English. I must let fly in the Saturday about it. The other day a poor lady who had enjoyed Sans Gêne at the Lyceum and was duly ashamed of herself pleaded for you most pathetically. "*Of course* she's not Réjane; but," &c., &c., &c. She had observed a difference, and preferred you, but took it for granted that her preference was the shameful penalty of her English simplicity and ignorance. I sometimes lay people in ashes who go on like this. You are, on a moderate computation, about sixty times as good an actress as Réjane, especially in grip and technique; but all that goes for nothing against the assumption that Paris, the least artistic place in the universe, is the centre of all art, especially stage art.

I am rambling frightfully: in another moment I shall tear this up in a rage. When I am tired and out of sorts I cant finish a speech or a letter: I drag on mechanically repeating the dullest things. The reason is that I want to say tender things to you and *wont* go away until I say them; and yet I *cant* say them because my soul is shrouded in mists and my heart clogged. If you would just touch the spring it would all flow fast enough; but you prefer to desert me and remain obstinately at a distance.

776

What will happen about marriage is probably this. As soon as it is realized that people are learning how to do without it, it will be considerably modified, as in America, by a great extension of divorce. The English will never abolish marriage. They never abolish things; but they circumvent them more unscrupulously than any other nation. At present it is far better for two people who do not mean to devote themselves to a regular domestic, nursery career to maintain a clandestine connection than to run the risks of marriage. But if the divorce laws were so extended that a marriage could be dissolved as easily as a business partnership, then everybody would marry even if they only contemplated a year's association: in fact most marriages would be "only for a year, mind," and would last a lifetime. In that way we shall have more marriages than ever through the virtual abolition of marriage by divorce. Divorce is the Achilles heel of marriage. But at present the old system has the support of women because they are not economically independent of men. If you earned your living by keeping a man's house for him and bearing and bringing up his children you would feel strongly the life-and-death importance to you of an iron law and a fierce public opinion to guarantee you against being dropped and turned out of doors when he was tired of you personally. Marriage is not the man's hold on the woman, but the woman's on the man, and she will hold on to it like grim death until, like you, she gets paid for her work. At present she's an amateur, and does everything as badly as most amateurs.

And now I *must* stop. I suppose you are not coming to Croydon tomorrow to see the last of The Man of Destiny?

GBS

To ELLEN TERRY

[U(B)/10; X/117]

29 Fitzroy Square W
2nd July 1897

No, [I'm] not altogether sorry [you are ill]; for when you are well you don't care for anybody (that's the glory of health—its iron-heartedness) but when you are ill, you become foolish, and love me. Heaven send you continual bad health, my dearest Ellen, so that you may lie at home writing to me instead of making love to Napoleon and that stupid Lyceum audience.

Don't trouble about "The Man of Destiny." *All* plays are thrown away on the stage: do you think even *that* piece would not be as much a secret between you and me as it is now if it were played for a thousand nights at the Lyceum or the Théâtre Français? It might have forced my Strange Lady to be no longer strange to me if it had been rehearsed; but when that plan was baffled, the matter concerned me no further. Words cannot express my indifference to all this external business at Croydon. If I could stay away tomorrow without seeming to slight the company, it would not occur to me to go. As to H.I. (of *him* you are thinking, I know), serve him right. If all this theatre business mattered I should say that he has thrown *you* away, a blacker crime than the throwing away of 50,000,000,000,000 Men of Destiny. But you, also, cannot be thrown away. A few people know, though none of them know so well as I do. Dearest love: send me one throb of your heart whilst it is still tender with illness. It will be hard again on Monday; so be quick, quick, quick.

G. Bernard Shaw

To ELLEN TERRY

[U(A)/10; X/117]

29 Fitzroy Square W
4th July 1897

[Tommaso Salvini (1829–1916) was a celebrated Italian tragedian, noted for his Othello (played in New York to Edwin Booth's Iago), Paolo in Silvio Pellico's *Francesca da Rimini*, and Orosmane in Voltaire's *Zaïre*. Charles Surface is a character in Sheridan's *The School for Scandal*. Don Felix is a character in Susannah Centlivre's *The Wonder, A Woman Keeps a Secret*, a play which was extremely successful in the eighteenth century. Sophie Larkin (1833–1903), popular actress of the 1870s and 1880s, and best known for her marathon appearance in H.J.Byron's long-running *Our Boys*, performed minor comedy rôles in her late years. Henry Howe (1812–96) had performed at the Haymarket Theatre for nearly forty years before joining Irving in 1881.]

Oh Lord, Ellen, I've been to see "The Man of Destiny." It's just as well, perhaps; for I should perhaps have thought, if I hadn't seen it, that my noble brothers the critics were cutting it up, whereas I now boil with indignation at their corrupt friendliness. Picture to yourself the worst you ever feared for it; raise that worst to nightmare absurdity and horror; multiply it by ten; and then imagine even that result ruined by an attack of utter panic on the part of the company in which each made the other's speeches when he (or she) could think of anything to say at all, and then you will have some faint guess of what it was like. I was only seen to smile twice; and that was when a rowdy little kitten, fluffy but disreputable, appeared in the vineyard and was chivied by the innkeeper, and when it subsequently revenged itself by unexpectedly walking in again at one of Murray Carson's most Marengoesque moments and staring at him as if it could not understand how a man could go on in a way that no sane cat would dream of.

But it is not the blundering & incompetence that makes me feel criminal at these performances. As long as people are really *trying* (and they were really trying with pitiable sincerity last night) I have an enormous patience with them. The dreadful thing is the impossibility to them of getting on terms of real intimacy and enjoyment with my stuff. I can compare the effect to nothing but that made by our Italian opera people twenty years ago when they first tried Wagner, and had a theory that his music was very wonderful and strange and important & original, but could not for the life of them catch the melody or follow the harmony of it. The sub-lieutenant understood vaguely that he had a comic part; but he *could* not be comic, though ordinarily he is an arrant clown. Once, when by pure accident he hit on the right delivery of a line, the instantaneous response from the bewildered and miserable house both excited and disconcerted him. The applause at the end— half goodnature to the actors, half a perplexed tribute to my reputation—was like a groan: it was more pathetic by far than a vigorous hooting would have been. There was something insane & ghastly about the business; for since the dialogue does not consist of obvious jokes (which must either come off or be perceptibly muffed) but has, apart from its comedy, as continuous a grammatical sense as any blue-book, it sounded at once serious and inexplicable, like a dream-play. Fortunately the audience was humble in its agony, and mutely respected Napoleon for saying things it could not understand. It would even make a mouselike attempt to shew its appreciation now & then; but each time it shrunk back lest it should be taking seriously something that was perhaps one of my dazzling jokes. An agonizing experience for the author, Ellen; but an intensely interesting one for the critic.

As to your health, what you don't realize is, that the playing-every-night system is only possible for *routine* acting. You are a frightfully strong woman; and you have been a good deal spared by the superficiality, discontinuity & ready-madeness of the Portia-Beatrice business at the Lyceum. But even Shakspere can't be played every night with impunity. If you had really played that headless man scene in Cymbeline every night at full pitch you would either have broken down in the second week, or else have been by this time a mere wreck, capable of being set to work only by coarsening ruinous stimulants. Duse does not attempt to play every night; and I have seen Duse, when she was only playing twice a week, positively reeling with a dose of morphia. Salvini in America resolutely refused to play more than four times a week even when money was raining in. Barry Sullivan, a strictly temperate man, persisted in playing every night, with Charles Surface or Don Felix for resting parts; but he at last degenerated frightfully and had a shower of paralytic strokes. Sara Bernhardt, though she has reduced her business to the most mechanical routine possible, is a worn out hack tragedienne, almost as terrible of aspect as Sophie Larkin. I have seen a good deal myself of the touring platform man (& woman), the Trade Union organizer, the Socialist, Temperance & Salvation apostles who speak almost every night. It is a ruinous business always: the only people who can keep it up with impunity are the easy, phlegmatic ones who amble through it in a quite unexciting way. For instance, Howe could, I imagine, have played twice a day for a hundred years without turning a hair: I never saw him flurried except one night as Flamborough in "Olivia" at the Lyceum, when he happened to be very drunk indeed. Now you are not that sort of person: you lay hold of your part with a tremendous nervous grip. It is not seen on the stage, because you come on with the grip ready fixed; but when you recite, you have to come on the platform first as Ellen Terry (with, oh, what bamboozling tricks & manners!), and then, when you attack the inevitable "Stay, gaoler, stay," a *critic* can see the clutch taking place, like the stringing of a bow. Well, at that rate it is useless to plan out hundreds of consecutive nights of "Sans Gêne": you can't do it. With H. I. it is quite different: he has no grip at all, comparatively, just as he has no voice, and therefore doesn't lose it. The condition in which he works is a somnambulistic one: he hypnotises himself into a sort of dreamy energy, and is intoxicated by the humming of his words in his nose. Besides, he escapes the terrible fatigue of thought & intellectual self-consciousness through having no brains. Wyndham *has* brains; but he, too, has found the somnambulistic method & the artificial voice. All that they need to get into the vein is a particular sort of dinner. But they pay the penalty too: they get older and muzzier and dreamier; and their flashes of genius become more delirious & shortwinded as they go on. Wyndham has been pulled up by something like a stroke on the stage. Now you have none of their reliefs & resources. Try the dinner system, and long before it has made you fat and coarse (forgive these blasphemies, dear Ellen)

& destroyed your delicacy & charm, the degeneration will present itself to you as *illness* and inability to act, & stop you. What is happening to you now is Nature's forcible interference to prevent you from killing yourself with overwork; and I rejoice in it. I don't want you to play every night; and if H. I. were wise he would prepare for the time when he will have either to stop or to keep the Lyceum open to [meet] at least its expenses for two or three nights a week with *drama* alone, independently of himself & you. *There's* a sermon for you. Now I promise not to write again until my book is a little more advanced!

GBS

To ELLEN TERRY

[U(E, E, & A)/10; X/117]

29 Fitzroy Square W
11th July 1897

[Shaw's *Saturday Review* article on 10th July was a notice of Réjane's current London season; in it he enumerated the many fine performers (Alma Murray, Ada Rehan, Mrs Charles Calvert, Mrs Kendal, etc.) who rarely were seen in the London theatre, and expressed his gratitude that foreign performers "look in upon us occasionally for an advertisement." The "extra Saturday article" was a review on the 17th of Sydney Grundy's *The Silver Key*, which opened at Her Majesty's (Shaw erroneously says the Haymarket) on 10th July. Ellen appeared as Portia in special performances of *The Merchant of Venice* on the 15th (evening) and 17th (matinée), presented by Irving for the Conference of Librarians.

Laurence Irving (1872–1914), Sir Henry's younger son, lost his life in the *Empress of Ireland* when it sank in the St Lawrence. The play Shaw asked Ellen to send was *Peter the Great*. When it was produced at the Lyceum on 1st January 1898, Shaw reviewed the playscript only, for the Lyceum management had not sent reviewer's tickets to the *Saturday Review*, and Shaw had respected "the appeal to one to stay away." (But see letter of 27th December 1897 to Ellen Terry.)

The Women's Jubilee Dinner and Soirée, given by one hundred distinguished women to one hundred distinguished men, in the Grafton Galleries on 14th July, was arranged by Mrs Humphry Ward and a committee which included Ellen Terry. Shaw attended, but as he had turned down Janet Achurch's invitation, it is not clear whose guest he was. Frederick Temple Blackwood (1826–1902), first Marquess of Dufferin and Ava, diplomatist and administrator, during his long career was undersecretary for India, governor-general of Canada and, later, of India, and ambassador at Paris.]

(Beginning of first attempt)

Oh most presumptuous, how do *you* know—you, who never go to the theatre? If you leave this world without knowing me, you will be sent back after a million years of unspeakable purgatory to accomplish that destiny; for there will always be some lonely Adam looking at the world amid millions of blind creatures stumbling about through their dreams, and cursing him when they trip over his foot; and you were made different to other women in order that you might be that lonely Adam's Eve. . . .

[Balance of text is torn away.]

29 Fitzroy Square W
12th July 1897

(Beginning of second attempt)

Inhuman Ellen! I tried twice to answer your letter; and both times you led me into an extra Saturday article. Why do you suppose I run from time to time to rest this weary head in your lap? To water my dry soul at the fountain of life, not to explain to you why Rejane's company is excellent or why Alma Murray has my good word.

29 Fitzroy Square W
14th July 1897

(Final attempt)

It serves you right: why do you overwork *me* with your critical conundrums. It has ended in my writing a Saturday article about you and your methods under cover of noticing the Haymarket play. A more fearful dissection and demonstration of your methods has never been penned. By the way, I ought to see Portia before I correct the proof. But the Lyceum would fall on my head, and bury me with the fainting Stoker & the prostrate Henry if I presented myself.

Send me along Master Lawrence's play if you like. If I steal the plot my version will be so Shawified that nobody will recognize it; and if I have anything critical to say about it you can say it as from yourself. Even if he finds out he won't mind: people always like to be read. If H. does not produce it, the Independent Theatre is always there to fall back on.

Talking of that, Charrington is taking out a Doll's House tour; and he's going to try "Candida" on the provincial dog. He wants somebody who can play Prossy (a character in "Candida" which you forget, probably) and Mrs Linden in the Ibsen play. I suggested Edy. Would she go, do you think? It will be a pretty miserable tour—start at

782

Aberdeen after 12 hours travelling; but she might pick up something from Charrington; and Janet would keep her in gossip for a twelve-month to come.

(TURN OVER)

Now that you *have* turned over, I don't know that I have anything to say that will bear writing down. I am at present scudding close reefed before a gale. Oh why won't women be content to leave their stars in the heavens and not want to tear them down and hang them round their necks with a gold ring! Why does their pleasure turn to pain and their love to hate without their knowing that it has happened? I will put an end to it all by marrying. Do you know a reasonably healthy woman of about sixty, accustomed to plain vegetarian cookery, and able to read & write enough to forward letters when her husband is away, but otherwise uneducated? Must be plain featured, and of an easy, unjealous temperament. No relatives, if possible. Must not be a lady. One who has never been in a theatre preferred. Separate rooms.

This soirée is a nuisance. Only one woman invited me to the dinner (Janet) and I made her invite the editor [H. W. Massingham] of the Chronicle instead, after first dazzling the committee by about fifteen shilling's worth of effusive telegraphed regrets from Lord Dufferin. She who invited me to the soirée frightened me by getting into a sort of heart paroxysm on Monday after the opera [Meyerbeer's *Les Huguenots*, at Covent Garden] because I foolishly pointed out to her (without the least malice—even with the tenderest regret) that she was beginning to dislike me, and not a word have I heard since, in spite of my message of enquiry. Can you give me the address of the nearest monastery? Your deliberately getting ill tonight (I had fully intended to carry you away off H's arm & leave him staring in the midst of the distinguished ones) is the last straw.

GBS

To CHARLOTTE PAYNE-TOWNSHEND

[A/2; X/151]

29 Fitzroy Square W
13th July 1897

I have an iron ring round my chest, which tightens and grips my heart when I remember that you are perhaps still tormented. Loosen it, oh ever dear to me, by a word to say that you slept well and have never been better than today. Or else lend me my fare to Australia, to Siberia, to the mountains of the moon, to any place where I can torment nobody but myself. I am sorry—not vainly sorry; for I have done a good morning's work, but painfully, wistfully, affectionately sorry that you were hurt; but if you had seen my mind you would not have been hurt. I am so certain of that that I am in violently, brutally high spirits in spite of that iron ring. Write me something happy, but only a few words; and don't sit down to *think* over them. What you think is all wrong.

GBS

P.S. I am going out to lunch & to Grant Richards's shop. If you send a line between, say, 4 & 5.30 (after which I think I will go off for a thousand leagues on the bike) I shall be here to receive it. Oh, the ring, the ring: hasten to ease it a little: it clutched me bitterly just then.

To ELLEN TERRY

[U(A)/10; X/117]

29 Fitzroy Square W
16th July 1897

[The "secret" was Laurence Irving's *Peter the Great*. Shaw instantly passed the news on to Golding Bright. Dorothy Tennant (d. 1926) was married to the famous African explorer Sir Henry Morton Stanley (1841–1904), whose autobiography she edited in 1909. Mrs Charles Kean was the actress Ellen Tree (1806–80). In the *Saturday Review* on 17th July, Shaw reported: "Miss Terry, as we all know, went on the stage in her childhood, and not only 'picked up' her profession, but was systematically taught it by Mrs. Charles Kean . . ."]

A secret! Good: we must paragraph it at once; and H.I. must confirm the rumor by announcing it from the stage on the last night of the season. I saw Laurence at the Dinner-Soirée; but as I don't know him I did not speak to him. But I told everybody that he had written a magnificent play, which was the right thing to do for him under the circumstances. I made the acquaintance of Ted, who won my heart with great ease, though I have no doubt he made abundant fun of me with the other Heavenly Twin when my back was turned.

Your last autograph letter not only got delayed in posting, but lost half of itself on the way. I only got the last sheet, beginning in the middle of a sentence. A cruel robbery.

784

I have always said that there are only two really sympathetic women in London—yourself & Dorothy Tennant (Mrs Stanley). Dorothy is the more sympathetic of the twain; for she has just *rested* me by getting me all alone and talking to me for an hour and a half. This should be an example to selfish people who shut themselves up and get ill all by themselves. I suppose I mayn't go to Winchelsea. I am almost dying for a little sea air. However, hasten away to rest & health, with my heart's blessing.

If there really is a part for you in Laurence's play, send it to me and I'll study it for you & save you a lot of trouble. Ask his leave if you like.

Tomorrow you will open the Saturday with dread & shut it with shrieks of indignation. Used Mrs Charles Kean to throw things at you?

GBS

P.S. Don't tire yourself by trying to write to me—at least not more than five or six pages.

To ELLEN TERRY

[U(A)/10; X/117]

29 Fitzroy Square W
20th July 1897

[Edith Craig had been engaged by the Charringtons for their tour of *Candida* and *A Doll's House* (the latter was performed at the Islington Grand all that week). She played Prossy again in the Stage Society production in 1900. Theodor Leschetizsky (1830–1915) was a composer and teacher of piano, whose pupils included Paderewski and Ossip Gabrilówitsch.]

Edy is going to have a very difficult job of it with Mrs Linden, because Janet is so loathingly sick of rehearsing it with new Lindens that she wants Edy to get through with only one rehearsal. And the effort of swallowing all those words will be bad for Prossy. However, we must make the best of it.

The only difficulty about Prossy will be the usual difficulty—want of muscle in the enunciation of the words. When people intend to play the piano in public, they play scales for several hours a day for years. A pupil of Leschetitsky (Paderewski's master) comes before the public with steel fingers, which give a quite peculiar quality and penetration even to pianissimo notes. An actress should practise her alphabet in just the same way, and come before the public able to drive a nail up to the head with one touch of a consonant. For want of this athleticism,

785

people get driven to slow intonings, and woolly execution. Now for Prossy I want extreme snap in the execution: every consonant should have a ten pound gun hammer spring in it, also great rapidity & certainty of articulation. Of course Edy has not got all that yet; but I shall get more of it out of her than she dreams of troubling herself for at present. Young people don't realize what a tremendous deal of work it takes to make a very small effect. But she starts with a good deal in hand that one looks in vain for elsewhere. Her expression is, if anything, too expressive normally, like Forbes Robertson's. Her voice is quite her own. But she needs to work & use her head a good deal; for she is like a boy in her youth & virginity, and cannot fall back on "emotional" effects which are really only the incontinences of a hysterical and sexually abandoned woman, but which pull a great many worthless & stupid actresses through leading parts in vulgar drama. So she will—fortunately for herself—get nothing cheap. I have told her that if I can do anything for her in the way of going over the part with her I will make time to do it. But probably she will not be able to make time for it. Still, if it can be done, I will fit myself into it somehow. A rehearsal (at Queen's Gate Hall) takes three hours. We begin at 11 tomorrow & should get finished a little after 2. I can put off writing the Saturday article (not yet begun, alas!) until the evening. Consequently, since you go to bed (don't you?) in the afternoon, I could lunch in the neighborhood & call at Barkston Gardens from half past three to half past five, if that would be any use. A couple of police-men on the stairs would be sufficient to prevent my attempting to see you by force. I do not see how she could call here without dislocating her day too frightfully. I have not proposed this to her, because she may feel—and be right in feeling—that she had better be satisfied with what she can pick up at rehearsal, and have all the rest of the time to herself. Just find out what she thinks; and if she wants a private rehearsal, propose my coming round as above, as a brilliant idea of your own. I can "hear her" over Mrs Linden if she likes, when my hand is in. If I can do anything else or anything more, say what; and I'll do it. But don't let her suppose that I doubt her perfect ability to look after herself. Far be such presumption from my mind!

How are you?

In haste, ever dearest Ellen,

your

GBS

786

To CHARLOTTE PAYNE-TOWNSHEND

[A/2]

29 Fitzroy Square W
21st July 1897

Heavy day before me—not a second to write—Rehearsal 10, Vestry 3 to 7, Saturday article in the evening. Love & blessing.

GBS

To JANET ACHURCH

[T/1 (C/4)]

29 Fitzroy Square W
Midnight—23rd July 1897

Wretch!—to drag me all the way to Islington for such an inconceivably bad performance. I declare before outraged Heaven that acting is to you and Charrington not an honest night's work, but a form of reckless self-indulgence. You'd much better have got me to rehearse "A Doll's House" than "Candida": it's all gone to the deepest devil. Rank is literally on his last legs: it is time for C.C. to change to Krogstad, and I strongly advise you to take a turn at Ellen [error for Christine Linden?]. You have driven a red hot harrow over my heart & soul: I will never enter a theatre again.

GBS

To ELLEN TERRY

[U(A)/10; X/117]

29 Fitzroy Square W
27th July 1897

[Inspired apparently by the Calvert-Achurch production of *Antony and Cleopatra*, Shaw had promised Forbes-Robertson a play about Cæsar and Cleopatra for himself and Mrs Patrick Campbell (see also letter of 8th September 1897 to Ellen Terry). Work on the play was not commenced until 23rd April 1898. In Forbes-Robertson's production of *Hamlet* in October, at the Lyceum, the Ghost and Osric were played by Ian Robertson and John (later Sir John) Martin Harvey. Jean de Reszke (1850–1925), Polish operatic tenor, was unrivalled in his dramatic interpretations and vocal brilliance in Wagnerian parts. He reigned at Covent Garden from 1888 until his retirement in 1901. Henry Duff Traill (1842–1900), journalist and critic, was an editorial writer for the *Daily Telegraph* (1882–97).
The father of Ellen Terry's son and daughter was Edward William Godwin

787

(1833–86), an archaeologist, architect, and theatre designer, with whom Ellen lived in retirement from 1868 to 1874, following the dissolution of her unfortunate marriage with the painter G. F. Watts.

Gertrude Kingston (1866–1937), actress-manager, made her professional début in Sarah Thorne's Margate company, and first appeared in London with Beerbohm Tree in Robert Buchanan's *Partners* (1888). Irving had engaged her to appear as the Queen of Naples in *Madame Sans-Gêne*. In later years she became a close friend of Shaw, who wrote *Great Catherine* (1913) for her. She also created the rôles of Aurora in *How He Lied to Her Husband* (London, 1905) and Ermyntrude in *The Inca of Perusalem* (1916), and starred in revivals of *Captain Brassbound's Conversion* (1912), *You Never Can Tell* (as Mrs Clandon, 1922), and *Getting Married* (as Mrs George, 1922).]

The "Candida" people are off to Aberdeen at last; and I have struck Saturday work for a month or two; so now I have nothing to do but get my seven plays through the press; write the prefaces to the two volumes; read the proof sheets of the Webbs' great book "Problems of Democracy" [*i.e., Industrial Democracy*] (doesn't it sound succulent?); answer two years' arrears of letters; and write a play & a few articles & Fabian tracts or so before October. Holiday times, dearest Ellen, holiday times!

Johnstone F. R. is in tribulation over his "Hamlet." He turned up here the other day beating his breast, and wanting to know whether I couldn't write a nicer third act for "The Devil's Disciple," since Cleopatra was not ready for Campbell-patra. I wrote him out a lovely cast for "Hamlet," including Teddy as Osric (if Edward Craig Esquire will so far condescend). Will you, however, give Ted this hint. Courtenay Thorpe lately played the Ghost, and made a hit in it. I put him down for it in my suggested cast; but I sincerely hope that F. R. won't take the suggestion, because it is (or may be) important to me to have Thorpe free for "Candida." In that case, Ted, with his pathetic voice, might play the Ghost himself, if Thorpe has broken the tradition sufficiently to make the notion acceptable. At all events, put it into Ted's head that it is a possible thing; so that if he gets chatting with F. R. or anyone else in the affair, he may say that his three parts are Hamlet (of course), the Ghost & Osric.

I am certain I could make "Hamlet" a success by having it played as Shakspere meant it. H. I. makes it a sentimental affair of his own; and this generation has consequently never seen the real thing. However, I am afraid F. R. will do the usual dreary business in the old way, & play the bass clarinet for four hours on end, with disastrous results.

788

Lord! how I would make that play jump along at the Lyceum if I were manager. I'd make short work of that everlasting "room in the castle." You should have the most beautiful old English garden to go mad in, with the flowers to pluck fresh from the bushes, and a trout stream of the streamiest and ripplingest to drown yourself in. I'd make such a scene of "How all occasions do inform against me!"—Hamlet in his travelling furs on a heath like a polar desert, and Fortinbras and his men "going to their graves like beds"—as should never be forgotten. I'd make lightning & thunder (comedy & tragedy) of the second & third acts: the people should say they had never seen such a play before. I'd—but no matter.

I was at the opera last night: "Tristan." O Ellen, Ellen, Ellen, think of it! De Reszke, at 48, playing his *second* season of Tristan, to a perfectly crazy house, and cursing himself in his old age for not doing what I told him years ago when I cannonaded the Opera and himself just as I now cannonade the Lyceum & Henry. And now Henry capitulates and orders a play [*The Medicine Man*, performed at the Lyceum on 4th May 1898] from the musical critic of The World (my successor Hichens) and Traill. In a year or two or three, you and he will be doing what I have told you, and saying, like De Reszke, "Why, oh why didn't we realize the godlike wisdom of this extraordinary man before!"

You need not be anxious about Edy: she will take care of herself & of the rest very efficiently. She has inherited your social powers & would be worth £20 a week in the company even if she didn't act at all. And she has lots of acting in her, though she has been much neglected technically by an unnatural mother. Charrington began, as usual, with the most elaborate and ingenious theories of what she must be (founded on masterly surveys of the Terry character, the Lyceum art, and her father's nature) but she bowled him out in no time, and it ended in his being so glad to have her in the company that if he were not by nature a hopelessly monogamic person, and so violent a partisan of his wife that he would be furiously jealous on her account if any other woman infringed her rights to his exclusive devotion, Heaven knows what might not happen. Edy made all the difference in the world in the comfort of the rehearsals: there was no strain in them for me. I am afraid I got on her nerves and hampered her—I always do; for I sit there apparently intently and sufferingly watching the most agonising maltreatment of my piece, when I am really taking things quite easily—but she never failed in tact for a moment; and I positively have not a notion whether she thinks that all the Aynesworth-Emery tales from the Haymarket fell leagues short of the horrible reality, or whether she thinks me the most inocuously amiable ass of an author who was ever laughed at by a company. Similarly, I haven't the ghost of a notion of what she really thinks of Thorpe or Janet or Charrington, although she is perfectly easy and unguarded & spontaneous in her ways. So you may leave her to herself with perfect tranquillity: she's the only member of the company that needs no looking after.

She is of course a little too young for Mrs Linden; but I am firmly persuaded that I could make her play it miles better in six rehearsals than it has ever been played before. Probably she will be the best on record as it is. She only wants to be shewn a few trumpery little tricks—mostly turns of the head & other methods of escape from perpetual profile—to get on capitally. Then she says "Ah'll" for "I'll" occasionally without a pang of remorse; but it's so pretty in effect that not for worlds would I call her attention to it. It is like her aunt Marion's trick of saying "doant," which is Irish for "don't," and much better than "downt," à la Gertrude Kingston.

I suppose I am going to Wales on Friday. My address there will be The Argoed, Penalt, Monmouth.

Are you reviving with the ozone?

GBS

To GRAHAM WALLAS

[B/13]

29 Fitzroy Square W
27th July 1897

[Wallas had just announced his engagement to Ernest Radford's sister Ada (1859–1934), whom he married in December. Shaw thus became the only unmarried member of the Fabian "old gang."]

Well, I'll be damned! Is the date fixed?

GBS

To ELLEN TERRY

[U(A)/10; X/117.e]

The Argoed. Penallt. Monmouth
5th August 1897

[Shaw was spending a six weeks' holiday with the Webbs and Charlotte Payne-Townshend in much the same manner as in the previous year. Lionel

Belmore (1868–1953) was a competent supporting performer, well known both in London and in the United States; in his later years he played character parts in more than a hundred American motion pictures. "Bo" was a sobriquet bestowed upon Beatrice Webb by her relatives.

William Archer, reviewing *The Man of Destiny* in *St Paul's* on 31st July, labelled the play a nondescript eccentricity which "represents nothing, illustrates nothing, typifies nothing, caricatures nothing." Confessing that at one point he actually fell asleep, he inquired of the author: "Now, frankly, my dear Shaw, if Mr. G.R. Sims had introduced such a piece of mechanical and meaningless claptrap into an Adelphi melodrama, what would the *Saturday Review* have said? And why should that in G.B.S. be a stroke of genius which in G.R.S. would be flat idiocy? And, taking it all in all, *is* this a play of which your critical intelligence can approve?"]

Just another line in the fresh morning before breakfast. If you have never been here it is no use describing this country to you. Dorking & Surrey are to it what Tottenham Court Road is to the 15th century. You not only have all the ordinary naturalnesses & freshnesses of Nature; but you have a deliberate poetic beauty. The god who made this country was an artist, who moulded his hills so that their lines run down into the valleys quite magically, and trimmed them with tufted woods so that not an acre *glares*, however warm the sun is. The fellow who turned out Dorking was a bank holiday tradesman in comparison.

It is a lovely morning, and from this lawn, 800 feet above the Wye, I can see away across it over the forest of Dean. There is not a cloud in the sky except a few toy white ones; and yet it is thundering away like mad, peal after peal, over eastward. And now they are just dropping a gauze over the horizon, and the tree under which I am sitting has shivered & sighed, as if it were catching cold. So perhaps we shall have some Rheingold effects presently.

Oh Lord, Ellen, I am so tired, even in the morning. I get out of bed so tired that I am in despair until I have braced myself with tubbing. When I sit down my back gets tired: when I jump up, I get giddy & have to catch hold of something to save myself from falling. Miss P.T. has brought down hammocks. Two days in one without a thought or a pen would re-establish me; but I haven't the energy to fix them up. I can only rest myself by thinking that *you* are in a hammock, and writing to you.

Before I left town I got a letter from Charrington. He said that Edy was too sympathetic for my notion of Prossy, but that a Terry couldn't be otherwise than sympathetic, and there was no use in trying to alter it. However, I am quite content with that account. I quite meant that the part should come out sympathetic *in spite of itself*, which is exactly what it seems to have done by C's account. He is wrong about Edy: she can do a hard bit of character well enough: at least she did it in Pinero's whatsitsname—"Bygones," is it? He said that Janet was very good in the scenes with Morell in the second act (it was evident at rehearsal that she would be), but that in the great final speech she sat there articulating staccato, and religiously imitating my way of doing it until he could hardly hold himself back from getting up & stopping the play. Burgess, the comic father [Lionel Belmore], was the success of the evening; and the drunken scene in the third act carried Aberdeen off its feet so that every exit was followed by a minute's uproarious applause. On the other hand, the poet was quite as misunderstood as he was in his own family, and this, Charrington says, was not Thorpe's fault, but Aberdeen's. He says nothing about himself.

They are to play the piece at Eastbourne & Bournemouth. See it if you can, & tell me about it; probably I shant see it at all, though there is some question of my going over to Leamington with Miss P.T. What are you wondering about us? She is getting used to me now, I think. Down at Dorking there was a sort of earthquake, because she had been cherishing a charming project of at last making me a very generous & romantic proposal—saving it up as a sort of climax to the proofs she was giving me every day of her regard for me. When I received that golden moment with shuddering horror & wildly asked the fare to Australia, she was inexpressibly taken aback, and her pride, which is considerable, was much startled—Excuse me one moment: she is calling me from her window. Tableau.

* * * * * *

Now I am all right. She threw me out two waterproof packets, looking like Army Stores. I found a hammock in each; and I have actually suspended them both from this tree, taking care to put one so high that nobody but myself will be able to get into it. And now I am swinging in that hammock, with your letter to answer, and "Arms & The Man" to prepare for the printer as soon as I feel disposed to work.

The tiredness, by the way, is *maladie du pays*: it is wearing off; and in a day or two I shall be sublime.

Well, as I was saying, that revelation of my self centredness as a mere artistic machine was a shock; but now she says "What a curious person you are!" or "What an utter brute you are!" as the humor takes her; and we live an irreproachable life in the bosom of the Bo family. By the way we have had one desertion—Graham Wallas has

792

suddenly got engaged to a Miss Radford. They all succumb sooner or later: I alone remain (and will die) faithful to myself and Ellen.

Just imagine this fifty pound business [Janet Achurch had borrowed £50 from Charlotte]. Can you imagine a more morally *thriftless* thing to do than to take advantage of a rich woman being fond of me and of a play of mine being in the repertory to extract money, knowing all the time what she must think of the transaction and what I must feel about it. We had a council of the family over it here when the fatal telegram arrived, Mrs Webb being absent (she has not come down yet). Webb was goodnatured & sensible—said "Yes: that's about what it was bound to cost you if you wish to be friendly. I'd give a fiver myself under the circumstances, which is about the equivalent out of my income of £50 out of yours." But I obstinately refused to consent not to withdraw "Candida" unless she [Charlotte] pledged herself to accept repayment from me out of my future profits (if any) as dramatic author; and I wrote to J. to explain to her that she had sold her monopoly for £50, as I should now have no right to allow any personal considerations to stand between that debt & its repayment, and will accept the first good offer I get for its production in London whether she is in the cast or not. On receiving this terrible intimation, Janet will weep, attempt suicide, write me an abusive letter, declare herself a wretch unworthy to live, and telegraph for £10 more to meet a pressing engagement. Is it not amazing—that histrionic character (or want of character) that *appreciates* every sort of heroism and nobility in the most exalted and affectionate spirit, and that cannot in its own proper person resist a five pound note any more than a cat can resist a penn'orth of fried fish.

Oh, I must do some work this morning. I have the proofs of "Mrs Warren" all but the last few pages. When they come I'll send you a spare set; & you must tell me what you think of it. By the way, that stupid old "Widowers' Houses" is not so bad as I thought: Ive made it quite presentable with a little touching up. Did you see Archer's column of weary & disgusted vituperation of "The Man of Destiny" in "St Paul's." I intended to send it to you; but I find Ive left it in the pocket of a London coat. No news from Forbes: he'll never touch "The D.'s D." unless he is driven to it by flat play-bankruptcy. Mustn't begin another sheet—

ever—
GBS

To ELLEN TERRY

[A/6]

The Argoed. Penallt. Monmouth
7th August 1897

Proofs of the last of "Mrs Warren" just come. Will you look through the play (excuse the roughness of a first proof) and send it back to me. The post is just going; and there is no further communication with this place for fortyeight hours.

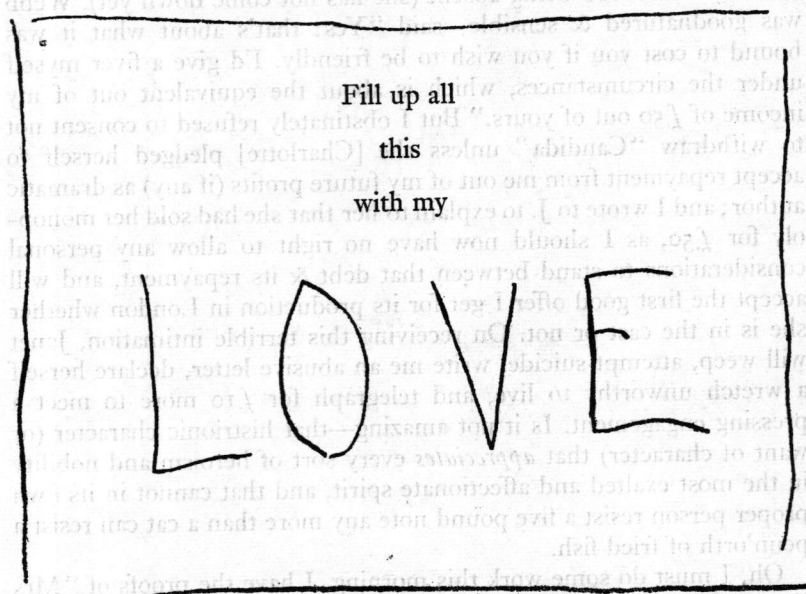

Fill up all this with my

LOVE

GBS

To ELLEN TERRY

[U(A)/10; X/117]

The Argoed. Penallt. Monmouth
10th August 1897

[*Madame attend monsieur* (1872) was a one-act play by Henri Meilhac and Ludovic Halévy.]

That's what they all want—a play in which pretty lies will make as much effect as awful truths. But it's impossible. You have seen all my plays now (except Widowers' Houses?). The hand is the same, the

794

heart is the same (none at all), the brain is the same, the man is the same; but you see how different the play is when it grapples with life unconditionally.

You are wrong, believe me, about the long speeches. The easiest thing to do in public is a monologue. It is sheer want of practice that makes actors self-mistrustful when they are asked to deliver a speech or tell a story on the stage instead of asking or answering questions, or throwing sentences at one another's heads. Why does nobody ever fail as Hamlet? Because he has long speeches. Remember, the nation is trained to hear sermons. The real difficulty in that scene is not Mrs Warren's talking, but Vivie's listening. Bless you, I've made speeches hours long to casual wayfarers who could go away when they pleased; and they all stopped at least half an hour, though I am by no means as attractive a speaker as you are an actress. They would not have stood ten minutes of duologue. Do you know "Madame attend Monsieur"? It is virtually a monologue. Of course, a flimsy, unreal subject wont stand long speeches; but if you have the right stuff, the speeches can't be too long.

I have a lot of other things to say; but it is time to go to post. Imagine! I've been a week here, and I've only finished the second act of "Arms & The Man" (the revision for the printer). It is a stupendous job.

The Weekly Sun says that you have gone to Winchelsea, where you have a cottage, and that H.I. has gone to Somewhereelse, where Mrs Pat. has a cottage. Such is journalistic tact.

GBS

To JANET ACHURCH

The Argoed. Penallt. Monmouth
19th August 1897

[T/1 (A/4)]

[The multiple copyrighting performance did not occur. *The Philanderer* and *You Never Can Tell* received copyright performances, a week apart, at the Bijou Theatre, Bayswater, in March 1898. George Alexander Redford (d. 1916) was the examiner of plays for the Lord Chamberlain; he subsequently became film censor. Redford did object to *Mrs Warren's Profession*, as will be seen in later correspondence (1898).

The anonymous critic of the *Northern Figaro*, Aberdeen, on 7th August, had written of the première performance of *Candida*: "I don't think we'll be much troubled with Mr. Shaw's comedy, for a comedy to be popular requires to have some life in it. It takes one quite a long time to understand what it is all about, and even then it is not very clear. . . . I was sorry for Miss Achurch, she had such an uncongenial part to play, she certainly did her best with it, but I don't think she will ever say that 'Candida' is her favourite part. . . . There was not a large audience in the theatre on Friday, and I noticed that they did not even know when they should laugh or keep silent. At the end the actors were cheered for getting through the performance so efficiently."]

I had my doubts about the susceptibility of Leamington; but the reason I didn't go is that the labor of preparing the plays for the press has assumed unexpected and colossal dimensions. I have worked without intermission ever since I came here; and the result is, "Arms & The Man" and one act of "Candida" ready for the printer—not a line more, as I live by vegetables! Can you tell me roughly where the play wants mending; for I am now at work on it, and must make the alterations this month or never. I enclose you a memorandum of the changes I have made in the first act. The first one is to meet the objection that has always been made—that the children are sprung on the audience to their utter surprise in the last scene for the first time. The others speak for themselves. The rest of the work I have been doing consists in replacing the scenic specifications and stage directions by descriptions for the benefit of the general reader. For instance the beginning of the act is an elaborate description of the whole Hackney district; then a description of Victoria Park; and finally a description of the parsonage and the room. The passages of description which are meant to replace the effect of the acting will be most illuminating to theatrical posterity.

As to Thorpe, there is nothing for it but to let him sow his wild oats in the part. Who else can you get? Esmond wouldn't go on tour with you: he will stick to London authorially and actorially. Lawrence Irving would hardly fit into your company either; and it is of the company you must think. You will find it hard to get a young leading man whose connexion with you will present so good a balance of advantage (over all the plays) for both sides. However, if you can better him, better him by all means. Only don't throw him over for the sake of adding twopennorth to the effect of Candida; for he makes a good deal of difference in the other plays.

My present plan as to copyrighting is to get up (or get you to get up) a performance consisting of an act of Mrs Warren, an act of The Philanderer, and an act of "You Never Can Tell." All the rest are secured. If Redford objects to Mrs W. I shall ask him to blue pencil what he objects to, or make Mrs W. a washerwoman or a pickpocket

796

or whatever will enable him to license enough of the text to protect me.

Do let me know where you are. As I have before timidly observed, I mislaid your itinerary.

There was a champion criticism of "Candida" in the Northern Figaro, so sincerely stupid that I have a mind to reprint it in my preface. Did you see it?

Nora's photograph looks very like Elizabeth Barrett Browning.

GBS

To EDITH CRAIG

[A/6]

The Argoed. Penallt. Monmouth
20th August 1897

[Ellen Terry saw *Candida* at Eastbourne on 26th August, and informed Shaw on the 30th that "it comes out on the stage even better than when one reads it. It is absorbingly interesting every second . . . Even the audience understood it all. . . . Only *one* thing struck me at the time as wrong. Towards quite the end of a play to say 'Now let's sit down and talk the matter over.' Several people took out their watches and some of them left to catch a train, or a drink! And it interrupted the attention of all of us who stayed."]

My dear Miss Craig

Will you send me a line to remind me of the business in the scene with Eugene at the place where you say "Pray are you flattering me or flattering yourself." Do you go back to the typewriter at the end of that speech or at "I'll leave the room, Mr Mb: I really will. It's not proper." I want to get it right for the printer.

Also, if you have accumulated any effective gags, you might let me have them for inclusion in the volume.

All the accounts I have received agree that you and Burgess saved the piece from utter ruin, and that Prossy (as Wyndham foresaw) was the popular favorite.

Please make your mother tell me what you thought of the performance; and then bring her to Eastbourne [to see it] so that she can tell me what she thinks herself.

yours sincerely
G. Bernard Shaw

The Argoed. Penallt. Monmouth
26th August 1897

[A/4; X/135]

[Herbert Stuart Stone (1871–1915) and Hannibal Ingalls Kimball (1874–1933) founded their publishing firm in Chicago in 1893. They went their separate ways in 1896, and Stone formed Herbert S. Stone & Company, which published Shaw's work in America until 1904. Stone perished in the *Lusitania* sinking.]

This letter of yours comes well, Grant Richards, from a man who has been bounding idly up the Jungfrau and down the Matterhorn to an exhausted wretch who, after a crushing season, has slaved these four weeks for four hours a day at your confounded enterprise. I have sent three plays to the printer, transmogrified beyond recognition, made more thrilling than any novel; and he has only sent me proofs of one, of which it has cost me endless letters & revises to get the page right, to teach him how to space letters for emphasis, and how to realize that I mean my punctuation to be followed.

I had no idea of the magnitude of the job. Anything like a holiday is out of the question for me. Must I endure in addition the insults of a publisher for whom I am preparing, with unheard-of toil, a gigantic triumph? Read "Mrs Warren"; and then blush for your impatience if you can.

Stone & Kimball's offer, as described to me in your letter of the 9th Apl (doubtless negligently and lazily composed before going up the river) mentioned neither the price nor the royalty after 10,000 copies. The latter I assume to be 20%: the former not less than 75 cents at least. A princely affluence will accrue to S. & K. on these terms; but I desire to make the fortune of one American publisher in order that I may spend the rest of my life in plundering all the others.

Shall I draw them an agreement? If they prefer to do it themselves, warn them that I wont assign copyright, but simply give them exclusive leave to publish in the U.S. for 5 years.

yrs, overworked to madness
G. Bernard Shaw

To GRANT RICHARDS

The Argoed. Penallt. Monmouth
[C/4; X/135]   28th August 1897

[*Carlyle and Balzac were notorious as proof revisionists.*]

By the way, a good many of the corrections so far (I have only sent
back one sheet, and that chiefly to get the page right and to settle about
spacing the letters for emphasized words instead of italicizing them)
are corrections of [Edward] Clark's departures from my copy, in spite
of my straitest injunctions, in the matter of punctuation. However, I
am now knocking righteousness into his head; and I shall feel deeply
humiliated if my corrections are not under rather than over the
Carlyle-Balzac average. I'll presently send you a sheet with the corrections of Clark's misdemeanors in red ink, and of my own in black. You
may charge me for all corrections over and above 95% of the total cost
of production.

GBS

P.S. Have you seen the translation of Diderot's "Neveu de Rameau"
just published by Macmillan? The paper on which it is printed is the
sort of thing we want for the plays, except that it might be well to have
it toned instead of white.

I am doing a sparkling study of Napoleon by way of preface to "The
Man of Destiny."

To FLORENCE FARR

The Argoed. Penallt. Monmouth
[A/4; X/115]   8th September 1897

[*The Poisoned Garden* appears to be an error for *The Poison Flower*, John
Todhunter's dramatic sketch, based on Hawthorne's short story "Rappa-
cini's Daughter," in which Florence Farr appeared at a matinée at the
Vaudeville Theatre on 15th June 1891. Dame Marie Tempest (1864–1942)
had been trained as a singer and made her earliest appearances in light opera.
In 1899 she forsook music, and eventually became one of London's most
popular performers in modern comedy.]

It is frightful—appalling—how the time rushes by here. I have not
drawn rein for a day; and yet "You Never Can Tell" is not ready for
the printer. It is the dullest trash I ever revised: "Widowers' Houses"
is worth fifty such.

There is nothing mysterious or peculiar to yourself in the fact that you get work only when people want you and not when you want them. That is everybody's experience. But it is by the failures that you gain the power to pick up the windfalls. If you had learnt the whole repertory of Sarah Bernhardt, Duse and Ellen Terry and practised them until you had been refused a chance of appearing in them by every manager in London, the failures of the Poisoned Garden and the Comedy of Sighs would have been personal successes for you, just as Marie Tempest achieved her position by appearing in a ghastly and ludicrous failure called "The Fay o' Fire" [by Henry Herman] at the Opéra Comique [in 1885]. I never had anything accepted; but if I had never written the five long novels and the bushel of articles that were refused I should not have been able to do the work that finally offered itself to me. If you change your name you will simply throw away the advantage of what you have done. Your belief in the miraculous is irrepressible. Probably I wont succeed in persuading you that there is no charm at work to be counteracted by some ceremony (changing your name and throwing a pinch of salt over your left shoulder come to the same thing); but I can only tell you again that you must keep on knocking your head against the stone wall until it gives way. Only, remember the saying "Knock, and it shall be opened to you." There's no use in waiting if you dont knock, or in thinking that the knocking is no use because the door will certainly open somewhere quite out of earshot of the knocks. Besides, the chances are enormously against a haphazard offer hitting on a haphazard vacancy. If you offer your services as dramatic critic to the Saturday Review, they will decline simply because they have a critic already; and the refusal is no more disparaging than your refusal of a coster's offer of a vegetable that you happen to have in the pantry. Wait for the usual fifteen years or so and you will fit yourself in somewhere.

I am alarmed to hear of your treatment of the 700 pounder. Why overdo things?

The wind has changed to the east; and "You Never Can Tell" has bored me to death. I am in the most disagreeable humor possible.

GBS

To ELLEN TERRY

The Argoed. Penallt. Monmouth
[U(A)/10; X/117]   8th September 1897

[The "Julia" reference is not to the jealous heroine of *The Philanderer*, but to her prototype, Jenny Patterson. John Ferguson Nisbet (1851–99) was

800

dramatic critic of *The Times* from 1882 until his death. The play about a "west end gentleman" and an "east end dona" took fifteen years to germinate, emerging in 1912 as *Pygmalion*. *Rejected Addresses* (1812) was a celebrated collection of parodies, by James and Horace Smith, of poets of the day. The lines quoted by Shaw (accurate except for the substitution of "spend" for "pass") are from "The Beautiful Incendiary," a parody of W.R. Spencer (1769–1834), a popular writer of *vers de société*, whose poetry was well known to contemporary readers.]

You can't imagine how it terrifies me to date a letter. It is incredible how the days fly past, like the telegraph poles on a railway journey. The 8th of September actually gone and still a whole four act play to be revised! And what a play! Oh, Ellen, Ellen, did you really read "You Never Can Tell"? *Could* anyone read it? It maddens me. I'll have my revenge in the preface by offering it as a frightful example of the result of trying to write for the theatre de nos jours.

Oh, I do not neglect "the material at hand." At my side people do not suffer from cold neglect: life is one long scene sometimes: at others it is as placid as possible. I make it a habit when I get restless over my work to seize the nearest woman and squeeze all the breath out of her stays. She does not feel neglected under these circumstances, nor is she much scandalized after the first few shocks. And when she does anything for me I always have a stock of fantastic complaints to make of it which are much more interesting than if I insulted her with delicate acknowledgments. It is not the small things that women miss in me, but the big things. My pockets are always full of the small change of lovemaking; but it is magic money, not real money. Mrs Webb, who is a remarkably shrewd woman, explains her freedom from the fascination to which she sees all the others succumb, by saying "You cannot fall in love with a *sprite*; and Shaw is a sprite in such matters, not a real person." Perhaps you can divine the truth in this: I am too lazy to explain it now, even if I understood it. It is certainly true: I am fond of women (or one in a thousand, say); but I am in earnest about quite other things. To most women one man and one lifetime make a world. I require whole populations and historical epochs to engage my interests seriously and make the writing machine (for that is what G.B.S. is) work at full speed and pressure: love is only diversion and recreation to me. Doubtless, dear Ellen, you've observed that you can't act things perfectly until you have got beyond them, and so have nothing to fear from them. That's why the women who fall in love with me worry me and torment me and make scenes (which they can't act) with me and suffer misery & destroy their health & beauty, whilst you, who could do without me as easily as I do without Julia (for instance) are my blessing and refuge, and really care more for *everybody* (including myself) than Julia cared for me. It is also, alas! why I act the lover so diabolically well that even the women who are clever enough to understand that such a person as myself might exist, can't bring themselves to believe that I am that person. My *impulses* are so prettily played—oh, *you* know: you wretch, you've done it often enough yourself.

Do you notice that this letter was begun on the 8th. Well, it's now the 14th; and that miserable play "You Never Can Tell" is not yet *half* ready. If only I could hurry it and still trust my work! For what I want to get at, you understand, is the preface, or rather the two prefaces. I am full of it, overripe and ready for it; and yet I must stick to this steady slow slow slow SO slow testing and correcting and punctuating and recasting of mere trivialities. It is frightful, and I want to have my finger in the Webbs' work too; for they also are struggling against time with the completion of a huge task for which our three wits would be all too few. It's the trifles that eat up time. Have you never wished that you could keep a ghost to do that part of your work that is within the reach of ordinary intelligence & industry? Nonsense, 'tis bootless to exclaim!

I rejoice to infer that you had fine weather for your drive. Here the fine weather has only just begun. This house—oh, by the way, the address now is Moorcroft Penallt Monmouth—has a garden close and some charm about it, and life here is softer. The woodpeckers are hammering like leprechaun cobblers all round, and keeping me industrious by the sound. And then your letter has just arrived, and I perceive from it that your holiday has renewed the fountain of your youth. I sent you a hasty scrawl yesterday about "Hamlet." I gave Forbes a description of what the end ought to be like—Fortinbras with a winged helmet, and Hamlet carried off on the shields, with the "ordnance shot off within" just as the wily William planned it. Nisbett in the Times describes the scene almost in my own terms; so that my idea seems to have come off; so you see, madam, I am not a dreamer who doesn't understand the practical exigencies of the stage, and the sooner you send Peter along the better. I suppose F.R. couldn't afford the snow scene, with Fortinbras on the march and Hamlet in his travelling furs; so Henry can have a present of that. I saw his Hamlet once—many years ago (the object of my visit being Ophelia). It was frightfully bad. He hadn't got hold of his classic style then: that began with Claude Melnotte [in *The Lady of Lyons*, 1888], which I saw incidentally whilst I was looking at Pauline [played by Ellen Terry].

Are you going to do Peter on the road? You should. Think of how much anxiety it will save you if you have your difficulties with the words settled before the first night in London. Mansfield produces "The Devil's Disciple" at the 5th Avenue Theatre on the 6th Oct, after an experiment or two with it in the provinces. Ah, if you only *would* play a matinee of it with Forbes, I would actually go to see it (a compliment I haven't paid Candida). Besides, I would teach that rapscallionly flower girl of his something. "Cæsar & Cleopatra" has been driven clean out of my head by a play I want to write for them in which he shall be a west end gentleman and she [Mrs Patrick Campbell] an east end dona in an apron and three orange and red ostrich feathers.

I see you wont tell me anything about Prossy. It would be seething the kid in its mother's milk, I suppose; but still I do want to know in general terms whether my style of work fits her.

It is luncheon hour, and there's a visitor.

That letter would not have surprised anybody at the hotel. Did you ever read "Rejected Addresses"? I only remember three lines from "Lady Elizabeth Mugg."

—for who would not slavery hug,
to spend but one exquisite hour
in the arms of Elizabeth Mugg!

I should write the same about you if there were any rhyme to Ellen. I love you soulfully & bodyfully, properly and improperly, every way that a woman can be loved.

GBS

To RICHARD MANSFIELD

[G.u/3]

[The Argoed. Penallt. Monmouth]
[8th September 1897]

[Shaw's letter of 8th September to Mansfield has not survived, although an extract from it was published in Paul Wilstach's *Richard Mansfield: The Man and the Actor* (1909): "I was much hurt by your contemptuous refusal of 'A Man of Destiny,' not because I think it one of my masterpieces, but because Napoleon is nobody else but Richard Mansfield himself. I studied the character from you, and then read up Napoleon and found that I had got him exactly right." Shaw, however, preserved his draft of the postscript to the letter.]

PS Your letter of the 19th August has just arrived. The moral of the figures is that you should break the back of this provincial sharing business by building a theatre for yourself, and pay me 15% instead of 10. It is no use trying to beat down the authors: the managers can only do that by a solemn covenant not to bid over a certain figure, which covenant they would all break next day. As to my own terms I am astonished at my moderation. I ought to have 25% to cover the risk of dealing with a genius void of conscience and the incarnation of caprice. However, if you want a trial on the road to feel how the play works, and are content to make the experiment in some modest town for the sake of the piece to your expenses, I am quite willing to forego my fees. But if the trial trip is to be made in Chicago before enthusiastic 1200 dollar houses, then you would simply be robbing the deserving poor if you cut off my tantième. Therefore let us put it this way. If the first six public performances of The Devil's Disciple are made experimentally in second class towns, no author's fees need be paid except for performances at which they would amount to $500 or more, in which case they shall be paid in full. By this arrangement you will only pay me when the house is at least $500, at which figure you will be able to bear the extortion. This management of course only applies to these tentative preliminary performances, and will not affect the full operation of our agreement from the date of the New York production or of the 7th performance, whichever shall take place first.

[On 27th September, five days before the world première of *The Devil's Disciple* in the Hermanus Bleecker Hall, Albany, N.Y., Mansfield replied:

"My dear Shaw.

"We play your D.D. at Albany on Friday next—your ideas concerning our expenses are funny. Why do you not come over here—stay with us a while & receive a liberal education? When I take your D.D. to Albany—seventy people in all—soldiers & supers—town band & military—calciums & scenery etc etc how much, pray, do you imagine our expenses to be? Do you really think $500 will cover them?

"That is why when we pay an author 10% unless the business is very large we can't afford to keep the play on, whereas had he been satisfied with less he might reap more honor & glory & more money in the end. À propos de ça—it will be—in case the D.D. does not catch on immediately—quite impossible to work it into a success—as owing to your extraordinary affection for Miss Marbury there will be no possibility of disguising the receipts. You insist upon employing an officer from the other camp at *our* headquarters & do you expect the other camp to make a secret of our returns?

"Miss Marbury is in the employ of Mr Frohman and Mr Frohman *has no scruples*. It is exceedingly annoying that you cannot be made to see reason in this matter—employ anybody you please—but not a person whose interests

804

are diametrically opposed to *mine*, & *I* have to play your play, —it is neither fair nor honorable. There are plenty of good agents here.

"Your remarks about my acting have greatly amused Mr Palmer & lots of other people. Your opinion is probably the reflection of Miss Janet Achurch. Why don't you ask somebody else. I wish I were the business head you imagine. I wish you would write jolly straightforward letters & not such a lot of *rot*."

Appended to the letter is an estimate by A. M. Palmer and his business manager, a Mr Dillon, of credits and debits for the production:

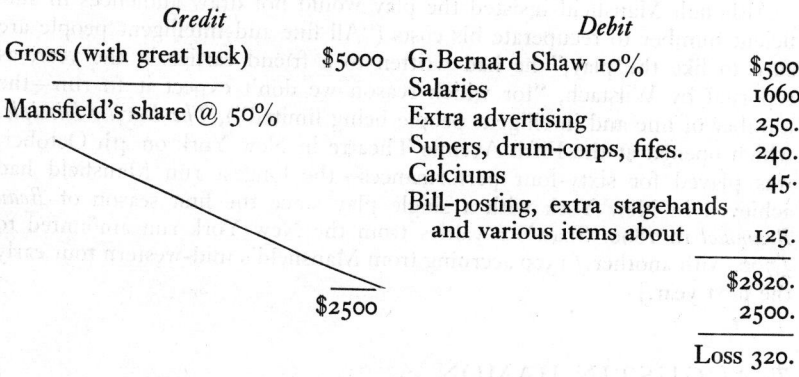

Credit		Debit	
Gross (with great luck)	$5000	G. Bernard Shaw 10%	$500
		Salaries	1660
Mansfield's share @ 50%		Extra advertising	250.
		Supers, drum-corps, fifes.	240.
		Calciums	45.
		Bill-posting, extra stagehands and various items about	125.
			$2820.
	$2500		2500.
			Loss 320.

"This makes no allowance whatever for costumes scenery etc.—or any pay whatever for R. M's work!"

Beneath this Mansfield has added a postscript: "Mr Palmer tells me that no one can pay 10% to an author & live in New York, & that your play will have to appear & disappear unless by some extraordinary chance it should play to extraordinary business. The above is average business of a N.Y. *success*. Fair terms, such terms as Mr Palmer has always paid & living terms for the Actor and Manager, are: 4% to $4000 & 7% on all over" (BM).

Despite Mansfield's entreaties, Shaw adamantly clung to his terms. On 29th October, Elisabeth Marbury wrote to him:

"I note that your decision is against making any change at present on the royalties, but there are one or two points I must explain to you. I presume that the reason Mr. Mansfield [originally] consented to 10% was because he did not realize that he was going to acquire such a successful property, and he doubtless felt willing to pay 10% for an occasional performance. As for Mr. Mansfield getting other terms from the theatre I believe he is thoroughly truthful when he says the theatre only gives him 50%. This is the inevitable arrangement in every New York theatre unless by chance Mr. Mansfield takes the theatre at a rental of £560 which may be the case. You see the expenses of a theatre in this country are infinitely greater than in London. The good theatres here are in constant demand, so they never have any difficulty in booking strong attractions even at 50%. It is for this reason the theatres make no concessions. Now, as for Mr. Mansfield building a theatre, he has tried this and it was an absolute failure, because he is thoroughly incapable of managing anything, even himself. I shall watch however the details of your contract closely and keep you advised. I confess it will make me feel most unhappy if I see that Mr. Mansfield changes his bill. You must remember he has a good deal of vanity and likes to show himself off in different characters, so we have not only his cupidity to fight but also his conceit" (Unpublished letter, privately owned).

Although Mansfield insisted the play would not draw audiences in sufficient number to recuperate his costs ("All fine and intelligent people are sure to like the play," he had written to a friend earlier in the year, as reported by Wilstach, "for which reason we don't expect it to run—the number of fine and intelligent people being limited"), *The Devil's Disciple*, which opened at the Fifth Avenue Theatre in New York on 4th October, was played for sixty-four performances—the longest run Mansfield had achieved in New York with a single play since the first season of *Beau Brummel* in 1890. Shaw's royalties from the New York run amounted to £700, with another £1300 accruing from Mansfield's mid-western tour early the next year.]

To AUGUSTIN HAMON

[S/1]

[The Argoed. Penallt. Monmouth]
11th September 1897

[Hamon had just become the editor of the Socialist journal *L'Humanité Nouvelle*. "The Illusions of Socialism," of which "several fragments" had been published, in a German translation, in *Die Zeit* (Vienna) on 24th and 31st October 1896, was published in *L'Humanité Nouvelle*, in a French translation, in August 1900.]

Mon cher Hamon

Mais sans doute je ne la connais pas du tout, votre "Humanité Nouvelle." Personne ne sait mieux que vous que c'est toujours de la vieille Humanité qu'il s'agit. La Nouvelle Humanité ne se souciera pas de revues.

On vient de publier ici "Forecasts of the Coming Century," un volume d'essais par plusieurs esprits forts Socialistes. Pas un traitre mot du coming century ne s'y trouve; mais il contient une de mes plus brillantes sorties metaphysiques (on se tarde de mourir avant d'en finir) qui s'appelle "The Illusions of Socialism." Quelques fragments en ont paru dans "Die Zeit" (journal Viennois); mais pour éblouir l'Europe il faut une traduction Française toute complète. Or, je n'ai

806

SEASON OF

MR. RICHARD
MANSFIELD,

—IN—

THE DEVIL'S DISCIPLE.

By G. BERNARD SHAW.

ACT I.—In Timothy Dudgeon's house. *Morning.*

ACT II.—SCENE 1—In Anderson's house. *Early evening.*
SCENE 2—In Anderson's house. *Later.*

There is no intermission between Scenes 1 and 2.)

ACT III.—SCENE 1—A waiting-room in the prison at Websterbridge.
SCENE 2—The council-chamber.
SCENE 3—The market square.

The action takes place in New Hampshire, in the year 1777.

The Scenery is by Mr. Richard Marston.

THE PERSONS IN THE DRAMA ARE:

ANTHONY ANDERSON, Presbyterian minister....................Mr. JOHNSON

JUDITH ANDERSON, his wife......................Miss BEATRICE CAMERON

MRS. ANNIE DUDGEON, widow of Timothy.........................Miss MONK

RICHARD DUDGEON, her elder son.............................Mr. MANSFIELD

CHRISTOPHER DUDGEON, her younger son....................Mr. ANDREWS

UNCLE WILLIAM DUDGEON) her { ....Mr. GRIFFITH
UNCLE TITUS DUDGEON....) brothers-in-law, { ....Mr. LEFEVRE

ESSIE, natural daughter of the late Peter Dudgeon, hanged for rebellion;
Miss BRISCOE

LAWYER HAWKINS...Mr. HUNTER

GENERAL BURGOYNE...Mr. FORREST

MAJOR SWINDON...Mr WEAVER

REV. MR. BRUDENELL, Chaplain ....Mr. COURTENAY

A SERGEANT...Mr. KINGDON

Also Mrs. William Dudgeon, Mrs. Titus Dudgeon, Soldiers,
Officers, Townspeople, etc.

Intermission between Acts I. and II. eight minutes.
No intermission between Scenes 1 and 2 in Act II.
Intermission between Acts II. and III. six minutes.
Intermission between Scenes 1 and 2 in Act III. two minutes.
Intermission between Scenes 2 and 3 in Act III. four minutes.

pas le temps de vous écrire un article exprès pour l'Humanité Nouvelle; mais pourquoi ne pas traduire "The Illusions of Socialism" pour enrager vos abonnés socialistes?

Merci bien de m'avoir envoyé votre compte rendu du Congrès International. Vous le faites trop d'honneur en gaspillant votre talent sur une telle farce. Ce n'est pas de la Nouvelle Humanité, cela. C'est franc Adam et Eve, n'est ce pas?

Excusez du peu mon Français Irlandais. Probablement vous ne pourrez pas en comprendre deux sentences; mais n'importe! je n'entends qu'une poignée de main bien cordiale pour vous ressouvenir de

> yours sincerely
> G. Bernard Shaw

To GRANT RICHARDS

[B/4; X/135]

[The Argoed. Penallt.] Monmouth
25th September 1897

Grant Richards, my boy, do not deceive yourself. Ibsen's plays sell at three & sixpence the volume of three plays. The first issue of a new play at 5/- by Heinemann fetches the rent of Ibsen's unique European position, which I have not yet reached. The point of a six shilling volume is the length of time it takes to read. The man who buys a six shilling book expects that he will not have to buy another for several Sundays; and he looks strictly to the quantity of matter supplied. Now a play is a very short business owing to the dialogueiness of it; and that is why every attempt to charge more than eighteenpence for a single play fails in England. The six shilling public will just go the seven shillings for our two volumes: make it ten, and you will not sell a thousand copies all told. At the three & six you will not lose; and you *may* land a really large circulation. An édition de luxe—two volumes in a case for a guinea—is the only real business alternative; and that would not pay *you*, as your interest does not lie in getting a reputation for that sort of thing, especially in connection with "Mrs Warren's Profession." Our original plan is the right one, and the only one in which there is any money. Sit tight therefore & trust my judgment. I mean this book to break out far beyond "my public": that is why I'm squandering hard work on it.

> G. Bernard Shaw

808

To WILLIAM ROTHENSTEIN

[A/6]

29 Fitzroy Square W
5th October 1897

[Sir William Rothenstein (1872–1945), who gained a reputation at the turn of the century for his remarkable series of portrait drawings and lithographs, became principal of the Royal College of Art in 1920. In 1897 he had embarked on a project of issuing *English Portraits*, a monthly series of portfolios of lithographed drawings, published by Richards; the drawings later were issued in a bound volume (1898). The two dozen subjects included Shaw, Hardy, Irving, James, Gissing, Sargent, and Pinero. A truncated passage from Shaw's "Mr Grundy's Improvements on Dumas" (*Saturday Review*, 17th July 1897) was incorporated in the note on Ellen Terry which preceded her portrait. Shaw provided a special note (unsigned) for Archer's portrait.]

On the occasion of the production of "The Silver Key" at the Haymarket three months or so ago, I wrote a lot about Ellen Terry which ought to do exactly (part of it) for what you want. Will you look at it and see whether it will do; for I feel incapable of writing another word about her: she's a frightfully difficult subject. How soon do you want the stuff anyhow?

As I am now settled in town again, you can have that sitting on any morning—Monday, Friday, Saturday or Sunday for choice—that may be convenient. But give me a few days notice if you can.

GBS

To CHARLOTTE PAYNE-TOWNSHEND

[A/2]

[29 Fitzroy Square W]
[Undated: *c*. 6th October 1897]

Oh insufferable infant!

If she bores you, come up here: you will be well received; but it will be dull for you; so dont come unless you can do no better.

GBS

P.S. If you dont come before 9.30, I shall conclude you are not coming. I ought to take a bit of a walk before going to bed—will see you home if you come.

To CHARLOTTE PAYNE-TOWNSHEND

29 Fitzroy Square W
7th October 1897

[B/2]

I have caught about 17 separate colds since I saw you; but I have not identified any of them with yours.

The infant is really going too far. Where am I to spend my evenings? Send me back the proof.

I escaped the Criterion last night through some providential hitch about my ticket, which didn't come. Sat at home and worked—a 14 hour day.

I am just at present furious because the hellborn printer has not sent my Saturday proof, which I wanted particularly to dispose of tonight; as I have promised Rothenstein a sitting early tomorrow.

Tomorrow evening is Webb's, isnt it?

I nearly called this afternoon, but refrained out of regard for the feelings of the infant. [Charlotte's sister Mary at this time intensely disliked Shaw.]

Damn the printer—blast him, curse him, burn him, double-damn him!

It is so lonely, cursing all by myself.

GBS

To CHARLOTTE PAYNE-TOWNSHEND

29 Fitzroy Square W
8th October 1897

[B/2]

[Ernest E. Williams had lectured to the Fabian Society that evening on "Socialism and [Tariff] Protection." After the birth of her daughter Cecily in 1896, Mary Cholmondeley suffered a series of miscarriages and never had another child.]

I presume Webb explained that we had forgotten all about the Fabian meeting. I had to go, as it was important that Williams and his Protection gospel should be looked after. We scattered his limbs on the blast.

Has the infant conceived again, or has her husband eloped? Let me know if she goes away tomorrow. I think I shall have to go to the Comedy Theatre [to see H. V. Esmond's *One Summer's Day*], but am not quite sure.

GBS

To GRANT RICHARDS

[A/4; X/135]

29 Fitzroy Square W
8th October 1897

[Despite Shaw's statement about attaining a circulation of one thousand copies of *The Quintessence of Ibsenism*, the publisher's extant royalty statements indicate that the work had sold about double this quantity in England by 1897.]

Dear G.R.

You have an india rubber mind: as fast as I stretch it to the TWO volumes, it contracts to one. If it were a question of 3/6 and 5, or even 6 shillings, I should not hesitate to go the larger figure; but it is a question between SEVEN shillings and TEN. Ten is a prohibitive price: you wont sell your 2000 copies at it—perhaps not even 1000; whereas at seven you will either sell upwards of 10,000 or the whole project will be a failure. I tell you the next price to seven shillings is a guinea for the two volumes in a case, which would get you a pornographic reputation.

My old circulation of 1000 was attained when I was comparatively unknown by an essay on "Ibsenism," with an unpopular title. And that was not a ten shilling circulation, but a half crown one.

I object strenuously to gilt tops.

If on thinking this over, you still feel suicidal, I am not sure that my best plan will not be to back my opinion by manufacturing the book myself, taking over Clark's contract from you and getting you to publish on commission. At any rate, it is a thing to be considered. There is an enormous section of bookbuyers who regard 10/- as a price absolutely outside their means, and 7/- within it. Evans's notion that they will give ten as soon as seven only applies to people who will give fifteen as soon as ten. 7/- is only silver: 10/- is gold. I believe in going for a large circulation, even if the paper is cheapened. Anyhow, Globe 8vo is too small for a big price, unless it is *de luxe*.

Do think it over a bit. The enterprise is really not worth undertaking at all if you limit your aim to 2000 circulation: at least not from my point of view. Allowing me the moderate tariff of £25 for the prefaces, I should get £25 apiece for the plays. It takes six months to write a play. Therefore the dramatic author would get less than £1 a week— say five shillings less than a dock laborer—4½d an hour for writing masterpieces. It's sweating. Sell 10,000 at 7/- and I shall get 1/3¾ an hour. Do you grudge me that modest reward?

yrs arithmetically
G. Bernard Shaw

53—B.S. I

To HENRY ARTHUR JONES

29 Fitzroy Square W
12th October 1897

[X/124]

[Jones's *The Liars* opened at the Criterion on 6th October. In the *Saturday Review* on 9th October, Shaw reviewed it from the privately printed copy of the play sent to him by Jones, commenting: "I am sure 'The Liars' must be an extremely diverting play on the stage. But I have not seen it there. Mr. Wyndham's acting-manager wrote to ask whether I would come if I were invited. I said Yes. Accordingly I was *not* invited. The shock to my self-esteem was severe and unexpected. I desire it to be distinctly understood, however, that I forgive everybody."

Falkner and Lady Jessica are characters in *The Liars*. T.B. Thalberg (1866-1947) had appeared in Jones's *The Physician* (1897) and was currently appearing in *The Liars*. Mary Moore (1862-1931) was associated with Charles Wyndham (whom she married in 1916) throughout most of her career. She appeared in many of Jones's plays, produced by Wyndham, including *The Case of Rebellious Susan*, *The Physician*, *The Liars*, and *Mrs Dane's Defence* (1900). The Society of Authors was founded in 1884. Shaw became a member in August 1897.]

My dear H.A.J.

My notice drew a stall for tomorrow like a cork. The omission was an accident; and the honest truth is that I took advantage of it purposely to escape the performance. I shall enjoy seeing Falkner and Lady Jessica turned into Thalberg and Mary Moore—just exactly as much as I should enjoy seeing you skinned alive. If you will write a comedy in which all the characters are merely our actors in disguise and then have the luck to find the originals disengaged for casting, I'll go out and see them eagerly. But not on any other terms. It will end in your having to do what I am doing—throwing the theatre to the devil, and trying to do with my pen what the actors can't do.

Will you look at the enclosed letter from the Society of Authors? I see that you are chairman of the dramatic sub-committee; and it seems to me that we ought to try to work up some sort of an organization with a view to getting a *minimum* price established for plays, and putting a stop to the ridiculous jobbing of "rights" that goes on at present through the silliness and ignorance of the authors. . . .* The difficulty is, of course, to find time for Trade Union work; but one feels that it ought to be done. It is all very well for you or me to pit our individual wit and strength against Irving and Wyndham and the rest; but the small fry are bound to crumple up without an organization behind

* The ellipses were made by Doris Arthur Jones, in her biography of her father.

them. We also want to fight the system of forcing collaboration on authors, whereby some fool of an actor-manager spoils a man's play in order that he may collar half the percentage. . . .

Mansfield has just proved to me by figures that he must lose $300 on every performance of The Devil's Disciple unless I reduce my percentage from 10 to 4. I have replied in terms sufficient to stand him on his head for a fortnight.

yours ever
G. Bernard Shaw

To CHARLOTTE PAYNE-TOWNSHEND

[A/2]

29 Fitzroy Square W
13th October 1897

[Charlotte was in Leicester, visiting her sister. She returned that night or on the morning of the 14th. The Brahms concert was performed at the home of an acquaintance named Max Hecht.]

How is it to be done? Vestry from 3 to 6.30 or perhaps 7. That means a rush from my Saturday article to St Martin's Lane & back to St Pancras. At 9 I have to be in Belsize Park Gardens to hear a private performance of two Brahms quintets which I cannot miss without outrageous offence, considering the circumstances under which I promised to attend.

Tomorrow I shall probably have to read "You Never Can Tell" to Hawtrey. If you can give me lunch (that is, if you are not going until the evening train) I could come then; but otherwise I seem to be locked up as tightly as a man can be.

I shall be at St Martin's Lane from 2 to half past 2 today; but there will be a lot of people & I shall be gobbling my dinner & my vestry minutes all the time—useless for talking. If by any chance the vestry gets its business done before 6, I might rush down to you for a few minutes; but there is hardly the ghost of a chance of that, as we have some contentious business on.

Damn!

GBS

813

To CHARLOTTE PAYNE-TOWNSHEND

[A/2; X/151.e]

29 Fitzroy Square W
15th October 1897

[Charlotte had left London again that afternoon, and was absent for a week. *The Devil's Disciple* was not produced in London until October 1907, at which time Dick Dudgeon was played by Harley Granville-Barker. Halma was one of Mrs Carr Shaw's favourite pastimes. On this occasion she apparently was playing the game by herself, pretending to be all four contestants.]

Oh, what a day!

First I sat, or rather stood to Rothenstein until he completed his drawing of me for his December set of lithographs. On biking back I got plunged into a mass of urgent messages about "The Devil's Disciple." I finally ascertain, at Miss Marbury's London office, that the play is wanted for "a first class production in London with John Drew in the leading part," but whether by Drew himself or Charles Frohman is left uncertain. Answer wanted immediately. I go in search of Forbes Robertson; can't find him; send him a letter to say that he must make up his mind now or never, giving him until midnight. It is now nearly 11; and the wretch has not replied. Bourchier is also on the warpath. The moral of the Drew offer, if it comes from Frohman is, beyond all doubt, that the success of "The D's D" is solid pecuniarily. If from Drew, it may mean simply that the part has knocked him over.

As I have to read "You Never Can Tell" tomorrow all in one stretch to Hawtrey I thought it best to make a desperate attempt to get my voice into order. I descended on my unfortunate mother's peaceful Halma foursome (her two hands against her two feet) and sang, mostly fortissimo, all "The Messiah," the Selection Day program of the 1894 Handel Festival, an album of German songs, and finally an almost exhaustive selection from "Das Rheingold." I now feel equal to the four acts. The worst of it is that as Forbes Robertson is evidently depending on a midnight visit from me, I shant get to bed in good time.

There was no Fabian.

It is most inconvenient having Adelphi Terrace shut up. I have nowhere to go, nobody to talk to. I tried Mrs Salt last night; but she was out; so I fell back on Edward Garnett & Nelly Heath, who were supping together.

I have to go to the Camberwell [Métropole] Theatre on Monday [to see Louis N. Parker's *The Vagabond King*], and the Avenue on Tuesday.

814

My new vestry committee is a Wednesday one; so I shall now vestrify *every* Wednesday.

"Fahr'wohl, mein treues Herz: zu tausend gute Nacht" (quotation from the Lieder Album).

I ought to be correcting "Widowers' Houses" instead of writing this. Positively haven't done my work today—only written a few letters.

GBS

To CHARLOTTE PAYNE-TOWNSHEND

[A/2]

29 Fitzroy Square W
~~17th~~ 18th October 1897
(what IS the date?)

[The Avenue Theatre had offered a triple-bill on the 16th: E. J. Malyon and Charles James's *The Lady Burglar*, Arthur Matthison's *More Than Ever*, and W. Gayer Mackay's musical fantasy *The Mermaids*. David Irvine, a Scotsman, wrote several books on Wagner, one of which, "*Parsifal*" *and Wagner's Christianity*, was reviewed by Shaw on 27th May 1899 in the *Morning Leader* and on 9th June in the *Daily Chronicle*. The "Italian lady" (see also letter of 7th November 1897 to Charlotte), who presumably had seen the Charringtons' production of *Candida*, has not been identified, but it is interesting to note that, in the *Evening Standard* on 28th November 1944, Shaw revealed he had borrowed Candida's name "from an Italian lady I never met: Candida Bartolucci, afterwards a British marchioness."

Robert Charles Phillimore (1871–1919), one of several wealthy young men who assisted the Webbs in their early work, was the eldest son of the first Lord Phillimore. He joined the Fabian Society in 1893, served as a Progressive member of the St Pancras Vestry, later was London County Councillor for Deptford. In 1895 he married Lucy Fitzpatrick, known to her friends as "Lion," who was for most of her life an ardent social worker. The Phillimores lived at Radlett, Hertfordshire.]

I wish the Devil's Disciple were lost in the bottomless pit. This rumor of "success" has brought me perfectly loathsome congratulations from the people who commiserate me for my worthy achievements.

Tree has taken away "The D's D" to Glasgow to read in the train. Hawtrey declares "You Never Can Tell" the best play he ever heard—at which point I bolted.

I was wrong about the Avenue. It was on Saturday—tomorrow (Tuesday) I shall be free. On Wednesday I dine with Massingham to meet David Irvine the Wagnerite.

815

"You Never Can Tell" contained a gross oversight and an absurd error which all the Haymarket rehearsals & my revision and your correction failed to detect.

This morning came an appalling letter from my Italian lady—"I have seen your play. It is beautiful. I am coming to London to congratulate you."

I must rush off to the vestry committee.

GBS

P.S. I biked to Radlett yesterday with Wallas & Ada Radford. In your absence I think I shall fall in love with Mrs Phillimore.

To GRANT RICHARDS

29 Fitzroy Square W
[A/4; X/135.e]   23rd October 1897

Dear G.R.

I return a couple more sheets—all I've got—for press. If you look at pp 17, 25, 6 & 7 you will see that I have made a faint protest against the whiteness of some of the lines. You might suggest to them that they need not justify to avoid dividing a word at the end—that it is better to divide a word than to have a loose line making a streak of whitey grey through the black. Caxton would have printed your name Gr-ant Richa-rds at the end of a line sooner than spoilt his page with rivers of white. The great thing is to get the color even. Besides, since we are substituting spaced letters for italic in underlined words, it is important that the spacing should be regular and rather narrow, so as to make the spacing distinctive. If "Mrs Warren" has to wait until "The Philanderer" is built up out of the ruins of "Widowers Houses" (otherwise I dont see how they are to get the pagination right) we might as well get another revise, to see whether my attempts to blacken the sentences have proved disastrous or not.

GBS

To CHARLOTTE PAYNE-TOWNSHEND

[10 Adelphi Terrace WC]
[A/2]   26th October 1897. 3.38 p.m.

This weather has shattered my nerves. I have to work all this evening at the square; and I now want somebody to waste my time and keep

816

my brains quiet until five, when I shall go home to write a few letters before posthour. So I came here. On the stairs I met Martha [the domestic]. I said "Is Miss Townshend at home, Charlotte?" [Shaw's error] as usual. She said you were not. *Now* what's to be done?

My mother has contrived that she and the domestic shall both be out all the evening; so that there will be nobody there to answer the door if I absent myself. My program is fortunately one which will tie me to the house. I shall finish my article & send back Webb's preface [to *Industrial Democracy*]; and then tomorrow will be clear for my own preface (to Vol II) and for the vestry.

Oh, that play last night! [R.C.Carton's *The Tree of Knowledge*, at the St James's Theatre.] Five acts—five headaches—stale as last years bread.

I do not know where the devil to go—what the devil to do! I have a mind not to see you again until I am quit of this brutalizing idiocy of dramatic criticism. As you see by Stratford & Moorcroft I am only tolerable when it stops. A theatrical journalist loafing round is bad for any woman.

All the same you need not have selected this particular afternoon to go out.

Damn!

GBS

To CHARLOTTE PAYNE-TOWNSHEND

29 Fitzroy Square W
[A/2; X/151.e]   29th October 1897

A curious thing happened to me last night. In the afternoon I got a telegram from some old friends asking me to dine with them at the Metropole, or at least to see them afterwards, as they were starting for India in the morning. I couldnt dine, as my work kept me until past ten here. It was 10.45 when I reached the Turkish Bath clock in Northumberland Avenue. I *willed* to cross the street to the Metropole; but to my astonishment my legs suddenly walked off with me through the railway arches to Adelphi Terrace. The big staircase light was blazing Eddystonianly through the night; but all the rooms were dark except two bedrooms at the top, one of them yours. So I returned to the Metropole and interviewed my people there.

If anything makes you unhappy, pluck it out, and go on to the next.

817

Unhappiness is a warning to move on, not to sit down. When you are no longer unhappy, you will be where I am.

I must be off to the Fabian.

GBS

To CHARLOTTE PAYNE-TOWNSHEND

29 Fitzroy Square W

[A/2]
31st October 1897

[Charlotte had just gone to Paris to visit her friends the Heseltines. Presumably these were John Postle Heseltine (1843–1929), a trustee of the National Gallery from 1893, and his wife Sarah. Shaw had met Philip Dalmas at the home of the Salts in February 1896.]

Just a line on a matter of business.

There is a young American musician—a Philadelphian genius—the only American I ever met without an American accent—at present starving in Paris in the usual way. His name is Philip Dalmas, 15 rue Gustave Courbet. A couple of years ago or thereabouts he appeared in England with some people near Manchester who were mad about Walt Whitman. He was a Whitmanite; and they brought him one day to see Edward Carpenter. Carpenter took to him, and he joined the sandal making village set, and met Mrs Salt, to whom he played many glorious compositions, covering himself with the splendor of genius. Mrs Salt insisted on his being brought to me in my musical-critic capacity. He came, and played me his great Sonata Appassionata. I listened attentively, and pointed out where it all came from, theme by theme, and how it had grown. It was mostly Beethoven. He had a vigorous bass voice, and was full of talent—an interesting young man, on the whole, and remarkably *un*American. Having totally beggared him as far as the sonata went, I took him on to a meeting of the Wagner Society and then lost sight of him. He presently went to Paris to study singing. How he lived I dont know—I think by subsidies from rich American friends who had taken his destiny in hand to train him as a pianist. He came over here to get his own way; but they followed him; objected to his socialist acquaintances and his taking to singing & composition; and dropped him. He is a mysterious scoundrel anyhow, and keeps things dark, I believe.

However, he has just written to Mrs Salt saying that he wants pupils.

818

She mentioned the matter to me, and it occurred to me that as you are staying with some Americans in Paris, you might by chance find one of them in want of music lessons. If so, mention his name and address. Most likely he wont teach them anything; but he will take their money, and if they are colossally rich he will interest them as a genius and get another spell of endowment out of them. He is about 22 years of age.

I have passed nearly a dozen sheets of the first volume of the plays for press, and am laboring at the preface to the second. Both prefaces will be of the most flashing brilliancy.

If you had been in town yesterday you could have come with me to Kent to inspect a gigantic fever hospital [Dartford Smallpox Hospital], 2½ as large as St Thomas's.

If you had been in town today, you could have given me lunch. The Webbs are away. Mrs Salt & I have had a rare time of it playing duets—especially the 8th symphony.

GBS

To JANET ACHURCH

[T/1 (A/4)]

29 Fitzroy Square W
1st November 1897

[The prospectus for *Plays Pleasant and Unpleasant* was a four-page brochure which Richards had prepared and Shaw had extensively revised. The volumes did not appear until the following April.]

My dear Janet

Have you got among your press cuttings an agonized notice of "Candida" from the Northern Figaro? If you have, will you lend it to me: I've mislaid my copy.

I have for a long time wanted to remonstrate with you about two things. First, the way you destroy every chance of getting "Candida" produced by persistently telling the press that it is going to be done presently in London. Of course everybody concludes that the market is closed. If only you had played the game properly, and told everybody that nobody in London would touch the play, and that only for you and the I.T. it would never have seen the light even in the provinces, you would have made such an interesting case of it that the way would have been clear by this time. But you *will* play Government tricks when you're in opposition. Making all due allowance for congenital

819

mendacity, I still think you ought to be able to see that the strength of your position lies in its commercial weakness, and its unequalled opportunities of making capital out of persecution.

Second, and more important, your diction is in such an unholy abyss of mannerism that London will not stand you unless you drop it. When I saw "Doll's House" for the second time at Islington, you inflicted such torments on me with every syllable you uttered that my affection for you finally came out by the roots. I really cannot love a woman with a sawmill at each corner of her mouth. Miss P.T., who had been tremendously impressed by her first visit at the Globe, was utterly confounded, and could not believe that it was the same woman. The last time I saw you everything went well until you made a scene about something—I forget what. Immediately you started both sawmills, fixed your eyes in a ghastly stare, and became a frightful ventriloquizing somnambulist, like the ghost of Cleopatra. This is no doubt extremely thrilling to your own diaphragm; but the effect on the innocent spectator is atrocious: it deprived me of the power of remonstrating with you; removed me miles away; set me asking myself whether it was really you or some nightmarish simulacrum of the once adorable Janet. It is that that has prevented me from going to see "Candida": I daren't face it. It is all the fault of that cursed Cleopatra. You have begun to *act*; and now it's all up with you. You complain of Thorpe's want of simplicity and sincerity and then burlesque his worst artificialities.

I enclose you the prospectus of the plays, as it has an important bearing on "Candida." The books will be out in the middle of January —at all events early in February. After that the novelty will be gone. Between this and then something might be done; for there is now no doubt that "The Devil's Disciple" has swept the board in New York: the average receipts at the first seven performances were over £250; and the press, which hedged a little at first as to the public liking the play, is now prostrate before Mansfield (I wish, by the way, they'd send me some of my fees: I have not seen the color of the money yet). This has had a perceptible effect here, especially as Charles Frohman offers to undertake the London production and bring over John Drew to play Richard. It ought to be possible for you to get someone to venture on a week of matinées. A regular evening production with all the houses will fail: the select matinée business will enable you to repeat the success of "Little Eyolf." If you grab at anything more, you will probably stamp yourself as a confirmed failure, instead of establishing yourself as a sure draw for a high class audience in a high class play.

820

At the Court they are in such a hole that they have just jumped Parker's "Vagabond King" into the bill from Camberwell.

Hawtrey, who has been in a state of excitement about "You Never Can Tell" might be on for matinées at the Comedy—an excellent theatre for the purpose.

Have you finished the tour yet?

GBS

To CHARLOTTE PAYNE-TOWNSHEND

[E/2]

29 Fitzroy Square W
4th November 1897

It's past midnight: I have worked since morning towards leisure for a letter; but now I must allow myself no more than I can get on this [visiting] card. What news have I? Charrington has paid me what he borrowed: his tour is over, and his debts on it only £240! "The Devil's Disciple" has really been a sensational success: the royalties for the first week have come, and I am richer than ever I was in my life before—actually £314 in the bank to my credit. It is cold here, but splendidly fine; but you escaped some hideous weather by going. I like to think of you germinating in Paris rather than suffering here; but I miss you in lots of ways. Shant spare you anything: it is my one virtue with women that I never spare them.

GBS

To CHARLOTTE PAYNE-TOWNSHEND

[B/2; X/151.e]

29 Fitzroy Square W
7th November 1897

[Massingham's boy was Harold John Massingham (1888–1952), who contributed to *The Nation* (1916–24), which was then edited by his father, and who was the author of more than fifty books, most of them on nature subjects. On 6th November 1897 *The Academy* printed a list, "based upon a consensus of opinion gathered from the staff," of forty suggested members for a proposed British Academy of Letters. Readers instantly bombarded the editor with alternative names. Shaw wrote two letters (published on 13th and 20th November), in which he indulged in some sharp criticism of Henry James, and bravely suggested the inclusion of Oscar Wilde (who was nominated also by H. G. Wells).]

Oh what a Sunday! Work in the morning—the eternal preface. Webb's to lunch: Massingham there with his boy, dressed like a newly painted pillar box, rousing maternal instincts in Beatrice, and Trevelyan afterwards. Webb, Trev. & I biked (B's steed being disabled) to Clapham Common & back through Battersea Park, whence I rode to the Metropole to see my Italian, who shivered like a steel filing confronted with a powerful magnet. We were chaperoned by a young man who turned out to be a brother of my old flame Katie Samuel. She is now a Montreal matron & goes in for political agitation. From the Metropole I fled, almost leaving my garment behind, to Lady C.C. [Colin Campbell], who wanted to consult me about professional business. Then I came home & drudged at the preface & wrote a letter to "The Academy" on their proposed Academy of Letters. Finally it struck 12; I finished my indispensable letters, and must now finish this & go to bed. I wish you could stay in Paris & that I could get there in quarter of an hour. I feel that you are much better & brighter there; but it is damnably inconvenient to have you out of my reach. Why dont you get introduced to Coquelin & tell him that Mansfield of New York plays a superb Coquelin part in a play called "Arms & The Man."—This is a spartan life—but no matter.

GBS

To CHARLOTTE PAYNE-TOWNSHEND

[B/2; X/151.e]

29 Fitzroy Square W
14th November 1897

[Charlotte, upon her return from Paris, had restlessly continued her peregrinations by proceeding straight to Radlett to visit the Phillimores. Shaw, ever practical, turned his accident to account by making it the subject of his article "On Pleasure Bent" in the *Saturday Review* on 20th November. After the heavy critical duties of the previous week, he reported, "I felt that I must have a real experience of some kind, under conditions, especially as regards fresh air, as unlike those of the stalls as possible. After some consideration it occurred to me that if I went into the country, selected a dangerous hill, and rode down it on a bicycle at full speed in the darkest part of the night, some novel and convincing piece of realism might result. It did."]

Ever dearest

I had a toss on the big hill on my way home; but I was not hurt except for a black eye & a cut face; so do not be alarmed by the bloodcurdling account I am sending to Mrs Phillimore. A woman got into my way when I was going fast down the hill. I managed to twist the bike round her safely; but the twist was too much for its balance, and after charging on swaying more & more widely it literally wiped the road with my left cheek. I am a ludicrous spectacle—like a badly defeated prizefighter. I rode on gorily to Edgware; called on a doctor there; got stitched up; & rode home. Visits were of course out of the question, not that I am not as fit as ever—positively the better for the adventure in nerve—but because I am too hideous to be looked at. The surgery would have interested you. I am glad I got just enough hurt to make you tender to me.

GBS

To GRAHAM WALLAS

[B/13]

29 Fitzroy Square W
16th November 1897

[Wallas, a member of the London School Board, was seeking re-election in Hoxton, and campaigning for support in Hoxton and Haggerston. George Turner (1872–1926), a young Fabian who had just drafted Tract No. 73, *The Case for State Pensions in Old Age*, and who later became an officer of the London County Council, was Wallas's campaign secretary. The election provided material for the still-invalided critic's article, "The Board School Playground," in the *Saturday Review* on 27th November.]

Will you tell Turner that I cant orate on Saturday. I have been taking my annual bicycle accident; and the left side of my face is temporarily obliterated. At present I look like a fearfully punished prizefighter at the end of the hundredth round; and there is no chance of my getting nearer to respectability than the end of the fiftieth by Saturday afternoon. The precise damages that disqualify me are a gash in the cheek, another under the eyebrow (both stitched), an unheard-of black eye, and a blending of the collection by a varnish of blood, clay, and collodion on a background of dirty face with such effect that by merely nodding to me publicly in Hoxton you would put yourself with absolute certainty at the bottom of the poll.

GBS

To CHARLOTTE PAYNE-TOWNSHEND

[B/2; X/151]

29 Fitzroy Square W
29th November 1897

[Shaw had attended a matinée of R.L. Stevenson and W.E. Henley's *Admiral Guinea*, produced by the New Century Theatre, at the Avenue. Charlotte had been performing secretarial services for Shaw, as had Kate Salt.]

As I did not see you at the theatre today I became possessed with a notion that the sudden sharp cold had given you neuralgia. The performance lasted until just six; and I had to rush away with Grant Richards after it. At 9, I called at the terrace & was confronted by Farmer [Charlotte's second servant] & Martha, who informed me that you had been out all the afternoon, which at least disposed of the disablement-by-neuralgia theory.

I shall not intrude on my secretary tomorrow. If she desires to resume her duties, doubtless she will come to me.

You shall not be worried into any more headaches. I am now a perfect gentleman, and, until further notice, am,

yours respectfully
G.B.S.

To MRS HUMPHRY WARD

[B/23]

29 Fitzroy Square W
1st December 1897

Dear Mrs Humphry Ward

If once I begin dining out I am a lost man. The very first thing you would do would be to ask me to take down some lady whose invitations I had scorned on pretence of not going into society, always dressing like a navvy, and not being fit company for ladies and gentlemen. Or else it will be somebody I dont know and dont want to know; and I shall have to sit sipping a glass of water & talking to her whilst she eats murdered animals. Why, good heavens! your house is the one place in London where I am certain not to be able to get five minutes conversation with you. No, I wont go to dinner—wont, wont, wont, wont, wont, wont, WON'T. Even if I would, are these the sort of manners you would tolerate at your dinner parties? I wonder at you.

yrs, deeply injured
G. Bernard Shaw

824

[29 Fitzroy Square W]
1st December 1897

[Henry Lowenfeld (1859–1931), an Austrian who had made a fortune out of Kop's ale, was manager of the Prince of Wales's Theatre, where his production of *La Poupée* (music by E. Audran) had been running for more than a year. On 12th November he had written to Shaw: "I have a new composer, whom I think very talented and am trying to find a book for him to compose the music for a Comic Opera. Would it suit your purpose to sell me the right to use your 'Chocolate Cream Soldier' piece (I have stupidly forgot the name of it) for this purpose? Shakespeare and other authors have been used in the same way, why therefore should Bernard Shaw object, or does he wish to occupy an entirely abnormal position? Anyhow kindly let me have your views on the subject . . ." (BM).

Victor Mapes (1870–1943), American playwright and journalist, Paris correspondent for the New York *Sun* (1892–96) and dramatic critic of the New York *World* (1898–99), was stage-manager for Daniel Frohman at the Lyceum Theatre, New York, in 1897. As Mapes had written only one play, *La Comtesse de Lisne* (1895), in French, produced in Paris, it is unlikely that Shaw would have known of him prior to Lowenfeld's putting forth his name as possible librettist. Shaw's belief that "the piece contains hardly any material for music" is ironic in view of the successful adaptation of the play by Oskar Straus as *Der tapfere Soldat* (*The Chocolate Soldier*) in 1908.]

Dear Lowenfeld

I have been all this time recovering from the shock of your proposal to make a Comic Opera of "Arms & the Man." How c^d you possibly make it more of a Comic Opera than it is at present?

Seriously, the piece contains hardly any material for music. I daresay Mozart could set it if you could get at him; but your new composer would find it impossible to do anything but interpolate a few numbers with "lyrics" by Mapes or somebody, with the effect that your "Comic Opera" would have all the ponderousness of a serious comedy & all the absurdity of a burlesque. Besides, where will you find comic opera singers who are sufficiently finished comedians to handle so difficult a play. You may take my word for it that the idea would not work.

By the way will you make my excuses to Mrs Lowenfeld for my lost opportunities of calling. I am forced to forego all social joys: I am now 15 years in arrear with my afternoon calls, & people have either to drop me altogether or to give me a privilege for bad manners.

yrs sinc[erely]
[G. Bernard Shaw]

To CHARLOTTE PAYNE-TOWNSHEND

29 Fitzroy Square W

[A/2; X/151]   3rd December 1897

[Charlotte had proposed that Shaw accompany her and Mrs Phillimore to Dieppe.]

Certainly the proposed treat is a rare one. I am to embark in a piercing wind, with lifeboats capsizing and ships foundering in all directions; to go to a watering place in the depth of winter with nothing to do and nowhere to go; I am to be chaperoned by two women, each determined that the other shall seduce me and each determined that I shall not seduce her; I am to sleep in a foreign hotel with the window open and no bedclothes—perhaps without even a lock to the door to protect me; and next day I am to embark again for four hours more of seasickness. No, thank you. I am comfortable as I am: j'y'suis et j'y'reste. If you go alone, you will be company for the invalid. If I went alone, she would be company for me. But I bar the seaside *à trois*.

My appointment with Waring last night was for 9.30. I *was* late—45 minutes late—did not get home until nearly 2.

No use in looking for human sympathy from me. I have turned the switch, and am your very good friend, but as hard as nails.

GBS

To CHARLOTTE PAYNE-TOWNSHEND

29 Fitzroy Square W

[C/2; X/151]   6th December 1897

[Presumably irked by Shaw's response, Charlotte left for Dieppe on 5th December without troubling to inform him of her departure.]

Secretary required tomorrow, not later than eleven.

GBS

To CHARLOTTE PAYNE-TOWNSHEND

29 Fitzroy Square W

[A/2; X/151]   8th December 1897

What do you mean by this inconceivable conduct? Do you forsake *all* your duties—even those of secretary? Is it not enough that I have

826

returned without a complaint to my stark and joyless life? Must I also go back to writing my own articles, and wasting half hours between the sentences with long trains of reflection? Not a word: not a sign! I send you instructions to arrive at eleven; and *wait* for you instead of beginning by myself, so perfect is my faith in your arrival. I get your shawl, your footwarmer: I sweep the hearth to make the fire look nice for you, and am openly grinned at by the domestic for my pains! Is Dieppe China (assuming that you are there)? Are there no stamps? has the post been abolished? have all the channel steamers foundered?

Go, then, ungrateful wretch: have your heart's desire: find a Master —one who will spend your money, and rule in your house, and order your servants about, and forbid you to ride in hansoms because it's unladylike, and remind you that the honor of his name is in your keeping, and decline in your name any further acquaintance with me, and consummate his marriage in the church lest the housemaid should regard his proceedings as clandestine. Protect yourself for ever from freedom, independence, love, unfettered communion with the choice spirits of your day, a lofty path on which to go your own way and keep your own counsel, and all the other blessings which 999 women cry for and the thousandth cries to get away from. But at least tell me when youre *not* coming; and say whether I am to get a new secretary or not.

GBS

To JANET ACHURCH

29 Fitzroy Square W

[T/1 (A/4)] 9th December 1897

[William Mollison (1861–1911), actor-manager, who had performed in Manchester as Henry IV to Beerbohm Tree's Falstaff and as Enobarbus in the Calvert-Achurch *Antony and Cleopatra*, played Macbeth in the Manchester revival on 22nd January 1898. When the production was transferred to the Métropole, Camberwell, Janet was replaced by Eleanor Calhoun.]

Janet, Janet, Janet

Is there any use in remonstrating?

Is Charrington to be ruined? Is Nora to make clinical observations when she comes back? Who is to play Candida?

Very well: I will tell everybody—tell Miss Townshend, Mrs Webb,

827

Mrs Phillimore, Archer, Ellen Terry, everybody whose knowledge will inflict the most exquisite cruelty on you.

When you came in tonight you were Janet, desirable and adorable. After dinner you were a rowdy, unpresentable wretch. Finally you were inarticulate—nearly as inarticulate as the time before. And I came to propose that you should go to my dentist to be prepared for Manchester!!

Three thirds of a tumbler is half a pint; Macbeth will be on the 22nd Jan; from this to then is 43 days; 43 half pints is $21\frac{1}{2}$ pints; $21\frac{1}{2}$ pints is 10.2/3 quarts, or about $2\frac{1}{2}$ gallons—or over nine gallons a year—say £35.

Useless to hang up the portrait again: it is no longer the least bit like you.

You talk of women *suffering*. When you see me like that, you will—if you ever cared for what I am—know what suffering is for the first time in your life. When I was a child of less than Nora's age, I saw the process in my father; and I have never felt anything since. I learnt soon to laugh at it; and I have laughed at everything since. Presently, no doubt, I shall learn to laugh at you. What else can I do?

No use, dear Janet: I can't be your taskmaster and schoolmaster any longer. If I could expend fifty pounds a week in keeping you luxuriously dulled and disciplined, with punctual splendours of dress and dinner and society to be faced in fine condition, I might be of some use. But as it is, I can only make myself uselessly disagreeable and load my heart with a crown of sword points. Let us drop the subject and say goodbye whilst there is still some Janet left to say goodbye to. The only service a friend can really render is to keep up your courage by holding up to you a mirror in which you can see a noble image of yourself. The moment the image loses its elevation, then away with that friend: however remorseful he may be, he has become a malignant influence on your life. I held up the mirror in which Janet was beautiful as long as I could, in private and in print: now I've held it up with Janet inarticulate and rowdy. Avoid me now as you would the devil; for from this time I will destroy your self respect if you let me near you. Restore the image, and look at it in a new, clean mirror—the archangel's with the purple wings, perhaps: mine is spoiled and done for. I am growing old and cowardly and selfish: it's sufficient that I loved you when I was young. Now I can do nothing but harm unless I say farewell, farewell, farewell, farewell, farewell, farewell, farewell, farewell.

GBS

828

Lucy Carr Shaw and Reginald Roberts in *Shamus O'Brien*
(Broadway Theatre, New York, January 1897)

To MRS RICHARD MANSFIELD

[A/21; X/141]

29 Fitzroy Square W
10th December 1897

[The "trustworthy eye-witnesses" included Elisabeth Marbury and Benjamin Tucker. Lucy Carr Shaw had also been in New York during this year, appearing in Villiers Stanford's *Shamus O'Brien*, which opened at the Broadway Theatre on 5th January 1897, and which subsequently toured the country; there is, however, no evidence that she was still in New York when *The Devil's Disciple* opened on 4th October. The Rev. Mr Anderson was played by Benjamin Johnson (1866-1928), a well-known stock company performer who appeared with Mansfield's company from 1896 to 1898.]

My dear Mrs Mansfield

Thank you for the Philadelphia notices. I informed myself as to the New York production by private reports from trustworthy eye-witnesses, with the result that I very nearly wrote to you about the way in which your business has been spoiled by your monster of a husband. Get divorced, my dear Mrs Mansfield, get divorced. However, you shall have your revenge. In the next play, it is you that shall have the actor-proof part, and he that shall have the uphill work. We shall see then whether he will fascinate New York by carrying hot kettles about the stage. I shall cross the Atlantic someday and play the executioner myself; and on that occasion *Anderson will arrive too late*.

You may take the extreme and tender care with which he lays you down on the stage after the kiss as the measure of his sense of the tremendous effect you would make by carrying out my directions. Observe how everyone admires his acting—*his* acting, if you please, with the coat—the business which I arranged for him and which would produce its effect equally if it were done by a roasting jack. But when it comes to *your* effect: oh no, thank you! And then I am told that *you* spoiled the scene at its climax. Fortunately I asked how, and learnt that the actor-manager had suddenly lost faith in my stagecraft when it went to somebody else's credit. What is to be done with such a man? Can you wonder at my disowning, disclaiming, repudiating him?

I find also that Anderson, who should gain strong sympathy from his first word onward, is introduced as a canting snuffling burlesque Plymouth Brother in the beginning. But that *may* be Mr Whatshisname's fault. The business of the kiss is Richard's and nobody else's—except of course yours. You could have remonstrated—are there no pokers or carving knives in the house to give emphasis to your protests?

I strongly recommend you to drop the part & play Essie, or retire from the play altogether. Without that particular stroke it is a thankless business. If the end of the second act produces the right effect, the sympathy goes from the woman for her mistake about Anderson: whenever I have read it here the women have always been disgusted at her little faith. It is extremely difficult to hold up the horror of the court-martial scene against Burgoyne & the rest, and to be made the butt of such a cruel effect as his "that will do very nicely" when she takes refuge in agonized prayer under the gallows (I understand that this has been totally missed, though it is one of the most appalling things in the play). Nevertheless, these scenes would be worth the labor they must cost, if you could fix the audience's interest in you by striking home in the scene of the arrest. As it is—well, as it is, I say again, divorce him, divorce him, divorce him. And then you shall have a play all to yourself, cramful of irresistible effects.

yrs sincerely
G. Bernard Shaw

To ELLEN TERRY

[U(A)/10; X/117]

29 Fitzroy Square W
24th December 1897

[Charlotte Payne-Townshend had translated Gabriele d'Annunzio's one-act play *Sogno d'un mattina di Primavera*. There is no record of production or publication of the translation. Jessie Millward (1861–1932), William Terriss's leading lady and mistress, had suffered the shock of having him die in her arms. She and Terriss had appeared together in a number of melodramas at the Adelphi since 1885, including G. R. Sims's *Harbour Lights*, Dion Boucicault's *The Shaughraun*, and William Gillette's *Secret Service* (in which they were performing at the time of Terriss's murder).

At the 14th annual dinner of the Playgoers' Club, in the Hotel Cecil on 13th February 1898, Shaw acknowledged Cecil Raleigh's toast to "The Press." There is, however, no evidence that he carried out his threat to harass Irving.]

Now I swear that you never mentioned Annunzio's name to me in your life. I believe you have multitudes of lovers, and in writing to them you forget which is which. However, it dont matter if youve read the play: Miss P. T's version is only a translation. Only, if you get very tired of the Lyceum, and the Savoy, you can go round to 10 Adelphi Terrace (door round the corner, opposite the Caledonian Hotel, with a lamp inscribed "London School of Economics") and get a cup of tea & an hour's rest on pretence of calling about a reputed version of the Spring Morning's Dream. Miss P.T. is a restful person, plain, greeneyed, very ladylike, completely demoralized by contact with my ideas, forty, with nice rooms on a solid basis of £4000 a year, independent & unencumbered, and not so very plain either when you are in her confidence. So whenever you want to run away and hide, probably the last place you will be sought for in is the London School of Economics & Political Science. She will be pretty curious about you, not only on the usual grounds of your celebrity, but because she has discovered that "work" & "important business" on my part sometimes means writing long letters to you. (N.B. She doesnt know that I have mentioned her Annunzio project to you.)

My calculations are quite put out by the unforeseen extinction of Terriss [on 16th December]. I was scheming to get the D's D. produced with him in the part, and Jessie as Judith. The alternative was a Waring-Bourchier combination—Bourchier to play Burgoyne. And now Terriss is only a name and a batch of lies in the newspapers, and Waring goes to the Adelphi in his place. However, Waring may need stronger plays than Terriss, who was a play in himself; so perhaps Jessie may play Judith yet. If I invest the author's fees from the New York run in County Council stock I shall have £20 a year for my old age. They run to £850. I roll in gold. I am a man of wealth & consideration. I will take a theatre presently, and engage Henry for eccentric comedy.

I cannot understand why you didn't get Laurence [Irving] or Courtenay Thorpe to play Alexis [in *Peter the Great*] instead of importing an American [Robert Taber].

And now prithee, dear Ellen, what is to be done for you tomorrow and the day after, with no post? On the 28th I go down to Shakespearland (address care of Sir G.O. Trevelyan Bt M.P.—I suppose that is correct—Welcombe, Stratford on Avon—however, it doesnt matter, as you wont have time to write to me & I'll have to write to you) for a few days. I am casting about for some deadly means of provoking Henry to strike me off the press list, so that I may astonish him by a magnificent notice of the play without having seen it.

The Playgoers Club always want to get me to attend their annual dinner and respond to the toast of The Press. This time they urge that as Sir Henry Irving is going to respond for the drama, I cannot refuse. The prospect of blighting the traitor's oratory is too tempting: I *have* *accepted*, ha! ha!; so let him tremble. My whole speech will not be

831

about "my dear friend, Miss Ellen Terry." That is, unless she buys mercy for him in the meantime by letting me kiss the tip of her little finger.

GBS

To JULIAN STURGIS

29 Fitzroy Square W
25th December 1897

[G.u/2]

[Julian Sturgis (1848–1904), American-born author and dramatist, wrote the libretti for Goring Thomas's *Nadeshda* (1885) and Sullivan's *Ivanhoe*. Shaw, reviewing *Ivanhoe* in *The World* on 4th February 1891, had written: "If the noble dialogue of Scott is not more suitable for English music than the fustian of Mr. Sturgis, then so much the worse for English music. . . . I protest, in the name of my own art of letters, against a Royal English Opera which begins by handing over a literary masterpiece for wanton debasement at the hands of a journeyman hired for the job."]

Dear Sir

There is no difficulty about the dialogue. Even in 18th century opera, the libretto is not in continuous symmetrical rhymed lines. It consists of "dry dialogue," set to conventional phrases accompanied by a few chords on the harpsichord (recitativo secco), now obsolete; and impassioned rhetorical speeches with full orchestral treatment (recitativo stromentato), as an exordium to the set piece in regular metre with rhymes and musical form to correspond. Nowadays the instrumented recitative has developed enormously (old fashioned people still explain their objection to Wagner's works by saying that they are "all recitative"); and the set pieces have either disappeared altogether, or are handled in such a way that if the rhymes were all altered in delivery into ludicrously dissimilar sounds, nobody would notice it. As to the metre, that has always been freely altered by composers. I well remember the disgust of William Morris when a musical Socialist sang him a new setting of the lines ["The March of the Workers," in *The Commonweal*, February 1885] he wrote to the tune of "John Brown." They began—

<blockquote>
"Hark, the rolling of the thunder!
Lo, the clouds and lo thereunder! &c"
</blockquote>

(metrically equivalent to the original
"glory, glory hallelujah").

832

In the new setting they went like this.

> "Hark, the rolling—the rolling of the thunder!
> Lo, the clouds—the clouds and lo thereunder! &c"

Yet this was abject fidelity to the poet compared to what many eminent composers have done.

Take two very strong instances of the music exactly following the verse metre, and making the need for the rhyme as strong as it ever can be in music—"La ci darem" [*Don Giovanni*] and "Yankee Doodle." Here the rhymes "mano" & "lontano," "pony" and "maccaroni" are obviously required. And yet if they had been introduced to us by a singer who substituted "il braccio" for "le mano" and "jackass" for "pony," the rhymes would not have been missed by 95% of the people who would miss them at once without the music. Wagner's Nibelungen tetralogy is rhymeless; but who has ever enjoyed it any the less? The truth is that poets use metre and rhyme only to enhance the purely musical effect of their verse. When they collaborate with a musician, you are bringing coals to Newcastle in trying to make your words musical in the technical sense. The only rhyme that tells in music is musical rhyme: for example, the three notes at the end of the first & third strains (lines) in Meyerbeer's "Shadow Dance" [*Dinorah*]. Now comes the question, may you then write in the style of Whittaker's Almanack with every confidence that it will do as well as the style of Shakespear? The answer is, of course, No; but the objection to Whittaker is not in the least that he is rhymeless and metrically irregular, but solely that his words record unrelated (i.e., *dry*) facts, whereas music can only express feeling. Not until words are so charged with emotion that they crave to glow into music as a heated stick glows into flame, or until the rhetorical force of them demands the stroke of the drum or the crash of the brass for satisfying emphasis are they of any use to the truly dramatic musician. *That* is what you must bring your composer, whether in rhyme & regular measure or not does not matter a rap.

To illustrate, "Thirty days hath September" &c *cannot* be made into music, because it expresses no feeling; but "Multiplication is vexation" is quite well suited for music, because it expresses a very marked mood of botheration and impatience. I cite it to shew that the feeling expressed need not be at all sublime or tender or heroic. So long as it *is* feeling, and not mere statement or calculation or argument, it is material for the musician. Even good comedies make good libretti, because, though the music cannot touch *wit*, it can express the gaiety

833

and tenderness which run all through the finest comedy. Mozart's settings of Beaumarchais and Molière (Le Nozze di Figaro & Don Giovanni) are wonderful examples.

If you have caught my point, you will now see why it is that the most illiterate balderdash suits a musician better than verse, however highly polished, epigrammatic, and witty, which is not rhetorically powerful or movingly emotional. Balderdash *can* express emotion, however inconsequently or ungrammatically. "When other lips" [*The Bohemian Girl*] and "Let me like a soldier fall" [*Maritana*] are frightful balderdash; but they gave Balfe & Wallace just what they wanted. Don Cæsar's "breast expanding to the ball" is outrageously funny to a critical reader; but to the musician it is as available as any better expressed *élan* of courage. Whereas Don Cæsar's *witticisms* are quite useless. Moral: give the composer the right passional material in words which will set the whole literary world laughing at you rather than the wrong historical or intellectual material in a form that will outlast Hudibras or Larouchefoucauld's maxims.

By the way, do not forget that if you bring a composer a string of verses, suitable or not, he can, if he is fool enough (which he generally is), compose a set of tunes which will fit your lines and syllables; for *any* word pattern can be fitted with a sound pattern. "Thirty days hath &c" can be fitted to Mozart's "Qui sdegno" [Italian version of *Die Zauberflöte*] as neatly as "Multiplication is vexation" to Offenbach's "Falsacappa, voici ma prise" [*Les Brigands*] or Handel's "Blessing & honor, glory & power, be unto Him &c" [*Messiah*]. That's your danger. You may extract from your novel a highly readable & even actable historical play, containing not one stroke that can become music. But nine out of ten composers, if they get the commission, will conscientiously manacle it to a score made up of very pretty & ingenious sound patterns, and will never know why the thing fails, as it must fail, when it comes to the footlights. Unless you can get hold of a Mozart or a Wagner, it is of the utmost importance that you should know what the musician needs better than he is at all likely to know it himself.

If the novel you are adapting is really prosaic it wont do for an opera. I assume, however, that it is really dramatic in the poetic, not the "historical" sense. In that case you may possibly find speeches in it which may be set as they stand. Shakespear's prose is better than his verse: you would never dream of paraphrasing "What a piece of work is man!" in the metre of "Twinkle, twinkle, little star," nor the magnificent dramatic speeches in "The Pilgrim's Progress," nor

834

Walt Whitman's "Mystic Trumpeter." Get someone to sing you (as an easy modern instance) the prologue from Leoncavallo's "Pagliacci," and you will see how entirely unnecessary it is to hamper your periods with rhyme or Procrustean metres. If when the composer gets to work, some bit of sentiment suggested by you turns into a minuet in his head, then he can easily ask for a bit of trim verse, & you can supply it. Unless the collaboration is a real one, with lots of give & take both ways in it, it can hardly be very successful.

If I were writing a libretto I should cast it in phrases (set down as lines) of a distinctly metrical character, but without any attempt at regularity. Each phrase would be a good line in some measure or other, or a rhetorical point; but as to the lengths I should be as free as Whitman. I should be careful to make the measure dance or languish or stalk loftily or creep mysteriously according to the feeling, as suggestively as possible for the musician; and occasionally I should no doubt bring it to a symmetrical lyric with rhymes. But you can see by looking at Handel's "Messiah" and his "Acis & Galatea" what can be done both ways. The Bible, the freest parts of Goethe's "Faust," Blake's prophetic books, Whitman & Edward Carpenter, will set lots of irregular but metrical ideas running through your head. Finally, look at the specific form academically designed for music—the ode (Dryden, for example). There you will find the free form you want. Its old bones are quite susceptible of resurrection & adaptation to dramatic purposes.

This is all I know about it—at least all I can express in a hasty letter without referring you to particular operas with which you may not be acquainted. By far the most suggestive book on the subject is Wagner's "Opera & Drama" (I think it's Vol II of Ashton Ellis's translation of the Prose Works); but it is long, and runs off rather into special pleading for the alliterative verse of the Nibelung Ring. You ought to read it someday: indeed all his writings are perfect mines of suggestion for the artist.

Excuse the length of this letter; but your order was too large to be executed, even cursorily, in any smaller space.

yrs faithfully
[G. Bernard Shaw]

835

To ELLEN TERRY

29 Fitzroy Square W
[U(A)/10; X/117]   27th December 1897

[Oscar Barrett (1846–1941) was the author of numerous works for the musical stage, including the pantomime *Aladdin* and the comic opera *The Kangaroo Girl* (1897). The pantomime Shaw attended at Drury Lane on the 27th was *The Babes in the Wood* by Arthur Sturgess and Arthur Collins, starring the comedian Dan Leno. Arthur Bourchier had produced Herman Merivale's *The Queen's Proctor* (an adaptation of Sardou's *Divorçons*) at the Royalty on 2nd June 1896. *A Scrap of Paper* (1861), adapted by J. P. Simpson from Sardou's *Les Pattes de mouche*, was first performed by the Kendals in 1875, and revived on several occasions, their latest production having been in 1893.

Irving's gesture, bringing Jessie Millward a bunch of violets and then escorting her to Terriss's funeral, was a generous one, for her position, as Terriss's mistress, "was such in the eyes of society as to preclude her presence" (Laurence Irving, *Henry Irving: The Actor and His World*, 1951). The journalist Eliza Aria, in her memoirs (*My Sentimental Self*, 1922), recalled: "There was not a member of the theatrical world, in the crowd which followed the murdered man to his resting-place, who did not fall in worshipful admiration of Irving when they noted the tenderness which went to his shepherding."

Ellen Terry, who had been touring the provinces with Irving most of the autumn, had no marriage plans. On 1st November, referring cryptically to the fact that she had been receiving letters from an elderly Scottish admirer, she had jested in a postscript: "When I get to Edinburgh I'm going to marry a man (and *Scotch* at that!), rich, and old. Then I butter the stairs, and wear a widow's cap next day!"]

Pity me, Ellen: I am going to the pantomime. However, it might have been worse. Barrett might have invited me to the Garrick; but happily he didn't: so I shall get off with Drury Lane.

Do you mean to say that Wyndham should play the D's D. himself? It would be impossible: he's too old; and he has not the peculiar fascination. But he would be admirable as the husband: it would suit him to a hair's breadth. Are you quite sure that you are up to date about the Bourchiers? Five years ago, when Violet was a *seconda donna* at the Lyceum, and he half amateur, half farceur, I should have agreed; but now things are altered. Bourchier is not only a very clever and effective comedian; but his physical power and completeness gives him a large range: he can play light & heavy, gallant and ridiculous, normal and eccentric. Violet, who has just sent me (and probably you) her portrait on a Xmas card with the very latest Parisian blouse on (six

836

guineas in the Chaussée d'Antin) has also developed into a personality of the first striking rank. Their adaptation of "Divorçons," whatever else it was, was certainly not underplayed: there has been nothing like it since the Kendals in "A Scrap of Paper." The woman's part in the D's D. would not suit her; but she could do it without disaster; and there can be no doubt about Bourchier's making a good—even a very imposing—Burgoyne. I put their merits strongly because I know how extraordinarily the landscape changes from five years to five years. That pair will cut a figure, I assure you. And B. is no such bad diplomatist either—did you appreciate his noble tribute to H.I. in the Morning Post correspondence [on "The Stage as a Profession," to which discussion Shaw had contributed on 29th November], which meant: "Good people: you think Sir H.I. is still the colossally rich man of business. You're wrong: he has lost money: he's only a nobly poor artist: hip, hip, hurrah for his fine qualities; and let us hope that the Lyceum is not really on its last legs."? Further, he has slipped in front of all the rest whilst they were explaining to one another what an amateur & booby he was. Keep your eye on that ménage, Ellen: you underrate it. Or am I an ass?

I should like to get the piece on at the Adelphi with Waring in order to secure Jessie's part for her. H.I. scored nobly by standing by her at the funeral: had it been his case, Lady Irving would have been in the position of Mrs Terriss; and you would have been—probably taking a nice drive through Richmond Park with me, or perhaps [with] that villain that you persuaded me you were going to marry the other day. Jessie must have been consoled a little; for she adores H.I., and always reserved his claims, as an intellectual prince, before Terriss's, greatly to William's indignation; for he knew that Henry was intellectually an imposter, nothing like so hardheaded as himself.

I must break off to catch the post. I go to Welcombe tomorrow afternoon. Dont break off your friendship with Henry on my account: I'll let him alone, under compulsion. What a nasty letter this is, isnt it? No matter: my heart is true to Ellen, and even to Ellen's wicked friends for her sake.

GBS

To GRANT RICHARDS

Welcombe. Stratford on Avon
[A/4]   29th December 1897

Dear G.R.

I return to town on Saturday. Up to the 6 o'clock post on Friday, proofs can be addressed as above.

I am not sure that we ought not to make a further experiment with the title page. Ask them to set it up in Great Primer (I think that's what they call the biggest fount of Caslon) instead of capitals, & let us see it. No other change except the change of type to be made. The fact is, the caps are too big for so small a page; and the smaller caps dont look black enough. I imagine great primer, in black or red (we mustn't have black *and* red) will be a success.

yrs ever
G. Bernard Shaw

To ELLEN TERRY

Welcombe. Stratford on Avon
[U(A)/10; X/117]   31st December 1897

[Sir George Trevelyan's "gigantic house" is now a luxury hotel. William Pember Reeves (1857–1932), a New Zealander who left his post of Minister of Labour, Education, and Justice to come to London as Agent-General, was a Fabian. He became director of the London School of Economics in 1908.]

This is how I break my promises to write to you by every post. The moment I get away to the country, there is nothing to stop my work; and it accordingly becomes incessant. This is a gigantic house, with sixteen hall doors, rooms that no man has ever counted, a conservatory like the Crystal Palace, 76 bath rooms, and 1300 miles of corridor, with every door the exact counterpart of every other door, so that we have to crumble bread as we walk, like the child in the fairy story, so as to find our way back to the eating room. By a violent effort, a corner of the place has been made humanly habitable; and in this corner now dwell Trevelyan junior (our host), the Webbs, the Reeveses (Reeves is Agent General for New Zealand, where he was a shining light of the Fabian Ministry which set our variety of Socialism on foot there) and myself. I correct proofs of the plays, and read up the subject of Peter. When I set aside an hour to write to you, they drag me off to bicycle to Warwick, or to go to Stratford and scatter innumerable sixpences on the relics of the immortal William. I return tomorrow afternoon, having only written you one letter.

I really dont like the notion of your pretending to be Catherine I. You see, she had one talent and one accomplishment. She could get round people; and she could act. Just like you! And she never cared a straw for anybody. I wonder is that like you! When she found she could cure Peter's headaches, and beg off his victims, she set up in the business; and when anybody was condemned to be impaled, or knouted, or beheaded, he or she promptly retained the Empress as intercessor at a handsome fee; so that she made no end of money out of her mercy, the quality of which was carefully strained. It dropped like the gentle dew of a showerbath when you paid her to pull the string. When Peter had her lover chopped up, and took her for a nice drive round the scaffold, she contemplated the spectacle like the Cheshire cat, smiling. When he put the poor fellow's head in a bottle of brandy and set it on her bedroom mantelpiece, she hung her pads on it, quite unruffled. When Peter died (shouldnt be at all surprised if she poisoned him) she dragged Eudoxia, who had survived two martyrdoms, out of her convent & flung her into a dungeon, a fact which disposes of Laurence's pretty romance—really taken from her conduct towards the Queen of Prussia, whom she wanted to get round. When she was rid of Peter, she made one glorious plunge into unlimited brandy and impropriety, and had such a roaring time of it that she killed herself inside of two years. And now, by the infinite irony of fate, she is to be revived again in the person of my Ellen, and I am to pretend to like it.

I was to have written to you last night; but they made me read the Devil's Disciple instead. The nervous effort of firing off those three acts all in one breath of course undid all my holiday. When I went to bed I dreamt that I had to play an important part with Forbes Robertson in a drama which I didnt know. It was necessary—I dont know why—that I should bluff it out at all hazards, and improvise my part. Whilst I was remonstrating about it, F.R's call came, and he bounded on the stage (a street, with a great tower & a harbor at the end—all real, not scenery) and I had to follow & begin. My first utterance, delivered from the top of the tower to him as he stood below on the quay, made him shriek with laughter; and I was anticipating utter disaster when I noticed that nobody was listening to us, and then the dream changed.

Yes: the curse of London is its dirt. Also its lack of *light*. (The Agent General, snoring on the sofa, is going to wake—yes: there he

839

goes). My much ridiculed Jaegerism is an attempt at cleanliness & porousness: I want my body to breathe. I have long resigned myself to dust & dirt & squalor in external matters: if seven maids with seven mops swept my den for half a century they would make no impression on it; but I always have the window wide open night & day; I shun cotton & linen & all fibrous fabrics that collect odors, as far as my person is concerned; and I never eat dead—oh, I forgot: you do. Shame! Now I must get back to my work. Choose that new house with a nice gate lodge or gamekeeper's cottage, communicating by a secret passage with the best bedroom: I'll find a tenant for it. Success tomorrow, oh ever dearest, for you & even for him. I can't write: I am too Ellen-hungry.

GBS

Index of Recipients

Roche, Vivie, 298
Rothenstein, William, 809
Russell, John Francis, 335

Salt, Henry S., 219
Samuel, Katie, 88
Samuels, H.B., 339
Sanders, William, 206
Sandham, Isabel, 204, 205, 253
Scott, Clement, 496
Seligman, De Witt J., 174
Seymour, Henry, 109
Shaw, Georgina (Mrs R.F.), 407, 425
Shaw, Lucinda Elizabeth, 11
Shaw, Lucinda Frances, 7, 8
Shaw, R. Frederick, 132
Shorter, Clement, 210, 280, 482
Sims, G.R., 20, 38
Smith, Alexander, 79, 89, 95, 112
Smith, Elder & Co., 39
Smoke Abatement Institute, 54
Southam, Ethel, 49, 50
Sparling, Henry Halliday, 148
Spry, G.W., 349
Standring, George, 211, 212
Star, The, 197, 199
Stead, William T., 170, 445, 448, 450
Stepniak, Sergius, 227, 323
Sturgis, Julian, 832
Sutton, R., 193
Swan Sonnenschein, William, 166, 167, 178, 179, 180, 181
Swan Sonnenschein & Co., 116, 117, 120, 122, 123, 124, 128, 129, 130, 143, 159, 160

Terry, Ellen, 342, 344, 346, 348, 564, 572, 608, 615, 621, 633, 641, 642, 646, 650, 653, 657, 661, 665, 667, 670, 672, 675, 679, 692, 694, 701, 704, 708, 710, 712, 719, 721, 728, 729, 730, 731, 733, 734, 737, 740, 741, 742, 744, 747, 750, 752, 759, 760, 762, 763, 767, 770, 772, 774, 776, 777, 778, 781, 784, 785, 787, 790, 794, 800, 830, 836, 838
Thomas, C., 329
Townshend, C. Uniakce, 12, 14
Truth, 230
Tucker, Benjamin R., 597

Unidentified Correspondents, 53, 54, 176, 242, 246, 474
Unwin, T. Fisher, 193, 201, 283, 286, 292, 329, 551, 556, 573, 595, 598, 607

Virtue, James, 42

Walker, Emery, 217, 225, 299, 305, 308, 343, 541
Walker, Mrs Emery, 114
Wallas, Graham, 190, 235, 343, 366, 368, 398, 404, 421, 790, 823
Ward, Mrs Humphry, 824
Waugh, Arthur, 436, 446
Webb, Beatrice (Potter), 267, 407, 452
Webb, Philip, 714
Webb, Sidney, 306, 358, 361, 364
Wedd, Nathaniel, 182, 186, 207
Whelen, Frederick, 406, 419, 715
White, Arnold, 21, 32
White, R.F., & Son, 33
Wilde, Oscar, 384
Woodruff, George B., 60

Yates, C.D., 436

GENERAL INDEX

COMPILED BY ERIC J. BATSON

Aeschylus, 570
Agnesi, Luigi, 9, 11
Aladdin, 721
Alan's Wife: *see* Bell, Florence
Albemarle, The, 352
Alcestis: *see* Todhunter
Alexander, George, 470, 472, 479, 480,
    535, 567, 568, 591, 633, 741
Alexandra: *see* Voss
Allen, George (& Co.), 116, 542
Allen, Grant, 449, 451
    The Woman Who Did, 489, 493
Allen and Unwin, Ltd., 542
All's Well That Ends Well: *see* Shakes-
    peare
Alma-Tadema, L., 657
Alone (Simpson and Merivale), 115,
    634
Alps and Balkans: *see* Shaw, *Arms and
    the Man*
Amber Heart, The: *see* Calmour
Ambient, Mark: *see Christina*
American Women: *see* Women: Ameri-
    can
Anarchism, 109, 184, 307
Anarchist, The, 109
Ancient Buildings, Society for the Pro-
    tection of, 343
Anderson, Mary, 320, 565, 601, 617
Androcles and the Lion: *see* Shaw
Angelico, Fra, 87
Anonymity, 221–3, 497
Antony and Cleopatra: *see* Shakespeare
Archer, Lt.-Col. Charles, 272
Archer, Frances (Mrs William Archer),
    127, 239, 430, 615
Archer, Thomas, 324–5, 400, 402, 540
Archer, William, 111, 118, 125, 153,
    208, 210, 213, 215, 222, 225, 239,
    250, 254, 272, 285, 290, 294, 305,
    382, 383, 386, 403, 424, 439, 477,
    500, 513, 540, 571, 580, 602, 607,
    628, 648, 683, 685, 694, 711, 713,
    809, 828
    early activities, 465
    his pessimism and diffidence, 238
    his incorruptibility, 320, 322, 324,
        327–8
    his controversiality, 401

Archer, William—*contd.*
    his rationalistic secularism, 588
    meeting with Shaw, 125
    assisted by Shaw as art critic, 145–7
    dramatic collaboration with Shaw,
        175–6, 386
    urged by Shaw to write plays, 395,
        402
    on Shaw's synthesising, 588
    reaction to *Widowers' Houses*, 372–3,
        425
    reaction to *Arms and the Man*, 425
    reviews *The Man of Destiny*, 791
    critical of Shaw's Ibsenism, 314–18
    as Ibsen translator, 289, 294, 599
    and *Little Eyolf*, 592, 594, 602
    critical of Ellen Terry in *Cymbeline*,
        673, 679
    lectures on the history of the Stage,
        662, 664
    on "The Theatres," 386
    edits *The Theatrical World* (1894),
        467, 472, 473, 530
Architecture, 714
    Italian, 310
Area Belle, The (Brough and Halliday),
    657, 741
Argus, The (Melbourne), 7, 586, 592
Aria, Eliza, 836
Aristophanes, 570
Armitage, Edward, 186–7
Arms and the Man: *see* Shaw
Armstrong, Florence, 209
Arnold, Sir Edwin, 287–9
Art and artists, 220, 309–12, 490
Art Journal, 42, 282
Art Workers' Guild, 305, 308
Ashwell, Lena, 712
Asquith, Herbert Henry (later Earl of
    Oxford and Asquith), 364–5, 587
As You Like It: *see* Shakespeare
Atheism, 302
Audiences, 462
Audran, Edmond: *La Poupée*, 825
Augier, Emile, 570
Austin, Alfred, 750, 760
Austin, John, 726
Austin, Louis F., 321–2, 755

Aveling, Edward, 81, 121, 139-40, 168, 210, 241, 359, 379
The Scarlet Letter, 237, 240
Aveling, Mrs Edward: *see* Marx, Eleanor
Aynesworth, Allan, 759, 789

Bach, Johann Sebastian, 118-19, 121
Bach choir, 118, 121
Backer-Gröndahl, Agathe, 503
Bacon, Francis, 109
Baird, Dorothea, 744
Balfe, Michael: *The Bohemian Girl*, 8, 58, 834
Balfour, A. J., 221, 224, 268-9, 587
Ballads, 58
Balzac, H. de, 799
Bancroft, Lady: *see* Wilton, Marie
Bandmann, D. E., 50, 52
Barker, Henry A., 164-6
Barker, H. Granville: *see* Granville-Barker
Barnby, Sir Joseph, 57-8
Barnhill, J. B.: *see* "McCall, E."
Barrett, George, 175-6
Barrett, Oscar, 836
Barrett, Wilson, 118-19, 175-6, 290, 617, 643, 710, 722, 765, 768, 770
The Sign of the Cross, 588, 589
Barrie, J. M.: *Becky Sharp*, 478
Barrington, Rutland, 412
Barry, M. Maltman, 358
Bartolucci, Candida, 815
Barton, Dr J. Kingston, 18, 35, 132, 141-2, 568, 569
Barwick, W. J., 768
Baum, F. C., 364, 366
Bax, E. Belfort, 164, 183, 233, 236, 241
Bayreuth Festival: *see* Wagner, R.: Bayreuth Festival
Beaconsfield, Benjamin Disraeli, Earl of, 761
Beardsley, Aubrey, 446, 549, 571-2
Beatty, Mazzini, 20, 137-8, 142, 160
Beatty, Octavius, 156-7
Beatty, Pakenham, 19, 20, 140, 169, 250, 374, 388, 390, 395, 467, 559, 587
forces his attentions on Lucy Shaw, 150-2

Beatty, Pakenham—*contd.*
satirised in *An Unsocial Socialist*, 137-8
To My Lady and Other Poems, 20
Marcia, 137-8
Beatty, Mrs Pakenham ("Ida"), 137-9, 140-2, 144-5, 148, 149, 150-1, 156-7, 159-60, 163-4, 467
Beau Austin (Henley and Stevenson), 638
Beau Brummel: *see* Fitch
Beauchamp, John, 385-6
Beaumarchais, P.-A. Caron de, 465
Le Mariage de Figaro, 327, 834
Beauty and the Beast, 8
Bebel, A., 355, 359
Becky Sharp: *see* Barrie
Bedford, Duke of, 171
Beerbohm, Max, 704
Beerbohm Tree: *see* Tree, H. Beerbohm
Beere, Mrs Bernard, 412, 472
Beethoven, Ludwig van, 48, 323, 445, 505, 666, 699, 818
Beeton, Henry R., 235, 237
Beggars, 728
Behnke, Emil, 366
Bell, Chichester, 34, 42
Bell, Florence (Mrs Hugh Bell): *Alan's Wife*, 393-4, 401-2
Bell Telephone Co., 25
Bellini, Vincenzo: *La Sonnambula*, 8, 12
Belmore, Lionel, 790-1
Bendall, E. A., 669
"Bennett, C. H., and Co." (article) *see* Shaw: other works
Benson, Sir Frank, 286-8
Bentinck, Lord George, 228-9
Bentley, George, 24-5, 29-30, 60, 74
Bentley, Richard (and Son), 24-5, 26, 38-9, 48, 59-60
Bentham, Jeremy, 185
Beringer, Mrs Oscar: *Salvé*, 580
Berlioz, Hector, 36, 58
Bernhardt, Sarah, 529, 598, 765, 776, 780, 800
Besant, Annie, 112-13, 139, 168, 170, 210, 233, 236, 270, 273, 274, 431, 505, 636
Besant, Sir Walter: sequel to *A Doll's House*, 237, 239

Burns, John, 177, 184, 271, 291, 355, 359, 361, 362, 382, 390, 399, 420, 577, 768
Burrows, Herbert, 254, 277, 365, 578
Burt, Thomas, 364
Buss, Frances M., 228
Butler, Samuel (1612–80): *Hudibras*, 834
Butler, Samuel (1835–1902), 300, 326
  Luck or Cunning?, 300
Butterfield, Charles R., 388
Butterfield, Mrs C. R.: *see* Shaw, Lucy
Bygones: *see* Pinero
Byles, Sir William, 376
Byron, Lord, 52
Byron, Henry J., 630

Cade, Jack, 212
Cæsar and Cleopatra: *see* Shaw
Caine, Sir Thomas Hall, 584
  The Manxman, 710
Calhoun, Eleanor, 475, 477
Call, Annie Payson, 695
Calmour, A. C.: *The Amber Heart*, 348
Calvert, Mrs Charles, 720, 781
Calvert, Louis, 720, 736, 771, 787
Cambridge University, 186
Cameron, Beatrice (Mrs Richard Mansfield), 441, 494, 499, 503, 508, 511, 523, 524, 637, 638, 643, 717, 738, 829
Camille, 658, 731, 732
Campbell, Lady Colin, 226, 289, 322, 396, 409, 822
Campbell, James Dykes, 87
Campbell, Mrs Patrick (Beatrice Stella Tanner), 334, 495, 500, 510, 622, 665, 671, 755, 756, 761, 787, 795
  note on, 564
  first meeting with, 684
  lack of engagements, 763
  suitability for Mrs Warren, 412
  foreseen as Eliza Doolittle, 803
  as Mrs Tanqueray, 610
  as Juliet, 564, 565, 655
  in *Little Eyolf*, 694, 702, 707, 708, 709, 713
Candid Friend, The, 99
Candida: *see* Shaw
Capital: *see* Marx, Karl

Capital punishment: *see* Punishment: capital
Capitalism, 172–3, 457, 632
Captain Brassbound's Conversion: *see* Shaw
Carl Rosa Opera Company, 581
Carlisle, Lady, 581
Carlyle, Thomas, 799
  Sartor Resartus, 642
Carpenter, Edward, 637, 640, 818, 835
  Forecasts of the Coming Century, 637
Carpenter, Major Wallace, 8, 9, 11
Carr, Comyns, 744, 745
Carré, M.: *see Mirette*
Carroll, the Rev. William George, 4
Carson, S. Murray, 773, 774: *see also Rosemary*
Carte, R. D'Oyly, 346–7, 473
Carte, Mrs R. D'Oyly: *see* Lenoir, Helen
  The Squire of Dames, 567
  The Tree of Knowledge, 817
Case of Rebellious Susan, The: *see* Jones
Cashel Byron's Profession (novel): *see* Shaw
Cassell & Co., 193
Caste: *see* Robertson, T. W.
Cathcart, J. L., 653
Cathedrals, 208: *see also* Milan; Peterborough; Strasbourg; Ulm
Catherine I (of Russia), 839
Catriona: *see* Stevenson
Cavendish, Ada, 9, 11
Caxton, William, 816
Cecil, Arthur, 175–6
Cellier, A.: *Dorothy*, 330
Cenci, The: *see* Shelley
Censorship: *see* Pigott, E. F. S.
Centlivre, Susannah: *The Wonder, a Woman Keeps a Secret*, 778
Central Democratic Club, 183
Century Co. (New York), 329–30
Cetewayo, 192
Chairman's Handbook, The: *see* Palgrave
Chamberlain, Joseph, 183, 185, 326, 359
Champion, Henry Hyde, 101–2, 115, 140, 145, 167, 180, 233, 351, 361–363, 365
  Unionist intrigue, 356–9

849

850

857

Irving, Sir Henry, 31, 175, 187, 342, 391, 434, 486, 539, 553, 639, 640, 654, 665, 667, 668, 699, 701, 720, 722, 730, 741, 768, 770, 773, 781, 782, 784, 795, 812, 830, 831
  knighthood, 734
  hypnotic state, 780
  at Terriss's funeral, 837
  as Charles I, 290
  as Hamlet, 788, 802
  as Lear, 661
  as Richard III, 692, 747, 753, 773
  and *Cymbeline*, 652, 653, 665
  in *Mme Sans-Gêne*, 743
  public execration of Shaw, 347
  attack on *The Quintessence of Ibsenism*, 346
  Shaw's criticism of, 747, 751
  Shaw's essay on, 465
  meeting with Shaw, 670, 672
  says Ellen Terry in love with Shaw, 732
  and *The Man of Destiny*, 609, 616, 620, 622, 630, 641, 643, 644, 650, 663, 667, 668, 669, 718, 745, 747, 752, 753, 755, 759, 760, 762, 763, 777
Irving, H. B., 744, 746, 773
Irving, Laurence (son of Henry Irving), 773, 796
  Godefroi and Yolande, 608
  Peter the Great, 781, 784, 892, 803, 831, 839
Irving, Laurence (grandson of Henry Irving): *Henry Irving*, 752, 836
"Isophily": *see* Girdlestone
Italian exhibition (1888), 196
Ivanhoe: see Scott, Sir W.; and Sullivan, Sir A.

"Jack the Ripper": *see* Whitechapel murders
Jackson, Harry, 515, 517
Jaeger, Dr Gustav, 138, 569
James, Henry, 821
  Guy Domville, 470, 473
Janotha, Natalia, 270
Jarvis, Rose, 575, 578
Jaurès, Jean-Léon, 742, 743

"J.C." (i.e. Jesus Christ): *see* Shaw: pseudonyms
Jerome, J. K.: *see Prude's Progress*
Jesting Apostle: see Winsten
Jevons, W. S., 193
Jewett, Henry, 441
John Bull's Other Island: see Shaw
John Gabriel Borkman: see Ibsen
Johns, C. H., 141
Johnson, Benjamin, 829
Johnson, D., 587
Johnson, Laura, 334
Johnson, Sam, 4, 710, 711
Johnson, Dr Samuel, 258
Johnson, W. P., 378–9, 381–2, 389–90
Johnston, Frances: *see* Hoey, Mrs Cashel
Joint Committee of Socialist Bodies: *see* Socialism
Jones, Henry Arthur, 387, 420, 424, 429, 461, 473, 606, 607, 631
  The Crusaders, 383
  Judah, 459, 468, 471, 475
  The Liars, 812
  The Masqueraders, 429, 443
  Michael and His Lost Angel, 585, 590 591
  Mrs Dane's Defence, 812
  The Physician, 737, 812
  The Case of Rebellious Susan, 466, 474, 812
Jonson, Mrs G. C. Ashton: *see* Leighton, Dorothy
Journalism, 192, 628: *see also* Anonymity
Journeys End in Lovers' Meeting (Hobbes and Moore), 710, 711
Joyce, the Rev. J.: *Scientific Dialogues*, 461, 462
Joynes, J. L., 190, 219
Juan, Don, 278
Judah: see Jones
Julius Cæsar: see Shakespeare
Justice, 81, 100, 169, 254, 341, 350–1
Justice, La, 355, 359

Katherine and Petruchio: see Garrick
Kean, Charles, 654, 763
Kean, Mrs Charles: *see* Tree, Ellen
Kean, Edmund, 751, 764

Napoleon: *see* Shaw: *The Man of Destiny*; and Sloane, W. M.: *The Life of Napoleon Bonaparte*

Nation, The (London), 185

National Reformer, the, 300, 303

National Secular Society, 67, 300, 590

National Telephone Co., 42

Need, 676

Neilson, Julia, 478

"Nelson, Alec" (*pseud.*): *see* Aveling, E. B.

Nerves, 615

Nesbit, Edith (Mrs Hubert Bland), 149–150, 425

Neveu de Rameau, Le: see Diderot

New Age, 455

New Century Theatre, 740

New Magdalen, The: see Collins

New Men and Old Acres: see Taylor, T.

New Monthly Magazine, 53, 69, 79

New Review, 436, 444, 447

New Shakspere Society, 79

New Woman, The: see Grundy

Newcombe, Bertha, 417, 518, 580, 593, 618, 628, 690, 697, 699
  relationship with Shaw, 544–5, 546–7, 552, 554, 568–9

Newman, John Henry, Cardinal, 259, 300, 302

Newman & Co., 43

Newton, Sir Isaac, 168

Nicholas Nickleby: see Dickens

Night with a Nihilist, A: see Hodgson

Nicholls, Harry, 175–6

"Nicholls, Jem": *see* Shaw: pseudonyms

Nicoll, D. J., 339–40

Nietzsche, F. W., 620, 621

Nisbet, J. F., 800, 802

Nordau, Max: *Degeneration*, 541, 544, 545, 547, 550, 561

Norman, Sir Henry, 146, 424, 608

North London Press, 244

Notorious Mrs Ebbsmith, The: see Pinero

Novel Review, 330, 335

Novikoff, Olga, 171, 172

"Nunquam" (*pseud.*): *see* Blatchford

Nutt, Alfred, 373

Nutt, David, Ltd., 373

Oakeshott, J., 275, 360

Oberammergau Passion Play, 253, 255–256, 259

O'Connor, T. P., 183, 185, 189, 192, 233, 241, 244, 390, 424

O'Connor, Mrs T. P., 188
  attempt to educate Shaw, 195

Odd, to Say the Least of It: see Rose

Odette: see Sardou

O'Donoghue, D. J., 209

O'Driscoll, Florence, 241, 362, 366

Offenbach, J.: *Les Brigands*, 834

Ohnet, G.: *Le Maître de forges*, 324, 325, 327, 384

Old Mortality: see Scott, Sir Walter

Olivia: see Wills, W. G.

Olivier, Sydney (later Baron Olivier), 235, 236, 243, 275, 351, 399, 424, 452, 453, 489, 496, 501, 512
  A Freedom in Fetters, 470

"On Going to Church" (essay): *see* Shaw

One And All, 21

Oneida Creek Community, 230, 232

One Summer's Day: see Esmond

Opera, 21, 211
  Covent Garden, 190

Originality, 242–3

Osgood, J. R., 161–2,

O'Shea, Katharine ("Kitty"), 274

Othello: see Shakespeare

Oughterard (family seat of the Shaws), 9, 10, 11

Our Corner, 112, 125, 165, 550

Our Mutual Friend: see Dickens

Our Partnership: see Webb, B.

Out of Court: see Hoey, Mrs Cashel

Overton, Charles, 429, 431–2, 434

Oxford and Asquith, Earl of: *see* Asquith

Paderewski, I. J., 589, 590, 785

Paepe, César de, 249

Paget, H. M., 723

Pagliacci: see Leoncavallo

Paine, Thomas, 590

Palace of Truth, The: see Gilbert, W. S.

Palgrave, Sir Reginald F. D.: *The Chairman's Handbook*, 664

863

864

865

870